# Principles of Database Management

## The Practical Guide to Storing, Managing and Analyzing Big and Small Data

*Principles of Database Management* provides students with the comprehensive database management information to understand and apply the fundamental concepts of database design and modeling, database systems, data storage and the evolving world of data warehousing, governance and more. Designed for those studying database management for information management or computer science, this illustrated textbook has a well-balanced theory–practice focus and covers the essential topics, from established database technologies up to recent trends like Big Data, NoSQL and analytics. On-going case studies, drill-down boxes that reveal deeper insights on key topics, retention questions at the end of every section of a chapter, and connections boxes that show the relationship between concepts throughout the text are included to provide the practical tools to get started in database management.

Key features include:

- Full-color illustrations throughout the text.
- Extensive coverage of important trending topics, including data warehousing, business intelligence, data integration, data quality, data governance, Big Data and analytics.
- An online playground with diverse environments, including MySQL for querying; MongoDB; Neo4j Cypher; and a tree structure visualization environment.
- Hundreds of examples to illustrate and clarify the concepts discussed that can be reproduced on the book's companion online playground.
- Case studies, review questions, problems and exercises in every chapter.
- Additional cases, problems and exercises in the appendix.

"Although there have been a series of classical textbooks on database systems, the new dramatic advances call for an updated text covering the latest significant topics, such as Big Data analytics, NoSQL and much more. Fortunately, this is exactly what this book has to offer. It is highly desirable for training the next generation of data management professionals."

– Jian Pei, *Simon Fraser University*

"I haven't seen an as up-to-date and comprehensive textbook for database management as this one in many years. *Principles of Database Management* combines a number of classical and recent topics concerning data modeling, relational databases, object-oriented databases, XML, distributed data management, NoSQL and Big Data in an unprecedented manner. The authors did a great job in stitching these topics into one coherent and compelling story that will serve as an ideal basis for teaching both introductory and advanced courses."

– Martin Theobald, *University of Luxembourg*

"This is a very timely book with outstanding coverage of database topics and excellent treatment of database details. It not only gives very solid discussions of traditional topics such as data modeling and relational databases, but also contains refreshing contents on frontier topics such as XML databases, NoSQL databases, Big Data and analytics. For those reasons, this will be a good book for database professionals, who will keep using it for all stages of database studies and works."

– J. Leon Zhao, *City University of Hong Kong*

"This accessible, authoritative book introduces the reader the most important fundamental concepts of data management, while providing a practical view of recent advances. Both are essential for data professionals today."

– Foster Provost, *New York University, Stern School of Business*

"This guide to big and small data management addresses both fundamental principles and practical deployment. It reviews a range of databases and their relevance for analytics. The book is useful to practitioners because it contains many case studies, links to open-source software, and a very useful abstraction of analytics that will help them choose solutions better. It is important to academics because it promotes database principles which are key to successful and sustainable data science."

– Sihem Amer-Yahia, *Laboratoire d'Informatique de Grenoble*; Editor-in-Chief, *The VLDB Journal (International Journal on Very Large DataBases)*

"This book covers everything you will need to teach in a database implementation and design class. With some chapters covering Big Data, analytic models/methods and NoSQL, it can keep our students up to date with these new technologies in data management-related topics."

– Han-fen Hu, *University of Nevada, Las Vegas*

# Principles of Database Management

## The Practical Guide to Storing, Managing and Analyzing Big and Small Data

Wilfried Lemahieu
KU Leuven, Belgium

Seppe vanden Broucke
KU Leuven, Belgium

Bart Baesens
KU Leuven, Belgium; University of Southampton, United Kingdom

CAMBRIDGE
UNIVERSITY PRESS

**CAMBRIDGE**
UNIVERSITY PRESS

University Printing House, Cambridge CB2 8BS, United Kingdom

One Liberty Plaza, 20th Floor, New York, NY 10006, USA

477 Williamstown Road, Port Melbourne, VIC 3207, Australia

314–321, 3rd Floor, Plot 3, Splendor Forum, Jasola District Centre, New Delhi – 110025, India

79 Anson Road, #06–04/06, Singapore 079906

Cambridge University Press is part of the University of Cambridge.

It furthers the University's mission by disseminating knowledge in the pursuit of education, learning, and research at the highest international levels of excellence.

www.cambridge.org
Information on this title: www.cambridge.org/9781107186125
DOI: 10.1017/9781316888773



First published 2018

Printed and bound in Great Britain by Clays Ltd, Elcograf S.p.A.

*A catalog record for this publication is available from the British Library.*

*Library of Congress Cataloging-in-Publication Data*
Names: Lemahieu, Wilfried, 1970– author. | Broucke, Seppe vanden, 1986– author. | Baesens, Bart, author.
Title: Principles of database management : the practical guide to storing, managing and analyzing big and small data / Wilfried Lemahieu, Katholieke Universiteit Leuven, Belgium, Seppe vanden Broucke, Katholieke Universiteit Leuven, Belgium, Bart Baesens, Katholieke Universiteit Leuven, Belgium.
Description: First edition. | New York, NY : Cambridge University Press, 2018. | Includes bibliographical references and index.
Identifiers: LCCN 2018023251 | ISBN 9781107186125 (hardback : alk. paper)
Subjects: LCSH: Database management.
Classification: LCC QA76.9.D3 L454 2018 | DDC 005.74–dc23
LC record available at https://lccn.loc.gov/2018023251

ISBN 978-1-107-18612-5 Hardback

Additional resources for this publication at www.cambridge.org/Lemahieu

# BRIEF CONTENTS

# CONTENTS

# ABOUT THE AUTHORS

Bart was born in Bruges (Belgium). He speaks West-Flemish, Dutch, French, a bit of German, some English, and can order a beer in Chinese. Besides enjoying time with his family, he is also a diehard Club Brugge soccer fan. Bart is a foodie and amateur cook and loves a good glass of wine overlooking the authentic red English phone booth in his garden. Bart loves traveling; his favorite cities are San Francisco, Sydney, and Barcelona. He is fascinated by World War I and reads many books on the topic. He is not a big fan of being called "Professor Baesens", shopping, vacuuming, long meetings, phone calls, admin, or students chewing gum during their oral exam on database management. He is often praised for his sense of humor, although he is usually more modest about this.

Bart is a professor of Big Data and analytics at KU Leuven (Belgium) and a lecturer at the University of Southampton (United Kingdom). He has done extensive research on Big Data and analytics, credit risk modeling, fraud detection, and marketing analytics. He has written more than 200 scientific papers and six books. He has received various best paper and best speaker awards. His research is summarized at www.dataminingapps.com.

Seppe was born in Jette (Brussels, Belgium), but has lived most of his life in Leuven. Seppe speaks Dutch, some French, English, understands German, and can order a beer in Chinese (and unlike Bart he can do so in the right intonation, having studied Mandarin for three years). He is married to Xinwei Zhu (which explains the three years of Mandarin). Besides spending time with family, Seppe enjoys traveling, reading (Murakami to Bukowski to Asimov), listening to music (Booka Shade to Miles Davis to Claude Debussy), watching movies and series, gaming, and keeping up with the news. He is not a fan of any physical activity other than walking way too fast through Leuven. Seppe does not like vacuuming (this seems to be common with database book authors), bureaucracy, meetings, public transportation (even though he has no car) or Windows updates that start when he is teaching or writing a book chapter.

Seppe is an assistant professor at the Faculty of Economics and Business, KU Leuven, Belgium. His research interests include business data mining and analytics, machine learning, process management, and process mining. His work has been published in well-known international journals and presented at top conferences. Seppe's teaching includes advanced analytics, Big Data, and information management courses. He also frequently teaches for industry and business audiences. See www.seppe.net for further details.

Wilfried was born in Turnhout, Belgium. He speaks Dutch, English, and French, and can decipher some German, Latin, and West-Flemish. Unable to order a beer in Chinese, he has perfected a "looking thirsty" facial expression that works in any language. He is married to Els Mennes, and together they produced three sons – Janis, Hannes, and Arne – before running out of boys' names. Apart from family time, one of Wilfried's most cherished pastimes is music. Some would say he is stuck in the eighties, but his taste ranges from Beethoven to Hendrix and from Cohen to The Cure. He also likes traveling, with fond memories of Alaska, Bali, Cuba, Beijing, the Swiss Alps, Rome, and Istanbul. He enjoys many different genres of movies, but is somewhat constrained by his wife's bias toward tearful-kiss-and-make-up-at-the-airport scenes. His sports watch contains data (certainly no Big Data!) on erratic attempts at running, swimming, biking, and skiing. Wilfried has no immediate aversion to vacuuming, although his fellow household members would claim that his experience with the matter is mainly theoretical.

Wilfried is a full professor at the Faculty of Economics and Business (FEB) of KU Leuven, Belgium. He conducts research on (big) data storage, integration, and analytics; data quality; business process management and service orchestration, often in collaboration with industry partners. Following his position of Vice Dean for Education at FEB, he was elected as Dean in 2017. See www.feb.kuleuven.be/wilfried.lemahieu for further details.

# PREFACE

Congratulations! By picking up this book, you have made the first step in your journey through the wonderful world of databases. As you will see in this book, databases come in many different forms – from simple spreadsheets or other file-based attempts and hierarchical structures, to relational, object-oriented, and even graph-oriented ones – and are used across the world throughout a variety of industry sectors to manage, store, and analyze data.

This book is the result of having taught an undergraduate database management class and a postgraduate advanced database management class for more than ten years. Throughout the years we have found no textbook that covers the material in a comprehensive way without becoming flooded by theoretical detail and losing focus. Hence, after we teamed up together, we decided to start writing a book ourselves. This work aims to offer a complete and practical guide covering all the governing principles of database management, including:

- end-to-end coverage, starting with legacy technologies to emerging trends such as Big Data, NoSQL databases, analytics, data governance, etc.;
- a unique perspective on how lessons learned from past data management could be relevant in today's technology setting (e.g., navigational access and its perils in CODASYL and XML/OO databases);
- a critical reflection and accompanying risk management considerations when implementing the technologies considered, based on our own experiences participating in data and analytics-related projects with industry partners in a variety of sectors, from banking to retail and from government to the cultural sector;
- a solid balance between theory and practice, including various exercises, industry examples and case studies originating from diverse and complementary business practices, scientific research, and academic teaching experience.

The book also includes an appendix explaining our "online playground" environment, where you can try out many concepts discussed in the book. Additional appendices, including an exam bank containing several cross-chapter questions and references to our YouTube lectures, are provided online as well.

We hope you enjoy this book and that you, the reader, will find it a useful reference and trusted companion in your work, studies, or research when storing, managing, and analyzing small or Big Data!

## Who This Book is For

We have tried to make this book complete and useful for both novice and advanced database practitioners and students alike. No matter whether you're a novice just beginning to work with database management systems, a versed SQL user aiming to brush up your knowledge of underlying concepts or theory, or someone looking to get an update on newer, more modern database approaches, this book aims to familiarize you with all the necessary concepts. Hence, this book is well suited for:

- under- or postgraduate students taking courses on database management in BSc and MSc programs in information management and/or computer science;
- business professionals who would like to refresh or update their knowledge on database management; and
- information architects, database designers, data owners, data stewards, database administrators, or data scientists interested in new developments in the area.

Thanks to the exercises and industry examples throughout the chapters, the book can also be used by tutors in courses such as:

- principles of database management;
- database modeling;
- database design;
- database systems;
- data management;
- data modeling;
- data science.

It can also be useful to universities working out degrees in, for example, Big Data and analytics.

## Topics Covered in this Book

This book is organized in four main parts. Chapters 1–4 address preliminary and introductory topics regarding databases and database design, starting with an introduction to basic concepts in Chapter 1, followed by a description of common database management system types and their architecture in Chapter 2. Chapter 3 discusses conceptual data modeling, and Chapter 4 provides a management overview of the different roles involved in data management and their responsibilities.

Part II (Chapters 5–11) then takes a dive into the various types of databases, from legacy pre-relational and relational database management systems into more recent approaches such as object-oriented, object-relational, and XML-based databases in Chapters 8–10, ending with a solid and up-to-date overview of NoSQL technologies in Chapter 11. This part also includes a comprehensive overview of the Structured Query Language (SQL) in Chapter 7.

In Part III, physical data storage, transaction management, and database access are discussed in depth. Chapter 12 discusses physical file organization and indexing, whereas Chapter 13 elaborates on physical database organization and business continuity. This is followed by an overview on the basics of transaction management in Chapter 14. Chapter 15 introduces database access mechanisms and various database application programming interfaces (APIs). Chapter 16 concludes this part of the book by zooming in on data distribution and distributed transaction management.

Chapters 17–20 form the last part of the book. Here, we zoom out and elaborate on data warehousing and emerging interest areas such as data governance, Big Data, and analytics. Chapter 17 discusses data warehouses and business intelligence in depth; Chapter 18 covers managerial concepts such as data integration, data quality, and data governance; Chapter 19 provides an in-depth overview of Big Data and shows how a solid database set-up can form the cornerstone of a modern analytical environment. Chapter 20 concludes this part and the book by examining different types of analytics.

By the end of the book, you will have gained a strong knowledge of all aspects that make up a database management system. You will be able to discern the different database systems, and to contrast their advantages and disadvantages. You will be able to make the best (investment) decisions through conceptual, logical, and physical data modeling, all the way to Big Data and analytical applications. You'll have gained a strong understanding of SQL, and will also understand how database management systems work at the physical level – including transaction management and indexing. You'll understand how database systems are accessed from the outside world and how they can be integrated with other systems or applications. Finally, you'll also understand the various managerial aspects that come into play when working with databases, including the roles involved, data integration, quality, and governance aspects, and you will have a clear idea on how the concept of database management systems fits in the Big Data and analytics story.

## How to Read this Book

This book can be used as both a reference manual for more experienced readers wishing to brush up their skills and knowledge regarding certain aspects, as well as an end-to-end overview on the whole area of database management systems. Readers are free to read this book cover to cover, or to skip certain chapters and start directly with a topic of interest. We have separated the book clearly into different parts and chapters so readers should have little trouble understanding the global structure of the book and navigating to the right spot. Whenever a topic is expanded upon in a later chapter or re-uses concepts introduced in an earlier chapter, we include clear "Connections" boxes so readers can (re-)visit earlier chapters for a quick refresher before moving on, or move ahead to other places in the book to continue their learning trail.

The following overview provides some common "reading trails", depending on your area of interest:

- Newcomers wishing to get up to speed quickly with relational database systems and SQL: start with Part I (Chapters 1–4), then read Chapters 6–9.
- Experienced users wishing to update their knowledge on recent trends: read Chapter 11, and then Chapters 15–20.
- Daily database users wishing to have high-level knowledge about database systems: Part I (Chapters 1–4) is for you.
- Managers wishing to get a basic overview on fundamental concepts and a broad idea of managerial issues: start with Part I (Chapters 1–4), then move on to Chapters 17, 18, 19, and 20.
- Professors teaching an undergraduate course in database management: Parts I and II.
- Professors teaching a postgraduate course in advanced database management: Parts III and IV.

The recommended chapters for each of these profiles, together with some others (which will be discussed in Chapter 4), are summarized in the table.

| Chapter | Newcomers | Experienced users | Database users | Managers | Professor (undergraduate course) | Professor (postgraduate course) | Information architect | Database designer | Database administrator | Data scientist |
|---|---|---|---|---|---|---|---|---|---|---|
| 1 | X | | X | X | X | | X | X | X | |
| 2 | X | | X | X | X | | X | X | X | |
| 3 | X | | X | X | X | | X | X | X | |
| 4 | X | | X | X | X | | X | X | X | |
| 5 | | | | | X | | | X | X | |
| 6 | X | | | | X | | | X | X | |
| 7 | X | | | | X | | | X | X | |
| 8 | X | | | | X | | | X | X | |
| 9 | X | | | | X | | | X | X | |
| 10 | | | | | X | | | X | X | |
| 11 | | X | | | X | | | X | X | X |
| 12 | | | | | | X | | X | X | |
| 13 | | | | | | X | | X | X | |
| 14 | | | | | | X | | | X | |
| 15 | | X | | | | X | | | | |
| 16 | | X | | | | X | | | X | |
| 17 | | X | | X | | X | | | X | X |
| 18 | | X | | X | | X | | | X | X |
| 19 | | X | | X | | X | | | X | X |
| 20 | | X | | X | | X | | | | X |

Every chapter aims to strike a balance between theory and practice, so theoretical concepts are often alternated with examples from industry in small "Drill Down" boxes that provide more background knowledge or an interesting story to illustrate a concept. We also include theoretical discussions on pros and cons of a specific technique or technology. Each chapter closes with a set of exercises to test your understanding. Both multiple-choice and open questions have been included.

## Cross-Chapter Case Study: Sober

Throughout the book we use an encompassing case (about a fictional self-driving car taxi company called "Sober") that will be revisited and expanded in each chapter. When reading the book from cover to cover you'll therefore be able to learn together with the people at Sober, experiencing how their database management system evolves from a simple small-scale system toward a more modern and robust set-up as they continue to grow. This way, the different chapters also form a cohesive whole from a practical perspective, and you'll see how all the technologies and concepts fit together.

## Additional Material

We are also happy to refer you to our book website at www.pdbmbook.com. The site includes additional information such as updates, PowerPoint slides, video lectures, additional appendices, and a Q&A section. It also features a hands-on, online environment where readers can play around with a MySQL relational database management system using SQL, explore NoSQL database systems, and other small examples without having to install anything. You'll find a guide in the Appendix that will set you on your way.

## Acknowledgments

It is a great pleasure to acknowledge the contributions and assistance of various colleagues, friends, and fellow database management lovers in the writing of this book. This book is the result of many years of research and teaching in database management.

We first would like to acknowledge our publisher, Cambridge University Press, for accepting our book proposal about two years ago. We would like to thank Lauren Cowles for supervising the entire process. We first met Lauren in August 2016 in San Francisco, discussing the book details during dinner (crab cakes paired with Napa white) while overlooking an ensemble of sunbathing seals. This turned out to be the perfect setting for initiating a successful partnership. We are also thankful to everyone at Cambridge University Press for their help in the editing, production, and marketing processes.

Gary J. O'Brien deserves a special mention as well. His careful proofreading of the text proved invaluable. Although opening a Word document with Gary's comments sometimes felt like being thrown in the ocean knowing sharks had been spotted, the mix of to-the-point remarks with humorous notes made the revision a truly enjoyable experience.

We would like to thank professor Jacques Vandenbulcke, who was the first to introduce us to the magical world of database management. Jacques' exquisite pedagogical talent can only be surpassed by his travel planning skills. His legacy runs throughout the entire book, not only in terms of database concepts and examples, but also travel experiences (e.g., the Basilica Cistern on the front cover, Meneghetti wine).

We would also like to acknowledge the direct and indirect contributions of the many colleagues, fellow professors, students, researchers, business contacts, and friends with whom we collaborated during the past years. We are grateful to the active and lively database management community for providing various user fora, blogs, online lectures, and tutorials that proved very helpful.

Last but not least, we are grateful to our partners, kids, parents, and families for their love, support, and encouragement! We trust they will read this book from the first page to the last, which will yield ample topics for lively and interesting discussions at the dinner table.

We have tried to make this book as complete, accurate, and enjoyable as possible. Of course, what really matters is what you, the reader, think of it. Please share your views by getting in touch. The authors welcome all feedback and comments, so do not hesitate to let us know your thoughts.

***Front cover:*** The cover picture represents the Basilica Cistern, an immense subterranean water storage facility built in the sixth century by the Romans in Istanbul. Why this picture? Well, overall it is a spectacular location in a truly magnificent city, which throughout its history has been a meeting point of cultures, civilizations, and, literally, continents. However, more to the point, it is definitely a storage infrastructure organized as rows and columns, which even involves replication and mirroring, not to mention historical data. In addition, it contained one of the most famous primary keys ever: 007, as it featured prominently in the James Bond movie *From Russia With Love*.

**Sober**

1000‰ Driven by Technology

Sober is a new taxi company deploying self-driving cars to provide cab services. Although it operates its own fleet of self-driving cabs, people can also register their cars as Sober cabs and have them provide taxi services whenever they are not using their cars. For the latter, Sober also wants to keep track of the car owners.

Sober offers two types of taxi services: ride-hailing and ride-sharing. Ride-hailing is a service whereby customers can hail a taxi so they can be picked up and driven to their destination for a time- and distance-based fee. The hailing is an immediate, on-demand service and requests can be made with the Sober App. With just one tap on the screen, a customer can request a cab from anywhere, receive an estimated wait time, and a notification when the car has arrived. Besides the Sober App, users can also hail Sober cabs by hand-waving them as they see them pass, in which case Sober's deep-learning based image recognition system identifies the wave gesture as a cab request. For each use of the ride-hail service, Sober wants to store the time of pick-up and drop-off, the location of pick-up and drop-off, the ride duration, the distance, the number of passengers, the fee, the type of request (via Sober App or hand-waving) and the number and name of the lead customer (the one who pays). The maximum number of passengers for a ride-hail service is six.

Ride-sharing is another service offered by Sober, which requires more careful planning. It can also be referred to as carpooling and aims at reducing costs, traffic congestion, and the carbon footprint. Because of the planning, both Sober and its customers can negotiate the fee whereby more customers per cab means a lower fee per customer (flexible pricing). To provide an eco-friendly incentive, Sober pledges to plant a tree for each customer who books 20 uses of the Sober ride-sharing service. For each ride-share service, Sober wants to store the time of pick-up and drop-off, the location of pick-up and drop-off, the ride duration, the distance, the number and names of all customers, and the upfront negotiated fee. The maximum number of passengers for a ride-share service is ten.

Due to the novelty of the self-driving car technology, accidents cannot be 100% ruled out. Sober also wants to store information about accident dates, location, and damage amounts per car.

# Part I

# Databases and Database Design

# 1 Fundamental Concepts of Database Management

## Chapter Objectives

In this chapter, you will learn to:

- understand the differences between the file versus database approach to data management;
- discern the key elements of a database system;
- identify the advantages of database systems and database management.

**Opening Scenario**

Since Sober is a startup company, it must carefully decide how it will manage all its data. The company is thinking about storing all its data in Word documents, Excel files, and maybe some other files (e.g., Notepad) as well.

In this chapter, we discuss the fundamental concepts of database management. Many ideas presented here are elaborated in later chapters. We kick off by reviewing popular applications of database technology, and follow this by defining key concepts such as a database and a database management system, or DBMS. Next, we step back in time and discuss the file-based approach and contrast it with the database approach to data management. We then zoom into the elements of a database system. We conclude by discussing the advantages of database design.

## 1.1 Applications of Database Technology

Data are everywhere and come in different shapes and volumes. These data need to be stored and managed using appropriate data management or database technologies. Think about the storage and retrieval of traditional numeric and alphanumeric data in an application developed to keep track of the number of products in stock. For each product, the product number, product name, and available quantity needs to be stored. Replenishment orders need to be issued as soon as the quantity drops below the safety limit. Every replenishment order has an order number, order date, supplier number, supplier name, and a set of product numbers, names, and quantities.

Database technology is not just for traditional numeric and alphanumeric data. It can also store multimedia data such as pictures, audio, or video – YouTube and Spotify support the querying of music based upon artist, album, genre, playlist, or record label. Biometric data, including fingerprints and retina scans, are often used for security, such as border control as you enter a country.

Information is also gathered by wearables, such as a Fitbit or an Apple Watch, which continuously monitor and analyze your health and fitness. *Geographical information systems (GIS)* applications, such as Google Maps, store and retrieve all types of spatial or geographical data.

Database technology can also store and retrieve *volatile* data. One example is high-frequency trading, where automated, algorithmic platforms are used by investment banks or hedge funds to process a large number of orders at extremely high speed based upon events happening in the environment or macro-economy. Another example is sensors monitoring the key parameters of a nuclear reactor, whereby an automatic system shutdown may be enacted if certain thresholds are hit.

You may have heard the term *Big Data*, referring to the huge amounts of data being gathered and analyzed by companies such as Google, Facebook, and Twitter. Look at Walmart, America's largest retailer with over 11,000 locations worldwide, $4.8 billion in annual sales and over 100 million customers per week. Its point-of-sale (POS) database system stores an enormous amount of data such as which customer bought what products, in what quantities, at which location, and at what time. All these data can then be intelligently analyzed using analytical data modeling to reveal unknown but interesting purchase patterns, such as which products are frequently purchased together. Better still, certain analysis techniques allow one to make predictions about the future (e.g., which customers are most likely to respond positively to a sales promotion). We discuss this in more detail in Chapter 20.

These are just a few examples of database applications; many others exist.

**Retention Questions**

- Give some examples of applications of database technology.

**Drill Down**

The Internet of Things (IoT) provides many examples of Big Data applications. Moocall is a Dublin-based startup providing sensors for farmers to reduce the mortality rates of calves and cows during birthing. The sensor is attached to the cow's tail. They measure specific movements of the tail triggered by labor contractions as the calving begins. These sensor data are then sent through the Vodafone IoT network to a farmer's smartphone. Using an app, the farmer gets up-to-date information about the calving process and can intervene or call a vet when needed. The app can generate alerts, and includes a herd management facility. This technology improves both the farmer's productivity and the survival probabilities of calves and cows during the birthing process.

## 1.2 Key Definitions

We have briefly introduced the concept of a database by exploring the various types of databases you may encounter every day. A **database** can be defined as a collection of related data items within a specific business process or problem setting. Consider a purchase order system, where you have data items such as products, suppliers, and purchase orders. Each data item has characteristics: a product has a product number, product name, and product color; a supplier has a supplier name and a supplier address; a purchase order has a reference number and date. These data items are also related. A product can be supplied by one or more suppliers. A purchase

**Connections**

In Chapter 2 we discuss the internal architecture of a DBMS. We also provide a categorization of DBMSs along various dimensions.

order is always connected to exactly one supplier. A supplier can supply one or more products. These are examples of relationships between the data items that should be adequately captured by a database. A database has a target group of users and applications. An inventory manager uses our purchase order system to manage the inventory and issue purchase orders; a product manager uses it for monitoring trends in product sales.

**Retention Questions**

- Define the following concepts:
  - database
  - DBMS
  - database system

A **database management system (DBMS)** is the software package used to define, create, use, and maintain a database. It typically consists of several software modules, each with their own functionality, as we discuss in Chapter 2. Popular DBMS vendors are Oracle, Microsoft, and IBM. MySQL is a well-known open-source DBMS. The combination of a DBMS and a database is then often called a **database system**.

**Drill Down**

Gartner[1] estimated the total DBMS market value at $35.9 billion for 2015, which represented an 8.7% growth when compared to 2014. According to the IDC, the overall market for database management solutions is estimated to reach over $50 billion by 2018.

## 1.3 File versus Database Approach to Data Management

Before we further explore database technology, let's step back and see how data management has evolved. This will give us a proper understanding of the legacy problems many companies are still facing.

### 1.3.1 The File-Based Approach

In the early days of computing, every application stored its data into its own dedicated files. This is known as a file-based approach and is illustrated in Figure 1.1.

Suppose we have a traditional invoicing application, written in a programming language such as COBOL or C, that makes use of customer information such as customer number, customer name, VAT code, etc., stored in a separate file. A separate application, such as a customer relationship management (CRM) system, makes use of a different file containing the same data. Finally, a third application (GIS) stores information such as customer number, customer name, and ZIP code in yet another file. The data files only contain the data themselves; the data definitions and descriptions are included in each application separately. An application can make use of one or more files. As more applications are developed with corresponding data files, this file-based approach to data management will cause serious problems.

Since each application uses its own data files and many applications use similar data, duplicate or redundant information will be stored, which is a waste of storage resources. If this is not appropriately managed there is a danger that customer data will be updated in only one file and not elsewhere, resulting in inconsistent data. In this file-based approach to data management there is a strong coupling, or dependency, between the applications and the data. A structural change in

[1] https://blogs.gartner.com/merv-adrian/2016/04/12/dbms-2015-numbers-paint-a-picture-of-slow-but-steady-change.

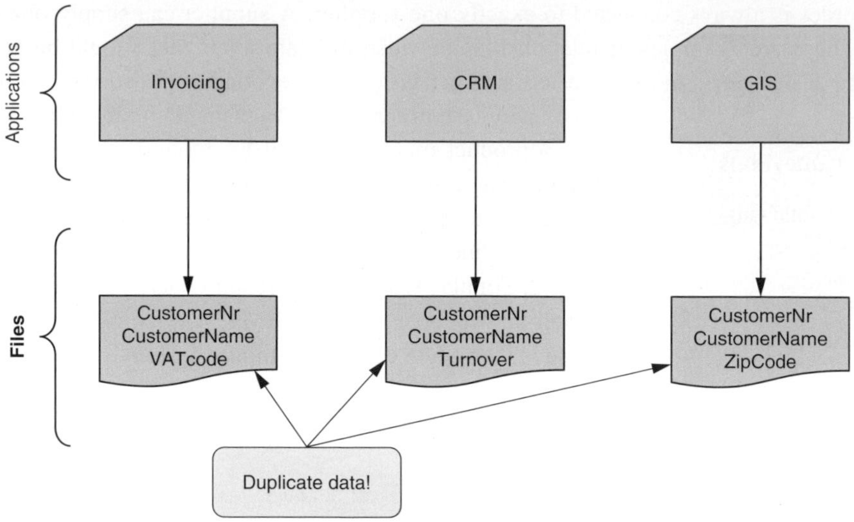


**Figure 1.1** File-based approach to data management.

a data file necessitates changes in all applications that use it, which is not desirable from a maintenance perspective. It is hard to manage *concurrency control* (i.e., the simultaneous access by different users or applications to the same data without conflicts). For example, if one application performs a cash transfer while another application calculates the account balance, and the data operations of both applications are interleaved for efficiency, this can easily lead to inconsistent data in cases where there are no adequate concurrency control facilities provided. Since the applications each work independently with their own ecosystem of data files, it is difficult and expensive to integrate applications aimed at providing cross-company services. Although this file approach to data management has serious disadvantages, many firms still struggle with "*legacy*" file-based systems in their current information and communications technology (ICT) environment.

### 1.3.2 The Database Approach

The emergence of database technology provided a new paradigm for data management. In this **database approach**, all data are stored and managed centrally by a DBMS, as illustrated in Figure 1.2.

The applications now directly interface with the DBMS instead of with their own files. The DBMS delivers the desired data at the request of each application. The DBMS stores and manages two types of data: raw data and metadata. **Metadata** refers to the data definitions that are now stored in the catalog of the DBMS. This is a key difference to the file-based approach. The metadata are no longer included in the applications, but are now properly managed by the DBMS itself. From an efficiency, consistency, and maintenance perspective, this approach is superior.

Another key advantage of the database approach is the facilities provided for data querying and retrieval. In the file-based approach, every application had to explicitly write its own query and access procedures. Consider the following example in pseudo-code:

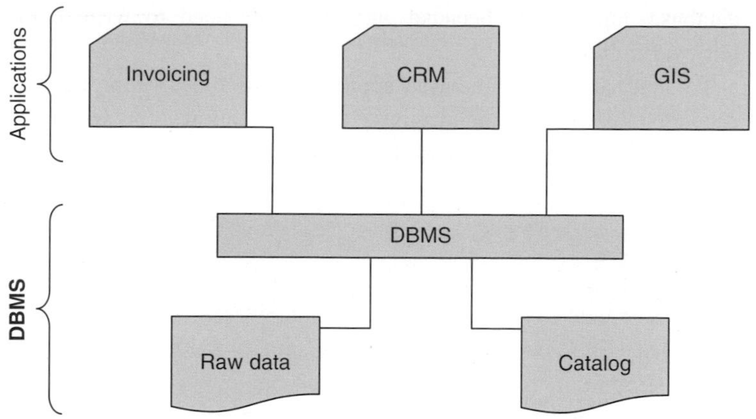


**Figure 1.2** Database approach to data management.

```
Procedure FindCustomer;
Begin
      open file Customer.txt;
      Read(Customer)
      While not EOF(Customer)
            If Customer.name='Bart' Then
                  display(Customer);
            EndIf
      Read(Customer);
      EndWhile;
End;
```

Here, we first open a Customer.txt file and read the first record. We then implement a while loop that iterates through each record in the file until the end of the file is reached (indicated by EOF (Customer)). If the desired information is found (Customer.name='Bart'), it will be displayed. This requires a lot of coding. Because of the tight coupling between data and applications, many procedures would be repeated in various applications, which is again not very appealing from a maintenance perspective. As noted, DBMSs provide database languages that facilitate both data querying and access. A well-known language, which we discuss extensively in Chapter 7, is Structured Query Language (SQL). SQL can be used to formulate database queries in a structured and user-friendly way, and is one of the most popular data querying standards used in the industry. An example SQL query that gives the same output as our pseudo-code above could be:

```
SELECT *
FROM Customer
WHERE
name = 'Bart'
```

Here, you only need to specify what information you want. In our case, we want all customer information for customer 'Bart'. This SQL query will then be executed by the DBMS in a transparent way. In the database approach, we only need to specify which data we are interested in, and no longer how we should access and retrieve them. This facilitates the development of

**Retention Questions**

- Contrast the file versus database approach to data management.

database applications because we no longer need to write complex data retrieval procedures.

To summarize, the file-based approach results in a strong application–data dependence, whereas the database approach allows for applications to be independent from the data and data definitions.

**Drill Down**

One of the key disadvantages of a file-based approach to data management is that the data typically sit all over the organization in silos; therefore, an overall, comprehensive view is lacking. For example, the city of Amsterdam has data spread across 12,000 different datasets. Because of the lack of integration, no one knows exactly how many bridges span Amsterdam's famous canals, because each of the city's individual districts has its own data and no overall comprehensive database is available. It turned out that many of these siloed datasets adopted their own data definition of a bridge, which further complicates matters. See http://sloanreview.mit.edu/case-study/lessons-from-becoming-a-data-driven-organization.

## 1.4 Elements of a Database System

In this section we discuss database model versus instances, data models, the three-layer architecture, the role of the catalog, the various types of database users, and DBMS languages.

### 1.4.1 Database Model versus Instances

In any database implementation, it is important to distinguish between the description of the data, or data definitions, and the actual data. The **database model** or **database schema** provides the description of the database data at different levels of detail and specifies the various data items, their characteristics, and relationships, constraints, storage details, etc.[2] The database model is specified during database design and is not expected to change frequently. It is stored in the catalog, which is the heart of the DBMS. The **database state** then represents the data in the database at a particular moment. It is sometimes also called the *current set of instances*. Depending upon data manipulations, such as adding, updating, or removing data, it typically changes on an ongoing basis.

The following are examples of data definitions that are an essential part of the database model stored in the catalog.

**Database model**

Student (number, name, address, email)
Course (number, name)
Building (number, address)
...

We have three data items: Student, Course, and Building. Each of these data items can be described in terms of its characteristics. A student is characterized by a number, name, address, and email; a course by a number and name; and a building by a number and address.

[2] We consider the terms *model* and *schema* as synonyms.

| STUDENT | | | |
|---|---|---|---|
| Number | Name | Address | Email |
| 0165854 | Bart Baesens | 1040 Market Street, SF | Bart.Baesens@kuleuven.be |
| 0168975 | Seppe vanden Broucke | 520, Fifth Avenue, NY | Seppe.vandenbroucke@kuleuven.be |
| 0157895 | Wilfried Lemahieu | 644, Wacker Drive, Chicago | Wilfried.Lemahieu@kuleuven.be |

| COURSE | |
|---|---|
| Number | Name |
| D0I69A | Principles of Database Management |
| D0R04A | Basic Programming |
| D0T21A | Big Data & Analytics |

| BUILDING | |
|---|---|
| Number | Address |
| 0600 | Naamsestraat 69, Leuven |
| 0365 | Naamsestraat 78, Leuven |
| 0589 | Tiensestraat 115, Leuven |

**Figure 1.3** Example database state.

Figure 1.3 shows an example of a corresponding database state. You can see the database includes data about three students, three courses, and three buildings.

### 1.4.2 Data Model

A database model comprises different data models, each describing the data from different perspectives. A good data model is the start of every successful database application. It provides a clear and unambiguous description of the data items, their relationships, and various data constraints from a particular perspective. Several types of data models will be developed during a database design process.

A **conceptual data model** provides a high-level description of the data items (e.g., supplier, product) with their characteristics (e.g., supplier name, product number) and relationships (e.g., a supplier can supply products). It is a communication instrument between the information architect (see Chapter 4) and business user to make sure the data requirements are adequately captured and modeled. Therefore, the conceptual data model should be implementation-independent, user-friendly, and close to how the business user perceives the data. It will usually be represented using an Enhanced Entity Relationship (EER) model or an object-oriented model, as we discuss in Chapter 3.

A **logical data model** is a translation or mapping of the conceptual data model toward a specific implementation environment. The logical data items may still be understood by business users, but are not too far removed from the physical data organization. Depending upon the ICT environment available, it can be a hierarchical (see Chapter 5), CODASYL (see Chapter 5), relational (see Chapters 6 and 7), object-oriented (see Chapter 8), extended relational (see Chapter 9), XML (see Chapter 10), or NoSQL model (see Chapter 11).

The logical data model can be mapped to an internal data model that represents the data's physical storage details. It clearly describes which data are stored where, in what format, which indexes are provided to speed up retrieval, etc. It is therefore highly DBMS-specific. We discuss internal data models in Chapters 12 and 13.

**Connections**

In Chapter 3 we discuss the EER and UML conceptual data models in more detail. Later chapters cover logical (and sometimes external) data models: the hierarchical and CODASYL model in Chapter 5, the relational model in Chapters 6 and 7, the object-oriented model in Chapter 8, the extended relational model in Chapter 9, the XML data model in Chapter 10 and various NoSQL data models in Chapter 11. Chapters 12 and 13 elaborate on internal data models.

The **external data model** contains various subsets of the data items in the logical model, also called views, tailored toward the needs of specific applications or groups of users.

### 1.4.3 The Three-Layer Architecture

The **three-layer architecture** is an essential element of every database application and describes how the different underlying data models are related.[3] It is illustrated in Figure 1.4.

We start with the conceptual/logical layer. Here, we have the conceptual and logical data models. Both focus on the data items, their characteristics, and relationships without bothering too much about the actual physical DBMS implementation. The conceptual data model should be a user-friendly, implementation-independent, and transparent data model, constructed in close collaboration between the information architect and business user(s). It will be refined to a logical data model based upon the implementation environment.

In the external layer we have the external data model, which includes views offering a window on a carefully selected part of the logical data model. A **view** describes the part of the database that a particular application or user group is interested in, hiding the rest of the database. It is used to control data access and enforce security. The views will be tailored to the data needs of an application or (group of) user(s). A view can serve one or more applications. Consider a view offering only student information to a student registration application, or a view offering only building information to a capacity planning application.

The **internal layer** includes the **internal data model**, which specifies how the data are stored or organized physically. Ideally, changes in one layer should have no to minimal impact on the others. It should be possible to physically reorganize the data with little impact on the conceptual/logical or external layer (physical data independence). Likewise, changes to the conceptual/logical layer can be made with minimal impact on the external layer (logical data independence). We elaborate on both types of data independence in Section 1.5.1.

Figure 1.5 illustrates the three-layer architecture for a procurement business process. The conceptual/logical layer defines the data items such as Product, Customer, Invoice, and Delivery. The internal layer contains the physical storage details specifying how and where the data are stored. The external layer has three views offering specific information to the finance, customer service, and logistics departments. This three-layer database architecture has several advantages in efficiency, maintenance, performance, security, etc.

### 1.4.4 Catalog

The **catalog** is the heart of the DBMS. It contains the data definitions, or metadata, of your database application. It stores the definitions of the views, logical and internal data models, and synchronizes these three data models to ensure their consistency.[4]

[3] Some textbooks refer to the three-schema architecture instead of the three-layer architecture. We prefer the latter since we are working with four data models (conceptual data model, logical data model, internal data model, and external data model) spread across three layers. This should not be confused with a three-tier architecture, which we discuss in Chapter 15.

[4] The conceptual data model is typically not stored in the catalog.

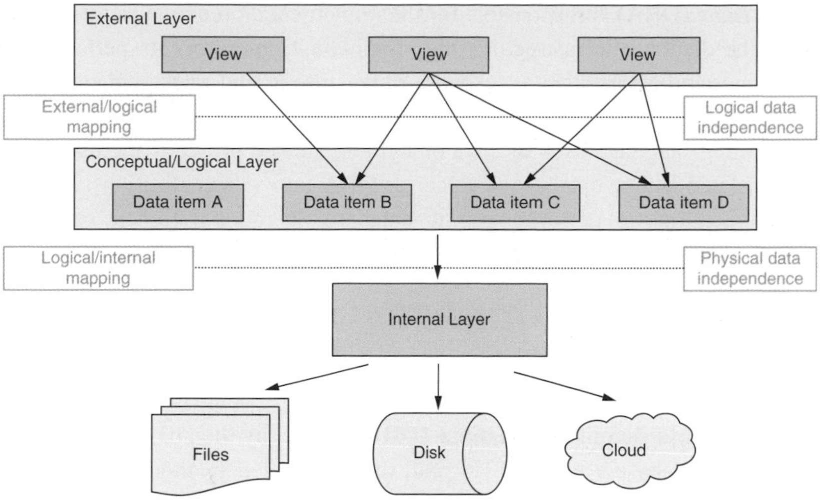


**Figure 1.4** The three-layer database architecture.

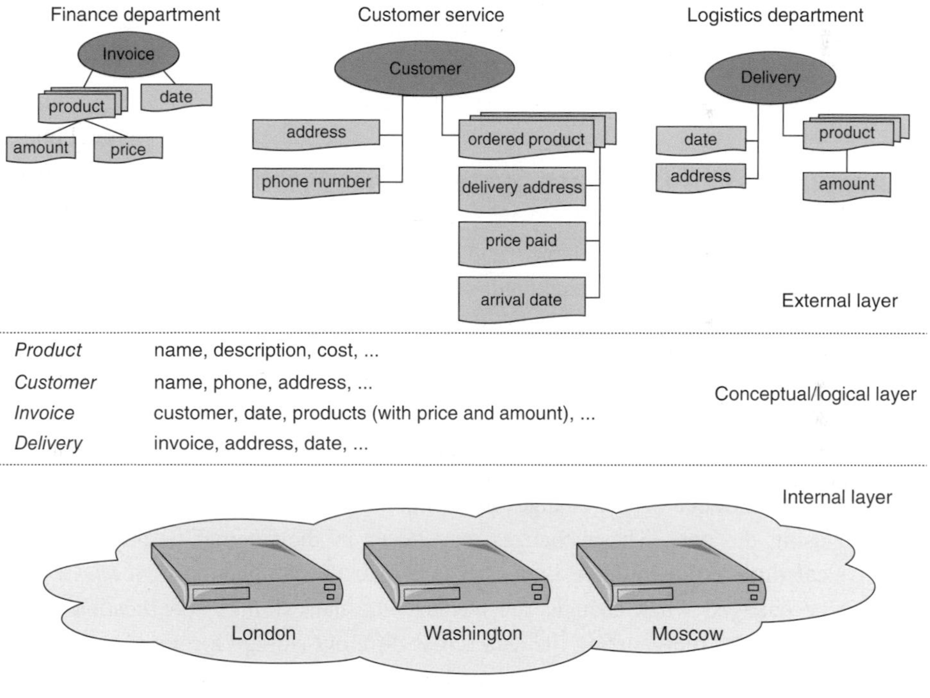


**Figure 1.5** Three-layer database architecture for a business procurement process.

### 1.4.5 Database Users

As we discuss more extensively in Chapter 4, various types of users interact with the database. An *information architect* designs the conceptual data model. He/she closely interacts with the *business user* to make sure the data requirements are fully understood and modeled. A database designer translates the conceptual data model into a logical and internal data model. The *database administrator* (DBA) is responsible for the implementation and monitoring of the database. He/she sets up the database infrastructure and continuously monitors its performance by inspecting key performance indicators such as response times, throughput rates, and storage space consumed (see Section 1.5.9). The *application developer* develops database applications in a general-purpose programming language such as Java or Python. He/she provides the data requirements, which are then translated by the database designer or DBA into view definitions. The business user will run these applications to perform specific database operations. He/she can also directly query the database using interactive querying facilities for reporting purposes.

### 1.4.6 Database Languages

Every DBMS comes with one or more accompanying database languages. The **data definition language (DDL)** is used by the DBA to express the database's external, logical, and internal data models. These definitions are stored in the catalog. The **data manipulation language (DML)** is used to retrieve, insert, delete, and modify data. DML statements can be embedded in a general-purpose programming language, or entered interactively through a front-end querying tool. SQL offers both DDL and DML statements for relational database systems (see Chapter 7).

**Retention Questions**

- What are the key elements of a database system?
- Discuss the three-layer architecture of a database application. Illustrate with an example.
- What is a catalog and why is it needed?

## 1.5 Advantages of Database Systems and Database Management

Databases, if adequately designed and managed, offer advantages such as data independence; managing structured, semi-structured, and unstructured data; database modeling; managing data redundancy; specifying integrity rules; concurrency control; backup and recovery facilities; data security and performance utilities. We elaborate on these elements in this section.

### 1.5.1 Data Independence

**Data independence** means changes in data definitions have minimal to no impact on the applications using the data. These changes may occur in the internal or the conceptual/logical layer. **Physical data independence** implies that neither the applications, views, or logical data model must be changed when changes are made to the data storage specifications in the internal data model. Consider reorganizing the data across different storage locations or media, the definition of new access paths or indexes, etc. The applications will keep running successfully, and may be even faster than they were before because of the physical reorganization of the data. To adequately guarantee physical data independence, the DBMS should provide interfaces between the logical and internal data models.

**Logical data independence** implies that software applications are minimally affected by changes in the conceptual or logical data model. Consider the example of adding new data items, characteristics, or relationships. The views in the external data model will act as a protective shield and mitigate the effect of these modifications on the applications. To guarantee logical data independence, the DBMS must provide interfaces between the conceptual/logical and external layer.

### 1.5.2 Database Modeling

A data model is an explicit representation of the data items together with their characteristics and relationships. It can also include integrity rules and functions. A conceptual data model should provide a formal and perfect mapping of the data requirements of the business process and is made in close collaboration with the business user. It is then translated into a logical data model and, finally, an internal data model. Unfortunately, a best-case scenario with perfect mapping is often unrealistic, and it is important that a data model's assumptions and shortcomings are clearly documented. Popular examples of data models are the hierarchical model, the CODASYL model, the (E)ER model, the relational model, and the object-oriented model. We discuss these more extensively in Chapters 5–8.

### 1.5.3 Managing Structured, Semi-Structured, and Unstructured Data

It is important to note that not all kinds of data can be described according to a formal logical data model. This is only possible for **structured data**, which was the only kind of data the earlier DBMS implementations focused on. With structured data, individual characteristics of data items can be identified and formally specified, such as the number, name, address, and email of a student, or the number and name of a course. The advantage is the ability to express integrity rules and in this way enforce the correctness of the data. As we will discuss in, e.g., Chapters 7–9, it also facilitates searching, processing, and analyzing data, because both the DBMS and the data processing applications have fine-grain control over the data. They can, for example, discriminate between a series of characters representing a student's name and a student's address. In this way, it becomes possible to retrieve, for example, all the names of students that live in New York.

With **unstructured data**, there are no finer-grain components in a file or series of characters that can be interpreted in a meaningful way by a DBMS or application. Consider a long text document containing the biographies of famous New York citizens. In this plain text it is possible to search for the terms "name", "student", and "New York" occurring closely together, but it is impossible to assess whether they pertain to students who lived in New York, students who were born in New York or maybe even students for which the text explains they always wore the same sweater, with the imprint "New York" on it. Moreover, it is not possible to retrieve only the series of characters that represent these students' names. In spite of that, many recent database management systems provide facilities to efficiently store and search such full-text documents. This is especially important, since the volume of unstructured data largely surpasses that of structured data in most organizations. These unstructured data may contain lots of useful information, if they can be extracted efficiently. Consider improving customer interaction by storing and analyzing complaints letters, classifying legal documents according to their content, or assessing the market's sentiment toward a new product by analyzing tweets that refer to the product. Moreover, modern-day DBMSs are not restricted to storing and managing unstructured textual data, but other kinds of data as well, such as still images, video, and audio.

Finally, it should be stressed that not all data are completely structured or completely unstructured. In later chapters we will discuss how recent DBMS types, such as XML databases (Chapter 10) and NoSQL databases (Chapter 11), aim explicitly at dealing efficiently with **semi-structured data**. These are data that have a certain structure, but the structure may be very irregular or highly volatile. Typical examples are individual users' webpages on a large social media platform, or resumé documents in a human resources database, which may loosely exhibit the same structure, but which do not comply entirely with a single, rigid format.

### 1.5.4 Managing Data Redundancy

One of the key drawbacks of the file-based approach to data management is undesirable duplication of data, which can easily lead to inconsistent data. In the database approach, redundant data can be successfully managed. Duplication of data can be desirable in distributed environments to improve data retrieval performance by providing local access to data rather than using resource-intensive network connections. The DBMS is now responsible for the management of the redundancy by providing synchronization facilities to safeguard data consistency. As an example, an update of a local data copy will be automatically propagated to all duplicate data copies stored at other locations. Compared to the file approach, the DBMS guarantees correctness of the data. It also requires no user intervention and is much more efficient and less error-prone.

### 1.5.5 Specifying Integrity Rules

Data integrity rules can also be explicitly defined. These rules can be used to enforce the correctness of the data. Syntactical rules specify how the data should be represented and stored. Examples are: customerID should be represented as an integer (e.g., 100, 125, and 200 are correct, but 1.20 or 2a are not); birth date should be stored as month, day, and year (e.g., 02/27/1975 is correct, but 27/02/1975 is not). Semantic rules focus on the semantic correctness or meaning of the data. Examples are: customerID should be unique; account balance should be bigger than 0; and a customer cannot be deleted if he/she has pending invoices. In the file-based approach, these integrity rules have to be embedded in every single application. In the database approach, they are specified as part of the conceptual/logical data model and are stored centrally in the catalog. This substantially improves the efficiency and maintainability of the applications since the integrity rules are now directly enforced by the DBMS whenever anything is updated. In the file-based approach, the applications themselves have to explicitly manage all integrity rules, resulting into a lot of duplication of code, with the accompanying risk of inconsistencies.

### 1.5.6 Concurrency Control

A DBMS has built-in facilities to support concurrent or parallel execution of database programs, which allows for good performance. A key concept is a database transaction that is a sequence of read/write operations, considered to be an atomic unit in the sense that either all operations are executed or none at all (more details on transactions are provided in Chapter 14). Typically, these read/write operations can be executed at the same time by the DBMS. However, this should be carefully supervised to avoid inconsistencies. Let's illustrate this with an example (Table 1.1).

**Table 1.1** Illustrating concurrency control

| Time | T1 | T2 | Balance |
|---|---|---|---|
| t1 | | Begin transaction | \$100 |
| t2 | Begin transaction | read(balance) | \$100 |
| t3 | read(balance) | balance = balance + 120 | \$100 |
| t4 | balance = balance – 50 | write(balance) | \$220 |
| t5 | write(balance) | End transaction | \$50 |
| t6 | End transaction | | \$50 |

Table 1.1 shows two database transactions: T1 and T2. T1 updates the account balance by withdrawing \$50. T2 deposits \$120. The starting balance is \$100. If both transactions were to run sequentially, instead of in parallel, the ending balance should be \$100 – \$50 + \$120 = \$170. If the DBMS interleaves the actions of both transactions, we get the following. T2 reads the balance at t2 and finds it is \$100. T1 reads the balance at t3 and finds it is \$100. At t3, T2 updates the balance to \$220. However, it still needs to write (or save) this value. At t4, T1 calculates the balance as \$100 – \$50 = \$50 whereas T2 saves the balance, which now becomes \$220. T1 then saves the balance as \$50 at t5. It overwrites the value of \$220 with \$50, after which both transactions are ended. Since T1 updates the balance based on the value it had before the update by T2, and then writes the updated balance after T2 is finished, the update effect of T2 is lost. It is as if transaction T2 did not take place. This is commonly called a lost-update problem. The DBMS should avoid the inconsistencies that emanate from the interference between simultaneous transactions.

To ensure database transactions are processed in a reliable way, the DBMS must support the *ACID* (**A**tomicity, **C**onsistency, **I**solation, **D**urability) properties. *Atomicity*, or the all-or-nothing property, requires that a transaction should either be executed in its entirety or not at all. *Consistency* assures that a transaction brings the database from one consistent state to another. *Isolation* ensures that the effect of concurrent transactions should be the same as if they had been executed in isolation. Finally, *durability* ensures that the database changes made by a transaction declared successful can be made permanent under all circumstances.

**Connections**

Chapter 14 introduces the basics of transactions, transaction management, recovery, and concurrency control. It describes how the interplay between these concepts guarantees concurrent access by different users to shared data. Chapter 16 then further elaborates on this by reviewing distributed transaction management.

## 1.5.7 Backup and Recovery Facilities

A key advantage of using databases is the availability of backup and recovery facilities. These facilities can be used to deal with the effect of loss of data due to hardware or network errors, or bugs in system or application software. Typically, backup facilities can perform either a full or incremental backup. In the latter case, only the updates since the previous backup will be considered. Recovery facilities allow restoration of data to a previous state after loss or damage.

## 1.5.8 Data Security

Data security can be directly enforced by the DBMS. Depending on the business application considered, some users have read access, while others have write access to the data (role-based functionality). This can also be further refined to certain parts of the data. Trends such as e-business, B2B (business-to-business), B2C (business-to-consumer), and CRM stress the importance of data security because they increasingly expose databases to internal and external parties. Consider the example of vendor-managed inventory (VMI), where a company can get access to inventory details of its downstream supply chain partner. Using the right security policies should enforce that only read access is provided and no information from competitor products can be retrieved. Data access can be managed via logins and passwords assigned to users or user accounts. Each account has its own authorization rules that can again be stored in the catalog.

### 1.5.9 Performance Utilities

**Retention Questions**

- What are the advantages of database systems and database management?
- What is data independence and why is it needed?
- What are integrity rules? Illustrate with examples.
- What is the difference between structured, semi-structured, and unstructured data?
- Define the ACID properties in a transaction management context.

Three key performance indicators (KPIs) of a DBMS are: response time; throughput rate; and space utilization. The response time denotes the time elapsed between issuing a database request (e.g., a query or update instruction) and the successful termination thereof. The throughput rate represents the transactions a DBMS can process per unit of time. Space utilization refers to the space utilized by the DBMS to store both the raw data and the metadata. A high-performing DBMS is characterized by quick response times, high throughput rates, and low space utilization.

DBMSs come with various types of utilities aimed at improving these three KPIs. Examples are utilities to distribute and optimize data storage, to tune indexes for faster query execution, to tune queries to improve application performance, or to optimize buffer management (buffering is instrumental to the exchange of data and updates between internal memory and disk storage). These utilities are typically managed by the DBA.

## Summary

We started this chapter by summarizing some key applications of database technology. We defined the concepts of a database, DBMS, and database system. We then reviewed the file approach to data management and contrasted it with the database approach. We reviewed the elements of database systems. We also discussed the advantages of database systems and database management.

**Scenario Conclusion**

Now that Sober understands the dangers of storing data in files and the benefits of using databases, it has invested in database technology.

## Key Terms List

**ACID**
**catalog**
**conceptual data model**
**data definition language (DDL)**
**data independence**
**data manipulation language (DML)**
**database**
**database approach**
**database management system (DBMS)**
**database model**
**database schema**
**database state**
**database system**
**external data model**
**file-based approach**
**internal data model**
**internal layer**
**logical data independence**
**logical data model**
**metadata**
**physical data independence**
**semi-structured data**
**structured data**
**three-layer architecture**
**unstructured data**
**view**

## Review Questions

**1.1.** Which statement is **not correct**?

a. The file-based approach to data management causes the same information to be stored separately for different applications.
b. In a file-based approach to data management, the data definitions are included in each application separately.
c. In a file-based approach to data management, different applications could be using older and newer versions of the same data.
d. In a file-based approach to data management, a change in the structure of a data file is easily handled because each application has its own data files.

**1.2.** Which statement is **not correct**?

a. In a database approach, applications don't have their own files, but all applications access the same version of the data by interfacing with the DBMS.
b. In a database approach, the data definitions or metadata are stored in the applications accessing the data.
c. In a database approach, there is typically less storage needed compared to the file approach.
d. In a database approach, maintenance of data and metadata is easier.

**1.3.** Which statement is **not correct**?

a. In a file-based approach, every application has its own query and access procedures, even if they want to access the same data.
b. SQL is a database language to manage DBMSs without having to write a substantial amount of programming code.
c. SQL is a database language that focuses on how to access and retrieve the data.
d. SQL is a database language that allows different applications to access different subsets of the data necessary for each application.

**1.4.** Which statement is **not correct**?

a. In a conceptual data model, the data requirements from the business should be captured and modeled.
b. A conceptual data model is implementation-dependent.
c. A logical data model translates the conceptual data model to a specific implementation environment.
d. Examples of implementations of logical data models are hierarchical, CODASYL, relational, or object-oriented models.

**1.5.** Complete the following sentence, choosing the right words in positions **A** and **B**. A(n) . . .**A**. . . data model is the mapping of a(n) . . .**B**. . . data model to a model that describes which data are stored where and in what format.

a. A: internal, B: logical.
b. A: conceptual, B: internal.
c. A: logical, B: internal.
d. A: logical, B: conceptual.

**1.6.** What concept specifies the various data items, their characteristics, and relationships, constraints, storage details, etc. and is specified during the database design?

a. Database model.
b. Catalog.

c. Database state.
d. None of the above.

**1.7.** Which statement regarding the database state is **correct**?

a. The database state represents the data in the database when the database is first created.
b. The database state changes when data are updated or removed.
c. The database state specifies the various data items, their characteristics, and relationships, and is specified during the database design.
d. The database state is stored in the catalog.

**1.8.** Complete this sentence: In the three-layer architecture, between the external layer and the conceptual/logical layer, there is . . .

a. physical data independence.
b. logical data independence.
c. no independence, they are basically the same thing.
d. the internal layer.

**1.9.** Which statement is **correct**?

Statement A: The middle layer of the three-layer architecture consists of both the conceptual data model and the logical data model. The logical data model is physically implemented in the internal layer.

Statement B: The top level of the three-layer architecture is the external layer. Views for one or more applications always offer a window on the complete logical model.

a. Only sentence A is right.
b. Only sentence B is right.
c. Sentences A and B are right.
d. Neither A nor B is right.

**1.10.** Which statement is **correct**?

Statement A: DDL is the language used to define the logical data model, but no other data models.

Statement B: SQL is a DML language to retrieve, insert, delete, and modify data. It is stored in the catalog.

a. Only A.
b. Only B.
c. A and B.
d. Neither A nor B.

**1.11.** Which statement is **correct**?

Statement A: Physical data independence implies that neither the applications nor the views or logical data model must be changed when changes are made to the data storage specifications in the internal data model.

Statement B: Logical data independence implies that software applications are minimally affected by changes in the conceptual or logical data model.

a. Only A.
b. Only B.
c. A and B.
d. Neither A nor B.

**1.12.** Consider this rule: "An employee of a department can never earn more than the manager of the department." This is an example of a:

a. syntactical integrity rule.
b. semantical integrity rule.

## Problems and Exercises

1.1E Discuss examples of database applications.

1.2E What are the key differences between the file-based and database approaches to data management?

1.3E Discuss the elements of a database system.

1.4E What are the advantages of database systems and database management?

# 2 Architecture and Categorization of DBMSs

## Chapter Objectives

In this chapter, you will learn to:

- identify the key components of a DBMS architecture;
- understand how these components work together for data storage, processing, and management;
- categorize DBMSs based upon data model, degree of simultaneous access, architecture, and usage.

**Opening Scenario**

To kick-start its business, Sober purchased the customer database of Mellow Cab, a firm that recently stepped out of the taxi business. Unfortunately, the database has been handed over in a legacy CODASYL format that Sober is not familiar with. Sober also needs a new database to store transaction details whenever passengers book either a ride-hailing or ride-sharing service. Other data (e.g., multimedia) are an option they are interested in. Sober wants to continuously store the location of its taxis and periodically review hot-spot pick-up and drop-off locations. Sober is looking at ways to manage all these data sources in the optimal way.

As discussed in Chapter 1, a DBMS supports the creation, usage, and maintenance of a database. It consists of several modules, each with their specific functionality, that work together according to a predefined architecture. In this chapter, we zoom into this internal architecture and provide a categorization of DBMSs along various dimensions. The overview of the chapter is straightforward. We start by discussing the components that together make up a DBMS. Next, we provide a classification of DBMSs in terms of data model, degree of simultaneous access, architecture, and usage.

## 2.1 Architecture of a DBMS

As discussed before, a DBMS needs to support various types of data management-related activities, such as querying and storage. It also must provide interfaces to its environment. To achieve both of these goals, a DBMS is composed of various interacting modules that together make up the **database management system architecture**. Figure 2.1 shows an overview of the key components of a DBMS architecture. We review each component in more detail in what follows.

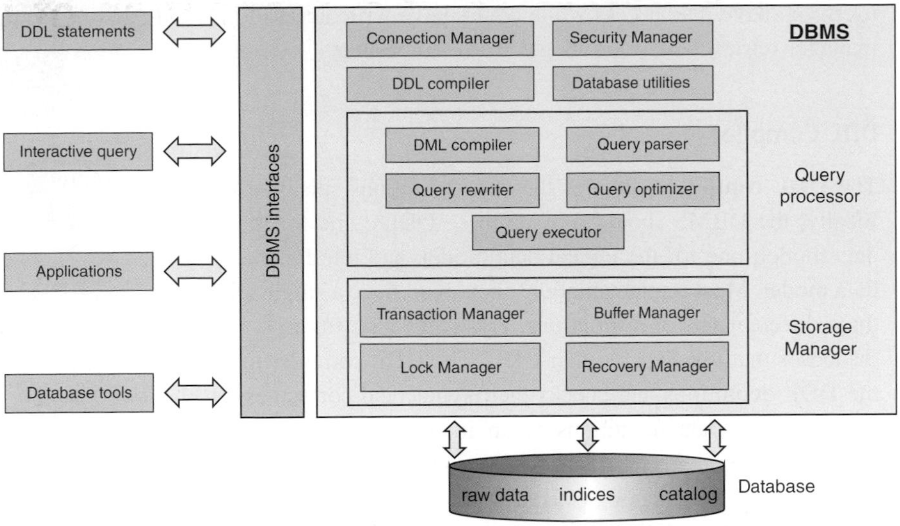


**Figure 2.1** Architecture of a database management system (DBMS).

Figure 2.1 is by no means exhaustive. Depending upon the vendor and implementation, some components may be left out and others added. On the left, you can see various ways of interacting with the DBMS. **DDL statements** create data definitions that are stored in the catalog. **Interactive queries** are typically executed from a front-end tool, such as a command-line interface, simple graphical user interface, or forms-based interface. Applications interact with the DBMS using **embedded DML statements**. Finally, the *database administrator* (DBA) can use various database tools to maintain or fine-tune the DBMS. To facilitate all these usages, the DBMS provides various interfaces that invoke its components. The most important components are: the connection manager; the security manager; the DDL compiler; various database utilities; the query processor; and the storage manager. The query processor consists of a DML compiler, query parser, query rewriter, query optimizer, and query executor. The storage manager includes a transaction manager, buffer manager, lock manager, and recovery manager. All these components interact in various ways depending upon which database task is executed. The database itself contains the raw data or database state and the catalog with the database model and other metadata, including the indexes that are part of the internal data model providing quick access to the data. In the rest of this section we discuss each component more extensively.

### 2.1.1 Connection and Security Manager

The **connection manager** provides facilities to set-up a database connection. It can be set-up locally or through a network, the latter being more common. It verifies the logon credentials, such as user name and password, and returns a connection handle. A database connection can run either as a single process or as a thread within a process. Remember, a thread represents an execution path within a process and represents the smallest unit of processor scheduling. Multiple threads can run within a process and share common resources such as memory. The security manager verifies whether a user has the right privileges to execute the database actions required. For example, some users can have read access while others have write access to certain parts of the data. The security manager retrieves these privileges from the catalog.

### 2.1.2 DDL Compiler

The **DDL compiler** compiles the data definitions specified in DDL. Ideally, the DBMS should provide three DDLs: one for the internal data model; one for the logical data model; and one for the external data model. Most implementations, however, have a single DDL with three different sets of instructions. This is the case for most relational databases that use SQL as their DDL. The DDL compiler first parses the DDL definitions and checks their syntactical correctness. It then translates the data definitions to an internal format and generates errors if required. Upon successful compilation, it registers the data definitions in the catalog, where they can be used by all the other components of the DBMS.

**Connections**

Chapter 7 discusses how SQL can be used to define a logical and external data model in a relational environment. Chapter 13 reviews how SQL can be used to define an internal data model.

### 2.1.3 Query Processor

The **query processor** is one of the most important parts of a DBMS. It assists in the execution of database queries such as retrieval of data, insertion of data, update of data, and removal of data from the database. Although most DBMS vendors have their own proprietary query processor, it usually includes a DML compiler, query parser, query rewriter, query optimizer, and query executor.

#### 2.1.3.1 DML Compiler

The **DML compiler** compiles the data manipulation statements specified in DML. Before we explain its functioning, we need to elaborate on the different types of DML. As discussed in Chapter 1, DML stands for data manipulation language. It provides a set of constructs to select, insert, update, and delete data.

The first data manipulation languages developed were predominantly **procedural DML**. These DML statements explicitly specified how to navigate in the database to locate and modify the data. They usually started by positioning on one specific record or data instance and navigating to other records using memory pointers. Procedural DML is also called **record-at-a-time DML**. DBMSs with procedural DML had no query processor. In other words, the application developer had to explicitly define the query optimization and execution him/herself. To write efficient queries, the developer had to know all the details of the DBMS. This is not a preferred implementation since it complicates the efficiency, transparency, and maintenance of the database applications. Unfortunately, many firms are still struggling with procedural DML applications due to the legacy DBMSs still in use.

**Declarative DML** is a more efficient implementation. Here, the DML statements specify which data should be retrieved or what changes should be made, rather than how this should be done. The DBMS then autonomously determines the physical execution in terms of access path and navigational strategy. In other words, the DBMS hides the implementation details from the application developer, which facilitates the development of database applications. Declarative DML is usually

**set-at-a-time DML**, whereby sets of records or data instances can be retrieved at once and provided to the application. Only the selection criteria are provided to the DBMS; depending on the actual database state, zero, one, or many records will qualify. A popular example of declarative DML is SQL, which we discuss extensively in Chapter 7.

Many applications work with data stored in a database. To access a database and work with it, DML statements will be directly embedded in the host language. The host language is the general-purpose programming language that contains the (non-database related) application logic. Obviously, both host language and DML should be able to successfully interact and exchange data.

As an example, think about a Java application that needs to retrieve employee data from a database. It can do this by using SQL, which is one of the most popular querying languages used in the industry nowadays. In the following Java program, the SQL DML statements are highlighted in bold face.

```
import java.sql.*;
public class JDBCExample1 {
public static void main(String[] args) {
try {
  System.out.println("Loading JDBC driver...");
  Class.forName("com.mysql.jdbc.Driver");
  System.out.println("JDBC driver loaded!");
} catch (ClassNotFoundException e) {
  throw new RuntimeException(e);
}
String url = "jdbc:mysql://localhost:3306/employeeschema";
String username = "root";
String password = "mypassword123";
String query = "select E.Name, D.DName " +
"from employee E, department D " +
"where E.DNR = D.DNR;";
Connection connection = null;
Statement stmt = null;
try {
  System.out.println("Connecting to database");
  connection = DriverManager.getConnection(url, username, password);
  System.out.println("MySQL Database connected!");
  stmt = connection.createStatement();
  ResultSet rs = stmt.executeQuery(query);
  while (rs.next()) {
    System.out.print(rs.getString(1));
    System.out.print("");
    System.out.println(rs.getString(2));
  }
  stmt.close();
} catch (SQLException e) {
  System.out.println(e.toString());
```

```
} finally {
  System.out.println("Closing the connection.");
  if (connection != null) {
  try {
  connection.close();
} catch (SQLException ignore) {}}}}
```

Without going into any language or syntax specifics, this Java application first initiates a database connection with a given username and password. Next, the application executes an SQL query that asks for the employee names together with their department names. It then iterates through the results, whereby at each step the employee name and corresponding department name are displayed on the screen.

Embedding DML statements into a host language is not as straightforward as it may at first seem. The data structures of the DBMS and the DML may differ from the data structures of the host language. In our example, we used Java, which is an object-oriented host language, and combined it with MySQL, which is a relational DBMS using SQL DML. The mapping between object-oriented and relational concepts is often called the impedance mismatch problem. It can be solved in various ways. First, we can choose a host language and DBMS with comparable data structures. In other words, we combine Java with an object-oriented DBMS, which allows transparent retrieval and storage of data. As an alternative, we could also opt to use middleware to map the data structures from the DBMS to the host language and vice versa. Both options have their pros and cons and are discussed more extensively in Chapter 8.

**Connections**

Chapter 5 introduces hierarchical and CODASYL data models which both assume procedural, record-at-a-time DML. Chapter 7 reviews SQL, which is declarative, set-at-time DML.

Figure 2.2 shows the impedance mismatch problem. On the left, we have a Java class Employee with characteristics such as EmployeeID, Name, Gender, and DNR (which is the department number). It also has "getter" and "setter" methods to implement the object-oriented principle of information hiding. To the right, we have the corresponding SQL DDL that essentially stores information in a tabular format.

**Java**

```
public class Employee {
private int EmployeeID;
private String Name;
private String Gender;
private int DNR;

public int getEmployeeID() {
return EmployeeID;
}
public  void  setEmployeeID( int id ) {
this.EmployeeID = id;
}
public String getName() {
return Name;
}
public void setName( String name ) {
this.Name = name;
}
...}
```

**SQL**

```
CREATE TABLE Employee (
'EmployeeID' INT NOT NULL,
'Name' VARCHAR(45) NULL,
'Gender' VARCHAR(45) NULL,
'DNR' INT NULL)
```

| EmployeeID | Name | Gender | DNR |
|---|---|---|---|
| 100 | Bart Baesens | Male | 2 |
| 110 | Wilfried Lemahieu | Male | 4 |
| 120 | Seppe vanden Broucke | Male | 6 |
| ... | | | |

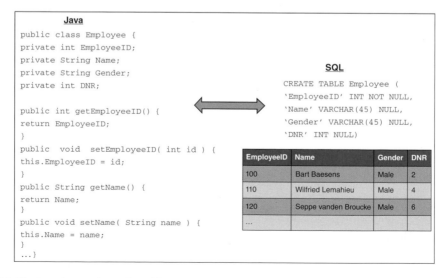

**Figure 2.2** The impedance mismatch problem.

The DML compiler starts by extracting the DML statements from the host language. It then closely collaborates with the query parser, query rewriter, query optimizer, and query executor for executing the DML statements. Errors are generated and reported if necessary.

#### 2.1.3.2 Query Parser and Query Rewriter

The query parser parses the query into an *internal representation format* that can then be further evaluated by the system. It checks the query for syntactical and semantical correctness. To do so, it uses the catalog to verify whether the data concepts referred to are properly defined there, and to see whether the integrity rules have been respected. Again, errors are generated and reported if necessary. The **query rewriter** optimizes the query, independently of the current database state. It simplifies it using a set of predefined rules and heuristics that are DBMS-specific. In a relational database management system, nested queries might be reformulated or flattened to join queries. We discuss both types of queries more extensively in Chapter 7.

#### 2.1.3.3 Query Optimizer

The **query optimizer** is a very important component of the query processor. It optimizes the query based upon the current database state. It can make use of predefined indexes that are part of the internal data model and provide quick access to the data. The query optimizer comes up with various query execution plans and evaluates their cost (in terms of resources required) by aggregating the estimated number of input/output operations, the plan's estimated CPU processing cost and the plan's estimated execution time into the total estimated response time. A good execution plan should have a low response time. It is important to note that the response time is estimated and not exact. The estimates are made using catalog information combined with statistical inference procedures. Empirical distributions of the data are calculated and summarized by their means, standard deviations, etc. Coming up with accurate estimates is crucial in a good query optimizer. Finding an optimal execution path is essentially a classical search or optimization problem whereby techniques such as dynamic programming can be used. As already mentioned, the implementation of the query optimizer depends upon the type of DBMS and the vendor, and is a key competitive asset.

#### 2.1.3.4 Query Executor

The result of the query optimization procedure is a final execution plan which is then handed over to the query executor. The **query executor** takes care of the actual execution by calling on the storage manager to retrieve the data requested.

### 2.1.4 Storage Manager

The **storage manager** governs physical file access and as such supervises the correct and efficient storage of data. It consists of a transaction manager, buffer manager, lock manager, and recovery manager. Let's zoom in for more detail.

#### 2.1.4.1 Transaction Manager

The **transaction manager** supervises the execution of database transactions. Remember, a database transaction is a sequence of read/write operations considered to be an atomic unit.

The transaction manager creates a schedule with interleaved read/write operations to improve overall efficiency and execution performance. It also guarantees the atomicity, consistency, isolation and durability or ACID properties in a multi-user environment (see Chapter 1). The transaction manager will "commit" a transaction upon successful execution, so the effects can be made permanent, and "rollback" a transaction upon unsuccessful execution, so any inconsistent or bad data can be avoided.

#### 2.1.4.2 Buffer Manager

The **buffer manager** is responsible for managing the buffer memory of the DBMS. This is part of the internal memory, which the DBMS checks first when data need to be retrieved. Retrieving data from the buffer is significantly faster than retrieving them from external disk-based storage. The buffer manager is responsible for intelligently caching the data in the buffer for speedy access. It needs to continuously monitor the buffer and decide which content should be removed and which should be added. If data in the buffer have been updated, it must also synchronize the corresponding physical file(s) on disk to make sure updates are made persistent and are not lost. A simple buffering strategy is based upon data locality that states that data recently retrieved are likely to be retrieved again. Another strategy uses the 20/80 law, which implies that 80% of the transactions read or write only 20% of the data. When the buffer is full, the buffer manager needs to adopt a smart replacement strategy to decide which content should be removed. Furthermore, it must be able to serve multiple transactions simultaneously. Hence, it closely interacts with the lock manager to provide concurrency control support.

#### 2.1.4.3 Lock Manager

The **lock manager** is an essential component for providing concurrency control, which ensures data integrity at all times. Before a transaction can read or write a database object, it must acquire a lock which specifies what types of data operations the transaction can carry out. Two common types of locks are read and write locks. A **read lock** allows a transaction to read a database object, whereas a **write lock** allows a transaction to update it. To enforce transaction atomicity and consistency, a locked database object may prevent other transactions from using it, hence avoiding conflicts between transactions that involve the same data. The lock manager is responsible for assigning, releasing, and recording locks in the catalog. It makes use of a *locking protocol*, which describes the locking rules, and a lock table with the lock information.

#### 2.1.4.4 Recovery Manager

The **recovery manager** supervises the correct execution of database transactions. It keeps track of all database operations in a logfile, and will be called upon to undo actions of aborted transactions or during crash recovery.

**Connections**

Chapter 14 elaborates further on the activities of the transaction, buffer, lock, and recovery managers.

### 2.1.5 DBMS Utilities

Besides the components we discussed before, a DBMS also comes with various utilities. A **loading utility** supports the loading of the database with information from a variety of sources, such as another DBMS, text files, Excel files, etc. A **reorganization utility** automatically reorganizes the data for improved performance. **Performance monitoring utilities** report various key performance indicators (KPIs), such as storage space consumed, query response times, and transaction throughput rates to monitor the performance of a DBMS. **User management utilities** support the creation of user groups or accounts, and the assignment of privileges to them. Finally, a **backup and recovery utility** is typically included.

### 2.1.6 DBMS Interfaces

A DBMS needs to interact with various parties, such as a database designer, a database administrator, an application, or even an end-user. To facilitate this communication, it provides various **user interfaces** such as a *web-based interface*, a *stand-alone query language interface*, a *command-line interface*, a *forms-based interface*, a *graphical user interface*, a *natural language interface*, an *application programming interface* (API), an *admin interface*, and a *network interface*.

Figure 2.3 shows an example of the MySQL Workbench interface. You can see the navigator window with the management, instance, performance, and schemas section. The query window provides an editor to write SQL queries. In our case, we wrote a simple SQL query to ask for all information from the product table. The results window displays the results of the execution of the query. The log window provides a log with actions and possible errors.

**Retention Questions**

- What are the key components of a DBMS?
- What is the difference between procedural and declarative DML?
- Give some examples of DBMS utilities and interfaces.

## 2.2 Categorization of DBMSs

Given the proliferation of DBMSs available, in this section we introduce a categorization according to various criteria. We discuss categorization of DBMSs based upon data model, simultaneous

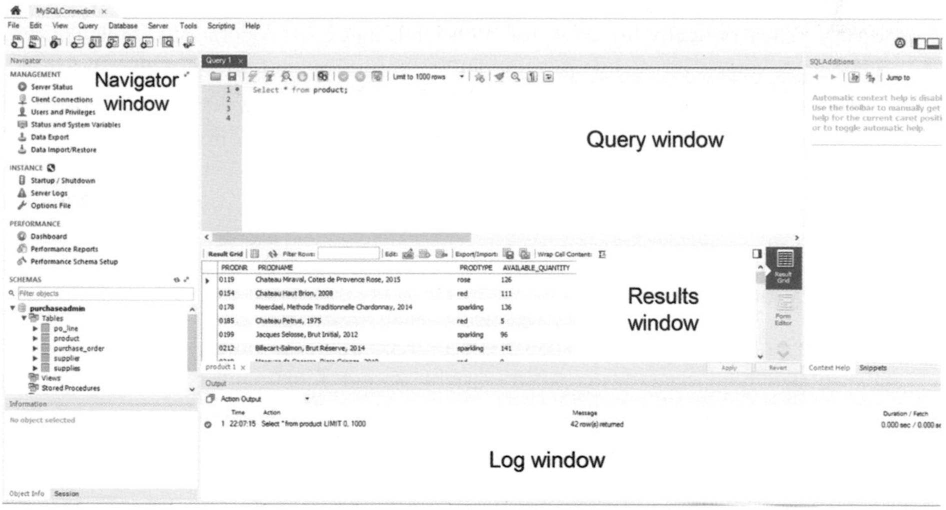


**Figure 2.3** MySQL interface.

access, architecture, and usage. Note that our categorization is not to be interpreted in an exhaustive or exclusive way. It can thus be that a DBMS falls into multiple categories simultaneously. Other categories may also be considered.

## 2.2.1 Categorization Based on Data Model

Throughout the past decades, various types of data models have been introduced for building conceptual and logical data models. We briefly summarize them here and provide more detail in later chapters.

### 2.2.1.1 Hierarchical DBMSs

**Hierarchical DBMSs** were one of the first DBMS types developed, and adopt a tree-like data model. The DML is procedural and record-oriented. No query processor is included. The definitions of the logical and internal data model are intertwined, which is not desirable from a usability, efficiency, or maintenance perspective. Popular examples are IMS from IBM and the Registry in Microsoft Windows.

### 2.2.1.2 Network DBMSs

**Network DBMSs** use a network data model, which is more flexible than a tree-like data model. One of the most popular types are CODASYL DBMSs, which implement the CODASYL data model. Again, the DML is procedural and record-oriented, and no query processor is available. Consequently, the definitions of the logical and internal data models are also intertwined. Popular examples are CA-IDMS from Computer Associates, UDS from Siemens Nixdorf, DMS 1100 from Unisys, and Image from HP. Both hierarchical and CODASYL DBMSs are legacy database software.

### 2.2.1.3 Relational DBMSs

**Relational DBMSs (RDBMSs)** use the relational data model and are the most popular in the industry. They typically use SQL for both DDL and DML operations. SQL is declarative and set oriented. A query processor is provided to optimize and execute the database queries. Data independence is available thanks to a strict separation between the logical and internal data model. This makes it very attractive to develop powerful database applications. Popular examples are MySQL, which is open-source and maintained by Oracle, the Oracle DBMS also provided by Oracle, DB2 from IBM, and Microsoft SQL Server from Microsoft.

### 2.2.1.4 Object-Oriented DBMSs

**Object-oriented DBMSs (OODBMSs)** are based upon the object-oriented data model. An object encapsulates both data (also called variables) and functionality (also called methods). When combining an OODBMS with an object-oriented programming language (e.g., Java, Python), there is no impedance mismatch since the objects can be transparently stored and retrieved from the database. Examples of OODBMSs are db4o, which is an open-source OODBMS maintained by Versant, Caché from Intersystems, and GemStone/S from GemTalk Systems. OODBMSs are not very popular in the industry, beyond some niche markets, due to their complexity.

#### 2.2.1.5 Object-Relational/Extended Relational DBMSs

An **object-relational DBMS (ORDBMS)**, also commonly called an **extended relational DBMS (ERDBMS)**, uses a relational model extended with object-oriented concepts, such as user-defined types, user-defined functions, collections, inheritance, and behavior. Hence, an ORDBMS/ ERDBMS shares characteristics with both an RDBMS and an OODBMS. As with pure relational DBMSs, the DML is SQL, which is declarative and set oriented. A query processor is available for query optimization. Most relational DBMSs such as Oracle, DB2, and Microsoft SQL Server incorporate object-relational extensions.

#### 2.2.1.6 XML DBMSs

**XML DBMSs** use the XML data model to store data. XML is a data representation standard. Here you can see an example of an XML fragment.

```
<employee>
      <firstname>Bart</firstname>
      <lastname>Baesens</lastname>
      <address>
            <street>Naamsestraat</street>
            <number>69</number>
            <zipcode>3000</zipcode>
            <city>Leuven</city>
            <country>Belgium</country>
      </address>
      <gender>Male</gender>
</employee>
```

You can see we have various tags, such as employee, firstname, lastname, etc. The address tag is further subdivided into street, number, zip code, city, and country tags. It is important that every <tag> is properly closed with a </tag>. An XML specification essentially represents data in a hierarchical way. Figure 2.4 shows the tree corresponding to our XML specification.

XML is a very popular standard to exchange data between various applications. Native XML DBMSs (e.g., BaseX, eXist) store XML data by using the logical, intrinsic structure of the XML document. More specifically, they map the hierarchical or tree structure of an XML document to a physical storage structure. XML-enabled DBMSs (e.g., Oracle, IBM DB2) are existing RDBMSs or ORDBMSs that are extended with facilities to store XML data and structured data in an integrated and transparent way. Both types of DBMSs also provide facilities to query XML data.

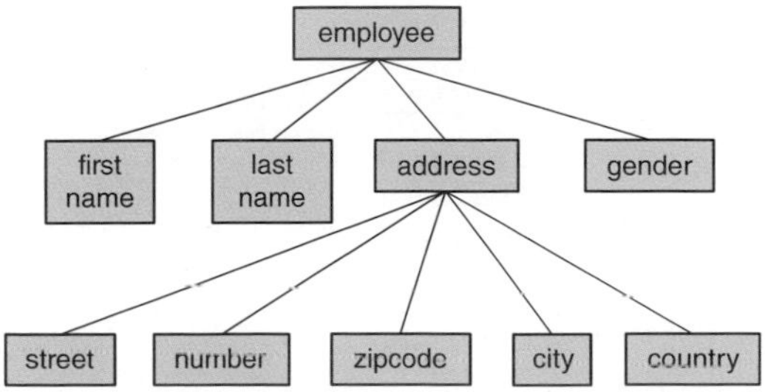


**Figure 2.4** Tree-based XML representation.

#### 2.2.1.7 NoSQL DBMSs

Finally, the last few years brought us a realm of new database technologies targeted at storing big and unstructured data. These are often referred to using the umbrella term **not-only SQL (NoSQL)** databases with popular examples such as Apache Hadoop or Neo4j. As we explain in Chapter 11, NoSQL databases can be classified according to data model into key–value stores, tuple, or document stores, column-oriented databases, and graph databases. However, even within such subcategories, the heterogeneity of the members is quite high. The common denominator of all NoSQL databases is that they attempt to make up for some shortcomings of relational DBMSs in terms of scalability and the ability to cope with irregular or highly volatile data structures.

**Connections**

Chapter 5 reviews both hierarchical and network DBMSs. Chapters 6 and 7 discuss relational DBMSs. Object-oriented DBMSs are covered in Chapter 8, whereas Chapter 9 reviews object-relational DBMSs. XML DBMSs are introduced in Chapter 10. Chapter 11 discusses NoSQL DBMSs.

### 2.2.2 Categorization Based on Degree of Simultaneous Access

DBMSs can also be categorized based upon the degree of **simultaneous access**. In a **single-user system**, only one user at a time is allowed to work with the DBMS. This is not desirable in a networked environment. **Multi-user systems** allow multiple users to simultaneously interact with the database in a distributed environment, as illustrated in Figure 2.5 where three clients are being served by three server instances or threads.

To do so successfully, the DBMS should support multi-threading and provide facilities for concurrency control. A dispatcher component then typically distributes the incoming database requests among server instances or threads.

### 2.2.3 Categorization Based on Architecture

The architectural development of DBMSs is similar to that of computer systems in general. In a **centralized DBMS architecture**, the data are maintained on a centralized host, e.g., a mainframe system. All queries will then have to be processed by this single host.

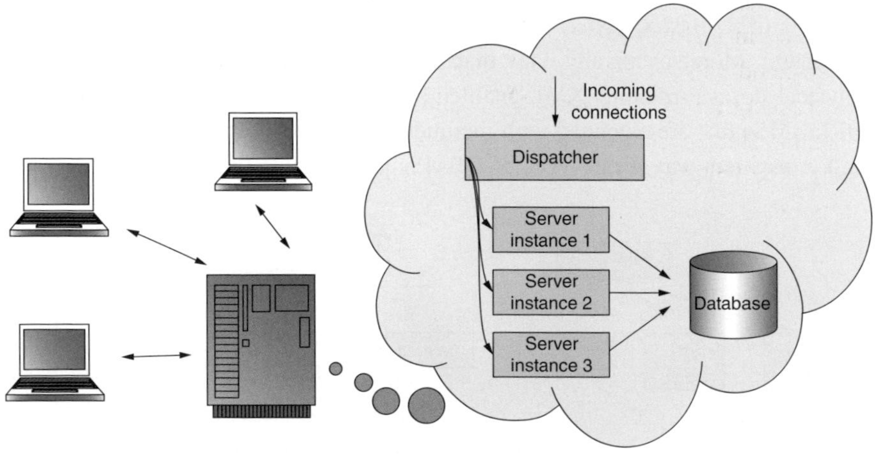


**Figure 2.5** Simultaneous access to a DBMS.

In a **client–server DBMS architecture**, active clients request services from passive servers. A *fat client variant* stores more processing functionality on the client, whereas a *fat server variant* puts more on the server.

The **n-tier DBMS architecture** is a straightforward extension of the client–server architecture. A popular example is a client with GUI (graphical user interface) functionality, an application server with the various applications, a database server with the DBMS and database, and a web server for the web-based access. The communication between these various servers is then handled by middleware.

In a **cloud DBMS architecture**, the DBMS and database are hosted by a third-party cloud provider. The data can then be distributed across multiple computers in a network. Although this is sometimes a cost-effective solution, depending on the context it can perform less efficiently in terms of processing queries or other database transactions. Popular examples are the Apache Cassandra project and Google's BigTable.

A **federated DBMS** is a DBMS that provides a uniform interface to multiple underlying data sources such as other DBMSs, file systems, document management systems, etc. By doing so, it hides the underlying storage details (in particular the distribution and possible heterogeneity of data formats and data management functionality) to facilitate data access.

An **in-memory DBMS** stores all data in internal memory instead of slower external storage such as disk-based storage. It is often used for real-time purposes, such as in Telco or defense applications. Periodic snapshots to external storage can be taken to support data persistence. A popular example of an in-memory DBMS is SAP's Hana product.

### 2.2.4 Categorization Based on Usage

DBMSs can also be categorized based on usage. In what follows, we discuss operational versus strategic usage, Big Data and analytics, multimedia DBMSs, spatial DBMSs, sensor DBMSs, mobile DBMSs, and open-source DBMSs.

**On-line transaction processing (OLTP) DBMSs** focus on managing operational or transactional data. Think of a point-of-sale (POS) application in a supermarket, where data about each purchase transaction such as customer information, products purchased, prices paid, location of the purchase, and timing of the purchase need to be stored. In these settings, the database server must be able to process lots of simple transactions per unit of time. Also, the transactions are initiated in real-time, simultaneously, by many users and applications, hence the DBMS must have good support for processing a high volume of short, simple queries. **On-line analytical processing (OLAP) DBMSs** focus on using operational data for tactical or strategical decision-making. Here, a limited number of users formulates complex queries to analyze huge amounts of data. The DBMS should support the efficient processing of these complex queries, which often come in smaller volumes.

Big data and analytics are all around these days (see Chapters 19 and 20). IBM projects that we generate 2.5 quintillion bytes of data every day. This is a lot compared to traditional database applications. Hence, new database technologies have been introduced to efficiently cope with Big Data. NoSQL is one of these newer technologies. **NoSQL databases** abandon the well-known and popular relational database schema in favor of a more flexible, or even schema-less, database structure. This is especially handy to store unstructured information such as emails, text documents, Twitter tweets, Facebook posts, etc. One of their key advantages is that they also scale more easily in terms of storage capacity. We already mentioned four popular types of

NoSQL database technologies, classified according to data model: key–value-based databases such as CouchDB; document-based databases such as MongoDB; column-based databases such as Cassandra; and graph-based databases such as Neo4j. We discuss these in more detail in Chapter 11.

**Multimedia DBMSs** allow for the storage of multimedia data such as text, images, audio, video, 3D games, CAD designs, etc. They should also provide content-based query facilities such as "find images of Bart" or "find images of people who look like Bart". Streaming facilities should also be included to stream multimedia output. These are very resource-intensive transactions that may require specific hardware support. Note that multimedia data are usually stored as a binary large object (BLOB), supported by most modern-day commercial DBMSs.

A **spatial DBMS** supports the storage and querying of spatial data. This could include both 2D objects (e.g., points, lines, and polygons) and 3D objects. Spatial operations such as calculating distances or relationships between objects (e.g., whether one object is contained within another, intersects with another, is detached from another, etc.) are provided. Spatial databases are a key building block of geographical information systems (GIS). Most commercial DBMS vendors offer facilities for spatial data management.

A **sensor DBMS** manages sensor data such as biometric data obtained from wearables, or telematics data which continuously record driving behavior. Ideally, it has facilities to formulate application-specific queries such as spatial–temporal queries that ask for the shortest path between two locations given the current state of the traffic. Most modern-day DBMSs provide support for storing sensor data.

**Mobile DBMSs** are the DBMSs running on smartphones, tablets, and other mobile devices. They should always be online, have a small footprint, and be able to deal with limited processing power, storage, and battery life. Depending upon the context, they could connect and synchronize to a central DBMS. Ideally, they should be capable of handling queries and support self-management without the intervention of a DBA. Some popular examples are: Oracle Lite, Sybase SQL Anywhere, Microsoft SQL Server Compact, SQLite, and IBM DB2 Everyplace.

**Retention Questions**

- How can DBMSs be categorized based on data model?
- How can DBMSs be categorized based on usage?

Finally, **open-source DBMSs** are DBMSs for which the code is publicly available and can be extended by anyone. This has the advantage of having a large development community working on the product. They are very popular for small business settings and in developing countries where budgets are limited. Most of the open-source DBMSs can be obtained from www.sourceforge.net, which is a well-known website for open-source software. Some examples are: MySQL, which is a relational DBMS maintained by Oracle; PostgresSQL, which is also relational and maintained by the PostgresSQL Global Development Group; Twig, which is an object-oriented DBMS maintained by Google; and Perst, which is also an OODBMS maintained by McObject.

**Drill Down**

Spotify streams more than 24 million songs to more than 40 million users worldwide. It needed a database solution which ensures data availability at all times, even in the event of crashes or bugs. It turned to Apache Cassandra as the database technology of choice since its cloud-based architecture ensures high availability.

### Drill Down

Gartner[1] estimates that by 2018 more than 70% of new applications will be developed using open-source DBMSs. This clearly illustrates that open-source solutions have significantly matured into viable and robust alternatives to their commercial counterparts.

## Summary

In this chapter we first zoomed in on the architecture of a DBMS. We discussed the components that together comprise a DBMS. We illustrated how they collaborate for data storage, processing, and management.

Next, we provided a categorization of DBMSs in terms of data model, degree of simultaneous access, architecture, and usage. This categorization is by no means exhaustive or exclusive since a DBMS can support various functionalities simultaneously. It is just handy to set the stage for the later chapters that provide more detail.

### Scenario Conclusion

The CODASYL customer database Sober received from Mellow Cab is an example of a network database. To retrieve the customer information, Sober will have to work with record-at-a-time and procedural DML, which is not efficient. Another option is that Sober could load the data into an RDBMS where it could access it in a more friendly way using SQL, which is set-at-time and declarative DML. If it would also like to store images of its taxis and other multimedia data, it could even contemplate using an ORDBMS instead. Storing the location of Sober's taxis is an example of a Big Data application where NoSQL databases can come in handy. Alternatively, a DBMS capable of storing sensor data can be considered as well. To continuously monitor the geographical positioning of its fleet, Sober might consider the development of a GIS built on top of a spatial database. The transaction information about ride-hailing and ride-sharing taxis should be stored using an OLTP database, whereas the analysis of hot-spot pick-up and drop-off locations could be implemented using OLAP facilities.

## Key Terms List

**backup and recovery utility**
**buffer manager**
**centralized DBMS architecture**
**client–server DBMS architecture**
**cloud DBMS architecture**
**connection manager**
**database management system architecture**
**DDL compiler**
**DDL statements**
**declarative DML**

[1] www.forbes.com/sites/benkerschberg/2016/03/08/how-postgres-and-open-source-are-disrupting-the-market-for-database-management-systems/#1d9cca320a3d.

**DML compiler**
**embedded DML statements**
**extended relational DBMS (ERDBMS)**
**federated DBMS**
**hierarchical DBMSs**
**in-memory DBMS**
**interactive queries**
**loading utility**
**lock manager**
**mobile DBMSs**
**multimedia DBMSs**
**multi-user systems**
**network DBMSs**
**Not-only SQL (NoSQL)**
**n-tier DBMS architecture**
**object-oriented DBMS (OODBMS)**
**object-relational DBMS (ORDBMS)**
**on-line analytical processing (OLAP) DBMSs**
**on-line transaction processing (OLTP) DBMSs**
**open-source DBMSs**
**performance monitoring utilities**
**procedural DML**
**query executor**
**query optimizer**
**query parser**
**query processor**
**query rewriter**
**read lock**
**record-at-a-time DML**
**recovery manager**
**relational DBMSs (RDBMS)**
**reorganization utility**
**sensor DBMS**
**set-at-a-time DML**
**simultaneous access**
**single-user system**
**spatial DBMS**
**storage manager**
**transaction manager**
**user interface**
**user management utilities**
**write lock**
**XML DBMS**

## Review Questions

**2.1.** Which of these is part of the query processor in the architecture of a DBMS?

a. DDL compiler.
b. DML compiler.
c. Transaction manager.
d. Security manager.

**2.2.** Which of these is **not** part of the storage manager in the DBMS architecture?

a. Connection manager.
b. Transaction manager.
c. Buffer manager.
d. Recovery manager.

**2.3.** Which statement(s) is/are correct?

Statement A: The DDL compiler compiles data definitions specified in DDL. It is possible that there is only one DDL with three instruction sets.

Statement B: The first step of the DDL compiler is to translate the DDL definitions.

a. Only A.
b. Only B.

c. A and B.
d. Neither A nor B.

**2.4.** Which statement(s) is/are correct?

Statement A: There is no query processor available in procedural DML.

Statement B: With procedural DML, the DBMS determines the access path and navigational strategy to locate and modify the data specified in the query.

a. Only A.
b. Only B.
c. A and B.
d. Neither A nor B.

**2.5.** Evaluate the following statements:

1. Record-at-a-time DML means that the query gets recorded from the user at the time the user inputs the query and then gets processed.
2. Record-at-a-time DML means that navigating the database starts with positioning on one specific record and going from there onwards to other records.
3. Set-at-a-time DML means that the query gets set beforehand and then gets processed by the DBMS.
4. Set-at-a-time DML means that many records can be retrieved in one DML statement.

a. 1 and 3 are right.
b. 2 and 3 are right.
c. 1 and 4 are right.
d. 2 and 4 are right.

**2.6.** Which statement(s) is/are correct?

Statement A: The impedance mismatch problem can be solved by using middleware to map data structures between the DBMS and the DDL statements.

Statement B: An object-oriented host language such as Java combined with a document-oriented DBMS such as MongoDB does not require mapping objects to documents and vice versa.

a. Only A.
b. Only B.
c. A and B.
d. Neither A nor B.

**2.7.** Which statement(s) is/are correct?

Statement A: The query parser optimizes and simplifies a query and then passes it on to the query executor.

Statement B: In the DBMS architecture, the storage manager takes care of concurrency control.

a. Only A.
b. Only B.
c. A and B
d. Neither A nor B.

**2.8.** Fill in the gaps in the following sentences:

When, during crash recovery, aborted transactions need to be undone, that is a task of the ...**A**...

The part of the storage manager that guarantees the ACID properties is the ...**B**...

a. A: lock manager, B: recovery manager.
b. A: lock manager, B: lock manager.
c. A: recovery manager, B: buffer manager.
d. A: recovery manager, B: transaction manager.

**2.9.** CODASYL is an example of . . .

a. a hierarchical DBMS.
b. a network DBMS.
c. a relational DBMS.
d. an object-oriented DBMS.

**2.10.** Which of the following DBMS types is **not** a classification based on a data model?

a. Hierarchical DBMS.
b. Network DBMS.
c. Cloud DBMS.
d. Object-relational DBMS.

**2.11.** Which statement(s) is/are correct?

Statement A: In a hierarchical DBMS, DML is declarative and set oriented with a query processor.

Statement B: In a relational DBMS, there is data independence between the conceptual and internal data model.

a. Only A.
b. Only B.
c. A and B.
d. Neither A nor B

**2.12.** If you want to use a DBMS architecture that can access multiple data sources itself and provides a uniform interface hiding the low-level details, the most appropriate DBMS would be a(n). . .

a. n-tier DBMS.
b. cloud DBMS.
c. client–server DBMS.
d. federated DBMS.

**2.13.** Which statement(s) is/are correct?

Statement A: An OLTP system is able to cope with real-time, simultaneous transactions that the database server is able to process in a large volume.

Statement B: An OLAP system uses large amounts of operational data to run complex queries on and provide insights for tactical and strategic decision-making.

a. Only A.
b. Only B
c. A and B.
d. Neither A nor B.

**2.14.** Which statement(s) is/are correct?

Statement A: Native XML DBMSs map the hierarchical structure of an XML document to a physical storage structure, because they are able to use the intrinsic structure of an XML document.

Statement B: XML-enabled DBMSs are able to store XML data in an integrated and transparent way, because they are able to use the intrinsic structure of an XML document.

a. Only A.
b. Only B.
c. A and B.
d. Neither A nor B.

## Problems and Exercises

2.1E What are the key components of a DBMS architecture and how do they collaborate?

2.2E What is the difference between procedural and declarative DML?

2.3E Why is it important that a DBMS has a good query optimizer?

2.4E Give some examples of DBMS utilities and interfaces.

2.5E How can DBMSs be categorized in terms of the following?

- data model
- degree of simultaneous access
- architecture
- usage

# 3 Conceptual Data Modeling Using the (E)ER Model and UML Class Diagram

## Chapter Objectives

In this chapter, you will learn to:

- understand the different phases of database design: conceptual design, logical design, and physical design;
- build a conceptual data model using the ER model and understand the limitations thereof;
- build a conceptual data model using the EER model and understand the limitations thereof;
- build a conceptual data model using the UML class diagram and understand the limitations thereof.

**Opening Scenario**

Sober has decided to invest in a new database and begin a database design process. As a first step, it wants to formalize the data requirements in a conceptual data model. Sober asks you to build both an EER and a UML data model for its business setting. It also wants you to extensively comment on both models and properly indicate their shortcomings.

In this chapter we start by zooming out and reviewing the database design process. We elaborate on conceptual, logical, and physical database design. We continue the chapter with conceptual design, which aims at elucidating the data requirements of a business process in a formal way. We discuss three types of conceptual data models: the ER model; the EER model; and the UML class diagram. Each model is first defined in terms of its fundamental building blocks. Various examples are included for clarification. We also discuss the limitations of the three conceptual data models and contrast them in terms of their expressive power and modeling semantics. Subsequent chapters continue from the conceptual data models of this chapter and map them to logical and internal data models.

## 3.1 Phases of Database Design

Designing a database is a multi-step process, as illustrated in Figure 3.1. It starts from a **business process**. As an example, think about a B2B procurement application, invoice handling process, logistics process, or salary administration. A first step is **requirement collection and analysis**, where the aim is to carefully understand the different steps and data needs of the process. The information architect (see Chapter 4) will collaborate with the business user to elucidate the database requirements. Various techniques can be used, such as interviews or

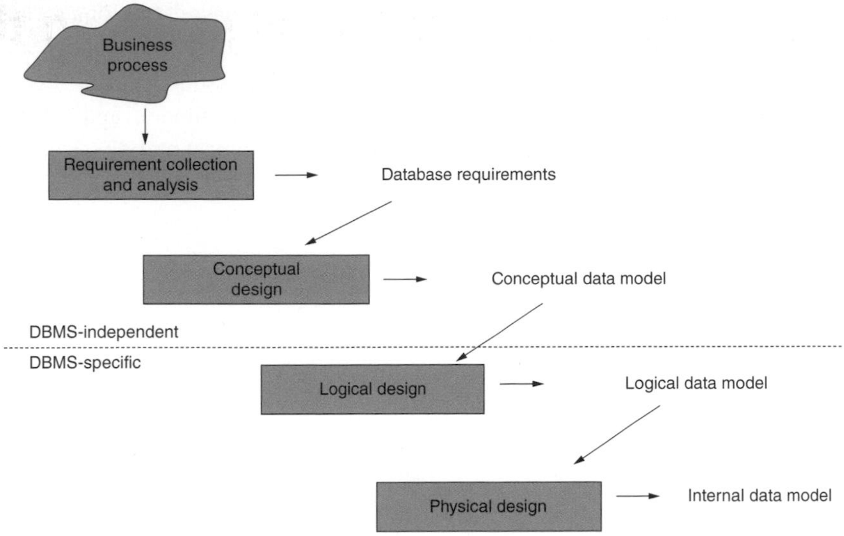


**Figure 3.1** The database design process.

surveys with end-users, inspections of the documents used in the current process, etc. During the conceptual design, both parties try to formalize the data requirements in a **conceptual data model**. As mentioned before, this should be a high-level model, meaning it should be both easy to understand for the business user and formal enough for the database designer who will use it in the next step. The conceptual data model must be user-friendly, and preferably have a graphical representation such that it can be used as a handy communication and discussion instrument between both information architects and business users. It should be flexible enough that new or changing data requirements can easily be added to the model. Finally, it must be DBMS- or implementation-independent since its only goal is to adequately and accurately collect and analyze data requirements. This conceptual model will also have its limitations, which should be clearly documented and followed up during application development.

**Connections**

We discuss logical data models in Chapter 5 (hierarchical and CODASYL model), Chapters 6 and 7 (relational model), Chapter 8 (object-oriented model), Chapter 9 (extended relational model), Chapter 10 (XML model), and Chapter 11 (NoSQL models). Internal data models are covered in Chapters 12 and 13.

Once all parties have agreed upon the conceptual data model, it can be mapped to a logical data model by the database designer during the logical design step. The logical data model is based upon the data model used by the implementation environment. Although at this stage it is already known what type of DBMS (e.g., RDBMS, OODBMS, etc.) will be used, the product itself (e.g., Microsoft, IBM, Oracle) has not been decided yet. Consider a conceptual EER model that will be mapped to a logical relational model since the database will be implemented using an RDBMS. The mapping exercise can result in a loss of semantics which should be properly documented and followed up during application development. It might be possible that additional semantics can be added to further enrich the logical data model. Also, the views of the external data model can be designed during this logical design step.

In a final step, the logical data model can be mapped to an internal data model by the database designer. The DBA can also give some recommendations regarding performance during this physical design step. In this step, the

DBMS product is known, the DDL is generated, and the data definitions are stored in the catalog. The database can then be populated with data and is ready for use. Again, any semantics lost or added during this mapping step should be documented and followed up.

In this chapter, we elaborate on the ER model, EER model, and UML class diagram for conceptual data modeling. Subsequent chapters discuss logical and physical database design.

## 3.2 The Entity Relationship Model

The **entity relationship (ER)** model was introduced and formalized by Peter Chen in 1976. It is one of the most popular data models for conceptual data modeling. The ER model has an attractive and user-friendly graphical notation. Hence, it has the ideal properties to build a conceptual data model. It has three building blocks: entity types, attribute types, and relationship types. We elaborate on these in what follows. We also cover weak entity types and provide two examples of ER models. This section concludes by discussing the limitations of the ER model.

**Drill Down**

Peter Pin-Shan Chen is a Taiwanese-American computer scientist who developed the ER model in 1976. He has a PhD in computer science/applied mathematics from Harvard University and held various positions at MIT Sloan School of Management, UCLA Management School, Louisiana State University, Harvard, and National Tsing Hua University (Taiwan). He is currently a Distinguished Career Scientist and faculty member at Carnegie Mellon University. His seminal paper "The Entity–Relationship Model: Toward A Unified View of Data" was published in 1975 in *ACM Transactions on Database Systems*. It is considered one of the most influential papers within the field of computer software. His work initiated the research field of conceptual modeling.

### 3.2.1 Entity Types

An entity type represents a business concept with an unambiguous meaning to a particular set of users. Examples of entity types are: supplier, student, product, or employee. An entity is one particular occurrence or instance of an entity type. Deliwines, Best Wines, and Ad Fundum are entities from the entity type supplier. In other words, an entity type defines a collection of entities that have similar characteristics. When building a conceptual data model, we focus on entity types and not on individual entities. In the ER model, entity types are depicted using a rectangle, as illustrated in Figure 3.2 for the entity type SUPPLIER.

### 3.2.2 Attribute Types

An **attribute type** represents a property of an entity type. As an example, name and address are attribute types of the entity type supplier. A particular entity (e.g., Deliwines) has a value for each of

**Figure 3.2** The entity type SUPPLIER.

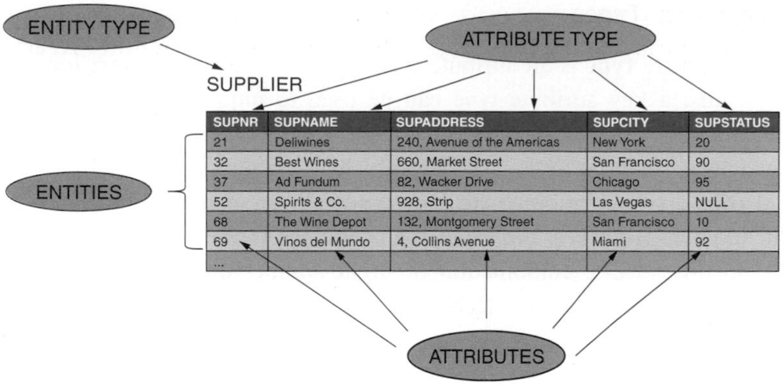


**Figure 3.3** Entity relationship model: basic concepts.

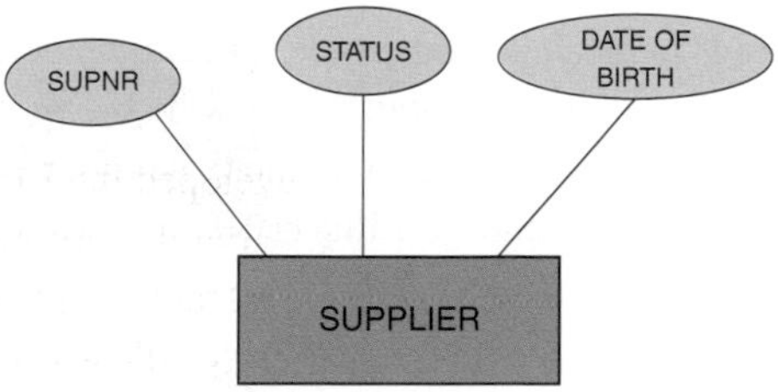


**Figure 3.4** The entity type SUPPLIER with attribute types SUPNR, STATUS, and DATE OF BIRTH.

its attribute types (e.g., its address is 240, Avenue of the Americas). An attribute type defines a collection of similar attributes, or an attribute is an instance of an attribute type. This is illustrated in Figure 3.3. The entity type SUPPLIER has attribute types SUPNR (supplier number), SUPNAME (supplier name), SUPADDRESS (supplier address), SUPCITY (supplier city), and SUPSTATUS (supplier status). Entities then correspond to specific suppliers such as supplier number 21, Deliwines, together with all its other attributes.

In the ER model, we focus on attribute types and represent them using ellipses, as illustrated in Figure 3.4 for the entity type SUPPLIER and attribute types SUPNR, STATUS, and DATE OF BIRTH.

In the following subsections we elaborate on attribute types and discuss domains, key attribute types, simple versus composite attribute types, single-valued versus multi-valued attribute types and derived attribute types.

#### 3.2.3.1 Domains

A **domain** specifies the set of values that may be assigned to an attribute for each individual entity. A domain for gender can be specified as having only two values: male and female. Likewise, a date domain can define dates as day, followed by month, followed by year. A domain can also contain null values. A null value means that a value is not known, not applicable, or not relevant. It is thus not the same as the value 0 or as an empty string of text " ". Think about a domain email address that allows for null values in case the email address is not known. By convention, domains are not displayed in an ER model.

#### 3.2.3.2 Key Attribute Types

A **key attribute type** is an attribute type whose values are distinct for each individual entity. In other words, a key attribute type can be used to uniquely identify each entity. Examples are: supplier number, which is unique for each supplier; product number, which is unique for each product; and social security number, which is unique for each employee. A key attribute type can also be a combination of attribute types. As an example, suppose a flight is identified by a flight number. However, the same flight number is used on each day to represent a particular flight. In this case, a combination of flight number and departure date is needed to uniquely identify flight entities. It is clear from this example that the definition of a key attribute type depends upon the business setting. Key attribute types are underlined in the ER model, as illustrated in Figure 3.5.

#### 3.2.3.3 Simple versus Composite Attribute Types

A **simple or atomic attribute type** cannot be further divided into parts. Examples are supplier number or supplier status. A **composite attribute type** is an attribute type that can be decomposed into other meaningful attribute types. Think about an address attribute type, which can be further decomposed into attribute types for street, number, ZIP code, city, and country. Another example is name, which can be split into first name and last name. Figure 3.6 illustrates how the composite attribute types address and name are represented in the ER model.

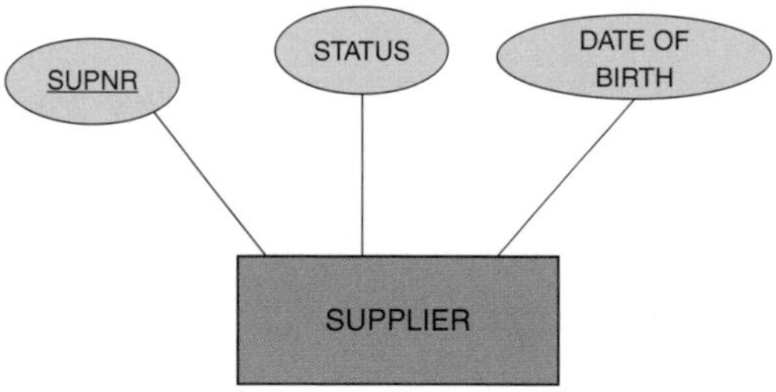


**Figure 3.5** The entity type SUPPLIER with key attribute type SUPNR.

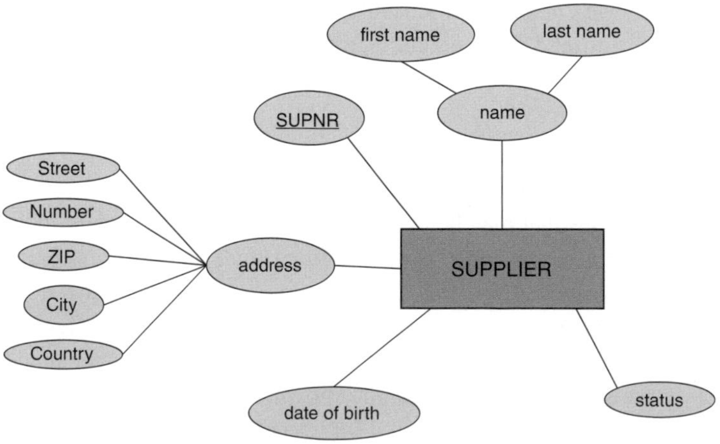


**Figure 3.6** The entity type SUPPLIER with composite attribute types address and name.

#### 3.2.3.4 Single-Valued versus Multi-Valued Attribute Types

A **single-valued attribute** type has only one value for a particular entity. An example is product number or product name. A **multi-valued attribute type** is an attribute type that can have multiple values. As an example, email address can be a multi-valued attribute type as a supplier can have multiple email addresses. Multi-valued attribute types are represented using a double ellipse in the ER model, as illustrated in Figure 3.7.

#### 3.2.3.5 Derived Attribute Type

A **derived attribute type** is an attribute type that can be derived from another attribute type. As an example, age is a derived attribute type since it can be derived from birth date. Derived attribute types are depicted using a dashed ellipse, as shown in Figure 3.8.

### 3.2.4 Relationship Types

A **relationship** represents an association between two or more entities. Consider a particular supplier (e.g., Deliwines) supplying a set of products (e.g., product numbers 0119, 0178, 0289, etc.).

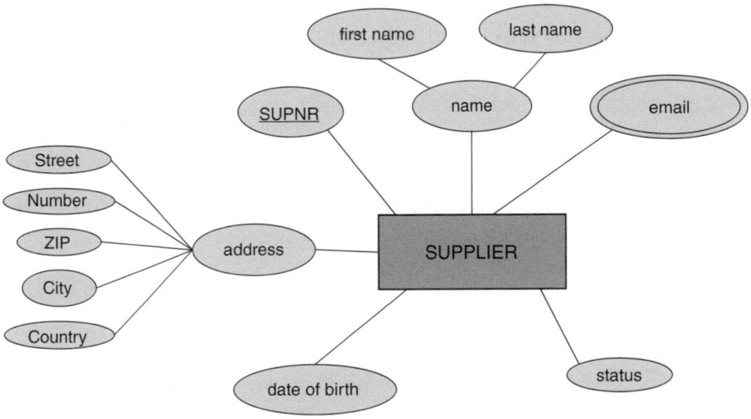


**Figure 3.7** The entity type SUPPLIER with multi-valued attribute type email.

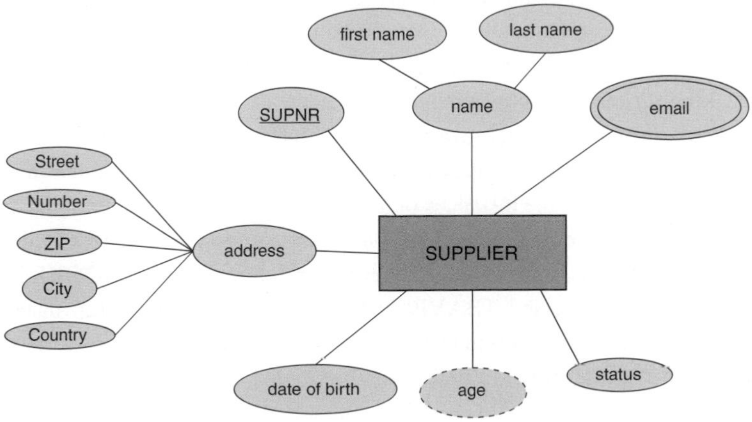


**Figure 3.8** The entity type SUPPLIER with derived attribute type age.

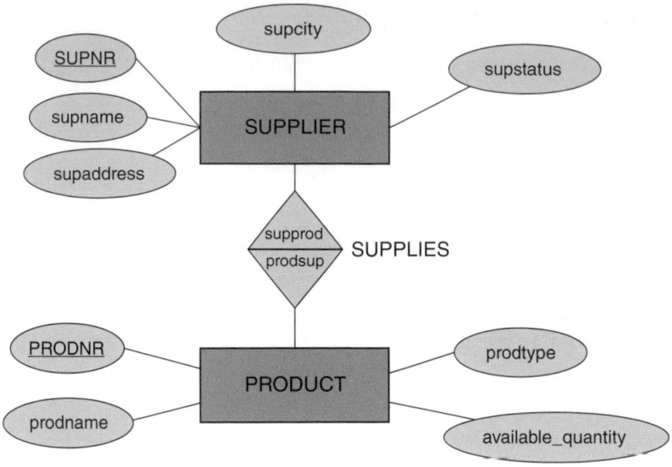


**Figure 3.9** Relationship type in the ER model.

A **relationship type** then defines a set of relationships among instances of one, two, or more entity types. In the ER model, relationship types are indicated using a rhombus symbol (see Figure 3.9). The rhombus can be thought of as two adjacent arrows pointing to each of the entity types specifying both directions in which the relationship type can be interpreted. Figure 3.9 shows the relationship type SUPPLIES between the entity types SUPPLIER and PRODUCT. A supplier can supply products (as indicated by the downwards arrow) and a product can be supplied by suppliers (as indicated by the upwards arrow). Each relationship instance of the SUPPLIES relationship type relates one particular supplier instance to one particular product instance. However, similar to entities and attributes, individual relationship instances are not represented in an ER model.

In the following subsections we elaborate on various characteristics of relationship types, such as degree and roles, cardinalities, and relationship attribute types.

#### 3.2.4.1 Degree and Roles

The **degree** of a relationship type corresponds to the number of entity types participating in the relationship type. A unary or recursive relationship type has degree one. A binary relationship type has two participating entity types whereas a ternary relationship type has three participating entity types. The **roles** of a relationship type indicate the various directions that can be used to interpret it. Figure 3.9 represents a binary relationship type since it has two participating entity types (SUPPLIER and PRODUCT). Note the role names (supprod and prodsup) that we have added in each of the arrows making up the rhombus symbol.

Figures 3.10 and 3.11 show two other examples of relationship types. The SUPERVISES relationship type is a unary or recursive relationship type, which models the hierarchical relationships between employees. In general, the instances of a unary relationship relate two instances of the same entity type to one another. The role names *supervises* and *supervised by* are added for further clarification. The second example is an example of a ternary relationship type BOOKING between the entity types TOURIST, HOTEL, and TRAVEL AGENCY. Each relationship instance represents the interconnection between one particular tourist, hotel, and travel agency. Role names can also be added but this is less straightforward here.

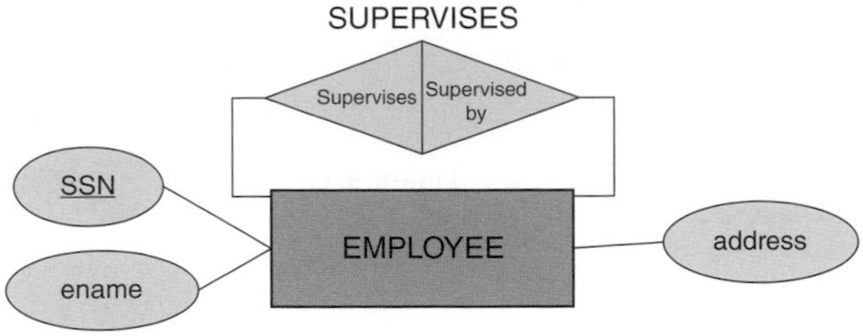


**Figure 3.10** Unary ER relationship type.

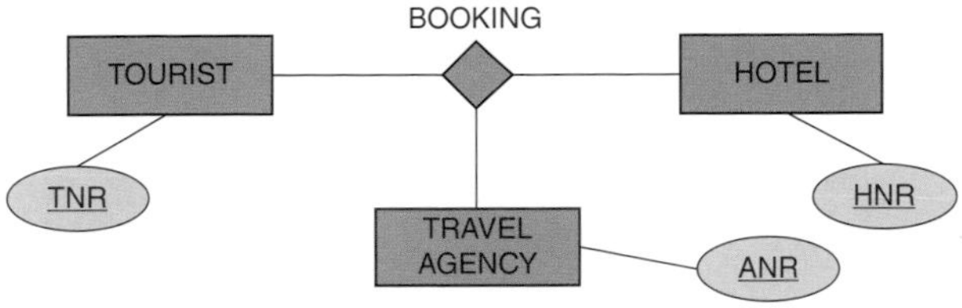


**Figure 3.11** Ternary ER relationship type.

### 3.2.4.2 Cardinalities

Every relationship type can be characterized in terms of its **cardinalities**, which specify the minimum or maximum number of relationship instances that an individual entity can participate in. The minimum cardinality can either be 0 or 1. If it is 0, it implies that an entity can occur without being connected through that relationship type to another entity. This can be referred to as **partial participation** since some entities may not participate in the relationship. If the minimum cardinality is 1, an entity must always be connected to at least one other entity through an instance of the relationship type. This is referred to as **total participation** or **existence dependency**, since all entities need to participate in the relationship, or in other words, the existence of the entity depends upon the existence of another.

The maximum cardinality can either be 1 or N. In the case that it is 1, an entity can be involved in only one instance of that relationship type. In other words, it can be connected to at most one other entity through that relationship type. In case the maximum cardinality is N, an entity can be connected to at most N other entities by means of the relationship type. Note that N represents an arbitrary integer number bigger than 1.

Relationship types are often characterized according to the maximum cardinality for each of their roles. For binary relationship types, this gives four options: 1:1, 1:N, N:1, and M:N.

Figure 3.12 illustrates some examples of binary relationship types together with their cardinalities. A student can be enrolled for a minimum of one course and a maximum of M courses. Conversely, a course can have minimum zero and maximum N students enrolled. This is an example of an N:M relationship type (also called many-to-many relationship type). A student can be assigned to minimum zero and maximum one master's thesis. A master's thesis is assigned to minimum zero and maximum one student. This is an example of a 1:1 relationship type. An employee can manage minimum zero and maximum N projects. A project is managed by minimum one and maximum one, or in other words exactly one employee. This is an example of a 1:N relationship type (also called one-to-many relationship type).

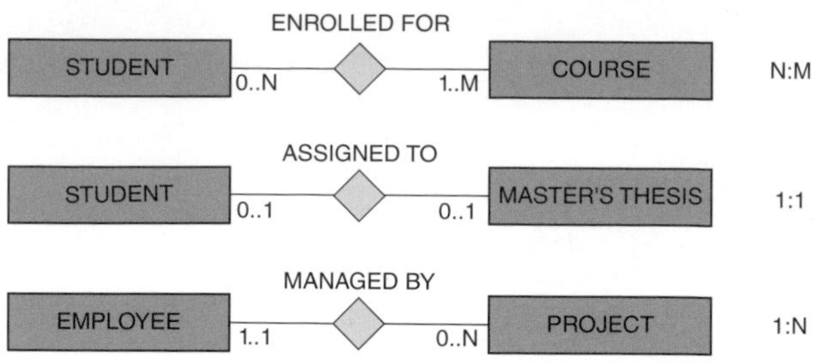


**Figure 3.12** ER relationship types: examples.

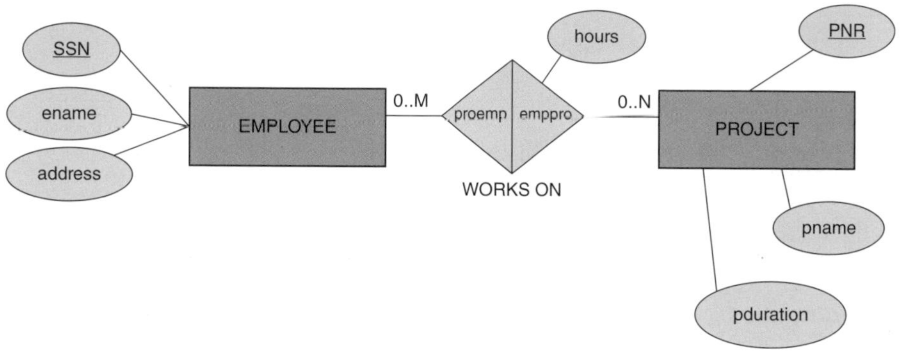


**Figure 3.13** Relationship type with attribute type.

#### 3.2.4.3 Relationship Attribute Types

Like entity types, a relationship type can also have attribute types. These attribute types can be migrated to one of the participating entity types in case of a 1:1 or 1:N relationship type. However, in the case of an M:N relationship type, the attribute type needs to be explicitly specified as a relationship attribute type.

This is illustrated in Figure 3.13. The attribute type *hours* represents the number of hours an employee worked on a project. Its value cannot be considered as the sole property of an employee or of a project; it is uniquely determined by a combination of an employee instance and project instance – hence, it needs to be modeled as an attribute type of the WORKS ON relationship type which connects employees to projects.

### 3.2.5 Weak Entity Types

A **strong entity** type is an entity type that has a key attribute type. In contrast, a **weak entity type** is an entity type that does not have a key attribute type of its own. More specifically, entities belonging to a weak entity type are identified by being related to specific entities from the **owner entity type**, which is an entity type from which they borrow an attribute type. The borrowed attribute type is then combined with some of the weak entity's own attribute types (also called partial keys) into a key attribute type. Figure 3.14 shows an ER model for a hotel administration.

A hotel has a hotel number (HNR) and a hotel name (Hname). Every hotel has a unique hotel number. Hence, HNR is the key attribute type of Hotel. A room is identified by a room number (RNR)

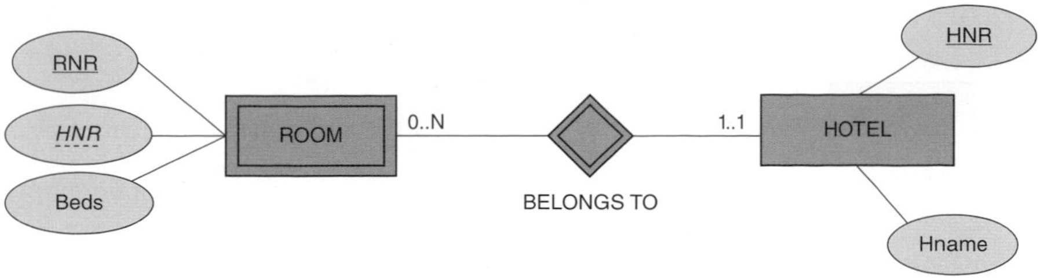


**Figure 3.14** Weak entity types in the ER model.

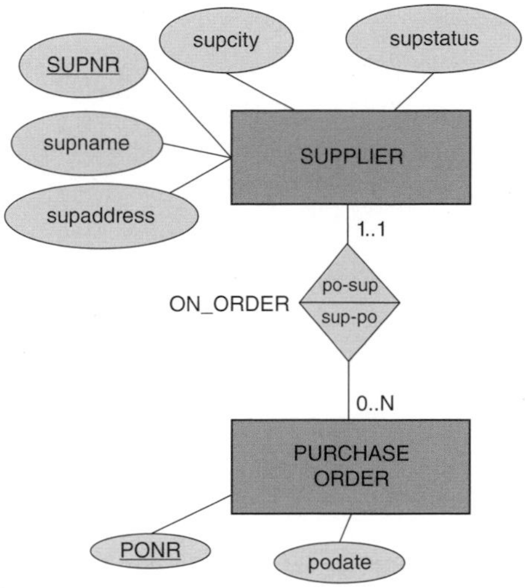


**Figure 3.15** Weak versus existence-dependent entity type in the ER model.

and a number of beds (Beds). Within a particular hotel, each room has a unique room number but the same room number can occur for multiple rooms in different hotels. Hence, RNR as such does not suffice as a key attribute type. Consequently, the entity type ROOM is a weak entity type since it cannot produce its own key attribute type. More specifically, it needs to borrow HNR from HOTEL to come up with a key attribute type which is now a combination of its partial key RNR and HNR. Weak entity types are represented in the ER model using a double-lined rectangle, as illustrated in Figure 3.14. The rhombus representing the relationship type through which the weak entity type borrows a key attribute type is also double-lined. The borrowed attribute type(s) is/are underlined using a dashed line.

Since a weak entity type needs to borrow an attribute type from another entity type, its existence will always be dependent on the latter. For example, in Figure 3.14, ROOM is existence-dependent on HOTEL, as also indicated by the minimum cardinality of 1. Note, however, that an existence-dependent entity type does not necessarily imply a weak entity type. Consider the example in Figure 3.15. The PURCHASE ORDER entity type is existence-dependent on SUPPLIER, as indicated by the minimum cardinality of 1. However, in this case PURCHASE ORDER has its own key attribute type, which is purchase order number (PONR). In other words, PURCHASE ORDER is an existence-dependent entity type but not a weak entity type.

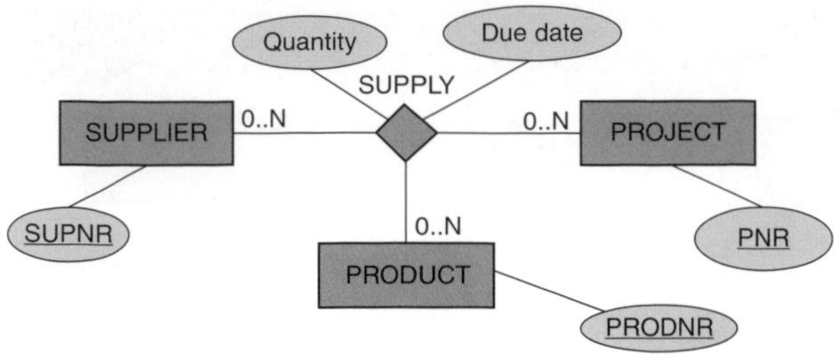


**Figure 3.16** Ternary relationship type: example.

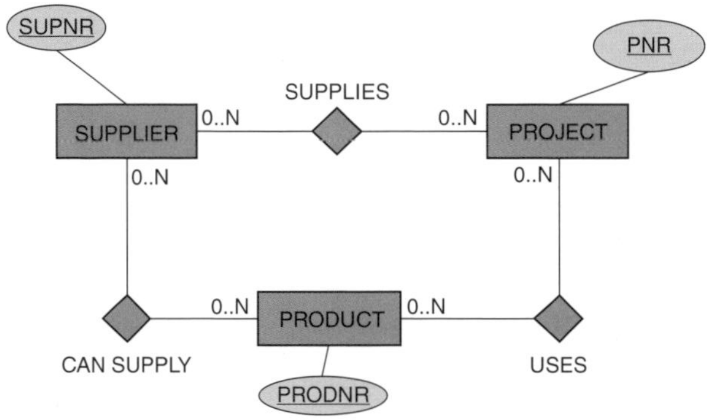


**Figure 3.17** Ternary versus binary relationship types.

### 3.2.6 Ternary Relationship Types

The majority of relationship types in an ER model are binary or have only two participating entity types. However, higher-order relationship types with more than two entity types, known as **ternary relationship types**, can occasionally occur, and special attention is needed to properly understand their meaning.

Assume that we have a situation in which suppliers can supply products for projects. A supplier can supply a particular product for multiple projects. A product for a particular project can be supplied by multiple suppliers. A project can have a particular supplier supply multiple products. The model must also include the quantity and due date for supplying a particular product to a particular project by a particular supplier. This is a situation that can be perfectly modeled using a ternary relationship type, as you can see in Figure 3.16.

A supplier can supply a particular product for 0 to N projects. A product for a particular project can be supplied by 0 to N suppliers. A supplier can supply 0 to N products for a particular project. The relationship type also includes the quantity and due date attribute types.[1]

An obvious question is whether we can also model this ternary relationship type as a set of binary relationship types, as shown in Figure 3.17.

We decomposed the ternary relationship type into the binary relationship types "SUPPLIES" between SUPPLIER and PROJECT, "CAN SUPPLY" between SUPPLIER and PRODUCT, and

[1] Some textbooks put the cardinalities of each entity type next to the entity type itself instead of at the opposite side as we do. For ternary relationship types, this makes the notation less ambiguous. However, we continue to use our notation because this is the most commonly used.

SUPPLY

| Supplier | Product | Project |
|---|---|---|
| Peters | Pencil | Project 1 |
| Peters | Pen | Project 2 |
| Johnson | Pen | Project 1 |

SUPPLIES

| Supplier | Project |
|---|---|
| Peters | Project 1 |
| Peters | Project 2 |
| Johnson | Project 1 |

USES

| Product | Project |
|---|---|
| Pencil | Project 1 |
| Pen | Project 1 |
| Pen | Project 2 |

CAN SUPPLY

| Supplier | Product |
|---|---|
| Peters | Pencil |
| Peters | Pen |
| Johnson | Pen |

**Figure 3.18** Ternary versus binary relationship types: example instances.

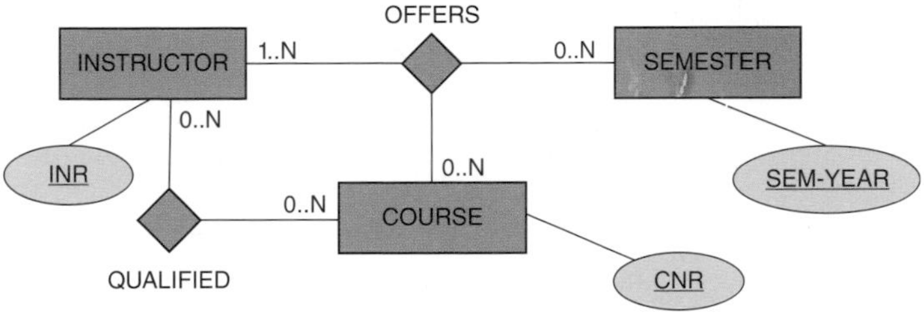


**Figure 3.19** Ternary relationship type in the ER model.

"USES" between PRODUCT and PROJECT. We can now wonder whether the semantics of the ternary relationship type is preserved by these binary relationship types. To properly understand this, we need to write down some relationship instances. Say we have two projects: Project 1 uses a pencil and a pen, and Project 2 uses a pen. Supplier Peters supplies the pencil for Project 1 and the pen for Project 2, whereas supplier Johnson supplies the pen for Project 1.

Figure 3.18 shows the relationship instances for both cases. At the top of the figure are the relationship instances that would be used in a ternary relationship type "SUPPLY". This can be deconstructed into the three binary relationship types: "SUPPLIES", "USES", and "CAN SUPPLY".

From the "SUPPLIES" relationship type, we can see that both Peters and Johnson supply to Project 1. From the "CAN SUPPLY" relationship type, we can see that both can also supply a pen. The "USES" relationship type indicates that Project 1 needs a pen. Hence, from the binary relationship types, it is not clear who supplies the pen for Project 1. This is, however, clear in the ternary relationship type, where it can be seen that Johnson supplies the pen for Project 1. By decomposing the ternary relationship types into binary relationship types, we clearly lose semantics. Furthermore, when using binary relationship types, it is also unclear where we should add the relationship attribute types such as quantity and due date (see Figure 3.16). Binary relationship types can, however, be used to model additional semantics.

Figure 3.19 shows another example of a ternary relationship type between three entity types: INSTRUCTOR with key attribute type INR representing the instructor number; COURSE with key attribute type CNR representing the course number; and SEMESTER with key attribute type SEM-YEAR representing the semester year. An instructor can offer a course during zero to N semesters. A course during a semester is offered by one to N instructors. An instructor can offer zero to N courses during a semester. In this case, we also added an extra binary relationship type QUALIFIED between INSTRUCTOR and COURSE to indicate what courses an instructor is qualified to teach. Note that, in this way, it is possible to model the fact that an instructor may be qualified for more courses than the ones she/he is actually teaching at the moment.

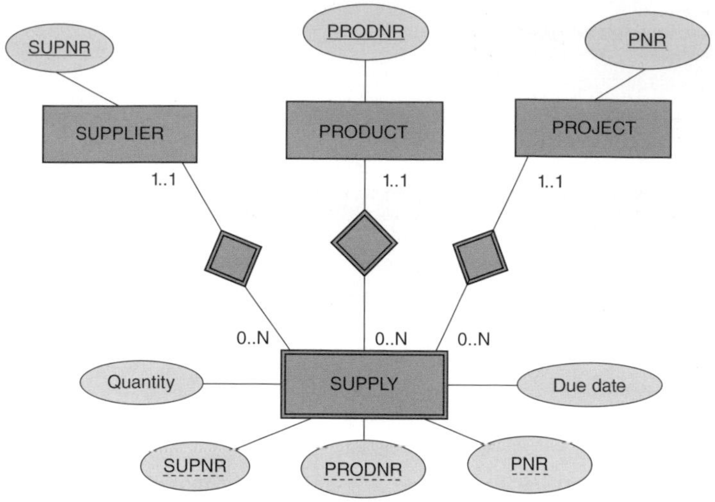


**Figure 3.20** Modeling ternary relationship types as binary relationship types.

Another alternative to model a ternary relationship type is by using a weak entity type as shown in Figure 3.20. The weak entity type SUPPLY is existence-dependent on SUPPLIER, PRODUCT, and PROJECT, as indicated by the minimum cardinalities of 1. Its key is a combination of supplier number, product number, and project number. It also includes the attribute types *quantity* and *due date*. Representing a ternary relationship type in this way can be handy in case the database modeling tool only supports unary and binary relationship types.

## 3.2.7 Examples of the ER Model

Figure 3.21 shows the ER model for a human resources (HR) administration. It has three entity types: EMPLOYEE, DEPARTMENT, and PROJECT. Let's read some of the relationship types. An employee works in minimum one and maximum one, so exactly one, department. A department has minimum one and maximum N employees working in it. A department is managed by exactly one employee. An employee can manage zero or one department. A department is in charge of zero to N projects. A project is assigned to exactly one department. An employee works on zero to N projects. A project is being worked on by zero to M employees. The relationship type WORKS ON also has an attribute type hours, representing the number of hours an employee worked on a project. Also note the recursive relationship type to model the supervision relationships between employees. An employee supervises zero to N employees. An employee is supervised by zero or one employees.

Figure 3.22 shows another example of an ER model for a purchase order administration. It has three entity types: SUPPLIER, PURCHASE ORDER, and PRODUCT. A supplier can supply zero to N products. A product can be supplied by zero to M suppliers. The relationship type SUPPLIES also includes the attribute types purchase_price and deliv_period. A supplier can have zero to N purchase orders on order. A purchase order is always assigned to one supplier. A purchase order can have one to N purchase order lines with products. Conversely, a product can be included in zero to M purchase orders. In addition, the relationship type PO_LINE includes the quantity of the order. Also note the attribute types and key attribute types of each of the entity types.

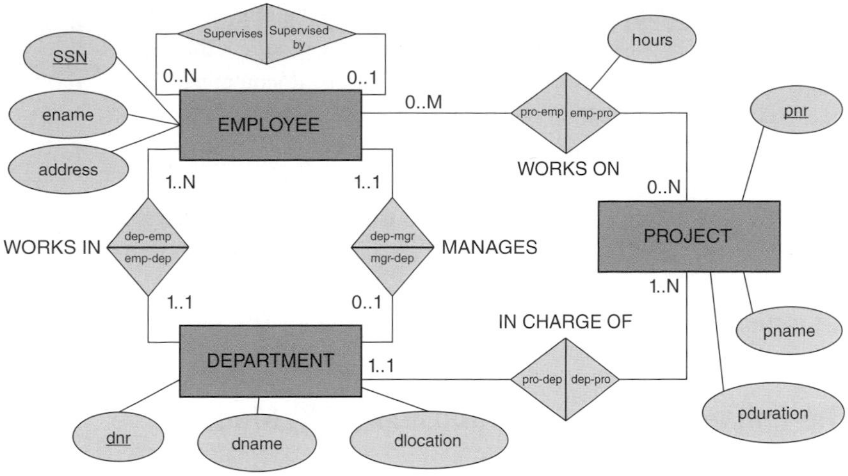


**Figure 3.21** ER model for HR administration.

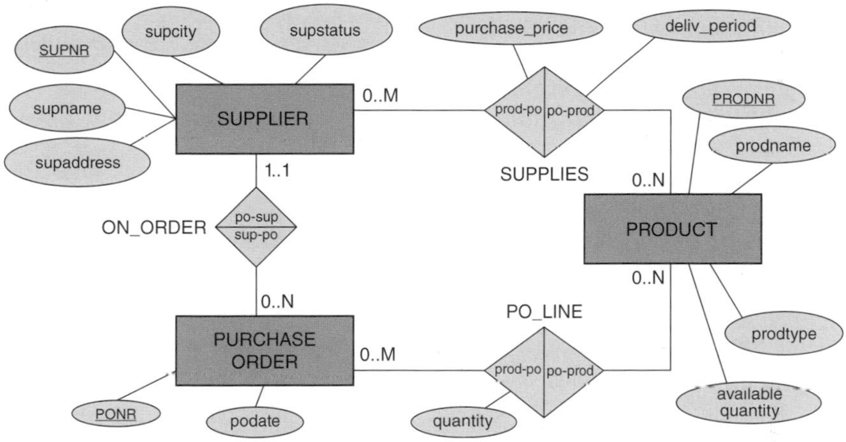


**Figure 3.22** ER model for purchase order administration.

## 3.2.8 Limitations of the ER Model

Although the ER model is a very user-friendly data model for conceptual data modeling, it also has its limitations. First of all, the ER model presents a temporary snapshot of the data requirements of a business process. This implies that **temporal constraints**, which are constraints spanning a particular time interval, cannot be modeled. Some example temporal constraints that cannot be enforced are: a project needs to be assigned to a department after one month, an employee cannot return to a department of which he previously was a manager, an employee needs to be assigned to a department after six months, a purchase order must be assigned to a supplier after two weeks. These rules need to be documented and followed up with application code.

Another shortcoming is that the ER model cannot guarantee consistency across multiple relationship types. Some examples of business rules that cannot be enforced in the ER model are: an employee should work in the department that he/she manages, employees should work on projects assigned to departments to which the employees belong, and suppliers can only be assigned to purchase orders for products they can supply. Again, these business rules need to be documented and followed up with application code.

Furthermore, since domains are not included in the ER model, it is not possible to specify the set of values that can be assigned to an attribute type (e.g., hours should be positive; prodtype must be red, white, or sparkling, supstatus is an integer between 0 and 100). Finally, the ER model also does not support the definition of functions (e.g., a function to calculate an employee's salary).

**Retention Questions**

- What are the key building blocks of the ER model?
- Discuss the attribute types supported in the ER model.
- Discuss the relationship types supported in the ER model.
- What are weak entity types and how are they modeled in the ER model?
- Discuss the limitations of the ER model.

## 3.3 The Enhanced Entity Relationship (EER) Model

The **Enhanced Entity Relationship model or EER model** is an extension of the ER model. It includes all the modeling concepts (entity types, attribute types, relationship types) of the ER model, as well as three new additional semantic data modeling concepts: specialization/generalization, categorization, and aggregation. We discuss these in more detail in the following subsections.

### 3.3.1 Specialization/Generalization

The concept of **specialization** refers to the process of defining a set of subclasses of an entity type. The set of subclasses that form a specialization is defined on the basis of some distinguishing characteristic of the entities in the superclass. As an example, consider an ARTIST superclass with subclasses SINGER and ACTOR. The specialization process defines an "IS A" relationship. In other words, a singer is an artist. Also, an actor is an artist. The opposite does not apply. An artist is not necessarily a singer. Likewise, an artist is not necessarily an actor. The specialization can then establish additional specific attribute types for each subclass. A singer can have a music style attribute type. During the specialization, it is also possible to establish additional specific relationship types between each subclass and other entity types. An actor can act in movies. A singer can be part of a band. A subclass inherits all attribute types and relationship types from its superclass.

**Generalization**, also called **abstraction**, is the reverse process of specialization. Specialization corresponds to a top-down process of conceptual refinement. As an example, the ARTIST entity type can be specialized or refined in the subclasses SINGER and ACTOR. Conversely, generalization corresponds to a bottom-up process of conceptual synthesis. As an example, the SINGER and ACTOR subclasses can be generalized in the ARTIST superclass.

Figure 3.23 shows how our specialization can be represented in the EER model. An artist has a unique artist number and an artist name. The ARTIST superclass is specialized in the subclasses SINGER and ACTOR. Both SINGER and ACTOR inherit the attribute types ANR and aname from ARTIST. A singer has a music style. An actor can act in zero to N movies. Conversely, in a movie one to M actors can act. A movie has a unique movie number and a movie title.

A specialization can be further qualified in terms of its disjointness and completeness constraints. The **disjointness constraint** specifies what subclasses an entity of the superclass can belong to. It can be set to either disjoint or overlap. A **disjoint specialization** is a specialization where an

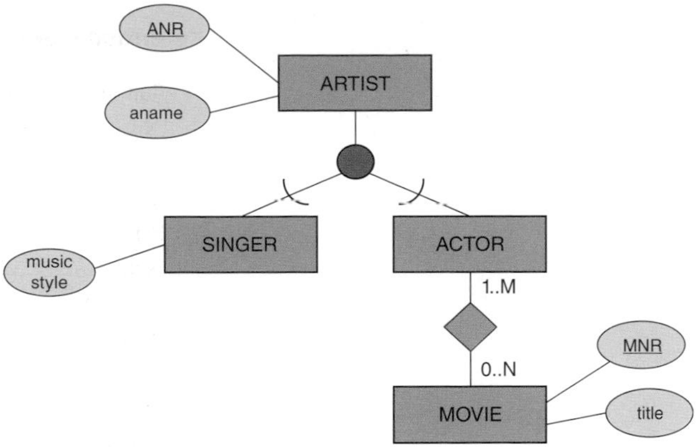


**Figure 3.23** Example of EER specialization.

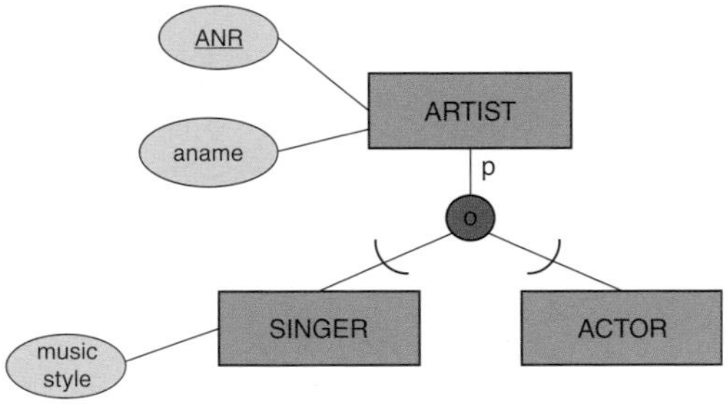


**Figure 3.24** Example of partial (p) specialization with overlap (o).

entity can be a member of at most one of the subclasses. An **overlap specialization** is a specialization where the same entity may be a member of more than one subclass. The **completeness constraint** indicates whether all entities of the superclass should belong to one of the subclasses or not. It can be set to either total or partial. A **total specialization** is a specialization where every entity in the superclass must be a member of some subclass. A **partial specialization** allows an entity to only belong to the superclass and to none of the subclasses. The disjointness and completeness constraints can be set independently, which gives four possible combinations: disjoint and total; disjoint and partial; overlapping and total; and overlapping and partial. Let's illustrate this with some examples.

Figure 3.24 gives an example of a partial specialization with overlap. The specialization is partial since not all artists are singers or actors; think about painters, for example, which are not included in our EER model. The specialization is overlap since some artists can be both singers and actors.

Figure 3.25 illustrates a total disjoint specialization. The specialization is total, since according to our model all people are either students or professors. The specialization is disjoint, since a student cannot be a professor at the same time.

A specialization can be several levels deep: a subclass can again be a superclass of another specialization. In a specialization hierarchy, every subclass can only have a single superclass and inherits the attribute types and relationship types of all its predecessor superclasses all the way up to the root of the hierarchy. Figure 3.26 shows an example of a specialization hierarchy. The STUDENT subclass is further specialized in the subclasses BACHELOR, MASTER, and PHD. Each of those subclasses inherits the attribute types and relationship types from STUDENT, which inherits both in turn from PERSON.

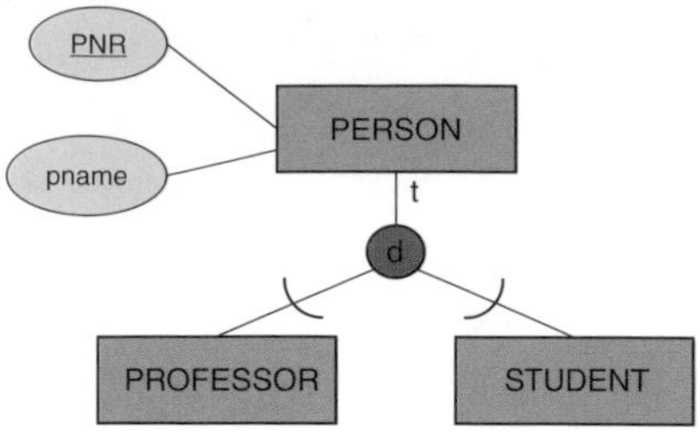


**Figure 3.25** Example of total (t) and disjoint (d) specialization.

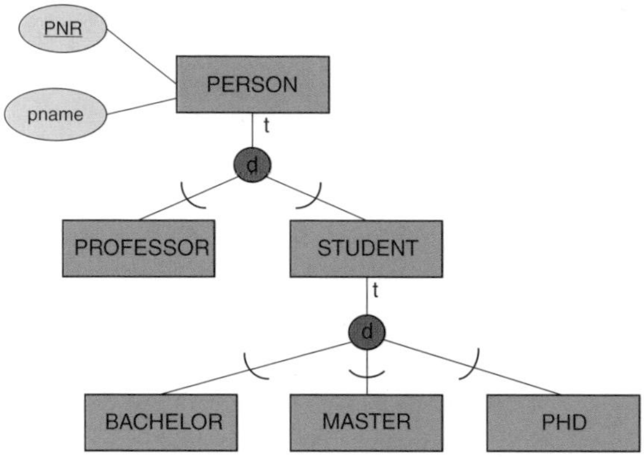


**Figure 3.26** Example of specialization hierarchy.

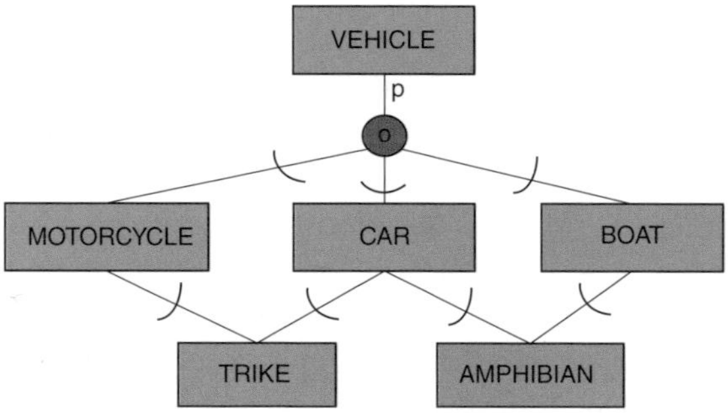


**Figure 3.27** Example of specialization lattice.

In a specialization lattice, a subclass can have multiple superclasses. The concept in which a shared subclass or a subclass with multiple parents inherits from all of its parents is called multiple inheritance. Let's illustrate this with an example.

Figure 3.27 shows a specialization lattice. The VEHICLE superclass is specialized into MOTORCYCLE, CAR, and BOAT. The specialization is partial and with overlap. TRIKE is a shared subclass of MOTORCYCLE and CAR and inherits the attribute types and relationship types from both. Likewise, AMPHIBIAN is a shared subclass of CAR and BOAT and inherits the attribute types and relationship types from both.

### 3.3.2 Categorization

**Categorization** is the second important modeling extension of the EER model. A category is a subclass that has several possible superclasses. Each superclass represents a different entity type.

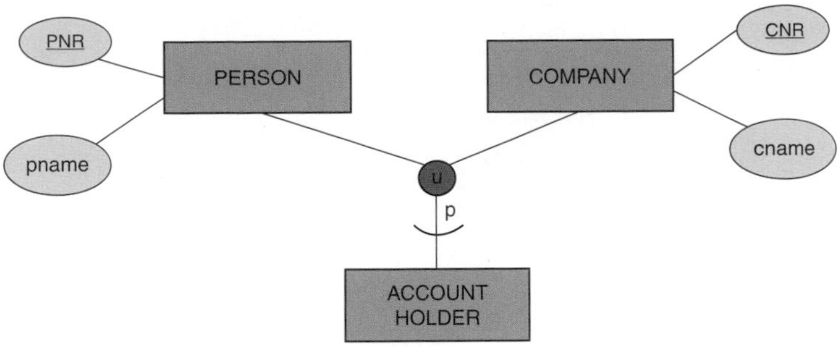


**Figure 3.28** EER categorization.

The category then represents a collection of entities that is a subset of the union of the superclasses. Therefore, a categorization is represented in the EER model by a circle containing the letter "u" (from union) (see Figure 3.28).

**Inheritance** in the case of categorization corresponds to an entity inheriting only the attributes and relationships of that superclass of which it is a member. This is also referred to as **selective inheritance**. Similar to a specialization, a categorization can be *total* or *partial*. In a **total categorization**, all entities of the superclasses belong to the subclass. In a **partial categorization**, not all entities of the superclasses belong to the subclass. Let's illustrate this with an example.

Figure 3.28 shows how the superclasses PERSON and COMPANY have been categorized into an ACCOUNT HOLDER subclass. In other words, the account holder entities are a subset of the union of the person and company entities. Selective inheritance in this example implies that some account holders inherit their attributes and relationships from person, whereas others inherit them from company. The categorization is partial as represented by the letter "p". This implies that not all persons or companies are account holders. If the categorization had been total (which would be represented by the letter "t" instead), then this would imply that all person and company entities are also account holders. In that case, we can also model this categorization using a specialization with ACCOUNT HOLDER as the superclass and PERSON and COMPANY as the subclasses.

### 3.3.3 Aggregation

**Aggregation** is the third modeling extension provided by the EER model. The idea here is that entity types that are related by a particular relationship type can be combined or aggregated into a higher-level aggregate entity type. This can be especially useful when the aggregate entity type has its own attribute types and/or relationship types.

Figure 3.29 gives an example of aggregation. A consultant works on zero to N projects. A project is being worked on by one to M consultants. Both entity types and the corresponding relationship type can now be aggregated into the aggregate concept PARTICIPATION. This aggregate has its own attribute type, date, which represents the date at which a consultant started working on a project. The aggregate also participates in a relationship type with CONTRACT. Participation should lead to a minimum of one and maximum of one contract. Conversely, a contract can be based upon one to M participations of consultants in projects.

### 3.3.4 Examples of the EER Model

Figure 3.30 presents our earlier HR administration example (see Figure 3.21), but now enriched with some EER modeling concepts. More specifically, we partially specialized EMPLOYEE into

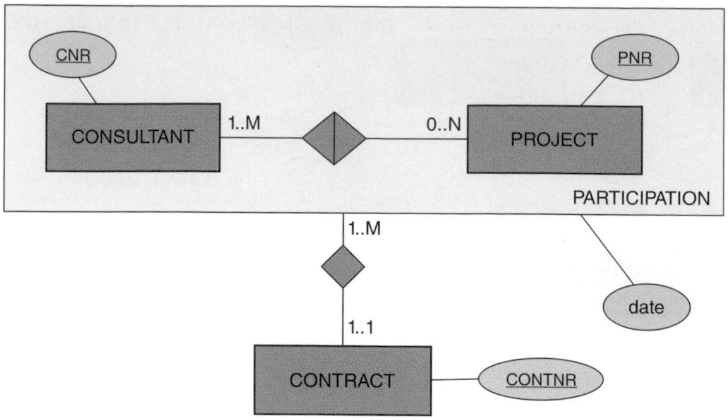


**Figure 3.29** EER aggregation.

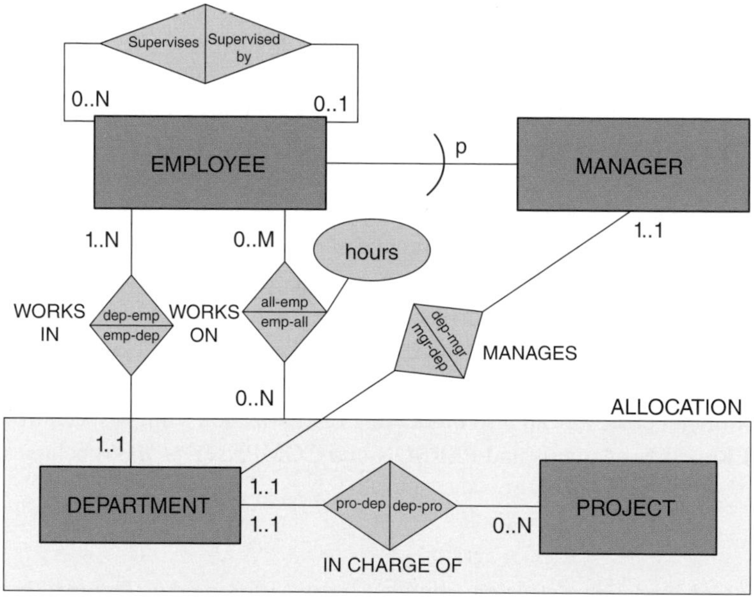


**Figure 3.30** EER model for HR administration.

MANAGER. The relationship type MANAGES then connects the MANAGER subclass to the DEPARTMENT entity type. DEPARTMENT and PROJECT have been aggregated into ALLOCATION. This aggregate then participates in the relationship type WORKS ON with EMPLOYEE.[2]

## 3.3.5 Designing an EER Model

To summarize, an EER conceptual data model can be designed according to the following steps:

1. Identify the entity types.
2. Identify the relationship types and assert their degree.

[2] We introduced the aggregation in the EER model for illustration purposes. However, since every project is assigned to exactly one department, we could also remove the aggregate ALLOCATION and draw a relationship type between EMPLOYEE and PROJECT.

**Retention Questions**

- What modeling extensions are provided by the EER model? Illustrate with examples.
- What are the limitations of the EER model?

3. Assert the cardinality ratios and participation constraints (total versus partial participation).
4. Identify the attribute types and assert whether they are simple or composite, single- or multi-valued, derived or not.
5. Link each attribute type to an entity type or a relationship type.
6. Denote the key attribute type(s) of each entity type.
7. Identify the weak entity types and their partial keys.
8. Apply abstractions such as generalization/specialization, categorization, and aggregation.
9. Assert the characteristics of each abstraction such as disjoint or overlapping, total or partial.

Any semantics that cannot be represented in the EER model must be documented as separate business rules and followed up using application code. Although the EER model offers some new interesting modeling concepts such as specialization/generalization, categorization, and aggregation, the limitations of the ER model unfortunately still apply. Hence, temporal constraints still cannot be modeled, the consistency among multiple relationship types cannot be enforced and attribute type domains or functions cannot be specified. Some of these shortcomings are addressed in the UML class diagram, which is discussed in the next section.

## 3.4 The UML Class Diagram

The **Unified Modeling Language (UML)** is a modeling language that assists in the specification, visualization, construction, and documentation of artifacts of a software system.[3] UML is essentially an object-oriented system modeling notation which focuses not only on data requirements, but also on behavioral modeling, process, and application architecture. It was accepted as a standard by the Object Management Group (OMG) in 1997 and approved as an ISO standard in 2005. The most recent version is UML 2.5, introduced in 2015. To model both the data and process aspects of an information system, UML offers various diagrams such as use case diagrams, sequence diagrams, package diagrams, deployment diagrams, etc. From a database modeling perspective, the class diagram is the most important. It visualizes both classes and their associations. Before we discuss this in more detail, let's first provide a recap of object orientation (OO).

### 3.4.1 Recap of Object Orientation

Two important building blocks of OO are classes and objects. A **class** is a blueprint definition for a set of objects. Conversely, an **object** is an instance of a class. In other words, a class in OO corresponds to an entity type in ER, and an object to an entity. Each object is characterized by both variables and methods.[4] Variables correspond to attribute types and variable values to attributes in the EER model. The EER model has no equivalent to methods. You can think of an example class Student and an example object student Bart. For our student object, example variables could be the

[3] See www.omg.org/spec/UML/2.5 for the most recent version.

[4] In the UML model, variables are also referred to as attributes and methods as operations. However, to avoid confusion with the ER model (where attributes represent instances of attribute types), we will stick to the terms variables and methods.

> **Connections**
>
> We discuss object orientation in greater detail in Chapter 8.

student's name, gender, and birth date. Example methods could be calcAge, which calculates the age of the student based upon the birth date; isBirthday to verify whether the student's birthday is today; hasPassed(courseID), which verifies whether the student has passed the course represented by the courseID input parameter, etc.

**Information hiding** (also referred to as encapsulation) states that the variables of an object can only be accessed through either getter or setter methods. A getter method is used to retrieve the value of a variable, whereas a setter method assigns a value to it. The idea is to provide a protective shield around the object to make sure that values are always correctly retrieved or modified by means of explicitly defined methods.

Similar to the EER model, inheritance is supported. A superclass can have one or more subclasses which inherit both the variables and methods from the superclass. As an example, Student and Professor can be a subclass of the Person superclass. In OO, method overloading is also supported. This implies that various methods in the same class can have the same name, but a different number or type of input arguments.

### 3.4.2 Classes

In a UML class diagram, a class is represented as a rectangle with three sections. Figure 3.31 illustrates a UML class SUPPLIER. In the upper part, the name of the class is mentioned (e.g., SUPPLIER), in the middle part the variables (e.g., SUPNR, Supname), and in the bottom part the methods (e.g., getSUPNR). You can compare this with the corresponding ER representation in Figure 3.2.

Example methods are the getter and setter methods for each of the variables. The method getSUPNR is a getter method that retrieves the supplier number of a particular supplier object, whereas the method setSUPNR(newSUPNR) assigns the value newSUPNR to the SUPNR variable of a supplier object.

### 3.4.3 Variables

Variables with unique values (similar to key attribute types in the ER model) are not directly supported in UML. The reason is because a UML class diagram is assumed to be implemented using an OODBMS in which every object created is assigned a unique and immutable object identifier (OID) that it keeps during its entire lifetime (see Chapter 8). Hence, this OID can be used to uniquely identify objects and no other variables are needed to serve as a key. To explicitly enforce the uniqueness constraint of a variable, you can use OCL, as we discuss in Section 3.4.9.2.

UML provides a set of primitive types such as string, integer, and Boolean, which can be used to define variables in the class diagram. It is also possible to define your own data types or domains

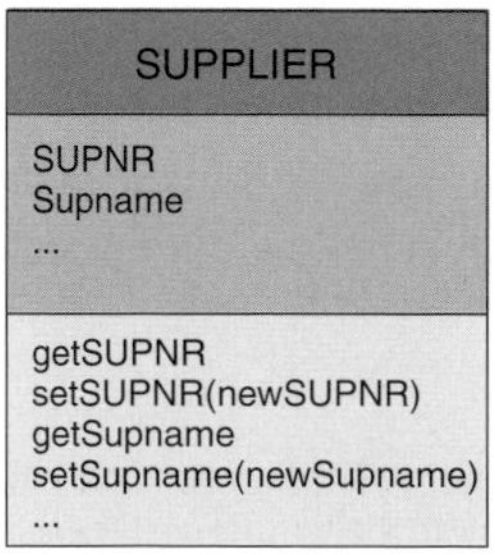


**Figure 3.31** UML class.

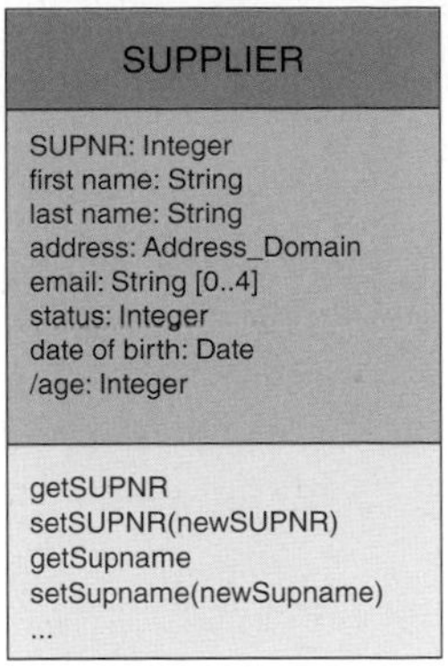


**Figure 3.32** UML class with refined variable definitions.

and use them. This is illustrated in Figure 3.32. The variables SUPNR and status are defined as integers. The variable address is defined using the domain Address_Domain.

Composite variables (similar to composite attribute types in the ER model) can be tackled in two ways. A first option is to decompose them into their parts. In our example, we decomposed Supname into first name and last name. Another alternative is by creating a new domain as we did for the address variable.

Multi-valued variables can also be modeled in two ways. A first option is to indicate the multiplicity of the variable. This specifies how many values of the variable will be created when an object is instantiated. In our example, we specified that a supplier can have 0 to 4 email addresses. An infinite number of email addresses can be defined as "email: String[*]". Another option is by using an aggregation, as we discuss in what follows.

Finally, derived variables (e.g., age) need to be preceded by a forward slash.

### 3.4.4 Access Modifiers

In UML, **access modifiers** can be used to specify who can access a variable or method. Example choices are: private (denoted by the symbol "–"), in which case the variable or method can only be accessed by the class itself; public (denoted by the symbol "+"), in which case the variable or method can be accessed by any other class; and protected (denoted by the symbol "#"), in which case the variable or method can be accessed by both the class and its subclasses. To enforce the concept of information hiding, it is recommended to declare all variables as private and access them using getter and setter methods. This is illustrated in Figure 3.33, where all variables are private and all methods public.

You can compare this with the corresponding ER representation in Figure 3.2. From this comparison, it is already clear that UML models more semantics than its ER counterpart.

### 3.4.5 Associations

Analogous to relationship types in the ER model, classes can be related using **associations** in UML. Multiple associations can be defined between the same classes. Also, unary (or reflexive) and n-ary (e.g., ternary) associations are possible. An association corresponds to a relationship type in the ER model, whereas a particular occurrence of an association is referred to as a link that corresponds to a relationship in the ER model.

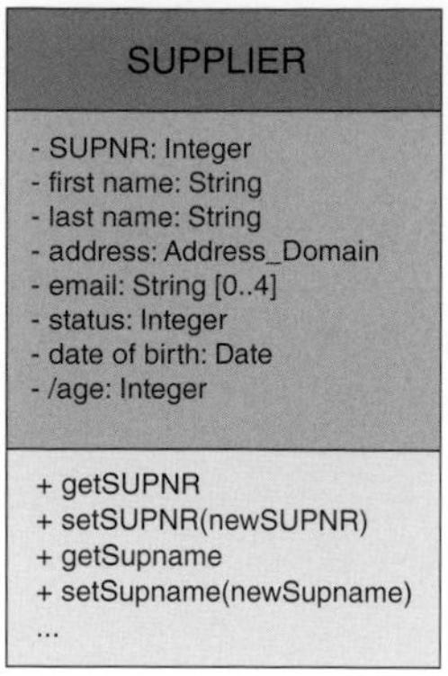


**Figure 3.33** Access modifiers in UML.

**Table 3.1** UML multiplicities versus ER cardinalities

| UML class diagram multiplicity | ER model cardinality |
|---|---|
| * | 0..N |
| 0..1 | 0..1 |
| 1..* | 1..N |
| 1 | 1..1 |

An association is characterized by its multiplicities, which indicate the minimum and maximum number of participations of the corresponding classes in the association. Hence, this corresponds to the cardinalities we discussed in the ER model. Table 3.1 lists the options available and contrasts them with the corresponding ER model cardinalities. An asterisk (*) is introduced to denote a maximum cardinality of N.

In what follows, we elaborate further on associations and discuss association classes, unidirectional versus bidirectional associations, and qualified associations.

#### 3.4.5.1 Association Class

If an association has variables and/or methods on its own, it can be modeled as an **association class**. The objects of this class then represent the links of the association. Consider the association between SUPPLIER and PRODUCT as depicted in Figure 3.34. The association class SUPPLIES has two variables: the purchase price and delivery period for each product supplied by a supplier. It can also have methods such as getter and setter methods for these variables. Association classes are represented using a dashed line connected to the association.

#### 3.4.5.2 Unidirectional versus Bidirectional Association

Associations can be augmented with direction reading arrows, which specify the direction of querying or navigating through it. In a **unidirectional association**, there is only a single way of navigating, as indicated by the arrow. Figure 3.35 gives an example of a unidirectional association between the classes SUPPLIER and PURCHASE_ORDER. It implies that all purchase orders can be retrieved through a supplier object. Hence, according to this model, it is not possible to navigate from a purchase order object to a supplier object. Also note the multiplicities of the association.

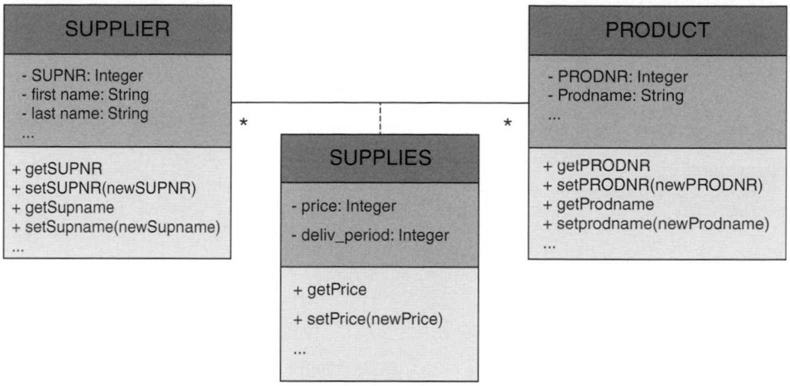


**Figure 3.34** Association class.

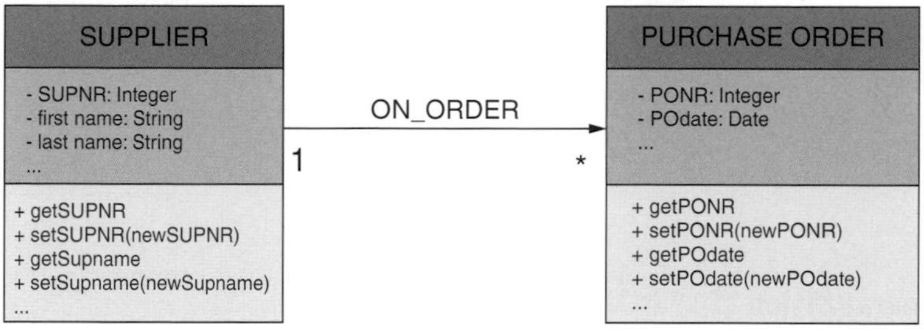


**Figure 3.35** Unidirectional association.

In a **bidirectional association**, both directions are possible, and hence there is no arrow. Figure 3.34 is an example of a bidirectional association between the classes SUPPLIER and PRODUCT. According to this UML class diagram, we can navigate from SUPPLIER to PRODUCT as well as from PRODUCT to SUPPLIER.

### 3.4.5.3 Qualified Association

A **qualified association** is a special type of association that uses a qualifier to further refine the association. The qualifier specifies one or more variables that are used as an index key for navigating from the qualified class to the target class. It reduces the multiplicity of the association because of this extra key. Figure 3.36 gives an example.

We have two classes, TEAM and PLAYER. They are connected using a 1:N relationship type in the ER model (upper part of the figure) since a team can have zero to N players and a player is always related to exactly one team. This can be represented in UML using a qualified association by including the position variable as the index key or qualifier (lower part of the figure). A team at a given position has zero or one players, whereas a player always belongs to exactly one team.

Qualified associations can be used to represent weak entity types. Figure 3.37 shows our earlier example of ROOM as a weak entity type, being existence-dependent on HOTEL. In the UML class diagram, we can define room number as a qualifier or index key. In other words, a hotel combined with a given room number corresponds to zero or one room, whereas a room always belongs to one hotel.

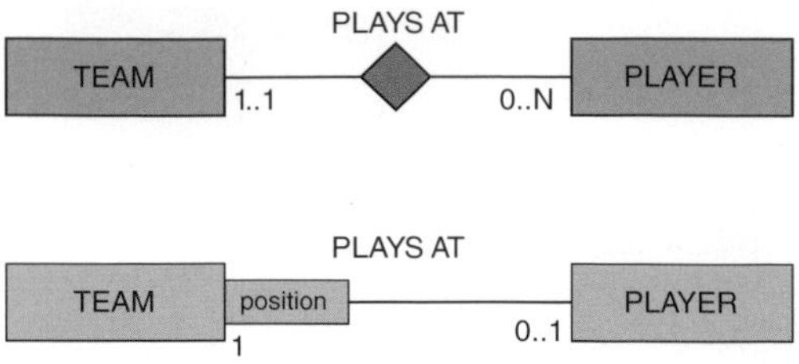


**Figure 3.36** Qualified association.

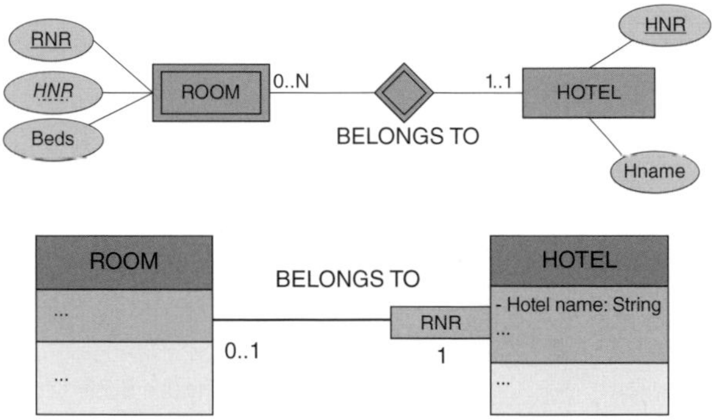


**Figure 3.37** Qualified associations for representing weak entity types.

### 3.4.6 Specialization/Generalization

Similar to the EER model, UML also supports specialization or generalization relationships. Figure 3.38 shows the UML representation of our earlier EER specialization of Figure 3.24 with ARTIST, SINGER, and ACTOR.

The hollow triangle represents a specialization in UML. The specialization characteristics such as total/partial or disjoint/overlap can be added next to the triangle. UML also supports multiple inheritance where a subclass can inherit variables, methods, and associations from multiple superclasses.

### 3.4.7 Aggregation

Similar to EER, aggregation represents a composite to part relationship whereby a composite class contains a part class. Two types of aggregation are possible in UML: shared aggregation (also referred to as aggregation) and composite aggregation (also referred to as composition). In shared aggregation, the part object can simultaneously belong to multiple composite objects. In other words, the maximum multiplicity at the composite side is undetermined. The part object can also occur without belonging to a composite object. A shared aggregation thus represents a rather loose coupling between both classes. In composite aggregation or composition, the part object can only belong to one composite. The maximum multiplicity at the composite side is 1. According to the original UML standard, the minimum multiplicity can be either 1 or 0. A minimum cardinality of 0 can occur in case the part can belong to another composite. Consider two composite aggregations – one between engine and boat and one between engine and car. Since an engine can only belong to either a car or a boat, the minimum cardinality from engine (the part) to boat and car will be 0, respectively. A composite aggregation represents a tight coupling between both classes, and the part

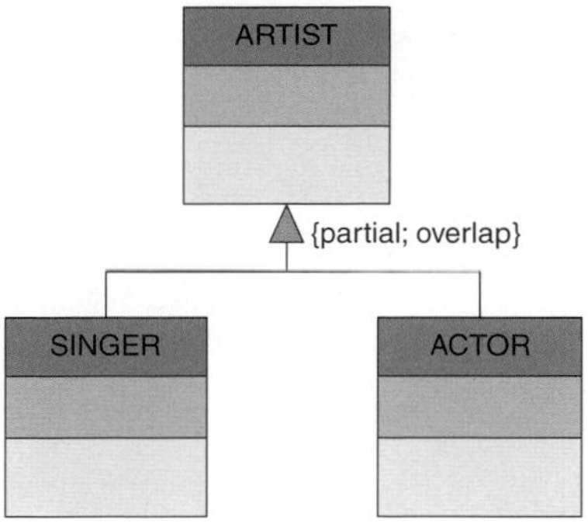


Figure 3.38 Specialization/generalization in UML.

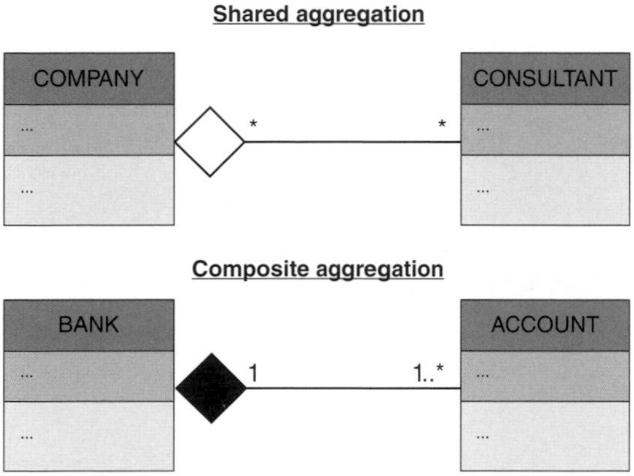


Figure 3.39 Shared versus composite aggregation in UML.

object will be automatically removed when the composite object is removed. Note that a part object can also be deleted from a composite before the composite is deleted.

Figure 3.39 illustrates both concepts. A shared aggregation is indicated by a hollow diamond and a composite aggregation by a filled diamond. We have a shared aggregation between COMPANY and CONSULTANT. A consultant can work for multiple companies. When a company is removed, any consultants that worked for it remain in the database. We have a composite aggregation between BANK and ACCOUNT. An account is tightly coupled to one bank only. When the bank is removed, all connected account objects disappear as well.

### 3.4.8 UML Example

Figure 3.40 shows our earlier EER HR example of Figure 3.30 in UML notation. It has six classes including two association classes (Manages and Works_On). Note the different variables and methods for each of the classes. The access modifiers for each of the variables have been set to private so as to enforce information hiding. Getter and setter methods have been added for each of the variables. We also included a shared aggregation between DEPARTMENT and LOCATION and between PROJECT and LOCATION. Hence, this implies that location information is not lost upon removal of a department or project. We have two unidirectional associations: between EMPLOYEE and PROJECT, and between DEPARTMENT and PROJECT. The unary association

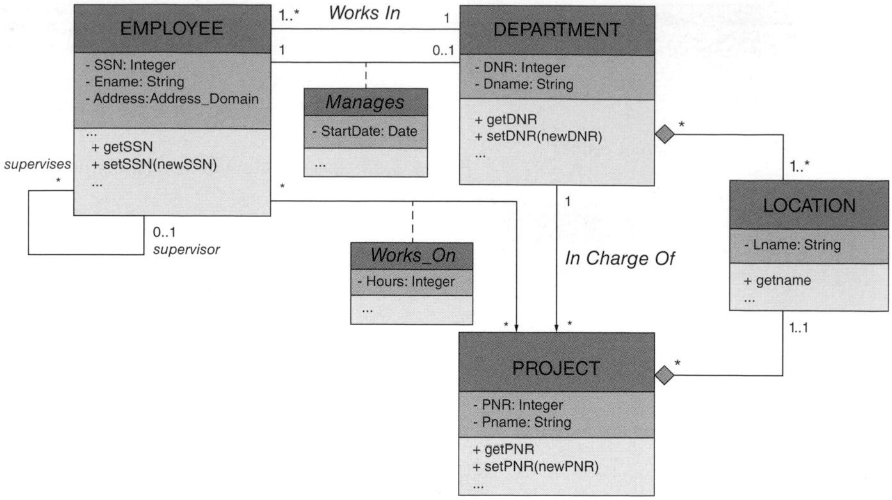


**Figure 3.40** HR example in UML.

for the EMPLOYEE class models the supervision relationship. When you contrast this UML class diagram with the EER model of Figure 3.30, it is clear that the former has a lot more semantics embedded.

## 3.4.9 Advanced UML Modeling Concepts

UML offers various advanced modeling concepts to further add semantics to our data model. In the following subsections, we discuss the changeability property, the object constraint language (OCL), and the dependency relationship.

### 3.4.9.1 Changeability Property

The **changeability property** specifies the type of operations that are allowed on either variable values or links. Three common choices are: default, which allows any type of edit; addOnly, which only allows additional values or links to be added (no deletions); and frozen, which allows no further changes once the value or link is established. You can see this illustrated in Figure 3.41.

The supplier and purchase order number are both declared as frozen, which means that once a value has been assigned to either of them it can no longer change. The languages variable of the SUPPLIER class defines a set of languages a supplier can understand. It is defined as addOnly since languages can only be added and not removed from it. Also note the addOnly characteristic that was added to the ON_ORDER association. It specifies that for a given supplier, purchase orders can only be added and not removed.

### 3.4.9.2 Object Constraint Language (OCL)

The **object constraint language (OCL)**, which is also part of the UML standard, can be used to specify various types of constraints. The OCL constraints are defined in a declarative way. They specify what must be true, but not how this should be accomplished. In other words, no control flow

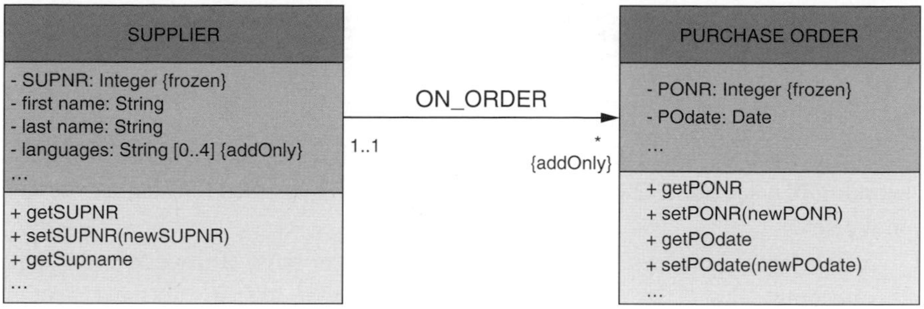


**Figure 3.41** Changeability property in UML.

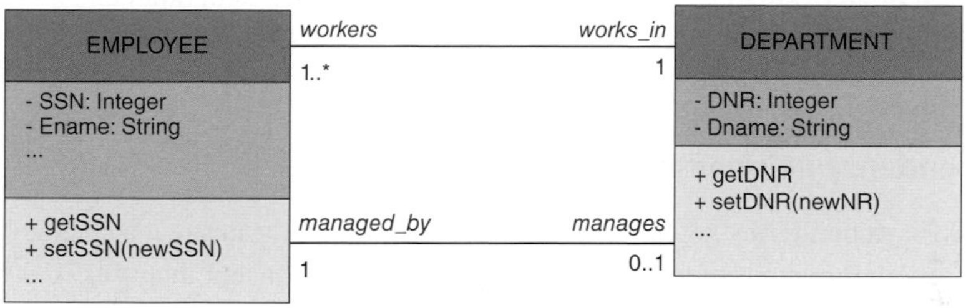


**Figure 3.42** OCL constraints in UML.

or procedural code is provided. They can be used for various purposes, such as to specify invariants for classes, to specify pre- and post-conditions for methods, to navigate between classes, or to define constraints on operations.

A class invariant is a constraint that holds for all objects of a class. An example could be a constraint specifying that the supplier status of each supplier object should be greater than 100:

```
SUPPLIER: SUPSTATUS>100
```

Pre- and post-conditions on methods must be true when a method either begins or ends. For example, before the method *withdrawal* can be executed, the balance must be positive. After it has been executed, the balance must still be positive.

OCL also supports more complex constraints. Figure 3.42 illustrates the two classes EMPLOYEE and DEPARTMENT. These two classes are connected with two associations to define which employee works in which department and which employee manages what department. Note the role names that have been added to both associations. Various constraints can now be added. A first constraint states that a manager of a department should have worked there for at least ten years:

```
Context: Department
invariant: self.managed_by.yearsemployed>10
```

The context of this constraint is the DEPARTMENT class. The constraint applies to every department object, hence the keyword invariant. We use the keyword self to refer to an object of the DEPARTMENT class. We then used the role name managed_by to navigate to the EMPLOYEE class and retrieve the yearsemployed variable.

A second constraint states: a department should have at least 20 employees:

```
Context: Department
invariant: self.workers→size() >20
```

The context is again DEPARTMENT. Note that self.workers returns the set of employees working in a specific department. The size method is then used to calculate the number of members in the set.

A final constraint says: A manager of a department must also work in the department. In OCL, this becomes:

```
Context: Department
Invariant: self.managed_by.works_in=self
```

From these examples, it is clear that OCL is a very powerful language that adds a lot of semantics to our conceptual data model. For more details on OCL, refer to www.omg.org/spec/OCL.

#### 3.4.9.3 Dependency Relationship

In UML, **dependency** defines a "using" relationship that states that a change in the specification of a UML modeling concept may affect another modeling concept that uses it. It is denoted by a dashed line in the UML diagram. An example could be when an object of one class uses an object of another class in its methods, but the referred object is not stored in any variable. This is illustrated in Figure 3.43.

We have two classes, EMPLOYEE and COURSE. Let's say an employee can take courses as part of a company education program. The EMPLOYEE class includes a method, tookCourse, that determines whether an employee took a particular course represented by the input variable CNR. Hence, an employee object makes use of a course object in one of its methods. This explains the dependency between both classes.

### 3.4.10 UML versus EER

Table 3.2 lists the similarities between both the UML class diagram and the EER model. From the table, it can be seen that the UML class diagram provides a richer set of semantics for modeling than the EER model. The UML class diagram can define methods that are not supported in the EER model. Complex integrity constraints can be modeled using OCL, which is also not available in the EER model.

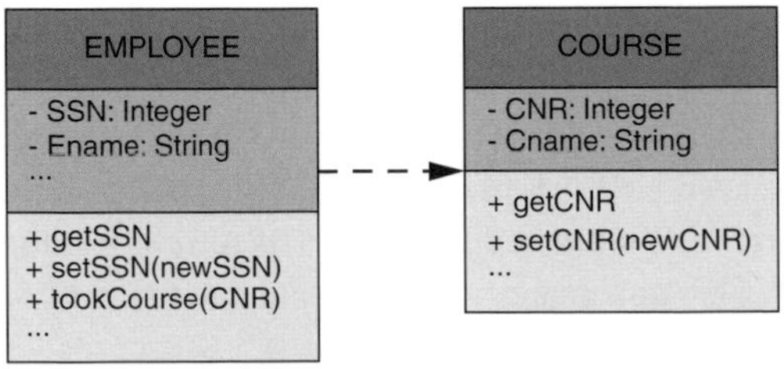


**Figure 3.43** Dependency relationship in UML.

**Retention Questions**

- What are the key concepts of object orientation (OO)?
- Discuss the components of a UML class diagram.
- How can associations be modeled in UML?
- What types of aggregation are supported in UML?
- What advanced modeling concepts are offered by UML?
- Contrast the UML class diagram with the EER model.

**Table 3.2** UML versus EER concepts

| UML class diagram | | EER model | |
|---|---|---|---|
| Class | | Entity type | |
| Object | | Entity | |
| Variable | | Attribute type | |
| Variable value | | Attribute | |
| Method | | – | |
| Association | | Relationship type | |
| Link | | Relationship | |
| Qualified association | | Weak entity type | |
| Specialization/generalization | | Specialization/generalization | |
| Aggregation | | Aggregation (composite/shared) | |
| OCL | | – | |
| Multiplicity | * | Cardinality | 0..N |
| | 0..1 | | 0..1 |
| | 1..* | | 1..N |
| | 1 | | 1..1 |

**Drill Down**

Some popular examples of conceptual modeling tools are: Astah (Change Vision), Database Workbench (Upscene Productions), Enterprise Architect (Sparx Systems), ER/Studio (Idera), and Erwin Data Modeler (Erwin). These tools typically provide facilities to build a conceptual model (e.g., EER or UML class diagram) and then automatically map it to a logical or internal data model for various target DBMS platforms. Most of them also include reverse engineering facilities whereby an existing internal data model can be turned back into a conceptual data model.

## Summary

In this chapter we discussed conceptual data modeling using the ER model, EER model, and UML class diagram. We started the chapter by reviewing the phases of database design: requirement collection and analysis, conceptual design, logical design, and physical design. The aim of a conceptual model is to formalize the data requirements of a business process in an accurate and user-friendly way. The ER model is a popular technique for conceptual data modeling. It has the following building blocks: entity types, attribute types, and relationship types. The EER model offers three additional modeling constructs: specialization/generalization, categorization, and aggregation. The UML class diagram is an object-oriented conceptual data model and consists of classes, variables, methods, and associations. It also supports specialization/generalization and aggregation, and offers various advanced modeling concepts such as the changeability property, object constraint language, and dependency relationships. From a pure semantic perspective, UML is richer than both ER and EER. In subsequent chapters, we elaborate on how to proceed to both logical and physical design.

### Scenario Conclusion

Figure 3.44 shows the EER model for our Sober scenario case. It has eight entity types. The CAR entity type has been specialized into SOBER CAR and OTHER CAR. Sober cars are owned by Sober, whereas other cars are owned by customers. The RIDE entity type has been specialized into RIDE HAILING and RIDE SHARING. The shared attribute types between both subclasses are put in the superclass: RIDE-NR (which is the key attribute type), PICKUP-DATE-TIME, DROPOFF-DATE-TIME, DURATION, PICKUP-LOC, DROPOFF-LOC, DISTANCE, and FEE. Note that DURATION is a derived attribute type since it can be derived from PICKUP-DATE-TIME and DROPOFF-DATE-TIME. DISTANCE is not a derived attribute type since there could be multiple routes between a pick-up location and a drop-off location. Three attribute types are added to the RIDE HAILING entity type: PASSENGERS (the number of passengers), WAIT-TIME (the effective wait time), and REQUEST-TIME (Sober App request or hand wave). The LEAD_CUSTOMER relationship type is a 1:N relationship type between CUSTOMER and RIDE HAILING, whereas the BOOK relationship type is an N:M relationship type between CUSTOMER and RIDE SHARING. A car (e.g., Sober or other car) can be involved in zero to N accidents, whereas an accident can have one to M cars (e.g., Sober or other car) involved. The DAMAGE AMOUNT attribute type is connected to the relationship type because it is dependent upon the car and the accident.

As discussed in this chapter, our EER model has certain shortcomings. Since the EER model is a snapshot in time, it cannot model temporal constraints. Examples of temporal constraints that cannot be enforced by our EER model are: the pick-up-date-time should always precede the drop-off-date-time; a customer cannot book a ride-hailing and ride-sharing service that overlap in time.

The EER model cannot guarantee the consistency across multiple relationship types. An example of a business rule that cannot be enforced in the EER model is: a customer cannot book a ride-hailing or ride-sharing service with his/her own car.

The EER model does not support domains – for example, we cannot specify that the attribute type PASSENGERS is an integer with a minimum value of 0 and a maximum value of 6.

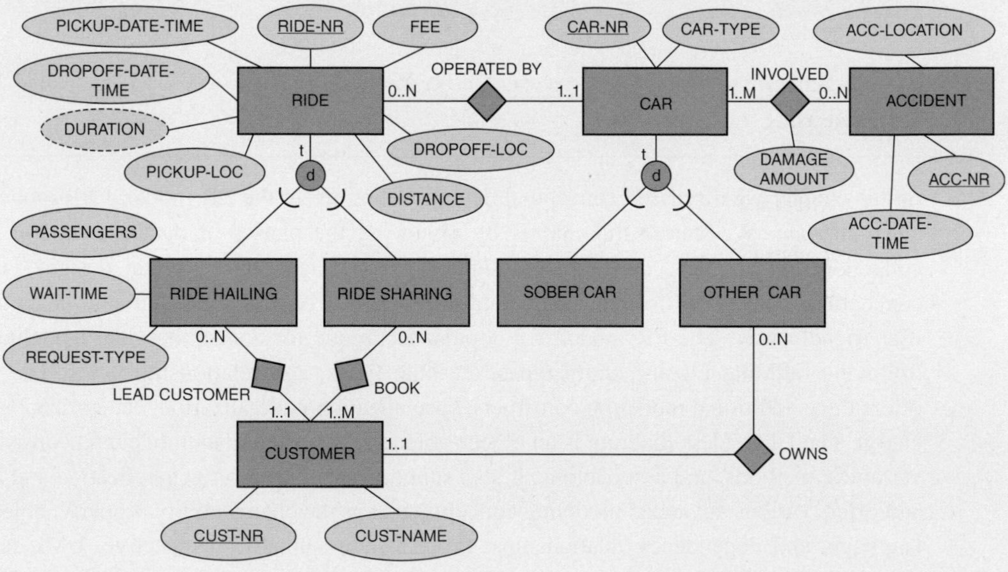


**Figure 3.44** EER model for Sober.

Furthermore, our EER model does not specify that the maximum number of passengers for a ride-share service is ten or that the WAIT-TIME is only relevant for Sober App requests and should be zero in case of hand-wave requests.

Figure 3.45 shows the UML class diagram for Sober. It has nine classes. The class INVOLVED is an association class between CAR and ACCIDENT. To enforce information hiding, the access modifiers of all variables have been set to private. Getter and setter methods are used to access them. We also added the following additional methods:

- In the RIDE class: CalcDuration which calculates the derived variable duration.
- In the RIDE-SHARING class: NumberOfCustomers, which returns the number of customers for a ride-share service.
- In the CUSTOMER class: Top5CustomersHail and Top5CustomersShare, which returns the top five customers for ride-hailing and ride-sharing services, respectively.
- In the CAR class: NumberOfRides, which returns the number of rides a car has serviced.
- In the SOBER CAR class: NumberOfSoberCars, which returns the number of Sober cars in the database.
- In the INVOLVED association class: GenerateReport, which returns a report of which cars have been involved in what accident.
- In the ACCIDENT class: Top3AccidentHotSpots and Top3AccidentPeakTimes, which return the top three most common accident locations and timings, respectively.

All associations have been defined as bidirectional, which implies that they can be navigated in both directions. We set the changeability property of the number variables (e.g., RIDE-NR, CAR-NR, etc.) to frozen, which means that once a value has been assigned to any of them, it can no longer be changed.

We can now enrich our UML model by adding OCL constraints. We define a class invariant for the RIDE HAILING class, which specifies that the number of passengers for a ride-hail service should be less than six:

```
RIDE-HAILING: PASSENGERS ≤ 6
```

Remember that the maximum number of passengers for a ride-share service is ten. This can be defined using the following OCL constraint:[5]

```
Context: RIDE SHARING
invariant: self.BOOK→size() ≤ 10
```

The constraint applies to every ride-sharing object, hence the keyword invariant. Other OCL constraints can be added for further semantic refinement.

The UML specification is semantically richer than its EER counterpart. As an example, both passenger constraints cannot be enforced in the EER model. The UML class diagram also specifies the domains (e.g., integer, string, etc.) for each of the variables and includes methods, both of which were not possible in the EER model.

Sober is now ready to proceed to the next stage of database design in which the conceptual data model will be mapped to a logical model.

[5] We could have defined two different role names for the association BOOK to represent its two directions. However, for the sake of simplicity, we use BOOK to refer to the association from the direction of RIDE SHARING to CUSTOMER.

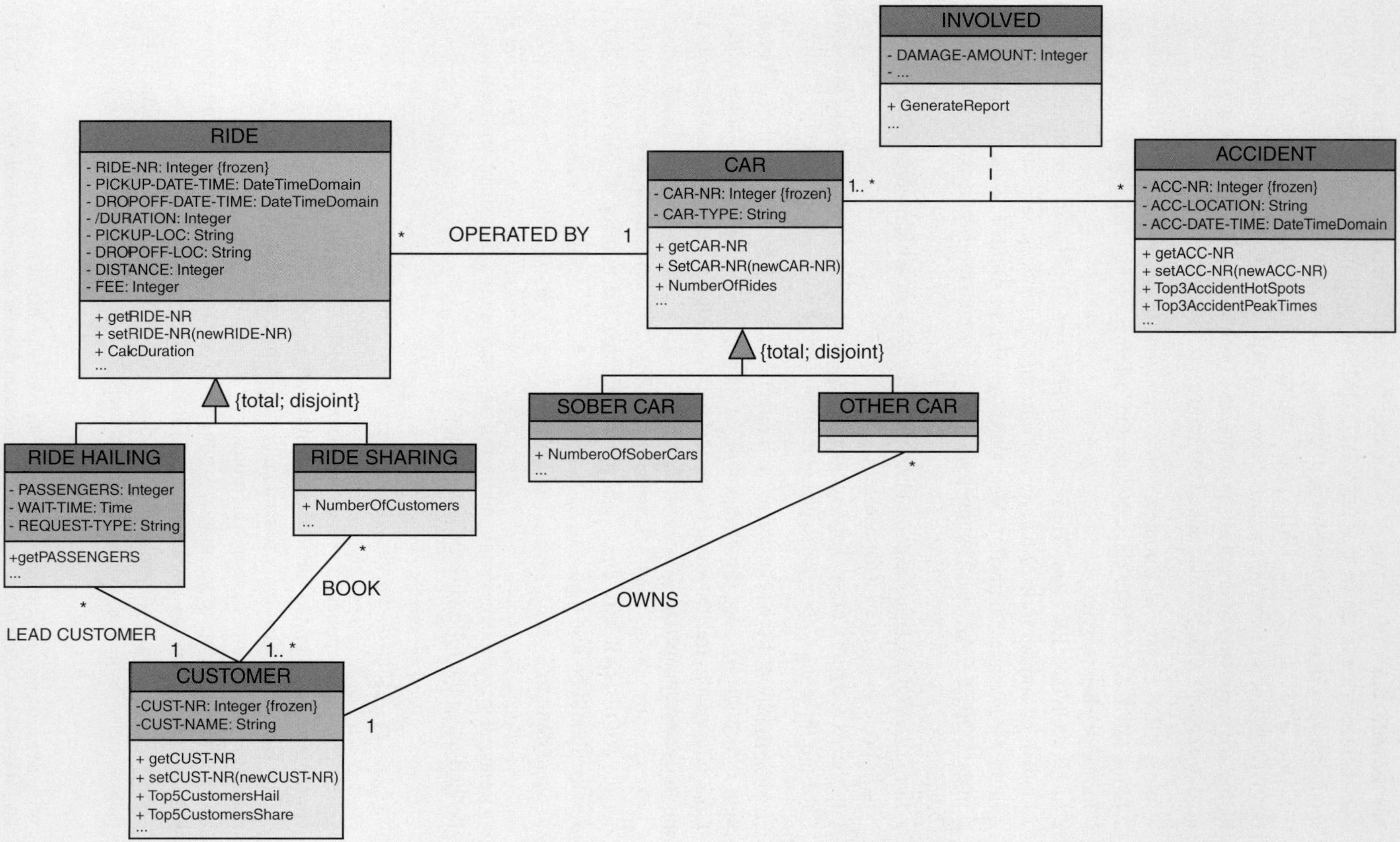


**Figure 3.45** UML class diagram for Sober.

## Key Terms List

abstraction
access modifiers
aggregation
association class
associations
attribute type
bidirectional association
business process
cardinalities
categorization
changeability property
class
class invariant
completeness constraint
composite attribute type
conceptual data model
degree
dependency
derived attribute type
disjoint specialization
disjointness constraint
domain
Enhanced Entity Relationship (EER) model
entity relationship (ER) model
entity type
existence dependency
generalization
information hiding
inheritance
key attribute type
multi-valued attribute type
object
object constraint language (OCL)
overlap specialization
owner entity type
partial categorization
partial participation
partial specialization
qualified association
relationship
relationship type
requirement collection and analysis
roles
selective inheritance
simple or atomic attribute type
single-valued attribute
specialization
strong entity type
temporal constraints
ternary relationship types
total categorization
total participation
total specialization
unidirectional association
Unified Modeling Language (UML)
weak entity type

## Review Questions

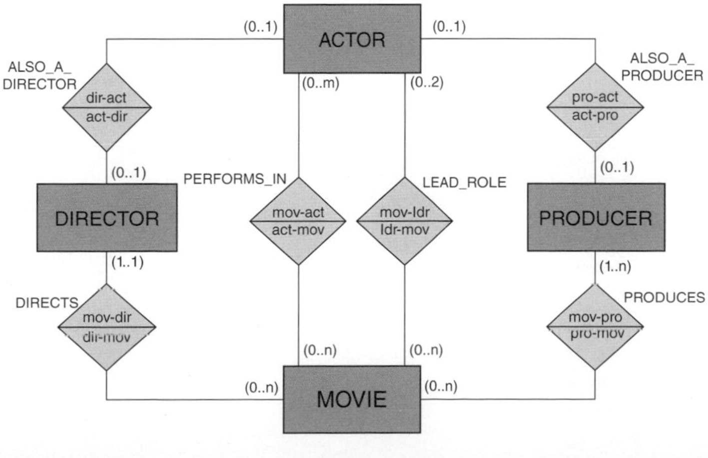

**3.1.** Given the ER model above, which of the following statements is **correct**?

a. A movie can have as many lead actors as there are actors in the movie.
b. PRODUCER is an existence-dependent entity type.
c. A director of a movie can also act in the same movie.
d. A movie can have multiple actors, producers, and directors.

**3.2.** In the movie ER model above, we focus on the binary relationship "PRODUCES". Suppose we add an attribute type that indicates the time that each producer spent on producing each movie called "WORKING HOURS". Which of the following scenarios is possible?

a. We can migrate the attribute type "WORKING HOURS" to the "MOVIE" entity type.
b. We can migrate the attribute type "WORKING HOURS" to the "PRODUCER" entity type.
c. We can migrate the attribute type "WORKING HOURS" to either one of the linked entity types.
d. We can add the attribute type "WORKING HOURS" to the relationship type PRODUCES.

**3.3.** Which statement is **correct**?

a. In the case a ternary relationship type is represented as three binary relationship types, then semantics will get lost.
b. A ternary relationship type can always be represented as three binary relationship types without loss of semantics.
c. Three binary relationship types between three entity types can always be replaced by one ternary relationship type between the three participating entity types.
d. A ternary relationship type cannot have attribute types.

**3.4.** Which statements are **correct**?

a. A weak entity type can only have one attribute type.
b. A weak entity type is always existence-dependent.
c. An existence-dependent entity type is always a weak entity type.
d. An existence-dependent entity type always participates in a 1:1 relationship type.

**3.5.** Given the following ER model:

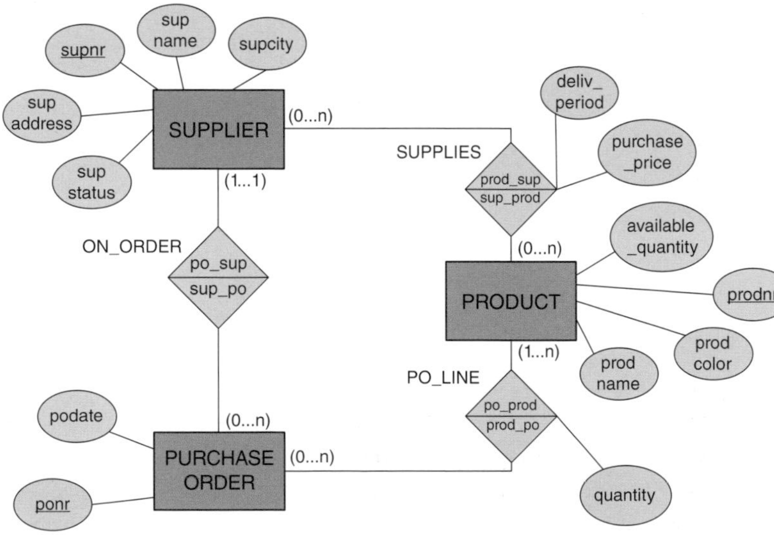

which statement is **not correct**?

a. The ER model does not enforce that a supplier can only have purchase orders outstanding for products he/she can actually supply.
b. The ER model has both weak and existence-dependent entity types.
c. According to the ER model, a supplier cannot have more than one address.
d. According to the ER model, there can be suppliers that supply no products and have no purchase orders outstanding.

**3.6.** Given the following EER specialization:

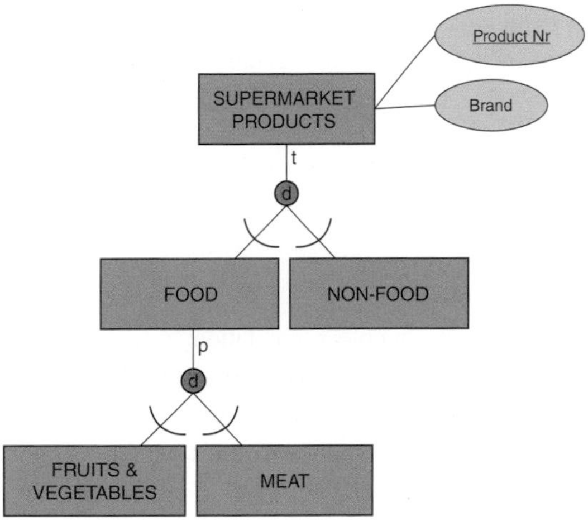


which of the following statements is **correct**?

a. A supermarket product can be a food and non-food product at the same time.
b. There are certain supermarket products that are not fruits and vegetables, not meat and not non-food.
c. All food products are either fruits and vegetables or meat.
d. A meat product does not have any attribute types.

**3.7.** Given the following EER categorization:

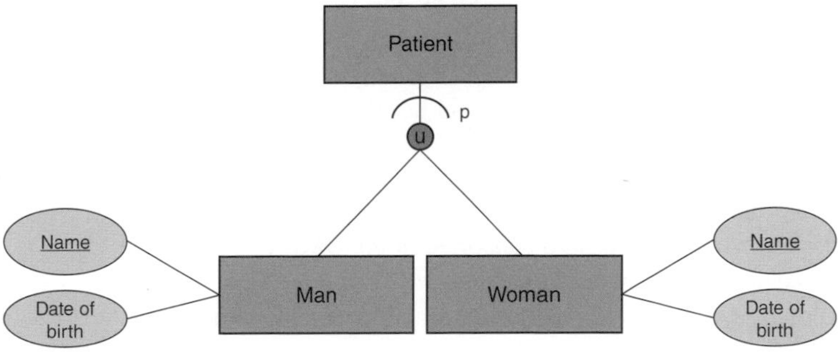


which statement is **correct**?

a. All men and women are patients.
b. A patient only inherits the "Name" and "Date of birth" attribute types from the superclass that the current entity belongs to.

c. The categorization can also be represented as a specialization.
d. The categorization can also be represented as an aggregation.

**3.8.** Which one of the following is an example of a **disjoint** and **partial** specialization?

a. HUMAN → VEGETARIAN + NON-VEGETARIAN
b. HUMAN → BLONDE + BRUNETTE
c. HUMAN → LOVES FISH + LOVES MEAT
d. HUMAN → UNIVERSITY DEGREE + COLLEGE DEGREE

**3.9.** Which of the following statements is **correct**?

a. An aggregation cannot have attribute types.
b. An aggregation cannot participate in a relationship type.
c. An aggregation should both have attribute types and participate in one or more relationship types.
d. An aggregation can have attribute types and participate in relationship types.

**3.10.** Which statement is **correct**?

a. A class is an instance of an object.
b. A class only has variables.
c. Inheritance is not supported in object orientation.
d. Information hiding (also referred to as encapsulation) states that the variables of an object can only be accessed through either getter or setter methods.

**3.11.** Which variable types are not directly supported in UML?

a. Composite variables.
b. Multi-valued variables.
c. Variables with unique values (similar to key attribute types in the ER model).
d. Derived variables.

**3.12.** Which of the following statements is **not correct**?

a. In UML, access modifiers can be used to specify who can have access to a variable or method.
b. A private access modifier (denoted by the symbol "–") is used in the case that the variable or method can only be accessed by the class itself.
c. A public access modifier (denoted by the symbol "+") is used in the case that the variable or method can be accessed by any other class.
d. A protected access modifier (denoted by the symbol "#") is used in the case that the variable or method can be accessed by both the class and its superclasses.

**3.13.** Which statement is **correct**?

a. An association is an instance of a link.
b. Only binary associations are supported in the UML class diagram.
c. An association is always bidirectional.
d. Qualified associations can be used to represent weak entity types.

**3.14.** A composite aggregation...

a. has a maximum multiplicity of 1 and a minimum multiplicity of 0 or 1 at the composite side.
b. has a maximum multiplicity of n and a minimum multiplicity of 0 at the composite side.
c. has a maximum multiplicity of n and a minimum multiplicity of 0 or 1 at the composite side.
d. has a maximum multiplicity of 1 and a minimum multiplicity of 1 at the composite side.

**3.15.** Which statement is **not correct**?

a. The changeability property specifies the type of operations that are allowed on either variable values or links.
b. OCL constraints are defined in a procedural way.
c. OCL constraints can be used for various purposes, such as to specify invariants for classes, to specify pre- and post-conditions for methods, to navigate between classes or to define constraints on operations.
d. In UML, dependency defines a "using" relationship that states that a change in the specification of a UML modeling concept may affect another modeling concept that uses it.

## Problems and Exercises

3.1E Fitness company "Conan" wants to set-up a database for its members and trainers. One of the aims is to record information about which members participated in which sessions and which trainers supervised which sessions.

Conan operates various fitness centers in various cities. Every center is characterized by a unique name (e.g., Fitplaza, my6pack). Every center has an address and one or more rooms (you can consider address as atomic). Every room has a maximum capacity. Within a center, each room has a unique number such as 1, 2, 3, etc.

People can register for individual or group sessions in different centers. Each group session requires exactly one trainer. Individual sessions are done without a trainer. For each person, we want to store the first name, family name, and birth date. You can assume that the combination of first name, family name, and birth date is unique. For each trainer, the diploma is also recorded. A person can be a trainer in one session and participant in another session (either individual or group session). The model should also include information about people (e.g., prospects) that have not participated in any sessions yet, or trainers (e.g., interns) that have not supervised any group sessions yet.

For each session, the date and starting hour should be recorded. For group sessions, also the type should be stored (e.g., aerobics, bodystyling, etc.). Sessions can start at the same time on the same day but in different rooms of a center or in different centers. At a given start hour of a given day, at most one individual or group session can start in a given room of a given center.

Make an EER model and UML class diagram to model the data requirements for Conan. Comment on the limitations of both models.

3.2E Recently, the European Union made funds available to set-up a cross-national research database that stores information concerning scientific articles of researchers working at institutions in the EU. Science Connect is the company that will be setting up this database.

The system will store information regarding scientific staff (persons) and research institutions. Both are uniquely identified by a person ID and an institution code, respectively. The following is also recorded for each person: a phone number, keywords that identify his/her key research topics and the institution he/she works for. A person can be an author of one article and a reviewer of another peer-reviewed article at the same time.

The database will store the following information concerning scientific articles. Each scientific article is uniquely identified by a DOI (a document object identifier), and the system also stores the title and the authors of the article. In the case of multiple authors, the position of each author is stored. Science Connect distinguishes between two types of scientific articles: a scientific article is either a peer-reviewed paper or a technical report. The system stores the citation count of peer-reviewed papers and who reviewed the paper. A technical report is always published by a single research institution, while research institutions can of course publish multiple technical reports.

The system keeps track of the different scientific publishers (e.g., IEEE, Elsevier). A publisher is identified by name. A publisher can publish multiple journals to which research institutions can subscribe. These journals are given a name by the publisher (e.g., *Decision Support Systems*). Publishers can have journals with the same name as other publishers; e.g., it is possible that both IEEE and Elsevier have a journal with the title *Management Science*. The impact factor, which measures the scientific impact of a journal, is also stored.

Finally, only peer-reviewed papers are published in journals, not technical reports.

Make an EER model and UML class diagram to model the data requirements. Comment on the limitations of both models.

3.3E One of your (hipster) acquaintances thinks he has the next billion-dollar startup idea for an app: Pizza Delivery with Entertainment. He heard from other people that you are following the course on database management, and asks you to design the EER model. Afterwards, he will use the EER model to ask programmers to implement the app.

He explains the basic functionality of the app as follows: customers can order pizzas from restaurants to be delivered to a specific address, and if they want to, they can choose a special "entertainment order". When an order is an entertainment order, the delivery person stays with the customer after delivering the pizza and entertains the customers (e.g., by singing, making jokes, doing magic tricks, etc.) for a certain amount of time.

Now follows a detailed explanation of the range of capabilities of the app: when people create an account for the app and become app users, they have to indicate their birthday and fill in their name and address. Every user should also be uniquely identifiable.

Once the account is created, the users should be presented with three options: the first option in the app is to select "business owner". Of these business owners, we also ask them to provide their LinkedIn account so we can add them to our professional network. Every business owner can own a number of pizza restaurants. Of these pizza restaurants, we want to register the zip code, address, phone number, website, and the opening hours.

Each pizza restaurant can offer a number of pizzas. Of those pizzas, we want to keep the name (margarita, quattro stagioni, etc.), the crust structure (for example, classic Italian crust, deep dish crust, cheese crust), and the price. While two pizzas from different pizza restaurants may have the same name, they will not be exactly the same as the taste will be different, and thus should be considered unique. Moreover, pizzas should be distinguishable even if they have the same price, e.g., a pizza margarita from Pizza Pronto in New York which costs $12 must be distinguishable from a pizza margarita from Pizza Rapido in Singapore, which also costs $12.

The second option in the app is to select "hungry customer". For these hungry customers, we need a delivery address. Hungry customers can make orders for pizzas. Each order gets assigned an ID, and we want our app to log the date and time when the order was placed. We also allow the hungry customer to indicate the latest time of delivery, and ask how many people the order is for. An order can be for one or more pizzas.

Also, a special type of order can be made: the entertainment order. Not every order has to be an entertainment order. But when a hungry customer indicates that he or she wants to be entertained while eating the pizza, we not only want to register all the regular order information, but also the type of entertainment the user requests, and for how long (a duration).

The third option in the app to select is that of "entertainer". When users select entertainer, they need to provide a stage name, write a short bio about themselves, and indicate their price per 30 minutes. Every entertainment order is fulfilled by exactly one entertainer. Every entertainer can choose for which pizza restaurant(s) he/she wants to work. For each pizza restaurant an entertainer wants to work with, he/she should indicate his/her availability by day (Monday, Tuesday, Wednesday, etc.).

Make an EER model and UML class diagram to model the data requirements. Comment on the limitations of both models.

3.4E Attracted by the success of Spotify, a group of students wants to build its own music streaming website called Musicmatic. Being economists, they are unaware of the specificities of databases and have therefore asked you to create an EER model.

A large number of songs will be made available through their website, and the following information on each song needs to be stored: title, year, length, and genre. Also, artist information will be added, including date of birth, name and a URL to a website (e.g., Wikipedia page) with additional information on the artist. You can assume an artist is uniquely identified by his/her name, and that a song always belongs to exactly one artist. The Musicmatic students also point out that songs having the same title are possible, and only the combination of song and artist can be assumed to be unique.

The database will also have to store information on the people using Musicmatic. It was decided to only discriminate between two types of users: the regular users who will be able to buy music, and the business users who will deliver the content (upload the music). The following information is recorded on each user: (unique) ID, name, and address. Business users will also have a VAT number.

The students want to offer a flexible service, and decided business users can only upload individual songs. These songs are classified either as singles or hits, and regular users can directly buy the singles. Otherwise, people can compose an album consisting of multiple hits (no singles). The position of each hit in the album is stored as a track number in the database. Note that the album of regular users can be turned into a suggestion to other regular users with similar purchasing behavior.

Finally, a user can be a regular user on some occasions (e.g., when downloading a single or album), and a business user at other times (e.g., when uploading self-made songs to Musicmatic).

Make an EER model and UML class diagram to model the data requirements. Comment on the limitations of both models.

3.5E Recently, a new social network site, Facepage, was founded. Given the current trends, the managers of Facepage are convinced that this will be the new hype in the near future.

When new users want to join Facepage, they first need to fill in a form with their personal information (i.e., ID, name, email, and date of birth). A user has a unique ID. Afterwards, an account is created. An account is uniquely identified by an account number, automatically generated by the database system. The user needs to specify which type of account he/she prefers: a business account or a personal account. A business account is specifically designed to support companies in their marketing campaigns. When a user decides to open a business account, he/she has to specify the name of the company. Users with a business account pay a monthly fee. When a user opts for a personal account, he/she can keep in touch with other Facepage users. Only personal accounts can send or receive friend requests.

Maintaining multiple accounts, regardless of the purpose, is a violation of Facepage's Terms of Use. If a user already has a personal (business) account, then Facepage cannot allow the user to create an additional personal or business account for any reason.

Each account can create several pages. While each page must be administrated by exactly one account, personal accounts can be granted privileges (e.g., to write something on the wall of friends, adjust some information) to pages belonging to other personal accounts. For each page, the page name and the number of visits are logged. For each account, no two pages can exist with the same name. Users with a business profile can create a special type of page: an advertisement page. This page records several features, like the bounce rate, the click-through rate, and the conversion rate. The bounce rate is the percentage of visitors on the page that leave immediately. The click-through rate is the percentage of visitors that click on a certain banner on the page. The conversion rate is the percentage of visitors that accomplish the intended goal, like a purchase or a transaction.

Make an EER model and UML class diagram to model the data requirements for Facepage. Comment on the limitations of both models.

# 4 Organizational Aspects of Data Management

## Chapter Objectives

In this chapter, you will learn to:

- identify the basic concepts of data management;
- understand the role and importance of catalogs, metadata, data quality, and data governance;
- identify key roles in database modeling and management;
- understand the differences between an information architect, database designer, data owner, data steward, database administrator, and data scientist.

**Opening Scenario**

Sober realizes that the success of its entire business model depends on data, and it wants to make sure the data are managed in an optimal way. The company is looking at how to organize proper data management and wondering about the corresponding job profiles to hire. The challenge is twofold. On the one hand, Sober wants to have the right data management team to ensure optimal data quality. On the other hand, Sober only has a limited budget to build that team.

In this chapter, we zoom into the organizational aspects of data management. We begin by elaborating on data management and review the essential role of catalogs and metadata, both of which were introduced in Chapter 1. We then discuss metadata modeling, which essentially follows a similar database design process to that which we described in Chapter 3. Data quality is also extensively covered in terms of both its importance and its underlying dimensions. Next, we introduce data governance as a corporate culture to safeguard data quality. We conclude by reviewing various roles in data modeling and management, such as information architect, database designer, data owner, data steward, database administrator, and data scientist.

## 4.1 Data Management

**Data management** entails the proper management of data and the corresponding data definitions or metadata. It aims at ensuring that (meta-)data are of good quality and thus a key resource for effective and efficient managerial decision-making. In the following subsections we first review catalogs, the role of metadata, and the modeling thereof. This is followed by a discussion on data quality and data governance.

### 4.1.1 Catalogs and the Role of Metadata

The importance of good metadata management cannot be understated. In the past this was often neglected, resulting in significant problems when applications needed to be updated or maintained. In the file-based approach to data management, the metadata were stored in each application separately, creating the issues discussed in Chapter 1. Just as with raw data, metadata are also data that need to be properly modeled, stored, and managed. Hence, the concepts of data modeling should also be applied to metadata in a transparent way. In a DBMS approach, metadata are stored in a catalog, sometimes also called a data dictionary or data repository, which constitutes the heart of the database system. This facilitates the efficient answering of questions such as which data are stored *where* in the database? Who is the owner of the data? Who has access to the data? How are the data defined and structured? Which transactions work with which data? Are the data replicated and how can consistency be guaranteed? Which integrity rules are defined? How frequently are backups made? The catalog can be an integral part of a DBMS or a standalone component that must be updated manually. The integrated solution is preferred and is more prevalent in modern DBMSs.

The **catalog** provides an important source of information for end-users, application developers, and the DBMS itself. Remember, the data definitions are generated by the DDL compiler. The DML compiler and query processor use the metadata to solve queries and determine the optimal access path (see Chapter 2).

The catalog should provide support for various functionalities. It should implement an extensible metamodel for the description of the metadata. It should have facilities to import and export the data definitions and provide support for maintenance and re-use of metadata. The integrity rules stored should be continuously monitored and enforced whenever the raw data are updated. By doing so, the catalog guarantees that the database is always in a consistent and correct state. It should support facilities for user access by clearly defining which user has access to which metadata. A catalog also stores statistics about the data and its usage. These are extensively used by the DBA for performance monitoring and tuning. Also, the query optimizer of the DBMS relies on these statistics to determine the optimal execution path of a query.

**Drill Down**

Different vendors may adopt different names for the catalog. For example, in Oracle it is referred to as the data dictionary, in SQL server as the system catalog, in DB2 as the DB2 catalog or system catalog, and in MySQL as the information schema.

### 4.1.2 Metadata Modeling

**Connections**

In Chapter 7 we discuss how to design a relational database for a catalog and illustrate how it can be defined and queried using SQL.

A **metamodel** is a data model for metadata. A metamodel determines the type of metadata that can be stored. Just as with raw data, a database design process can be used to design a database storing metadata (see Chapter 3). As already discussed, the first step is to design a conceptual model of the metadata. This can be either an EER model or a UML model. Figure 4.1 shows an example of a metamodel that in this case is an EER conceptual model of an EER model. The relationship types $R_1$ and $R_2$ model the relationship between an attribute and an entity or relationship. The relationship type $R_3$ specifies which entities participate in which relationships. The relationship type $R_4$ is a ternary

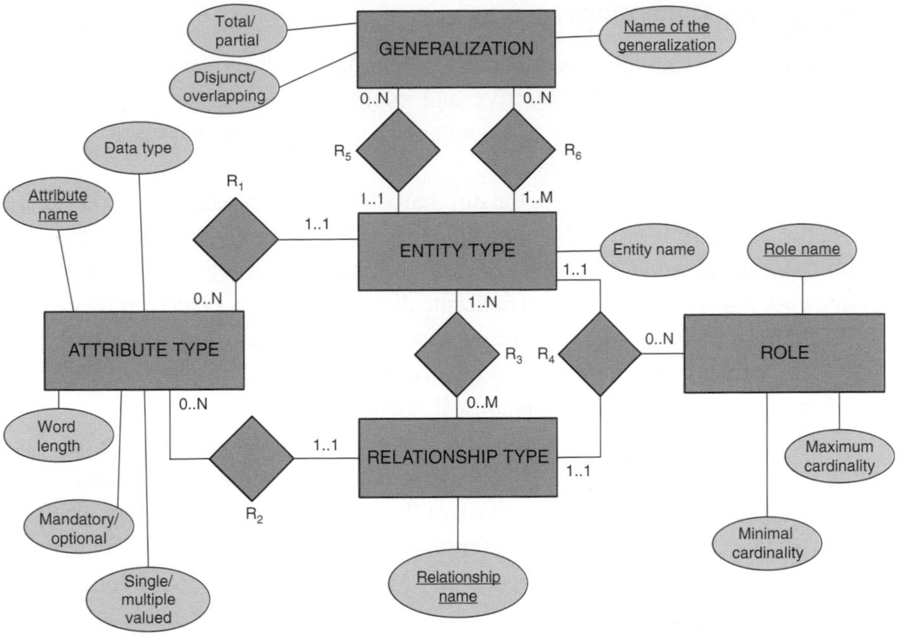


**Figure 4.1** EER conceptual model of an EER model.

relationship type between entity type, relationship type, and role. $R_5$ and $R_6$ model the entities that participate in a generalization, as either a superclass or a subclass. We assume that every generalization has one superclass ($R_5$) and one or more subclasses ($R_6$).

### 4.1.3 Data Quality

**Data quality (DQ)** is often defined as “fitness for use”, which implies the relative nature of the concept. Data of acceptable quality in one decision context may be perceived to be of poor quality in another decision context, even by the same business user. For instance, the extent to which data are required to be complete for accounting tasks may not be required for analytical sales prediction tasks.

Data quality determines the intrinsic value of the data to the business. Information technology only serves as a magnifier for this intrinsic value. Hence, high-quality data combined with effective technology comprises a great asset, but poor-quality data combined with effective technology is an equally great liability. This is sometimes also called the GIGO – Garbage In, Garbage Out – principle, stating that bad data result in bad decisions, even with the best technology available. Decisions made based on useless data have cost companies billions of dollars. A popular example of this is the address of a customer. It is estimated that approximately 10% of customers change their address annually. Obsolete customer addresses can have substantial consequences for mail order companies, package delivery providers, or government services.

Poor DQ impacts organizations in many ways. At the operational level, it affects customer satisfaction, increases operational expenses, and will lead to lower employee job satisfaction. Similarly, at the strategic level, it affects the quality of the decision-making process. The magnitude of DQ problems is exacerbated by the exponential increase in the size of databases. This qualifies DQ management as one of the most important business challenges in today’s data-based economy.

#### 4.1.3.1 Data Quality Dimensions

Data quality is a multidimensional concept in which each dimension represents a single aspect or construct, comprising both objective and subjective perspectives.[1] Some aspects are absolute, whereas others depend on the task and/or experience of the data user. Therefore, it is useful to define DQ in terms of its dimensions.

A **DQ framework** categorizes the different dimensions of data quality. Different DQ frameworks exist, but a prevalent one is the framework given by Wang *et al.*[2] It is represented in Table 4.1 and shows the different DQ dimensions grouped into four categories.[3] The motivation behind the framework was to capture a broad conceptualization of DQ as perceived by data consumers (instead of ICT professionals) since they are the ones using the data. The framework provides a means to measure, analyze, and improve data quality in a valid way. It was built using a two-stage survey combined with well-established empirical research methods.

The **intrinsic category** represents the extent to which data values conform to the actual or true values. It denotes that data should have good quality. The **contextual category** measures the extent to which data are appropriate to the task of the data consumer. Obviously, this can vary in time and across data consumers. The **representation category** indicates the extent to which data are presented in a consistent and interpretable way. Hence, it relates to the format and meaning of data. The **access category** represents the extent to which data are available and obtainable in a secure manner. This is especially important in today's networked environment, with data being distributed across various platforms. Each category has multiple dimensions, as is illustrated in Table 4.1. High-quality data should be intrinsically good, contextually appropriate for the task, clearly represented, and accessible to the data consumer.

Some dimensions (e.g., accuracy and objectivity) lend themselves to objective assessment that is intrinsic to the data themselves, independently from the context in which the data are used. Other dimensions cannot be measured in absolute terms and vary with the usage context or task at hand. We now discuss some of the most important DQ dimensions in Table 4.1.

##### *Accuracy*

**Accuracy** refers to whether the data values stored for an object are the correct values. For example, suppose the value for birth date of a customer is February 27, 1975. If a customer database has a BIRTH_DATE data element that expects dates in US format, a date of 02/27/1975 would be correct. A date of 02/27/1976 would be incorrect because it is the wrong value. A date of 27/02/1975 would also be incorrect because it follows a European instead of a US representation. This example also illustrates that the accuracy dimension is heavily correlated with other DQ dimensions. Often, after root cause analysis, a quality issue initially labeled as an accuracy problem will turn out, for example, to be a matter of representation (e.g., US versus European notation) or **timeliness** (e.g., customer address is obsolete).

##### *Completeness*

Another crucial dimension is the completeness of data. The **completeness** dimension can be viewed from at least three perspectives: schema completeness, column completeness, and population

[1] Moges H.T., Dejaeger K., Lemahieu W., Baesens B., A multidimensional analysis of data quality for credit risk management: New insights and challenges, *Information and Management*, 2013; 50(1): 43–58.

[2] Wang R.Y., Strong, D.M. Beyond accuracy: What data quality means to data consumers, *Journal of Management Information Systems*, 1996; 12(4).

[3] The actual dimensions within these categories differ slightly from the original framework and are based on the work of Moges et al. (2013).

**Table 4.1** Data quality dimensions

| Category | DQ dimensions | Definitions |
|---|---|---|
| **Intrinsic** | Accuracy | The extent to which data are certified, error-free, correct, flawless, and reliable |
| | Objectivity | The extent to which data are unbiased, unprejudiced, based on facts, and impartial |
| | Reputation | The extent to which data are highly regarded in terms of their sources or content |
| **Contextual** | Completeness | The extent to which data are not missing and cover the needs of the tasks and are of sufficient breadth and depth for the task at hand |
| | Appropriate-amount | The extent to which the volume of data is appropriate for the task at hand |
| | Value-added | The extent to which data are beneficial and provide advantages from their use |
| | Relevance | The extent to which data are applicable and helpful for the task at hand |
| | Timeliness | The extent to which data are sufficiently up-to-date for the task at hand |
| | Actionable | The extent to which data are ready for use |
| **Representation** | Interpretable | The extent to which data are in appropriate languages, symbols, and the definitions are clear |
| | Easily understandable | The extent to which data are easily comprehended |
| | Consistency | The extent to which data are continuously presented in the same format |
| | Concisely represented | The extent to which data are compactly represented, well presented, well organized, and well formatted |
| | Alignment | The extent to which data are reconcilable (compatible) |
| **Access** | Accessibility | The extent to which data are available, or easily and swiftly retrievable |
| | Security | The extent to which access to data is restricted appropriately to maintain their security |
| | Traceability | The extent to which data are traceable to the source |

**Table 4.2** Column completeness

| ID | Forename | Surname | Birth date | Email |
|---|---|---|---|---|
| 1 | Bart | Baesens | 27/02/1975 | Bart.Baesens@kuleuven.be |
| 2 | Wilfried | Lemahieu | 08/03/1970 | Null |
| 3 | Seppe | vanden Broucke | 09/11/1986 | Null |
| 4 | John | Edward | 14/20/1955 | Null |

completeness. By *schema completeness*, we mean the degree to which entity types and attribute types are missing from the schema. An example of a schema completeness problem could be a missing ORDER entity type or a missing Email address attribute type. *Column completeness* considers the degree to which there exist missing values in a column of a data table. An example of a column completeness problem could be a missing value for a customer's birth date. *Population completeness* indicates the degree to which the necessary members of a population are present or not. An example of a population completeness problem could be that important supplier entities are missing for the SUPPLIER entity type.

Table 4.2 gives an example of three column completeness problems. Although the null values seem identical at first sight, there could be various reasons for this. For example, suppose Wilfried Lemahieu has no email address – then this is not then an incompleteness problem. If Seppe vanden

Broucke has an email address, but it is not known, this would be an incompleteness problem. Finally, we do not know if John Edward has an email address, so we do not have enough information to determine whether this is an incompleteness problem.

*Consistency*

The **consistency** dimension can also be viewed from several perspectives. For example, one can be concerned about the consistency of redundant or duplicated data in one table or in multiple tables: different data elements representing the same real-world concept should be consistent with one another. Another perspective would be the consistency between two related data elements. For example, the name of the city and the postal code should be consistent. Consistency can also refer to consistency of format for the same data element used in different tables. Otherwise, two values can be both correct and unambiguous, but still cause problems – for example, the values New York and NY may both refer to the same city. These examples of inconsistencies will typically be symptomatic for underlying problems with other DQ dimensions, such as accuracy or completeness.

*Accessibility*

The **accessibility** dimension reflects the ease of retrieving the data from the underlying data sources. Often, there will be a tradeoff between the security and accessibility dimensions. The more measures are in place to enhance security, the more obstacles may be introduced to obtain access to the data. Such tradeoffs are common between DQ dimensions. Another example is the possible tradeoff between timeliness and completeness; the higher the pressure to deliver the data promptly, the fewer measures can be taken to detect and resolve missing values.

#### 4.1.3.2 Data Quality Problems

Data quality is a multidimensional concept. Hence, DQ problems can arise in various ways. The following are common causes of poor DQ:

- Multiple data sources: multiple sources with the same data may produce duplicates – a problem of consistency.
- Subjective judgment in data production: data production using human judgment (e.g., opinions) can cause the production of biased information – a problem of objectivity.
- Limited computing resources: lack of sufficient computing resources and/or digitalization may limit the accessibility of relevant data – a problem of accessibility.
- Volume of data: large volumes of stored data make it difficult to access needed information in a reasonable time – a problem of accessibility.
- Changing data needs: data requirements change on an ongoing basis due to new company strategies or the introduction of new technologies – a problem of relevance.
- Different processes using and updating the same data – a problem of consistency.

These causes of DQ problems have always existed to a certain extent, since the beginning of the digital era. However, initially most data processing applications and database systems existed in relative isolation, as so-called silos. This was far from an ideal situation from a company-wide data-sharing perspective, but at least the producers and consumers of the data were largely the same people or belonged to the same department or business unit. One was mostly aware of which DQ issues existed with one's own data and people would often deal with them in an ad-hoc manner, based on familiarity with the data. However, with the advent of business process integration, company-wide data-sharing, and using data from various operational systems for strategic decision-making, the data producers and consumers have been largely decoupled. Therefore, people responsible for entering the data are not fully aware of the DQ requirements of the people using the data, or of the different business processes in which the data are used. Moreover, different tasks using the same data may have very distinct DQ requirements.

### 4.1.4 Data Governance

Due to the DQ problems we introduced in the previous section, organizations are increasingly implementing company-wide data governance initiatives *to measure, monitor, and improve* the DQ dimensions that are relevant to them. To manage and safeguard DQ, a **data governance** culture should be put in place assigning clear roles and responsibilities. The aim of data governance is to set-up a company-wide controlled and supported approach toward DQ accompanied by DQ management processes. The core idea is to manage data as an asset rather than a liability, and adopt a proactive attitude toward data quality. To succeed, it should be a key element of a company's corporate governance and supported by senior management. Worldwide international regulatory institutions have further amplified the importance of data governance through business-specific compliance guidelines. For example, the Basel and Solvency Accords provide clear guidelines for data governance within a credit risk and insurance context.[4]

Different frameworks have been introduced for DQ management and improvement. Some are rooted in (general) quality management while others focus explicitly on data quality. Another category of frameworks focuses on the maturity of DQ management processes. They aim at assessing the maturity level of DQ management to understand best practices in mature organizations and identify areas for improvement. Popular examples of such frameworks include: Total Data Quality Management (TDQM), Total Quality Management (TQM), Capability Maturity Model Integration (CMMI), ISO 9000, Control Objectives for Information and Related Technology (CobiT), Data Management Body of Knowledge (DMBOK), Information Technology Infrastructure Library (ITIL), and Six Sigma. Most frameworks are scientifically grounded and consider the perspective and knowledge of various data stakeholders across different industries.

> **Connections**
>
> Data quality and data governance are discussed further in Chapter 18. This chapter also zooms in on the realm of technologies that exist to integrate data from multiple sources and the different tradeoffs these technologies entail regarding the DQ dimensions.

As an example, the TDQM framework is illustrated in Figure 4.2.[5] A TDQM cycle consists of four steps – *define, measure, analyze*, and *improve* – which are performed iteratively. The *define* step identifies the pertinent DQ dimensions, using, e.g., the framework in Table 4.1. These can then be quantified using metrics in the *measure* step. Some example metrics are: the percentage of customer records with incorrect address (accuracy); the percentage of customer records with missing birth date (completeness); or an indicator specifying when customer data were last updated (timeliness). The *analyze* step tries to identify the root cause for the diagnosed DQ problems. These can then be remedied in the *improve* step. Example actions could be: automatic and periodic verification of

[4] Baesens B., Roesch D., Scheule H., *Credit Risk Analytics: Measurement Techniques, Applications and Examples in SAS*, Wiley, 2016.

[5] Wang R.Y. A product perspective on Total Data Quality Management. *Communications of the ACM*, 1998; 41(2).

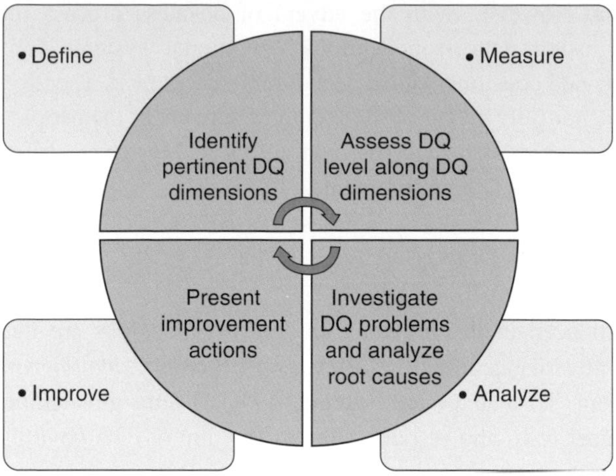


**Figure 4.2** Total Data Quality Management.

customer addresses, the addition of a constraint that makes birth date a mandatory data field, and the generation of alerts when customer data have not been updated during the previous six months.

If actual DQ improvement is not an option in the short term for reasons of technical constraints or strategic priorities, it is sometimes a partial solution to annotate the data with explicit information about its quality. Such DQ metadata can be stored in the catalog, possibly with other metadata. In this way, the DQ issues are not resolved, but at least data consumers across the organization are aware of them and can take the necessary precautions as part of their task execution. For example, credit risk models could incorporate an additional risk factor to account for uncertainty in the data, derived from DQ metadata. Unfortunately, many companies still ignore DQ problems because of a lack of perceived added value. Hence, many data governance efforts (if any) are mostly reactive and ad-hoc, only addressing the DQ issues as they occur.

**Retention Questions**

- Discuss some of the key dimensions of data quality.
- How can data governance contribute to better data quality?

## 4.2 Roles in Data Management

In this section we discuss various job profiles within the context of data management. We introduce the information architect, database designer, data owner, data steward, database administrator, and data scientist. Each of these roles are essential in ensuring high DQ and transforming data into actual business value. Depending upon the size of the database and the company, multiple profiles may be merged into one job description.

### 4.2.1 Information Architect

The **information architect** (also called **information analyst**) designs the conceptual data model, preferably in dialogue with the business users. He/she bridges the gap between the business processes and the IT environment and closely collaborates with the database designer, who may assist in choosing the type of conceptual data model (e.g., EER or UML) and the database modeling tool.

### 4.2.2 Database Designer

The **database designer** translates the conceptual data model into a logical and internal data model. He/she also assists the *application developers* in defining the views of the external data model. To facilitate future maintenance of the database applications, the database designer should define company-wide uniform naming conventions when creating the various data models.

### 4.2.3 Data Owner

Every data field in every database in the organization should be *owned* by a **data owner**, who has the authority to ultimately decide on the access to, and usage of, the data. The data owner could be the original producer of the data, one of its consumers, or a third party. The data owner should be able to fill in or update its value, which implies the data owner has knowledge of the meaning of the field and has access to the current correct value (e.g., by contacting a customer, by looking into a file, etc.). Data owners can be requested by data stewards (see the next subsection) to check or complete the value of a field, as such correcting a DQ issue.

### 4.2.4 Data Steward

**Data stewards** are the DQ experts in charge of ensuring the quality of both the actual business data and the corresponding metadata. They assess DQ by performing extensive and regular data quality checks. These checks involve, among other evaluation steps, the application or calculation of DQ indicators and metrics for the most relevant DQ dimensions. They are also in charge of taking initiative and further acting upon the results. A first type of action to be taken is the application of *corrective measures*. However, data stewards are not in charge of correcting data themselves, as this is typically the responsibility of the data owner. The second type of action to be taken upon the results of the DQ assessment involves a deeper investigation into the *root causes* of the DQ issues detected. Understanding these causes may allow designing *preventive measures* that aim at eradicating DQ problems. Preventive measures may include modifications to the operational information systems where the data originate (e.g., making fields mandatory, providing drop-down lists of possible values, rationalizing the interface, etc.). Also, values entered in the system may immediately be checked for validity against predefined integrity rules and the user may be requested to correct the data if these rules are violated. For instance, a corporate tax portal may require employees to be identified based upon their social security number, which can be checked in real-time by contacting the social security number database. Implementing such preventive measures requires the close involvement of the IT department in charge of the application. Overall, preventing erroneous data from entering the system is often more cost-efficient than correcting errors afterwards. However, care should be taken not to slow down critical processes because of non-essential DQ issues in the input data.

### 4.2.5 Database Administrator

The **database administrator (DBA)** is responsible for the implementation and monitoring of the database. Example activities include: installing and upgrading the DBMS software; backup and recovery management; performance tuning and monitoring; memory management; replication management; security and authorization. A DBA closely collaborates with *network and system* *managers*. He/she also interacts with database designers to reduce operational management costs and guarantee agreed service levels (e.g., response times and throughput rates).

**Connections**

We discuss data science further in Chapter 20, where we also elaborate more on the skill set of a data scientist.

**Drill Down**

The Bureau of Labor Statistics[6] shows that DBAs usually have a bachelor's degree in an information- or computer-related subject such as computer science. Their 2015 median pay was $81,710 per year. Triggered by the massive growth in data, the employment of DBAs is projected to grow 11% from 2014 to 2024, which is faster than the average for all occupations.

### 4.2.6 Data Scientist

**Data scientist** is a relatively new job profile within the context of data management. He/she analyzes data using state-of-the-art analytical techniques to provide new insights into, for example, customer behavior. A data scientist has a multidisciplinary profile combining ICT skills (e.g., programming) with quantitative modeling (e.g., statistics), business understanding, communication, and creativity.

**Retention Questions**

- Discuss the job profiles in data management. Which ones can be combined?
- What differentiates a data owner from a data steward?
- What are the key characteristics of a data scientist?

## Summary

In this chapter we zoomed into the organizational aspects of data management. We clarified the critical role of metadata and the appropriate modeling thereof. We reviewed data quality and illustrated how data governance can contribute to it. We concluded by reviewing key roles in data management: information architect, database designer, data owner, data steward, database administrator, and data scientist.

**Scenario Conclusion**

Now that Sober has a better idea about the importance of good metadata and data quality, it has put in place a data governance initiative inspired by the Total Data Quality Management framework.[7] It will also assign clear roles and responsibilities for data management. However, since Sober is a startup company and has limited budgets, it must combine some of these. Sober hired two data management profiles: one will be working as an information architect, database designer, data owner, and DBA; the second will take on the roles of data steward and data scientist. Both will be combined in a data management business unit and will need to collaborate closely.

[6] www.bls.gov/ooh/computer-and-information-technology/database-administrators.htm.

[7] Wang R.Y., A product perspective on Total Data Quality Management. *Communications of the ACM*, 1998; 41(2).

## Key Terms List

access category
accessibility
accuracy
catalog
completeness
consistency
contextual category
data governance
data management
data owner
data quality (DQ)
data scientist
data steward
database administrator (DBA)
database designer
DQ frameworks
information analyst
information architect
intrinsic category
metamodel
representation category
timeliness

## Review Questions

**4.1.** Which of the following statements is **correct**?

a. The catalog forms the heart of a database. It can be an integral part of the DBMS or a standalone component.
b. The catalog makes sure the database continues to be correct by, among other measures, specifying all integrity rules.
c. The catalog describes all metadata components that are defined in the metamodel.
d. All of the above are correct.

**4.2.** A data steward notices that part of the database contains values in a different language. Which type of data quality error is this?

a. Intrinsic.
b. Contextual.
c. Representational.
d. Accessibility.

**4.3.** Is the following statement true or false? "The accuracy of a database depends on its representational and contextual characteristics."

a. True.
b. False.

**4.4.** Why can data incompleteness prove to be useful information?

a. We can track down faults in the database model, such as updating errors that cause inconsistencies.
b. We can track down the source of the incompleteness and thereby eliminate the cause thereof.
c. We can track down certain patterns in the incomplete fields, which can lead to more information about a certain user.
d. All of the above.

**4.5.** Which of the following statements is **not correct**?

a. Subjectivity can cause data quality issues.
b. Consistency issues can arise due to sharing data across multiple departments.

c. Data quality can always be measured objectively.
d. All aspects of data quality need to be checked regularly, as every change in the database or even the company can lead to unforeseen issues.

## Problems and Exercises

4.1E Discuss the importance of metadata modeling and catalogs.

4.2E Define data quality and discuss why it is an important concept. What are the most important data quality dimensions? Illustrate with examples.

4.3E Discuss the Total Data Quality Management (TDQM) data governance framework and illustrate with examples.

4.4E Discuss and contrast the various roles in data management. Clearly indicate the key activities and skills required. Discuss which job profiles can be combined.

# Part II

# Types of Database Systems

# 5 Legacy Databases

## Chapter Objectives

In this chapter, you will learn to:

- understand why it is important to know the basic concepts of legacy databases;
- identify the basic building blocks and limitations of the hierarchical model;
- identify the basic building blocks and limitations of the CODASYL model.

**Opening Scenario**

Sober purchased the customer database of Mellow Cab, who recently stepped out of the taxi business after many years at the top. Since Mellow Cab started in the mid-1970s, it was still using outdated database technology. It used CODASYL to store and manage its customer data. Sober is not familiar with this technology and wants to understand its limitations before deciding to either continue with it or invest in a modern DBMS.

In this chapter we briefly zoom into legacy database technologies and their logical data models. Although these are outdated and semantically inferior to modern database technologies, there are three reasons to review them. Firstly, many firms still struggle with legacy databases due to historical implementations and limited IT budgets – hence, knowing the basic characteristics of these models is essential to the maintenance of the corresponding database applications and the potential migration to modern DBMSs. Secondly, understanding the basics of these legacy models will contribute to better understanding the semantical richness of newer database technologies. Finally, the concept of procedural DML and navigational access originally introduced by these legacy models has also been adopted by more recent databases such as OODBMSs.

In this chapter we cover both the hierarchical and CODASYL data models. Throughout the discussion, we extensively discuss the expressive power and limitations of both models.

## 5.1 The Hierarchical Model

The **hierarchical model** is one of the first data models developed. The model originated during the Apollo moon missions program conducted by NASA. To manage the huge amount of data collected, IBM developed the Information Management System or IMS DBMS (1966–1968). There is no formal description available and it has lots of structural limitations. Therefore, it is considered **legacy**.

The two key building blocks of the hierarchical model are record types and relationship types. A **record type** is a set of records describing similar entities. Think about a product record type or a supplier record type. A record type has zero, one, or more records. It consists of fields or data items. A product record type has a field product number, a field product name, a field product color, etc.

A **relationship type** connects two record types. It models the relationships between record types. Only hierarchical structures are allowed – or in other words only 1:N relationship types can be modeled. Hence, a parent record can have multiple child records according to the same relationship type, but a child record has at most one parent record. A record type can be a parent in multiple parent–child relationship types, but it can participate in at most one relationship type as a child. Relationship types can be nested (i.e., a child record type can be a parent in another parent–child relationship type, which allows building hierarchical structures). The root record type is the record type that sits at the top of the hierarchy, whereas a leaf record type sits at the bottom of the hierarchy.

Figure 5.1 shows an example of a parent–child relationship type. A parent record can be connected to minimal 0 and maximal N child records. A child record can be connected to minimum one and maximum one parent. Hence, a child record is always connected to exactly one parent. No other cardinalities are supported in the hierarchical model, which makes it very restrictive in terms of expressive power. Remember that a relationship type is always summarized in terms of its maximum cardinalities. In our case, we can say that the hierarchical model supports only 1:N relationship types.

Figure 5.2 shows an example of a simple hierarchical model. We have three record types: department, employee, and project. The department record type has three data fields: department number, department name, and department location. The department record type participates in two

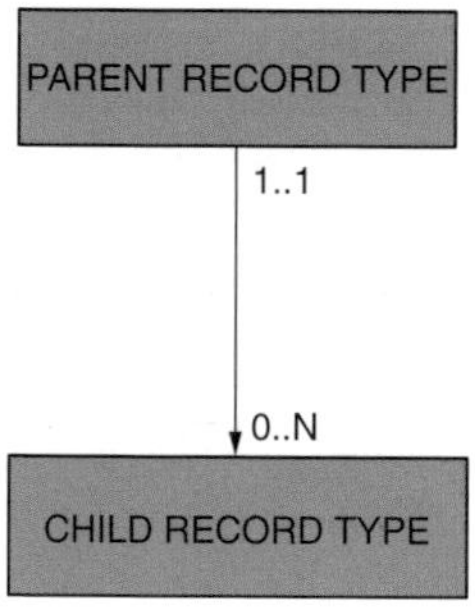


**Figure 5.1** Parent–child relationship type.

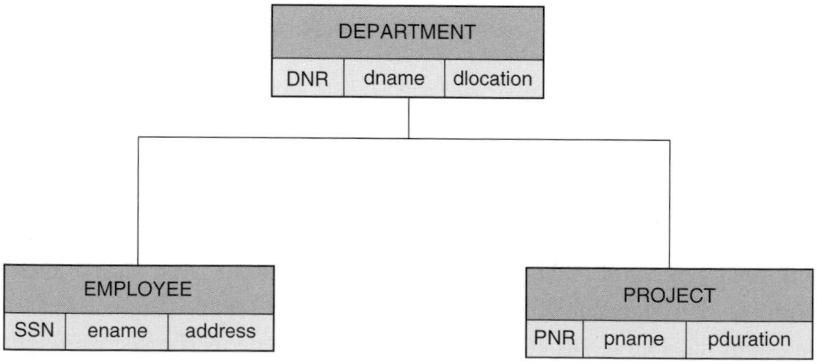


**Figure 5.2** Example of a parent–child relationship type.

parent–child relationship types. A department can have zero to N employees. An employee is always connected to one department. A department can work on zero to N projects. A project is always worked on by exactly one department. This is a very simple hierarchical structure. Department is the root record type, and both employee and project are the leaf record types.

In the hierarchical model, all record data need to be retrieved by navigating down from the root node of the hierarchical structure. In other words, the DML adopted is procedural, which is not efficient. The hierarchical model is also very rigid and limited in expressive power since it allows only 1:N relationship types. There is no support to model N:M or 1:1 relationship types. Hence, these must be implemented using workarounds. To implement an N:M relationship type, we can assign one record type as the parent and the other as the child record type. In other words, we transform the network structure into a tree structure, which will obviously involve a loss of semantics. Any relationship type attributes (e.g., number of hours an employee worked on a project) will be put in the child record type. This solution creates **redundancy**, which is dependent upon both the amount of data in the child record type and the value of the maximum cardinality of the "child to parent" role in the original N:M relationship type. Let's illustrate this with an example: we have an N:M relationship type between project and employee. Put differently, an employee can work on zero to N projects, whereas a project can be worked upon by zero to M employees. To implement this in the hierarchical model, we need to map it to a 1:N relationship type, which is obviously not ideal. Hence, we can opt to make *project* the parent and *employee* the child record type. Figure 5.3 shows some example records for this implementation.

**Connections**

Chapter 2 discusses the differences between procedural and declarative DML.

Project number 10 has three employees working on it: employee 110, employee 120, and employee 145. You can also see that employee 110 works on all three projects – projects 10, 15, and 20. Hence, the data of employee 110 are replicated for each project she works on, which is inefficient from both a storage and maintenance perspective. If the data of employee 110 is updated in one relation, it must also be updated in the other relations or inconsistent data will occur. Note that the number of hours an employee worked on a project can be put in the child record type.

An alternative to implementing an N:M relationship type is to create two hierarchical structures and connect them using a **virtual child record type** and a **virtual parent–child relationship type**. Pointers can then be used to navigate between both structures. The relationship type attributes can be put in the virtual child record type. This solution has no more redundancy since multiple virtual children can refer to one parent.

Figure 5.4 illustrates our earlier N:M relationship type between employee and project, but now implemented using virtual child and **virtual parent record types**. The virtual children have

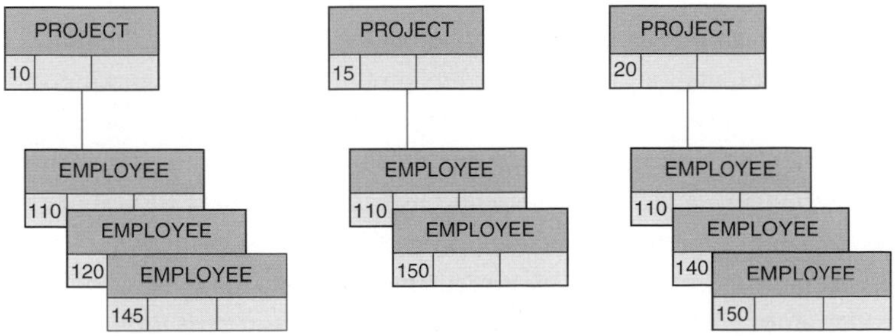


**Figure 5.3** Implementing N:M relationship types in the hierarchical model.

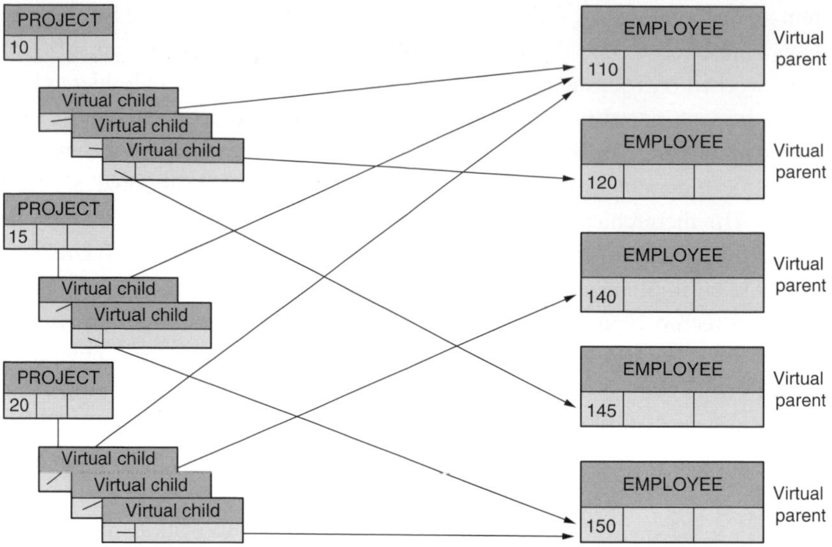


**Figure 5.4** Virtual child and virtual parents for N:M relationship types.

pointers to virtual parents. Although this solution has no more redundancy, it is rather artificial and difficult to maintain.

The 1:1 relationship types are a special case of a 1:N relationship type with N equal to 1. This cardinality cannot be enforced as such in the hierarchical model. Hence, the application programs should take care of this, which is not efficient because we are now forced to include part of the data definitions in our applications, which hampers maintenance and consistency. The hierarchical model only allows relationship types of degree 2, or in other words with two participating record types. Recursive (or unary) relationship types with degree 1 or relationship types with more than two record types need to be implemented using virtual child record types. Finally, the maximum and minimum cardinality from child to parent is 1. A child therefore cannot be disconnected from its parent. This implies that once a parent record is removed, then all connected child records are also removed, creating an "on delete cascade" effect.

> **Connections**
>
> Cascading deletes are discussed in more detail in the context of SQL in Chapter 7.

Figure 5.5 shows an example of a hierarchical data model for an HR administration business process. It includes two connected hierarchical structures. *Department* is the root record type of the first hierarchy and *employee* of the second hierarchy. A department can work on zero to N projects. A project is being worked on by exactly one department. The *works on* record type is a virtual child to implement the N:M relationship type between project and employee. It also includes the *hours worked* data item, which represents the number of hours an employee spent working on a project. The *manager* virtual child record type refers to the employee record type. Note that according to this implementation, a department can have more than one manager since a department parent record can be connected to between zero and N manager child records. The *works at* virtual child models the relationship type between department and employee. Zero to N employees can work in a department. The *manages* virtual child models a recursive relationship type which specifies the supervision relationships among employees. An employee can manage zero to N other employees.

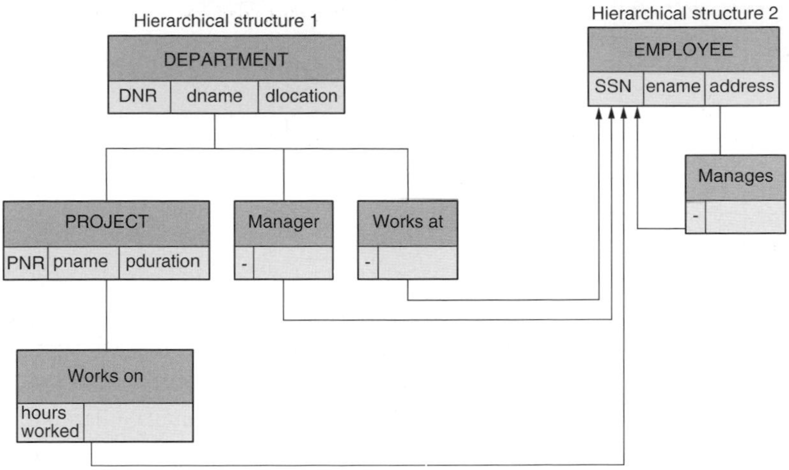


**Figure 5.5** Hierarchical model for HR administration.

**Retention Questions**

- What are the key concepts of the hierarchical model?
- What cardinalities are supported when modeling relationship types?
- What are the limitations of the hierarchical model?

This model is not user-friendly and is difficult to interpret. It also has various model limitations. More specifically, our model does not guarantee that each department has exactly one manager. According to our model, a department can have zero managers or more than one manager. We also cannot enforce that a department has at least one employee since it is possible that a department parent record has zero *works at* child records. Hence, according to our model, it is possible that a department has zero employees. Most of these constraints or rules have to be directly embedded in the application programs, which is not optimal.

**Drill Down**

On May 25, 1961, President John F. Kennedy declared his ambition to put an American on the moon by the end of the decade. The Apollo program was launched and various firms collaborated to accomplish the mission. North American Aviation, together with IBM, were tasked to build an automated system capable of managing large bills of material for the construction of the spacecraft. To this end, they developed a hierarchical database system called Information Control System and Data Language/Interface (ICS/DL/I). After Apollo 11 landed on the moon on July 20, 1969, ICS was rebranded as Information Management System/360 (IMS/360) and made available to the industry.

## 5.2 The CODASYL Model

The **CODASYL model** was the next data model developed by the Data Base Task Group of the **CO**nference on **DA**ta **SY**stem **L**anguages in 1969, so not that much later than the hierarchical model. It has various popular software implementations, such as IDMS from Cullinet Software, which was later acquired by Computer Associates and rebranded as CA-IDMS. It is an

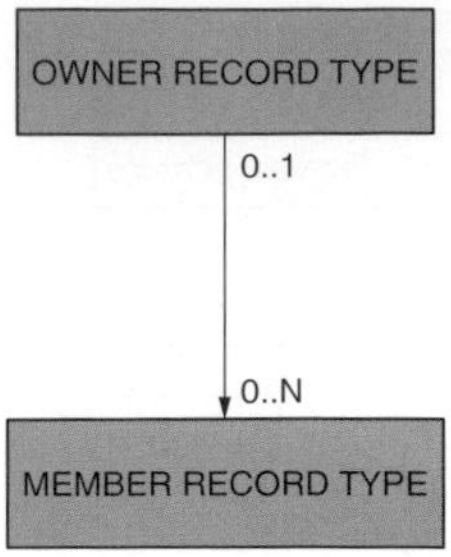


**Figure 5.6** CODASYL set type.

implementation of the network model that originally included record types and links, and supported 1:1, 1:N, and N:M relationship types. However, the CODASYL model only includes record types, set types, and 1:N relationship types. Although this may sound similar to the hierarchical model at first sight, there are some clear differences, which we will illustrate. Similar to the hierarchical model, the CODASYL model is considered to be legacy and has lots of structural limitations.

The two key building blocks of the CODASYL model are record types and set types. Just as in the hierarchical model, a record type is a set of records describing similar entities. It has zero, one, or more records or record occurrences. It consists of various data items. As an example, a supplier record type can have data items such as supplier number, supplier name, etc. The CODASYL model provides support for both vectors and repeated groups. A **vector** is a multi-valued attribute type (i.e., an atomic data item for which a record can have multiple values). For example, if a supplier can have multiple email addresses, then this can be modeled using a vector. A **repeated group** is a composite data item for which a record can have multiple values or a composite multi-valued attribute type. For example, if a supplier can have multiple addresses each with their street name, number, zip code, city, and country, then this can be modeled using a repeated group. The support for vectors and repeated groups is the first difference with the hierarchical model.

A **set type** models a 1:N relationship type between an **owner record type** and a **member record type**. A set type has a set occurrence for each record occurrence of the owner record type, together with all member records. Hence, a set occurrence has one owner record and zero, one, or more member records. It is important to note that the CODASYL interpretation of a set does not completely correspond to the concept of a set as we know it in mathematics. Remember, in mathematics a set is defined as a collection with similar elements and without ordering. However, a CODASYL set has both owner and member records and it is also possible to order the member records.

Figure 5.6 shows a CODASYL set type with the corresponding cardinalities. An owner record can be connected to a minimum of zero and maximum of N member records. A member record can be connected to a minimum of zero and maximum of one owner records.[1] Hence, a member record can exist without being connected to an owner record or can be disconnected from its owner. This is a key difference with the hierarchical model. A record type can be a member record type in multiple set types, which allows the creation of network structures. In the hierarchical model, a child record type can only be connected to one parent record type. Finally, multiple set types may be defined between the same record types, which is another difference to the hierarchical model.

CODASYL data models are usually represented using a network or **Bachman diagram**. Charles Bachman was one of the important contributors of the CODASYL model.

[1] Note that CODASYL can also support a minimum cardinality of 1 using specific DDL options.

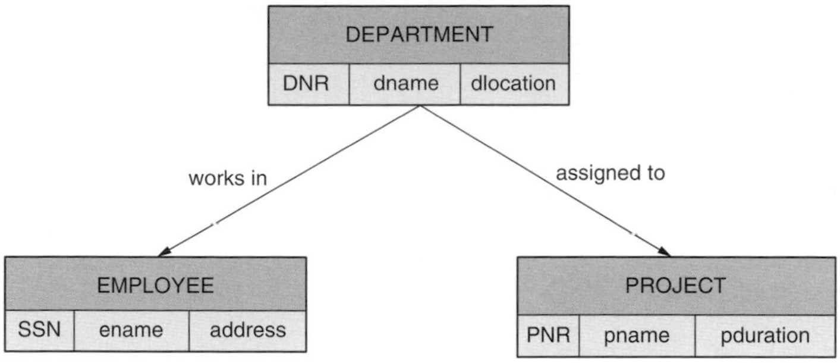


**Figure 5.7** Bachman diagram.

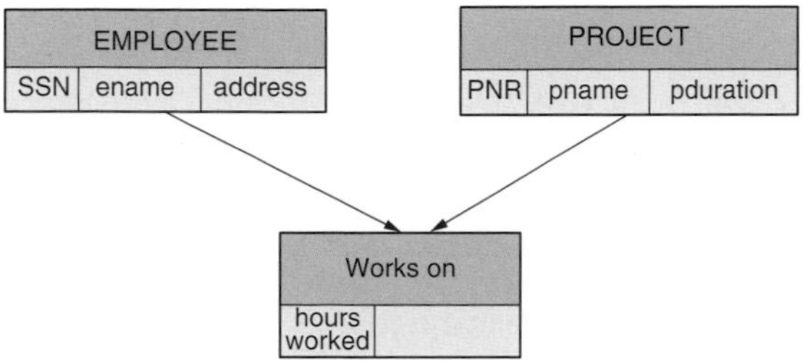


**Figure 5.8** Implementing N:M relationship types in CODASYL.

Figure 5.7 shows an example. We have three record types: department, employee, and project. A department has zero to N employees. An employee works in a minimum of zero and maximum of one department. A department can work on zero to N projects. A project is assigned to a minimum of zero and maximum of one department.

As with the hierarchical model, 1:1 relationship types must be enforced or modeled in the application programs, which should enforce that an owner record can only be connected to at most one member record. As with the hierarchical model, the addition of these semantic constraints to the application programs is not desirable from a maintenance perspective (see also Chapter 1). N:M relationship types need to be also modeled using a workaround. As an example, consider the N:M relationship type between employee and project (see Figure 5.8). Remember, an employee can work on zero to M projects, whereas a project can be allocated to zero to N employees. A member record (e.g., a project) can only belong to one set occurrence of a specific set type, hence we cannot just define a set type between the corresponding record types (e.g., employee and project). One option is to introduce a **dummy record type** that is included as a member record type in two set types having as owners the record types of the original N:M relationship type. This dummy record type can then also contain the attributes of the relationship type, if any.

Figure 5.8 illustrates how the N:M relationship type between employee and project can be modeled in CODASYL by introducing a dummy record type, *works on*, which also includes the attribute type of the relationship, *hours worked*, representing the number of hours that an employee worked on a project.

Figure 5.9 illustrates how this works with some example records. You can see that employee 120 only works on project 10, whereas employee 150 works on projects 15 and 20. You can also see that project 15 is allocated to employees 110 and 150.

This implementation of N:M relationship types has serious implications for data usage. Suppose we have a query that asks for all projects an employee is working on. To solve this query, we first

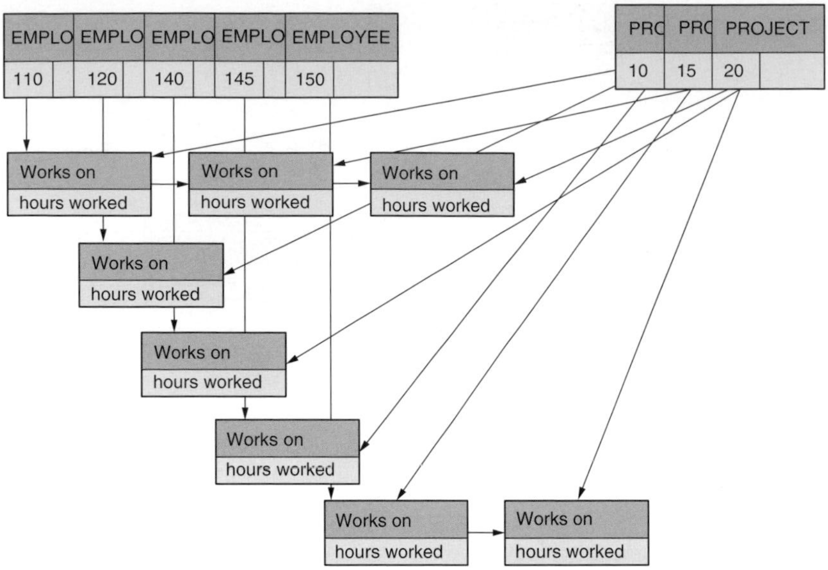


**Figure 5.9** Implementing N:M relationship types in CODASYL: example records.

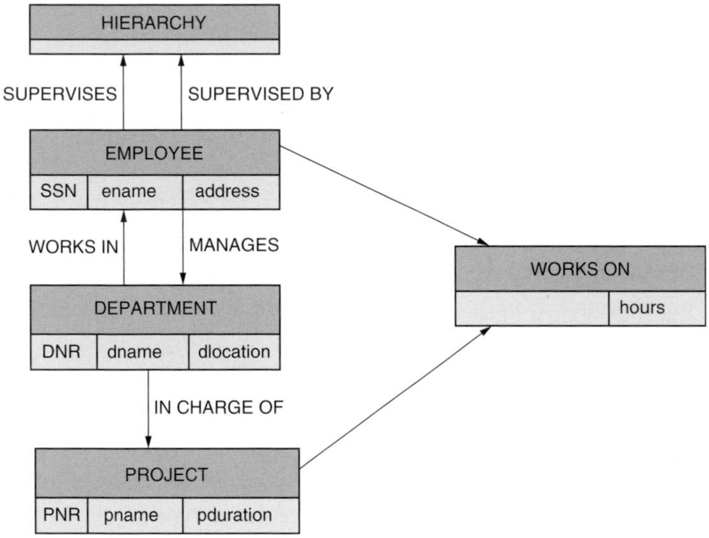


**Figure 5.10** CODASYL model for HR administration.

need to select a set in the set type between *employee* and *works on*. For each member record, we then need to determine the owner record in the set type between *project* and *works on*. If another query asks for all employees working on a particular project, then we need to navigate the other way around. Again, this is an example of procedural DML since we must explicitly work out a procedure to solve our query by working with one record at a time.

As we already mentioned, CODASYL allows logical ordering of the member records of a set. An example order could be alphabetically, or based upon birth date. This can be useful for data manipulation. For the root member record type, the system can act as the owner, which is then called a singular or system owned set type with only one set occurrence.

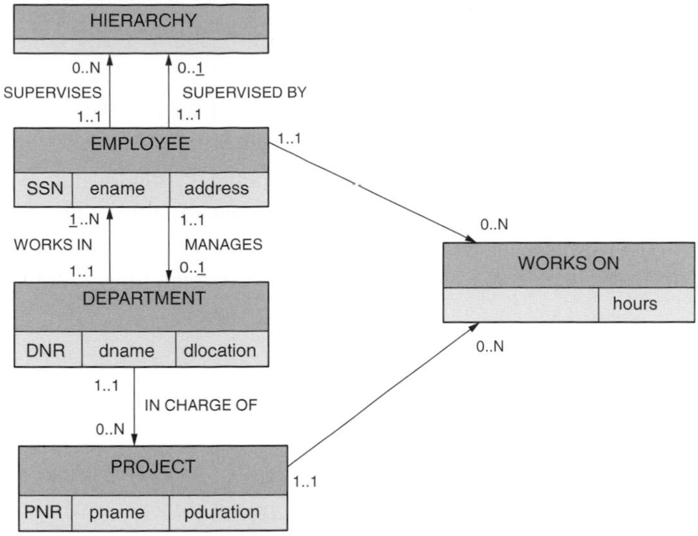


**Figure 5.11** CODASYL model for HR administration: desired cardinalities.

CODASYL provides no support for recursive set types with only one participating record type. A dummy record type needs to be introduced that is then defined as a member in two set types, each having as owner the record type of the recursive relationship. Note this again implies extensive navigation when manipulating the data. Additionally, no set types with more than two participating record types are supported.

Figure 5.10 shows the CODASYL implementation of our HR administration example. The *works on* dummy record type models the N:M relationship type between *employee* and *project*. The *hierarchy* dummy record type implements a recursive relationship type modeling the supervision relationships between employees. The set type *supervises* models which colleagues an employee supervises. The set type *supervised by* represents the supervisor of an employee. Two set types are defined between employee and department. The *works in* set type models which employee works in what department. The *manages* set type models which employee manages what department. Finally, the set type *in charge of* between department and project models which projects a department works on.

Figure 5.11 shows the cardinalities as we ideally would like them to be. The underlined cardinalities cannot be enforced by the CODASYL model.

Again, our CODASYL model has some important shortcomings to note. According to our CODASYL model an employee can be managed by multiple employees, which is not desirable. The model does not enforce that an employee can manage at most one department. It also does not enforce that a department has a minimum of one employee. Unfortunately, all of these constraints and rules need to be embedded in the application programs.

### Retention Questions

- What are the key concepts of the CODASYL model?
- What cardinalities are supported when modeling relationship types?
- What are the limitations of the CODASYL model?

### Drill Down

The website http://db-engines.com provides monthly rankings of database management systems according to their popularity. It illustrates that both IMS (hierarchical DBMS) and IDBMS (CODASYL DBMS), although declining in popularity, are still relevant nowadays, with IMS ranking higher than IDMS.

## Summary

In this chapter we reviewed legacy database technology. We discussed the key building blocks and limitations of the hierarchical and CODASYL data models. The semantics of both of these models are too restricted for efficient modeling (e.g., 1:1, N:M, and recursive relationship types). This shortcoming has serious implications for the development of the application programs that are now responsible for some of the data constraints. As discussed in Chapter 1, this is not a desirable or efficient way of working. In later chapters we review more advanced database paradigms.

### Scenario Conclusion

Sober reviewed the CODASYL database model of Mellow Cab in detail. It included record types for customer, cab ride, and car. The company saw how the N:M relationship type between customer and cab ride for ride-sharing (a customer can book zero to N cab rides and a cab ride can be booked or shared by zero to M customers) had to be mapped using an extra dummy record type. Also, the set type between cab ride and car did not allow enforcing that a cab ride should be serviced by exactly one car. Furthermore, all data need to be retrieved using procedural DML, which is not efficient. Given all these shortcomings, Sober has decided to invest in a more sophisticated DBMS.

## Key Terms List

**Bachman diagram**
**CODASYL model**
**dummy record type**
**hierarchical model**
**legacy**
**member record type**
**owner record type**
**record type**
**redundancy**
**relationship type**
**repeated group**
**set type**
**vector**
**virtual child record type**
**virtual parent record type**
**virtual parent–child relationship type**

## Review Questions

**5.1.** A bank needs to store the following information: customer names, customer addresses, city of a branch, number of accounts, account IDs, and account balances. How many record types do you need to construct a hierarchical database with this information?

a. One.
b. Three.
c. Four.
d. Five.

**5.2.** If a hierarchical model contains N:M relationship types that have been integrated by repeating the child nodes where necessary, what are the dangers of updating the database?

a. Slower retrieval of data.
b. Creating data inconsistency.
c. Creating unnecessary records.
d. All of the above.

**5.3.** The human resources department of a university wants to make sure that every course has exactly one main professor. How can they implement this constraint using the CODASYL framework?

a. They introduce an extra set type called "is-main-professor-of" between record types "professor" and "course".
b. They introduce an "is-main-professor" record type between record types "professor" and "course" to model the correct relationship.
c. They introduce "main professor" as a data item in the record type "professor".
d. It is impossible to model this constraint in CODASYL.

**5.4.** In CODASYL, a multi-valued composite attribute type can be represented as a . . .

a. record type.
b. data item.
c. vector.
d. repeated group.

**5.5.** How can the CODASYL framework correctly model a family tree, taking into account that every child has to have (at least) two parents?

a. Use a set type "is parent of" between record types "parent" and "child".
b. Use a dummy record type "is parent of" between record types "parent" and "child".
c. List the parents as a vector in the data item set of every child.
d. We cannot model this constraint with the CODASYL framework.

## Problems and Exercises

5.1E Contrast the hierarchical model with the CODASYL model in terms of
- attribute types supported;
- relationship types and cardinalities supported.

5.2E Make a hierarchical and CODASYL model for the fitness company "Conan" discussed in Chapter 3. Contrast both models and discuss their limitations. Give examples of semantics that cannot be enforced. Compare the models with the ER, EER, and UML models of Chapter 3.

# 6 Relational Databases

*The Relational Model*

## Chapter Objectives

In this chapter, you will learn to:

- understand the basic concepts of the relational model;
- differentiate between different types of keys and identify their role in the relational model;
- understand how normalization can be used to make sure a relational data model has no redundancies or inconsistencies;
- map a conceptual ER model to a relational model and identify any loss of semantics;
- map a conceptual EER model to a relational model and identify any loss of semantics.

### Opening Scenario

Starting from the EER conceptual data model developed in Chapter 3, Sober wants to proceed to the next step of database design. The company wants to map the EER model to a logical relational model and needs to understand what semantics gets lost in the mapping process.

Relational databases implement the relational model, which is one of the most popular logical and internal data models in use nowadays. It was first formalized by Edgar F. Codd in his seminal paper "A relational model of data for large shared data banks", which appeared in the well-respected journal *Communications of the ACM* in 1970. In this chapter we first introduce the basic concepts of the relational model and then formally define them in the next section. This is followed by an overview of the different types of keys, which are an essential building block of the relational model. The relational constraints are summarized next, followed by an example of a relational data model. Normalization will also be reviewed as a procedure to remove redundancies and anomalies from a relational data model. After having introduced the need for normalization and some informal guidelines, we zoom into functional dependencies and prime attribute types and discuss how both can be used during a multi-step normalization procedure. To conclude, we discuss how to map both ER and EER conceptual data models to a logical relational data model. The next chapter then zooms into SQL, which is the DDL and DML used by relational databases.

### Drill Down

Edgar F. Codd was an English computer scientist (19 August 1923–18 April 2003) who laid the foundation of the relational model while working for IBM. He received the Turing Award in

1981 and was inducted as a Fellow of the Association for Computing Machinery (ACM) in 1994. His seminal paper, "A relational model of data for large shared data banks", was published in *Communications of the ACM* in 1970 and laid the foundations of the relational model as we know it today. IBM was initially reluctant to implement the relational model as they feared it would cannibalize its revenue from its hierarchical IMS DBMS. Codd managed to convince some of the IBM customers about the potential of the relational model such that they put pressure on IBM for a commercial implementation of it. After some first implementations that were not fully compliant with Codd's original ideas, IBM released SQL/DS (Structured Query Language/ Data System) in 1981 as its first commercial SQL-based RDBMS. Codd also coined the term on-line analytical processing (OLAP), which we introduced in Chapter 1.

## 6.1 The Relational Model

The **relational model** is a formal data model with a sound mathematical foundation, based on *set theory* and *first-order predicate logic*.[1] Unlike the ER and EER models, the relational model has no standard graphical representation, which makes it unsuitable as a conceptual data model. Given its solid theoretical underpinning, the relational model is commonly adopted to build both logical and internal data models. Many commercial RDBMSs exist which implement the relational model. Popular examples are Microsoft SQL Server, IBM DB2, and Oracle. In what follows, we discuss its basic concepts and formal definitions. We also elaborate on keys, which are a fundamental building block of the relational model and summarize the relational constraints. We conclude with an example of a relational data model.

**Drill Down**

The top ten DBMSs in use according to http://db-engines.com are usually dominated by RDBMSs such as Oracle (commercial), MySQL (open-source), Microsoft SQL Server (commercial), PostgreSQL (open-source), IBM's DB2 (commercial), Microsoft Access (commercial), and SQLite (open-source). Other popular RDBMSs are Teradata (commercial), SAP Adaptive Server (commercial), and FileMaker (commercial).

### 6.1.1 Basic Concepts

In the relational model, a database is represented as a collection of relations. A **relation** is defined as a set of *tuples* that each represent a similar real-world entity such as a product, a supplier, an employee, etc. (see Figure 6.1). A **tuple** is an ordered list of attribute *values* that each describe an aspect of this entity, such as supplier number, supplier name, supplier address, etc.

A relation can be visualized as a table of values. Figure 6.1 illustrates a relation SUPPLIER. Table names (e.g., SUPPLIER) and column names (e.g., SUPNR, SUPNAME) are used to help in interpreting the meaning of the values in each row. Each tuple corresponds to a row in the table.

[1] See the online appendix at www.pdbmbook.com for a discussion on relational algebra and relational calculus, which are two formal languages underlying the relational model.

SUPPLIER

| SUPNR | SUPNAME | SUPADDRESS | SUPCITY | SUPSTATUS |
|---|---|---|---|---|
| 21 | Deliwines | 240, Avenue of the Americas | New York | 20 |
| 32 | Best Wines | 660, Market Street | San Francisco | 90 |
| 37 | Ad Fundum | 82, Wacker Drive | Chicago | 95 |
| 52 | Spirits & Co. | 928, Strip | Las Vegas | NULL |
| 68 | The Wine Depot | 132, Montgomery Street | San Francisco | 10 |
| 69 | Vinos del Mundo | 4, Collins Avenue | Miami | 92 |
| ... | | | | |

**Figure 6.1** Basic concepts of the relational model.

**Table 6.1** Correspondence between EER model and relational model

| ER model | Relational model |
|---|---|
| Entity type | Relation |
| Entity | Tuple |
| Attribute type | Column name |
| Attribute | Cell |

An example of a tuple for the SUPPLIER relation in Figure 6.1 is (21, Deliwines, "240, Avenue of the Americas", "New York", 20).

Attribute types (e.g., SUPNR, SUPNAME) can be seen as the column names. Each attribute corresponds to a single cell. A relation corresponds to an entity type in the EER model, a tuple to an entity, an attribute type to a column and an attribute to a single cell. The correspondence between the ER and relational model is summarized in Table 6.1.

To facilitate understanding, it is recommended to use meaningful names for each relation and its attribute types. Here you can see some examples of relations:

```
Student (Studentnr, Name, HomePhone, Address)
Professor (SSN, Name, HomePhone, OfficePhone, Email)
Course (CourseNo, CourseName)
```

The student relation has attribute types Studentnr, Name, HomePhone, and Address; the professor relation has attribute types SSN, Name, HomePhone, OfficePhone and Email; and the course relation has attribute types CourseNo and CourseName. The meaning of the relations and their attribute types is clear from the naming.

### 6.1.2 Formal Definitions

Before we can formally define a relation, we need to introduce the concept of a domain. A **domain** specifies the range of admissible values for an attribute type. For example, a domain can consist of all integer values between 1 and 9999 and can be used to define the attribute type SUPNR. Other examples are a gender domain, which contains the values male and female, and a time domain which defines time as day (e.g., 27) followed by month (e.g., 02) followed by year (e.g., 1975). Each attribute type of a relation is defined using a corresponding domain.

A domain can be used multiple times in a relation. Assume we define a domain representing integer values between 1 and 9999. Let's say we then want to build a relation BillOfMaterial representing which product is made up of which other product in what quantity. Think of a bike (with product number 5) consisting of two wheels (product number 10), a wheel in turn consisting

BillOfMaterial

| MAJORPRODNR | MINORPRODNR | QUANTITY |
|---|---|---|
| 5 | 10 | 2 |
| 10 | 15 | 30 |

**Figure 6.2** Example tuples for BillOfMaterial relation.

of 30 spokes (product number 15), etc. This can be represented as a relation BillOfMaterial with majorprodnr, representing the composite object, minorprodnr, representing the part object, and the quantity as follows:

```
BillOfMaterial(majorprodnr, minorprodnr, quantity)
```

with corresponding tuples (Figure 6.2).

Our domain can now be used to define the attribute types majorprodnr and minorprodnr. An advantage of using a domain here is that if the product numbers ever have to change, such as between 1 and 99999, then this change should only be done in the domain definition, which significantly improves the maintainability of our relational model.

A *relation* $R(A_1, A_2, A_3, \ldots A_n)$ (e.g., SUPPLIER(SUPNR, SUPNAME, ...)) can now be formally defined as a set of $m$ tuples $r = \{t_1, t_2, t_3, \ldots t_m\}$ whereby each *tuple* $t$ is an ordered list of $n$ values $t = <v_1, v_2, v_3, \ldots v_n>$ corresponding to a particular entity (e.g., a particular supplier). Each value $v_i$ is an element of the corresponding domain, $dom(A_i)$, or is a special NULL value. A NULL value means that the value is missing, irrelevant, or not applicable. Some example tuples for the student, professor, and course relations are as follows:

```
Student(100, Michael Johnson, 123 456 789, 532 Seventh Avenue)
Professor(50, Bart Baesens, NULL, 876 543 210, Bart.Baesens@kuleuven.be)
Course(10, Principles of Database Management)
```

It is important to note that a relation essentially represents a set. Hence, there is no logical ordering of tuples in a relation. A relation also does not have any duplicate tuples. There is, however, an ordering to the values within a tuple based upon how the relation was defined.

The domain constraint of the relational model states that the value of each attribute type A must be an atomic and single value from the domain dom(A). Suppose we have a relation COURSE with attribute types coursenr, coursename, and study points:

```
COURSE(coursenr, coursename, study points)
```

Two example tuples could be:

```
(10, Principles of Database Management, 6)
(10, {Principles of Database Management, Database Modeling}, 6)
```

The first tuple is correct, specifying coursenr 10, Principles of Database Management with 6 study points. The second tuple is incorrect, as it specifies 2 values for the coursename: Principles of Database Management and Database Modeling.

A relation R of degree $n$ on the domains $dom(A_1)$, $dom(A_2)$, $dom(A_3)$, ..., $dom(A_n)$ can also be alternatively defined as a subset of the Cartesian product of the domains that define each of the attribute types. Remember, the *Cartesian product* specifies all possible combinations of values from the underlying domains. Of all these possible combinations, the current relation state represents only the valid tuples that represent a specific state of the real world.

| Domain Product ID |
|---|
| 001 |
| 002 |
| 003 |
| … |

X

| Domain Product Color |
|---|
| Blue |
| Red |
| Black |

X

| Domain Product Category |
|---|
| A |
| B |
| C |

| ProductID | Product Color | Product Category |
|---|---|---|
| 001 | Blue | A |
| 001 | Blue | B |
| 001 | Blue | C |
| 001 | Red | A |
| 001 | Red | B |
| 001 | Red | C |
| … | | |

**Figure 6.3** A relation is a subset of the Cartesian product of its domains.

You can see this illustrated in Figure 6.3. We have three domains: productID defined as an integer between 1 and 9999, product color defined as either blue, red, or black, and product category defined as either A, B, or C. The Cartesian product of these three domains then simply lists all possible combinations as shown in the bottom table. Our relation R will then be a subset of all these combinations.

### 6.1.3 Types of Keys

Keys are a very important concept in the relational model to uniquely identify tuples as well as to establish relationships between relations. In what follows, we discuss different types of keys and their usage.

#### 6.1.3.1 Superkeys and Keys

As we already mentioned, a relation is a set of tuples. Hence, per the mathematical definition of a set, all tuples in a relation must be distinct. No two tuples can have the same combination of values for all their attribute types. A **superkey** is defined as a subset of attribute types of a relation R with the property that no two tuples in any relation state should have the same combination of values for these attribute types. In other words, a superkey specifies a uniqueness constraint in the sense that no two distinct tuples in a state can have the same value for the superkey. Every relation has at least one default superkey – the set of *all* its attribute types. A superkey can have redundant attribute types. As an example, for the relation Student, (Studentnr, Name, HomePhone) is a superkey, but note that both Name and HomePhone are redundant and Studentnr is a superkey as such.

A key K of a relation scheme R is a superkey of R with the additional property that removing any attribute type from K leaves a set of attribute types that is no superkey of R. Hence, a key does not have any redundant attribute types and is also called a minimal superkey. For our student relation, Studentnr is a key. The key constraint states that every relation must have at least one key that allows one to uniquely identify its tuples.

#### 6.1.3.2 Candidate Keys, Primary Keys, and Alternative Keys

In general, a relation may have more than one key. As an example, a product relation may have both a unique product number and a unique product name. Each of these keys is called a **candidate key**.

**Connections**

In Chapters 12 and 13 we discuss how primary keys can be used to define indexes as part of the internal data model.

One of them is designated as the **primary key** of the relation. In our product example, we can make prodnr the primary key. The primary key is used to identify tuples in the relation and to establish connections to other relations (see Section 6.1.3.3). It can also be used for storage purposes and to define indexes in the internal data model (see Chapter 13). The attribute types that make up the primary key should always satisfy a NOT NULL constraint. Otherwise, it would not be possible to identify some tuples. This is called the entity integrity constraint. The other candidate keys are then referred to as **alternative keys**. In our example, productname can be defined as an alternative key. Optionally, a NOT NULL constraint can also be specified for the other attribute types, such as the alternative keys.

### 6.1.3.3 Foreign Keys

Like relationship types in the EER model, relations in the relational model can be connected. These connections are established through the concept of a **foreign key**. A set of attribute types FK in a relation $R_1$ is a foreign key of $R_1$ if two conditions are satisfied. First, the attribute types in FK have the same domains as the primary key attribute types PK of a relation $R_2$. Next, a value FK in a tuple $t_1$ of the current state $r_1$ either occurs as a value of PK for some tuple $t_2$ in the current state $r_2$ or is NULL. These conditions for a foreign key specify a so-called referential integrity constraint between two relations $R_1$ and $R_2$.

On the left in Figure 6.4, you can see our EER relationship type ON_ORDER, which says: A supplier can have minimum zero and maximum N purchase orders, whereas a purchase order is always connected to a minimum of one and maximum of one – or in other words exactly one – supplier. How can we now map this EER relationship type to the relational model? A first attempt could be to add purchase order number as a foreign key to the SUPPLIER table. However, since a supplier can have multiple purchase orders, this would create a multi-valued attribute type, which is not allowed in the relational model. A better option is to include supplier number as a foreign key in the PURCHASE_ORDER table, since every purchase order is connected to exactly one supplier. Since the minimum cardinality is 1, this foreign key should be declared as NOT NULL. In our example, you can see that purchase order number 1511 is supplied by supplier number 37 whose

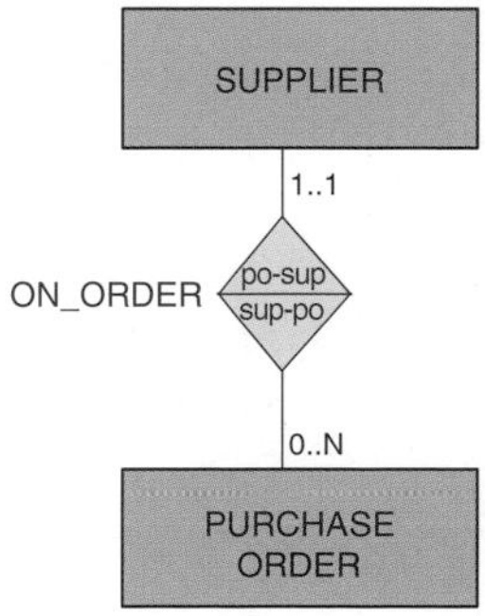


SUPPLIER

| SUPNR | SUPNAME | SUPADDRESS | SUPCITY | SUPSTATUS |
|---|---|---|---|---|
| ... | | | | |
| 37 | Ad Fundum | 82, Wacker Drive | Chicago | 95 |
| 94 | The Wine Crate | 330, McKinney Avenue | Dallas | 75 |
| ... | | | | |

PURCHASE_ORDER

| PONR | PODATE | *SUPNR* |
|---|---|---|
| 1511 | 2015-03-24 | 37 |
| 1512 | 2015-04-10 | 94 |
| ... | | |

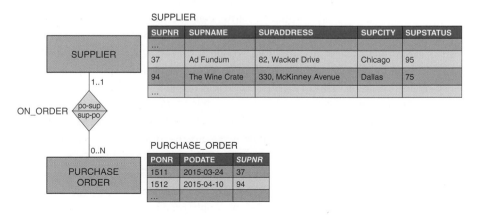

**Figure 6.4** Foreign keys: example 1.

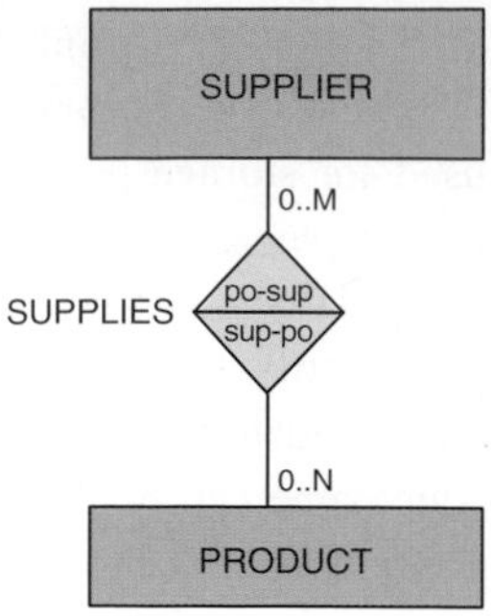


SUPPLIER

| SUPNR | SUPNAME | SUPADDRESS | SUPCITY | SUPSTATUS |
|---|---|---|---|---|
| 21 | Deliwines | 240, Avenue of the Americas | New York | 20 |
| 32 | Best Wines | 660, Market Street | San Francisco | 90 |
| ... | | | | |

PRODUCT

| PRODNR | PRODNAME | PRODTYPE | AVAILABLE_QUANTITY |
|---|---|---|---|
| 0119 | Chateau Miraval, Cotes de Provence Rose, 2015 | rose | 126 |
| 0154 | Chateau Haut Brion, 2008 | red | 111 |
| ... | | red | 5 |

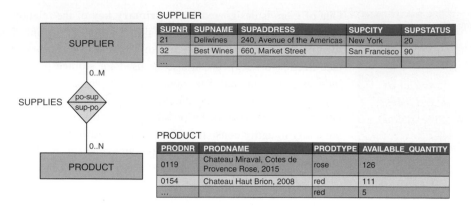

**Figure 6.5** Foreign keys: example 2.

SUPPLIES

| *SUPNR* | *PRODNR* | PURCHASE_PRICE | DELIV_PERIOD |
|---|---|---|---|
| ... | | | |
| 68 | 0327 | 56.99 | 4 |
| ... | | | |
| 21 | 0289 | 17.99 | 1 |
| 21 | 0327 | 56.00 | 6 |
| 21 | 0347 | 16.00 | 2 |
| ... | | | |
| 69 | 0347 | 18.00 | 4 |
| 84 | 0347 | 18.00 | 4 |
| ... | | | |

**Figure 6.6** Foreign keys: example 3.

name is Ad Fundum, and purchase order number 1512 is supplied by supplier number 94 which is The Wine Crate.

Figure 6.5 shows another example. We have an N:M relationship type between SUPPLIER and PRODUCT. A supplier can supply zero to N products, whereas a product can be supplied by zero to M suppliers. How can we map this N:M relationship type to the relational model? We could add a foreign key PRODNR to the SUPPLIER table. However, since a supplier can supply multiple products, this would create a multi-valued attribute type, which is not allowed. Alternatively, we could also add SUPNR as a foreign key to the PRODUCT relation. Unfortunately, the same problem arises since a product can be supplied by multiple suppliers.

The solution is to create a new relation SUPPLIES, which includes two foreign keys, SUPNR and PRODNR, that together make up the primary key of the relation as illustrated in Figure 6.6.

Note that we also added the attribute types of the EER relationship type to this relation: PURCHASE_PRICE and DELIV_PERIOD. You can see that this relation perfectly models the N:M cardinalities. Supplier number 21 can supply product numbers 289, 327, and 347. Vice versa, product number 347 can be supplied by supplier numbers 21, 69, and 84.

**Table 6.2** Overview of relational constraints

| | |
|---|---|
| Domain constraint | The value of each attribute type A must be an atomic and single value from the domain dom(A). |
| Key constraint | Every relation has a key that allows one to uniquely identify its tuples. |
| Entity integrity constraint | The attribute types that make up the primary key should always satisfy a NOT NULL constraint. |
| Referential integrity constraint | A foreign key FK has the same domain as the primary key PK attribute type(s) it refers to and occurs as a value of either PK or NULL. |

### 6.1.4 Relational Constraints

The relational model supports various integrity constraints on the values of the attribute types. These constraints aim to ensure that the data are always correct and consistent. The RDBMS will have to take care that the integrity constraints are always checked and violations reported if the database state is updated. Table 6.2 summarizes all relational constraints we have discussed thus far.

**Connections**

In Chapter 9 we discuss how triggers and stored procedures can be used to implement more advanced types of constraints.

### 6.1.5 Example Relational Data Model

Here you can see an example of a relational data model for the purchase order administration discussed in Chapter 3:

**SUPPLIER**(<u>SUPNR</u>, SUPNAME, SUPADDRESS, SUPCITY, SUPSTATUS)
**PRODUCT**(<u>PRODNR</u>, PRODNAME, PRODTYPE, AVAILABLE QUANTITY)
**SUPPLIES**(<u>*SUPNR*</u>, <u>*PRODNR*</u>, PURCHASE_PRICE, DELIV_PERIOD)
**PURCHASE_ORDER**(<u>PONR</u>, PODATE, *SUPNR*)
**PO_LINE**(<u>*PONR*</u>, <u>*PRODNR*</u>, QUANTITY)

The relational model includes five relations: SUPPLIER, PRODUCT, SUPPLIES, PURCHASE_ORDER, and PO_LINE. Each relation has a set of corresponding attribute types. Note that primary keys are underlined and foreign keys have been put in italics. As an example, the foreign keys SUPNR and PRODNR in the SUPPLIES relation refer to the primary keys SUPNR and PRODNR in the SUPPLIER and PRODUCT relation, respectively. In Section 6.4 we discuss in detail how to map the conceptual ER model of Figure 3.22 to the above relational model. Figure 6.7 shows an example of a corresponding relational database state. Note that each tuple has atomic and single values for each of its attribute types as required by the domain constraint.

**Retention Questions**

- Discuss the similarities and differences between the EER and the relational model.
- What are the different types of keys in the relational model? Why are they needed? Illustrate with examples.
- What are the most important relational constraints? Illustrate with examples.

## 6.2 Normalization

**Normalization** of a relational model is a process of analyzing the given relations to ensure they do not contain any redundant data. The goal of normalization is to ensure that no anomalies can occur

SUPPLIER

| SUPNR | SUPNAME | SUPADDRESS | SUPCITY | SUPSTATUS |
|---|---|---|---|---|
| 21 | Deliwines | 240, Avenue of the Americas | New York | 20 |
| 32 | Best Wines | 660, Market Street | San Francisco | 90 |
| ... | | | | |

PRODUCT

| PRODNR | PRODNAME | PRODTYPE | AVAILABLE_QUANTITY |
|---|---|---|---|
| 0119 | Chateau Miraval, Cotes de Provence Rose, 2015 | rose | 126 |
| 0384 | Dominio de Pingus, Ribera del Duero, Tempranillo, 2006 | red | 38 |
| ... | | | |

SUPPLIES

| *SUPNR* | *PRODNR* | PURCHASE_PRICE | DELIV_PERIOD |
|---|---|---|---|
| 21 | 0119 | 15.99 | 1 |
| 21 | 0384 | 55.00 | 2 |
| ... | | | |

PURCHASE_ORDER

| PONR | PODATE | *SUPNR* |
|---|---|---|
| 1511 | 2015-03-24 | 37 |
| 1512 | 2015-04-10 | 94 |
| ... | | |

PO_LINE

| *PONR* | *PRODNR* | QUANTITY |
|---|---|---|
| 1511 | 0212 | 2 |
| 1511 | 0345 | 4 |
| ... | | |

**Figure 6.7** Example relational database state.

during data insertion, deletion, or update. A step-by-step procedure needs to be followed to transform an unnormalized relational model to a normalized relational model. In what follows, we start by discussing the data anomalies that can occur when working with an unnormalized relational model. Next, we outline some informal normalization guidelines. This is followed by defining two concepts that are fundamental building blocks of a normalization procedure: functional dependencies and prime attribute types. Both will then be extensively used when discussing the normalization forms in Section 6.2.3.

### 6.2.1 Insertion, Deletion, and Update Anomalies in an Unnormalized Relational Model

Figure 6.8 shows an example of a relational data model in which we only have two relations with all the information. The SUPPLIES relation also includes all the attribute types for SUPPLIER, such as supplier name, supplier address, etc., and all the attribute types for PRODUCT, such as product number, product type, etc. You can also see that the PO_LINE relation now includes purchase order date and supplier number. Both relations contain duplicate information that may easily lead to inconsistencies. In the SUPPLIES table, for example, all supplier and product information is repeated for each tuple, which creates a lot of redundant information. Because of this redundant information, this relational model is called an unnormalized relational model. At least three types of anomaly may arise when working with an unnormalized relational model: an insertion anomaly, a deletion anomaly, and an update anomaly.

An **insertion anomaly** can occur when we wish to insert a new tuple in the SUPPLIES relation. We must then be sure to each time include the correct supplier (e.g., SUPNR, SUPNAME, SUPADDRESS, etc.) and product (e.g., PRODNR, PRODNAME, PRODTYPE, etc.) information. Furthermore, in this unnormalized relational model, it is difficult to insert a new product for which there are no suppliers yet, or a new supplier who does not supply anything yet since the primary key is a combination of SUPNR and PRODNR, which can thus both not be NULL (entity integrity

SUPPLIES

| SUPNR | PRODNR | PURCHASE_PRICE | DELIV_PERIOD | SUPNAME | SUPADDRESS | ... | PRODNAME | PRODTYPE | ... |
|---|---|---|---|---|---|---|---|---|---|
| 21 | 0289 | 17.99 | 1 | Deliwines | 240, Avenue of the Americas | | Chateau Saint Estève de Neri, 2015 | Rose | |
| 21 | 0327 | 56.00 | 6 | Deliwines | 240, Avenue of the Americas | | Chateau La Croix Saint-Michel, 2011 | Red | |
| ... | | | | | | | | | |

PO_LINE

| PONR | PRODNR | QUANTITY | PODATE | SUPNR |
|---|---|---|---|---|
| 1511 | 0212 | 2 | 2015-03-24 | 37 |
| 1511 | 0345 | 4 | 2015-03-24 | 37 |
| ... | | | | |

**Figure 6.8** Unnormalized relational data model.

SUPPLIER

| SUPNR | SUPNAME | SUPADDRESS | SUPCITY | SUPSTATUS |
|---|---|---|---|---|
| 21 | Deliwines | 240, Avenue of the Americas | New York | 20 |
| 32 | Best Wines | 660, Market Street | San Francisco | 90 |
| ... | | | | |

PRODUCT

| PRODNR | PRODNAME | PRODTYPE | AVAILABLE_QUANTITY |
|---|---|---|---|
| 0119 | Chateau Miraval, Cotes de Provence Rose, 2015 | rose | 126 |
| 0384 | Dominio de Pingus, Ribera del Duero, Tempranillo, 2006 | red | 38 |
| ... | | | |

SUPPLIES

| *SUPNR* | *PRODNR* | PURCHASE_PRICE | DELIV_PERIOD |
|---|---|---|---|
| 21 | 0119 | 15.99 | 1 |
| 21 | 0384 | 55.00 | 2 |
| ... | | | |

PURCHASE_ORDER

| PONR | PODATE | *SUPNR* |
|---|---|---|
| 1511 | 2015-03-24 | 37 |
| 1512 | 2015-04-10 | 94 |
| ... | | |

PO_LINE

| *PONR* | *PRODNR* | QUANTITY |
|---|---|---|
| 1511 | 0212 | 2 |
| 1511 | 0345 | 4 |
| ... | | |

**Figure 6.9** Normalized relational data model.

constraint). A **deletion anomaly** can occur if we were to delete a particular supplier from the SUPPLIES relation. Consequently, all corresponding product data may get lost as well, which is not desirable. An **update anomaly** can occur when we wish to update the supplier address in the SUPPLIES relation. This would necessitate multiple updates with the risk of inconsistency.

Figure 6.9 shows another example relational data model and state for the purchase order administration. Let's see how our insertion, deletion, and update operations work out here. Inserting a new tuple in the SUPPLIES relation can be easily done since the supplier name, address, etc. and the product name, product type, etc. are only stored once in the relations SUPPLIER and PRODUCT. Inserting a new product for which there are no supplies yet, or a new supplier who does not supply anything yet, can be accomplished by adding new tuples to the PRODUCT and SUPPLIER relation. Deleting a tuple from the SUPPLIER relation will not affect any product tuples in the PRODUCT relation. Finally, if we wish to update the supplier address, we only need to do one single update in the SUPPLIER table. As there are no inconsistencies or duplicate information in this relational model, it is also called a normalized relational model.

To have a good relational data model, all relations in the model should be normalized. A formal normalization procedure can be applied to transform an unnormalized relational model into a normalized form. The advantages are twofold. At the logical level, the users can easily understand the meaning of the data and formulate correct queries (see Chapter 7). At the implementation level, the storage space is used efficiently and the risk of inconsistent updates is reduced.

### 6.2.2 Informal Normalization Guidelines

Before we start discussing a formal step-by-step normalization procedure, let's review some informal normalization guidelines. First, it is important to design a relational model in such a way that it is easy to explain its meaning. Consider the following example:

```
MYRELATION123(SUPNR, SUPNAME, SUPTWITTER, PRODNR, PRODNAME, ...)
```

The name of the relation is not very meaningful. Hence, a better alternative would be:

```
SUPPLIER(SUPNR, SUPNAME, SUPTWITTER, PRODNR, PRODNAME, ...)
```

Next, attribute types from multiple entity types should not be combined in a single relation, so as to not cloud its interpretation. When looking back at the above relation, both supplier and product information are mixed. Hence, a better alternative would be to create two relations, SUPPLIER and PRODUCT, whereby the former looks like:

```
SUPPLIER(SUPNR, SUPNAME, SUPTWITTER,...)
```

Finally, avoid excessive amounts of NULL values in a relation. For example, assume that SUPTWITTER has many NULL values because not many suppliers have a Twitter account. Hence, keeping it in the SUPPLIER relation implies a waste of storage capacity. A better option might be to split up the SUPPLIER relation in two relations: SUPPLIER and SUPPLIER-TWITTER, whereby the latter includes supplier number as a foreign and primary key and SUPTWITTER as follows:

```
SUPPLIER(SUPNR, SUPNAME, ...)
SUPPLIER-TWITTER(SUPNR, SUPTWITTER)
```

As we discuss in Chapter 7, both relations can then be joined in case we want combined information from a supplier.

**Connections**

Chapter 7 discusses join queries which allow combination of information from two or more relations.

### 6.2.3 Functional Dependencies and Prime Attribute Types

Before we can start discussing various normalization steps, we need to introduce two important concepts: functional dependency and prime attribute type.

A **functional dependency** $X \rightarrow Y$ between two sets of attribute types X and Y implies that a value of X uniquely determines a value of Y. We also say that there is a functional dependency from X to Y or that Y is functionally dependent on X. As an example, the employee name is functionally dependent upon the social security number:

```
SSN → ENAME
```

In other words, a social security number uniquely determines an employee name. The other way around does not necessarily apply, since multiple employees can share the same name, hence one employee name may correspond to multiple social security numbers. A project number uniquely determines a project name and a project location:

```
PNUMBER → {PNAME, PLOCATION}
```

Project name and project location are thus functionally dependent upon project number. The number of hours an employee worked on a project is functionally dependent upon both the social security number and the project number

```
{SSN, PNUMBER} → HOURS
```

Note that if X is a candidate key of a relation R, this implies that Y is functionally dependent on X for any subset of attribute types Y of R.

A **prime attribute type** is another important concept that is needed in the normalization process. A prime attribute type is an attribute type that is part of a candidate key. Consider the following relation:

```
R1(SSN, PNUMBER, PNAME, HOURS)
```

The key of the relation is a combination of SSN and PNUMBER. Both SSN and PNUMBER are prime attribute types, whereas PNAME and HOURS are non-prime attribute types.

### 6.2.4 Normalization Forms

Normalization of a relational model is a process of analyzing the given relations based on their functional dependencies and candidate keys to minimize redundancy and insertion, deletion, and update anomalies. The normalization procedure entails various *normal form tests* which are typically sequentially evaluated. Unsatisfactory relations that do not meet the normal form tests are decomposed into smaller relations.

#### 6.2.4.1 First Normal Form (1 NF)

The **first normal form (1 NF)** states that every attribute type of a relation must be atomic and single-valued. Hence, no composite or multi-valued attribute types are tolerated. This is the same as the domain constraint we introduced earlier.

Consider the following example:

```
SUPPLIER(SUPNR, NAME(FIRST NAME, LAST NAME), SUPSTATUS)
```

This relation is not in 1 NF as it contains a composite attribute type NAME that consists of the attribute types FIRST NAME and LAST NAME. We can bring it in 1 NF as follows:

```
SUPPLIER(SUPNR, FIRST NAME, LAST NAME, SUPSTATUS)
```

In other words, composite attribute types need to be decomposed in their parts to bring the relation in 1 NF.

Suppose we have a relation DEPARTMENT. It has a department number, a department location and a foreign key referring to the social security number of the employee who manages the department:

| DNUMBER | DLOCATION | *DMGRSSN* |
|---|---|---|
| 15 | {New York, San Francisco} | 110 |
| 20 | Chicago | 150 |
| 30 | {Chicago, Boston} | 100 |

↓ 1 NF

DEPARTMENT

| DNUMBER | *DMGRSSN* |
|---|---|
| 15 | 110 |
| 20 | 150 |
| 30 | 100 |

DEP-LOCATION

| *DNUMBER* | DLOCATION |
|---|---|
| 15 | New York |
| 15 | San Francisco |
| 20 | Chicago |
| 30 | Chicago |
| 30 | Boston |

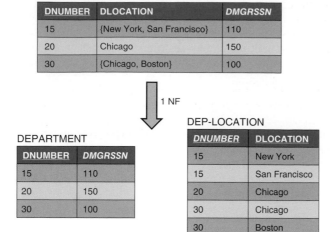

**Figure 6.10** First normal form: the unnormalized relation (above) is decomposed into two relations (below) by ensuring there are no composite or multi-valued attribute types.

DEPARTMENT(DNUMBER, DLOCATION, *DMGRSSN*)

Assume now that a department can have multiple locations and that multiple departments are possible at a given location. The relation is not in 1 NF since DLOCATION is a multi-valued attribute type. We can bring it in 1 NF by removing DLOCATION from department and putting it into a new relation DEP-LOCATION together with DNUMBER as a foreign key:

DEPARTMENT(DNUMBER, *DMGRSSN*)
DEP-LOCATION(*DNUMBER*, DLOCATION)

The primary key of this new relation is then the combination of both, since a department can have multiple locations and multiple departments can share a location. Figure 6.10 illustrates some example tuples. You can see that department number 15 has two locations: New York and San Francisco. Department number 30 also has two locations: Chicago and Boston. The two lower tables bring it in the 1 NF since every attribute type of both relations is now atomic and single-valued. To summarize, multi-valued attribute types (e.g., DLOCATION) should be removed and put in a separate relation (e.g., DEP-LOCATION) along with the primary key (e.g., DNUMBER) of the original relation (e.g., DEPARTMENT) as a foreign key. The primary key of the new relation is then the combination of the multi-valued attribute type and the primary key of the original relation (e.g., DNUMBER and DLOCATION).

Let's give another example. Say we have a relation R1 with employee information such as SSN, ENAME, DNUMBER, DNAME, and PROJECT, which is a composite attribute type consisting of PNUMBER, PNAME and HOURS:

R1(SSN, ENAME, DNUMBER, DNAME, PROJECT(PNUMBER, PNAME, HOURS))

We assume an employee can work on multiple projects and multiple employees can work on the same project. Hence, we have a multi-valued composite attribute type PROJECT in our relation R1. In other words, both conditions of the first normal form are clearly violated. To bring it in first normal form, we create two relations R11 and R12 where the latter includes the project attribute types together with SSN as a foreign key:

R11(SSN, ENAME, DNUMBER, DNAME)
R12(*SSN*, PNUMBER, PNAME, HOURS)

The primary key of R12 is then the combination of SSN and PNUMBER, since an employee can work on multiple projects and multiple employees can work on a project.

#### 6.2.4.2 Second Normal Form (2 NF)

Before we can start discussing the **second normal form (2 NF)**, we need to introduce the concepts of full and partial functional dependency. A functional dependency X → Y is a **full functional dependency** if removal of any attribute type A from X means that the dependency does not hold anymore. For example, HOURS is fully functionally dependent upon both SSN and PNUMBER:

```
SSN, PNUMBER → HOURS
```

More specifically, to know the number of hours an employee worked on a project, we need to know both the SSN of the employee and the project number. Likewise, project name is fully functionally dependent upon project number:

```
PNUMBER → PNAME
```

A functional dependency X → Y is a partial dependency if an attribute type A from X can be removed from X and the dependency still holds. As an example, PNAME is partially functionally dependent upon SSN and PNUMBER:

```
SSN, PNUMBER → PNAME
```

It only depends upon PNUMBER, not on SSN.

A relation R is in the 2 NF if it satisfies 1 NF and every non-prime attribute type A in R is fully functionally dependent on any key of R. In case the relation is not in second normal form, we must decompose it and set up a new relation for each partial key together with its dependent attribute types. Also, it is important to keep a relation with the original primary key and any attribute types that are fully functionally dependent on it. Let's illustrate this with an example.

Say we have a relation R1 with attribute types SSN, PNUMBER, PNAME, HOURS:

```
R1(SSN, PNUMBER, PNAME, HOURS)
```

It contains both project information and information about which employee worked on what project for how many hours. The assumptions are as follows: an employee can work on multiple projects; multiple employees can work on the same project; and a project has a unique name. The relation R1 is in 1 NF since there are no multi-valued or composite attribute types. However, it is not in 2 NF. The primary key of the relation R1 is a combination of SSN and PNUMBER. The attribute type PNAME is not fully functionally dependent on the primary key, it only depends on PNUMBER. HOURS, however, is fully functionally dependent upon both SSN and PNUMBER. Hence, we need to remove the attribute type PNAME and put it in a new relation R12, together with PNUMBER:

```
R11(SSN, PNUMBER, HOURS)
R12(PNUMBER, PNAME)
```

The relation R11 can then be called WORKS-ON(SSN, PNUMBER, HOURS) and the relation R12 can be referred to as PROJECT(PNUMBER, PNAME).

Figure 6.11 illustrates how to bring a relation into 2 NF with some example tuples. Note the redundancy in the original relation. The name "Hadoop" is repeated multiple times, which is not

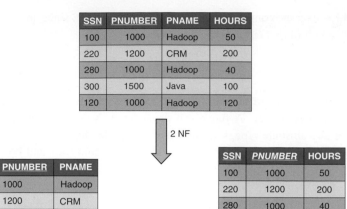

| SSN | PNUMBER | PNAME | HOURS |
|---|---|---|---|
| 100 | 1000 | Hadoop | 50 |
| 220 | 1200 | CRM | 200 |
| 280 | 1000 | Hadoop | 40 |
| 300 | 1500 | Java | 100 |
| 120 | 1000 | Hadoop | 120 |

2 NF

| PNUMBER | PNAME |
|---|---|
| 1000 | Hadoop |
| 1200 | CRM |
| 1500 | Java |

| SSN | *PNUMBER* | HOURS |
|---|---|---|
| 100 | 1000 | 50 |
| 220 | 1200 | 200 |
| 280 | 1000 | 40 |
| 300 | 1500 | 100 |
| 120 | 1000 | 120 |

**Figure 6.11** Second normal form: the unnormalized relation (above) is decomposed into two relations (below) by ensuring every non-prime attribute type is fully functionally dependent on the primary key.

desirable from a storage perspective. Also, if we would like to update it (e.g., from "Hadoop" to "Big Data"), then multiple changes need to take place. This is not the case for the two normalized relations at the bottom, where the update should only be done once in the PROJECT relation.

### 6.2.4.3 Third Normal Form (3 NF)

To discuss the **third normal form (3 NF)**, we need to introduce the concept of **transitive dependency**. A functional dependency X → Y in a relation R is a transitive dependency if there is a set of attribute types Z that is neither a candidate key nor a subset of any key of R, and both X → Z and Z → Y hold. A relation is in the 3 NF if it satisfies 2 NF and no non-prime attribute type of R is transitively dependent on the primary key. If this is not the case, we need to decompose the relation R and set up a relation that includes the non-key attribute types that functionally determine the other non-key attribute types. Let's work out an example to illustrate this.

The relation R1 contains information about employees and departments as follows:

```
R1(SSN, ENAME, DNUMBER, DNAME, DMGRSSN)
```

The SSN attribute type is the primary key of the relation. The assumptions are as follows: an employee works in one department; a department can have multiple employees; and a department has one manager. Given these assumptions, we have two transitive dependencies in R. DNAME is transitively dependent on SSN via DNUMBER. In other words, DNUMBER is functionally dependent on SSN, and DNAME is functionally dependent on DNUMBER. Likewise, DMGRSSN is transitively dependent on SSN via DNUMBER. In other words, DNUMBER is functionally dependent on SSN and DMGRSSN is functionally dependent on DNUMBER. DNUMBER is not a candidate key nor a subset of a key. Hence, the relation is not in 3 NF. To bring it in 3 NF, we remove the attribute types DNAME and DMGRSSN and put them in a new relation R12 together with DNUMBER as its primary key:

```
R11(SSN, ENAME, DNUMBER)
R12(DNUMBER, DNAME, DMGRSSN)
```

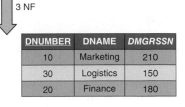

| SSN | NAME | DNUMBER | DNAME | *DMGRSSN* |
|---|---|---|---|---|
| 10 | O'Reilly | 10 | Marketing | 210 |
| 22 | Donovan | 30 | Logistics | 150 |
| 28 | Bush | 10 | Marketing | 210 |
| 30 | Jackson | 20 | Finance | 180 |
| 12 | Thompson | 10 | Marketing | 210 |

3 NF

| SSNR | NAME | *DNUMBER* |
|---|---|---|
| 10 | O'Reilly | 10 |
| 22 | Donovan | 30 |
| 28 | Bush | 10 |
| 30 | Jackson | 20 |
| 12 | Thompson | 10 |

| DNUMBER | DNAME | *DMGRSSN* |
|---|---|---|
| 10 | Marketing | 210 |
| 30 | Logistics | 150 |
| 20 | Finance | 180 |

**Figure 6.12** Third normal form: the unnormalized relation (above) is decomposed into two relations (below) by ensuring no non-prime attribute types are transitively dependent on the primary key.

The relation R11 can be called EMPLOYEE(SSN, ENAME, DNUMBER) and the relation R12 can be referred to as DEPARTMENT(DNUMBER, DNAME, DMGRSSN).

Figure 6.12 shows some example tuples for both the unnormalized and normalized relations. Note the redundancy in the unnormalized case, where the values "marketing" for DNAME and "210" for DMGRSSN are repeated multiple times. This is not the case for the normalized relations where these values are only stored once.

### 6.2.4.4 Boyce–Codd Normal Form (BCNF)

We can now discuss the **Boyce–Codd normal form (BCNF)**, also referred to as the 3.5 normal form (3.5 NF). Let's first introduce another concept. A functional dependency X → Y is called a **trivial functional dependency** if Y is a subset of X. An example of a trivial functional dependency is between SSN and NAME, and SSN:

```
SSN, NAME → SSN
```

A relation R is in the BCNF provided that for *each* of its non-trivial functional dependencies X → Y, X is a superkey – that is, X is either a candidate key or a superset thereof. It can be shown that the BCNF is stricter than the 3 NF. Hence, every relation in BCNF is also in 3 NF. However, a relation in 3 NF is not necessarily in BCNF. Let's give an example.

Suppose we have a relation R1 with attribute types SUPNR, SUPNAME, PRODNR, and QUANTITY:

```
R1(SUPNR, SUPNAME, PRODNR, QUANTITY)
```

It models information about which supplier can supply what products in what quantities. The assumptions are as follows: a supplier can supply multiple products; a product can be supplied by multiple suppliers; and a supplier has a unique name. Therefore, SUPNR and PRODNR are a superkey of the relation. Further, we have a non-trivial functional dependency between SUPNR and SUPNAME. The relation is thus not in BCNF. To bring it in BCNF we remove SUPNAME from R1 and put it in a new relation R12 together with SUPNR as the primary key:

```
R11(SUPNR, PRODNR, QUANTITY)
R12(SUPNR, SUPNAME)
```

The relation R11 can be called SUPPLIES and the relation R12 can be referred to as SUPPLIER.

**Drill Down**

The Boyce–Codd normal form was developed in 1974 by Raymond F. Boyce and Edgar F. Codd.

### 6.2.4.5 Fourth Normal Form (4 NF)

We can conclude by discussing the **fourth normal form (4 NF)**. First, we introduce the concept of a **multi-valued dependency**. There is a multi-valued dependency from X to Y, $X \rightarrow\rightarrow Y$, if and only if each X value exactly determines a set of Y values, independently of the other attribute types. A relation is in the 4 NF if it is in BCNF and for every one of its non-trivial multi-valued dependencies $X \rightarrow\rightarrow Y$, X is a superkey – that is, X is either a candidate key or a superset thereof. Let's illustrate it with an example.

Suppose we have a relation R1 including information about courses, instructors and textbooks:

**Connections**

In Chapter 17, we come back to normalization in the context of data warehousing. We discuss there how a controlled degree of denormalization can be tolerated to improve data retrieval performance in this type of setting.

```
R1(course, instructor, textbook)
```

The assumptions are as follows: a course can be taught by different instructors; and a course uses the same set of textbooks for each instructor. Hence, we have a multi-valued dependency between course and textbook. In other words, each course exactly determines a set of textbooks, independently of the instructor. To bring it in 4 NF, we create two relations: R11 with course and textbook; and R12 with course and instructor:

```
R11(course, textbook)
R12(course, instructor)
```

Figure 6.13 shows some example tuples for the unnormalized and normalized relations. You can spot the redundancy in the former case. Suppose a new textbook were added to the course Database Management. In the

| COURSE | INSTRUCTOR | BOOK |
|---|---|---|
| Database Management | Baesens | Database cookbook |
| Database Management | Lemahieu | Database cookbook |
| Database Management | Baesens | Databases for dummies |
| Database Management | Lemahieu | Databases for dummies |

4 NF

| COURSE | INSTRUCTOR |
|---|---|
| Database Management | Baesens |
| Database Management | Lemahieu |

| COURSE | BOOK |
|---|---|
| Database Management | Database cookbook |
| Database Management | Databases for dummies |

**Figure 6.13** Fourth normal form: the unnormalized relation (above) is decomposed into two relations (below) by ensuring that for every one of the non-trivial multi-valued dependencies $X \rightarrow\rightarrow Y$, X is a superkey.

**Table 6.3** Overview of normalization steps and dependency

| Normal form | Type of dependency | Description |
|---|---|---|
| 2 NF | Full functional dependency | A functional dependency $X \rightarrow Y$ is a full functional dependency if removal of any attribute type A from X means that the dependency does not hold anymore. |
| 3 NF | Transitive functional dependency | A functional dependency $X \rightarrow Y$ in a relation R is a transitive dependency if there is a set of attribute types Z that is neither a candidate key nor a subset of any key of R, and both $X \rightarrow Z$ and $Z \rightarrow Y$ hold. |
| BCNF | Trivial functional dependency | A functional dependency $X \rightarrow Y$ is called trivial if Y is a subset of X. |
| 4 NF | Multi-valued dependency | A dependency $X \rightarrow\rightarrow Y$ is multi-valued if and only if each X value exactly determines a set of Y values, independently of the other attribute types. |

**Retention Questions**

- What is normalization and why is it needed?
- Discuss the various normalization forms and illustrate with examples.

unnormalized case, this would imply adding as many tuples as there are instructors teaching it, or two in our case. In the normalized case, only one tuple needs to be added.

Table 6.3 concludes this section by reviewing the various normalization steps and the types of dependencies considered.

## 6.3 Mapping a Conceptual ER Model to a Relational Model

There exists a plethora of database modeling tools that allow the database designer to draw an (E)ER model and automatically generate a relational data model from it. If the correct translation rules are applied, the resulting relational model will automatically be normalized. Therefore, although the translation can be automated, it is useful to study these rules in detail. They provide us with valuable insights into the intricacies of good database design and the consequences of certain design decisions, by linking relational concepts to their (E)ER counterparts. In this section, we discuss how to map a conceptual ER model to a relational model. After that, we move on to mapping EER constructs.

### 6.3.1 Mapping Entity Types

The first step is to map each entity type into a relation. Simple attribute types can be directly mapped. A composite attribute type needs to be decomposed into its component attribute types. One of the key attribute types of the entity type can be set as the primary key of the relation.

You can see this illustrated in Figure 6.14. We have two entity types: EMPLOYEE and PROJECT. We create relations for both:

```
EMPLOYEE(SSN, address, first name, last name)
PROJECT(PNR, pname, pduration)
```

The EMPLOYEE entity type has three attribute types: SSN, which is the key attribute type; address, which is considered as an atomic attribute type; and ename, which is a composite attribute type consisting of first name and last name. The PROJECT entity type also has three attribute types:

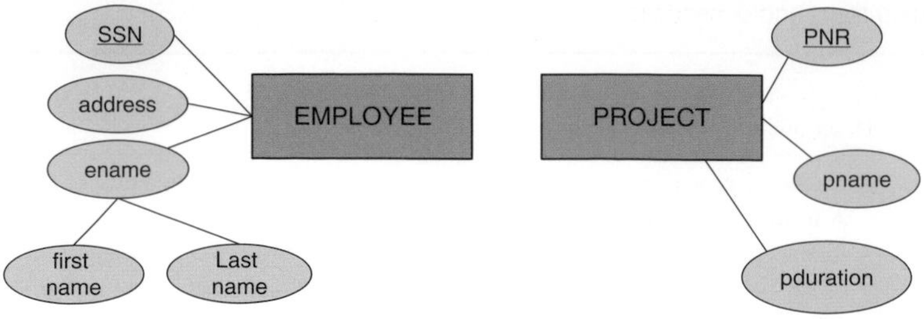


**Figure 6.14** Mapping entity types to relations.

PNR, which is the key attribute type; pname; and pduration. You can see that both key attribute types SSN and PNR have been mapped to the primary keys of both relations. Also, note that the ename composite attribute type has been decomposed into first name and last name in the relation EMPLOYEE.

## 6.3.2 Mapping Relationship Types

Once we have mapped the entity types, we can continue with the relationship types. The mapping depends upon the degree and cardinalities, as we illustrate in what follows.

### 6.3.2.1 Mapping a Binary 1:1 Relationship type

For a binary 1:1 relationship type, we create two relations – one for each entity type participating in the relationship type. The connection can be made by including a foreign key in one of the relations to the primary key of the other. In case of existence dependency, we put the foreign key in the existence-dependent relation and declare it as NOT NULL. The attribute types of the 1:1 relationship type can then be added to the relation with the foreign key.

Let's consider the MANAGES relationship type between EMPLOYEE and DEPARTMENT, as depicted in Figure 6.15.

Remember, an employee manages either zero or one department, whereas a department is managed by exactly one employee, which means DEPARTMENT is existence-dependent on EMPLOYEE. We create relations for both entity types and add the corresponding attribute types as follows:

```
EMPLOYEE(SSN, ename, address)
DEPARTMENT(DNR, dname, dlocation)
```

The question now is: How do we map the relationship type? One option would be to add a foreign key DNR to the EMPLOYEE relation, which refers to the primary key DNR in DEPARTMENT as follows:

```
EMPLOYEE(SSN, ename, address, DNR)
DEPARTMENT(DNR, dname, dlocation)
```

This foreign key can be NULL, since not every employee manages a department. Let's now find out how many of the four cardinalities of the relationship type are correctly modeled, using Figure 6.16.

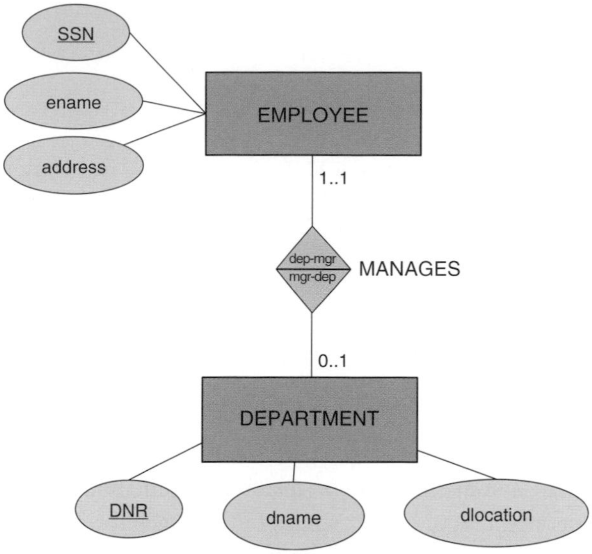


**Figure 6.15** Mapping 1:1 ER relationship types to the relational model.

EMPLOYEE(<u>SSN</u>, ename, address, *DNR*)

| | | | |
|---|---|---|---|
| 511 | John Smith | 14 Avenue of the Americas, New York | 001 |
| 289 | Paul Barker | 208 Market Street, San Francisco | 003 |
| 356 | Emma Lucas | 432 Wacker Drive, Chicago | NULL |
| 412 | Michael Johnson | 1134 Pennsylvania Avenue, Washington | NULL |
| 564 | Sarah Adams | 812 Collins Avenue, Miami | 001 |

DEPARTMENT(<u>DNR</u>, dname, dlocation)

| | | |
|---|---|---|
| 001 | Marketing | 3th floor |
| 002 | Call center | 2nd floor |
| 003 | Finance | basement |
| 004 | ICT | 1st floor |

**Figure 6.16** Example tuples for mapping a 1:1 relationship type.

We start from DEPARTMENT. Can a department have zero managers? Yes, this is the case for department number 2, the Call Center, which has no manager assigned as its department number 002 does not appear in the DNR column of the EMPLOYEE table. Also, the ICT department has no manager. Can a department have more than one manager? Yes, this is the case for department number 001, marketing, which has two managers: employee 511, John Smith, and employee 564, Sarah Adams. Can an employee manage zero departments? Yes, this is the case for Emma Lucas and Michael Johnson. Can an employee manage more than one department? No, since the

EMPLOYEE(<u>SSN</u>, ename, address)

| | | |
|---|---|---|
| 511 | John Smith | 14 Avenue of the Americas, New York |
| 289 | Paul Barker | 208 Market Street, San Francisco |
| 356 | Emma Lucas | 432 Wacker Drive, Chicago |

DEPARTMENT(<u>DNR</u>, dname, dlocation, *SSN*)

| | | | |
|---|---|---|---|
| 001 | Marketing | 3th floor | 511 |
| 002 | Call center | 2nd floor | 511 |
| 003 | Finance | basement | 289 |
| 004 | ICT | 1st floor | 511 |

**Figure 6.17** Example tuples for mapping a 1:1 relationship type.

EMPLOYEE relation is normalized and the foreign key DNR should thus be single-valued, as required by the first normal form. To summarize, out of the four cardinalities, only two are supported. Moreover, this option generates a lot of NULL values for the DNR foreign key, as there are typically many employees who are not managing any department.

Another option would be to include SSN as a foreign key in DEPARTMENT, referring to SSN in EMPLOYEE:

```
EMPLOYEE(SSN, ename, address)
DEPARTMENT(DNR, dname, dlocation, SSN)
```

This foreign key should be declared as NOT NULL, since every department should have exactly one manager. Let's now also look at the other cardinalities, using Figure 6.17.

Can you have employees that manage zero departments? Yes, this is the case for Emma Lucas since her SSN 356 does not appear in the SSN column of the DEPARTMENT table. Can we make sure that an employee manages at most one department? In fact, we cannot! As you can see, John Smith manages three departments. Hence, out of the four cardinalities, three are supported. This option is to be preferred above the previous one, although it is not perfect. The semantics lost in the mapping should be documented and followed up using application code.

#### 6.3.2.2 Mapping a Binary 1:N Relationship Type

Binary 1:N relationship types can be mapped by including a foreign key in the relation corresponding to the participating entity type at the N-side of the relationship type (e.g., the EMPLOYEE relation in Figure 6.18). The foreign key refers to the primary key of the relation corresponding to the entity type at the 1-side of the relationship type (e.g., the DEPARTMENT relation in Figure 6.18). Depending upon the minimum cardinality, the foreign key can be declared as NOT NULL or NULL ALLOWED. The attribute types (e.g., starting date in Figure 6.18) of the 1:N relationship type can be added to the relation corresponding to the participating entity type.

The WORKS_IN relationship type is an example of a 1:N relationship type. An employee works in exactly one department, whereas a department can have one to N employees working in it. The attribute type starting date represents the date at which an employee started working in a department. As with 1:1 relationships, we first create the relations EMPLOYEE and DEPARTMENT for both entity types:

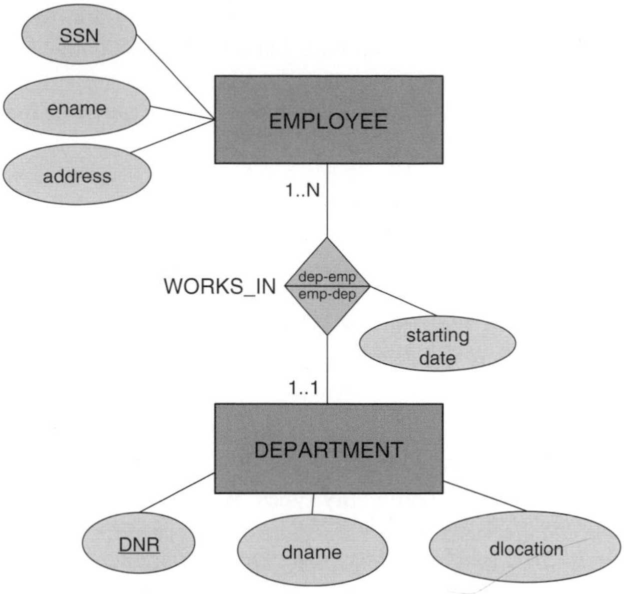


**Figure 6.18** Mapping 1:N ER relationship types to the relational model.

EMPLOYEE(SSN, ename, address, starting date, *DNR*)

| | | | | |
|---|---|---|---|---|
| 511 | John Smith | 14 Avenue of the Americas, New York | 01/01/2000 | 001 |
| 289 | Paul Barker | 208 Market Street, San Francisco | 01/01/1998 | 001 |
| 356 | Emma Lucas | 432 Wacker Drive, Chicago | 01/01/2010 | 002 |

DEPARTMENT(DNR, dname, dlocation)

| | | |
|---|---|---|
| 001 | Marketing | 3th floor |
| 002 | Call center | 2nd floor |
| 003 | Finance | basement |
| 004 | ICT | 1st floor |

**Figure 6.19** Example tuples for mapping a 1:N relationship type.

```
EMPLOYEE(SSN, ename, address)
DEPARTMENT(DNR, dname, dlocation)
```

We can again explore two options to establish the relationship type in the relational model. Since a department can have multiple employees, we cannot add a foreign key to it as this would create a multi-valued attribute type, which is not tolerated in the relational model. That's why we add DNR as a foreign key to the EMPLOYEE relation.

```
EMPLOYEE(SSN, ename, address, starting date, DNR)
DEPARTMENT(DNR, dname, dlocation)
```

Since the minimum cardinality is one, this foreign key is defined as NOT NULL, ensuring that an employee works in exactly one department. What about the other cardinalities? We can find out using Figure 6.19.

Can a department have more than one employee? Yes, this is the case for the marketing department, which has two employees – John Smith and Paul Barker. Can we guarantee that every department has at least one employee? In fact, we cannot. The finance and ICT departments have no employees. Out of the four cardinalities, three are supported. Note that the attribute type starting date has also been added to the EMPLOYEE relation.

#### 6.3.2.3 Mapping a Binary M:N Relationship Type

M:N relationship types are mapped by introducing a new relation R. The primary key of R is a combination of foreign keys referring to the primary keys of the relations corresponding to the participating entity types. The attribute types of the M:N relationship type can also be added to R.

The WORKS_ON relationship type shown in Figure 6.20 is an example of an M:N relationship type. An employee works on zero to N projects, whereas a project is being worked on by zero to M employees. We start by creating relations for both entity types. We cannot add a foreign key to the EMPLOYEE relation as this would give us a multi-valued attribute type since an employee can work on multiple projects. Likewise, we cannot add a foreign key to the project relation, as a project is being worked on by multiple employees. In other words, we need to create a new relation to map the ER relationship type WORKS_ON:

```
EMPLOYEE(SSN, ename, address)
PROJECT(PNR, pname, pduration)
WORKS_ON(SSN, PNR, hours)
```

The WORKS_ON relation has two foreign keys, SSN and PNR, which together make up the primary key and, therefore, cannot be NULL (entity integrity constraint). The hours attribute type is also added to this relation.

Figure 6.21 shows some example tuples of the EMPLOYEE, PROJECT, and WORKS_ON relations.

All four cardinalities are successfully modeled. Emma Lucas does not work on any projects, whereas Paul Barker works on two projects. Projects 1002 and 1004 have no employees assigned, whereas project 1001 has two employees assigned.

Now let's see what happens if we change the assumptions as follows: an employee works on at least one project and a project is being worked on by at least one employee. In other words, the minimum cardinalities change to 1 on both sides. Essentially, the solution remains the same and you

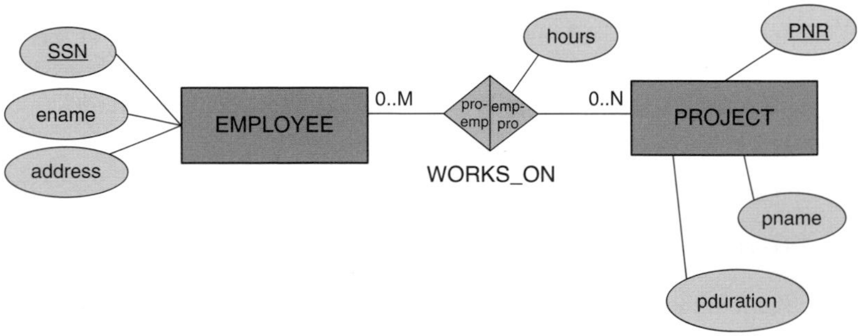


**Figure 6.20** Mapping M:N ER relationship types to the relational model.

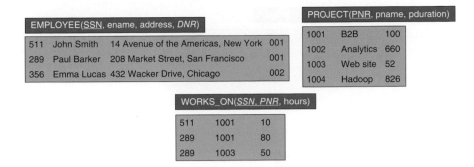

EMPLOYEE(SSN, ename, address, *DNR*)

| | | | |
|---|---|---|---|
| 511 | John Smith | 14 Avenue of the Americas, New York | 001 |
| 289 | Paul Barker | 208 Market Street, San Francisco | 001 |
| 356 | Emma Lucas | 432 Wacker Drive, Chicago | 002 |

PROJECT(PNR, pname, pduration)

| | | |
|---|---|---|
| 1001 | B2B | 100 |
| 1002 | Analytics | 660 |
| 1003 | Web site | 52 |
| 1004 | Hadoop | 826 |

WORKS_ON(*SSN*, *PNR*, hours)

| | | |
|---|---|---|
| 511 | 1001 | 10 |
| 289 | 1001 | 80 |
| 289 | 1003 | 50 |

**Figure 6.21** Example tuples for mapping an M:N relationship type.

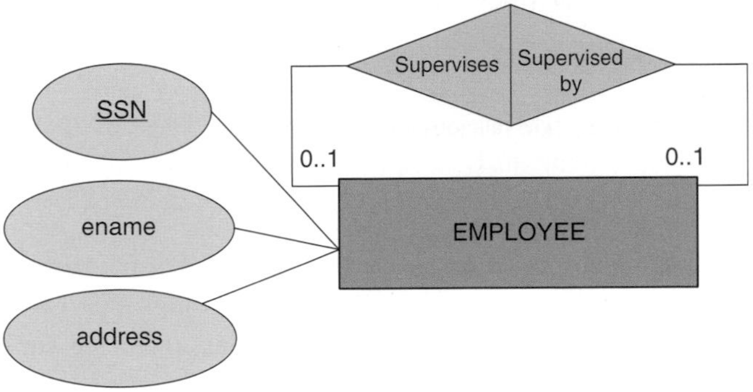


**Figure 6.22** Mapping unary relationship types to the relational model.

can see that none of the minimum cardinalities are supported since Emma Lucas is not working on any projects and projects 1002 and 1004 have no employees assigned. Out of the four cardinalities, only two are supported! This will require close follow-up during application development to make sure these missing cardinalities are enforced by the applications instead of the data model.

### 6.3.2.4 Mapping Unary Relationship Types

Unary or recursive relationship types can be mapped depending upon the cardinality. A recursive 1:1 or 1:N relationship type can be implemented by adding a foreign key referring to the primary key of the same relation. For an N:M recursive relationship type, a new relation R needs to be created with two NOT NULL foreign keys referring to the original relation. It is recommended to use role names to clarify the meaning of the foreign keys. Let's illustrate this with some examples.

Figure 6.22 shows a 1:1 unary relationship type modeling the supervision relationships between employees. It can be implemented in the relational model by adding a foreign key – supervisor – to the EMPLOYEE relation, which refers to its primary key – SSN – as follows:

```
EMPLOYEE(SSN, ename, address, supervisor)
```

The foreign key can be NULL since, according to the ER model, it is possible that an employee is supervised by zero other employees. Since the foreign key cannot be multi-valued, an employee cannot be supervised by more than one other employee. This is illustrated in Figure 6.23.

EMPLOYEE(<u>SSN</u>, ename, address, *supervisor*)

| | | | |
|---|---|---|---|
| 511 | John Smith | 14 Avenue of the Americas, New York | 289 |
| 289 | Paul Barker | 208 Market Street, San Francisco | 412 |
| 356 | Emma Lucas | 432 Wacker Drive, Chicago | 289 |
| 412 | Dan Kelly | 668 Strip, Las Vegas | NULL |

**Figure 6.23** Example tuples for mapping a unary 1:1 relationship type.

EMPLOYEE(<u>SSN</u>, ename, address)

| | | |
|---|---|---|
| 511 | John Smith | 14 Avenue of the Americas, New York |
| 289 | Paul Barker | 208 Market Street, San Francisco |
| 356 | Emma Lucas | 432 Wacker Drive, Chicago |
| 412 | Dan Kelly | 668 Strip, Las Vegas |

SUPERVISION(<u>*Supervisor*, *Supervisee*</u>)

| | |
|---|---|
| 289 | 511 |
| 289 | 356 |
| 412 | 289 |
| 412 | 511 |

**Figure 6.24** Example tuples for mapping a unary N:M relationship type.

Some employees do not supervise other employees, like Emma Lucas. However, some employees supervise more than one other employee, like Paul Barker who supervises both John Smith and Emma Lucas. To summarize, out of the four cardinalities, three are supported by our model.

Let's now change one assumption as follows: an employee can supervise at least zero, at most N other employees. The relational model stays the same, with supervisor as the foreign key referring to SSN:

```
EMPLOYEE(SSN, ename, address, supervisor)
```

In this case, all four cardinalities can be perfectly captured by our relational model.

Let's now set both maximum cardinalities to N and M, respectively. In other words, an employee can supervise zero to N employees, whereas an employee can be supervised by zero to M employees. We can no longer add a foreign key to the EMPLOYEE relation as this would result in a multi-valued attribute type. Hence, we need to create a new relation, SUPERVISION, with two foreign keys, Supervisor and Supervisee, which both refer to SSN in EMPLOYEE:

```
EMPLOYEE(SSN, ename, address)
SUPERVISION(Supervisor, Supervisee)
```

Since both foreign keys make up the primary key, they cannot be NULL.

All four cardinalities are perfectly supported (see Figure 6.24). Emma Lucas and John Smith are not supervising anyone, and Dan Kelly is not being supervised by anyone (both minimum cardinalities = 0). Paul Barker and Dan Kelly supervise two employees each (maximum cardinality N) and John Smith is being supervised by both Paul Barker and Dan Kelly (maximum cardinality M). Note, however, that if one or both minimum cardinalities had been 1, then the relational model would have essentially stayed the same such that it could not accommodate this. Hence, these minimum cardinalities would again have to be enforced by the application programs, which is not an efficient solution.

### 6.3.2.5 Mapping *n*-ary Relationship Types

To map an *n*-ary relationship type, we first create relations for each participating entity type. We then also define one additional relation R to represent the *n*-ary relationship type and add foreign keys referring to the primary keys of each of the relations corresponding to the participating entity types. The primary key of R is the combination of all foreign keys which are all NOT NULL. Any attribute type of the *n*-ary relationship can also be added to R. Let's illustrate this with an example.

The relationship type BOOKING (Figure 6.25) is a ternary relationship type between TOURIST, BOOKING, and TRAVEL AGENCY. It has one attribute type: price. The relational model has relations for each of the three entity types together with a relation BOOKING for the relationship type:

```
TOURIST(TNR, ...)
TRAVEL_AGENCY(ANR, ...)
HOTEL(HNR, ...)
BOOKING(TNR, ANR, HNR, price)
```

The primary key of the BOOKING relation is the combination of the three foreign keys, as illustrated. It also includes the price attribute. All six cardinalities are perfectly represented in the relational model.

The relationship type OFFERS (Figure 6.26) is a ternary relationship type between Instructor, Course, and Semester. An instructor offers a course during zero to N semesters. During a semester, a course should be offered by at least one and at most N instructors. During a semester, an instructor can offer zero to N courses. As with the previous example, the relational model has one relation per entity type and one relation for the relationship type:

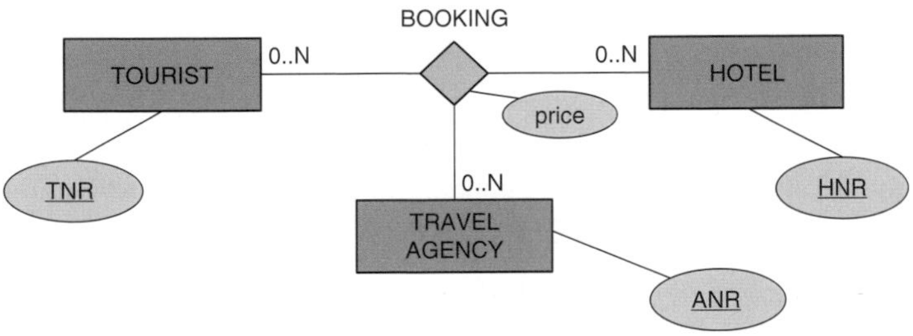


**Figure 6.25** Mapping *n*-ary relationship types to the relational model.

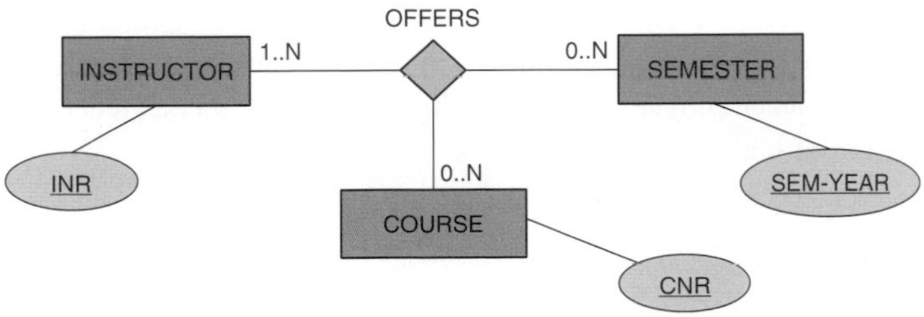


**Figure 6.26** Mapping *n*-ary relationship types to the relational model.

| INSTRUCTOR(INR, iname, ....) | |
|---|---|
| 10 | Bart |
| 12 | Wilfried |
| 14 | Seppe |

| COURSE(CNR, cname, ....) | |
|---|---|
| 100 | Database Management |
| 110 | Analytics |
| 120 | Java Programming |

| SEMESTER(SEM-YEAR, ....) |
|---|
| 1-2015 |
| 2-2015 |
| 1-2016 |

| OFFERS(*INR, CNR, SEM-YEAR*) | | |
|---|---|---|
| 10 | 100 | 1-2015 |
| 12 | 100 | 1-2016 |
| 10 | 120 | 1-2015 |
| 14 | 120 | 1-2015 |

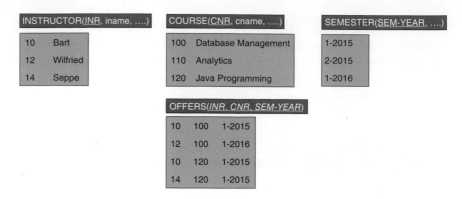

**Figure 6.27** Example tuples for mapping an *n*-ary relationship type.

```
INSTRUCTOR(INR, ...)
COURSE(CNR, ...)
SEMESTER(SEM-YEAR, ...)
OFFERS(INR,CNR,SEM-YEAR)
```

Let's have a look at the cardinalities. Figure 6.27 shows some example tuples. Note that course number 110, Analytics, is not offered during any semester. Some other courses are not offered in all semesters. Hence, the minimum cardinality of 1, stating that during a semester a course should be offered by at least one instructor, cannot be guaranteed by the relational model.

### 6.3.3 Mapping Multi-Valued Attribute Types

For each multi-valued attribute type, we create a new relation R. We put the multi-valued attribute type in R together with a foreign key referring to the primary key of the original relation. Multi-valued composite attribute types are again decomposed into their components. The primary key can then be set based upon the assumptions.

Let's say we have a multi-valued attribute type phone number (Figure 6.28). An employee can have multiple phones. We create a new relation EMP-PHONE:

```
EMPLOYEE(SSN, ename, address)
EMP-PHONE(PhoneNr, SSN)
```

It has two attribute types: PhoneNr and SSN. The latter is a foreign key referring to the EMPLOYEE relation. If we assume that each phone number is assigned to only one employee, then the attribute type PhoneNr suffices as a primary key of the relation EMP-PHONE.

Let's now change the assumption such that a phone number can be shared by multiple employees. Hence, PhoneNr is no longer appropriate as a primary key of the relation. Also, SSN cannot be assigned as a primary key since an employee can have multiple phone numbers. Hence, the primary key becomes the combination of both PhoneNr and SSN:

```
EMPLOYEE(SSN, ename, address)
EMP-PHONE(PhoneNr, SSN)
```

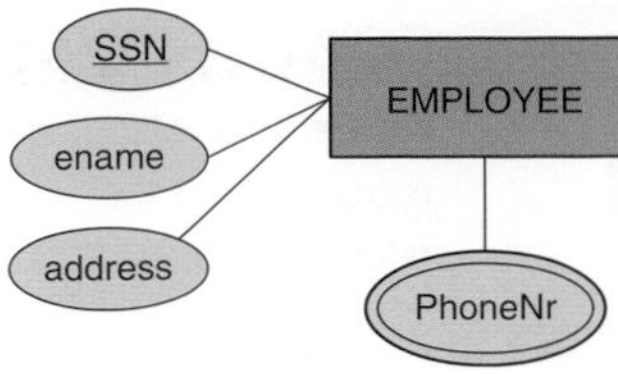


**Figure 6.28** Mapping multi-valued attribute types to the relational model.

EMPLOYEE(SSN, ename, address, *DNR*)

| | | | |
|---|---|---|---|
| 511 | John Smith | 14 Avenue of the Americas, New York | 001 |
| 289 | Paul Barker | 208 Market Street, San Francisco | 001 |
| 356 | Emma Lucas | 432 Wacker Drive, Chicago | 002 |

EMP-PHONE(PhoneNr, *SSN*)

| | |
|---|---|
| 900-244-8000 | 511 |
| 900-244-8000 | 289 |
| 900-244-8002 | 289 |
| 900-246-6006 | 356 |

**Figure 6.29** Example tuples for mapping a multi-valued attribute type.

Some example tuples are depicted in Figure 6.29, where you can see that tuples 1 and 2 of the EMP-PHONE relation have the same value for PhoneNr, whereas tuples 2 and 3 have the same value for SSN. This example illustrates how the business specifics can help define the primary key of a relation.

### 6.3.4 Mapping Weak Entity Types

Remember, a weak entity type is an entity type that cannot produce its own key attribute type and is existence-dependent on an owner entity type. It should be mapped into a relation R with all its corresponding attribute types. Next, a foreign key must be added referring to the primary key of the relation corresponding to the owner entity type. Because of the existence dependency, the foreign key is declared as NOT NULL. The primary key of R is then the combination of the partial key and the foreign key.

Figure 6.30 illustrates our earlier example. Room is a weak entity type and needs to borrow HNR from Hotel to define a key attribute type, which is the combination of RNR and HNR.

We can map both entity types to the relational model as follows:

```
Hotel (HNR, Hname)
Room (RNR, HNR, beds)
```

Room has a foreign key, HNR, which is declared as NOT NULL and refers to Hotel. Its primary key is the combination of RNR and HNR.

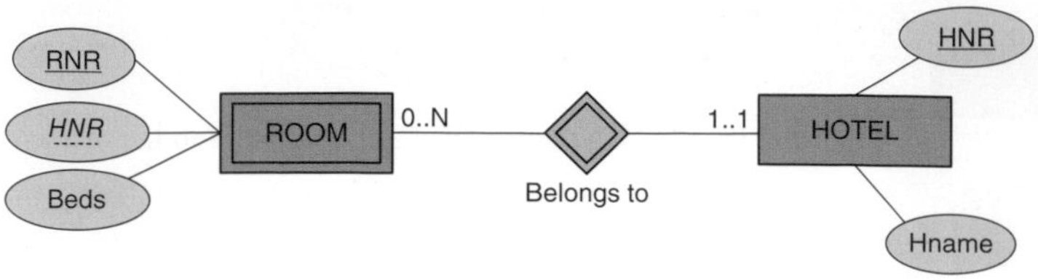


**Figure 6.30** Mapping weak entity types to the relational model.

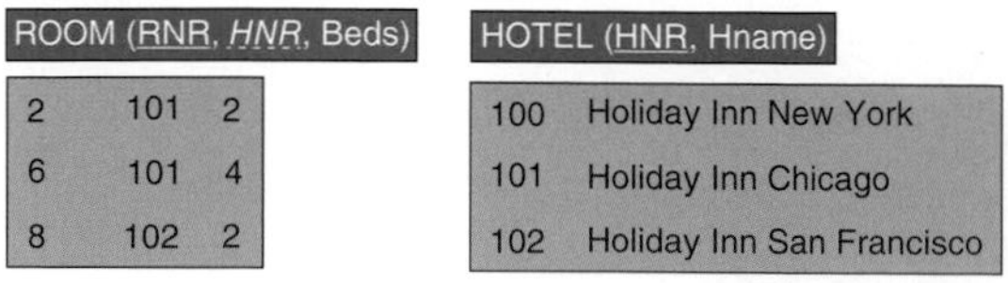
ROOM (RNR, HNR, Beds)
2 101 2
6 101 4
8 102 2
HOTEL (HNR, Hname)
100 Holiday Inn New York
101 Holiday Inn Chicago
102 Holiday Inn San Francisco

**Figure 6.31** Example tuples for mapping a weak entity type.

**Table 6.4** Mapping an ER model to a relational model

| ER model | Relational model |
|---|---|
| Entity type | Relation |
| Weak entity type | Foreign key |
| 1:1 or 1:N relationship type | Foreign key |
| M:N relationship type | New relation with two foreign keys |
| *n*-ary relationship type | New relation with *n* foreign keys |
| Simple attribute type | Attribute type |
| Composite attribute type | Component attribute types |
| Multi-valued attribute type | Relation and foreign key |
| Key attribute type | Primary or alternative key |

Some example tuples are depicted in Figure 6.31. All four cardinalities are nicely supported by the relational model.

### 6.3.5 Putting it All Together

Up to now we have extensively discussed how to map the ER model to a relational model. Table 6.4 summarizes how the key concepts of both models are related.

Here you can see the resulting relational model for our employee administration ER model as discussed in Chapter 3:

- EMPLOYEE (SSN, ename, streetaddress, city, sex, dateofbirth, MNR, DNR)
  - MNR foreign key refers to SSN in EMPLOYEE, NULL ALLOWED
  - DNR foreign key refers to DNR in DEPARTMENT, NOT NULL
- DEPARTMENT (DNR, dname, dlocation, MGNR)
  - MGNR: foreign key refers to SSN in EMPLOYEE, NOT NULL
- PROJECT (PNR, pname, pduration, DNR)
  - DNR: foreign key refers to DNR in DEPARTMENT, NOT NULL

- WORKS_ON (SSN, PNR, HOURS)
  - SSN foreign key refers to SSN in EMPLOYEE, NOT NULL
  - PNR foreign key refers to PNR in PROJECT, NOT NULL

Let's briefly discuss it. The primary key of the EMPLOYEE relation is SSN. It has two foreign keys: MNR, which refers to SSN and implements the recursive SUPERVISED BY relationship type; and DNR, which refers to DEPARTMENT and implements the WORKS_IN relationship type. The former is NULL ALLOWED, whereas the latter is not. The primary key of DEPARTMENT is DNR. It has one foreign key MGNR which refers to SSN in EMPLOYEE and implements the MANAGES relationship type. It cannot be NULL. The primary key of PROJECT is PNR. The foreign key DNR refers to DEPARTMENT. It implements the IN CHARGE OF relationship type and cannot be NULL. The WORKS_ON relation is needed to implement the M:N relationship type between EMPLOYEE and PROJECT. Its primary key is made up of two foreign keys referring to EMPLOYEE and PROJECT respectively. It also includes the relationship type attribute HOURS representing how many hours an employee worked on a project.

**Retention Questions**

- Illustrate how an ER entity type can be mapped to the relational model.
- Illustrate how ER relationship types with varying degrees and cardinalities can be mapped to the relational model. Discuss the loss of semantics where appropriate.

Our relational model is not a perfect mapping of our ER model. Some of the cardinalities have not been perfectly translated. More specifically, we cannot guarantee that a department has at minimum one employee (not counting the manager). Another example is that the same employee can be a manager of multiple departments. Some of the earlier-mentioned shortcomings for the ER model still apply here. We cannot guarantee that a manager of a department also works in the department. We also cannot enforce that employees should work on projects assigned to departments to which they belong.

## 6.4 Mapping a Conceptual EER Model to a Relational Model

The EER model builds upon the ER model by introducing additional modeling constructs such as specialization, categorization, and aggregation (see Chapter 3). In this section we discuss how these can be mapped to the relational model.

### 6.4.1 Mapping an EER Specialization

EER specializations can be mapped in various ways. A first option is to create a relation for the superclass and each subclass, and link them with foreign keys. An alternative is to create a relation for each subclass and none for the superclass. Finally, we can create one relation with all attribute types of the superclass and subclasses and add a special attribute type. Let's explore these options in more detail, with some examples.

Figure 6.32 shows an EER specialization of ARTIST into SINGER and ACTOR. The specialization is partial since not all artists are either a singer or an actor. It also has overlap, since some singers can also be actors. An artist has an artist number and an artist name. A singer has a music style.

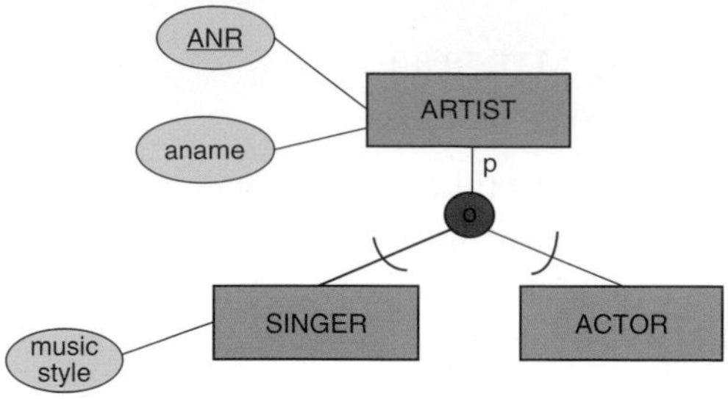


**Figure 6.32** Example EER specialization with superclass ARTIST and subclasses SINGER and ACTOR.

**Figure 6.33** Example tuples for option 1.

In our first option (option 1), we create three relations: one for the superclass and two for the subclasses:

```
ARTIST(ANR, aname, ...)
SINGER(ANR, music style, ...)
ACTOR(ANR, ...)
```

We add a foreign key ANR to each subclass relation that refers to the superclass relation. These foreign keys then also serve as primary keys.

Figure 6.33 illustrates option 1 with some example tuples. This solution works well if the specialization is partial. Not all artists are included in the subclass relations. For example, Claude Monet is only included in the superclass relation and not referred to in any of the subclass relations. In the case that the specialization had been total instead of partial, then we could not have enforced it with this solution. The overlap characteristic is also nicely modeled. You can see that Madonna is referenced both in the SINGER and ACTOR relations. If the specialization had been disjoint instead of overlap, then again we could not have enforced it with this solution.

Let's now change the specialization to total instead of partial. In other words, we assume all artists are either singers or actors. Option 1 would not work well for this since there could be ARTIST tuples which are not referenced in either the SINGER or ACTOR relation. In this case, a better option (option 2) to map this EER specialization only creates relations for the subclasses as follows:

SINGER(ANR, aname, music style, ...)

| | | | |
|---|---|---|---|
| 2 | Madonna | Pop music | ... |
| 12 | Andrea Bocelli | Classical music | |

ACTOR(ANR, aname, ...)

| | | |
|---|---|---|
| 6 | Tom Cruise | ... |
| 2 | Madonna | |

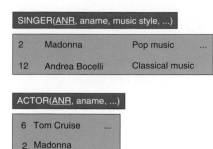

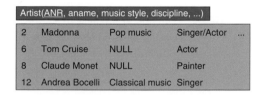

**Figure 6.34** Example tuples for option 2.

Artist(ANR, aname, music style, discipline, ...)

| | | | | |
|---|---|---|---|---|
| 2 | Madonna | Pop music | Singer/Actor | ... |
| 6 | Tom Cruise | NULL | Actor | |
| 8 | Claude Monet | NULL | Painter | |
| 12 | Andrea Bocelli | Classical music | Singer | |

**Figure 6.35** Example tuples for option 3.

```
SINGER(ANR, aname, music style, ...)
ACTOR(ANR, aname, ...)
```

The attribute types of the superclass have been added to each of the subclass relations.

Figure 6.34 illustrates some example tuples for option 2. This solution only works for a total specialization. The overlap characteristic can also be supported. You can see that Madonna is included in both relations. Note, however, that this creates redundancy. If we would also store her biography, picture, etc., then this information needs to be added to both relations, which is not very efficient from a storage perspective. This approach cannot enforce a specialization to be disjoint since the tuples in both relations can overlap.

Another option (option 3) is to store all superclass and subclass information into one relation:

```
ARTIST(ANR, aname, music style, ..., discipline)
```

An attribute type discipline is then added to the relation to indicate the subclass.

Figure 6.35 shows some example tuples for option 3. The values that can be assigned to the attribute type discipline depend upon the characteristics of the specialization. Hence, all specialization options are supported. Note that this approach can generate a lot of NULL values for the subclass-specific attribute types (music style in our case).

In a specialization lattice, a subclass can have more than one superclass as you can see illustrated in Figure 6.36. A PhD student is both an employee and a student. This can be implemented in the relational model by defining three relations: EMPLOYEE, STUDENT, and PHD-STUDENT:

```
EMPLOYEE(SSN, ...)
STUDENT(SNR, ...)
PHD-STUDENT(SSN, SNR, ...)
```

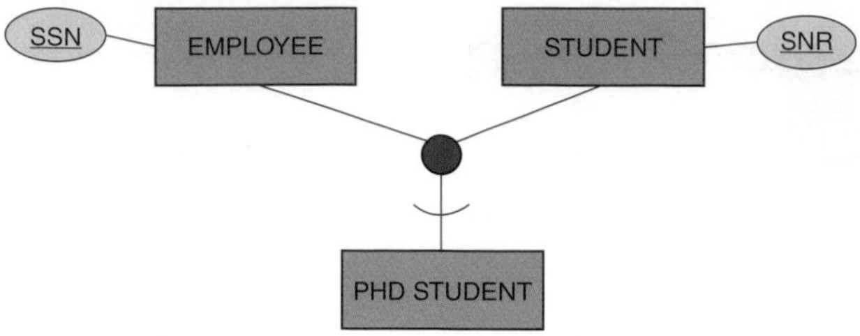


**Figure 6.36** Example of an EER specialization lattice.

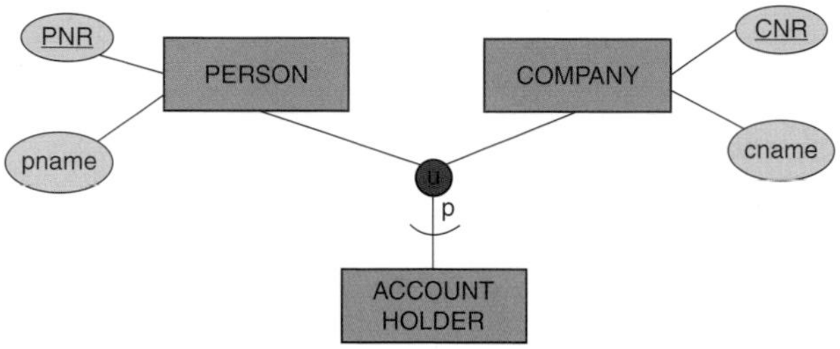


**Figure 6.37** Example of an EER categorization with superclasses PERSON and COMPANY, and category ACCOUNT HOLDER.

The primary key of the latter is a combination of two foreign keys referring to EMPLOYEE and STUDENT, respectively. This solution does not support total specialization, since we cannot enforce that all employee and student tuples are referenced in the PHD-STUDENT relation.

## 6.4.2 Mapping an EER Categorization

Another extension provided by the EER model is the concept of a categorization. As shown in Figure 6.37, the category subclass is a subset of the union of the entities of the superclasses.

Therefore, an account holder can be either a person or a company. This can be implemented in the relational model by creating a new relation ACCOUNT-HOLDER that corresponds to the category and adding the corresponding attribute types to it as follows:

```
PERSON(PNR, ..., CustNo)
COMPANY(CNR, ..., CustNo)
ACCOUNT-HOLDER(CustNo, ...)
```

We then define a new primary key attribute, CustNo, also called a surrogate key, for the relation that corresponds to the category. This surrogate key is then added as a foreign key to each relation corresponding to a superclass of the category. This foreign key is declared as NOT NULL for a total categorization and NULL ALLOWED for a partial categorization. In the case that the superclasses happen to share the same key attribute type, this one can be used and there is no need to define a surrogate key.

This is illustrated in Figure 6.38. In our case the categorization is partial since Wilfried and Microsoft are not account holders, hence the NULL values. This solution is not perfect: we cannot guarantee that the tuples of the category relation are a subset of the union of the tuples of the superclasses. As an example, customer number 12 in the ACCOUNT-HOLDER relation does not appear in either the PERSON or the COMPANY relation. Moreover, we cannot avoid that a tuple in

PERSON(PNR, pname, ... , *CustNo*)

| | | | |
|---|---|---|---|
| 122 | Bart | ... | 6 |
| 124 | Seppe | | 8 |
| 126 | Wilfried | | NULL |

COMPANY(CNR, cname, ... , *CustNo*)

| | | | |
|---|---|---|---|
| 1006 | Microsoft | ... | NULL |
| 1008 | SAS | | 10 |

ACCOUNT-HOLDER (CustNo, ... )

| | |
|---|---|
| 6 | ... |
| 8 | |
| 10 | |
| 12 | |

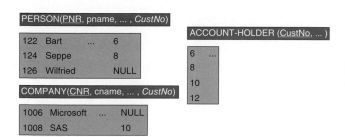

**Figure 6.38** Example tuples for mapping a categorization.

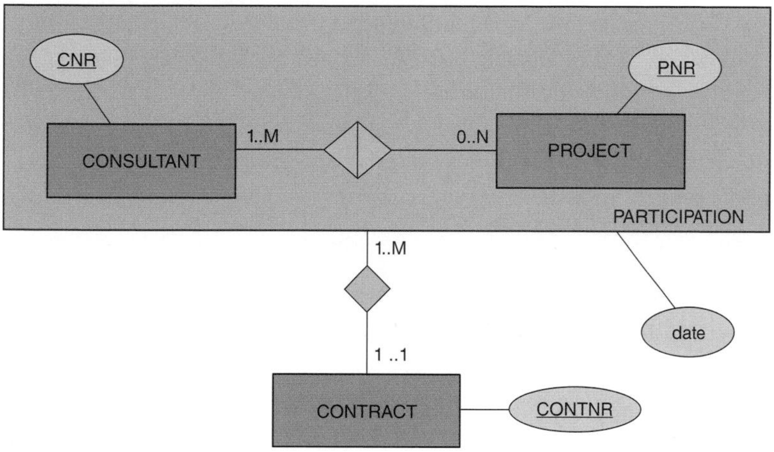


**Figure 6.39** Example of an EER aggregation.

the PERSON relation and a tuple in the COMPANY relation would have the same value for CustNo, which means they would refer to the same ACCOUNT-HOLDER tuple. In that case, this account holder would be a person and a company at the same time, which is incorrect as well.

### 6.4.3 Mapping an EER Aggregation

Aggregation is the third extension provided by the EER model. In Figure 6.39 we have aggregated the two entity types CONSULTANT and PROJECT and their relationship type into an aggregate called PARTICIPATION. This aggregate has an attribute type date and participates in a 1:M relationship type with the entity type CONTRACT.

This can be implemented in the relational model by creating four relations: CONSULTANT, PROJECT, PARTICIPATION, and CONTRACT:

```
CONSULTANT(CNR, ...)
PROJECT(PNR, ...)
PARTICIPATION(CNR, PNR, CONTNR, date)
CONTRACT(CONTNR, ...)
```

The PARTICIPATION relation models the aggregation. Its primary key is a combination of two foreign keys referring to the CONSULTANT and PROJECT relations. It includes a NOT NULL foreign key to the CONTRACT relation to model the relationship type. It also includes the attribute type date.

**Retention Questions**

- Discuss how the EER concepts of specialization, categorization, and aggregation can be mapped to the relational model. Illustrate with examples and clarify what semantics may get lost in the mapping.

## Summary

In this chapter we have discussed the relational model as one of the most popular data models used in the industry today. After formally introducing its basic building blocks, we elaborated on different types of keys. Next, we reviewed various relational constraints that ensure the data in the relational database have the desired properties. Normalization was extensively covered. First, we illustrated the need to guarantee no redundancy or anomalies in the data model. Functional dependencies and prime attribute types were introduced as important concepts during the normalization procedure, which brings the data model into the first normal form, second normal form, third normal form, Boyce–Codd normal form, and fourth normal form. We concluded by discussing how both ER and EER conceptual data models can be mapped to a logical relational model. We extensively discussed the semantics that get lost during the mapping by using plenty of examples. In the next chapter, we zoom into Structured Query Language (SQL), which is the DDL and DML of choice for relational databases.

### Scenario Conclusion

Following the mapping procedure outlined in this chapter, the EER conceptual data model for Sober can be mapped to the following logical relational model (primary keys are underlined; foreign keys are in italics):

- **CAR** (CAR-NR, CARTYPE)
- **SOBER CAR** (*S-CAR-NR*)
  - FOREIGN KEY S-CAR-NR refers to CAR-NR in CAR; NULL NOT ALLOWED
- **OTHER CAR** (*O-CAR-NR*, *O-CUST-NR*)
  - FOREIGN KEY O-CAR-NR refers to CAR-NR in CAR; NULL NOT ALLOWED
  - FOREIGN KEY O-CUST-NR refers to CUST-NR in CUSTOMER; NULL NOT ALLOWED
- **ACCIDENT** (ACC-NR, ACC-DATE-TIME, ACC-LOCATION)
- **INVOLVED** (*I-CAR-NR, I-ACC-NR*, DAMAGE AMOUNT)
  - FOREIGN KEY I-CAR-NR refers to CAR-NR in CAR; NULL NOT ALLOWED
  - FOREIGN KEY I-ACC-NR refers to ACC-NR in ACCIDENT; NULL NOT ALLOWED
- **RIDE** (RIDE-NR, PICKUP-DATE-TIME, DROPOFF-DATE-TIME, DURATION, PICKUP-LOC, DROPOFF-LOC, DISTANCE, FEE, *R-CAR-NR*)
  - FOREIGN KEY R-CAR-NR refers to CAR-NR in CAR; NULL NOT ALLOWED
- **RIDE HAILING** (*H-RIDE-NR*, PASSENGERS, WAIT-TIME, REQUEST-TYPE, *H-CUST-NR*)
  - FOREIGN KEY H-RIDE-NR refers to RIDE-NR in RIDE; NULL NOT ALLOWED
  - FOREIGN KEY H-CUST-NR refers to CUST-NR in CUSTOMER; NULL NOT ALLOWED
- **RIDE SHARING** (*S-RIDE-NR*)
  - FOREIGN KEY S-RIDE-NR refers to RIDE-NR in RIDE; NULL NOT ALLOWED
- **CUSTOMER** (CUST-NR, CUST-NAME)
- **BOOK** (*B-CUST-NR, B-S-RIDE-NR*)

- FOREIGN KEY B-CUST-NR refers to CUST-NR in CUSTOMER; NULL NOT ALLOWED
- FOREIGN KEY B-S-RIDE-NR refers to S-RIDE-NR in RIDE SHARING; NULL NOT ALLOWED

The relational model has ten relations. Both EER specializations (RIDE into RIDE HAILING and RIDE SHARING; CAR into SOBER CAR and OTHER CAR) have been mapped using option 1; a separate relation was introduced for the superclass and for each of the subclasses. The reason we chose option 1 is that both superclasses participated in relationship types: RIDE with CAR and CAR with ACCIDENT. Although both specializations are total and disjoint in the EER model, this cannot be enforced in the relational model. Hence, it is possible to have a tuple in the CAR relation which is not referenced in either the SOBER CAR or OTHER CAR relation, which makes the specialization partial. Likewise, it is perfectly possible to have the same CAR referenced both in the SOBER CAR and OTHER CAR relations, which makes the specialization overlap. The four EER cardinalities of the OPERATED BY, LEAD CUSTOMER, and OWNS relationship types can be perfectly mapped to the relational model. The minimum cardinalities of 1 of the EER relationship types BOOK and INVOLVED cannot be enforced in the relational model. For example, it is perfectly possible to define an accident, by adding a new tuple to ACCIDENT, without any car involved.

## Key Terms List

**alternative keys**
**Boyce–Codd normal form (BCNF)**
**candidate key**
**deletion anomaly**
**domain**
**first normal form (1 NF)**
**foreign key**
**fourth normal form (4 NF)**
**full functional dependency**
**functional dependency**
**insertion anomaly**
**multi-valued dependency**
**normalization**
**primary key**
**prime attribute type**
**relation**
**relational model**
**second normal form (2 NF)**
**superkey**
**third normal form (3 NF)**
**transitive dependency**
**trivial functional dependency**
**tuple**
**update anomaly**

## Review Questions

**6.1.** Consider the following (normalized) relational model (primary keys are underlined, foreign keys are in italics).

**EMPLOYEE**(<u>SSN</u>, ENAME, EADDRESS, SEX, DATE_OF_BIRTH, *SUPERVISOR, DNR*)
SUPERVISOR*: foreign key refers to* <u>SSN</u> in EMPLOYEE, *NULL value allowed*
DNR: *foreign key refers to* <u>DNR</u> in DEPARTMENT, *NULL value not allowed*

**DEPARTMENT**(DNR, DNAME, DLOCATION, *MGNR*)
MGNR: *foreign key refers to* SSN in EMPLOYEE, *NULL value not allowed*
**PROJECT**(PNR, PNAME, PDURATION, *DNR*)
DNR: *foreign key refers to* DNR in DEPARTMENT, *NULL value not allowed*
**WORKS_ON**(*SSN*, *PNR*, HOURS)
SSN: *foreign key refers to* SSN in EMPLOYEE, *NULL value not allowed*
PNR: *foreign key refers to* PNR in PROJECT, *NULL value not allowed*

Which statement is **correct**?

a. According to the model, a supervisor cannot supervise more than one employee.
b. According to the model, an employee can manage multiple departments.
c. According to the model, an employee can work in multiple departments.
d. According to the model, an employee should always work on projects assigned to his/her department.

**6.2.** Which of the following statements is **correct**?

a. A foreign key of a relation A cannot refer to the primary key of the same relation A.
b. A relation cannot have more than one foreign key.
c. Every relation must have a foreign key.
d. A foreign key can be NULL.

**6.3.** Consider a data model for the Olympics storing information about countries and athletes. There is a 1:N relationship type between country and athlete and an athlete always has to belong to exactly one country. A relational data model containing only one table leads to:

a. Unnecessary replication of data about athletes.
b. Unnecessary replication of data about countries.
c. Unnecessary replication of data about athletes and countries.
d. No unnecessary replication of data.

**6.4.** The following relational model represents an HRM system of a consultancy firm. The primary keys are underlined; foreign keys are in italic font.

Consultant (ConsultantID, Date of Birth, Expertise)
Assigned_to (*ConsultantID*, *ProjectID*) *ConsultantID* refers to ConsultantID in Consultant; *ProjectID* refers to ProjectID in Project
Project (ProjectID, Description, Type, *Company*) *Company* refers to Name in Company
Company (Name, Location)

Suppose a new consultant is hired and immediately assigned to a new training project at a new firm and to two other, already-existing projects. How many rows (tuples) must be added to the database to reflect this change?

a. 1.
b. 3.
c. 5.
d. 6.

**6.5.** Consider the following (normalized) relational model (primary keys underlined; foreign keys in italics):

EMPLOYEE (SSN, ENAME, EADDRESS, SEX, DATE_OF_BIRTH, *SUPERVISOR*, *DNR*)
SUPERVISOR: *foreign key, refers to* SSN in EMPLOYEE, *NULL value allowed*
DNR: *foreign key, refers to* DNR in DEPARTMENT, *NULL value not allowed*
DEPARTMENT (DNR, DNAME, DLOCATION, *MGNR*)
MGNR: *foreign key, refers to* SSN in EMPLOYEE, *NULL value not allowed*

PROJECT (PNR, PNAME, PDURATION, *DNR*)
DNR: *foreign key, refers to* DNR in DEPARTMENT, *NULL value not allowed*
WORKS_ON (*SSN, PNR*, HOURS)
SSN: *foreign key, refers to* SSN in EMPLOYEE, *NULL value not allowed*
PNR: *foreign key, refers to* PNR in PROJECT, *NULL value not allowed*

Which statement is **not correct?**

a. A department always has exactly one manager.
b. Every employee must always be supervised by exactly one other employee.
c. Every project is always assigned to exactly one department.
d. According to the model, an employee can work in another department than he/she manages.

**6.6.** Consider the following relational model (primary keys are underlined, foreign keys in italics):

STUDENT (student number, student name, street name, street number, zip code, city)
ENROLLED (*student number, course number*)
COURSE (course number, course name)
PROFESSOR (professor number, professor name)
TEACHES (*course number, professor number*)

Which statement is **correct**?

a. The model does not allow a course to be taught by multiple professors.
b. The model can be further normalized.
c. The model does not allow a professor to teach multiple courses.
d. The model does not allow a course to be followed by multiple students.

**6.7.** A relation is in 3 NF if it satisfies 2 NF and . . .

a. no non-prime attribute type of R is transitively dependent on the primary key.
b. no prime attribute type of R is transitively dependent on the primary key.
c. no primary key of R is transitively dependent on a prime attribute type.
d. no non-primary key of R is transitively dependent on a prime attribute type.

**6.8.** Which statement is **correct**?

a. The Boyce–Codd normal form is more strict than the fourth normal form.
b. The Boyce–Codd normal form is more strict than the third normal form.
c. The second normal form is more strict than the Boyce–Codd normal form.
d. The first normal form is more strict than the Boyce–Codd normal form.

**6.9.** Consider the following generalization/specialization.

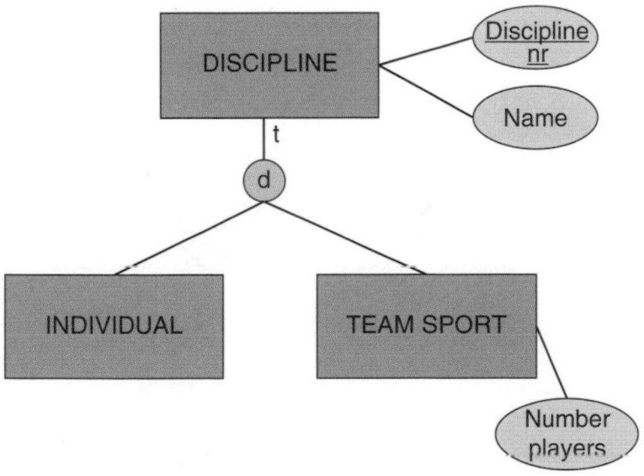

Suppose we represent this generalization/specialization by the following relational model:

Discipline (<u>Disciplinenr</u>, Name)
Individual sport (<u>*Disciplinenr*</u>) *Disciplinenr* refers to Disciplinenr in Discipline
Teamsport (<u>*Disciplinenr*</u>, Number players) *Disciplinenr* refers to Disciplinenr in Discipline

Consider the following four statements:

1. The relational model does not allow one to enforce the completeness constraint; the disjointness constraint can be enforced.
2. The relational model does not allow one to enforce both the completeness constraint and the disjointness constraint.
3. By dropping the relation "Discipline" in the relational model, the completeness constraint can be enforced.
4. The relational model allows the specialization to be partial.

Which of the following options is **correct**?

a. Statements 1 and 2 are both correct.
b. Statements 1 and 4 are both incorrect.
c. Only statement 1 is incorrect, the other statements are correct.
d. Only statement 4 is incorrect, the other statements are correct.

**6.10.** Consider the following EER model.

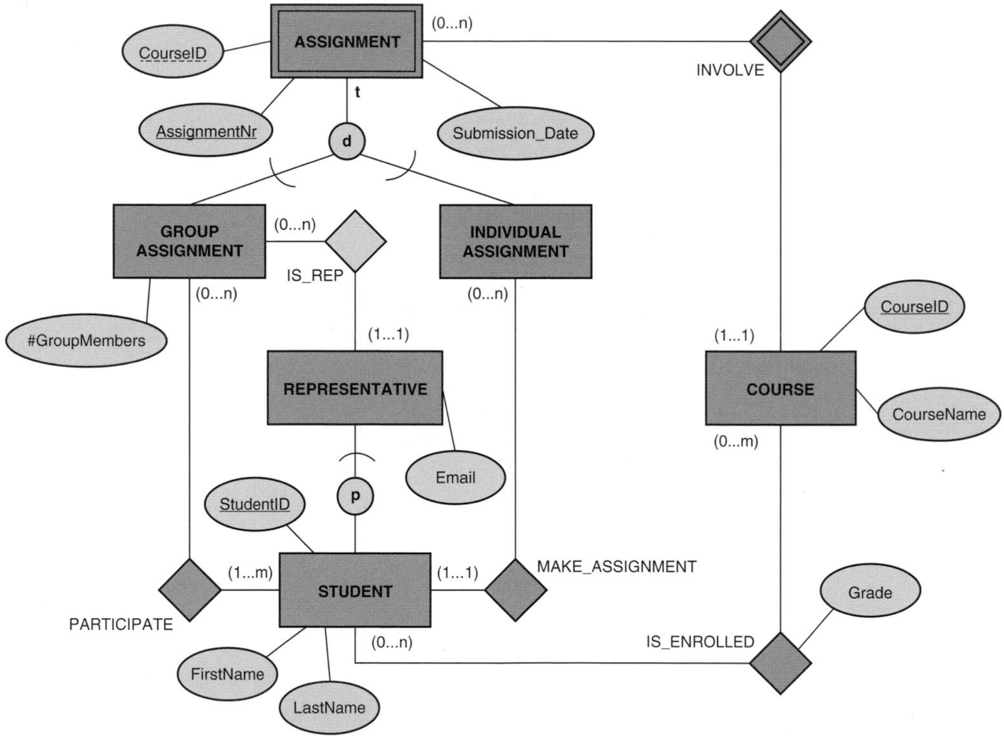


Which statement is **correct**?

a. When mapping the EER relationship type IS_ENROLLED between COURSE and STUDENT to the relational model, a new relation needs to be introduced. The relation is identified by GRADE as its primary key.

b. When mapping the EER relationship type INVOLVE between COURSE and ASSIGNMENT to the relational model, a new relation needs to be introduced. The 1..1 cardinalities of this relationship type cannot be enforced in the relational model.
c. When mapping the EER relationship type PARTICIPATE between GROUP ASSIGNMENT and STUDENT to the relational model, a new relation needs to be introduced. The four cardinalities of this EER relationship type can be perfectly mapped to the relational model.
d. The partial inheritance relationship between STUDENT and REPRESENTATIVE can be perfectly mapped to the relational model by the following two relations: STUDENT(StudentID, FirstName, LastName) and REPRESENTATIVE (S-StudentID, Email) whereby S-StudentID refers to StudentID in STUDENT.

**6.11.** Consider the following ER model for a course administration.

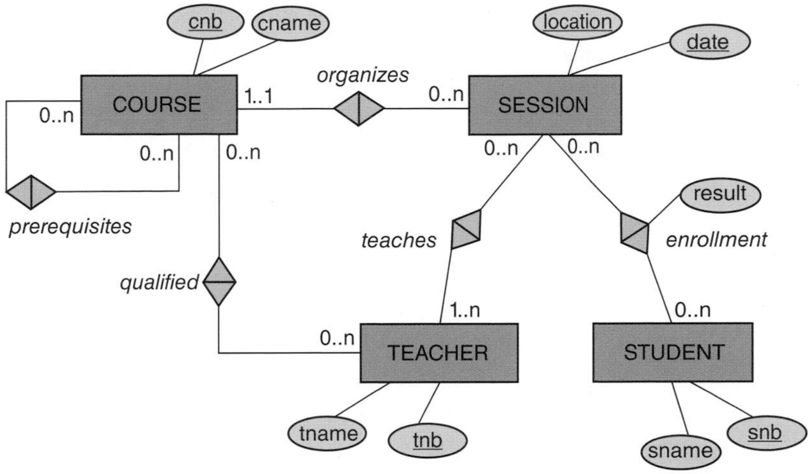


Which statement is **not correct**?

a. When mapping the ER relationship type *teaches* between Session and Teacher to the relational model, a new relation needs to be introduced. The four cardinalities of this ER relationship type can be perfectly mapped to the relational model.
b. When mapping the ER relationship type *organizes* between Course and Session to the relational model, the primary key "cnb" of the Course relation will be included as a NOT NULL foreign key in the Session relation. The four cardinalities of this ER relationship type can be perfectly mapped to the relational model.
c. When mapping the ER relationship type *enrollment* between Session and Student to the relational model, a new relation needs to be introduced. The four cardinalities of this ER relationship type can be perfectly mapped to the relational model.
d. Both the ER and the relational model cannot enforce that a teacher can only teach sessions of courses for which he/she is qualified.

## Problems and Exercises

6.1E A library database records the authors and the publisher of each book. Normalize the following relation and indicate the primary and foreign key attribute types:

R (ISBN, title, author(name, date_of_birth), publisher(name, address(streetnr, streetname, zipcode, city)), pages, price)

The assumptions are:

- each book has a unique ISBN number;
- each author has a unique name;
- each publisher has a unique name;
- a book can have multiple authors;
- an author can write more than one book;
- a publisher can publish more than one book;
- a book has only one publisher;
- a publisher has only one address.

Suppose that one book can have multiple publishers. How can you extend your model to accommodate this? Where would you put the attribute type "number_of_copies"?

6.2E Given the following assumptions:

- a flight has a unique flight number, a passenger has a unique name, a pilot has a unique name;
- a flight is always handled by one airline;
- a flight can have multiple passengers, a passenger can be on multiple flights;
- a flight has one pilot, a pilot can operate multiple flights;
- a flight is always handled by exactly one airplane;

normalize the following relation:

Flight (Flightnumber, Flighttime, airline (airlinename), passenger (passengername, gender, date of birth), pilot (pilotname, gender, date of birth), departure_city, arrival_city, airplane (planeID, type, seats))

6.3E Given the following EER model for an electricity market:

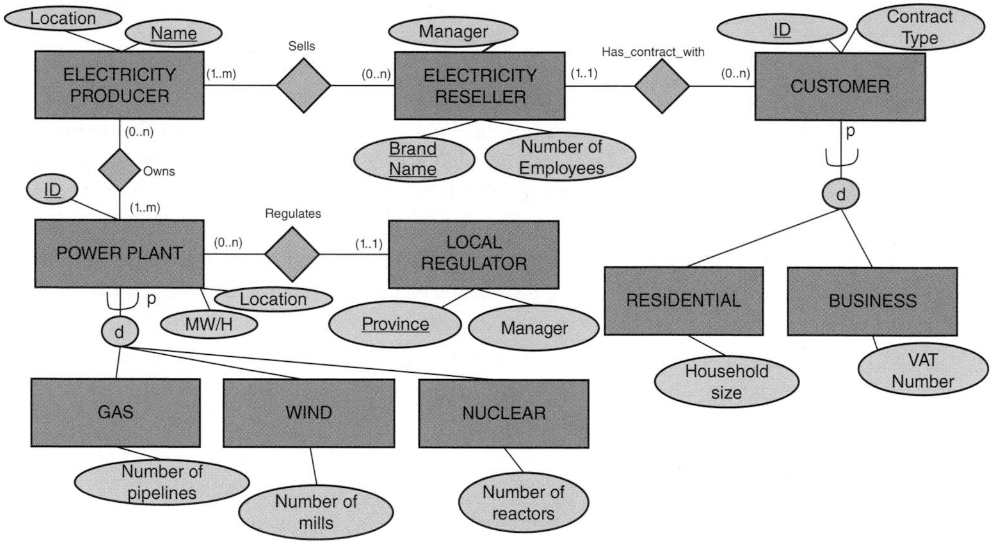


- discuss some examples of semantics that cannot be enforced by the EER model;
- map the model to a relational model representation. Discuss the possible loss of semantics. Clearly indicate the primary–foreign key relationships and specify NOT NULL declarations where necessary.

6.4E Given the following EER model for an airline business:

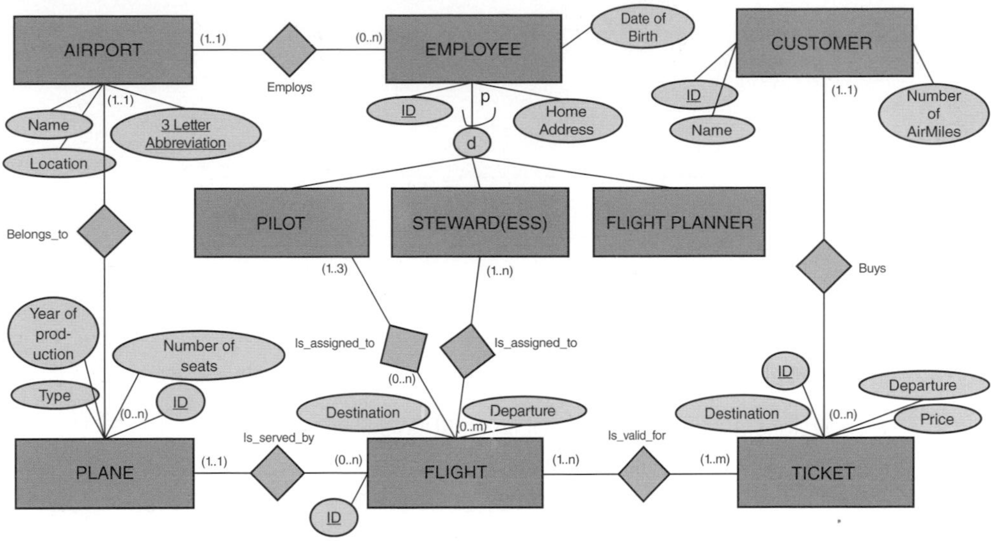


- discuss some examples of semantics that cannot be enforced by the EER model;
- map the model to a relational model representation. Discuss the possible loss of semantics. Clearly indicate the primary–foreign key relationships and specify NOT NULL declarations where necessary.

6.5E Given the following EER model for a driving school company:

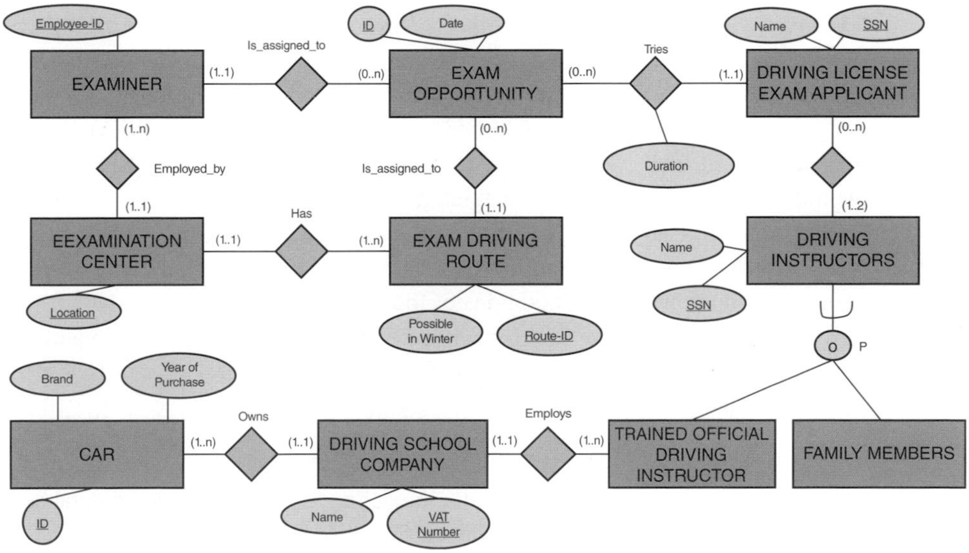


- discuss some examples of semantics that cannot be enforced by the EER model;
- map the model to a relational model representation. Discuss the possible loss of semantics. Clearly indicate the primary–foreign key relationships and specify NOT NULL declarations where necessary.

# 7 Relational Databases

*Structured Query Language (SQL)*

## Chapter Objectives

In this chapter, you will learn to:

- understand the importance of SQL in an RDBMS environment;
- use SQL as a data definition language (DDL);
- use SQL as a data manipulation language (DML) for retrieving, inserting, deleting, and updating data;
- define and use views in SQL;
- define indexes in SQL;
- use SQL for granting and revoking privileges;
- understand how SQL can be used to manage metadata.

### Opening Scenario

The relational model adopted by Sober needs to serve various information needs. For example, the insurance firm of the company requests an overview of all accidents together with the number of Sober cars involved and the average damage amount per accident. As part of its customer relationship management (CRM) program, the company wants to retrieve the customer with the maximum wait time and offer him or her a free ride-hailing service. Furthermore, Sober also would like to find out which customers have never booked any of its services and target them with a promotion campaign. To implement its eco-friendly tree-planting program, Sober needs to know which customers booked more than 20 Sober ride-sharing services. Finally, the company remembers that one of the limitations of the EER conceptual data model was that it is perfectly possible that customers book either a ride-hailing or ride-sharing service with their own car. To safeguard its data quality, Sober wants to periodically check that this is not the case in its relational database.

In the previous chapter, we dealt with the modeling aspects of relational databases. In this chapter, we elaborate on SQL, which is the lingua franca of RDBMSs and one of the most popular data definition and manipulation languages in use in the industry nowadays. Its core functionality is implemented, with only some minor variations, throughout all RDBMS products. We discuss the SQL language constructs to express a relational model and to formulate queries that retrieve and modify the data in a relational database.

First, we provide an overview of the SQL data definition language (SQL DDL) to define a relational data model. We also discuss how the SQL data manipulation language (SQL DML) can be used for data manipulation such as retrieving data, updating data, inserting new data and deleting existing data. We then elaborate on SQL views and SQL indexes, which are part of the external and internal data model, respectively. We also illustrate how SQL can be used for authorization by granting or revoking privileges to users or user accounts. We conclude by illustrating how SQL can be used for managing metadata.

## 7.1 Relational Database Management Systems and SQL

As explained in the previous chapter, relational databases are based upon the relational data model and managed by a **relational database management system**, or RDBMS. **Structured Query Language**, or **SQL**,[1] is the language used for both data definition and data manipulation. It is one of the most popular database languages currently in use in the industry. It what follows, we elaborate on its key characteristics and position it in terms of the three-layer database architecture discussed in Chapter 1.

### 7.1.1 Key Characteristics of SQL

Various versions of the SQL standard have been introduced, starting with the first, SQL-86 in 1986, and the most recent one in 2016 (SQL:2016). It was accepted as a standard for relational data definition and manipulation by the American National Standards Institute (ANSI) in 1986 and by the International Organization for Standardization (ISO) in 1987. Note that each relational database vendor provides its own implementation (also called SQL dialect) of SQL, in which the bulk of the standard is typically implemented and complemented with some vendor-specific add-ons.

> **Connections**
>
> In Chapter 2 we discussed the difference between procedural, record-at-a-time DML (as is used in hierarchical and CODASYL DBMSs) and declarative, set-at-a-time DML (as is used in SQL-based RDBMSs).

SQL is primarily set-oriented and declarative (see Chapter 2). In other words, as opposed to record-oriented database languages, SQL can retrieve and manipulate many records at a time (i.e., it operates on sets of records instead of individual records). Furthermore, you only need to specify which data to retrieve, in contrast to procedural database languages, which also require you to explicitly define the navigational access path to the data.

SQL can be used both interactively from a command prompt or executed by a program, written in a particular programming language (Java, Python, and many others). In that case, the general-purpose programming language is called the host language to the SQL code. Figure 7.1 shows an example of using SQL interactively in a MySQL environment. MySQL is an open-source RDBMS that can be freely downloaded from the web. It is very popular in the industry. In this screenshot you can see that a query has been entered in the query window at the top. We explain in Section 7.3.1.7 how this query works, but it basically selects all product numbers and product names of products for which more than one order line is outstanding. The query can then be executed and the result displayed in the result window below. Other RDBMSs, such as Microsoft SQL Server, Oracle, and IBM DB2, also provide facilities to execute queries in an interactive way whereby a user can enter SQL queries, run them, and evaluate the results.

[1] SQL is sometimes also pronounced as SEKWEL.

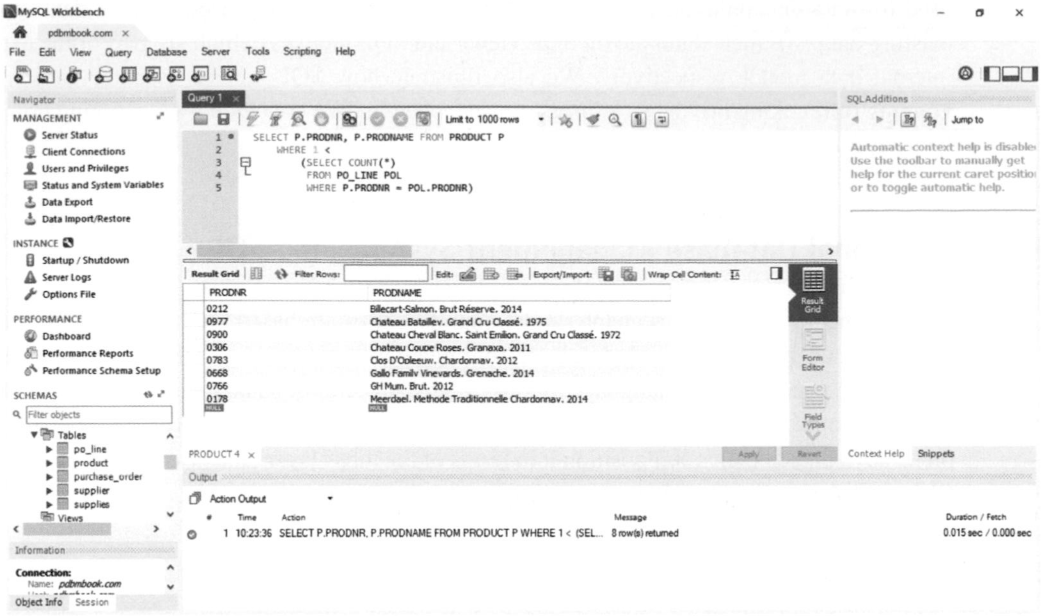


**Figure 7.1** Example of interactive SQL.

Figure 7.2 illustrates the same query, but now executed by a host language – Java in this case. You can see the Java program at the top and the corresponding results in the console window below. DBMSs typically expose many application programming interfaces (APIs) through which client-applications (written in Java, for example) that wish to utilize the services provided by a DBMS can access and query a DBMS. Chapter 15 takes a detailed look at such APIs. For now, it is important to keep in mind that most of these rely on SQL as the main language to express queries to be sent to the DBMS.

> **Connections**
>
> Chapter 15 takes a closer look at the various ways of accessing database systems using different types of database application programming interfaces, or APIs.

In most RDBMS environments, SQL is implemented as a **free-form language**. In other words, no special indentation is required as is the case for languages such as Python or COBOL. Most SQL implementations are case insensitive. It is, however, recommended to adopt a consistent formatting style (e.g., always write table names in uppercase) to facilitate the understanding and maintenance of your SQL queries.

> **Drill Down**
>
> In 2015, Stack Overflow (www.stackoverflow.com) conducted a survey about the most popular application development languages. Based upon 26,086 respondents, it was shown that SQL ranked second, just behind JavaScript. The survey clearly illustrated that despite continuous threats from new technologies (e.g., NoSQL; see Chapter 11), SQL is still standing its ground as the most important data definition and manipulation language. It also showed that knowledge of SQL has a positive impact on your salary.

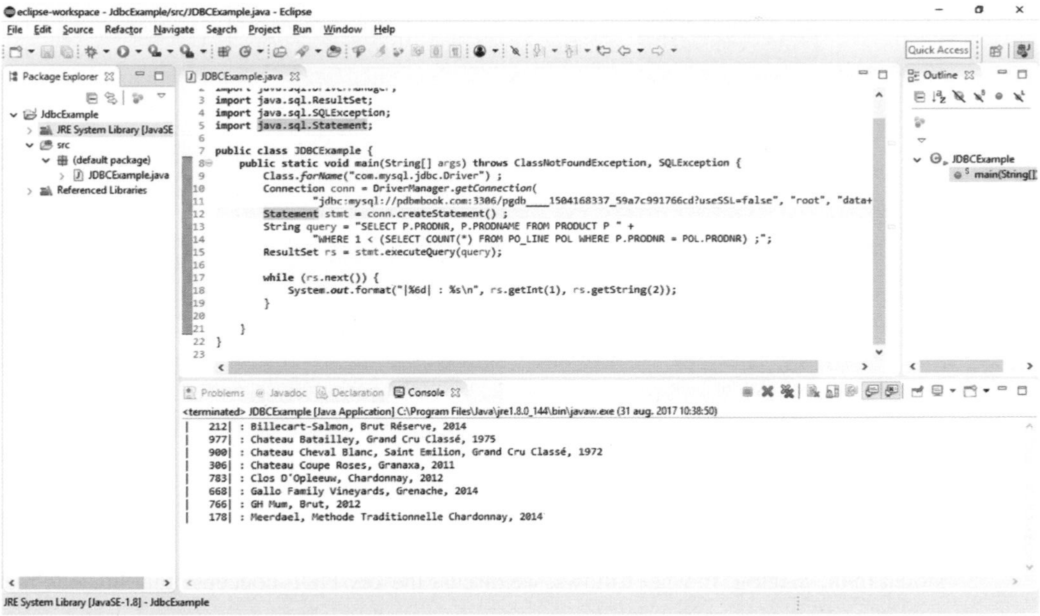


**Figure 7.2** Example of a Java program with an SQL statement.

### 7.1.2 Three-Layer Database Architecture

Figure 7.3 illustrates the positioning of SQL across the three-layer database architecture we introduced in Chapter 1. At the internal data model layer, we find the SQL database, SQL tablespace, and SQL index definitions.[2] At the logical data model layer, we have the SQL table definitions, whereby a table corresponds to a relation from the relational model. At the external data model layer, SQL views are defined that essentially offer a tailored set of data for one or more applications or queries. The queries can be implemented in a host language or in an interactive environment. Remember, these layers should be connected, but loosely coupled such that a change in one layer has minimal to no impact on all other layers above (see Chapter 1).

The SQL DDL and DML statements are clearly separated to successfully implement the three-layer database architecture.

**Connections**

Chapter 1 discussed the advantages and implications of using a three-layer database architecture.

**Retention Questions**

- What are the key characteristics of SQL?
- Discuss the positioning of SQL across the three-layer database architecture.

## 7.2 SQL Data Definition Language

As discussed in Chapter 1, the data definition language (DDL) is used by the database administrator (DBA) to express the database's logical, internal, and external data models. These definitions are

[2] Newer versions of the SQL standard no longer focus on the internal data model.

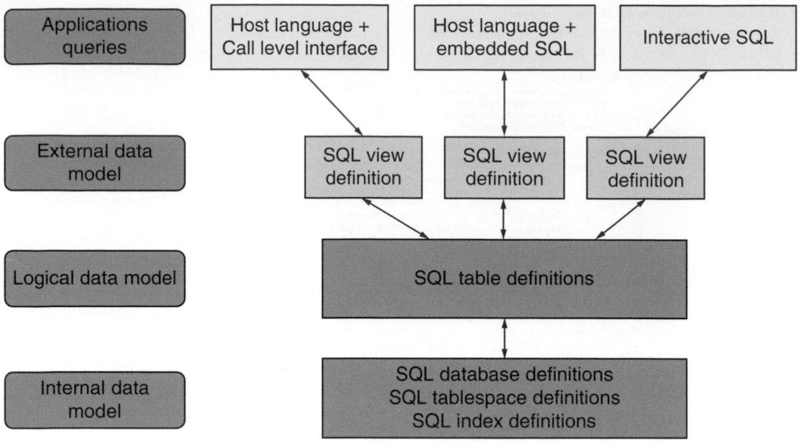


**Figure 7.3** SQL and the three-layer database architecture.

stored in the catalog. In what follows, we discuss the key DDL concepts and illustrate them with an example. We revisit referential integrity constraints and elaborate on how to drop or alter database objects.

### 7.2.1 Key DDL Concepts

A key concept to start off with is the **SQL schema**. This is a grouping of tables and other database objects such as views, constraints, and indexes which logically belong together. An SQL schema is defined by a schema name and includes an **authorization identifier** to indicate the user, or user account, who owns the schema. Such users can perform any action they want within the context of the schema. A schema is typically defined for a business process or context such as a purchase order or HR system. Here, you can see the SQL definition of a schema called purchase whereby BBAESENS is assigned as the owner:

```
CREATE SCHEMA PURCHASE AUTHORIZATION BBAESENS
```

Once we have defined a schema, we can start creating SQL tables. An SQL table implements a relation from the relational model. It typically has multiple columns, one per attribute type, and multiple rows, one for each tuple. An SQL table can be created using the CREATE TABLE statement followed by the name of the table. Below you can see two examples. The first one creates a table PRODUCT which is assigned to the default schema. The second example creates a table PRODUCT within the PURCHASE schema. It is recommended to explicitly assign a new table to an already-existing schema to avoid any confusion or inconsistencies.

```
CREATE TABLE PRODUCT ...
CREATE TABLE PURCHASE.PRODUCT ...
```

An SQL table has various columns – one per attribute type. As an example, our SQL table PRODUCT can have columns such as PRODNR, PRODNAME, PRODTYPE, etc. Each of these columns has a corresponding data type to represent the format and range of possible values. Table 7.1 gives some examples of commonly used SQL data types.

Table 7.1 SQL data types

| Data type | Description |
|---|---|
| CHAR(n) | Holds a fixed length string with size *n* |
| VARCHAR(n) | Holds a variable length string with maximum size *n* |
| SMALLINT | Small integer (no decimal) between –32,768 and 32,767 |
| INT | Integer (no decimal) between –2,147,483,648 and 2,147,483,647 |
| FLOAT(n,d) | Small number with a floating decimal point. The total maximum number of digits is *n* with a maximum of *d* digits to the right of the decimal point. |
| DOUBLE(n,d) | Large number with a floating decimal point. The total maximum number of digits is *n* with a maximum of *d* digits to the right of the decimal point. |
| DATE | Date in format YYYY-MM-DD |
| DATETIME | Date and time in format YYYY-MM-DD HH:MI:SS |
| TIME | Time in format HH:MI:SS |
| BOOLEAN | True or false |
| BLOB | Binary large object (e.g., image, audio, video) |

These data types might be implemented differently in various RDBMSs, and it is recommended to check the user manual for the options available.

In SQL it is also possible for a user to define a data type or domain. This can be handy when a domain can be re-used multiple times in a table or schema (e.g., see our BillOfMaterial example in Chapter 6). Changes to the domain definition then only need to be done once, which greatly improves the maintainability of your database schema. Here you can see an example of a domain PRODTYPE_DOMAIN, which is defined as a variable number of characters of which the value is either white, red, rose, or sparkling:

```
CREATE DOMAIN PRODTYPE_DOMAIN AS VARCHAR(10)
CHECK (VALUE IN ('white', 'red', 'rose', 'sparkling'))
```

If you would decide later to also include beer, then this can be easily added to the list of admissible values. Note, however, that some RDBMSs such as MySQL do not support the concept of an SQL domain.

SQL column definitions can be further refined by imposing column constraints (see also Chapter 6). The primary key constraint defines the primary key of the table. Remember, a primary key should have unique values and null values are thus not tolerated (entity integrity constraint). A foreign key constraint defines a foreign key of a table, which typically refers to a primary key of another (or the same) table, thereby restricting the range of possible values (referential integrity constraint). A **UNIQUE** constraint defines an alternative key of a table. A **NOT NULL** constraint prohibits null values for a column. A **DEFAULT** constraint can be used to set a default value for a column. Finally, a **CHECK** constraint can be used to define a constraint on the column values. All these constraints should be set in close collaboration between the database designer and business user.

### 7.2.2 DDL Example

Let's now illustrate the DDL concepts discussed before with an example. Figure 7.4 shows an ER model for a purchase order administration which we will also use to illustrate both SQL DDL and SQL DML in this chapter. Let's spend some time understanding it. We have three entity types: SUPPLIER, PURCHASE ORDER, and PRODUCT. A supplier has a unique supplier number,

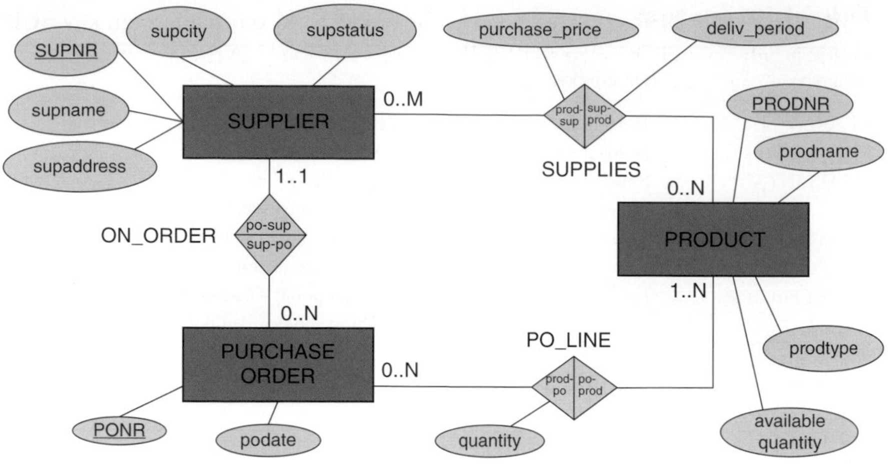


**Figure 7.4** Example ER model.

which is its key attribute type. It is also characterized by a supplier name, supplier address, supplier city, and supplier status. A purchase order has a unique purchase order number, which is its key attribute type. It also has a purchase order date. A product has a unique product number, which is its key attribute type. It also has a product name, product type, and available quantity.

Let's look at the relationship types. A supplier can supply minimum zero and maximum N products. A product is supplied by minimum zero and maximum M suppliers. The SUPPLIES relationship type has two attribute types: purchase_price and deliv_period, representing the price and period for a particular supplier to supply a particular product. A supplier has minimum zero and maximum N purchase orders on order. A purchase order is on order with minimum one and maximum one – in other words, exactly one – supplier. PURCHASE ORDER is existence-dependent on SUPPLIER. A purchase order can have several purchase order lines, each for a particular product. This is the relationship type between PURCHASE ORDER and PRODUCT. A purchase order can have minimum one and maximum N products as purchase order lines. Vice versa, a product can be included in minimum zero and maximum N purchase orders. The relationship type is characterized by the quantity attribute type, representing the quantity of a particular product in a particular purchase order.

The corresponding relational tables for our ER model then become (primary keys are underlined; foreign keys are in italics):

**SUPPLIER**(SUPNR, SUPNAME, SUPADDRESS, SUPCITY, SUPSTATUS)

**PRODUCT**(PRODNR, PRODNAME, PRODTYPE, AVAILABLE_QUANTITY)

**SUPPLIES**(*SUPNR*, *PRODNR*, PURCHASE_PRICE, DELIV_PERIOD)

**PURCHASE_ORDER**(PONR, PODATE, *SUPNR*)

**PO_LINE**(*PONR*, *PRODNR*, QUANTITY)

The SUPPLIER and PRODUCT table correspond to the SUPPLIER and PRODUCT entity types. The SUPPLIES table is needed to implement the N:M relationship type between SUPPLIER and PRODUCT. Its primary key is a combination of two foreign keys: SUPNR and PRODNR. It also includes both the PURCHASE_PRICE and DELIV_PERIOD, which were the attribute types of the relationship type SUPPLIES. The PURCHASE_ORDER table corresponds to the

PURCHASE_ORDER entity type in the ER model. It also has a foreign key SUPNR, which refers to the supplier number in the SUPPLIER table. The PO_LINE table implements the N:M relationship type between PURCHASE_ORDER and PRODUCT. Its primary key is again a combination of two foreign keys: PONR and PRODNR. The QUANTITY attribute type is also included in this table.

The DDL definition for the SUPPLIER table becomes:

```
CREATE TABLE SUPPLIER
      (SUPNR CHAR(4) NOT NULL PRIMARY KEY,
      SUPNAME VARCHAR(40) NOT NULL,
      SUPADDRESS VARCHAR(50),
      SUPCITY VARCHAR(20),
      SUPSTATUS SMALLINT)
```

The SUPNR is defined as CHAR(4) and set to be the primary key. We could have also defined it using a number data type, but let's say the business asked us to define it as four characters so to also accommodate some older legacy product numbers, which may occasionally include alphanumeric symbols. SUPNAME is defined as a NOT NULL column.

The PRODUCT table can be defined as follows:

```
CREATE TABLE PRODUCT
      (PRODNR CHAR(6) NOT NULL PRIMARY KEY,
       PRODNAME VARCHAR(60) NOT NULL,
           CONSTRAINT UC1 UNIQUE(PRODNAME),
       PRODTYPE VARCHAR(10),
           CONSTRAINT CC1 CHECK(PRODTYPE IN ('white', 'red', 'rose', 'sparkling')),
       AVAILABLE_QUANTITY INTEGER)
```

In the PRODUCT table, the PRODNR column is defined as the primary key. The PRODNAME column is defined as NOT NULL and UNIQUE. Hence, it can be used as an alternative key. The PRODTYPE column is defined as a variable number of characters up to ten. Its values should either be white, red, rose, or sparkling. The AVAILABLE_QUANTITY column is defined as an integer.

The DDL for the SUPPLIES table is:

```
CREATE TABLE SUPPLIES
      (SUPNR CHAR(4) NOT NULL,
      PRODNR CHAR(6) NOT NULL,
      PURCHASE_PRICE DOUBLE(8,2)
         COMMENT 'PURCHASE_PRICE IN EUR',
      DELIV_PERIOD INT
         COMMENT 'DELIV_PERIOD IN DAYS',
      PRIMARY KEY (SUPNR, PRODNR),
      FOREIGN KEY (SUPNR) REFERENCES SUPPLIER (SUPNR)
           ON DELETE CASCADE ON UPDATE CASCADE,
      FOREIGN KEY (PRODNR) REFERENCES PRODUCT (PRODNR)
           ON DELETE CASCADE ON UPDATE CASCADE)
```

The SUPPLIES table has four columns. First, the SUPNR and PRODNR are defined. The PURCHASE_PRICE is defined as DOUBLE(8,2). It consists of a total of eight digits with two digits after the decimal point. The DELIV_PERIOD column is assigned the INT data type. The primary key is then defined as a combination of SUPNR and PRODNR. The foreign key relationship is then also specified. Neither of the foreign keys can be null since they both make up the primary key of the table. The ON UPDATE CASCADE and ON DELETE CASCADE statements are discussed below.

Next, we have the PURCHASE_ORDER table:

```
CREATE TABLE PURCHASE_ORDER
      (PONR CHAR(7) NOT NULL PRIMARY KEY,
      PODATE DATE,
      SUPNR CHAR(4) NOT NULL,
      FOREIGN KEY (SUPNR) REFERENCES SUPPLIER (SUPNR)
            ON DELETE CASCADE ON UPDATE CASCADE)
```

The PURCHASE_ORDER table is defined with the PONR, PODATE, and SUPNR columns. The latter is again a foreign key.

We conclude our database definition with the PO_LINE table:

```
CREATE TABLE PO_LINE
      (PONR CHAR(7) NOT NULL,
      PRODNR CHAR(6) NOT NULL,
      QUANTITY INTEGER,
      PRIMARY KEY (PONR, PRODNR),
      FOREIGN KEY (PONR) REFERENCES PURCHASE_ORDER (PONR)
            ON DELETE CASCADE ON UPDATE CASCADE,
      FOREIGN KEY (PRODNR) REFERENCES PRODUCT (PRODNR)
            ON DELETE CASCADE ON UPDATE CASCADE);
```

It has three columns: PONR, PRODNR, and QUANTITY. Both PONR and PRODNR are foreign keys and make up the primary key of the table.

### 7.2.3 Referential Integrity Constraints

Remember, the referential integrity constraint states that a foreign key has the same domain as the primary key it refers to and occurs as either a value of the primary key or NULL (see Chapter 6). The question now arises of what should happen to foreign keys in the case that a primary key is updated or even deleted. As an example, suppose the supplier number of a SUPPLIER tuple is updated or the tuple is deleted in its entirety. What would have to happen to all other referring SUPPLIES and PURCHASE_ORDER tuples? This can be specified by using various referential integrity actions. The ON UPDATE CASCADE option says that an update should be cascaded to all referring tuples. Similarly, the ON DELETE CASCADE option says that a removal should be cascaded to all referring tuples. If the option is set to RESTRICT, the update or removal is halted if referring tuples exist. SET NULL implies that all foreign keys in the referring tuples are set to NULL. This obviously assumes that a NULL value is allowed. Finally, SET DEFAULT means that the foreign keys in the referring tuples should be set to their default value.

This is illustrated in Figure 7.5. We have listed some tuples of the SUPPLIER table. Let's focus on supplier number 37, whose name is Ad Fundum. This supplier has four referring SUPPLIES

SUPPLIER

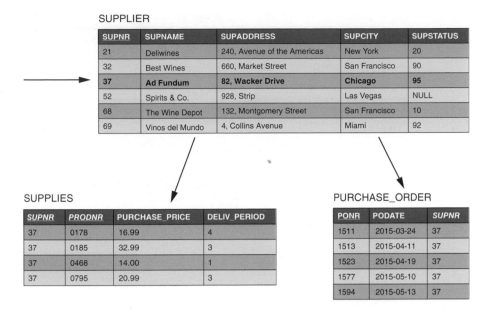

| SUPNR | SUPNAME | SUPADDRESS | SUPCITY | SUPSTATUS |
|---|---|---|---|---|
| 21 | Deliwines | 240, Avenue of the Americas | New York | 20 |
| 32 | Best Wines | 660, Market Street | San Francisco | 90 |
| **37** | **Ad Fundum** | **82, Wacker Drive** | **Chicago** | **95** |
| 52 | Spirits & Co. | 928, Strip | Las Vegas | NULL |
| 68 | The Wine Depot | 132, Montgomery Street | San Francisco | 10 |
| 69 | Vinos del Mundo | 4, Collins Avenue | Miami | 92 |

SUPPLIES

| *SUPNR* | *PRODNR* | PURCHASE_PRICE | DELIV_PERIOD |
|---|---|---|---|
| 37 | 0178 | 16.99 | 4 |
| 37 | 0185 | 32.99 | 3 |
| 37 | 0468 | 14.00 | 1 |
| 37 | 0795 | 20.99 | 3 |

PURCHASE_ORDER

| PONR | PODATE | *SUPNR* |
|---|---|---|
| 1511 | 2015-03-24 | 37 |
| 1513 | 2015-04-11 | 37 |
| 1523 | 2015-04-19 | 37 |
| 1577 | 2015-05-10 | 37 |
| 1594 | 2015-05-13 | 37 |

**Figure 7.5** Referential integrity actions.

tuples and five referring PURCHASE_ORDER tuples. Suppose now that we update the supplier number to 40. In the case of an ON UPDATE CASCADE constraint, this update will be cascaded to all nine referring tuples where the supplier number will thus also be updated to 40. In the case of an ON UPDATE RESTRICT constraint, the update will not be allowed because of the referring tuples. If we now remove supplier number 37, then an ON DELETE CASCADE option will also remove all nine referring tuples. In the case of an ON DELETE RESTRICT constraint, the removal will not be allowed. The constraints can be set individually for each foreign key in close collaboration with the business user.

### 7.2.4 DROP and ALTER Command

The **DROP** command can be used to drop or remove database objects (e.g., schemas, tables, views, etc.). It can also be combined with the CASCADE and RESTRICT options. Some examples are:

```
DROP SCHEMA PURCHASE CASCADE
DROP SCHEMA PURCHASE RESTRICT
DROP TABLE PRODUCT CASCADE
DROP TABLE PRODUCT RESTRICT
```

The first statement drops the purchase schema. The CASCADE option indicates that all referring objects such as tables, views, indexes, etc. will also be automatically dropped. If the option had been RESTRICT, such as in the second example, the removal of the schema will be refused if there are still referring objects (e.g., tables, views, indexes). The same reasoning applies when dropping tables.

The **ALTER** statement can be used to modify table column definitions. Common actions are: adding or dropping a column; changing a column definition; or adding or dropping table constraints. Here you can see two examples:

SUPPLIER

| SUPNR | SUPNAME | SUPADDRESS | SUPCITY | SUPSTATUS |
|---|---|---|---|---|
| 21 | Deliwines | 240, Avenue of the Americas | New York | 20 |
| 32 | Best Wines | 660, Market Street | San Francisco | 90 |
| ... | | | | |

PRODUCT

| PRODNR | PRODNAME | PRODTYPE | AVAILABLE_QUANTITY |
|---|---|---|---|
| 0119 | Chateau Miraval, Cotes de Provence Rose, 2015 | rose | 126 |
| 0154 | Chateau Haut Brion, 2008 | red | 111 |
| ... | | red | 5 |

SUPPLIES

| *SUPNR* | *PRODNR* | PURCHASE_PRICE | DELIV_PERIOD |
|---|---|---|---|
| 21 | 0289 | 17.99 | 1 |
| 21 | 0327 | 56.00 | 6 |
| ... | | | |

PURCHASE_ORDER

| PONR | PODATE | *SUPNR* |
|---|---|---|
| 1511 | 2015-03-24 | 37 |
| 1512 | 2015-04-10 | 94 |
| ... | | |

PO_LINE

| *PONR* | *PRODNR* | QUANTITY |
|---|---|---|
| 1511 | 0212 | 2 |
| 1511 | 0345 | 4 |
| ... | | |

**Figure 7.6** Example relational database state.

**Retention Questions**

- Discuss how SQL DDL can be used to define schemas, tables, and domains.
- What types of referential integrity actions are supported in SQL?
- What is the purpose of the SQL DROP and ALTER commands?

```
ALTER TABLE PRODUCT ADD PRODIMAGE BLOB
ALTER TABLE SUPPLIER ALTER SUPSTATUS SET DEFAULT '10'
```

The first one adds the PRODIMAGE column to the PRODUCT table and defines it as **a binary large object**, or **BLOB**. The second example assigns a default value of 10 to the SUPSTATUS column.

Once we have finalized the data definitions, we can compile them so that they can be stored in the catalog of the RDBMS. The next step is to start populating the database. Figure 7.6 shows some examples of tuples listed for the various tables we defined earlier. We continue with the relational database for a wine purchase administration whereby the products represent wines.

## 7.3 SQL Data Manipulation Language

The data manipulation language (DML) retrieves, inserts, deletes, and modifies data (see Chapter 1). From a DML perspective, SQL defines four statements. The SELECT statement retrieves data from the relational database. The UPDATE and INSERT statements modify and add data. Finally, the DELETE statement removes data. We examine each of these separately in the following subsections.

### 7.3.1 SQL SELECT Statement

We start with the SQL SELECT statement. You can see the full syntax illustrated below.

```
SELECT component
FROM component
[WHERE component]
[GROUP BY component]
[HAVING component]
[ORDER BY component]
```

By using the options listed, we can ask very specific and complex questions of the database. It is important to note that the result of an SQL SELECT statement is a multiset, not a set. Remember, in a set there are no duplicates and the elements are not ordered. In a **multiset** (sometimes also called *bag*), the elements are also not ordered. However, there can be duplicate elements in a multiset. As an example, you can think of a set {10, 5, 20}, and a multiset {10, 5, 10, 20, 5, 10}, where the elements 5 and 10 each occur multiple times. SQL will not automatically eliminate duplicates in the result. There are various reasons for this. First, duplicate elimination is an expensive operation. Next, the user may also want to see duplicate tuples in the query result. Finally, duplicates may also be considered by aggregate functions as we illustrate in Section 7.3.1.2.

In what follows, we discuss simple queries; queries with **aggregate functions**; queries with GROUP BY/HAVING; queries with ORDER BY; join queries; nested queries; correlated queries; queries with ALL/ANY; queries with EXISTS; queries with subqueries in SELECT/FROM; and queries with set operations.

**Drill Down**

You can follow along with the queries below by using the SQL environment in the online playground (see the Appendix for more details).

#### 7.3.1.1 Simple Queries

Simple queries are SQL statements that retrieve data from only one table. In other words, the FROM component in the SELECT statement contains only one table name. The SELECT component then extracts the columns required. It can contain various expressions which generally refer to the names of the columns we are interested in:[3]

```
Q1: SELECT SUPNR, SUPNAME, SUPADDRESS, SUPCITY, SUPSTATUS
    FROM SUPPLIER
```

Q1 selects all information from the SUPPLIER table. In other words, it provides a complete table dump. In the case that all columns of a table are requested, SQL provides a handy shortcut notation:

```
Q1: SELECT * FROM SUPPLIER
```

The result is displayed in Figure 7.7.

It is also possible to select only a few columns:

```
Q2: SELECT SUPNR, SUPNAME FROM SUPPLIER
```

[3] We number all queries as Q1, Q2, Q3, etc., so we can easily refer to them.

| SUPNR | SUPNAME | SUPADDRESS | SUPCITY | SUPSTATUS |
|---|---|---|---|---|
| 21 | Deliwines | 240, Avenue of the Americas | New York | 20 |
| 32 | Best Wines | 660, Market Street | San Francisco | 90 |
| 37 | Ad Fundum | 82, Wacker Drive | Chicago | 95 |
| 52 | Spirits & Co. | 928, Strip | Las Vegas | NULL |
| 68 | The Wine Depot | 132, Montgomery Street | San Francisco | 10 |
| 69 | Vinos del Mundo | 4, Collins Avenue | Miami | 92 |

**Figure 7.7** Result for Q1.

| SUPNR | SUPNAME |
|---|---|
| 21 | Deliwines |
| 32 | Best Wines |
| 37 | Ad Fundum |
| 52 | Spirits & Co. |
| 68 | The Wine Depot |
| 69 | Vinos del Mundo |

**Figure 7.8** Result for Q2.

| SUPNR |
|---|
| 32 |
| 32 |
| 37 |
| 37 |
| 37 |
| 37 |
| 37 |
| 68 |
| 69 |
| 94 |

**Figure 7.9** Result for Q3.

| SUPNR |
|---|
| 32 |
| 37 |
| 94 |
| 68 |
| 69 |

**Figure 7.10** Result for Q4.

As shown in Figure 7.8, this query selects the supplier number and supplier name from the SUPPLIER table.

Q3 selects the supplier number from the PURCHASE_ORDER table. Since a supplier can have multiple purchase orders outstanding, the same supplier number can appear multiple times in the result, as illustrated in Figure 7.9. Remember, the result of an SQL query is a multiset, that's why we see supplier numbers 32 and 37 appearing multiple times.

```
Q3: SELECT SUPNR FROM PURCHASE_ORDER
```

Q4 adds the DISTINCT option. This option removes duplicates and makes sure that only distinct values are shown in the result (see Figure 7.10).

```
Q4: SELECT DISTINCT SUPNR FROM PURCHASE_ORDER
```

Q5 shows that we can also include simple arithmetic expressions in the SELECT statement. It selects the supplier number, product number, and delivery period divided by 30 from the SUPPLIES

| SUPNR | PRODNR | MONTH_DELIV_PERIOD |
|---|---|---|
| 21 | 0119 | 0.0333 |
| 21 | 0178 | NULL |
| 21 | 0289 | 0.0333 |
| 21 | 0327 | 0.2000 |
| 21 | 0347 | 0.0667 |
| 21 | 0384 | 0.0667 |
| ... | ... | ... |

**Figure 7.11** Result for Q5.

| SUPNR | SUPNAME | SUPSTATUS |
|---|---|---|
| 32 | Best Wines | 90 |
| 68 | The Wine Depot | 10 |

**Figure 7.12** Result for Q6.

table. Remember, the delivery period was expressed in days, so if we divide it by 30 we can approximate it in terms of months. Note that we also added MONTH_DELIV_PERIOD as an alias or shortcut name to the calculation.

```
Q5: SELECT SUPNR, PRODNR, DELIV_PERIOD/30 AS MONTH_DELIV_PERIOD
  FROM SUPPLIES
```

Figure 7.11 displays the result of Q5.

The SQL queries we discussed thus far only include a SELECT and FROM component. A missing WHERE clause indicates there is no condition on the actual tuple selection. When a WHERE clause is added to the SQL statement, it specifies selection conditions to indicate which table rows should be selected. Several operators can be used in the WHERE clause, such as: comparison operators, Boolean operators, the BETWEEN operator, the IN operator, the LIKE operator, and the NULL operator. Let's illustrate this with some examples.

Q6 selects the supplier number and supplier name from the SUPPLIER table of all suppliers living in San Francisco.

```
Q6: SELECT SUPNR, SUPNAME
  FROM SUPPLIER
  WHERE SUPCITY = 'San Francisco'
```

The result is shown in Figure 7.12.

Q7 selects the supplier number and supplier name from the SUPPLIER table of all suppliers living in San Francisco and whose status is higher than 80. Note that both conditions are combined with a Boolean AND operator.

```
Q7: SELECT SUPNR, SUPNAME
  FROM SUPPLIER
  WHERE SUPCITY = 'San Francisco' AND SUPSTATUS > 80
```

The result is shown in Figure 7.13.

Q8 selects the supplier number, name and status from the SUPPLIER table of all suppliers whose status is between 70 and 80 (see Figure 7.14).

```
Q8: SELECT SUPNR, SUPNAME, SUPSTATUS
  FROM SUPPLIER
  WHERE SUPSTATUS BETWEEN 70 AND 80
```

| SUPNR | SUPNAME | SUPSTATUS |
|---|---|---|
| 32 | Best Wines | 90 |

**Figure 7.13** Result for Q7.

| SUPNR | SUPNAME | SUPSTATUS |
|---|---|---|
| 94 | The Wine Crate | 75 |

**Figure 7.14** Result for Q8.

| PRODNR | PRODNAME |
|---|---|
| 0178 | Meerdael, Methode Traditionnelle Chardonnay, 2014 |
| 0199 | Jacques Selosse, Brut Initial, 2012 |
| 0212 | Billecart-Salmon, Brut Réserve, 2014 |
| 0300 | Chateau des Rontets, Chardonnay, Birbettes |
| 0494 | Veuve-Cliquot, Brut, 2012 |
| 0632 | Meneghetti, Chardonnay, 2010 |
| ... | .... |

**Figure 7.15** Result for Q9.

| PRODNR | PRODNAME |
|---|---|
| 0300 | Chateau des Rontets, Chardonnay, Birbettes |
| 0783 | Clos D'Opleeuw, Chardonnay, 2012 |
| 0178 | Meerdael, Methode Traditionnelle Chardonnay, 2014 |
| 0632 | Meneghetti, Chardonnay, 2010 |

**Figure 7.16** Result for Q10.

| SUPNR | SUPNAME | SUPSTATUS |
|---|---|---|
| 52 | Spirits & Co. | NULL |

**Figure 7.17** Result for Q11.

Q9 selects the product number and product name of all products whose product type is either white or sparkling. Note the use of the IN operator which combines the strings "white" and "sparkling" into a set.

```
Q9: SELECT PRODNR, PRODNAME
  FROM PRODUCT
  WHERE PRODTYPE IN ('WHITE', 'SPARKLING')
```

The result of Q9 is shown in Figure 7.15.

Q10 illustrates the use of the percentage sign as a *wildcard* representing zero or more characters. Another popular wildcard is the underscore (_), which is a substitute for a single character. In our example, we select the product number and product name of all products having the string CHARD as part of their product names. This selects all the chardonnay wines, as you can see in Figure 7.16.

```
Q10: SELECT PRODNR, PRODNAME
   FROM PRODUCT
   WHERE PRODNAME LIKE '%CHARD%'
```

The keyword NULL can also be handy when formulating queries. For example, Q11 selects the supplier number and supplier name of all suppliers whose status is NULL (see Figure 7.17).

```
Q11: SELECT SUPNR, SUPNAME, SUPSTATUS
     FROM SUPPLIER
     WHERE SUPSTATUS IS NULL
```

#### 7.3.1.2 Queries with Aggregate Functions

Several expressions can be added to the SELECT statement to ask for more specific information. These may also include aggregate functions used to summarize information from database tuples. Popular examples are COUNT, SUM, AVG, VARIANCE, MIN/MAX, and STDEV. Let's work out some examples using the tuples illustrated in Figure 7.18.

The query

```
Q12: SELECT COUNT(*)
     FROM SUPPLIES
     WHERE PRODNR = '0178'
```

selects the number of tuples in the SUPPLIES table where the product number equals 178. For our example (see Figure 7.18), the result of this query will be the number 5. Note the use of the COUNT operator.

Q13 selects the number of NOT NULL purchase price values in the SUPPLIES table for tuples where the product number equals 178. The result will be the number 4, referring to the values 16.99, 17.99, 16.99, and 18. Note that the value 16.99 is counted twice here.

```
Q13: SELECT COUNT(PURCHASE_PRICE)
     FROM SUPPLIES
     WHERE PRODNR = '0178'
```

If we want to filter out duplicates, then we can add the keyword DISTINCT to the query, which will result in the value 3:

```
Q14: SELECT COUNT(DISTINCT PURCHASE_PRICE)
     FROM SUPPLIES
     WHERE PRODNR = '0178'
```

The query

```
Q15: SELECT PRODNR, SUM(QUANTITY) AS SUM_ORDERS
     FROM PO_LINE
     WHERE PRODNR = '0178'
```

| SUPNR | PRODNR | PURCHASE_PRICE | DELIV_PERIOD |
|---|---|---|---|
| ... | | | |
| 21 | 0178 | NULL | NULL |
| 37 | 0178 | 16.99 | 4 |
| 68 | 0178 | 17.99 | 5 |
| 69 | 0178 | 16.99 | NULL |
| 94 | 0178 | 18.00 | 6 |
| ... | | | |
| | | | |

**Figure 7.18** Example tuples of SUPPLIES table.

| PONR | PRODNR | QUANTITY |
|---|---|---|
| ... | | |
| 1512 | 0178 | 3 |
| 1538 | 0178 | 6 |
| ... | | |

**Figure 7.19** Example tuples of PO_LINE table.

| SUPNR | PRODNR | PURCHASE_PRICE | DELIV_PERIOD |
|---|---|---|---|
| ... | | | |
| 21 | 0178 | NULL | NULL |
| 37 | 0178 | 16.99 | 4 |
| 68 | 0178 | 17.99 | 5 |
| 69 | 0178 | 16.99 | NULL |
| 94 | 0178 | 18.00 | 6 |
| ... | | | |

**Figure 7.20** Example tuples of SUPPLIES table.

selects the product number and sum of the quantities (as calculated by SUM(QUANTITY)) of all PO_LINE tuples of which the product number equals 178. The result of this query is 0178 and the value 9, which equals 3 plus 6, as illustrated for the sample tuples in Figure 7.19.

The query

```
Q16: SELECT SUM(QUANTITY) AS TOTAL_ORDERS
     FROM PO_LINE
```

simply adds up all quantities of the PO_LINE table, which results in the value 173.

Q17 selects the product number and average purchase price (as calculated by AVG(PURCHASE_PRICE)) from the SUPPLIES table (see Figure 7.20) for all tuples where the product number equals 178. The result of this query is a weighted average price since duplicate values will not be filtered out in the calculation. More specifically, since supplier number 37 and 69 both adopt a price of 16.99, this price will be counted twice, resulting in a weighted average price of (16.99 + 17.99 + 16.99 + 18.00)/4, or 17.4925. Hence, the result of this query will be the values 0178 and 17.4925.

```
Q17: SELECT PRODNR, AVG(PURCHASE_PRICE) AS WEIGHTED_AVG_PRICE
     FROM SUPPLIES
     WHERE PRODNR = '0178'
```

If we are interested in an unweighted average, then we need to add the DISTINCT option, as shown in Q18. Here the value 16.99 will only be counted once, resulting in an average of (16.99 + 17.99 + 18.00)/3, or 17.66.

```
Q18: SELECT PRODNR, AVG(DISTINCT PURCHASE_PRICE)
     AS UNWEIGHTED_AVG_PRICE
     FROM SUPPLIES
     WHERE PRODNR = '0178'
```

The variance, which represents the average squared deviation from the average, can also be calculated using VARIANCE(PURCHASE_PRICE), as shown in Q19.

```
Q19: SELECT PRODNR, VARIANCE(PURCHASE_PRICE)
     AS PRICE_VARIANCE FROM SUPPLIES
     WHERE PRODNR = '0178'
```

| PRODNR | PRICE_VARIANCE |
|---|---|
| 0178 | 0.25251875000000024 |

**Figure 7.21** Result for Q19.

| PRODNR | LOWEST_PRICE | HIGHEST_PRICE |
|---|---|---|
| 0178 | 16.99 | 18.00 |

**Figure 7.22** Result for Q20.

The result is displayed in Figure 7.21.

Q20 selects the product number, minimum price (calculated using MIN(PURCHASE_PRICE)), and maximum price (calculated using MAX(PURCHASE_PRICE)) of all SUPPLIES tuples for which the product number equals 178. This results in the values 16.99 and 18, as shown in Figure 7.22.

```
Q20: SELECT PRODNR, MIN(PURCHASE_PRICE) AS LOWEST_PRICE,
   MAX(PURCHASE_PRICE) AS HIGHEST_PRICE
   FROM SUPPLIES
   WHERE PRODNR = '0178'
```

#### 7.3.1.3 Queries with GROUP BY/HAVING

Let's add some more complexity to our queries by using a GROUP BY/HAVING clause. The idea here is to apply aggregate functions to subgroups of tuples in a table, where each subgroup consists of tuples that have the same value for one or more columns. By using the GROUP BY clause, rows are grouped when they have the same value for one or more columns and the aggregation is applied to each group separately, instead of to the table as a whole, as in the previous examples. The HAVING clause can then be added to retrieve the values of only those groups that satisfy specified conditions. It can only be used in combination with a GROUP BY clause and can include aggregate functions such as SUM, MIN, MAX, and AVG. Let's start with the following query as an illustration:

```
Q21: SELECT PRODNR
   FROM PO_LINE
   GROUP BY PRODNR
   HAVING COUNT(*) >= 3
```

This query retrieves the product numbers with at least three outstanding orders. If you look at the PO_LINE table in Figure 7.23, you see that both product numbers 212 and 900 satisfy the condition.

The GROUP BY PRODNR clause makes groups based upon the product number. You can see those groups represented in Figure 7.24. We have a group for product number 212, for product number 178, and so on. The HAVING COUNT(*) >= 3 clause counts how many tuples are in each group and sees whether this is more than or equal to 3, in which case the product number will be reported. For the group with product number 212, the COUNT(*) gives 3, and since this is more than or equal to 3, the product number 212 will be reported. For the group with product number 178, the COUNT(*) results in 2 such that no output will be generated. Therefore, the resulting output will be PRODNR 212 and 900, as shown in Figure 7.25.

Q22 assumes we want to retrieve the product numbers of products where the total order quantity exceeds 15. This can again be done using a GROUP BY/HAVING clause. The SQL query will be:

| PONR | PRODNR | QUANTITY |
|---|---|---|
| 1511 | 0212 | 2 |
| 1512 | 0178 | 3 |
| 1513 | 0668 | 7 |
| 1514 | 0185 | 2 |
| 1514 | 0900 | 2 |
| 1523 | 0900 | 3 |
| 1538 | 0178 | 6 |
| 1538 | 0212 | 15 |
| 1560 | 0900 | 9 |
| 1577 | 0212 | 6 |
| 1577 | 0668 | 9 |
| … | .. | … |

**Figure 7.23** Example tuples from the PO_Line table.

GROUP BY

| PONR | PRODNR | QUANTITY |
|---|---|---|
| 1511 | 0212 | 2 |
| 1577 | 0212 | 6 |
| 1538 | 0212 | 15 |

| PONR | PRODNR | QUANTITY |
|---|---|---|
| 1512 | 0178 | 3 |
| 1538 | 0178 | 6 |

| PONR | PRODNR | QUANTITY |
|---|---|---|
| 1513 | 0668 | 7 |
| 1577 | 0668 | 9 |

| PONR | PRODNR | QUANTITY |
|---|---|---|
| 1514 | 0900 | 2 |
| 1523 | 0900 | 3 |
| 1560 | 0900 | 9 |

| PONR | PRODNR | QUANTITY |
|---|---|---|
| 1514 | 0185 | 2 |

**Figure 7.24** Illustrating the GROUP BY function.

| PRODNR |
|---|
| 0212 |
| 900 |

**Figure 7.25** Result of Q21.

```
Q22: SELECT PRODNR, SUM(QUANTITY) AS QUANTITY
     FROM PO_LINE
     GROUP BY PRODNR
     HAVING SUM(QUANTITY) > 15
```

Figure 7.26 illustrates how this query works. First, groups are made based upon the product number. The HAVING SUM(QUANTITY) > 15 clause then calculates the sum of the quantities within each group, and if this is bigger than 15 the product number and quantity will be reported in the output. Note that you cannot include this kind of selection criterion simply in the WHERE clause, since the WHERE clause expresses selection conditions on individual tuples in the table. Instead, the HAVING clause defines selection conditions on *groups* of tuples, based on a specified aggregate value calculated over each group.

As you can see in Figure 7.26, the product number 212 group has three entries, for which the total outstanding quantity is 23; the product number 668 has two entries, for which the total outstanding quantity is 16. This result will be output as shown in Figure 7.27.

Note that a GROUP BY clause can also be used without a HAVING clause, e.g., to show the total number of outstanding orders for each individual product.

GROUP BY

| PONR | PRODNR | QUANTITY |
|---|---|---|
| 1511 | 0212 | 2 |
| 1577 | 0212 | 6 |
| 1538 | 0212 | 15 |
| | SUM | 23 |

| PONR | PRODNR | QUANTITY |
|---|---|---|
| 1512 | 0178 | 3 |
| 1538 | 0178 | 6 |
| | SUM | 9 |

| PONR | PRODNR | QUANTITY |
|---|---|---|
| 1513 | 0668 | 7 |
| 1577 | 0668 | 9 |
| | SUM | 16 |

| PONR | PRODNR | QUANTITY |
|---|---|---|
| 1514 | 0185 | 2 |
| | SUM | 2 |

| PONR | PRODNR | QUANTITY |
|---|---|---|
| 1514 | 0900 | 2 |
| 1523 | 0900 | 3 |
| 1560 | 0900 | 9 |
| | SUM | 14 |

**Figure 7.26** Illustrating the GROUP BY function.

| PRODNR | QUANTITY |
|---|---|
| 0212 | 23 |
| 0668 | 16 |

**Figure 7.27** Result of Q22.

### 7.3.1.4 Queries with ORDER BY

By using the ORDER BY statement, SQL allows the user to order the tuples in the result of a query by the values of one or more columns. Each column specified in the SELECT clause can be used for ordering and you can sort by more than one column. The default sorting mode is ascending. Depending upon the commercial implementation, NULL values may appear first or last in the sorting. Q23 retrieves a list of outstanding purchase orders, ordered ascending by date and descending by supplier number:

```
Q23: SELECT PONR, PODATE, SUPNR
     FROM PURCHASE_ORDER
     ORDER BY PODATE ASC, SUPNR DESC
```

The result is shown in Figure 7.28.

Q24 selects the product number, supplier number, and purchase price of all SUPPLIES tuples where the product number is 0178. The result is sorted by purchase price in a descending mode. The number 3 in the ORDER BY statement refers to the third column which is PURCHASE_PRICE. Note that in this implementation the NULL values appear last (see Figure 7.29).

```
Q24: SELECT PRODNR, SUPNR, PURCHASE_PRICE
     FROM SUPPLIES
     WHERE PRODNR = '0178'
     ORDER BY 3 DESC
```

The GROUP BY and ORDER BY clauses are quite often confused, although they serve completely different purposes. The GROUP BY clause denotes the groups of tuples over which an aggregate function is applied. The ORDER BY clause has no effect on the actual tuple selection, but denotes the order in which the query result is presented.

| PONR | PODATE | SUPNR |
|---|---|---|
| 1511 | 2015-03-24 | 37 |
| 1512 | 2015-04-10 | 94 |
| 1513 | 2015-04-11 | 37 |
| 1514 | 2015-04-12 | 32 |
| ... | | |

**Figure 7.28** Result of Q23.

| PRODNR | SUPNR | PURCHASE_PRICE |
|---|---|---|
| 0178 | 94 | 18.00 |
| 0178 | 68 | 17.99 |
| 0178 | 37 | 16.99 |
| 0178 | 69 | 16.99 |
| 0178 | 21 | NULL |

**Figure 7.29** Result of Q24.

### 7.3.1.5 Join Queries

Until now, we only discussed simple SQL queries through which data were retrieved from a single table. **Join queries** allow the user to combine, or join, data from multiple tables. The FROM clause then specifies the names of the tables containing the rows we want to join. The conditions under which the rows of different tables can be joined must be stated. These conditions are included in the WHERE clause. As with simple queries, it is possible to specify which columns from each table should be reported in the end result.

In SQL, the same name (e.g., SUPNR) can be used for two or more columns, provided the columns are in different tables (e.g., SUPPLIER and SUPPLIES). If the FROM component of a join query refers to two or more tables containing columns with the same name, we must qualify the column name with the table name to prevent ambiguity. This can be done by prefixing the table name to the column name (e.g., SUPPLIER.SUPNR).

An SQL join query without a WHERE component (e.g., SELECT * FROM SUPPLIER, SUPPLIES) corresponds to the Cartesian product of both tables, whereby all possible combinations of rows of both tables are included in the end result. However, this is typically not desired and join conditions can be specified in the WHERE component to ensure that correct matches are made.

There are different types of joins. In what follows, we discuss both inner and outer joins.

*Inner Joins*

Let's assume that we start from the SUPPLIER table, which contains supplier number, name, address, city and status, and the SUPPLIES table which contains supplier number, product number, purchase price, and delivery period. You now want to retrieve the supplier number, name, and status from the SUPPLIER table along with the product numbers they can supply and corresponding price. To do this, we first list the tables from which we need information:

```
SUPPLIER(SUPNR, SUPNAME, ..., SUPSTATUS)
SUPPLIES(SUPNR, PRODNR, PURCHASE_PRICE, ...)
```

Figures 7.30 and 7.31 show some example tuples from both tables. Note that each table also contains additional information we do not need. We have two tables with corresponding information that we need to combine or join in a specific way. The question is how?

First, note that there are columns in each table with the same name (SUPNR). Instead of using the verbose SUPPLIER.SUPNR and SUPPLIES.SUPNR notation, we use a shorthand notation. In this

| SUPNR | SUPNAME | SUPADDRESS | SUPCITY | SUPSTATUS |
|---|---|---|---|---|
| 32 | Best Wines | | | 90 |
| 68 | The Wine Depot | | | 10 |
| 84 | Wine Trade Logistics | | | 92 |
| ... | | | | |

**Figure 7.30** Example tuples from SUPPLIER table.

| *SUPNR* | *PRODNR* | PURCHASE_PRICE | DELIV_PERIOD |
|---|---|---|---|
| 32 | 0474 | 40.00 | 1 |
| 32 | 0154 | 21.00 | 4 |
| 84 | 0494 | 15.99 | 2 |
| ... | | | |

**Figure 7.31** Example tuples from SUPPLIES table.

| R.SUPNR | R.SUPNAME | R.SUPSTATUS | S.SUPNR | S.PRODNR | S.PURCHASE_PRICE |
|---|---|---|---|---|---|
| 21 | Deliwines | 20 | 21 | 0119 | 15.99 |
| 32 | Best Wines | 90 | 21 | 0119 | 15.99 |
| 37 | Ad Fundum | 95 | 21 | 0119 | 15.99 |
| 52 | Spirits & Co. | NULL | 21 | 0119 | 15.99 |
| ... | | | | | |
| 32 | Best Wines | 90 | 32 | 0154 | 21.00 |
| 37 | Ad Fundum | 95 | 32 | 0154 | 21.00 |
| 52 | Spirits & Co. | NULL | 32 | 0154 | 21.00 |
| ... | | | | | |
| 69 | Vinos del Mundo | 92 | 94 | 0899 | 15.00 |
| 84 | Wine Trade Logistics | 92 | 94 | 0899 | 15.00 |
| 94 | Vinos del Mundo | 75 | 94 | 0899 | 15.00 |

**Figure 7.32** Incorrect matches due to a missing join condition.

case, we will add R, referring to the SUPPLIER table, and S, referring to the SUPPLIES table. This gives us R.SUPNR and S.SUPNR to differentiate both supplier numbers. Therefore, our first attempt to solve the question using an SQL query reads:

```
Q25: SELECT R.SUPNR, R.SUPNAME, R.SUPSTATUS, S.SUPNR, S.PRODNR,
     S.PURCHASE_PRICE
     FROM SUPPLIER R, SUPPLIES S
```

What is this query doing? Since we have no WHERE component, it will make the Cartesian product of both tables by combining every possible tuple from the SUPPLIER table with every possible tuple from the SUPPLIES table. This results in incorrect matches, as illustrated in Figure 7.32. For example, you can see that supplier number 32, which is Best Wines, from the SUPPLIER table is now combined with supplier number 21 from the SUPPLIES table, and many other incorrect matches. This is clearly not what we want!

To solve this we need to carefully define under which conditions the join can take place by adding a WHERE clause to our SQL join query. With an additional WHERE clause our SQL join query reads as follows:

```
Q26: SELECT R.SUPNR, R.SUPNAME, R.SUPSTATUS, S.PRODNR, S.PURCHASE_PRICE
    FROM SUPPLIER R, SUPPLIES S
    WHERE R.SUPNR = S.SUPNR
```

| R.SUPNR | R.SUPNAME | R.SUPSTATUS | S.SUPNR | S.PRODNR | S.PURCHASE_PRICE |
|---|---|---|---|---|---|
| 21 | Deliwines | 20 | 21 | 0119 | 15.99 |
| 21 | Deliwines | 20 | 21 | 0178 | NULL |
| 21 | Deliwines | 20 | 21 | 0289 | 17.99 |
| 21 | Deliwines | 20 | 21 | 0327 | 56.00 |
| 21 | Deliwines | 20 | 21 | 0347 | 16.00 |
| 21 | Deliwines | 20 | 21 | 0384 | 55.00 |
| 21 | Deliwines | 20 | 21 | 0386 | 58.99 |
| 21 | Deliwines | 20 | 21 | 0468 | 14.99 |
| 21 | Deliwines | 20 | 21 | 0668 | 6.00 |
| 32 | Best Wines | 90 | 32 | 0154 | 21.00 |
| 32 | Best Wines | 90 | 32 | 0474 | 40.00 |
| 32 | Best Wines | 90 | 32 | 0494 | 15.00 |
| 32 | Best Wines | 90 | 32 | 0657 | 44.99 |
| 32 | Best Wines | 90 | 32 | 0760 | 52.00 |
| 32 | Best Wines | 90 | 32 | 0832 | 20.00 |
| 37 | Ad Fundum | 95 | 37 | 0178 | 16.99 |
| ... | | | | | |

**Figure 7.33** Correct matchings with a join condition.

In this query the tuples can be joined only if the supplier numbers are identical. This is why it is called an **inner join**. You can see that the matchings are correct in the resulting tuples shown in Figure 7.33. The data of supplier number 21 from the SUPPLIER table are correctly joined with the data of supplier number 21 from the SUPPLIES table, and likewise for the other suppliers.

Here you can see another equivalent way of expressing an SQL join query using the INNER JOIN keyword. Both queries Q26 and Q27 give identical results.

```
Q27: SELECT R.SUPNR, R.SUPNAME, R.SUPSTATUS, S.PRODNR, S.PURCHASE_PRICE
   FROM SUPPLIER AS R INNER JOIN SUPPLIES AS S
   ON (R.SUPNR = S.SUPNR)
```

It is also possible to join data from more than two tables. Assume we are interested in the following: for each supplier with outstanding purchase orders, retrieve supplier number and name, together with the purchase order numbers, their date, and the product numbers, names, and quantities specified in these purchase orders. We can again start by listing all the tables needed. We now need data from four tables: SUPPLIER, PRODUCT, PURCHASE_ORDER, and PO_LINE. We need to use the primary–foreign key relationships to specify our join conditions to ensure that correct matches are made. Our SQL join query becomes:

```
Q28: SELECT R.SUPNR, R.SUPNAME, PO.PONR, PO.PODATE, P.PRODNR,
   P.PRODNAME, POL.QUANTITY
   FROM SUPPLIER R, PURCHASE_ORDER PO, PO_LINE POL, PRODUCT P
   WHERE (R.SUPNR = PO.SUPNR)
   AND (PO.PONR = POL.PONR)
   AND (POL.PRODNR = P.PRODNR)
```

Again, note the shorthand notation that we use to refer to the tables. The WHERE clause specifies all the join conditions. It should be noted that since data from four tables need to be joined, this query is very resource-intensive. The result is displayed in Figure 7.34.

In SQL, it is possible to join rows that refer to the same table twice. In this case, we need to declare alternative table names, called aliases. The join condition is then meant to join the table with

| R.SUPNR | R.SUPNAME | PO.PONR | PO.PODATE | P.PRODNR | P.PRODNAME | POL.QUANTITY |
|---|---|---|---|---|---|---|
| 37 | Ad Fundum | 1511 | 2015-03-24 | 0212 | Billecart-Salmon, Brut Réserve, 2014 | 2 |
| 37 | Ad Fundum | 1511 | 2015-03-24 | 0345 | Vascosassetti, Brunello di Montalcino, 2004 | 4 |
| 37 | Ad Fundum | 1511 | 2015-03-24 | 0783 | Clos D'Opleeuw, Chardonnay, 2012 | 1 |
| 37 | Ad Fundum | 1511 | 2015-03-24 | 0856 | Domaine Chandon de Briailles, Savigny-Les-Beaune, 2006 | 9 |
| 94 | The Wine Crate | 1512 | 2015-04-10 | 0178 | Meerdael, Methode Traditionnelle Chardonnay, 2014 | 3 |
| ... | | | | | | |

**Figure 7.34** Result of Q28.

| SUPNR | SUPNAME | SUPADDRESS | SUPCITY | SUPSTATUS |
|---|---|---|---|---|
| 21 | Deliwines | 240, Avenue of the Americas | New York | 20 |
| 32 | Best Wines | 660, Market Street | San Francisco | 90 |
| 37 | Ad Fundum | 82, Wacker Drive | Chicago | 95 |
| 52 | Spirits & Co. | 928, Strip | Las Vegas | NULL |
| 68 | The Wine Depot | 132, Montgomery Street | San Francisco | 10 |
| 69 | Vinos del Mundo | 4, Collins Avenue | Miami | 92 |

**Figure 7.35** Example tuples from the SUPPLIER table.

| SUPNAME | SUPNAME | SUPCITY |
|---|---|---|
| Best Wines | The Wine Depot | San Francisco |

**Figure 7.36** Result of Q29.

itself by matching the tuples that satisfy the join condition. Suppose we want to retrieve all pairs of suppliers who are located in the same city. We need data from only one table: SUPPLIER. However, we need to join this table with itself to solve the question. The SQL query becomes:

```
Q29: SELECT R1.SUPNAME, R2.SUPNAME, R1.SUPCITY
   FROM SUPPLIER R1, SUPPLIER R2
   WHERE R1.SUPCITY = R2.SUPCITY
   AND (R1.SUPNR < R2.SUPNR)
```

Note that we introduced two aliases, R1 and R2, to refer to the SUPPLIER table. The join condition is now based upon matching SUPCITY. However, there is another condition added: R1.SUPNR < R2.SUPNR. What would be the rationale for this?

Figure 7.35 shows a dump of the SUPPLIER table, which is the same for both R1 and R2. If we omit the condition R1.SUPNR < R2.SUPNR, then the query result will also include duplicates such as: Deliwines, Deliwines; Best Wines, Best Wines; Ad Fundum, Ad Fundum; Best Wines, The Wine Depot; The Wine Depot, Best Wines, etc., because these have matching values for SUPCITY. To filter out these meaningless duplicates, we added the condition R1.SUPNR < R2.SUPNR. Only one result remains then: Best Wines (whose SUPNR is 32) and The Wine Depot (whose SUPNR is 68), which are both located in San Francisco (see Figure 7.36).

Any condition can be added to the join condition. Suppose we want to select the names of all suppliers who can supply product number 0899. We need data from two tables, SUPPLIER and SUPPLIES, which should again be joined. The SQL query becomes:

```
Q30: SELECT R.SUPNAME
   FROM SUPPLIER R, SUPPLIES S
   WHERE R.SUPNR = S.SUPNR
   AND S.PRODNR = '0899'
```

| SUPNAME |
|---|
| DeliWines |
| DeliWines |
| DeliWines |
| The Wine Depot |

**Figure 7.37** Result of Q31 without DISTINCT option.

| SUPNAME |
|---|
| DeliWines |
| The Wine Depot |

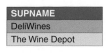

**Figure 7.38** Result of Q31 with DISTINCT option.

The result of it is The Wine Crate.

Remember, the result of an SQL query is a multiset, which may contain duplicates. If we want to eliminate duplicates from the result, we can use the keyword DISTINCT. Assume the following request: Retrieve the names of all the suppliers who can supply at least one type of rose wine. To answer this question, we need data from three tables: SUPPLIER, SUPPLIES, and PRODUCT. In some cases, a supplier can supply more than one type of rose wine, and may appear multiple times in the result. This can be avoided by using the DISTINCT option, as in the following query:

```
Q31: SELECT DISTINCT R.SUPNAME
   FROM SUPPLIER R, SUPPLIES S, PRODUCT P
   WHERE S.SUPNR = R.SUPNR
   AND S.PRODNR = P.PRODNR
   AND P.PRODTYPE = 'ROSE'
```

You can see the result of the same query both without (Figure 7.37) and with (Figure 7.38) a DISTINCT option. Since Deliwines supplies multiple rose wines, it appears multiple times in the result of the first query.

A join condition can also be combined with any of the earlier SQL constructs we discussed. This allows for the building of very powerful SQL queries answering complex business questions. Let's consider the following example: find the product number, name, and total ordered quantity for each product that is specified in a purchase order. We need data from two tables: PRODUCT and PO_LINE. The SQL query becomes:

```
Q32: SELECT P.PRODNR, P.PRODNAME, SUM(POL.QUANTITY)
   FROM PRODUCT P, PO_LINE POL
   WHERE P.PRODNR = POL.PRODNR
   GROUP BY P.PRODNR
```

This query first joins both tables based upon corresponding product number. The GROUP BY clause then groups the join result by corresponding product number. For each group, the product number, product name, and sum of the order line quantity are reported. You can see the result in Figure 7.39.

### *Outer Joins*

The joins we have covered thus far are all examples of inner joins. This means that we always require an exact match before a tuple can be reported in the output. An outer join can be used when we want to keep all the tuples of one or both tables in the result of the JOIN, regardless of whether or

| PRODNR | PRODNAME | SUM(POL.QUANTITY) |
|---|---|---|
| 0178 | Meerdael, Methode Traditionnelle Chardonnay, 2014 | 9 |
| 0185 | Chateau Petrus, 1975 | 2 |
| 0212 | Billecart-Salmon, Brut Réserve, 2014 | 23 |
| 0295 | Chateau Pape Clement, Pessac-Léognan, 2001 | 9 |
| 0306 | Chateau Coupe Roses, Granaxa, 2011 | 11 |
| ... | | |

**Figure 7.39** Result of Q32.

| SUPNR | SUPNAME | SUPADDRESS | SUPCITY | SUPSTATUS |
|---|---|---|---|---|
| 68 | The Wine Depot | | | |
| 21 | Deliwines | | | |
| 94 | The Wine Crate | | | |
| ... | | | | |

**Figure 7.40** Example tuples from SUPPLIER table.

| *SUPNR* | *PRODNR* | PURCHASE_PRICE | DELIV_PERIOD |
|---|---|---|---|
| 21 | 0119 | 15.99 | 1 |
| 21 | 0289 | 17.99 | 1 |
| 68 | 0178 | 17.99 | 5 |
| ... | | | |

**Figure 7.41** Example tuples from SUPPLIES table.

| R.SUPNR | R.SUPNAME | R.SUPSTATUS | S.PRODNR | S.PURCHASE_PRICE |
|---|---|---|---|---|
| 21 | Deliwines | 20 | 0119 | 15.99 |
| 21 | Deliwines | 20 | 0178 | NULL |
| ... | | | | |
| 37 | Ad Fundum | 95 | 0795 | 20.99 |
| **52** | **Spirits & Co.** | **NULL** | **NULL** | **NULL** |
| 68 | The Wine Depot | 10 | 0178 | 17.99 |
| ... | | | | |

**Figure 7.42** Result of Q33.

not they have matching tuples in the other table. Three types of outer joins exist; a **left outer join**, a **right outer join**, and a **full outer join**. Let's work out some examples.

In a left outer join, each row from the left table is kept in the result; if no match is found in the other table it will return NULL values for these columns. Consider the following example: retrieve number, name, and status of all suppliers, and, if applicable, include number and price of the products they can supply. In other words, we want the information of all the suppliers, even if they cannot supply any products at all. This can be solved using an outer join between the SUPPLIER and SUPPLIES table as follows:

```
Q33: SELECT R.SUPNR, R.SUPNAME, R.SUPSTATUS, S.PRODNR, S.PURCHASE_PRICE
   FROM SUPPLIER AS R LEFT OUTER JOIN SUPPLIES AS S
   ON (R.SUPNR = S.SUPNR)
```

The LEFT OUTER JOIN clause indicates that all tuples from the SUPPLIER table should be included in the result, even if no matches can be found in the SUPPLIES table. Figures 7.40 and 7.41 illustrate some example tuples from both the SUPPLIER and SUPPLIES table. The result of the OUTER JOIN query is displayed in Figure 7.42.

Note the tuple in bold face. This is supplier number 52, Spirits & Co. This supplier has no corresponding SUPPLIES tuples. It could be a new supplier for which no supplies have yet been entered in the database. Because of the LEFT OUTER JOIN clause, this supplier is now appearing in the end result with NULL values for the missing columns of the SUPPLIES table.

In a right outer join, each row from the right table is kept in the result, completed with NULL values if necessary. Assume we have the following request: select all product numbers, together with the product name and total ordered quantity, even if there are currently no outstanding orders for a product. This can be answered using a RIGHT OUTER JOIN between the tables PRODUCT and PO_LINE. The SQL query becomes:

```
Q34: SELECT P.PRODNR, P.PRODNAME, SUM(POL.QUANTITY) AS SUM
   FROM PO_LINE AS POL RIGHT OUTER JOIN PRODUCT AS P
   ON (POL.PRODNR = P.PRODNR)
   GROUP BY P.PRODNR
```

The PO_LINE and PRODUCT table are joined using a right outer join based on product number. This means that all products will be included, even if they are not included in any purchase order line. Next, the GROUP BY clause will make groups in this join table. For each group, the product number, product name, and sum of the quantity will be reported. You can see the result of this in Figure 7.43. Note that for product number 0119, which is Chateau Miraval, the quantity is NULL. Also for product numbers 154, 199, and 0289, the quantity is NULL. These are now included in the end result because of the outer join.

Finally, in a FULL OUTER JOIN each row of both tables is kept in the result, if necessary completed with NULL values.

### 7.3.1.6 Nested Queries

SQL queries can also be **nested**. In other words, complete SELECT FROM blocks can appear in the WHERE clause of another query as illustrated in Figure 7.44. The subquery, or inner block, is nested in the outer block. Multiple levels of nesting are allowed. Typically, the query optimizer starts by executing the query in the lowest-level inner block. Subqueries try to solve queries in a step-by-step, sequential way.

| P.PRODNR | P.PRODNAME | SUM |
|---|---|---|
| 0119 | Chateau Miraval, Cotes de Provence Rose, 2015 | NULL |
| 0154 | Chateau Haut Brion, 2008 | NULL |
| 0178 | Meerdael, Methode Traditionnelle Chardonnay, 2014 | 9 |
| 0185 | Chateau Petrus, 1975 | 2 |
| 0199 | Jacques Selosse, Brut Initial, 2012 | NULL |
| 0212 | Billecart-Salmon, Brut Réserve, 2014 | 23 |
| … | | |

**Figure 7.43** Result of Q34.

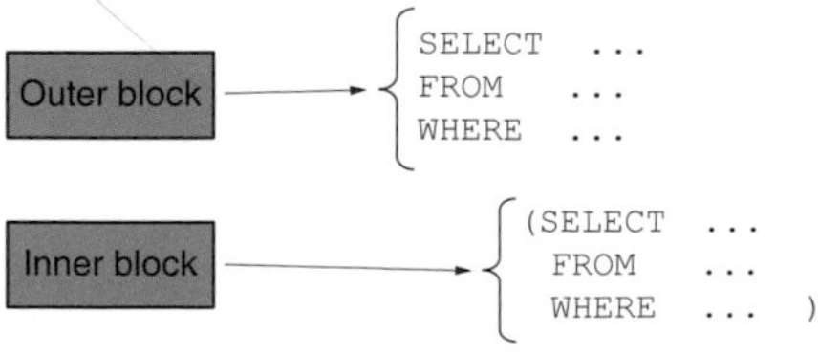


**Figure 7.44** Nesting SQL queries.

Let's work out some examples. Assume we want to find the name of the supplier with whom purchase order number 1560 is placed. We need data from two tables: SUPPLIER and PURCHASE_ORDER. We can now formulate a nested SQL query as follows:

```
Q34: SELECT SUPNAME
            FROM SUPPLIER
            WHERE SUPNR =
                  (SELECT SUPNR
                   FROM PURCHASE_ORDER
                   WHERE PONR = '1560')
```

To solve this query, the query optimizer first solves the inner block, which is:

```
SELECT SUPNR
FROM PURCHASE_ORDER
WHERE PONR = '1560'
```

The result of this inner block is 32, which is a scalar. That's why this is sometimes also referred to as a scalar subquery. We can now solve the outer block query, which becomes:

```
SELECT SUPNAME
FROM SUPPLIER
WHERE SUPNR = 32
```

The result of this query is Best Wines. Note that this query can also be solved using an inner join, as discussed before.

Consider the following example: retrieve product number and name for each product that exceeds the available quantity of product 0178. We only need one table to solve this question: PRODUCT. The nested SQL query becomes:

```
Q35: SELECT PRODNR, PRODNAME
            FROM PRODUCT
            WHERE AVAILABLE_QUANTITY >
                  (SELECT AVAILABLE_QUANTITY
                   FROM PRODUCT
                   WHERE PRODNR = '0178')
```

Again, the inner block is solved first:

```
SELECT AVAILABLE_QUANTITY
FROM PRODUCT
WHERE PRODNR = '0178'
```

This is again a scalar subquery resulting in the scalar 136. The outer block now becomes:

```
SELECT PRODNR, PRODNAME
FROM PRODUCT
WHERE AVAILABLE_QUANTITY > 136
```

You can see the result of Q35 in Figure 7.45.

The WHERE component of an outer SELECT block can contain an IN operator, followed by a new inner SELECT block. Let's say you want to

**Connections**

Although the query results will be the same, the performance of different query types such as join queries or nested queries will depend, among other things, on the internal data model, the characteristics of the data (e.g., the number of rows in a table) and the availability of physical constructs such as indexes. Chapters 12 and 13 provide details on the interplay between physical database organization and query performance.

| PRODNR | PRODNAME |
|---|---|
| 0212 | Billecart-Salmon, Brut Réserve, 2014 |
| 0347 | Chateau Corbin-Despagne, Saint-Emilion, 2005 |
| 0474 | Chateau De La Tour, Clos-Vougeot, Grand cru, 2008 |
| 0885 | Chateau Margaux, Grand Cru Classé, 1956 |
| 0899 | Trimbach, Riesling, 1989 |

**Figure 7.45** Result of Q35.

| SUPNAME |
|---|
| Deliwines |
| Ad Fundum |
| The Wine Depot |
| Vinos del Mundo |
| The Wine Crate |

**Figure 7.46** Result of Q36.

retrieve all supplier names who can supply product 0178. To solve this, we need data from the SUPPLIER and SUPPLIES table. The nested SQL query becomes:

```
Q36: SELECT SUPNAME
     FROM SUPPLIER
     WHERE SUPNR IN
          (SELECT SUPNR
           FROM SUPPLIES
           WHERE PRODNR ='0178')
```

Again, the inner block is solved first, which is:

```
SELECT SUPNR
FROM SUPPLIES
WHERE PRODNR ='0178'
```

The result of this inner block is no longer a scalar, but a multiset of values: 21, 37, 68, 69, and 94. The outer block can then be evaluated, which now becomes:

```
SELECT SUPNAME
FROM SUPPLIER
WHERE SUPNR IN (21, 37, 68, 69, 94)
```

This query results in the supplier names depicted in Figure 7.46.

As already mentioned, multiple levels of nesting are allowed. Assume we want to retrieve the names of all suppliers who can supply at least one type of rose wine. This can be solved using a query with two subqueries:

```
Q37: SELECT SUPNAME
     FROM SUPPLIER
     WHERE SUPNR IN
          (SELECT SUPNR
           FROM SUPPLIES
           WHERE PRODNR IN
                (SELECT PRODNR
                 FROM PRODUCT
                 WHERE PRODTYPE = 'ROSE'))
```

To execute this query, the RDBMS starts at the lowest level of nesting, so it first solves the subquery:

```
SELECT PRODNR
FROM PRODUCT
WHERE PRODTYPE = 'ROSE'
```

This results in the values 0119, 0289, and 0668, which are the product numbers of rose wines. The second subquery becomes:

```
SELECT SUPNR
FROM SUPPLIES
WHERE PRODNR IN (0119, 0289, 0668)
```

The result of this subquery is 21, 21, 21, and 68. Finally, the outer block can be processed, which results in Deliwines and The Wine Depot. Note that this query can also be solved using an inner join across the tables SUPPLIER, SUPPLIES, and PRODUCT.

Here is another example of a nested query. We are interested in finding the product names that supplier number 32 as well as supplier number 84 can supply. To solve this query, we need information from both the PRODUCT and SUPPLIES table. The nested SQL query becomes:

```
Q38: SELECT PRODNAME
   FROM PRODUCT
   WHERE PRODNR IN
     (SELECT PRODNR
     FROM SUPPLIES
     WHERE SUPNR = '32')
  AND PRODNR IN
     (SELECT PRODNR
     FROM SUPPLIES
     WHERE SUPNR = '84')
```

We now have two subqueries at the same level. If the computing architecture supports it, both subqueries can be executed in parallel, which allows us to speed up query execution. The result of the first subquery is 0154, 0474, 0494, 0657, 0760, and 0832. The result of the second subquery is 0185, 0300, 0306, 0347, 0468, 0494, 0832, and 0915. Since the results of both subqueries are combined using a Boolean AND operator, only the numbers 0494 and 0832 remain, which correspond to product names “Veuve-Cliquot, Brut, 2012” and “Conde de Hervías, Rioja, 2004”, respectively.

#### 7.3.1.7 Correlated Queries

In all previous cases, the nested subquery in the inner select block could be entirely solved before processing the outer select block. This is no longer the case for **correlated nested queries**. Whenever a condition in the WHERE clause of a nested query references some column of a table declared in the outer query, the two queries are said to be correlated. The nested query is then evaluated once for each tuple (or combination of tuples) in the outer query. Let’s give some examples.

Assume we want to retrieve the product numbers of all products with at least two orders. This is a very simple request at first sight. We need data from two tables: PRODUCT and PO_LINE. The question can be solved using the following correlated SQL query:

```
Q39: SELECT P.PRODNR
     FROM PRODUCT P
          WHERE 1 <
               (SELECT COUNT(*)
               FROM PO_LINE POL
               WHERE P.PRODNR = POL.PRODNR)
```

As previously, the RDBMS starts by evaluating the inner select block first, which reads:

```
SELECT COUNT(*)
FROM PO_LINE POL
WHERE P.PRODNR = POL.PRODNR
```

This is an example of a correlated query, because the inner block refers to table P, which is declared in the outer block. Hence, this subquery cannot be processed, because the variable P and thus P.PRODNR are not known here. To solve this correlated query the RDBMS iterates through each product tuple of the PRODUCT table declared in the outer block and evaluates the subquery for the given tuple each time. Let's give an example.

Figure 7.47 shows some example tuples from the PRODUCT table. Remember, the tuples in a table are not ordered. The first product has product number 0212. The subquery is now evaluated with this product number. In other words, it becomes:

```
SELECT COUNT(*)
FROM PO_LINE POL
WHERE 0212 = POL.PRODNR
```

The result of this subquery is 3, as you can see in the PO_LINE table (Figure 7.48). Since 3 is bigger than 1, the product number 0212 will be reported in the output. This process is then repeated for all other product numbers, resulting in product numbers 0212, 0977, 0900, 0306, 0783, 0668, 0766, and 0178 as the output of Q39. Basically, a correlated SQL query implements a looping

| PRODNR | PRODNAME |
|---|---|
| 0212 | Billecart-Salmon, Brut Réserve, 2014 |
| 0289 | Chateau Saint Estève de Neri, 2015 |
| 0154 | Chateau Haut Brion, 2008 |
| 0295 | Chateau Pape Clement, Pessac-Léognan, 2001 |
| ... | |

**Figure 7.47** Example tuples from the PRODUCT table.

| PONR | PRODNR | QUANTITY |
|---|---|---|
| ... | | |
| 1511 | 0212 | 2 |
| ... | | |
| 1538 | 0212 | 15 |
| ... | | |
| 1577 | 0212 | 6 |
| ... | | |

**Figure 7.48** Example tuples from the PO_LINE table.

mechanism, looping through the subquery for each tuple of the table defined in the outer query block.

Correlated queries can answer very complex requests such as the following: retrieve number and name of all the suppliers who can supply a product at a price lower than the average price of that product, together with the number and name of the product, the purchase price, and the delivery period. The query needs information from three tables: SUPPLIER, SUPPLIES, and PRODUCT:

```
Q40: SELECT R.SUPNR, R.SUPNAME, P.PRODNR, P.PRODNAME, S1.PURCHASE_PRICE,
  S1.DELIV_PERIOD
  FROM SUPPLIER R, SUPPLIES S1, PRODUCT P
  WHERE R.SUPNR = S1.SUPNR
     AND S1.PRODNR = P.PRODNR
     AND S1.PURCHASE_PRICE <
            (SELECT AVG(PURCHASE_PRICE)
            FROM SUPPLIES S2
            WHERE P.PRODNR = S2.PRODNR)
```

The first part of Q40 starts by specifying the join conditions using the primary–foreign key relationships. The second part then ensures that the price of the product is lower than the average price charged by all suppliers for the same product using a correlated subquery referring to the PRODUCT table P defined in the outer SELECT block. It is thus evaluated for every product tuple separately.

Figure 7.49 shows a visual representation of the query's functioning. Note that we use two appearances of the SUPPLIES table: S1 in the outer block and S2 in the correlated inner block. You can see that product number 0178 can be supplied by supplier number 37 at a price of 16.99, which is clearly lower than the average of all prices charged by suppliers for product number 0178.

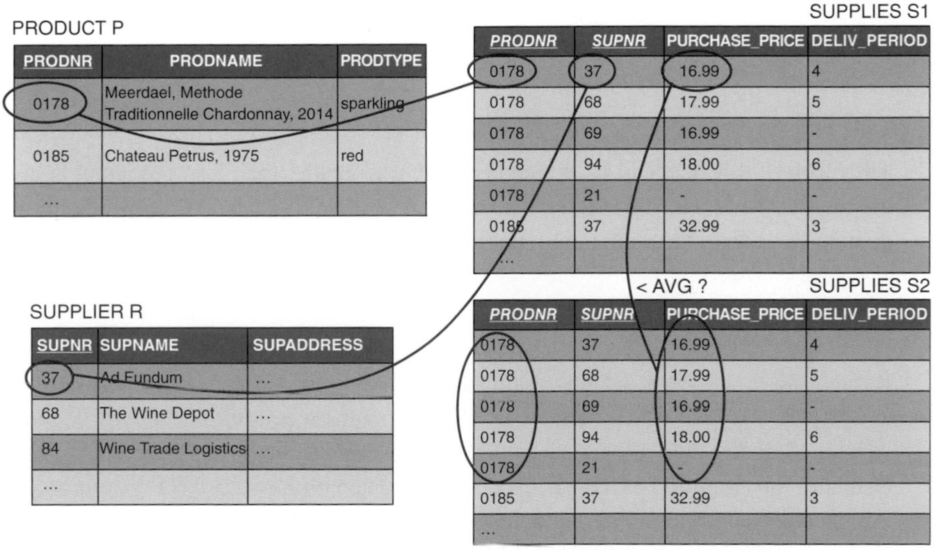


**Figure 7.49** Illustrating Q40.

| P1.PRODNR | Result of Inner Query block | < 3? | Output |
|---|---|---|---|
| 0119 | 41 | No | No |
| 0154 | 40 | No | No |
| 0178 | 39 | No | No |
| ... | ... | ... | ... |
| 0899 | 3 | No | No |
| 0900 | 2 | Yes | Yes |
| 0915 | 1 | Yes | Yes |
| 0977 | 0 | Yes | Yes |

**Figure 7.50** Illustrating Q41.

Let's now assume we are interested in finding the three highest product numbers. This can be easily accomplished using an ORDER BY clause, but that will list all product numbers, which may not be very useful if you have many products. A correlated query can provide a better solution:

```
Q41: SELECT P1.PRODNR
     FROM PRODUCT P1
     WHERE 3 >
                 (SELECT COUNT(*)
                 FROM PRODUCT P2
                 WHERE P1.PRODNR < P2.PRODNR)
```

Essentially, this query counts for each product the number of products with a higher product number. If this number is strictly smaller than three, the product number belongs to the three highest product numbers and will be reported. Put differently, there is no product with a product number higher than the highest product number. There is only one product number which is higher than the second highest product number, and two product numbers which are higher than the third highest product number. The results of this correlated query are the product numbers 0915, 0977, and 0900.

Figure 7.50 illustrates the functioning of Q41. The inner query block is evaluated for each product number separately. For product number 0119, which happens to be the smallest product number, the inner query becomes:

```
SELECT COUNT(*)
FROM PRODUCT P2
WHERE 0119 < P2.PRODNR
```

The result of this query is 41, which is clearly not smaller than 3 so no output is given. For product numbers 0900, 0915, and 0977, the inner block will yield 2, 1, and 0, respectively, which are all less than 3. Therefore, these product numbers will be output.

#### 7.3.1.8 Queries with ALL/ANY

Besides the IN operator, which we already discussed, the **ANY** and **ALL** operators can also be used to compare a single value to a multiset. The comparison condition v > ALL V returns TRUE if the value v is greater than all the values in the multiset V. If the nested query does not return a value, it evaluates the condition as TRUE. The comparison condition v > ANY V returns TRUE if the value v is greater than at least one value in the multiset V. If the nested query does not return a value, it evaluates the whole condition as FALSE. Note that the comparison condition = ANY(...) is hence equivalent to using the IN operator.

Consider the following example: retrieve the names of the suppliers who charge the highest price for the product with product number 0668. This query needs information from both the SUPPLIER and SUPPLIES table. It can be solved using a nested query with the ALL operator as follows:

```
Q42: SELECT SUPNAME
   FROM SUPPLIER
   WHERE SUPNR IN
      (SELECT SUPNR
      FROM SUPPLIES
      WHERE PRODNR = '0668'
       AND PURCHASE_PRICE >= ALL
          (SELECT PURCHASE_PRICE
          FROM SUPPLIES
          WHERE PRODNR = '0668'))
```

The query has two levels of nesting. First, we start with the deepest level of nesting and execute the subquery:

```
SELECT PURCHASE_PRICE
FROM SUPPLIES
WHERE PRODNR = '0668'
```

The results of this subquery are the prices 6.00 and 6.99. The next subquery then becomes:

```
SELECT SUPNR
FROM SUPPLIES
WHERE PRODNR = '0668'
AND PURCHASE_PRICE >= ALL (6.00, 6.99)
```

The result of this subquery is 68. We can now finally evaluate the outer SELECT block, which becomes:

```
SELECT SUPNAME
FROM SUPPLIER
WHERE SUPNR IN (68)
```

The result will then be The Wine Depot.

Figure 7.51 visualizes the functioning of Q42. You can see that The Wine Depot, which is supplier number 68, can supply product number 0668 at a price of 6.99, which is higher than or equal to all other prices – in this case 6.99 and 6.00.

Assume we are interested in the following information: retrieve number, name, city, and status for each supplier who has the highest status of all the suppliers located in the same city. The SQL query becomes:

```
Q43: SELECT R1.SUPNR, R1.SUPNAME, R1.SUPCITY, R1.SUPSTATUS
   FROM SUPPLIER R1
   WHERE R1.SUPSTATUS >= ALL
      (SELECT R2.SUPSTATUS
       FROM SUPPLIER R2
       WHERE R1.SUPCITY = R2.SUPCITY)
```

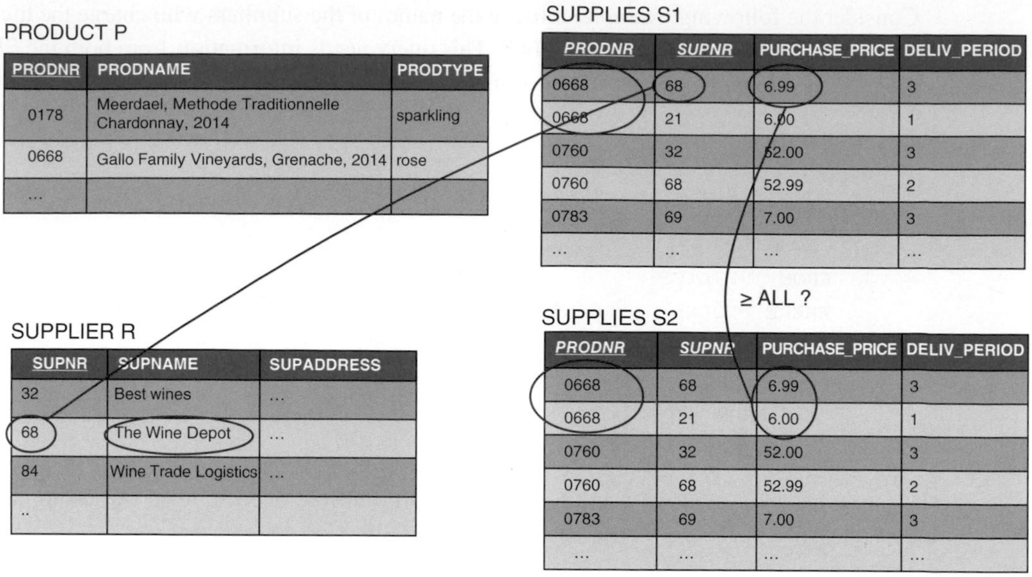


**Figure 7.51** Functioning of Q42.

| SUPNR | SUPNAME | SUPCITY | SUPSTATUS |
|---|---|---|---|
| 21 | Deliwines | New York | 20 |
| 32 | Best Wines | San Francisco | 90 |
| 37 | Ad Fundum | Chicago | 95 |
| 69 | Vinos del Mundo | Miami | 92 |
| 84 | Wine Trade Logistics | Washington | 92 |
| 94 | The Wine Crate | Dallas | 75 |

**Figure 7.52** Result of Q43.

This is an example of the ALL operator in combination with a correlated query. It is quite self-explanatory, since it selects the supplier number, name, city, and status of a supplier R1 where the status is higher than or equal to the status of all suppliers R2 which are located in the same city as supplier R1. The result is displayed in Figure 7.52.

Let's now also illustrate the ANY operator. Suppose we want to retrieve the names of the suppliers who do not charge the lowest price for product number 0178. This can be solved with the following SQL query:

```
Q44: SELECT SUPNAME
    FROM SUPPLIER
    WHERE SUPNR IN
             (SELECT SUPNR
              FROM SUPPLIES
              WHERE PRODNR = '0178' AND PURCHASE_PRICE > ANY
                    (SELECT PURCHASE_PRICE
                     FROM SUPPLIES
                     WHERE PRODNR = '0178'))
```

This is a double nested query and we can start again with the lowest-level subquery, which is:

```
SELECT PURCHASE_PRICE
FROM SUPPLIES
WHERE PRODNR = '0178'
```

The answer to this subquery is the multiset with elements NULL, 16.99, 17.99, 16.99, and 18.00. The next subquery then becomes:

```
SELECT SUPNR
FROM SUPPLIES
WHERE PRODNR = '0178' AND
PURCHASE_PRICE > ANY (NULL, 16.99, 17.99, 16.99, 18.00)
```

The ANY operator returns TRUE if the purchase price is greater than at least one value in the multiset. The result of this query then becomes 68 and 94. The outer SELECT block can now be run, which gives the supplier names The Wine Depot and The Wine Crate.

#### 7.3.1.9 Queries with EXISTS

The EXISTS function is another handy feature in SQL. It allows us to check whether the result of a correlated nested query is empty or not. The result is a Boolean value: TRUE or FALSE. In general, EXISTS returns TRUE if there is at least one tuple in the result of the nested query, or otherwise returns FALSE. Vice versa, the NOT EXISTS function returns TRUE if there are no tuples in the result of the nested query, or otherwise returns FALSE. Because the EXISTS function only evaluates whether or not a nested query outputs any rows, it is unimportant what is specified in the SELECT component. Hence, one commonly uses SELECT * for the subquery.

Consider the following example: retrieve the names of the suppliers who can supply product number 0178. This can be easily solved by using either a join or nested subquery as we discussed before. Here we present a third alternative using the EXISTS function as follows:

```
Q44: SELECT SUPNAME
   FROM SUPPLIER R
   WHERE EXISTS
      (SELECT *
      FROM SUPPLIES S
      WHERE R.SUPNR = S.SUPNR
      AND S.PRODNR = '0178')
```

You can clearly see that the subquery is correlated, as it refers to the SUPPLIER table R defined in the outer select block. For each supplier, the correlated subquery is evaluated. As soon as it returns a result, the EXISTS function will evaluate to TRUE, and the supplier name will be reported. You can see the result of this query displayed in Figure 7.53.

The EXISTS function allows for complex requests such as the following: retrieve name, address, and city for each supplier who can supply all products. This question can be solved using a double correlated query with two NOT EXISTS functions as follows:

| SUPNAME |
|---|
| Deliwines |
| Ad Fundum |
| The Wine Depot |
| Vinos del Mundo |
| The Wine Crate |

**Figure 7.53** Result of Q44.

```
Q45: SELECT SUPNAME, SUPADDRESS, SUPCITY
    FROM SUPPLIER R
    WHERE NOT EXISTS
            (SELECT *
             FROM PRODUCT P
             WHERE NOT EXISTS
                  (SELECT *
                   FROM SUPPLIES S
                   WHERE R.SUPNR = S.SUPNR
                   AND P.PRODNR = S.PRODNR))
```

This query looks for all suppliers for whom there exist no products they cannot supply. Remember, the NOT EXISTS function evaluates to TRUE if the subquery does not return a result. This query starts from a specific supplier and then looks for all products that the supplier cannot supply. If there are no products the supplier cannot supply, then it means that he/she can supply all products and the supplier name will be reported. In our example, this query returns zero rows as there are no suppliers who can supply all products.

#### 7.3.1.10 Queries with Subqueries in SELECT/FROM

Besides the WHERE component, subqueries can also appear in the SELECT or FROM component. Assume that we want to retrieve the product number, name, and total ordered quantity of each product, even if a product has no outstanding orders. We have solved this earlier using an outer join. An alternative is the following query:

```
Q46: SELECT P.PRODNR, P.PRODNAME,
    (SELECT SUM(QUANTITY) FROM PO_LINE POL
    WHERE P.PRODNR = POL.PRODNR) AS TOTALORDERED
    FROM PRODUCT P
```

In this query, we have a subquery in the SELECT component. This subquery results in a scalar representing the total ordered quantity for a specific product. As with the outer join, if no match can be found in the PO_LINE table, a NULL value will be generated for the SUM (QUANTITY) expression. This is the case for product number 0523, as you can see in Figure 7.54.

Subqueries can also appear in the FROM component. Consider the following example: retrieve all numbers of products where the difference between the maximum and minimum price is strictly bigger than 1. This can be solved as follows:

| PRODNR | PRODNAME | TOTALORDERED |
|---|---|---|
| 0212 | Billecart-Salmon, Brut Réserve, 2014 | 23 |
| 0795 | Casa Silva, Los Lingues, Carmenere, 2012 | 3 |
| 0915 | Champagne Boizel, Brut, Réserve, 2010 | 13 |
| 0523 | Chateau Andron Blanquet, Saint Estephe, 1979 | NULL |
| 0977 | Chateau Batailley, Grand Cru Classé, 1975 | 11 |
| ... | | |

**Figure 7.54** Result of Q46.

| PRODNR | MINPRICE | MAXPRICE |
|---|---|---|
| 0178 | 16.99 | 18.00 |
| 0199 | 30.99 | 32.00 |
| 0300 | 19.00 | 21.00 |
| 0347 | 16.00 | 18.00 |
| 0468 | 14.00 | 15.99 |

**Figure 7.55** Result of Q47.

```
Q47: SELECT M.PRODNR, M.MINPRICE, M.MAXPRICE FROM
     (SELECT PRODNR, MIN(PURCHASE_PRICE) AS MINPRICE,
     MAX(PURCHASE_PRICE) AS MAXPRICE
     FROM SUPPLIES GROUP BY PRODNR) AS M
     WHERE M.MAXPRICE-M.MINPRICE > 1
```

You can see that the FROM component has a table subquery which calculates the minimum and maximum price for each product. It uses a GROUP BY clause to accomplish this. The subquery assigns the aliases MINPRICE and MAXPRICE to the corresponding columns, and the alias M to the overall result. These can then be used in the outer query as you can see illustrated. The result of this query is given in Figure 7.55.

#### 7.3.1.11 Queries with Set Operations

Standard SQL also supports set operations such as UNION, INTERSECT, and EXCEPT to combine the results of multiple SELECT blocks. Let's first refresh how these set operations work. Consider the following two sets, A and B:

A = {10, 5, 25, 30, 45}
B = {15, 20, 10, 30, 50}

The result of A UNION B is the set of all values that are either in A or in B, or in other words {5, 10, 15, 20, 25, 30, 45, 50}. The result of A INTERSECT B is the set of all values that are in A and B, or in other words {10, 30}. The result of A EXCEPT B is the set of all values that are in A but not in B, or in other words {5, 25, 45}. Hence, when applied to an SQL query, the result of the UNION operation is a table that includes all tuples that are in one of the SELECT blocks, or both. The result of the INTERSECT operation is a table that includes all tuples that are in both SELECT blocks. The result of the EXCEPT operation is a table that includes all tuples that are in the first SELECT block but not in the second. Duplicate tuples are by default eliminated from the result, unless the ALL operator is added.

It is important to highlight that when using the UNION, INTERSECT, or EXCEPT operation, all SELECT statements must be *union compatible*, i.e., they should select the same number of attribute types and the corresponding attribute types should have compatible domains. Note that not all commercial RDBMSs support these set operations.

| SUPNR | SUPNAME |
|---|---|
| 21 | Deliwines |
| 84 | Wine Trade Logistics |

**Figure 7.56** Result of Q48.

Consider the following example: retrieve number and name of suppliers who are located in New York or who can supply product number 0915. This query can be solved as follows:

```
Q48: SELECT SUPNR, SUPNAME
   FROM SUPPLIER
   WHERE SUPCITY = 'New York'
   UNION
   SELECT R.SUPNR, R.SUPNAME
   FROM SUPPLIER R, SUPPLIES S
   WHERE R.SUPNR = S.SUPNR
   AND S.PRODNR = '0915'
   ORDER BY SUPNAME ASC
```

Observe how the results of both queries are combined using the UNION operator. To successfully accomplish this, both SELECT blocks should be union compatible in the sense that they ask for the same columns (e.g., SUPNR, SUPNAME and R.SUPNR, R.SUPNAME). The result is also sorted by supplier name by adding an ORDER BY clause to the end of the last SELECT block. The result is given in Figure 7.56.

Assume that we change the query as follows: retrieve number and name of suppliers who are located in New York and who can supply product number 0915. Both SELECT blocks remain the same as you can see illustrated, but are now combined with the INTERSECT instead of UNION operation. The result of this query is NULL.

```
Q49: SELECT SUPNR, SUPNAME
   FROM SUPPLIER
   WHERE SUPCITY = 'NEW YORK'
   INTERSECT
   SELECT R.SUPNR, R.SUPNAME
   FROM SUPPLIER R, SUPPLIES S
   WHERE R.SUPNR = S.SUPNR
   AND S.PRODNR = '0915'
   ORDER BY SUPNAME ASC
```

To conclude, consider the following request: retrieve the number of the suppliers who cannot currently supply any product. This can be solved using two SELECT blocks combined with an EXCEPT operation as follows:

```
Q50: SELECT SUPNR
   FROM SUPPLIER
   EXCEPT
   SELECT SUPNR
   FROM SUPPLIES
```

This query selects all supplier numbers which appear in the SUPPLIER table, but not in the SUPPLIES table. The result of Q50 is supplier number 52.

### 7.3.2 SQL INSERT Statement

The SQL INSERT statement adds data to a relational database. The following statement inserts a new tuple into the PRODUCT table:

```
INSERT INTO PRODUCT VALUES
('980', 'Chateau Angelus, Grand Clu Classé, 1960', 'red', 6)
```

The values are entered according to the order in which the columns have been defined using the CREATE TABLE statement. The next statement is equivalent, but also explicitly mentions the column names. This is recommended to avoid any confusion.

```
INSERT INTO PRODUCT(PRODNR, PRODNAME, PRODTYPE, AVAILABLE_QUANTITY) VALUES
('980', 'Chateau Angelus, Grand Clu Classé, 1960', 'red', 6)
```

It is also possible to specify only a few column names as follows:

```
INSERT INTO PRODUCT(PRODNR, PRODNAME, PRODTYPE) VALUES
('980', 'Chateau Angelus, Grand Clu Classé, 1960', 'red')
```

The values for the unspecified columns then become NULL (if NULL is allowed) or the DEFAULT value (if a default value has been defined). In our example, the above INSERT query is equivalent to:

```
INSERT INTO PRODUCT(PRODNR, PRODNAME, PRODTYPE, AVAILABLE_QUANTITY) VALUES
('980', 'Chateau Angelus, Grand Clu Classé, 1960', 'red', NULL)
```

The following statement adds three tuples to the PRODUCT table:

```
INSERT INTO PRODUCT(PRODNR, PRODNAME, PRODTYPE, AVAILABLE_QUANTITY) VALUES
('980', 'Chateau Angelus, Grand Clu Classé, 1960', 'red', 6),
('1000', 'Domaine de la Vougeraie, Bâtard Montrachet', Grand cru, 2010', 'white', 2),
('1002', 'Leeuwin Estate Cabernet Sauvignon 2011', 'white', 20)
```

It is important to respect all constraints defined (NOT NULL, referential integrity, etc.) when adding new tuples to a table. Otherwise, the INSERT will be rejected by the DBMS and an error notification will be generated.

An INSERT statement can also be combined with a subquery. The following example inserts the supplier numbers of all suppliers that cannot supply any products in a new table INACTIVE-SUPPLIERS:

```
INSERT INTO INACTIVE-SUPPLIERS(SUPNR)
SELECT SUPNR
   FROM SUPPLIER
   EXCEPT
   SELECT SUPNR
   FROM SUPPLIES
```

### 7.3.3 SQL DELETE Statement

Data can be removed using the SQL DELETE statement. The following example removes the product tuple with product number 1000 from the PRODUCT table:

```
DELETE FROM PRODUCT
WHERE PRODNR = '1000'
```

The next statement removes all supplier tuples from the SUPPLIER table where the supplier status is NULL:

```
DELETE FROM SUPPLIER
WHERE SUPSTATUS IS NULL
```

The DELETE statement can include subqueries. The following example removes all product numbers from the SUPPLIES table of products that have the string "CHARD" as part of their product name. This will remove the chardonnay wines in the SUPPLIES table.

```
DELETE FROM SUPPLIES
WHERE PRODNR IN (SELECT PRODNR
                 FROM PRODUCT
                 WHERE PRODNAME LIKE '%CHARD%')
```

A DELETE statement can also contain correlated subqueries. This is illustrated in the next example, which removes suppliers from the SUPPLIER table that have no corresponding tuples in the SUPPLIES table:

```
DELETE FROM SUPPLIER R
WHERE NOT EXISTS
      (SELECT PRODNR
       FROM SUPPLIES S
       WHERE R.SUPNR = S.SUPNR)
```

The next example is a self-referencing DELETE. It removes all SUPPLIES tuples where the purchase price is strictly bigger than twice the average purchase price for a specific product:

```
DELETE FROM SUPPLIES S1
WHERE S1.PURCHASE_PRICE >
      (SELECT 2*AVG(S2.PURCHASE_PRICE)
       FROM SUPPLIES S2
       WHERE S1.PRODNR = S2.PRODNR)
```

Removing all tuples from the PRODUCT table can be done as follows:

```
DELETE FROM PRODUCT
```

As discussed before, the removal of tuples should be carefully considered as this may impact other tables in the database. As an example, consider removing a supplier that still has connected SUPPLIES or PURCHASE_ORDER tuples. Earlier we spoke about referential integrity constraints which keep the database in a consistent state in case of removal of one or more referenced tuples. Remember, the ON DELETE CASCADE option cascades the delete operation to the referring tuples, whereas the ON DELETE RESTRICT option prohibits removal of referenced tuples.

### 7.3.4 SQL UPDATE Statement

Modifications to data can be made using the SQL UPDATE statement. The following example sets the available quantity to 26 for product number 0185 in the PRODUCT table:

```
UPDATE PRODUCT
SET AVAILABLE_QUANTITY = 26
WHERE PRODNR = '0185'
```

**Retention Questions**

- Given an example of an SQL query with GROUP BY.
- What is the difference between an inner join and an outer join? Illustrate with an example.
- What are correlated queries? Illustrate with an example.
- What's the difference between the ALL and ANY operator? Illustrate with an example.

The next UPDATE statement sets the supplier status to the default value for all suppliers:

```
UPDATE SUPPLIER
SET SUPSTATUS = DEFAULT
```

UPDATE statements can include subqueries. Suppose we want to add seven days to the delivery period for all supplies of the supplier Deliwines:

```
UPDATE SUPPLIES
SET DELIV_PERIOD = DELIV_PERIOD + 7
WHERE SUPNR IN (SELECT SUPNR
                 FROM SUPPLIER
                 WHERE SUPNAME = 'Deliwines')
```

An UPDATE statement can also contain correlated subqueries. The following UPDATE statement guarantees that supplier number 68 can supply all its products at the minimum price and delivery period.

```
UPDATE SUPPLIES S1
SET (PURCHASE_PRICE, DELIV_PERIOD) =
(SELECT MIN(PURCHASE_PRICE), MIN(DELIV_PERIOD)
FROM SUPPLIES S2
WHERE S1.PRODNR = S2.PRODNR)
WHERE SUPNR = '68'
```

An UPDATE statement can be combined with an ALTER TABLE statement. The ALTER TABLE statement below adds a column SUPCATEGORY with default value Silver to the SUPPLIER table. An UPDATE statement is then used to set the values of this new column. In the case that the supplier status is between 70 and 90, a Gold status is assigned. In the case that it is higher than 90, it is set to Platinum. Note the use of the CASE statement, which allows us to implement if-then-else operations in SQL:

```
ALTER TABLE SUPPLIER ADD SUPCATEGORY VARCHAR(10) DEFAULT 'SILVER'
UPDATE SUPPLIER
SET SUPCATEGORY =
CASE WHEN SUPSTATUS >=70 AND SUPSTATUS <=90 THEN 'GOLD'
WHEN SUPSTATUS >=90 THEN 'PLATINUM'
ELSE 'SILVER'
END
```

The result is shown in Figure 7.57.

| SUPNR | SUPNAME | SUPADDRESS | SUPCITY | SUPSTATUS | SUPCATEGORY |
|---|---|---|---|---|---|
| 21 | Deliwines | 20, Avenue of the Americas | New York | 20 | SILVER |
| 32 | Best Wines | 660, Market Street | San Francisco | 90 | GOLD |
| 37 | Ad Fundum | 82, Wacker Drive | Chicago | 95 | PLATINUM |
| 52 | Spirits & Co. | 928, Strip | San Francisco | NULL | SILVER |
| 68 | The Wine Depot | 132, Montgomery Street | Las Vegas | 10 | SILVER |
| 69 | Vinos del Mundo | 4, Collins Avenue | Miami | 92 | PLATINUM |
| 84 | Wine Trade Logistics | 100, Rhode Island Avenue | Washington | 92 | PLATINUM |
| 94 | The Wine Crate | 330, McKinney Avenue | Dallas | 75 | GOLD |

**Figure 7.57** Result of SQL UPDATE.

As with the DELETE statement, an UPDATE statement can affect other tables in the database. Again, this depends upon the ON UPDATE referential integrity actions that have been set during table definition.

## 7.4 SQL Views

SQL views are part of the external data model. A **view** is defined by means of an SQL query and its content is generated upon invocation of the view by an application or by another query. In this way, it can be considered as a virtual table without physical tuples. Views offer several advantages. By hiding complex queries, such as join queries or correlated queries from their users, views facilitate ease of use. They can also provide data protection by hiding columns or tuples from unauthorized users. Views allow for logical data independence, which makes them a key component in the three-layer database architecture (see Chapter 1).

Views can be defined using the CREATE VIEW statement. Here you can see three examples:

```
CREATE VIEW TOPSUPPLIERS
AS SELECT SUPNR, SUPNAME FROM SUPPLIER
WHERE SUPSTATUS > 50

CREATE VIEW TOPSUPPLIERS_SF
AS SELECT * FROM TOPSUPPLIERS
WHERE SUPCITY = 'San Francisco'

CREATE VIEW ORDEROVERVIEW(PRODNR, PRODNAME, TOTQUANTITY)
AS SELECT P.PRODNR, P.PRODNAME, SUM(POL.QUANTITY)
FROM PRODUCT AS P LEFT OUTER JOIN PO_LINE AS POL
ON (P.PRODNR = POL.PRODNR)
GROUP BY P.PRODNR
```

The first view is called TOPSUPPLIERS and offers the supplier number and supplier name of all suppliers whose status is greater than 50. The second view refines the first by adding an additional constraint: SUPCITY = "San Francisco". The third view is called ORDEROVERVIEW. It contains the product number, product name, and total ordered quantity of all products. Note that the left outer join in the view definition ensures that products with no outstanding orders are included in the result.

Once the views have been defined, they can be used in applications or other queries as follows:

```
SELECT * FROM TOPSUPPLIERS_SF

SELECT * FROM ORDEROVERVIEW
WHERE PRODNAME LIKE '%CHARD%'
```

The first query selects all tuples from the view TOPSUPPLIERS_SF, which we defined earlier. The second query retrieves all tuples from the ORDEROVERVIEW view where the product name contains the string "CHARD".

The RDBMS automatically modifies queries that query views into queries on the underlying base tables. Suppose we have our view TOPSUPPLIERS and a query which uses it as follows:

```
CREATE VIEW TOPSUPPLIERS
AS SELECT SUPNR, SUPNAME FROM SUPPLIER
WHERE SUPSTATUS > 50
```

```
SELECT * FROM TOPSUPPLIERS
WHERE SUPCITY= 'Chicago'
```

Both view and query can be modified into the following query, which works directly on the SUPPLIER table:

```
SELECT SUPNR, SUPNAME
FROM SUPPLIER
WHERE SUPSTATUS > 50 AND SUPCITY='Chicago'
```

This is often referred to as query modification. View materialization is an alternative strategy for DBMSs to perform queries on views, in which a physical table is created when the view is first queried. To keep the materialized view table up-to-date, the DBMS must implement a synchronization strategy whenever the underlying base tables are updated. Synchronization can be performed as soon as the underlying base tables are updated (immediate view maintenance) or it can be postponed until just before data are retrieved from the view (deferred view maintenance).

Some views can be updated. In this case, the view serves as a window through which updates are propagated to the underlying base table(s). Updatable views require that INSERT, UPDATE, and DELETE statements on the view can be unambiguously mapped to INSERTs, UPDATEs, and DELETEs on the underlying base tables. If this property does not hold, the view is read only.

Let's reconsider our view ORDEROVERVIEW, which we defined earlier:

```
CREATE VIEW ORDEROVERVIEW(PRODNR, PRODNAME, TOTQUANTITY)
AS SELECT P.PRODNR, P.PRODNAME, SUM(POL.QUANTITY)
FROM PRODUCT AS P LEFT OUTER JOIN PO_LINE AS POL
ON (P.PRODNR = POL.PRODNR)
GROUP BY P.PRODNR
```

The following UPDATE statement tries to set the total ordered quantity to 10 for product number 0154.

```
UPDATE VIEW ORDEROVERVIEW
SET TOTQUANTITY = 10
WHERE PRODNR = '0154'
```

Since there are multiple ways to accomplish this update, the RDBMS will generate an error. A view update is feasible when only one possible update on the base table(s) can accomplish the desired update effect on the view. In other words, this is an example of a view which is not updatable.

Various requirements can be listed for views to be updatable. They typically depend upon the RDBMS vendor. Common examples are: no DISTINCT option in the SELECT component; no aggregate functions in the SELECT component; only one table name in the FROM component; no correlated subquery in the WHERE component; no GROUP BY in the WHERE component; and no UNION, INTERSECT, or EXCEPT in the WHERE component.

Another issue may arise in the case that an update on a view can be successfully performed. More specifically, in the case that rows are inserted or updated through an updatable view, there is the chance that these rows no longer satisfy the view definition. Hence, the rows cannot be retrieved through the view anymore. The WITH CHECK option allows us to avoid such undesired effects by checking the UPDATE and INSERT statements for conformity with the view definition. To

**Connections**

We will return to views in Chapter 20, where we will use them as a mechanism to safeguard privacy and security in a Big Data and analytics setting.

illustrate this, consider the following two examples of UPDATE statements on our TOPSUPPLIERS view, which has now been augmented with a WITH CHECK option.

```
CREATE VIEW TOPSUPPLIERS
AS SELECT SUPNR, SUPNAME FROM SUPPLIER
WHERE SUPSTATUS > 50
WITH CHECK OPTION
```

```
UPDATE TOPSUPPLIERS
SET STATUS = 20
WHERE SUPNR = '32'
```

```
UPDATE TOPSUPPLIERS
SET STATUS = 80
WHERE SUPNR = '32'
```

**Retention Questions**

- What are SQL views and what can they be used for?
- What is a view WITH CHECK option? Illustrate with an example.

The first UPDATE will be rejected by the RDBMS because the supplier status of supplier 32 is updated to 20, whereas the view requires the supplier status to be greater than 50. The second update statement will be accepted by the RDBMS because the new supplier status is bigger than 50.

## 7.5 SQL Indexes

**Connections**

In Chapter 13 we elaborate more on designing the internal data model in SQL. We also discuss different types of indexes for speeding up data retrieval.

Indexes are part of the internal data model. Although we elaborate more on them in Chapters 12 and 13, we briefly highlight some key concepts here.

An **index** provides a fast access path to the physical data to speed up the execution time of a query. It can be used to retrieve tuples with a specific column value quickly, rather than having to read the entire table on disk. Indexes can be defined over one or more columns.

Indexes can be created in SQL using the CREATE INDEX statement. Below you can see some examples:

```
CREATE INDEX PRODUCT_NAME_INDEX
ON PRODUCT(PRODNAME ASC)
```

```
CREATE INDEX SUPSTATUS_INDEX
ON SUPPLIER(SUPSTATUS DESC)
```

```
DROP INDEX SUPSTATUS_INDEX
```

```
CREATE UNIQUE INDEX PRODUCT_UNIQUE_NAME_INDEX
ON PRODUCT(PRODNAME ASC)
```

```
CREATE UNIQUE INDEX PRODUCT_UNIQUE_NR_NAME_INDEX
ON PRODUCT(PRODNR ASC, PRODNAME ASC)
```

```
CREATE INDEX SUPPLIER_NAME_CLUSTERING_INDEX
ON SUPPLIER(SUPNAME ASC) CLUSTER
```

**Retention Questions**

Give some examples of how indexes can be created in SQL.

The first statement creates an index for the PRODNAME column, whereby the index entries are stored in ascending order. This index is useful for queries retrieving products by product name. The second example creates an index for the supplier status. Indexes can be removed using the DROP statement as illustrated. The keyword UNIQUE can be added to enforce that the values in the index are unique and do not allow duplicate index entries. The next example defines a composite index on the PRODNR and PRODNAME columns. The last example is a clustered index that enforces that the tuples in a table are physically ordered according to the index key, which is supplier name in our case. There can only be one clustered index per table, as the tuples can only be stored in one order. If a table has no clustered index, then its tuples are stored in a random order.

## 7.6 SQL Privileges

SQL also provides facilities to manage privileges. A **privilege** corresponds to the right to use certain SQL statements such as SELECT or INSERT on one or more database objects. Privileges can be granted or revoked. Both the database administrator and schema owner can grant or revoke privileges to/from users or user accounts. They can be set at account, table, view, or column level. Table 7.2 provides an overview.

Some examples of privilege statements in SQL are:

```
GRANT SELECT, INSERT, UPDATE, DELETE ON SUPPLIER TO BBAESENS
GRANT SELECT (PRODNR, PRODNAME) ON PRODUCT TO PUBLIC
REVOKE DELETE ON SUPPLIER FROM BBAESENS
GRANT SELECT, INSERT, UPDATE, DELETE ON PRODUCT TO WLEMAHIEU WITH GRANT OPTION
GRANT REFERENCES ON SUPPLIER TO SVANDENBROUCKE
```

The first example grants SELECT, INSERT, UPDATE, and DELETE privileges on the SUPPLIER table to user BBAESENS. The second grants a SELECT privilege on the PRODNR and PROD-NAME columns of the PRODUCT table to all public users. The third statement revokes the earlier granted DELETE privilege on the SUPPLIER table from user BBAESENS. The fourth statement grants SELECT, INSERT, UPDATE, and DELETE privileges on the PRODUCT table to user WLEMAHIEU, whereby the WITH GRANT allows the user WLEMAHIEU to grant the privileges to others. The fifth statement grants the user SVANDENBROUCKE the privilege to define referential integrity constraints that refer to the SUPPLIER table. Note that this privilege allows

**Table 7.2** Privileges in SQL

| Privilege | Explanation |
|---|---|
| SELECT | Provides retrieval privilege |
| INSERT | Gives insert privilege |
| UPDATE | Gives update privilege |
| DELETE | Gives delete privilege |
| ALTER | Gives privilege to change the table definition |
| REFERENCES | Provides the privilege to reference the table when specifying integrity constraints |
| ALL | Provides all privileges (DBMS-specific) |

> **Retention Questions**
>
> What facilities does SQL provide to manage privileges? Illustrate with examples.

inferring certain information from the SUPPLIER table, even if no privileges are granted to actually query the table. For example, a foreign key constraint in another table that refers to SUPNR in the SUPPLIER table can be used to verify whether a certain supplier exists.

It is important to stress that SQL privileges are often combined with views to exert fine-grained control over the (sub)set of rows and columns in a table that can be accessed by a particular user. For example, the view definition and access privilege below can be used to express that user WLEMAHIEU can only access the SUPNR and SUPNAME columns in the SUPPLIERS table, and only for suppliers located in New York:

```
CREATE VIEW SUPPLIERS_NY
AS SELECT SUPNR, SUPNAME FROM SUPPLIERS
WHERE SUPCITY = 'New York'
GRANT SELECT ON SUPPLIERS_NY TO WLEMAHIEU
```

## 7.7 SQL for Metadata Management

Since most DBMSs in use are relational, the catalog itself can also be implemented as a relational database. Hence, this implies that SQL can be used to define and manage metadata. To illustrate this, let's first start from an EER conceptual model for a relational model, as illustrated in Figure 7.58. It includes the following entity types: TABLE, COLUMN, KEY, PRIMARY KEY, and FOREIGN KEY. KEY is a superclass of the entity types PRIMARY KEY and FOREIGN KEY. The specialization is total and overlapping. A table has a unique table name. COLUMN is a weak entity type since its key is a combination of Tablename and Columnname. Hence, the same column name can be used in multiple tables. Relationship type R1 says that a table can have zero to N columns, whereas a column always belongs to exactly one table. R2 indicates that a column can correspond to zero or

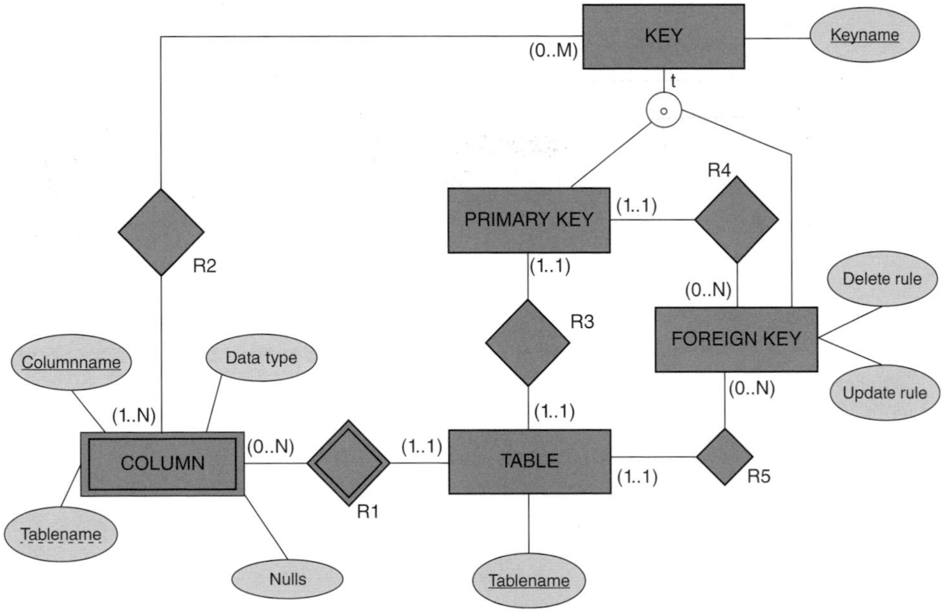


**Figure 7.58** EER conceptual model of a relational model.

M keys (e.g., a primary and a foreign key) and a key to between one and N columns. R3 specifies the relationship type between a table and its primary key. R4 models the relationship type between a foreign key and the corresponding primary key. R5 indicates what table a foreign key belongs to.

Using the mapping rules explained in Chapter 6, we can now map this EER model to the following relational model (primary keys are underlined and foreign keys are in italics):

```
Table(Tablename, ...)
Key(Keyname, ...)
Primary-Key(PK-Keyname, PK-Tablename, ...)
     PK-Keyname is a foreign key referring to Keyname in Key;
     PK-Tablename is a foreign key referring to Tablename in Table
Foreign-Key(FK-Keyname, FK-Tablename, FK-PK-Keyname, Update-rule, Delete-
rule, ...)
     FK-Keyname is a foreign key referring to Keyname in Key;
     FK-Tablename is a foreign key referring to Tablename in Table;
     FK-PK-Keyname is a foreign key referring to PK-Keyname in Primary-Key
Column(Columnname, C-Tablename, Data type, Nulls, ...)
     C-Tablename is a foreign key referring to Tablename in Table
Key-Column(KC-Keyname, KC-Columnname, KC-Tablename, ...)
     KC-Keyname is a foreign key referring to Keyname in Key;
     (KC-Columnname, KC-Tablename) is a foreign key referring to
     (Columnname, C-Tablename) in Column;
```

The above provides only a partial representation of a typical catalog's definitions. It focuses on information about the data structure (structural metadata), which is admittedly the most crucial type of metadata in most database settings. However, as explained in Chapter 4, a catalog may contain other types of metadata as well, such as information about database users and their access privileges, or statistical information about data usage. In some specific cases, catalogs even contain information about the quality of the data (data quality metadata) or about their meaning (semantic metadata).

Once the catalog has been successfully implemented, it can be populated and queried using SQL, just as when working with raw data. The following SQL query retrieves all column information of the SUPPLIER table:

**Connections**

Chapter 4 discussed the importance of metadata modeling and the role of the catalog, which is one of the essential components of a DBMS.

```
SELECT *
FROM Column
WHERE Tablename = 'SUPPLIER'
```

The next SQL query retrieves the primary key of the SUPPLIER table, the names of the foreign keys referring to it, together with their tables and delete rules.

```
SELECT PK.PK-Keyname, FK.FK-Keyname, FK.FK-Tablename,
FK.Delete-rule
FROM Primary-Key PK, Foreign-Key FK
WHERE PK.PK-Tablename = 'SUPPLIER'
AND PK.PK-Keyname = FK.FK-PK-Keyname
```

**Retention Questions**

How can SQL be used for metadata management? Illustrate with examples.

This clearly illustrates the power and beauty of SQL in an RDBMS environment. Using the same SQL DDL and SQL DML to manage both raw data and metadata contributes to the productivity and efficiency of database users when working with relational databases.

## Summary

In this chapter we discussed SQL as one of the most important data definition and data manipulation languages for relational databases. We started by introducing the basic concepts of SQL and positioned it in terms of the three-level database architecture outlined in Chapter 1. We then elaborated on the SQL DDL instructions that can be used to either create or remove database objects (e.g., schemas, tables, domains). We extensively discussed SQL DML instructions by reviewing the SELECT, INSERT, DELETE, and UPDATE statements. We also covered SQL views, which are part of the external data model in a relational environment. SQL indcxes, which belong to the internal data model, were also discussed, as was granting and revoking SQL privileges. We concluded by reviewing how SQL can be used to manage relational metadata in a transparent way. Given its widespread use and popularity, various extensions have been added to SQL for specific applications such as data warehousing, handling XML documents, and analytics. We discuss these in more detail in subsequent chapters.

### Scenario Conclusion

For its insurance firm, Sober needs to provide an overview of all accidents together with the number of Sober cars involved and the average damage amount per accident. This information can be retrieved using the following SQL query:

```
SELECT ACC-NR, ACC-DATE-TIME, ACC-LOCATION, COUNT(*), AVG(DAMAGE AMOUNT)
FROM ACCIDENT, INVOLVED, CAR, SOBER CAR
WHERE
ACC-NR=I-CAR-NR AND
I-ACC-NR=CAR-NR AND
CAR-NR=S-CAR-NR
GROUP BY(ACC-NR)
```

As part of its customer relationship management (CRM) program, Sober wants to retrieve the customer with the maximum wait time and offer him or her a free ride-hailing service. This information can be retrieved using the following SQL query:

```
SELECT CUST-NR, CUST-NAME
FROM CUSTOMER
WHERE CUST-NR IN
     (SELECT H1.CUST-NR
     FROM RIDE HAILING H1
     WHERE NOT EXISTS
          (SELECT * FROM RIDE HAILING H2
           WHERE H2.WAIT-TIME > H1.WAIT-TIME))
```

To find out which customers have never booked any of its services, the following SQL query can be used:

```
SELECT CUST-NR, CUST-NAME
FROM CUSTOMER
WHERE CUST-NR NOT IN (SELECT H-CUST-NR FROM RIDE HAILING)
AND
CUST-NR NOT IN (SELECT B-CUST-NR FROM BOOK)
```

The next SQL query retrieves the number and names of all customers who booked more than 20 Sober ride-sharing services:

```
SELECT CUST-NR, CUST-NAME
FROM CUSTOMER
WHERE 20 ≤ (SELECT COUNT(*)
            FROM BOOK
            WHERE CUST-NR=B-CUST-NR)
```

Remember, for each of these customers Sober pledged to plant a tree as part of its eco-friendly program.

As part of its data quality program, Sober wants to enforce that it is not possible for customers to book either a ride-hailing or ride-sharing service using their own car. The following SQL query retrieves the customer number and name, ride number and car number of customers that booked a ride-sharing service with their own car:

```
SELECT CUST-NR, CUST-NAME, RIDE-NR, CAR-NR
FROM CUSTOMER, BOOK, RIDE SHARING, RIDE, CAR, OTHER CAR
WHERE
CUST-NR=B.CUST-NR AND
B-S-RIDE-NR=S-RIDE-NR AND
S-RIDE-NR=RIDE-NR AND
R-CAR-NR=CAR-NR AND
CAR-NR=O-CAR-NR AND
O-CUST-NR=CUST-NR
```

A similar query can be used to find out which customers booked a ride-hailing service with their own car.

## Key Terms List

**aggregate functions**
**ALL**
**ALTER**
**ANY**
**authorization identifier**
**AVG**
**BETWEEN**
**binary large object (BLOB)**
**CHECK constraint**
**correlated nested queries**
**COUNT**
**DELETE**
**DISTINCT**
**DROP**

**EXCEPT**
**EXISTS**
**free-form language**
**FROM**
**full outer join**
**GROUP BY**
**IN**
**index**
**inner join**
**INSERT**
**INTERSECT**
**join queries**
**left outer join**
**LIKE**
**multiset**
**nested query**
**NOT EXISTS**
**NOT NULL constraint**
**ON DELETE CASCADE**
**ON UPDATE CASCADE**
**ORDER BY**
**privilege**
**relational database management system (RDBMS)**
**RESTRICT**
**right outer join**
**SELECT**
**SET DEFAULT**
**SET NULL**
**SQL**
**SQL schema**
**Structured Query Language (SQL)**
**SUM**
**UNION**
**UNIQUE constraint**
**UPDATE**
**VARIANCE**
**view**
**WHERE**

## Review Questions

**7.1.** The following table with purchase orders is created:

```
CREATE TABLE PURCHASE_ORDER
            (PONR CHAR(7) NOT NULL PRIMARY KEY,
             PODATE DATE,
             SUPNR CHAR(4) NOT NULL,
             FOREIGN KEY (SUPNR) REFERENCES SUPPLIER (SUPNR)
                   ON DELETE CASCADE ON UPDATE CASCADE);
```

What happens upon deletion of a supplier?

a. All purchase order records tied to that supplier are also deleted.
b. The SUPNR of this supplier is replaced by a NULL value in PURCHASE_ORDER.
c. The SUPNR of this supplier is deleted in PURCHASE_ORDER.
d. The SUPNR of this supplier is only deleted in SUPPLIER.

**7.2.** We're interested in wine stores. Therefore, we want to retrieve the SUPNR and SUPNAME of each store which contains "wine" in its store name. Which of the following queries can we use?

a.
```
SELECT SUPNR, SUPNAME
FROM SUPPLIER
WHERE SUPNAME = "WINE"
```

b.
```
SELECT SUPNR, SUPNAME
FROM SUPPLIER
WHERE SUPNAME IS "%WINE%"
```

c. 
```
SELECT SUPNR, SUPNAME
FROM SUPPLIER WHERE
SUPNAME LIKE "%WINE%"
```

d. 
```
SELECT SUPNR, SUPNAME
FROM SUPPLIER
WHERE SUPNAME IS "WINE"
```

**7.3.** Take the following extract from SUPPLIES:

| *SUPNR* | *PRODNR* | PURCHASE_PRICE | DELIV_PERIOD |
|---|---|---|---|
| 37 | 0185 | 32.99 | 3 |
| 84 | 0185 | 33.00 | 5 |
| 94 | 0185 | 32.99 | 1 |

We want to retrieve the fastest delivery time for product 0185. We type the following query:

```
SELECT PRODNR, MIN(DELIV_PERIOD) AS MIN_DELIV_PERIOD
FROM SUPPLIES
WHERE PRODNR = '0185'
```

What are the results? If you believe the query is correct, select answer a, otherwise choose which results you believe will be retrieved.

a.

| SUPNR | MIN_DELIV_PERIOD |
|---|---|
| 94 | 1 |

b.

| SUPNR | MIN_DELIV_PERIOD |
|---|---|
| 37 | 3 |

c.

| SUPNR | MIN_DELIV_PERIOD |
|---|---|
| 37 | 1 |

d.

| SUPNR | MIN_DELIV_PERIOD |
|---|---|
| 37 | 1 |
| 84 | 1 |
| 94 | 1 |

**7.4.** Consider the following query:

```
SELECT *
FROM PRODUCT
WHERE PRODTYPE='red'
ORDER BY AVAILABLE_QUANTITY DESC, PRODNAME
```

Which of the following answers is **correct**?

a.

| PRODNR | PRODNAME | PRODTYPE | AVAILABLE_QUANTITY |
|---|---|---|---|
| 474 | Chateau De La Tour, Clos-Vougeot, Grand cru, 2008 | red | 147 |
| 885 | Chateau Margaux, Grand Cru Classé, 1956 | red | 147 |
| 347 | Chateau Corbin-Despagne, Saint-Emilion, 2005 | red | 145 |
| 832 | Conde de Hervías, Rioja, 2004 | red | 121 |
| ... | ... | ... | ... |
| 331 | Chateau La Commanderie, Lalande-de-Pomerol, 1998 | red | 3 |
| 219 | Marques de Caceres, Rioja Crianza, 2010 | red | 0 |

b.

| PRODNR | PRODNAME | PRODTYPE | AVAILABLE_QUANTITY |
|---|---|---|---|
| 885 | Chateau Margaux, Grand Cru Classé, 1956 | red | 147 |
| 474 | Chateau De La Tour, Clos-Vougeot, Grand cru, 2008 | red | 147 |
| 347 | Chateau Corbin-Despagne, Saint-Emilion, 2005 | red | 145 |
| 832 | Conde de Hervías,Rioja, 2004 | red | 121 |
| 347 | Chateau Corbin-Despagne, Saint-Emilion, 2005 | red | 145 |
| 832 | Conde de Hervías, Rioja, 2004 | red | 121 |
| ... | ... | ... | ... |
| 331 | Chateau La Commanderie, Lalande-de-Pomerol, 1998 | red | 3 |
| 219 | Marques de Caceres, Rioja Crianza, 2010 | red | 0 |
| | | | |

c.

| PRODNR | PRODNAME | PRODTYPE | AVAILABLE_QUANTITY |
|---|---|---|---|
| 219 | Marques de Caceres, Rioja Crianza, 2010 | red | 0 |
| 331 | Chateau La Commanderie, Lalande-de-Pomerol, 1998 | red | 3 |
| 185 | Chateau Petrus, 1975 | red | 5 |
| 523 | Chateau Andron Blanquet, Saint Estephe, 1979 | red | 13 |
| ... | ... | ... | ... |
| 474 | Chateau De La Tour, Clos-Vougeot, Grand cru, 2008 | red | 147 |
| 885 | Chateau Margaux, Grand Cru Classé, 1956 | red | 147 |

d.

| PRODNR | PRODNAME | PRODTYPE | AVAILABLE_QUANTITY |
|---|---|---|---|
| 795 | Casa Silva, Los Lingues, Carmenere, 2012 | red | 105 |
| 523 | Chateau Andron Blanquet, Saint Estephe, 1979 | red | 13 |
| 977 | Chateau Batailley, Grand Cru Classé, 1975 | red | 21 |
| ... | ... | ... | ... |
| 847 | Seresin, Merlot, 1999 | red | 41 |
| 345 | Vascosassetti, Brunello di Montalcino, 2004 | red | 64 |

**7.5.** We want to retrieve all unique supplier numbers and statuses of suppliers who have at least one outstanding purchase order. Which query is **correct**?

a.
```
SELECT DISTINCT R.SUPNR, R.SUPSTATUS
FROM SUPPLIER R, PURCHASE_ORDER O
```

b.
```
SELECT DISTINCT R.SUPNR, R.SUPSTATUS
FROM SUPPLIER R, PURCHASE_ORDER O
WHERE (R.SUPNR = O.SUPNR)
```

c.
```
SELECT DISTINCT R.SUPNR, R.SUPSTATUS
FROM SUPPLIER R, PURCHASE_ORDER O
WHERE (R.SUPNR = O.PONR)
```

d.
```
SELECT R.SUPNR, R.SUPSTATUS
FROM PURCHASE_ORDER R
```

**7.6.** Consider the following query:

```
SELECT P.PRODNR, P.PRODNAME, P.AVAILABLE_QUANTITY, SUM(L.QUANTITY)
AS ORDERED_QUANTITY
FROM PRODUCT AS P LEFT OUTER JOIN PO_LINE AS L
ON (P.PRODNR=L.PRODNR)
GROUP BY P.PRODNR
```

Which of the following statements is **not correct**?

a. The query retrieves the product number, product name, and available quantity of each product thanks to the left outer join.

b. The query retrieves for each product the total ordered quantity.
c. The query result can never contain NULL values.
d. If we remove the GROUP BY statement and P.PRODNR, P.PRODNAME, P.AVAILABLE_QUANTITY from the SELECT statement, the query will result in one row containing the total outstanding ordered quantity over all products in column "ORDERED_QUANTITY".

**7.7.** Consider following query:

```
SELECT DISTINCT P1.PRODNR, P1.PRODNAME
FROM PRODUCT P1, SUPPLIES S1
WHERE P1.PRODNR = S1.PRODNR AND
1 <= (SELECT COUNT(*) FROM SUPPLIES S2
  WHERE S2.SUPNR <> S1.SUPNR AND P1.PRODNR=S2.PRODNR)
ORDER BY PRODNR
```

The query retrieves:

a. The number and name of all products that can only be supplied by one supplier.
b. The number and name of all products that cannot be supplied by any supplier.
c. The number and name of all products that can be supplied by more than one supplier.
d. The number and name of all products that can be supplied by all suppliers.

**7.8.** Which of the following queries selects the name of the supplier, corresponding order number, and total ordered quantity of the order that has the maximum total quantity ordered.

a.
```
SELECT R1.SUPNAME, POL1.PONR, SUM(POL1.QUANTITY)
FROM SUPPLIER R1, PURCHASE_ORDER PO1, PO_LINE POL1
WHERE R1.SUPNR = PO1.SUPNR AND PO1.PONR = POL1.PONR
GROUP BY POL1.PONR
HAVING SUM(POL1.QUANTITY) >= ANY
     (SELECT SUM(POL2.QUANTITY)
     FROM SUPPLIER R2, PURCHASE_ORDER PO2, PO_LINE POL2
     WHERE R2.SUPNR = PO2.SUPNR AND PO2.PONR = POL2.PONR
     GROUP BY POL2.PONR)
```

b.
```
SELECT R1.SUPNAME, POL1.PONR, SUM(POL1.QUANTITY)
FROM SUPPLIER R1, PURCHASE_ORDER PO1, PO_LINE POL1
WHERE R1.SUPNR = PO1.SUPNR AND PO1.PONR = POL1.PONR
GROUP BY POL1.PONR
HAVING SUM(POL1.QUANTITY) <= ALL
     (SELECT SUM(POL2.QUANTITY)
     FROM SUPPLIER R2, PURCHASE_ORDER PO2, PO_LINE POL2
     WHERE R2.SUPNR = PO2.SUPNR AND PO2.PONR = POL2.PONR
     GROUP BY POL2.PONR)
```

c.
```
SELECT R1.SUPNAME, POL1.PONR, SUM(POL1.QUANTITY)
FROM SUPPLIER R1, PURCHASE_ORDER PO1, PO_LINE POL1
WHERE R1.SUPNR = PO1.SUPNR AND PO1.PONR = POL1.PONR
GROUP BY POL1.PONR
HAVING SUM(POL1.QUANTITY) >= ALL
     (SELECT SUM(POL2.QUANTITY)
     FROM SUPPLIER R2, PURCHASE_ORDER PO2, PO_LINE POL2
     WHERE R2.SUPNR = PO2.SUPNR AND PO2.PONR = POL2.PONR
     GROUP BY POL2.PONR)
```

d.
```
SELECT R1.SUPNAME, POL1.PONR, SUM(POL1.QUANTITY)
FROM SUPPLIER R1, PURCHASE_ORDER PO1, PO_LINE POL1
WHERE R1.SUPNR = PO1.SUPNR AND PO1.PONR = POL1.PONR
GROUP BY POL1.PONR
HAVING SUM(POL1.QUANTITY) <= ANY
     (SELECT SUM(POL2.QUANTITY)
     FROM SUPPLIER R2, PURCHASE_ORDER PO2, PO_LINE POL2
     WHERE R2.SUPNR = PO2.SUPNR AND PO2.PONR = POL2.PONR
     GROUP BY POL2.PONR)
```

**7.9.** Consider the following SQL query:

```
SELECT SUPNAME, SUPADDRESS, SUPCITY
FROM SUPPLIER R
WHERE NOT EXISTS
     (SELECT *
     FROM PRODUCT P
     WHERE EXISTS
          (SELECT *
          FROM SUPPLIES S
          WHERE R.SUPNR = S.SUPNR
          AND P.PRODNR = S.PRODNR));
```

This query selects:

a. The supplier name, supplier address, and supplier city of all suppliers who cannot supply any products.
b. The supplier name, supplier address, and supplier city of all suppliers who cannot supply all products.
c. The supplier name, supplier address, and supplier city of all suppliers who can supply at least one product.
d. The supplier name, supplier address, and supplier city of all suppliers who can supply all products.

**7.10.** Consider the following query:

```
SELECT P.PRODNR, P.PRODNAME
FROM PRODUCT P
WHERE EXISTS
     (SELECT *
     FROM PO_LINE POL
     WHERE P.PRODNR = POL.PRODNR
     GROUP BY POL.PRODNR
     HAVING SUM(POL.QUANTITY) > P.AVAILABLE_QUANTITY)
```

The query retrieves:

a. The name and number of the product with the highest ordered quantity.
b. The name and number of all products that are ordered and do not exceed their available quantity.
c. The name and number of all products that are ordered and exceed their available quantity.
d. The name and number of the product with the lowest ordered quantity.

**7.11.** Consider following query:

```
SELECT CS.CURRENT_STOCK - O.ORDERED AS NEW_STOCK
FROM (SELECT SUM(P.AVAILABLE_QUANTITY) AS CURRENT_STOCK
```

```
FROM PRODUCT P) AS CS,
(SELECT SUM(POL.QUANTITY) AS ORDERED
FROM PO_LINE POL) AS O
```

The output of the query represents:

a. A table summarizing for each product the increase in stock after the ordered products are delivered.
b. A table summarizing for each product the decrease in stock after the ordered products are delivered.
c. A scalar, summarizing the total quantity of products in stock after all the ordered products are delivered.
d. A scalar, summarizing the decrease in total available quantity of all products after the ordered products are delivered.

**7.12.** Given the task to retrieve the numbers of all suppliers who can supply products 0832 and 0494, which query is **correct**?

a.
```
SELECT DISTINCT SUPNR
FROM SUPPLIES
WHERE PRODNR IN (0832, 0494)
```

b.
```
SELECT SUPNR
FROM SUPPLIES
WHERE PRODNR = 0832
UNION ALL
SELECT SUPNR
FROM SUPPLIES
WHERE PRODNR = 0494
```

c.
```
SELECT SUPNR
FROM SUPPLIES
WHERE PRODNR = 0832
INTERSECT
SELECT SUPNR
FROM SUPPLIES
WHERE PRODNR = 0494
```

d.
```
SELECT UNIQUE SUPNR
FROM SUPPLIES
WHERE PRODNR IN (0832, 0494)
```

**7.13.** Consider the following View definition and update statement:

```
CREATE VIEW TOPPRODUCTS(PRODNR,PRODNAME,QUANTITY) AS
SELECT PRODNR, PRODNAME, AVAILABLE_QUANTITY
FROM PRODUCT WHERE AVAILABLE_QUANTITY>100
WITH CHECK OPTION
UPDATE TOPPRODUCTS
SET QUANTITY=80
WHERE PRODNR=0153
```

What will be the result of this?

a. The update can be successfully made but only the PRODUCT table will be updated.
b. The update can be successfully made and both the View and PRODUCT table will be updated.

c. The update will be halted because of the WITH CHECK OPTION.
d. The update can be successfully made but only the View will be updated.

**7.14.** Compare the following two queries:

1.
```
SELECT COUNT(DISTINCT SUPNR)
FROM PURCHASE_ORDER
```

2.
```
SELECT COUNT(SUPNR)
FROM PURCHASE_ORDER
```

Which of the following statements is correct?

a. Result query 1 is always = result query 2 because PURCHASE_ORDER contains only unique purchase orders.
b. Result query 1 is always ≤ result query 2 because the DISTINCT operator counts only unique SUPNRs.
c. Result query 1 is always ≥ result query 2 because query 1 sums the number of purchase orders per supplier while query 2 sums the number of purchase orders in total.
d. Result query 1 is sometimes ≥ and sometimes ≤ result query 2 because the result depends on the number of suppliers and the number of purchase orders.

**7.15.** Consider the following query:

```
SELECT PRODNR, AVG(QUANTITY) AS AVG_QUANTITY
FROM PO_LINE
GROUP BY PRODNR
HAVING SUM(QUANTITY) < 15
```

What is the result?

a. The query returns the PRODNR and average QUANTITY of each purchase order that has fewer than 15 purchase order lines.
b. The query returns the PRODNR and average QUANTITY of each product that has fewer than 15 purchase order lines.
c. The query returns the PRODNR and average QUANTITY of each product that has fewer than 15 orders.
d. The query returns the PRODNR and average QUANTITY of each purchase order that has fewer than 15 orders.

**7.16.** Consider the following query:

```
SELECT PRODNAME
FROM PRODUCT
WHERE PRODNR IN
     (SELECT PRODNR
      FROM SUPPLIES
      WHERE SUPNR IN
           (SELECT SUPNR
            FROM SUPPLIER
            WHERE SUPCITY = 'New York'))
      AND PRODNR IN
     (SELECT PRODNR
      FROM SUPPLIES
      WHERE SUPNR IN
```

```
(SELECT SUPNR
 FROM SUPPLIER
 WHERE SUPCITY = 'Washington'))
```

What is the result?

a. The query retrieves the product name of each product that has a supplier in New York or Washington.
b. The query retrieves the product name of each product that has both a supplier in New York and a supplier in Washington.
c. The query retrieves the product name of each product along with all possible supplier cities.
d. The query incorrectly combines every product name and supplier city.

**7.17.** We want to retrieve the available quantity of each ordered product of supplier Ad Fundum. Which of the following queries is correct?

a.
```
SELECT PRODNR, AVAILABLE_QUANTITY
FROM PRODUCT
WHERE PRODNR IN
         (SELECT PRODNR
          FROM PO_LINE) AND
   SUPNR IN
         (SELECT SUPNR
          FROM SUPPLIER
          WHERE SUPNAME='Ad Fundum')
```

b.
```
SELECT PRODNR, AVAILABLE_QUANTITY
FROM PRODUCT
WHERE SUPNR IN
      (SELECT SUPNR
      FROM SUPPLIER
      WHERE SUPNAME='Ad Fundum')
```

c.
```
SELECT PRODNR, AVAILABLE_QUANTITY
FROM PRODUCT
WHERE PRODNR IN
      (SELECT PRODNR
      FROM PO_LINE
      WHERE PONR IN
           (SELECT PONR
           FROM PURCHASE_ORDER
           WHERE SUPNR IN
                (SELECT SUPNR
                FROM SUPPLIER
                WHERE SUPNAME='Ad Fundum')))
```

d.
```
SELECT PRODNR, AVAILABLE_QUANTITY
FROM PRODUCT
WHERE PRODNR =
      (SELECT PRODNR
      FROM PO_LINE
      WHERE PONR =
           (SELECT PONR
            FROM PURCHASE_ORDER
```

```
WHERE SUPNR =
      (SELECT SUPNR
      FROM SUPPLIER
      WHERE SUPNAME='Ad Fundum')))
```

**7.18.** Consider the following SQL query:

```
SELECT P1.PRODNR
       FROM PRODUCT P1
       WHERE 5 <=
             (SELECT COUNT(*)
              FROM PRODUCT P2
              WHERE P1.PRODNR < P2.PRODNR)
```

This query selects:

a. The five highest product numbers.
b. The five lowest product numbers.
c. All product numbers except for the five lowest product numbers.
d. All product numbers except for the five highest product numbers.

**7.19.** Consider the following query:

```
SELECT R1.SUPNAME, R1.SUPNR, COUNT(*)
FROM PURCHASE_ORDER PO1, SUPPLIER R1
WHERE PO1.SUPNR = R1.SUPNR
GROUP BY R1.SUPNR
HAVING COUNT(*) >= ALL
     (SELECT COUNT(*)
     FROM PURCHASE_ORDER PO2, SUPPLIER R2
     WHERE PO2.SUPNR = R2.SUPNR
     GROUP BY R2.SUPNR)
```

The query retrieves:

a. The name, number, and total outstanding orders of all suppliers that have outstanding orders.
b. The name, number, and total outstanding orders of all suppliers that have outstanding orders, except for the supplier(s) with the fewest outstanding orders.
c. The name, number, and total outstanding orders of the supplier with the most outstanding orders.
d. The name, number, and total outstanding orders of the supplier with the fewest outstanding orders.

**7.20.** Consider the following query:

```
SELECT P.PRODNR, P.PRODNAME
FROM PRODUCT P
EXCEPT
SELECT POL.PRODNR
FROM PO_LINE POL
```

The query retrieves:

a. The number and name of all the products with no outstanding order.
b. The number and name of all the products that are ordered.
c. The query will not execute because both queries do not select the same columns.
d. The query will not execute because both queries do not select the same rows.

**7.21.** Consider following query:

```
SELECT P1.PRODNR, P1.PRODNAME, S1.SUPNR, S1.PURCHASE_PRICE
FROM PRODUCT P1, SUPPLIES S1
WHERE P1.PRODNR = S1.PRODNR
AND NOT EXISTS
     (SELECT *
     FROM PRODUCT P2, SUPPLIES S2
     WHERE P2.PRODNR = S2.PRODNR
     AND P1.PRODNR = P2.PRODNR
     AND S1.PURCHASE_PRICE > S2.PURCHASE_PRICE)
```

and the following statements:

1. For each product, the supplier number of the supplier who can supply the product for the cheapest price is retrieved.
2. For each product, the supplier number of the supplier who supplies the product for the highest price is retrieved.
3. For each product, exactly one tuple is returned.
4. For each product, more than one tuple can be returned.

Which statements are true?

a. 1 and 3.
b. 1 and 4.
c. 2 and 3.
d. 2 and 4.

**7.22.** Consider the following query:

```
SELECT R.SUPNAME, (SELECT COUNT(PO.PODATE)
                   FROM PURCHASE_ORDER PO
                   WHERE R.SUPNR = PO.SUPNR) AS SUMMARY
FROM SUPPLIER R
```

The query selects:

a. The name and total number of outstanding orders of all suppliers that have at least one outstanding order.
b. The name and total number of outstanding orders of all suppliers.
c. The supplier name and order date of each of his/her outstanding orders.
d. The supplier name and order date of each of his/her outstanding orders. If a supplier does not have an outstanding order, she/he will be included in the output with a null value for the "SUMMARY" column.

## Problems and Exercises

7.1E Write an SQL query that retrieves each supplier who can deliver product 0468 within one or two days, accompanied by the price of the product and the delivery period.

7.2E Write an SQL query that returns the average price and variance per product.

7.3E Write an SQL query that retrieves all pairs of suppliers who supply the same product, along with their product purchase price if applicable.

7.4E Write a nested SQL query to retrieve the supplier name of each supplier who supplies more than five products.

7.5E Write an SQL query to retrieve the supplier number, supplier name, and supplier status of each supplier who has a higher supplier status than supplier number 21.

7.6E Write a correlated SQL query to retrieve the number and status of all suppliers, except for the three suppliers with the lowest supplier status.

7.7E Write a correlated SQL query to retrieve all cities with more than one supplier.

7.8E Write an SQL query to retrieve name, number, and total outstanding orders of all suppliers that have outstanding orders, except for the supplier(s) with the fewest outstanding orders.

7.9E Write an SQL query using EXISTS to retrieve the supplier numbers and names of all suppliers that do not have any outstanding orders.

7.10E Create a view SUPPLIEROVERVIEW that retrieves, for each supplier, the supplier number, the supplier name, and the total amount of quantities ordered. Once created, query this view to retrieve suppliers for whom the total ordered quantity exceeds 30.

7.11E Write an SQL query that retrieves the total available quantity of sparkling wines. Make sure to display this quantity as "TOTAL_QUANTITY".

7.12E Write a query to select all supplier numbers, together with their supplier name and total number of outstanding orders for each supplier. Include all suppliers in the result, even if there are no outstanding orders for that supplier at the moment.

7.13E Write an SQL query that returns the SUPNR and number of products of each supplier who supplies more than five products.

7.14E Write an SQL query that reports the average delivery time for each supplier who supplies products.

7.15E Write a nested SQL query to retrieve all purchase order numbers of purchase orders that contain either sparkling or red wine.

7.16E Write a correlated SQL query to retrieve the three lowest product numbers.

7.17E Write an SQL query with ALL or ANY to retrieve the name of the product with the highest available quantity.

7.18E Write an SQL query using EXISTS to retrieve the supplier name and number of the supplier who has the lowest supplier number.

# 8 Object-Oriented Databases and Object Persistence

## Chapter Objectives

In this chapter, you will learn to:

- use advanced concepts of object orientation, such as method overloading, inheritance, method overriding, polymorphism, and dynamic binding;
- identify various strategies to ensure object persistence;
- understand the key components of an OODBMS;
- understand the ODMG standard and its object model;
- use the ODMG object definition language (ODL) to define object types;
- use the ODMG object query language (OQL) to formulate queries;
- implement the ODMG standard through language bindings;
- evaluate OODBMSs against RDBMSs.

**Opening Scenario**

Sober has noted that many database applications are being developed using programming languages such as Java, Python, and C++. It found out that many languages are based on the object-oriented paradigm. The company wants to know what this entails and whether this could have any implications and/or potential for its database and choice of DBMS.

The object-oriented (OO) paradigm was first introduced by programming languages such as C++, Eiffel, and Smalltalk. Due to its expressive modeling power and formal semantics, the principles of OO have also been widely used in software development methodologies. However, for data storage and management, the adoption of OO proved less straightforward. In this chapter, we discuss various approaches to object persistence. First, we refresh the basic concepts of OO, many of which have been covered in Chapter 3. This will be followed by a discussion of advanced OO concepts such as method overloading, inheritance, method overriding, polymorphism, and dynamic binding. Next, we review the basic principles of object persistence. We then discuss object-oriented database management systems (OODBMSs), which is the core of this chapter. We conclude with evaluating OODBMSs and demonstrating their impact on the emergence of object-relational mapping (ORM) frameworks, which facilitate the persistence of objects into RDBMSs. Due to its popularity and ease of use, we use Java as the OO language for the examples.

## 8.1 Recap: Basic Concepts of OO

In **object-oriented (OO)** programming, an application consists of a series of objects that request services from each other. Each object is an instance of a class that contains a blueprint description of all the object's characteristics. Contrary to procedural programming, an object bundles both its variables (which determine its state) and its methods (which determine its behavior) in a coherent way. Let's consider an example of a class Employee defined in Java:

```
public class Employee {

private int EmployeeID;
private String Name;
private String Gender;
private Department Dep;

public int getEmployeeID() {
   return EmployeeID;
}
public void setEmployeeID( int id ) {
   this.EmployeeID = id;
}
public String getName() {
   return Name;
}
public void setName( String name ) {
   this.Name = name;
}
public String getGender() {
   return Gender;
}
public void setGender( String gender ) {
   this.Gender = gender;
}
public Department getDep() {
   return Dep;
}
public void setDep( Department dep) {
   this.Dep = dep;
}
}
```

In the example above, you can see a class Employee with four variables: EmployeeID, Name, Gender, and Dep, which represents the department where the employee works. Each variable comes with a getter and setter method, which allow retrieval or modification of the variable's value, respectively. Other methods can also be added as needed (e.g., to calculate an employee's salary). The getter and setter methods are also called **accessor methods** and implement the concept of **information hiding**, also called **encapsulation**. The main idea is to make variables private to the class, so they are not directly accessible from outside of the class. This gives the programmer control over how and when variables can be accessed. Encapsulation offers several advantages that make it standard recommended practice for all classes. For example, you can use the accessor methods to check for validity before changing a variable's value. If an invalid value is provided, the programmer can decide how to handle it, such as by adjusting it or throwing an exception. The concept of encapsulation enforces a strict separation between interface and implementation. The **interface** consists of the signatures of the methods. The **implementation** is then based upon the object's variables and method definitions and is kept hidden from the outside world.

**Retention Questions**

- What is the difference between an object and a class? Illustrate with examples.
- What is information hiding and why is it important?

Once the class has been defined, we can create objects from it. The following code snippet illustrates how we can create three Employee objects and set their names.

```
public class EmployeeProgram {
   public static void main(String[] args) {
     Employee Bart = new Employee();
     Employee Seppe = new Employee();
     Employee Wilfried = new Employee();
     Bart.setName("Bart Baesens");
     Seppe.setName("Seppe vanden Broucke");
     Wilfried.setName("Wilfried Lemahieu");
   }
}
```

**Connections**

We already discussed the basic concepts of OO in Chapter 3, when we introduced the UML conceptual data model.

## 8.2 Advanced Concepts of OO

In this section we elaborate on advanced concepts of OO. We discuss method overloading, inheritance, method overriding, polymorphism, and dynamic binding.

### 8.2.1 Method Overloading

**Method overloading** refers to using the same name for more than one method in the same class. The OO language environment can then determine which method you are calling, provided the number or type of parameters is different in each method. This is illustrated in the following example.

```
public class Book {
String title;
String author;
boolean isRead;
int numberOfReadings;

public void read(){
    isRead = true;
    numberOfReadings++;
}
```

```
public void read(int i){
    isRead = true;
    numberOfReadings += i;
}
}
```

Here you have one method with the name "read" and no parameters, and a second method with the name "read" and one integer parameter. To Java, these are two different methods, so you will have no duplication errors. As expected, if the parameter i equals 1 then read(1) will have the same effect as read(). Method overloading is a handy feature when defining constructors for a class. A **constructor** is a method that creates and returns a new object of a class. By using method overloading, various constructors can be defined, each with their own specific set of input parameters. Consider a Student class with two constructor methods: Student(String name, int year, int month, int day) and Student(String name). The former takes both the name and date of birth as its input argument, whereas the latter only takes the name and leaves the date of birth unspecified. By defining these two constructors and using method overloading, Student objects can be created when the date of birth is known or unknown.

### 8.2.2 Inheritance

**Inheritance** represents an "is a" relationship. For example, a Student is a Person, so the class Student could be a subclass of the Person class. An Employee is a Person too, so Employee could be another subclass of Person. An undergraduate is a student and a graduate is a student, so you can create two additional subclasses of the class Student. Staff and Faculty might be subclasses of the class Employee. A possible class hierarchy for this inheritance example is shown in Figure 8.1. Each subclass inherits both the variables and methods from the superclass. A subclass can also introduce new variables and methods. Below, you can see the definitions of the Person and Employee class in Java. The Person superclass has a name variable, a constructor method and getter/setter methods. The Employee class is a subclass of the Person class. Note the use of the extends keyword which specifies the inheritance relationship. The Employee subclass also defines two additional variables: the id variable and an Employee object which represents the manager of the employee. It also includes a constructor method and the necessary getter and setter methods to enforce information hiding.

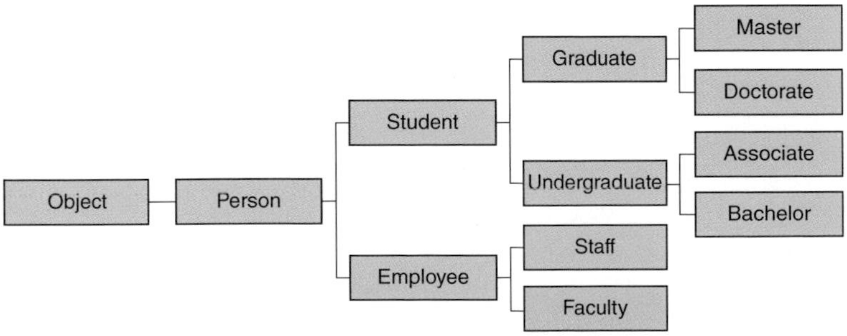


**Figure 8.1** Example inheritance hierarchy.

```
public class Person {
private String name;

public Person(String name) {
this.setName(name);
}
public String getName() {
return this.name;
}
public void setName(String name) {
this.name = name;
}
}
public class Employee extends Person {
private Employee manager;
private int id;

public Employee( String name, Employee manager, int empID ) {
super(name);
this.setManager(manager);
this.setEmployeeID(empID);
}
public Employee getManager() {
return manager;
}
public void setManager(Employee manager) {
this.manager = manager;
}
public int getEmployeeID() {
return id;
}
private void setEmployeeID(int employeeID) {
this.id = employeeID;
}
}
```

### 8.2.3 Method Overriding

As previously noted, subclasses inherit both variables and methods from their superclass. This means that if the Student class has a calculateGPA() method, then Graduate and Undergraduate will have this method as well. The subclasses can, however, override the method with a new, specialized implementation. This is called **method overriding**. This is not related to method overloading discussed earlier in this chapter. Consider the calculateGPA() method from the Student class. Assume the Student class has a grades variable that contains all the student's grades (e.g., stored in an array). The calculateGPA() method then just calculates the average of these grades as follows:

```
public double calculateGPA(){
double sum = 0;
int count = 0;
for (double grade: this.getGrades()){
sum += grade;
count++;
}
return sum/count;
}
```

Now, suppose graduate students only get credit for grades above a certain minimum. For example, only grades of 80% and higher are accepted, and courses with a grade below 80% must be repeated. Then for the Graduate class, you might want to calculate the GPA based only on those higher grades. To do this, you can override the calculateGPA() method and change the implementation by adding an if (grade > 80){} statement as follows:

```
public double calculateGPA(){
double sum = 0;
int count = 0;
for (double grade: this.getGrades()){
if (grade > 80){
sum += grade;
count++;
}
}
return sum/count;
}
```

This will make sure that graduate students have their grades properly calculated.

### 8.2.4 Polymorphism and Dynamic Binding

**Polymorphism** refers to the ability of objects to respond differently to the same method. It is a key concept in OO programming and is closely related to inheritance. Because inheritance models an "is a" relationship, one object can take on the variables and behavior of more than one class. According to the class hierarchy of the Person example, a Master is a Graduate, a Graduate is a Student, and a Student is a Person, so depending on the functionality desired, the OO environment might consider a particular Master object as a Master, a Graduate, a Student, or a Person, because, after all, a Master is still a Person.

Every method must be bound or mapped to its implementation. There are two types of binding. **Static binding** binds a method to its implementation at compile time. In contrast to static binding, **dynamic binding** means that the binding of methods to the appropriate implementation is resolved at runtime, based on the object and its class. It is also called *virtual method invocation* and is the binding used for methods to allow for polymorphism. When a method is overridden, multiple implementations can be called, depending on the object in question. During execution, the OO environment will first check the object class that the reference object points to for the method implementation. If it does not exist, the system will look to the superclass. It will check the superclass above that if it still finds no match, and so on throughout the entire class hierarchy. By searching from the bottom up, the most specific implementation, or the one from the class lowest in the hierarchy, will be the one used. Consider again the example of the GPA calculation, which calculates the average of all grades for most Student objects and the average of grades above a threshold for graduate students. Suppose you create a PersonProgram class to run your main method:

```
public class PersonProgram {
public static void main(String[] args){
Student john = new Master("John Adams");
john.setGrades(0.75,0.82,0.91,0.69,0.79);
Student anne = new Associate("Anne Philips");
anne.setGrades(0.75,0.82,0.91,0.69,0.79);
System.out.println(john.getName() + ": " + john.calculateGPA());
System.out.println(anne.getName() + ": " + anne.calculateGPA());
}
}
```

You have two Student objects: John is a Master (subclass of Graduate) and Anne is an Associate (subclass of Undergraduate). To compare easily, assume they both have the same grades for five courses. When your main method reaches the print statements, it will first call the getName() method for each object. For John, none of the Master class, the Graduate class, or the Student class contain a getName() method. Therefore, the Master object inherits the getName() method directly from the Person class. Next, it must call the calculateGPA() method for John. The Master class does not contain a calculateGPA() method, but the Graduate class, the superclass of Master, does. Dynamic binding looks at the type of object that John is: a Master and, hence, a Graduate. Therefore, the calculateGPA() method from the Graduate class is called. For Anne, the same decision process occurs. There is no getName() method in the subclasses, so the class hierarchy is considered to find that Anne is an Associate, which is an Undergraduate, which is a Student, which is a Person, and the getName() method from the Person class is called. For her GPA, neither Associate nor Undergraduate has a calculateGPA() method, so the Student version of the method is called for Anne. The output will then be as follows:

```
John Adams: 0.865
Anne Philips: 0.792
```

Since John is a master student, which is a subclass of Graduate, only the marks above 0.8 will be averaged so the result will be $(0.82+0.91)/2=0.865$. Since Anne is an associate, which is a subclass of Undergraduate, her average will be calculated as $(0.75+0.82+0.91+0.69+0.79)/5=0.792$. It shows two different GPAs, despite having the same grades, because dynamic method invocation allows different versions of the methods to be called depending on the object calling it.

We can conclude the discussion on advanced concepts of OO. Note that besides Java these concepts are also commonly available in other OO programming languages such as C++, Python, and C#.

### Retention Questions

- What is method overloading and why do we use it?
- Discuss the relationship between method overriding and inheritance.
- What is the difference between static and dynamic binding?

## 8.3 Basic Principles of Object Persistence

During OO program execution, a distinction can be made between transient and persistent objects. A **transient object** is only needed during program execution and can be discarded when the program terminates. It only resides in internal memory. As an example, think about graphical user interface (GUI) objects. A **persistent object** is one that should survive program execution. Its state should be made persistent using external storage media. Consider Employee objects or Student objects created and/or manipulated by the program.

Various strategies can ensure object persistence. **Persistence by class** implies that all objects of a particular class will be made persistent. Although this method is simple, it is inflexible because it does not allow a class to have any transient objects. **Persistence by creation** is achieved by extending the syntax for creating objects to indicate at compile time that an object should be made persistent. **Persistence by marking** implies that all objects will be created as transient. An object can then be marked as persistent during program execution (at runtime). **Persistence by inheritance** indicates that the persistence capabilities are inherited from a predefined persistent class. Finally, **persistence by reachability** starts by declaring the root persistent object(s). All objects referred to (either directly or indirectly) by the root object(s) will then be made persistent as well. This strategy is adopted by the Object Database Management Group (ODMG) standard, as we will discuss in Section 8.4.2.

Ideally, a persistence environment should support **persistence orthogonality**, which implies these properties: persistence independence, type orthogonality, and transitive persistence. With **persistence independence**, the persistence of an object is independent of how a program manipulates it. The same code fragment or function can be used with both persistent and transient objects. Hence, the programmer does not need to explicitly control the movement of objects between main memory and secondary storage as this is automatically taken care of by the system. **Type orthogonality** ensures that all objects can be made persistent, despite their type or size. This prevents the programmer from having to write customized persistence routines and getting sidetracked. Finally, **transitive persistence** refers to persistence by reachability as we discussed earlier. An environment supporting persistence orthogonality allows for improved programmer productivity and maintenance.

### 8.3.1 Serialization

Persistent programming languages were a first attempt to equip programming languages with the ability to preserve data across multiple executions of a program. This usually boiled down to extending an OO language with a set of class libraries for object persistence. One approach to do so is by using a mechanism called **serialization**, which translates an object's state into a format that can be stored (for example, in a file) and reconstructed later. In Java, this can be accomplished as follows:[1]

[1] We assume the Employee class implements the `java.io.Serializable` interface, which is part of the `java.io` package.

```
public class EmployeeProgram {
      public static void main(String[] args) {
            Employee Bart = new Employee();
            Employee Seppe = new Employee();
            Employee Wilfried = new Employee();
            Bart.setName("Bart Baesens");
            Seppe.setName("Seppe vanden Broucke");
            Wilfried.setName("Wilfried Lemahieu");
            try {
            FileOutputStream fos = new FileOutputStream("myfile.ser");
            ObjectOutputStream out = new ObjectOutputStream(fos);
            out.writeObject(Bart);
            out.writeObject(Seppe);
            out.writeObject(Wilfried);
            out.close;
            }
      catch (IOException e){ e.printStackTrace();}
      }
}
```

The above program creates three employee objects – Bart, Seppe, and Wilfried – and sets the "name" variable. We now wish to make all three objects persistent. The ObjectOutputStream class will serialize an object to a file, myfile.ser, using the writeObject method. The objects will be stored as a sequence of bytes, including the object's variables and their types. Here, Java will apply persistence by reachability. This implies that if the employee objects would have references to address objects, department objects, etc. then these will also be made persistent in myfile.ser. Once stored, the object can be deserialized from the file and recreated in internal memory using the class ObjectInputStream.

**Connections**

Serialization suffers from many disadvantages of the file-based approach to data management, as we discussed in Chapter 1.

Serialization is one of the simplest strategies to achieve persistence. However, this approach suffers from the same disadvantages as the file-based approach to data management, as discussed in Chapter 1 (e.g., application-data dependence, redundancy, inconsistent updates, no transaction support, etc.). Another significant problem relates to the object identity that is lost. Suppose we store information about lecturer and course objects. Bart and Wilfried both teach database management, whereas Seppe and Bart both teach basic programming. This can be visualized in the object graph of Figure 8.2.

**Retention Questions**

- What is the difference between a transient and a persistent object?
- What strategies can be adopted to ensure object persistence?
- What is meant by persistence orthogonality?

Assume we now serialize both the database management and basic programming course objects. This means the information for the Bart lecturer object will be duplicated. Upon deserialization, the Bart lecturer object will also be duplicated in internal memory, which can lead to inconsistencies when its values are changed during program execution. Hence, a better alternative would be to work with an object-oriented DBMS, as explained in what follows.

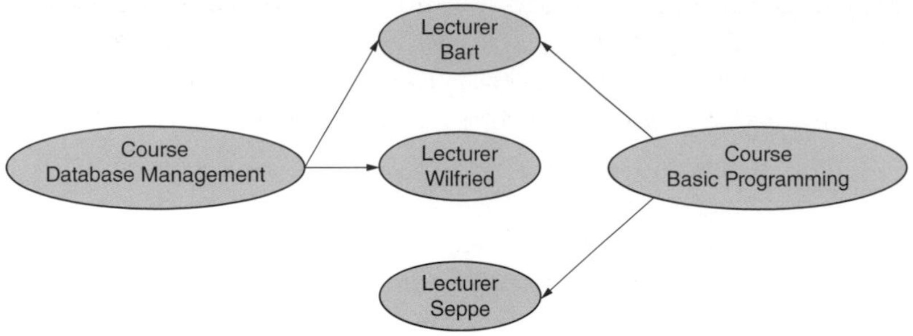


**Figure 8.2** Example object graph.

## 8.4 OODBMS

**Object-oriented DBMSs (OODBMS)** store persistent objects in a transparent way. They originated as extensions to object-oriented programming languages, such as C++ and Smalltalk, which included class libraries to make objects persistent. These libraries were then gradually extended with database facilities, such as querying, concurrency control, and transaction management. Initially, since these libraries and extensions were programming language-dependent, no universal standard (e.g., similar to SQL in relational databases) was available to explain the heterogeneous OODBMS landscape.

OODBMSs support persistence orthogonality, whereby the same data model is used for transient and persistent objects with no need to map to an underlying relational structure. They come with all the facilities of a traditional DBMS, such as a data definition and data manipulation language, query facilities, transaction management, concurrency control, backup and recovery facilities, etc. OODBMSs guarantee the ACID properties discussed in Chapter 1 for all persistent objects.

**Drill Down**

According to http://db-engines.com, the most popular OODBMSs are: Caché (commercial), DB4o (open-source), ObjectStore (commercial), Versant Object Database (commercial), and Matisse (commercial). Note that none of these ranks in the top 50 of most popular DBMSs used in industry. This clearly indicates that OODBMSs are targeted at niche applications.

### 8.4.1 Object Identifiers

In an OODBMS, every object has a unique and immutable **object identifier (OID)**, which it keeps during its entire lifetime. These OIDs are used to uniquely identify an object. No two objects can have the same identifier, and each object has only one identifier. An OID differs from a primary key in a relational database setting. A primary key depends upon the state of a tuple, whereas an OID is not dependent on an object's state. A primary key can be updated, whereas an OID never changes. A primary key has a unique value for each tuple within a relation, while an OID is unique within the entire OO environment.

In most commercial implementations, the OIDs will remain invisible to the user. They are typically system generated. The OIDs are used to identify objects and to create and manage references between objects. The references can implement relationship types, as discussed earlier.

By using these OIDs, it becomes possible that an object is shared by various other objects by simply referring to its OID. This reduces the number of updates when objects have their variable values or state changed. Because of the extensive use of these OIDs, the OO model is often called an *identity-based model*. The relational model is a *value-based model* since it uses primary and foreign keys, which are based on actual data values.

A difference can be made between **object equality** and **object identity**. Two objects are said to be equal when the values of their variables are the same. However, this does not automatically imply that their OIDs are the same. A further distinction can be made between shallow and deep equality. To illustrate both concepts, assume we have a purchase order object with some variables including a list of references to OIDs of related purchase order line objects. **Shallow equality** implies that two purchase order objects have the same values for their variables (e.g., purchase order number, purchase order date, supplier number, etc.). **Deep equality** implies that two purchase order objects have the same values for their variables and all their referred purchase order line objects have the same values for their variables. Two objects are said to be identical or equivalent when their OIDs are the same. Even though the values of an object's variables may change, its identity always remains.

### 8.4.2 ODMG Standard

The **Object Database Management Group (ODMG)** was formed in 1991 by a group of OO database vendors to define standards for working with OODBMSs. Its name was changed to *Object Data Management Group* in 1998 to expand its coverage to both OODBMSs and object-relational mapping standards. The primary goal was to promote portability and interoperability for object persistence by introducing a data definition and data manipulation language for OODBMSs, similar to the role SQL fulfills toward RDBMSs. The application developer should be able to use only one language for dealing with both transient and persistent objects. The group introduced five subsequent versions of the standard, the most recent being ODMG 3.0 in 2000 (!), which consists of these key components:

- *object model*, which provides a standard object model for object-oriented databases;
- *object definition language (ODL)*, which specifies object definitions (classes and interfaces);
- *object query language (OQL)*, which allows defining SELECT queries;
- *language bindings* (e.g., for C++, Smalltalk, and Java), which allow retrieval and manipulation of object data from within an OO programming language.

Although the group disbanded in 2001, many concepts and ideas put forward have been implemented in modern OODBMSs, and in so-called object-relational mapping frameworks.

### 8.4.3 Object Model

The **object model** serves as the backbone of the ODMG standard. It provides a common model to define classes, variables or attributes, behavior, and object persistence. Its two basic building blocks are objects and literals. Contrary to an object, a **literal** has no OID and cannot exist on its own. It represents a constant value and is typically embedded in an object. Three types of literals are supported: atomic, collection, and structured literals. Examples of **atomic literals** are short (short integer), long (long integer), double (real number), float (real number), boolean (true or false), char, and string. A **collection literal** can model a collection of elements. ODMG defines the following collection literals:

- set: unordered collection of elements without duplicates;
- bag: unordered collection of elements which may contain duplicates;
- list: ordered collection of elements;
- array: ordered collection of elements indexed;
- dictionary: unordered sequence of key–value pairs without duplicates.

A **structured literal** consists of a fixed number of named elements. ODMG has predefined the following structured literals: date, interval, time, and timestamp. User-defined structures are also supported, such as Address:

```
struct Address{
string street;
integer number;
integer zipcode;
string city;
string state;
string country;
};
```

In contrast to literals, objects have an OID. Their state is determined by their attributes and relationships, whereas their behavior is specified by several operations. All ODMG objects implement a set of generic operations such as "copy" (to create a copy of an object), "delete" (to remove an object), and "same_as" (to compare the identity of two objects), which have been defined in an Object interface. A further distinction can be made between *atomic objects*, which cannot be decomposed in a meaningful way; *structured objects*, which can be built-in (e.g., date, interval, time, timestamp, etc.) or user-defined; and *collection objects*.

### 8.4.4 Object Definition Language (ODL)

The **object definition language (ODL)** is a data definition language (DDL) to define the object types that conform to the ODMG object model. It is independent of any programming language. Similar to an SQL schema being portable across RDBMSs, an ODL schema can be implemented using multiple ODMG-compliant OODBMSs.

Here you can see an example ODL definition for the employee administration we discussed earlier:

```
class EMPLOYEE
(extent employees
 key SSN)
{
attribute string SSN;
attribute string ENAME;
attribute struct ADDRESS;
attribute enum GENDER {male, female};
attribute date DATE_OF_BIRTH;
```

```
relationship set<EMPLOYEE> supervises
inverse EMPLOYEE:: supervised_by;
relationship EMPLOYEE supervised_by
inverse EMPLOYEE:: supervises;
relationship DEPARTMENT works_in
inverse DEPARTMENT:: workers;
relationship set<PROJECT> has_projects
inverse PROJECT:: has_employees;
string GET_SSN();
void SET_SSN(in string new_ssn);
...
}

class MANAGER extends EMPLOYEE
(extent managers)
{
attribute date mgrdate;
relationship DEPARTMENT manages
inverse DEPARTMENT:: managed_by
}

class DEPARTMENT
(extent departments
 key DNR)
{
attribute string DNR;
attribute string DNAME;
attribute set<string> DLOCATION;
relationship set<EMPLOYEE> workers
inverse EMPLOYEE:: works_in;
relationship set<PROJECT> assigned_to_projects
inverse PROJECT:: assigned_to_department;
relationship MANAGER managed_by
inverse MANAGER:: manages;
string GET_DNR();
void SET_DNR(in string new_dnr);
...
}

class PROJECT
(extent projects
 key PNR)
{
attribute string PNR;
attribute string PNAME;
attribute string PDURATION;
relationship DEPARTMENT assigned_to_department
```

```
inverse DEPARTMENT:: assigned_to_projects;
relationship set<EMPLOYEE> has_employees
inverse EMPLOYEE:: has_projects;
string GET_PNR();
void SET_PNR(in string new_pnr);
}
```

A class is defined using the keyword "class". The "extent" of a class is the set of all current objects of the class. A variable is declared using the keyword "attribute". An attribute's value can be either a literal or an OID. Operations or methods can be defined by their name followed by parentheses. The keywords "in", "out", and "inout" are used to define the input, output, and input/output parameters of the method. The return types are also indicated, whereby "void" indicates that the method returns nothing. To support the concept of encapsulation, it is recommended to add getter and setter methods for each attribute. Only the operations' signatures are defined; their implementation is provided through the language bindings, as we will discuss in what follows. The "extends" keyword indicates the generalization relationship between MANAGER and EMPLOYEE. Remember that a subclass inherits the attributes, relationships, and operations from the superclass. In ODMG a class can have at most one superclass, so no multiple inheritance of classes is supported.[2]

Relationships can be defined using the keyword "relationship".[3] Only unary and binary relationships with cardinalities of 1:1, 1:N, or N:M are supported in ODMG. Ternary (or higher) relationships and relationship attributes must be decomposed by introducing extra classes and relationships. Every relationship is defined in a bidirectional way, using the keyword "inverse" through which both directions have names assigned to facilitate navigation. For example, consider the following 1: N relationship between EMPLOYEE and DEPARTMENT:

```
relationship DEPARTMENT works_in
inverse DEPARTMENT:: workers;
```

The name "works_in" will be used to navigate from EMPLOYEE to DEPARTMENT, whereas the name "workers" is the inverse relationship used to navigate from DEPARTMENT to EMPLOYEE. The latter then becomes:

```
relationship set<EMPLOYEE> workers
inverse EMPLOYEE:: works_in;
```

Since a department can have multiple employees, we used a set to model the collection of employees working in a department. Other collection types such as a bag or list can also implement the relation. For example, a list could be useful if we want to order the employees based on their age.

An N:M relationship can be implemented by defining collection types (set, bag, etc.) in both classes participating in the relationship. Consider this N:M relationship between EMPLOYEE and PROJECT:

```
relationship set<PROJECT> has_projects
inverse PROJECT:: has_employees;
relationship set<EMPLOYEE> has_employees
inverse EMPLOYEE:: has_projects;
```

[2] Similar to Java, ODMG *does* support multiple inheritance of interfaces.
[3] A relationship in the ODMG standard corresponds to what we called a relationship type in the (E)ER model.

This contrasts with the relational model, where a new relation must be introduced.

Based upon the relationships defined, the OODBMS will take care of the referential integrity by ensuring that both sides of the relationship remain consistent. For example, when adding a project to the set "has_projects" of an employee, the OODBMS will also add the employee to the set "has_employees" of the corresponding project.

## 8.4.5 Object Query Language (OQL)

**Object query language (OQL)** is a declarative, non-procedural query language. It is based upon the SQL SELECT syntax combined with OO facilities such as dealing with object identity, complex objects, path expressions, operation invocation, polymorphism, and dynamic binding. It can be used for both navigational (procedural) and associative (declarative) access.

### 8.4.5.1 Simple OQL Queries

A **navigational query** explicitly navigates from one object to another. Here, the application program is responsible for explicitly specifying the navigation paths. This makes it similar to procedural database languages that came with hierarchical and CODASYL DBMSs, discussed in Chapter 5. A navigational OQL query can start from a named object. Assume we have an Employee object named Bart. The following OQL query:

```
Bart.DATE_OF_BIRTH
```

returns the date of birth of Bart as a literal.

If we are interested in the address, we can write:

```
Bart.ADDRESS
```

which returns the address of Employee object Bart as a structure. If we are only interested in the city, the query can be refined to:

```
Bart.ADDRESS.CITY
```

Note how we use the dot operator (.) for navigation.

An **associative query** returns a collection (e.g., a set or bag) of objects located by the OODBMS. We can also start from the *extent*, which represents the set of all persistent objects of a class. The most straightforward associative OQL query then simply retrieves all objects of an extent:

```
employees
```

### 8.4.5.2 SELECT FROM WHERE OQL Queries

If we want more specific information, we can write an OQL query with the following syntax:

```
SELECT... FROM ... WHERE
```

As with SQL, the SELECT clause indicates the information we are interested in. The FROM clause refers to the extent(s) where the information should be retrieved from. The WHERE clause can define specific conditions. By default, an OQL query returns a bag. If the keyword DISTINCT is used, a set is returned. Queries with ORDER BY return a list. Associative OQL queries can also include navigation paths.

Consider the following example:

```
SELECT e.SSN, e.ENAME, e.ADDRESS, e.GENDER
FROM employees e
WHERE e.ENAME="Bart Baesens"
```

This query returns the SSN, name, address, and gender of all objects of the extent employees where the name is equal to "Bart Baesens". Note that the extent employees has been bound to a variable e as a shortcut notation.

Suppose now that the Employee class has a method age that calculates the age of an employee based upon the date of birth. We can then extend our previous query:

```
SELECT e.SSN, e.ENAME, e.ADDRESS, e.GENDER, e.age
FROM employees e
WHERE e.ENAME="Bart Baesens"
```

Besides literal values, an OQL query can also return objects:

```
SELECT e
FROM employees e
WHERE e.age > 40
```

The above query will return a bag of employee objects whose age is above 40.

### 8.4.5.3 Join OQL Queries

Just as in SQL, multiple classes can be joined. This can be accomplished by traversing the paths as defined in the ODL schema. The following query retrieves all information of employees working in the ICT department.

```
SELECT e.SSN, e.ENAME, e.ADDRESS, e.GENDER, e.age
FROM employees e, e.works_in d
WHERE d.DNAME="ICT"
```

The variable d gets bound to the department object based upon following the path e.works_in. Contrary to SQL, you can see no join condition. Instead, the traversal path e.works_in ensures the correct department information is used. Multiple traversal paths can be used in an OQL query. Consider the following query:

```
SELECT e1.ENAME, e1.age, d.DNAME, e2.ENAME, e2.age
FROM employees e1, e1.works_in d, d.managed_by e2
WHERE e1.age > e2.age
```

This query selects the name and age of all employees with a younger manager, the name of the department they work in, and the name and age of their manager.

### 8.4.5.4 Other OQL Queries

Like SQL, OQL provides support for subqueries, GROUP BY/HAVING, and aggregate operators such as COUNT, SUM, AVG, MAX, and MIN. For example, the number of employees can be determined using this simple query:

```
count(employees)
```

The EXISTS operator can also be used. The following query retrieves information about employees working on at least one project:

```
SELECT e.SSN, e.ENAME
FROM employees e
WHERE EXISTS e IN (SELECT x FROM projects p WHERE p.has_employees x)
```

Suppose both the EMPLOYEE and MANAGER class each have their own operation salary(). Consider this OQL query:

```
SELECT e.SSN, e.ENAME, e.salary
FROM employees e
```

This query will calculate the salary for all employee objects. Thanks to polymorphism and dynamic binding, the correct implementation of the salary method will be invoked at runtime for both MANAGER and regular EMPLOYEE objects.

The OQL language provides no explicit support for INSERT, UPDATE, and DELETE operations. These have to be directly implemented in the class definitions instead, as discussed in Section 8.4.6.

### 8.4.6 Language Bindings

A key difference between relational and OO database management systems is that the latter cannot be used without a particular programming language. ODMG language bindings provide implementations for the ODL and OQL specifications in popular OO programming languages such as C++, Smalltalk, or Java. The object manipulation language (OML) is kept language-specific to accomplish a full and transparent handling of both transient objects in internal memory, and persistent objects in the database. As mentioned before, the goal is that the programmer can use only one language transparently for both application development and database manipulation.

For the Java language binding, for instance, this goal entails that Java's type system will also be used by the OODBMS, that the Java language syntax is respected (and therefore should not be modified to accommodate the OODBMS), and that the OODBMS should handle management aspects based on Java's object semantics. For instance, the OODBMS should be responsible for persisting objects when they are referenced by other persistent objects; this is what we called persistence by reachability earlier in this chapter.

The ODMG Java language binding describes two core ways to indicate that a Java class should be persistence-capable: either existing Java classes are made persistence-capable, or Java class definitions are generated from the ODL class definitions. The ODMG Java API is contained in the package org.odmg. The entire API consists of interfaces, so the actual implementation is up to the OODBMS vendor, with the implementation of the org.odmg.Implementation interface forming the main entry point for the client application and exposing the methods listed in Table 8.1.

For the mapping of the ODMG object model to Java, an ODMG object type maps into a Java object type. The ODMG atomic literal types map into their respective Java primitive types. There are no structured literal types in the Java binding. The object model definition of a structure maps into a Java class. The Java binding also includes several collection interfaces (DMap, DSet) that extend their respective Java counterparts.

**Table 8.1** Methods of the org.odmg.Implementation interface

| Method | Meaning |
|---|---|
| org.odmg.Transaction currentTransaction() | Get the current Transaction for the thread. |
| org.odmg.Database getDatabase(java.lang.Object obj) | Get the Database that contains the object obj. |
| java.lang.String getObjectId(java.lang.Object obj) | Get a String representation of the object's identifier. |
| org.odmg.DArray newDArray() | Create a new DArray object. |
| org.odmg.Database newDatabase() | Create a new Database object. |
| org.odmg.DBag newDBag() | Create a new DBag object. |
| org.odmg.DList newDList() | Create a new DList object. |
| org.odmg.DMap newDMap() | Create a new DMap object. |
| org.odmg.DSet newDSet() | Create a new DSet object. |
| org.odmg.OQLQuery newOQLQuery() | Create a new OQLQuery object. |
| org.odmg.Transaction newTransaction() | Create a Transaction object. |

The following code snippet provides an example of using the ODMG Java language binding (note that age is now considered as an attribute and no longer as a method for what follows):

```
import org.odmg.*;
import java.util.Collection;
// org.odmg.Implementation as implemented by a particular vendor:
Implementation impl = new com.example.odmg-vendor.odmg.Implementation();
Database db = impl.newDatabase();
Transaction txn = impl.newTransaction();

try {
    db.open("my_database", Database.OPEN_READ_WRITE);
    txn.begin();
    OQLQuery query = new OQLQuery(
         "select e from employees e where e.lastName = \"Lemahieu\"");
    Collection result = (Collection) query.execute();
    Iterator iter = result.iterator();
    while (iter.hasNext()){
        Employee employee = (Employee) iter.next();
        // Update a value
        employee.age += 1;
    }
    txn.commit();
    db.close();
} catch (Exception e) {}
```

This code starts by creating an ODMG implementation object which is then used to construct a database object. We open the database my_database for read and write access and initiate a transaction. An OQL query object is defined to retrieve all EMPLOYEE objects of employees whose last name is Lemahieu. The query is then

**Retention Questions**

- What are object identifiers and why are they needed in an OODBMS?
- What are the key components of the ODMG standard?
- Discuss the ODMG object model.
- Contrast ODMG ODL against SQL DDL.
- What types of queries can be solved using ODMG OQL? How is it different from queries in SQL?

executed and the results stored in a collection object. Next, an iterator object is defined to loop through the collection of query results. For each employee in the collection, the age is increased by one unit.[4] The transaction is then committed, implying that the updates are made persistent. The database object is then properly closed.

**Drill Down**

Delta Airlines serves more than 170 million customers per year. In the event of irregular operations (e.g., due to severe weather), Delta needs an efficient application to reroute crew members, and for this they need to process a huge load of data in real-time. Efficient caching that allows quick saving and retrieval of objects is essential for this. Delta wanted a solution that was capable of storing C++ objects in a persistent way and retrieving them like regular objects with no intermediate mapping that would hamper the performance. For this, they turned to OODBMSs and used ObjectStore.

## 8.5 Evaluating OODBMSs

OODBMSs offer several advantages. First, they store complex objects and relationships in a transparent way. The identity-based approach allows for improved performance when performing complex queries involving multiple interrelated objects, avoiding expensive joins. By using the same data model as the programming language to develop database applications, the impedance mismatch problem is no longer an issue. In addition, developers can be more productive as they are confronted with only a single language and data model.

Still, the success of OODBMSs has been limited to niche applications characterized by complex, nested data structures where an identity-based, instead of value-based, method of working pays off. An example is the processing of scientific datasets by CERN in Switzerland, where data access follows predictable patterns. The widespread use and performance of RDBMSs, however, proved hard to displace: the (ad-hoc) query formulation and optimization procedures of OODBMSs are often inferior to relational databases, which all adopt SQL as their primary database language combined with a powerful query optimizer. When compared to RDBMSs, OODBMSs are not as well developed in terms of robustness, security, scalability, and fault tolerance. They also do not provide a transparent implementation of the three-layer database architecture. More specifically, most OODBMSs provide no support for defining external database models, such as views in the relational model.

In addition, despite efforts made by the ODMG, the uniform standards proposed were not widely implemented by vendors, who were quick to realize that the concepts of an OODBMS and object persistence as such are not the same, hence the name change from ODMG to the Object *Data* Management Group (still abbreviated ODMG) in 1998. The aim was to focus on the standardization of an API for object persistence, still according to the same ODMG principles, regardless of whether the underlying data store was an RDBMS or an OODBMS. In hindsight,

[4] For the sake of this illustration, we assume that age is defined as an attribute here and not as a method.

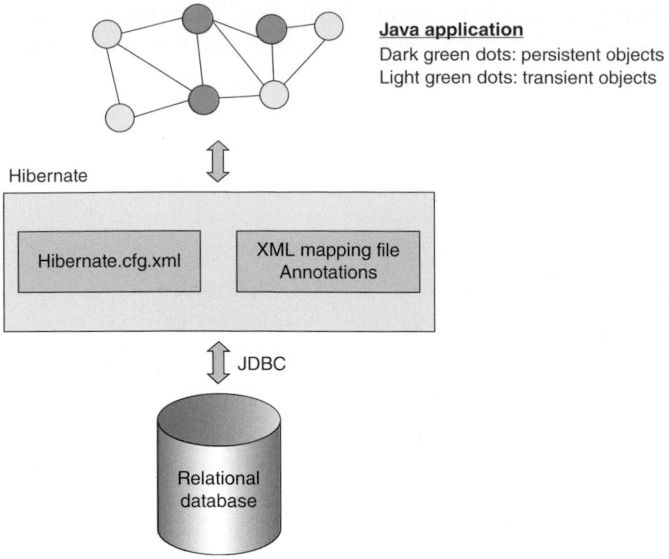


**Figure 8.3** Hibernate architecture.

this is probably the most important contribution of the ODMG, even though the standard itself was abandoned over time.

The ODMG effort inspired the creation of a series of persistence APIs for the Java programming language (which we extensively discuss in Chapter 15), which are the APIs used by most OODBMSs today, rather than the ODMG standard. However, most mainstream database applications will typically be built using an OO programming language in combination with an RDBMS. In such an environment, a persistence API works with an **object-relational mapping (ORM)** framework, which is used as middleware to facilitate the communication between both environments: the OO host language and the RDBMS. An ORM framework tackles the impedance problem between an OO application and an RDBMS by directly mapping objects to relational concepts and vice versa. Every object that needs to be made persistent can be mapped by the ORM to one or more tuples in a relational database without having to implement vendor-specific interfaces or classes. The ORM provides full support of all CRUD (create, read, update, and delete) database operations. A key advantage of using an object-relational mapper is that the developer does not need to understand and master all details of relational database design and advanced SQL query tuning. This allows the developer to focus on the OO paradigm only. All database interactions are directly handled and optimized by the ORM, whereas the developer is solely confronted with objects and OO concepts. Ideally, this will result in more compact application code, a potential decrease in database calls, more efficient queries, and greater portability across database platforms.

Different ORM implementations exist for various programming languages, with Hibernate being one of the most popular choices for the Java programming language, providing support for most commercial relational database platforms such as MySQL, Oracle, Sybase, and others. Figure 8.3 provides a high-level outline of the Hibernate architecture. We elaborate each of these components in more detail in Chapters 10 and 15.

**Connections**

Chapter 15 deals with database access and APIs in depth, and will revisit the concept of object-relational mapping in more detail. Chapter 10 covers XML, which can define the mappings as illustrated in Figure 8.3.

One key distinction to remember between ORM and OODBMSs is that the ORM acts as a middleware layer between a relational DBMS and a host language, which follows an OO paradigm. The usage of an ORM framework should be regarded as a more advanced form of relational database access.

## Summary

In this chapter we started by reviewing the basic concepts of object orientation. This was followed by a discussion of advanced OO concepts such as method overloading, inheritance, method overriding, polymorphism, and dynamic binding, all illustrated in Java. We then introduced the basic principles of object persistence and reviewed serialization as a first attempt to equip programming languages with the ability to preserve data across multiple executions of a program. This brought us to OODBMSs, where we started by introducing object identifiers, which play a key role in identifying objects. The ODMG standard was covered next, and we discussed its object model, the object definition language (ODL), the object query language (OQL) and its implementation through language bindings. We concluded with a critical review of OODBMSs by contrasting them to RDBMSs and introducing object-relational mapping frameworks (ORMs).

### Scenario Conclusion

Now that Sober understands the basic principles of OO, object persistence, and OODBMSs, it can properly weigh the benefits versus risks of these technologies. Although the company was initially charmed by the ability to model complex objects, they considered the lack of a good and easy-to-use query language (compared to, e.g., SQL in RDBMSs) combined with the absence of a transparent three-layer database architecture as the main motivation to not pursue any of these technologies at the moment. Sober may, however, reconsider this once they have grown into a mature data-aware organization.

## Key Terms List

**accessor methods**
**associative query**
**atomic literal**
**collection literal**
**constructor**
**deep equality**
**dynamic binding**
**encapsulation**
**implementation**
**information hiding**
**inheritance**
**interface**
**literal**
**method overloading**
**method overriding**
**navigational query**
**Object Data Management Group**
**object definition language (ODL)**
**object equality**
**object identifier (OID)**
**object identity**
**object model**
**object query language (OQL)**
**object-relational mapping (ORM)**

**object-oriented (OO)**
**object-oriented DBMS (OODBMS)**
**persistence by class**
**persistence by creation**
**persistence by inheritance**
**persistence by marking**
**persistence by reachability**
**persistence independence**
**persistence orthogonality**
**persistent object**
**polymorphism**
**serialization**
**shallow equality**
**static binding**
**structured literal**
**transient object**
**transitive persistence**
**type orthogonality**

## Review Questions

**8.1.** Which of the following statements is **not correct**?

a. Objects are blueprints of classes. "Human", "Employee", and "Sale" are examples of objects.
b. Objects are instances of classes. The people "Bart Baesens", "Wilfried Lemahieu", and "Seppe vanden Broucke" could be instances of the class "Person".
c. Objects store both a piece of information and ways to manipulate this information.
d. A class can be instantiated into several objects.

**8.2.** Which statement about "Encapsulation" is **correct**?

a. Encapsulation refers to storing a value in a variable, and never changing it again. This way its value is safe forever.
b. Encapsulation refers to storing a value variable, and making it impossible to retrieve it.
c. Encapsulation refers to controlling the way a variable is accessed by forcing users to use getter/setter methods that prevent misuse of the variable.
d. Encapsulation implies that the methods of a class are not accessible to the other classes.

**8.3.** In Java, what is method overloading?

a. Putting so much code in a method that its functionality becomes hard to understand.
b. Using two methods with the same name, but a different number (and/or different type) of arguments.
c. Offering the user of your class all possible methods that he/she would like to perform on the variables the class offers.
d. Making sure that every method uses all variables of the class.

**8.4.** Which statement is **correct**?

a. Dynamic binding means that objects are allowed to take the form of either the class they are an instance of, or any of its subclasses.
b. In an inheritance structure with a parent class "Animal" and subclass "Chicken" at most one of these classes is allowed to have a method with the name "makeNoise".
c. Different subclasses of a parent class can all have different implementations of methods with the same name, number of parameters, and parameter types.
d. Static binding occurs at runtime whereas dynamic binding occurs at compile time.

**8.5.** Objects should be made persistent when. . .

a. you need them over multiple program executions.
b. you only need them during one program execution, and then never again.

**8.6.** Which statement is **not correct**?

a. Persistence by marking implies that all objects will be created as persistent. An object can then be marked as transient at compile time.
b. Persistence by class implies that all objects of a particular class will be made persistent.
c. Persistence by creation is achieved by extending the syntax for creating objects to indicate at compile time that an object should be made persistent.
d. Persistence by inheritance indicates that the persistence capabilities are inherited from a predefined persistent class.

**8.7.** Which statement about object identifiers (OIDs) is **correct**?

a. The OID of an object remains the same during the entire lifetime of the object.
b. An OID is the same as a primary key in a relational database setting.
c. Two objects with the same values always have the same OID.
d. Each literal is defined by an OID according to the ODMG standard.

**8.8.** Which of the following statements about ODL is **correct**?

a. ODL is only optimized for Java objects.
b. The extent of a class is the set of all current instances.
c. Many-to-many relationships cannot be expressed using ODL.
d. Unary, binary, and ternary relationships are supported in ODL.

**8.9.** What statement about OQL is **not correct**?

a. OQL is a declarative, non-procedural query language.
b. Join queries are not supported in OQL.
c. OQL can be used for both navigational (procedural) as well as associative (declarative) access.
d. The OQL language provides no explicit support for INSERT, UPDATE, and DELETE operations.

**8.10.** What is **not** an advantage of OODBMSs?

a. They allow storing objects and relationships in a transparent way.
b. They solve the impedance mismatch problem by using the same data model as the programming language.
c. Scalability and fault tolerance of OODBMSs is far better than that of their relational counterparts.
d. The identity-based approach allows for improved performance when performing complex queries involving multiple interrelated objects, avoiding expensive joins.

## Problems and Exercises

8.1E What is the relationship between polymorphism and dynamic binding? Illustrate with an example.

8.2E Discuss various strategies to ensure object persistence. When would you use what strategy? What are the key properties a persistence environment should support?

8.3E What are object identifiers? Why are they used by OODBMSs? What is the difference with primary keys in an RDBMS?

8.4E What are literals in the ODMG model? What types of literals are supported? How are literals mapped in Java? Illustrate with examples.

8.5E What types of relationships and cardinalities are supported in ODMG?

8.6E Contrast OQL with SQL.

8.7E Explain the following query in detail.

```
SELECT e1.ENAME, e1.age, d.DNAME, e2.ENAME, e2.age
FROM employees e1, e1.works_in d, d.managed_by e2
WHERE e1.age > e2.age
```

How would you solve a similar query in SQL?

8.8E Contrast OODBMSs versus RDBMSs in terms of:

- handling of complex objects;
- query performance;
- implementation of the three-layer database architecture;
- adoption in industry.

# 9 Extended Relational Databases

## Chapter Objectives

In this chapter, you will learn to:

- identify the shortcomings of the relational model;
- define and use triggers and stored procedures;
- understand how RDBMSs can be extended with OO concepts such as user-defined types, user-defined functions, inheritance, behavior, polymorphism, collection types, and large objects;
- define and use recursive SQL queries.

### Opening Scenario

Now that Sober has decided to continue with its relational model, the company was wondering whether it could enrich it with some smart extensions. It wondered whether it would be possible to make the RDBMS more active so it can autonomously take initiative for action when case-specific situations occur. Although Sober was not entirely convinced about OODBMSs and decided not to continue with them, they appreciate some of the OO concepts introduced. They are wondering whether it would be possible to have a best-of-both-worlds approach, whereby they could enrich their relational model with some of the OO concepts they learned about.

In this chapter, we revisit RDBMSs, which are very popular in industry. We start by refreshing the key building blocks of the relational model and discuss its limitations. We then look at the ways of extending relational databases, starting with reviewing triggers and stored procedures as two key mechanisms to make RDBMSs more active. Next, we introduce object-relational DBMSs (ORDBMSs). In contrast to the OODBMSs in Chapter 8, ORDBMSs build on a relational engine, but they extend RDBMSs with object-oriented (OO) characteristics. We conclude with recursive queries, which are a powerful extension to the SQL language.

## 9.1 Limitations of the Relational Model

The relational data model, and the RDBMS implementations thereof, have been very successful for managing well-structured numerical and alphanumerical data. One of the major reasons for this is the mathematical simplicity and soundness of the relational model. As discussed in Chapter 6, its two key building blocks are tuples and relations. A tuple is a composition of values of attribute types that describe an entity. It can be created by using a tuple constructor. A relation is a mathematical set of tuples describing similar entities. It can be created by using a set constructor. As also mentioned in Chapter 6, the relational model requires all relations to be normalized. Data about entities can be fragmented across multiple relations, which are connected using primary–foreign key relationships. Since the latter are based on actual, observable data values, the relational model is also called a value-based model, as opposed to the OO model, which is an identity-based model where references are made using unobservable object identifiers. Another reason for the success of RDBMSs is the availability of SQL, which is an easy-to-learn, descriptive, and non-navigational data manipulation language (DML) (see Chapter 7).

Despite the popularity of the relational model in industry, the emergence of applications dealing with complex objects (e.g., multimedia, geospatial information systems (GIS), genomics, time series, the internet of things, etc.) stretched its limits and unveiled its shortcomings. In what follows, we elaborate on this.

A first concern relates to the normalization itself. Due to the normalization, the relational model has a flat structure whereby relations can only be connected by using primary–foreign key relationships. This puts a heavy burden on the performance of database applications if the complexity of the data model increases, since expensive joins are needed to defragment the data before it can be successfully used and manipulated. Modeling concepts such as specialization, categorization, and aggregation cannot be directly supported. This clearly negatively affects code efficiency and maintenance.

Another shortcoming relates to the fact that the relational model supports only two type constructors: the tuple constructor and the set constructor. The former can only be used on atomic values, which implies that composite attribute types cannot be directly modeled. The latter can only be used on tuples, so multi-valued attribute types cannot be supported. Both constructors are not orthogonal and cannot be used in a nested way. Complex objects cannot be directly modeled but need to be broken down into simple, manageable objects of which the data can then be spread across multiple relations.

A next limitation concerns the inability to model behavior or store functions to work with the data within the DBMS runtime environment. If this would be possible, then applications can share and invoke these functions, reducing network traffic and unnecessary replication of code. Besides data independence, this would also allow support of functional independence, whereby the implementation of a function stored in the database can change without the applications using it being affected.

Finally, in their basic form, RDBMSs offer very poor support to deal with specific data, such as audio, video, or text files, which are often encountered in modern-day applications.

To address the above shortcomings, RDBMSs have been extended with additional functionality. In what follows, we discuss active and OO extensions. We also review recursive SQL queries that allow for more complex query formulation, which is another way to cope with some structural limitations of the relational model.

**Connections**

The relational model is discussed in detail in Chapter 6. Chapter 7 covers SQL, whereas OODBMSs are reviewed in Chapter 8.

**Retention Questions**

- Discuss the key limitations of the relational model. Illustrate with examples.

## 9.2 Active RDBMS Extensions

Traditional RDBMSs are **passive**, in the sense that they only execute transactions explicitly invoked by users and/or applications. Most modern-day RDBMSs are **active**, since they can autonomously take initiative for action if specific situations occur. Two key components of active RDBMSs are triggers and stored procedures.

### 9.2.1 Triggers

A **trigger** is a piece of SQL code consisting of declarative and/or procedural instructions and stored in the catalog of the RDBMS. It is automatically activated and run (also called fired) by the RDBMS whenever a specific event (e.g., insert, update, delete) occurs and a specific condition is evaluated as true. In contrast to CHECK constraints discussed in Chapter 7, triggers can also reference attribute types in other tables. Therefore, one of their applications is to enforce complex semantic constraints that cannot be captured in the basic relational model. Triggers are defined in SQL using this syntax:

```
CREATE TRIGGER trigger-name
BEFORE | AFTER trigger-event ON table-name
[ REFERENCING old-or-new-values-alias-list ]
[ FOR EACH { ROW | STATEMENT } ]
[ WHEN (trigger-condition) ]
trigger-body;
```

Let's illustrate this with a few examples. Assume we have these two relational tables:

```
EMPLOYEE(SSN, ENAME, SALARY, BONUS, JOBCODE, DNR)
DEPARTMENT(DNR, DNAME, TOTAL-SALARY, MGNR)
```

Remember that the foreign key DNR in EMPLOYEE refers to DNR in DEPARTMENT and the foreign key MGNR refers to the SSN of the department manager in EMPLOYEE. The wage of an employee consists of both a fixed salary and a variable bonus. The JOBCODE attribute type refers to the type of job the employee is assigned to. The attribute type TOTAL-SALARY in DEPARTMENT contains the total salary of all employees working in a department and should be updated whenever a new employee is assigned to a particular department. This can be accomplished with the following SQL trigger:[1]

```
CREATE TRIGGER SALARYTOTAL
AFTER INSERT ON EMPLOYEE
FOR EACH ROW
WHEN (NEW.DNR IS NOT NULL)
UPDATE DEPARTMENT
SET TOTAL-SALARY = TOTAL-SALARY + NEW.SALARY
WHERE DNR = NEW.DNR
```

This is an example of an **after trigger**, since it first inserts the employee tuple(s) and then executes the trigger body, which adjusts the attribute type TOTAL-SALARY in DEPARTMENT. The trigger is executed for each row or tuple affected by the INSERT and first verifies if the DNR of the new employee tuple is NULL or not before the update is performed.

A **before trigger** is always executed before the triggering event (in this case the INSERT operation on EMPLOYEE) can take place. Assume we now also have a relational table WAGE defined as follows:

[1] We could also create a view on the DEPARTMENT table that calculates the total salary, but let's assume we want to maintain TOTAL-SALARY as an actually stored value, e.g., for performance reasons.

```
WAGE(JOBCODE, BASE_SALARY, BASE_BONUS)
```

For each value of JOBCODE, this table stores the corresponding base salary and bonus. We can now define the following before trigger:

```
CREATE TRIGGER WAGEDEFAULT
BEFORE INSERT ON EMPLOYEE
REFERENCING NEW AS NEWROW
FOR EACH ROW
SET (SALARY, BONUS) =
(SELECT BASE_SALARY, BASE_BONUS
FROM WAGE
WHERE JOBCODE = NEWROW.JOBCODE)
```

This before trigger first retrieves the BASE_SALARY and BASE_BONUS values for each new employee tuple and then inserts the entire tuple in the EMPLOYEE table. Triggers have various advantages:

- automatic monitoring and verification if specific events occur (e.g., generate message if bonus is 0);
- modeling extra semantics and/or integrity rules without changing the user front-end or application code (e.g., salary should be $>$ 0, bonus cannot be bigger than salary);
- assign default values to attribute types for new tuples (e.g., assign default bonus);
- synchronic updates if data replication occurs;
- automatic auditing and logging, which may be hard to accomplish in any other application layer;
- automatic exporting of data (e.g., to the web).

However, they should also be approached with care and oversight because they may cause:

- hidden functionality, which may be hard to follow-up and manage;
- cascade effects leading to an infinite loop of a trigger triggering another trigger, etc.;
- uncertain outcomes if multiple triggers for the same database object and event are defined;
- deadlock situations (e.g., if the event causing the trigger and the action in the trigger body pertain to different transactions attempting to access the same data – see Chapter 14);
- debugging complexities since they do not reside in an application environment;
- maintainability and performance problems.

Given the above considerations, it is very important to extensively test triggers before deploying them in a production environment.

Some RDBMS vendors also support **schema-level triggers** (also called DDL triggers) which are fired after changes are made to the DBMS schema (such as creating, dropping, or altering tables, views, etc.). Most RDBMS vendors offer customized implementations of triggers. It is recommended to check the manual and explore the options provided.

## 9.2.2 Stored Procedures

A **stored procedure** is a piece of SQL code consisting of declarative and/or procedural instructions and stored in the catalog of the RDBMS. It must be invoked explicitly by calling it from an application or command prompt. This is the key difference with triggers, which are implicitly “triggered”.

Consider this example of a stored procedure:

```
CREATE PROCEDURE REMOVE-EMPLOYEES
(DNR-VAR IN CHAR(4), JOBCODE-VAR IN CHAR(6)) AS
BEGIN
DELETE FROM EMPLOYEE
WHERE DNR = DNR-VAR AND JOBCODE = JOBCODE-VAR;
END
```

This stored procedure takes two input variables, DNR-VAR and JOBCODE-VAR, whose values can be passed on from the application. It will then remove all employee tuples from the EMPLOYEE table which have the specified values for both variables. As an example, consider this JDBC call:[2]

```
import java.sql.CallableStatement;
...
CallableStatement cStmt = conn.prepareCall("{ call REMOVE-EMPLOYEES(?, ?)} ");
cStmt.setString(1, "D112");
cStmt.setString(2, "JOB124");
cStmt.execute();
...
```

We start by importing the package java.sql.CallableStatement (see Chapter 15) which is needed to execute stored procedures. We then create a new CallableStatement object using the Connection object "conn" and the method prepareCall(). The two question marks represent the input parameters and can be set in the Java program. In our case, we use the setString() method to set the (String) values of the parameters and execute the stored procedure using the execute() method. This call will ensure that all employees who work in department D112 and whose jobcode is JOB124 will be removed from the EMPLOYEE table. Note that a stored procedure can also return results to the Java program, which can then be processed using a JDBC Resultset object (see Chapter 15 for details).

Stored procedures have various advantages:

- Similar to OODBMSs, they store behavior in the database. The stored procedure can be compiled upfront, so no compilation is required at runtime, which contributes to better performance.
- They can reduce network traffic since less communication is needed between the application and DBMS. Calculations on large subsets of the database can be performed "close to the data" in the RDBMS runtime environment, rather than transferring large volumes of data over the network to be processed in the application layer.
- They can be implemented in an application-independent way and can be easily shared across applications and/or invoked from different programming languages.
- They improve data and functional independence, and can implement customized security rules (e.g., a user can have permission to execute a stored procedure, without having permission to read from the underlying tables or views).

**Retention Questions**

- What is the difference between triggers and stored procedures? When would you use which extension? What are the risks of using these extensions?

[2] We discuss JDBC extensively in Chapter 15. For the moment, it suffices to say that JDBC allows Java programs to interact with a relational database by introducing a set of classes (e.g., `CallableStatement` in our example).

- They can be used as a container for several SQL instructions that logically belong together.
- They are easier to debug compared to triggers, since they are explicitly called from the application.

Like triggers, the main disadvantage is their maintainability.

**Drill Down**

Some opponents of triggers and stored procedures often cite that their usage can cause a butterfly effect – i.e., a butterfly flapping its wings in New Mexico (similar to adding a trigger or stored procedure to a database) can cause a hurricane in China (similar to the crash of an application or ecosystem of applications).

## 9.3 Object-Relational RDBMS Extensions

We discussed OODBMSs in Chapter 8. Although they offer several advantages, such as storing complex objects and relationships in a transparent way, and bypassing the impedance mismatch, few success stories have been reported in the industry. This is because they are perceived as very complex to work with, which is largely caused by the absence of a good, standard, DML such as SQL for RDBMSs, and the lack of a transparent three-layer database architecture. Object-relational DBMSs (ORDBMSs) try to combine the best of both worlds. The idea is to keep the relation as the fundamental building block and SQL as the core DDL/DML, but extend them with the following set of OO concepts:

- user-defined types (UDTs);
- user-defined functions (UDFs);
- inheritance;
- behavior;
- polymorphism;
- collection types;
- large objects (LOBs).

**Connections**

Chapter 8 discusses the key concepts of OODBMSs. ORDBMSs build on these concepts by adding them as extensions to an RDBMS.

Note that most ORDBMS vendors only implement a selection of these options, possibly combined with customized extensions. Therefore, it is recommended to check the DBMS manual to know what extensions it supports. Popular examples of ORDBMSs include PostgreSQL (open-source) and the most recent DBMS products provided by major relational vendors such as Oracle, Microsoft, and IBM.

**Drill Down**

One of the first open-source ORDBMSs developed is POSTGRES, initially released on July 8, 1996. The code forms the basis of PostgreSQL and was also commercialized as Illustra, later purchased by Informix, which was in turn acquired by IBM.

### 9.3.1 User-Defined Types

Standard SQL only provides a limited set of data types such as: char, varchar, int, float, double, date, time, boolean (see Chapter 7). These standard data types are insufficient to model complex objects.

If we could specialize these data types, or even define new data types combined with the necessary operations on them, we could solve this problem. As the term suggests, **user-defined types (UDTs)**[3] define customized data types with specific properties. Five types of UDTs can be distinguished as follows:

- Distinct data types: extend existing SQL data types.
- Opaque data types: define entirely new data types.
- Unnamed row types: use unnamed tuples as attribute values.
- Named row types: use named tuples as attribute values.
- Table data types: define tables as instances of table types.

#### 9.3.1.1 Distinct Data Types

A **distinct data type** is a user-defined data type that specializes a standard, built-in SQL data type. The distinct data type inherits all the properties of the SQL data type used for its definition. Consider these two examples:

```
CREATE DISTINCT TYPE US-DOLLAR AS DECIMAL(8,2)
CREATE DISTINCT TYPE EURO AS DECIMAL(8,2)
```

We defined two distinct types US-DOLLAR and EURO as numbers with six digits before the decimal and two digits after the decimal. We can now use both when defining attribute types in a table ACCOUNT as follows:

```
CREATE TABLE ACCOUNT
(ACCOUNTNO SMALLINT PRIMARY KEY NOT NULL,
...
AMOUNT-IN-DOLLAR US-DOLLAR,
AMOUNT-IN-EURO EURO)
```

One of the key advantages of distinct types is that they can be used to prevent erroneous calculations or comparisons. For example, if we had defined both AMOUNT-IN-DOLLAR and AMOUNT-IN-EURO as Decimal(8,2), then values of both attribute types can be added and compared without any problem, which is clearly not meaningful. By using a distinct type, we can only add and/or compare between amounts either in euros or dollars.

Once a distinct data type has been defined, the ORDBMS will automatically create two casting functions: one to cast or map the values of the user-defined type to the underlying, built-in type, and the other to cast or map the built-in type to the user-defined type. Suppose we now wish to retrieve all account tuples where the amount in euros is bigger than 1000 and write this SQL query:

```
SELECT *
FROM ACCOUNT
WHERE AMOUNT-IN-EURO > 1000
```

This query will not successfully execute and an error will be thrown. The reason is that we have a type incompatibility between AMOUNT-IN-EURO whose data type is EURO and 1000 whose data

[3] User-defined types are sometimes also referred to as abstract data types (ADTs).

type is DECIMAL. To successfully do the comparison, we should first cast 1000 to the EURO data type using the ORDBMS generated Euro() casting function as follows:

```
SELECT *
FROM ACCOUNT
WHERE AMOUNT-IN-EURO > EURO(1000)
```

#### 9.3.1.2 Opaque Data Types

An **opaque data type** is an entirely new, user-defined data type, not based upon any existing SQL data type. Some examples are data types for image, audio, video, fingerprints, text, spatial data, RFID tags, or QR codes. These opaque data types will also require their own user-defined functions to work with them. Once defined, they can be used anywhere a standard SQL data type can be used, such as table definitions or queries. Defining opaque data types directly in the database allows multiple applications to share them efficiently, rather than each application independently having to provide its own implementation for them. Here you can see an example of this:

```
CREATE OPAQUE TYPE IMAGE AS <...>
CREATE OPAQUE TYPE FINGERPRINT AS <...>

CREATE TABLE EMPLOYEE
  (SSN SMALLINT NOT NULL,
  FNAME CHAR(25) NOT NULL,
  LNAME CHAR(25) NOT NULL,
  ...
  EMPFINGERPRINT FINGERPRINT,
  PHOTOGRAPH IMAGE)
```

#### 9.3.1.3 Unnamed Row Types

An **unnamed row type** includes a composite data type in a table by using the keyword ROW. It consists of a combination of data types such as built-in types, distinct types, opaque types, etc. Note that since no name is assigned to the row type, it cannot be re-used in other tables and needs to be explicitly redefined wherever it is needed. It can also not be used to define a table. Here you can see an example of two unnamed row types to define the name and address of an employee:

```
CREATE TABLE EMPLOYEE
  (SSN SMALLINT NOT NULL,
  NAME ROW(FNAME CHAR(25), LNAME CHAR(25)),
  ADDRESS ROW(
   STREET ADDRESS CHAR(20) NOT NULL,
   ZIP CODE CHAR(8),
   CITY CHAR(15) NOT NULL),
  ...
  EMPFINGERPRINT FINGERPRINT,
  PHOTOGRAPH IMAGE)
```

#### 9.3.1.4 Named Row Types

A **named row type** is a user-defined data type that groups a coherent set of data types into a new composite data type and assigns a meaningful name to it. Once defined, the named row type can be used in table definitions, queries, or anywhere else a standard SQL data type can be used. Named row types store complete rows of data in one variable and can also be used as the type for input or output parameters of SQL routines and/or functions (see Section 9.3.2). The usage of (un)named row types implies the end of the first normal form, as we discussed in Chapter 6. Remember, 1 NF allowed no composite attribute types in a relation. ORDBMSs drop this requirement in favor of more modeling flexibility. Unlike unnamed row types, named row types can be used to define tables. As an example, we can define a named row type ADDRESS:

```
CREATE ROW TYPE ADDRESS AS
(STREET ADDRESS CHAR(20) NOT NULL,
ZIP CODE CHAR(8),
CITY CHAR(15) NOT NULL)
```

This can then be used to define our EMPLOYEE table:

```
CREATE TABLE EMPLOYEE
 (SSN SMALLINT NOT NULL,
  FNAME CHAR(25) NOT NULL,
  LNAME CHAR(25) NOT NULL,
  EMPADDRESS ADDRESS,
  ...
  EMPFINGERPRINT FINGERPRINT,
  PHOTOGRAPH IMAGE)
```

The individual components of the named row type can then be accessed using the dot (.) operator as in this query:[4]

```
SELECT LNAME, EMPADDRESS
FROM EMPLOYEE
WHERE EMPADDRESS.CITY = 'LEUVEN'
```

This query retrieves the last name and full address of all employees who live in the city of Leuven. Another example is:

```
SELECT E1.LNAME, E1.EMPADDRESS
FROM EMPLOYEE E1, EMPLOYEE E2
WHERE E1.EMPADDRESS.CITY = E2.EMPADDRESS.CITY
AND E2.SSN = '123456789'
```

This query returns the last name and full address of all employees who live in the same city as the employee with SSN equal to 123456789.

[4] The individual components of an unnamed row type can also be accessed using the dot (.) operator.

#### 9.3.1.5 Table Data Types

A **table data type** (or typed table) defines the type of a table. The latter refers to a table definition, much like a class in OO. It's used to instantiate various tables with the same structure. Consider this example:

```
CREATE TYPE EMPLOYEETYPE AS
 (SSN SMALLINT NOT NULL,
 FNAME CHAR(25) NOT NULL,
 LNAME CHAR(25) NOT NULL,
 EMPADDRESS ADDRESS
 ...
 ...
 EMPFINGERPRINT FINGERPRINT,
 PHOTOGRAPH IMAGE)
```

The EMPLOYEETYPE table data type can now be used to define two tables, EMPLOYEE and EX-EMPLOYEE, as follows:

```
CREATE TABLE EMPLOYEE OF TYPE EMPLOYEETYPE PRIMARY KEY (SSN)
CREATE TABLE EX-EMPLOYEE OF TYPE EMPLOYEETYPE PRIMARY KEY (SSN)
```

A column of a table type definition can also refer to another table type definition using the keyword REF, as follows:

```
CREATE TYPE DEPARTMENTTYPE AS
 (DNR SMALLINT NOT NULL,
 DNAME CHAR(25) NOT NULL,
 DLOCATION ADDRESS
 MANAGER REF(EMPLOYEETYPE))
```

This assumes that the ORDBMS supports row identifications. When a department table is defined using the DEPARTMENTTYPE type, its MANAGER attribute type will contain a reference or pointer to an employee tuple of a table whose type is EMPLOYEETYPE. Note that these references represent the ORDBMS counterpart of OIDs in OODBMSs. However, unlike OIDs, the references used in ORDBMSs can be explicitly requested and visualized to the user. As we will see in Section 9.3.6 later in this chapter, the reference can be replaced by the actual data it refers to by means of the DEREF (from dereferencing) function.

Note that some ORDBMS vendors make no distinction between named row types and table data types, but only support a CREATE TYPE function, which can then define either columns in tables or an entire table.

### 9.3.2 User-Defined Functions

Every RDBMS comes with a set of built-in functions, for example MIN(), MAX(), AVG(). **User-defined functions (UDFs)** allow users to extend these by explicitly defining their own functions to enrich the functional capability of the RDBMS, similar to methods in OODBMSs. These UDFs can work on both built-in and user-defined data types. Every UDF will consist of a name, with the input and output arguments, and the implementation. The implementation can be written by using proprietary procedural extensions of SQL, which are provided by most RDBMS vendors, or by using external programming languages such as C, Java, or Python.

The UDFs are stored in the ORDBMS and hidden from the applications, which contributes to the property of encapsulation or information hiding (see Chapter 8). The implementation of a UDF can change without affecting the applications that use it. Most ORDBMSs will overload UDFs, which implies that UDFs operating on different data types can have the same name. When a UDF is called by an application, the ORDBMS will invoke the correct implementation based upon the data types specified.

Three types of UDFs can be distinguished: sourced functions, external scalar functions, and external table functions.

A **sourced function** is a UDF based on an existing, built-in function. They are often used in combination with distinct data types. Assume we define the distinct data type MONETARY as follows:

```
CREATE DISTINCT TYPE MONETARY AS DECIMAL(8,2)
```

We can then use it in our EMPLOYEE table definition:

```
CREATE TABLE EMPLOYEE
  (SSN SMALLINT NOT NULL,
  FNAME CHAR(25) NOT NULL,
  LNAME CHAR(25) NOT NULL,
  EMPADDRESS ADDRESS,
  SALARY MONETARY,
  ...
  EMPFINGERPRINT FINGERPRINT,
  PHOTOGRAPH IMAGE)
```

Let's now define a sourced UDF to calculate the average:

```
CREATE FUNCTION AVG(MONETARY)
RETURNS MONETARY
SOURCE AVG(DECIMAL(8,2))
```

The name of the sourced function is AVG(MONETARY), the return data type is MONETARY, and the source function is the built-in function AVG(DECIMAL). We can now invoke this function by using this query:

```
SELECT DNR, AVG(SALARY)
FROM EMPLOYEE
GROUP BY DNR
```

This query selects the department number and average salary per department as calculated using the sourced UDF we defined earlier.

Both **external scalar** and **external table functions** are functions that contain explicitly defined functionality, written in an external host language (e.g., Java, C, Python). The difference is that the former returns a single value or scalar, whereas the latter returns a table of values.

### 9.3.3 Inheritance

The relational model is a flat model since, besides a primary–foreign key connection between tables, no other explicit relationships are allowed. Hence, no superclass–subclass relationships and thus no inheritance are supported. An ORDBMS extends an RDBMS by providing explicit support for inheritance, both at the level of a data type and a typed table.

#### 9.3.3.1 Inheritance at Data Type Level

Inheritance at data type level implies that a child data type inherits all the properties of a parent data type and can then be further specialized by adding specific characteristics. Let's revisit the following example to define an ADDRESS data type consisting of a street address, zip code, and city:

```
CREATE ROW TYPE ADDRESS AS
  (STREET ADDRESS CHAR(20) NOT NULL,
  ZIP CODE CHAR(8),
  CITY CHAR(15) NOT NULL)
```

We can now specialize this by creating a subtype INTERNATIONAL_ADDRESS which also adds the country:

```
CREATE ROW TYPE INTERNATIONAL_ADDRESS AS
  (COUNTRY CHAR(25) NOT NULL) UNDER ADDRESS
```

Remember, specialization always assumes an "is a" relationship, which applies in our case, since an international address is an address. We can use this in our EMPLOYEE table definition as follows:

```
CREATE TABLE EMPLOYEE
  (SSN SMALLINT NOT NULL,
  FNAME CHAR(25) NOT NULL,
  LNAME CHAR(25) NOT NULL,
  EMPADDRESS INTERNATIONAL_ADDRESS,
  SALARY MONETARY,
  ...
  EMPFINGERPRINT FINGERPRINT,
  PHOTOGRAPH IMAGE)
```

We can now write this SQL query:

```
SELECT FNAME, LNAME, EMPADDRESS
FROM EMPLOYEE
WHERE EMPADDRESS.COUNTRY = 'Belgium'
AND EMPADDRESS.CITY LIKE 'Leu%'
```

This query asks for the names and addresses of all employees who live in a city in Belgium starting with the three characters "Leu". Note that the definition of the INTERNATIONAL_ADDRESS data type does not explicitly include the CITY attribute type, but the latter will be inherited from its superclass ADDRESS, where it is defined.

#### 9.3.3.2 Inheritance at Table Type Level

We can now also apply the concept of inheritance to table types. Assume we have this definition for EMPLOYEETYPE:

```
CREATE TYPE EMPLOYEETYPE AS
  (SSN SMALLINT NOT NULL,
  FNAME CHAR(25) NOT NULL,
  LNAME CHAR(25) NOT NULL,
  EMPADDRESS INTERNATIONAL_ADDRESS
  ...
  ...
  EMPFINGERPRINT FINGERPRINT,
  PHOTOGRAPH IMAGE)
```

We can now create various subtypes for it, such as ENGINEERTYPE and MANAGERTYPE:

```
CREATE TYPE ENGINEERTYPE AS
  (DEGREE CHAR(10) NOT NULL,
  LICENSE CHAR(20) NOT NULL) UNDER EMPLOYEETYPE
CREATE TYPE MANAGERTYPE AS
  (STARTDATE DATE,
  TITLE CHAR(20)) UNDER EMPLOYEETYPE
```

The inheritance relationship is specified using the keyword UNDER. Both ENGINEERTYPE and MANAGERTYPE inherit the definition properties from EMPLOYEETYPE. As you can see, a supertype can have multiple subtypes. However, most RDBMSs will not support multiple inheritance, and a subtype can have at most one supertype. The table type hierarchy can be multiple levels deep and cannot contain any cyclic references. The type definitions can then be used to instantiate tables. Obviously, the table hierarchy should correspond to the underlying type hierarchy, as follows:

```
CREATE TABLE EMPLOYEE OF TYPE EMPLOYEETYPE PRIMARY KEY (SSN)
CREATE TABLE ENGINEER OF TYPE ENGINEERTYPE UNDER EMPLOYEE
CREATE TABLE MANAGER OF TYPE MANAGERTYPE UNDER EMPLOYEE
```

Note that the primary key is only defined for the maximal supertable and inherited by all subtables in the hierarchy. The definition of inheritance has implications for data manipulation. Suppose we have this query:

```
SELECT SSN, FNAME, LNAME, STARTDATE, TITLE
FROM MANAGER
```

This query targets the MANAGER table and asks for the SSN, FNAME, LNAME (from the EMPLOYEE table) and the STARTDATE and TITLE (both from the MANAGER table). The ORDBMS will automatically retrieve these data elements from the right table. Suppose we now have the following query:

```
SELECT SSN, FNAME, LNAME
FROM EMPLOYEE
```

This query will retrieve the SSN, FNAME, and LNAME of all employees, including the managers and engineers. Tuples added to a subtable are automatically visible to queries on the supertable. If we want to exclude the subtables, we should use the keyword ONLY, as follows:

```
SELECT SSN, FNAME, LNAME
FROM ONLY EMPLOYEE
```

### 9.3.4 Behavior

One of the key characteristics of objects in an OO environment is that they encapsulate both data, which determine their state, and methods, which characterize their behavior. An ORDBMS will also store behavior in the database. This can be done implicitly by defining triggers, stored procedures, or UDFs, as we discussed in previous sections. More explicitly, an ORDBMS can include the signature or interface of a method in the definitions of data types and tables. Only this interface is made visible to the outside world; the implementation remains hidden, enforcing the concept of information hiding. This behavior can then be considered as virtual columns in a table. Let's consider the following example:

```
CREATE TYPE EMPLOYEETYPE AS
  (SSN SMALLINT NOT NULL,
  FNAME CHAR(25) NOT NULL,
  LNAME CHAR(25) NOT NULL,
  EMPADDRESS INTERNATIONAL_ADDRESS,
  ...
  ...
  EMPFINGERPRINT FINGERPRINT,
  PHOTOGRAPH IMAGE,
  FUNCTION AGE(EMPLOYEETYPE) RETURNS INTEGER)
```

We have now explicitly defined a function, AGE, that has an input parameter of type EMPLOYEETYPE and returns the age represented as an integer. We can now define a table EMPLOYEE:

```
CREATE TABLE EMPLOYEE OF TYPE EMPLOYEETYPE
PRIMARY KEY (SSN)
```

We can then write this SQL query to retrieve the SSN, FNAME, LNAME, and PHOTOGRAPH of all employees whose age equals 60:

```
SELECT SSN, FNAME, LNAME, PHOTOGRAPH
FROM EMPLOYEE
WHERE AGE = 60
```

Note this query will invoke the AGE function to calculate the age. An outside user does not even need to know whether AGE was implemented as a virtual column (i.e., a function) or as a real column.

### 9.3.5 Polymorphism

A subtype inherits both the attribute types and functions of its supertype. It can also override functions to provide more specialized implementations. This implies that the same function call can invoke different implementations, depending upon the data type it is related to. This property is polymorphism, which was also discussed in Chapter 8. Consider the following example:

```
CREATE FUNCTION TOTAL_SALARY(EMPLOYEE E)
RETURNING INT
AS SELECT E.SALARY
```

The TOTAL_SALARY function takes one employee tuple as input and returns the salary as an integer. We can now further specialize this function in the manager subtype:

```
CREATE FUNCTION TOTAL_SALARY(MANAGER M)
RETURNING INT
AS SELECT M.SALARY + <monthly_bonus>
```

The <monthly_bonus> part refers to a manager-specific add-on that can be implemented as desired. We now have two versions for the TOTAL_SALARY function: one for regular employees and one for managers. Suppose we now write this query:

```
SELECT TOTAL_SALARY FROM EMPLOYEE
```

This query will retrieve the TOTAL_SALARY for all employees, both managers and non-managers. The ORDBMS will ensure that, depending upon the tuple, the right implementation is used.

### 9.3.6 Collection Types

ORDBMSs also provide type constructors to define collection types. A collection type can be instantiated as a collection of instances of standard data types or UDTs. The following collection types can be distinguished:

- Set: unordered collection, no duplicates
- Multiset or bag: unordered collection, duplicates allowed
- List: ordered collection, duplicates allowed
- Array: ordered and indexed collection, duplicates allowed

Note that the usage of collection types again implies the end of the first normal form as we discussed it in Chapter 6. Consider the following type definition:

```
CREATE TYPE EMPLOYEETYPE AS
  (SSN SMALLINT NOT NULL,
  FNAME CHAR(25) NOT NULL,
  LNAME CHAR(25) NOT NULL,
  EMPADDRESS INTERNATIONAL_ADDRESS,
  ...
  EMPFINGERPRINT FINGERPRINT,
  PHOTOGRAPH IMAGE,
  TELEPHONE SET (CHAR(12)),
  FUNCTION AGE(EMPLOYEETYPE) RETURNS INTEGER)
```

The EMPLOYEETYPE makes use of a SET construct to model the assumption that an employee can have multiple telephone numbers. In the traditional relational model, this had to be modeled by introducing a new relation with SSN and TELEPHONE where both also make up the primary key (assuming an employee can have multiple phone numbers and a phone number can be shared among multiple employees). Let's now create the EMPLOYEE table as follows:

```
CREATE TABLE EMPLOYEE OF TYPE EMPLOYEETYPE (PRIMARY KEY SSN)
```

We can now write this query:

```
SELECT SSN, FNAME, LNAME
FROM EMPLOYEE
WHERE '2123375000' IN (TELEPHONE)
```

This query will retrieve the SSN and name of all employees who have a telephone number with digits 2123375000. Note the use of the IN operator to verify whether the specified digits belong to the set.

The definition of sets and their usage in queries can give rise to a situation in which the result consists of sets of sets that need to be sorted afterwards. Consider the following query:

```
SELECT T.TELEPHONE
FROM THE (SELECT TELEPHONE FROM EMPLOYEE) AS T
ORDER BY T.TELEPHONE
```

Notice the usage of the keyword THE in the above query. This will transform the result of the subquery into a set of atomic values that can be sorted afterwards using the ORDER BY instruction. This will give us an ordered list of telephone numbers of all the employees.

Let's now also create a DEPARTMENTTYPE type:

```
CREATE TYPE DEPARTMENTTYPE AS
  (DNR CHAR(3) NOT NULL,
  DNAME CHAR(25) NOT NULL,
  MANAGER REF(EMPLOYEETYPE),
  PERSONNEL SET (REF(EMPLOYEETYPE))
```

Note the use of the REF operator for both MANAGER and PERSONNEL. The former contains a reference or pointer to a manager employee tuple, whereas the latter contains a set of references to the employees working in the department. Instead of a set, we could have also used an array or list to store the employee tuples in a specific order. We can now instantiate this type:

```
CREATE TABLE DEPARTMENT OF TYPE DEPARTMENTTYPE (PRIMARY KEY DNR)
```

If we would run the following query to retrieve personnel data from a specific department:

```
SELECT PERSONNEL
FROM DEPARTMENT
WHERE DNR = '123'
```

then we would get a set of meaningless references. We can, however, use the DEREF function to get access to the actual data:

```
SELECT DEREF(PERSONNEL).FNAME, DEREF(PERSONNEL).LNAME
FROM DEPARTMENT
WHERE DNR = '123'
```

Note the use of the dot operator to navigate. In a classical RDBMS environment, this query had to be solved by using a time-consuming value-based join between the DEPARTMENT and the EMPLOYEE tables. The support for navigational access by means of path expressions will affect the design of the query processor in an ORDBMS.

### 9.3.7 Large Objects

Many multimedia database applications make use of large data objects such as audio, video, photos, text files, maps, etc. Traditional relational database systems provide no adequate support for this. ORDBMSs introduce **large objects (LOBs)** to deal with such items. To improve physical storage efficiency, the LOB data will be stored in a separate table and tablespace (see Chapter 13). The base table then includes a LOB indicator that refers to this location. Also, queries will return these indicators. ORDBMSs typically support various types of LOB data such as the following:

- **BLOB (binary large object):** a variable-length binary string whose interpretation is left to an external application.
- **CLOB (character large object):** variable-length character strings made up of single-byte characters.
- **DBCLOB (double byte character large object):** variable-length character strings made up of double-byte characters.

Many ORDBMSs will also provide customized SQL functions for LOB data. Examples are functions to search in image or video data or access text at a specified position.

**Retention Questions**

- Discuss the key concepts of object-relational RDBMS extensions. Illustrate with examples.

## 9.4 Recursive SQL Queries

Recursive queries are a powerful SQL extension that allow formulation of complex queries. In particular, they compensate for the somewhat cumbersome way in which hierarchies are modeled in the relational model by means of foreign keys. Querying such hierarchies until an arbitrary level or depth is not easy in standard SQL, but can be facilitated to a great extent by means of recursive queries. Consider the hierarchy among employees in a firm from Figure 9.1.

Let's assume we store this in a table Employee defined as:

```
Employee(SSN, Name, Salary, MNGR)
```

Note that MNGR is a NULL-ALLOWED foreign key referring to SSN. According to Figure 9.1, this table has the tuples shown in Figure 9.2.

Let's now assume we would like to write a query to find all subordinates of a given employee. This can be solved with this recursive SQL query:

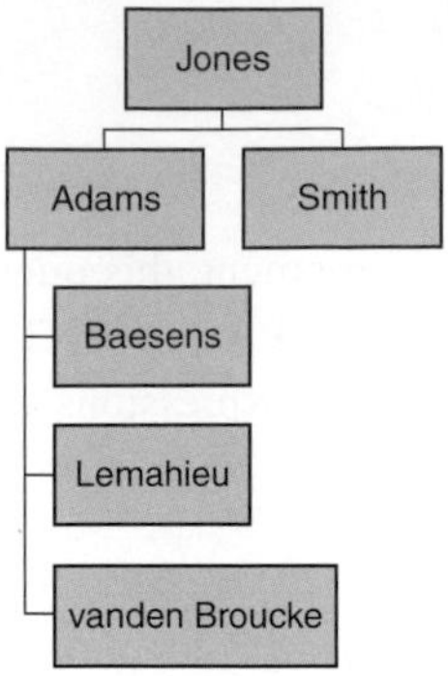


**Figure 9.1** Hierarchy of employees.

| SSN | Name | Salary | *MNGR* |
|---|---|---|---|
| 1 | Jones | 10.000 | NULL |
| 2 | Baesens | 2.000 | 3 |
| 3 | Adams | 5.000 | 1 |
| 4 | Smith | 6.000 | 1 |
| 5 | vanden Broucke | 3.000 | 3 |
| 6 | Lemahieu | 2.500 | 3 |

**Figure 9.2** Tuples based on Figure 9.1.

```
WITH SUBORDINATES(SSN, NAME, SALARY, MNGR, LEVEL) AS
(SELECT SSN, NAME, SALARY, MNGR, 1
FROM EMPLOYEE
WHERE MNGR=NULL)
UNION ALL
(SELECT E.SSN, E.NAME, E.SALARY, E.MNGR, S.LEVEL+1
 FROM SUBORDINATES AS S, EMPLOYEE AS E
 WHERE S.SSN=E.MNGR)
SELECT * FROM SUBORDINATES
ORDER BY LEVEL
```

This recursive query defines a temporary view SUBORDINATES which will be used to store the intermediate results. Such a view always contains three parts:

1. The base or anchor query that contains the seed of our recursive query:

   ```
   SELECT SSN, NAME, SALARY, MNGR, 1
   FROM EMPLOYEE
   WHERE MNGR=NULL
   ```

   This query will select the CEO as the starting point for the recursion (i.e., Jones in our case). Other employees could be selected as starting points as well.

2. The recursive query that references the view we are defining:

   ```
   SELECT E.SSN, E.NAME, E.SALARY, E.MNGR, S.LEVEL+1
    FROM SUBORDINATES AS S, EMPLOYEE AS E
    WHERE S.SSN=E.MNGR
   ```

| SSN | NAME | SALARY | *MNGR* | LEVEL |
|---|---|---|---|---|
| 1 | Jones | 10.000 | NULL | 1 |

**Figure 9.3** Results of base query.

| SSN | NAME | SALARY | *MNGR* | LEVEL |
|---|---|---|---|---|
| 3 | Adams | 5.000 | 1 | 2 |
| 4 | Smith | 6.000 | 1 | 2 |

**Figure 9.4** Results of the first recursive step.

| SSN | NAME | SALARY | *MNGR* | LEVEL |
|---|---|---|---|---|
| 2 | Baesens | 2.000 | 3 | 3 |
| 5 | vanden Broucke | 3.000 | 3 | 3 |
| 6 | Lemahieu | 2.500 | 3 | 3 |

**Figure 9.5** Results of the second iteration of the recursive step.

| SSN | NAME | SALARY | *MNGR* | LEVEL |
|---|---|---|---|---|
| 1 | Jones | 10.000 | NULL | 1 |
| 3 | Adams | 5.000 | 1 | 2 |
| 4 | Smith | 6.000 | 1 | 2 |
| 2 | Baesens | 2.000 | 3 | 3 |
| 5 | vanden Broucke | 3.000 | 3 | 3 |
| 6 | Lemahieu | 2.500 | 3 | 3 |

**Figure 9.6** Results of full recursive SQL query.

3. The keyword UNION ALL between the two queries to join both result sets

Note that we also include a variable LEVEL to calculate the hierarchical level of each employee.

Upon execution, the base or anchor query returns the results shown in Figure 9.3.

The first recursive step is then run to figure out the direct subordinates of Jones and add them to the view. This will return the results shown in Figure 9.4.

The recursive step is then activated repeatedly until no more rows can be added to the view. The second iteration of the recursive step uses the set of the previous step as the input value and returns the results shown in Figure 9.5.

The full result of the recursive SQL query then becomes what is shown in Figure 9.6.

Suppose we are now interested in the subordinates of Adams, then we must adjust the base query as follows:

```
WITH SUBORDINATES(SSN, NAME, SALARY, MNGR, LEVEL) AS
(SELECT SSN, NAME, SALARY, MNGR, 1
FROM EMPLOYEE
WHERE NAME='ADAMS')
UNION ALL
(SELECT E.SSN, E.NAME, E.SALARY, E.MNGR, S.LEVEL+1
 FROM SUBORDINATES AS S, EMPLOYEE AS E
 WHERE S.SSN=E.MNGR)
SELECT * FROM SUBORDINATES
ORDER BY LEVEL
```

**Retention Questions**

- What is a recursive SQL query? In what situations can it be used?

## Summary

In this chapter we have discussed three extensions to traditional RDBMSs: active extensions, object-oriented extensions, and recursive SQL queries. The first two focus on extending the RDBMS with concepts such as triggers, stored procedures, user-defined types, user-defined functions, etc. A key benefit of this is that it allows sharing and re-use of code across applications. The re-use stems from the ability to extend the database with functionality now stored centrally, rather than replicated in each application.

ORDBMSs extend RDBMSs with OO facilities. They capture some of the benefits of OO while retaining the relation as the fundamental building block. Hence, they provide a softer leap for those interested in combining the best of both worlds. However, disbelievers argue that one of the key benefits of RDBMSs was their simplicity and purity, which is lost when using an ORDBMS. On the other hand, OO purists are not happy with the OO extensions provided, since the relation is still the key concept, rather than a pure OO class. In industry, ORDBMSs have had modest success, with most companies only implementing a carefully selected set of extensions.

Finally, we also discussed recursive SQL queries, which allow for more complex data retrieval. They do not improve the expressiveness of RDBMSs in the way the other two extensions do, but instead extend the SQL language in such a way that some inadequacies of the relational paradigm are alleviated. Recursive queries partially make up for the cumbersome way hierarchies are represented and navigated in relational databases.

Many extensions discussed in this chapter have been implemented in various ways by ORDBMS vendors. Some implement them partially or even add more specific functionality. Hence, it is recommended to explore the options available to a particular system.

### Scenario Conclusion

Remember that in the relational model of Sober, the DURATION attribute type of the relation RIDE was a derived attribute type (see Chapter 6). It can be calculated by subtracting the pick-up time from the drop-off time. Now that Sober has learned about triggers, it has defined this after trigger:

```
CREATE TRIGGER CALCDURATION
AFTER INSERT ON RIDE
FOR EACH ROW
WHEN (NEW.PICKUP-DATE-TIME IS NOT NULL AND NEW.DROPOFF-DATE-TIME IS NOT NULL)
UPDATE RIDE
SET DURATION = NEW.DROPOFF-DATE-TIME - NEW.PICKUP-DATE-TIME
```

The advantage of using this trigger, rather than manually entering a value for the DURATION attribute type, is that the value is always correctly calculated. Note that if a value for DURATION is manually inserted, then this trigger will override it since it is an *after* trigger and thus first inserts the new tuples before executing the trigger body.

Sober decided not to implement any stored procedures because it might complicate the maintenance of Sober's database applications.

In the current relational model, Sober has treated the PICKUP-LOC, DROPOFF-LOC, and ACC-LOCATION attribute types as atomic attribute types. Now that it has learned about named row types, it has defined the following named row type instead:

```
CREATE ROW TYPE ADDRESS AS
(STREET ADDRESS CHAR(20) NOT NULL,
ZIP CODE CHAR(8),
CITY CHAR(15) NOT NULL)
```

This can then be used in the RIDE table:

```
CREATE TABLE RIDE
  (RIDE-NR INT NOT NULL,
  ...,
  PICKUP-LOC ADDRESS,
  DROPOFF-LOC ADDRESS,
  ...)
```

By doing so, Sober can ask more detailed queries. As an example, suppose the company wants to retrieve all ride-hailing services with drop-off location in San Francisco. It can now do this with the following SQL query:

```
SELECT *
FROM RIDE HAILING, RIDE
WHERE
H-RIDE-NR=RIDE-NR AND
DROPOFF-LOC.CITY='San Francisco'
```

Sober also decided to store the email addresses of its customers for marketing purposes. Since a customer can have multiple email addresses (e.g., professional and private), it will make use of a SET collection type as follows:

```
CREATE TABLE CUSTOMER
  (CUST-NR INT NOT NULL,
  CUST-NAME VARCHAR(30) NOT NULL,
  EMAIL SET (CHAR(20)),
)
```

Finally, Sober wants to store a high-resolution image of each of its Sober cars and an extensive report of each accident that took place. It can now do this using the BLOB and CLOB data types discussed in this chapter.

## Key Terms List

**active**
**after trigger**
**before trigger**
**BLOB (binary large object)**
**CLOB (character large object)**
**DBCLOB (double byte character large object)**
**distinct data type**

**external scalar function**
**external table function**
**large objects (LOBs)**
**named row type**
**opaque data type**
**passive**
**schema-level triggers**
**sourced function**
**stored procedure**
**table data type**
**trigger**
**unnamed row type**
**user-defined functions (UDFs)**
**user-defined types (UDTs)**

## Review Questions

**9.1.** Which statement is **correct**?

a. In the relational model, the tuple constructor can only be used on atomic values and the set constructor can only be used on tuples.
b. In the relational model, the tuple constructor allows defining composite attribute types.
c. In the relational model, the set constructor allows defining multi-valued attribute types.
d. In the relational model, the tuple and set constructor can be used in a nested way.

**9.2.** Which of the following is not an advantage of triggers?

a. Triggers support automatic monitoring and verification in case of specific events or situations.
b. Triggers allow avoidance of deadlock situations.
c. Triggers allow modeling extra semantics and/or integrity rules without changing the user front-end or application code.
d. Triggers allow performance of synchronic updates in case of data replication.

**9.3.** The key difference between stored procedures and triggers is that:

a. Stored procedures are explicitly invoked whereas triggers are implicitly invoked.
b. Stored procedures cannot have input variables whereas triggers can.
c. Stored procedures are stored in the data catalog, whereas triggers are not.
d. Stored procedures are more difficult to debug than triggers.

**9.4.** Which of the following is **correct**?

a. A distinct data type is a user-defined data type which specializes a standard, built-in SQL data type.
b. An opaque data type is an entirely new, user-defined data type, which is not based upon any existing SQL data type.
c. An unnamed row type allows inclusion of a composite data type in a table by using the keyword ROW.
d. A named row type is a user-defined data type that groups a coherent set of data types into a new composite data type and assigns a meaningful name to it.
e. All of the above are correct.

**9.5.** Which of the following is **correct**?

a. User-defined functions (UDFs) can only work on user-defined data types.
b. A sourced function is a user-defined function (UDF) that is based on an existing, built-in function.
c. User-defined functions (UDFs) can only be defined in SQL.
d. User-defined functions (UDFs) must be stored in the application, and not in the catalog.

**9.6.** An ORDBMS will typically support inheritance...

a. only at tuple level.
b. only at data type level.
c. only at table type level.
d. at both data type and table type level.

**9.7.** Which of these statements is **correct**?

a. A set is an ordered collection with no duplicates.
b. A bag is an unordered collection which may contain duplicates.
c. A list is an ordered collection which cannot contain duplicates.
d. An array is an unordered collection which can contain duplicates.

**9.8.** Which data type can be used to store image data?

a. BLOB.
b. CLOB.
c. DBCLOB.
d. None of the above.

**9.9.** Recursive queries are a powerful SQL extension which allow formulation of complex queries such as...

a. queries that need to combine data from multiple tables.
b. queries that need to get access to multimedia data.
c. queries that need to navigate through a hierarchy of tuples.
d. queries that have multiple subqueries.

**9.10.** In industry, ORDBMSs have...

a. been very successful since they replaced RDBMSs as the mainstream database technology.
b. had modest success, with most companies only implementing a carefully selected set of extensions.
c. not been successful at all.

## Problems and Exercises

9.1E Give some examples of triggers and stored procedures for the purchase order database we discussed in Chapter 6. Discuss the advantages and disadvantages of both extensions.

9.2E Contrast an ORDBMS against
- an RDBMS;
- an OODBMS.

Give examples of applications where each of these can be used.

9.3E What is the impact of ORDBMSs on normalization?

9.4E What are the different types of UDTs that can be supported by ORDBMSs? Illustrate with examples.

9.5E What are the different types of UDFs that can be supported by ORDBMSs? Illustrate with examples.

9.6E Consider a table hierarchy with supertable STUDENT and subtables BACHELOR_STUDENT, MASTER_STUDENT and PHD_STUDENT. Both bachelor and master students pass when they achieve at least 50%. PhD students pass when they achieve at least 70%. Illustrate using an SQL query how polymorphism can be useful.

9.7E Discuss the following collection types: set, multiset, list, and array. Illustrate with examples.

9.8E How are large objects handled by ORDBMSs? Illustrate with examples.

9.9E Discuss how triggers, stored procedures, object-relational extensions, and recursive queries are supported in modern-day DBMSs provided by, e.g., Oracle, IBM, and Microsoft.

9.10E Consider the following relational model:

COURSE(coursenr, coursename, *profnr*) – profnr is a foreign key referring to profnr in PROFESSOR

PROFESSOR(profnr, profname)

PRE-REQUISITE(*coursenr*, *pre-req-coursenr*) – coursenr is a foreign key referring to coursenr in COURSE; pre-req-coursenr is a foreign key referring to coursenr in COURSE

The PRE-REQUISITE relation essentially models a recursive N:M relationship type for COURSE, since a course can have multiple prerequisite courses and a course can be a prerequisite for multiple other courses.

Write a recursive SQL query to list all prerequisite courses for the course "Principles of Database Management".

# 10 XML Databases

## Chapter Objectives

In this chapter, you will learn to:

- understand the basic concepts of XML, Document Type Definition, XML Schema Definition, Extensible Stylesheet Language, namespaces, and XPath;
- process XML documents using the DOM and SAX APIs;
- store XML documents using a document-oriented, data-oriented, or hybrid approach;
- grasp the key differences between XML and relational data;
- map between XML documents and (object-)relational data using table-based mapping, schema-oblivious mapping, schema-aware mapping, and SQL/XML;
- search XML data using full-text search, keyword-based search, structured search using XQuery, and semantic search using RDF and SPARQL;
- use XML for information exchange in combination with message-oriented middleware (MOM) and web services;
- understand other data representation formats such as JSON and YAML.

### Opening Scenario

For regulatory and insurance purposes, Sober needs to store a report for each accident. The report should include the date, the location (including GPS coordinates), a summary of what happened and the individuals involved. Furthermore, for each individual Sober needs to know:

- the name;
- whether he/she is a driver driving a Sober car or not, a pedestrian, or a cyclist;
- whether he/she was injured.

The report should also include information about aid provided, such as police or ambulance assistance. Sober would like to know the best way to store this report.

In this chapter, we discuss how to store, process, search, and visualize XML documents, and how DBMSs can support this. We start by looking at the XML data representation standard and discuss related concepts such as DTDs and XSDs for defining XML documents, XSL for visualizing or transforming XML documents, and namespaces to provide for a unique naming convention. This is followed by introducing XPath, which uses path expressions to navigate through XML documents. We review the DOM and SAX API to process XML documents. Next, we cover both the document- and data-oriented approach for storing XML documents. We extensively highlight the key differences between the XML and relational data model. Various mapping methods between XML and (object-)relational data are discussed: table-based mapping, schema-oblivious mapping, schema-aware mapping, and the SQL/XML extension. We also present various ways to search XML data: full-text search, keyword-based search, structured search, XQuery, and semantic search. We then illustrate how XML can be used for information exchange, both at the company level using RPC and message-oriented middleware and between companies using SOAP or REST-based web services. We conclude by discussing some other data representation standards, such as JSON and YAML.

## 10.1 Extensible Markup Language

In what follows we discuss the basic concepts of XML. This is followed by a review of Document Type Definition and XML Schema definition, which can both be used to specify the structure of an XML document. Extensible Stylesheet Language is covered next. Namespaces are discussed as a means to avoid name conflicts. The section concludes by introducing XPath as a simple, declarative language that uses path expressions to refer to parts of an XML document.

### 10.1.1 Basic Concepts

**Extensible Markup Language (XML)** was introduced by the World Wide Web Consortium (W3C) in 1997.[1] It is essentially a simplified subset of the Standard Generalized Markup Language (SGML), which is a meta-markup language that can be used to define markup languages. The development of XML was triggered by the emergence of the World Wide Web and the need to exchange information and machine-processable documents between various web applications and across heterogeneous data sources. The XML standard is aimed at storing and exchanging complex, structured documents.

Like HTML, XML data are enclosed between tags, which are used to annotate a document's content, hence the term "markup". However, whereas HTML comes with a fixed set of predefined tags, users can define new tags in XML, hence the name *Extensible* Markup Language. Consider the following example:

```
<author>Bart Baesens</author>
```

The combination of a start tag (<author>), content (Bart Baesens), and end tag (</author>) is called an **XML element**. Note that XML is case-sensitive, so <author> is different than <Author> or <AUTHOR>. Tags can be nested and make the data self-descriptive as follows:

```
<author>
<name>
<firstname>Bart</firstname>
<lastname>Baesens</lastname>
</name>
</author>
```

[1] www.w3.org/XML.

Start tags can contain attribute values, such as the following

```
<author email="Bart.Baesens@kuleuven.be">Bart Baesens</author>
```

All attribute values (including numbers!) must be quoted using either single or double quotes. An element may have several attributes, but each attribute name can only occur once within an element to avoid ambiguity. An obvious question then becomes when to use an attribute instead of defining an additional XML element. An alternative to the above example is:

```
<author>
<name>Bart Baesens</name>
<email>Bart.Baesens@kuleuven.be</email>
</author>
```

The latter option is better in case email is a multi-valued attribute type or if we would like to add more metadata, as follows:

```
<author>
<name>Bart Baesens</name>
<email use="work">Bart.Baesens@kuleuven.be</email>
<email use="private">Bart.Baesens@gmail.com</email>
</author>
```

This example defines two email addresses, and an additional attribute is included to define the context thereof. This specification is semantically richer than the one we used before.

Besides the ability to define one's own tags, another crucial difference with HTML is already apparent from even these small examples. Whereas the predefined tags in HTML aim at specifying the *layout* of the content (e.g., "bold," "italic" etc.), the self-defined XML tags can be used to describe the document structure. Each bit of content can be labeled with metadata for how it should be interpreted by a human or a software application. Therefore, whereas an HTML document represents unstructured data that can only be "shown" on the screen with a particular layout, XML documents represent structured information that can be processed by a computer system in much more detail (i.e., an application "knows" whether a series of characters represents a name rather than an email address).[2] As we will discuss in Section 10.1.2, it is also possible to prescribe the structure of certain document types and validate individual documents for conformance with this structure, much like the data entered in a relational database is validated against the database model or schema.

**Connections**

The general distinction between structured data, unstructured data, and semi-structured data was discussed in Chapter 1.

XML elements can have no content at all, in which case the start and closing tag can be combined:

```
<author name="Bart Baesens"/>
```

This is a concise representation equivalent to:

```
<author name="Bart Baesens"></author>
```

[2] The structure of XML documents is somewhat less strict and more volatile than that of, e.g., relational data. Therefore, the term semi-structured data is also used in reference to XML. We come back to this later in this chapter.

Comments can be included between <!-- and --> tags:

```
<!--This is a comment line -->
```

Comments can be useful for clarification (e.g., for developers), or to edit out a portion of the XML code during debugging. They are not processed by the XML parser.

Processing instructions are enclosed between <? and ?> tags. A common example is an instruction referring to the XML version and text encoding format:

```
<?xml version="1.0" encoding="UTF-8"?>
```

UTF-8 is a Unicode standard that covers nearly all characters, punctuation, and symbols in the world. It can process, store, and transport text independent of platform and language.

The following example illustrates an XML definition for a wine cellar with two wines:

```
<?xml version="1.0" encoding="UTF-8"?>
<winecellar>
   <wine>
      <name>Jacques Selosse Brut Initial</name>
      <year>2012</year>
      <type>Champagne</type>
      <grape percentage="100">Chardonnay</grape>
      <price currency="EURO">150</price>
      <geo>
         <country>France</country>
         <region>Champagne</region>
      </geo>
      <quantity>12</quantity>
   </wine>
   <wine>
      <name>Meneghetti White</name>
      <year>2010</year>
      <type>white wine</type>
      <grape percentage="80">Chardonnay</grape>
      <grape percentage="20">Pinot Blanc</grape>
      <price currency="EURO">18</price>
      <geo>
         <country>Croatia</country>
         <region>Istria</region>
      </geo>
      <quantity>20</quantity>
   </wine>
</winecellar>
```

This example illustrates the typical structure of XML documents. A wine cellar consists of wines. Every wine is characterized by its name, year, type, grape composition, price, geographic location (country and region), and quantity. The comprehensibility of an XML document depends on the adoption of proper formatting rules as depicted in Table 10.1. An XML document satisfying these

**Table 10.1** XML formatting rules

| XML formatting rule | Bad example | Good example |
|---|---|---|
| Only one root element is allowed | `<winecellar>`<br>`<wine>`<br>`<name>Jacques Selosse`<br>`Brut Initial</name>`<br>`</wine>`<br>`</winecellar>`<br><br>`<winecellar>`<br>`<wine>`<br>`<name>Meneghetti`<br>`White</name>`<br>`</wine>`<br>`</winecellar>` | `<winecellar>`<br>`<wine>`<br>`<name>Jacques Selosse`<br>`Brut Initial</name>`<br>`</wine>`<br>`<wine>`<br>`<name>Meneghetti`<br>`White</name>`<br>`</wine>`<br>`</winecellar>` |
| Every start tag should be closed with a matching end tag | `<winecellar>`<br>`<wine><name>Jacques`<br>`Selosse Brut Initial`<br>`</winecellar>` | `<winecellar>`<br>`<wine><name>Jacques`<br>`Selosse Brut Initial`<br>`</name></wine>`<br>`</winecellar>` |
| No overlapping tag sequence or incorrect nesting of tags | `<winecellar>`<br>`<wine><name>Jacques`<br>`Selosse Brut Initial`<br>`</winecellar>`<br>`</wine>`<br>`</name>` | `<winecellar>`<br>`<wine><name>Jacques`<br>`Selosse Brut Initial`<br>`</name></wine>`<br>`</winecellar>` |

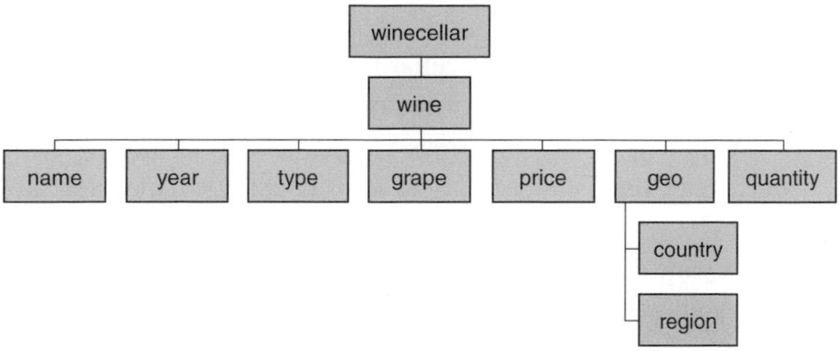


**Figure 10.1** Tree representation of an XML document.

rules is referred to as **well formed**. A simple way to check if an XML document is well formed is by verifying that it can be successfully opened in a web browser.

Since XML elements can be nested, every XML document can be represented as a tree, as illustrated in Figure 10.1. The root of the tree is the element *winecellar*. The element *wine* is the child of *winecellar*. The elements *name*, *year*, *type*, *grape*, *price*, *geo*, and *quantity* are children of *wine*. All these elements are also descendants of *winecellar*. The ancestors of *country* and *region* are *geo*, *wine*, and *winecellar*. The elements *name*, *year*, *type*, *grape*, *price*, *geo*, and *quantity* are siblings.

### 10.1.2 Document Type Definition and XML Schema Definition

**Document Type Definition (DTD)** and **XML Schema Definition (XSD)** formally specify the structure of an XML document. Both define the tag set, the location of each tag, and how they can be nested. An XML document that complies with a DTD or XSD is referred to as **valid**. Note that defining a DTD or XSD for an XML document is not mandatory. However, a document without a DTD or XSD can only be guaranteed to be **well-formed**, i.e., to satisfy the overall syntax of XML documents. A valid XML document is certified to comply with the structural prescriptions of a specific document type (e.g., an invoice, a purchase order, or a wine cellar listing), which is a much stronger property than just being well-formed. Being well-formed is a prerequisite for being valid.

Here you can see the DTD definition for our wine cellar example:

```
<?xml version="1.0" encoding="UTF-8"?>
<!DOCTYPE winecellar [
<!ELEMENT winecellar (wine+)>
<!ELEMENT wine (name, year, type, grape*, price, geo, quantity)>
<!ELEMENT name (#PCDATA)>
<!ELEMENT year (#PCDATA)>
<!ELEMENT type (#PCDATA)>
<!ELEMENT grape (#PCDATA)>
<!ATTLIST grape percentage CDATA #IMPLIED>
<!ELEMENT price (#PCDATA)>
<!ATTLIST price currency CDATA #REQUIRED>
<!ELEMENT geo (country, region)>
<!ELEMENT country (#PCDATA)>
<!ELEMENT region (#PCDATA)>
<!ELEMENT quantity (#PCDATA)>
]>
```

A few things are worth mentioning:

- The root element is defined as <!DOCTYPE winecellar [. . .]>
- <!ELEMENT winecellar (wine+)> implies that a wine cellar can have one or more wines. The modifier + refers to one or more (e.g., wine+) whereas * refers to zero or more (e.g., wine*).
- <!ELEMENT wine (name, year, type, grape*, price, geo, quantity)> specifies all the wine attributes.
- grape* refers to the fact that a wine can be assembled from zero or more grapes (as is the case for the Meneghetti wine). If we would define it as grape+, we enforce that a wine is assembled from one or more grapes.
- Attributes are specified using <!ATTLIST... >. The keyword #IMPLIED (e.g., for grape percentage) indicates that the attribute value is optional, whereas #REQUIRED (e.g., for price currency) indicates a compulsory value. #FIXED can be used for a constant value.
- CDATA refers to character data not parsed by the XML parser, whereas PCDATA refers to character data parsed by the XML parser. Tags inside PCDATA text will be parsed as regular XML tags, whereas tags inside CDATA will be considered as strings.

- Key attribute types can be defined using the ID keyword. For example, this declaration:

```
<!ATTLIST wine winekey ID #REQUIRED>
```

  requires that each wine has a unique value for the attribute type winekey in the XML document. An IDREF (IDREFS) attribute type can also be defined to refer to the value (values) of some ID attribute type defined elsewhere in the XML document. Although this sounds similar to a primary–foreign key relationship in the relational model, both ID and IDREF are untyped, which means that an IDREF can refer to any ID within the XML document.

The DTD can be included in the XML document or stored in an external file with *.dtd extension:

```
<!DOCTYPE winecellar SYSTEM "winecellar.dtd">
```

The keyword SYSTEM indicates that the DTD is only accessible to a limited set of authors. An alternative is PUBLIC, if the DTD should be accessible to a broader audience. An advantage of storing the DTD in an external file is that it can be referred to and shared by multiple XML documents.

**Drill Down**

Some popular examples of DTDs are: MathML (mathematics markup language) for mathematical expressions; CML (chemical markup language) for describing molecules; Legal XML for court records; XHTML (XML-based HTML) for web pages, and PMML (predictive modeling markup language) for describing analytical models.

A key disadvantage of DTD is that it only supports character data. No support for integers, dates, or other complex types is provided. Also note that a DTD is not defined using XML syntax, which further inhibits its adoption. Both shortcomings are addressed by XML Schema, which provides a semantically richer way of defining XML document types.

XML Schema supports various data types and user-defined types. Its modeling toolkit has been inspired by both relational and object-oriented data modeling and provides modeling concepts similar to primary–foreign keys, domains, cardinalities, complex and user-defined data types, supertype–subtype relationships, etc.

Here you can see an example XML Schema Definition (XSD) for our wine cellar example:

```
<?xml version="1.0" encoding="UTF-8" ?>
<xs:schema xmlns:xs="http://www.w3.org/2001/XMLSchema">
<xs:element name="winecellar">
<xs:complexType>
<xs:sequence>
<xs:element name="wine" maxOccurs="unbounded" minOccurs="0">
<xs:complexType>
<xs:sequence>
<xs:element type="xs:string" name="name"/>
<xs:element type="xs:short" name="year"/>
<xs:element type="xs:string" name="type"/>
<xs:element name="grape" maxOccurs="unbounded" minOccurs="1">
<xs:complexType>
```

```
<xs:simpleContent>
<xs:extension base="xs:string">
<xs:attribute type="xs:byte" name="percentage" use="optional"/>
</xs:extension>
</xs:simpleContent>
</xs:complexType>
</xs:element>
<xs:element name="price">
<xs:complexType>
<xs:simpleContent>
<xs:extension base="xs:short">
<xs:attribute type="xs:string" name="currency" use="optional"/>
</xs:extension>
</xs:simpleContent>
</xs:complexType>
</xs:element>
<xs:element name="geo">
<xs:complexType>
<xs:sequence>
<xs:element type="xs:string" name="country"/>
<xs:element type="xs:string" name="region"/>
</xs:sequence>
</xs:complexType>
</xs:element>
<xs:element type="xs:byte" name="quantity"/>
</xs:sequence>
</xs:complexType>
</xs:element>
</xs:sequence>
</xs:complexType>
</xs:element>
</xs:schema>
```

A few things are worth noting:

- XML Schema is more verbose than DTD.
- An XSD is a well-formed XML document itself. Just like the catalog in an RDBMS consists of relational data that prescribe the structure of the user database, an XSD is an XML document that prescribes the structure of other XML documents.
- XML Schema instructions start with the prefix "xs:", which refers to the corresponding namespace (see Section 10.1.4).
- The <xs:complexType> tag specifies that *winecellar* is a complex element which consists of a sequence of *wine* child elements as defined by the <xs:sequence> tag.
- Minimum and maximum cardinalities can be specified using minOccurs and maxOccurs.
- Various data types are supported such as xs:string, xs:short, xs:byte, etc.
- A *wine* is also a complex element that consists of a sequence of child elements, such as *name*, *year*, *type*, etc.

- *Grape* is a complex element defined as an extension of a simple type and contains no further elements, as indicated by the <xs:simpleContent> tag. The extension is defined by the tag <xs:extension> with the base type: xs:string. An optional attribute type percentage with data type xs:byte is also included. Price is defined in a similar way.
- *Geo* is defined as a complex type that is a sequence of country and region.
- Like DTD, XML Schema also supports ID, IDREF, and IDREFS attribute types.

As with DTDs, XSDs can be stored in the XML document itself or in an external file with an *.xsd extension.

To facilitate working with XML documents, DTD, and XML Schema, tools are available that automatically check whether an XML document or XSD is well-formed (see Table 10.1), and validate an XML document against a DTD or XSD.[3]

### 10.1.3 Extensible Stylesheet Language

XML documents focus on the content of the information, whereas other standards, such as HTML, describe the representation or layout of information. **Extensible Stylesheet Language (XSL)** can be used to define a stylesheet specifying how XML documents can be visualized in a web browser.

XSL encompasses two specifications: **XSL Transformations (XSLT)** and **XSL Formatting Objects (XSL-FO)**. The former is a language that transforms XML documents to other XML documents, HTML webpages, or plain text; the latter is a language to specify formatting semantics (e.g., to transform XML documents to PDFs). XSL-FO was discontinued in 2012, so we will proceed with XSLT in the following.

An XSLT stylesheet specifies the set of rules to transform XML documents. It will be processed by an XSLT processor that will first inspect the data in the XML file to make sure it is well-formed (checked against the factors listed in Table 10.1) and, optionally, valid (checked against the DTD or XSD). It will then apply the transformation rules and write the result to an output stream.

Two common types of XSLT transformations can be distinguished. The first one transforms an XML document to another XML document with a different structure. Suppose that in our wine cellar example we are interested in generating a summary document that only includes the name and quantity of each wine. We can then define the following XSLT stylesheet:

```
<?xml version="1.0" encoding="UTF-8"?>
<xsl:stylesheet version="1.0" xmlns:xsl="http://www.w3.org/1999/XSL/Transform">
<xsl:template match="/">
<winecellarsummary>
<xsl:for-each select="winecellar/wine">
<wine>
<name><xsl:value-of select="name"/></name>
<quantity><xsl:value-of select="quantity"/></quantity>
</wine>
</xsl:for-each>
</winecellarsummary>
</xsl:template>
</xsl:stylesheet>
```

[3] For a freely available online tool, see www.freeformatter.com.

A few things are worth noting:

- An XSLT stylesheet is a well-formed XML document itself.
- XSLT tags are represented using the prefix xsl:, which refers to the corresponding namespace (see Section 10.1.4).
- An XSLT stylesheet consists of templates, which are transformation rules defining what action to perform to what element. The <xsl:template> tag contains the rules to apply when a specified node in the document tree is matched, whereby match="/" refers to the whole XML document. We could have worked out an alternative solution by using <xsl:template match="wine"> instead.
- The <xsl:for-each select="winecellar/wine"> statement essentially implements a for loop that iterates through each wine of the wine cellar. The statement "winecellar/wine" is an XPath expression used for navigational purposes (see Section 10.1.5).
- The statements <xsl:value-of select="name"/> and <xsl:value-of select="quantity"/> then retrieve the name and quantity of each wine.

If we now run this XSLT stylesheet on our XML document using an XSLT processor,[4] we will get this result:

```
<?xml version="1.0" encoding="UTF-8"?>
<winecellarsummary>
   <wine>
      <name>Jacques Selosse Brut Initial</name>
      <quantity>12</quantity>
   </wine>
   <wine>
      <name>Meneghetti White</name>
      <quantity>20</quantity>
   </wine>
</winecellarsummary>
```

Another popular application of XSLT is to transform an XML document to an HTML page that can be displayed in a web browser. Most web browsers have built-in facilities to transform an XML document with an XSLT stylesheet into an HTML page. Below you can see an XSLT stylesheet that transforms our wine cellar XML document to HTML format:

```
<?xml version="1.0" encoding="UTF-8"?>
<html xsl:version="1.0" xmlns:xsl="http://www.w3.org/1999/XSL/Transform">
   <body style="font-family:Arial;font-size:12pt;background-color:#ffff">
<h1>My Wine Cellar</h1>
<table border="1">
    <tr bgcolor="#f2f2f2">
       <th>Wine</th>
       <th>Year</th>
       <th>Quantity</th>
    </tr>
```

[4] See www.freeformatter.com for a freely available online XSLT processor.

```
      <xsl:for-each select="winecellar/wine">
      <tr>
        <td><xsl:value-of select="name"/></td>
        <td><xsl:value-of select="year"/></td>
        <td><xsl:value-of select="quantity"/></td>
     </tr>
     </xsl:for-each>
  </table>
  </body>
  </html>
```

A few things are worth noting:

- Every HTML document starts with an <html> and <body> tag.
- <h1> defines an HTML header.
- A visual table format can be defined using the <table>, <th> (referring to table header), <tr> (referring to table row), and <td> (referring to table data or table cell) tags.
- The expression "winecellar/wine" is an XPath expression (see Section 10.1.5) used for navigational purposes.
- We implement a for loop using <xsl:for-each select="winecellar/wine"> and select the corresponding values using for example <xsl:value-of select="name"/>.

If we now process our XML data with this stylesheet, we will obtain this HTML code:

```
<html>
   <body style="font-family:Arial;font-size:12pt;background-color:#ffff">
      <h1>My Wine Cellar</h1>
      <table border="1">
         <tr bgcolor="#f2f2f2">
            <th>Wine</th>
            <th>Year</th>
            <th>Quantity</th>
         </tr>
         <tr>
            <td>Jacques Selosse Brut Initial</td>
            <td>2012</td>
            <td>12</td>
         </tr>
         <tr>
            <td>Meneghetti White</td>
            <td>2010</td>
            <td>20</td>
         </tr>
      </table>
   </body>
</html>
```

This can be represented in a web browser (e.g., Google Chrome) as shown in Figure 10.2.

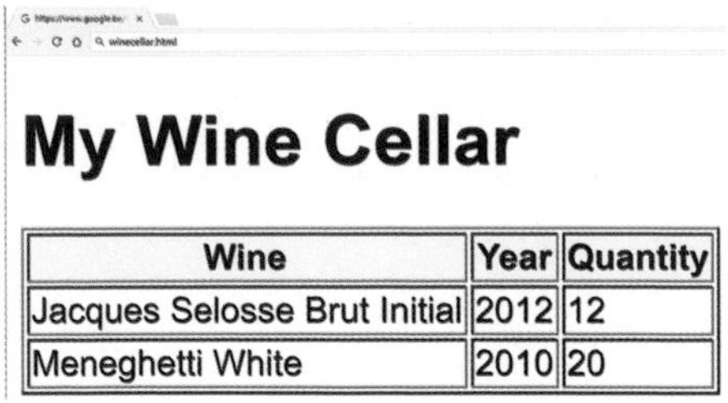


**Figure 10.2** Google Chrome representation of the wine cellar.

A key advantage of using stylesheets is the decoupling of information content from information visualization, so the underlying information needs to be stored only once, but can be represented in various ways, depending on the user or device (e.g., mobile phone) just by applying a different stylesheet.

### 10.1.4 Namespaces

Since XML allows every user to define his/her own tags, name conflicts can arise. Consider the tag <element>, which can either refer to a chemical element, mathematical element of a set or even a part of an XML Schema specification. Note that this is not the case in HTML, since all HTML tags have been defined by the World Wide Web Consortium (W3C).

To avoid name conflicts, XML has introduced the concept of a **namespace**. The idea is to introduce prefixes to XML elements to unambiguously identify their meaning. These prefixes typically refer to a URI (uniform resource identifier) that uniquely identifies a web resource such as a URL (uniform resource locator). The URL does not need to refer to a physically existing webpage; it is just used as a unique identifier. All tags and attributes associated with the same prefix belong to the same namespace and should be unique. Namespaces can be defined as follows:

```
<winecellar xmlns:Bartns="www.dataminingapps.com/home.html">
```

The above example defines a namespace called “Bartns”, which refers to the URL www.dataminingapps.com/home.html. Tags can now be prefixed:

```
<bartns:wine>
<bartns:name>Jacques Selosse Brut Initial</bartns:name>
<bartns:year>2012</bartns:year>
</bartns:wine>
```

Multiple namespaces can be defined and used within a single XML document. A default name space can be defined:

```
<winecellar xmlns="www.dataminingapps.com/defaultns.html">
```

All XML tags without any prefix will then be assumed to belong to this default namespace. Note that in our earlier examples we already made use of namespaces for, respectively, XML Schema tags and stylesheet tags, as the following two code snippets illustrate:

```
<xs:schema xmlns:xs="http://www.w3.org/2001/XMLSchema">

<xsl:stylesheet version="1.0" xmlns:xsl="http://www.w3.org/1999/XSL/Transform">
```

### 10.1.5 XPath

**XPath** is a simple declarative language that uses path expressions to refer to parts of an XML document. XPath considers an XML document as an ordered tree whereby every element, attribute, or text fragment corresponds to a node of the tree. An XPath expression starts from a context node and then navigates from there onwards. Every navigation step results in a node or list of nodes that can then be used to continue the navigation. Predicates can be added to tailor the navigation.

In what follows, we will discuss examples of XPath expressions. This expression selects all wine elements from our winecellar example:

```
doc("winecellar.xml")/winecellar/wine
```

The doc( ) expression is used to return the root of a named document. Note that navigating using the "/" symbol always selects one level down. "//" can be used to skip multiple levels of nodes and search through all descendants of a node.

If we are only interested in a particular wine, we can use an index:

```
doc("winecellar.xml")/winecellar/wine[2]
```

This expression will select all details of the second wine in our wine cellar XML document, which is the Meneghetti white wine information in our example. Note that the indexing starts at 1 and not at 0, as is the case in, e.g., Java.

Predicates can be added between square brackets:

```
doc("winecellar.xml")/winecellar/wine[ price > 20] /name
```

This will select the names of all wines with a price greater than 20 (which will return Jacques Selosse Brut Initial in our example).

XPath provides facilities to select attribute values, move between ancestors, descendants, siblings, combine multiple paths, etc. It also includes various operators for mathematical computations and Boolean comparisons. XPath is an essential part of the XSLT standard, where it is also used for navigational purposes, as we discussed before.

**Retention Questions**

- What is XML and what can it be used for?
- What is the difference between DTD and XML Schema?
- What is XSLT and what can it be used for?
- Why can namespaces be useful?
- Give an example of an XPath expression and discuss its meaning.

## 10.2 Processing XML Documents

The information in an XML document can be used by an application for further processing. Figure 10.3 shows a generic outline of the processing steps involved. A first step is using an XSLT stylesheet and XSLT processor to translate the XML document to the XML format required by the application. The XML parser will check whether the XML document is well-formed (see Table 10.1) and valid according to the corresponding DTD or XSD. The application will then process the parsed XML code using an API, such as the DOM API or SAX API.

The **DOM API** is a tree-based API and will represent the XML document as a tree in internal memory. It was developed by the World Wide Web Consortium. DOM provides various classes with methods to navigate through the tree and do various operations such as adding, moving, or removing elements. It is especially useful to facilitate direct access to specific XML document parts

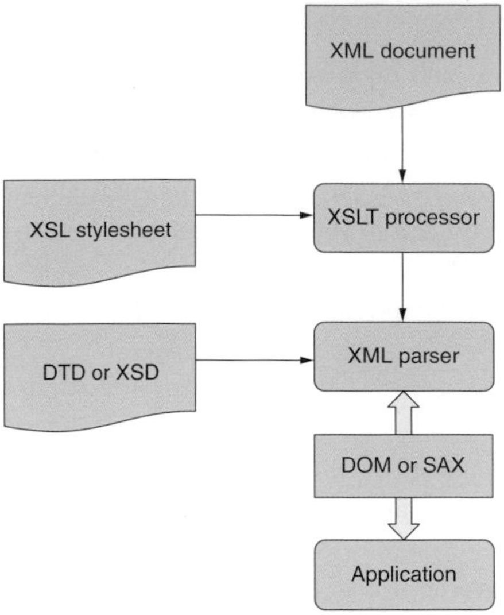


**Figure 10.3** Processing an XML document.

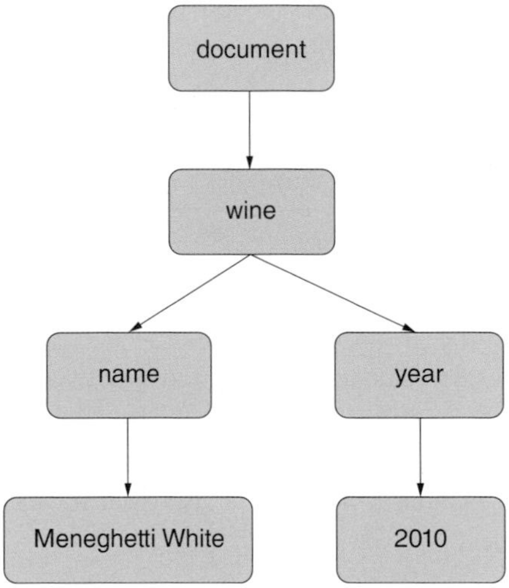


**Figure 10.4** DOM tree.

and when a high number of data manipulations are needed. However, it can get too memory intensive when handling large XML documents.

As an example, consider this XML fragment

```
<wine>
<name>Meneghetti White</name>
<year>2010</year>
</wine>
```

with corresponding DOM tree as illustrated in Figure 10.4.

The **SAX API (simple API for XML)** is an event-based API. The XML document will be represented as a stream of events:

```
start document
start element: wine
start element: name
text: Meneghetti
end element: name
start element: year
text: 2010
end element: year
end element: wine
end document
```

This stream can then be directly passed on to the application, which will use an event handler to process the events. When compared to DOM, SAX has a smaller memory footprint, since no tree needs to be built, and is more scalable for processing large XML documents. It is excellent for sequential access, but less suited to supporting direct random access to specific parts of the XML document. It also performs worse than DOM if heavy data manipulation occurs.

Both DOM and SAX have been implemented in various programming languages such as C++, Java, Perl, Python, etc. Some languages provide combined support. The JAXP (Java API for XML processing) is one of the Java XML APIs which includes an XML parser, XSLT processor, and both DOM and SAX access facilities to XML documents for Java applications. This implies that the XML parser and XSLT processor can be easily updated or changed with no effect on the applications using them. Also note that both DOM and SAX are low-level APIs which are often used by higher-level APIs to further facilitate XML access, such as JAXB (Java API for XML binding) which converts XML elements and attributes to a Java object hierarchy (and vice versa).

**Retention Questions**

- Summarize the key differences between the DOM and SAX API.
- How does the StAX API relate to the DOM and SAX API?

DOM and SAX are two XML access methods that can be thought of as opposites. **StAX (streaming API for XML)** was defined as a more recent compromise between both, and originated from the Java programming community. As opposed to SAX, which pushes the data to the application using events, StAX allows the application to pull the required data from the XML document using a cursor mechanism. The latter is positioned at a particular point within the XML document and can be explicitly moved forward by the application, pulling the information on an "as needed" basis.

## 10.3 Storage of XML Documents

**Connections**

Chapter 1 discusses the disadvantages of the file-based approach to data management, as opposed to the database approach.

XML documents are stored as semi-structured data. A first option would be to store XML documents as files on a web server, similar to HTML pages. Although this option is simple, it will be cumbersome in terms of maintenance, data manipulation, and structured search.

A better alternative could be a content or document management system aimed at editing, storing, and maintaining complex, hierarchically structured documents. These systems are usually built on top of a DBMS (e.g., hierarchical, relational, or OO), which is hidden from the end-user. They come with various facilities such as editors, authoring tools, workflow systems, and publishing tools, and often provide full-text search capabilities. Another option is an XML server or XML DBMS specifically designed to "natively" store XML documents and provide support for all related XML standards, such as DTD, XML Schema, XPath, etc. It also includes advanced facilities for indexing, querying using XQuery (see Section 10.6.3), transaction management, security, concurrency control, backup, and recovery. XML documents can also be stored in an (object-) relational database using either a document- or data-oriented approach. We will discuss both in more detail in what follows.

### 10.3.1 The Document-Oriented Approach for Storing XML Documents

In the **document-oriented approach**, an XML document will be stored as either a BLOB (binary large object) or CLOB (character large object) in a table cell. The RDBMS considers these objects as one chunk of "black box" data and provides facilities for efficient storage, retrieval, and querying. The latter is usually based upon full text search features provided through an object-relational extension. This can also include automatic indexing based on keywords. To facilitate direct access to XML document elements, some (O)RDBMSs have introduced an XML data type as part of the SQL/XML extension, which offers methods to parse and manipulate XML content including XML to SQL data type mappings. We discuss this further in the section on SQL/XML.

The document-oriented approach is simple and compact, and needs no DTD or XSD for the XML document to do the mapping. It is especially well suited for storing static content that is not frequently updated, such as letters, reports, purchase orders, or contracts. A drawback of this approach is the poor integration with traditional relational SQL query processing.

### 10.3.2 The Data-Oriented Approach for Storing XML Documents

According to the **data-oriented approach**, an XML document will be decomposed into its constituting data parts which will be spread across a set of connected (object-)relational tables. This approach is also called **shredding** and is recommended in the case of highly structured documents and fine-granular queries targeting individual XML elements. The corresponding set of tables will focus on capturing the data elements accurately, so the document structure itself becomes less relevant. The DBMS or separate middleware can do the back-and-forth translation between the XML data and the relational data. A further distinction can be made between schema-oblivious shredding, which starts from the XML document itself, and schema-aware shredding, which starts from a DTD or XSD. We will discuss both in more detail in Sections 10.5.2 and 10.5.3.

The major advantage of this approach is that SQL queries can now directly access and manipulate individual XML elements. The entire XML document can be reconstructed by using SQL joins. Note, however, that extensive joins might hamper the performance. An alternative could be to use an object-relational DBMS which provides facilities (e.g., nesting, collection types) to foster a closer resemblance between the data structure and the XML document structure. We will elaborate more on this in Section 10.5.

**Connections**

Chapter 9 discusses object-relational DBMSs.

### 10.3.3 The Combined Approach for Storing XML Documents

This **combined approach**, also called **partial shredding**, combines the document- and data-oriented approaches for storing XML documents. Some parts of the XML document will be stored as BLOBs, CLOBs, or XML objects, whereas other parts will be shredded and stored in relational tables. This approach combines the best of both worlds. SQL views can then be defined to reconstruct the entire XML document. Most DBMSs provide facilities to automatically determine the optimal level of decomposition. As an example, consider a car insurance claim XML document. The details of the claimant and car (e.g., name, birth date, license plate, etc.) can be stored in relational tables, while the description of the accident, photos, etc. can be stored as BLOBs, CLOBs, or XML objects.

Note that the mapping approaches discussed above can be implemented either using middleware or by the DBMS itself, in which case it is referred to as an **XML-enabled DBMS**.

**Retention Questions**

- Discuss and contrast the document-oriented, data-oriented, and combined approach for storing XML documents. Give recommendations for when to use each approach.

**Drill Down**

According to http://db-engines.com, the most popular Native XML DBMSs are: MarkLogic (commercial), Virtuoso (open-source), Sedna (open-source), BaseX (open-source), and Tamino (commercial). Note, however, that none of these ranks in the top 20.

## 10.4 Differences Between XML Data and Relational Data

Both the relational model and XML represent data in a *structured* way (or in a semi-structured way in the case of XML). However, the structuring elements and the semantics that can (and cannot) be expressed in both are very different. Before we tackle the mapping between XML and (object-)relational data, we must briefly overview some major differences in the way each deals with structure.

**Connections**

The basic principles of the relational model were discussed in Chapter 6. Object-relational DBMSs were covered in Chapter 9.

To begin with, remember that the building block of the relational model is a mathematical relation that consists of zero, one, or more unordered tuples. Each tuple consists of one or more attributes. The relational model does not implement any type of ordering. This is different in the XML model, where the ordering of the elements can be meaningful (e.g., the ordering of the different paragraphs in a contract). To implement this ordering in a relational database an extra attribute type must be added. In an object-relational database the ordering can be implemented using a list collection type.

According to the first normal form, the relational model does not support the concept of nested relations. As discussed before, XML data are typically hierarchically structured, and hence are all about nesting, which creates a mapping problem. This is not an issue in object-relational databases, since they provide direct support to model complex objects using nested relations.

Another requirement of the first normal form is that attribute types cannot be multi-valued. XML allows the same child element to appear multiple times. As an example, an author can have multiple email addresses. To map this to the relational model, an additional table and primary–foreign key relationship will have to be defined which will create additional overhead. Multi-valued attribute types can be implemented in object-relational databases using any of the collection types (set, multiset, list, array) discussed before.

**Retention Questions**

- Summarize the key differences between XML data and relational data. Illustrate with an example.

A relational database only provides support for atomic data types, such as integer, string, date, etc. XML DTDs define aggregated types but provide no support for these atomic data types since all numbers, text, and dates are stored as (P)CDATA. The latter can be appropriately defined using XML Schema which supports both atomic and aggregated types. Aggregated types can be directly modeled in object-relational databases using user-defined types.

Finally, XML data are semi-structured. This implies that XML documents can include certain anomalies or peculiarities in their structure. For example, it is possible that some elements are missing (e.g., a customer without an address) or have variable length. The introduction of a new tag, or change to the DTD or XSD, will necessitate a re-generation of the relational tables.

## 10.5 Mappings Between XML Documents and (Object-) Relational Data

In this section we review various ways of mapping XML documents to (object-)relational data so they can be easily stored, managed, and queried using an (O)RDBMS. We discuss table-based mapping, schema-oblivious mapping and schema-aware mapping, and conclude by introducing SQL/XML.

### 10.5.1 Table-Based Mapping

A **table-based mapping** specifies strict requirements to the structure of the XML document: it should be a perfect reflection of the database structure. The back-and-forth mapping becomes straightforward. Here you can see an example XML document:

```
<database>
<table>
<row>
<column1> data </column1>
<column2> data </column2>
...
</row>
<row>
<column1> data </column1>
<column2> data </column2>
...
</row>
...
</table>
<table>
...
</table>
...
</database>
```

> **Connections**
>
> Updatable SQL views were discussed in Chapter 7.

The actual data are stored as the content of the column elements. As an alternative, it can also be stored as column attribute values in the row elements, such as <row column1=data column2=data. . ./>. Most tools will use more meaningful names than table, column, row, etc.

The key advantage of this approach is its simplicity, given the perfect one-to-one mapping that implies that data can be transferred efficiently from the XML document to the relational tables and vice versa. The document structure itself can be implemented using an updatable SQL view (instead of actual tables), which will facilitate the data transfer.

The technique also allows you to extract XML data from the database, whereby the document structure corresponds to the result of an SQL query.

The major disadvantage relates to the rigid structure imposed on the XML document. This can be partly mitigated by using XSLT to tailor the document according to the requirements of a specific application.

The table-based mapping approach is frequently used to serialize and transfer data from one DBMS to another DBMS. Another example concerns web forms, whereby the data entered are stored in an XML document that can then be imported into the DBMS directly.

## 10.5.2 Schema-Oblivious Mapping

A **schema-oblivious mapping/shredding** transforms an XML document without the availability of a DTD or XSD. This situation could occur for irregular XML documents that do not abide to a common schema. Therefore, we need to think about a very general, high-level schema to assist in the mapping. One common approach is to transform the document to a tree structure, whereby the nodes represent the data in the document. The tree can then be mapped to a relational model in various ways. A first option is to create one relational table:

```
CREATE TABLE NODE(
ID CHAR(6) NOT NULL PRIMARY KEY,
PARENT_ID CHAR(6),
TYPE VARCHAR(9),
LABEL VARCHAR(20),
VALUE CLOB,
FOREIGN KEY (PARENT_ID) REFERENCES NODE (ID)
CONSTRAINT CC1 CHECK(TYPE IN ("element", "attribute"))
)
```

The idea here is to assign a unique identifier to each element or attribute type. The PARENT_ID attribute type is a self-referencing foreign key referring to the parent of the element or attribute type. The TYPE attribute type indicates whether the tuple relates to an element or attribute type. The LABEL attribute type specifies the XML tag name of the element or name of the attribute type. The VALUE attribute type is the text value of the element or attribute type. An additional ORDER attribute type can be added to the table to record the order of the children.

As an example, consider this XML specification:

```
<?xml version="1.0" encoding="UTF-8"?>
<winecellar>
   <wine winekey="1">
      <name>Jacques Selosse Brut Initial</name>
      <year>2012</year>
      <type>Champagne</type>
      <price>150</price>
   </wine>
   <wine winekey="2">
      <name>Meneghetti White</name>
      <year>2010</year>
      <type>white wine</type>
      <price>18</price>
   </wine>
</winecellar>
```

This will result in the tuples in the NODE table shown in Figure 10.5.

XPath or XQuery (see Section 10.6.3) queries can then be translated into SQL queries, of which the result can be translated back to XML. As an example, consider our previous XPath query:

```
doc("winecellar.xml")/winecellar/wine[price > 20]/name
```

This can now be translated into:

```
SELECT N2.VALUE
FROM NODE N1, NODE N2
WHERE
N2.LABEL="name" AND
N1.LABEL="price" AND
CAST(N1.VALUE AS INT)> 20 AND
N1.PARENT_ID=N2.PARENT_ID
```

**Connections**

Chapter 9 discusses recursive SQL queries.

Note that the CAST() function is needed to cast the VARCHAR into an INT so the mathematical comparison can be done. The generation of this SQL query from the XPath expression can be taken care of by a middleware tool. Note, however, that not all XPath queries can be translated to SQL.

| ID | PARENT_ID | TYPE | LABEL | VALUE |
|---|---|---|---|---|
| 1 | NULL | element | winecellar | NULL |
| 2 | 1 | element | wine | NULL |
| 3 | 2 | attribute | winekey | 1 |
| 4 | 2 | element | name | Jacques Selosse Brut Initial |
| 5 | 2 | element | year | 2012 |
| 6 | 2 | element | type | Champagne |
| 7 | 2 | element | price | 150 |
| 8 | 1 | element | wine | NULL |
| 9 | 8 | attribute | winekey | 2 |
| 10 | 8 | element | name | Meneghetti White |
| 11 | 8 | element | year | 2010 |
| 12 | 8 | element | type | white wine |
| 13 | 8 | element | price | 18 |

**Figure 10.5** Example tuples in the NODE table.

An example of this is a search through all descendants of a node at different levels using the XPath // operator. The latter cannot be expressed adequately in SQL unless the extension of recursive SQL queries is used.

Although a single relational table gives a very compact representation, it will require extensive querying resources since every single navigation step requires a self-join on this table. Various alternatives can be considered by creating more tables storing information separately about elements, attributes, siblings, etc. The optimal design depends upon the type of queries executed. The mapping can be further facilitated by making use of object-relational extensions (e.g., nesting constructs, collection types) to avoid extensive normalization, which risks over-shredding the XML data across too many relations.

Note that due to extensive shredding, the reconstruction of the XML document from the (object-)relational data can get quite resource intensive. Some middleware solutions offer a DOM API or SAX API on top of the DBMS. XML applications can then access the relational data through these APIs without the need to have a physical XML document. The (object-)relational data are offered as a virtual XML document. A related option is to use materialized views to store the XML documents.

**Connections**

Chapter 7 discusses materialized views.

### 10.5.3 Schema-Aware Mapping

A **schema-aware mapping** transforms an XML document based on an already existing DTD or XSD. The availability of a DTD or XSD will facilitate the definition of a corresponding database schema. The following steps can be taken to generate a database schema from a DTD or XSD:

1. Simplify the DTD or XSD as much as possible.
2. Map every complex element type (consisting of other element types or mixed content) to a relational table, or user-defined type in the case of an ORDBMS, with corresponding primary key.
3. Map every element type with mixed content to a separate table where the (P)CDATA is stored. Connect this table to the parent table using a primary–foreign key relationship.
4. Map single-valued attribute types, or child elements that occur only once, with (P)CDATA content to a column in the corresponding relational table. When starting from an XSD, choose the SQL data type that most closely resembles the XML Schema data type (e.g., xs:short to SMALLINT). Null values are allowed if the attribute type or child elements are optional.
5. Map multi-valued attribute types, or child elements that can occur multiple times, with (P)CDATA content to a separate table. Use a primary–foreign key relationship to connect this table to the parent table. In an object-relational DBMS, collection types can be used as an alternative.
6. For each complex child element type, connect the tables corresponding to the child and parent element types using a primary–foreign key relationship.

Note that the above guidelines are only to be rules of thumb. Often the number of relational tables generated from a DTD or XSD will be further minimized by allowing some denormalization to avoid expensive joins when the data need to be retrieved.[5] Shredding is a very complicated process with many possible solutions. The best option depends upon the requirements of the applications that use the data.

[5] Denormalization can be achieved by combining two or more normalized tables into one. By doing so, join queries will execute faster since now only one table needs to be considered. However, this comes at a price of redundant data and possibly inconsistent data as well if not appropriately managed.

The following steps can be taken to generate a DTD or XSD from a database model or schema:

1. Map every table to an element type.
2. Map every table column to an attribute type or child element type with (P)CDATA in the case of DTD, or most closely resembling data type in case of XML Schema (e.g., SMALLINT to xs:short).
3. Map primary–foreign key relationships by introducing additional child element types. Object-relational collections can be mapped to multi-valued attribute types or element types which can occur multiple times.

Annotations with mapping information can be added to the DTD or XSD. Most vendors will also offer user-friendly visualization facilities to clarify the mapping.

### 10.5.4 SQL/XML

**SQL/XML** was introduced in 2003, with revisions in 2006, 2008, and 2011. It is basically an extension of SQL that introduces:

- a new XML data type with a corresponding constructor that treats XML documents as cell values in a column of a relational table, and can be used to define attribute types in user-defined types, variables and parameters of user-defined functions;
- a set of operators for the XML data type;
- a set of functions to map relational data to XML.

SQL/XML includes no rules for shredding XML data into SQL format, as we discussed before.

Here you can see an example of an SQL/XML DML instruction:

```
CREATE TABLE PRODUCT(
PRODNR CHAR(6) NOT NULL PRIMARY KEY,
PRODNAME VARCHAR(60) NOT NULL,
PRODTYPE VARCHAR(15),
AVAILABLE_QUANTITY INTEGER,
REVIEW XML)
```

The table PRODUCT has been extended with a column REVIEW with data type XML. We can now insert values into this table:

```
INSERT INTO PRODUCT VALUES("120", "Conundrum", "white", 12,
XML(<review><author>Bart Baesens</author><date>27/02/2017</date>
<description>This is an excellent white wine with intriguing aromas of
green apple, tangerine and honeysuckle blossoms.</description><rating
max-value="100">94</rating></review>)
```

As mentioned, SQL/XML can be used to represent relational data in XML format. It provides a default mapping whereby the names of tables and columns are translated to XML elements and row elements are included for each table row. As a byproduct, it will add the corresponding DTD or XSD. SQL/XML also includes facilities to represent the output of SQL queries in a tailored XML format. The instruction XMLElement defines an XML element using two input arguments: the name of the XML element and the column name, which represents its content as follows:

```
SELECT XMLElement("sparkling wine", PRODNAME)
FROM PRODUCT
WHERE PRODTYPE="sparkling"
```

This query will give this result:[6]

```
<sparkling_wine>Meerdael, Methode Traditionnelle Chardonnay, 2014
</sparkling_wine>
<sparkling_wine>Jacques Selosse, Brut Initial, 2012</sparkling_wine>
<sparkling_wine>Billecart-Salmon, Brut Réserve, 2014</sparkling_wine>
...
```

The above shows how the values of the PRODNAME column have been enclosed between <sparkling_wine> and </sparkling_wine> tags.

XMLElement instructions can be nested and the XMLAttributes instruction can be added as a subclause to specify the attributes of XML elements:

```
SELECT XMLElement("sparkling wine", XMLAttributes(PRODNR AS "prodid"),
XMLElement("name", PRODNAME), XMLElement("quantity", AVAILABLE_QUANTITY))
FROM PRODUCT
WHERE PRODTYPE="sparkling"
```

The result will then become:

```
<sparkling_wine prodid="0178">
<name>Meerdael, Methode Traditionnelle Chardonnay, 2014</name>
<quantity>136</quantity>
</sparkling_wine>
<sparkling_wine prodid="0199">
<name>Jacques Selosse, Brut Initial, 2012</name>
<quantity>96</quantity>
</sparkling_wine>
...
```

The above query can be reformulated using the XMLForest instruction, which generates a list of XML elements as children of a root element:

```
SELECT XMLElement("sparkling wine", XMLAttributes(PRODNR AS "prodid"),
XMLForest(PRODNAME AS "name", AVAILABLE_QUANTITY AS "quantity"))
FROM PRODUCT
WHERE PRODTYPE="sparkling"
```

XMLAgg is an aggregate function similar to COUNT, MIN, or MAX in standard SQL, and can generate a list of XML elements from a collection of elements in combination with a GROUP BY statement:

```
SELECT XMLElement("product", XMLElement(prodid, P.PRODNR),
XMLElement("name", P.PRODNAME), XMLAgg("supplier", S.SUPNR))
```

[6] These queries can only be executed when using a DBMS that supports SQL/XML.

```
FROM PRODUCT P, SUPPLIES S
WHERE P.PRODNR=S.PRODNR
GROUP BY P.PRODNR
```

This query will append all supplier numbers of suppliers that can supply a particular product under the corresponding product information:

```
<product>
<prodid>178</prodid>
<name>Meerdael, Methode Traditionnelle Chardonnay</name>
<supplier>21</supplier>
<supplier>37</supplier>
<supplier>68</supplier>
<supplier>69</supplier>
<supplier>94</supplier>
</product>
<product>
<prodid>199</prodid>
<name>Jacques Selosse, Brut Initial, 2012</name>
<supplier>69</supplier>
<supplier>94</supplier>
</product>
...
```

The result of an SQL/XML query can also be a combination of both relational and XML data types, as this query illustrates:

```
SELECT PRODNR, XMLElement("sparkling wine", PRODNAME), AVAILABLE_QUANTITY
FROM PRODUCT
WHERE PRODTYPE="sparkling"
```

The result of this will be:

```
0178, <sparkling_wine>Meerdael, Methode Traditionnelle Chardonnay,
2014</sparkling_wine>, 136
0199, <sparkling_wine>Jacques Selosse, Brut Initial, 2012</sparkling_wine>, 96
0212, <sparkling_wine>Billecart-Salmon, Brut Réserve, 2014
</sparkling_wine>, 141
...
```

SQL/XML also includes functions to concatenate a list of XML values (XMLConcat), generate an XML comment (XMLComment) or processing instruction (XMLPI), serialize an XML value to a character or binary string (XMLSerialize), perform a non-validating parse of a character string to produce an XML value (XMLParse) and to create an XML value by modifying the properties of the root item of another XML value (XMLROOT). Despite its potential, most vendor implementations of SQL/XML are proprietary and incompatible with each other.

Some tools will also support a **template-based mapping** in which SQL statements can be directly embedded in XML documents using a tool-specific delimiter (e.g., <selectStmt>) as follows:

**Retention Questions**

- Discuss the table-based mapping for mapping between XML documents and (object-)relational data. Illustrate with an example and discuss the advantages and disadvantages.
- Discuss the schema-oblivious mapping for mapping between XML documents and (object-) relational data. Illustrate with an example and discuss the advantages and disadvantages.
- Discuss the schema-aware mapping for mapping between XML documents and (object-)relational data. Illustrate with an example and discuss the advantages and disadvantages.
- What is SQL/XML and what can it be used for? Illustrate with an example.

```
<?xml version="1.0" encoding="UTF-8"?>
<sparklingwines>
<heading>List of Sparkling Wines</heading>
<selectStmt>
SELECT PRODNAME, AVAILABLE_QUANTITY FROM PRODUCT WHERE
PRODTYPE="sparkling";
</selectStmt>
<wine>
<name> $PRODNAME </name>
<quantity> $AVAILABLE_QUANTITY </quantity>
</wine>
</sparklingwines>
```

The tool will then execute the query and generate this output:

```
<?xml version="1.0" encoding="UTF-8"?>
<sparklingwines>
<heading>List of Sparkling Wines</heading>
<wine>
<name>Meerdael, Methode Traditionnelle Chardonnay, 2014</name>
<quantity>136</quantity>
</wine>
<wine>
<name>Jacques Selosse, Brut Initial, 2012</name>
<quantity>96</quantity>
</wine>
..
</sparklingwines>
```

The approaches discussed in this subsection generate a variety of XML documents based upon the same underlying relational data.

**Drill Down**

Given the amount of unstructured and textual data they are working with, the media and publishing industry are frequent customers of XML databases. As an example, for more than 140 years, the Press Association (PA) served as the UK's main provider of fast and accurate news. PA provides different types of information such as news, sports data, and weather forecasts, and various types of multimedia content (images and video). Since XML is one of their key technologies, they needed an XML-enabled DBMS such as MarkLogic to merge a large volume of structured and unstructured data in a transparent and efficient way.

## 10.6 Searching XML Data

Whereas SQL is used to query relational data, different techniques exist to directly query XML data. Some exploit the structured aspect of XML, much like SQL does with relational data, whereas others merely treat XML documents as plain text, not taking the inherent structure into account. We discuss the respective options in this section.

### 10.6.1 Full-Text Search

A first option is to treat XML documents as textual data and conduct a brute force **full-text search**. This approach does not take into account any tag structure or information. It can be applied to XML documents that have been stored as files (e.g., in a file or content management system) or as BLOB/CLOB objects in a DBMS. Note that many DBMSs offer full-text search capabilities by means of object-relational extensions. The same method can also be applied to search in HTML documents, emails, or other text documents. A major drawback is that it does not formulate semantically rich queries targeting individual XML elements and/or join XML data with relational data.

### 10.6.2 Keyword-Based Search

A **keyword-based search** assumes that the XML document is complemented with a set of keywords describing the document metadata, such as file name, author name, date of last modification, keywords summarizing document content, etc. These keywords can then be indexed by text search engines to speed-up information retrieval. The document itself is still stored in a file or BLOB/CLOB format. Although this approach is semantically richer than the previous one, it still does not unleash the full expressive power of XML for querying.

### 10.6.3 Structured Search With XQuery

**Structured search** methods make use of structural metadata, which relates to the actual document content. To clarify the difference between document metadata and structural metadata, consider a set of XML documents describing book reviews. The document metadata describe properties of the document, such as author of the review document (e.g., Wilfried Lemahieu) and creation date of the document (e.g., June 6, 2017). The structural metadata describe the role of individual content fragments within the overall document structure. Examples of structural metadata are: "title of book" (e.g., describing the content fragment "Analytics in a Big Data World"), "author of book" (e.g., describing the content fragment "Bart Baesens"), rating (e.g., describing the content fragment "excellent"), and "review" (describing the actual review text).

Structured search queries offer more possibilities than both full-text and keyword-based search methods since we can now also query document content by means of the structural metadata. In this way, we can search for reviews of just books authored by Bart Baesens, instead of all documents somehow containing the text string "Bart Baesens", as with full-text search. Also, we can retrieve only the title of the qualifying books, instead of the entire review documents.

The **XQuery** language formulates structured queries for XML documents. The queries can take both the document structure and the actual elements' content into account. XPath path expressions are used to navigate through the document structure and to retrieve the children, parents, ancestors, descendants, siblings, and references of an XML element. Also, the ordering of the elements can be accounted for. XQuery complements the XPath expressions with constructs to refer to and compare the content of elements. Here, the syntax is somewhat similar to SQL. An XQuery statement is formulated as a **FLWOR** (pronounced as "flower") instruction as follows:

```
FOR $variable IN expression
LET $variable:=expression
WHERE filtercriterion
ORDER BY sortcriterion
RETURN expression
```

Consider this example:

```
LET $maxyear:=2012
RETURN doc("winecellar.xml")/winecellar/wine[year <$maxyear]
```

This query will return all wine elements (including all attributes and children) of wines that are older than 2012. Note how the LET instruction is used to assign the value 2012 to the variable "maxyear". The RETURN instruction will return the query result.

The FOR instruction implements an iteration as follows:

```
FOR $wine IN doc("winecellar.xml")/winecellar/wine
ORDER BY $wine/year ASCENDING
RETURN $wine
```

The $wine variable will iterate through each wine element of the wine cellar. As in SQL, the ORDER BY instruction can be used for sorting. In our example, we will sort the wines based upon ascending year.

Similar to SQL, the WHERE clause allows for further refinement:

```
FOR $wine IN doc("winecellar.xml")/winecellar/wine
WHERE $wine/price < 20 AND $wine/price/@currency="EURO"
RETURN <cheap_wine> { $wine/name, $wine/price} </cheap_wine>
```

The above query will select wine elements whose price is cheaper than 20 euros. Remember that currency was an attribute of the XML element price. XML attributes can be referred to by preceding their name with an "@" in the query. Also note that we added the new tag <cheap_wine> to the result.

XQuery also supports join queries. Assume we have an XML document winereview.xml that contains wine reviews and ratings. Wines are also identified by their "winekey". We can now formulate this XQuery join query:

```
FOR $wine IN doc("winecellar.xml")/wine
    $winereview IN doc("winereview.xml")/winereview
WHERE $winereview/@winekey=$wine/@winekey
RETURN <wineinfo> {$wine, $winereview/rating} </wineinfo>
```

This will connect every "wine" XML element to every "winereview/rating" XML element and encloses the result between the <wineinfo> and </wineinfo> tags.

Most of the SQL constructs (e.g., aggregation functions, DISTINCT, nested queries, ALL, ANY) are supported in XQuery, including the definition of user-defined functions. The W3C also provided a recommendation to extend XQuery with update operations such as INSERT, DELETE, REPLACE, RENAME, and TRANSFORM. More details can be found at www.w3.org.

### 10.6.4 Semantic Search With RDF and SPARQL

The concept of **semantic search** emanates from the broader context of the semantic web. The goal is to get a better understanding of the relationships behind the links between web resources as identified by their URI. This will allow asking more semantically complicated queries, such as:

Give me all spicy, ruby colored red wines with round texture raised in clay soil and Mediterranean climate which pair well with cheese.

Imagine you have to solve this query on data formatted in HTML. It would take a tremendous effort to find reliable sources and then (manually) scrape and integrate the data. One reason is because HTML makes use of untyped links which convey no semantically meaningful information about the relationship behind the link. The semantic web technology stack tries to overcome this by introducing components such as RDF, RDF Schema, OWL, and SPARQL, which are all combined to provide a formal description of concepts, terms, and their relationships. We will elaborate on these in this subsection.

**Resource Description Framework (RDF)** provides the data model for the semantic web and was developed by the World Wide Web Consortium.[7] It encodes graph-structured data by attaching a semantic meaning to the relationships. An RDF data model consists of statements in subject–predicate–object format, which are also known as triples. Some examples are shown in Table 10.2.

The table states that Bart's name is Bart Baesens and he likes Meneghetti White, which has a citrusy flavor and pairs with fish. The idea is now to represent the subjects and predicates using URIs, and the objects using URIs, or literals, as shown in Table 10.3.[8]

By using URIs, a universal unique identification – which cannot be established using database specific primary keys – becomes possible. Data items identified with URIs can be easily dereferenced over the web. Note that the predicate refers to a vocabulary or *ontology* which is a model defining the various concepts and their relationships. In our example we developed our own wine ontology. The success of an ontology depends upon how widely it is supported.

**Drill Down**

Examples of popular ontologies are the Dublin Core Ontology (http://dublincore.org) for describing metadata, and the Friend Of A Friend (FOAF) ontology (www.foaf-project.org) to describe people's social relationships, interests, and activities.

An RDF data model can be visualized as a directed, labeled graph (Figure 10.6).

RDF data can be serialized in different ways. One possible representation is the XML format, by means of RDF/XML, as you can see here for the first two triples of Table 10.2:

[7] www.w3.org/RDF. [8] The URIs in our example are fictitious.

**Table 10.2** Example RDF triples

| Subject | Predicate | Object |
|---|---|---|
| Bart | Name | Bart Baesens |
| Bart | Likes | Meneghetti White |
| Meneghetti White | Tastes | Citrusy |
| Meneghetti White | Pairs | Fish |

**Table 10.3** Representing subjects and predicates using URIs and objects using URIs or literals in RDF

| Subject | Predicate | Object |
|---|---|---|
| www.kuleuven.be/Bart.Baesens | http://mywineontology.com/#term_name | "Bart Baesens" |
| www.kuleuven.be/Bart.Baesens | http://mywineontology.com/#term_likes | www.wine.com/MeneghettiWhite |
| www.wine.com/MeneghettiWhite | http://mywineontology.com/#term_tastes | "Citrusy" |
| www.wine.com/MeneghettiWhite | http://mywineontology.com/#term_pairs | http://wikipedia.com/Fish |

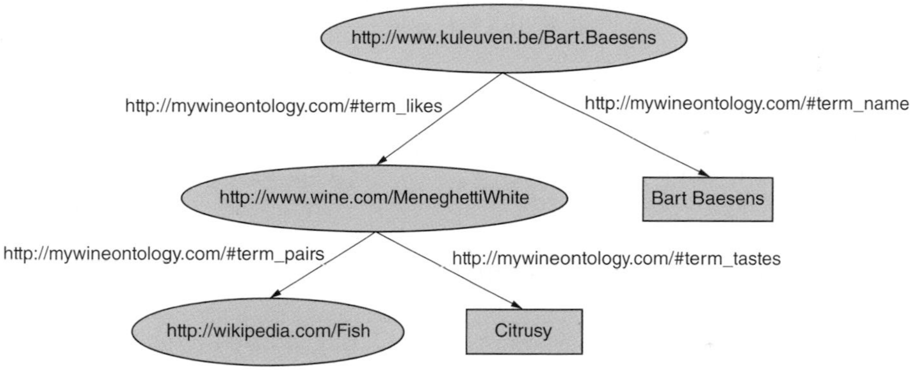


**Figure 10.6** Example RDF graph.

```
<?xml version="1.0"?>
<rdf:RDF xmlns:rdf="http://www.w3.org/TR/PR-rdf-syntax/"
xmlns:myxmlns="http://mywineontology.com/">
<rdf:Description rdf:about="www.kuleuven.be/Bart.Baesens">
<myxmlns:name>Bart Baesens</myxmlns:name>
<myxmlns:name:likes rdf:resource="www.wine.com/MeneghettiWhite"/>
</rdf:Description>
</rdf:RDF>
```

The RDF data model is easy to understand and use. Hence, it is one of the key technologies to realize the concept of so-called **linked data** by using a simple representation to connect existing information via the re-use of URIs. It provides a powerful mechanism to mash distributed and heterogeneous data into one overall semantic model. **RDF Schema** enriches RDF by extending its vocabulary with classes and subclasses, properties and subproperties, and typing of properties. **Web Ontology Language (OWL)** is an even more expressive ontology language which

**Retention Questions**

- Discuss the advantages and disadvantages of searching XML data using full-text search.
- Discuss the advantages and disadvantages of searching XML data using keyword-based search.
- Discuss the advantages and disadvantages of searching XML data using XQuery.
- Discuss the advantages and disadvantages of searching XML data using semantic search with RDF and SPARQL.

implements various sophisticated semantic modeling concepts.[9] See www.w3.org/OWL for more details.

RDF data can be queried using **SPARQL**, which is a recursive acronym for "SPARQL Protocol and RDF Query Language".[10] SPARQL is based upon matching graph patterns against RDF graphs. Two examples of SPARQL queries are:

```
PREFIX: mywineont: <http://mywineontology.com/>
SELECT ?wine
WHERE {?wine, mywineont:tastes, "Citrusy"}

PREFIX: mywineont: <http://mywineontology.com/>
SELECT ?wine, ?flavor
WHERE {?wine, mywineont:tastes, ?flavor}
```

The first query retrieves all wines that taste citrusy, whereas the second query retrieves all wines together with their flavors. The PREFIX keyword is SPARQL's version of a namespace declaration. Names beginning with ? represent variables (e.g., ?name, ?wine). The WHERE clause essentially specifies a graph pattern. The result of a SPARQL query is a set of bindings for the variables in the SELECT clause shown in tabular format. SPARQL is a semantically rich query language that allows us to extract RDF subgraphs using complex graph patterns and even construct new RDF graphs. It allows us to formulate complex queries and perform semantic search. A drawback is the complexity of the technology stack needed, which gives it a heavy implementation footprint.

## 10.7 XML for Information Exchange

Besides modeling and storing (semi-)structured data, XML also has great potential to exchange information between two or more databases or applications, or information systems of different partners in an e-business setting, such as purchase orders, product catalogs, or invoices. Ideally, all collaborating parties first agree upon a common DTD or XSD concerning the information to be exchanged. These schema definitions are more frequently specified at industry level, facilitating global information exchange. Two common technologies to exchange XML-based information are message-oriented middleware (MOM) and web services.

### 10.7.1 Message-Oriented Middleware

**Enterprise application integration (EAI)** refers to the set of activities aimed at integrating applications within a specific enterprise environment. As an example, think about the integration between enterprise resource planning (ERP), supply chain management (SCM) and customer relationship management (CRM) applications. This integration can be facilitated by two types of middleware solutions. A first option concerns **remote procedure call (RPC)** technologies in which communication between applications is established through procedure calls. Popular examples are RMI and DCOM. The idea is that an object invokes a method from a remote object on another

[9] The acronym for Web Ontology Language is OWL and not WOL, as it is easier to remember and suggests wisdom.
[10] www.w3.org/TR/rdf-sparql-query/#sparqlDefinition.

server. For example, Java provides a built-in mechanism to perform RPC, called Java RMI (Java remote method invocation).

RPC is usually synchronous, which implies that the calling object/application must wait to continue further processing until the called object/application returns an answer. Hence, RPC creates a strong coupling between interacting objects/applications. **Message-oriented middleware (MOM)** provides an alternative that may be more suitable in a heterogeneous environment. The integration is established by exchanging XML messages between the parties involved. An example could be an XML purchase order:

```
<purchaseorder id="12345" purchaseorderdate="2017-06-08">
<supplier>Deliwines</supplier>
<wine>Meneghetti White</wine>
<quantity>12</quantity>
...
</purchaseorder>
```

**Connections**

A broader discussion on data integration and application integration techniques and patterns, as well as the tradeoffs between different approaches, is provided in Chapter 18.

As opposed to RPC, MOM works in an asynchronous way, which implies that the calling object/application does not need to wait for an answer from the called object/application. This establishes a loose coupling that facilitates the integration in a highly heterogeneous environment. This also requires guarantees of reliable messaging, so no messages get delivered more than once or get lost.

### 10.7.2 SOAP-Based Web Services

Besides EAI technologies, which focus on integrating applications within a company-specific context, interactions, and collaboration between applications of different companies are also needed in a globalized e-business setting. Modern companies typically operate as partners in a cross-company integrated value chain. This requires that IT applications be integrated using sophisticated B2B (business-to-business) integration technologies. Since the more traditional RPC and MOM technologies proved unsuitable for an inter-organizational setting, a new technology stack was introduced that relied on so-called web services.

**Web services** can be defined as self-describing software components, which can be published, discovered, and invoked through the web. The main components needed to leverage web services for B2B integration are SOAP, as an exchange format, and WSDL, to describe the service offerings. Each of these is based upon XML, as we will discuss in this subsection.

**SOAP** stands for "Simple Object Access Protocol," although the W3 standards body has dropped the use of the name as an acronym in later revisions of the standard in favor of just using "SOAP" as is. The basic idea behind SOAP is to provide an XML-based messaging framework that is extensible (new features can be easily added), neutral (SOAP messages can travel on top of HTTP[11] and many other protocols), and independent (it can be used independently of the programming language and architecture at hand). These aspects make SOAP very versatile, although slower and more verbose than other RPC standards, because XML messages can quickly grow large. Here you can see an example of a SOAP message:

[11] HTTP (HyperText Transfer Protocol) was originally conceived as the interaction protocol between web browsers and web servers, but it may serve multiple purposes. HTTP is being maintained by the W3C. See www.w3.org/Protocols for further details.

```
<?xml version="1.0" encoding="utf-8"?>
<soap:Envelope xmlns:xsi="http://www.w3.org/2001/XMLSchema-instance"
xmlns:xsd="http://www.w3.org/2001/XMLSchema"
xmlns:soap="http://schemas.xmlsoap.org/soap/envelope/">
<soap:Body>
<GetQuote xmlns="http://www.webserviceX.NET/">
<symbol>string</symbol>
</GetQuote>
</soap:Body>
</soap:Envelope>
```

As you can see, it consists of a header (which is optional) and body (which is compulsory). The header contains application-specific information (e.g., for security or transaction management). The body contains an XML encoded payload, which supports both MOM-style and RPC-style interactions. The body can be an actual document (e.g., a purchase order), or a method call with corresponding parameters. In our example, the SOAP message calls the GetQuote web service available on www.webserviceX.NET with a string input parameter referring to a stock symbol (e.g., The Coca-Cola Co.).[12]

Before a SOAP message can be sent to a web service, it must be clear which type(s) of incoming messages the service understands and what messages it can send in return. The web service must define its supported functionality. This is the goal of **Web Services Description Language (WSDL)**, which is an XML-based language used to describe the interface or functionalities offered by a web service. Here you can see part of the WSDL document for our stock quote web service:[13]

```
<?xml version="1.0" encoding="UTF-8"?>
<wsdl:definitions xmlns:wsdl="http://schemas.xmlsoap.org/wsdl/"
targetNamespace="http://www.webserviceX.NET/"
xmlns:http="http://schemas.xmlsoap.org/wsdl/http/"
xmlns:soap12="http://schemas.xmlsoap.org/wsdl/soap12/"
xmlns:s="http://www.w3.org/2001/XMLSchema"
xmlns:soap="http://schemas.xmlsoap.org/wsdl/soap/"
xmlns:tns="http://www.webserviceX.NET/"
xmlns:mime="http://schemas.xmlsoap.org/wsdl/mime/"
xmlns:soapenc="http://schemas.xmlsoap.org/soap/encoding/"
xmlns:tm="http://microsoft.com/wsdl/mime/textMatching/">
<wsdl:types>
<s:schema targetNamespace="http://www.webserviceX.NET/"
elementFormDefault="qualified">
<s:element name="GetQuote">
<s:complexType>
<s:sequence>
<s:element type="s:string" name="symbol" maxOccurs="1" minOccurs="0"/>
</s:sequence>
</s:complexType>
```

[12] The website www.webservicex.net hosts a number of small web services and serves over six million requests a day.
[13] See www.webservicex.net/stockquote.asmx?WSDL for the full specification.

```
</s:element>
<s:element name="GetQuoteResponse">
<s:complexType>
<s:sequence>
<s:element type="s:string" name="GetQuoteResult" maxOccurs="1" minOccurs="0"/>
</s:sequence>
</s:complexType>
</s:element>
<s:element type="s:string" name="string" nillable="true"/>
</s:schema>
</wsdl:types>
...
<wsdl:message name="GetQuoteSoapIn"><wsdl:part name="parameters"
element="tns:GetQuote"/></wsdl:message>
<wsdl:message name="GetQuoteSoapOut"><wsdl:part name="parameters"
element="tns:GetQuoteResponse"/></wsdl:message>
<wsdl:message name="GetQuoteHttpGetIn"><wsdl:part name="symbol"
type="s:string"/></wsdl:message>
<wsdl:message name="GetQuoteHttpGetOut"><wsdl:part name="Body"
element="tns:string"/></wsdl:message>
...
<wsdl:portType name="StockQuoteSoap"><wsdl:operation
name="GetQuote"><wsdl:documentation
xmlns:wsdl="http://schemas.xmlsoap.org/wsdl/">Get Stock quote for a
company Symbol</wsdl:documentation><wsdl:input
mcssagc="tns:CctQuoteSoapIn"/><wsdl:output
message="tns:GetQuoteSoapOut"/></wsdl:operation></wsdl:portType>
...
</wsdl:definitions>
```

Every web service is represented as a set of so-called port types that define a set of abstract operations. Every operation has an input message (which can be the SOAP message, as shown earlier) and optional output message corresponding to its return value. Every message specifies the attributes and their types using XML Schema. Port types can be mapped to an implementation (port) by specifying the corresponding URL. Hence, the same WSDL document can refer to multiple implementations.

Standardized procedure calls between applications based upon simple request/response communication are not enough to automate e-business applications. E-business transactions typically take place according to a predefined process model, in which each activity in the process may be realized by a different web service. Hence, the execution of such a process requires the *orchestration* of a set of web services, possibly belonging to different interacting partners. Also here, XML plays a central role.

As an example, consider a purchasing process with the following activities: select supplier, create purchase order, confirm purchase order, shipment of goods, receipt of goods, send invoice, payment, etc. Some of these activities are executed sequentially, while others can be parallelized. Although web services can automate these process steps, the order in which they need to be executed needs to be specified upfront to guarantee a successful overall execution. This can be specified using an orchestration language, which is typically also XML based. A popular example is WS-BPEL (Web Services Business Process Execution Language). One step further would be to standardize the process itself. An example is RosettaNet, which defines a set of RosettaNet partner interface processes (PIPs) based upon standardized XML documents and document exchange sequences for various processes such as retrieving inventory data, consulting product catalogs, placing product orders, etc.

### 10.7.3 REST-Based Web Services

Due to the verbosity and heaviness of SOAP, a new web service standard, called **REST (Representational State Transfer)**, has been gaining traction in recent years. REST is built directly on top of HTTP and is completely stateless and light, in terms of bandwidth consumption. The idea behind REST stems from the realization that most web services just provide simple request–reply functionality, for which HTTP is already perfectly suited. Extra standards, such as SOAP, which add extra overhead and complexity, are not needed in many contexts. REST has been adopted by most websites offering an API. It is well suited for basic, ad-hoc web services. In addition, as the standard is tightly coupled with HTTP, it has become the architecture of choice by "modern" web companies (e.g., social networks) to provide APIs with which third-party developers can develop applications. A shift is taking place in which developers can be seen first constructing a REST API (API-first development) and then building their own applications and websites around this API. One of the biggest differences between REST and SOAP is that SOAP is communication agnostic (remember that SOAP messages can be transferred on top of HTTP or any other network protocol), whereas REST is tightly integrated with HTTP and "embraces" the protocol. The HTTP protocol is the complete exchange protocol, meaning that REST basically instructs programmers to use the same protocol as your web browser uses to access websites, with the difference being that web servers will not return HTML data to be rendered by a web browser, but structured data that can be parsed by a computer. This can be in XML and other formats, but with the difference that this XML message will contain none of the SOAP-defined tags. A REST request looks similar to a normal HTTP request:

```
GET /stockquote/IBM HTTP/1.1
Host: www.example.com
Connection: keep-alive
Accept: application/xml
```

This is a normal HTTP GET request for the URI /stockquote/IBM sent to the host www.example.com. The server can then respond with a formatted representation of stock information (e.g., XML):

```
HTTP/1.0 200 OK
Content-Type: application/xml
<StockQuotes>
<Stock>
<Symbol>IBM</Symbol>
<Last>140.33</Last>
<Date>22/8/2017</Date>
<Time>11:56am</Time>
<Change>-0.16</Change>
<Open>139.59</Open>
```

```
<High>140.42</High>
<Low>139.13</Low>
<MktCap>135.28B</MktCap>
<P-E>11.65</P-E>
<Name>International Business Machines</Name>
</Stock>
</StockQuotes>
```

GET and POST are the most commonly used HTTP methods. In fact, your browser will typically execute GET requests to request a document from a web server specified by its URL, and will perform POST requests to send web forms to the server.

Unlike SOAP, REST does not have an official standard, so different APIs may apply different conventions in terms of how they deal with the HTTP methods listed previously. Additionally, REST specifies no formatting language or standard for the actual request and response messages to represent data, so the server may answer the GET /stockquote/IBM request shown previously using XML or newer data representation formats such as JSON, YAML (see Section 10.8), or even a plain English description of the stock information. Nowadays, companies such as Twitter, Facebook, and PayPal are all providing a REST interface to access their services, information, and functionalities (Facebook calls this their "Graph API", but it works the same way). Because there is no real REST standard, conventions might differ among implementations, so you will need to browse through the API documentation of each service you want to access, though they all agree on using simple HTTP-based request–response communication.

Despite the potential of REST, SOAP remains in wide use, especially in enterprise environments that have a strong need for its versatility.

### 10.7.4 Web Services and Databases

Web service technology also affects the interaction with databases. A web service can make use of an underlying database to perform its functionality. The database itself can also act as a web service provider or web service consumer.

Stored procedures can be extended with a WSDL interface and published as web services. The corresponding database functionality can then be invoked from other applications by sending the appropriate SOAP message (or using REST as an alternative) to the port of the database system. In the case that the stored procedure consists of a SELECT operation, the results can be mapped to an XML (using e.g., SQL/XML) or other format (see Section 10.8) and returned to the calling application.

Database systems can also act as service consumers. Stored procedures or triggers can include calls to external web services. This augments their possibilities. Other external data sources, such as hosted by web service-enabled database systems, can be queried and the results retrieved in XML format, which can then be stored (possibly after being converted into a relational format). Besides data, external functionality can be invoked. An example could be a third-party web service that converts amounts stored locally in euros to amounts in dollars. Another example is a trigger that monitors (local) stock data, and if the safety stock level is reached automatically generates a (e.g., SOAP) message with a purchase order to the web service hosted by the supplier.

Working in a worldwide database-enabled web services setting will also have implications for transaction management. Consider a web service for travel booking. If this service already

**Retention Questions**

- Discuss the key characteristics of message-oriented middleware (MOM).
- Contrast SOAP- versus REST-based web services.
- Discuss the impact of web service technology on the interaction with databases.

booked a hotel and rental car, but can find no flights, then the whole transaction needs to be rolled back and the hotel and car bookings canceled. The web service technology stack does not include any overseeing distributed transaction management to accomplish this. To deal with this, orchestration languages such as WS-BPEL have introduced the concept of compensating actions. The idea is to extend the process definition with activities that should be executed if the process, or part thereof, cannot be successfully finished. In this way, a "manual" rollback mechanism is implemented. The latter is dealt with in more detail in Chapter 16.

## 10.8 Other Data Representation Formats

In recent years, especially with the rise of "modern" web frameworks such as Ruby on Rails, a shift has been occurring toward simpler data description languages such as JSON and YAML. The latter are primarily optimized for data interchange and serialization instead of representing documents, as is the case for XML.

**JavaScript Object Notation (JSON)** provides a simple, lightweight representation of data whereby objects are described as name–value pairs.[14] Here you can see the JSON specification of our wine cellar example:

```
{
  "winecellar": {
    "wine": [
      {
        "name": "Jacques Selosse Brut Initial",
        "year": "2012",
        "type": "Champagne",
        "grape": {
          "_percentage": "100",
          "__text": "Chardonnay"
        },
        "price": {
          "_currency": "EURO",
          "__text": "150"
        },
        "geo": {
          "country": "France",
          "region": "Champagne"
        },
        "quantity": "12"
      },
```

[14] http://json.org.

```
        {
         "name": "Meneghetti White",
         "year": "2010",
         "type": "white wine",
         "grape": [
           {
             "_percentage": "80",
             "__text": "Chardonnay"
           },
           {
             "_percentage": "20",
             "__text": "Pinot Blanc"
           }
         ],
         "price": {
           "_currency": "EURO",
           "__text": "18"
         },
         "geo": {
           "country": "Croatia",
           "region": "Istria"
         },
         "quantity": "20"
       }
      ]
    }
  }
```

A few things are worth mentioning:

- JSON provides two structured types: objects and arrays. The root node of a JSON document must be an object or an array.
- Every object is encapsulated between brackets ({}) and consists of an unordered set of name–value pairs separated by commas (,). A colon (:) separates the name from the value. Values can be nested and a value can be of primitive type (see below), an object, or an array.
- Arrays represent an ordered collection of values and are enclosed within square brackets ([]), with values being separated by commas.
- Attributes of XML elements are mapped using underscores (e.g., "_percentage": "100"). The content of the XML element is then indicated using the keyword text (e.g., "__text": "Chardonnay"). This may vary depending upon the implementation.
- These primitive types are supported: string, number, Boolean, and null.

Similar to XML, it can be seen that JSON is human and machine readable based upon a simple syntax, and also models the data in a hierarchical way. Analogous to DTD and XML Schema, the structure of a JSON specification can be defined using JSON Schema. JSON is, however, less verbose and includes support for ordered elements by means of arrays. Unlike XML, JSON is not a markup language and is not extensible. Its primary usage is for data (rather than document) exchange and serialization of (e.g., JavaScript, Java) objects. The popularity of JSON grew due to the increased usage of JavaScript on the web (e.g., in AJAX applications, see Chapter 15). JSON documents can be simply parsed in JavaScript using the built-in eval() function with the JSON string as its input argument. The JavaScript interpreter will then construct the corresponding object with properties as defined by the JSON string. As an alternative, most modern web browsers also include native and fast JSON parsers.

**YAML Ain't a Markup Language (YAML)** is a superset of JSON with additional capabilities, such as support for relational trees (which allow referring to other nodes in the YAML document), user-defined types, explicit data typing, lists, and casting.[15] These extensions make it a better solution for object serialization since it can stay closer to the original class definition, facilitating the deserialization. YAML has been defined based upon concepts from programming languages such as C, Perl, and Python, combined with some ideas from XML. Our wine cellar YAML specification looks as follows:

```
winecellar:
 wine:
  -
   name: "Jacques Selosse Brut Initial"
   year: 2012
   type: Champagne
   grape:
    _percentage: 100
    __text: Chardonnay
   price:
    _currency: EURO
    __text: 150
   geo:
    country: France
    region: Champagne
   quantity: 12
  -
   name: "Meneghetti White"
   year: 2010
   type: "white wine"
   grape:
    -
   _percentage: 80
     __text: Chardonnay
    -
   _percentage: 20
     __text: "Pinot Blanc"
   price:
    _currency: EURO
     __text: 18
```

[15] www.yaml.org.

```
geo:
 country: Croatia
 region: Istria
quantity: 20
```


A few things are worth mentioning:

- In contrast to JSON, YAML uses inline and white space delimiters instead of square brackets. Important to note is that the indentation should be done by means of one or more spaces and never with tabulation.
- In terms of structured types, YAML works with mappings, which are sets of unordered key–value pairs separated by a colon and a mandatory space (: ), and sequences that correspond to arrays and are represented using a dash and a mandatory space (- ). YAML uses indentation to represent nesting. Keys are separated from values by a colon and an arbitrary number of spaces.
- As in JSON, attributes of XML elements are mapped using underscores (e.g., _percentage: 100). The content of the XML element is then indicated using the keyword text (e.g., __text: Chardonnay). This may vary depending upon the implementation.
- In terms of primitive data types, YAML supports numbers, strings, Boolean, dates, timestamps, and null.
- The usage of quotes is optional since everything is treated as a string.

When compared against XML, both JSON and YAML are far less technically mature. There is no good equivalent to XPath, which as we discussed before facilitates path-based navigation through XML documents and is one of the key building blocks of XQuery. Mature and standardized SQL/JSON or SQL/YAML counterparts to SQL/XML are not available. Another distinction concerns the concept of namespaces, which is well developed and extensively used in XML, making it easily extensible compared to JSON and YAML where namespace support is lacking. Hence, XML is still the language of choice for many commercial tools and applications.

**Retention Questions**

- Contrast JSON against YAML.
- How do JSON and YAML compare against XML?

## Summary

In this chapter we introduced the basic concepts of XML as a data representation format. We discussed how Document Type Definition and XML Schema Definition can be used to specify the structure of an XML document. We also covered Extensible Stylesheet Language, namespaces, and XPath. We reviewed various ways of processing XML documents using the DOM and SAX APIs. We then elaborated on storing XML documents using a document-oriented, data-oriented, or hybrid approach. We listed the key differences between XML and relational data and then discussed how to map between XML documents and (object-)relational data using a table-based mapping, schema-oblivious mapping, schema-aware mapping, and SQL/XML. We discussed various ways of searching XML data using full-text search, keyword-based search, structured search using XQuery, and semantic search using RDF and SPARQL. We illustrated how XML can be used for information exchange in combination with message-oriented middleware and web services. We concluded by reviewing other data representation formats such as JSON and YAML.

### Scenario Conclusion

Now that Sober has learned about XML, it has decided to use this technology for its accident reports. An example XML report could then look as follows:

```
<report>
<date>Friday September 13th, 2017</date>
<location>
<name>Broadway, New York</name>
<GPS_latitude>41.111547</GPS_latitude>
<GPS_longitude>-73.858381</GPS_longitude>
</location>
<summary>Collision between 2 cars, 1 cyclist and 1 pedestrian.</summary>
<actor>
<driver injured="yes" Sobercar="yes">John Smith</driver>
<driver injured="no" Sobercar="no">Mike Doe</driver>
<pedestrian injured="yes">Sarah Lucas</pedestrian>
<cyclist injured="no">Bob Kelly</cyclist>
</actor>
<aid>
<police>NYPD</police>
<ambulance>Broadway Hospital</ambulance>
</aid>
</report>
```

Sober chose XML Schema to define its XML report since it is semantically richer than DTD. An example XML Schema specification for the above report could look as follows:

```
<?xml version="1.0" encoding="UTF-8" ?>
<xs:schema xmlns:xs="http://www.w3.org/2001/XMLSchema">
<xs:element name="report">
<xs:complexType>
<xs:sequence>
<xs:element type="xs:string" name="date"/>
<xs:element name="location">
<xs:complexType>
<xs:sequence>
<xs:element type="xs:string" name="name"/>
<xs:element type="xs:float" name="GPS_latitude"/>
<xs:element type="xs:float" name="GPS_longitude"/>
</xs:sequence>
</xs:complexType>
</xs:element>
<xs:element type="xs:string" name="summary"/>
<xs:element name="actor">
<xs:complexType>
```

```
<xs:sequence>
<xs:element name="driver" maxOccurs="unbounded" minOccurs="0">
<xs:complexType>
<xs:simpleContent>
<xs:extension base="xs:string">
<xs:attribute type="xs:string" name="injured" use="optional"/>
<xs:attribute type="xs:string" name="Sobercar" use="optional"/>
</xs:extension>
</xs:simpleContent>
</xs:complexType>
</xs:element>
<xs:element name="pedestrian" maxOccurs="unbounded" minOccurs="0">
<xs:complexType>
<xs:simpleContent>
<xs:extension base="xs:string">
<xs:attribute type="xs:string" name="injured"/>
</xs:extension>
</xs:simpleContent>
</xs:complexType>
</xs:element>
<xs:element name="cyclist" maxOccurs="unbounded" minOccurs="0">
<xs:complexType>
<xs:simpleContent>
<xs:extension base="xs:string">
<xs:attribute type="xs:string" name="injured"/>
</xs:extension>
</xs:simpleContent>
</xs:complexType>
</xs:element>
</xs:sequence>
</xs:complexType>
</xs:element>
<xs:element name="aid">
<xs:complexType>
<xs:sequence>
<xs:element type="xs:string" name="police"/>
<xs:element type="xs:string" name="ambulance"/>
</xs:sequence>
</xs:complexType>
</xs:element>
</xs:sequence>
</xs:complexType>
</xs:element>
</xs:schema>
```

Sober will also define two XSLT stylesheets:

- one to transform its XML reports to an XML format tailored to its insurance firm;
- one to transform its XML reports to HTML which can then be displayed in a web browser on the Sober intranet.

If Sober wants to list all actors for a specific accident, it can use this XPath expression:

```
doc("myreport.xml")/report/actor
```

Sober also plans to use SQL/XML to add the report to the relational ACCIDENT table:

```
CREATE TABLE ACCIDENT(
ACC-NR INT NOT NULL PRIMARY KEY,
ACC-DATE-TIME DATETIME NOT NULL,
ACC-LOCATION VARCHAR(15),
REPORT XML)
```

## Key Terms List

**combined approach**
**data-oriented approach**
**Document Type Definition (DTD)**
**document-oriented approach**
**DOM API**
**enterprise application integration (EAI)**
**Extensible Markup Language (XML)**
**Extensible Stylesheet Language (XSL)**
**FLWOR**
**full-text search**
**JavaScript Object Notation (JSON)**
**keyword-based search**
**linked data**
**message-oriented middleware (MOM)**
**namespace**
**partial shredding**
**RDF Schema**
**remote procedure call (RPC)**
**Resource Description Framework (RDF)**
**REST (Representational State Transfer)**
**SAX API (simple API for XML)**
**schema-aware mapping**
**schema-oblivious mapping/shredding**
**semantic search**
**shredding**
**SOAP**
**SPARQL**
**SQL/XML**
**StAX (streaming API for XML)**
**structured search**
**table-based mapping**
**template-based mapping**
**valid**
**Web Ontology Language (OWL)**
**Web services**
**Web Services Description Language (WSDL)**
**well-formed**
**XML element**
**XML Schema Definition (XSD)**
**XML-enabled DBMS**
**XPath**
**XQuery**
**XSL Formatting Objects (XSL-FO)**
**XSL Transformations (XSLT)**
**YAML Ain't a Markup Language (YAML)**

## Review Questions

**10.1.** XML focuses on the...

a. content of documents.
b. representation of documents.

**10.2.** Which statement is **correct**?

a. Using XSLT, an XML document can be transformed to another XML document.
b. Using HTML, an XML document can be transformed to an XSLT document.
c. Using XML, an XSLT document can be transformed to an XML document.
d. Using DTD, an XML document can be transformed to an HTML document.

**10.3.** Which of the following statements about XML Schema is **not correct**?

a. It is more verbose than DTD.
b. It allows specification of minimum and maximum cardinalities.
c. Various data types are supported such as xs:string, xs:short, xs:byte, etc.
d. It is not defined using XML syntax.

**10.4.** Which of the following statements is **not correct** about XPath?

a. It is a simple, declarative language.
b. It considers an XML document as a set of XML elements.
c. It uses path expressions to refer to parts of an XML document.
d. Every navigation step results in a node or list of nodes which can then be used to continue the navigation.

**10.5.** In the case that an application needs to process large XML documents in a sequential way, it is recommended to use the...

a. DOM API.
b. SAX API.

**10.6.** A key difference between XML data and relational data is that...

a. relational data assume atomic data types, whereas XML data can consist of aggregated types.
b. relational data are ordered, whereas XML data are unordered.
c. relational data can be nested, whereas XML data cannot be nested.
d. relational data can be multi-valued, whereas XML data cannot be multi-valued.

**10.7.** Consider the following table, which maps an XML document to a relational database:

```
CREATE TABLE NODE(
ID CHAR(6) NOT NULL PRIMARY KEY,
PARENT_ID CHAR(6),
TYPE VARCHAR(9),
LABEL VARCHAR(20),
VALUE CLOB,
FOREIGN KEY (PARENT_ID) REFERENCES NODE (ID)
CONSTRAINT CC1 CHECK(TYPE IN ("element", "attribute"))
)
```

Which statement is **correct**?

a. The above table assumes the presence of a DTD or XSD before the mapping can take place.
b. The table will require extensive querying resources since every single (e.g., XPath) navigation step requires a self-join on this table.

c. Using the above table, every XPath expression can be translated to a corresponding SQL query.
d. The table is not entirely normalized and still contains redundant information.

**10.8.** What statement about SQL/XML is **not correct**?

a. It introduces a new XML data type.
b. It includes facilities for mapping relational data to XML.
c. It includes rules for shredding XML data into SQL.
d. The result of an SQL/XML query can be a combination of both relational and XML data types.

**10.9.** What statement about XQuery is **not correct**?

a. It allows making use of both the document structure and its content.
b. It does not allow joining information from different XML documents.
c. It uses XPath expressions to navigate through the document.
d. The end results can be sorted.

**10.10.** In an enterprise application integration (EAI) context, asynchronous communication between objects and/or applications can be achieved by means of. . .

a. remote procedure call (RPC).
b. message-oriented middleware (MOM).

**10.11.** Which of the following statements is **not correct**?

a. An RDF data model consists of statements which are in subject–predicate–object format.
b. RDF allows use of database-specific primary keys to identify resources.
c. An RDF data model can be visualized as a directed, labeled graph.
d. RDF Schema enriches RDF by extending its vocabulary with classes and subclasses, properties and subproperties, and typing of properties.

**10.12.** Which of the following are properties of SPARQL?

a. It is based upon matching graph patterns.
b. It can query RDF graphs.
c. It provides support for namespaces.
d. All of the above.

**10.13.** A key benefit of REST when compared to SOAP for web services is that. . .

a. REST has an official standard.
b. REST only allows XML for exchanging requests and responses.
c. REST is communication agnostic, whereas SOAP is tightly integrated with HTTP.
d. REST is built directly on top of HTTP and is less verbose and heavy than SOAP.

**10.14.** When compared against XML, both JSON and YAML are. . .

a. not human readable.
b. unable to provide support for ordered elements such as arrays.
c. less technically mature.
d. much more verbose.

## Problems and Exercises

10.1E Consider our purchase order administration example from Chapter 3. Remember, a purchase order can have multiple purchase order lines, each corresponding to a particular product. A purchase order is also assigned to exactly one supplier. Develop a DTD and XML Schema for a purchase order and contrast both. Work out an example of an XML purchase order document with four purchase order lines. Illustrate how XPath can be used to retrieve specific elements of this purchase order.

10.2E Using the purchase order example of Question 1, illustrate how the DOM and SAX APIs would process the XML document differently.

10.3E Discuss and contrast the various approaches that can be used to search XML data.

10.4E Discuss how XML can be used for information exchange.

10.5E Represent the purchase order XML document of Question 1 in JSON and YAML. Contrast the three representations against each other.

10.6E Consider the most recent (O)RDBMS products provided by Oracle, IBM, and Microsoft. Discuss and contrast their support in terms of:

- storing XML documents (document-oriented approach, data-oriented approach, or combined approach);
- table-based mapping facilities;
- schema-oblivious mapping facilities;
- schema-aware mapping facilities;
- SQL/XML;
- searching facilities for XML data (full-text search, keyword-based search, XQuery, RDF, and SPARQL);

# 11 NoSQL Databases

## Chapter Objectives

In this chapter, you will learn:

- what is meant by "NoSQL" and how this movement differs from earlier approaches;
- to understand the differences between key–value-, tuple-, document-, column-, and graph-based databases;
- about the defining characteristics of NoSQL databases, such as their capability to scale horizontally, their approach toward data replication and how this relates to eventual consistency, their APIs, and how they are queried and interacted with;
- how to query NoSQL databases, using MapReduce, Cypher, and other approaches.

Sober has been happily using its relational database system for quite a while now, but is experiencing some limits of its existing system. In particular, due to the growth of its mobile applications (now serving many users simultaneously), some queries are performing slower, causing users to wait a few seconds when working with the app. Sober's database administrators have identified that this is mainly due to the normalized approach of its relational database model, causing many queries to involve joining tables, which results in bottlenecks when thousands of users are hailing cabs simultaneously.

Another issue is that the mobile developers regularly want to experiment with new features (to do so, a "beta" version of the app is rolled out to a subset of users), though given the emphasis on data consistency put forward by RDBMSs, changing existing data schemas so they can handle new data fields is a time-intensive effort. The app developers are not very familiar with this, causing back-and-forth between the development team and the database administrators.

Given these new issues, Sober is thinking of different scenarios to handle its growth. One option would be to roll out additional servers to handle the increased usage, but keep using the RDBMS system to do so. Another possibility would be to explore a NoSQL database solution. Sober's database administrator has heard about newer approaches such as MongoDB, Cassandra, and others, which offer strong scaling opportunities and a schema-free approach to data management.

Relational database management systems (RDBMSs) put a lot of emphasis on keeping data consistent. They require a formal database schema, and new data or modifications to existing data are not accepted unless they comply with this schema in terms of data type, referential integrity, etc.

Sometimes this focus on consistency may become a burden, because it induces (in some cases unnecessarily) overhead and hampers scalability and flexibility. In this chapter, we discuss a series of non-relational database management systems that focus specifically on being highly scalable in a distributed environment: NoSQL databases. We discuss in turn key–value stores, tuple, and document stores, column-oriented databases, and graph databases, and show how they deviate from the typical relational model, and which concepts they utilize to achieve a high scalability. We will also see how this high scalability often comes with a cost as well, such as strong querying facilities being absent, or not being able to provide strong consistency guarantees.

## 11.1 The NoSQL Movement

If one thing becomes apparent from this chapter, it is that the label "NoSQL" covers a very broad and diverse category of DBMSs. There probably isn't a single concept or statement that applies to each system, except that they all somehow attempt to overcome certain inherent limitations of the traditional RDBMS. Therefore, before tackling NoSQL databases, we discuss the settings in which these limitations manifest themselves.

### 11.1.1 The End of the "One Size Fits All" Era?

RDBMSs pay a lot of attention to data consistency and compliance with a formal database schema. New data or modifications to existing data are not accepted unless they satisfy constraints represented in this schema in terms of data types, referential integrity, etc. The way in which RDBMSs coordinate their transactions guarantees that the entire database is consistent at all times (the ACID properties; see Section 14.5 in Chapter 14). Consistency is usually a desirable property; one normally wouldn't want erroneous data to enter the system, nor for a money transfer to be aborted halfway through, with only one of the two accounts updated.

Yet sometimes this focus on consistency may become a burden, because it induces (sometimes unnecessarily) overhead and hampers scalability and flexibility. RDBMSs are at their best when performing intensive read/write operations on small- or medium-sized datasets, or when executing larger batch processes, but with only a limited number of simultaneous transactions. As the data volumes or the number of parallel transactions increase, capacity can be increased by **vertical scaling** (also called scaling up), i.e., by extending storage capacity and/or CPU power of the database server. However, there are hardware-induced limitations to vertical scaling.

Therefore, further capacity increases need to be realized by **horizontal scaling** (also known as scaling out), with multiple DBMS servers being arranged in a cluster. The respective nodes in the cluster can balance workloads among one another and scaling is achieved by adding nodes to the cluster, rather than extending the capacity of individual nodes. Such a clustered architecture is an essential prerequisite to cope with the enormous demands of recent evolutions such as Big Data (analytics), cloud computing, and all kinds of responsive web applications. It provides the necessary performance, which cannot be realized by a single server, but also guarantees availability, with data being replicated over multiple nodes and other nodes taking over their neighbor's workload if one node fails.

However, RDBMSs are not good at extensive horizontal scaling. Their approach toward transaction management and their urge to keep data consistent at all times induces a large coordination overhead as the number of nodes increases. In addition, the rich querying functionality may be overkill in many Big Data settings, where applications merely need high capacity to "put" and "get" data items, with no demand for complex data interrelationships nor selection criteria. Also, Big Data settings often focus on semi-structured data or on data with a very volatile structure (consider sensor data, images, audio data and so on), where the rigid database schemas of RDBMSs are a source of inflexibility.

None of this means that relational databases will become obsolete soon. However, the "one size fits all" era, where RDBMSs were used in nearly any data and processing context, seems to have come to an end. RDBMSs are still the way to go when storing up to medium-sized volumes of highly structured data, with strong emphasis on consistency and extensive querying facilities. Where massive volumes, flexible data structures, scalability, and availability are more important, other systems may be called for. This need resulted in the emergence of NoSQL databases.

### 11.1.2 The Emergence of the NoSQL Movement

The term "NoSQL" has become overloaded throughout the past decade, so the moniker now relates to many meanings and systems. The name "NoSQL" itself was first used in 1998 by the NoSQL Relational Database Management System, a DBMS built on top of input/output stream operations as provided by Unix systems. It implements a full relational database to all effects, but foregoes SQL as a query language.

**Drill Down**

The NoSQL Relational Database Management System itself was a derivative of an even earlier database system, called RDB. Like RDB, NoSQL follows a relational approach to data storage and management, but opts to store tables as regular textual files. Instead of using SQL to query its data, NoSQL relies on standard command-line tools and utilities to select, remove, and insert data.

The system has been around for a long time and has nothing to do with the more recent "NoSQL movement" discussed in this chapter.

**Drill Down**

The home page of the NoSQL Relational Database Management System even explicitly mentions it has nothing to do with the "NoSQL movement".

The modern **NoSQL** movement describes databases that store and manipulate data in other formats than tabular relations, i.e., non-relational databases. The movement should have more appropriately been called NoREL, especially since some of these non-relational databases actually provide query language facilities close to SQL. Because of such reasons, people have changed the original meaning of the NoSQL movement to stand for "not only SQL" or "not relational" instead of "not SQL".

What makes NoSQL databases different from other, legacy, non-relational systems that have existed since as early as the 1970s? The renewed interest in non-relational database systems stems from Web 2.0 companies in the early 2000s. Around this period, up-and-coming web companies, such as Facebook, Google, and Amazon, were increasingly being confronted with huge amounts of data to be processed, often under time-sensitive constraints. For example, think about an instantaneous Google search query, or thousands of users accessing Amazon product pages or Facebook profiles simultaneously.

Often rooted in the open-source community, the characteristics of the systems developed to deal with these requirements are very diverse. However, their common ground is that they try to avoid, at least to some extent, the shortcomings of RDBMSs in this respect. Many aim at near-linear horizontal scalability, which is achieved by distributing data over a cluster of database nodes for the sake of performance (parallelism and load balancing) and availability (replication and failover management). A certain measure of data consistency is often sacrificed in return. A term frequently used in this respect is **eventual consistency**; the data, and respective replicas of the same data item, will become consistent in time after each transaction, but continuous consistency is not guaranteed.

The relational data model is cast aside for other modeling paradigms, which are typically less rigid and better able to cope with quickly evolving data structures. Often, the API (application programming interface) and/or query mechanism are much simpler than in a relational setting. The Comparison Box provides a more detailed comparison of the typical characteristics of NoSQL databases against those of relational systems. Note that different categories of NoSQL databases exist and that even the members of a single category can be very diverse. No single NoSQL system will exhibit all of these properties.

## Comparison Box

| | Relational databases | NoSQL databases |
|---|---|---|
| **Data paradigm** | Relational tables | Key–value (tuple) based<br>Document based<br>Column based<br>Graph based<br>XML, object based (see Chapter 10)<br>Others: time series, probabilistic, etc. |
| **Distribution** | Single-node and distributed | Mainly distributed |
| **Scalability** | Vertical scaling, harder to scale horizontally | Easy to scale horizontally, easy data replication |
| **Openness** | Closed and open-source | Mainly open-source |
| **Schema role** | Schema-driven | Mainly schema-free or flexible schema |
| **Query language** | SQL as query language | No or simple querying facilities, or special-purpose languages |
| **Transaction mechanism** | ACID: Atomicity, Consistency, Isolation, Durability | BASE: Basically Available, Soft state, Eventually consistent |
| **Feature set** | Many features (triggers, views, stored procedures, etc.) | Simple API |
| **Data volume** | Capable of handling normal-sized datasets | Capable of handling huge amounts of data and/or very high frequencies of read/write requests |

In the remainder of this chapter, we will look closely at some NoSQL databases, and classify them according to their data model. XML databases and object-oriented DBMSs, which could also be kinds of NoSQL databases, were already discussed extensively in previous chapters. Therefore, we will focus on key–value-, tuple-, document-, column-, and graph-based databases. Besides their data model, we will also discuss other defining characteristics of NoSQL databases, such as their capability to scale horizontally; their approach toward data replication and how this relates to eventual consistency; and NoSQL DBMS APIs and how they are interacted with and queried.

**Connections**

For a discussion on object-oriented database management systems (OODBMSs), see Chapter 8. For XML databases, see Chapter 10. Both can also be regarded as kinds of NoSQL databases.

## 11.2 Key–Value Stores

**Key–value stores** have been around for decades, since the early days of Unix in the 1970s. A key–value-based database stores data in a format that is easy to understand, i.e., as (key, value) pairs. The keys are unique and represent the sole "search" criterion to retrieve the corresponding value. This approach maps directly to a data structure also present natively in the majority of programming languages, namely that of a hash map, or hash table, or dictionary as they're also called. For example, Java provides the HashMap class which allows storing arbitrary objects (in internal memory in this case) based on a single "key":

**Retention Questions**

- What is meant by vertical scaling and horizontal scaling?
- Which type of scaling are RDBMSs not good at? Why?
- What does the NoSQL movement describe? Is this an appropriate name?
- List the differences between relational databases and NoSQL databases.

```
import java.util.HashMap;
import java.util.Map;
public class KeyValueStoreExample {
        public static void main(String... args) {
                // Keep track of age based on name
                Map<String, Integer> age_by_name = new HashMap<>();

                // Store some entries
                age_by_name.put("wilfried", 34);
                age_by_name.put("seppe", 30);
                age_by_name.put("bart", 46);
                age_by_name.put("jeanne", 19);

                // Get an entry
                int age_of_wilfried = age_by_name.get("wilfried");
                System.out.println("Wilfried's age: " + age_of_wilfried);

                // Keys are unique
                age_by_name.put("seppe", 50); // Overrides previous entry
        }
}
```

### 11.2.1 From Keys to Hashes

To make the data structure of a hash map more efficient, its keys (such as "bart", "seppe" and so on in the example above) are hashed by means of a so-called **hash function**. A hash function is a

**Connections**

We will also look into hashing in more detail in the chapters on physical file organization and physical database organization (Chapters 12 and 13).

**Connections**

In practice, the address resulting from the hash function will often be a relative address, from which the absolute address can be easily derived. Also, there exist different solutions if too many keys map to the same address (collision). This is treated in more detail in Chapter 12.

function that takes an arbitrary value of arbitrary size and maps it to a key with a fixed size, which is called the hash value, hash code, hash sum, or simply the hash.

Good hash functions must satisfy a number of properties, i.e., they should be:

- deterministic: hashing the same input value must always provide the same hash value. A typical example of a simple hash function is taking the remainder after dividing the key–value by a prime number (nonnumeric keys are first converted to an integer format).
- uniform: a good hash function should map the inputs evenly over its output range, to prevent so-called "collisions" between closely related pairs of inputs (two inputs leading to the same hash value).
- defined size: it is desirable that the output of a hash function has a fixed size, which makes it easier to store the data structure efficiently (every key takes a known, fixed amount of space).

The reason hashes allow for efficient storage and lookup of entries is because each hash can be mapped to a space in computer memory, allowing for rapid, exact lookup of a key. Figure 11.1 illustrates this concept.

In Figure 11.1, we use a trivial hash function that converts keys to a double-digit value. When storing the key–value pair (bart, 46), the hash value of the key will be calculated: hash(bart) = 07. The value "46" will then be stored on address 07. Conversely, when a user wishes to retrieve the value for key "bart", the lookup in memory can be performed immediately based on hash (bart) = 07. In Figure 11.1 we store the original unhashed key next to the actual value in memory, which is not required (as we use the hash of the original key to perform the lookup), but can be helpful in case you wish to retrieve the set of all keys with a given value associated to them. Note that the whole hash table must be scanned in that case, resulting in linear (non-immediate) lookup times.

## 11.2.2 Horizontal Scaling

Now that we've explained the concept of hashes, we can introduce a first key characteristic of NoSQL databases: the fact that they are built with horizontal scalability support in mind and can be easily distributed. The reason follows from the nature of hash tables themselves. Consider a very large hash table. Naturally, there is a limit to the number of entries that can be stored on a single machine. Luckily, since the nature of a hash function is to spread inputs uniformly over its output range, it is easy to create an index over the hash range that can spread out the hash table over different locations.

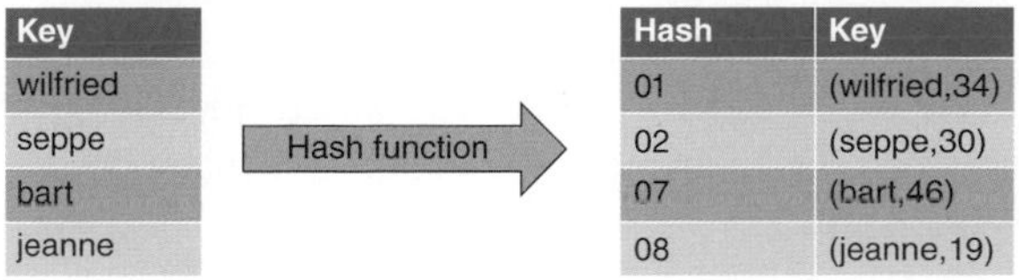


**Figure 11.1** Simple example of a hash function.

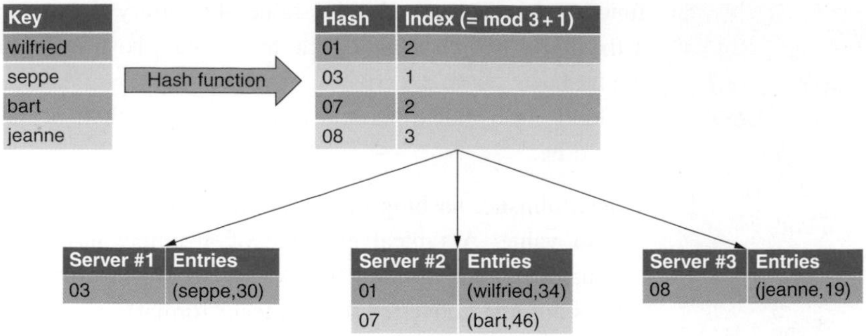


**Figure 11.2** Key–value pairs are spread over multiple servers.

Expanding the example above, imagine that our hash table of ages exceeds the limits of our computer's memory. We decide to bring two more computers into the mix, over which our hash table must now be distributed. We need to spread our hashes over three servers, which can be done easily using the mathematical modulo (the remainder after division) of each hash. For example: index(hash) = mod(hash, nrServers) + 1 in the example shown in Figure 11.2. Hash 08 divided by three has a remainder of 2, which results in index 3 after adding 1. This whole operation can be regarded as another hash function, so that every key ("wilfried", "seppe" and so on) is now hashed to a server identifier ("Server #1," "#2" and "#3"). It is worth emphasizing that the concept of hashing can be used to convert keys to locations or addresses within a node or server, and can be used to assign or distribute values over a list of resources, such as multiple servers, as illustrated by Figure 11.2.

There are other techniques besides hashing to distribute values over resources, such as using a separate routing server that will distribute data over a cluster of resources. Regardless of the actual technique, distributing the data over different nodes means we partition the data into separate sets, each of which are attributed to a different node. This practice of partitioning is also known as **sharding** and an individual partition is often called a **shard**.

### 11.2.3 An Example: Memcached

A famous, early example of a NoSQL database (as in NoSQL, the movement) built on the ideas above is **Memcached**. Memcached implements a distributed memory-driven hash table (a key–value store), which is placed in front of a traditional database to speed up queries by caching recently accessed objects in internal memory. In that sense, Memcached is a caching solution rather than a persistent database, but its API inspired many follow-up projects that do allow persistent key–value stores. The Memcached hash table can grow very large (several gigabytes) and can be scaled horizontally across multiple servers in a data center. To prevent hash tables from growing too large, old entries are discarded to make room for new ones.

**Drill Down**

Memcached was originally developed by LiveJournal, but was quickly picked up by other companies such as YouTube, Reddit, Facebook, Twitter, Wikipedia, and many others, thanks to the software being free and open-source.

Memcached has many client libraries in many languages. The example below illustrates a trivial Java program using the popular SpyMemcached library:

```
import java.util.ArrayList;
import java.util.List;
import net.spy.memcached.AddrUtil;
import net.spy.memcached.MemcachedClient;

public class MemCachedExample {
  public static void main(String[] args) throws Exception {
    List<String> serverList = new ArrayList<String>() {
      {
        this.add("memcachedserver1.servers:11211");
        this.add("memcachedserver2.servers:11211");
        this.add("memcachedserver3.servers:11211");
      }
    };

    MemcachedClient memcachedClient = new MemcachedClient(
        AddrUtil.getAddresses(serverList));

    // ADD adds an entry and does nothing if the key already exists
    // Think of it as an INSERT
    // The second parameter (0) indicates the expiration - 0 means no expiry
    memcachedClient.add("marc", 0, 34);
    memcachedClient.add("seppe", 0, 32);
    memcachedClient.add("bart", 0, 66);
    memcachedClient.add("jeanne", 0, 19);

    // It is possible to set expiry dates: the following expires in three seconds:
    memcachedClient.add("short_lived_name", 3, 19);
    // Sleep 5 seconds to make sure our short-lived name is expired
    Thread.sleep(1000 * 5);

    // SET sets an entry regardless of whether it exists
    // Think of it as an UPDATE-OR-INSERT
    memcachedClient.add("marc", 0, 1111); // <- ADD will have no effect
    memcachedClient.set("jeanne", 0, 12); // <- But SET will

    // REPLACE replaces an entry and does nothing if the key does not exist
    // Think of it as an UPDATE
    memcachedClient.replace("not_existing_name", 0, 12); // <- Will have no effect
    memcachedClient.replace("jeanne", 0, 10);

    // DELETE deletes an entry, similar to an SQL DELETE statement
    memcachedClient.delete("seppe");

    // GET retrieves an entry
    Integer age_of_marc = (Integer) memcachedClient.get("marc");
    Integer age_of_short_lived = (Integer) memcachedClient.get("short_lived_name");
```

```
        Integer age_of_not_existing = (Integer) memcachedClient.get("not_existing_name");
        Integer age_of_seppe = (Integer) memcachedClient.get("seppe");
        System.out.println("Age of Marc: " + age_of_marc);
        System.out.println("Age of Seppe (deleted): " + age_of_seppe);
        System.out.println("Age of not existing name: " + age_of_not_existing);
        System.out.println("Age of short lived name (expired): " + age_of_short_lived);

        memcachedClient.shutdown();

    }
}
```

**Connections**

Memcached is also often placed on top of an existing Hibernate-driven project (see Chapter 15) to cache queries to an existing relational database, which is especially helpful in cases where such queries take substantial time (for example, for queries involving many joins).

It is important to note that – with Memcached – it is the client's responsibility to distribute the entries among the different servers in the Memcached pool (in the example above, we have provided three servers). That is: the client decides to which server each key – and hash – should be mapped, for example by using a mechanism similar to the modulo hashing function illustrated above. With the SpyMemcached Java library, this is taken care of automatically once multiple servers are passed to the client object. Also, Memcached provides no data redundancy. That means that if a server goes down, all the entries stored on that node will be lost. Despite this, Memcached remains very popular as a caching solution, especially because many middleware libraries exist that allow you to put it on top of a web server (to cache recently requested pages) or on top of an existing Hibernate-driven project (see Chapter 15).

## 11.2.4 Request Coordination

In the simplest case, such as with Memcached, it is the duty of the client to make sure requests to store and retrieve key–value pairs are routed to the desired node which will store the data (i.e., by directly contacting and "talking to" that node over the network). However, starting from the basic key–value architecture it is possible to move such duties from the client to the nodes themselves. Many NoSQL implementations, such as Cassandra, Google's BigTable, Amazon's DynamoDB, CouchDB, Redis, and CouchBase – to name a few – do so. In such a set-up, all nodes often implement the same functionality and can all perform the role of **request coordinator**: i.e., the responsible party to route requests to the appropriate destination node and relay back the result status of the operation.

Since any node can act as a request coordinator, and clients can send requests to any of such nodes, it is necessary that all nodes remain informed at all times of the other nodes in the network. This problem is addressed through a **membership protocol**: each node talks to the network to retrieve a membership list and keep its view of the whole network up to date. This protocol allows all nodes to know about the existence of other nodes, and is the fundamental underlying protocol on top of which other functionality can be built.

Each membership protocol contains two sub-components, called **dissemination** and **failure detection**, which can be accomplished simultaneously or implemented using separate logic. The most naïve way to implement a membership protocol would be by using a network multicast, in which each node would send out an "are you (still) there and part of my network?" request to all other members in a node's known network, but this solution is inefficient and scales badly. Therefore, implementation in practice commonly uses dissemination protocols that mimic how rumors or gossip are spread in social networks, or how viruses spread in an epidemic. The basic idea behind this dissemination involves periodic, pairwise communication, with the information exchanged in such interaction being bounded. When two nodes interact, the state of the node (i.e., the node's current view on the network) being most out of date will be updated to reflect the state of the other party. When a node is added to the network, it will contact a known existing node to announce its arrival, which will then be spread throughout the network. When a node is removed from the network, it will not respond anymore when contacted by a random, different node. The latter node can then spread this information about this node being down further through the network. In this way, failure detection is handled.

### 11.2.5 Consistent Hashing

Thanks to the membership protocol, nodes are (eventually) aware of one another. Following this, they can now partition hashed key–value pairs among them. This can be done using the same technique in which each hash can be mapped to a specific node using the modulo operator. In practice, however, more **consistent hashing** schemes are often used, which avoid having to remap each key to a new node when nodes are added or removed.[1]

Let's explain this concept in more detail. Recall Figure 11.2 on the usage of the modulo operator to distribute keys over a list of servers. The hash function used to distribute keys over a set of servers can be expressed as:

$h(key) = key \% n$ With % the modulo operator and $n$ the number of servers.

Imagine now that we have a situation where ten keys are distributed over three servers ($n = 3$). The table in Figure 11.3 outlines what happens when a server is removed ($n = 2$) or added ($n = 4$).

Note how, upon removal or addition of a server, many items have to be moved to a different server (the highlighted entries in Figure 11.3). That is, increasing $n$ from three to four causes $1 - n/k = 70\%$ of the keys to be moved. If there had been ten servers ($n = 10$) and 1000 items (keys), then the number of keys that would have to be moved when adding another server equals $1 - 10/1000$, or 99% of all items. Clearly, this is not a desirable outcome in set-ups where servers are likely to be removed or added.

A consistent hashing scheme resolves this issue. At the core of a consistent hashing set-up is a so-called **"ring"-topology**, which is basically a representation of the number range [0,1] as illustrated in Figure 11.4.

In this set-up, all servers (three servers with identifiers 0, 1, 2) are hashed to place them in a position on this ring (Figure 11.5).

To distribute the keys, we follow a similar mechanism in which we first hash each key to a position on the ring, and store the actual key–value pair on the first server that appears clockwise of the hashed point on the ring. For instance, for key 3, we obtain a position of 0.78, which ends up being stored on server 0 (Figure 11.6).

[1] The SpyMemcached example illustrated earlier in fact uses a consistent hashing mechanism as well.

| | n | | |
|---|---|---|---|
| key | 3 | 2 | 4 |
| 0 | 0 | 0 | 0 |
| 1 | 1 | 1 | 1 |
| 2 | 2 | 0 | 2 |
| 3 | 0 | 1 | 3 |
| 4 | 1 | 0 | 0 |
| 5 | 2 | 1 | 1 |
| 6 | 0 | 0 | 2 |
| 7 | 1 | 1 | 3 |
| 8 | 2 | 0 | 0 |
| 9 | 0 | 1 | 1 |

**Figure 11.3** Keys are distributed over three nodes using a simple hashing function. Which hashes would change when removing or adding a node?

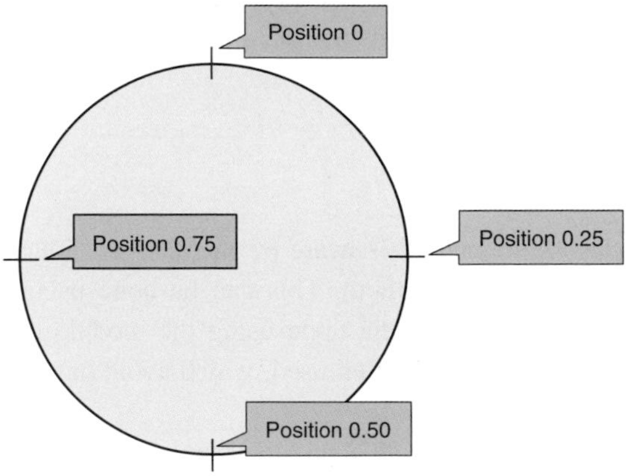


**Figure 11.4** A consistent hashing scheme starts from a ring topology.

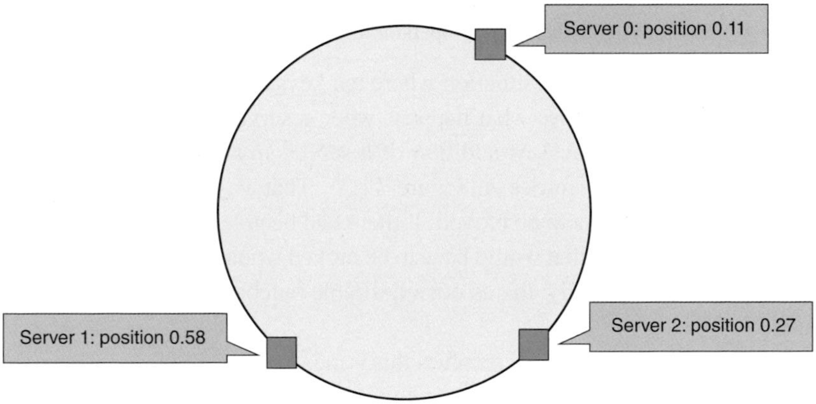


**Figure 11.5** Server identifiers are hashed and placed on the ring.

Because of the uniformity property of a "good" hash function, roughly $1/n$ key–value pairs will end up being stored on each server. This time, however, most of the key–value pairs will remain unaffected if a machine is added or removed. For instance, say we add a new server to the ring, only the keys positioned on the highlighted section of the ring in Figure 11.7 would have to be moved to the new server.

Typically, the fraction of keys that need to be moved when using this set-up is about $k/(n + 1)$ – i.e., a much smaller fraction than was the case for modulo-based hashing.

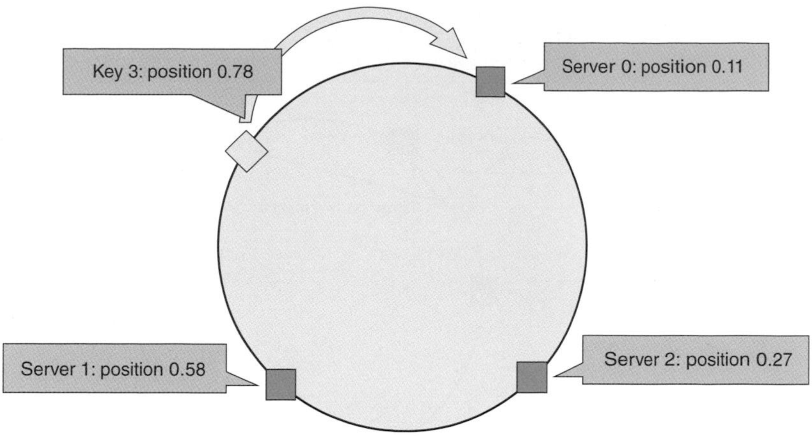


**Figure 11.6** Keys are hashed as well and stored in the next occurring server (clockwise order).

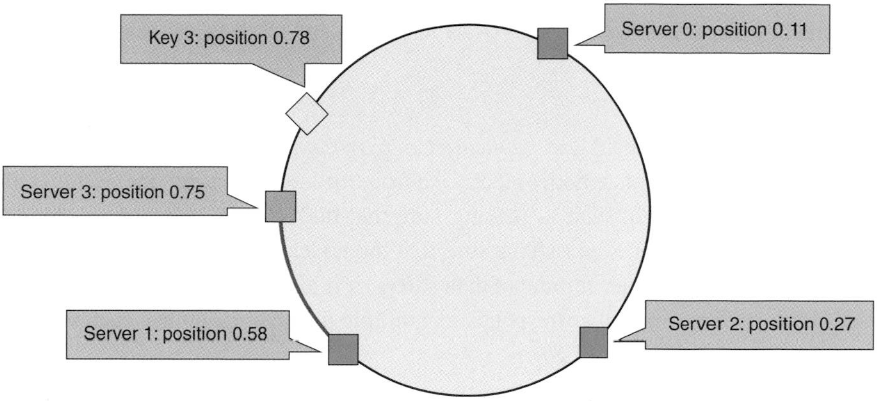


**Figure 11.7** In case a server joins the network, only a small fraction of keys need to be moved.

### 11.2.6 Replication and Redundancy

The basic consistent hashing procedure as described above is still not ideal. First, if two servers end up being mapped close to one another, one of these nodes will end up with few keys to store (as the distance between the two nodes on the ring is small). Second, if a server is added to the ring, we see that all of the keys moved to this new node originate from just one other server.

Luckily, the mechanism of consistent hashing allows us to deal with these issues in an elegant manner. Instead of mapping a server $s$ to a single point on our ring, we map it to multiple positions, called **replicas**. For each physical server $s$, we hence end up with $r$ (the number of replicas) points on the ring, with everything else working like before. By using this mechanism, we increase the uniformity with which key–value pairs will end up being distributed to servers, and can also ensure that an even lower number of keys must be moved when a server is added to a cluster.

Note, however, this concept has nothing to do with **redundancy**. Each replica for a node still represents *the same physical instance*. Many vendors refer to this concept as **virtual nodes**, as the nodes placed on the ring correspond to a lower number of real, physical nodes. To handle **data replication or redundancy**, many vendors extend the consistent hashing mechanism outlined

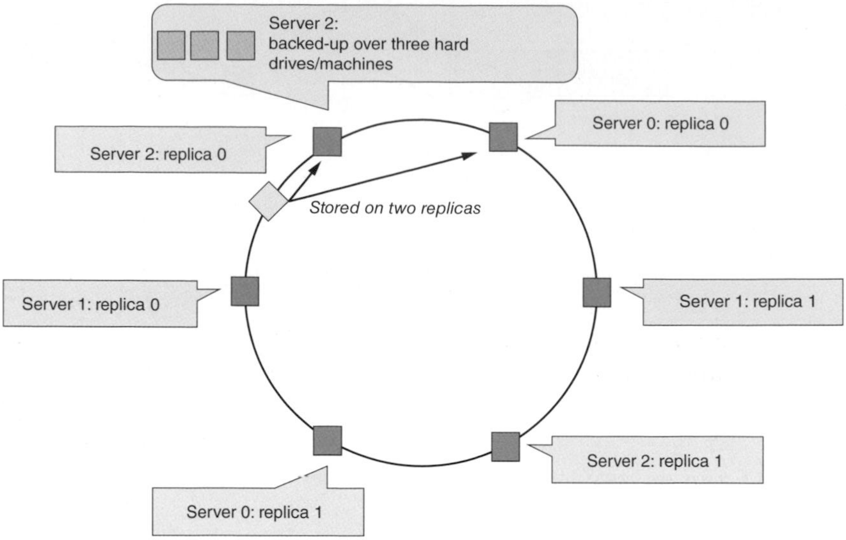


**Figure 11.8** Replication (virtual) nodes create a more uniform topology, whereas data replication ensures data safety in the event of faults.

above so key–value pairs are *duplicated across multiple nodes*, for instance by storing the key–value pair on two or more nodes clockwise from the key's position on the ring. Other constraints can be considered as well, such as making sure that the (virtual) nodes correspond to actual different physical machines, or even making sure that the nodes are present in different data centers. Finally, to ensure an even greater amount of data safety, it is also possible to set up a full redundancy scheme in which each node itself corresponds to multiple physical machines each storing a fully redundant copy of the data (Figure 11.8).

### 11.2.7 Eventual Consistency

Recall that the membership protocol does not guarantee that every node is aware of every other node *at all times*, but guarantees that up-to-date information will spread through the network so it will reach a consistent state over time, i.e., in which all nodes possess up-to-date information regarding the current layout of the network. This affects read and write operations that clients perform, as they must deal with the fact that the state of the network might not be perfectly consistent at any moment in time, though will eventually become consistent at a future point in time. Many NoSQL databases guarantee so-called eventual consistency. Contrary to traditional relational databases, which enforce ACID (Atomicity, Consistency, Isolation, and Durability) on their transactions, most NoSQL databases follow the **BASE principle** (Basically Available, Soft state, Eventually consistent).

**Connections**

The principles of ACID are explained in much more detail in Chapter 14, where we talk about transaction management.

The BASE acronym was originally conceived by Eric Brewer, who is also known for formulating the **CAP theorem**, which states that a distributed computer system, such as the one we've looked at above, cannot guarantee the following three properties simultaneously: consistency (all nodes see the same data simultaneously); availability (guarantees that every request receives a response indicating a success or failure result); and partition tolerance (the system continues to work even if nodes go down or are added). Stand-alone RDBMSs needn't bother with partition tolerance, because there is only a single node, so they can focus on consistency and availability. Distributed RDBMSs will typically attempt to enforce consistency at all costs in a multi-node setting, which may affect *availability* if individual nodes cannot be reached.

As stated above, most NoSQL databases, but not all, sacrifice the *consistency* part of CAP in their set-up, instead striving for eventual consistency, indicating that the system will become consistent over time, once all inputs to that system stop. The full BASE acronym stands for:

- Basically Available, indicating that NoSQL databases adhere to the availability guarantee of the CAP theorem;
- Soft state, indicating that the system can change over time, even without receiving input (since nodes continue to update each other);
- Eventually consistent, indicating that the system will become consistent over time but might not be consistent at a particular moment.

The impact of eventual consistency becomes immediately apparent when we look closely at write and read requests. Imagine that our client wishes to store a key–value pair "(bart, 32)" in the ring topology described above. The node receiving this request maps the hash of this key to, for example, three node replicas (corresponding to different physical servers), and contacts these nodes to store this key in their storage. The original receiving node can then send a response to the client immediately, wait until at least one replica answers with a positive reply ("the replica is up and stored the entry"), wait until all replicas reply, or wait until a quorum of at least half of the replicas reply. The latter is oftentimes called quorum consistency. In the case that a replica is down and does not reply, the request receiving node can keep the request around to retry the operation later, or rely on the membership protocol to spread the information in case at least one of the replicas received the entry.

If our client wishes to retrieve a key–value pair, a similar mechanism is applied, but some nodes might contain an outdated version of the entry compared to others. Again, the request-receiving node can then take immediate action and instruct the outdated nodes to update their entry, or again wait until the membership protocol takes care of things on its own.

Note, however, that although eventual consistency is typically associated with NoSQL databases, a fair number of them hold on to stronger consistency and ACID-like transactions.

**Connections**

Eventual consistency and BASE transactions will return and will be discussed in more detail in Chapter 16.

**Drill Down**

When choosing a NoSQL system, it is important to know whether a choice regarding consistency policy is available. If the database system supports eventual consistency only, then the application must handle the possibility of reading inconsistent data. This is not as easy as it sounds since this responsibility is then left to the application developer, who then has to consider questions such as "What happens if a database read returns an arbitrarily old value?" Handling such cases can take up a lot of developer time. Google addressed the pain points of eventual consistency in a paper on its distributed F1 database and noted:

"We also have a lot of experience with eventual consistency systems at Google. In all such systems, we find developers spend a significant fraction of their time building extremely complex and error-prone mechanisms to cope with eventual consistency and handle data that may be out of date. We think this is an unacceptable burden to place on developers and that consistency problems should be solved at the database level."[2]

Hence, we've seen newer NoSQL systems move away from the eventual consistency idea.

### 11.2.8 Stabilization

As we've explained above, because the partitioning of hashes over nodes depends on the number of nodes available, it is required to repartition hashes over nodes if this amount changes. The operation that repartitions hashes over nodes if nodes are added or removed is called **stabilization**, and should preferably be as efficient as possible to reduce network overhead or waiting time. If a consistent hashing scheme is being applied, the number of fluctuations in the hash–node mappings will be minimized, hence leading to a shorter stabilization period.

If a node gets added or permanently removed, each node's membership list will eventually get updated, which instructs that node to investigate its list of entries it is holding and remap its keys. In the optimal case, a key still belongs to the same node and no action must be taken. If a node is no longer responsible for an entry, it can use the partitioning scheme to figure out which node or nodes are now responsible and send the entry to those. Note that if a node is removed, entries can only be deleted from the to-be-removed node once they are present in their new, correct, location. Again, it is relevant to note this stabilization operation takes time, so the planned removal of a node can still take some time before the node can actually be removed from the network.

### 11.2.9 Integrity Constraints and Querying

In this section, we have attempted to provide a comprehensive overview of the defining elements of key–value stores. It must be stressed that this category of NoSQL databases still represents a very diverse gamut of systems. As already explained, some systems are full-blown DBMSs in their own right, whereas others are merely used as caches in front of a (relational) DBMS. Some have the hash values refer to internal memory addresses, whereas others use persistent memory. A typical property is that only limited query facilities are offered, with an interface that often comes down to simple put() and get() instructions, with the key as the defining, single-hit parameter. Such APIs can be offered, for example, as a SOAP or REST interface. Also, there are limited to zero means to enforce structural constraints on the data. The DBMS remains agnostic to the internal structure, if any, of the "values" in the key–value pairs: these are treated as opaque objects and as a consequence they cannot be subject to search criteria. Moreover, no relationships, let alone referential integrity constraints or

**Retention Questions**

- How do key–value stores store their data?
- Which properties should a good hash function adhere to?
- In which way does a key–value store allow for better horizontal scalability?
- What is request coordination? When is it needed?
- What is consistent hashing? Which issues does it solve?
- Explain eventual consistency in the context of the CAP theorem.
- What is meant by stabilization?
- Which query operations does a typical key–value store support?

[2] Corbett, J., Dean, J., Epstein, M. et al. Spanner: Google's globally-distributed database. In Proceedings of OSDI '12: Tenth Symposium on Operating System Design and Implementation, Hollywood, CA, October 2012.

database schema, can be defined over the respective elements stored in the database. New key–value pairs are simply added, without impact on the other data. The DBMS treats them as completely independent and any constraints or relationships are to be managed and enforced entirely at application level. Therefore, the main feature of key–value stores is their ability to offer a very efficient and scalable, yet simple, environment for storing and retrieving unrelated data elements. In this capacity, they are also often used as a foundation layer to systems with more complex functionalities.

## 11.3 Tuple and Document Stores

Now that we have explained the basic concepts of key–value stores, we can easily make the jump to other types of NoSQL databases, such as the tuple store. A **tuple store** is essentially the same thing as a key–value store, with the difference that it does not store pairwise combinations of a key and a value, but instead stores a unique key together with a vector of data. To expand upon our earlier example, an entry in a tuple store could look like this:

```
marc -> ("Marc", "McLast Name", 25, "Germany")
```

There is no requirement of each tuple in the tuple store having the same length or semantic ordering, meaning that the handling of data is completely schema-less. Unlike relational databases, where each table is defined under a particular schema, tuple stores simply allow you to start adding any sort of rows, and leaves the handling and checking of those up to the application. Various NoSQL implementations do, however, permit organizing entries in semantical groups, often called collections or even tables, which is basically an extra namespace defined over the keys. For instance, a collection "Person" might hold these two entries:

```
Person:marc -> ("Marc", "McLast Name", 25, "Germany")
Person:harry -> ("Harry", "Smith", 29, "Belgium")
```

And another collection "Book" might hold the following single entry:

```
Book:harry -> ("Harry Potter", "J.K. Rowling")
```

Making the jump from a tuple store to a document-based NoSQL database is easily done. Rather than storing a tuple-based structure (unlabeled and ordered), **document stores** store a collection of attributes labeled and unordered, representing items that are semi-structured. For instance, a book can be described using this collection of attributes:

```
{
   Title       = "Harry Potter"
   ISBN        = "111-1111111111"
   Authors     = [ "J.K. Rowling" ]
   Price       = 32
   Dimensions  = "8.5 x 11.0 x 0.5"
   PageCount   = 234
   Genre       = "Fantasy"
}
```

Again, most implementations allow organizing items in tables or collections. Just like with key–value or tuple stores, no schema needs to be defined over the items in a collection. Instead, a structure is imposed by the internal structure of the documents – for instance, as a (nested) collection of attributes as illustrated above. Most modern NoSQL databases represent documents using the JSON standard (JavaScript Object Notation), which includes numbers, strings, Booleans, arrays, objects, and null as its basic types. For instance, a book can be represented using JSON as follows:

> **Connections**
>
> More details regarding the JSON standard and other representations such as XML can be found in Chapter 10.

```
{
    "title": "Harry Potter",
    "authors": [ "J.K. Rowling", "R.J. Kowling"],
    "price": 32.00,
    "genres": [ "fantasy"],
    "dimensions": {
        "width": 8.5,
        "height": 11.0,
        "depth": 0.5
    },
    "pages": 234,
    "in_publication": true,
    "subtitle": null
}
```

Other commonly found representations are BSON (Binary JSON), YAML (YAML Ain't Markup Language) and even XML. In that sense, XML databases can be considered an example of document stores, and hence be considered a NoSQL database as well.

### 11.3.1 Items with Keys

Since document stores store collections of attributes, it is possible to include an item's key directly in this collection of attributes, though many of the concepts such as hashing and partitioning we've seen before remain present. Most NoSQL document stores will allow you to store items in tables (collections) in a schema-less manner, but will enforce that a primary key be specified over each table to uniquely identify each item in the collection. This can be done by leaving it up to the end-user to indicate which attribute should be used as the unique key (e.g., "title" in a collection of books), such as with Amazon's DynamoDB, or by predefining an always-present primary key attribute itself. MongoDB, for instance, uses "_id" as the primary key attribute in an item, which can be set by the user or left out. If left out, MongoDB will auto-generate a unique, random identifier for the item. Just as with key–value stores, the primary key will be used as a partitioning key to create a hash and determine where the data will be stored.

### 11.3.2 Filters and Queries

We've seen that document stores deal with semi-structured items. They impose no particular schema on the structure of items stored in a particular collection, but assume that items nevertheless exhibit an implicit structure following from their representational format, representing a collection of attributes, using JSON, XML, etc.

Just as with key–value stores, the primary key of each item can be used to rapidly retrieve a particular item from a collection, but since items are composed of multiple attributes, most document stores can retrieve items based on simple filters as well. Therefore, they typically also offer a richer API than key–value stores, with functionality to query and manipulate document content. To illustrate a basic example, the Java code below shows how you can connect to a MongoDB instance, insert some documents, query, and update them:

```
import org.bson.Document;
import com.mongodb.MongoClient;
import com.mongodb.client.FindIterable;
import com.mongodb.client.MongoDatabase;
import java.util.ArrayList;

import static com.mongodb.client.model.Filters.*;
import static java.util.Arrays.asList;

public class MongoDBExample {
    public static void main(String... args) {
        MongoClient mongoClient = new MongoClient();
        MongoDatabase db = mongoClient.getDatabase("test");

        // Delete all books first
        db.getCollection("books").deleteMany(new Document());

        // Add some books
        db.getCollection("books").insertMany(new ArrayList<Document>() {{
          add(getBookDocument("My First Book", "Wilfried", "Lemahieu",
                    12, new String[]{"drama"}));
          add(getBookDocument("My Second Book", "Seppe", "vanden Broucke",
                    437, new String[]{"fantasy", "thriller"}));
          add(getBookDocument("My Third Book", "Seppe", "vanden Broucke",
                    200, new String[]{"educational"}));
          add(getBookDocument("Java Programming for Database Managers",
                    "Bart", "Baesens",
                    100, new String[]{"educational"}));
        }});

        // Perform query
        FindIterable<Document> result = db.getCollection("books").find(
                        and(
                                eq("author.last_name", "vanden Broucke"),
                                eq("genres", "thriller"),
                                gt("nrPages", 100)));

        for (Document r: result) {
            System.out.println(r.toString());
            // Increase the number of pages:
            db.getCollection("books").updateOne(
                    new Document("_id", r.get("_id")),
                    new Document("$set",
                      new Document("nrPages", r.getInteger("nrPages") + 100)));
```

```
        }

        mongoClient.close();
    }

    public static Document getBookDocument(String title,
            String authorFirst, String authorLast,
            int nrPages, String[] genres) {
        return new Document("author", new Document()
                                .append("first_name", authorFirst)
                                .append("last_name", authorLast))
                        .append("title", title)
                        .append("nrPages", nrPages)
                        .append("genres", asList(genres));
    }
}
```

This example works as follows: first, we set up a MongoClient and MongoDatabase to establish a connection to MongoDB. Next, we use the deleteMany() method to delete all entries in the "books" collection. This method needs a filter condition, but since we wish to delete all entries we pass a blank document here. Next, we add some books using the insertMany() method. Each book is constructed using a static helper method (getBookDocument()), which creates a new document with the fields "author", "title", "nrPages", and "genres". Note that fields of documents can be documents themselves, such as the "author" field consisting of "first_name" and "last_name". MongoDB will use a dot (".") to indicate such fields, so that the full identifier of "first_name" becomes "author.first_name". After inserting some books, we perform a simple query using the find() method and passing a conjunctive (and) condition containing three clauses: the "author.last_name" should equal "vanden Broucke", the genres should contain "thriller" (the "eq" filter gets used to search through a list in this case), and the number of pages should be greater than 100. For each document in the result set, we use the updateOne() method to set the number of pages to a new value.

Running this code will produce this result:

```
Document{{_id=567ef62bc0c3081f4c04b16c,
author=Document{{first_name=Seppe, last_name=vanden Broucke}}, title=My
Second Book, nrPages=437, genres=[fantasy, thriller]}}
```

**Drill Down**

We use MongoDB here as it remains one of the most well-known and widely used implementations of a document store. In case you're wondering where MongoDB stands in the "eventual consistency" story as discussed before, know that MongoDB is strongly consistent by default: if you write data and read it back out, you will always be able to read the result of the write you just performed (if the write succeeded). This is because MongoDB is a so-called "single-master" system where all reads go to a primary node by default. If you do optionally enable reading from the secondary nodes, then MongoDB becomes eventually consistent where it's possible to read out-of-date results.

This is the theory; the actual story is somewhat more complicated than this. In various MongoDB versions, researchers were able to show that MongoDB's implementation of a strong consistency model was broken (this happened in 2013, 2015, and again recently in 2017[3]). Versions 3.4.1 and 3.5.1 are finally consistent with no bugs, though this shows that end-users should be very attentive when adopting a NoSQL database.

**Drill Down**

The online playground contains a MongoDB version of the wine database, which you can query through its JavaScript shell (see the Appendix for more details).

Apart from basic filtering and query operations, most NoSQL document stores support more complex queries (e.g., with aggregations). For example, the Java code below shows how you can perform a query that shows the total number of pages across all books, grouped by author:

```
// Perform aggregation query
AggregateIterable<Document> result = db.getCollection("books")
       .aggregate(asList(
              new Document("$group",
                     new Document("_id", "$author.last_name")
                            .append("page_sum", new Document("$sum", "$nrPages")))));
for (Document r: result) {
     System.out.println(r.toString());
}
```

Running this code on the Java example above will yield this result:

```
Document{{_id=Lemahieu, page_sum=12}}
Document{{_id=vanden Broucke, page_sum=637}}
Document{{_id=Baesens, page_sum=100}}
```

Although NoSQL databases are built with scalability and simplicity in mind, running individual queries with many query criteria, sorting operators, or aggregations can still be relatively slow, even when no relational joining is performed. The reason for this is that every filter (such as "author. last_name = Baesens") entails a complete collection or table scan (i.e., a scan of every document item in the collection) to figure out which documents match the query statements. The primary key defined for every item forms a notable exception, as this key functions as a unique partitioning index making efficient retrieval of items possible.

To speed up other, more complex operations, most document structures allow defining indexes over collections, in a manner very similar to table indexes in a relational database. Defining indexes over collections makes it easy to traverse a collection and perform efficient matching

[3] See https://jepsen.io/analyses for the detailed analysis. Jepsen also stress tests and evaluates many other NoSQL vendors and is a fantastic resource to use as a guide when making a NoSQL-related decision.

> **Connections**
>
> Indexing will be discussed in more detail in Chapters 12 and 13.

operations, at a cost of storage, as storing the index itself will also take up some amount of storage space. Many document storage systems can define a variety of indexes, including unique and non-unique indexes, composite indexes, which are composed of multiple attributes, and even specialized indexes, such as geospatial indexes (when an attribute represents geospatial coordinates), or text-based indexes (when an attribute represents a large text field).

### 11.3.3 Complex Queries and Aggregation with MapReduce

Based on the explanation above, you might notice that document stores exhibit many similarities to relational databases, including query, aggregation, and indexing facilities. One notable aspect missing from most document stores, however, is that of relations between tables. To illustrate this concept, say we start from our book example above, but that we get a request to store more information about each author, rather than just modeling it as a list of string values per book like we did before.

One way to tackle this problem is to just model the concept of an author as a document on its own, and continue to store it in an author list per book, meaning that instead of the following:

```
{
    "title": "Databases for Beginners",
    "authors": ["J.K. Sequel", "John Smith"],
    "pages": 234
}
```

we model a book item like this:

```
{
    "title": "Databases for Beginners",
    "authors": [
      {"first_name": "Jay Kay", "last_name": "Sequel", "age": 54},
      {"first_name": "John", "last_name": "Smith", "age": 32} ],
    "pages": 234
}
```

This concept is referred to by MongoDB and other vendors as "**embedded documents**", and is what we've been applying to our Java example above as well. This idea has the benefit that queries on "linked items" (authors to books, in this case) work just as normal attributes would. For instance, it is possible to perform an equality check on "authors.first_name = John". The downside of this approach, however, is that it can quickly lead to data duplication, and can make it cumbersome to perform an update to an author's information because every book containing that author entry will have to be updated.

> **Connections**
>
> See Chapters 6 and 9 for more information on relational databases and normalization.

Readers familiar with the chapters on relational databases would see this as a strong case for normalization, and would advise creating two collections: one for books and one for authors.

Books can then contain items like the following:

```
{
    "title": "Databases for Beginners",
    "authors": ["Jay Kay Rowling", "John Smith"],
    "pages": 234
}
```

And for the authors collection:

```
{
    "_id": "Jay Kay Rowling",
    "age": 54
}
```

This approach, however, has the downside that most document stores will force you to resolve complex relational queries "by hand" at the level of your application code. For instance, say we would like to retrieve a list of books for which the author is older than a particular age. In many document stores, this is impossible through a single query. Instead, users are advised to first perform a query to retrieve all authors older than the requested age, and then retrieve all titles per author. Contrary to relational databases, this operation will involve many round-trips to the document store to fetch additional items.

This way of working might seem limiting at first, but remember that document stores are geared toward storing a large number of documents across many nodes, especially in cases where the amount or velocity of data is so high that relational databases would not be able to keep up. To perform complex queries and aggregations, most analytics-oriented document stores offer ways to query the dataset through map–reduce operations. **MapReduce** is a well-known programming model made popular by Google and subsequently implemented by Apache Hadoop, an open-source software framework for distributed computing and storage of large datasets.

**Connections**

We mainly focus on MapReduce in what follows. Hadoop and the wider field of Big Data and analytics are discussed in Chapters 19 and 20.

The main innovative aspects of MapReduce do not come from the map-and-reduce paradigm itself, as these concepts were long known in functional programming circles, but rather from the idea of applying these functions in a manner incredibly scalable and fault-tolerant. A map–reduce pipeline starts from a series of key–value pairs (k1,v1) and maps each pair to one or more output pairs. Note, therefore, that multiple output entries per input entry can be produced. This operation can easily be run in parallel over the input pairs. Next, the output entries are shuffled and distributed so all output entries belonging to the same key are assigned to the same worker (in most distributed set-ups, workers will correspond to different physical machines). These workers then apply a reduce function to each group of key–value pairs having the same key, producing a new list of values per output key. The resulting final outputs are then (optionally) sorted per key k2 to produce the final outcome.

Let's illustrate a map–reduce pipeline using a simple example. Imagine we would like to get a summed count of pages for books per genre. Assuming each book has one genre, we can resolve this in a relational database setting using this SQL query:

```
SELECT genre, SUM(nrPages) FROM books
GROUP BY genre
ORDER BY genre
```

Assume now we are dealing with a large collection of books. Using a map–reduce pipeline, we can tackle this query by first creating a list of input key–value pairs corresponding to the records we want to process:

| **k1** | **v1** |
|---|---|
| 1 | {genre: education, nrPages: 120} |
| 2 | {genre: thriller, nrPages: 100} |
| 3 | {genre: fantasy, nrPages: 20} |
| ... | ... |

Each worker will now start working on an input entry, and will apply its *map* operation. Here, the map function is a simple conversion to a genre–nrPages key–value pair:

```
function map(k1, v1)
    emit output record (v1.genre, v1.nrPages)
end function
```

Our workers will hence have produced the following three output lists (example with three workers below), with the keys now corresponding to genres:

| **Worker 1** | |
|---|---|
| **k2** | **v2** |
| education | 120 |
| thriller | 100 |
| fantasy | 20 |

| **Worker 2** | |
|---|---|
| **k2** | **v2** |
| drama | 500 |
| education | 200 |

| **Worker 3** | |
|---|---|
| **k2** | **v2** |
| education | 20 |
| fantasy | 10 |

Next, a working operation will be started per unique key k2, for which its associated list of values will be reduced. For instance, (education,[120,200,20]) will be reduced to its sum, 340:

```
function reduce(k2, v2_list)
    emit output record (k2, sum(v2_list))
end function
```

The final output list hence looks as follows:

| **k2** | **v3** |
|---|---|
| education | 340 |
| thriller | 100 |
| drama | 500 |
| fantasy | 30 |

This final list can then be sorted based on k2 or v3 to produce the desired result.

Depending on the query, it might require careful thought to produce the desired result. For instance, if we would like to retrieve an average page count per book for each genre, it seems plausible to rewrite our reduce function as such:

```
function reduce(k2, v2_list)
   emit output record (k2, sum(v2_list) / length(v2_list))
end function
```

Just as before, after mapping the input list, our workers will have produced the following three output lists:

| Worker 1 | |
|---|---|
| k2 | v2 |
| education | 120 |
| thriller | 100 |
| fantasy | 20 |

| Worker 2 | |
|---|---|
| k2 | v2 |
| drama | 500 |
| education | 200 |

| Worker 3 | |
|---|---|
| k2 | v2 |
| education | 20 |
| fantasy | 10 |

which are now reduced to averages as follows:

| k2 | v3 |
|---|---|
| education | (120 + 200 + 20)/3 = 113.33 |
| thriller | 100/1 = 100.00 |
| drama | 500/1 = 500.00 |
| fantasy | (20 + 10)/2 = 15.00 |

This example serves well to illustrate another powerful concept of the map–reduce pipeline, namely the fact that the *reduce operation can happen more than once, and can already start before all mapping operations have finished*. This is especially helpful when the output data are too large to be reduced at once, or when new data arrive later on.

Using the same averaging example, imagine that two workers have already finished mapping the first couple of input rows like so:

| Worker 1 | |
|---|---|
| k2 | v2 |
| education | 20 |
| education | 50 |
| education | 50 |
| thriller | 100 |
| fantasy | 20 |

| Worker 2 | |
|---|---|
| k2 | v2 |
| drama | 100 |
| drama | 200 |
| drama | 200 |
| education | 100 |
| education | 100 |

Instead of sitting around until all mappers have finished, our reducers can already start to produce an intermediate reduced result:

| k2 | v3 |
|---|---|
| education | (20 + 50 + 50 + 100 + 100)/5 = 64.00 |
| thriller | 100/1 = 100.00 |
| drama | (100 + 200 + 200)/3 = 166.67 |
| fantasy | (20)/1 = 20.00 |

Now let's say that the next batch arrives, which is mapped as follows:

| k2 | v2 |
|---|---|
| education | 20 |
| fantasy | 10 |

However, if we would reduce this set with our previously reduced set, *we would get the following, wrong, result*:

| Previously reducedset | |
|---|---|
| k2 | v3 |
| education | 64.00 |
| thriller | 100.00 |
| drama | 166.67 |
| fantasy | 20.00 |

| New set | |
|---|---|
| k2 | v2 |
| education | 20 |
| fantasy | 10 |

| Reduces to (WRONG!) | |
|---|---|
| k2 | v3' |
| thriller | 100 / 1 = 100.00 |
| drama | 166.67 / 1 = 166.67 |
| education | (64 + 20) / 2 = 42.00 |
| fantasy | (20 + 10) / 2 = 15.00 |

This illustrates a particularly important aspect of the MapReduce paradigm. To obtain the actual correct result, we need to rewrite our map and reduce functions:

```
function map(k1, v1)
     emit output record (v1.genre, (v1.nrPages, 1))
end function

function reduce(k2, v2_list)
     for each (nrPages, count) in v2_list do
          s = s + nrPages * count
          newc = newc + count
     repeat
     emit output record (k2, (s/newc, newc))
end function
```

Our mapping function now produces the following result. Note that the values are now a pair of pages and the literal number "1" (a counter keeping track of the number of items in the so-far-reduced average):

| Worker 1 | |
|---|---|
| k2 | v2 |
| education | 20, 1 |
| education | 50, 1 |
| education | 50, 1 |
| thriller | 100, 1 |
| fantasy | 20, 1 |

| Worker 2 | |
|---|---|
| k2 | v2 |
| drama | 100, 1 |
| drama | 200, 1 |
| drama | 200, 1 |
| education | 100, 1 |
| education | 100, 1 |

| Worker 3 | |
|---|---|
| k2 | v2 |
| education | 20, 1 |
| fantasy | 10, 1 |

If we reduce the first two lists, we get:

| First reduced list | |
|---|---|
| k2 | v3 |
| education | 64.00, 5 |
| thriller | 100.00, 1 |
| drama | 166.67, 3 |
| fantasy | 20.00, 1 |

If we now reduce this list with the last set, we get a correct, final result:

| First reduced list | |
|---|---|
| **k2** | **v3** |
| education | 64.00, 5 |
| thriller | 100.00, 1 |
| drama | 166.67, 3 |
| fantasy | 20.00, 1 |

| New set | |
|---|---|
| **k2** | **v2** |
| education | 20, 1 |
| fantasy | 10, 1 |

| Reduces to (CORRECT) | |
|---|---|
| **k2** | **v3'** |
| thriller | (100) / (1), 1 |
| drama | (166.67 * 3) / (3), 3 |
| education | (64 * 5 + 20 * 1) / (5+1), 6 |
| fantasy | (20 * 1 + 10 * 1) / (1+1), 2 |

This example highlights *two very important criteria* regarding the reduce function. Since this function can be called multiple times on partial results:

1. The reduce function should output the same structure as emitted by the map function, since this output can be used again in an additional reduce operation.
2. The reduce function should provide correct results even if called multiple times on partial results.

As a final example, we close with a famous one (almost every NoSQL database or Big Data technology supporting the MapReduce paradigm uses this example as an introductory one): to count the number of occurrences of each word in a document:

```
function map(document_name, document_text)
     for each word in document_text do
          emit output record (word, 1)
     repeat
end function

function reduce(word, partial_counts)
     emit output record (word, sum(partial_counts))
end function
```

You might be tempted to change the map function so that it already aggregates the sum per word it has found in its given document (in "document_text"). However, it is advisable to *not* include this reduce logic in your map function and to keep the mapping simple. Imagine, for instance, that a worker were confronted with a huge list of words exceeding its local memory, in which case it would never be able to perform the aggregation and return its output list. By iterating the words one by one and emitting an output record per word, the mapping function is guaranteed to finish. The job scheduler can then inspect the size of the stored, emitted records to decide whether it needs to split up the list among different reduce jobs. As we've seen before, this is possible since reduce functions are written so they can be applied on partial results.

Let's return to our MongoDB based Java examples to illustrate the concept of MapReduce in practice. We will implement an aggregation query that returns the average number of pages per genre, but now taking into account that books can have more than one genre associated to them. The following code fragments set up a new database for us to use:

```
import org.bson.Document;
import com.mongodb.MongoClient;
import com.mongodb.client.MongoDatabase;
import java.util.ArrayList;
import java.util.List;
import java.util.Random;

import static java.util.Arrays.asList;
```

```
public class MongoDBAggregationExample {
    public static Random r = new Random();

  public static void main(String... args) {
    MongoClient mongoClient = new MongoClient();
    MongoDatabase db = mongoClient.getDatabase("test");

    setupDatabase(db);
    for (Document r: db.getCollection("books").find())
        System.out.println(r);

    mongoClient.close();
  }

  public static void setupDatabase(MongoDatabase db) {
    db.getCollection("books").deleteMany(new Document());

    String[] possibleGenres = new String[] {
                "drama", "thriller", "romance", "detective",
                "action", "educational", "humor", "fantasy" };

     for (int i = 0; i < 100; i++) {
          db.getCollection("books").insertOne(
                     new Document("_id", i)
                     .append("nrPages", r.nextInt(900) + 100)
                     .append("genres",
                        getRandom(asList(possibleGenres), r.nextInt(3) + 1)));
     }
  }

  public static List<String> getRandom(List<String> els, int number) {
    List<String> selected = new ArrayList<>();
    List<String> remaining = new ArrayList<>(els);
    for (int i = 0; i < number; i++) {
          int s = r.nextInt(remaining.size());
          selected.add(remaining.get(s));
          remaining.remove(s);
    }
    return selected;
  }
}
```

Running this code will set up a random books database and print out the following list of inserted items:

```
Document{{_id=0, nrPages=188, genres=[action, detective, romance]}}
Document{{_id=1, nrPages=976, genres=[romance, detective, humor]}}
Document{{_id=2, nrPages=652, genres=[thriller, fantasy, action]}}
Document{{_id=3, nrPages=590, genres=[fantasy]}}
Document{{_id=4, nrPages=703, genres=[educational, drama, thriller]}}
Document{{_id=5, nrPages=913, genres=[detective]}}
...
```

Let us now construct our aggregation query. If we performed this query manually, a basic solution would look as follows:

```
public static void reportAggregate(MongoDatabase db) {
	Map<String, List<Integer>> counts = new HashMap<>();
	for (Document r: db.getCollection("books").find()) {
		for (Object genre: r.get("genres", List.class)) {
			if (!counts.containsKey(genre.toString()))
				counts.put(genre.toString(), newArrayList<Integer>());
			counts.get(genre.toString()).add(r.getInteger("nrPages"));
		}
	}
	for (Entry<String, List<Integer>> entry: counts.entrySet()) {
		System.out.println(entry.getKey() + " --> AVG = " +
				sum(entry.getValue()) / (double) entry.getValue().size());
	}
}

private static int sum(List<Integer> value) {
	int sum = 0;
	for (int i: value) sum += i;
	return sum;
}
```

In the code fragment above, we loop through all books in the collection, iterate over its genres, and keep track of all page counts per genre in a hashmap structure. This code produces this result:

```
romance --> AVG = 497.39285714285717
drama --> AVG = 536.88
detective --> AVG = 597.1724137931035
humor --> AVG = 603.5357142857143
fantasy --> AVG = 540.0434782608696
educational --> AVG = 536.1739130434783
action --> AVG = 398.9032258064516
thriller --> AVG = 513.5862068965517
```

This code will scale badly once we are dealing with millions of books. If the list of genres is known beforehand, we can also optimize this query somewhat by performing the aggregation per genre directly in MongoDB itself:

```
public static void reportAggregate(MongoDatabase db) {
	String[] possibleGenres = new String[] {
			"drama", "thriller", "romance", "detective",
			"action", "educational", "humor", "fantasy" };

	for (String genre: possibleGenres) {
		AggregateIterable<Document> iterable =
			db.getCollection("books").aggregate(asList(
				new Document("$match", new Document("genres", genre)),
```

```
                    new Document("$group", new Document("_id", genre)
                        .append("average", new Document("$avg", "$nrPages")))));

                for (Document r: iterable) {
                    System.out.println(r);
                }
        }
}
```

which produces a similar output:

```
Document{{_id=drama, average=536.88}}
Document{{_id=thriller, average=513.5862068965517}}
Document{{_id=romance, average=497.39285714285717}}
Document{{_id=detective, average=597.1724137931035}}
Document{{_id=action, average=398.9032258064516}}
Document{{_id=educational, average=536.1739130434783}}
Document{{_id=humor, average=603.5357142857143}}
Document{{_id=fantasy, average=540.0434782608696}}
```

Assume we have millions of books in our database and we do not know the number of genres beforehand. First looping through all books to fetch all possible genres and then constructing a list of averages per genre would be very time-consuming, so it makes sense to rewrite our logic using a map–reduce approach.

In MongoDB, the map and reduce functions should be supplied using JavaScript code, and using the following prototypes. For map:

```
function() {
   // No arguments, use "this" to refer to the
   // local document item being processed
   emit(key, value);
}
```

and for reduce:

```
function(key, values) {
   return result;
}
```

Let's start with building the map function. We need to map each incoming document item to a number of key–value pairs. Because we want to create aggregate page counts per genre, our key will be the genre of an item, with its value being a pair composed of the current running average and the number of items used to create the average, similar to the example above:

```
function() {
      var nrPages = this.nrPages;
      this.genres.forEach(function(genre) {
            emit(genre, {average: nrPages, count: 1});
      });
}
```

The reduce function will then take a list of values and output a new, averaged result. Remember the two requirements of the reduce function as listed above: the reduce function should output the same structure as emitted by the map function, and the reduce function should continue to work even if called multiple times on partial results, as MongoDB will run this function as many times as necessary:

```
function(genre, values) {
      var s = 0;
      var newc = 0;
      values.forEach(function(curAvg) {
            s += curAvg.average * curAvg.count;
            newc += curAvg.count;
      });
      return {average: (s / newc), count: newc};
}
```

We can then implement these JavaScript functions in our Java code example as follows, by passing them as plain strings to the mapReduce() method:

```
public static void reportAggregate(MongoDatabase db) {
       String map = "function() {  " +
                    " var nrPages = this.nrPages; " +
                    " this.genres.forEach(function(genre) {  " +
                    " emit(genre, {average: nrPages, count: 1}); " +
                    " }); " +
                    "} ";
       String reduce = "function(genre, values) {  " +
                    " var s = 0; var newc = 0; " +
                    " values.forEach(function(curAvg) {  " +
                    " s += curAvg.average * curAvg.count; " +
                    " newc += curAvg.count; " +
                    " }); " +
                    " return {average: (s / newc), count: newc}; " +
                    "} ";
       MapReduceIterable<Document> result = db.getCollection("books")
            .mapReduce(map, reduce);
       for (Document r: result)
             System.out.println(r);
}
```

Running this code gives us the same result as before, now achieved in a map–reduce fashion:

```
Document{{_id=action, value=Document{{average=398.9032258064516, count=31.0}}}}
Document{{_id=detective, value=Document{{average=597.1724137931035, count=29.0}}}}
Document{{_id=drama, value=Document{{average=536.88, count=25.0}}}}
Document{{_id=educational, value=Document{{average=536.1739130434783, count=23.0}}}}
Document{{_id=fantasy, value=Document{{average=540.0434782608696, count=23.0}}}}
```

```
Document{{_id=humor, value=Document{{average=603.5357142857143, count=28.0}}}}
Document{{_id=romance, value=Document{{average=497.39285714285717, count=28.0}}}}
Document{{_id=thriller, value=Document{{average=513.5862068965517, count=29.0}}}}
```

### 11.3.4 SQL After All...

We have seen how map–reduce-based operations can help perform complex queries and aggregations in document stores, even though these document stores do not support relational structures directly.

Based on the map–reduce examples shown above, it becomes apparent that many traditional GROUP BY-style SQL queries are convertible to an equivalent map–reduce pipeline. That is the reason many Hadoop vendors and document store implementations express queries using an SQL interface (most often using a subset of the SQL language), offering users a more familiar way of working rather than requiring them to think in map–reduce logic.

Some document stores, such as Couchbase, also allow you to define foreign keys in document structures and to perform join operations directly in queries. This means that the following query is possible using Couchbase N1QL (Couchbase's SQL dialect):

```
SELECT books.title, books.genres, authors.name
FROM books
JOIN authors ON KEYS books.authorId
```

With this kind of functionality, one can wonder where traditional relational databases end and where the NoSQL way of thinking begins. This is exactly why the line between the two has become blurred over the years, and why we see vendors of relational databases catching up and implementing some of the interesting aspects that made NoSQL databases, and document stores especially, popular in the first place. These aspects include:

- focus on horizontal scalability and distributed querying;
- dropping schema requirements;
- support for nested data types or allowing to store JSON directly in tables;
- support for map–reduce operations;
- support for special data types, such as geospatial data.

This comes backed by a strong querying backend and SQL querying capabilities. For example, recent versions of the open-source PostgreSQL database allow you to execute the following statements:

```
CREATE TABLE books (data JSONB);
INSERT INTO books (data) VALUES
('
      {
      "title": "Beginners Guide to Everything",
      "genres": ["educational", "fantasy"],
      "price": 200,
      }
');
SELECT DISTINCT data->>'title' AS titles FROM books;
```

**Retention Questions**

- What is the difference between a tuple store and a key–value store in terms of data representation?
- What is the difference between a tuple store and a document store in terms of data representation?
- Which types of queries do typical document stores such as MongoDB provide? How are more complex queries handled?

In the first statement a new table is created (books) containing one field (data) of the type **JSONB** (the "B" stands for "binary"). The non-binary JSON data type stores an exact copy of the input text, which must be processed every time a query is run over this field. JSONB data, on the other hand, are stored in a decomposed binary format that makes it slightly slower to store (since the textual JSON representation must be converted to a binary format), but significantly faster to process in subsequent calls, as no reparsing is needed. Next, we can insert plain JSON objects using a normal INSERT statement. Finally, we can perform a SELECT query to select all distinct "title" fields (using the ->> syntax). In the background, PostgreSQL takes care of query optimization and planning.

## 11.4 Column-Oriented Databases

A **column-oriented DBMS** is a DBMS that stores data tables as sections of columns of data, rather than as rows of data as in most DBMS implementations. Such an approach has advantages in some areas, such as marketing analytics, business intelligence-focused systems, and clinical data systems (i.e., systems where aggregates are regularly computed over large numbers of similar data items). Columns with many null values, known as sparse data, can be dealt with more efficiently, without wasting storage capacity for the empty cells.

Note that being column oriented, rather than row oriented, is a decision that stands quite orthogonal to the type of data being stored. This means that relational databases can be both row and column oriented, and so can key–value or document stores. However, since the need for column-oriented data structures became apparent, along with the need for non-relational databases, column-oriented database systems are categorized as a form of NoSQL.

To illustrate the basic workings of a column-oriented database, imagine a database system containing these rows:

| Id | Genre | Title | Price | Audiobook price |
|---|---|---|---|---|
| 1 | fantasy | My first book | 20 | 30 |
| 2 | education | Beginners guide | 10 | null |
| 3 | education | SQL strikes back | 40 | null |
| 4 | fantasy | The rise of SQL | 10 | null |

A row-based system is designed to efficiently return data for an entire row, which matches the common use case in which users wish to retrieve information about a particular object or entity, such as a book with Id 3. By storing a row's data in a single block on the hard drive, along with related rows, the system can quickly retrieve rows.

**Connections**

See Chapters 12 and 13 for more information on indexing.

However, such systems are not efficient at performing operations that apply to the entire dataset, as opposed to a particular row. For example, if we want to find all records in our example with a price above 20, we would need to seek through each row to find the matching ones. Most database systems speed up such operations by means of database indexes.

For instance, we could define an index on price, which would be stored as an index mapping column values to a tuple of identifiers:

| Price value | Record identifiers |
|---|---|
| 10 | 2,4 |
| 20 | 1 |
| 40 | 3 |

By sorting the index, we can obtain huge time savings because we avoid scanning the whole dataset, using the index to retrieve only those rows that satisfy the query. However, maintaining an index also adds overhead, especially when new data enter the database. New data require the index to be updated in addition to the actual data objects.

In a column-oriented database, all values of a column are placed together on the disk, so our example table would be stored in this way:

```
Genre:             fantasy:1,4   education:2,3
Title:             My first...:1  Beginners...:2   SQL Strikes..:3   The rise...:4
Price:             20:1          10:2,4           40:3
Audiobook price:   30:1
```

In this way, one particular column matches the structure of a normal index in a row-based system – an iteration of possible values together with the record identifiers holding that value. However, the need for separate indexes disappears here, as the primary keys for each column are the data values themselves, mapping directly to record identifiers (i.e., genre "fantasy" maps to records 1 and 4). Operations such as "find all records with price equal to 10" can now be executed directly in a single operation. Other aggregation operations (sums, averages, etc.) over columns can be sped up in this manner as well.

Moreover, null values do not take up storage space anymore; only cells that contain an actual value are present in the storage scheme. The latter is illustrated in the example, where only a small minority of the books is available as an audiobook. Therefore, only very few cells in the column "Audiobook price" will have a non-null value. All these nulls are effectively "stored" in the row-oriented format, but not in the column-oriented version.

There are also disadvantages to this approach. To begin with, retrieving all attributes pertaining to a single entity becomes less efficient. It is also clear that joining operations will be slowed down considerably, because every column must now be scanned to find values belonging to a certain foreign record identifier rather than being able to immediately retrieve a particular record by its identifier directly. Many column-oriented databases, such as Google Big-Table, group commonly joined tables by defining "column groups," avoiding frequent time-intensive join operations.

**Retention Questions**

- What is a column-oriented database?
- Which advantages do column-oriented databases offer compared with row-based ones?

**Drill Down**

Other notable implementations of column stores include Cassandra, HBase, and Parquet. Parquet is a columnar storage format gaining traction in the data science community as an alternative format to CSV (comma separated value) or other row-oriented formats, as it greatly improves data science workflows, since these often include the need to perform dataset-wide aggregations (imagine for instance the calculation of a simple correlation metric between values from two columns). Data science workflows are mostly read, but not write, intensive.

## 11.5 Graph-Based Databases

Of all the categories of NoSQL databases, graph-based databases may become the most significant in the future. **Graph databases** apply graph theory to the storage of records. In computer science and maths, **graph theory** entails the study of graphs – mathematical structures used to model pairwise relations between objects. Graphs consist of **nodes** (or points, or vertices) and **edges** (or arcs, or lines) that connect nodes. Arcs can be uni- or bidirectional. In recent years, graph structures have become popular due to being capable of modeling social networks. For instance, Figure 11.9 depicts three nodes with edges representing a "follows"-relation as you'd find in a social network such as Twitter or Facebook.

Figure 11.9 shows that everyone follows Seppe, Seppe follows Bart, and Bart follows Wilfried. Graph structures are used in many areas of mathematics, computer science, data science, and operations research to solve a variety of problems, such as routing problems, network flow modeling, etc.

The reason why graph databases are an interesting category of NoSQL is because, contrary to the other approaches, they actually go the way of increased relational modeling, rather than doing away with relations. That is, one-to-one, one-to-many, and many-to-many structures can easily be modeled in a graph-based way. Consider books having many authors and vice versa. In an RDBMS, this would be modeled by three tables: one for books, one for authors, and one modeling the many-to-many relation. A query to return all book titles for books written by a particular author would then look as follows:

```
SELECT book.title
FROM book, author, books_authors
WHERE author.id = books_authors.author_id
  AND book.id = books_authors.book_id
  AND author.name = "Bart Baesens"
```

In a graph database, this structure would be represented as shown in Figure 11.10.

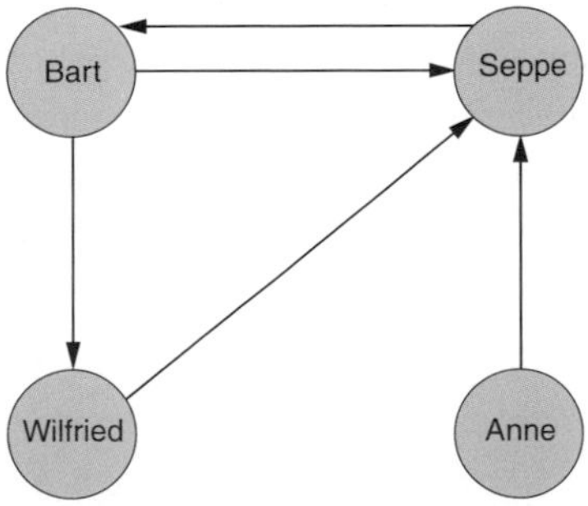


**Figure 11.9** A simple social network represented as a graph.

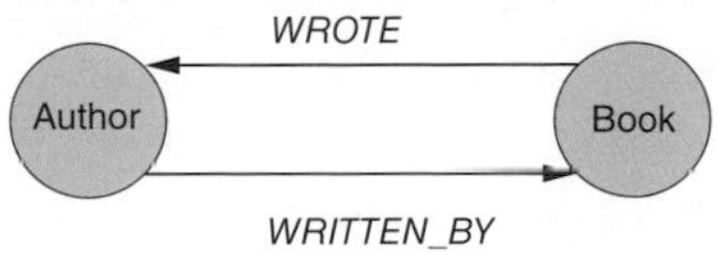


**Figure 11.10** Capturing the relations between an author and book.

The related query to fetch the desired list of books becomes more straightforward as well:

```
MATCH (b:Book)<-[ :WRITTEN_BY]-(a:Author)
WHERE a.name = "Bart Baesens"
RETURN b.title
```

**Drill Down**

Monsanto is an international agricultural company producing seeds. With the world population continuously growing and more land needed for housing, less farmland is left for feeding people. Hence, it is important to develop new crop species (e.g., corn) with improved yield that can feed more people given the limited land available. To this end, Monsanto invested in genomics to carefully unravel genetic traits of plants.

Before graph databases were available, Monsanto used a relational database to store its gene data, which consisted of 11 connected tables representing 900 million rows of data. One of the commonly used queries requested information about the entire tree of ancestors for a single plant. Solving this query using the relational database design resulted in massive, resource-intensive joins with long response times. To speed up these query times, Monsanto invested in graph databases which turned out to be a superior alternative to model and query genetic relationships between plants.

Here, we're using the **Cypher query language**, the graph-based query language introduced by Neo4j, one of the most popular graph databases.

**Drill Down**

Other notable implementations of graph databases include AllegroGraph, GraphDB, InfiniteGraph, and OrientDB. We'll continue to use Neo4j and Cypher in this section.

In a way, a graph database is a hyper-relational database, where JOIN tables are replaced by more interesting and semantically meaningful relationships that can be navigated (*graph traversal*) and/or queried, based on graph pattern matching. We will continue to use Neo4j to work out some examples and topics in the following subsections, starting with an overview of Cypher, Neo4j's query language. However, note that graph databases differ in terms of representation of the underlying graph data model. Neo4j, for instance, supports nodes and edges having a type (book) and a number of attributes (title), next to a unique identifier. Other systems are geared toward speed and scalability and only support a simple graph representation.

**Drill Down**

FlockDB, for instance, developed by Twitter, only supports storing a simplified directed graph as a list of edges having a source and destination identifier, a state (normal, removed, or archived), and an additional numeric "position" to help with sorting results. Twitter uses FlockDB to store social graphs (who follows whom, who blocks whom – refer back to Figure 11.9) containing billions of edges and sustaining hundreds of thousands of read queries per second. Obviously, graph database implementations position themselves regarding the tradeoff between speed and data expressiveness.

**Drill Down**

The online playground contains a Neo4j database for our book reading club. You can use the same queries as the ones in this chapter to follow along (see the Appendix for more details).

### 11.5.1 Cypher Overview

Like SQL, Cypher is a declarative, text-based query language, containing many similar operations to SQL. However, because it is geared toward expressing patterns found in graph structures, it contains a special MATCH clause to match those patterns using symbols that look like graph symbols as drawn on a whiteboard.

Nodes are represented by parentheses, symbolizing a circle:

```
()
```

Nodes can be labeled if they need to be referred to elsewhere, and be further filtered by their type, using a colon:

```
(b:Book)
```

Edges are drawn using either -- or -->, representing an undirected line or an arrow representing a directional relationship respectively. Relationships can also be filtered by putting square brackets in the middle:

```
(b:Book)<-[ :WRITTEN_BY]-(a:Author)
```

Let's look at some examples. This is a basic SQL SELECT query:

```
SELECT b.*
FROM books AS b;
```

It can be expressed in Cypher as follows:

```
MATCH (b:Book)
RETURN b;
```

Alternatively, OPTIONAL MATCH can be used and works just like MATCH does, except that if no matches are found, OPTIONAL MATCH will use a null for missing parts of the pattern.

ORDER BY and LIMIT statements can be included as well:

```
MATCH (b:Book)
RETURN b
ORDER BY b.price DESC
LIMIT 20;
```

WHERE clauses can be included explicitly, or as part of the MATCH clause:

```
MATCH (b:Book)
WHERE b.title = "Beginning Neo4j"
RETURN b;

MATCH (b:Book {title:"Beginning Neo4j"})
RETURN b;
```

JOIN clauses are expressed using direct relational matching. The following query returns a list of distinct customer names who purchased a book written by Wilfried Lemahieu, are older than 30, and paid in cash:

```
MATCH (c:Customer)-[ p:PURCHASED] ->(b:Book)<-[ :WRITTEN_BY]-(a:Author)
WHERE a.name = " Wilfried Lemahieu"
  AND c.age > 30
  AND p.type = "cash"
RETURN DISTINCT c.name;
```

**Connections**

For an overview on recursive queries and other extensions in SQL, see Chapter 9.

Where graph databases really start to shine is in tree-based structures. Imagine we have a tree of book genres, and books can be placed under any category level. Performing a query to fetch a list of all books in the category "Programming" and all its subcategories can become problematic in SQL, even with extensions that support recursive queries.

Yet, Cypher can express queries over hierarchies and transitive relationships of any depth simply by appending a star * after the relationship type and providing optional min/max limits in the MATCH clause:

```
MATCH (b:Book)-[:IN_GENRE]->(:Genre)
              -[:PARENT*0..]-(:Genre {name:"Programming"})
RETURN b.title;
```

All books in the category "Programming," but also in any possible subcategory, sub-subcategory, and so on, will be retrieved. The latter type of problem is often called the "friend-of-a-friend" problem.

## 11.5.2 Exploring a Social Graph

Here, we'll try to explore a social graph for a book-reading club, modeling genres, books, and readers in the structure shown in Figure 11.11.

We start by inserting some data using Cypher queries. You can do this using the Neo4j web console or using Neo4j's JDBC driver. Note that CREATE statements require you to specify a relation direction, but the actual direction (i.e., using -> or <-) does not matter in this example as we will query all relations as unidirectional ones later:

```
CREATE (Bart:Reader {name:'Bart Baesens', age:32})
CREATE (Seppe:Reader {name:'Seppe vanden Broucke', age:30})
CREATE (Wilfried:Reader {name:'Wilfried Lemahieu', age:40})
CREATE (Marc:Reader {name:'Marc Markus', age:25})
```

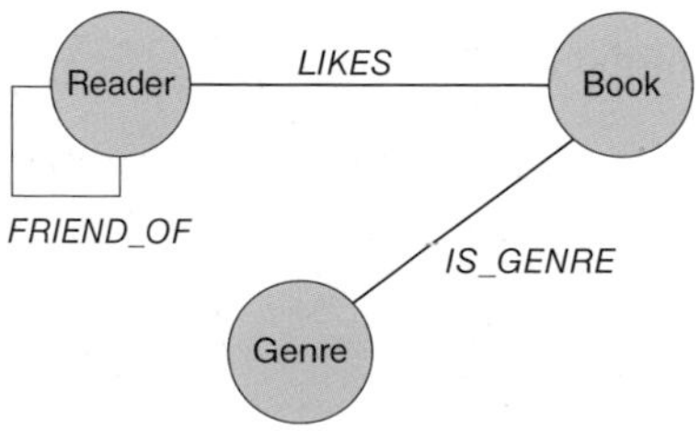


**Figure 11.11** Metadata structure of our social graph.

```
CREATE (Jenny:Reader { name:'Jenny Jennifers', age:26} )
CREATE (Anne:Reader { name:'Anne HatsAway', age:22} )
CREATE (Mike:Reader { name:'Mike Smith', age:18} )
CREATE (Robert:Reader { name:'Robert Bertoli', age:49} )
CREATE (Elvis:Reader { name:'Elvis Presley', age:76} )
CREATE (Sandra:Reader { name:'Sandra Mara', age:12} )

CREATE (Fantasy:Genre { name:'fantasy'} )
CREATE (Education:Genre { name:'education'} )
CREATE (Thriller:Genre { name:'thriller'} )
CREATE (Humor:Genre { name:'humor'} )
CREATE (Romance:Genre { name:'romance'} )
CREATE (Detective:Genre { name:'detective'} )

CREATE (b01:Book { title:'My First Book'} )
CREATE (b02:Book { title:'A Thriller Unleashed'} )
CREATE (b03:Book { title:'Database Management'} )
CREATE (b04:Book { title:'Laughs, Jokes, and More Jokes'} )
CREATE (b05:Book { title:'Where are my Keys?'} )
CREATE (b06:Book { title:'A Kiss too Far'} )
CREATE (b07:Book { title:'A Wizardly Story'} )
CREATE (b08:Book { title:'A Wizardly Story 2: Order of the SQL'} )
CREATE (b09:Book { title:'Laughing and Learning'} )
CREATE (b10:Book { title:'A Murder in Fantasyville'} )
CREATE (b11:Book { title:'Without you I am Nothing'} )
CREATE (b12:Book { title:'How to be Romantic: a Guide'} )
CREATE (b13:Book { title:'Why Boring is Good'} )
CREATE (b14:Book { title:'An Unsolved Problem for Detective Whiskers'} )
CREATE (b15:Book { title:'Mathematics for the Rest of Us'} )
CREATE (b16:Book { title:'The Final Book I ever Wrote'} )
CREATE (b17:Book { title:'Who Says Love is Outdated?'} )
CREATE (b18:Book { title:'A Chainsaw Massacre'} )

CREATE
 (b01)-[ :IS_GENRE] ->(Education),
 (b02)-[ :IS_GENRE] ->(Thriller),
 (b03)-[ :IS_GENRE] ->(Education),
 (b04)-[ :IS_GENRE] ->(Humor),
 (b05)-[ :IS_GENRE] ->(Humor), (b05)-[ :IS_GENRE] ->(Detective),
 (b06)-[ :IS_GENRE] ->(Humor), (b06)-[ :IS_GENRE] ->(Romance),
  (b06)-[ :IS_GENRE] ->(Thriller),
 (b07)-[ :IS_GENRE] ->(Fantasy),
 (b08)-[ :IS_GENRE] ->(Fantasy), (b08)-[ :IS_GENRE] ->(Education),
 (b09)-[ :IS_GENRE] ->(Humor), (b09)-[ :IS_GENRE] ->(Education),
 (b10)-[ :IS_GENRE] ->(Detective), (b10)-[ :IS_GENRE] ->(Thriller),
  (b10)-[ :IS_GENRE] ->(Fantasy),
 (b11)-[ :IS_GENRE] ->(Humor), (b11)-[ :IS_GENRE] ->(Romance),
```

```
  (b12)-[ :IS_GENRE]->(Education), (b12)-[ :IS_GENRE]->(Romance),
  (b13)-[ :IS_GENRE]->(Humor), (b13)-[ :IS_GENRE]->(Education),
  (b14)-[ :IS_GENRE]->(Humor), (b14)-[ :IS_GENRE]->(Detective),
  (b15)-[ :IS_GENRE]->(Education),
  (b16)-[ :IS_GENRE]->(Romance),
  (b17)-[ :IS_GENRE]->(Romance), (b17)-[ :IS_GENRE]->(Humor),
  (b18)-[ :IS_GENRE]->(Thriller)
CREATE
  (Bart)-[ :FRIEND_OF]->(Seppe),
  (Bart)-[ :FRIEND_OF]->(Wilfried),
  (Bart)-[ :FRIEND_OF]->(Jenny),
  (Bart)-[ :FRIEND_OF]->(Mike),
  (Seppe)-[ :FRIEND_OF]->(Wilfried),
  (Seppe)-[ :FRIEND_OF]->(Marc),
  (Seppe)-[ :FRIEND_OF]->(Robert),
  (Seppe)-[ :FRIEND_OF]->(Elvis),
  (Wilfried)-[ :FRIEND_OF]->(Anne),
  (Wilfried)-[ :FRIEND_OF]->(Mike),
  (Marc)-[ :FRIEND_OF]->(Mike),
  (Jenny)-[ :FRIEND_OF]->(Anne),
  (Jenny)-[ :FRIEND_OF]->(Sandra),
  (Anne)-[ :FRIEND_OF]->(Mike),
  (Anne)-[ :FRIEND_OF]->(Elvis),
  (Mike)-[ :FRIEND_OF]->(Elvis),
  (Robert)-[ :FRIEND_OF]->(Elvis),
  (Robert)-[ :FRIEND_OF]->(Sandra)
CREATE
  (Bart)-[ :LIKES]->(b01), (Bart)-[ :LIKES]->(b03),
  (Bart)-[ :LIKES]->(b05), (Bart)-[ :LIKES]->(b06),
  (Seppe)-[ :LIKES]->(b01), (Seppe)-[ :LIKES]->(b02),
  (Seppe)-[ :LIKES]->(b03), (Seppe)-[ :LIKES]->(b07),
  (Wilfried)-[ :LIKES]->(b01), (Wilfried)-[ :LIKES]->(b05),
  (Wilfried)-[ :LIKES]->(b06), (Wilfried)-[ :LIKES]->(b10),
  (Marc)-[ :LIKES]->(b03), (Marc)-[ :LIKES]->(b11),
  (Marc)-[ :LIKES]->(b13), (Marc)-[ :LIKES]->(b15),
  (Jenny)-[ :LIKES]->(b08), (Jenny)-[ :LIKES]->(b09),
  (Jenny)-[ :LIKES]->(b12), (Jenny)-[ :LIKES]->(b14),
  (Anne)-[ :LIKES]->(b14), (Anne)-[ :LIKES]->(b15),
  (Anne)-[ :LIKES]->(b17), (Anne)-[ :LIKES]->(b18),
  (Mike)-[ :LIKES]->(b05), (Mike)-[ :LIKES]->(b07),
  (Mike)-[ :LIKES]->(b11), (Mike)-[ :LIKES]->(b17),
  (Robert)-[ :LIKES]->(b04), (Robert)-[ :LIKES]->(b10),
  (Robert)-[ :LIKES]->(b12), (Robert)-[ :LIKES]->(b13),
  (Elvis)-[ :LIKES]->(b03), (Elvis)-[ :LIKES]->(b06),
  (Elvis)-[ :LIKES]->(b14), (Elvis)-[ :LIKES]->(b16),
```

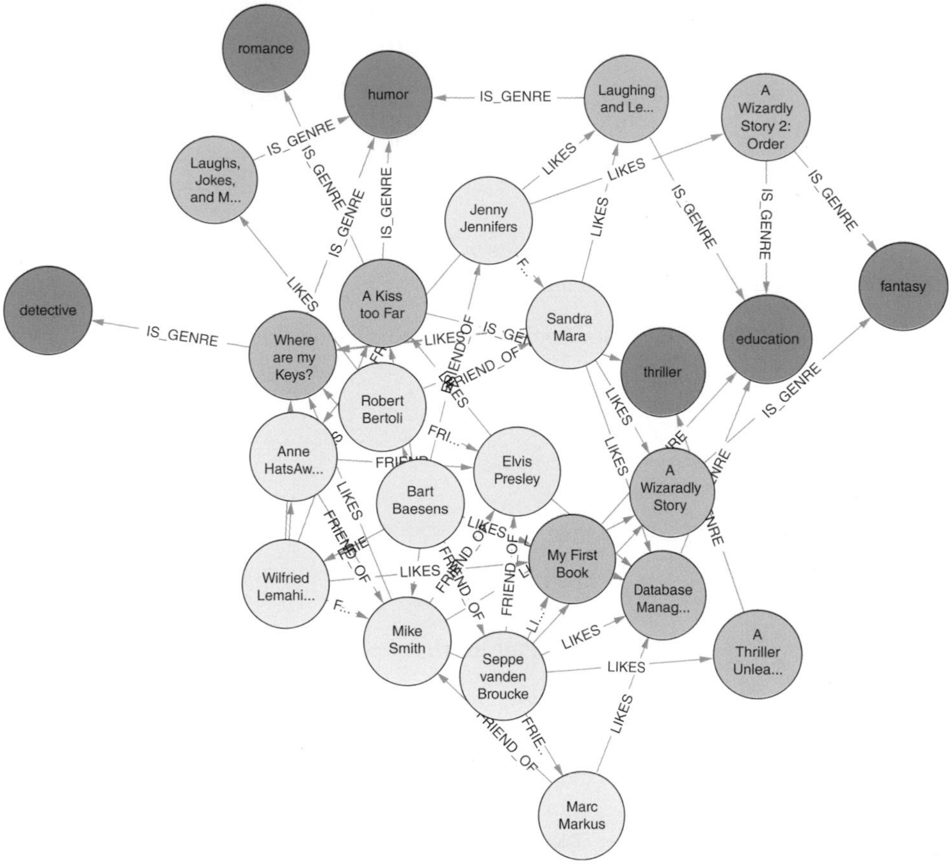


Figure 11.12 Our complete social graph.

```
(Sandra)-[ :LIKES]->(b03), (Sandra)-[ :LIKES]->(b05),
(Sandra)-[ :LIKES]->(b07), (Sandra)-[ :LIKES]->(b09)
```

Our complete social graph now looks as depicted in Figure 11.12.

Let us start now to answer queries. For instance: who likes romance books? Because there is only one type of relationship between each node type, we can drop the square brackets colon-selector. Note also the usage of --()-- to perform a non-directional query.

```
MATCH (r:Reader)--(:Book)--(:Genre {name:'romance'})
RETURN r.name
```

Returns:

```
Elvis Presley
Mike Smith
Anne HatsAway
Robert Bertoli
Jenny Jennifers
Marc Markus
```

```
Elvis Presley
Wilfried Lemahieu
Bart Baesens
```

Who are Bart's friends that liked humor books?

```
MATCH (me:Reader)--(friend:Reader)--(b:Book)--(g:Genre)
WHERE g.name = 'humor'
  AND me.name = 'Bart Baesens'
RETURN DISTINCT friend.name
```

Can you recommend humor books that Seppe's friends liked and Seppe has not liked yet?

```
MATCH (me:Reader)--(friend:Reader),
      (friend)--(b:Book),
      (b)--(genre:Genre)
WHERE NOT (me)--(b)
  AND me.name = 'Seppe vanden Broucke'
  AND genre.name = 'humor'
RETURN DISTINCT b.title
```

Get a list of people with books Bart liked, sorted by most liked books in common:

```
MATCH (me:Reader)--(b:Book),
      (me)--(friend:Reader)--(b)
WHERE me.name = 'Bart Baesens'
RETURN friend.name, count(*) AS common_likes
ORDER BY common_likes DESC
```

Note that we are applying an aggregation operator, "count". In Cypher, grouping for aggregation is implicit, meaning that as soon as you use an aggregation function, all non-aggregated columns (friend.name in the example above) will be used as grouping keys. Hence, the query returns:

```
friend.name           common_likes
Wilfried Lemahieu     3
Seppe vanden Broucke  2
Mike Smith            1
```

Now let's get a list of pairs of books having more than one genre in common. The following query:

```
MATCH (b1:Book)--(g:Genre)--(b2:Book)
WHERE common_genres > 1
RETURN b1.title, b2.title, count(*) AS common_genres
```

fails as "common_genres" in the WHERE clause is placed before its actual definition. To resolve this, we can use the WITH clause to put the definition upfront, as so:

```
MATCH (b1:Book)--(g:Genre)--(b2:Book)
WITH b1, b2, count(*) AS common_genres
WHERE common_genres > 1
RETURN b1.title, b2.title, common_genres
```

**Connections**

In the context of semantical representation, it is interesting to make the link to Chapter 10, where RDF (Resource Description Framework) and the SPARQL query language were discussed. As RDF models intrinsically represent a labeled, directed multi-graph, many graph databases natively support RDF statements and SPARQL as a query language. Neo4j plugins exist for SPARQL as well, though the vendor mainly continues to back Cypher as its primary query language.

**Retention Questions**

- What is a graph database? How does it represent data?
- Which query language does Neo4j use? In which ways does it differ from SQL?

Now let's say we'd like to retrieve pairs of books that have no genres in common. At first, this seems easy enough:

```
MATCH (b1:Book)--(g:Genre)--(b2:Book)
WITH b1, b2, count(*) AS common_genres
WHERE common_genres = 0
RETURN b1.title, b2.title, common_genres
```

However, this query will return zero results. This is not due to the fact that there are no pairs of books with no common genres, but rather since the MATCH clause will only select completely matching patterns. Since pairs of books that have no common genre in between will not have a "--(g:Genre)--" relationship by definition, the MATCH clause selects nothing at all, causing no rows to be returned. To resolve this issue, we can use the OPTIONAL MATCH, which will replace missing parts of a pattern with nulls, which we can then use in the WHERE clause.

```
MATCH (b1:Book), (b2:Book)
WITH b1, b2
OPTIONAL MATCH (b1)--(g:Genre)--(b2)
WHERE g IS NULL
RETURN b1.title, b2.title
```

Remember that different graph database implementations support different data models. Some graph databases will also allow end-users to impose schemas – for example, to constrain the types of edges that can occur between certain nodes (plugins to do so are available for Neo4j as well).

Though graph databases have not become as widely adopted as relational DBMSs by a long shot, it is interesting to note they have succeeded in various, niche application domains (e.g., Twitter using FlockDB to store its social graph). Likewise, graph databases are frequently applied in domains such as location-based services, where many topological entities and algorithms can be represented as, or work over, a graph, such as finding the shortest route among two locations. Graph databases are also applied to construct recommender systems (think of recommending books that your friends like), social media (suggest followers or find common friends), and knowledge-based systems to provide a semantical representation of resources and rules.

## 11.6 Other NoSQL Categories

Besides the main categories we have covered above, among which are key–value stores, tuple and document stores, column-oriented databases, and graph-based databases, several other, niche, NoSQL databases exist. In many cases, these are geared specifically toward storing and querying

**Connections**

See Chapter 8 for object-oriented databases and Chapter 10 for XML databases.

specialized types of data or structures. Two of these, XML and object-oriented databases, were discussed earlier.

Other types include:

- Database systems to deal with time series and streaming events, such as Event Store and Axibase. Such systems represent data as a series of immutable events over time, making it easier to support use cases such as event monitoring, complex event processing, or real-time analytics. Typically, availability and performance are of high concern for such systems.
- Database systems to store and query geospatial data, supporting geospatial operators following the DE-9IM model, which defines relations between polygons as them being equal, touching, disjoint, contained, covered, or intersecting. For example, you can express a "within radius" query as follows:

```
SELECT name, type, location,
  ST_Distance_Sphere(Point(-70, 40), location) AS distance_in_meters
FROM restaurants
WHERE type = "french cuisine"
ORDER BY distance_in_meters
LIMIT 10
```

- Database systems such as BayesDB, which lets users query the probable implication of their data (for example, to derive which fields in a table are the main predictors to estimate a certain outcome) and simulate what-if scenarios using a Bayesian query language, such as:

```
SIMULATE gdp -- simulate gross domestic product
FROM countries -- using table with information on countries
-- given the following:
GIVEN population_million = 1000, continent = 'asia'
LIMIT 10; -- run 10 simulations
```

**Retention Questions**

- Which NoSQL databases exist? List some niche NoSQL databases geared toward a particular context.

## Summary

This chapter has discussed NoSQL databases, a group of database management systems that have become quite popular throughout the past decade, and represents a shift in thinking toward schema-less structures, horizontal scalability, and non-relational data models and querying facilities.

We note, however, that the explosion of popularity of NoSQL data storage layers should be put into perspective, considering their limitations. Most NoSQL implementations have yet to prove their true worth in the field (most are very young and in development). Most implementations sacrifice ACID concerns in favor of being eventually consistent, and the lack of relational support makes expressing some queries or aggregations particularly difficult, with map–reduce interfaces being offered as a possible, but harder to learn and use, alternative.

Combined with the fact that RDBMSs do provide strong support for transactionality, durability, and manageability, quite a few early adopters of NoSQL were confronted with some sour lessons.

**Drill Down**

For some well-known examples of such "sour lessons", see the FreeBSD maintainers speaking out against MongoDB's lack of on-disk consistency support,[4] Digg struggling with the NoSQL Cassandra database after switching from MySQL,[5] and Twitter facing similar issues as well (which also ended up sticking with a MySQL cluster for a while longer),[6] or the fiasco of HealthCare.gov, where the IT team also went with a badly suited NoSQL database.[7]

It would be an over-simplification to reduce the choice between RDBMSs and NoSQL databases to a choice between consistency and integrity on the one hand, and scalability and flexibility on the other. The market of NoSQL systems is far too diverse for that. Still, this tradeoff will often come into play when deciding on taking the NoSQL route. We see many NoSQL vendors focusing again on robustness and durability. We also observe traditional RDBMS vendors implementing features that let you build schema-free, scalable data stores inside a traditional RDBMS, capable of storing nested, semi-structured documents, as this seems to remain the true selling point of most NoSQL databases, especially those in the document store category.

**Drill Down**

Some vendors have already adopted "NewSQL" as a term to describe modern relational database management systems that aim to blend the scalable performance and flexibility of NoSQL systems with the robustness guarantees of a traditional DBMS.

Expect the future trend to continue toward adoption of such "blended systems", except for use cases that require specialized, niche DBMSs. In these settings, the NoSQL movement has rightly taught users that the one-size-fits-all mentality of relational systems is no longer applicable and should be replaced by finding the right tool for the job. For instance, graph databases arise as being "hyper-relational" databases, which makes relations first-class citizens next to records themselves rather than doing away with them altogether. We've seen how such databases express complicated queries in a straightforward way, especially where one must deal with many, nested, or hierarchical relations between objects.

[4] www.ivoras.net/blog/tree/2009-11-05.a-short-time-with-mongodb.html.

[5] www.forbes.com/2010/09/21/cassandra-mysql-software-technology-cio-network-digg.html.

[6] https://techcrunch.com/2010/07/09/twitter-analytics-mysql.

[7] https://gigaom.com/2013/11/25/how-the-use-of-a-nosql-database-played-a-role-in-the-healthcare-gov-snafu.

## Comparison Box

| | Traditional SQL RDBMSs | NoSQL databases | Blended systems, "NewSQL" |
|---|---|---|---|
| **Relational** | Yes | No | Yes |
| **SQL** | Yes | No, though can come with own query languages | Yes |
| **Column stores** | No | Yes | Yes |
| **Scalability** | Limited | Yes | Yes |
| **Consistency model** | Strong | Eventually consistent, though some efforts to enforce stronger consistency | Strongly consistent for the most part |
| **BASE (Basically Available, Soft state, and Eventually consistent)** | No | Yes | No |
| **Handles large volumes of data** | No | Yes | Yes |
| **Schema-less** | No | Yes | No, though can store and query free-structured fields |

## Scenario Conclusion

After performing a thorough evaluation of NoSQL database systems, Sober's team decides to implement the following approach. First, the decision is made to continue using the RDBMS-based set-up at the core of its operations, as the database administrators show that the strong ACID approach, maturity, and data consistency enforcement of such systems cannot be bested by existing NoSQL systems. On the other hand, the mobile app development team is given the go-ahead to use MongoDB to handle the increased workload coming from mobile users. The document store will be used as an operational support system to handle incoming queries from many simultaneous users and to develop and prototype new experimental features. Finally, Sober plans to look at graph databases for more analytical purposes in the near future – for instance to identify users who frequently hail cabs together, or wish to go to similar destinations. The marketing team especially is interested in this approach to enrich their customer profiling activities.

## Key Terms

**BASE principle**
**CAP theorem**
**column-oriented DBMS**
**consistent hashing**
**Cypher**
**data redundancy**
**data replication**
**dissemination**
**document stores**
**edges**
**embedded documents**
**eventual consistency**

failure detection
graph-based databases
graph theory
hash function
horizontal scaling
JSONB
key–value stores
MapReduce
membership protocol
Memcached
nodes
redundancy
replicas
request coordinator
ring topology
shard
sharding
stabilization
tuple stores
vertical scaling
virtual nodes

## Review Questions

**11.1.** Which of the following statements describes NoSQL databases best?

a. A NoSQL database offers no support for SQL.
b. NoSQL databases do not support joins.
c. NoSQL databases are non-relational.
d. NoSQL databases are not capable of dealing with large datasets.

**11.2.** Which of the following is **not** an example of a NoSQL database?

a. Graph-based databases.
b. XML-based databases.
c. Document-based databases.
d. All three can be regarded as NoSQL databases.

**11.3.** Which of the following is **not** a property of a good hash function for use in key–value-based storage structures?

a. A hash function should always return the same output for the same input.
b. A hash function should return an output of fixed size.
c. A good hash function should map its inputs as evenly as possible over the output range.
d. Two hashes from two inputs that differ little should also differ as little as possible.

**11.4.** Which of the following is **correct**?

a. The fact that most NoSQL databases adopt an eventual consistency approach is due to the CAP theorem, which states that strong consistency cannot be obtained when availability and partitioning have to be ensured.
b. Replicas in a distributed NoSQL environment relate to making periodic backups of the database to a second system.
c. Stabilization relates to the waiting time between the start-up of a NoSQL system and when the system becomes available to receive user queries.
d. Some relational constructs, such as the many-to-many relationship, are harder to express using graph databases.

**11.5.** Which of the following is **correct**?

a. Document stores require users to define document schemas before data can be inserted.
b. Document stores require that you perform all filtering and aggregation logic in your application.

c. Document stores are built on the same ideas as key–value- and tuple-based database systems.
d. Document stores do not provide SQL-like capabilities.

**11.6.** When are column-oriented databases more efficient?

a. When many columns of a single group need to be fetched at the same time.
b. When inserts are performed where all of the row data are supplied at the same time.
c. When aggregates need to be calculated over many or all rows in the dataset.
d. When a lot of joins need to be performed in queries.

**11.7.** Which of the following statements is **not correct**?

a. Graphs are mathematical structures consisting of nodes and edges.
b. Graph models are not capable of modeling many-to-many relationships.
c. Edges in graphs can be uni- or bidirectional.
d. Graph databases work particularly well on tree-like structures.

**11.8.** What does the following Cypher query express?

```
OPTIONAL MATCH (user:User)-[ :FRIENDS_WITH]-(friend:User)
WHERE user.name = "Bart Baesens"
RETURN user, count(friend) AS NumberOfFriends
```

a. Get the node for Bart Baesens and a count of all his friends, but only if at least one FRIENDS_WITH relation exists.
b. Get the node for Bart Baesens and a count of all his friends, even if no FRIENDS_WITH relation exists.
c. This query will fail if Bart Baesens is FRIENDS_WITH himself.
d. Get the node for Bart Baesens and all his friends.

**11.9.** Using Cypher, how do you get a list of all movies Wilfried Lemahieu has liked, when he has given at least four stars?

a.
```
SELECT (b:User)--(m:Movie)
WHERE b.name = "Wilfried Lemahieu"
AND m.stars >= 4
```

b.
```
MATCH (b:User)-[ l:LIKES]-(m:Movie)
WHERE b.name = "Wilfried Lemahieu"
AND m.stars >= 4
RETURN m
```

c.
```
MATCH (b:User)-[ l:LIKES]-(m:Movie)
WHERE b.name = "Wilfried Lemahieu"
AND l.stars >= 4
RETURN m
```

d.
```
MATCH (b:User)--(m:Movie)
WHERE b.name = "Wilfried Lemahieu"
AND l.stars >= 4
RETURN m
```

**11.10.** What does the following Cypher query express?

```
MATCH (bart:User {name:'Bart'})-[ :KNOWS*2]->(f)
WHERE NOT((bart)-[ :KNOWS]->(f))
RETURN f
```

a. Return all of Bart's friends, and their friends as well.
b. Do not return Bart's friends, but return their friends.
c. Do not return Bart's friends, but return their friends if Bart does not know them.
d. Return Bart's friends who have exactly one other friend.

## Problems and Exercises

11.1E Write map and reduce functions to perform an aggregation with a MAX function, instead of the AVG and SUM examples we have discussed in this chapter.

11.2E Assume you have a list of people and people they are following on Twitter:

```
Seppe -> Bart Wilfried An
Bart -> Wilfried Jenny An
Wilfried -> Bart An
Jenny -> Bart An Seppe
An -> Jenny Wilfried Seppe
```

Write a map–reduce pipeline that outputs a list of commonly followed people per pair of people. E.g.: (Wilfried, Seppe) -> (Bart, An).

11.3E Using the Neo4j book club database in this chapter, can you do the following using Cypher queries?

- Find a list of books no-one likes.
- Find all pairs of people that have no liked books in common.
- Find the genre with the most liked books.
- Find the person who has the most likes in common with a given, other person.

11.4E One newer and promising NoSQL database is VoltDB, as it tries to combine the best aspects of RDBMSs and the NoSQL movement. Its documentation states the following:

> As a fully ACID, distributed SQL database, VoltDB must either commit or rollback 100% of all transactions. There can be no partial applications, which means the changes made by all SQL statements must be complete and visible at all live replicas, or none of the changes can be visible. A transaction commits once VoltDB confirms it has successfully completed at all replicas of all involved partitions. Once a transaction is confirmed at all replicas, VoltDB sends a confirmation message to the calling client.
> VoltDB must confirm transactions that have completed at all replicas for a given partition. If a given partition is unable to confirm it completed a transaction within a user-specified time, VoltDB's cluster membership consensus kicks in and one or more nodes are removed from the cluster. The result is that all replicas move in lockstep. They do the same transactions, in the same order, as fast as they can. If they fall out of lockstep they are actively ejected from the cluster. Note this is different from systems that require a quorum of replicas to do a write. There are benefits and tradeoffs to the VoltDB approach that are intentional.

Link this explanation to concepts we have discussed in this chapter. How does VoltDB achieve transaction consistency? Why might the "lockstep" approach of VoltDB be better than the "quorum"-based approach?

11.5E Apart from using a map–reduce pipeline to write complex queries in MongoDB, it also provides an "aggregate" command through which you can define an aggregation pipeline consisting of several stages (filtering, limiting, grouping, and sorting), as we've discussed in the chapter. Would it be possible to write the following query:

```
SELECT genre, SUM(nrPages) FROM books
GROUP BY genre
ORDER BY genre
```

also as an "aggregate" command instead of using a map–reduce pipeline? For which types of queries would aggregation become harder in MongoDB?

11.6E A fun programming exercise is to implement a basic gossip membership protocol. You can even simulate this locally in one program, so you don't have to run it over a network of computers. Remember that the basic idea of gossip-based dissemination involves periodic, pairwise communication, with the information exchanged in such interaction being bounded. When two nodes interact, the state of the node (i.e., the node's current view on the network) being most out of date will be updated to reflect the state of the other party. Try to implement a very basic version of such gossip protocol in any programming language (adding a visualization is even better).

# Part III

# Physical Data Storage, Transaction Management, and Database Access

# 12 Physical File Organization and Indexing

## Chapter Objectives

In this chapter, you will learn to:

- grasp the basic principles of storage hardware and physical database design;
- understand how data items can be organized into stored records;
- identify various methods for primary and secondary file organization;

**Opening Scenario**

Now that Sober has its relational logical data model from Chapter 6 ready, it wants to understand how it can be physically implemented. The company is also wondering whether there exist any physical means to speed up the response times of frequently used queries.

This chapter focuses on the most important principles pertaining to the physical organization of records and files. As such, it can be considered as the prerequisite to Chapter 13, which applies these principles in the context of physical database organization. In this way Chapters 12 and 13 are complementary in covering all facets of physical database design – the translation of a logical data model into an internal data model, including the design of indexes to speed up data access.

First, we present some overall properties of *storage devices* and the impact of the mechanicals of hard disk drives on the performance aspects of data retrieval. After that, we overview the mapping of logical modeling constructs onto physical concepts, and thus of the logical data model onto the internal model. Then, we briefly discuss *record organization*, covering the different alternatives to organize physical data records, consisting of individual data fields. After that comes the main body of this chapter, focusing on *file organization* and covering methods to organize records into physical files, as well as techniques to efficiently search for records with certain characteristics. We discuss several approaches, such as sequential files, hashing and the use of different index types, including $B^+$-trees. Chapter 13 follows on from this chapter, applying the insights gained from the file organization section to the particular context of *physical database organization*.

## 12.1 Storage Hardware and Physical Database Design

Physical database design pertains to the design of an internal data model and to the way in which the logical database concepts discussed in the previous chapters are realized

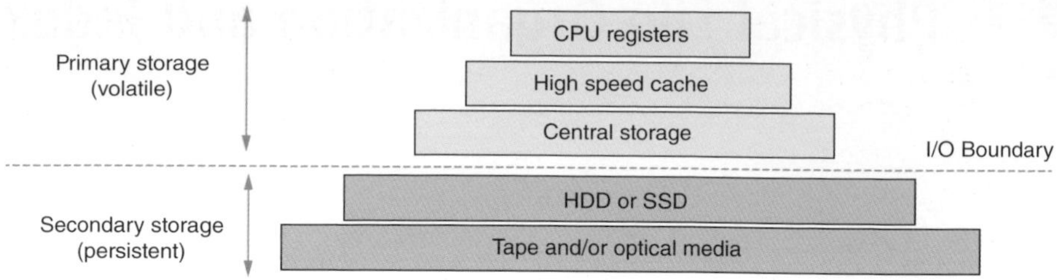


**Figure 12.1** The storage hierarchy.

physically as stored records, physical files, and, ultimately, a physical database. In this chapter, we assume a relational database setting unless noted otherwise, although most concepts apply to other database types as well.[1]

> **Connections**
>
> Chapter 6 discusses the basic concepts of the relational model.

### 12.1.1 The Storage Hierarchy

Before discussing the actual database files, we briefly focus on the storage devices on which these files reside. This section deals with the individual storage device, and we come back to storage hardware in the next chapter when we discuss storage device pooling and the overall architecture of enterprise storage subsystems.

A computer system's memory can be looked upon as a hierarchy (Figure 12.1), with high-speed memory that is very expensive and limited in capacity at the top, and slower memory that is relatively cheap and much larger in size at the bottom. The top of the hierarchy is the central processing unit (CPU) with its registers, in which the mathematical and logical processor operations are executed. Most often, some high-speed cache memory is physically integrated with the CPU and/or with the motherboard that contains the CPU. Cache memory operates at nearly the same speed as the CPU. Below that, we have **central storage**, which is also referred to as internal memory or main memory. It consists of memory chips (also called random access memory, or RAM), of which the performance is expressed in nanoseconds. Each individual byte in central storage has its own address and is directly referable by the operating system. The entirety of the memory described so far is called **primary storage**. This type of memory is considered **volatile memory**, which means its content is cleared when the power is turned off. Volatile memory certainly has its role in a database system, as it contains the database buffer as well as the runtime code of the applications and DBMS. However, the memory we will focus on in this chapter is **secondary storage**, which consists of **persistent storage media**, retaining its content even without being powered. The physical database files reside in secondary storage. The most important secondary storage device is still the hard disk drive (HDD), although solid state drives (SSD) based on flash memory are catching up quickly.

> **Connections**
>
> Chapter 2 elaborates on the architecture of a DBMS and also includes a discussion on the database buffer.

[1] Some very specific aspects regarding physical database organization, which are particular to a certain type of DBMS, are dealt with in the chapter discussing that DBMS type (e.g., physical aspects of NoSQL databases).

Primary and secondary storage are divided by what's known as the **I/O boundary**. This means that all memory above this boundary, although slower than the CPU, still operates at speeds that make it efficient for the CPU to "wait" until data are retrieved from primary storage. In comparison, secondary storage is much slower. The speed of HDDs and SSDs is typically expressed in milliseconds. It is not efficient for the CPU to wait until the interaction with secondary storage is completed. Rather, the CPU will switch to another task or thread until the requested data are copied from secondary storage to primary storage or until data that were manipulated in primary storage become persistent in secondary storage. The exchange of data between secondary storage and primary storage is called **I/O** (input/output) and is supervised by the operating system.[2] The operating system signals when the I/O task is completed, such that the CPU can continue processing the data.

Still lower in the hierarchy, we have even slower storage technology such as optical drives (e.g., rewritable DVD or Blu-ray) and tape, which mainly serve as media for backup and archiving, rather than being considered a directly accessible layer in the storage hierarchy.

In what follows, and unless noted otherwise, we assume a HDD as the storage medium for the physical database. Given their capacity and cost, hard disks are still the preferred medium for most database settings for the time being. Still, in-memory database technology, directly exploiting central storage for database purposes, is gaining momentum for particular high-performance applications. Hybrid solutions exist as well, caching part of the physical database in RAM for higher performance, as is the case with, e.g., the Memcached NoSQL database discussed in Chapter 11. Moreover, flash memory can be expected to take over from hard disk technology in the not too distant future, but at present the supported capacity is still limited in comparison to hard disk storage.

We'll now look at the internals of an HDD, as its physical concepts impact the way in which we deal with file organization and physical database design. That being said, much of the discussion in this chapter is applicable to SSDs, and sometimes in-memory databases, as well.

### 12.1.2 Internals of Hard Disk Drives

Hard disk drives store their data on circular platters, which are covered with magnetic particles (Figure 12.2). A HDD also contains a **hard disk controller**, which is circuitry that oversees the drive's functioning and that interfaces between the disk drive and the rest of the system.

Reading from and writing to hard disks comes down to magnetizing and demagnetizing the spots on these platters to store binary data. HDDs are **directly accessible storage devices (DASDs)**, which means that every location on a platter should be individually addressable and directly reachable to access its content.[3] Since a platter is two-dimensional, movement in two dimensions should be supported by the HDD's mechanicals. The first dimension of movement is disk rotation. For that purpose, the platters, or sometimes only a single platter, are secured on a **spindle**, which rotates at a constant speed. Movement in a second dimension is realized by positioning the **read/write heads** on arms, which are fixed to an **actuator**. There is a set of read/write heads for each

[2] To this end, the operating system implements a *file system* that keeps track of which file (fragment) is positioned where on the storage devices. However, as we discuss in the next chapter, high-performance DBMSs often bypass the operating system's file system, directly accessing and managing the data on the storage devices.

[3] This is in contrast to tape storage, which is only sequentially accessible (SASD: sequentially accessible storage device); the entire tape has to be read until the section containing the required data is reached.

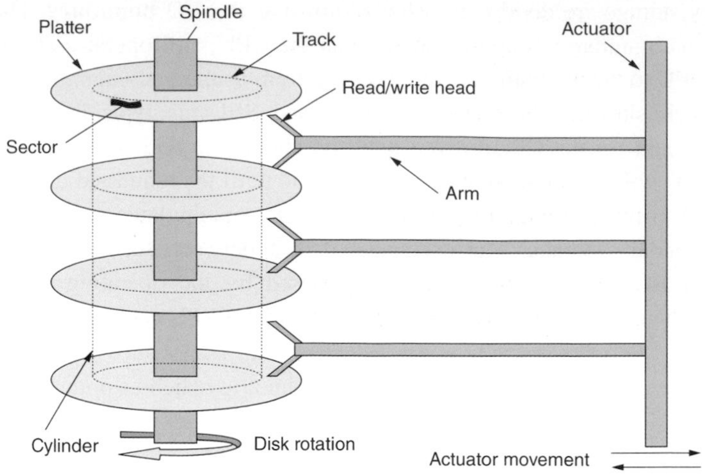


**Figure 12.2** Internals of a hard disk drive.

writable platter surface. The actuator, along with the arms and the read/write heads, can be moved toward or away from the center of the disks. By combining disk rotation with actuator movement, each individual section of the disk is directly reachable.

The magnetic particles on the platters are organized in concentric circular **tracks**, with each track consisting of individual **sectors**. The sector is the smallest addressable unit on a HDD. Traditionally, the standard sector size was 512 bytes, but many more recent HDDs have sector sizes of up to 4096 bytes. Also, for reasons of efficiency, it often occurs that the operating system or the HDD itself does not directly address individual sectors, but rather addresses so-called **disk blocks** (aka *clusters*, *pages*, or *allocation units*), which consist of two or more physically adjacent sectors. By addressing disk blocks encompassing multiple sectors, the number of required addresses and the amount of overhead can be reduced. In what follows, we make abstraction from these distinctions and always use the generic term *disk block*, or *block* for short, to refer to an addressable unit of hard disk storage capacity, consisting of one or more adjacent physical sectors.

When organizing physical files on disk blocks and tracks, it is important to keep the mechanicals of the movement in a HDD in mind. Indeed, reading from a block, or writing to a block, identified by its block address comes down to the following. First, the actuator needs to be moved in such a way that the read/write heads are positioned above the track that contains the desired block. The time necessary to position the actuator is called the **seek time**. All sectors on the same track of a platter can then be read without additional seeks. Moreover, since all read/write heads are positioned on arms above one another, all tracks at the same distance from the center on the respective platter surfaces can be read without additional seeks. Such a set of tracks, with the same diameter, is called a **cylinder**. Once the heads are positioned appropriately, one must wait until the desired sector has rotated under the read/write head of that platter surface. The time required for that is called the **rotational delay** or **latency**. Finally, the data can be read or written. The **transfer time** depends on the block size, the density of the magnetic particles and the rotation speed of the disks.

The response time to retrieve a disk block from a disk drive can be summarized as follows:

- response time = service time + queuing time;
- service time = seek time + rotational delay + transfer time.

We will not discuss the queuing time at this point; it pertains to the waiting time until the device is actually free from other jobs, and depends upon task scheduling, system workload, and facilities for parallelism. Some of these aspects are tackled in the next chapter and in later chapters. The transfer time itself is typically fixed and depends on the hardware properties of the disk drive. Still, physical file organization can be optimized in such a way that the expected seek time and, to a lesser extent, rotational delay are minimized and this may have a considerable impact on overall performance of a database system. For that reason, we discriminate between the expected service time for random block accesses ($T_{rba}$) and the expected service time for sequential block accesses ($T_{sba}$). $T_{rba}$ refers to the expected time to retrieve or write a disk block independently of the previous read/write. $T_{sba}$ denotes the expected time to sequentially retrieve a disk block with the read/write head already in the appropriate position from a previous read/write to a physically adjacent disk block:

- $T_{rba} = \text{Seek} + \text{ROT}/2 + \text{BS}/\text{TR}$
- $T_{sba} = \text{ROT}/2 + \text{BS}/\text{TR}$

$T_{rba}$ is equal to the sum of the expected seek time, the rotational delay, and the transfer time. The seek time depends upon the number of cylinders to be traversed. Hard disk manufacturers tend to provide an average value – "average seek time" – expressed in milliseconds in their descriptions of a drive model. The expected rotational delay is calculated as one-half of the time required for a full disk rotation (ROT), also expressed in milliseconds. If the manufacturer provides the rotation speed of the drive in rotations per minute (RPM), then ROT (in milliseconds) = $(60 \times 1000)/\text{RPM}$. The last term in the above equation represents the transfer time, which is equal to the block size (BS) divided by the transfer rate TR. The transfer rate is expressed in megabytes per second (MBps) or mega*bits* per second (Mbps). For $T_{sba}$, the expression is similar, with omission of the seek term.

For example, for a HDD with the following characteristics:

Average seek time: 8.9 ms
Spindle speed: 7200 rpm
Transfer rate: 150 MBps
Block size: 4096 bytes

we have the following results:

- $T_{rba} = 8.9\text{ ms} + 4.167\text{ ms} + 0.026\text{ ms} = 13.093\text{ ms}$
- $T_{sba} = 4.167\text{ ms} + 0.026\text{ ms} = 4.193\text{ ms}$

From this example, it is recommended to organize physical files onto tracks and cylinders in a way that seeks and, to a lesser extent, rotational delay are minimized as much as possible. This objective is a leading theme throughout most of this and the next chapter.

**Drill Down**

Solid state drives (SSDs) are based on integrated circuitry (most often flash memory), rather than on magnetic disk technology. Unlike HDDs, SSDs have no moving mechanical components and therefore have lower access times than HDDs and are, in several aspects, more robust. In particular, read performance of SSDs is much better than with HDDs. On the other hand, most elements mentioned with respect to HDDs also apply to SSDs: SSDs are accessible through the same controller types and I/O commands as traditional HDDs. The concepts of file system, blocks, sequential block access, and random block access apply as well.

One problem of SSDs (especially in the early days) is that their blocks can only sustain a limited number of writes before they go bad, whereas most HDDs fail due to mechanical failure, not blocks going bad. This has some implications for physical data management in the sense that the DBMS or operating system will make sure not to overwrite the same sector too many times. Modern SSDs will include firmware which transparently organizes data to protect the drive, so this is less of an issue when using newer drives. This technique is called wear leveling. Therefore, whereas a file that is updated on a HDD will generally be rewritten into its original location, a new version of a file on an SSD will typically be written to a different location.

Some SSDs are not based on persistent flash memory, but on volatile DRAM (dynamic random access memory) circuitry. Such SSDs are characterized by even faster access times. However, in contrast to flash memory, DRAM does not retain its content in the case of a power outage. Therefore, DRAM-based SSDs are typically equipped with an internal battery or external power supply, which lasts long enough to persist its content into a backup storage facility in case of power failure. Finally, hybrid drives exist as well, combining SSD and HDD technology in a single unit, using the SSD as a cache for the most frequently accessed data.

### 12.1.3 From Logical Concepts to Physical Constructs

The main focus of this and the next chapter is on how a database is realized as a set of physical files and other constructs. The purpose is mostly to optimize update and retrieval efficiency by minimizing the number of required block accesses, especially random block accesses. An optimal tradeoff is pursued between efficient update/retrieval and efficient use of storage space. The main focus is on the physical organization of *structured* data, by translating logical structures into physical ones. Chapter 18, dealing with data integration, also discusses the indexing and searching of unstructured data.

Physical database design comes down to the translation of a logical data model into an internal data model, also called the physical data model. This translation takes the physical properties of the storage media into account, as well as the statistical properties of the data and the types of operations (search, insert, update, delete) that are executed on them. The internal data model should provide adequate support for the most frequent and/or most time-critical operations. Figure 12.3 recapitulates the three-layer database architecture and the position of the internal data model in it. As discussed in Chapter 1, this approach guarantees physical data independence.

**Connections**

Chapter 1 discusses the three-layer database architecture, logical, and physical data independence.

The logical data model does not contain any concrete implementation-related specifications, but it does make an assumption about the actual type of DBMS used to implement the model physically. As already stated, we focus on a relational database setting although most aspects in the discussion on physical record and file organization are applicable to other DBMS types as well.

If we position the logical data model next to the internal data model, we can compare the corresponding concepts in each of them, which are to be translated from logical into physical structures. We use both the "generic" terminology of a logical data model and the more specific terminology of a relational model. In general, a logical model defines entity records, or just records for short, as instances of entity record types (or record types for short). A record is described by its

**Table 12.1** Logical and internal data model concepts

| Logical data model (general terminology) | Logical data model (relational setting) | Internal data model |
|---|---|---|
| Attribute type and attribute | Column name and (cell) value | Data item or field |
| (Entity) record | Row or tuple | Stored record |
| (Entity) record type | Table or relation | Physical file or dataset |
| Set of (entity) record types | Set of tables or relations | Physical database or stored database |
| Logical data structures | Foreign keys | Physical storage structures |

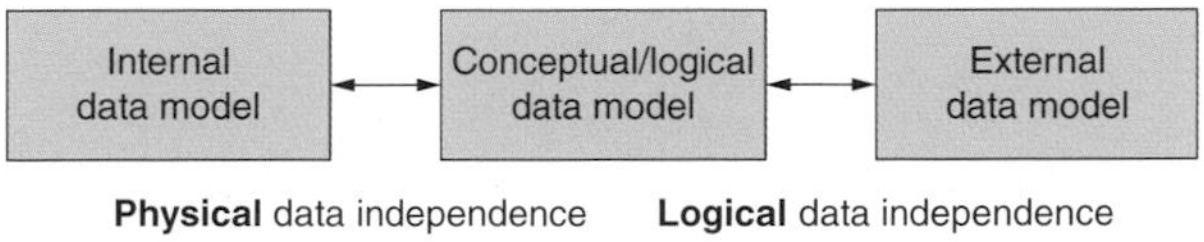


**Figure 12.3** Position of the internal data model.

attributes. In a relational setting, we speak of a logical database as a set of tables or relations. A table consists of rows or tuples, which contain values (aka cell values, as they represent values to the individual cells in a relational table), described by the corresponding column names (see Chapter 6). The internal data model denotes how the former concepts can be realized physically on storage media and also defines physical structures that allow for these concepts to be accessed in an efficient way.

**Connections**

Chapter 6 discusses the basic concepts of the relational model.

The corresponding physical concepts are represented in Table 12.1. A **data item** (also called field) is a collection of bits or characters that represents a specific value on a physical storage medium. A **stored record** is a collection of data items that pertain to the same real-world entity and that represent all attributes of this entity. In this way, it is the physical representation of a tuple in a relational table. A **physical file** (also called *dataset*) is a collection of stored records that represent similar real-world entities, such as students, wines, or purchase orders. It implements a relational table or, in general, all instances of a logical record type. In most cases, all records in a physical file have a similar structure and contain data items that represent the same set of attribute types. On some occasions, it may be required to combine stored records representing different real-world concepts into a single file. In that case, the records in the file may be different in structure and attribute types and we speak of a **mixed file**. Moreover, physical files may contain additional structures, such as indexes and pointers (see Section 12.3.5) to efficiently search and/or update the file and its contents.

Finally, a **physical database** (also called *stored database*) is an integrated collection of stored files. In this way, it contains data items and stored records describing different kinds of real-world entities (e.g., suppliers and purchase orders) as well as their interrelationships (e.g., the fact that a particular purchase order is placed with a particular supplier). The logical structures that model the relationships between record types, such as the foreign keys in a relational model, also yield a physical representation. A stored database contains physical storage structures to represent these logical interrelations, as well as to support the efficient retrieval and manipulation of stored records according to these interrelations (e.g., to execute a join query in a relational setting).

To conclude this discussion, we present the example of a simple conceptual data model, which is translated into a relational logical data model and, ultimately, into an internal data model

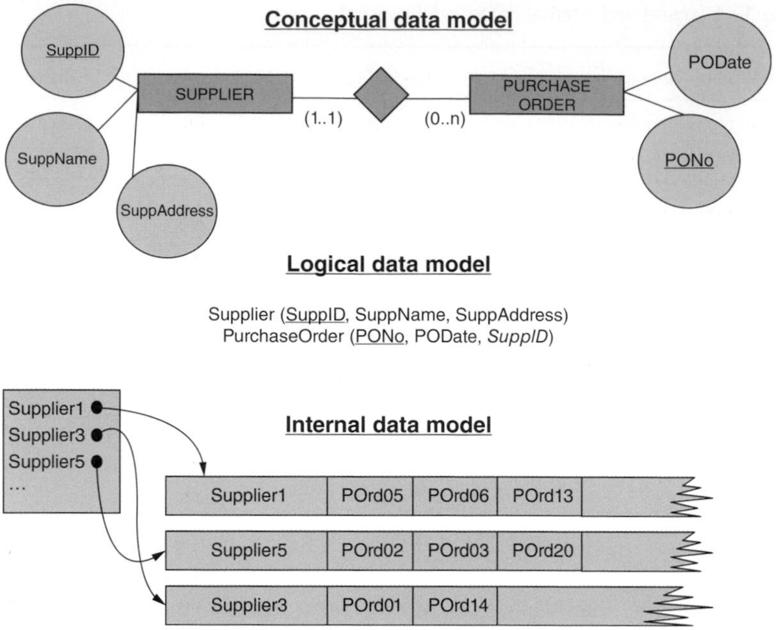


**Figure 12.4** Example of conceptual, logical, and internal data model.

(Figure 12.4). The relationship type between a supplier and his/her corresponding purchase orders is represented by means of a foreign key in the relational data model. In the internal data model, it is implemented by storing a supplier record physically adjacent to its purchase order records. If supplier records and the corresponding purchase orders are often retrieved together, this contiguous organization is beneficial, as they can be retrieved with a consecution of sequential block accesses, thus avoiding more inefficient random block accesses. In addition, a separate index is provided, which allows one to efficiently look up the supplier in question. The latter refers to the suppliers not by means of physical contiguousness, but by means of *pointers*.

It is important to note that Figure 12.4 provides just one possible way of physically realizing the logical data model. Depending on the storage device and the statistical properties of the data and queries (number of tuples, average number of purchase orders per supplier, most frequently executed query types, etc.) other physical models may be more appropriate. For example, if purchase orders are only rarely retrieved according to the supplier, but mostly according to the PODate, an index over the POdate is more appropriate. Moreover, at all levels (stored record, physical file and physical database) either direct physical contiguity or the indirection of pointers can be used to relate constructs (data items, stored record, index entries, etc.) to one another.

In the rest of this chapter we discuss the different possible approaches. We start with a brief overview of some elements of physical record organization, such as the way in which data items are organized into stored records. Then, we deal with file organization and indexing, including the organization of stored records into physical files. In the next chapter we focus on physical

### Retention Questions

- What is meant by storage hierarchy?
- Discuss the basic functioning of a hard drive.
- Discuss how the following logical data model concepts can be mapped to physical data model concepts in a relational setting: attribute type and attribute; (entity) record; (entity) record type; set of (entity) record types; logical data structures. Illustrate with examples.

database organization, with an emphasis on how physical storage structures can enhance the efficiency of querying data in a single table, as well as across tables, by means of a join query.

## 12.2 Record Organization

**Connections**

Chapter 6 discusses the various data types in a relational database setting. Chapter 9 reviews the BLOB and CLOB data types.

*Record organization* refers to the organization of data items into stored records. Each data item embodies an attribute of a particular real-world entity that is represented by the stored record. The physical implementation of the data item is a series of bits; the actual format depends on the attribute's data type. Typical data types in a relational database setting were discussed in Chapter 6. They include numeric data types (e.g., integer and float), character strings of variable or fixed length (e.g., character or varchar), date and time-related data types (e.g., date, time, timestamp), and the Boolean data type to represent truth values. In many cases, the data types BLOB and CLOB are also supported in order to capture large chunks of binary data and text data respectively (see Chapter 9). We only briefly highlight some aspects pertaining to organizing data items into stored records, as a database administrator typically has only limited impact on how this is realized in a particular DBMS. We focus on the following techniques: *relative location*, *embedded identification*, and the use of *pointers and lists*.

The simplest, and most widespread, technique for record organization is **relative location**. Here, only the attributes are stored. The data items that represent the attributes of the same entity are stored on physically adjacent addresses. The corresponding attribute types are not stored with them; they are determined implicitly by the relative ordering in which the data items occur, based on metadata about record structure in the catalog.[4] In this way, each data item can be identified by its relative location. This is the simplest and most efficient approach in terms of storage space. Figure 12.5 shows a partial relational table definition and the corresponding record structure.

While relative location is the most common approach, it becomes somewhat problematic if the record structure is highly irregular (e.g., if many attributes are not always present in each record). In that case, the relative location cannot be used to determine which data item corresponds to which attribute. A solution could be to always retain empty storage space for the missing attributes, but this is obviously not efficient in terms of storage use if the irregularities are very frequent. An alternative solution is **embedded identification**. Here, the data items representing attributes are always preceded by the attribute type. Only non-empty attributes of the record are included (Figure 12.6). Because the attribute types are registered explicitly, missing attributes are not a problem and there is no need to store the attributes in a fixed order to identify them. The obvious disadvantage is the extra storage space required for the attribute types, but for highly irregular records this approach is still more efficient than relative location. Note that this way of working, with explicitly embedded metadata on attribute types, is quite similar to the approaches in languages for semi-structured data such as XML and JSON.

**Connections**

Chapter 10 discusses XML and JSON.

[4] In a purely file-based approach, without the use of a DBMS, this information has to be encoded in every separate application that uses the data, instead of in the DBMS's catalog (see Chapter 1).

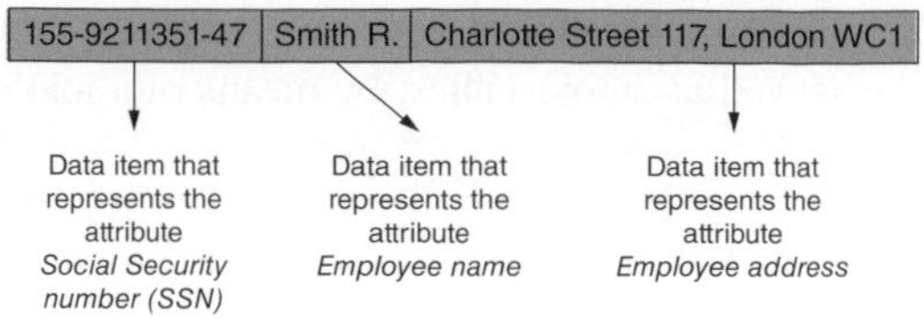


```
CREATE TABLE EMPLOYEE
      (SSN ...
      EMPLOYEE NAME ...
      EMPLOYEE ADDRESS ...
      ...
      );
```

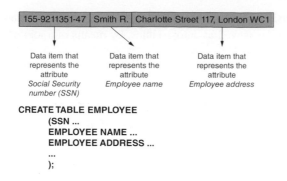

**Figure 12.5** Example of record organization with relative location.

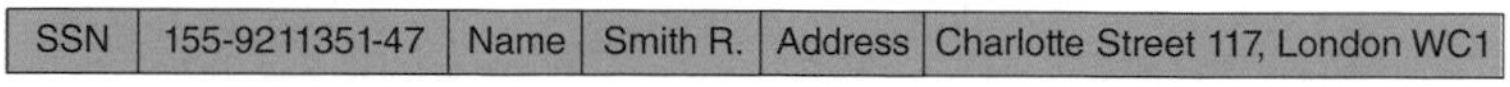


**Figure 12.6** Example of record organization with embedded identification.

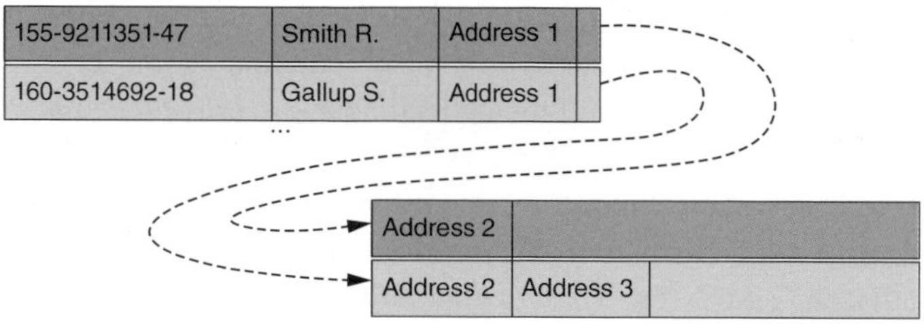


**Figure 12.7** Example of record organization with pointers and lists.

A third option is to use **pointers** and **lists**. These are discussed in more detail in Section 12.3, but can also be used for the sake of record organization. There are different possibilities. Figure 12.7 shows an example in which only attributes are stored. There is a regular record structure, except for the fact that the number of addresses may be different for each person. Therefore, for each person, one address is stored physically adjacent to the other data items; but if a person has multiple addresses, a pointer is included that refers to the storage location where the other addresses are positioned. In this way, irregularities can be dealt with without affecting the overall record structure.

This is just one example of dealing with **variable-length records**. This variability can have different causes. A first cause may be one or more attribute types that have a data type with variable length (e.g., the VARCHAR type). A second possible cause is that one or more attribute types may be multi-valued, as is the case with the Address attribute type in the example above. A third possibility is that certain attribute types are optional and occur only for some entities, as discussed previously. A fourth possible reason for variable-length records is when we have a mixed file containing different kinds of records (e.g., both supplier and purchase order records).

Another alternative for dealing with variable length records is to use **delimiters** that explicitly separate the respective attributes. Yet another possibility is to use an indirect structure, consisting of pointers, which themselves have a fixed length and are stored physically next to one another. In this way, the record has a regular format, but the pointers point to the location of the actual data items, which may have a variable length. This level of indirection is used very often when dealing with

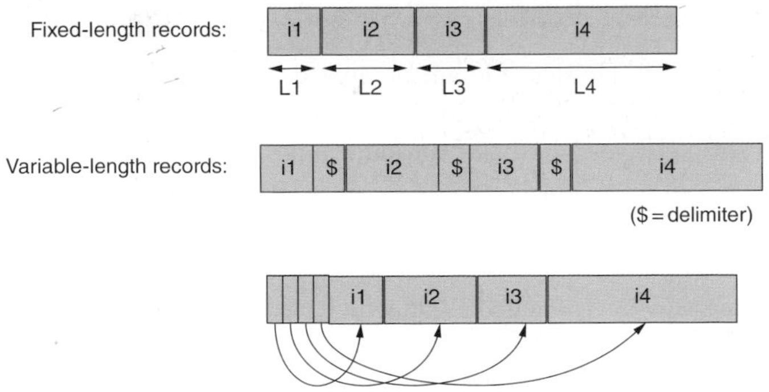


**Figure 12.8** Dealing with fixed- and variable-length records.

BLOB and CLOB data. BLOB and CLOB data types are mostly stored separately from the other data types, as they are much larger in size and thus require other methods to be stored and retrieved efficiently. In that way, a record can contain the actual values of regular data types such as integer and character, as well as pointers to "large" data items, with the actual BLOB and CLOB values stored in a separate file or file area. In Figure 12.8, we show some typical organizations of both fixed-length and variable-length records.

A last important concept in the context of record organization is the **blocking factor** (BF). The latter indicates how many records are stored in a single disk block.[5] For a file with fixed-length records, BF is calculated as follows:

$$BF = \lfloor BS/RS \rfloor$$

In this formula, BS denotes the block size and RS is the record size, both represented in bytes. The floor function $\lfloor x \rfloor$ rounds down the $x$ value to an integer. For variable-length records, BF denotes the average number of records in a block. The blocking factor is an important value when organizing physical records for efficient access, as it determines how many records are retrieved with a single read operation, without intermediate seeks and/or rotational delay.

**Retention Questions**

- Discuss and contrast different techniques to organize data items into stored records.

## 12.3 File Organization

Physical file organization pertains to the organization of stored records into physical files or datasets. We first introduce some introductory concepts such as search keys and the distinction between primary and secondary file organization, before tackling the actual file organization techniques.

[5] Given the typical size of records and disk blocks, in most cases at least one entire record will fit in a single disk block. In the rare cases where the record size is larger than the block size, a single record will span multiple blocks. A pointer can be included with the record data to refer to the next block containing data items from the same record.

### 12.3.1 Introductory Concepts: Search Keys, Primary, and Secondary File Organization

**Connections**

Chapter 7 discusses SQL.

The records in a physical file are organized in such a way that they can be retrieved efficiently according to one or more search keys. A **search key** is a single attribute type, or set of attribute types, whose values determine the criteria according to which records are retrieved. Most often, these criteria are formulated by means of a query language, such as SQL in the case of relational databases.

A search key can be a primary key or candidate key, in which case the search only yields a single result since no two stored records can have the same primary or candidate key value in a physical file.[6] Examples of such unique search keys are a customer ID, a license plate number, the combination of a flight number and the date of departure, etc. For example, a search key "customerID" with value "0285719" would yield only a single record, or none at all if there is no record with such a key value in the file.

Although primary keys are often used to retrieve data, a search key can just as well consist of one or more non-key attribute types. Indeed, one often needs to retrieve data according to other criteria, which do not represent unique identifiers. For example, the "class" of a flight seat (economy class, business class, first class, etc.) is a search key that can be used to retrieve seats, but the result is not necessarily unique and may contain many seats. A search key can be composite. For example, the search key (country, gender) with values (USA, F) yields all female customers that live in the USA. Finally, search keys can also be used to specify range queries. These are queries that retrieve all records in which some attribute value is between a lower and upper limit, such as all customers with a search key value for "YearOfBirth" between 1980 and 1990.

Apart from the above, there are typically also attribute types in a stored record that are never, or only rarely, used as search keys. They can, however, be retrieved to provide additional information to a record that was selected according to other criteria. For example, a customer's street address may never be used as a search key, but can be displayed as part of the result if the customer was retrieved according to the customerID or the year of birth. The file organization methods we discuss in this chapter aim at optimizing record access according to primary keys, according to other candidate keys and/or according to non-key attribute types we consider as relevant and frequent search keys.

We distinguish between two categories of file organization methods. First, there are methods that determine the physical positioning of stored records on a storage medium. We call them **primary file organization methods**. Examples we discuss are heap files, random file organization, and indexed sequential file organization. Some methods require a **linear search** on the entire file for records that match the search key: each record in the file is retrieved and assessed against the search key. Yet, the more advanced methods specify a relationship between a record's search key and its physical location. This improves retrieval speed considerably, as it allows directly accessing the storage locations that contain records that correspond to the search key, thus avoiding a full linear search. **Hashing** and **indexing** are the primary techniques to establish such a relationship. When implementing a physical file, the records are physically organized according to the primary file organization method.

[6] If the primary key or candidate is composite, they could have the same value for one or more component attribute types of the key, but never for the entirety of the key attribute types.

Since the primary file organization impacts the physical ordering of the records, we can apply only one primary file organization on a particular physical file, at least if we want to avoid duplicating the file. Hence, it is important to organize the file according to the search key that is most often used, or most time-critical, for retrieving the file's records. However, in most cases we want to be able to retrieve records from the same file according to different criteria. For example, sometimes we want to retrieve customers according to their customerID, sometimes according to their country or gender, or sometimes according to the combination of both country and gender. Therefore, we need **secondary file organization methods**, which provide constructs to efficiently retrieve records according to a search key that was not used for the primary file organization. Secondary file organization methods do not impact a record's physical location and invariably use some kind of index, called a **secondary index**.

In what follows, we first deal with the most important primary organization methods, starting with heap files. Then, we overview the different uses of pointers to improve physical file organization. We conclude with a discussion of secondary indexes and some particularly important index types, such a B-trees and $B^+$-trees.

## 12.3.2 Heap File Organization

The most basic primary file organization method is the **heap file**. New records are inserted at the end of the file; there is no relationship between a record's attributes and its physical location. Consequently, adding records is fairly efficient, but retrieving a particular record or set of records according to a search key is not. The only option is to do a linear search, scanning through the entire file, and to retain the records that match the selection criteria. If a single record is sought according to its primary key, the scanning continues until the record is found, or until the end of the file is reached, meaning that the record is not present. For a file with NBLK blocks, it takes on average NBLK/2 sequential block accesses to find a record.[7] Still, the more requests occur for records that turn out not to be in the file, the more searches will happen until the end of the file, requiring NBLK block accesses. Searching records according to a non-unique search key also requires scanning the entire file, hence NBLK block accesses. Deleting a record often comes down to just flagging it as "deleted". The records are then physically removed upon periodical reorganization of the file.

## 12.3.3 Sequential File Organization

With **sequential file organization**, records are stored in ascending or descending order of a search key. This is often the primary key, but a non-unique search key (i.e., a non-key attribute type or set of attribute types) can also be used as ordering criterion. An advantage this has over heap files is that it becomes much more efficient to retrieve the records in the order determined by this key, since it requires only sequential block accesses. Moreover, as with heap files, individual records can still be retrieved by means of a linear search, but now a more effective stopping criterion can be used, since the search key is the same as the attribute type(s) that determine(s) the order of the records. If the records are organized in ascending/descending order of this key, the linear search can be terminated once the first higher/lower key value than the required one is found; one can be assured that no more

[7] NBLK stands for number of blocks.

matching records exist in the remainder of the file. In addition, and even more importantly, if the sequential file is stored on a direct access storage device such as a HDD, a **binary search** technique can be used, which in the case of large files is far more efficient than a linear search. A binary search algorithm is applied recursively, halving the search interval with each iteration. For a unique search key K, with values $K_j$, the algorithm to retrieve a record with key value $K_\mu$ is as follows:

- `Selection criterion: record with search key value` $K_\mu$
- `Set l = 1; h = number of blocks in the file (suppose the records are in ascending order of the search key K)`
- `Repeat until h` $\leq$ `l`
  - `i = (l + h) / 2, rounded to the nearest integer`
  - `Retrieve block i and examine the key values` $K_j$ `of the records in block i`
    - `if any` $K_j = K_\mu$ → `the record is found!`
    - `else if` $K_\mu >$ `all` $K_j$ → `continue with l = i + 1`
    - `else if` $K_\mu <$ `all` $K_j$ → `continue with h = i - 1`
    - `else record is not in the file`

The expected number of block accesses to retrieve a record according to its primary key in a sequential file of NBLK blocks by means of a linear search is still NBLK/2 sequential block accesses. If, on the other hand, binary search is used, the expected number is $\log_2$(NBLK) random block accesses, which is much more efficient for high values of NBLK. Note that the binary search algorithm needs to be modified slightly when searching according to a non-unique search key. In that case, a few additional sequential block accesses may be called for, to retrieve all successive records with the same search key value.

For example, let's examine a sequential file with the following properties:

Number of records (NR): 30,000
Block size (BS): 2048 bytes
Record size (RS): 100 bytes

The blocking factor (BF) can be calculated in the following way: BF $= \lfloor BS/RS \rfloor = \lfloor 2048/100 \rfloor = 20$. Each block contains 20 records and thus the required number of blocks NBLK to store the 30,000 records is 1500.

If a single record is retrieved according to its primary key by means of a linear search, the expected number of required block accesses is $1500/2 = 750$ sequential block accesses. On the other hand, if a binary search is used, the expected number of block accesses is $\log_2(1500) \approx 11$ random block accesses. Even though random block accesses take more time than sequential block accesses, the binary search algorithm is much more efficient to search sequential files than scanning sequential files or heap files.

Then again, updating a sequential file is more cumbersome than updating a heap file, since now the records must be kept in order and new records cannot just be added at the end of the file. Updates are often executed in batch; they are organized according to the same ordering attribute type(s) as the actual sequential file and then the entire file is updated in a single run. A possible alternative is to place newly added records, as well as records for which the value of the ordering attribute type(s) is updated, in a separate "overflow" file (the latter organized as a heap file). Deleted records can just be flagged, without being physically removed. In this way, the file only has to be reorganized periodically, if the overflow file becomes too large. Overflow is discussed more extensively in Section 12.3.4. In a database setting, sequential files are often combined with one or more indexes, resulting in the indexed sequential file organization method (see Section 12.3.5).

### 12.3.4 Random File Organization (Hashing)

The main disadvantage of sequential file organization is that many other records need to be accessed to retrieve a single required record. This problem is somewhat alleviated with binary search, but even then the number of unnecessary record retrievals may become quite large. With **random file organization** (also called *direct file organization* or *hash file organization*), there exists a direct relationship between the value of the search key and a record's physical location. In this way, a record can be retrieved with one, or at most a few, block accesses if the key value is provided.

#### 12.3.4.1 Key-to-Address Transformation

The relationship described above is based on hashing. A hashing algorithm defines a **key-to-address transformation**, such that the record's physical address can be calculated from its key value. Each time a new record is to be added to the file, this transformation is applied to its key, returning the physical address where the record should be stored (at least, if that address is still available, as discussed below). If later on the record is to be retrieved based on this search key, applying the same transformation to the key returns the address where the record can be found. Clearly, this approach is only feasible on a direct access storage device.

As discussed in Chapter 11, variations of the hashing technique can be applied in multiple contexts. Hashing is used in programming languages to map key values to addresses in internal memory (e.g., an array data type). The recent wave of NoSQL databases often relies on a variant, consistent hashing, to evenly distribute and replicate data records over the respective database nodes in a cluster setting. In what follows, we focus on the use of hashing to transform record keys into physical addresses of a persistent storage device, most often a hard disk drive. This approach is most effective when using a primary key or other candidate key as a search key, for reasons that are clarified later in this section.

> **Connections**
>
> Chapter 11 discusses NoSQL databases and also introduces hashing.

A key-to-address transformation consists of several steps, as represented in Figure 12.9. First, the key is converted into an integer numerical format, if it isn't an integer already. For instance, non-integer numerical values can be rounded or alphanumerical keys can be turned into an integer by means of the characters' position in the alphabet or their ASCII codes. Then, the actual hashing algorithm is applied, where the integer key values are transformed into a spread of numbers of roughly the same magnitude as the desired addresses. The more uniformly these keys are distributed over this range of numbers, the better. Note that, quite often, the generated addresses do not pertain to individual record addresses, but rather to a contiguous area of record addresses, called a **bucket**. A bucket contains one or more stored record slots. Its size can be defined at will, but can also be aligned to the physical characteristics of the storage device, such as an integer number of disk blocks, tracks, or cylinders. The hashing algorithm can take on many forms, ranging from a simple hash function to more complex algorithms. However, it invariably consists of a consecution of

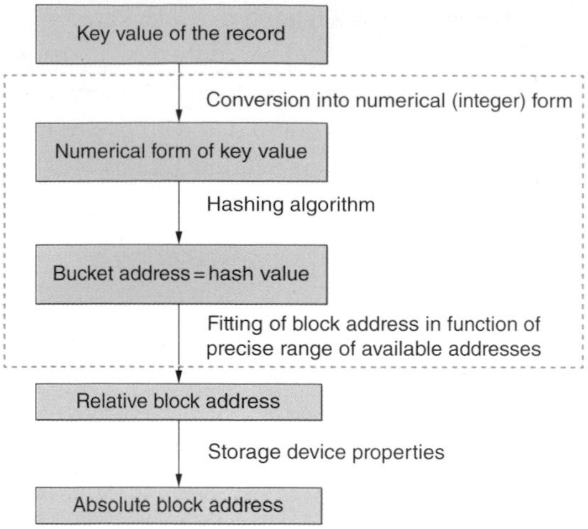


**Figure 12.9** Key-to-address transformation.

mathematical operations, applied to a numerical representation of the key and returning a hash value that corresponds to a bucket address. In a next step, this bucket address is translated into an actual block address. For that purpose, it is multiplied by a constant that "compresses" the generated hash values into the exact range of desired block addresses. The latter is still a ***relative*** **block address**, that is, relative to the first block of the file.

A final step, which is governed by the file system and therefore can be considered beyond the scope of the key-to-address transformation, is the translation of the relative block address into an ***absolute*** **address** consisting of a device number, cylinder number, track number, and block number. If a bucket spans multiple physical blocks, retrieving a record according to its key comes down to a single random block access to the first block in the bucket as determined by the key-to-address transformation. This is possibly followed by one or more sequential block accesses until the entire bucket is retrieved and the record is found.

A very important consideration with respect to hashing is that it cannot guarantee that all keys are mapped to different hash values, hence bucket addresses. Whereas its purpose is indeed to distribute all keys evenly over the available address space, several records may be assigned to the same bucket. In that case, we speak of a **collision** and the corresponding records are called **synonyms**. Collisions are not a problem per se, since a single bucket normally consists of multiple record slots, but if there are more synonyms than slots for a certain bucket, the bucket is said to be in **overflow**. As discussed later in this section, there are different ways of dealing with overflow, but regardless of the actual overflow-handling method, it inevitably causes some records to be stored on a different location than where they were initially expected according to the key-to-address transformation. Hence, additional block accesses are needed to retrieve overflow records and therefore overflow should be avoided as much as possible so as not to jeopardize performance. For that reason, a hashing algorithm should be chosen that distributes the keys as evenly as possible over the respective bucket addresses, thus reducing the risk of overflow.

Many hashing techniques have been developed for transforming key values into addresses, such as *division*, *digit analysis*, *mid-square*, *folding*, and *base transformation*. We illustrate the hashing approach by one of them: division. This is one of the simplest hashing techniques, yet in most circumstances it performs remarkably well. With the division technique, the numerical

| Series 1 | | | Series 2 | | |
|---|---|---|---|---|---|
| Key value | Division by 20 | Division by 23 | Key value | Division by 20 | Division by 23 |
| 3000 | 00 | 10 | 3000 | 00 | 10 |
| 3001 | 01 | 11 | 3025 | 05 | 12 |
| 3002 | 02 | 12 | 3050 | 10 | 14 |
| 3003 | 03 | 13 | 3075 | 15 | 16 |
| 3004 | 04 | 14 | 3100 | 00 | 18 |
| 3005 | 05 | 15 | 3125 | 05 | 20 |
| 3006 | 06 | 16 | 3150 | 10 | 22 |
| 3007 | 07 | 17 | 3175 | 15 | 01 |
| 3008 | 08 | 18 | 3200 | 00 | 03 |
| 3009 | 09 | 19 | 3225 | 05 | 05 |
| 3010 | 10 | 20 | 3250 | 10 | 07 |
| 3011 | 11 | 21 | 3275 | 15 | 09 |
| 3012 | 12 | 22 | 3300 | 00 | 11 |
| 3013 | 13 | 00 | 3325 | 05 | 13 |
| 3014 | 14 | 01 | 3350 | 10 | 15 |
| 3015 | 15 | 02 | 3375 | 15 | 17 |
| 3016 | 16 | 03 | 3400 | 00 | 19 |
| 3017 | 17 | 04 | 3425 | 05 | 21 |
| 3018 | 18 | 05 | 3450 | 10 | 00 |
| 3019 | 19 | 06 | 3475 | 15 | 02 |

**Figure 12.10** Impact of hashing technique and key set distribution on number of collisions.

form of the key is divided by a positive integer M. The remainder of the division[8] becomes the record address:

$$\text{address}(\text{key}_i) = \text{key}_i \bmod M$$

The choice of M is very important; if M is inappropriate for the key set at hand, many collisions, and therefore extensive overflow, will be the result. Common factors between the key values and M should be avoided. For this reason, the chosen M is often a prime number. For example, Figure 12.10 shows two series of key values, each time with the remainder of division by 20 and by 23. For the first series, both 20 and 23 result in a nearly uniform distribution of remainders, and address values, so they would both be adequate as M. However, in the second series, division by 20 yields a much worse distribution, with many records attributed to bucket addresses 00, 05, 10, and 15, whereas other buckets remain empty. Yet, division by the prime number 23 again results in a nearly uniform distribution. For a particular key set, one prime number may still perform better than another, so ideally multiple candidates are tested. Most often, a prime number is chosen that is close to, but a bit larger than, the number of available addresses, yielding roughly as many values as the number of required addresses. The next step in

[8] The mathematical operator that takes the remainder after a division is called the *modulo*, abbreviated as "mod."

the key-to-address transformation then multiplies them by a factor (a bit) smaller than 1, such that they fit perfectly into the actual address space (see Figure 12.9).

#### 12.3.4.2 Factors that Determine the Efficiency of Random File Organization

The efficiency of a hashing algorithm for a certain dataset is ultimately measured by the expected number of random and sequential block accesses to retrieve a record. Several factors have an impact on this efficiency. Retrieving a non-overflow record requires only a single random block access to the first block of the bucket denoted by the hashing algorithm. It is possibly followed by one or more sequential block accesses if the bucket consists of multiple physical blocks. To retrieve an overflow record, additional block accesses are required, hence the *percentage of overflow records*, as well as the *overflow-handling technique* affect the performance. The former denotes how many records are in the overflow; the latter determines where records that do not fit in the bucket as determined by the hashing algorithm are stored and how many block accesses are required to retrieve them. We first discuss the parameters that impact the percentage of overflow records. After that, we briefly present some overflow-handling techniques.

As illustrated in Figure 12.10, the percentage of overflow records depends on how appropriate the hashing algorithm is to the key set. In many cases, the key values are not distributed evenly; gaps and clusters may occur, even more so if records are frequently added and deleted. It is up to the hashing algorithm to map this irregularly distributed key set as evenly as possible onto a set of addresses. The term "random" file organization is somewhat misleading in this context: the aim is *not* to assign records to storage addresses according to a random statistical distribution function. With a random distribution, any record would have the same chance to be assigned to any physical address in the available range. However, the real aim is to achieve a **uniform distribution**, spreading the set of records evenly over the set of available buckets, because this would minimize the chance of overflow and, therefore, performance degradation. Yet, in practice, the best-performing hashing algorithms closely approximate the results of a theoretical random distribution, rather than the ideal of a uniform distribution. The statistical properties of a random distribution can be used by the file designer to estimate the expected percentage of overflow records. Moreover, theoretically, a perfectly uniform distribution would require only as many record slots as there are records to be stored. Still, the reality of less-than-uniform distributions implies that more record slots are needed, because some buckets are fuller than others and the only way to avoid too extensive an overflow is to provide more record slots than strictly necessary. The following formula expresses the required number of buckets (NB) as the *number of records* (NR) divided by the *bucket size* (BS) and the *loading factor* (LF):

$$\text{NB} = \lceil NR/(BS \times LF) \rceil$$

The number of records is determined by the dataset. The bucket size indicates the number of record slots in a bucket. The tradeoff here is that the larger the bucket size, the smaller the chance of overflow will be. On the other hand, a larger bucket means more additional sequential block accesses to retrieve all non-overflow records in the bucket. Therefore, the blocking factor, which is the number of records in a single block, plays a role as well. Finally, the **loading factor** represents the average number of records in a bucket divided by the bucket size and indicates how "full" every bucket is on average. In this way, the loading factor embodies the tradeoff between efficient use of storage capacity and retrieval performance. A lower loading factor results in less overflow, and hence better performance, but also more wasted storage space. A higher loading factor has the

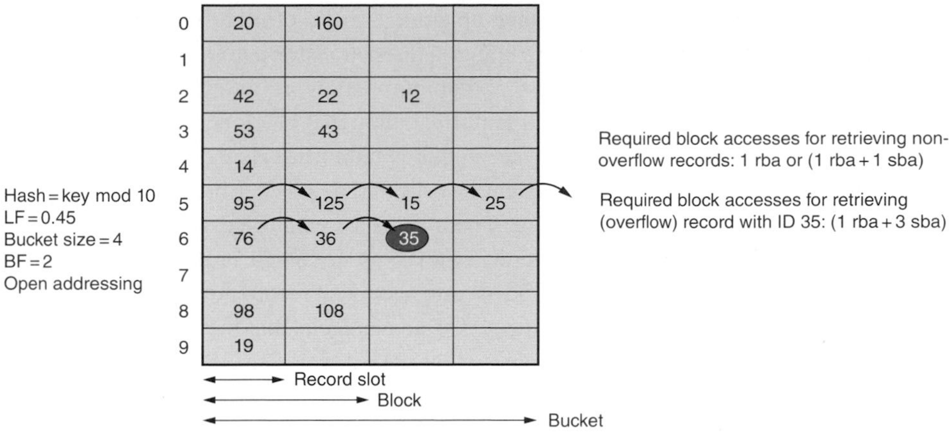


**Figure 12.11** Impact of overflow on retrieval performance.

opposite effect. In practice, the loading factor is often set between 0.7 and 0.9 to balance storage efficiency with performance. Clearly, the random file organization is most effective on a unique search key, thus a primary key or other candidate key. Hashing can also be applied to non-unique search keys, but in that case there are more records with the same key value and, hence, more collisions. The risk of overflow then depends on the average number of records sharing the same search key value, and on the distribution of this number.

The second main factor impacting the performance of random file organization is the way in which overflow records are stored and retrieved, known as the **overflow-handling technique**. There are different approaches here, with overflow records being stored either in the **primary area** or in a separate **overflow area**. The primary area is the address space that also contains the non-overflow records; some techniques direct overflow records toward partially empty buckets of the primary area. Other techniques use a separate overflow area that only contains overflow records. The standard key-to-address algorithm does not apply in the overflow area.

To discuss all techniques would be far too much detail, but let's examine the small example in Figure 12.11 that illustrates how the combination of an inadequate transformation and inappropriate overflow handling may have a negative effect on retrieval performance. The simplified file contains 18 records, with numeric keys 12, 14, 15, 19, etc. There are ten buckets, with a bucket size of four. The blocking factor is two and each bucket spans two physical blocks. Suppose we use **open addressing** as a simple overflow-handling technique. With open addressing, overflow records are stored in the primary area, more particularly in the next free slot after the full bucket where the record would normally have been stored according to the key-to-address transformation. A "mod 10" key-to-address transformation is used, yielding ten possible bucket addresses. The resulting key distribution is far from uniform, and does not even come close to a random distribution, resulting in bucket 5 being overly stacked, whereas other buckets remain empty. Thus, despite the low loading factor of 0.45, we already have an overflow record. Indeed, the record with key 35 would normally have been stored in bucket 5, but since this bucket is already filled with other records (95, 125, etc.), the next free slot is used, in bucket 6. Retrieving record 35 now requires one random block access plus three sequential block accesses, whereas retrieving a non-overflow record would require at most one sequential block access in addition to the random block access. So indeed, overflow has a negative impact on performance. Moreover, so far record 35 is the only overflow record, but if more records are added, record 35 may take up storage space of other records that would rightfully be directed to bucket 6 according to the key-to-address transformation (e.g., a newly added record 86). Consequently, such records may also end up in overflow, resulting in a domino effect of more and more records being out of place and requiring additional block accesses for retrieval.

An alternative overflow-handling technique is **chaining**. Here, overflow records are stored in a separate overflow area, with subsequent records that overflow from the same bucket being chained together by pointers. Such a structure, where items are connected sequentially by pointers, is called a **linked list**. It can be used in several contexts, as discussed in detail in Section 12.3.6.2. In the context of hashing, linked lists can be used to access all records overflowing from the same bucket by following the pointers between them. The advantage is that they do not clutter the primary area, and therefore cannot cause additional overflow. The downside is that accessing linked lists results in additional random block accesses. Yet another overflow-handling technique is to use a second hashing algorithm, different to the primary one, to determine the location of overflow records.

To conclude the discussion on hashing, it is important to note that so far we have assumed that the number of records does not increase or decrease significantly over time, which means the number of insertions is more or less equal to the number of deletions. If the number of records decreases over time, the storage capacity will not be used efficiently after a while. Even worse, if the number of records increases, many buckets will be in overflow, resulting in degrading performance. In both cases, the key-to-address transformation is not adequate anymore because of the changed number of records. A new transformation must be chosen, and the entire file should be rearranged according to the newly generated hash values. Luckily, several **dynamic hashing** techniques exist that allow for a file to shrink or grow without the need for it to be completely rearranged. It is beyond the scope of this overview to discuss these techniques in detail.

### 12.3.5 Indexed Sequential File Organization

While random file organization, if applied adequately, is probably the most effective technique to retrieve individual records by their search key value, it is very inefficient if many records are to be retrieved *in a certain order* (e.g., sorted according to that same key, or if records are to be retrieved according to a range of key values). For example, for retrieving all customers in order of their customerID it would be inadequate because all customer records are scattered throughout the file according to the hashing algorithm, requiring a multitude of random block accesses.[9] In comparison, sequential file organization would be much more efficient for this task, since all records are already ordered according to customerID and just need to be retrieved sequentially. An **indexed sequential file organization** method reconciles both concerns: in many situations, it is only marginally less efficient in directly retrieving individual records than random file organization and it still allows for records to be stored in ascending or descending order of the search key, to cater for efficient sequential access.

#### 12.3.5.1 Basic Terminology of Indexes

Indexed sequential file organization combines sequential file organization with the use of one or more indexes. To this end, the file is divided into different **intervals** or **partitions**. Each interval is

[9] In practice, in such a situation the records would probably be retrieved in the (random) order in which they are stored, and then sorted afterwards. Still, this also induces a considerable amount of overhead.

represented by an **index entry**, which contains the search key value of the first record in the interval, as well as a pointer to the physical position of the first record in the interval. Depending on the case, this pointer may be realized as a **block pointer** or a **record pointer**. A block pointer refers to the physical block address of the corresponding record. A record pointer consists of the combination of a block address and a record ID or offset within this block and refers to an actual record. An index itself is then a sequential file, ordered according to the search key values. The index consists of entries with the following format:

```
Index entry = <search key value, block pointer or record pointer>
```
[10]

The search key can be atomic (e.g., a customer ID) or composite (e.g., the combination of year of birth and gender). In the case of composite search keys, the key values in the index entries are composite as well (e.g., <(1980, M), pointer>; <(1976, F), pointer>). For simplicity, we use examples with atomic keys hereafter, but all claims are valid for composite keys as well.

In addition, we discriminate between **dense indexes** and **sparse indexes**. A dense index has an index entry for every possible value of the search key that it indexes. Therefore, if the search key is a unique key (e.g., primary key or other candidate key), a dense index has an index entry for each separate record. If the search key is a non-key attribute type or combination of attribute types, a dense index has an index entry for every *group* of records with the same value for that attribute type (s). A sparse index, on the other hand, has an index entry for only some of the search key values. Each entry refers to a group of records and there are fewer index entries than with a dense index. Dense indexes are generally faster, but require more storage space and are more complex to maintain than sparse indexes.

With an indexed sequential file organization, both sequential access, based on the physical order of the records, and random access, based on the index, are supported. Different configurations, with one or more index levels, are possible. We discuss the most typical examples in the following subsections.

#### 12.3.5.2 Primary Indexes

With **primary index** file organization, the data file is ordered on a unique key (this can be a primary key or another candidate key) and an index is defined over this unique search key. For now, we work with only a single index level – multilevel indexes are covered in Section 12.3.5.4. An example is given in Figure 12.12. It depicts a file with intervals of four records. Each interval corresponds to a single disk block; hence the blocking factor is four. The records are ordered according to the primary key CustomerID. For each interval, there is an index entry, consisting of the key of the first record in the interval and a pointer referring to the disk block that contains the records in the interval. There is an index entry for each disk block, and not for each key value, so the index is sparse. To retrieve a record according to the required key value, say 12111, a binary search is executed on the index to retrieve the pointer to the block that should contain the corresponding record, at least if it is present in the file. This is the third block in the example. In this way, instead of searching the entire file with data records, only the index and a single block of the actual data file need to be accessed; either the record is found in that block, or it isn't present

[10] From now on, we just use the term "pointer" and make abstraction from the distinction between record pointer and block pointer.

**Table 12.2** Required block accesses for linear search, binary search, and index-based search

| | |
|---|---|
| Linear search | NBLK sba |
| Binary search | $\log_2$(NBLK) rba |
| Index-based search | $\log_2$(NBLKI) + 1 rba, with NBLKI << NBLK |

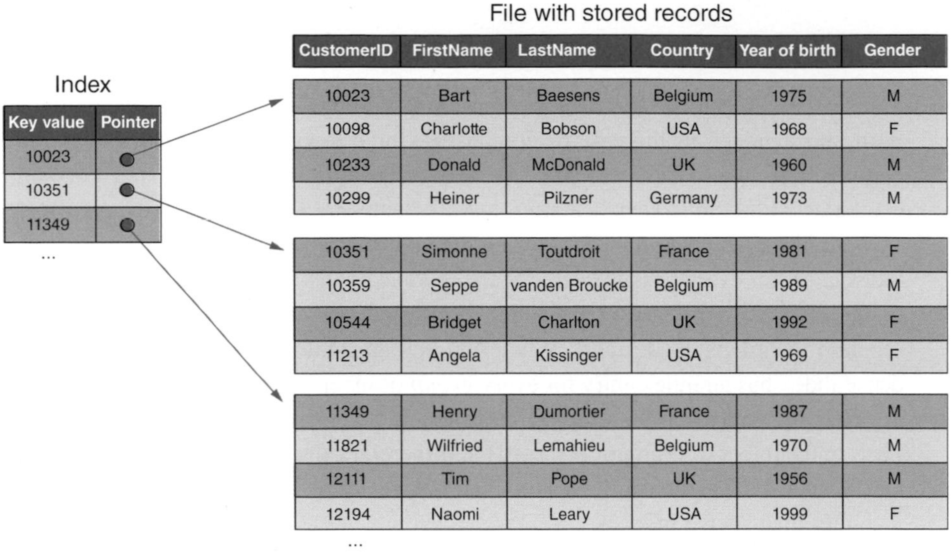

File with stored records
CustomerID FirstName LastName Country Year of birth Gender
10023 Bart Baesens Belgium 1975 M
10098 Charlotte Bobson USA 1968 F
10233 Donald McDonald UK 1960 M
10299 Heiner Pilzner Germany 1973 M
10351 Simonne Toutdroit France 1981 F
10359 Seppe vanden Broucke Belgium 1989 M
10544 Bridget Charlton UK 1992 F
11213 Angela Kissinger USA 1969 F
11349 Henry Dumortier France 1987 M
11821 Wilfried Lemahieu Belgium 1970 M
12111 Tim Pope UK 1956 M
12194 Naomi Leary USA 1999 F
Index
Key value Pointer
10023
10351
11349


**Figure 12.12** Example of primary index.

in the file. Additionally, the index entries are much smaller than the actual stored records. This means an index file occupies considerably fewer disk blocks than the data file and can be searched much quicker.

The expected number of block accesses to retrieve a single record using a primary index amounts to $\log_2$(NBLKI) random block accesses for a binary search on the index, with NBLKI representing the number of blocks in the index. One additional random block access is needed to retrieve the actual record, assuming the intervals correspond to individual disk blocks. We summarize the required block accesses for respectively linear search, binary search, and indexed search in Table 12.2.

Let's apply this to the same example as the one used for sequential file organization (i.e., a file consisting of 1500 blocks and a block size of 2048 bytes). Remember that the expected number of block accesses to retrieve an individual record by means of a linear search amounted to 750 sequential block accesses, whereas a binary search on the data file required only 11 random block accesses. If we assume index entries of 15 bytes (e.g., a key of 10 bytes and a block address of 5 bytes), then the blocking factor of the index is $\lfloor 2048/15 \rfloor = 136$. NBLKI is then $\lceil 1500/136 \rceil = 12$ blocks. A binary search on the index requires $\log_2(12) + 1 \approx 5$ random block accesses. Moreover, indexing becomes even more advantageous in comparison to pure sequential organization as the file sizes grow larger than the one in the rather small file in the example.

On the other hand, if many records are to be retrieved, it may be more efficient to process the entire file in a single run, requiring NBLK sequential block accesses, rather than consecutively

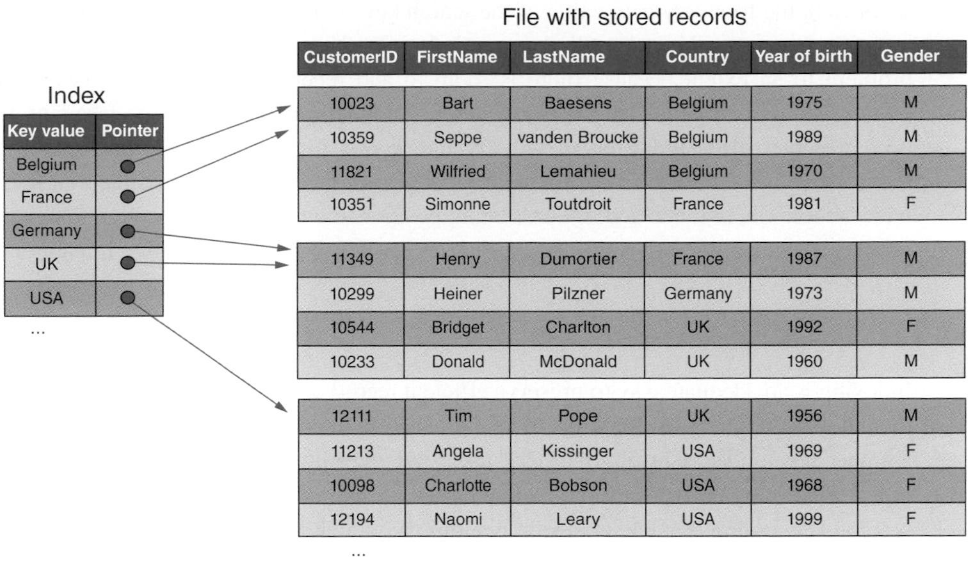
File with stored records
CustomerID FirstName LastName Country Year of birth Gender
10023 Bart Baesens Belgium 1975 M
10359 Seppe vanden Broucke Belgium 1989 M
11821 Wilfried Lemahieu Belgium 1970 M
10351 Simonne Toutdroit France 1981 F
11349 Henry Dumortier France 1987 M
10299 Heiner Pilzner Germany 1973 M
10544 Bridget Charlton UK 1992 F
10233 Donald McDonald UK 1960 M
12111 Tim Pope UK 1956 M
11213 Angela Kissinger USA 1969 F
10098 Charlotte Bobson USA 1968 F
12194 Naomi Leary USA 1999 F
...
Index
Key value Pointer
Belgium
France
Germany
UK
USA
...

**Figure 12.13** Example of clustered index.

searching for the individual records by means of the index, resulting in random block accesses. Also, note that the previous remark regarding the complexity of updating a sequential file in comparison to a heap file also holds for an indexed sequential file. Moreover, we now have the added complexity that the index itself is a sequential file as well, which needs to be updated along with insertions and deletions in the actual data file.

#### 12.3.5.3 Clustered Indexes

A **clustered index** is similar to a primary index, with the difference that the ordering criterion and therefore the search key is a non-key attribute type or set of attribute types, instead of a primary or candidate key. Consequently, the search key values do not uniquely identify a single record.[11] Each index entry consists of a search key value, as well as the address of the first block that contains records with this key value (see Figure 12.13). If there is an index entry for each unique value of the search key, the index is dense. If only some search key values are indexed, the index is sparse. The search process is the same as with a primary index, except additional sequential block accesses may be required after the first random block access to the data file, to retrieve all subsequent records with the same search key value. In the example, a clustered index is defined over the search key "Country". A search for all records with "UK" as the value for Country requires random block accesses to search the index and retrieve the second block in the file, which is the first to contain customers from the UK. In addition, a sequential block access to the third block is required, which contains UK customers as well.

Just like primary indexes, clustered indexes have the additional complexity of keeping the index up to date if records in the data file are inserted or deleted, or if their search key value is updated (e.g., a customer moves from Belgium to France). A frequently used variation is to start a new block

[11] Sometimes also alternative terminology is used, where the term clustered index pertains to indexes over both unique and non-unique search keys. In that case, one speaks of unique and non-unique clustered indexes.

in the data file for every new value of the search key. This is less efficient in terms of storage space, as many blocks will not be filled up entirely. On the other hand, it alleviates the maintenance problem to an extent because there is room to add records with the same key value to a block without reorganizing the data file or the index. Another option to avoid too frequent file reorganization, which is also applicable to primary indexes, is to provide a separate overflow section for records that cannot be stored in the appropriate position in the regular sequential file. However, as with random file organization, records being positioned on a different location than where they were initially expected results in additional block accesses, which has a negative impact on performance.

### 12.3.5.4 Multilevel Indexes

Indexing is an adequate way to preserve efficient record access for larger file sizes, but at some point the index itself may grow too large to be searched efficiently. In that case, one may need to introduce a higher-level index. Creating an index-to-an-index results in **multilevel indexes**. In practice, many index levels may occur; we illustrate the case with two index levels in Figure 12.14. Each index is searched according to a binary search, yielding a pointer to the appropriate block in the lower-level index. The lowest-level index yields a pointer to the appropriate block in the data file. In the case of a primary index, all block accesses are random block accesses. With a clustered index, additional sequential block accesses on the data file may be called for to retrieve subsequent records with the same search key value. Note that the number of random block accesses on the higher-level indexes remains limited, since they are sparse indexes and can be kept limited in size thanks to the multiple levels. In addition, higher-level indexes can often be kept and searched in-memory, resulting in even more efficient processing.

To conclude, it needs to be stressed that there is only one way to physically order a file, unless the file is duplicated. A primary index and clustered index can never occur together for the same file and it is important to choose the most appropriate index to base the physical ordering of the records on. Nevertheless, in addition to a primary index or a clustered index, it is possible to create additional indexes over other search keys. These are called secondary indexes and have no impact on the

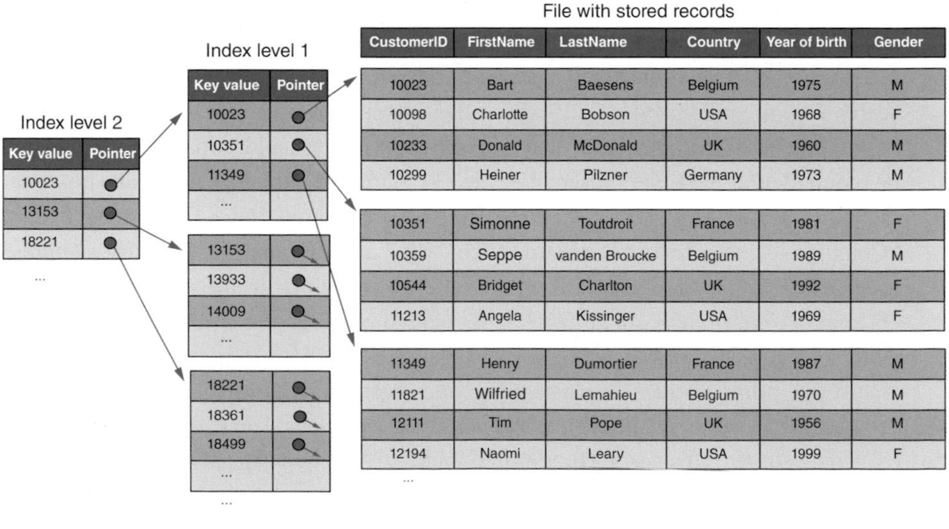


**Figure 12.14** Example of multilevel index.

physical ordering of the records, but do allow speeding up retrieval according to criteria other than the one used for the primary file organization. The use of indexes for secondary file organization is discussed in Section 12.3.7. Also, all remarks made with respect to maintenance of indexes are even more pertinent in the case of multiple index levels. As we will see in Section 12.3.8, B-trees and $B^+$-trees provide a more flexible mechanism in terms of keeping the index up to date without the need to frequently restructure the index files.

## 12.3.6 List Data Organization (Linear and Nonlinear Lists)

This section provides a brief overview of several techniques under the common denominator "list data organization methods". These techniques are used in different contexts, first as a main organization method, but also to organize overflow records or indexes. This section overviews the general concepts; some important elements were or will be treated in more detail in other sections of this chapter.

A **list** can be defined as an *ordered set of elements*. If each element has exactly one successor, except for the last element in the list, we call it a linear list. A linear list can be used to represent sequential data structures. All other types of lists are called **nonlinear lists**. These can be used to represent tree data structures and other types of directed graphs.

In what follows, we only focus on the use of lists to represent sequential data structures and tree data structures. In both, the ordering can be represented by means of either *physical contiguity* of the data records or by means of *pointers*.

### 12.3.6.1 Linear Lists

A **linear list** embodies a sequential data structure and can be represented in two ways. If the logical ordering of the records is expressed by means of physical contiguity, we have the sequential file organization method already discussed in this chapter. If, on the other hand, the logical ordering of the records is represented physically by means of pointers, we speak of a linked list.

The simplest linked list method is the **one-way linked list**. In this method, records are physically stored in an arbitrary order, or sorted according to another search key. A logical sequential ordering is then represented by means of pointers, with each record containing a "next" pointer to the physical location of its logical successor. The pointers are *embedded* as additional fields in the stored records. To process the list, the first record is retrieved, the pointer to the next record is followed and so on, until a record is reached that contains an end-of-list indicator instead of a "next" pointer. The one-way linked list is illustrated in Figure 12.15. The physical addresses are represented by numbers (10, 11, 12, etc.). The search keys that determine the logical ordering of the records are represented by letters (A, B, C, etc.). As can be seen, each record contains a pointer to its logical successor; the logical order is independent from the

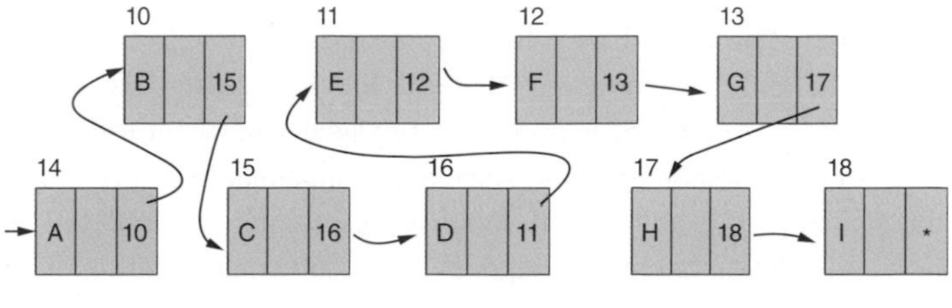


**Figure 12.15** Example of a one-way linked list.

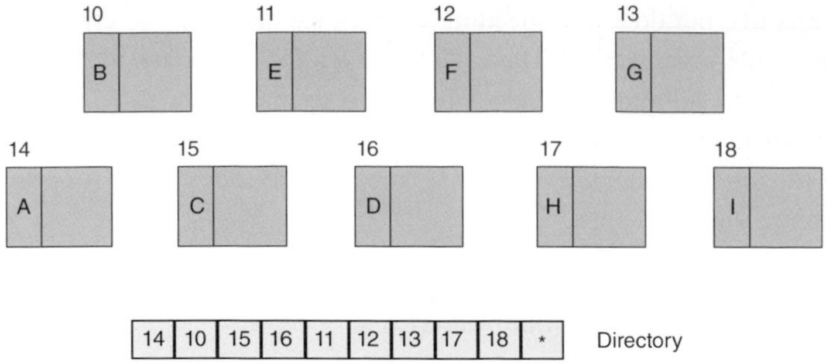


**Figure 12.16** Example of a directory.

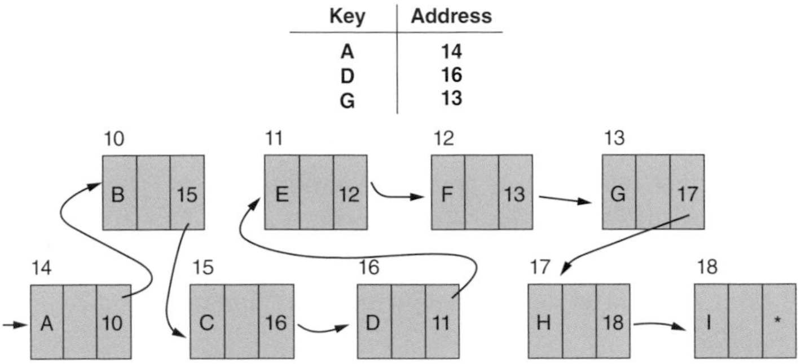


**Figure 12.17** Example of linked list with index.

physical ordering of the records. The end-of-list is indicated by an asterisk (*). Alternatively, the last record may contain a pointer that points back to the head of the list, such that the list can be processed from any starting position. Linked lists make it possible to define one or more logical orderings over the same set of records, independently of their physical ordering. They are often used to chain overflow records together.

A possible disadvantage of the above approach is that all records must be retrieved, even if only part of the list needs to be processed, because the pointers to navigate the list are embedded in the records. An alternative is to store the pointers separately in a *directory* (not to be confused with directories in a file system). A **directory** (Figure 12.16) is a file that defines the relationships between the records in another file. As the pointers are much smaller than the actual data records, by storing them in a separate file navigating them requires fewer block accesses and, hence, less time. Also, adding, updating, and deleting pointers is much easier in a separate file.

Another variant is to combine a linked list with indexed addressing. The records are distributed into intervals, with each interval being represented by an index entry. The index allows for directly accessing the first record of an interval, without passing through all the records in previous intervals (see Figure 12.17).

To calculate the expected retrieval time of a linked list, we can use the same formulas we used for sequential file organization. The only difference is that all block accesses are random block accesses, since the logical successor of a record is no longer physically adjacent to its predecessor. Also, the impact of blocking is limited to non-existent, since the chance that logically related records are stored physically in the same block is quite small. Without discussing this in detail, it is worth noting that also the insertion and deletion of records requires quite some manipulation, including the

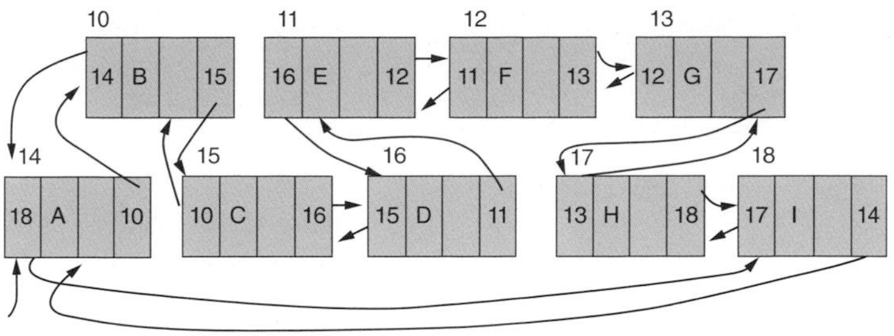


**Figure 12.18** Example of two-way linked list.

updating of pointers to preserve the logical ordering. It is very common to not actually delete a record, but to just flag it as "deleted" to avoid part of this manipulation. This comes at the cost of storage space, because no space is released upon record deletion.

Two disadvantages of a one-way linked list are the inability to return to a record's predecessor in an efficient way and the fact that, if one of the pointers is lost or damaged, the logical sequence of the list cannot be reconstructed. Both disadvantages are resolved with the **two-way linked list** method. In a two-way linked list, each record contains a "prior" pointer as well as a "next" pointer (Figure 12.18). In this way, the list can be processed efficiently in both directions. Moreover, the "prior" pointers add a measure of redundancy that can be exploited to reconstruct the logical ordering if a pointer in the "other" direction is lost or damaged. Just like with the one-way linked list, a variant with a directory or an index is also possible.

#### 12.3.6.2 Tree Data Structures

A tree consists of a set of nodes and edges with the following properties:

- There is exactly one *root* node.
- Every node, except for the root, has exactly one *parent node.*
- Every node has zero, one, or more *children* or *child nodes.*
- Nodes with the same parent node are called *siblings.*
- All children, children-of-children, etc. of a node are called the node's *descendants.*
- A node without children is called a *leaf node.*
- The tree structure consisting of a non-root node and all of its descendants is called a *subtree* of the original tree.
- The nodes are distributed in *levels*, representing the distance from the root. The root node has level 0; the level of a child node is equal to the level of its parent plus 1. All siblings have the same level.
- A tree where all leaf nodes are at the same level is called *balanced.* In that case, the path from the root node to any leaf node has the same length. If leaf nodes occur at different levels, the tree is said to be *unbalanced.*

Tree data structures are relevant in several ways. First, they may provide a physical representation of a logical hierarchy or tree structure. Examples are a hierarchy of employees, where all nodes in the tree then represent a similar kind of real-world entity, or the hierarchical relationships between suppliers, purchase orders, and purchase order lines, where the nodes in the tree now represent different kinds of real-world entities. A second, and even more important, application of tree data structures is when they do not correspond to the physical representation of a logical hierarchy, but

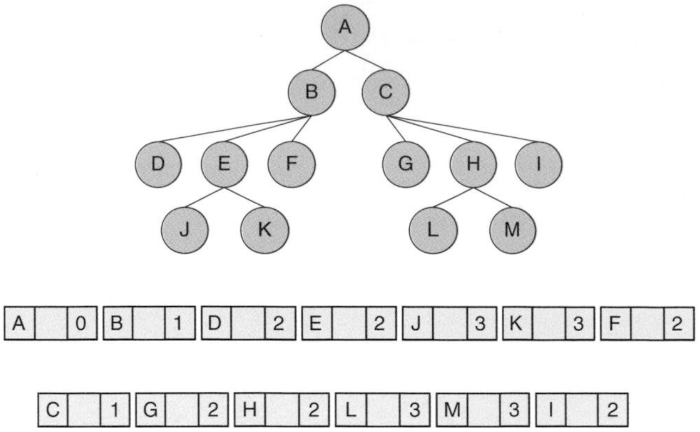


**Figure 12.19** Example of tree structure represented as a physically contiguous list.

when they provide a purely physical index structure to speed up the search and retrieval of records by navigating the interconnected nodes of the tree. We denote this type of tree structure with the general term *search tree*. The most well-known representatives of this class are the B-tree and B$^+$-tree, which are dealt with in more detail in Section 12.3.8.

In what follows, we overview the general aspects of tree data structures. A first way to implement them is by means of physical contiguity, where the physical position of the records, along with additional information, expresses the tree structure. The tree nodes are typically stored in a "top–down–left–right" sequence: first the root, then the root's first child, then the child's first child if it exists, etc. If a node has no more children, its next sibling (from left to right) is stored. If a node has no more siblings, its parent's next sibling is stored. In order to reconstruct the tree structure, each node's level needs to be included explicitly, because the physical contiguity of two nodes does not discriminate between a parent–child and sibling–sibling relationship. Figure 12.19 illustrates how a logical tree structure is represented physically in this way. The letters represent the record keys, the numbers denote the level in the tree for the physical records. Such a representation is only navigable in a sequential way. For example, it is not possible to directly navigate from node B to node C without passing through all of B's descendants.

A *linked list* can also be used to represent a tree structure. Here, physical contiguity is complemented with pointers to improve navigability. The nodes are stored in the same physical sequence as described previously but, in addition, each node has a pointer to its next sibling, if the latter exists. This is illustrated in Figure 12.20. In this way, both parent–child and sibling–sibling navigation are supported, respectively by accessing the physically subsequent record and following the pointer. Also, there is no need to store each node's level: this information can be inferred from the physical positions and the pointers. Still, for reasons of efficiency, a single bit is often added to each node, indicating whether the node is a leaf node (bit = 0) or not (bit = 1).

Many variations of the above exist, where the physical ordering of the nodes can be kept entirely independent from the tree structure; both parent–child and sibling–sibling relations are represented by pointers (Figure 12.21a). In some cases, other pointers (e.g., child–parent pointers, Figure 12.21b) are included as well, to accommodate for navigability in all directions of the tree.

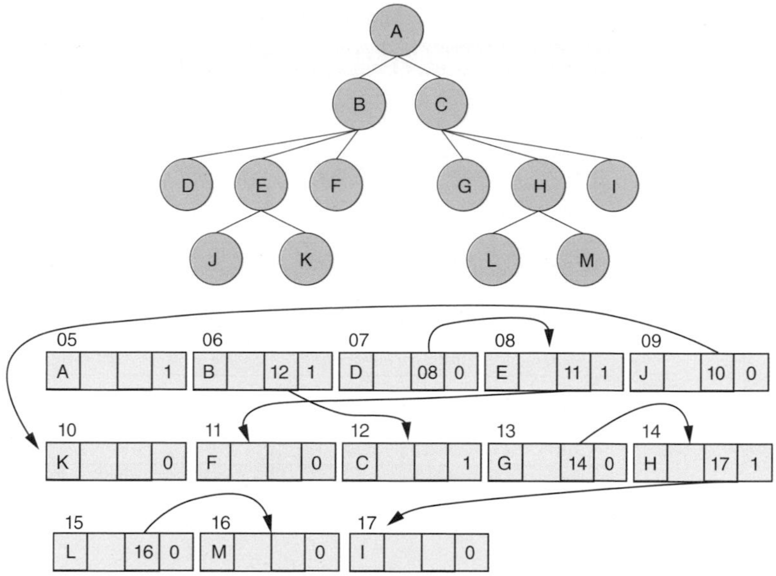


**Figure 12.20** Example of tree structure represented as a linked list.

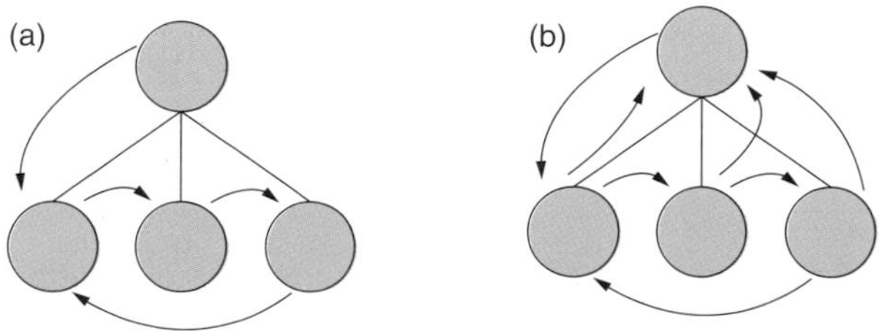


**Figure 12.21** Alternative formats to represent tree structures with pointers.

## 12.3.7 Secondary Indexes and Inverted Files

The previous sections described different techniques for primary file organization aimed at organizing records physically in such a way that they can be retrieved efficiently according to a particular search key. However, in most contexts, access to the same dataset might occur according to different criteria or search keys. Only one of these can be used as a basis for physically ordering the data, unless multiple copies of the same file are held, with different ordering criteria, which is obviously not efficient in terms of storage space. For example, the aforementioned Customers dataset could be queried according to both the unique CustomerID or the non-unique Country. The data are either ordered according to CustomerID (resulting in a primary index on this attribute type) or according to Country (resulting in a clustered index on Country). Yet, complementary techniques are needed to speed up access to data according to those search keys that had no impact on the physical ordering of the data. These techniques, which we refer to as secondary file organization, always involve indexes, called secondary indexes.

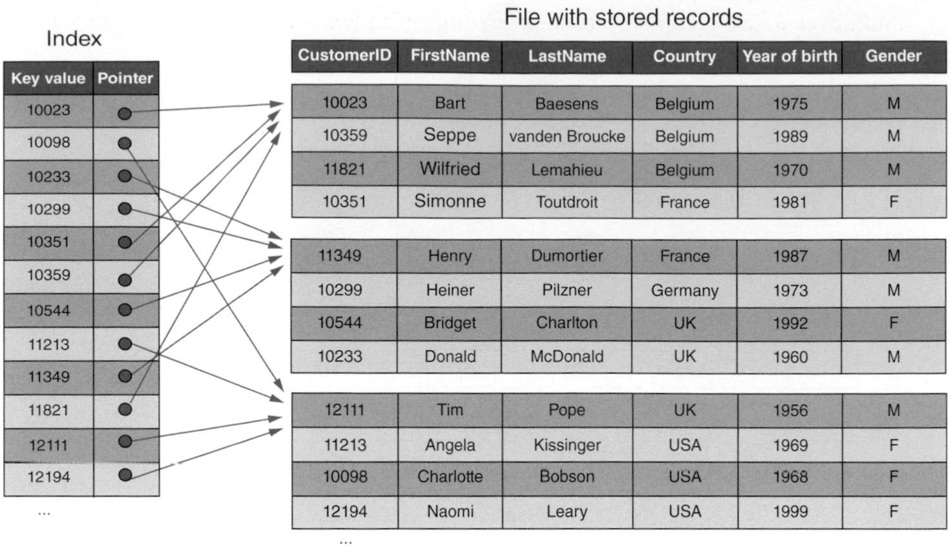


**Figure 12.22** Example of secondary index.

### 12.3.7.1 Characteristics of Secondary Indexes

In contrast to a primary index or a clustered index, a secondary index is based on an attribute type or set of attribute types that is/are not used as ordering criteria of the actual data file. There can only be a single primary or clustered index for a data file, but in addition there can be several secondary indexes. Secondary indexes can also be combined with other primary file organization techniques, such as random file organization or heap files.

A secondary index's search key can be atomic or composite, consisting of multiple attribute types. It can be either a primary key or other candidate key, or a non-key attribute type or combination of attribute types. In the former case, the search key uniquely identifies a single record. In the latter case, it yields selection criteria to retrieve zero, one, or more records. The index itself is again a sequential file that can be searched by means of the binary search technique.

Overall, the index entries have the following format: <key value, record pointer, or block pointer>. If the search key is unique (i.e., it is a primary key or a candidate key), there is one index entry for each key value, and hence record, in the data file. The index, therefore, is dense.[12] Each entry contains the key value and a pointer to the record or block with this key value (Figure 12.22).

If the search key is non-unique, multiple records correspond to a particular key value. In that case, there are several possibilities. One option is to have a dense index, with an index entry for each record and thus multiple entries with the same key value. A more commonly used alternative is to add a level of indirection, with each index entry referring to a separate block that contains all pointers to records with the corresponding search key value. In that case, we speak of an **inverted file**, as discussed in the next section. Also, as was the case with primary and clustered indexes, additional index levels can be created on top of a lowest-level secondary index, resulting in a

[12] A sparse index is not useful in the context of secondary indexes, because the file is not physically ordered in the appropriate way. As a consequence, records for which the search key value was not in the index cannot be retrieved through consecutive sequential block accesses to the data file.

multilevel index. We come back to multilevel indexes later in this chapter, when we deal with B-trees and $B^+$-trees (Section 12.3.8).

Before continuing, let's assess the pros and cons of secondary indexes. They are additional constructs that need to be updated if the data file changes, but the performance increase they offer may be even bigger than with primary or clustered indexes. Indeed, because the data file is not ordered according to the search key of a secondary index, it would not be possible to conduct a binary search on the data file itself, and a full linear search of the file would be required if a secondary index was not available.

For example, let's explore once more the sample file with 30,000 records and 1500 blocks, which we introduced earlier. Suppose we are using a secondary index, defined over a unique search key. The index contains 30,000 index entries, one for each search key value. If we assume an index entry size of 15 bytes, the blocking factor of the index is again 136. In that case, NBLKI equals $\lceil 30{,}000/136 \rceil = 221$ blocks. The expected number of block accesses to retrieve a record by means of the secondary index then amounts to $\log_2(221) + 1 \approx 9$ random block accesses. Without a secondary index, it would take a full file scan, hence on average $1500/2 = 750$ sequential block accesses, to find a record according to the search key.

#### 12.3.7.2 Inverted Files

As discussed in the previous section, an inverted file defines an index over a non-unique, non-ordering search key of a dataset. There is one index entry per key value and hence each entry may refer to multiple records with that same key value. The index entries have the following format: <key value, block address>. The block address refers to a block containing record pointers or block pointers to all records with that particular key value. This is illustrated in Figure 12.23.

In comparison to the previous calculations with respect to index usage, this approach requires an additional random block access to the block with pointers to records that correspond to an index entry. However, it allows avoiding the creation of a large, dense index. Also, as discussed in the

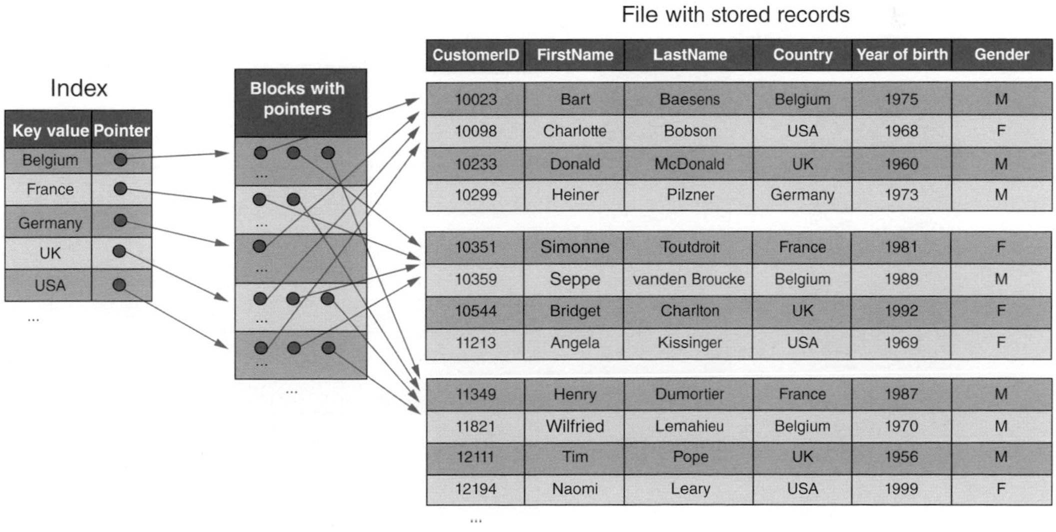


**Figure 12.23** Example of inverted file.

next chapter, queries that involve multiple attribute types can be executed efficiently by taking the intersection of the blocks with pointers corresponding to an individual attribute type. For example, if two indexes exist, one on Country and one on Gender, then all males living in the UK can be retrieved by taking the intersection between the block with "UK" pointers and the block with "male" pointers. The resulting set of pointers refers to data rows with a "UK" value for Country and an "M" value for Gender.

#### 12.3.7.3 Multicolumn Indexes

The previous sections stated that a search key can be either atomic or composite, and that the same indexing principles pertain to both atomic and composite search keys. In this section we show an example of an index over a composite search key, resulting in a so-called multicolumn index. If certain combinations of attribute types are often used together in a query, it can be advantageous to create a multicolumn index over these attribute types, to speed up retrieval according to combinations of their values. This principle can be applied to primary, clustered, and secondary indexes. In the case of a secondary index, if the composition of the indexed attribute types is not a primary key nor a candidate key, the inverted file approach can be used, as discussed in the previous section. An example is given in Figure 12.24. The search key consists of the Country and Gender attribute types, and all index entries consist of combinations of (Country, Gender) values. Since the combination is non-unique and since the data records are not sorted according to the search key, the inverted file approach is used, with intermediate blocks containing all pointers to data records with a certain (Country, Gender) combination.

Note that the index can be used to efficiently retrieve all records with the desired (Country, Gender) values. For the rows depicted in the example, all males living in the UK can be retrieved with a binary search on the index, a random block access to the appropriate block with pointers and two more block accesses to the data file, according to these pointers.

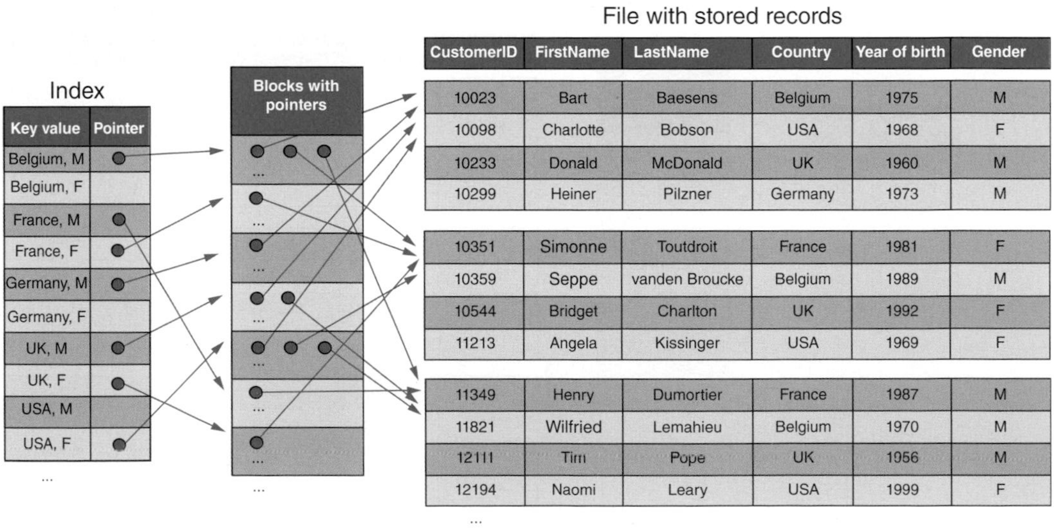


**Figure 12.24** Example of multicolumn index.

Also, all people living in a certain country, regardless of their gender, can be retrieved efficiently, since all index entries pertaining to the same country are adjacent. For example, retrieving all persons (male and female) living in the UK requires a binary search on the index, followed by two block accesses to the blocks with pointers (one for males and one for females) and three more block accesses to the data file, according to these pointers. However, retrieving all males regardless of the country will not be so efficient, since all index entries for people with the same gender are scattered throughout the index. A binary search is not possible, so the entire index has to be scanned linearly. This is a consequence of the way in which multicolumn indexes are sorted, with the attribute types in rightmost columns taking on all their consecutive values, whereas the values in the leftmost columns are kept stable. Using a multicolumn index to retrieve data according to a search key that involves only a subset of the index's columns is therefore mainly efficient if the leftmost index columns are used.

#### 12.3.7.4 Other Index Types

Many database vendors also introduced other types of indexes, to accommodate specific purposes or data retrieval tasks. For example, **hash indexes** provide a secondary file organization method that combines hashing with indexed retrieval. The index entries have the same format as in a normal secondary index; they consist of <key value, pointer> pairs. Yet, the index is organized not as a sequential file, but as a hash file. Applying the hash function to the search key yields the index block where the corresponding index entry can be found. Based on the pointer in this entry, the actual record(s) can be retrieved.

Another index type worth mentioning is the **bitmap index**. Bitmap indexes are mostly efficient for attribute types with only a limited set of possible values. Instead of these values, bitmap indexes contain a row ID and a series of bits – one bit for each possible value of the indexed attribute type. For each entry, the bit position that corresponds to the actual value for the row at hand is set to 1. The row IDs can be mapped to record pointers. Bitmap indexes for the "Country" and "Gender" attribute types from Figure 12.24 are represented in Figure 12.25.

When looked at vertically, each column can be considered as a bitmap or bit vector indicating which tuples have the values indicated by the column. By applying Boolean operations to bit vectors from multiple bitmap indexes, it becomes very efficient to identify records that satisfy certain

| RowID | Belgium | USA | UK | Germany | France |
|---|---|---|---|---|---|
| 0 | 1 | 0 | 0 | 0 | 0 |
| 1 | 0 | 1 | 0 | 0 | 0 |
| 2 | 0 | 0 | 1 | 0 | 0 |
| 3 | 0 | 0 | 0 | 1 | 0 |
| 4 | 0 | 0 | 0 | 0 | 1 |
| 5 | 1 | 0 | 0 | 0 | 0 |
| 6 | 0 | 0 | 1 | 0 | 0 |
| 7 | 0 | 1 | 0 | 0 | 0 |
| 8 | 0 | 0 | 0 | 0 | 1 |
| 9 | 1 | 0 | 0 | 0 | 0 |
| 10 | 0 | 0 | 1 | 0 | 0 |
| 11 | 0 | 1 | 0 | 0 | 0 |

| RowID | M | F |
|---|---|---|
| 0 | 1 | 0 |
| 1 | 0 | 1 |
| 2 | 1 | 0 |
| 3 | 1 | 0 |
| 4 | 0 | 1 |
| 5 | 1 | 0 |
| 6 | 0 | 1 |
| 7 | 0 | 1 |
| 8 | 1 | 0 |
| 9 | 1 | 0 |
| 10 | 1 | 0 |
| 11 | 0 | 1 |

**Figure 12.25** Example of bitmap indexes.

criteria, such as male customers that live in the UK. For attribute types with a limited number of different values, bitmap indexes can be stored efficiently by means of compression techniques.

A final example of a specific index type is the **join index** as supported by some RDBMSs. The latter is a multicolumn index that combines attribute types from two or more tables in such a way that it contains the precalculated result of a join between these tables. In this way, join queries can be executed very efficiently.

## 12.3.8 B-Trees and B$^+$-Trees

B-trees and B$^+$-trees are tree-structured index types that are heavily used in many commercial database products. Before discussing them in detail, we position them in the general context of multilevel indexes and search trees.

### 12.3.8.1 Multilevel Indexes Revisited

As discussed previously, multilevel indexes are very useful for speeding up data access if the lowest-level index itself becomes too large to be searched efficiently. An index can be considered as a sequential file and building an index-to-the-index improves the access to this sequential file. This higher-level index is, again, a sequential file to which an index can be built and so on. This principle can be applied to primary, clustering, and secondary indexes. The lowest-level index entries may contain pointers to disk blocks or individual records. Each higher-level index contains as many entries as there are blocks in the immediately lower-level index. Each index entry consists of a search key value and a reference to the corresponding block in the lower-level index. Index levels can be added until the highest-level index fits entirely within a single disk block. In this context, we speak of a first-level index, second-level index, third-level index, etc.

The performance gain induced by higher-level indexes is because an individual index is searched according to the binary search technique. With a binary search on a single index, the search interval, consisting of disk blocks, is reduced by a factor of two with every iteration and therefore it requires approximately $\log_2(\text{NBLKI})$ random block accesses to search an index consisting of NBLKI blocks. One additional random block access is needed to the actual data file. With a multilevel index, the search interval is reduced by a factor **BFI** with every index level, BFI being the blocking factor of the index. BFI denotes how many index entries fit within a single disk block, resulting in a single entry for the higher-level index. This reduction factor is also called the *fan-out* of the index. Searching a data file according to a multilevel index then requires $\lceil \log_{\text{BFI}}(\text{NBLKI}) + 2 \rceil$ random block accesses, with NBLKI denoting the number of blocks in the first-level index. This formula can be derived as follows:

- We need to add index levels until the highest-level index fits within a single disk block.
- The number of required blocks for index level i can be calculated as follows: $\text{NBLKI}_i = \lceil \text{NBLKI}_{i-1}/\text{BFI} \rceil$ for i = 2,3,. . .
- By applying the previous formula (i – 1) times, we derive that $\text{NBLKI}_i = \lceil \text{NBLKI}/\left(\text{BFI}^{i-1}\right) \rceil$ for i = 2,3,. . . and with NBLKI the number of blocks in the lowest-level index.
- For the highest-level index, consisting of only one block, it then holds that $1 = \lceil \text{NBLKI}/\left(\text{BFI}^{h-1}\right) \rceil$, with h denoting the highest index level.
- Therefore, $h - 1 = \lceil \log_{\text{BFI}}(\text{NBLKI}) \rceil$ and hence $h = \lceil \log_{\text{BFI}}(\text{NBLKI}) + 1 \rceil$.

- The number of block accesses to retrieve a record by means of a multilevel index then corresponds to a random block access for each index level, plus a random block access to the data file, which thus equals $\lceil \log_{BFI}(NBLKI) + 2 \rceil$.

BFI is typically much higher than two, so using a multilevel index is more efficient than a binary search on a single-level index.

Let's apply these insights to the same 30,000 records sample file. Suppose we retain the lowest-level index from the secondary index example (i.e., a secondary index over a unique search key). The index entries are 15 bytes in size and BFI is 136. The number of blocks in the first-level index (NBLKI) = 221. The second-level index then contains 221 entries and consumes $\lceil 221/136 \rceil = 2$ disk blocks. If a third index level is introduced, it contains two index entries and fits within a single disk block.[13] Searching a record by means of the multilevel index requires four random block accesses; three to the respective index levels and one to the actual data file. This can also be calculated as follows: $\lceil \log_{136}(221) + 2 \rceil = 4$. Remember that nine random block accesses were required when only using the lowest-level index.

A multilevel index can be considered as a so-called **search tree**, with each index level representing a level in the tree, each index block representing a node, and each access to the index resulting in navigation toward a subtree in the tree, hence reducing the search interval. The problem is that multilevel indexes may speed up data retrieval, but large multilevel indexes require a lot of maintenance if the data file is updated. Hence, traditional multilevel indexes have quite a negative impact on update performance of the database. For that reason, so-called B-trees and $B^+$-trees are a better alternative: they keep the essence of a search tree, but leave some space in the tree nodes (i.e., disk blocks) to accommodate for inserts, deletions, and updates in the data file without having to rearrange the entire index. We discuss these in the next sections.

#### 12.3.8.2 Binary Search Trees

> **Drill Down**
>
> The online playground provides visualization of several tree-based data structures (i.e., binary search trees, B-trees, and $B^+$-trees) as discussed in this chapter (see the Appendix for more details).

The functioning of B-trees and $B^+$-trees is easier to grasp if we first introduce the concept of **binary search trees**. A binary search tree is a physical tree structure in which each node has at most two children. Each tree node contains a search key value and a maximum of two pointers to children. Both children are the root nodes of subtrees, with one subtree only containing key values that are lower than the key value in the original node, and the other subtree only containing key values that are higher.

Navigating a binary search tree is very similar to applying the binary search technique already discussed in the context of sequential file organization. Here also, search efficiency is improved by "skipping" half of the search key values with every step, rather than linearly navigating all key values. Now the search space is not narrowed by splitting the physical range of addresses in half, as

[13] In practice, it would probably be more efficient to use only a second-level and first-level index, with the second-level index maintained and searched in internal memory.

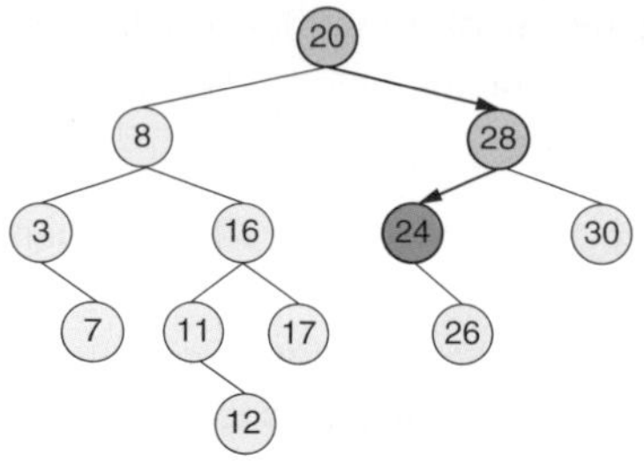


**Figure 12.26** Example of binary search tree.

with the binary search technique, but by navigating a tree structure, and in each node choosing between a "left" and a "right" subtree. More concretely, suppose a search key K is used with values $K_i$. To find the node with search key value $K_\mu$, the key value $K_i$ in the root node is compared to $K_\mu$. If $K_i = K_\mu$, the search key is found. If $K_i > K_\mu$, then the pointer to the root of the "left" subtree with only key values lower than $K_i$ is followed. Otherwise, if $K_i < K_\mu$, the pointer to the root of the "right" subtree is followed. This subtree contains only key values higher than $K_i$. The same procedure is applied recursively to the chosen subtree until the node with $K_\mu$ is found or until a leaf node is reached, meaning that the key value $K_\mu$ is not present in the tree. This is illustrated in Figure 12.26, with $K_\mu = 24$. The appropriate node is found after three steps, whereas a linear search would have taken nine steps in this case. As already discussed in the context of binary search, this performance gain becomes larger as the number of key values increases.

The performance could be increased even further if each node contained more than one key value and more than two children. In that case, with an equal total number of key values, the height of the tree would be reduced and therefore the average and maximal number of steps would be lower. This exact consideration is the basis of the B-tree concept, as discussed in the next section.

### 12.3.8.3 B-Trees

A **B-tree** is a tree-structured index. B-trees can be considered as variations of search trees that are explicitly designed for hard disk storage. In particular, each node corresponds to a disk block and nodes are kept between half full and full to cater for a certain dynamism of the index, hereby accommodating changes in the data file without the need for too extensive rearrangements of the index.

Every node contains a set of **search key values**, a set of **tree pointers** that refer to child nodes and a set of **data pointers** that refer to data records, or blocks with data records, that correspond to the search key values. The data records are stored separately and are not part of the B-tree. A B-tree of order k holds the following properties:

- Every non-leaf node is of the following format:[14] $<P_0, <K_1, Pd_1>, P_1, <K_2, Pd_2>, \ldots <K_q, Pd_q>, P_q>$, with $q \leq 2k$. Every $P_i$ is a tree pointer: it points to another node in the tree. This node is the root of the subtree that $P_i$ refers to. Every $Pd_i$ is a data pointer: it points to the record with key value $K_i$,[15] or to the disk block that contains this record.
- A B-tree is a *balanced* tree; all leaf nodes are at the same level in the tree. Every path from the root of the B-tree to any leaf node thus has the same length, which is called the *height* of the B-tree. Leaf nodes have the same structure as non-leaf nodes, except that all their tree pointers $P_i$ are null.

[14] Some authors define the order differently and state a B-tree of this format to be of order 2k instead of k.

[15] As always, a search key can be atomic or composite, combining multiple attribute types. $K_i$ may represent a single atomic or single composite key value.

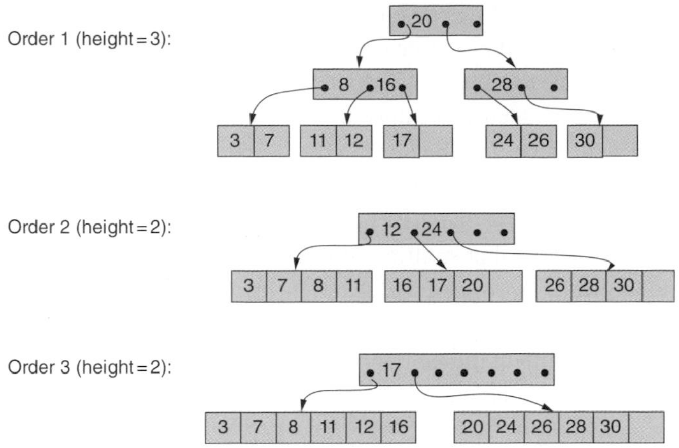


**Figure 12.27** Examples of a B-tree.

- Within a node, the property holds that $K_1 < K_2 < \ldots < K_q$.
- For every key value X in the subtree referred to by $P_i$, the following holds:
  - $K_i < X < K_{i+1}$ for $0 < i < q$
  - $X < K_{i+1}$ for $i = 0$
  - $K_i < X$ for $i = q$
- The B-tree's root node has a number of key values, and an equal number of data pointers, that varies between 1 and 2k. The number of tree pointers and child nodes then varies between 2 and 2k + 1.
- All "normal" nodes (i.e., internal nodes: non-root and non-leaf nodes) have a number of key values and data pointers between k and 2k. The number of tree pointers and child nodes varies between k + 1 and 2k + 1.
- Every leaf node has a number of key values and data pointers between k and 2k and no tree pointers.

Hence, every non-leaf node with q key values should have q data pointers and q + 1 tree pointers to child nodes. If the indexed search key is non-unique, a level of indirection is introduced, similar to the inverted file approach discussed in Section 12.3.7.2. The data pointers $Pd_i$ then don't point to the records directly, but to a block containing pointers to all records satisfying the search key value $K_i$. Figure 12.27 provides a few simple examples to illustrate the principles of B-trees, with varying order and height. The numbers represent key values $K_i$, whereas the arrows represent tree pointers $P_i$. The data pointers $Pd_i$ are not depicted so as not to clutter the illustration, but in reality there is a data pointer for every key value.

A B-tree is searched starting from the root. If the desired key value X is found in a node (say $K_i = X$), then the corresponding data record(s) can be accessed in the data file by following the data pointer $Pd_i$. If the desired value is not found in the node, a tree pointer is followed to the subtree that contains the appropriate range of key values. More precisely, the subtree pointer $P_i$ to be followed is the one corresponding to the smallest value of i for which $X < K_{i+1}$. If $X >$ all $K_i$ then the tree pointer $P_{i+1}$ is followed. The same procedure is repeated for this subtree and so on, until the desired key value is found in a node or until a leaf node is reached, meaning that the desired search key value is not present. This approach is again very similar to a binary search algorithm, but since the number of tree pointers is much higher than two, the fan-out and therefore search efficiency is much higher than with a binary search.

The capacity of a node equals the size of a disk block, and all nodes, except for the root, are filled to at least 50%. Hence, a B-tree uses the storage capacity efficiently, but still leaves room for additions to the data file without the need for impactful rearrangements of the index structure. If data records, and hence key values, are added, the empty space in a node is filled up. If all nodes in the appropriate subtree for that key value are already filled to capacity, a node is split into two half-full nodes. Both will be sibling children of the original node's parent. If, upon deletion of records and key values, a node becomes less than half full, it is merged with one of its siblings to produce a node filled to at least 50%. Note that splitting or merging a node also impacts the parent node, where a tree pointer and key value are added or deleted, respectively. Therefore, a node split or merger at the parent's level may be called for as well. In rare cases, these changes may work their way up to the root node, but even then the number of changes is limited to the height of the B-tree. This is still substantially less than the required changes if the index had been organized as a sequential file.

It is very complex to make exact predictions about the required number of block accesses when searching a B-tree. There are many possible configurations, every node may contain between k and 2k key values (except for the root), and the tree may assume different shapes depending on node splits and mergers. For example, in Figure 12.27, searching for key value 24 requires three random block accesses in the first B-tree, one block access in the second B-tree, and two block accesses in the third tree. Searching for key value 17 requires three, two, and one block accesses, respectively. The height of the tree, and hence the maximum number of random block accesses to find a certain key value in the tree, will decrease as the order of the tree increases. Note also that a B-tree being *balanced* is an important property in this context. With a non-balanced tree, the path from root to leaf node would not be the same for all leaf nodes, resulting in even more variation in search time.

Finally, it is worth mentioning that sometimes B-trees are also used as a primary file organization technique, hence organizing the actual data file as a search tree. The nodes then still contain search key values and tree pointers. However, instead of data pointers, they contain the actual data fields of the records that correspond to the search key values. This approach can be very efficient with small files and records with a very limited number of fields. Otherwise, the number of tree levels quickly becomes too large for efficient access.

**Drill Down**

B-trees were originally invented in 1971 by Rudolf Bayer and Edward McCreight, who then worked for Boeing Research Labs. It is not entirely clear what the "B" stands for; according to Edward McCreight it could be multiple things: "Boeing," "balanced", and even "Bayer" (Rudolf Bayer was the senior author of the two). However, as he stated at the 24th Symposium on Combinatorial Pattern Matching in 2013: "The more you think about what the B in B-trees means, the better you understand B-trees".

#### 12.3.8.4 B$^+$-Trees

Most DBMS implementations use indexes based on **B$^+$-trees** rather than B-trees. The main difference is that in a B$^+$-tree, only the leaf nodes contain data pointers. In addition, all key values that exist in the non-leaf nodes are repeated in the leaf nodes, such that every key value occurs in a

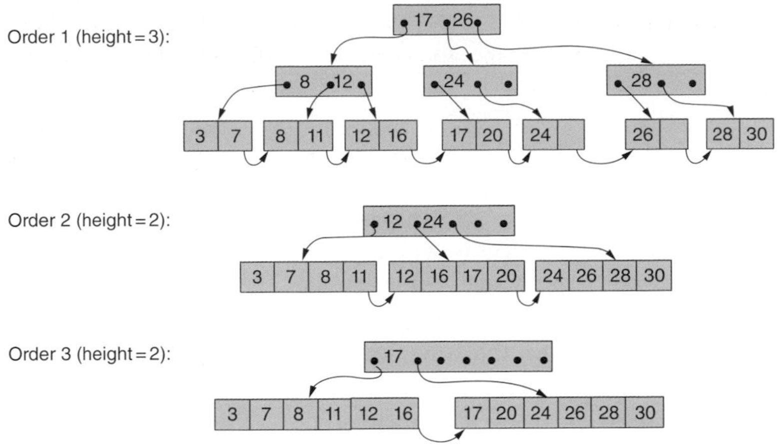


**Figure 12.28** Examples of a B⁺-tree.

leaf node, along with a corresponding data pointer. The higher-level nodes only contain a subset of the key values present in the leaf nodes. Finally, every leaf node of a $B^+$-tree also has one tree pointer, pointing to its next sibling. In this way, the latter tree pointers create a linked list of leaf nodes, sequentially arranging all leaf nodes according to the key values they contain.

Figure 12.28 presents some simple $B^+$-tree examples, with the same order and search key values as the B-tree example. Again, the data pointers, which now only exist in the leaf nodes, are not represented. In contrast to the B-trees, the $B^+$-trees contain some redundancy in their search key values. Note also the "next" tree pointers in the leaf nodes. Sometimes "previous" pointers are present as well.

Searching and updating a $B^+$-tree occurs in a similar way as with a B-tree. Since only the leaf nodes contain data pointers, every search must continue until the leaf nodes, which was not the case with B-trees. Still, $B^+$-trees are often more efficient, because the non-leaf nodes do not contain any data pointers, so with the same block size their order can be higher than with a B-tree. As a consequence, the height of a $B^+$-tree is often smaller, resulting in fewer block accesses to search the tree. In most cases, the leaf nodes of a $B^+$-tree, which *do* contain data pointers, have a different order than the other tree nodes.

Also, the "next" tree pointers in the leaf nodes, in combination with the fact that all search key values and data pointers are present in the leaf nodes, provide for an additional way of traversing the tree. The tree is then not navigated top-down, but by accessing several leaf nodes consecutively, starting from a leftmost leaf node and following the next pointers between them. The latter allows for more efficient processing of *range queries*, as discussed in the next chapter.

It is worth noting that other variants exist as well. In particular, there are variations on the ***fill factor***, which denotes how "full" a non-leaf node must be, which is 50% for standard B-trees and $B^+$-trees. For example, a B-tree with a fill factor of two-thirds is often called a B*-tree.

### Retention Questions

- What are the differences between primary and secondary file organization?
- Discuss and contrast the most important primary file organization methods.
- Discuss and contrast the most important secondary file organization methods.
- Discuss and contrast B-trees and $B^+$-trees.

## Summary

In this chapter we dealt with different aspects pertaining to physical file organization. First, we presented the characteristics of storage devices and how these affect the performance of physical data access. Then, we discussed the organization of, respectively, stored records and physical files. We distinguished between primary and secondary file organization methods. In this context, special attention was paid to different types of indexes and the ways in which they improve search performance. B-trees and $B^+$-trees in particular were discussed as index types that often occur in DBMS products. The next chapter builds on these findings to discuss physical database organization, with the physical database consisting of a set of physical files and indexes.

**Connections**

Chapter 13 applies the principles of record organization and file organization in the context of physical database organization. It also comes back to the topic of storage hardware, discussing how individual storage devices are clustered and managed as larger entities, called enterprise storage subsystems.

### Scenario Conclusion

Now that Sober has learned about various file organization methods, it has decided to physically implement each relational table using the indexed sequential file organization method. Moreover, to speed up the execution time of its queries it has decided to define the following indexes:

| Table | Index |
|---|---|
| CAR(CAR-NR, CARTYPE) | Primary index on CAR-NR; secondary index on CARTYPE |
| SOBER CAR(S-CAR-NR) | Primary index on S-CAR-NR |
| OTHER CAR(O-CAR-NR, O-CUST-NR) | Primary index on O-CAR-NR |
| ACCIDENT(ACC-NR, ACC-DATE-TIME, ACC-LOCATION) | Clustered index on ACC-LOCATION |
| INVOLVED(I-CAR-NR, I-ACC-NR, DAMAGE AMOUNT) | Primary index on I-CAR-NR, I-ACC-NR; secondary index on DAMAGE AMOUNT |
| RIDE(RIDE-NR, PICKUP-DATE-TIME, DROPOFF-DATE-TIME, DURATION, PICKUP-LOC, DROPOFF-LOC, DISTANCE, FEE, R-CAR-NR) | Clustered index on PICKUP-LOC; secondary index on FEE |
| RIDE HAILING(H-RIDE-NR, PASSENGERS, WAIT-TIME, REQUEST-TYPE, H-CUST-NR) | Clustered index on WAIT-TIME: secondary on PASSENGERS |
| RIDE SHARING(S-RIDE-NR) | Primary index on S-RIDE-NR |
| CUSTOMER(CUST-NR, CUST-NAME) | Primary index on CUST-NR |
| BOOK(B-CUST-NR, B-S-RIDE-NR) | Primary index on B-CUST-NR, B-S-RIDE-NR |

## Key Terms List

absolute address
actuator
binary search
binary search trees
bitmap index
block pointer
blocking factor
blocking factor of the index (BFI)
B-tree
$B^+$-trees
bucket
central storage
chaining
clustered index
collision
cylinder
data item
data pointers
delimiters
dense indexes
directly accessible storage devices (DASDs)
directory
disk blocks
dynamic hashing
embedded identification
hard disk controller
hash indexes
hashing
heap file
I/O
I/O boundary
index entry
indexed sequential file organization
indexing
intervals
inverted file
join index
key-to-address transformation
latency
linear list
linear search
linked list
lists
loading factor
mixed file
multilevel indexes
nonlinear list
one-way linked list
open addressing
overflow
overflow area
overflow-handling technique
partitions
persistent storage media
physical database
physical file
pointers
primary area
primary file organization methods
primary index
primary storage
random file organization
read/write heads
record pointer
relative block address
relative location
rotational delay
search key
search key values
search tree
secondary file organization methods
secondary index
secondary storage
sectors
seek time
sequential file organization
sparse indexes
spindle
stored record
synonyms
tracks
transfer time
tree pointers
uniform distribution
variable length records
volatile memory

## Review Questions

**12.1.** What does DASD stand for?

a. Database appropriate storage device.
b. Directly accumulative storage device.
c. Directly accessible storage device.
d. Data accumulative storage device.

**12.2.** When translating a logical data model into an internal data model, what should be taken into account?

a. The physical storage properties.
b. The types of operations that will be executed on the data.
c. The size of the database.
d. All of the above should be taken into account.

**12.3.** How is a row/tuple translated into an internal data model?

a. Data item.
b. Stored record.
c. Dataset.
d. Physical storage structure.

**12.4.** When can the relative location technique for record organization be problematic?

a. When there are many missing values in records.
b. When there is a large number of records.
c. When there are many different data types.
d. When there are a lot of relations.

**12.5.** In which of these cases can we make use of delimiters to separate attributes?

a. The data are stored in mixed files.
b. Some attributes have data types that can have variable lengths as input.
c. Some attributes are multi-valued.
d. All of the above.

**12.6.** Why is the blocking factor important to know?

a. For calculating the seek time of a hard disk drive.
b. For achieving efficient access to records.
c. For determining the maximum size of the database.
d. None of the above.

**12.7.** Which of the following statements with regards to search keys is **not correct**?

a. A search key can be composite, meaning that it can consist of a combination of values.
b. A search key needs to be a unique identifier of a record.
c. A search key can be used to retrieve all records of which a certain attribute type falls within a range.
d. A search key determines the criteria for retrieving records.

**12.8.** Which of the following file organization methods is **not** a primary file organization method?

a. Linked lists.
b. Sequential file organization.
c. Heap files.
d. Hash file organization.

**12.9.** Which of the following statements with regards to random file organization is **correct**?

a. In order to avoid overflow, the hashing algorithm that distributes keys to bucket addresses needs to be carefully chosen.
b. A higher loading factor leads to less overflow but also more wasted storage space.
c. Retrieving a record only requires a single block access, more particularly a random block access to the first block of the bucket indicated by the hashing algorithm.
d. Division, a hashing technique that divides the key by a positive integer M and takes the remainder as the record address, frequently performs very poorly.

**12.10.** Which of the following statements with regards to indexed sequential file organization is **correct**?

a. The search key of a sparse index is a unique key (i.e., a primary key or candidate key).
b. Sparse indexes are generally faster than dense indexes.
c. Entries of dense indexes always refer to a group of records.
d. Dense indexes are more complex to maintain than sparse indexes.

**12.11.** Which of the following statements is **correct**?

a. Secondary file organization methods make insertion and deletion of records a lot easier.
b. An important application of tree data structures is when they provide a physical index structure to speed up retrieval of records.
c. An advantage of one-way linked lists, where each record contains a pointer to its logical successor, is that not all records must be retrieved any longer, because frequently only part of the list needs to be processed.
d. An inverted file defines an index over a unique, ordered search key of the dataset.

**12.12.** Which of the following statements with regards to search trees, B-trees, and $B^+$-trees is **correct**?

a. An unbalanced B-tree allows for additional performance gain by reducing the height of the tree.
b. B-trees are a primary file organization method and directly impact the physical location of records.
c. Search trees are a good alternative to B-trees and $B^+$-trees because they allow for better maintenance.
d. The performance gain of binary search trees over linear search trees becomes larger as the number of key values increases.

## Problems and Exercises

12.1E What is the I/O boundary? Where are databases situated with regards to this boundary?

12.2E What is the expected time for a sequential block access and the expected time for a random block access given a hard disk drive with the following characteristics?
- Average seek time = 7.5 ms
- Spindle speed = 5400 rpm
- Transfer rate = 200 MBps
- Block size = 512 bytes

12.3E If a food delivery service wants to gather the personal information of new clients and uses an online form in which all fields are required to be filled in, which record organization technique would be preferred for this purpose? Why would this be the best choice? And what if not all fields were mandatory?

12.4E How can we improve the speed of physically retrieving a record based on a search key?

12.5E What is the difference between a bucket address, a relative block address, and an absolute block address when talking about key-to-address transformation (a hashing algorithm)?

12.6E Discuss the advantages and disadvantages of secondary indexes. When would it be useful to maintain a secondary index?

12.7E Discuss the differences between and (dis)advantages of heap files, sequential files, and random file organization.

# 13 Physical Database Organization

## Chapter Objectives

In this chapter, you will learn to:

- grasp the basic concepts of physical database organization;
- identify various database access methods;
- understand how individual devices can be pooled and managed as so-called enterprise storage subsystems;
- understand the importance of business continuity.

**Opening Scenario**

Now that Sober knows what indexes it needs, it wants to understand how these indexes can be implemented in SQL. The company is also curious to find out how the query optimizer works and how it decides on the access path to the data for a given query. Sober wonders what type of storage hardware it should adopt. Finally, the company wants to figure out how it can guarantee its uninterrupted functioning, despite possible planned or unplanned downtime of the hard- and software.

This chapter deals with physical database organization in its broadest sense. A primary focus is on physical database design – the translation of a logical data model into an internal data model, including the design of indexes to speed up data access. In this respect, this chapter builds on the insights gained from Chapter 12 in relation to physical record and file organization. However, we also zoom out to other concerns of physical data storage, such as technological and management aspects, as well as the important area of business continuity.

First, we discuss the concepts of *tablespaces* and *index spaces*, as well as other basic building blocks of physical database organization. The principles of file organization acquired in the previous chapter are then applied in the context of *database organization*. Here, we deal with the role of the *query optimizer* and how the latter uses indexes and other techniques to determine the optimal *access plan* to execute a query. We also pay particular attention to different alternatives for *join implementation*. In the second half of this chapter, we return to storage hardware, but now from a more global perspective than in Chapter 12. We deal with *RAID technology* and different approaches to *networked storage*, such as SAN and NAS. We conclude with a discussion on how these techniques can be applied in the context of *business continuity*. By no means do we claim exhaustiveness with respect to the topics covered in this chapter. Rather, we aim to provide the reader with a broad perspective on the many angles and concerns of physical data storage and management. Just like in Chapter 12, we assume a relational database setting unless noted otherwise, although most concepts apply to other database types as well.

## 13.1 Physical Database Organization and Database Access Methods

Physical database organization focuses on conceiving the internal data model. Therefore, this section applies the principles discussed in the previous chapter with respect to the physical organization of individual records and files, but adds provisions for efficient retrieval of related records belonging to different record types or datasets, as is the case with, e.g., a join query in SQL. In addition, it focuses on how the generic file organization principles are implemented in the concrete setting of a database management system, particularly a relational DBMS. As a starting point, it is advised to re-visit the discussion related to Table 12.1 in the previous chapter, which presented the mapping between logical data model and internal data model concepts.

> **Connections**
>
> Chapter 6 discusses relational DBMSs. Join SQL queries were introduced in Chapter 7. Physical record organization and file organization were dealt with in Chapter 12. This chapter also overviewed the physical properties of storage devices (and particularly hard disk drives [HDDs]) and their impact on the respective file organization techniques.

It should be stressed that the more recent versions of SQL do not impose any standardization on the internal data model or on the way in which a logical relational data model is implemented physically. Different DBMS vendors all have their own approaches in improving DBMS performance by means of different file organization techniques, index types, database access methods, join implementations, and tuning facilities. Speaking of "the" physical database organization method is thus meaningless and the reader is encouraged to carefully examine a particular DBMS's configuration and tuning manual for specifics. Still, the following sections aim at providing an overview of some widely applied principles with respect to physical database design and the impact of certain design decisions on performance. We focus on index design, different possible access paths given particular properties of queries, tables and indexes, and different ways of efficiently implementing join queries.

### 13.1.1 From Database to Tablespace

We can discriminate between the user databases and the system database. The user databases have a physical structure that is determined by the database designer and contain data that represents an organization's state. The system database's structure is predefined by the database vendor and holds the catalog tables that support the DBMS's exploitation. In its most simple incarnation, a physical user database is a collection of index files and data files, organized according to the principles of record organization and file organization discussed in the previous chapter. However, many DBMS implementations introduce an additional level of indirection between a logical database and the physical data files, called a **tablespace**.

A tablespace can be considered as a physical container of database objects. It consists of one or more physical files, often with the option of distributing the files over multiple storage devices. In smaller-scale database systems, the files are managed by the operating system's file system, whereas high performance DBMSs often manage the files themselves, interacting directly with the storage

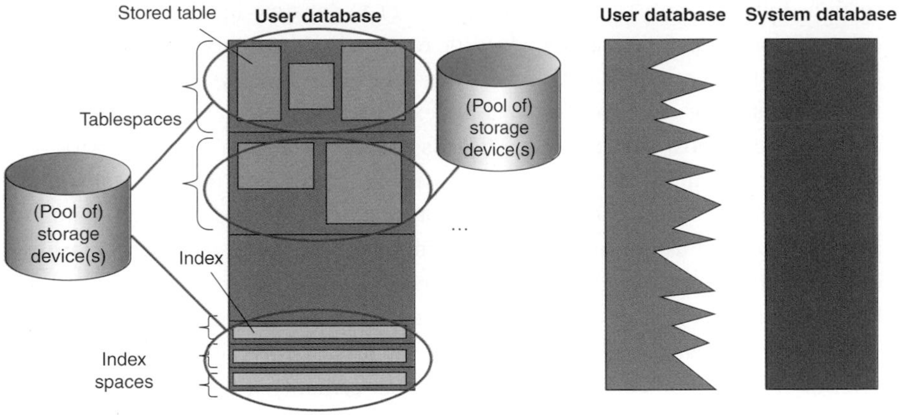


**Figure 13.1** Stored tables, indexes, tablespaces, and index spaces.

devices, bypassing the overhead of the operating system's file management features. Every logical table is assigned to a tablespace to be persisted physically. We then speak of a **stored table**. A stored table occupies one or more disk blocks or pages[1] in the tablespace. A tablespace can contain indexes as well, although sometimes separate **index spaces** are used for this purpose.

The use of tablespaces as a level of indirection when mapping stored tables onto physical files and storage devices provides a first important instrument to the database administrator to tune the DBMS's performance. For example, data from the same table can be distributed over multiple storage devices. Different subsets of the data can then be searched in parallel in the context of a single, complex query for improved performance. We call this **intra-query parallelism**. On the other hand, it can also be desirable to avoid involving multiple storage devices in the same query and rather to optimize the system for **inter-query parallelism**, where many simple queries can be executed in parallel. It is also possible to cluster data from multiple tables into a single tablespace to cater for efficient retrieval of strongly interrelated data.

**Connections**

Chapter 4 discussed the roles of the database designer and database administrator.

Physical database design comes down to attributing logical concepts to physical constructs, as illustrated in Figure 13.1. This is a joint responsibility of the database designer and the database administrator. A first decision pertains to the choice of storage devices. It can be a deliberate option to provide storage devices with different cost and performance characteristics, as not all logical tables require the same retrieval and/or update performance. Sometimes, several devices are pooled into larger entities for better performance and reliability, but also for more effective management, as discussed in Section 13.2. On the chosen storage devices, files are created which form the tablespaces and index spaces. In line with the aforementioned considerations, tables are then attributed to tablespaces. In this way, if desired, they can be distributed over multiple physical files. If the DBMS does not provide the indirection of tablespaces, tables are mapped directly onto data files. Some indexes are generated automatically by the DBMS according to the logical data model (e.g., to enforce uniqueness for all primary keys). Other indexes are created explicitly by the database administrator; we discuss the choices and criteria with respect to index design in detail in the next

[1] In file organization literature, the term "block" is used most often, but in actual database literature the term "page" is more frequent.

section. Indexes are assigned to tablespaces or to separate index spaces. Particularly in the latter case, secondary indexes can be added or removed without any impact on the physical data files. Remember that a primary or clustered index determines the physical ordering of the data records in a file, so creation or deletion of such an index deserves particular consideration.

Fortunately, most contemporary DBMSs are equipped with extensive performance-tuning facilities. These pertain to decisions with respect to distributing data and tables over storage media, detecting and resolving I/O problems of storage devices, providing index-tuning wizards to monitor and optimize the use of indexes, monitoring and optimizing the **access paths** involved in query execution, etc. Even though most DBMSs provide ample auto-configuring and self-tuning features, this responsibility remains to a very large extent with the database administrator. The number of parameters that can be manipulated by the latter is often very extensive; in the next sections, we offer an overview of some essential aspects, but certainly without claiming to be exhaustive.

### 13.1.2 Index Design

Although indexing was already discussed extensively in the previous chapter, it is useful to further focus on the question of which indexes to create in the context of actual database organization. On the one hand, indexes are probably *the* most important tuning instrument to the database designer and database administrator; it is discussed in the next section on database access methods how indexes directly impact the decisions made by the *query optimizer* with respect to how a query is implemented and optimized physically. On the other hand, there are also other reasons to define an index than just efficient query processing. This section focuses on the criteria a database designer can use to decide which indexes to create, and which indexes not to create. We start off by summarizing in Table 13.1 the respective index types presented in the previous chapter.

Since indexes belong to the internal data model, which is not part of the most recent versions of the SQL standard, there is no standard SQL syntax for index creation. Still, most DBMSs use a similar syntax, which looks as follows:

```
CREATE [UNIQUE]  INDEX INDEX_NAME
ON TABLE_NAME (COLUMN_NAME [ORDER] {, COLUMN_NAME [ORDER]})
[CLUSTER]
```

The UNIQUE and CLUSTER clauses are optional. We show some concrete examples, which are further explained in the discussion on index creation below:

a.
```
CREATE UNIQUE INDEX PRODNR_INDEX
ON PRODUCT(PRODNR ASC)
```

b.
```
CREATE INDEX PRODUCTDATA_INDEX
ON PRODUCT(PRODPRICE DESC, PRODTYPE ASC)
```

**Table 13.1** Summary of different index types

| Index type | Impacts physical ordering of tuples | Unique search key | Dense or sparse |
|---|---|---|---|
| **Primary** | Yes | Yes | Sparse |
| **Clustered** | Yes | No | Dense or sparse |
| **Secondary** | No | Yes | Dense |
| | | No | Dense or inverted file |

c.
```
CREATE INDEX PRODNAME_INDEX
ON PRODUCT(PRODNAME ASC)
CLUSTER
```

d.
```
CREATE INDEX PRODSUPPLIER_INDEX
ON PRODUCT(SUPPLIERNR ASC)
```

The main reasons for index creation are the following:

- *Efficient retrieval of rows according to certain queries or selection criteria*: An index can be created on any column or combination of columns in a table. As shown in the next section, retrieval is much more efficient for search keys that are indexed. Selection criteria aiming at a unique tuple can be supported by a primary index or by a secondary index on a candidate key – see index (a) above. Selection criteria targeting a set of tuples can be supported by a clustered index or by a secondary index on a non-key attribute type or combination of attribute types, as shown in indexes (c) and (b) respectively. In many cases, even if only some of the attribute types of a composite search key are indexed, retrieval performance will increase.
- *Efficient performance of join queries*: As stated previously, the join is one of the most expensive operations, performance wise, in query execution. Indexes can be used to perform the search for related tuples in both tables (i.e., tuples that match the join criteria) in a more efficient way. Such an index often involves a foreign key, as these are typical candidates to appear in join conditions. The latter is illustrated in index (d). More details are provided in Section 13.1.4.
- *Enforce uniqueness on a column value or combination of column values*: It would be very inefficient for a DBMS to enforce a uniqueness constraint on an attribute type or set of attribute types without using an index. In that case, every time a tuple is added or an attribute is updated, the DBMS would have to linearly scan the entire table to verify whether the uniqueness constraint has not been violated. Therefore, enforcing a uniqueness constraint requires that an index is created over the corresponding attribute type(s), such that the DBMS only has to search the index to make sure there are no duplicate values. We call such an index a *unique index*; it is denoted by the UNIQUE clause in the abovementioned syntax for query creation, as shown in index (a). A unique index is generated automatically for every primary key. Other unique indexes can be defined explicitly over other candidate keys by the database designer. If the unique attribute type or combination of attribute types determines the physical ordering of the rows in the table, the unique index is a primary index. If this is not the case, the unique index is a secondary index.
- *Logical ordering of rows in a table*: Every index is ordered in a certain way, according to the attribute type(s) it involves. This can be specified by means of the ASC (for ascending) or DESC (for descending) clause in the syntax. As such, the index also specifies a logical ordering on the actual tuples in the table, which contain, among others, these same attribute types. The number of secondary indexes that can be created is in theory only limited by the number of attribute types in a table. Thus, one can define numerous logical ordering criteria on the same physically ordered stored table. This is illustrated in all index examples above.
- *Physical ordering of rows in a table*: The ordering of the index entries can also be used to determine the physical order of the rows in a stored table. In that case, the values to the index's search key(s) determine the physical positioning of the respective rows on the disk. If every value or combination of values in the search key is unique, we have a primary index. Otherwise, it is a clustered index. Consequently, retrieving the tuples in this order (e.g., in the context of an ORDER BY clause in an SQL query) becomes very efficient. Also, as illustrated hereafter, range

queries can be performed more efficiently on attribute types for which such an index is available. Unfortunately, since it determines the physical ordering of the tuples, there can be only one such index (either a primary index or a clustered index) for every table. Hence, the choice of which attribute types to involve should be made very carefully, in light of the expected frequency and importance of this type of query. The clustering property can be set by the optional CLUSTER clause when creating an index – see index (c) in the above example.

Apart from a single primary or clustered index for every table, one can define as many secondary indexes as desired. However, every index also comes with a cost: it consumes storage capacity and may slow down update queries, as the corresponding indexes need to be updated as well. The database administrator must rely on statistical information in the catalog (see below), as well as his/her own experience to decide which indexes to create. Fortunately, because of the physical data independence discussed earlier, indexes can be added or deleted in light of altered requirements or new insights into data usage, without affecting the logical data model or applications. In addition, secondary indexes can be constructed or removed without affecting the actual data files. This is not the case for primary indexes and clustered indexes.

Attribute types that are typical candidates to be indexed are primary keys and other candidate keys to enforce uniqueness, foreign keys and other attribute types that are often used in join conditions, and attribute types that occur frequently as selection criteria in queries. Overall, it is better to avoid attribute types that are large or variable in size (e.g., large character strings or varchar attribute types), as these render index search and maintenance less efficient. Other pertinent factors are the size of the tables, as an index over a small table often induces more overhead than performance gain, and the proportion of retrieval and update queries. Typically, retrieval is sped up, whereas updates are slowed down.

**Connections**

Chapter 1 discussed physical data independence.

## 13.1.3 Database Access Methods

### 13.1.3.1 Functioning of the Query Optimizer

**Connections**

Chapter 5 introduced navigational DBMSs such as CODASYL. SQL was discussed in Chapter 7.

In contrast to legacy environments such as CODASYL, an essential characteristic of RDBMSs and other more recent DBMS types is that they *are non-navigational* (see Chapter 5). In this respect, SQL is a declarative query language in which a developer specifies *which* data are required, but not *how* the data are to be located and retrieved from the physical database files (see Chapter 7).

In many cases, different access paths exist to get to the same data, although the time to accomplish the retrieval task may vary greatly. For each query, it is the responsibility of the *optimizer* to translate the different possible ways of resolving the query into different *access plans* and to select the plan with the highest estimated efficiency. Modern **cost-based optimizers** calculate the optimal[2] access plan according to a set of built-in cost formulas similar to the ones discussed in Chapter 12 on file organization, as well as information such as the table(s) involved in the query, the available indexes, the statistical properties of the data in the tables, etc.

[2] In fact, real optimality cannot be guaranteed in most cases. The optimizer uses heuristics to determine the best access plan possible, based on the available information and within the boundaries of calculation time.

The respective steps of query execution and the role of the optimizer were already discussed in Chapter 2. In summary, the *query processor* is the DBMS component that assists in the execution of both retrieval and update queries against the database. It consists of a DML compiler, a query parser, a query rewriter, a query optimizer, and a query executor. The *DML compiler* first extracts the DML statements from the host language. The *query parser* then parses the query into an internal representation format and checks the query for syntactical and semantical correctness. This representation is rewritten by the *query rewriter*. The latter optimizes the query, independently of the current database state, by simplifying it according to a set of predefined rules and heuristics. Then the *query optimizer* kicks in. It optimizes the query, taking the current database state into account, as well as information in the catalog and available access structures such as indexes. The result of the query optimization procedure is a final access plan which is then handed over to the query executor for execution.

The DBMS maintains the following statistical data in its catalog, to be used by the optimizer to calculate the optimal access plan:

- Table-related data:
  - number of rows;
  - number of disk blocks occupied by the table;
  - number of overflow records associated with the table.
- Column-related data:
  - number of different column values;
  - statistical distribution of the column values.
- Index-related data:
  - number of different values for indexed search keys and for individual attribute types of composite search keys;
  - number of disk blocks occupied by the index;
  - index type: primary/clustered or secondary.
- Tablespace-related data:
  - number and size of tables in the tablespace;
  - device-specific I/O properties of the device on which the table resides.

It would lead us too far to discuss all elements in detail, but we illustrate a few essential aspects below. A first important concept is the **filter factor**, or FF for short.[3] An FF is associated with a **query predicate**. The query predicate specifies the selection condition with respect to a particular attribute type $A_i$ in the query, (e.g., "CustomerID = 11349" or "Gender = M" or "Year of Birth $\geq$ 1970"). The $FF_i$ of a query predicate represents the fraction of the total number of rows that is expected to satisfy the predicate associated with attribute type $A_i$. In other words, the FF denotes the chance that a particular row will be selected according to the query predicate. For queries over a single table,[4] the expected **query cardinality** (QC; the number of rows selected by the query) equals the **table cardinality** (TC; the number of rows in the table) multiplied by the *product of the filter factors of the respective search predicates* in the query:

$$QC = TC \times FF_1 \times FF_2 \times \ldots FF_n$$

[3] Other terms are used as well for this concept, e.g., the *selectivity* of a query.

[4] Join queries are discussed in a later section.

If no further statistical information is available, then an estimate for $FF_i$ is $1/NV_i$, with $NV_i$ representing the number of different values of attribute type $A_i$.

For example, suppose the Customer table as illustrated in Figure 12.24 contains 10,000 customers. Let's examine the following query:

```
SELECT CUSTOMERID
FROM CUSTOMERTABLE
WHERE COUNTRY = 'UK'
AND GENDER = 'M'
```

The TC = 10,000, as there are 10,000 rows in the table. Suppose the table contains 20 different countries and Gender has two values "M" and "F". In that case, $FF_{Country} = 0.05$ and $FF_{Gender} = 0.5$. The expected query cardinality can then be calculated as:

$$QC = 10{,}000 \times 0.05 \times 0.5 = 250$$

Thus, we expect 250 rows in the data file to have both the properties "Country = UK" and "Gender = M". Suppose the optimizer must choose between two access plans. A first option is an access plan in which all rows that satisfy "Country = UK" are retrieved, by means of an index over "Country". The second option is an access plan in which all rows that satisfy "Gender = M" are retrieved, by means of an index over "Gender". In the first case, the expected number of rows to be retrieved is $10{,}000 \times 0.05 = 500$. Since $QC = 250$, we expect half of these 500 to satisfy the query and half of them to be discarded (because they have the wrong value for "Gender"). In the second case, the expected number of rows to be retrieved is $10{,}000 \times 0.5 = 5000$. Of these, we expect only 250 to be retained and 4750 to be discarded because they have the wrong value for "Country". The first strategy will be considered as more efficient than the second, as fewer, in hindsight useless, record retrievals have to be performed. Yet, in fact, the situation is often a bit more complicated than that. For example, it could be that the records are sorted according to gender, which may make retrieval according to that criterion more efficient, because only sequential block accesses are performed. Also, additional statistical information could be available – for example, the fact that many more customers live in the UK than in any other country. In that case, the second alternative may turn out to be more efficient after all.

The latter illustrates an optimizer's "reasoning" over statistical data in the catalog, in combination with properties of the query at hand, to draw conclusions about the most efficient access path. In what follows, we discuss some typical situations in which a different access path may be chosen for the same query, depending on the physical table properties, availability, and type of indexes, for example.

#### 13.1.3.2 Index Search (with Atomic Search Key)

Let's first examine the situation with a single query predicate, in which the query involves a search key with only a single attribute type. If an index exists for this attribute type, an index search is usually the most efficient way of implementing the query. This approach is applicable to queries targeting a single value as well as range queries. Let's revisit the $B^+$-tree index example from Chapter 12, as depicted again in Figure 13.2. We assume the following range query:

```
SELECT *
FROM MY_TABLE
WHERE MY_KEY >= 12
AND MY_KEY <= 24
```

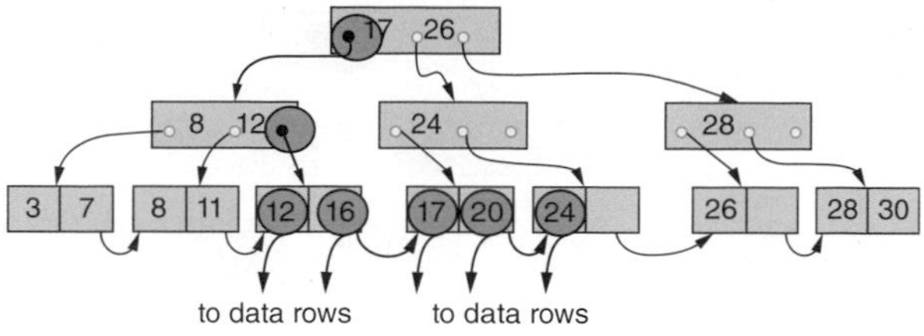


**Figure 13.2** Example of index search by means of a $B^+$-tree.

The index allows filtering which data rows should be retrieved, hence avoiding unnecessary retrievals and therefore greatly improving performance of query execution. The following steps are taken, as illustrated in Figure 13.2:

- Starting from the index's root node, descend the $B^+$-tree along the tree pointers according to the search key values onto the first leaf node that contains key values satisfying the search condition.
- From this leaf node, follow the data pointers to retrieve the data rows satisfying the search key values.
- Follow the "next" tree pointers[5] in the leaf nodes to subsequently access all nodes that contain key values still within the desired range of the search key. For each of these nodes, follow the data pointers to retrieve the corresponding data rows.

If the query involves only a single search key value, and not a range of values, an efficient alternative would be to organize the table according to the random file organization method, mapping search key values onto physical locations by means of hashing, instead of using an index. Note that this approach is not efficient in supporting range queries, where an interval of key values is used as a search criterion.

As to range queries, a primary or clustered index is even more efficient than a secondary index. Indeed, if the data records are stored in the same order as the search key, the $B^+$-tree's leaf nodes can be accessed by means of the "next" pointers and the data rows can be retrieved in the same order by means of sequential block accesses. On the other hand, applying the same procedure by means of a secondary index would result in all random block accesses on the data file, "jumping" back and forth because the data records are not in the appropriate physical order. This is illustrated in Figure 13.3. In such a case, the DBMS would probably first sort the pointers to the disk blocks to be accessed, according to their physical address, but this sorting also induces a certain amount of overhead.

#### 13.1.3.3 Multiple Index and Multicolumn Index Search

If the search key is composite, a similar approach is feasible, but other options exist as well, depending on the availability of single-column and/or multicolumn indexes, which cover all or part of the attribute types that occur in the query predicates.

If the indexed attribute types are the same as the attribute types in the search key, then the approach in the previous section is usually the most efficient. The **multicolumn index** then allows filtering out and retrieving only these data rows that satisfy the query. In most cases, it is not feasible

[5] This step is not needed if the query is not a range query but only uses a single search key value e.g., "MY_KEY = 12".

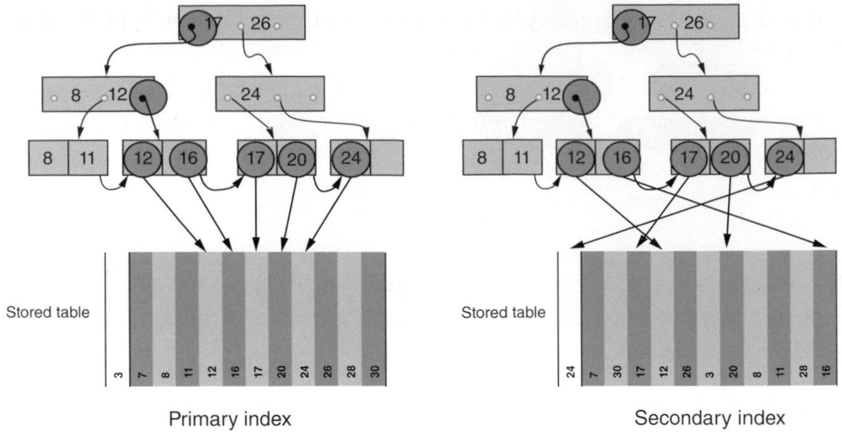


**Figure 13.3** Example of range query with primary versus secondary index.

to create a multicolumn index for every possible combination of search keys, as these indexes would become very large. Indeed, if we assume there are $n$ possible attribute types $A_i$ to be used in a search key (i = 1..$n$), with attribute type $A_i$ having $NV_i$ possible values, then a dense index created over all $A_i$ has $\prod_{i=1}^{n} NV_i$ entries.[6] If, instead, we create separate dense indexes over each individual attribute type, we have $n$ indexes with respectively $NV_i$ entries (i = 1..$n$). The total number of entries over all indexes is then only $\sum_{i=1}^{n} NV_i$, which is considerably lower.[7] For example, a search key with five attribute types, each with ten possible values, would yield a multicolumn index with 100,000 entries. When using single-column indexes instead, there would be five indexes, each with ten entries, thus 50 entries in total.

The case becomes even more complex if not only queries involving all search attribute types are executed, but also queries involving an arbitrary subset of these attribute types. As already explained in Chapter 12, to efficiently support these kinds of queries, a multicolumn index should have all attribute types involved in the query predicates in its leftmost columns. In order to support all possible queries with $n$ or fewer attribute types, multiple multicolumn redundant indexes could be created with the same $n$ attribute types, but with a different ordering of the columns. It can be proven that, to cater for all possible search keys with $n$ attribute types or less, $\binom{n}{\lceil n/2 \rceil}$ indexes are required.[8] For example, with three attribute types, $\binom{3}{2} = 3$ indexes are required. The index combinations ($A_1$, $A_2$, $A_3$), ($A_2$, $A_3$, $A_1$), and ($A_3$, $A_1$, $A_2$) accommodate for any query that includes $A_1$, $A_2$ and/or $A_3$. A few cases are illustrated below:

- A query involving $A_1$, $A_2$, and $A_3$ $\rightarrow$ any index can be used.
- A query involving $A_1$ and $A_3$ $\rightarrow$ use ($A_3$, $A_1$, $A_2$).
- A query involving $A_2$ and $A_3$ $\rightarrow$ use ($A_2$, $A_3$, $A_1$).
- A query involving only $A_1$ $\rightarrow$ use ($A_1$, $A_2$, $A_3$).

[6] $\prod_{i=1}^{n}$ refers to the mathematical "product" notation. $\prod_{i=1}^{n} NV_i$ equals $NV_1 \times NV_2 \times NV_3 \ldots \times NV_n$.

[7] $\sum_{i=1}^{n}$ refers to the mathematical "summation" notation. $\sum_{i=1}^{n} NV_i$ equals $NV_1 + NV_2 + NV_3 \ldots + NV_n$.

[8] $\binom{x}{y}$ refers to the mathematical "combination" notation. $\binom{x}{y}$ equals $\frac{x!}{y!(x-y)!}$.

It is clear from the formula that the number of possible attribute type combinations, and therefore the number of required indexes, grows quickly as the number of attribute types increases. For example, if we have five attribute types, this requires already ten redundant indexes over the same attribute types. Hence, multicolumn indexes are only appropriate for selective cases, such as queries that are executed very often or that are very time critical. As already explained, they are also used to enforce uniqueness constraints, but then the number of attribute types is limited and there is no need for redundant indexes.

Fortunately, an efficient alternative to a multicolumn index is to use multiple single-column indexes, or indexes with fewer columns, as already briefly discussed in Chapter 12. If we have a query of the following format:

```
SELECT *
FROM MY_TABLE
WHERE A1 = VALUE1
AND A2 = VALUE2
AND ...
AND An = VALUEn
```

and we have single-column indexes for every attribute type $A_i$, then the *intersection* can be taken between the sets of pointers in the index entries that correspond to the desired values of $A_i$. This intersection yields the pointers to all records that satisfy the query. On the other hand, for queries of the type:

```
SELECT *
FROM MY_TABLE
WHERE A1 = VALUE1
OR A2 = VALUE2
OR ...
OR An = VALUEn
```

we can take the *union* of the sets of pointers to yield the records that qualify.

As an example, Figure 13.4 illustrates the use of two indexes, one on Country and one on Gender, to execute the already familiar query:

```
SELECT CUSTOMERID
FROM CUSTOMERTABLE
WHERE COUNTRY = 'UK'
AND GENDER = 'M'
```

By taking the intersection between the set of pointers referring to people living in the UK and the set of pointers referring to males,[9] all pointers to males living in the UK can be identified. Note that this approach works best with record pointers, because then the selection can actually be made at record level. Since in this case every block contains both males and females, an index on Gender with just block pointers will not contribute to more selectivity on which blocks to access. Compare this example to the example with a multicolumn index on (Country, Gender) in Figure 12.24. An alternative approach, as supported by an increasing number of DBMS implementations, is the use of

[9] Note that, since both indexes are secondary indexes on non-key attribute types, we used the inverted file approach, associating each index entry with a block of pointers to all corresponding records, as discussed in Chapter 12.

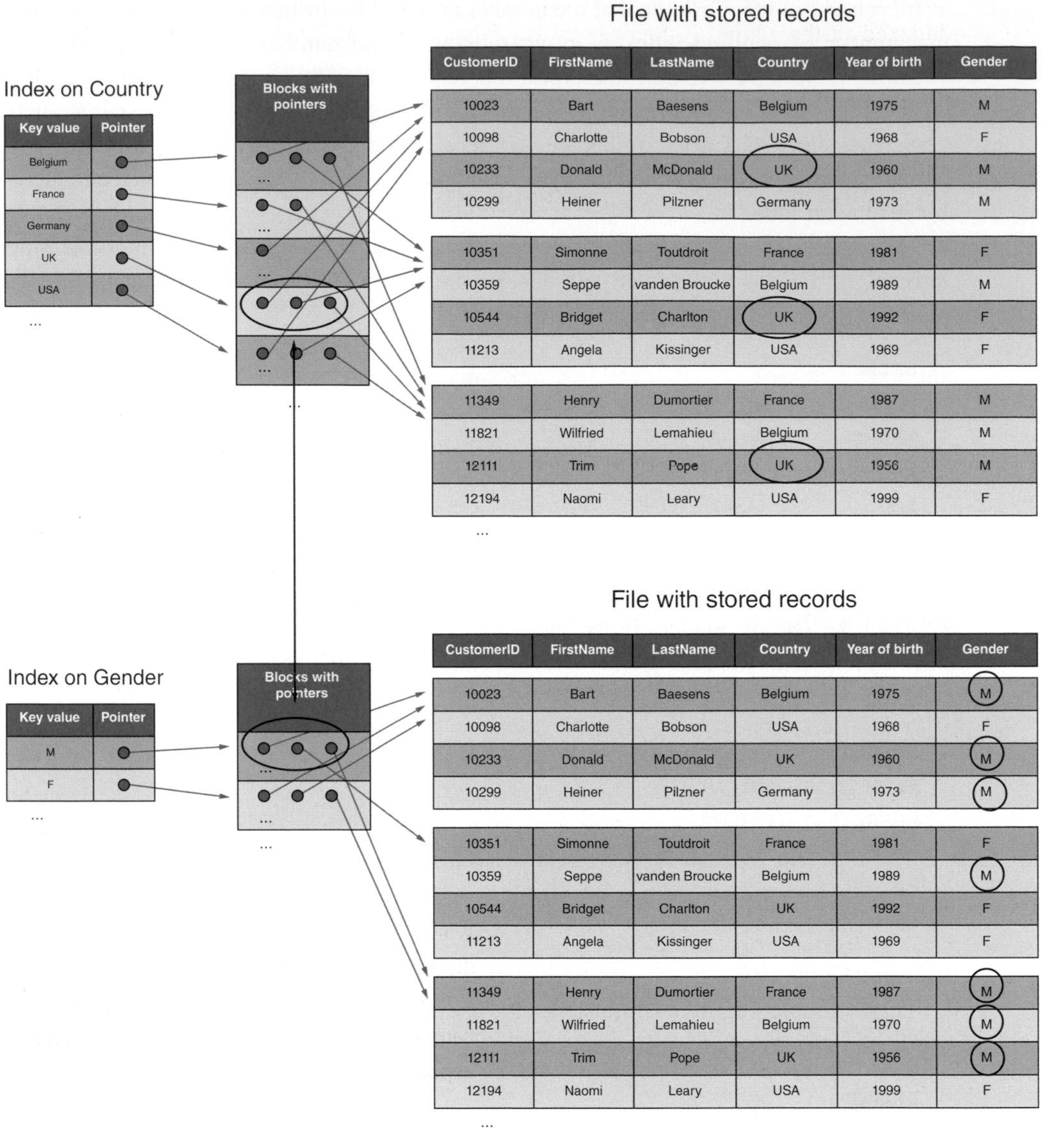


**Figure 13.4** Example of using two indexes to execute query with multiple predicates.

bitmap indexes. As discussed in Chapter 12, each bitmap denotes tuples with a certain attribute. By applying Boolean operations to bitmaps from multiple indexes, tuples that satisfy a combination of predicates can be identified.

Finally, it is also possible to use a *single index*, or a few indexes, that together cover only a subset of the attribute types involved in the search key. In that case, the index(es) can be used to retrieve only those records that satisfy the predicates associated with these attribute types. Each of these records has to be retrieved and tested for compliance with the predicates associated with the non-indexed attribute types. The efficiency of this approach depends largely on the filter factors of the query predicates associated with the indexed attribute types. The more selective these predicates, the fewer data rows will be retrieved in vain because they ultimately do not comply with the query predicates associated with the non-indexed attribute types. The most extreme case is that one of the indexed attribute types is the primary key or another candidate key; in that case, the total number of records to be retrieved is zero or one, so most of the inefficiency is mitigated anyway.

Let's resume the discussion considering the example in Figure 13.4. Suppose only the index on "Country" exists. In support of the same query, searching for all male customers in the UK, the index can be used to retrieve all data rows representing customers in the UK. For these rows, the "Gender" attribute type is inspected, resulting in two rows depicted in the example being retained (Gender = "M") and one row being discarded (Gender = "F"). If, on the other hand, only the index on "Gender" existed, we would have retrieved seven rows depicted in the example, each representing a male customer. After inspecting every one of these for the "Country" attribute type, only two would have been retained (Country = "UK") and five would have been discarded because they have the wrong country. If a multicolumn index had been used on (Country, Gender), two rows would have been retrieved, which both satisfy the query. No rows are retrieved unnecessarily. These results based on the limited set of rows depicted in the example align with the efficiency estimates made in Section 13.1.3.1. There, according to the filter factors, we saw that the selectivity, and therefore the efficiency of using the corresponding index, of the predicate associated with "Country" was much higher than the selectivity associated with the predicate on "Gender".

To summarize, the optimizer has complex decisions to make in the case of queries with many predicates. A multicolumn index over all these predicates is the most efficient alternative: its FF is equal to the query's FF, so only the data rows that satisfy the query are retrieved. Still, this approach becomes unfeasible if many attribute types are used in query predicates, as the indexes would become very large and, possibly, redundancy is required to accommodate for queries with predicates for only a subset of the attribute types. As an alternative, multiple indexes can be combined, if they exist, to cover as many query predicates as possible. This requires more indexes, but with a much lower total number of index entries than in the case of a composite index. Generally speaking, the more selective a query predicate's FF, the more desirable it is to use the index on the corresponding attribute type in the access plan. If the filter factors associated with non-indexed attribute types are in their turn very selective, many records are retrieved in vain, which is inefficient. Apart from these considerations, it is important to keep in mind that ultimately the number of block accesses determines the performance, not the number of rows retrieved. Thus, the impact of clustering always needs to be investigated, since despite what the filter factors indicate, using a primary index or a clustered index may be more efficient than using a secondary index, especially for range queries.

#### 13.1.3.4 Index-Only Access

In some cases, the optimizer might be extremely "lucky", in the sense that the query can be executed entirely without accessing the data files, based solely on information in the index. In that case, not only should the attribute types used in the search key be indexed, but also the attribute types that occur in the query's SELECT clause. For example, consider the following query:

```
SELECT LASTNAME
FROM CUSTOMERTABLE
WHERE COUNTRY = 'UK'
AND GENDER = 'M'
```

If there exists a multicolumn index, or a combination of single-column indexes, over the attribute types LastName, Country, and Gender, then the data in the index(es) suffice to yield the query result. In that case, access to the actual data rows can be avoided. This is especially efficient if the data rows consist of many attribute types, and take much more time to retrieve than index entries. Index-only access is thus an additional reason for creating multicolumn indexes. A particular application of index-only access is the use of a join index, as discussed in Section 12.3.7.4. Here, the result of a join query between two or more tables can be retrieved based on just the index, without accessing the respective base tables involved.

Of course, the more attribute types are included in the index, the higher the negative performance impact is on update queries, since the index entries need to be updated as well. Note that, because the data rows are not retrieved anyway, a primary or clustered index does not yield better performance than a secondary index for index-only access.

#### 13.1.3.5 Full Table Scan

If no index is available for the attribute type(s) and table(s) involved in the query, there is no other option than to linearly search the entire table for rows that satisfy the query. This means that all corresponding disk blocks in the tablespace will be retrieved, and their rows examined in main memory, even if they turn out not to contain any rows that satisfy the query. Thus, the higher the query's FF and/or the larger the table, the less efficient a full table scan will be. However, for very small tables, or for queries that require nearly all of a table's tuples anyway (e.g., range queries with a very extensive range), a full table scan might actually be more efficient than using an index, with all its overhead involved. In the specific situation in which the data records are ordered according to the attribute type(s) in the search key, a binary search on the actual data file can also be an efficient alternative to a linear search. These considerations can be a guide for the database designer or database administrator when deciding on the creation of indexes, obviously also taking into account how frequently the particular type of query will be executed.

Finally, it is important to note that several of the file organization techniques we discussed involve *overflow records*. If these techniques are applied in the context of physical database organization, we also need to deal with this overflow. We are confronted with overflow if a stored record is added or updated and does not "fit" in the position where it belongs according to the applicable file organization technique. The record is then placed in another location, according to the chosen overflow-handling technique. Overflow has a negative impact on the efficiency of a clustering index; the more rows are out of place; the more additional block accesses are needed to retrieve the data in the corresponding order. Clearly, if the number of overflow records becomes too high, the stored table needs to be reorganized.

### 13.1.4 Join Implementations

One of the key differences between database organization and just file organization is the fact that database organization should also cater for queries that involve multiple tables, by means of a join construct in SQL. A join query between two tables specifies selection criteria that relate tuples from the two tables to one another, according to a so-called join operator. It is one of the most time-consuming operations in an RDBMS and therefore deserves special attention. We restrict ourselves to the inner join. The general notation of an inner join between tables R and S is as follows:

**Connections**

Chapter 7 introduced join SQL queries.

$$R \underset{r(a)\ \theta\ s(b)}{\bowtie} S$$

**Table R**

| Employee | Payscale |
|---|---|
| Cooper | 1 |
| Gallup | 2 |
| O'Donnell | 1 |
| Smith | 2 |

**Table S**

| Payscale | Salary |
|---|---|
| 1 | 10000 |
| 2 | 20000 |

$R \bowtie_{r(payscale)=s(payscale)} S$

| Employee | Payscale | Salary |
|---|---|---|
| Cooper | 1 | 10000 |
| Gallup | 2 | 20000 |
| O'Donnell | 1 | 10000 |
| Smith | 2 | 20000 |

**Figure 13.5** Illustration of a join.

The θ-operator specifies the *join condition*, which is the criteria that determine which rows from table R are combined with which rows from table S. To this end, a set of attributes a of tuples r in R is compared to a set of attributes b of tuples s in S. The comparison operator may involve an equality such as r(a) = s(b) or an inequality such as r(a) ≥ s(b). In what follows, we limit ourselves to joins based on an equality condition.

The tuples in the individual tables are retrieved by means of one or more of the access methods outlined in the previous section (e.g., index search, table scan, etc.). The tuples that match according to the join condition are then combined into a unified result. This is illustrated in Figure 13.5. A join between $n$ tables with $n > 2$ is realized as a series of $(n - 1)$ consecutive joins between two tables.

Different techniques exist to physically implement a join; their efficiency depends on the properties of the tables and columns involved, as well as on the availability of indexes. We discuss three of the main techniques: the *nested-loop join*, the *sort-merge join*, and the *hash join*.

#### 13.1.4.1 Nested-Loop Join

With a **nested-loop join**, one of the tables is denoted as the *inner table* and the other becomes the *outer table*.[10] For every row in the outer table, all rows of the inner table are retrieved and compared to the current row of the outer table. If the join condition is satisfied, both rows are joined and put in an output buffer. The inner table is traversed as many times as there are rows in the outer table. The algorithm is as follows:

$R \bowtie_{r(a) = s(b)} S$

```
Denote S → outer table
For every row s in S do
    {for every row r in R do
        {if r(a) = s(b) then join r with s and place in output buffer}
    }
```

[10] The outer table is not to be confused with the concept of an outer join as discussed in Chapter 7. This overview on join implementations is limited to inner joins.

As mentioned above, the inner table is traversed as many times as there are rows in the outer table. Therefore, this approach is mainly effective if the inner table is very small or if the internal data model provides facilities for efficient access to the inner table, such as by means of a primary or clustered index over the join columns of the inner table. This approach is also more efficient if the filter factor of the other query predicates is very restrictive with respect to the rows that qualify in the inner table.

#### 13.1.4.2 Sort-Merge Join

With a sort-merge join, the tuples in both tables are first sorted according to the attribute types involved in the join condition. Both tables are then traversed in this order, with the rows that satisfy the join condition being combined and put in an output buffer. The algorithm is represented below:

$$R \bowtie_{r(a) = s(b)} S$$

```
Stage 1: sort R according to r(a)
         sort S according to s(b)

Stage 2: retrieve the first row r of R
         retrieve the first row s of S
         for every row r in R
            {while s(b) < r(a)
              read the next row s of S
              if r(a) = s(b) then join r with s and place in output buffer}
```

In contrast to a nested-loop join, every table is traversed only once. This approach is appropriate if many rows in both tables satisfy the query predicates and/or if there exist no indexes over the join columns. The sorting algorithm that is applied in stage 1 may be quite time consuming, hence a sort-merge join will be more efficient if the tuples in R and/or S are already physically ordered in the stored tables according to the attribute types used in the join condition.

#### 13.1.4.3 Hash Join

Finally, with a **hash join**, a hashing algorithm is applied to the values of the attribute types involved in the join condition for table R. Based on the resulting hash values, the corresponding rows are assigned to buckets in a hash file. The same hashing algorithm is then applied to the join attribute types of the second table S. If a hash value for S refers to a non-empty bucket in the hash file, the corresponding rows of R and S are compared according to the join condition. If the join condition is satisfied, the rows of R and S are joined and put in the output buffer. Still, given the possibility of collisions, rows with different column values may still be assigned to the same bucket, so not all rows assigned to the same bucket will necessarily satisfy the join condition. The performance of this approach depends on the size of the hash file. If, instead of a physical file, the hash structure can be maintained entirely in internal memory, a hash join can be very efficient.

**Retention Questions**

- Contrast primary indexes versus clustered indexes versus secondary indexes in terms of impact on physical ordering of tuples; unique search keys and sparseness.
- Elaborate on the functioning of the query optimizer.
- Discuss and contrast various types of database access methods. Discuss and contrast three techniques to physically implement a join.

## 13.2 Enterprise Storage Subsystems and Business Continuity

We continue this chapter on physical database organization by returning to the storage hardware. In contrast to the previous chapter, we will not focus on the individual storage devices, but rather on the broader aspect of pooling individual devices and managing them as so-called enterprise storage subsystems. First, we discuss disk arrays and RAID as a mechanism of combining multiple physical devices into a single, larger, logical device. Then, we deal with networked storage techniques such as SAN and NAS. We conclude with a discussion on how these techniques can be applied in the context of business continuity, which is a primary concern to most organizations.

### 13.2.1 Disk Arrays and RAID

Whereas the storage capacity of hard disk drives has increased tremendously over the last two decades, their performance has not increased at the same rate. Consequently, it is often more efficient to combine multiple smaller physical disk drives into one larger logical drive. The reason is twofold. First, distributing data over multiple physical drives allows for parallel retrieval, resulting in much improved performance. Second, each additional drive increases the risk of failure, but if a certain measure of data redundancy is introduced, this risk can be mitigated, and the reliability actually becomes much better than with a single physical drive. Both considerations are at the core of the **Redundant Array of Independent Disks (RAID)** concept (Figure 13.6).

RAID is a technology in which standard HDDs are coupled to a dedicated hard disk controller (the **RAID controller**) to make them appear as a single logical drive. The same can be realized by a software RAID controller, without dedicated hardware, but in that case the performance increase is lower. The following techniques are applied in RAID:

- **Data striping:** Subsections of a data file (called *strips*) are distributed over multiple disks to be read and written in parallel. The strips can consist of individual bits or entire disk blocks. With $n$ disks, bit or block $i$ is written to disk $(i \bmod n)+1$.

  With *bit-level* data striping, a byte is split into eight individual bits, to be distributed over the available disks. For example, four disks each contain two bits of the same byte. Disk 1 contains bits 1 and 5, disk 2 contains bits 2 and 6, etc. In that case, every disk participates in every read/write operation. The number of disk accesses per unit of time remains the same, but the number of bits retrieved in a single access increases with a factor equal to the number of disks, resulting in higher transfer rates for a single transfer.

  With *block-level* data striping, each block is stored in its entirety on a single disk, but the respective blocks of the same file are distributed over the disks. In this way, individual block accesses remain independent. Efficiency of a single block access is not increased, but different

**Figure 13.6** Example of a RAID set-up from the IBM Power S824L server.

processes can read blocks in parallel from the same logical disk, hence reducing the queuing time. Also, a single large process can read multiple blocks in parallel, hence reducing the total transfer time.

- **Redundancy:** Redundant data are stored along with the original data to increase reliability. The redundant data consist of error detection and correcting codes such as Hamming codes or parity bits. Parity bits are a very simple kind of error-detecting code, adding one redundant bit to a series of bits to ensure that the total number of 1 – bits in the series is either always even or always odd. In this way, individual bit errors can be detected. If a bit is not readable, its value can be derived from the other bits and the parity bit. It would lead us too far to discuss Hamming codes in detail, but it suffices to say that they provide stronger error-correcting capabilities than parity bits, but they are also more computationally heavy and induce more redundancy than parity bits.
- **Disk mirroring**: This is an extreme form of redundancy, where for each disk there is an exact copy, called the mirror, containing the same data. Note that, if the probability of a single disk failure is $p$, the probability of one of $n$ disks in a RAID set-up failing is $n$ times as high. However, when mirroring the disks, the chance of both copies failing is $p^2$, which is much lower than $p$. On the downside, mirroring consumes much more storage space than the error-correcting codes.

There exist multiple RAID configurations, called **RAID levels**. The term "level" here is somewhat misleading, as a higher level does not necessarily imply a "better" level. The levels should just be considered as different configurations, with a different combination of the abovementioned techniques, resulting in different characteristics in terms of performance and reliability. We summarize the properties of the respective original RAID levels in Table 13.2.

**Table 13.2** Overview of original RAID levels

| RAID level | Description | Fault tolerance | Performance |
|---|---|---|---|
| 0 | Block-level striping | No error correction | Improved read and write performance due to parallelism (multiple processes can read individual blocks in parallel) |
| 1 | Disk mirroring | Error correction due to complete duplication of data | Improved read performance: both disks can be accessed by different processes in parallel<br>Write performance is slightly worse, since data need to be written twice |
| 2 | Bit-level striping, with separate checksum disk | Error correction through Hamming codes | Improved read performance through parallelism<br>Slower write performance: calculation of checksum; checksum disk involved in every write may become a bottleneck |
| 3 | Bit-level striping, with parity bits on separate parity disk | Error correction through parity bits | Improved read performance through parallelism, especially for large, sequential transfers<br>Slower write performance: less calculation overhead than with RAID 2, but parity disk involved in every write may still become a bottleneck |
| 4 | Block-level striping, with parity bits on separate parity disk | Error correction through parity bits | No improved read performance for individual blocks, but support for efficient parallel block accesses<br>Slower write performance; see RAID 3 |
| 5 | Block level striping, with distributed parity bits | Error correction through parity bits | Read performance: see RAID 4<br>Better write performance than RAID 4: parity bits distributed over data disks, so no parity drive as bottleneck |

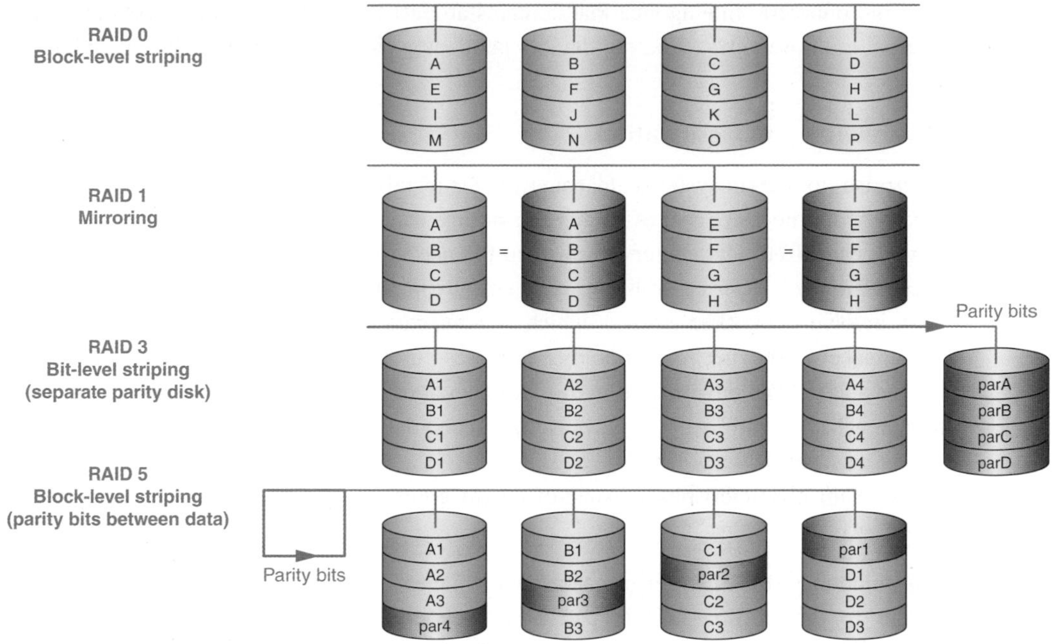


**Figure 13.7** Illustration of RAID levels 0, 1, 3, and 5.

Some typical raid levels are illustrated in Figure 13.7. The letters represent blocks; the combinations of letters and numbers represent bits in a block. The colored disks or disk sections denote redundancy.

RAID 0 is used if performance is more important than fault tolerance. RAID 1 is mostly used for very critical data – for example, the logfile of the DBMS. This configuration is the best in terms of continuity, as there is always an exact copy available in the event of disk failure. In contrast, the other RAID levels that include redundancy invariably require reading the other disks in order to reconstruct the data from a failed disk. On the other hand, the fault tolerance in RAID 1 comes at the cost of a higher degree of redundancy, therefore requiring more storage capacity. RAID 5 is quite popular overall, as it strikes a balance between read and write performance, storage efficiency, and fault tolerance.

Since the inception of the original RAID levels, some levels have become more or less obsolete, whereas others have been added. For example, RAID level 0+1 combines the properties of level 0 and 1. RAID level 6 aims at tolerance against two simultaneous disk failures. This can be realized by extending RAID level 5 with a second series of parity bits distributed across the drives, independent of the first one.

**Connections**

Chapter 14 discusses the logfile of a DBMS.

## 13.2.2 Enterprise Storage Subsystems

Whereas RAID technology already aims at pooling multiple physical hard disk drives into a single logical one, typical organization-wide storage solutions tend to take this idea even further. They combine storage devices, which will often be RAID based, into larger entities, called enterprise storage subsystems. A storage subsystem can be defined as a separate, external entity with a certain level of "onboard" intelligence that contains at least two storage devices. By "external" we mean external to the server(s) (i.e., the devices containing the CPUs that process the data).

#### 13.2.2.1 Overview and Classification

Enterprise storage subsystems emanate from the insight that the management cost of storage tends to exceed by far the sheer cost of purchasing storage hardware. In addition, the often-perceived rigor of purely centralized data centers resulted in the need for more flexible, distributed storage architectures, which still offer centralized management capabilities. Modern enterprise storage subsystems often involve networked storage, which is connected to high-end servers by means of high-speed interconnects. The network topology provides for transparent any-to-any connectivity between servers and storage devices and in this way functions as a "black box" of storage. It combines large storage capacity with features such as high-speed data transfer, high availability, and sophisticated management tools.

The main characteristics of state-of-the-art enterprise storage subsystems can be summarized as follows:

- accommodate for high performance data storage;
- cater for scalability, and in particular independent scaling of storage capacity and server capacity;
- support data distribution and location transparency;[11]
- support interoperability and data sharing between heterogeneous systems and users;
- reliability and near continuous availability;
- protection against hardware and software malfunctions and data loss, as well as abusive users and hackers;
- improve manageability and reduce management cost through centralized management of storage facilities, which may themselves be distributed.

We can classify the technologies for realizing storage subsystems according to three criteria: the *connectivity*, the *medium*, and the *I/O protocol*.

By **connectivity**, we refer to the way in which the storage devices are connected to processors and/or servers. These are illustrated in Figure 13.8.

- **Direct attach** refers to storage devices with a one-to-one connection between server and storage device.
- **Network attach** refers to storage devices in a many-to-many connection with the corresponding servers by means of network technology.

By *medium*, we refer to the physical cabling and corresponding low-level protocol to realize the abovementioned connectivity, i.e., to transfer data between storage medium and server. We discriminate between the following main technologies:

- **SCSI (Small Computer Systems Interface)**: This has been a standard to connect storage devices to servers and/or processors for decades, although in several incarnations. Despite the "small" in the naming, SCSI is currently mainly used for high-performance and high-capacity workstations

[11] Location transparency refers to the fact that the users and applications are insulated from the complexity of the data being distributed across multiple locations.

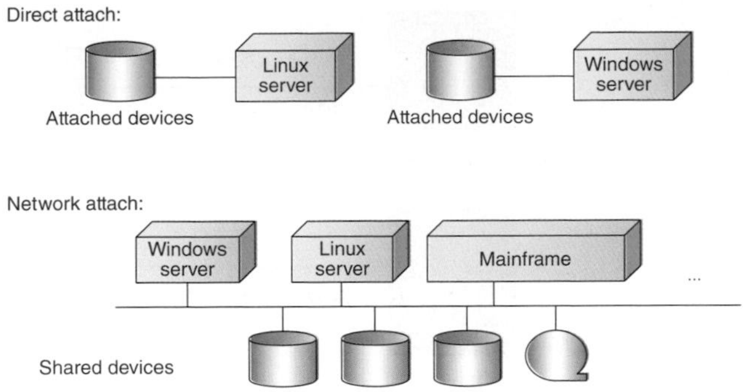


**Figure 13.8** Direct attach versus network attach.

and servers, whereas consumer devices often use other technologies such as Serial Advanced Technology Attachment (SATA). Without going into too much detail, it is important to note that the SCSI specification involves two elements: on the one hand, a *command set* to communicate with storage devices, and on the other hand, specifications for a *low-level protocol and cabling* to transfer SCSI commands and data between servers and storage devices. It is the latter that is relevant in this "medium" category; the command set belongs to the "I/O protocol" category discussed hereafter and can also be combined with other (non-SCSI) cabling.

- **Ethernet**: This is the long-standing standard medium for local area networks (LANs) and sometimes wide area networks (WANs), mostly in combination with the internet protocol stack TCP/IP (Transmission Control Protocol/Internet Protocol). It is not specifically aimed at storage-related data transfer.
- **Fibre Channel (FC)**: This is a more recent medium, developed specifically to connect high-end storage systems to servers. Originally, it was based on fiber-optic cable (hence the name), but nowadays it also supports other cabling such as copper wire. Depending on the vendor, different topologies (e.g., from point-to-point set-ups to more complex configurations with hubs and switches) are possible.

Whereas the abovementioned medium referred to the cabling and low-level protocol to transport bits in the context of storage-related traffic over a cable or network, the *I/O protocol* denotes the command set to communicate with the storage device. With this high-level protocol, the transported bits take the meaning of I/O requests exchanged between servers and storage devices. In this context, we discriminate between the following:

- **Block-level I/O protocols**: The I/O commands are defined at the level of requests for individual blocks on the storage device. The SCSI command set is widely used for this purpose. Originally, SCSI I/O commands could only be exchanged over SCSI cabling, but nowadays other media such as Fibre Channel and Ethernet can also be used for transporting SCSI commands.
- **File-level I/O protocols**: The commands are defined at the level of requests for entire files on the storage device. The protocol is device-independent, as it is situated at the file level and therefore not impacted by the physical block position of the data on the storage device. Widespread file-level I/O protocols are Network File System (NFS), originating in the UNIX and Linux world, and Common Internet File System (CIFS), also known as Server Message Block (SMB), mainly popular in Windows environments. Also, some internet application protocols can be positioned under this denominator, in particular HTTP (HyperText Transfer Protocol) and FTP (File Transfer Protocol).

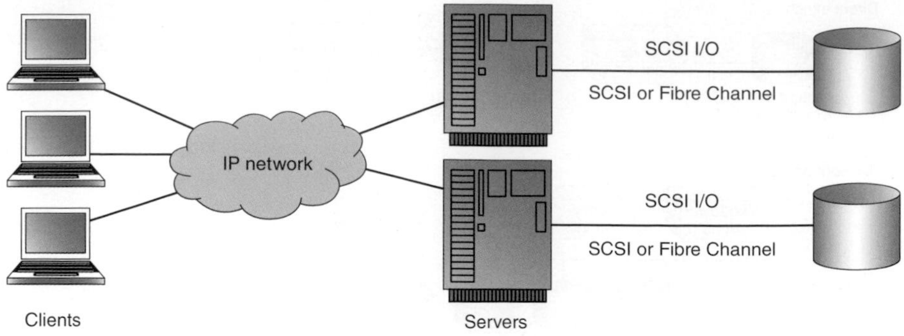


**Figure 13.9** Illustration of DAS.

Based on these three criteria, we can distinguish between the following storage architectures: Directly Attached Storage (DAS); Storage Area Network (SAN); Network Attached Storage (NAS); NAS gateway, and Storage over IP (iSCSI). We discuss each of these in more detail.

### 13.2.2.2 DAS (Directly Attached Storage)

With DAS, the storage devices (HDDs, but possibly also tape drives and others) are directly connected to individual servers (see Figure 13.9). A block-level I/O protocol is used; servers communicate with storage devices by means of SCSI I/O commands. Different options for the medium are possible: this could be a standard SCSI cable, but the SCSI commands can also be exchanged over point-to-point Fibre Channel or, although less common in this setting, an Ethernet cable. Each storage device is connected to a single server or, for the sake of failover,[12] to two separate servers. In this configuration, no network is used for traffic between servers and storage devices, although servers and clients can be connected to a standard IP-network for LAN or WAN functionality.

A DAS set-up is the simplest and least expensive solution. However, it does not offer out-of-the-box capabilities for centralized storage management and sharing unused disk capacity across servers.[13] Even more important, this approach is reasonably vulnerable to hardware failures in servers, storage devices, and cabling, since there is only a single path between individual servers and storage units. In the case of failure of any of these components, part of the data may not be reachable.

### 13.2.2.3 SAN (Storage Area Network)

In a SAN setting, all storage-related data transfer occurs over a dedicated network (see Figure 13.10). Again, servers and storage devices communicate by means of a block-level I/O protocol (i.e., SCSI commands), but now the network provides an any-to-any connectivity between servers and storage devices. Most often, Fibre Channel is used as a medium, with different possible network topologies. Ethernet-based SANs are possible as well, but these are discussed in Section 13.2.2.6. Apart from the separate storage network, clients and servers can communicate over a standard IP-based LAN or WAN.

[12] Failover means switching to a redundant or standby system in case of malfunction of the primary system.

[13] There are software-based solutions for all of this, but these are typically less efficient.

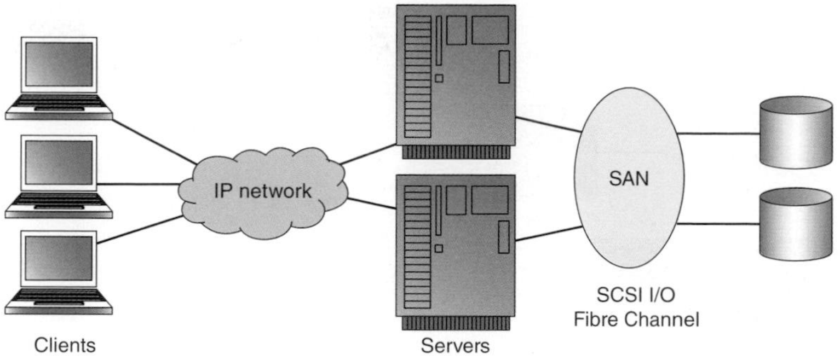


**Figure 13.10** Illustration of SAN.

A SAN set-up has some unmistakable advantages. Foremost, it is superior to DAS in terms of availability, given the any-to-any connectivity between servers and storage devices and the redundancy in access paths, given the network setting. The latter also facilitates data sharing, hence reducing unnecessary data redundancy. Note that data redundancy is not mitigated entirely, because redundant copies are still needed for reasons of availability (e.g., by means of RAID technology), but redundancy is not needed for the sake of providing the same data to multiple unconnected servers. A SAN is typically also the best solution in terms of performance; a first reason is the high-speed interconnections and the Fibre Channel medium that is very efficient for this purpose. A second reason is that the SAN relieves the actual LAN or WAN from storage-related traffic, resulting in higher network throughput for data processing-related tasks. An example here is the so-called *LAN-free backup*, where the often-large transfers between storage devices and backup[14] facilities are not routed over the LAN, but over the SAN. A third reason is that Fibre Channel-compatible storage devices come with some measure of onboard intelligence, allowing them to perform certain tasks autonomously, without interference by a server. An example here are so-called *server-free backups*, which can be performed entirely by the storage devices themselves, without burdening server performance. Other advantages are the flexibility and scalability of being able to make separate decisions about adding servers and storage devices to the SAN. These decisions are much more intertwined in a one-to-one setting. Given the network technology, a SAN is also able to bridge larger distances than direct connections between storage devices and servers. In addition, the connectivity between the devices offers possibilities for storage pooling and centralized management. On the other hand, SAN technology is still rather complex and expensive, with the added burden of ever-evolving standards of hardware and software. Hence, the SAN approach is mainly beneficial to larger organizations, with sufficient expertise and financial resources.

### 13.2.2.4 NAS (Network Attached Storage)

In contrast to SAN, NAS is essentially a quite straightforward and inexpensive way of organizing storage facilities into a network (Figure 13.11). A NAS device is often called a "NAS appliance" because of its relative simplicity. It is a specialized device for file storage that can be "plugged" straightforwardly into a TCP/IP-based LAN or WAN, hence the medium is Ethernet. To put it simply, a NAS device can be considered as a stripped-down file server[15] that consists of an

[14] We come back to different types of backup in Section 13.2.3.2.

[15] A file server stores and provides access to entire files that are shared in a network. This and other client–server configurations are discussed in more detail in Chapter 15.

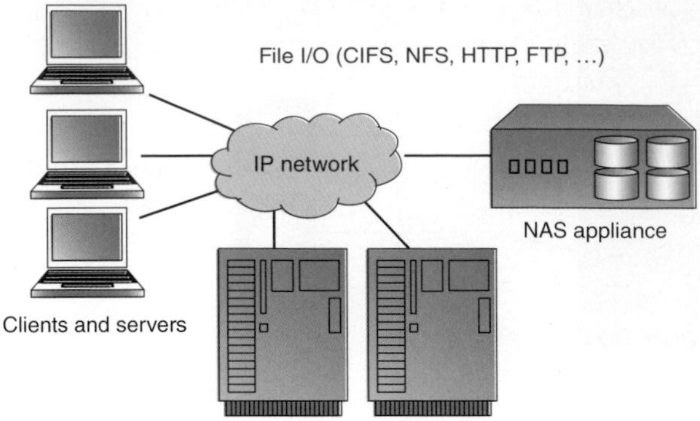


**Figure 13.11** Illustration of NAS.

integrated combination of a processor, operating system, and a set of hard disk drives. Yet, in contrast to a real server, there is no keyboard or screen, and the operating system is stripped to the bare minimum necessary for its sole purpose: serving files to the network. In this way, a NAS appliance is not only less expensive than a full-blown server, but there is also less complexity in the hardware and software that may cause failures. Also in contrast to a SAN, NAS devices are accessed through a file-level I/O protocol such as CIFS, NFS, or sometimes HTTP or FTP. The NAS offers a *file system*[16] to the network, with file requests being translated by the NAS's internal processor into SCSI block I/O commands onto the actual HDDs. This conversion is transparent to the outside world. From a client perspective, a NAS behaves similarly to a general-purpose file server. There exists a very extensive range of NAS devices; some have very limited functionality apart from basic file serving, whereas high-end NAS devices offer more advanced features such as automated backup and recovery, support for RAID, email-based error notifications, remote administration, etc.

The main advantage of NAS technology is that it offers very flexible, relatively simple and inexpensive facilities to add additional storage to the network in a "plug and play" fashion. In this way, it is good for file sharing on the network, possibly between different servers and platforms. Yet, performance is in most cases lower than with a SAN set-up. This is because all storage-related traffic passes over the standard LAN or WAN, rather than over a dedicated network. The file-level access makes life easy when the main aim is to share unstructured files on a network. On the downside, the indirection of file-level access being translated into block-level access is less efficient, especially to high-end DBMSs, which often prefer to directly access the raw storage devices at block level, hence bypassing the file system provided by the operating system or NAS device.

#### 13.2.2.5 NAS Gateway

A **NAS gateway** is similar to a NAS device, but without the HDDs; it consists of only a processor and a stripped-down operating system (Figure 13.12). On one side, a NAS gateway can be plugged into a TCP/IP-based LAN or WAN, whereas on the other it can be connected to external disk drives. This connection can be realized by either DAS or SAN technology. In this way, the NAS gateway receives file-level I/O requests from servers connected to the LAN or WAN and translates these into SCSI block I/O commands to access the external storage devices.

[16] See also the discussion on storage devices in Chapter 12.

In comparison to a normal NAS device, a NAS gateway offers more flexibility regarding the choice of disk drives, as well as more scalability, since it is not confined by the physical boundaries of the NAS box. More importantly, it allows plugging an existing disk array into a LAN or WAN, hence making its content accessible to the entire network. In this way, the same disk array becomes accessible by means of both file-level I/O through the NAS gateway, and block-level I/O via DAS or SAN. As such, a NAS gateway can yield a hybrid NAS/SAN environment in which an existing SAN can also be accessed at the file level from a LAN or WAN through the NAS gateway acting as a front-end.

#### 13.2.2.6 iSCSI/Storage Over IP

iSCSI, also called *internet SCSI* or, with a more general term, *Storage over IP*, offers a set-up that is similar to a SAN, but instead of Fibre Channel, the much more familiar Ethernet is used as a medium (Figure 13.13). SCSI block-level I/O commands are packaged and sent over a TCP/IP network. This network can be the normal LAN or WAN, or a separate network dedicated to storage, but still based on familiar LAN technology and protocols. This results in a SAN-like set-up, although iSCSI can also be used for a direct connection between server and storage device (DAS).

iSCSI solutions sit somewhere between SAN and NAS: they allow for block-level disk access like SAN, but they are Ethernet-based like NAS. Overall, they provide for a lower-cost alternative to SANs, since the Ethernet hardware is often less expensive than Fibre Channel. It is also possible to

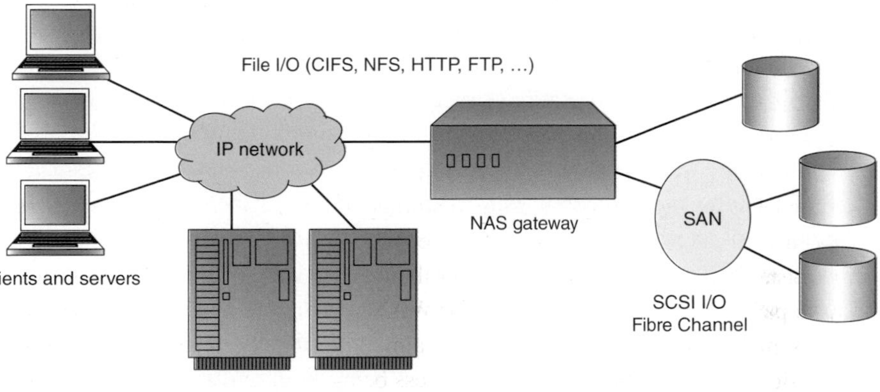


**Figure 13.12** Illustration of a NAS gateway.

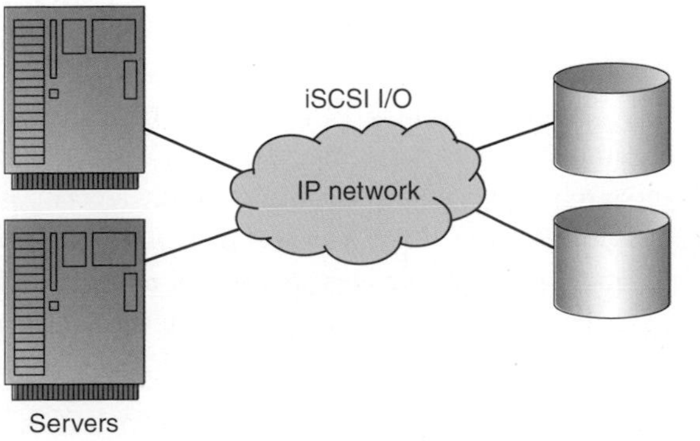


**Figure 13.13** Illustration of iSCSI.

**Table 13.3** Overview of DAS, SAN, NAS (gateway), and iSCSI

| Technology | Connectivity | Medium | I/O protocol |
|---|---|---|---|
| DAS | Direct attach | SCSI cable, point-to-point Fibre Channel (or Ethernet) | SCSI block-level I/O |
| SAN | Network attach | Fibre Channel | SCSI block-level I/O |
| NAS + NAS gateway | Network attach | Ethernet | File-level I/O |
| iSCSI | Network attach | Ethernet | SCSI block-level I/O |

re-use existing LAN components in this way. In addition, Ethernet technology is much more familiar to most than Fibre Channel, and less prone to incompatibilities and/or teething problems. For that reason, iSCSI is particularly popular in small- and medium-sized organizations in comparison to SANs. On average, iSCSI can also cover larger distances than FC-based SANs, but typically it is a bit slower than Fibre Channel.

To summarize this section on enterprise storage subsystems, we refer to Table 13.3 with the defining properties of each technology. Note that this overview provides the main categories in a continuously evolving landscape, and that many vendors offer variations and/or hybrid approaches as well.

**Drill Down**

Recently, the concept of *object storage* (aka object-based storage) has been put forward as an alternative to file-level and block-level storage. In fact, the object storage label is used for many different, although related, technologies, with as a common denominator the fact that they provide a means to store and retrieve chunks of data (objects) according to a single identifier that is unique across the entire storage space. The latter is in most cases a distributed system.

Object storage is often contrasted to the more traditional block- and file-level storage approaches, which both rely on a file system, with the files being organized in a hierarchy of folders. Files are associated with a path according to these folders, as well as with a limited amount of metadata (e.g., the file's creation date). With block-level I/O, the file system is external to the devices (e.g., in a storage area network), whereas with file-level I/O, it is internal (e.g., in a NAS appliance). However, object storage does away with hierarchical file systems altogether and persists chunks of data through a flat system of globally unique identifiers, not unlike the domain name system of the internet. In this way, the unwieldy file system structure can be avoided and objects of arbitrary size are stored and retrieved according to (only) their unique key, resulting in more speedy access. As a result, object storage is massively scalable, even to billions of objects, because the complexity of the file organization does not increase considerably as the number of objects grows. In addition, extensive user-definable metadata can be added, which offers improved capabilities for search and analytics.

The abovementioned principles have been implemented in different formats. First, object storage can refer to the organization of arrays of physical storage devices. A primary aim is to abstract away the lower storage layers from applications and users. Data are exposed and managed as variable-size objects instead of files or fixed-size physical disk blocks. A term often used in this context is RAIN (Redundant Array of Independent Nodes, as opposed to RAID), which organizes a collection of storages devices as a set of nodes in a cluster and exposes a simple "put" and "get" API on top of it to store and retrieve objects according to their ID, transparently offering features such as data replication and load balancing.

The same principles have been implemented in cloud storage offerings such as Amazon Simple Storage Service (S3) and OpenStack Swift. Here, the "put" and "get" functionality is typically offered via RESTful HTTP APIs (see also Chapter 10). Proprietary implementations also exist under the hood of well-known web-based platforms such as Spotify, Dropbox, and Facebook (the latter for photo storage by means of a product called Haystack).

Sometimes, the line between object storage technology and some NoSQL database products, notably key–value stores and document stores (see Chapter 11), is somewhat blurred. They have in common that an arbitrary chunk of data can be stored and retrieved according to a unique ID, possibly with the addition of some attribute–value pairs. However, the focus of object storage is more purely on storage capacity for fairly stable data and less on database functionality and rapidly changing data.

Overall, object storage is best suited for large datasets of unstructured data (e.g., web pages or multimedia data) in which the objects do not change too frequently. They are not really suited for more mainstream transactional database processing. Therefore, object storage should be considered as complementary to block and file storage, rather than as a substitute.

### 13.2.3 Business Continuity

We conclude this chapter with a brief discussion on **business continuity**. This is a very important topic to any business, which covers a very broad range of concerns related to ICT as well as organization and logistics. It is recommended to at least pinpoint some elements with respect to data and database functionality.

In the context of database management, business continuity can be defined as *an organization's ability to guarantee its uninterrupted functioning, despite possible planned or unplanned downtime of the hardware and software supporting its database functionality*. Planned downtime can be due to backups, maintenance, upgrades, etc. Unplanned downtime can be due to malfunctioning of the server hardware, the storage devices, the operating system, the database software, or business applications. A very specific, and extreme, aspect of business continuity is an organization's endurance against human- or nature-induced disasters. In that context, we speak of *disaster tolerance*.

#### 13.2.3.1 Contingency Planning, Recovery Point, and Recovery Time

An organization's measures with respect to business continuity and recovery from any calamities are formalized in a **contingency plan**. Without going into too much detail, a primary element of such a plan is the quantification of recovery objectives, considering an organization's strategic priorities:

- The *Recovery Time Objective (RTO)* specifies the amount of downtime that is acceptable after a calamity occurs. The estimated cost of this downtime provides guidance as to the investments an organization is prepared to make to keep this downtime as minimal as possible. The closer the RTO is to the calamity, the less downtime there will be, but also the higher the required investments in measures to restore database systems to a functioning state after planned or unplanned downtime. The RTO is different for each organization. For example, a worldwide online shop will push for zero downtime, as even the slightest downtime costs vast amounts in lost

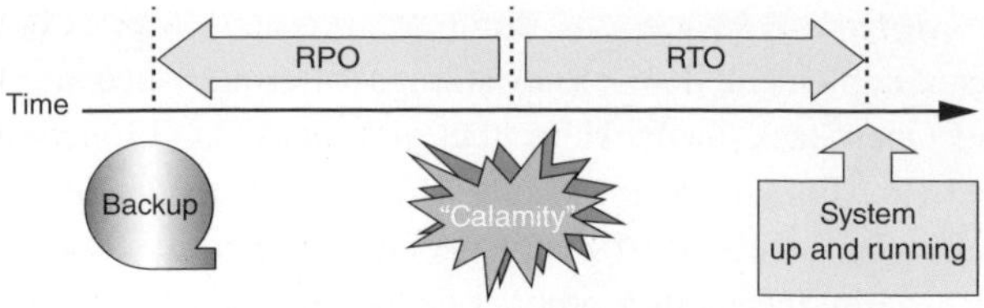


**Figure 13.14** Illustration of RPO and RTO.

sales. On the other hand, a secondary school may be able to cope with a few hours of downtime, so there is no need to make investments to recover from a calamity in a matter of minutes.

- *The Recovery Point Objective (RPO)* specifies the degree to which data loss is acceptable after a calamity. Or to put it differently, it specifies which point in time the system should be restored to, once the system is up and running again. The closer the RPO is to the time of the calamity, the fewer data will be lost, but also the higher the required investments in state-of-the-art backup facilities, data redundancy, etc. The RPO differs from organization to organization. For example, although a higher RTO is acceptable for a secondary school, its RPO is probably closer to zero, as loss of data with respect to, e.g., pupils' exam results is quite unacceptable. On the other hand, a weather observatory is better off with a low RTO than with a low RPO, as it is probably important to be able to resume observations as soon as possible, but a certain loss of past data from just before the calamity may be less dramatic.

The consequences of RPO and RTO are depicted in Figure 13.14.

The aim of a contingency plan is to minimize the RPO and/or RTO, or to at least guarantee a level that is appropriate to the organization, department, or process at hand. A crucial aspect in this context is to avoid **single points of failure**, as these represent the Achilles heel of the organization's information systems. With respect to database management, the following "points of failure" can be identified: *availability and accessibility of storage devices, availability of database functionality*, and *availability of the data themselves*. In each of these domains, some form of redundancy is called for to mitigate single points of failure. We discuss the respective domains in the following subsections.

### 13.2.3.2 Availability and Accessibility of Storage Devices

The availability and accessibility of storage devices was already covered when discussing RAID and enterprise storage subsystems. For example, networked storage, in addition to other considerations, avoids the single points of failure that a DAS set-up implies with respect to the connectivity between servers and storage devices. In addition, the different RAID levels impact not only the RPO by avoiding data loss through redundancy, but also the RTO. For example, the mirror set-up in RAID 1 allows for uninterrupted storage device access, as all processes can be instantaneously redirected to the mirror drive if the primary drive fails. In contrast, the redundancy in the format of parity bits in other RAID levels requires some time to reconstruct the data, if the content of one drive in the RAID configuration is damaged.

### 13.2.3.3 Availability of Database Functionality

Safeguarding access to storage devices is useless if the organization cannot guarantee a DBMS that is permanently up and running as well. A first, simple, approach here is to provide for **manual failover** of DBMS functionality. This means that a spare server with DBMS software is in standby, possibly with shared access to the same storage devices as the primary server. However, in case of a calamity, manual intervention is needed, initiating startup scripts, etc., to transfer the workload from the primary database server over to the backup server. This inevitably takes some time, hence pushing back the RTO.

A more complex and expensive solution, but with a much better impact on the RTO, is the use of **clustering**. In general, clustering refers to multiple interconnected computer systems working together to be perceived, in certain aspects, as a unity. The individual computer systems are denoted as the *nodes* in the cluster. The purpose of cluster computing is to improve performance by means of parallelism and/or availability through redundancy in hardware, software, and data. Cluster computing for the sake of performance is discussed in more detail in Chapter 11 on NoSQL databases, but it can also play an important role in the context of business continuity. Availability is guaranteed by automated failover, in that other nodes in the cluster are configured to take over the workload of a failing node without halting the system. In the same way, planned downtime can be avoided. A typical example here are *rolling upgrades*, where software upgrades are applied one node at a time, with the other nodes temporarily taking over the workload. The coordination of DBMS nodes in a cluster can be organized at different levels. It can be the responsibility of the operating system, which then provides specific facilities for exploiting a cluster environment. Several DBMS vendors also offer tailored DBMS implementations, with the DBMS software itself taking on the responsibility of coordinating and synchronizing different DBMS instances in a distributed setting.

**Connections**

Chapter 11 discusses NoSQL databases and cluster computing. Other aspects of cluster computing are tackled in Chapter 16.

#### 13.2.3.4 Data Availability

A last concern in the context of business continuity is the availability of the data themselves. Many techniques exist to safeguard data by means of *backup* and/or *replication*. These techniques all have a different impact on the RPO and RTO, resulting in a different answer to the respective questions "how much data will be lost since the last backup, in the case of a calamity ?" and "how long does it take to restore the backup copy ?" Of course, also here, a tighter RPO and/or RTO often comes at a higher cost. We present some typical approaches:

- **Tape backup**: With tape backup, the database files are copied periodically to a tape storage medium for safekeeping. Tape backup is still the least expensive backup solution. However, it is a time-consuming process, so the frequency is necessarily somewhat lower, which has a negative impact on the RPO. Therefore, tape backup is often combined with other precautions, such as maintaining multiple online copies of the logfile. The logfile is an essential tool in the context of transaction management and is discussed in more detail in Chapter 14. Restoring a backup copy from tape onto a functional database server after a calamity is a time-intensive process as well. Tape backup thus has an equally negative impact on the RTO as on the RPO.

**Drill Down**

Even although tape-based storage has existed for quite a while, it is still used frequently for archiving and backup of data. The Linear Tape-Open (LTO) consortium, composed of IBM, HP, and Quantum, the three big players in tape storage technology, has decided on a roadmap regarding future tape-based storage solutions. The roadmap goes all the way from LTO4 (able to store 800 GB on a tape cartridge and already available) to LTO10 (with the ability to store 120 TB!). Who's using it? Clients dealing with exponential data growth and a need for deep storage solutions. This includes media companies such as ABC, NBC, Comcast, ESPN, PBS, Showtime, Sony, and dozens of individual television stations around the world, as well as the health and banking industries.

- **Hard disk backup**: The process of making and restoring backups to/from hard disk is more efficient than tape backup because of the device characteristics, such as better access times and transfer rate. This has a positive impact on the RTO and possibly also on the RPO. Still, as to the latter, the frequency of backups not only depends on the characteristics of the backup medium, but also on the infrastructure within which the primary copy of the data resides. For example, the workload of the source system, and the possible performance impact on the latter, may be an important factor to determine backup frequency. As already discussed earlier in this chapter, storage networks, taking the burden of data and backup-related traffic from the LAN and from the servers, can be a solution here.
- **Electronic vaulting**: Creating backups is key to business continuity, but in most cases it is also essential to safeguard the backup copies at a remote site a sufficient distance from the primary site to avoid them both being involved in the same incident or disaster. A simple but error-prone approach here is to manually transport the offline tape backups to the remote site. A more efficient technique is electronic vaulting. Here, backup data are transmitted over a network to hard disk or tape devices at a secure vaulting facility or at an alternate data center. This process can be largely automated.
- **Replication and mirroring**: The techniques mentioned thus far are all asynchronous approaches; backup copies of the data are only created periodically. Therefore, whatever the frequency, there is always a certain amount of data loss and the RPO will never coincide with the moment of the calamity. To avoid data loss altogether, synchronous techniques are needed, maintaining redundant copies of the data in real-time. Two closely related terms in this context are replication and mirroring. Some authors consider them to be synonyms, some define them in slightly different ways. We refer to mirroring as the act of performing the same write operations on two or more identical disks simultaneously. Mirroring is always synchronous. The most well-known implementation of mirroring is RAID 1. Replication is the act of propagating data written to one device over a network onto another device. This can be done synchronously, semi-synchronously, or asynchronously. Many SAN and NAS implementations, and also DBMSs and dedicated replication servers,[17] feature replication facilities. Synchronous replication and mirroring provide near-real-time redundant copies of the data and thus cater for a very strict RPO. Of course, the tradeoff is the cost of the solution, but also the performance impact that real-time replication may have on the source system and sometimes the network. Asynchronous replication is more flexible in this respect.
- **Disaster tolerance**: To guarantee a tight RPO and RTO under any circumstances, remote data replication is needed to an actual second data center at a sufficiently distant location. The data can be replicated over a dedicated network (e.g., WAN) or over public lines. The same considerations

[17] Replication as a data integration technique is discussed in more detail in Chapter 18.

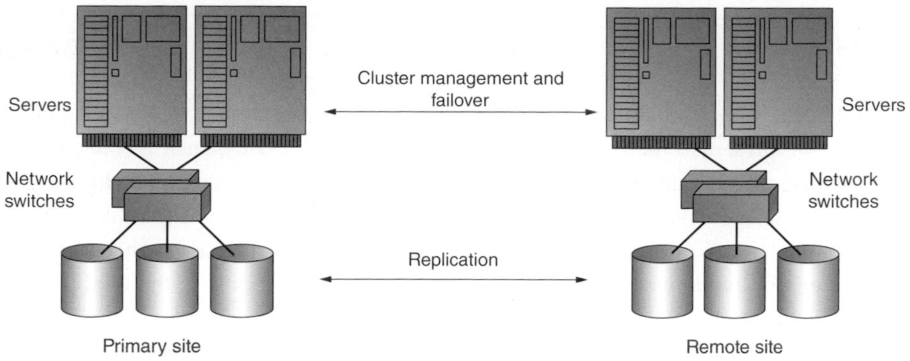


**Figure 13.15** Illustration of stretched cluster with primary and remote site.

exist with respect to synchronous versus asynchronous replication, with the addition that asynchronous replication is less sensitive to network latency, which may be an important factor, given the distance. The remote site should be fully operational, and in that case, it may also handle some workload to relieve the primary site, or at least be able to become fully operational in a very limited amount of time. This means that not only up-to-date data should be available, but also DBMS functionality should be up and running or at least on standby. In some implementations, both the primary and the backup DBMS are conceived as nodes in a cluster that spans both the primary and remote data center. We refer to this as a **stretched cluster**. In this way, failover, but also load balancing, for example, can be managed efficiently between the primary and backup facilities. This is illustrated in Figure 13.15. Of course, at each individual site there is still the need to mitigate single points of failure by providing redundant storage devices as well as servers, network components, power supplies, etc.

- **Transaction recovery**: As a final remark, it must be stressed that replicating the data alone does not always suffice to guarantee database integrity in the case of calamities. Also, the *transaction context* must be preserved. For example, suppose disaster strikes in a bank amid a set of database operations in which money is withdrawn from one account and is about to be transferred to another account. Even if the data files themselves were replicated synchronously from the primary site to the remote site, the remote database is not necessarily aware that a transaction was going on in which money was already retrieved from one account, but not yet deposited in the other account. This information, which is vital to the consistency of the database, is what we call the transaction context. If the overall data replication is coordinated at the DBMS level, and not at the operating system or network level, then typically the transaction context is also transferred between the DBMSs. One popular technique here is called *log shipping*. This means that the logfile, which keeps account of ongoing transactions, is replicated between both DBMSs. The remote DBMS can use this logfile for transaction recovery, i.e., to restore the context of the transactions that were ongoing at the primary site. Transaction recovery and the role of the logfile are discussed in detail in Chapters 14 and 16.

**Connections**

Chapter 14 discusses transaction management and the logfile of a DBMS. Chapter 16 focuses in more detail on transaction management, replication, and recovery in a distributed setting.

**Retention Questions**

- Discuss various ways of pooling and managing individual devices as so-called enterprise storage subsystems.
- Discuss how these techniques can be applied in the context of business continuity.

## Summary

In this chapter we dealt with a broad range of aspects pertaining to physical database organization. First, we presented the building blocks of physical databases, such as tablespaces and indexes. In this way, we built upon the insights into physical record organization and file organization from the previous chapter. We explained how the presence or absence of different index types affects query performance according to an optimal access path as determined by the query optimizer. We also focused on several ways of physically realizing join operations. In the final parts of the chapter, we returned to the hardware aspects of storage, discussing technologies such as RAID, SAN, and NAS. We concluded with an overview of some database-related concerns with respect to business continuity.

### Scenario Conclusion

Sober has now learned how it can implement the indexes defined in Chapter 6 using SQL. For example, the primary index on CAR-NR in CAR can be defined as follows:

```
CREATE UNIQUE INDEX CAR-NR_INDEX
ON CAR(CAR-NR ASC)
```

Likewise, the clustered index on ACC-LOCATION in ACCIDENT can be defined as follows:

```
CREATE INDEX ACC-LOCATION_INDEX
ON ACCIDENT(ACC-LOCATION ASC)
CLUSTER
```

The company now also has a good understanding of various database access methods and join implementations.

Since the company is a startup, it will kick off with a LAN with NAS appliances. As it continues to grow, it might switch to a full-blown SAN at a later stage.

To safeguard business continuity, Sober has decided to work out a contingency plan. This will include a secure vaulting facility using tape backup.

## Key Terms List

**access paths**
**block-level I/O protocol**
**business continuity**
**clustering**
**connectivity**
**contingency plan**
**cost-based optimizer**
**data striping**
**DAS (directly attached storage)**
**direct attach**
**disaster tolerance**
**disk mirroring**
**electronic vaulting**
**Ethernet**
**Fibre Channel (FC)**
**file-level I/O protocol**
**filter factor (FF)**
**hard disk backup**
**hash join**
**index spaces**
**inter-query parallelism**
**intra-query parallelism**

**iSCSI**
**manual failover**
**mirroring**
**multicolumn index**
**NAS (network attached storage)**
**NAS gateway**
**nested-loop join**
**network attach**
**query cardinality (QC)**
**query predicate**
**RAID controller**
**RAID levels**
**redundancy**
**Redundant Array of Independent Disks (RAID)**
**replication**
**SAN (storage area network)**
**SCSI (Small Computer Systems Interface)**
**single points of failure**
**sort-merge join**
**stored table**
**stretched cluster**
**table cardinality (TC)**
**tablespace**
**tape backup**
**transaction recovery**

## Review Questions

**13.1.** Which of the following statements is **correct**?

a. Current versions of SQL require a specific internal data model.
b. Current versions of SQL impose a specific physical implementation of internal data models.
c. Current versions of SQL require both a specific internal data model *and* a specific physical implementation of that data model.
d. Current versions of SQL do not impose any standardization on the internal data model or on the way in which a relational data model is implemented physically.

**13.2.** Which of the following statements is **not correct**?

a. Index creation can help improve the performance of join queries.
b. Indexing makes it harder to enforce uniqueness on a (combination of ) column(s).
c. An index implies a logical ordering of the rows in a table.
d. An index can be used to create a physical ordering of rows.

**13.3.** Which of the following statements is **not correct**?

a. The more selective a query predicate's FF, the less desirable it is to use the index on the corresponding attribute type in the access plan.
b. For range queries, a primary or clustered index is more efficient than a secondary index.
c. The number of block accesses determines the performance, not the number of rows retrieved.
d. The more attribute types are included in the index, the higher the performance impact is on update queries.

**13.4.** Given two tables R and S, which of the following join strategies is described by the following algorithm:

```
Denote S → outer table
For every row s in S do
     for every row r in R do
         { if r(a) = s(b) then join r with s and place in output buffer}
     }
```

a. Hash join.
b. Sort-merge join.
c. Nested-loop join.
d. None of the above.

**13.5.** Given two tables R and S, which of the following join strategies is described by the following algorithm:

```
Stage 1: sort R according to r(a)
         sort S according to s(b)

Stage 2: retrieve the first row r of R
         retrieve the first row s of S
         for every row r in R
            {while s(b) < r(a)
               read the next row s of S
               if r(a) = s(b) then join r with s and place in output buffer}
```

a. Hash join.
b. Sort-merge join.
c. Nested-loop join.
d. None of the above.

**13.6.** Which of the following statements is **correct?**

a. SQL is a declarative language, meaning that the programmer has to specify which data to retrieve and how the data are to be located and retrieved from the physical database files.
b. The filter factor of a predicate is the fraction of rows that contain a missing value for that predicate.
c. If no further statistical information about a predicate is available, the filter factor of that predicate can be estimated by dividing 1 by the number of different values the attribute type can have.
d. Table cardinality is another way of referring to the number of columns in a table.

**13.7.** Which statement is **not correct**?

a. RAID level 0 is used if performance is more important than fault tolerance.
b. To store the same amount of data, RAID 1 needs twice the amount of storage capacity compared to RAID 0.
c. RAID level 5 strikes a balance between read and write performance, storage efficiency, and fault tolerance.
d. Block-level striping as used in RAID 0 does not increase read performance.

**13.8.** Which statement is **not correct**?

a. It is often more efficient to combine multiple smaller physical disk drives into one larger logical drive because having multiple physical drives allows for parallel retrieval, which results in much more improved performance.
b. It is often more efficient to combine multiple smaller physical disk drives into one larger logical drive because reliability can be improved by introducing some measure of data redundancy.
c. With bit-level data striping, every disk participates in each read or write operation.
d. Using error-correcting codes for fault tolerance requires extra storage space, almost as much as when opting for disk mirroring.

**13.9.** Which statement is **not correct**?

a. The management of data storage is more expensive than the purchase of storage hardware, which is why businesses opt for enterprise storage subsystems.
b. "Network attach" refers to establishing a many-to-many connection between storage devices and the corresponding servers by means of network technology.
c. Although SCSI has been a popular medium for connecting storage devices to servers and/or processors in the past, nowadays it is not used for high-performance and high-capacity workstations and servers.
d. The SCSI I/O command set is a type of block-level I/O protocol which can be exchanged over SCSI, Ethernet, or Fibre Channel cabling.

**13.10.** Which statement is **not correct**?

a. A DAS does not offer out-of-the-box capabilities for centralized storage management and sharing unused disk capacity across servers.
b. A SAN is typically best in terms of performance because it often uses Fibre Channel, the LAN network is freed from storage-related traffic, and Fibre Channel-compatible storage devices have some onboard intelligence, which allows them to perform certain tasks autonomously, e.g., server-free backups.
c. Compared to SAN, a NAS is much less expensive and much simpler in software and hardware. However, it achieves performance similar to a NAS set-up.
d. A NAS gateway receives file-level I/O requests from servers connected to the LAN or WAN and translates these into SCSI block I/O commands to access the external storage devices; this latter connection can be organized by DAS or SAN technology.

**13.11.** Which statement is **not correct**?

a. A primary element of a contingency plan is the quantification of recovery objectives in RTO and RPO, given the organization's strategic priorities.
b. The only points of failure of a database system are the availability of database functionality and the availability of the data themselves.
c. The manual failover of DBMS functionality is a simple and not very expensive solution to guarantee the availability of DBMS functionality in the case of a calamity.
d. Rolling upgrades are an example of how to avoid downtime in a cluster computing set-up.

**13.12.** Statement 1: When opting for hard drive backups to maintain data availability in case of a calamity, the RPO depends on the underlying infrastructure. Choosing a SAN as a storage subsystem might be a solution here, as it keeps the burden of data and backup-related traffic from the LAN and from the servers.

Statement 2: Log shipping is a technique that is used for preserving the transaction context of a DBMS in the case of a calamity. The remote DBMS used for replication can use the primary log for restoring transactions that were ongoing at the primary site.

Which statements are correct or incorrect?

a. Both statements are correct.
b. Statement 1 is correct, statement 2 is incorrect.
c. Statement 1 is incorrect, statement 2 is correct.
d. Both statements are incorrect.

## Problems and Exercises

13.1E What is intra-query parallelism? How does the concept of a tablespace enable it?

13.2E Illustrate how SQL can be used to create an index called CUSTOMER_INDEX, on the table with name CUSTOMERS based on the CUSTOMER_AGE (descending) and CUSTOMER_ZIP-CODE (ascending) attribute types. Give a minimum of three reasons why choosing an appropriate index can be beneficial.

13.3E Discuss and compare three different techniques to physically implement a join.

13.4E Which three techniques are used in a RAID set-up? Which configuration of options of each of these three techniques is best used for very critical data, in terms of business continuity?

13.5E Along which three criteria can storage subsystems be classified? Situate the DAS, SAN, NAS, NAS gateway, and iSCSI approaches along each of these three criteria.

13.6E Suppose you work for a bank and have to create a contingency plan. Compare your RTO and RPO objectives with other businesses and organizations. What kind of RAID set-up would you choose? What kind of enterprise storage subsystem?

# 14 Basics of Transaction Management

## Chapter Objectives

In this chapter, you will learn to:

- understand the concepts of transactions, recovery, and concurrency control;
- identify the various steps of a transaction lifecycle as well as the DBMS components involved and the role of the logfile;
- discern different types of failures and how to deal with them;
- understand different types of concurrency problems as well as the importance of schedules, serial schedules, and serializable schedules;
- discern the differences between optimistic and pessimistic schedulers;
- grasp the importance of locking and locking protocols;
- understand the responsibility of the DBMS's transaction management facilities to ensure the ACID properties of a transaction.

### Opening Scenario

Since many users will interact simultaneously with Sober's database, the company wants to understand any problems that may occur. Furthermore, Sober also wants to mitigate the risks of various types of failures that may make its data incorrect.

The majority of databases in actual organizational settings are **multi-user databases**. This implies that many applications and users can access the data in the database in parallel. This concurrent access to the same data, if not managed properly, may induce different types of anomalies or unexpected problems. Moreover, various kinds of errors or calamities may occur in the respective DBMS components or its environment – such as the operating system, the applications interacting with the DBMS, or the storage subsystem – possibly rendering the database data into an inconsistent state. Fortunately, most database systems provide a realm of transparent, although often configurable, solutions to avoid or otherwise deal with such problems. In this way, the DBMS supports the ACID (Atomicity, Consistency, Isolation, Durability) properties already mentioned in Chapter 1. At the heart of these solutions are the concepts of **transactions and transaction management**, **recovery**, and **concurrency control**. In this chapter, we first introduce each of these concepts. Then, we focus in more detail on transaction management and the DBMS components involved. After that, we discuss recovery and the different techniques to deal with calamities in the DBMS or application program, as well as the storage media. Finally, we describe in detail how concurrency control techniques, in interplay with transaction management and recovery, guarantee seamless concurrent access by multiple users to shared data.

## 14.1 Transactions, Recovery, and Concurrency Control

A transaction is a set of database operations (e.g., a sequence of SQL statements in a relational database) induced by a single user or application that should be considered as one undividable unit of work. A typical example illustrating the importance of transactions is the transfer between two bank accounts of the same customer. This transfer should be considered as a single transaction, but actually involves at least two database operations; one update to debit the first account and a second update to credit the other account for the same amount. Users should only see a "before" and "after" of this logical unit of work, and should never be confronted with the possible inconsistent states that occur between the respective operations that are part of the transaction. Also, it should not be possible to terminate a transaction in such a way that the database remains in an inconsistent state, because some operations of a single transaction were executed successfully and others were not; otherwise, either the customer or the bank would be deprived. In other words, a transaction should always "succeed" or "fail" in its entirety. In the event of a failure, no effects whatsoever of partially executed statements should remain in the database. In this way, a transaction represents a set of database operations that renders the database from one consistent state into another consistent state. The inconsistent intermediate states that may occur during the execution of the transaction should remain hidden to users.

During transaction execution, different types of errors or problems may occur. There may be a hard disk failure; the application, operating system, or DBMS may crash or there may even be a power outage. Moreover, the transaction itself may run into an error (e.g., because of a division by zero). *Recovery* is the activity of ensuring that, whichever of the problems occurred, the database is returned to a consistent state without any data loss afterwards. In particular, for transactions that were completed successfully (i.e., committed transactions, see Section 14.2.1) the database system should guarantee that all changes are persisted into the database, even if one of the errors occurred between the moment when the DBMS (logically) signaled transaction completion and the moment when it (physically) updated the actual database files. In the same way, recovery involves ensuring that no effects remain of transactions that ended unsuccessfully; to the outside world, it should appear as if the unsuccessful transaction never happened.

Finally, even if every transaction by itself would bring the database from one consistent state into another, transactions do not exist in isolation. Transactions are frequently executed concurrently, on partially the same data. This interleaved execution of different transactions may introduce many interferences between the transactions, which bring about inconsistencies that would not exist if the transactions were executed **serially** (i.e., one after the other). However, a purely serial execution would, in most cases, require many transactions to wait for one another, and therefore would have a severely negative impact on transaction throughput and performance. It is therefore important to oversee a non-serial execution in such a way that interference problems between transactions are avoided or resolved. This activity, known as concurrency control, is the coordination of transactions that execute simultaneously on the same data so that they do not cause inconsistencies in the data because of mutual interference. Different strategies, with different tradeoffs, exist for this purpose, as explained in Section 14.4.

**Retention Questions**

- Define the following concepts: transaction, recovery, and concurrency control.

## 14.2 Transactions and Transaction Management

In this section, we first elaborate on delineating transactions and the transaction lifecycle. We then discuss the DBMS components involved in transaction management. We conclude by reviewing the essential role of the logfile in transaction management.

### 14.2.1 Delineating Transactions and the Transaction Lifecycle

A database application may uphold multiple operations, and even multiple ongoing transactions, at the same time. For a database system to be able to assess which operations belong to which transaction, it is necessary to specify the transaction boundaries – to **delineate** the transaction. This can be done in an implicit or an explicit way.

The program can mark the first operation of a new transaction explicitly by means of a **begin_transaction** instruction. Alternatively, without an explicit notification, the database management system will assume that the first executable SQL statement in a program execution thread denotes the start of a new transaction.[1] The transaction's operations are received by the transaction manager and put into a **schedule**, along with other ongoing transactions. Once the first operation is executed, the transaction is active.

The end of a transaction is marked explicitly by means of an **end_transaction** instruction. Upon completion of a transaction, it is to be decided whether the changes made by the transaction should be persisted into the database, or should be undone. If the transaction completed successfully, all changes made by the individual operations belonging to that transaction should be made permanent; the transaction is **committed**. After the transaction is committed, the changes become visible to other users and cannot be undone (unless, of course, another transaction would induce exactly the opposite changes afterwards). However, if the transaction is **aborted**, it means that an error or anomaly occurred during the transaction's execution. This anomaly may have happened at different levels (application, operating system, database system, see Section 14.3), but, whatever the cause, the transaction did not complete successfully. It is possible that the transaction, before being aborted, already made some partial changes to the database. In that case, a **rollback** of the transaction is required: all changes made by the transaction's respective operations should be undone in such a way that, after completion of the rollback, it appears as if the faulty transaction never happened.

**Drill Down**

In the context of loosely coupled systems and so-called long-running transactions (see Chapter 16), the principle of compensation is often applied. In that case, instead of the database system mechanically undoing any changes made by the transaction, a new transaction is issued that induces the exact opposite changes, or more generally, changes that somehow "make up" for the previous transaction. However, this is the responsibility of the application programmer rather than the database system.

[1] In this chapter we will assume a relational database environment, although many concepts equally apply to non-relational systems.

Let's examine the following simple example:

```
<begin_transaction>

UPDATE account
SET balance = balance - :amount
WHERE accountnumber = :account_to_debit

UPDATE account
SET balance = balance + :amount
WHERE accountnumber = :account_to_credit

<end_transaction>
```

This bank transfer between two accounts of the same customer can be considered a single logical unit of work that involves two database operations. The start of a new transaction is signaled by the <begin_transaction> instruction. In particular, two update operations are required, respectively to debit and credit the two accounts (in this case: two tuples in the same table) according to the same variable[2] :amount. The two account tuples involved are identified by the respective variables :account_to_debit and :account_to_credit. Once the <end_transaction> instruction is reached, the database system decides on the transaction's outcome. If everything went well, the transaction is committed; the changes are persisted into the database and the two updated balance values in the table become visible to the other database users and transactions. However, if thc transaction fails to complete successfully, or if an error occurred before the end_transaction instruction, the transaction is aborted. If, let's say, the first update operation was already completed before the anomaly occurred, this update needs to be rolled back and the original balance value is restored. After that, the two (unchanged) account tuples are made available again to other users and transactions; no traces of the faulty transaction should remain.

After the transaction is committed or aborted, a new transaction can be started, depending on the program logic. Alternatively, if the abort was the result of a program malfunction, the program itself may be terminated. If the program code does not contain explicit transaction delimiters, the database system will typically attempt to commit transactions induced by programs or procedures that completed successfully and abort transactions otherwise.

## 14.2.2 DBMS Components Involved in Transaction Management

**Connections**

We already briefly introduced the transaction manager in Chapter 2 when we discussed the architecture of a DBMS.

The main DBMS component responsible for coordinating transaction execution is called the **transaction manager**. Figure 14.1 depicts the functioning of the transaction manager in interaction with the other main components involved in transaction management: the scheduler, the stored data manager, the buffer manager, and the recovery manager.

The transaction manager informs the **scheduler** of new transactions that were presented to its input area (1). The scheduler plans the start of the transactions and the execution of their respective operations, aiming at optimizing KPIs such as query response times and transaction throughput rates. As soon as a transaction can be started, the recovery manager and the **stored data**

[2] Chapter 15 will discuss in more detail the mechanisms for passing variables as input to an SQL query.

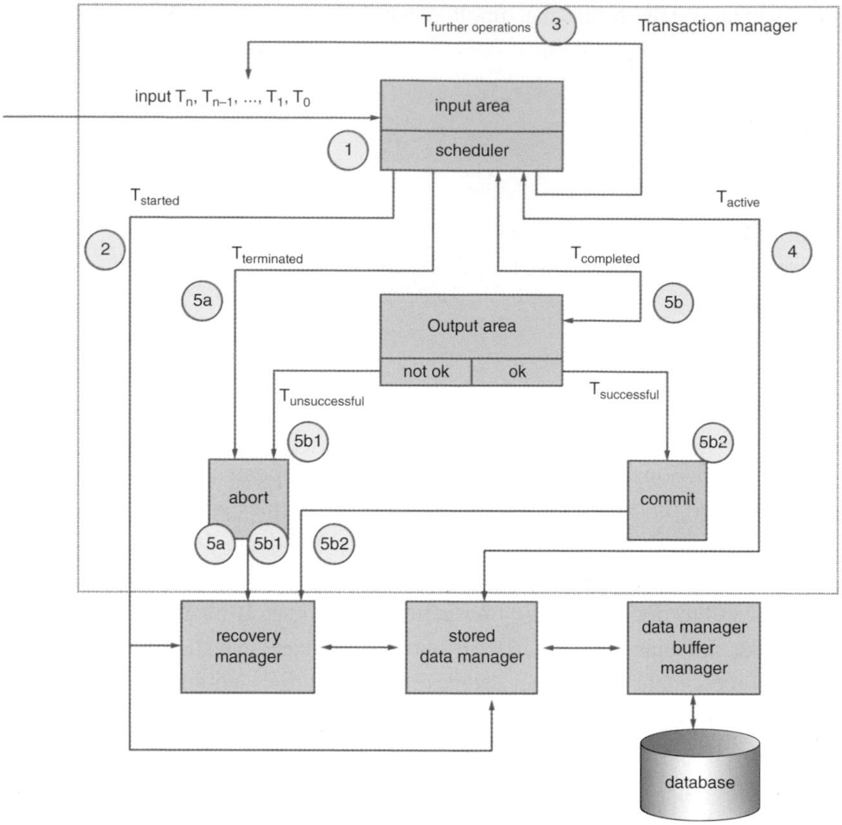


**Figure 14.1** DBMS components involved in transaction management.

> **Connections**
>
> Chapters 12 and 13 discuss physical database organization in more detail.

**manager** are notified (2). The stored data manager coordinates the I/O instructions and hence the physical interactions with the database files. However, for reasons of performance, physical file operations are not executed immediately when a database read or write instruction is received. Rather, a database buffer in (fast) internal memory is used as an intermediary, such that access to (slow) external memory can be postponed a bit. In this way, physical file operations can be buffered and are executed in an optimized way, according to physical file structure, parallel disk access, etc. In this context, the buffer manager is responsible for data exchange between the database buffer and the physical database files.

Once the transaction has started, its state is said to be active. As the input area receives the respective operations belonging to the transaction, as well as operations belonging to other active transactions, the scheduler plans their execution order (3). Upon execution, the operations trigger interaction with the database through the stored data manager (4). The latter informs the scheduler about the outcome of the execution. When a transaction has completed (5b), and if no calamities have occurred, the transaction reaches the committed state. Updates as induced by the transaction, which may still reside in the database buffer, can be considered as permanent and should be persisted into the physical database files. The recovery manager is invoked to coordinate this (5b2). If, however, the transaction was completed unsuccessfully because a problem was detected (5b1) or if the transaction was terminated before completion (5a), the transaction reaches an aborted state. If any (intermediate) changes were already written to disk, they should be undone. To coordinate the latter, again, the recovery manager is invoked.

### 14.2.3 The Logfile

Aside from the functional DBMS components described above, the **logfile** is a vital element in transaction management and recovery. Although the logfile essentially contains redundant data, this redundancy is of absolute importance if, for whatever reason, data are lost or damaged in the context of transaction execution. Should this occur, the recovery manager will attempt to recover the lost data by means of the registrations on the logfile. For each transaction and each operation, relevant information is registered on the logfile in **log records**. In this way, the logfile is a sequential file, consisting of log records that contain the following information:

- a unique log sequence number to identify the log record;
- a unique transaction identifier, relating the log registration to an individual transaction;
- a marking to denote the start of a transaction, along with the transaction's start time and an indication of whether the transaction is read only or read/write;
- identifiers of the database records involved in the transaction, as well as the operation(s) they were subjected to (*select*, *update*, *insert*, *delete*);
- **before images** of all records that participated in the transaction; these are the original values, before the records were updated. Before images are used to *undo* unwanted effects of failed transactions;
- **after images** of all records that were changed by the transaction; these are the new values, after the update. After images are used to *redo* changes that were not adequately persisted in the physical database files in the first place;
- the current state of the transaction (*active*, *committed*, or *aborted*).

The logfile may also contain **checkpoints**. These denote synchronization points – moments when buffered updates by active transactions, as present in the database buffer, are written to disk at once. In this context, it is important that all updates are registered on the logfile before they can be written to disk. This is called the **write ahead log strategy**. In this way, before images are always recorded on the logfile prior to the actual values being overwritten in the physical database files, in order to be prepared for a possible rollback. Moreover, a transaction should only attain the "committed" state after recording the necessary after images on the logfile, as well as the "commit" sign. Changes made by committed transactions can be redone afterwards if a problem occurred before all of its buffered updates could be written to disk.

Given the essential role of the logfile in the context of recovery, it is often duplicated (e.g., in a RAID level 1 configuration). The latter, in combination with other precautions, makes sure that, should a calamity occur, an intact copy of the logfile can be recovered at all times.

**Connections**

Chapter 13 discussed the RAID level 1 configuration.

**Retention Questions**

- Discuss the various steps in the transaction lifecycle.
- What DBMS components are involved in transaction management?
- What is the role of the logfile?

## 14.3 Recovery

In this section, we first elaborate on different types of failures that can occur when executing a transaction. We then discuss both system and media recovery, which are different recovery techniques that may be appropriate, depending on the type of failure.

### 14.3.1 Types of Failures

As previously mentioned, the correct execution of a transaction can be obstructed by several types of failures. To understand the modalities of recovery and the role of the recovery manager, it is useful to consider the actual failures that may occur. These can be classified into three broad categories, according to their causes: transaction failure, system failure, and media failure.

- A **transaction failure** results from an error in the logic that drives the transaction's operations (e.g., wrong input, uninitialized variables, incorrect statements, etc.) and/or in the application logic. As a consequence, the transaction cannot be completed successfully and should be aborted. This decision is typically made by the application or by the database system itself. If any tentative changes were made by the transaction, these should be rolled back.
- A **system failure** occurs if the operating system or the database system crashes due to a bug or a power outage, for example. This may result in loss of the primary storage's content and, consequently, the database buffer.
- **Media failure** occurs if the secondary storage (hard disk drive or in some cases flash memory) that contains the database files, and possibly the logfile, is damaged or inaccessible due to a disk crash, a malfunction in the storage network, etc. Although the transaction may have been logically executed correctly, and hence the application or user that induced the transaction was informed that the transaction was committed successfully, the physical files may not be able to capture or reflect the updates induced by the transaction.

In what follows, we discriminate between system recovery and media recovery. System recovery will be called for in the event of system failure and in some cases of transaction failure. Media recovery will be needed to cope with media failures.

### 14.3.2 System Recovery

Let's assume that a system failure occurs, causing loss of the database buffer's contents. Updates that resided in this buffer can be ascribed to transactions belonging to two possible categories: transactions that already had reached the committed state before the failure occurred, and transactions that were still in an active state. For each of these transactions, UNDO or REDO operations may be required, depending on which updates were already written to disk and which changes were still pending in the database buffer upon system failure. The latter is determined by the moment when the buffer manager last "flushed" the database buffer to disk. This moment is marked as a checkpoint on the logfile. The different possible situations are represented in Figure 14.2.

Figure 14.2 presents five transactions ($T_1$ to $T_5$) that are executed more or less simultaneously. Let's assume for now that the transactions do not interfere; we will cover concurrency control in Section 14.4. Suppose a checkpoint was registered on the logfile at time $t_c$, marking the last time

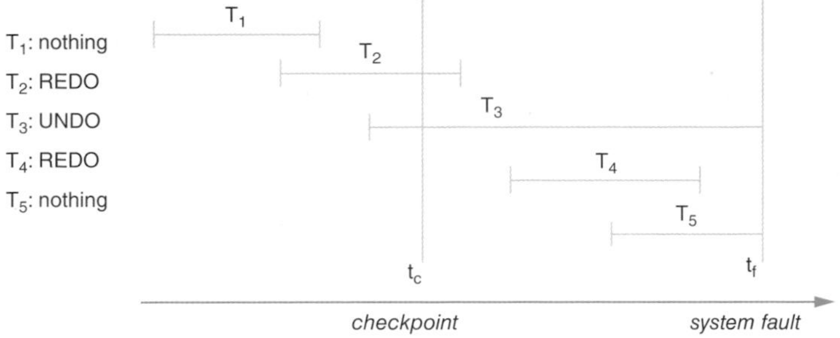


**Figure 14.2** Required UNDO and REDO operations upon system failure.

when pending updates in the database buffer were persisted into the physical database files. Later, at time $t_f$, a system fault occurred, resulting in loss of the database buffer.

Transaction $T_1$ committed before time $t_c$, when the checkpoint was registered. For this transaction, no recovery operations are required. Indeed, all the transaction's updates were already written to disk, so a REDO is not necessary. Moreover, since the transaction was successfully committed, no UNDO operations are required either.

Transaction $T_2$, was still active on time $t_c$. However, the transaction committed successfully before the actual system fault at time $t_f$. Since the transaction committed, but not all updates were written to disk before the database buffer was lost, a REDO is required to eventually persist all the transaction's updates.

Transaction $T_3$ was still active when the system fault occurred at time $t_f$. Some of its updates were still pending in the database buffer and disappeared by themselves when the buffer was lost. However, other updates, the ones made before $t_c$, were already written to disk. Since the transaction cannot continue because of the system fault, it cannot commit and must be aborted. The partial changes already written to disk must be rolled back by means of UNDO operations.

Transaction $T_4$ started after time $t_c$ and committed before the system fault at time $t_f$. Since all of its updates were still pending in the database buffer, a REDO is required to persist its effects into the database.

Transaction $T_5$ also started after $t_c$. Since the transaction was still active at time $t_f$, it cannot continue because of the system fault and will be aborted. However, since all its updates were still pending in the database buffer, they disappear along with the rest of the buffer's contents. No UNDO is required.

The logfile is indispensable to take account of which updates were made by which transactions (and when) in the above situations and to keep track of before images and after images. Based on this information, the recovery manager coordinates the required UNDO and REDO operations. Whereas the above-discussed system recovery focused on system failure, a similar reasoning can be applied in case of transaction failure. However, in that case, only the situations for $T_3$ and $T_5$ will occur, as a transaction will never be committed in the case of transaction failure.

Finally, it is important to note that different approaches to coordinate the flushing of the database buffer are available. In some situations, the buffer is simply flushed when it is "full" (i.e., without any involvement of the recovery manager). However, in many implementations, the recovery manager supervises this process and periodically instructs the buffer manager to flush (parts of) the buffer's content. In this case, many variations are possible. For example, if only pending updates from already committed transactions can be written to disk, there will never be a need for UNDO operations, but REDO operations may still be required. We call this a **deferred**

**update** or NO-UNDO/REDO policy. The opposite is the **immediate update policy**, which means that the database may be updated before a transaction is committed. A particular case here is if all of a transaction's buffered updates are persisted immediately upon transaction commit. We speak of an UNDO/NO-REDO policy, because a REDO will never be called for. Still, in most cases, such approaches would not be optimal from the perspective of physical file management and hence performance, so UNDO and REDO operations are an integral element of most implementations of system recovery.

### 14.3.3 Media Recovery

**Connections**

An extensive discussion of data redundancy and backup approaches, in the context of business continuity, was provided in Chapter 13. We briefly review some elements in this section, with an emphasis on recovery.

Media recovery is required if the physical database files and/or the logfile are unavailable or damaged due to a malfunction of the storage media or the storage subsystem (e.g., the storage network). Although many alternatives exist, media recovery is invariably based on some type of **data redundancy**: additional (redundant) copies of the files or data are stored on offline media (e.g., a tape vault) or online media (e.g., on an online backup hard disk drive, or even in a full-blown redundant database node).

Each solution typically entails a tradeoff between the cost to maintain the redundant data, along with its storage environment, and the time needed to recover the files and restore the system to a fully functional state. Considering this tradeoff, two techniques are often distinguished: mirroring and archiving. Note, however, that this classification is not absolute and that each technique has a myriad of variants; many hybrid approaches exist as well.

Disk mirroring[3] is a (near) real-time approach that writes the same data simultaneously to two or more physical disks. This can be implemented in different ways, with varying performance, by either software or hardware (e.g., by the operating system; by the hard disk controller in a RAID set-up; or by the components of a storage area network). The identical disks (as well as servers, etc.) can be located at the same premises or at separate locations, particularly for reasons of disaster recovery. Because of the real-time element, mirroring typically only requires limited **failover time** to have the system up and running again, with up-to-date data, after a media malfunction. However, the technology required is often costlier than archiving. In terms of performance, the duplicate writing may have a (limited) negative impact on write performance, but the redundant copy of the data can sometimes be exploited for parallel access, improving read performance. Aside from the physical file level, mirroring can also be realized at the database level, where not only the actual database files, but also the transaction state and the database system itself, are duplicated on different servers. This means the data and the transaction context can be preserved, i.e., transactions that are still active at the moment of a disk crash can failover to the redundant database server and continue their execution, instead of being aborted.

**Archiving** is an approach in which database files are periodically copied to other storage media, such as tape or another hard disk. Such a copy is called the **backup** copy. If the original file is damaged, the backup copy can be restored to recover the lost data. However, as the backup is only made periodically, the changes since the last copy will be missing. Therefore, there will be a tradeoff

[3] In fact, a further distinction can be made between mirroring and replication. For details, refer to Chapter 13.

between the cost (overhead and storage cost) of more frequent backups and the cost of lost data because of less frequent backups. In a database setting, if archiving is applied to the database files, then at least the logfile will often be mirrored, such that the older data as restored from the backup copy can be complemented with (a redo of) the more recent transactions as recorded in the logfile. This activity is called **rollforward recovery**. Besides the frequency, a backup strategy is typically subject to other parameters as well, such as the periodicity of an intermittent **full backup**, coupled with more frequent **incremental backups**, to capture the changes since the last full backup. A restore operation will then boil down to first restoring the last full backup, followed by chronologically restoring all incremental backups made since the last full backup. Other variation points that impact the tradeoff between cost and the time needed for recovery are: the choice of backup media (e.g., tape versus disk); whether the backup is offline or online; offsite or onsite backup, etc.

More recently, another tradeoff has come forward in the context of redundancy: the one between performance and consistency. As discussed in Chapter 11, several newly developed large scale (NoSQL) databases have redundancy at the core of their architecture, both for reasons of fault tolerance and for the sake of performance (parallel access). Moreover, performance is further increased by avoiding the transactional overhead required to keep the redundant copies of the same data item in sync at all times. Hence, such systems allow for a certain measure of temporary inconsistency, in return for increased performance. This transaction paradigm, referred to as eventual consistency, contrasts the approach of traditional relational databases, which typically favors absolute data consistency over performance. Moreover, many NoSQL database systems support multiple configurations, with a different positioning on the tradeoff between consistency and performance.

**Connections**

The particularities of eventual consistency and redundancy in the context of NoSQL databases are discussed further in Chapter 16.

**Retention Questions**

- Discuss the different types of failures and how to deal with them.

## 14.4 Concurrency Control

In this section, we start by illustrating typical concurrency problems such as the lost update problem, the uncommitted dependency problem, and the inconsistent analysis problem. We then define the concepts of a schedule and a serial schedule. Next, we review the constraints for a schedule to be serializable. We conclude by discussing both optimistic and pessimistic schedulers.

### 14.4.1 Typical Concurrency Problems

The scheduler, as a component of the transaction manager, is responsible for planning the execution of transactions and their individual operations. The most straightforward approach would be simply scheduling all transactions serially, according to the order in which they are submitted to the scheduler. In that way, all of a transaction's operations would be completed before a new transaction can be started, guaranteeing that no transactions can interfere with one another. Unfortunately, such a serial execution would be very inefficient, with many transactions waiting endlessly for their predecessors to finish, resulting in very poor response times and transaction throughput. The typical capabilities for parallel processing of both operating systems and storage systems would be vastly underexploited.

| *time* | $T_1$ | $T_2$ | $amount_x$ |
|---|---|---|---|
| $t_1$ | | begin transaction | 100 |
| $t_2$ | begin transaction | read($amount_x$) | 100 |
| $t_3$ | read($amount_x$) | $amount_x$ = $amount_x$ + 120 | 100 |
| $t_4$ | $amount_x$ = $amount_x$ - 50 | write($amount_x$) | 220 |
| $t_5$ | write($amount_x$) | commit | 50 |
| $t_6$ | commit | | 50 |

**Figure 14.3** Illustration of the lost update problem.

Instead, the scheduler will ensure that the operations of the respective transactions can be executed in an interleaved way, drastically increasing performance. Caution should be taken to not focus purely on parallelism, because interference problems would occur between transactions that access (and particularly those that update) the same data items. This would result in an inconsistent database which, in most cases,[4] is even less desirable than poor performance. Before presenting possible solutions, we first discuss the most typical interference problems that occur in the context of (lack of) concurrency control: the lost update problem, the uncommitted dependency problem, and the inconsistent analysis problem.

#### 14.4.1.1 Lost Update Problem

A **lost update problem** occurs if an otherwise successful update of a data item by a transaction is overwritten by another transaction that wasn't "aware" of the first update. This is illustrated in Figure 14.3: two transactions $T_1$ and $T_2$ have started around the same time. They both read the amount on the same account x. $T_1$ reduces the amount by 50, whereas $T_2$ increases the amount by 120. The execution of both transactions' operations is interleaved. Consequently, since $T_1$ uses a version of $amount_x$ that was read before it was updated by $T_2$, and since afterwards $amount_x$ is updated by $T_1$, the update by $T_2$ is "overwritten" and is completely lost. This is a first illustration of the fact that, even though two transactions may be completely correct by themselves, problems can still occur if the transactions interfere with one another.

#### 14.4.1.2 Uncommitted Dependency Problem (aka Dirty Read Problem)

If a transaction reads one or more data items that are being updated by another, as yet uncommitted, transaction, we may run into the **uncommitted dependency problem**. This is the case if the other transaction is ultimately aborted and rolled back, such that the first transaction ends up in a situation where it has read tentative values it never should have "seen" in the first place. This is illustrated in Figure 14.4: again, two transactions $T_1$ and $T_2$ have started around the same time. Both transactions read the amount on account x. $T_1$ reduces the amount by 50, whereas $T_2$ increases the same amount by 120. Both transactions are executed in an interleaved manner, although this time $T_1$ *is* aware of the update by $T_2$, since it reads $amount_x$ at time $t_5$, after it was written by $T_2$. Unfortunately, $T_2$ was still uncommitted at $t_5$ and is rolled back afterwards (at $t_6$), which means that no traces of it should

[4] As mentioned previously, many NoSQL database systems actually do allow for a certain measure of inconsistency, in return for increased performance. See Chapter 16 for details.

be left in the database state. In the meantime, however, $T_1$ has read, and possibly used, this "non-existent" value of $amount_x$.

#### 14.4.1.3 Inconsistent Analysis Problem

The **inconsistent analysis problem** denotes a situation in which a transaction reads partial results of another transaction that simultaneously interacts with (and updates) the same data items. The problem typically occurs when one transaction calculates an aggregate value based on multiple data items, whereas another transaction is concurrently updating some of these items. The example in Figure 14.5 involves three accounts x, y, and z. The initial amounts are respectively 100, 75, and 60. $T_1$ is to transfer $50 from account x to account z. $T_2$ calculates the sum of the three amounts. Both transactions are initiated at approximately the same time; the execution of their operations is interleaved. The problem is that $T_1$ subtracts an amount from account x when its value was already read by $T_2$, whereas $T_1$ adds an amount to account z before it will be read by $T_2$. Consequently, the $50 transferred by $T_1$ is included twice in the sum calculated by $T_2$ ; the result is 285 instead of 235.

Note that in this example, the final database state may not be inconsistent (the value of amount x, y, and z is what it ought to be), but the query result returned to a client application (the sum of amount x, y, and z) is nevertheless incorrect. In this way, the lost update problem always results in an inconsistent database state, whereas an uncommitted dependency or inconsistent analysis may yield either an inconsistent database state or an incorrect query result, depending on whether the incorrect value is stored into the database or returned to the client application.

| time | $T_1$ | $T_2$ | $amount_x$ |
|---|---|---|---|
| $t_1$ | | begin transaction | 100 |
| $t_2$ | | read($amount_x$) | 100 |
| $t_3$ | | $amount_x$ = $amount_x$ + 120 | 100 |
| $t_4$ | begin transaction | write($amount_x$) | 220 |
| $t_5$ | read($amount_x$) | | 220 |
| $t_6$ | $amount_x$ = $amount_x$ - 50 | rollback | 100 |
| $t_7$ | write($amount_x$) | | 170 |
| $t_8$ | commit | | 170 |

**Figure 14.4** Illustration of the uncommitted dependency problem.

| time | $T_1$ | $T_2$ | $amount_x$ | y | z | sum |
|---|---|---|---|---|---|---|
| $t_1$ | | begin transaction | 100 | 75 | 60 | |
| $t_2$ | begin transaction | sum = 0 | 100 | 75 | 60 | 0 |
| $t_3$ | read($amount_x$) | read($amount_x$) | 100 | 75 | 60 | 0 |
| $t_4$ | $amount_x$ = $amount_x$ - 50 | sum = sum + $amount_x$ | 100 | 75 | 60 | 100 |
| $t_5$ | write($amount_x$) | read($amount_y$) | 50 | 75 | 60 | 100 |
| $t_6$ | read($amount_z$) | sum = sum + $amount_y$ | 50 | 75 | 60 | 175 |
| $t_7$ | $amount_z$ = $amount_z$ + 50 | | 50 | 75 | 60 | 175 |
| $t_8$ | write($amount_z$) | | 50 | 75 | 110 | 175 |
| $t_9$ | commit | read($amount_z$) | 50 | 75 | 110 | 175 |
| $t_{10}$ | | sum = sum + $amount_z$ | 50 | 75 | 110 | 285 |
| $t_{11}$ | | commit | 50 | 75 | 110 | 285 |

**Figure 14.5** Illustration of the inconsistent analysis problem.

#### 14.4.1.4 Other Concurrency-Related Problems

There are other typical concurrency problems than the ones above. For example, **nonrepeatable read** (also known as **unrepeatable read**) occurs when a transaction $T_1$ reads the same row multiple times, but obtains different subsequent values, because another transaction $T_2$ updated this row in the meantime. Another somewhat related example are **phantom reads**. In this case, a transaction $T_2$ is executing insert or delete operations on a set of rows that are being read by a transaction $T_1$. It could be that, if $T_1$ reads the same set of rows a second time, additional rows turn up, or previously existing rows disappear, because they have been inserted or deleted by $T_2$ in the meantime.

### 14.4.2 Schedules and Serial Schedules

We define a *schedule* S as a set of *n* transactions, and a sequential ordering over the statements of these transactions, for which the following property holds:

For each transaction T that participates in a schedule S and for all statements $s_i$ and $s_j$ that belong to the same transaction T: if statement $s_i$ precedes statement $s_j$ in T, then $s_i$ is scheduled to be executed before $s_j$ in S.

In other words, the definition of a schedule implies that the schedule preserves the ordering of the individual statements *within* each respective transaction, whereas it allows an arbitrary ordering of the statements *between* transactions. Each alternate ordering yields a different schedule.

A schedule S is *serial* if all statements $s_i$ of the same transaction T are scheduled consecutively, without any interleave with statements from a different transaction. As a consequence, a set of *n* transactions yields *n*! different serial schedules.

If we assume that each transaction, if executed in complete isolation, is correct and the transactions in the schedule are independent from one another, then, logically, each serial schedule will be correct as well. A serial schedule guarantees that there will be no interferences between the transactions, which would result in database inconsistency. Yet, as previously stated, serial schedules prevent parallel transaction execution and put a heavy burden on performance. For that reason, they are undesirable by themselves; what we need is a *non-serial schedule that is still correct.*

### 14.4.3 Serializable Schedules

All examples in the previous section represented non-serial schedules, but they resulted in inconsistent database states, or at least incorrect query results. Therefore, these schedules were obviously incorrect. The question arises whether we can conceive non-serial schedules that are still correct. Suppose a non-serial schedule *is equivalent to (i.e., yields the same outcome as) a serial schedule*. This means that the final database state, as well as the query results returned to the client, are exactly the same. In that case, the non-serial schedule will still be correct, while at the same time typically much more efficient than the corresponding serial schedule. We call such a schedule **serializable**.

Formally, two schedules $S_1$ and $S_2$ (encompassing the same transactions $T_1, T_2, \ldots, T_n$) are equivalent if these two conditions are satisfied:

- For each operation $read_x$ of $T_i$ in $S_1$ the following holds: if a value x that is read by this operation was last written by an operation $write_x$ of a transaction $T_j$ in $S_1$, then that same operation $read_x$ of $T_i$ in $S_2$ should read the value of x, as written by the same operation $write_x$ of $T_j$ in $S_2$.

| | schedule $S_1$ serial schedule | | schedule $S_2$ non-serial schedule | |
|---|---|---|---|---|
| time | $T_1$ | $T_2$ | $T_1$ | $T_2$ |
| $t_1$ | | | begin transaction | |
| $t_2$ | begin transaction | | read(amount$_x$) | |
| $t_3$ | read(amount$_x$) | | amount$_x$ = amount$_x$ + 50 | |
| $t_4$ | amount$_x$ = amount$_x$ + 50 | | write(amount$_x$) | |
| $t_5$ | write(amount$_x$) | | | begin transaction |
| $t_6$ | read(amount$_y$) | | | read(amount$_x$) |
| $t_7$ | amount$_y$ = amount$_y$ - 50 | | | amount$_x$ = amount$_x$ × 2 |
| $t_8$ | write(amount$_y$) | | | write(amount$_x$) |
| $t_9$ | end transaction | | | read(amount$_y$) |
| $t_{10}$ | | begin transaction | | amount$_y$ = amount$_y$ × 2 |
| $t_{11}$ | | read(amount$_x$) | | write(amount$_y$) |
| $t_{12}$ | | amount$_x$ = amount$_x$ × 2 | | end transaction |
| $t_{13}$ | | write(amount$_x$) | read(amount$_y$) | |
| $t_{14}$ | | read(amount$_y$) | amount$_y$ = amount$_y$ - 50 | |
| $t_{15}$ | | amount$_y$ = amount$_y$ × 2 | write(amount$_y$) | |
| $t_{16}$ | | write(amount$_y$) | end transaction | |
| $t_{17}$ | | end transaction | | |

**Figure 14.6** Comparison of a serial and a non-serial schedule.

- For each value x that is affected by a write operation in these schedules, the last write operation write$_x$ in schedule $S_1$, as executed as part of transaction $T_i$, should also be the last write operation on x in schedule $S_2$, again as part of transaction $T_i$.

The example in Figure 14.6 compares a serial schedule $S_1$ to a non-serial schedule $S_2$. As can be seen, $S_2$ is not equivalent to $S_1$, because the read(amount$_y$) operation of $T_2$ in $S_1$ reads the value of amount$_y$ as written by $T_1$, whereas the same operation in $S_2$ reads the original value of amount$_y$. This is a violation of the first of the two conditions above. In this case, there does not exist any other serial schedule that is equivalent to $S_2$ either. Consequently, $S_2$ is not serializable and therefore not correct.

To test a schedule for serializability, a **precedence graph** can be used. Such a graph is drawn up in the following way:

- Create a node for each transaction $T_i$.
- Create a directed edge $T_i \rightarrow T_j$ if $T_j$ reads a value after it was written by $T_i$.
- Create a directed edge $T_i \rightarrow T_j$ if $T_j$ writes a value after it was read by $T_i$.
- Create a directed edge $T_i \rightarrow T_j$ if $T_j$ writes a value after it was written by $T_i$.

It can be proven that if the precedence graph contains a cycle, the schedule is not serializable. In the previous example, $S_2$ clearly contains a cycle.

### 14.4.4 Optimistic and Pessimistic Schedulers

Theoretically, each non-serial schedule could be continuously monitored for serializability, but this is not recommended in practice because of the overhead involved. Instead, the scheduler will apply a scheduling protocol that guarantees the ensuing schedule to be serializable. In general, we can distinguish between optimistic schedulers (applying optimistic protocols) and pessimistic schedulers (applying pessimistic protocols).

An **optimistic protocol** assumes that conflicts between simultaneous transactions are exceptional. This is the case, for example, when the transactions operate on more or less disjoint subsets of the database, or if most operations are read operations. With optimistic protocols, a transaction's operations are scheduled without delay. When the transaction has completed and is ready to commit, it is verified for conflicts with other transactions during its execution. If no conflicts are detected, the transaction is committed. Otherwise, it is aborted and rolled back. A rollback brings about quite a bit of overhead, so this approach is only feasible if the chances of conflicts are rather small.

On the other hand, a **pessimistic protocol** assumes it is very likely that transactions will interfere and cause conflicts. Therefore, the execution of a transaction's operations is somewhat delayed until the scheduler can schedule them in such a way that any conflicts are avoided, or at least made very unlikely. This delay will reduce the throughput to some extent, but the impact on performance will be lower than the impact of the numerous rollbacks that would otherwise occur, given the high risk of conflicts. A serial scheduler can be considered as an extreme case of a (very) pessimistic scheduler.

Both optimistic and pessimistic concurrency are applied in practice. The most well-known technique is **locking**. In the context of pessimistic concurrency, locking is used in a pre-emptive way to limit the simultaneity of transaction execution to some extent, with the locks indicating which transactions are allowed to access which data at a certain moment in time, and which transactions are required to wait, hence reducing the risk of conflicts. With optimistic concurrency, locks are not used to limit simultaneity, but to detect conflicts during transaction execution that will need to be resolved before transaction commit. For example, they will signal that a transaction ran into a dirty read problem, which will require the transaction to be rolled back.

Another popular technique to resolve concurrency issues is **timestamping**. Read and write timestamps are attributes associated with a database object. They indicate the last time at which the object was read and/or the last time it was written. By keeping track of these timing aspects, it is possible to enforce that a set of transactions' operations is executed in the appropriate order and hence guarantees serializability, or to verify afterwards whether serializability conditions were violated. In the remainder of this chapter we focus on locking and, for the most part, pessimistic concurrency; timestamping and optimistic concurrency are dealt with in more detail in Chapter 16, as they are applied often in the context of distributed and loosely coupled databases.

### 14.4.5 Locking and Locking Protocols

In this section, we first introduce the purposes of locking. We then review the Two-Phase Locking Protocol (2PL). Next, we zoom in on cascading rollbacks and discuss how to deal with deadlocks. We conclude by discussing isolation levels and lock granularity.

#### 14.4.5.1 Purposes of Locking

From the previous examples, it is clear that conflicts between transactions always emanate from two or more transactions accessing the same database object, with at least one of them *writing to* this object. If the same object is only *read* by multiple transactions at the same time, this can never be a cause of conflict, because no data are changed and therefore no inconsistencies can be incurred. For now, we assume that a database object corresponds to an individual tuple in a table. In Section 14.4.5.6, we will take other granularity levels into account, such as a column or an entire table.

The purpose of *locking* and *locking protocols* is to ensure that, in situations where different concurrent transactions attempt to access the same database object, access is only granted in such a

*Type of lock(s) currently held on object*

| *Type of lock requested* | *unlocked* | *shared* | *exclusive* |
|---|---|---|---|
| *unlock* | - | yes | yes |
| *shared* | yes | yes | no |
| *exclusive* | yes | no | no |

**Figure 14.7** Simple compatibility matrix with shared and exclusive locks.

way that no conflicts can occur. The latter is achieved by placing a *lock* on the object. We can look upon a lock as a variable that is associated with a database object, where the variable's value constrains the types of operations that are allowed to be executed on the object at that time. Operations that do not comply with these constraints are postponed for some time, until they are no longer in a position to cause any conflict. The *lock manager* is responsible for granting locks (*locking*) and releasing locks (*unlocking*). The lock manager applies a **locking protocol** that specifies the rules and conditions of when to lock and unlock database objects.

Many types of locks and locking protocols exist. In the most straightforward situation, we discriminate between shared locks (also called s-locks or read locks) and exclusive locks (also called x-locks or write locks). An **exclusive lock** means that a single transaction acquires the sole privilege to interact with that specific database object at that time; no other transactions are allowed to read from it or write to it until the lock is released. Therefore, the first transaction is able to both read and update the object, without any risk of conflicts with other transactions accessing the same object at the same time. On the other hand, if a transaction acquires a **shared lock**, this means that it gets the guarantee that no other transactions will update that same object for as long as the lock is held. As a consequence, the first transaction can read from the object without the risk of conflicts with other transactions that write to it. Still, other transactions may hold a shared lock on that same object as well. This is not a problem, since all transactions holding a shared lock on the same object are only allowed to read from it, which can never be a cause of conflict.

The above means that multiple transactions can acquire a lock on the same object, on the condition that these are all shared locks and, therefore, all the transactions can only read the object. If a transaction wants to update the object, an exclusive lock is required. The latter can only be acquired if no other transactions hold any lock on the object and, consequently, no other transactions can read or update the object at that time. These rules can be summarized in a **compatibility matrix**, as represented in Figure 14.7. The figure indicates which request will be granted for a particular database object (cf. the first column) based on the locks currently in place on that same object (cf. the first row). If a transaction's request cannot be granted, this means that the corresponding operation would cause a concurrency problem. The scheduler will put the transaction in a wait state until other transactions' locks on the same object are released. After that, the lock can be granted and the first transaction can continue without any risk of conflicts.

Locking and unlocking requests can be made explicitly by a transaction, or could remain implicit. In implicit requests, read and write operations will induce s-locks and x-locks, respectively, whereas a commit or rollback will result in an unlock instruction. The transaction manager interacts with the lock manager, requesting locks on behalf of individual transactions. If a lock is not granted, the corresponding operation is postponed by the scheduler. The lock manager implements a *locking protocol* as a set of rules to determine what locks can be granted in what situation. The compatibility matrix is a primary element of this locking protocol. The lock manager also uses a **lock table**. The latter contains information about which locks are currently held by which transaction; which transactions are waiting to acquire certain locks, etc.

The lock manager has an important responsibility with respect to "fairness" of transaction scheduling. Indeed, when an exclusive lock is released, the corresponding database object is in an unlocked state and a new lock can be granted to any of the waiting transactions. However, if a shared lock is released, it could be that other shared locks are still held by other transactions on that same object. The lock manager will have to decide whether additional shared locks can be granted on this object, or whether the shared locks should be gradually phased out in favor of transactions that are waiting to acquire an exclusive lock on the object. If an inappropriate priority schema is used, such situations could result in so-called **starvation**, with some transactions waiting endlessly for the required exclusive locks, whereas the other transactions continue normally.

#### 14.4.5.2 The Two-Phase Locking Protocol (2PL)

In practice, many locking protocols exist, but the most well known, and the most prevalent in a standalone database context, is **Two-Phase Locking (2PL)**. In addition to applying a compatibility matrix, the locking protocol also determines when lock and unlock instructions are allowed in a transaction's lifecycle.

The 2PL protocol entails the following rules:

1. Before a transaction can read a database object, it should acquire a shared lock on that object. Before it can update the object, it should acquire an exclusive lock.
2. The lock manager determines whether requested locks do not cause any conflicts and can be granted, based on the compatibility matrix. Transactions whose locking requests cannot be granted are put on hold until the request can be granted.
3. Acquiring and releasing locks occurs in two phases for each transaction: a growth phase in which new locks can be acquired but no locks can be released, and a shrink phase in which locks are gradually released, and no additional locks can be acquired. To put it in other words: all locking requests should precede the first unlock instruction.

According to the basic 2PL protocol, a transaction can already start releasing locks before it has attained the "committed" state, on the condition that no further locks are acquired after releasing the first lock. In most DBMS implementations, a variant to 2PL is applied, called **Rigorous 2PL**. The protocol specifies that the transaction holds all its locks until it is committed. Yet another variant is **Static 2PL** (aka **Conservative 2PL**). With this protocol, a transaction acquires all its locks right at the start of the transaction.[5] The different 2PL variants are represented schematically in Figure 14.8.

When applying the 2PL Protocol, concurrency problems such as the ones mentioned in Section 14.4.1 are avoided. Figure 14.9 illustrates how the lost update problem is resolved, because transaction $T_1$ has to wait until amount$_x$ is unlocked by $T_2$ before $T_1$ can acquire a write lock on it. As a consequence, $T_1$ is now aware of the update of amount$_x$ by $T_2$ and, consequently, the lost update problem is resolved. A similar reasoning can be applied for the inconsistent analysis problem.

[5] It is not always possible to predict which locks will be required – for example, if the next operations can only be determined based on the results of previous operations. In that case, all locks that *may* be needed should be requested, instead of all locks that will actually be needed.

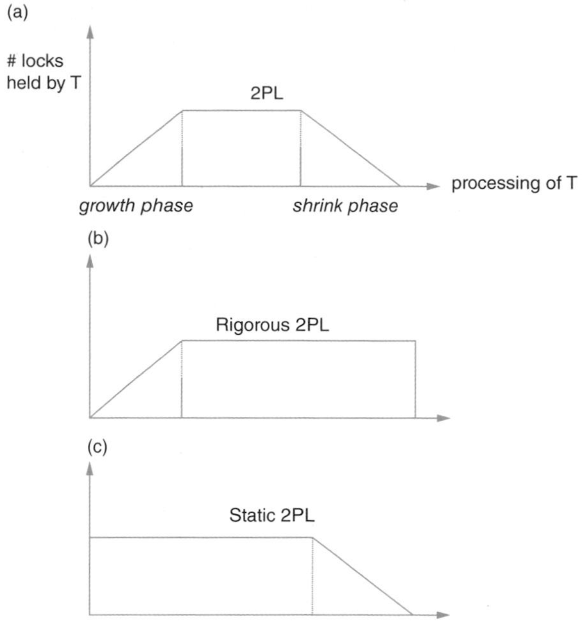


**Figure 14.8** Illustration of 2PL variants.

| *time* | $T_1$ | $T_2$ | $amount_x$ |
|---|---|---|---|
| $t_1$ | | begin transaction | 100 |
| $t_2$ | begin transaction | x-lock($amount_x$) | 100 |
| $t_3$ | x-lock($amount_x$) | read($amount_x$) | 100 |
| $t_4$ | wait | $amount_x$ = $amount_x$ + 120 | 100 |
| $t_5$ | wait | write($amount_x$) | 220 |
| $t_6$ | wait | commit | 220 |
| $t_7$ | wait | unlock($amount_x$) | 220 |
| $t_8$ | read($amount_x$) | | 220 |
| $t_9$ | $amount_x$ = $amount_x$ - 50 | | 220 |
| $t_{10}$ | write($amount_x$) | | 170 |
| $t_{11}$ | commit | | 170 |
| $t_{12}$ | unlock($amount_x$) | | 170 |

**Figure 14.9** Resolution of the lost update problem.

In the same way, Figure 14.10 illustrates how the uncommitted dependency problem is resolved by 2PL.

### 14.4.5.3 Cascading Rollbacks

Even if transactions are managed and scheduled according to a solid protocol, undesirable effects may still occur, emanating from the mutual impact between concurrency control and recovery. Let's revisit the uncommitted dependency problem in the context of 2PL. As can be seen in Figure 14.10, the problem is resolved if $T_2$ holds all its locks until it is rolled back.

However, with the basic 2PL Protocol, there is a shrink phase in which locks can already be released before the transaction commits or aborts. In that case, it is still possible for a transaction $T_1$ to read values written by $T_2$, with $T_2$ subsequently aborting. This is illustrated in Figure 14.11.

| time | $T_1$ | $T_2$ | $amount_x$ |
|---|---|---|---|
| $t_1$ | | begin transaction | 100 |
| $t_2$ | | x-lock($amount_x$) | 100 |
| $t_3$ | | read($amount_x$) | 100 |
| $t_4$ | begin transaction | $amount_x$ = $amount_x$ + 120 | 100 |
| $t_5$ | x-lock($amount_x$) | write($amount_x$) | 220 |
| $t_6$ | wait | rollback | 100 |
| $t_7$ | wait | unlock($amount_x$) | 100 |
| $t_8$ | read($amount_x$) | | 100 |
| $t_9$ | $amount_x$ = $amount_x$ - 50 | | 100 |
| $t_{10}$ | write($amount_x$) | | 50 |
| $t_{11}$ | commit | | 50 |
| $t_{12}$ | unlock($amount_x$) | | 50 |

**Figure 14.10** Resolution of the uncommitted dependency problem.

| time | $T_1$ | $T_2$ | $amount_x$ |
|---|---|---|---|
| $t_1$ | | begin transaction | 100 |
| $t_2$ | | x-lock($amount_x$) | 100 |
| $t_3$ | | read($amount_x$) | 100 |
| $t_4$ | begin transaction | $amount_x$=$amount_x$+120 | 100 |
| $t_5$ | x-lock($amount_x$) | write($amount_x$) | 220 |
| $t_6$ | wait | unlock ($amount_x$) | 220 |
| $t_7$ | read($amount_x$) | | 220 |
| $t_8$ | $amount_x$=$amount_x$-50 | rollback | 220 |
| $t_9$ | write($amount_x$) | | 170 |
| $t_{10}$ | commit | | 170 |
| $t_{11}$ | unlock($amount_x$) | | 170 |
| $t_{12}$ | | | |

**Figure 14.11** Illustration of the need for cascading rollbacks with basic 2PL.

Therefore, before any transaction $T_1$ can be committed, the DBMS should make sure that all transactions that made changes to data items that were subsequently read by $T_1$ are committed first. Even then, if a transaction $T_2$ is rolled back, all uncommitted transactions $T_u$ that have read values written by $T_2$ need to be rolled back as well to avoid the uncommitted dependency problem. In addition, all transactions that have in their turn read values written by the transactions $T_u$ need to be rolled back as well, and so forth. This escalating series of rollbacks is called a **cascading rollback**. Such rollbacks should be applied recursively – transactions that read data that were written by transactions marked for rollback in the previous step have to be rolled back as well and so on. It goes without saying that cascading rollbacks can be very time-consuming. The best way to avoid this is for all transactions to hold their locks until they have reached the "committed" state. Therefore, most DBMSs apply the Rigorous 2PL Protocol, or yet another variant, rather than basic 2PL.

#### 14.4.5.4 Dealing with Deadlocks

One of the disadvantages of protocols such as 2PL, including Rigorous 2PL, is that they may cause *deadlocks*. A deadlock occurs if two or more transactions are waiting for one another's locks to be released. Since each transaction holds one or more locks that are required by another transaction for it to be able to continue, all transactions remain in an endless wait state. We illustrate a deadlock situation with two transactions in the context of 2PL in Figure 14.12: $T_1$ holds an exclusive lock on

| *time* | $T_1$ | $T_2$ |
|---|---|---|
| $t_1$ | begin transaction | |
| $t_2$ | x-lock($amount_x$) | begin transaction |
| $t_3$ | read($amount_x$) | x-lock($amount_y$) |
| $t_4$ | $amount_x = amount_x - 50$ | read($amount_y$) |
| $t_5$ | write($amount_x$) | $amount_y = amount_y - 30$ |
| $t_6$ | x-lock($amount_y$) | write($amount_y$) |
| $t_7$ | wait | x-lock($amount_x$) |
| $t_8$ | wait | wait |

**Figure 14.12** Illustration of a deadlock.

$amount_x$, but later also requests a lock on $amount_y$. However, the latter is locked by $T_2$, which in turn requests a lock on $amount_x$. Neither transaction will ever acquire the requested lock and therefore both transactions will wait endlessly for one another. Of course, in practice, a deadlock will often involve more than two transactions.

There are multiple ways of dealing with deadlocks. One possibility is **deadlock prevention**, which is achieved by static 2PL. With static 2PL, a transaction must acquire all its locks upon the start. If this is not possible, no locks are granted and the transaction is put in a wait state until the locks can be acquired. In this way, deadlocks are avoided. However, throughput may be severely impacted for two reasons: locks are held longer than with basic 2PL and the transaction is forced to request all locks it *may* need for its execution, rather than acquiring the locks when they are actually needed.

In most practical cases, **deadlock, detection and resolution** is preferable over deadlock prevention. Deadlocks are detected according to a **wait-for graph**. A wait-for graph consists of nodes representing active transactions and directed edges $T_i \rightarrow T_j$ for each transaction $T_i$ that is waiting to acquire a lock currently held by transaction $T_j$. A deadlock exists only if the wait-for graph contains a cycle. Deadlock detection then comes down to an algorithm that, at fixed time intervals, inspects the wait-for graph for any cycles. Note that this time interval is an important parameter: too short an interval will cause a lot of unnecessary overhead, but with an interval that is too long, deadlocks will go unnoticed for quite some time.

Once a deadlock is detected, it still needs to be resolved. In this context, **victim selection** means choosing and aborting one of the transactions involved in the deadlock. Several criteria can be applied, such as different priorities of the transactions or the concern to select a transaction with a minimal number of updates to avoid the overhead of an extensive rollback when aborting the transaction.

#### 14.4.5.5 Isolation Levels

It often occurs that the level of transaction isolation offered by 2PL is too stringent with too negative an effect on transaction throughput. For many types of transactions, a limited amount of interference is acceptable if this implies a better throughput because fewer transactions have to be put in a wait state. For that reason, most DBMSs allow for different isolation levels, such as read uncommitted, read committed, repeatable read, and serializable.

Before we can discuss these respective isolation levels, it is necessary to introduce the concept of **short-term locks**. A short-term lock is only held during the time interval needed to complete the associated operation. This contrasts with **long-term locks**, which are granted and released according to a protocol, and are held for a longer time, until the transaction is committed. The use of short-term locks violates rule 3 of the 2PL Protocol, so serializability can no longer be

**Table 14.1** Isolation levels and their impact on concurrency problems

| Isolation level | Lost update | Uncommitted dependency | Inconsistent analysis | Nonrepeatable read | Phantom read |
|---|---|---|---|---|---|
| Read uncommitted | Yes | Yes | Yes | Yes | Yes |
| Read committed | No[6] | No | Yes | Yes | Yes |
| Repeatable read | No | No | No | No | Yes |
| Serializable | No | No | No | No | No |

guaranteed. Still, sometimes it is acceptable to use them, if this improves the throughput and the transaction type at hand isn't too sensitive to a certain amount of interference. The use of short-term and/or long-term locks results in different possible isolation levels. We discuss the most important ones below:

- **Read uncommitted** is the lowest isolation level. Long-term locks are not taken into account; it is assumed that concurrency conflicts do not occur or simply that their impact on the transactions with this isolation level are not problematic. This isolation level is typically only allowed for read-only transactions, which do not perform updates anyway.
- **Read committed** uses long-term write locks, but short-term read locks. In this way, a transaction is guaranteed not to read any data that are still being updated by a yet-uncommitted transaction. This resolves the lost update as well as the uncommitted dependency problem. However, the inconsistent analysis problem may still occur with this isolation level, as well as nonrepeatable reads and phantom reads.
- **Repeatable read** uses both long-term read locks and write locks. Thus, a transaction can read the same row repeatedly, without interference from insert, update, or delete operations by other transactions. Still, the problem of phantom reads remains unresolved with this isolation level.
- **Serializable** is the strongest isolation level and corresponds roughly to an implementation of 2PL. Now phantom reads are also avoided. Note that in practice, the definition of serializability in the context of isolation levels merely comes down to the absence of concurrency problems, such as nonrepeatable reads and phantom reads, and does not correspond entirely to the theoretical definition we provided in Section 14.4.3.

Table 14.1 provides an overview of these isolation levels and the resultant occurrence of concurrency problems.

#### 14.4.5.6 Lock Granularity

So far, we have not been specific as to which kind of database object can be subject to locking; in a relational database context, such database objects can be a tuple, a column, a table, a tablespace, a disk block, etc. There will always be a tradeoff though. On the one hand, locking at a fine-grained level (e.g., an individual tuple) has the least negative impact on throughput, because the only

[6] The lost update problem is defined somewhat differently by different authors. Depending on this definition, higher isolation levels (repeatable read or even serializable) may be needed to prevent lost updates.

| Type of lock requested \ Type of lock(s) currently held on object | unlocked | is-lock | ix-lock | s-lock | six-lock | x-lock |
|---|---|---|---|---|---|---|
| *unlocked* | - | yes | yes | yes | yes | yes |
| *is-lock* | yes | yes | yes | yes | yes | no |
| *ix-lock* | yes | yes | yes | no | no | no |
| *s-lock* | yes | yes | no | yes | no | no |
| *six-lock* | yes | yes | no | no | no | no |
| *x-lock* | yes | no | no | no | no | no |

**Figure 14.13** Compatibility matrix for an MGL Protocol.

transactions affected are those that concurrently try to access that very tuple. On the other hand, if many tuples are involved in the transaction, locking each individual tuple causes a lot of overhead in granting and releasing locks and keeping track of all locks held. In that case, locking at a coarse-grained level (e.g., an entire table) is more efficient overhead-wise, but may have a severe impact on throughput because transactions interacting with the same table may be put in a wait state, even if they access different tuples of that table. Because choosing the most appropriate level of lock granularity is not always easy, many DBMSs provide the option to have the optimal granularity level determined by the database system, depending on the required isolation level and the number of tuples involved in the transaction.

To guarantee serializability in a situation in which locks can be placed at multiple granularity levels, additional types of locks are required and the 2PL Protocol is to be extended into a **Multiple Granularity Locking Protocol** (MGL Protocol). The MGL Protocol is to ensure that the respective transactions that acquired locks on database objects that are interrelated hierarchically (e.g., tablespace–table–disk block–tuple) cannot conflict with one another. For example, it is to be avoided that if transaction $T_i$ holds an s-lock on a table, another transaction $T_j$ can acquire an x-lock on a tablespace that encompasses that table.

The MGL Protocol introduces additional types of locks: an **intention shared lock (is-lock)**, an **intention exclusive lock (ix-lock)** and a **shared and intention exclusive lock (six-lock)**. An is-lock only conflicts with x-locks; an ix-lock conflicts with both x-locks and s-locks. A six-lock conflicts with all other lock types, except for an is-lock. This is summarized in the compatibility matrix for an MGL Protocol, as represented in Figure 14.13.

Before a lock on object x can be granted, the lock manager needs to ascertain that no locks are held (or granted later) on coarser-grained database objects that encompass object x, and which may conflict with the lock type requested on x. To do so, an **intention lock** is placed on all coarser-grained objects encompassing x. In concrete, if a transaction requests an s-lock on a particular tuple, an is-lock will be placed on the tablespace, table, and disk block that contain that tuple. If a transaction requests an x-lock on a tuple, an ix-lock will be placed on the coarser-grained objects that contain that tuple. It could also be that a transaction intends to read a hierarchy of objects, but only aims at updating some of the objects in this hierarchy. In that case, a six-lock is required, which combines the properties of an s-lock and an ix-lock. The locks will only be granted if they do not cause any conflicts according to the MGL compatibility matrix.

According to the MGL Protocol, a transaction $T_i$ can lock an object that is part of a hierarchical structure, if the following constraints are satisfied:

1. All compatibilities are respected as represented in the compatibility matrix.
2. An initial lock should be placed on the root of the hierarchy.
3. Before $T_i$ can acquire an s-lock or an is-lock on an object x, it should acquire an is-lock or an ix-lock on the parent of x.
4. Before $T_i$ can acquire an x-lock, six-lock, or an ix-lock on an object x, it should acquire an ix-lock or a six-lock on the parent of x.
5. $T_i$ can only acquire additional locks if it hasn't released any locks yet (cf. 2PL).
6. Before $T_i$ can release a lock on x, it should have released all locks on all children of x.

Summarizing, according to the MGL Protocol, locks are acquired top-down, but released bottom-up in the hierarchy.

**Retention Questions**

- Discuss the different types of concurrency problems. Illustrate with an example.
- What is the relevance of schedules, serial schedules, and serializable schedules?
- What is the difference between optimistic and pessimistic schedulers?
- What is the purpose of locking?
- Discuss the Two-Phase Locking Protocol (2PL).
- What are cascading rollbacks? Illustrate with an example.
- How can we deal with deadlocks?
- What is the meaning of the following isolation levels: read uncommitted, read committed, repeatable read, and serializable?
- Discuss the impact of lock granularity.

## 14.5 The ACID Properties of Transactions

To conclude this chapter, we return to the ACID properties of transactions, which were already mentioned briefly in Chapter 1. ACID stands for Atomicity, Consistency, Isolation, and Durability. These represent four properties in the context of transaction management that are desirable to most conventional DBMSs. Note that, as we will see in Chapter 16, some particular settings like NoSQL databases may require other transaction paradigms such as BASE (Basically Available, Soft state, Eventually consistent).

*Atomicity* guarantees that multiple database operations that alter the database state can be treated as one indivisible unit of work. This means that either all changes as induced by a transaction's respective operations are persisted into the database, or none at all. This is the responsibility of the recovery manager, which will induce rollbacks where necessary, by means of UNDO operations, such that no partial traces of failed transactions remain in the database.

*Consistency* refers to the fact that a transaction, if executed in isolation, renders the database from one consistent state into another consistent state. The developer, who is to ensure that the application logic that drives the transactions is flawless, is primarily responsible for the consistency property. However, consistency is also an overarching responsibility of the DBMS's transaction management system, since lack of any of the other properties (atomicity, isolation and durability) will also result in an inconsistent database state.

*Isolation* denotes that, in situations in which multiple transactions are executed concurrently, the outcome should be the same as if every transaction were executed in isolation. This means that interleaved transactions should not interfere, nor should they present intermediate results to one another, before having reached a committed state. Guaranteeing isolation is the responsibility of the concurrency control mechanisms of the DBMS, as coordinated by the scheduler. The scheduler typically makes use of a locking protocol and interacts with a lock manager, although other optimistic and pessimistic concurrency control techniques exist as well.

**Retention Questions**

- Discuss the responsibility of the DBMS's transaction management facilities to ensure the ACID properties of a transaction.

*Durability* refers to the fact that the effects of a committed transaction should always be persisted into the database. If a calamity occurs after transaction commit but before the updates that reside in the database buffer are written to the physical files, the recovery manager is responsible for ensuring that the transaction's updates are eventually written to the database by means of REDO operations. Similarly, the recovery manager should safeguard the DBMS from the effects of damaged storage media through some form of data redundancy.

## Summary

This chapter discussed how DBMSs consider transactions as atomic units of work. First, we introduced the concepts of transaction management, recovery, and concurrency control. Then, we presented the respective DBMS components involved in transaction management, as well as the logfile. The latter keeps track of all operations performed by a transaction, for the sake of recovery. In this context, we discriminated between system recovery and media recovery. Then, we discussed how concurrency control aims at avoiding the calamities that may result from interference between two or more simultaneous transactions that act upon the same data. Two crucial concepts here are serializability and locking. In particular, we discussed the Two-Phase Locking Protocol. We then introduced additional variation points, such as different isolation levels between transactions and different granularity levels for locking. We concluded by revisiting the ACID properties, which represent four desirable principles that should be supported by a DBMS in the context of transaction management.

**Scenario Conclusion**

Sober has now gained a good understanding of the basics of transaction management. Although this will automatically be taken care of by the DBMS, it is good for the company to know how the DBMS's transaction management facilities work to ensure the ACID properties of all transactions that interact with its database.

## Key Terms List

**aborted**
**after images**
**archiving**
**backup**
**before image**
**begin_transaction**
**cascading rollback**
**checkpoints**
**committed**
**compatibility matrix**
**concurrency control**
**conservative 2PL**
**data redundancy**
**deadlock detection and resolution**
**deadlock prevention**
**deferred update**
**delineate**
**end_transaction**
**exclusive lock**
**failover time**

**full backup**
**immediate update policy**
**inconsistent analysis problem**
**incremental backups**
**intention exclusive lock (ix-lock)**
**intention lock**
**intention shared lock (is-lock)**
**lock table**
**locking**
**locking protocol**
**log records**
**logfile**
**long-term locks**
**lost update problem**
**media failure**
**multi-user database**
**Multiple Granularity Locking (MGL) Protocol**
**nonrepeatable read**
**optimistic protocol**
**pessimistic protocol**
**phantom reads**
**precedence graph**
**read committed**
**read uncommitted**
**recovery**
**repeatable read**
**rigorous 2PL**
**rollback**
**rollforward recovery**
**schedule**
**scheduler**
**serializable**
**serially**
**shared and intention exclusive lock (six-lock)**
**shared lock**
**short-term locks**
**starvation**
**static 2PL**
**stored data manager**
**system failure**
**timestamping**
**transaction**
**transaction failure**
**transaction management**
**transaction manager**
**Two-Phase Locking (2PL)**
**uncommitted dependency problem**
**unrepeatable read**
**victim selection**
**wait-for graph**
**write ahead log strategy**

## Review Questions

**14.1.** Which statement is **not correct**?

a. A transaction is a set of database operations (e.g., a consecution of SQL statements in a relational database), induced by a single user or application, that should be considered as one undividable unit of work.
b. Transactions typically exist in isolation, and cannot be executed concurrently with other transactions on the same data.
c. It should not be possible to terminate a transaction in such a way that the database remains in an inconsistent state, because some operations of a single transaction were executed successfully and others were not.
d. Recovery is the activity of ensuring that, whichever problem occurred, the database is returned to a consistent state afterwards, without any data loss.

**14.2.** When a transaction is aborted, it is important that. . .

a. all changes made by the individual operations belonging to that transaction should be made permanent.

b. a rollback of the transaction is executed: all changes made by the transaction's respective operations should be undone.

**14.3.** Which of the following DBMS components is involved in transaction management?

a. Scheduler.
b. Stored data manager.
c. Buffer manager.
d. Recovery manager.
e. All of the above.

**14.4.** Which statement is **not correct**?

a. The logfile contains all updates after they have been written to disk.
b. The logfile contains redundant data.
c. The logfile can be implemented as a sequential file.
d. The logfile is often duplicated, e.g., in a RAID level 1 configuration.

**14.5.** The following figure presents five transactions ($T_1$ until $T_5$) that are executed more or less simultaneously. Suppose a checkpoint was registered on the logfile at time $t_c$, marking the last time when pending updates in the database buffer were persisted into the physical database files. Later, at time $t_f$, a system fault occurred, resulting in loss of the database buffer.

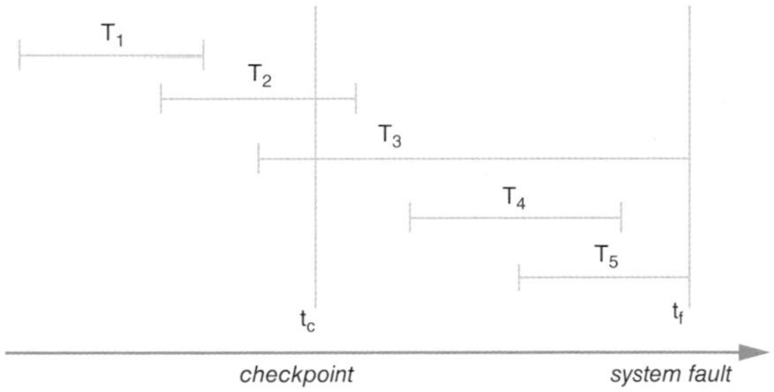


What recovery operations are required?

a. $T_1$: nothing; $T_2$: UNDO; $T_3$: REDO; $T_4$: REDO; $T_5$: nothing.
b. $T_1$: nothing; $T_2$: REDO; $T_3$: UNDO; $T_4$: REDO; $T_5$: nothing.
c. $T_1$: REDO; $T_2$: UNDO; $T_3$: REDO; $T_4$: nothing; $T_5$: nothing.
d. $T_1$: nothing; $T_2$: REDO; $T_3$: REDO; $T_4$: REDO; $T_5$: nothing.

**14.6.** Which statement is **not correct**?

a. Disk mirroring is a (near) real-time approach that writes the same data simultaneously to two or more physical disks.
b. Archiving is an approach in which database files are copied periodically to other storage media, such as tape or (another) hard disk.
c. Traditional relational databases allow for a certain measure of temporary inconsistency, in return for increased performance.
d. There is a tradeoff between the cost (overhead and storage cost) of more frequent backups and the cost of lost data because of less frequent backups.

**14.7.** Which statement is **not correct**?

a. A lost update problem occurs if an otherwise successful update of a data item by a transaction is overwritten by another transaction that wasn't "aware" of the first update.

b. If a transaction reads one or more data items that are being updated by another, as yet uncommitted, transaction, we may run into the uncommitted dependency problem.
c. The inconsistent analysis problem denotes a situation in which a transaction reads partial results of another transaction that simultaneously interacts with (and updates) the same data items.
d. The lost update problem does not always result in an inconsistent database state, whereas an uncommitted dependency or inconsistent analysis always yields an inconsistent database state.

**14.8.** If the precedence graph contains a cycle, the schedule is...

a. serializable.
b. not serializable.

**14.9.** Which statement is **not correct**?

a. An optimistic protocol assumes that conflicts between simultaneous transactions are exceptional.
b. A pessimistic protocol assumes it to be very likely that transactions will interfere and cause conflicts.
c. A serial scheduler can be considered as an extreme case of a (very) optimistic scheduler.
d. With optimistic concurrency, locks are not used to limit simultaneity, but to detect conflicts during transaction execution that will need to be resolved before transaction commit.

**14.10.** Which statement is **correct**?

a. Multiple transactions may hold a shared lock on the same object.
b. Multiple transactions may hold an exclusive lock on the same object.

**14.11.** Which statement is **not correct**?

a. Deadlock prevention can be achieved by static 2PL.
b. One approach for deadlock resolution is victim selection, which means choosing and aborting one of the transactions involved in the deadlock.
c. The use of short-term locks violates rule 3 of the 2PL Protocol, so serializability can no longer be guaranteed.
d. The read committed isolation level uses long-term read locks, but short-term write locks.

**14.12.** According to the MGL Protocol...

a. locks are acquired top-down, but released bottom-up in the hierarchy.
b. locks are acquired bottom-up, but released top-down in the hierarchy.

## Problems and Exercises

14.1E What DBMS components are typically involved in transaction management?

14.2E Discuss the lost update, uncommitted dependency, and inconsistent analysis problem. Illustrate with an example. Which ones result in an inconsistent database state?

14.3E What is the difference between a serial and serializable schedule and why is this difference important? How can a schedule be tested for serializability?

14.4E Discuss the difference between optimistic and pessimistic schedulers and the role of locking.

14.5E Work out the compatibility matrix illustrating which requests can be granted given the locks (shared or exclusive) currently held on a database object.

14.6E Discuss the Two-Phase Locking Protocol and the different variants thereof. Illustrate how this protocol can help address the lost update, uncommitted dependency, and inconsistent analysis problems.

14.7E What is a deadlock? Illustrate with an example.

14.8E Complete the following table by indicating which concurrency problems can occur based on the isolation level.

| Isolation level | Lost update | Uncommitted dependency | Inconsistent analysis | Nonrepeatable read | Phantom read |
|---|---|---|---|---|---|
| Read uncommitted | | | | | |
| Read committed | | | | | |
| Repeatable read | | | | | |
| Serializable | | | | | |

14.9E Work out the compatibility matrix for the MGL Protocol, illustrating which requests can be granted given the locks currently held on a database object.

14.10E Discuss the ACID properties of transaction management and the responsibility of the DBMS's transaction management system to ensure this.

# 15 Accessing Databases and Database APIs

## Chapter Objectives

In this chapter, you will learn:

- how database systems can be accessed from the outside world;
- what is meant by a database application programming interface (API);
- to understand the differences between proprietary versus universal APIs, between embedded versus call-level APIs, and early binding versus late binding;
- which universal database application programming interfaces are available to interact with database systems;
- how DBMSs play their role within the World Wide Web and the internet.

### Opening Scenario

Sober has decided on a relational DBMS vendor, has drawn up the relational schema to implement, and has verified that the database is working as planned by importing sample data and testing some SQL queries. However, a DBMS system does not live in isolation. Sober is planning to develop several applications that will have to connect to its DBMS. For instance, Sober is thinking about a website where customers can book cabs and retrieve their order history, and a mobile app that will have to fetch information from the DBMS. Finally, Sober is also planning to develop a desktop application for the customer support team that will be used internally, but also has to be able to access the same DBMS. Sober is still thinking about different options in terms of programming languages to develop these applications, but wonders how easy it will be for these applications to access the database in order to store and retrieve information from it.

In this chapter, we take a closer look at the forms of accessing database systems. Naturally, the manner of how a DBMS is interfaced with heavily depends on the system architecture it applies. Accessing a DBMS in a legacy mainframe set-up is different than interfacing with a DBMS in a client–server-based architecture, so we open this chapter with an overview of different database system architectures. Next, we turn our attention toward the different database application programming interfaces, or APIs for short. As the name suggests, a database API exposes an interface through which clients, third-party, and end-user applications can access, query, and manage the DBMS. Finally, we look at DBMSs' role and place within the World Wide Web, and how recent trends in this landscape are influencing and shaping the requirements imposed on DBMSs.

## 15.1 Database System Architectures

**Connections**

Refer to Chapter 2 for a quick introduction regarding DBMS architectures.

In Chapter 2, the different system architectures of DBMSs were already briefly mentioned. In what follows, we revisit the different ways a DBMS can be set up and placed in an overall information system. This will serve as important background information as the different ways in which a DBMS is located in an overall set-up will lead to the next logical question: how to access the DBMS within these different environments?

### 15.1.1 Centralized System Architectures

In a **centralized DBMS architecture**, all responsibilities of the DBMSs are handled by one centralized entity, meaning that the DBMS logic, the data themselves and the application logic and presentation logic (also called the user interface), are all handled by the same system.

Such a set-up was appealing in early implementations, such as the ones found on mainframes. Hence, a popular centralized DBMS architecture is that of mainframe database computing (also called host-based computing), where the execution of applications (the *application logic*), querying operations and storage of data (the DBMS) and even the presentation of results and the overall user interface (the *presentation logic*) are all happening on a central mainframe. Nevertheless, the concept of system access is still important in this form, as typically many workstations would connect to a mainframe system that can handle sessions for multiple users. Note, however, that no form of processing would occur on these workstations, often denoted as terminals: input commands are sent directly to the mainframe, which then performs the necessary computations and interactions with the DBMS on its side, and formats and returns the results together with the full composition (i.e., drawing of the user interface that the terminal would then depict to the end-user). The system access exists solely on a basic, raw level (see Figure 15.1). Such monolithic set-ups were common in the early growth of computing, as this was the most viable way to provide complex applications in a multi-user fashion. Nowadays, this system architecture has become rare, expensive, and difficult to maintain.

The rise of the PC introduced a paradigm shift in which it became possible to replace monolithic, heavy-weight mainframes with powerful, affordable, personal computers. Hence, another form of a centralized system architecture moves the complete DBMS stack, together with the application logic and the presentation logic (including drawing of the user interface), to a personal computer. In this set-up, the DBMS runs on the PC, as well as the application that uses the DBMS and the user interface that exposes it to the end-user.

In some cases, however, the database itself can also be stored on a separate file server, so the next scenario offers a first example of a *client–server architecture*. When the DBMS (here acting as the client) requests data, a request is sent to the file server (the server), which is responsible for file

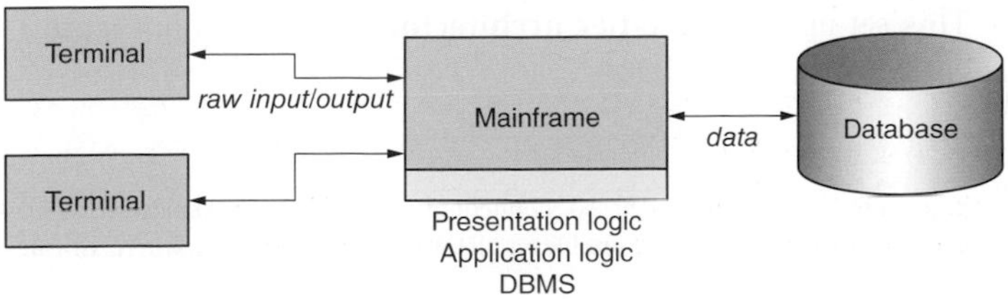


**Figure 15.1** A centralized database architecture running on a mainframe.

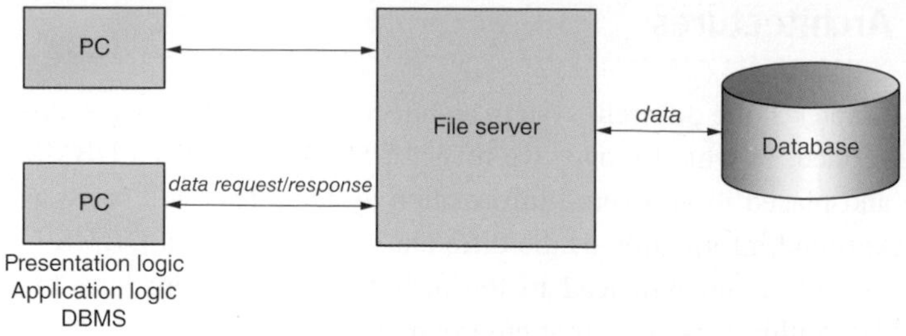


**Figure 15.2** Illustration of PC/file server-based computing.

storage and management, including the database files. The file server returns the requested files to the DBMS. Figure 15.2 illustrates this set-up. This can cause a lot of data exchange and network traffic to and from the file server, as entire files are transferred, potentially causing performance issues. In addition, maintenance concerns remain an issue in this set-up, as now a fleet of PCs must be maintained and kept up-to-date with the DBMS, application logic, and user interface functionality.

> **Connections**
>
> See Chapter 13 for an overview of file-level access techniques and storage architectures.

Nevertheless, this system is still relatively common, especially in environments where other (non-database) data files are served to the network, particularly in the form of unstructured data such as text documents or multimedia data.

### 15.1.2 Tiered System Architectures

Contrary to a centralized system, where either a mainframe or single PC handles all the workload, a **tiered system architecture** aims to decouple this centralized set-up by combining the computing capabilities of powerful central computers with the flexibility of PCs. The latter act as active clients, requesting services from the former, the passive server. Multiple variants of this architecture, also denoted as a **two-tier architecture** (or also a **client–server architecture**), exist. As illustrated in Figure 15.3, in the "fat" client variant, the presentation logic and application logic are handled by the client (i.e., the PC). This is common where it makes sense to couple an application's workflow (e.g., opening of windows, screens, and forms) with its look and feel (i.e., its front-end, the way it shows itself to the user). The DBMS, however, now runs fully on the database server. When an application running on a PC, the client, needs data or wishes to execute a query, a request is sent to the server, which will perform the actual database commands on its side before sending the results back.

In a second variant of this set-up, only the presentation logic is handled by the client. Applications and database commands are both executed on the server. This form is common when application logic and database logic are very tightly coupled or similar. This variant is denoted as a "fat" server, or a thin client architecture.[1]

It is possible to decouple application logic from the DBMS and place this in a separate layer (i.e., on an application server). This set-up is a **three-tier architecture**, illustrated in Figure 15.4.

[1] Following this line of reasoning, a centralized mainframe-based architecture with terminals connecting to it is sometimes denoted as a "dumb" client architecture, as it resembles a client–server architecture where all roles have been stripped away from the clients.

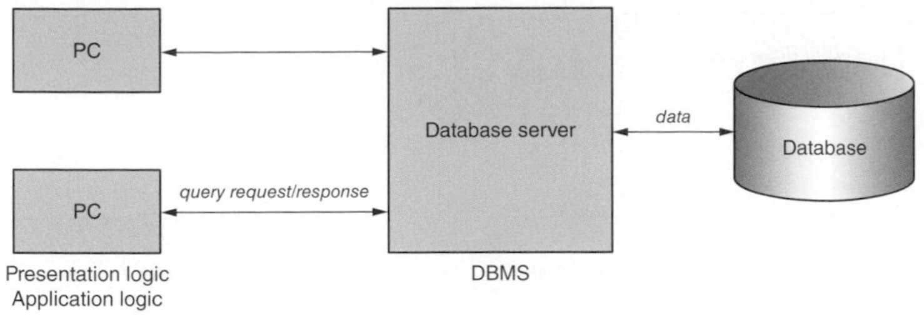


**Figure 15.3** Client–server architecture with "fat" clients.

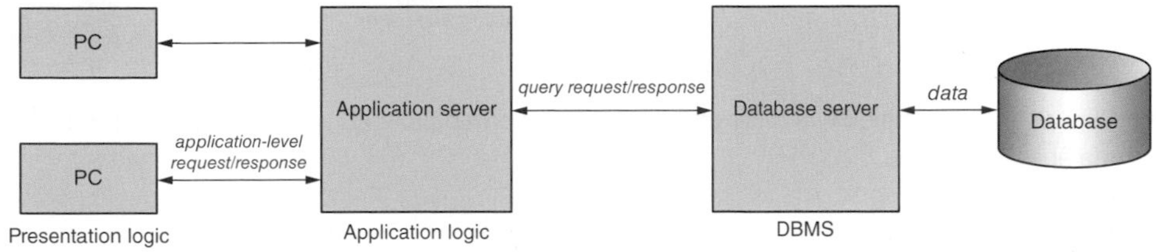


**Figure 15.4** Three-tier architecture.

This set-up allows different applications on the application server (e.g., a marketing application, a logistics application, an accounting application, etc.) to access the same database. If the applications on the application server, and/or the functionalities on the other tiers, are spread over multiple tiers, we speak of an **n-tier** architecture.

A common, modern example of an n-tier architecture consists of a web browser acting as the client (i.e., handling some of the presentation logic, drawing the user interface, and handling user inputs), which sends and receives web requests to a web server (an example of such a command can be the navigation toward an overview of recent orders for a retail website, as indicated by a URL). To prepare the result page to be sent back to the client, the web server can then initiate multiple queries to the database server – for instance, a query to get a list of recent orders for user "cust203" in the event that a user visits the page "www.myshop.com/orders/cust203". The results of this query are then used to construct the HTML source code of the web page (also handling part of the presentation logic), which is then sent back to the web browser, which will render and display the page to the user.

**Connections**

The ability to distribute a DBMS across different machines plays an important role in environments where scalability is a desirable trait. In Chapter 11 we saw how many NoSQL DBMSs are built specifically with this concern in mind – to be easily scalable across multiple machines. The general concept of DBMS and data distribution over multiple physical servers is discussed in Chapter 16.

In some set-ups, this decomposition is taken one step further, by only using the web server as a gateway intercepting requests from the web browser, which is then translated in a series of requests made to a separate application server, containing the actual business logic (Figure 15.5). In this set-up, the application server will perform the necessary queries to the database server, and return the results in a structured format to the web server, who can then (still) use these to construct a web page to send back to the browser. This set-up has the added benefit that the database server can be completely decoupled from the outside world, only allowing communication from and to the application server, adding a layer of security. This also allows for types of programs other

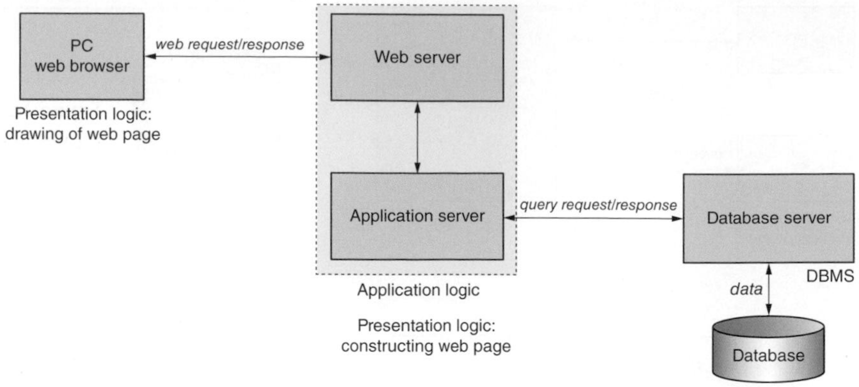


**Figure 15.5** Example of an n-tier architecture using a web browser, web and application server, and database server.

than web browsers to access the application server – for instance, a desktop application talking directly to the application server.

Note that what we show as a single "application server" or "database server" can in fact consist of multiple physical, distributed machines. This becomes especially relevant when talking about a cloud-based DBMS architecture, where the DBMS and database will be hosted by a third-party provider. The DBMS functionality and data can then be distributed across multiple computers.

**Retention Questions**

- Which types of database system architectures exist?
- What are the advantages of a tiered system architecture?

## 15.2 Classification of Database APIs

We have seen how, in a tiered DBMS system architecture, client applications can query database servers and receive the results. The question now remains how exactly such access is performed.

Client applications that wish to utilize the services provided by a DBMS are commonly programmed to use a specific **application programming interface (API)** provided by the DBMS. This database API exposes an interface through which client applications can access and query a DBMS. In a two-tiered client–server architecture with a fat client, this interface is present on the client's side, together with the application logic. In an n-tiered environment, the application server will contain the database API. The database server receives calls made by the clients through its server interface and executes the relevant operations before returning the results. In many cases, the client and server interfaces are implemented in the form of *network sockets*; a server runs on a specific computer and has a socket (a virtual endpoint in a two-way communication line managed by the underlying operating system) that is bound to a specific network port number. The server then waits, listening to the socket for a client to make a connection request. Once a connection is set up, the client and server can communicate over the network.

The main goal of database APIs is to expose an interface through which other parties can utilize the services provided by the DBMS, though the API can also serve additional objectives, such as hiding network-related aspects (e.g., by enabling clients to access a DBMS as if it were running locally). An additional benefit is that application programmers do not have to concern themselves

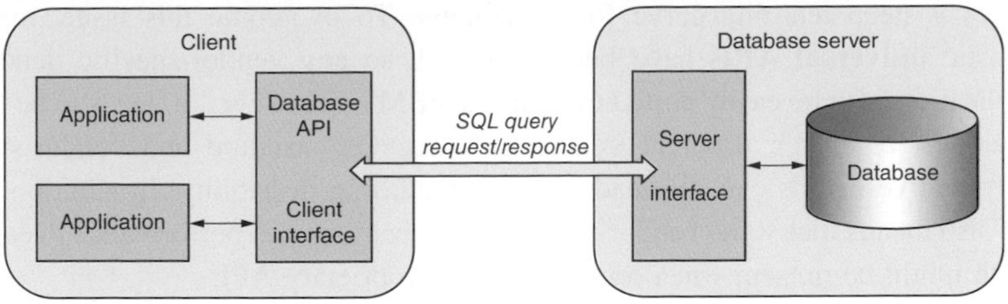


**Figure 15.6** Position of the database API.

with implementing a full communication protocol, but can focus on creating their applications and talking to the DBMS through a common language, SQL. The database API is then responsible to implement and handle the underlying protocols and formats. Figure 15.6 shows the position of the database API.

**Drill Down**

It is important to note that we discuss database APIs in this chapter: interfaces offered to programmers and system administrators to access and integrate DBMSs. Besides this, you'll see the term "API" being mentioned and used outside the realm of databases as well. Consider Facebook's graph API, Spotify's API, and so on. The goal of such "open APIs" is the same: to provide an interface to programmers, end-users, and application builders to utilize and query the services and data these parties are offering. The difference between these and the database APIs that we're discussing in this chapter is that Facebook does not provide a database API that would give third parties direct access to its underlying DBMS. Instead, these APIs operate at a higher level, offering a number of predetermined endpoints you can utilize. This does not mean that, underlyingly, no connection to a DBMS is made, but only that this is done in a way that is transparent to the API user. To provide an example: say you use Facebook's API to get a list of friends for a particular user. The "getFriends" service is something Facebook's API offers. To prepare the result, Facebook's API servers naturally have to perform queries to a database, so your API call will get translated behind the scenes to a number of internal queries, which are then performed using one of the database access APIs that we will discuss in what follows. The reason companies such as Facebook, Twitter, or Spotify do not expose a direct API to their database is not only due to security reasons, but also to make them easier to use: instead of having to know how Facebook organizes its databases and which SQL queries you should perform (something that might also change frequently), the Facebook API instead exposes a list of simple, high-level services you can use.

### 15.2.1 Proprietary versus Universal APIs

Most DBMS vendors include a **proprietary**, DBMS-specific API together with the DBMS software. The disadvantage of this approach is that client applications must be aware of the DBMS that will be utilized on the server side. If a different DBMS is to be used, the client application needs to be modified to interact with the new database API. Of course, a change of DBMS will not happen frequently, but nevertheless this creates an often undesirable dependency between application and DBMS. In addition, being able to write efficient application code "toward" yet another DBMS creates a steep learning curve for developers. To overcome this issue, many generic, vendor-agnostic **universal APIs** have been proposed, so any vendor-specific details are hidden away. Applications can be easily ported to multiple DBMSs. However, it needs to be noted that differences in support regarding different versions of the SQL standard and vendor-specific extensions or interpretative details can still lead to issues regarding portability. In addition, utilizing a universal API also means that some vendor-specific optimizations and performance tweaks cannot be utilized, which might be present when opting to use a proprietary API.

Both proprietary and universal APIs have their advantages and disadvantages. Most available DBMSs opt to provide a universal API according to one of the available standards, such as ODBC, JDBC, or ADO.NET, which will be discussed further on in this chapter.

## 15.2.2 Embedded versus Call-Level APIs

Besides proprietary and universal APIs, another taxonomy can be applied to categorize database APIs – namely whether they are embedded or operate at a call level. Understanding the differences between these two types is important, as they influence the way in which the API itself will be utilized by the user of the API to access the DBMS.

As the name suggests, an **embedded API** embeds SQL statements in the host programming language, or host language for short, meaning that the SQL statement(s) will end up being an integral part of the source code of a program. Before the program is compiled,[2] an "SQL pre-compiler" parses the SQL-related instructions and replaces these with source code instructions native to the host programming language used, invoking a separate code library. The converted source code is then sent to the actual compiler to construct a runnable program.

An advantage of embedded APIs is that the pre-compiler can perform specific syntax checks to make sure the embedded SQL is correct. The pre-compiler can also perform an early binding step (see the next section), which helps to generate an efficient query plan before the program is run, hence improving performance.

However, the facts that a pre-processing step is required and that the mixture between host-language code and SQL statements can lead to harder-to-maintain code have caused embedded database APIs to become a rarity in contemporary DBMS implementations. The SQLJ specification is one of the few remaining universal embedded API standards of importance these days, and was proposed by IBM, Oracle, Compaq, Informix, Sybase, and others to allow for the creation of embedded APIs to use in tandem with Java as the host language.

We will discuss SQLJ in more detail in Section 15.3.6. Still, SQLJ (and other embedded APIs) are not widely in use anymore, with **call-level APIs** being far more widespread. When interacting with such an API, SQL instructions are passed to the DBMS by means of direct calls to a series of procedures, functions, or methods as provided by the API to perform the necessary actions, such as setting up a database connection, sending queries, and iterating over the query result. Call-level APIs were developed in the early 1990s and standardized by the International Organization for Standardization (ISO) and International Electrotechnical Commission (IEC). The most widespread implementation of the standard is found in the **Open Database Connectivity (ODBC)** specification, which remains in wide use: many programming languages support the ODBC specification and many DBMS vendors provide APIs for it as well.

[2] Compilation means translating a program's source code into machine language so that it can be executed. A "compiler" is the program that performs this action.

### 15.2.3 Early Binding versus Late Binding

Another important pair of concepts to discuss when talking about database APIs is that of early versus late binding. SQL binding refers to the translation of SQL code to a lower-level representation that can be executed by the DBMS, after performing tasks such as validation of table and field names, checking whether the user or client has sufficient access rights and generating a query plan to access the physical data in the most performant way possible. Early versus late binding then refers to the actual moment when this binding step is performed.

The distinction between early and late binding coincides with the distinction between embedded and call-level APIs. That is, **early binding** typically occurs if a pre-compiler is used, which will then perform this binding step, and is therefore mostly paired with an embedded API.[3] This is beneficial in terms of performance, as the binding step happens (and thus consumes time) before the program is executed and not during the actual execution. Moreover, the binding only needs to be performed once, which can result in a significant performance benefit if the same query has to be executed many times afterwards. An additional benefit is that the pre-compiler can perform specific syntax checks and immediately warn the programmer if badly formatted SQL statements are present or table names are misspelled. In this way, errors are detected before the actual execution of the code, rather than causing the program to crash or malfunction because the errors occur during the execution.

**Late binding** performs the binding of SQL statements at runtime (i.e., during the actual execution of the application). The benefit of this approach is the additional flexibility it offers: SQL statements can be generated at runtime, so this is also called "dynamic SQL" rather than the "static SQL" as employed by early binding. A drawback of this approach is that syntax errors or authorization issues will remain hidden until the program is executed. The SQL statements will typically look like textual "strings" placed in the source code of the program, and are hence treated as such during compilation without additional checks taking place. This can make testing the application harder, though more feature-rich development environments can perform some of these static checks. An additional drawback is that late binding is less efficient, especially for queries that must be executed multiple times, because the binding is repeated with every execution of the query. However, this problem can be avoided by using "prepared" SQL statements, in which the database API can be instructed to perform the binding of a query once (though still at runtime), which can then be re-used multiple times within the same session of the program. As we will see later, most APIs provide support for parametrized prepared queries, so the same SQL statement can be executed using different input parameters – for example, subsequently retrieving different customers according to different values of the customerID. The DBMS will still try to optimize toward the most efficient query plan, even though the actual values for the input parameters are not yet given during the preparation of the statement.

When using an embedded API, the involvement of a pre-processor couples this API type to the use of early binding. For call-level APIs, late-binding will

**Connections**

For more information on stored procedures, see Chapter 9.

**Retention Questions**

- Explain what is meant by "proprietary" and "universal" APIs.
- Explain embedded versus call-level APIs, and early binding versus late binding. What is the relationship between these two pairs of terms?

[3] One notable exception is when stored procedures are used, which can combine early binding with call-level APIs, as we'll discuss a bit further on.

often be used. However, it is possible even when using call-level APIs to pre-compile SQL statements and call these at runtime, by defining such statements as "stored procedures" in the DBMS. The call-level API can then be used to indicate that a client application wishes to call a stored procedure, which is early-bound by the DBMS. Using this approach, early binding can be combined with call-level APIs, though one needs to define the stored procedures first, making the queries less "dynamic" in nature.

The overview table in the Comparison Box contrasts the usage of early and late binding with embedded and call-level APIs:

**Comparison Box**

| | Embedded APIs | Call-level APIs |
|---|---|---|
| **Early binding ("static" SQL)** | **Possible as a pre-compiler is used**<br>• Performance benefit, especially when the same query must be executed many times<br>• Pre-compiler detects errors before the actual execution of the code<br>• SQL queries must be known upfront | **Only possible through stored procedures** |
| **Late binding ("dynamic" SQL)** | **Not used with embedded APIs** | **Necessary as no pre-compiler is used**<br>• Flexibility benefit: SQL statements can be dynamically generated and used during execution<br>• Errors are only detected during the execution of the program<br>• Possibility to use prepared SQL statements to perform binding once during execution |

## 15.3 Universal Database APIs

Recall that most database vendors provide database access these days using a universal API standard, rather than only offering a proprietary access mechanism. Many different universal API standards have been proposed over the years, which differ in terms of them being embedded or call-level APIs, and in the programming languages they can be used in, and the functionalities they provide to the programmer working with them. In this section, we discuss the most prevalent universal API standards, starting with ODBC.

### 15.3.1 ODBC

**ODBC** stands for Open DataBase Connectivity. ODBC is an open standard, developed by Microsoft, with the aim to offer applications a common, uniform interface to various DBMSs. ODBC consists of four main components. First, the ODBC API itself is the universal interface through which client applications will interact with a DBMS. The ODBC API is a call-level API (using late binding, though stored procedure calls are supported as well), and exposes functions to set up a connection to a "data source", preparing an SQL statement, executing an SQL statement, calling a

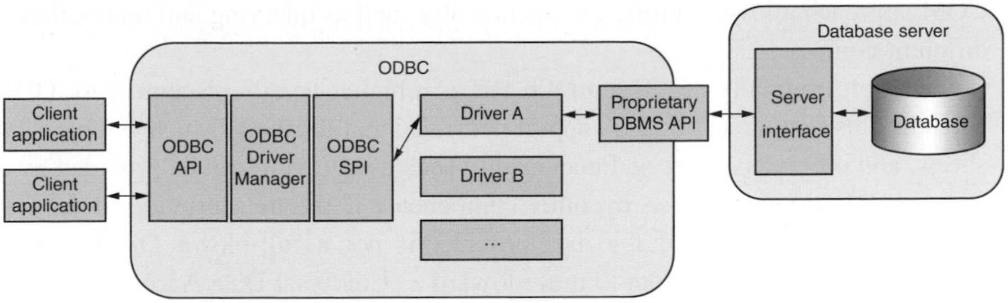


**Figure 15.7** Overview of the ODBC architecture.

stored procedure, fetching results and status messages, performing a transaction commit or rollback, getting error information, and querying metadata, closing a connection, and so on.

The ODBC driver manager, the second component of ODBC, is responsible for selecting the correct database driver (the third component) to communicate with a DBMS. A driver is a collection of routines that contain the actual code to communicate with a DBMS (potentially through an existing, proprietary DBMS API), and is provided by the DBMS vendor. The driver manager itself interacts with the drivers by means of a fourth component, the service provider interface, or SPI, a separate interface intended to be implemented by the DBMS vendor. Figure 15.7 provides an overview of the ODBC architecture.

A major benefit of ODBC is that it – as a universal API standard – allows applications to be easily ported between DBMSs or even between DBMS vendors, without having to modify the application's code (provided the vendors agree on an SQL standard). This is very similar to the role of a printer driver in an operating system: the printer driver translates generic "print" commands by the respective applications into calls toward a specific printer type, hence allowing for the printer to be replaced by another printer brand without altering applications' code. A drawback of ODBC lies mainly in the fact that the architecture is native to Microsoft-based platforms; an implementation for Linux exists, but vendor support is often lacking (as separate drivers must be provided), so ODBC remains mainly popular on Windows. Another drawback of ODBC is its age: ODBC is based on the C programming language, so it does not utilize the programmer-friendly object-oriented paradigm. Consequently, it exposes some complex resource management to the driver maintainer (i.e., the vendor implementing the DBMS driver). Another drawback compared to directly using a proprietary API is that the ODBC middleware introduces an extra layer of indirection and therefore some extra performance lag, though this is the case for other universal APIs as well.

## 15.3.2 OLE DB and ADO

ODBC remains an immensely popular offering to gain access to DBMSs in a uniform manner, even though Microsoft has also developed newer (and objectively better) APIs in recent times. **OLE DB** (originally an abbreviation for Object Linking and Embedding for DataBases, but now a name in itself) was a follow-up specification to ODBC to allow uniform access to a variety of data sources using Microsoft's Component Object Model (COM). COM is a programming framework for specifying software components, which represent highly modular and re-usable building blocks to applications running on a Microsoft platform. Compared to the more monolithic approach of ODBC, in which all the functionality regarding one DBMS was contained in a single driver, the

COM approach allows splitting up functionality such as querying and transaction management into different components.

Microsoft originally developed OLE DB as a higher-level replacement for ODBC, primarily by extending its feature set to also support non-relational databases, such as object databases, spreadsheets, and other data sources. Functionality such as querying can be provided by the data provider (e.g., an RDBMS), but also by other components if the data provider does not incorporate the functionality itself (e.g., if the data provider is not a full-blown DBMS). As such, OLE DB represents Microsoft's attempt to move toward a "Universal Data Access" approach, assuming that not all data can be stored in a relational database, so that integrating these data sources and offering unified access capabilities become highly relevant.[4]

OLE DB can also be combined with **ActiveX Data Objects (ADO)**, which provides a richer, more "programmer-friendly" programming model on top of OLE DB. The following code fragment shows an example of using OLE DB with ADO to access an SQL data source, such as a relational database. The first lines set up a connection to the database. Next, a query is performed, resulting in a result set that can be looped over:

```
Dim conn As ADODB.Connection
Dim recordSet As ADODB.Recordset

Set conn = New ADODB.Connection
conn.Open("my_database")

Set qry = "select nr, name from suppliers where status < 30"
Set recordSet = conn.Execute(qry)

Do While Not recordSet.EOF
 MsgBox(recordSet.Fields(0).Name & "= "& recordSet.Fields(0).Value & vbCrLf &
     recordSet.Fields(1).Name & "= "& recordSet.Fields(1).Value)
 recordSet.MoveNext
Loop

recordSet.Close
conn.Close
```

### 15.3.3 ADO.NET

After the introduction of Microsoft's .NET framework, OLE DB and ADO were merged and reworked thoroughly to form **ADO.NET**. The .NET framework was developed by Microsoft with the objective to perform a modern overhaul of all core components that make up the Windows and related technologies stack. It consists mainly of two large pieces of technology: the Common Language Runtime (CLR) and a set of class libraries.

The CLR provides an execution environment for .NET. Source code (written in a programming language that supports the CLR, such as C# or VB.Net) is compiled to an intermediate language, comparable to Java's byte code. This intermediate language is then compiled "just-in-time" to native machine code when an application is executed, managed by the CLR – "managed" here meaning

[4] This is in contrast to the "Universal Data Storage" approach we observed in extended relational DBMSs in Chapter 9, which aimed at extending database functionality to support storing any kind of (non-relational) data in an RDBMS as well.

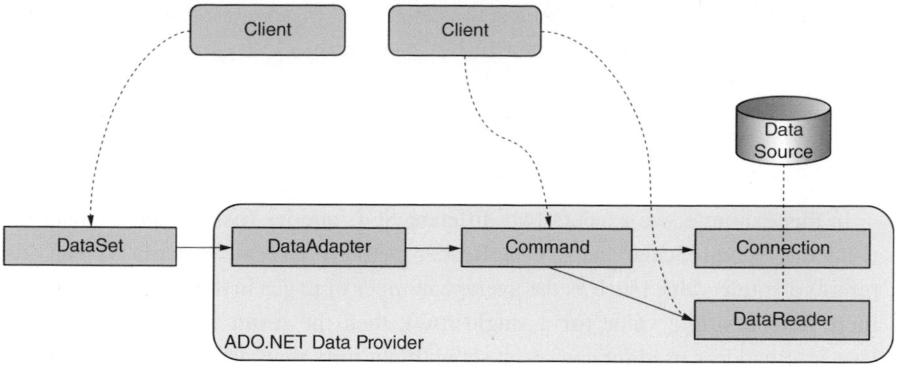


**Figure 15.8** Overview of ADO.NET classes.

that the CLR performs additional checks and tasks to ensure security, protect against crashes, perform memory management, and so on. Clearly, the .NET framework was heavily inspired by Java (together with its Java Virtual Machine). The .NET class libraries offer a hierarchy of libraries containing a plethora of generic, re-usable components, including components for I/O operations, threading and so on to GUI components (such as Windows Forms) or components offering data source access, such as those in ADO.NET.

Note that ADO.NET is quite different from OLE DB and ADO. Like OLE DB, ADO.NET breaks down all database-related access features into a set of components. To access data, ADO.NET offers a series of *data providers*, which are broken down into a series of objects handling creation of database connections, sending queries, and reading results. Figure 15.8 provides a summary of ADO.NET's classes.

The following C# code fragment shows the Connection, Command, and DataReader objects in action using the .NET Framework Data Provider for SQL Server (SqlClient):

```
String connectionString = "Data Source=(local);Initial Catalog=example;"
SqlConnection conn = new SqlConnection(connectionString)
conn.Open();

String query1 = "select avg(num_pages) from books";
String query2 = "select title, author from books where num_pages > 30";

SqlCommand command1 = conn.CreateCommand();
SqlCommand command2 = conn.CreateCommand();

command1.CommandText = query1;
command2.CommandText = query2;

int average_pages = command1.ExecuteScalar();
Console.Writeln(average_pages);

SqlDataReader dataReader = command2.ExecuteReader();

String title;
String author;

while (dataReader.Read()) {
 title = dataReader.GetString(0);
```

```
    author = dataReader.GetString(1);
    Console.Writeln(title + " by " + author);
  }

  dataReader.Close();
  conn.Close();
```

In this example, we execute two different SQL queries (using SqlCommand) and execute them using the ExecuteScalar and ExecuteReader methods. ExecuteScalar is typically used when a query returns a single value (such as the average number of pages in the example above). If a query returns more than a single value (or a single row), then the result is the first column of the first row. ExecuteReader is used for any result set with multiple rows and/or columns. ExecuteNonQuery (not shown in the example) is typically used for SQL statements without results (e.g., UPDATE, INSERT queries). For the query returning multiple rows and columns, we use an ADO.NET DataReader (an SqlDataReader object) to retrieve a read-only, forward-only stream of data from a database. Using this approach, results are returned as the query executes, and are stored on the client until you request them using the Read method of the DataReader (as shown in the example). By default, the DataReader stores only one row at a time in memory, reducing system overhead.

A DataAdapter provides an alternative approach that can be used to retrieve data from a data source and populate tables within a DataSet object. A DataAdapter can also persist changes made to the DataSet back to the underlying data source. To retrieve data and resolve changes, the DataAdapter will use various Command objects which will perform the requested operations toward the underlying data source: SelectCommand to read data from the data source into the DataSet and InsertCommand, UpdateCommand, and DeleteCommand to propagate updates from the DataSet back into the data source. A DataAdapter hence positions itself between a data source (which can be a relational database but may well be a file system or some other data source) and the DataSet containing the data themselves in a relational, tabular format. The DataSet object in ADO.NET is a complex structure, offering a hierarchy of sub-objects representing relations, tables, constraints, rows, fields, and more. An important aspect to note (especially when compared to an ADO Recordset object) is that a DataSet implements a so-called "disconnected" data source access model, meaning it resides on the client and will not retain a persistent connection to the backing data source. All data manipulations on a DataSet happen in-memory, with a connection only being opened when the data are initially retrieved from the data source and updates must be saved back to the persistent data source. Especially in web-based applications, this offers several benefits regarding scalability, as the web application can more easily serve a large number of users without maintaining persistent database connections for every session. When a DataSet is backed by a relational database, it can serve as an intelligent cached data structure, but a DataSet is also capable to work with non-relational data sources (by using a different DataAdapter) and can even combine multiple data sources by using multiple DataAdapters. Finally, programmers can also use DataSet objects without any backing data source, hence constructing tables, relations, fields and constraints completely "by hand", while still being free to persist these later on by then coupling a DataAdapter object. To summarize, a DataSet can exist completely independently from any data source and is not even aware about which data sources might exist. Necessary connections with data sources are made through short-lived sessions set up by one or more DataAdapters, either to persist data from a DataSet to a data store, or to load data from a data store

**Connections**

The impact of the "disconnected" approach as implemented in an ADO.NET DataSet on transaction management and concurrency control is discussed in more detail in Chapter 16.

into a DataSet. The following code fragment shows an example of using a DataSet with an SqlDataAdapter (the data adapter object for SQL Server):

```
// Create a DataAdapter object, based on a connection conn and a
// queryString, which will be used to retrieve data from the data
// source (behind the scenes, a SelectCommand will be created based on
// this query)
string queryString = "select title, author from books";
SqlDataAdapter ada = new SqlDataAdapter(queryString, conn);

// Create a DataSet object and fill it with data from the books table
// By invoking the fill method, the aforementioned SelectCommand
// containing the SELECT query will be executed against the data source
DataSet booksDataSet = new DataSet();
ada.Fill(booksDataSet, "myBooks");

// [ Work with the booksDataSet DataSet]

// Fetch the DataTable from the DataSet and loop over it
DataTable tbl = booksDataSet.Tables["myBooks"] ;
foreach (DataRow bookRow in tbl.Rows) {
  Console.WriteLine(bookRow["title"] );
}
```

Finally, it is worth emphasizing the large degree of backward-compatibility provided by ADO.NET. Next to data providers that can directly connect with SQL databases from various vendors (e.g., as illustrated by the SqlDataAdapter object in the example above, which works with SQL Server), data providers are available that can call existing ODBC APIs, as well as data providers that can call legacy OLE DB providers (which in turn might even call ODBC APIs).

## 15.3.4 Java DataBase Connectivity (JDBC)

Like ODBC, **Java DataBase Connectivity (JDBC)** offers a call-level database API. JDBC was heavily inspired by ODBC, so many concepts are the same, with an important difference being that JDBC was developed to be used in Java and geared only toward this programming language. This narrow focus, however, also helps to introduce many benefits, such as high portability (Java runs on a multitude of platforms) and the ability to program in an object-oriented manner. Database connections, drivers, queries, and results are all expressed as objects, based on uniform interfaces and hence exposing a uniform set of methods, no matter which DBMS is utilized. Figure 15.9 illustrates the JDBC architecture.

JDBC exposes a series of object interfaces through which drivers, connections, SQL statements, and results are expressed. Figure 15.10 provides an overview of JDBC's classes.

The DriverManager is a singleton object that acts as the basic service to manage JDBC drivers. To utilize a DBMS driver, it first must be registered with the DriverManager, using the registerDriver method. Once done, database connections can be created using one of the registered drivers by means of the getConnection method. This method takes a string as a parameter, representing a connection URL to indicate which DBMS one wishes to connect to, which should be of the form "jdbc:subprotocol:subname", e.g., "jdbc:sqlite:my_database". This method can also take optional username and password parameters. The following Java code snippet shows how to register a driver and set up a connection using the DriverManager:

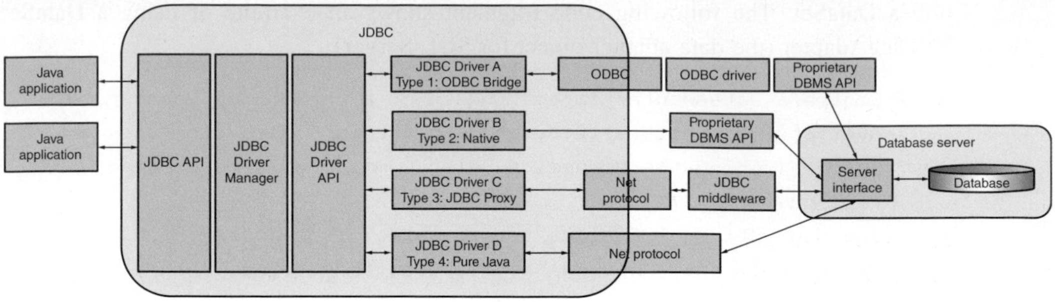


**Figure 15.9** Overview of the JDBC architecture.

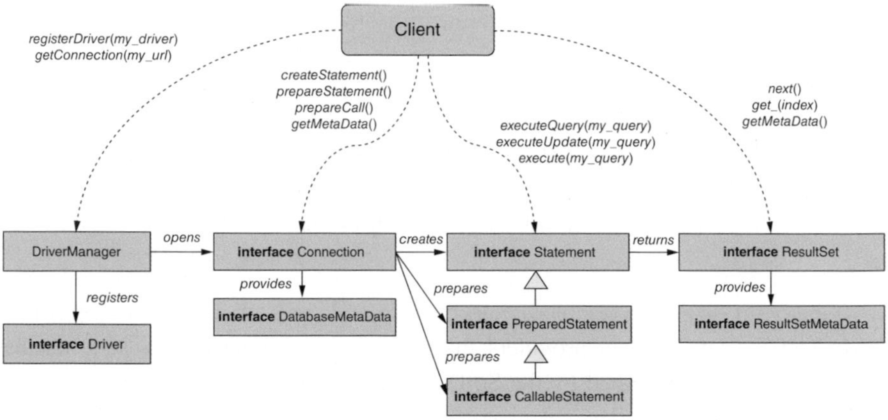


**Figure 15.10** Overview of JDBC's classes.

```
DriverManager.registerDriver(new org.sqlite.JDBC());
String dbURL = "jdbc:sqlite:my_database";
Connection conn = DriverManager.getConnection(dbURL);
if (conn != null) {
 System.out.println("Connected to the database");
 DatabaseMetaData dm = conn.getMetaData();
 System.out.println("Driver name: " + dm.getDriverName);
 conn.close();
}
```

Note that many drivers will also register themselves automatically, and version 4 of the JDBC standard even does away with the need to register drivers completely, as drivers supporting this version must be findable using a service location mechanism. Recent versions of JDBC also contain an alternative method to connect to a JDBC data source, by using the DataSource interface class, which uses Java's JNDI (Java Naming and Directory Interface) instead of a connection URL to connect to a DBMS, which has the advantage that a naming service can be used to look up the desired endpoint for a given data source name. Most examples online and in print still prefer to use the simpler approach above, however.

The driver objects registered with the DriverManager implement the Driver interface and enable the communication between the DriverManager and the DBMS. To implement the interface, database vendors can decide between different so-called driver "types". Type-1 drivers are also denoted as JDBC–ODBC bridge drivers. They do not communicate with a DBMS directly, but instead translate JDBC calls to corresponding ODBC calls, which will then be fed to the ODBC API, which, in turn, will use its ODBC drivers. The advantage of this approach is clear, as it allows re-use of existing ODBC drivers in JDBC. To do so, however, one needs to make sure the ODBC stack is present on the host system next to JDBC. In addition, using ODBC bridge drivers means that client applications will be harder to port to different (non-Microsoft) platforms, and that the number of "in-between" layers also negatively impacts performance. Type-2 drivers (JDBC–native API drivers), on the other hand, are completely written in Java, but will communicate to a DBMS using its "native" database API. This means this driver translates JDBC calls into native calls to the proprietary database API. As these APIs will commonly not be implemented in Java, this again means that native calls have to be made at some point, which might cause issues when portability is a concern. Type-3 drivers (JDBC–Net drivers) are completely written in Java. Here, the JDBC client will use standard networking sockets to communicate with an application server, which will convert the calls into a native database API call or will utilize a different JDBC type-1, 2, or 4 driver on its end. This driver type acts as a proxy, where a separate server will perform calls on the client's behalf. A type-4 driver, finally, is also completely written in Java and uses networking functionality, though here a direct connection is made with the database server. The driver communicates directly with the DBMS over the network, and hence offers both performance and portability. Table 15.1 provides a summary of the different JDBC driver types.

Opening a connection returns a Connection object, representing a session to a specific database. SQL statements will be executed and results returned within the context of such a connection. The createStatement method can be used to create SQL statements, with which an SQL query can be executed. The prepareStatement and prepareCall methods can be used to create objects representing prepared statements and stored procedure calls respectively. The getMetaData method can be used to obtain a separate object representing metadata describing the connection, such as the driver name and version used, the vendor name, and so on.

**Table 15.1** Summary of different JDBC driver types

| Driver type | Driver description | Advantages | Disadvantages |
|---|---|---|---|
| **Type 1** | JDBC–ODBC bridge driver | Backward compatible with existing ODBC drivers | Harder to port to different platforms, extra ODBC layer impacts performance |
| **Type 2** | JDBC–native API driver | Uses existing native DBMS APIs, less of a performance drawback | Portability remains an issue |
| **Type 3** | JDBC–Net driver | Uses existing native DBMS APIs over a network socket, hence acting as a proxy | Client portability is easier, though the fact that the application server still needs to call underlying native APIs can lead to a performance hit |
| **Type 4** | Pure Java driver | Direct network connection to DBMS and pure Java implementation leads to performance and portability | Not always available, creating a pure Java JDBC driver may incur extra programming effort from the vendor |

A Statement object represents an SQL instruction. Different methods are available to execute statements. For a SELECT query, the executeQuery method should be invoked, which returns a ResultSet representing the returned data. This method takes one parameter, namely the SQL query itself, passed as a string (a textual value). The following example shows the Statement object and executeQuery method in action:

```
Statement selectStatement = conn.createStatement("select title, num_pages from books")
ResultSet selectResult = selectStatement.executeQuery();
```

A ResultSet object contains the result of a SELECT query executed by a Statement object. Because SQL is a set-oriented language, the query result (the ResultSet object) will generally comprise multiple tuples. Host languages such as Java are essentially record-oriented: they cannot handle more than one record/tuple at a time. To overcome this so-called impedance mismatch, JDBC (like ODBC) exposes a **cursor mechanism** in order to loop through result sets. A cursor is a programmatic control structure that enables traversal over the records in a query result set, similar to a textual cursor as seen in a word processing application, where you can move the cursor line-by-line, with the cursor then indicating the current position in the text. Here, the database cursor keeps track of where we are in the result set, so that the tuples that result from an SQL query can be traversed and presented to the application code one by one.[5]

In JDBC, the rows of a ResultSet object can be iterated over using the "next" method, which moves the cursor to the next row if possible and returns a Boolean "true" value to indicate that the next row could be retrieved. When the end of the ResultSet is reached, "next" will return "false". For every row, fields can be retrieved using the get____-collection of "getter" methods (e.g., getInt, getFloat, getString, and so on), using either the name of the field as a parameter, or an integer representing the index of the field in the result row. Note that when the wrong data type is used to get a field, an error is raised at runtime, i.e., during the actual execution of the program. The following example shows the cursor mechanism and "getters" in action:

```
while (selectResult.next()) {
 String bookTitle = selectResult.getString("title"); // or: .getString(1);
 int bookPages = selectResult.getInt("num_pages"); // or: .getInt(2);
 System.out.println(bookTitle + "has" + bookPages + "pages");
}
```

For INSERT, UPDATE, or DELETE queries (or DDL queries), the executeUpdate method should be called. Here, the return value is not a ResultSet object, but an integer (a number) representing the number of affected rows (i.e., inserted, modified, or deleted). When the query type is not known beforehand, one can also invoke the generic "execute" method, which returns a Boolean value representing whether the just-executed query was a SELECT query, based on which the program can decide to call the getResultSet method to then fetch the actual result set.

```
String deleteQuery = "delete from books where num_pages <= 30";
Statement deleteStatement = conn.createStatement();
int deletedRows = deleteStatement.executeUpdate(deleteQuery);
System.out.println(deletedRows + "books were deleted");
```

[5] The naive approach of passing the complete result set to the client application is certainly undesirable as this might entail sending huge amounts of data (a `SELECT` in a huge table, for instance) to the client at once, leading to a congested computer network or out-of-memory errors.

The PreparedStatement interface extends Statement with functionalities to bind a query once and then execute it multiple times efficiently. Prepared statements also provide support to pass query parameters, which should then be instantiated using so called "setter methods" such as setInt, setString, and so on. Note here the usage of question marks ("?") inside of the SQL query to indicate that this represents a parameter value that will be bound later:

```
String selectQuery = "select * from books where num_pages > ? and num_pages < ? ";
Statement preparedSelectStatement = conn.prepareStatement(selectQuery);

int min_pages = 50;
int max_pages = 200;
// Set the value to the first parameter (1):
preparedSelectStatement.setInt(1, min_pages);
// Set the value to the second parameter (2):
preparedSelectStatement.setInt(2, max_pages);

ResultSet resultSet1 = preparedSelectStatement.executeQuery();

// Execute the same query a second time with different parameter values:
preparedSelectStatement.setInt(1, 10);
preparedSelectStatement.setInt(2, 20);
ResultSet resultSet2 = preparedSelectStatement.executeQuery();
```

CallableStatement extends PreparedStatement and offers support to execute stored procedures. It also provides facilities for passing "in", "out", and "inout" parameters. "In" parameters are comparable to prepared statement parameters and are also set using set____ methods; they can be used for passing "input values" from the application code to the stored procedure. By default, all parameters are "in" parameters. If some parameters are to be used for "output" from the stored procedure to the application code, they are "out" parameters and need to be registered explicitly using registerOutParameter. This method also takes an integer representing the order of the parameter in the query (which is necessary to refer to the appropriate parameter if multiple parameters are used) and a java.sql.Types object denoting the Java type of the parameter. "Inout" parameters, finally, can be used as both input and output parameters. The following code fragment shows these statements in action:

```
// "price_after_discount" is the name of the stored procedure we want to call
Statement preparedStProcCall = conn.prepareCall("{ call price_after_discount(?,?)}");

// The first parameter is an "in"-value:
double discountPercentage = 0.15;
preparedStProcCall.setDouble(1, discountPercentage);

// Indicate that the second parameter is an "out"-value of type FLOAT (a
// decimal value):
preparedStProcCall.registerOutParameter(2, java.sql.Types.FLOAT);

// Execute the stored procedure
preparedStProcCall.execute();

// Get the value of the second parameter
float priceAfterDiscount = preparedStProcCall.getFloat(2);
```

JDBC also supports the creation of updatable ResultSets, where rows in a ResultSet can be updated on the fly. In addition, ResultSets may provide richer navigation functionality than just moving to the next row. The following code fragment shows this in action:

```
String query = "select title, author, num_pages
        from books where num_pages > 100";

/* We pass some additional parameters here to createStatement to
indicate that we want to allow scrolling backward and forward through
the ResultSet, and that we want an updatable ResultSet: */
Statement stat = conn.createStatement(
  ResultSet.TYPE_SCROLL_SENSITIVE, ResultSet.CONCUR_UPDATABLE);

ResultSet resultSet = stat.executeQuery(query);

// Move the cursor to the first position and get out some information:
resultSet.first();
String title = resultSet.getString(1);
int numPages = resultSet.getInt(3);
String author = resultSet.getString("author");

// Move forward some rows:
resultSet.next();
resultSet.next();

// Update this row on the fly and propagate the update to the database:
resultSet.updateInt("num_pages", 85);
resultSet.updateRow();

// Move to row number 40:
resultSet.absolute(40);

// Insert a new row at this position:
resultSet.updateString(1, "New book");
resultSet.updateString(2, "D.B. Rowling");
resultSet.updateInt(3, 100);
resultSet.insertRow();

// Move back one row:
resultSet.previous();

// Delete this row:
resultSet.deleteRow();
```

Note that not all JDBC drivers support flexible cursor scrolling or updateable ResultSets as shown in the example above. Older, legacy drivers especially lack support for this. Here, one needs to perform additional INSERT, UPDATE, or DELETE queries manually to execute the desired changes.

More recent versions of JDBC also add the *RowSet* interface, which extends the *ResultSet* interface. RowSet objects can act as a wrapper around a normal ResultSet object, adding support for scrollable and updateable cursors even if the underlying DBMS driver does not support this, in

**Connections**

See Chapter 14 for more information on transactions and transaction management.

which case the RowSet interface will make sure that the necessary operations are executed. Another benefit of a RowSet is that it allows other objects to register themselves with a RowSet to receive updates they might be interested in. For instance, an object representing a table in a program's user interface can register itself to receive updates every time the row set changes, so it can immediately update itself and stay up-to-date (without adding a separate refresh button, for instance).

Another important role of JDBC's Connection object is the coordination of transactions. To do so, the Connection interface also defines commit, rollback, setTransactionIsolation, setAutoCommit, setSavepoint, and releaseSavepoint methods.

The JDBC API provides no explicit method to start a transaction. The decision to initiate a new transaction is made implicitly by the JDBC driver or the DBMS. The way transactions are committed depends on the "auto-commit" attribute of the Connection object, which can be set using the setAutoCommit method. When auto-commit is enabled, the JDBC driver will perform a commit after every individual SQL statement automatically. When auto-commit is disabled, the program itself is responsible for committing transactions using the commit or rollback methods. The setSavepoint and releaseSavepoint methods can be used to set a synchronization point in the current transaction (which can then be rolled back to) and release (i.e., remove) a synchronization point respectively. The following code fragment shows these methods in action.

```
// Disable auto-commit
myConnection.setAutoCommit(false);
Statement myStatement1 = myConnection.createStatement();
Statement myStatement2 = myConnection.createStatement();
Statement myStatement3 = myConnection.createStatement();
Statement myStatement4 = myConnection.createStatement();
myStatement1.executeUpdate(myQuery1);
myStatement2.executeUpdate(myQuery2);
// Create a save point
Savepoint mySavepoint = myConnection.setSavepoint();
myStatement3.executeUpdate(myQuery3);
// Roll back to earlier savepoint, myStatement3 will be undone
myConnection.rollback(mySavepoint);
// Now execute myStatement4
myStatement4.executeUpdate(myQuery4);
// Commit the transaction
myConnection.commit();
```

As a result, the updates as induced by myQuery1, myQuery2, and myQuery4 will be committed.

### 15.3.5 Intermezzo: SQL Injection and Access Security

Now that we have seen a set of examples of call-level APIs (the most common type of database API), you will have noted that all SQL queries are represented using standard strings, e.g., as normal Java strings when using JDBC. This means that no additional validation or syntax checking can be performed at compile time; a drawback of call-level APIs. This approach has, however, the benefit of allowing for dynamic queries in the form of strings that can be dynamically constructed by the program at runtime. Consider a user entering a search term in a search box to search for books, which is then used to construct a dynamic SQL statement. The following code fragment shows what this could look like (using Java and JDBC, but the principle is the same for ODBC and other call-level APIs as well):

```
BufferedReader br = new BufferedReader(new InputStreamReader(System.in));
System.out.println("Enter your search term: ");
String searchInput = br.readLine();

String selectQuery = "select * from books where upper(title) like '%" +
                      searchInput.toUpperCase() + "%'";
Statement stat = conn.createStatement();
ResultSet resultSet = stat.executeQuery(selectQuery);
```

When the user enters "database management", for instance, the "selectQuery" string in the example above would look as follows:

```
select * from books where upper(title) like '%DATABASE MANAGEMENT%'
```

At first sight, this example illustrates a strong aspect of call-level APIs, namely the possibility to dynamically construct SQL statements. Nevertheless, using simple string manipulation routines to construct SQL queries can also lead to potential security issues, especially when queries are constructed based on user input. Imagine what would happen if someone entered "' OR 1=1 --" as a name, causing the query to end up looking like this ("--" is used to indicate that the rest of the line is to be treated as a comment by many DBMSs):

```
select * from books where upper(title) like '%' OR 1=1 --%'
```

Without much effort, our user now has insight into the complete database table. This looks harmless, but one might just as well try the following:

```
select * from books where upper(title) like '%GOTCHA!'; DROP TABLE BOOKS; --%'
```

Many DBMS systems can send multiple SQL statements in one string, separated by semicolons. Our malicious user has now caused the complete books table to be dropped. This type of attack (to cause damage as well as to gain access to hidden information) is called **SQL injection**, as one injects malicious fragments into normal-looking SQL statements. Such attacks can cause a wide range of harm, and many websites and applications are vulnerable to it.

The solution, however, is rather simple. Whenever user input or external input is to be used in SQL statements, always make use of prepared statements, as discussed above. Virtually all call-level APIs (including all seen in this chapter) provide means to do so. For instance, in JDBC, we'd write our example as follows:

```
String searchInput = br.readLine();
String selectQuery = "select * from books where upper(title) like ?";
Statement stat = conn.prepareStatement(selectQuery);
stat.setString(1, "%" + searchInput.toUpperCase() + "%");
ResultSet resultSet = stat.executeQuery();
```

Since the SQL statement used in a prepared statement is bound by the driver, all parameters are sent to the driver as *literal values and not as executable portions of an SQL statement*, meaning you might end up searching for titles containing "GOTCHA!"; DROP TABLE BOOKS; --", but no harm can be done (probably no such books will be retrieved).

### 15.3.6 SQLJ

Today, JDBC remains widely popular, with a plethora of drivers available for the platform. It offers one of the most portable ways to access DBMSs (especially when using type-4 drivers), and provides fine-grained control over the execution of SQL statements. **SQLJ**, Java's embedded, static SQL API, was developed after JDBC, and allows embedding SQL statements directly into Java programs. The following code example illustrates this lineage, as some JDBC classes, such as the DriverManager, are still used in SQLJ:

```
// Create a connection and default SQLJ context
DriverManager.registerDriver(new oracle.jdbc.driver.OracleDriver());
Connection conn = DriverManager.getConnection(dbUrl);
DefaultContext.setDefaultContext(new DefaultContext(conn));

// Define an SQLJ iterator
#sql iterator BookIterator(String, String, int);

// Perform query and fetch results
BookIterator mybooks;
int min_pages = 100;
#sql mybooks = { select title, author, num_pages from books
       where num_pages >= :min_pages };

String title;
String author;
int num_pages;

#sql { fetch :mybooks into :title, :author, :num_pages};
while (!mybooks.endFetch()) {
  System.out.println(title + ' by '+ author + ': '+ num_pages);
  #sql { fetch :mybooks into :title, :author, :num_pages};
}
conn.close();
```

Note that, when using SQLJ, queries are no longer expressed as textual parameters (strings), but instead directly embedded in the Java source code. Hence, a pre-compiler will first convert these statements to native Java code (by converting them, for instance, to JDBC instructions), but will also perform a series of additional checks, such as checking whether our SQL statements are correctly spelled and all table fields are known. Arguments for embedded SQL statements are passed through host variables, which are variables that are defined in the programming language "hosting" the embedded API (Java in this case) and can then be referred to in SQL statements by prefixing their name with a colon, ":" to use as input variables (parameters for the query) or as output variables (to receive results from a query). The SQLJ pre-compiler will also perform additional checks based on the host variables used, e.g., to verify whether they have been defined in the Java code and whether all type definitions of the host variables used inside #sql{ . . . } statements match the database schema definition. For example, if the :num_pages parameter in the example above were defined as a decimal field in the DBMS, the SQLJ pre-compiler would complain about the fact that we're using integer (non-decimal) types for the min_pages and num_pages host variables instead of decimal floats as the database expects. These errors can then be resolved before the program is run. Such compile-time checking cannot be performed when using late-bound parameters such as those shown in the JDBC example above. Errors will then be thrown during the actual execution of the program, potentially causing additional debugging hassle.

However, as stated earlier, SQLJ and other embedded APIs have fallen out of use in recent years, and especially SQLJ never experienced the level of adoption seen by JDBC. One reason for this is its lack of support for dynamic SQL. A second reason lies in the extra cognitive overhead required from the programmer, as SQLJ statements look somewhat out of place compared to normal Java source code, and hence this requires the programmer to know how to combine Java with SQLJ. Another reason is that, at the time of SQLJ's development, new, large integrated development environments (IDEs) were just making their entrance into the Java ecosystem (such as Eclipse and NetBeans), which didn't play nicely with SQLJ statements sprinkled throughout Java code. A further reason is that the additional validations and compile-time safety checks as promised by the SQLJ pre-compiler didn't mature quickly, causing SQLJ to fall behind in adoption, especially since more high-level APIs (such as object-relational mappers, which will be discussed in Section 15.4) were right on the horizon as well. Nevertheless, whereas embedded database APIs in Java and other more recent languages never took off, they still remain the prevalent technology in the plethora of legacy database applications that are still around, written in older host languages such as COBOL. As many of these applications cannot be phased out yet and still need to be maintained, COBOL programmers with embedded SQL skills are actually sought-after profiles in some sectors.

### 15.3.7 Intermezzo: Embedded APIs versus Embedded DBMSs

At this point it is important to note that some call-level APIs might be easily confused with embedded APIs, especially for some database management systems that denote themselves as **embedded DBMSs**. One example is SQLite. In contrast to many other DBMSs, SQLite does not operate in a client–server environment. Instead, the DBMS is completely contained in a single library (written in C), which in turn is embedded into the application itself, so the DBMS becomes an integral part of the actual application.

Invoking the SQLite API from a host language, however, is performed in a call-level manner, not using an embedded API. No pre-compiler is present. The following code fragment shows how SQLite can be used in C – note the absence of embedded statements as was the case with SQLJ; everything is pure C code. The SQLite C library has been ported to many other languages as well, and today can be used by virtually every programming language available.

**Drill Down**

Even where a direct port of the SQLite library would be hard, the library itself has also been ported to be compatible with the JDBC standard, so you can use it in this set-up.

```
// Import the SQLite and standard C input/output libraries
#include <sqlite3.h>
#include <stdio.h>

int callback(void *, int, char **, char **);

// Main program:
int main(void) {
  sqlite3 *db;
  char *err_msg = 0;

  // Set up the connection to the database (stored in one file)
  int rc = sqlite3_open("my_database.db", &db);

  if (rc != SQLITE_OK) {
    sqlite3_close(db);
    return 1;
  }

  // Execute a query using sqlite3_exec, we specify a function
  // called "callback" to handle the result-rows if successful
  char *sql = "SELECT * FROM books ORDER BY title";
  rc = sqlite3_exec(db, sql, callback, 0, &err_msg);

  if (rc != SQLITE_OK ) {
    sqlite3_free(err_msg);
    sqlite3_close(db);
    return 1;
  }

  // Close the connection
  sqlite3_close(db);
  return 0;
}

// What should we do for every row in a result set?
int callback(void *Ignore, int num_cols, char **col_values, char **col_names) {
  // Iterate over the columns and show the name and value
  for (int i = 0; i < num_cols; i++)
    printf("%s = %s\n", col_names[ i] ,
      col_values[ i] ? col_values[ i] : "<NULL>");
  printf("\n");
  return 0;
}
```

The following fragment shows the SQLite Python port (available in the "sqlite3" Python library). Note the brevity of this implementation compared to the C program above: the "sqlite3" library contains additional methods (such as "execute") which are easier to use:

```
import sqlite3
conn = sqlite3.connect('my_database.db')
```

```
c = conn.cursor()

for row in c.execute('SELECT * FROM books ORDER BY title'):
  print row

conn.close()
```

**Drill Down**

Other embedded DBMSs than SQLite exist, though SQLite remains one of the most popular ones (it is used by web browsers, smartphone applications, and many other systems to store and query data in a simple single-file set-up). Other notable examples include Apache Derby (written in Java), LevelDB, SQL Anywhere, and H2. Most embedded databases offer ODBC and/or JDBC driver implementations as well.

### 15.3.8 Language-Integrated Querying

The lack of compile-time type checking and validation can make working with JDBC somewhat cumbersome at times. JDBC programs can be difficult to debug, can easily grow in size (JDBC interfaces expose a lot of methods that need to be called, even to execute simple queries), and miss syntactic and semantic SQL checks, since queries are expressed as simple Java strings.

With the above in mind, it is worth mentioning that some modern programming languages have started to incorporate language-native query expressions into their syntax (either directly or through the usage of an additional programming library), which can often operate on any collection of data (e.g., a database, but also XML documents or collection types). When targeting a DBMS, such expressions will typically be converted to an SQL statement, which can then, behind the scenes, be sent off to the target database server using JDBC or another API.

A good example of this approach can be found in the third-party library jOOQ. This project aims to provide the benefits of embedded SQL using pure Java, rather than resorting to an additional pre-compiler. To do so, a code generator is run first that inspects the database schema and reverse-engineers it into a set of Java classes representing tables, records, sequences, types, stored procedures, and other schema entities. These can then be queried and invoked using plain Java code, as illustrated by the following code fragment:

```
String sql = create.select(BOOK.TITLE, AUTHOR.NAME)
          .from(BOOK)
          .join(AUTHOR)
          .on(BOOK.AUTHOR_ID.equal(AUTHOR.ID))
          .where(BOOK.NUM_PAGES.greaterThan(100))
          .getSQL();
```

Note that the code generator has generated BOOK and AUTHOR classes. Since now only pure, plain Java code is used to express statements, IDEs do not need to be aware of a separate language, no pre-compiler is necessary, and the standard Java compiler can be used to perform type safety checks and generate compilation errors when necessary. For instance, if we would try to pass a string value to the generated greaterThan method of the BOOK.NUM_PAGES class, the Java compiler would throw an error indicating that such a method template does not exist. jOOQ can be combined to work in tandem with other APIs such as JDBC (for instance to perform the actual execution of an SQL string generated by jOOQ, as done in the code sample above).

Another project following a similar approach is QueryDSL, which also aims to add integrated querying capabilities into the Java host language, using pure Java expressions rather than resorting to a pre-compiler. Compared to jOOQ, QueryDSL steers even further away from raw SQL, as it aims to enable querying operations on any sort of collection, including databases, XML files, and other data sources. The following code fragment shows an example of QueryDSL applied on an SQL data source:

```
// Set up a new queryFactory given a certain configuration
// and data source, e.g., a relational database
SQLQueryFactory queryFactory =
  new SQLQueryFactory(configuration, dataSource);

// The QBook class will be generated by QueryDSL
QBook book = new QBook();

// Use the defined queryFactory together with the QBook
object to perform a select query
List<String> names = queryFactory.select(book.name)
                 .from(book)
                 .where(book.num_pages.gt(100))
                 .fetch();
```

**Retention Questions**

- What are some commonly used universal database APIs?
- Give an example of a call-level universal API and an embedded one. Which is more in use these days? Why?
- Explain the general set-up of ODBC; which functionality does it expose?
- Explain the general set-up of JDBC; which functionality does it expose?
- Is an embedded API the same as an embedded DBMS? Why/why not?
- What is meant by language-integrated querying?
- List some of the main differences between ADO.NET and its predecessors.

It is worth noting that this approach of providing host language native querying capabilities was originally made popular by Microsoft's LINQ (Language Integrated Query), a .NET framework component adding native querying capabilities to .NET programming languages. This includes a LINQ to SQL subcomponent which converts LINQ expressions to SQL queries, like the Java projects above. Just as with jOOQ and QueryDSL, LINQ to SQL also applies a mapping where database tables, columns, and other schema entities are mapped to classes to enable compile-time type checking and verification. The following code fragment shows a simple LINQ example (in C#):

```
var hugeBooks = from b in books
        where b.NumberOfPages >= 1000
        select b;
foreach (var book in hugeBooks) {
  Console.WriteLine(book.title + " is a huge book");
}
```

## 15.4 Object Persistence and Object-Relational Mapping APIs

So far, we have discussed several universal API technologies that can be used by client applications to access a variety of databases and even other data sources. We observe that many, recent, API technologies such as JDBC and ADO.NET represent database-related entities, such as fields,

**Connections**

Object persistence was already introduced in Chapter 8. In this section we further explore common object persistence APIs.

records, tables, in an object-oriented (OO) fashion, which makes it easy to integrate such entities in host applications already following an OO paradigm, which makes up a large proportion of applications written nowadays.

Instead of representing data-source related entities, such as a DataSet or ResultSet and so on, in a series of objects, one might also wonder if it is possible to approach this task from another angle. That is, we might want to represent domain entities, such as Book, Author, and so on, as plain objects using the representational capabilities and syntax of the programming language at hand. These objects can then be persisted behind the scenes to a database or another data source. It is exactly this approach that is described when we talk about **object persistence**.

Note that language-integrated query technologies (see jOOQ and LINQ in the previous section) apply similar ideas, namely to use the host programming language's validation and type safety checks, and OO structures to express queries directly within the host language environment, without resorting to a pre-compiler or SQL statements expressed as strings. We will see how object persistence APIs go a step further, as they also describe the full business domain (i.e., the definition of data entities) within the host language.

Nevertheless, to allow for efficient querying and retrieval of objects, such entities are frequently mapped to a relational database model using a so-called object-relational mapper (ORM), which we will also discuss in more detail below. It is not strictly necessary to utilize an ORM when utilizing the concept of object persistence (one might just as well serialize objects in plain text, XML files, or an OODBMS), though most APIs tightly couple both concepts as the efficiency and speed of relational DBMSs can then still be leveraged to offer fast object storage, retrieval, and modification, as well as guaranteeing transactional safety over such operations.

### 15.4.1 Object Persistence with Enterprise JavaBeans

Given Java's strong focus on OO programming and early support for strong data access fundamentals (e.g., through JDBC), as well as its focus on enterprise environments, it is no wonder that Java's ecosystem was an early adopter of object persistence, built on top of **Enterprise JavaBeans (EJB)**. A Java Bean (or Bean for short) is Java's term to refer to re-usable, modular, OO software components. Enterprise JavaBeans are "business" components that run within the Java Enterprise Edition (Java EE) platform. Java EE defines an open application model to develop n-tiered business applications, and is composed of several tiers or layers. The "client tier" contains client-side functionality. This can be a "standalone" Java application, a web browser, or a Java applet, which is a piece of Java code running in a web browser. The "web tier" defines web-oriented functionality, which can act as a bridge between the client tier (if the client tier consists of a web browser) and the "business tier", which contains the actual business logic (i.e., the Enterprise JavaBeans). The final "enterprise information system" tier contains the database system and other data stores. Figure 15.11 summarizes Java EE's tiered architecture.

One of the main objectives of the Java EE application model is to establish a clear decoupling between business logic and client applications, hence supporting re-usability and allowing EJB components to be accessed and used by several types of client applications and web services. Note that the Java EE platform also defines interfaces to handle email, XML processing, security aspects, etc., which are not discussed in full here.

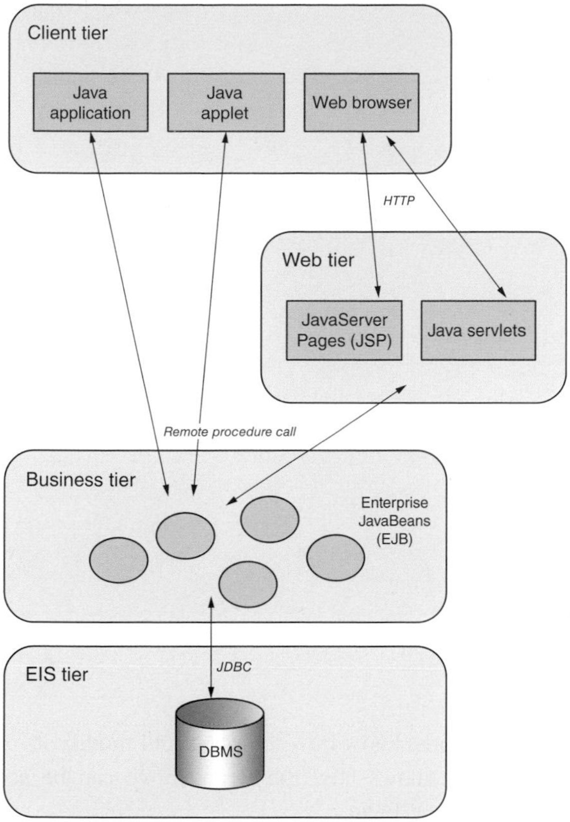


**Figure 15.11** Java EE application model overview.

As was already stated, Enterprise JavaBeans expand the concept of Java Beans, which encapsulate a piece of re-usable, modular logic. Beans are essentially nothing more than a normal Java class definition, following some additional rules. Beans must expose a default constructor without arguments (this makes it easy for outside frameworks to instantiate Beans – see the example below), their class properties must be accessible using getter and setter methods according to a standard naming convention (this allows easy inspection and updating of such properties by outside frameworks), and the class should be serializable, so outside frameworks can reliably store and restore a Bean's state. The following code sample shows a simple Java Bean definition:

```
public class BookBean implements java.io.Serializable {

  private String title = null;
  private int numPages = 0;
  private boolean inStock = false;

  /* Default constructor without arguments */

  public BookBean() {
  }

  /* Getters and setters */

  public String getTitle() {
```

```
        return title;
    }

    public void setTitle(String value) {
        this.title = value;
    }

    public boolean isInStock() {
        return inStock;
    }

    public void setInStock(boolean value) {
        this.inStock = value;
    }

    public int getNumPages() {
        return numPages;
    }

    public void setNumPages(int value) {
        this.numPages = value;
    }
}
```

Once a Java Bean is defined, outside frameworks know how to access and modify its properties. The following JavaServer Page code fragment shows how the Bean above can be accessed to generate an HTML page with information from the Bean.

```
<jsp:useBean id="book" class="BookBean" scope="page"/>

<html>
<body>
Title: <jsp:getProperty name="book" property="title"/><br/>
Still in stock? <jsp:getProperty name="book" property="inStock"/><br/>
</body>
</html>
```

**Drill Down**

JavaServer Pages (JSP) is a Java-based technology to create dynamically generated web pages.

The EJB standard extends the concept of Java Beans to utilize these components in a server environment.

The objective behind EJB is to define enterprise Java Beans that can be easily "plugged into" a server environment to extend its functionality. Enterprise Beans contain modular, re-usable pieces of business logic, such as how to calculate a book's price after applying a discount, to get a list of available books and so on. The following code snippet shows an example of a simple random number generator service enterprise Java Bean:

```
@Stateless
public class RandomNumberGeneratorService {
 private Random rand = new Random();
 public int generateRandomNumber(int min, int max) {
   return rand.nextInt((max - min) + 1) + min;
 }
}
```

Note the use of Java annotations (such as @Stateless) to describe the various EJB-related aspects and metadata of the enterprise Bean. For example, @Stateless indicates that no "conversation" should be kept open with the client application, i.e., that this class is a stateless session Bean, as it will be called later in this chapter.

Other components can then utilize this Bean as follows:

```
public class ServiceTest {
  @EJB // This annotation injects the service bean
  private RandomNumberGeneratorService randService;

  public void testGenerator() {
   int randomNumber = randService.generateRandomNumber(1,3);
   System.out.println("Random number" + randomNumber);
  }
}
```

The initial versions of EJB discriminate between three types of enterprise Beans: session Beans, message-driven Beans, and entity Beans. Session Beans are Beans that perform a task for a client. They represent a transient (hence non-persistent) object that handles part of the business logic of an application. Every instance of a session Bean is bound to a specific client, and – in most cases – has a short-lived timespan. Session Beans can be stateless or stateful. A stateless session Bean does not maintain a conversational state with the client, meaning that when a client invokes a method of a stateless Bean, the Bean's instance variables may contain a state specific to that client, but only for the duration of the invocation. When the method call is finished, the client-specific state is not retained. In a stateful session Bean, the instance variables represent the state of a unique client–Bean conversational session, which is retained for the full duration of the client–Bean interaction. If the client removes the Bean or terminates, the session ends, and the state disappears. Note that the EJB container (i.e., the EJB server managing the EJB components) will often be configured to re-use stateless session Beans over multiple invocations from different clients, instead of destroying and setting up a new stateless session Bean for each call. Even although the latter approach is possible, as stateless session Beans by definition do not assume or keep track of state over separate calls and hence can be removed and re-instantiated at will, keeping them around over multiple calls can easily support many clients or rapid calls. In this way, the overhead induced by new Bean instantiations can be avoided. Stateless session Beans therefore often provide better scalability than their stateful counterparts.

A message-driven Bean – the second enterprise Bean type – allows Java EE applications to process messages in an asynchronous manner. In terms of functionality, message-driven Beans are comparable to stateless session Beans, with the most important difference being that clients access message-driven Beans by sending an asynchronous message, meaning that the client will not block and wait until a reply comes in. This is in contrast to session Beans, which are invoked synchronously through (remote) procedure calls.

Contrary to session Beans, which represent a conversion with a client invoking a certain piece of business logic and are short-lived, entity Beans (the third type of enterprise Beans[6]) are persistent. These Beans represent the OO incarnation of business entities, such as a Book, a Customer, or an Order. Contrary to session Beans, entity Beans are not bound to a specific client, and their information should be retained (i.e., persisted) even after the application is stopped. Two approaches exist to ensure such persistence. The first, called Bean-managed persistence (BMP), leaves the implementation of the actual persistence code up to the programmer of the entity Bean itself, meaning that the Bean implementation will contain code (using JDBC, in most cases) to persist its state into, for instance, a relational database in the EIS tier. However, implementing such code can be a daunting, repetitive task. A second approach, called container-managed persistence (CMP), delegates this responsibility to the EJB container (i.e., the EJB server), which will generate all necessary database calls behind the scenes to retrieve and persist objects. The application programmer can then fully think in terms of objects and does not have to concern him/herself with writing SQL. In addition, it is possible to indicate which fields of the object should not be persisted, as well as how the primary key, forming the unique identifier for an object, should be composed. The following class provides an illustration of an (EJB 2) entity Bean definition using CMP:

```
public abstract BookBean implements javax.ejb.EntityBean {
   // instance fields (by default, these will not be persisted)
   EntityContext ejbContext;
   String thisWillNotBePersisted;

   // container-managed persistent fields are defined as abstract getters and setters
   public abstract void setTitle(String value);
   public abstract String getTitle();
   public abstract void setNumPages(int value);
   public abstract int getNumPages();

   // container-managed relationships
   public abstract void setAuthor(Author value);
   public abstract Author getAuthor();
}
```

This code sample also illustrates another aspect of CMP, namely the possibility to automatically manage relationships between entities, called container-managed relationships (CMR). When using CMR, one-to-one, one-to-many, many-to-one, and many-to-many relationships will be maintained by the container. For instance, the setAuthor method in the example above will be managed so the container updates all necessary foreign key fields, embodying the relationship between books and authors, in the underlying DBMS.

### 15.4.2 Object Persistence with the Java Persistence API

We have discussed a particular version of the EJB standard (EJB 2.0). As practitioners realized that many of the original EJB value propositions felt over-engineered, and simpler enterprise

[6] We discuss entity Beans for the historical perspective and because they make it easier to understand the present-day approaches. However, in recent versions of EJB (from EJB 3.0 onwards), entity Beans were superseded by the Java Persistence API (JPA), which serves a similar purpose, but as a separate specification and not necessarily within an EJB context. JPA is discussed in the next section.

**Table 15.2** Common annotations defined in the Java Persistence API

| Annotation | Description |
|---|---|
| @Entity | Declares a persistent POJO class. |
| @Table | Allows one to explicitly specify the name of the relational table to map the persistent POJO class to. |
| @Column | Allows one to explicitly specify the name of the relational table column. |
| @Id | Maps a persistent POJO class field to a primary key of a relational table. |
| @Transient | Allows one to define POJO class fields that are transient and should not be made persistent. |

frameworks such as Spring (an application framework) and **Hibernate** (to handle object persistence through object-relational mapping) came along, the need to update the EJB specification arose. Accordingly, the EJB 3.0 specification is a radical departure from its predecessors. It is heavily inspired by alternative application frameworks such as Spring in its use of "plain old Java objects" (POJOs), rather than a verbose and at times confusing combination of Java Beans and XML-based configuration files.[7] The **Java Persistence API** then forms the replacement for the entity Beans in EJB 3.0, which were removed altogether from this version of the standard.

**Drill Down**

Gavin King, creator of the Hibernate persistence framework, participated in the EJB 3.0 process and was one of the driving factors behind the new Java Persistence API (JPA).

Instead, the EJB 3.0 specification combines simple POJOs with an exhaustive set of annotations, replacing the verbose, cumbersome XML configuration files.[8] JPA allows POJOs to be easily persisted without requiring the classes to implement any interfaces or methods as the EJB 2.0 CMP specification required. In this way, the strengths of CMP are retained (transparent object persistence through object-relational mapping), but in a much more lightweight fashion.

Note that JPA itself is just a specification defining a set of interfaces and annotations, and hence requires an implementation to perform any actual persistence. Currently, most of the persistence vendors have released implementations of JPA, confirming its adoption, including Hibernate (now part of Red Hat), TopLink (Oracle), Kodo JDO (also by Oracle), Cocobase, and JPOX.

In this section we take a closer look at JPA. As said, JPA defines a set of annotations that adds persistence-aware functionality to any plain Java object. Table 15.2 enumerates some common annotations.

We will use these in a simple code example illustrating an application with two class definitions representing entities:

```
import java.util.List;
import javax.persistence.*;

@Entity // Book is an entity mapped to a table
@Table
```

[7] Many of EJB 2.0's components, including entity Beans, depend on such configuration files, for instance to determine how entity Beans are related to one another, though we have left out the details as we wish to focus on the newer EJB 3.0 (and beyond) standard.

[8] JPA still allows use of XML files to specify how Java classes map to a relational database, though using annotations is a much more fluid and programmer-friendly way to do so.

```
public class Book {

     @Id // Use id as the primary key
     // Generate id values automatically:
     @GeneratedValue(strategy = GenerationType.AUTO)
     private int id;
     private String title;

     // Define a many-to-many relation
     @ManyToMany(cascade = {CascadeType.ALL})
     private List<Author> authors;

     public Book(String title) {
          setTitle(title);
     }

     public String getTitle() {
          return title;
     }

     public void setTitle(String title) {
          this.title = title;
     }

     public List<Author> getAuthors() {
          return authors;
     }

     public void setAuthors(List<Author> authors) {
          this.authors = authors;
     }

     public String toString() {
          String r = "Book [id=" + id + ", title=" + title + "] ";
          for (Author a : getAuthors()) {
               r += "\nBy author: "+a.toString();
          }
          return r;
     }
}
```

```
import java.util.List;
import javax.persistence.*;

@Entity
@Table
public class Author {

     @Id
     @GeneratedValue(strategy = GenerationType.AUTO)
```

```
        private int id;
        private String name;

        // Many-to-many relation in the other direction
        @ManyToMany(cascade = {CascadeType.ALL})
        private List<Book> books;

        public Author(String name) {
              setName(name);
        }

        public String getName() {
              return name;
        }

        public void setName(String name) {
              this.name = name;
        }

        public List<Book> getBooks() {
              return books;
        }

        public void setBooks(List<Book> books) {
              this.books = books;
        }

        public String toString() {
              return "Author [id=" + id + ", name=" + name + "]";
        }
  }
```

The simplicity of JPA should become immediately apparent here. By using a handful of annotations, we have specified two persistable entities, linked with each other through a many-to-many relation. Hibernate and other JPA implementations will be smart enough to handle the setting up of an intermediate cross-table for us.

Next, we still use a single "persistence.xml" XML file to specify global configuration options. We have set up this example to use Hibernate (one of the popular implementations of the JPA standard) together with Derby, an embedded DBMS written in Java itself, created in memory for the purpose of this example:

```
<persistence xmlns:xsi="http://www.w3.org/2001/XMLSchema-instance"
        xsi:schemaLocation="http://java.sun.com/xml/ns/persistence/
        persistence_2_0.xsd"
        version="2.0" xmlns="http://java.sun.com/xml/ns/persistence">

<persistence-unit name="app">
 <!-- We have the following persistable classes: -->
 <class>Book</class>
 <class>Author</class>
```

```
  <!-- Settings to connect to the database -->
  <properties>
   <property name="hibernate.archive.autodetection" value="class" />
   <property name="hibernate.connection.driver_class"
        value="org.apache.derby.jdbc.EmbeddedDriver" />
   <property name="hibernate.connection.url"
        value="jdbc:derby:memory:myDB;create=true" />
   <property name="hibernate.show_sql" value="true" />
   <property name="hibernate.flushMode" value="FLUSH_AUTO" />
   <property name="hibernate.hbm2ddl.auto" value="create" />
  </properties>

 </persistence-unit>
 </persistence>
```

Next, a simple test class is created in which we set up an EntityManager object and insert some newly created objects. The EntityManager is responsible to create and remove persistent entity instances (i.e., objects):

```
import java.util.ArrayList;
import javax.persistence.*;

public class Test {

       public static void main(String[] args) {

              EntityManagerFactory emfactory =
                    Persistence.createEntityManagerFactory("app");

              EntityManager entitymanager = emfactory.createEntityManager();
              entitymanager.getTransaction().begin();

              final Author author1 = new Author("Seppe vanden Broucke");
              final Author author2 = new Author("Wilfried Lemahieu");
              final Author author3 = new Author("Bart Baesens");
              final Book book = new Book("My first book");

              book.setAuthors(new ArrayList<Author>(){{
                    this.add(author1);
                    this.add(author2);
              }});

              // Persist the book object, the first two authors will be
              // persisted as well as they are linked to the book
              entitymanager.persist(book);
              entitymanager.getTransaction().commit();

              System.out.println(book);

              // Now persist author3 as well
              entitymanager.persist(author3);
```

```
                entitymanager.close();
                emfactory.close();
        }
}
```

When the above is run, the following output appears:

```
Hibernate: create table Author (id integer not null, name varchar(255),
primary key (id))
Hibernate: create table Author_Book (Author_id integer not null, books_id
integer not null)
Hibernate: create table Book (id integer not null, title varchar(255),
primary key (id))
Hibernate: create table Book_Author (Book_id integer not null, authors_id
integer not null)
Hibernate: alter table Author_Book add constraint FK3wjtcus6sftdj8dfvthui6335
foreign key (books_id) references Book
Hibernate: alter table Author_Book add constraint FKo3f90h3ibr9jtq0u93mjgi5qd
foreign key (Author_id) references Author
Hibernate: alter table Book_Author add constraint FKt42qaxhbq87yfijncjfrs5ukc
foreign key (authors_id) references Author
Hibernate: alter table Book_Author add constraint FKsbb54ii8mmfvh6h2lr0vf2r7f
foreign key (Book_id) references Book

Hibernate: values next value for hibernate_sequence
Hibernate: values next value for hibernate_sequence
Hibernate: insert into Book (title, id) values (?, ?)
Hibernate: insert into Author (name, id) values (?, ?)
Hibernate: insert into Book_Author (Book_id, authors_id) values (?, ?)

Book [ id=1, title=My first book]
By author: Author [ id=0, name=Seppe vanden Broucke]
Author [ id=1, name=Wilfried Lemahieu]
Hibernate: values next value for hibernate_sequence
Author [ id=2, name=Bart Baesens]

Hibernate: insert into Author (name, id) values (?, ?)
```

Notice how Hibernate automatically creates our table definitions, and persists the objects.

So far, we have seen how JPA supports modification and persistence of objects, but the standard naturally also includes functionality to query and retrieve stored entities, also through the EntityManager. The EntityManager.find method is used to look up entities in the data store by the entity's primary key:

```
entitymanager.find(Author.class, 2)
```

The EntityManager.createQuery method can be used to query the datastore using Java Persistence query language queries:

```
entitymanager.createQuery(
        "SELECT c FROM Author c WHERE c.name LIKE :authName")
                    .setParameter("authName", "%vanden%")
                    .setMaxResults(10)
                    .getResultList()
```

The JPA query language (JPQL) closely resembles SQL, including support for SELECT, UPDATE, and DELETE statements (with FROM, WHERE, GROUP BY, HAVING, ORDER BY, and JOIN clauses). However, JPQL is simpler than SQL – it does not, for instance, support UNION, INTERSECT, and EXCEPT clauses. Why, then, the need for JPQL? The reason has to do with portability. Contrary to earlier approaches and universal APIs, where it was – in theory – easy to migrate an application to a different DBMS, differences in SQL support might still cause a client application to fail in new DBMS environments. JPQL tries to prevent this by inserting itself as a more pure, vendor-agnostic SQL, and will translate JPQL queries to appropriate SQL statements. Note that it is also still possible to use raw SQL statements should you wish to do so, using the createNativeQuery method:

```
entitymanager.createNativeQuery(
     "SELECT * FROM Author",
     Author.class).getResultList();
```

Like call-level APIs discussed earlier, JPA does not support compile-time checking and validation of queries. In other words, the following code will compile fine:

```
entitymanager.createQuery(
        "SELECT c FROM Author c WHERE c.INVALID LIKE :authName")
                    .setParameter("authName", 2)
                    .setMaxResults(10)
                    .getResultList()
```

but will spawn a runtime error once the application is run:

```
Exception in thread "main" java.lang.IllegalArgumentException:
org.hibernate.QueryException: could not resolve property: INVALID of:
Author [ SELECT c FROM Author c WHERE c.INVALID LIKE :authName]
```

A case can still be made for language-integrated query technologies as discussed earlier in this chapter. Note that QueryDSL, a Java project aiming to enrich Java with language-integrated querying capability (see above), is also able to work together with JPA:

```
JPQLQuery query = new JPAQuery(entityManager);

QAuthor author = QAuthor.author;

Author seppe = query.from(author)
  .where(author.name.eq("Seppe vanden Broucke"))
  .uniqueResult(author);
```

### 15.4.3 Object Persistence with Java Data Objects

**Connections**

The ODMG standard, which evolved from a standard for OODBMSs to a specification for object persistence, was discussed in Chapter 8.

Just as JPA, the **Java Data Objects (JDO)** API also arose from the failed adoption of the ODMG standard and the desire to "break out" object persistence capabilities from EJB. Unlike JPA, which is primarily targeted toward relational DBMS data stores, JDO is agnostic to the technology of the data store used.[9] To illustrate this, we will give an example of how JDO can be used to work with an OODBMS,[10] ObjectDB in this case.

When using JDO, the first step is to define the properties to connect to the underlying data store using a Properties object as follows (note that here too, an XML file can be used to initialize JDO):

```
Properties props = new Properties();
props.setProperty("javax.jdo.PersistenceManagerFactoryClass", "
        com.objectdb.jdo.PMF");
props.setProperty("javax.jdo.option.ConnectionURL",
        "objectdb://localhost/employee.odb");
props.setProperty("javax.jdo.option.ConnectionUserName", "root");
props.setProperty("javax.jdo.option.ConnectionPassword", "mypassword123");
```

Here you can see we connect to an underlying ObjectDB OODBMS. In the event that it does not exist yet, it will be created as soon as we start making objects persistent. A JDO application then continues by creating a PersistenceManager object using the PersistenceManagerFactory class as follows:

```
PersistenceManagerFactory pmf =
     JDOHelper.getPersistenceManagerFactory(props);
PersistenceManager pm = pmf.getPersistenceManager();
```

The PersistenceManager object will supervise the persistence, update, deletion, and retrieval of objects from the underlying data store.

Earlier versions of JDO used XML metadata files stored at predefined locations to specify the persistence options. Newer versions support Java annotations whereby Java classes can be annotated to further fine-tune their persistence options, similarly as done by JPA. JDO defines the @Persistent and @NotPersistent annotations to indicate which fields are persistent, whereas the @PrimaryKey annotation can be used to indicate the primary key. Consider the following example to illustrate this:

```
import java.util.Date;
import java.time.*;
import javax.jdo.annotations.IdGeneratorStrategy;
import javax.jdo.annotations.PersistenceCapable;
import javax.jdo.annotations.Persistent;
import javax.jdo.annotations.PrimaryKey;
```

[9] This being said, several vendors exist that provide JPA support to access non-relational DBMSs as well, such as ObjectDB (which implements an OODBMS on top of both the JPA and JDO APIs).

[10] See http://db.apache.org/jdo/index.html for more details about the JDO specification.

```
@PersistenceCapable
public class Employee {
  @PrimaryKey
  @Persistent(valueStrategy = IdGeneratorStrategy.IDENTITY)
  private long key;

  @Persistent
  private String firstName;

  @Persistent
  private String lastName;

  @Persistent
  private Date birthDate;
  private int age; // This attribute will not be persisted

  public Employee(String firstName, String lastName, Date birthDate) {
    this.firstName = firstName;
    this.lastName = lastName;
    setBirthDate(birthDate);
  }

  public Key getKey() {
    return key;
  }

  public String getFirstName() {
    return firstName;
  }

  public void setFirstName(String firstName) {
    this.firstName = firstName;
  }

  public String getLastName() {
    return lastName;
  }

  public void setLastName(String lastName) {
    this.lastName = lastName;
  }

  public Date getBirthDate() {
    return birthDate;
  }

  public void setBirthDate(Date birthDate) {
    this.birthDate = birthDate;
    LocalDate today = LocalDate.now();
    LocalDate birthday = birthDate.toInstant()
                            .atZone(ZoneId.systemDefault()).toLocalDate();
    Period p = Period.between(birthday, today);
```

```
        this.age = p.getYears();
    }

    public int getAge() {
        return age;
    }
}
```

The Java class definition starts by importing all the necessary classes and definitions including the JDO classes provided by the ObjectDB vendor and packaged in javax.jdo. The Employee class has four variables that will be persisted: a unique key, the firstName, the lastName, and the birth date, as well as one variable that will not (the age, which can be calculated from the birth date and hence does not need to be persisted). To implement the concept of encapsulation, the Employee class also has getter and setter methods for each of these variables. Note that JDO will not use these, but your application obviously can. The property valueStrategy = IdGeneratorStrategy.IDENTITY specifies that the next value of the key will automatically be created by the system, whereby uniqueness is ensured.

The below example illustrates how an Employee object can be made persistent in the underlying data store. We first initiate a transaction by creating a Transaction object. The makePersistent method can then be called on the Employee object to make it persistent. JDO implements persistence by reachability, so if the Employee object refers to other objects then those will be made persistent as well. The makePersistent method call is synchronous, meaning that the execution of the application will halt until the object(s) is/are saved and any accompanying data store indexes updated. JDO also includes a method makePersistentAll to save multiple objects (e.g., from a collection).

```
Transaction tx = pm.currentTransaction();
try {
    tx.begin();
    Employee myEmp = new Employee(
            "Bart","Baesens", new Date(1975, 2, 27));
    pm.makePersistent(myEmp);
    tx.commit();
} catch (Exception e) {}
finally {
    if (tx.isActive()) {
        tx.rollback();
    }
    pm.close();
}
```

Once created and stored, objects can be queried in various ways. A first, straightforward, way is to retrieve the entire extent or, in other words, all objects of a class. This can be done as follows:

```
Extent e = pm.getExtent(Employee.class, true);
Iterator iter = e.iterator();
while (iter.hasNext()){
    Employee myEmp = (Employee) iter.next();
    System.out.println("First name:" + myEmp.getFirstName());
}
```

The method getExtent is called on the PersistenceManager object. The first parameter indicates the class for which we would like to retrieve the objects (Employee.class in our case). The second parameter is a Boolean, indicating whether the system should also retrieve any objects of the subclasses. In other words, if we would have a subclass Manager of Employee, then the method call pm.getExtent(Employee.class, true) would also retrieve all Manager objects.

Like JPA, JDO comes with a query language called JDOQL or Java Data Objects Query Language. It basically supports two types of queries: declarative and single-string queries. A declarative query can be defined as follows:

```
Query q = pm.newQuery(Employee.class, "lastName == last_name");
q.declareParameters("string last_name");
List results = (List) q.execute("Smith");
```

This query retrieves all the employee objects for which the lastName is Smith. The results are stored in a list object that can then be further processed by the Java application.

We can also formulate this query as a single-string query, as follows:

```
Query q = pm.newQuery(
  "SELECT FROM Employee WHERE lastName == last_name" +
  " PARAMETERS string last_name");
List results = (List) q.execute("Smith");
```

### 15.4.4 Object Persistence in Other Host Languages

Java is not the only programming language whose ecosystem offers object persistence APIs through the concept of ORM. The Ruby on Rails ecosystem has made heavy use of the ActiveRecord library, and – according to some – was one of the driving factors behind the uptake of ORM libraries. The .NET framework also comes with the Entity Framework (EF), an object-relational mapper that enables .NET developers to work with relational data using domain-specific objects, i.e., comparable with JPA. The following code snippet shows the EF through a brief example, using the so-called “Code-First” approach (where the program source is the main authority for the definition of entity types, rather than an existing database):

```
public class Book
{
  public Book() {
  }
  public int BookId { get; set; }
  public string BookTitle { get; set; }
  public Author Author { get; set; }
}

public class Author
{
  public Author() {
  }
  public int AuthorId { get; set; }
```

```
    public string AuthorName { get; set; }
    // One-to-many books:
    public ICollection<Book> Books { get; set; }
}
```

After creating the entities (here as plain and simple C# class definitions), EF's Code-First approach also requires the definition of a "context class", a class that will serve as the coordinator for our data model. The context class should extend DbContext and expose DbSet properties for the types that you want to be part of the model, e.g., Book and Author in our example:

```
namespace EF_Example
{
    public class ExampleContext: DbContext
    {
        public ExampleContext(): base()
        {
        }
        public DbSet<Book> Books { get; set; }
        public DbSet<Author> Authors { get; set; }
    }
}
```

We can now create a simple program using our entities as follows:

```
class Program
{
    static void Main(string[] args)
    {
        using (var ctx = ExampleContext())
        {
            Author a = new Author() { AuthorName = "New Author" };
            Books b = new Book() { BookTitle = "New Book", Author = a };
            ctx.Books.Add(b); // No need to explicitly add the author
            // as it is linked to the book, it will be persisted as well
            ctx.SaveChanges();
            //...
        }
    }
}
```

It is worth noting that the EF is even less verbose than the JPA standard. Behind the scenes, the EF will create a database schema with two tables, and set up primary keys, foreign keys, and fields with appropriate data types. This seems like magic at first, were it not that the EF relies on several coding conventions to pull this off (rather than a set of annotations as in JPA). For instance, a primary key should be defined as a class field name Id or <class name>Id, such as "BookId" and "AuthorId" in the example above.

The following example shows an equivalent application in Python using the SQLAlchemy library, showing a many-to-many relation. Here, the many-to-many relation requires either the explicit definition of a separate association class, or a reference to a table in the DBMS without an associated class, as done in the example below:

```
from sqlalchemy import Table, Column, String, Integer, ForeignKey
from sqlalchemy.orm import relationship, backref
from sqlalchemy.ext.declarative import declarative_base
from sqlalchemy import create_engine
from sqlalchemy.orm import sessionmaker

Base = declarative_base()

book_author_table = Table('book_author', Base.metadata,
  Column('book_id', Integer, ForeignKey('books.id')),
  Column('author_id', Integer, ForeignKey('authors.id'))
)

class Book(Base):
  __tablename__ = 'books'
  id = Column(Integer, primary_key=True)
  title = Column(String)
  authors = relationship("Author",
    secondary=book_author_table,
    back_populates="books")

  def __repr__(self):
    return '[ Book: {} by {}] '.format(self.title, self.authors)

class Author(Base):
  __tablename__ = 'authors'
  id = Column(Integer, primary_key=True)
  name = Column(String)
  books = relationship("Book",
   secondary=book_author_table,
   back_populates="authors")

  def __repr__(self):
   return '[ Author: {}] '.format(self.name)

if __name__ == '__main__':
  engine = create_engine('sqlite://')
  session_maker = sessionmaker()
  session_maker.configure(bind=engine)
  session = session_maker()
  Base.metadata.create_all(engine)

  book1 = Book(title='My First Book')
  book2 = Book(title='My Second Book')
  author1 = Author(name='Seppe vanden Broucke')
  author2 = Author(name='Wilfried Lemahieu')
  author3 = Author(name='Bart Baesens')
```

```
  book1.authors.append(author1)
  book2.authors.append(author2)
  author3.books.append(book2)

  session.add_all([ book1, book2, author1, author2, author3] )
  session.flush() # Persist to DB

  query = session.query(Author).filter(Author.name.like('%vanden%'))
  for author in query:
    print(author)
    print(author.books)
```

Running this example will output:

```
[ Author: Seppe vanden Broucke]
[[ Book: My First Book by [[ Author: Seppe vanden Broucke]]]]
```

Note that SQLAlchemy is an exhaustive library containing support for complex relations, the possibility to perform a rawer ORM starting from an existing database schema, the possibility to allow for automatic DBMS schema migrations,[11] and more. The library is more comprehensive than we can possibly describe here, and remains a best-in-class example for solid object persistence and ORM support.

Finally, the following code fragment shows the same set-up using the Python Peewee library:

```
from peewee import *
from playhouse.fields import ManyToManyField

db = SqliteDatabase('')

class BaseModel(Model):
  class Meta:
    database = db

class Book(BaseModel):
  title = CharField()

  def __repr__(self):
    return '[ Book: {} by {}] '.format(self.title, [ a for a in self.authors] )

class Author(BaseModel):
  name = CharField()
  books = ManyToManyField(Book, related_name='authors')

  def __repr__(self):
    return '[ Author: {}] '.format(self.name)

BookAuthor = Author.books.get_through_model()
```

[11] Schema migration in the context of object persistence and ORM becomes important once programmers start changing entity class definitions (e.g., adding or removing fields) and want the ORM library to automatically adjust the DBMS schema to reflect these changes, without – obviously – starting from scratch and completely emptying the existing database. This is a complex task, even more so since different DBMS vendors require different approaches. Most ORM libraries have trouble with this, including the Hibernate framework, which does try to appeal to more complex enterprise environments where schema-changes are not uncommon.

```
if __name__ == '__main__':
  db.create_tables([ Book, Author, BookAuthor] )

  book1 = Book.create(title='My First Book')
  book2 = Book.create(title='My Second Book')
  author1 = Author.create(name='Seppe vanden Broucke')
  author2 = Author.create(name='Wilfried Lemahieu')
  author3 = Author.create(name='Bart Baesens')

  book1.authors.add(author1)
  book2.authors.add(author2)
  author3.books.add(book2)

  authors = Author.select().where(Author.name.
  contains('vanden'))

  for author in authors:
    print(author)
     for book in author.books:
       print(book)
```

### Retention Questions

- What is meant by object persistence and object-relational mapping?
- Describe the Java Persistence API and its relationship with Enterprise JavaBeans.
- What is the difference between the Java Persistence API and Java Data Objects?

## 15.5 Database API Summary

We have now seen how client applications that wish to utilize the services provided by a DBMS can use a wide range of database APIs to access and query a DBMS. We have discussed various types of universal database APIs, as well as APIs that aim to hide underlying DBMS and SQL aspects by representing domain entities as plain objects using the programming language representational capabilities and syntax, which can then be persisted behind the scenes to a database (or another data source).

The table in the comparison box lists the technologies discussed in a summarizing overview with their main characteristics.

### Retention Questions

- Contrast the universal APIs discussed in this chapter. Are they embedded or call-level? Which types of databases do they target, do they support early or late binding? What do they expose in the host programming language?

### Comparison Box

| Technology | Embedded or call-level | Early or late binding | Objects in host programming language represent | Data sources | Other |
|---|---|---|---|---|---|
| **ODBC** | Call-level | Late binding, though prepared SQL statements possible as well as calling stored procedures | A resultset with rows of fields | Mainly relational databases, though other structured tabular sources possible as well | Microsoft-based technology, not object-oriented, mostly outdated but still in wide use |

(cont.)

| Technology | Embedded or call-level | Early or late binding | Objects in host programming language represent | Data sources | Other |
|---|---|---|---|---|---|
| **JDBC** | Call-level | Late binding, though prepared SQL statements possible as well as calling stored procedures | A resultset with rows of fields | Mainly relational databases, though other structured tabular sources possible as well | Java-based technology, portable, still in wide use |
| **SQLJ** | Embedded | Early binding | A resultset with rows of fields | Relational databases supporting SQL | Java-based technology, uses a pre-compiler, mostly outdated |
| **Language-integrated Query Technologies** | Use an underlying call-level API | Use an underlying late-binding API | A resultset with rows of fields, sometimes converted to a plain collection of objects representing entities | Relational databases supporting SQL or other data sources | Examples: jOOQ and LINQ, work together with another API to convert expressions to SQL |
| **OLE DB and ADO** | Call-level | Late binding, though prepared SQL statements possible as well as calling stored procedures | A resultset with rows of fields | Mainly relational databases, though other structured tabular sources possible as well | Microsoft-based technology, backward compatible with ODBC, mostly outdated |
| **ADO.NET** | Call-level | Late binding, though prepared SQL statements possible as well as calling stored procedures | A resultset with rows of fields provided by a DataReader, or a DataSet: a collection of tables, rows, and fields, retrieved and stored by DataAdapters | Various data sources | Microsoft-based technology, backward compatible with ODBC and OLE DB, disconnected approach with DataSet |
| **Enterprise JavaBeans (EJB 2.0)** | Uses an underlying call-level API | Uses an underlying late-binding API | Java entity Beans as the main representation | Mainly relational databases, though other structured tabular sources possible as well | Java-based technology, works together with another API to convert expressions to SQL |
| **Java Persistence API (JPA in EJB 3.0)** | Uses an underlying call-level API | Uses an underlying late-binding API | Plain Java objects as the main representation | Mainly relational databases, though other structured tabular sources possible as well | Java-based technology, works together with another API to convert expressions to SQL |
| **Java Data Objects (JDO)** | Uses an underlying call-level API | Uses an underlying late-binding API | Plain Java objects as the main representation | Various data sources | Java-based technology |
| **ORM APIs (ActiveRecord, Entity Framework, SQL Alchemy)** | Use an underlying call-level API | Use an underlying late-binding API | Plain objects defined in the programming language as the main representation | Relational databases | Various implementations available for each programming language |

## 15.6 Database Access in the World Wide Web

Thanks to the internet, the situation has arisen that the world's information has become globally accessible through one, universal client application: the web browser. Originally, web browsers could only retrieve HTML documents from web servers and display those, but with a growing demand for more responsive, richer web applications, the capabilities of browsers have grown as well, with the web-first approach being very engrained nowadays.

**Drill Down**

A nice illustration of the omnipresence of web-based computing is that companies such as Google are distributing an operating system (ChromeOS) which directly boots into a web browser as a computing environment, without any native applications.

Naturally, the growing presence and capabilities of the internet have an impact on DBMSs. In the previous sections, it was already seen how Java EE and other n-tiered system architectures make the difference between the client, web, application, and DBMS tier. In this section, we take a closer look at some web technologies and how they interact with DBMS systems.

### 15.6.1 Introduction: the Original Web Server

As an introduction, let us first consider the most basic format by which a web browser can interact with a web server. In this most basic form, a web browser will send HTTP (HyperText Transfer Protocol) requests to a web server, which will reply with the content corresponding with the URL (the Uniform Resource Locator) the client requested. To allow for basic markup and layout aspects, this content is oftentimes formatted using HTML (HyperText Markup Language), though other content types can be requested and retrieved as well, such as XML, JSON, YAML, plain text, or even multimedia formats. Figure 15.12 illustrates this basic web client–server set-up.

### 15.6.2 The Common Gateway Interface: Toward Dynamic Web Pages

Originally, the main goal of the HTTP web browser–server set-up was to retrieve and display static documents. However, it rapidly became clear there was a need to access dynamic documents and

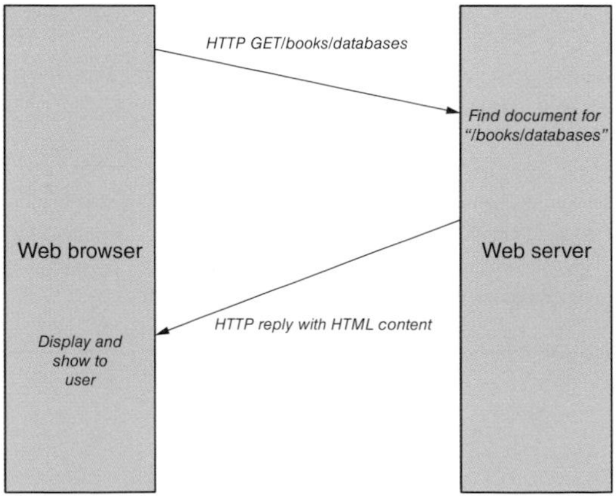


**Figure 15.12** A simple interaction between a web browser and server.

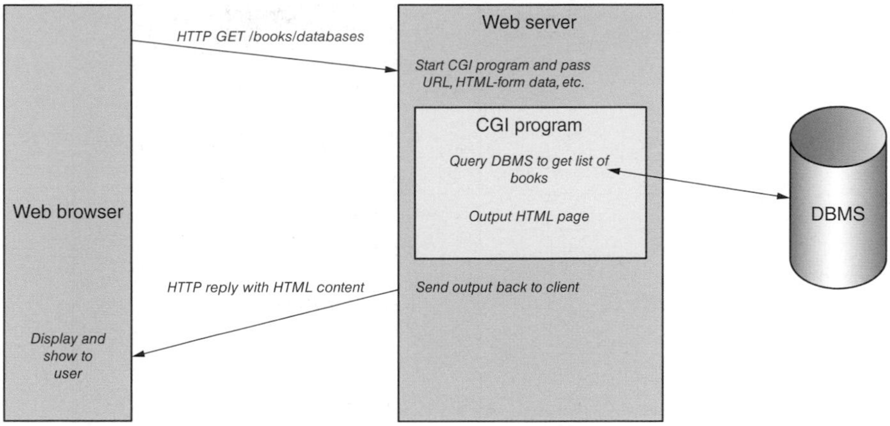


**Figure 15.13** Illustration of CGI.

visualize them in a web browser. For instance, when a user accesses the URL "/books/databases", we might wish for the web server to construct an HTML document "on-the-fly", performing a database query to get a list of currently available books in the category "databases", perhaps ranking them by their release date as well. Since it would be unwieldy to manually edit HTML documents every time a book gets added, is out of stock, or a ranking changes, the need for the dynamic construction of such documents becomes clear.

The **common gateway interface (CGI)** was proposed as one of the first technologies to construct dynamic pages. When a client now requests a URL, a program is started on the web server that receives the requested URL as well as several other contextual variables (e.g., the IP address of the client), and is responsible for generating the content (e.g., an HTML page) that will be sent to the client. CGI also allows for a first, basic form of interactivity, by means of so-called HTML Forms. These are created as part of the HTML markup and displayed to the user in the web browser (think of a username/password form on various websites, for instance, or a search field), which can then be submitted to a specific URL. The values filled in by the user will then be passed to the CGI program, which can use these values as parameters when querying the database (e.g., to retrieve all books by a certain author). The CGI program will then generate appropriate output (e.g., an HTML page containing a list of retrieved books).

Since CGI programs can be written in virtually any language, interpreted and easy-to-use languages such as Perl quickly became popular to implement CGI programs in. The popularity of CGI and dynamic web pages also led to the creation of PHP (PHP Hypertext Preprocessor[12]), which was and still is popular in the open-source community. PHP was meant to be used as a web-focused CGI "glue" language, as it made a series of common tasks, such as connecting to databases (using both proprietary APIs and universal APIs such as ODBC), working with received HTML Form data, and formatting HTML output, easy and programmer-friendly. Figure 15.13 illustrates the basic workings of CGI, with a DBMS in the back-end (note this can hence be considered as an n-tiered set-up).

[12] PHP is indeed the abbreviation of "PHP: Hypertext Preprocessor" and is therefore a recursive abbreviation. It does not get any nerdier than that.

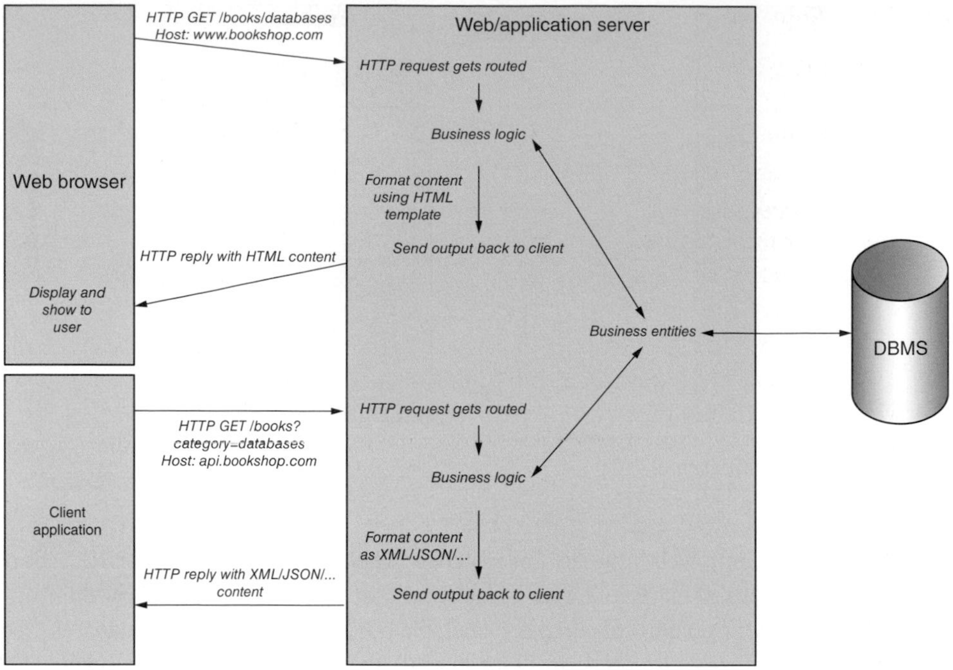


**Figure 15.14** Illustration of HTTP as the lingua franca for web browsers and other client applications.

The basic idea behind CGI still forms the basis for interactivity and dynamic documents found on the web today, though the actual implementation has changed and is now more flexible and efficient. In the original CGI implementation, every request from a client would lead to a new process being spawned, which negatively impacts scalability, and takes a high toll on system resources. Therefore, newer CGI-derived technologies (such as fastCGI) have been proposed over the years, as well as web servers that directly integrate the possibility to deliver dynamic web pages, without having to resort to external programs. Since the web server is a continuously running, threaded program capable of handling multiple simultaneous connections, it might just as well handle the creation of dynamic pages, so the reasoning goes.

This line of thinking was the basis behind JSP (JavaServer Pages), ASP (Active Server Pages), and ASP.NET. In many cases, the web server then actually becomes the "application server", as the web server is now the central entity handling business logic and business entity management, with HTTP as the main language spoken between the client and the server. This client will be a web browser in most cases, though HTTP is also rapidly replacing older remote protocols such as RMI, CORBA, and DCOM[13] to become the *lingua franca* of the net, which is made evident by the number of APIs offered by Google, Amazon, Facebook, and many others built on top of HTTP (these are moving away from the decoupled web and application tiers proposed by, e.g., the Java EE application model). Figure 15.14 illustrates this concept: a web application is responsible for the business logic, which interacts with business entities which in turn are persisted in a DBMS.

[13] These are all protocols to "remotely" invoke functionality, among other things, for a client to call on the functionality of an application server.

### 15.6.3 Client-Side Scripting: The Desire for a Richer Web

The HTTP protocol, with HTML pages, is limited regarding the interfaces that can be shown to end-users. The HTTP protocol relies heavily on repeated request–reply messages, whereas HTML only provides limited support for designing good-looking, fluid websites (HTML Form elements are relatively basic). This is less of a problem if the web content consists of only static pages, but it is an issue if the web browser is the client in an interactive database session. As such, the need for more support for dynamic, interactive elements on the side of the web browser also quickly arose, with various vendors such as Netscape and Microsoft rising to the occasion to propose **client-side scripting** languages such as JavaScript, VBScript, and JScript. These scripts are embedded inside HTML documents and interpreted and run by the web browser, which can then use these to flavor web pages shown to the user. A few simple examples can illustrate this: imagine a web page on which a user is asked to enter a telephone number in an input field. As HTML only supports[14] basic input fields, a round-trip to the web server must be made to check whether the formatting of the phone number is correct. If it is not, the web server shows the same page to the user again, with an error message, and is hopefully also kind enough to retain the values you might have entered in other fields to avoid having to fill in the whole form again – a burden on both the programmer and the end-user (this is why some web forms are so annoying). Also, the form suddenly "feels" like a slow web form, as a visible "refresh" of the page occurs once the user pushes the submit button and the server takes some time to process the HTTP request and send a reply, which the browser can then draw up again. By incorporating some client code in the web page, the execution of the phone form field validation check can be performed by the web browser itself, which can show a friendly error message while the user is filling in the form, only enabling the submit button when everything looks okay.[15]

The adoption of client-side scripting languages was – initially, at least – hampered by the different languages available, which all received different levels of support from different browser vendors, often even between different versions of a browser of the same vendor, making it hard for developers to pick a single language that would work reliably in all browsers. At the same time, client-side scripting languages could only go so far to enhance the experience of end-users, as their functionality was still inherently bound to the markup and layout capabilities of HTML. Another type of client-side program started to appear; these basically inject themselves into the web browser and then take over the complete functionality. Java's Applet technology, Microsoft's ActiveX controls, Windows Forms, and Adobe's Flash are all examples of such client-side plugins that were popular at one point in time.

Let us illustrate this system using **Java applets**. An "applet" is a normal Java program that runs in a special so-called sandbox, stripping away many permissions a normal Java program would have (such as full access to the local filesystem, for instance). It is started as follows: first, a browser requests a URL from a web server, which answers with an HTML document (which can be static) containing a special tag referring to the location of the packaged applet (another URL). A third-party plugin installed in the web browser knows how to interpret this tag, and will download the applet

[14] Though support for richer HTML forms is being proposed by standard bodies and being adopted by web browser vendors.

[15] This also means that we actually trust the client to perform this validation, which is a dangerous assumption to make as web browsers might have client-side scripting disabled or a malicious entity might try to send form details while forcefully ignoring client-side checks. Hence, client-side scripting is fine to enhance user experience, but does not resolve the programmer of the burden to perform an additional check on the server once data are received.

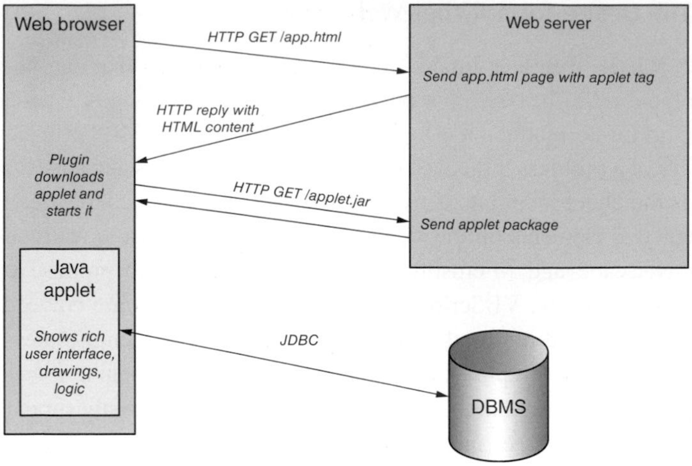


**Figure 15.15** Illustration of a Java applet directly accessing a DBMS.

package and start it. From that moment, the applet handles the full user interface, with (optionally) business logic and database access. Figure 15.15 illustrates this.

Remember that we have also seen when discussing Java's EE stack how applets can – instead of making a direct database connection as shown here – interact with Enterprise JavaBeans instead. Other equivalent technologies have similar set-ups. In general, a direct connection to the database from the client application is not recommended, as malicious entities might be able to reverse engineer the client application to try to gain access to the database and execute malicious queries.

## 15.6.4 JavaScript as a Platform

In recent years, client-side plugins such as applets, Flash, and ActiveX have mostly been pushed aside. The reasons for this are many: they require the installation of a separate plugin that might not be available for every browser or platform, they were confronted with several security issues over the years (even applets, which run in a sandboxed environment), they don't work well on mobile platforms (which are used by more and more web users), and standards such as HTML and CSS (Cascading Style Sheets), together with JavaScript, have evolved to the point that all major browser vendors support a solid, common stack, causing **JavaScript** to re-arise as the most popular choice for enriching web pages. JavaScript (not to be confused with Java) is a programming language originally meant to be embedded in web pages and executed by the web browser to enhance the user experience on a particular web page. As a simple example, think of filling out a web form where some validation (e.g., to check if all fields have been filled in) can be performed by the web browser (running a piece of JavaScript code) before having to send the form to the web server and incur additional waiting time for the next page to come in, as explained before.

JavaScript has seen a sudden increase in popularity in recent years. It can be argued that the main reason for the re-adoption of JavaScript was the rising usage of AJAX-based development techniques. **AJAX (Asynchronous JavaScript and XML)** was born as an ActiveX component, developed by Microsoft, but was rapidly implemented by other browser vendors as the "XMLHttpRequest" JavaScript object, originally created to perform asynchronous calls to URLs in the background with the expectation to receive back XML-formatted data. The utility of performing background HTTP requests remained largely unused until it started appearing in several

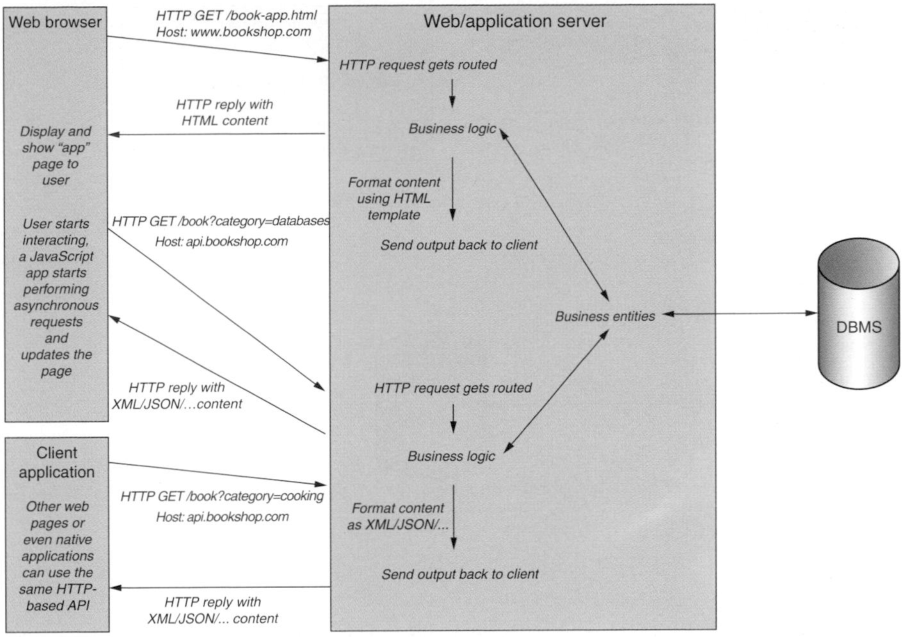


**Figure 15.16** Illustration of a rich JavaScript-based web application.

web apps, most notable Gmail in 2004 and Google Maps in 2005, using it to dynamically fetch updates from a web server to update parts of a web page without having to perform a complete new request, transmitting and redrawing the whole page. The technique was made popular thanks to JavaScript libraries, which aim to offer a set of functionalities that would work on all browsers, including the ability to perform asynchronous, background HTTP requests.

This, with the increasing feature set of HTML and CSS, has allowed for the development of true web applications that work as well as, and look and feel just as good as, native applications, and has become the development stack of choice for all modern web projects, even going so far as projects such as Node.JS, which enables JavaScript to be used as a server-side language as well. Figure 15.16 shows this set-up in action.

## 15.6.5 DBMSs Adapt: REST, Other Web Services, and a Look Ahead

The rising popularity of JavaScript and web-based APIs and protocols has caused many database vendors to incorporate standard web service related technologies, such as **REST (REpresentational State Transfer)** and **SOAP (Simple Object Access Protocol)** to offer querying APIs to outside clients. REST has become especially popular in recent NoSQL databases (see also Chapter 11), as it offers a simple querying interface on top of the standard HTTP protocol, making it easy for rich web applications to query and retrieve records directly from within the web browser (which then acts as the client directly connecting to the database server). This is represented in Figure 15.17. SOAP, on the other hand, is based on similar principles, but is more heavy-weight and relies on XML.

> **Connections**
>
> See Chapter 11 for a discussion on interacting with NoSQL databases, and Chapter 10 for further information on REST, JSON, XML, and SOAP.

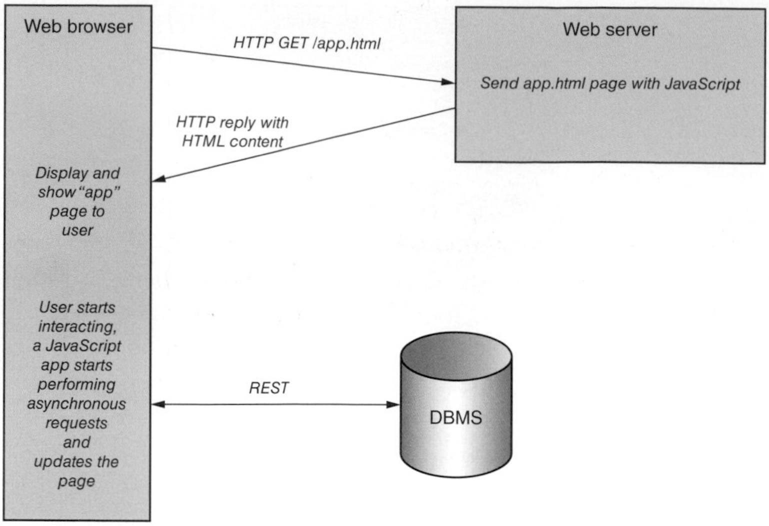


**Figure 15.17** Illustration of direct interaction between JavaScript and a DBMS.

As an example of using REST for database access, a JavaScript fragment embedded inside a web application can perform a synchronous HTTP call to the following endpoint (e.g., using Oracle's NoSQL data services):

```
http://database_server:8080/book_database/books/
```

The following answer is returned by the server, formatted as JSON, as a standard HTTP reply:

```
HTTP/1.1 200 OK
Content-Type: application/json
Transfer-Encoding: chunked

{
 "items":[
 { "id":7369,"title":"Book One"} ,
 { "id":7499,"title":"My Second Book"} ,
 { "id":7521,"title":"Third Book"}
 ] ,
 "hasMore":true,
 "limit":3,
 "offset":0,
 "count":3,
 "links":[
 { "rel":"self",
  "href":" http://database_server:8080/book_database/books/"} ,
 { "rel":"describedby",
  "href":"http://database_server:8080/ metadata-catalog/book_database/books/"} ,
 { "rel":"first",
  "href":"http://database_server:8080/book_database/books/"} ,
```

```
  { "rel":"next",
    "href":"http://database_server:8080/book_database/books/?offset=3"}
  ]
}
```

Next to actual records, note that the reply also contains additional metadata describing the result set, including whether more records can be fetched, and which URL endpoints can be used to fetch the next bunch of rows. This "pagination" approach is comparable to the "cursor" approaches as seen in JDBC, though the client application developer should be aware of the structure of the returned replies and how additional records should be requested.

Note that REST web services also often only expose very basic querying capabilities – in some cases also supporting filtering e.g., by specifying additional URL parameters:

```
http://database_server:8080/book_database/books/?filter={'id':{'gt':7400}}
```

Some DBMS systems also support defining SQL queries on the server side, which can then be called using a REST call, similar to stored procedures, e.g., a call to

```
http://database_server:8080/book_database/query/my_stored_query?param1=100
```

can then correspond to a complex query named "my_stored_query" which expects one parameter named "param1". Allowing a client to send a complete query string would be unwise, as here too requests can be spoofed by malicious entities so that a "raw SQL" request might end up looking as such:

```
http://database_server:8080/book_database/raw_query?sql=DROP TABLE books
```

Although REST and other web service-based technologies have become popular in recent years as web developers have wanted to access databases directly from a web browser, it is notable how many functionalities provided were already implemented years before in other universal APIs such as JDBC or ADO.NET. The key selling point of REST is its relative simplicity (as it is built on the HTTP protocol), which allows it to be called directly from a web browser (e.g., using JavaScript as a client-side scripting language). Nevertheless, the rising popularity of web-based applications, together with the interest in highly scalable NoSQL databases, is causing DBMS vendors to adapt their products: outdated protocols and APIs are replaced by web-based ones, and database users are putting more emphasis on scalability, speed, and schema flexibility, rather than schema enforcement, transaction support, etc. Similar trends are appearing in the world of Big Data and analytics and the Internet of things: there are many factors to keep in mind when choosing a database for such applications, which do not always align with the needs of other more traditional enterprise databases. Some of the most important considerations here are scalability, ability to ingest data at sufficient rates, schema flexibility, integration with analytics tools, and costs.

These aspects are causing DBMS vendors to adapt, though – as we already remarked in the chapter on NoSQL – the downsides of these approaches should be kept in mind. Many early adopters of NoSQL were confronted with some sour lessons, and we already see vendors focusing again on robustness and durability, combined with some of the more appealing aspects of NoSQL. Nevertheless, we can expect to see DBMS systems continue to evolve toward a wider adaption of web-based APIs.

**Retention Questions**

- What is the common gateway interface? Why is it important in dynamic web pages?
- What is meant by client-side scripting?
- How are DBMSs adopting new paradigms such as REST and other web service technologies?

## Summary

In this chapter, we have discussed the many ways in which DBMSs can be accessed from the outside world. Most database vendors these days provide several interfaces based on a universal API standard to do so. Through these APIs clients, third-party applications, and end-user applications can access, query, and manage the DBMS. There exists a long lineage of various APIs that can be implemented by DBMS vendors, all the way from Microsoft's ODBC to newer language-integrated query facilities and REST-based web services. This wide variety of offerings can make it somewhat confusing for a beginning programmer to decide which API one should use to access a DBMS, though remember that many of the universal APIs are built with backward compatibility in mind. In the Java ecosystem, JDBC and the Java Persistence API remain popular choices, while Microsoft's ecosystem gears heavily toward ADO.NET.

It is important to understand how database APIs form a necessary component to make databases accessible from the outside world. This should be done in a way that is portable and vendor-agnostic in the sense that one can easily switch vendors without having to change running applications. The latter is not always that straightforward, as an application might send vendor-specific SQL statements over an API which would cease to work when changing the DBMS on the other end. In addition, it is important to remark that database APIs form the cornerstone in an organization's integration exercises and projects as well. Firms often utilize a variety of database systems and vendors (e.g., a database for the customer relationship management system and a separate one for the order and sales system). It is only natural that for many use cases, systems will need to utilize data that might be spread out across different DBMSs. Think for instance about providing an overview of the number of orders a customer made from the sales database and showing this in the CRM system, or about a reporting application that has to combine and aggregate information from multiple data sources. Also in this setting, database APIs play an important role as they will form the "entry points" through which data can be accessed. Different strategies exist to tackle this integration problem – for instance by using a database API to fetch data from a different source when required, or by setting up a system in which information from one source gets copied over and loaded into a second database. These issues are heavily related to ETL (extracting, transforming and loading data) and EAI (enterprise application integration), something that will be discussed in depth in Chapter 18.

**Connections**

Data integration, data quality, and governance are discussed in detail in Chapter 18.

### Scenario Conclusion

After learning about the various universal database API standards that can be used to access databases, Sober decides to take a look at what its DBMS vendor is offering in terms of support. The vendor provides support for both the ODBC and JDBC API, opening up a broad range of possible ways for Sober to access its database. Since Sober is a relatively small company, the decision is made to go forward with JDBC. Sober's plan is to write the internal desktop applications for its employees in Java, where JDBC can be directly used to access the database and perform queries. For its website, Sober plans to adopt a Java-based web server, which can then also simply use JDBC to connect to the DBMS. For the mobile app, several options present themselves. The first is to use a native application for both Android and iOS. Since Android apps use Java as well, setting up a JDBC connection from within an Android app is easy. iOS, however, not being based on Java, has a harder time supporting JDBC in its apps. To work around this issue, Sober is considering setting up a REST-based web service on its web server which would perform queries on its end using JDBC, but send the results to the mobile app as JSON or XML over HTTP. Both the Android and iOS apps could then use this REST web service. However, since the development of this web service would take up extra development time, and since Sober does not have much experience with developing native Android or iOS apps in the first place, the decision is made to go for a responsive website, meaning that the website that customers open in a web browser on their computer can easily "scale down" on a smaller smartphone screen while remaining pleasant to use. By using this approach, Sober only needs to maintain one customer-facing web portal which can then serve both PC and mobile users, and where the DBMS is accessed by the same Java-based web server.

## Key Terms List

**ActiveX Data Objects (ADO)**
**ADO.NET**
**application programming interface (API)**
**Asynchronous JavaScript and XML (AJAX)**
**call-level APIs**
**centralized DBMS architecture**
**client–server architecture**
**client-side scripting**
**common gateway interface (CGI)**
**cursor mechanism**
**early binding**
**embedded API**
**embedded DBMSs**
**Enterprise JavaBeans (EJB)**
**Hibernate**
**Java applets**
**Java DataBase Connectivity (JDBC)**
**Java Data Objects (JDO)**
**Java Persistence API**
**JavaScript**
**language-native query expressions**
**late binding**
**n-tier architecture**
**object persistence**
**OLE DB**
**Open Database Connectivity (ODBC)**
**proprietary API**
**Representational State Transfer (REST)**
**Simple Object Access Protocol (SOAP)**
**SQL injection**
**SQLJ**
**three-tier architecture**
**tiered system architecture**
**two-tier architecture**
**universal API**

## Review Questions

**15.1.** Which of the following statements is **not correct**?

a. Embedded database APIs can use early binding.
b. Embedded database APIs can use late binding.
c. Call-level database APIs can use early binding.
d. Call-level database APIs can use late binding.

**15.2.** Which of the following statements is **not correct**?

a. One drawback of ODBC is that the architecture is mostly native to Microsoft-based platforms.
b. One drawback of ODBC is that application code needs to be modified every time a different driver needs to be used.
c. One drawback of ODBC is it is not using an object-oriented paradigm.
d. One drawback of ODBC is that performance can be worse compared to proprietary DBMS APIs.

**15.3.** Which of the following statements is **correct**?

a. JDBC drivers come in different types, which come with different tradeoffs in terms of portability and performance.
b. JDBC was originally developed to be used in the C++ programming language.
c. JDBC can only be used on Linux- and Unix-based systems.
d. Just like ODBC, JDBC does not expose programmer-friendly object classes to work with.

**15.4.** Which of the following statements is **not correct**?

a. Enterprise JavaBeans are components that establish a clear decoupling between business logic and client applications.
b. Enterprise JavaBeans extend the concept of Java Beans.
c. Three types of Enterprise JavaBeans exist, although one type is outdated now.
d. Session Beans represent an object-oriented representation of business entities and can be made persistent.

**15.5.** Which of the following statements is **not correct**?

a. The Java Persistence API arose as part of the specification of version 3.0 of the EJB standard.
b. The Java Persistence API is in itself just a specification defining a set of interfaces and annotations.
c. Java Data Objects are part of the Java Persistence API standard.
d. Java Data Objects are agnostic to the technology of the data store used.

**15.6.** Which of the following statements is **correct**?

a. The JPA query language (JPQL) supports more complex queries than SQL.
b. JPQL queries can differ depending on the underlying DBMS used.
c. One big advantage of JPQL is its portability.
d. One big advantage of JPQL is the fact that it supports compile-time checking and validation of queries.

**15.7.** Which of the following statements is **not correct**?

a. CGI was one of the first technologies that allowed for the construction of dynamic web pages.
b. CGI programs can be written in almost any programming language.
c. An important drawback of CGI was the fact that it could not handle database querying.
d. An advantage of CGI was that it could deal with user-supplied input, such as provided through HTML Forms.

**15.8.** Which of the following is not a client-side scripting language?

a. JavaScript.
b. VBScript.
c. JScript.
d. PHP.

**15.9.** Which JDBC driver type is implemented completely in Java and communicates directly with the vendor's DBMS through a network socket connection?

a. Type 1.
b. Type 2.

c. Type 3.
d. Type 4.

**15.10.** Which of the following statements is **not correct**?

a. SQLJ uses a pre-compiler to translate embedded SQL statements before invoking the Java compiler.
b. SQL syntax can be checked before runtime when using SQLJ.
c. JDBC uses SQLJ as an underlying technology.
d. Many IDEs do not have SQLJ support.

**15.11.** Which database access technique does the following C# statement illustrate?

```
public void Example() {
  DataClassesContext dc = new DataClassesContext();
  var q =
    from a in dc.GetTable<Order>()
    where a.CustomerName.StartsWith("Seppe")
    select a;
  dataGrid.DataSource = q;
}
```

a. JDBC.
b. ODBC.
c. Language-integrated queries.
d. None of the above.

**15.12.** Which of the following statements regarding JPA is **not correct**?

a. The JPA was meant as a replacement for entity Beans in EJB 2.0.
b. JPA relies heavily on annotations and convention-over-configuration.
c. JPA uses its own internal query language, but supports SQL as well.
d. All the statements above are correct.

## Problems and Exercises

15.1E Explain the differences between a centralized system and tiered system architecture.

15.2E What is meant by a “fat” client versus a “thin” one? Are web browsers fat or thin clients?

15.3E Explain the differences between “static” and “dynamic” SQL and how this relates to early and late binding.

15.4E DBMSs such as Microsoft Access, SQLite, and Apache Derby are often described as embedded databases. Does this mean they are accessed using embedded APIs? Explain why/why not.

15.5E OLE DB is often described as following a universal data access approach, rather than a universal data storage approach. What is meant by this?

15.6E One complaint against using JavaScript-heavy web applications that directly interface with a DBMS through REST or a similar technique is that they are, by default, less secure than using a traditional client–server–database set-up. Why do you think that is?

15.7E What are the different ways client-side applications can be enriched and made more interactive? Which technology stack is common today?

# 16 Data Distribution and Distributed Transaction Management

## Chapter Objectives

In this chapter, you will learn to:

- grasp the basics of distributed systems and distributed databases;
- discern key architectural implications of distributed databases;
- understand the impact of fragmentation, allocation, and replication;
- identify different types of transparency;
- understand the steps in distributed query processing;
- understand distributed transaction management and concurrency control;
- grasp the impact of eventual consistency and BASE transactions.

### Opening Scenario

As Sober envisions growing as part of its long-term strategy, it wants to have a careful understanding of the data implications involved. More specifically, the company wants to know if it would make sense to distribute its data across a network of offices and work with a distributed database. Sober wants to know the impact of data distribution on query processing and optimization, transaction management, and concurrency control.

In this chapter, we focus on the specifics of distributed databases (i.e., systems in which the data and DBMS functionality are distributed over different nodes or locations on a network). First, we discuss the general properties of distributed systems and offer an overview of some architectural variants of distributed database systems. Then, we tackle the different ways of distributing data over nodes in a network, including the possibility of data replication. We also focus on the degree to which the data distribution can be made transparent to applications and users. Then, we discuss the complexity of query processing and query optimization in a distributed setting. A next section is dedicated to distributed transaction management and concurrency control, focusing on both tightly coupled and loosely coupled settings. The last section overviews the particularities of transaction management in Big Data and NoSQL databases, which are often distributed in a cluster set-up, presenting BASE transactions as an alternative to the traditional ACID transaction paradigms.

## 16.1 Distributed Systems and Distributed Databases

Ever since the early days of computing, which were dominated by monolithic mainframes, distributed systems have had their place in the ICT landscape. A distributed computing system consists of several processing units or nodes with a certain level of autonomy, which are interconnected by a network and which cooperatively perform complex tasks. These complex tasks can be divided into subtasks as performed by the individual nodes.

The rationale behind distributed architectures and systems is grounded in the principle that the overhead of a monolithic system increases more than proportionally to the number of tasks and users. By dividing and distributing a complex problem into smaller, more manageable units of work, performed by semi-independent nodes, the complexity becomes, at least in theory, more manageable. This makes the system also more scalable; a monolithic system can only be extended within a limited capacity range, whereas (again, in theory) a distributed system's capacity can be increased indefinitely by just adding nodes to the system. Distribution of data and functionality often guarantees a certain measure of local autonomy and availability. For example, a sportswear chain organizing inventory information in a distributed system, with data pertaining to each local outlet being stored and maintained locally, allows for every outlet to remain operational if unavailability of the central system due to network failure occurs. This is especially pertinent where the distributed system is shared by several, partially independent parties (e.g., in a web services context).

The architectural complexity of distributed systems is typically much higher, compared to standalone systems. The latter also holds for **distributed database systems**, where data and data retrieval functionality are distributed over multiple data sources and/or locations. Part of the additional complexity is because most distributed database systems are designed to provide an integrated view of the distributed data; they attempt to offer a certain measure of **transparency** to users and application programs. This transparency refers to the often desirable property that the user is insulated from one or more aspects of the distribution. In other words, the user perceives the database as a standalone system to a certain extent, although the data are distributed over different locations and query processing, transaction management, concurrency control, etc. might consider different locations. For example, performing analytics across all outlets on the sportswear chain's inventory movements requires much less coordination if all inventory data are stored in a single centralized database, instead of it being spread geographically over several locations.

A distributed database environment may exist for different reasons in an organization. It could be a deliberate choice (e.g., for scalability or local autonomy of individual departments or business units), as mentioned above. However, more often than not, distributed architectures are merely a consequence of other factors (e.g., a merger or acquisition), or simply of consecutive investments in different database technologies, for technological and/or financial reasons. If data distribution is a deliberate choice, one of the main concerns will be to decide on optimal distribution criteria. Example criteria are performance (e.g., maximizing parallelism and/or minimizing network traffic) or local autonomy and availability (i.e., the ability to retain access to relevant local data, even if failures occur in the global system). The performance criterion is particularly relevant to the current wave of NoSQL database systems, where cluster computing is used to attain a near linear relationship between performance and the number of nodes. If the distribution aspect is the consequence of other factors, such

**Connections**

Refer to Chapter 11 for an overview on NoSQL databases.

**Retention Questions**

- What is the rationale behind distributed architectures and systems?
- What is meant by transparency in a distributed system?
- Where do distributed database environments emanate from?

as a merger, an additional concern will often be to deal with the heterogeneity of database management software, data models, and formats.

Regardless of the reason for the distribution, other important elements should be considered. Examples are the degree of transparency that is to be offered with respect to the distribution, how to deal with distributed query processing, the complexity of distributed transaction management (and, possibly, the added complexity of keeping replicated data consistent), and distributed concurrency control and recovery. In what follows, we deal with each of these concerns, but first we discuss the most important architectural variants of distributed databases.

## 16.2 Architectural Implications of Distributed Databases

In Chapter 15 we presented different database system architectures, including tiered architectures where presentation logic, application logic, and DBMS are spread over three or more tiers. However, particular to distributed databases is that the data and DBMS are distributed over multiple interconnected nodes. Within this realm of systems, there are still different possible architectures, as illustrated in Figure 16.1.

In a **shared-memory architecture**, multiple interconnected processors that run the DBMS software share the same central storage and secondary storage. As more processors are added, this shared central storage may become the bottleneck.

With a **shared-disk architecture**, each processor has its own central storage but shares secondary storage with the other processors. The disk sharing can be realized by, for example, a storage area network or network attached storage. Shared-disk architectures are typically more fault tolerant than shared-memory architectures. However, a possible bottleneck is the network that interconnects the disks with the processors.

**Connections**

Storage area networks and network attached storage were discussed in Chapter 13.

The most prevalent approach for distributed databases is the **shared-nothing architecture**. In this set-up, each processor has its own central storage and hard disk units. Data sharing occurs through the processors communicating with one another over the network, not by the processors directly accessing one another's central storage or secondary storage.

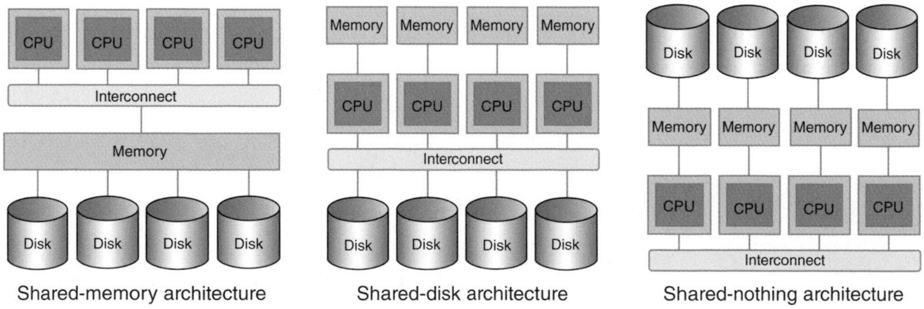


**Figure 16.1** Different distributed database architectures.

In most cases, the respective processors each run their own DBMS instance. However, there also exists DBMS software explicitly equipped to exploit the parallelism of multiple processors, with the single DBMS instance being distributed over multiple processor nodes.

Scalability can be achieved in two ways in a distributed database system: vertical scalability or horizontal scalability. In vertical scalability the capacity (CPU power, disk capacity) of individual nodes can be increased. There are certain hardware limitations to this. Horizontal scalability is achieved by adding nodes to the system. Here, the challenge is to keep the coordination overhead over the respective nodes as low as possible. It was discussed in Chapter 11 how NoSQL databases can achieve near linear horizontal scalability, for example, whereas traditional standalone databases are restricted to vertical scaling. Horizontal scaling of distributed RDBMSs may be problematic beyond a certain number of nodes because of the increased coordination cost (ensuring transaction atomicity, keeping different replicas of the same data item consistent, etc.). However, as we will see in Section 16.7 in this chapter, reducing coordination overhead to improve horizontal scalability may also come with a cost, in terms of less consistent data.

Some authors distinguish between distributed databases and **parallel databases**. With parallel databases, they refer to data distribution with only one purpose: performance. The performance gain is achieved through parallel access to the distributed data. As explained in Chapter 13, we can distinguish between **intra-query parallelism** (different subsets of the data are searched in parallel in the context of a single, complex query) and **inter-query parallelism** (many simple queries are executed in parallel). Parallel databases can have a shared-memory, shared-disk, or shared-nothing architecture. The nodes are relatively close to one another and are connected through a local area network (LAN). One then refers to distributed databases as database systems with a shared-nothing architecture, possibly with much larger distances between the nodes and wide area network (WAN) connectivity. The reason for the distribution can be performance, but also local autonomy, or a data integration project (e.g., in a merger or acquisition).

In what follows, we will use the broader term distributed database for both types of architectures and will not use the term parallel database. Furthermore, it is worth noting that if the respective nodes in a shared-nothing architecture each run an independent DBMS instance, and if the data are fragmented horizontally over these instances (see the next section), the term **federated database** is often used. The respective nodes in a federated database set-up may each run the same DBMS software, but it is also possible that the respective nodes contain different DBMS types. This is often the case if the federated database resulted from a data integration effort. One of the complexities will then be to have the different database APIs, data models, and database software interact seamlessly to provide a unified view of the distributed data.

**Retention Questions**

- Explain the following concepts: shared-memory architecture, shared-disk architecture, shared-nothing architecture.
- How can scalability be achieved in a distributed system?
- What is the difference between intra-query parallelism and inter-query parallelism?

## 16.3 Fragmentation, Allocation, and Replication

If data distribution is a deliberate choice, and not a consequence of an event like a merger or acquisition, one of the main concerns of a distributed database will be the criteria according to which to partition the data into subsets, called **fragments**, as well as the criteria to *allocate* these fragments to nodes or locations. Different concerns may come into play here. Some are performance related,

| CustomerID | FirstName | LastName | Country | Year of birth | Gender |
|---|---|---|---|---|---|
| 10023 | Bart | Baesens | Belgium | 1975 | M |
| 10098 | Charlotte | Bobson | USA | 1968 | F |
| 10233 | Donald | McDonald | UK | 1960 | M |
| 10299 | Heiner | Pilzner | Germany | 1973 | M |
| 10351 | Simonne | Toutdroit | France | 1981 | F |
| 10359 | Seppe | vanden Broucke | Belgium | 1989 | M |
| 10544 | Bridget | Charlton | UK | 1992 | F |
| 11213 | Angela | Kissinger | USA | 1969 | F |
| 11349 | Henry | Dumortier | France | 1987 | M |
| 11821 | Wilfried | Lemahieu | Belgium | 1970 | M |
| 12111 | Tim | Pope | UK | 1956 | M |
| 12194 | Naomi | Leary | USA | 1999 | F |

Horizontal fragmentation

Vertical fragmentation

**Figure 16.2** Global dataset as a basis for fragmentation examples.

such as maximizing query parallelism or minimizing network traffic. Others pertain to local autonomy (i.e., the ability of nodes to operate independently and to retain access to relevant local data, even if failures occur in the global system). A related concern is the decision on whether to *replicate* some or all of the data over multiple nodes, again for reasons of performance and/or availability. Obviously, the cost element will play a role as well – among others, network costs, server capacity, additional storage cost if data are replicated, etc. If data distribution was not a deliberate choice but was induced by external factors, there are often no or only very limited degrees of freedom regarding how to partition, allocate, and replicate the data.

The act of partitioning the global dataset into fragments is called **fragmentation**. We can distinguish between vertical fragmentation, horizontal fragmentation, and mixed fragmentation. To illustrate these concepts, we will use the global dataset with customer data, as illustrated in Figure 16.2.

## 16.3.1 Vertical Fragmentation

With **vertical fragmentation**, every fragment consists of a subset of the columns of the global dataset.[1] Vertical fragmentation is especially useful if only some of a tuple's attributes are relevant to a certain node. For example, a node responsible for order processing only needs the CustomerIDs and customer names, whereas a node performing data analytics on the customer data is mainly interested in demographic data such as country, year of birth, and gender. Both fragments contain the necessary columns (most often the primary key) to combine the respective vertical fragments with a JOIN construct if a view of the global dataset is required (see Figure 16.3).

[1] We use a table representation and terms such as rows and columns, but the different types of fragmentation also apply to non-relational DBMSs such as NoSQL databases.

| CustomerID | FirstName | LastName |
|---|---|---|
| 10023 | Bart | Baesens |
| 10098 | Charlotte | Bobson |
| 10233 | Donald | McDonald |
| 10299 | Heiner | Pilzner |
| 10351 | Simonne | Toutdroit |
| 10359 | Seppe | vanden Broucke |
| 10544 | Bridget | Charlton |
| 11213 | Angela | Kissinger |
| 11349 | Henry | Dumortier |
| 11821 | Wilfried | Lemahieu |
| 12111 | Tim | Pope |
| 12194 | Naomi | Leary |

| CustomerID | Country | Year of birth | Gender |
|---|---|---|---|
| 10023 | Belgium | 1975 | M |
| 10098 | USA | 1968 | F |
| 10233 | UK | 1960 | M |
| 10299 | Germany | 1973 | M |
| 10351 | France | 1981 | F |
| 10359 | Belgium | 1989 | M |
| 10544 | UK | 1992 | F |
| 11213 | USA | 1969 | F |
| 11349 | France | 1987 | M |
| 11821 | Belgium | 1970 | M |
| 12111 | UK | 1956 | M |
| 12194 | USA | 1999 | F |

**Figure 16.3** Illustration of vertical fragmentation.

## 16.3.2 Horizontal Fragmentation (Sharding)

According to **horizontal fragmentation**, each fragment consists of rows that satisfy a certain query predicate.[2] For example, in Figure 16.4 the rows are attributed to worldwide nodes according to the country of the customer (Country = "Belgium" or "France"; Country = "UK"; Country = "USA" etc.), so customer data for each country can be stored in the local branch. In this way, network traffic for queries on local customers is reduced and local availability is improved if network failure occurs. Note that all data pertaining to the same customer are now stored at the same node. A global view can be reconstructed with a UNION query over all the horizontal fragments.

Horizontal fragmentation is also applied in many NoSQL databases organized in a cluster set-up, where the horizontal fragments (called shards) are attributed to different nodes in the cluster. Typically, a measure of redundancy is introduced for performance and availability, so the shards on different nodes are not disjoint. In this context, the fragmentation criterion is mostly purely technical and has no business meaning. The sole purpose is to distribute the data as evenly as possible over the respective nodes for load balancing. This is often achieved by a form of randomization called consistent hashing.

**Connections**

Consistent hashing was discussed in Chapter 11.

## 16.3.3 Mixed Fragmentation

**Mixed fragmentation** combines horizontal with vertical fragmentation. Figure 16.5 illustrates a situation in which rows containing CustomerID, FirstName, and LastName are fragmented horizontally according to the customers' Country (note Country itself is not included as a column in the fragments). However, there is also vertical fragmentation, since all demographic

[2] See also Chapter 13.

| CustomerID | FirstName | LastName | Country | Year of birth | Gender |
|---|---|---|---|---|---|
| 10023 | Bart | Baesens | Belgium | 1975 | M |
| 10359 | Seppe | vanden Broucke | Belgium | 1989 | M |
| 11821 | Wilfried | Lemahieu | Belgium | 1970 | M |
| 10351 | Simonne | Toutdroit | France | 1981 | F |
| 11349 | Henry | Dumortier | France | 1987 | M |

| CustomerID | FirstName | LastName | Country | Year of birth | Gender |
|---|---|---|---|---|---|
| 10299 | Heiner | Pilzner | Germany | 1973 | M |

| CustomerID | FirstName | LastName | Country | Year of birth | Gender |
|---|---|---|---|---|---|
| 10544 | Bridget | Charlton | UK | 1992 | F |
| 10233 | Donald | McDonald | UK | 1960 | M |
| 12111 | Tim | Pope | UK | 1956 | M |

| CustomerID | FirstName | LastName | Country | Year of birth | Gender |
|---|---|---|---|---|---|
| 11213 | Angela | Kissinger | USA | 1969 | F |
| 10098 | Charlotte | Bobson | USA | 1968 | F |
| 12194 | Naomi | Leary | USA | 1999 | F |

**Figure 16.4** Illustration of horizontal fragmentation.

| CustomerID | FirstName | LastName |
|---|---|---|
| 10023 | Bart | Baesens |
| 10359 | Seppe | vanden Broucke |
| 11821 | Wilfried | Lemahieu |
| 10351 | Simonne | Toutdroit |
| 11349 | Henry | Dumortier |

| CustomerID | FirstName | LastName |
|---|---|---|
| 10299 | Heiner | Pilzner |

| CustomerID | FirstName | LastName |
|---|---|---|
| 10544 | Bridget | Charlton |
| 10233 | Donald | McDonald |
| 12111 | Tim | Pope |

| CustomerID | FirstName | LastName |
|---|---|---|
| 11213 | Angela | Kissinger |
| 10098 | Charlotte | Bobson |
| 12194 | Naomi | Leary |

| CustomerID | Country | Year of birth | Gender |
|---|---|---|---|
| 10023 | Belgium | 1975 | M |
| 10098 | USA | 1968 | F |
| 10233 | UK | 1960 | M |
| 10299 | Germany | 1973 | M |
| 10351 | France | 1981 | F |
| 10359 | Belgium | 1989 | M |
| 10544 | UK | 1992 | F |
| 11213 | USA | 1969 | F |
| 11349 | France | 1987 | M |
| 11821 | Belgium | 1970 | M |
| 12111 | UK | 1956 | M |
| 12194 | USA | 1999 | F |

**Figure 16.5** Illustration of mixed fragmentation.

data are allocated to a separate node (this time without horizontal fragmentation) to perform analytics on worldwide customer demographics. Each fragment also contains the primary key CustomerID, to be able to reconstruct a global view with a query containing JOIN and UNION operations.

Sometimes **derived fragmentation** is applied, which means that the fragmentation criteria belong to another table. For example, the customer data can be fragmented according to the sales total for that customer, as stored in a separate SALES table. In this way, separate fragments with, for example, high-volume, medium-volume, and low-volume customers can be created.

Decisions regarding data distribution must be made for all tables or, in a non-relational setting, datasets. It may be possible that fragments from multiple tables are attributed to the same node, e.g., with the CUSTOMER table being fragmented horizontally according to Country, and the rows from the INVOICES table being attributed to the same node as the corresponding customer to improve local autonomy.

The optimization of the data fragmentation and allocation to appropriate nodes according to one or more chosen criteria (performance, local autonomy, etc.) is typically very complex. There may not be a single optimal solution, or it may be impossible to compute this solution, but at least some heuristics, practical experience, and rules of thumb can underpin the choices made. Fortunately, if the distributed database environment offers sufficient levels of transparency (see below), some distribution properties can be tuned over time without affecting the overall functioning of the applications that make use of the database.

### 16.3.4 Replication

Data distribution entails the partitioning of the global dataset into smaller subsets, called fragments, which are then allocated to individual nodes. The subsets may or may not be disjoint. If the subsets overlap, or if there are multiple identical subsets allocated to different nodes, we have data replication. There may be different reasons for data replication:

Local autonomy: the same data are required to be stored locally by different nodes to be able to function independently.

Performance and scalability: using replication, different queries that involve the same data can be executed in parallel on different nodes.

Reliability and availability: if a node fails, other nodes containing the same data can take over the workload without interrupting normal operation.

Depending on the actual system, each of these concerns, or a combination, may be a valid reason for replication. For example, to the sportswear chain discussed earlier, local autonomy may be the main driver. In many Big Data settings, local autonomy is not an issue since the cluster of nodes always acts as one global system, but performance and availability are significant reasons for replication.

> **Connections**
>
> Chapter 13 already discussed how reliability and availability by itself may be a sufficient reason for different forms of data replication.

Replication also induces additional overhead and complexity, to keep the different replicas consistent and propagate updates to a data item to all its replicas. This propagation may be performed instantly (synchronous replication) or with some delay (asynchronous replication). As discussed in Section 16.7, the degree of *coupling* between the respective nodes (tight coupling versus looser coupling) often determines a tradeoff between keeping the replicas consistent at all times (inducing more overhead) and more asynchronous approaches to replication (requiring less overhead), resulting in a certain measure of data inconsistency.

### Retention Questions

- What is meant by fragmentation, allocation, and replication in a distributed environment?
- Discuss the different types of fragmentation.
- What could be reasons for data replication in a distributed environment?

### 16.3.5 Distribution and Replication of Metadata

Similar decisions to the ones on the distribution and replication of the actual data need to be made with respect to the *metadata*: will all metadata be centralized in a single catalog or will the metadata be fragmented and allocated to, e.g., the nodes that contain the data described by the metadata? Also, there is the question of whether some metadata must be replicated (e.g., in a set-up with both local catalogs and a global catalog). Replication is often desirable, since only a single global metadata catalog has a negative impact on the local autonomy of the database nodes, whereas only-local catalogs make it hard to perform global queries and interpret their results in a consistent manner. Of course, if global and local metadata catalogs exist, their consistency needs to be assured over time as well.

### Drill Down

One "distributed system" that is getting a lot of attention these days is "blockchains", as seen in, e.g., crypto currencies such as Bitcoin or digital ledgers. In essence, a blockchain is simply a distributed database that maintains a continuously growing list of records, called blocks. Each block contains a reference to a previous block, and the whole "chain" of blocks is managed by a peer-to-peer network which collectively agree to a system for validating new blocks. Because of this, blockchains are resistant to modification of data stored in the blocks. Once recorded, the data in any given block cannot be modified without the alteration of all subsequent blocks and the collusion of the network. Hence, a blockchain can serve as a distributed ledger that can record transactions between two parties in a verifiable, permanent, and efficient manner, and hence has caught the attention of many financial institutions.

## 16.4 Transparency

Transparency refers to the fact that, although the data and database functionality are physically distributed, the application and users are confronted with only a single logical database and are insulated (at least to a certain extent) from the complexities of the distribution. In this way, this transparency can be looked upon as an extension to the logical and physical data independence.

### Connections

Logical and physical data independence were discussed in Chapter 1.

Several types of transparency can be identified and may or may not be supported by a distributed database system. An important property is **location transparency**, which means that database users do not need to know on which node the required data resides. **Fragmentation transparency** refers to the fact that users can execute global queries without being concerned with the fact that distributed fragments will be involved, and need to be combined, to perform the query. **Replication transparency** means that different replicas of the same data item will be automatically kept consistent by the database system and updates to one replica will be propagated transparently (be it synchronously or asynchronously) to the other copies of the same data item.

One particular type of transparency, which is especially relevant in a federated database setting with different DBMS types or components from different vendors, is **access transparency**. This refers to the fact that the distributed database can be accessed and queried uniformly, regardless of the different database systems and APIs that may be involved. Access transparency is particularly an issue if the distributed database is the consequence of a database integration effort (e.g., in a merger), where one is confronted with a heterogeneous as-is situation. A key technique to realize access transparency is the use of universal database APIs as discussed in the previous chapter. However, in many cases, a universal API will be complemented by an additional layer of **wrappers** which form a shell around the respective data sources, insulating the users and applications from their heterogeneity and providing, e.g., a virtual unified database model over the distributed data sources.

**Connections**

Chapter 15 discussed different universal database APIs. Chapter 18 discusses aspects of federation as a data integration technique.

A last crucial type of transparency is **transaction transparency**. Here, the DBMS transparently performs distributed transactions involving multiple nodes as if they were transactions in a standalone system. Transparent handling of transaction execution requires extra coordination in a distributed setting. A first issue is concurrency control. The locking mechanisms discussed in Chapter 14 need to be extended to cater for locking and transaction consistency across multiple nodes or locations. In addition, care should be taken to avoid transactions that require locks across multiple locations ending up in a global deadlock. Different extensions to the Two-Phase Locking Protocol exist in this context. A second issue is recovery, where recovery mechanisms in a distributed setting need to be able to deal with additional types of problems, such as unavailability of a single node, messages not received, or failure of one or more communication links. Guaranteeing transaction atomicity requires coordination across multiple nodes that together execute a distributed transaction.

**Retention Questions**

- What is meant by transparency in a distributed environment?
- Discuss the different types of transparency.

In the next section we deal with querying data in distributed databases, whereas the last two sections of this chapter focus on distributed transaction management. First, different optimistic and pessimistic concurrency protocols are discussed, along with approaches to deal with atomicity of distributed transactions. The last section focuses explicitly on the particularities of transaction management in a Big Data setting, with high levels of data replication, as supported by NoSQL databases.

**Connections**

The basics of transaction management were introduced in Chapter 14. NoSQL databases were discussed in Chapter 11.

## 16.5 Distributed Query Processing

Query optimization becomes even more complex if queries are to be executed on data distributed over multiple nodes or locations. Ideally, location and fragmentation transparency are guaranteed by the DBMS, but even then the optimizer should consider not only the elements of a standalone setting (availability of indexes, sizes of the tables, statistics on data usage, and query execution as discussed in Chapter 13), but also the properties of the respective fragments, communication costs, and the location of the data in the network. Also, the necessary metadata may be distributed. Based on these

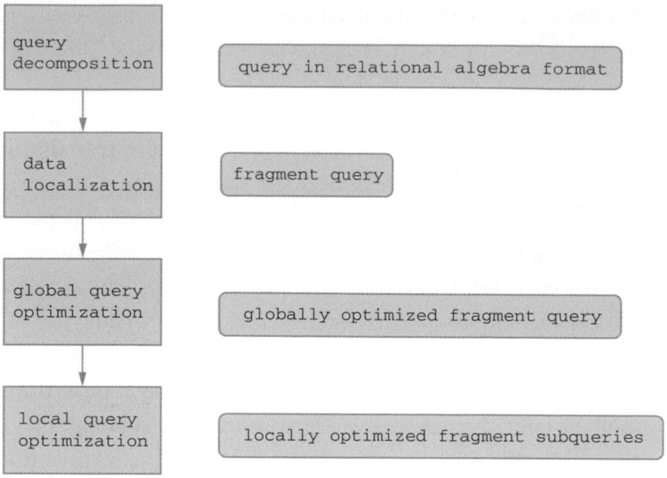


**Figure 16.6** Steps in distributed query processing.

> **Connections**
>
> Chapter 13 discusses query processing in a standalone database setting. Some typical approaches for query processing in NoSQL databases, and other retrieval techniques such as MapReduce, were presented in Chapter 11.

characteristics, both global (across all nodes) and local (within a single node) query optimization are needed. In this chapter, we focus on distributed query processing in a relational setting.

Usually, distributed query processing involves four steps: query decomposition, data localization, global query optimization, and local query optimization (Figure 16.6). The first and fourth step also exist in a standalone environment; the second and third step are particular to a distributed setting.

In the **query decomposition** step, the query is first analyzed for correctness: syntax and data types are verified, and column and table names are validated against the metadata in the catalog. The query is then represented in relational algebra and transformed into a **canonical form**,[3] which is most appropriate for further processing.

The **data localization** step entails the transformation of the query into a **fragment query**. The database fragments subjected to the query are identified, as well as their locations. Several reduction techniques are applied in such a way that fragments that are guaranteed to contain no data that satisfy the query predicate are omitted from the fragment query. In this way, unnecessary processing is avoided where possible.

During the **global query optimization** step, a cost model, based on statistical evidence, is used to evaluate different global strategies for query execution. The strategy with the lowest predicted cost is selected.

The results of the previous step determine which operations should be performed on which location. For each of these local operations, a **local query optimization** step determines the optimal strategy for local execution.

We illustrate the complexity of distributed query processing using the example in Figure 16.7. The most crucial element here is the global query optimization step. The example represents a situation in which we want to retrieve all purchase order numbers and the names of the suppliers associated with the purchase orders. The database is distributed over three locations: all supplier

[3] The canonical form is a mathematical expression of the query, according to the relational algebra that provides the mathematical underpinning of the relational model. For more information about relational algebra, see our online appendix at www.pdbmbook.com.

SUPPLIER (SUPNR, SUPNAME, SUPADDRESS, SUPSTATUS)
PURCHASEORDER (PONR, PODATE, *SUPPLIER*)
PRODUCT (PNR, PNAME, PCOLOR, PWEIGHT, WAREHOUSE, STOCK)
...

**Location 1:**

SUPPLIER table
SUPNR: 4 bytes
SUPNAME: 30 bytes
Entire row: 84 bytes
Number of rows: 1000

**Location 2:**

PURCHASEORDER table
PONR: 6 bytes
SUPPLIER: 4 bytes
Entire row: 16 bytes
Number of rows: 3000
On average, there are 200 suppliers with outstanding purchase orders

**Location 3:**

Query:
**SELECT** PONR, SUPNAME
**FROM** PURCHASEORDER PO, SUPPLIER S
**WHERE** PO.SUPPLIER = S.SUPNR

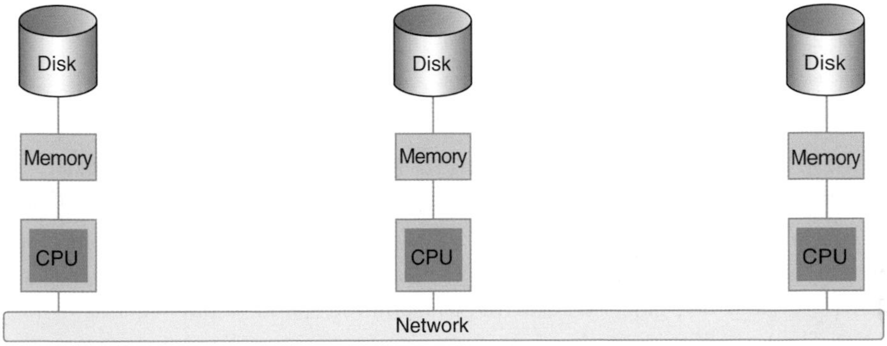


**Figure 16.7** Illustration of distributed query optimization.

data are in location 1, the purchase order and product data are maintained in location 2, and all other data are stored in location 3. The query originates from location 3, which is also where the query result should be delivered. We assume a shared-nothing architecture.

Figure 16.7 contains some quantitative and statistical data that further describe the situation. The optimal strategy will depend on the actual optimization criteria; one could minimize response time or network traffic, aim at equally balanced workloads over the respective servers, etc. Suppose the optimization criterion is minimal network traffic and, for simplicity, let's assume that each fragment corresponds to an individual table. We evaluate four possible strategies:

***Strategy 1:*** all tables are copied to location 3, which is also the location where all querying is performed. The total data transport amounts to $(1000 \times 84) + (3000 \times 16)$ bytes = 132,000 bytes.

***Strategy 2:*** the SUPPLIER table is copied to location 2, where it is joined with the PURCHASEORDER table. The query result is then sent to location 3. The data transport amounts to $(1000 \times 84) + (3000 \times (6 + 30))$ bytes = 192,000 bytes.

***Strategy 3:*** the PURCHASEORDER table is copied to location 1, where it is joined with the SUPPLIER table. The query result is sent to location 3. The data transport amounts to $(3000 \times 16)$ bytes + $(3000 \times (6 + 30))$ bytes = 156,000 bytes.

***Strategy 4:*** this strategy illustrates the *semi-join* technique. Here, projections[4] are used to reduce tables before sending them over the network and joining them with other tables. In location 2, a

[4] A projection is an operation in relational algebra that reduces the number of attributes in a tuple (i.e., it discards or excludes some of the attributes). For more information about relational algebra, see our online appendix at www.pdbmbook.com.

**Retention Questions**

- Discuss the different steps of distributed query processing. Illustrate with an example.

projection operation is executed to yield all numbers of suppliers associated with a purchase order. We estimate this operation will yield 200 supplier numbers. These numbers are copied to location 1, where a JOIN operation is executed to combine the supplier numbers with the corresponding supplier names. This intermediate result is copied to location 2, to process the query further. The final result is then sent to location 3. Here, the data transport amounts to only $(200 \times 4) + (200 \times (4 + 30)) + (3000 \times (6 + 30))$ bytes = 115,600 bytes.

If we only consider the four strategies mentioned above, and the optimization criterion is network traffic, the fourth strategy will be chosen. However, whereas the semi-join reduces the network traffic, a higher processing cost is incurred. Therefore, other strategies may be preferable if an optimization criterion other than network traffic is applied.

## 16.6 Distributed Transaction Management and Concurrency Control

There exists a large gamut of techniques to coordinate transactions in a distributed setting. Such transactions entail distinct subtransactions at individual nodes or locations, with a certain measure of autonomy. We speak of a global **transaction coordinator** and local **participants** in the distributed transaction.

Before discussing individual approaches, it is important to note that interdependence between, and the level of central control over, the participants in a distributed transaction may vary greatly from case to case. In a **tightly coupled** setting, this interdependence and central control are substantial. The distributed transaction is required to have roughly the same ACID properties as the transactions in a standalone setting as we discussed in Chapter 14. Such tight coupling is typically paired with synchronous communication between the transaction participants. Database connections remain open for the entire interaction. However, mobile devices, web services, and programming models geared toward **loose coupling**, such as .NET, also brought about the need for less tightly coupled distributed transaction paradigms. The interactions are based on asynchronous messaging and locally replicated data. Cached local updates are only synchronized periodically with the global system. Database connections are opened just long enough to synchronize data or to execute a query and retrieve the results, but are closed immediately afterward. The data can then be examined and, possibly, updated in a disconnected entity such as an ADO.NET DataSet (see Chapter 15). The database connection is briefly re-established if these updates are to be propagated to the database. Also, loosely coupled paradigms often apply some form of optimistic concurrency, rather than a pessimistic protocol. The latter approaches increase the local autonomy of transaction participants, and in many cases they also have a positive effect on transaction throughput and scalability. The consistency of the data, and especially consistency between different replicas of the same data item, may suffer to some extent.

In the next sections, we start with the more traditional approaches of distributed transaction management and concurrency control in a tightly coupled setting and then gradually move on to more loosely coupled paradigms. We conclude this chapter with transaction handling in NoSQL databases.

### 16.6.1 Primary Site and Primary Copy 2PL

In a distributed but tightly coupled setting, many (variations of) concurrency control techniques from a standalone database system are still applicable. Most of these techniques rely on locking. Three well-known approaches are primary site 2PL, primary copy 2PL, and distributed 2PL. We discuss the former two in this section and dedicate the next section to distributed 2PL.

**Primary site 2PL** comes down to applying the centralized Two-Phase Locking Protocol discussed in Chapter 14 in a distributed environment. In this approach, a single lock manager is responsible for lock management across all locations. Requests for acquiring and releasing locks for all participants should be directed by the transaction coordinator to this central lock manager. The latter applies the rules of 2PL, so serializability is guaranteed. The lock manager informs the coordinator when the required locks can be granted. Based on that, the coordinator will instruct the transaction participants to execute their subtransactions. A participant that has completed processing all its subtransaction's operations will notify the coordinator, who then instructs the central lock manager to release the corresponding locks.

The biggest advantage of primary site 2PL is its relative simplicity. In contrast to other solutions such as distributed 2PL (see Section 16.6.2), no global deadlocks can occur. An obvious disadvantage is that the central lock manager may become a bottleneck. There is no location autonomy: individual nodes cannot perform any local transactions without support from the central lock manager. Concentrating all locking activities with one node may also undermine reliability and availability. This shortcoming can be alleviated to some extent by including a backup location for registering locking data. If the primary site is down, the backup location takes over, and another location is dedicated to become the new backup site. However, the increased availability and reliability will come with a cost of decreased performance because of the additional overhead.

An extension of primary site 2PL is **primary copy 2PL**, which aims at further reducing the aforementioned disadvantages. Here, lock managers are implemented at different locations and maintain locking information pertaining to a predefined subset of the data. All requests for granting and releasing locks are directed to the lock manager responsible for that subset. In this way, the impact of a particular location going down will be less severe than with primary site 2PL, since only a subset of the data and transactions will be affected.

### 16.6.2 Distributed 2PL

With **distributed 2PL**, every site has its own lock manager, which manages all locking data pertaining to the fragments stored on that site. For global transactions that involve updates at $n$ different sites, there will be $n$ locking requests; $n$ confirmations about whether the locks are granted or not; $n$ notifications of local operations having completed; and $n$ requests to release the locks. In this way, location autonomy is respected, but there is a considerable increase in message exchanges, particularly so if the global transaction involves many participants. Also, global deadlocks and other undesirable circumstances may occur, which requires precautions to be included as additional rules to the basic 2PL.

More concretely, as long as the database has no replicated data, applying the basic 2PL Protocol guarantees serializability. Since the local schedules will be serializable, the global schedule, which is nothing more than the union of the local schedules, will be serializable as well. The latter no longer holds if certain data are replicated over different locations. There, the 2PL Protocol must be extended, as illustrated in Figure 16.8. The example represents a schedule with two global transactions

| | Location 1 ($L_1$) | | Location 2 ($L_2$) | |
|---|---|---|---|---|
| time | $T_{1.1}$ | $T_{2.1}$ | $T_{1.2}$ | $T_{2.2}$ |
| $t_1$ | | begin transaction | begin transaction | |
| $t_2$ | begin transaction | x-lock($amount_x$) | x-lock($amount_x$) | begin transaction |
| $t_3$ | x-lock($amount_x$) | read($amount_x$) | read($amount_x$) | x-lock($amount_x$) |
| $t_4$ | wait | $amount_x$ = $amount_x$ x 2 | $amount_x$ = $amount_x$-50 | wait |
| $t_5$ | wait | write($amount_x$) | write($amount_x$) | wait |
| $t_6$ | wait | commit | commit | wait |
| $t_7$ | wait | unlock($amount_x$) | unlock($amount_x$) | wait |
| $t_8$ | read($amount_x$) | | | read($amount_x$) |
| $t_9$ | $amount_x$ = $amount_x$-50 | | | $amount_x$ = $amount_x$ x 2 |
| $t_{10}$ | write($amount_x$) | | | write($amount_x$) |
| $t_{11}$ | commit | | | commit |
| $t_{12}$ | unlock($amount_x$) | | | unlock($amount_x$) |

**Figure 16.8** Illustration of problems with 2PL in the event of replicated data.

($T_1$ and $T_2$). Both transactions update the value of the same account x. This value is replicated, as it is stored on both the locations $L_1$ and $L_2$. $T_1$ subtracts 50 from the amount on account x, using the subtransactions $T_{1.1}$ (in $L_1$) and $T_{1.2}$ (in $L_2$). $T_2$, on the other hand, doubles the amount on account x, using subtransactions $T_{2.1}$ (in $L_1$) and $T_{2.2}$ (in $L_2$). The order in which the operations are executed is important. The global schedule as shown in the example results in inconsistent data: if the initial value of $amount_x$ is, say, 100, then the final value of $amount_x$ in $L_1$ is 150, whereas it is 100 in $L_2$. Still, the local schedules by themselves are serializable. The problem is that both schedules serialize $T_1$ and $T_2$ in a different order. This illustrates that to guarantee global consistency, an additional requirement needs to be imposed apart from the serializability of the local schedules. This requirement stipulates that conflicting operations should be executed in the same order across all schedules.

A second issue pertaining to 2PL is that it can give rise to **global deadlocks**. A global deadlock spans several locations. Consequently, it cannot be detected by individual local lock managers. We illustrate this in Figure 16.9. Two transactions ($T_1$ and $T_2$) process a money transfer between $account_x$ and $account_y$. The account data are stored in location $L_1$ and $L_2$ respectively. Transaction $T_1$ transfers 50 from $account_x$ to $account_y$ using subtransactions $T_{1.1}$ and $T_{1.2}$, whereas transaction $T_2$ transfers 30 from $account_y$ to $account_x$ using subtransactions $T_{2.1}$ and $T_{2.2}$. Although the schedule complies with 2PL, a global deadlock will occur. Whereas there are no cycles in the respective local wait-for graphs, the global wait-for graph, which combines the local ones, *does* contain a cycle, denoting a global deadlock. Therefore, deadlock detection in distributed 2PL requires the construction of a global wait-for graph, besides the local graph. A schedule is only deadlock free if not only the local graphs, but also the global graph contains no cycles.

In practice, there are different approaches to detect global deadlocks. For example, one location can be chosen as the central site to maintain the global wait-for graph. All local lock managers will periodically inform this central site of changes in their local wait-for graphs, to update the global wait-for graph. If one or more cycles are detected, the local lock managers will be informed accordingly and victim selection will determine which transaction(s) to abort and rollback to resolve the global deadlock.

### 16.6.3 The Two-Phase Commit Protocol (2PC)

Besides concurrency control, another concern with distributed transaction management is guaranteeing global transaction atomicity as part of the recovery strategy. Therefore, the mechanism for

| Transaction 1 ($T_1$) | Transaction 2 ($T_2$) |
|---|---|
| begin transaction | begin transaction |
| x-lock($account_x$) | x-lock($account_y$) |
| read($account_x$) | read($account_y$) |
| $account_x = account_x - 50$ | $account_y = account_y - 30$ |
| write($account_x$) | write($account_y$) |
| x-lock($account_y$) | x-lock($account_x$) |
| read($account_y$) | read($account_x$) |
| $account_y = account_y + 50$ | $account_x = account_x + 30$ |
| write($account_y$) | write($account_x$) |
| commit | commit |
| unlock($account_x$, $account_y$) | unlock($account_y$, $account_x$) |

**$Account_x$ is stored on Location 1**
**$Account_y$ is stored on Location 2**

| | Location 1 ($L_1$) | | Location 2 ($L_2$) | |
|---|---|---|---|---|
| Time | $T_{1.1}$ | $T_{2.2}$ | $T_{2.1}$ | $T_{1.2}$ |
| $t_1$ | begin transaction | | | |
| $t_2$ | x-lock($account_x$) | | begin transaction | |
| $t_3$ | read($account_x$) | | x-lock($account_y$) | |
| $t_4$ | $account_x = account_x - 50$ | | read($account_y$) | |
| $t_5$ | write($account_x$) | | $account_y = account_y - 30$ | |
| $t_6$ | | | write($account_y$) | x-lock($account_y$) |
| $t_7$ | | x-lock($account_x$) | | wait |
| $t_8$ | | wait | | wait |

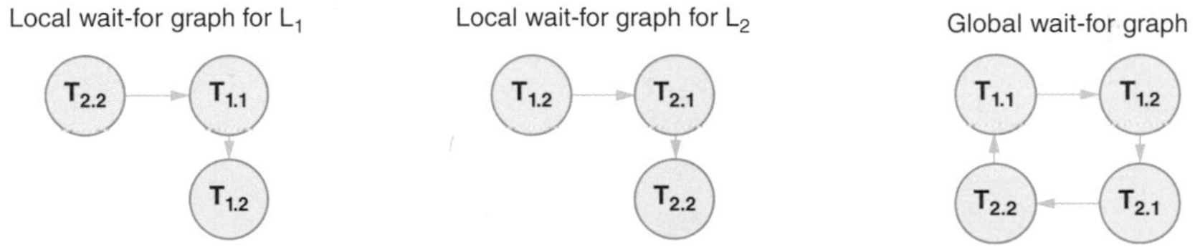


**Figure 16.9** Illustration of a global deadlock with distributed 2PL.

transaction commit and abort should guarantee that the global transaction can only attain a "committed" or "aborted" state if all its subtransactions have attained this same state. Also, care should be taken that individual locations that participate in a global transaction cannot get blocked because of a communication infrastructure malfunction or other calamity.

The **Two-Phase Commit Protocol (2PC Protocol)** was developed specifically to support transaction recovery in a distributed environment. The protocol derives its name from the fact that global transaction completion involves two phases: a **voting phase** in which all transaction participants "vote" about transaction outcome and a **decision phase** in which the transaction coordinator makes the final decision about the outcome. The protocol is illustrated in Figure 16.10.

In phase 1, the coordinator of the global transaction sends a *prepare* message to all transaction participants. The coordinator then waits until all participants have responded, or until a timeout period has passed. Upon receiving a prepare message, each participant assesses whether it can (locally) commit the transaction. If it can, then a *commit* vote is sent to the coordinator. In the opposite case, the participant sends an *abort* vote to the coordinator, after which it immediately aborts the local transaction.

In phase 2, the votes are counted by the coordinator and a final decision is made about transaction outcome. If all participants voted "commit", the coordinator decides to execute a global commit. It sends a "global commit" message to all participants, and enters the "committed" state. If at least one participant voted "abort", the coordinator decides to abort the transaction globally. It sends a "global

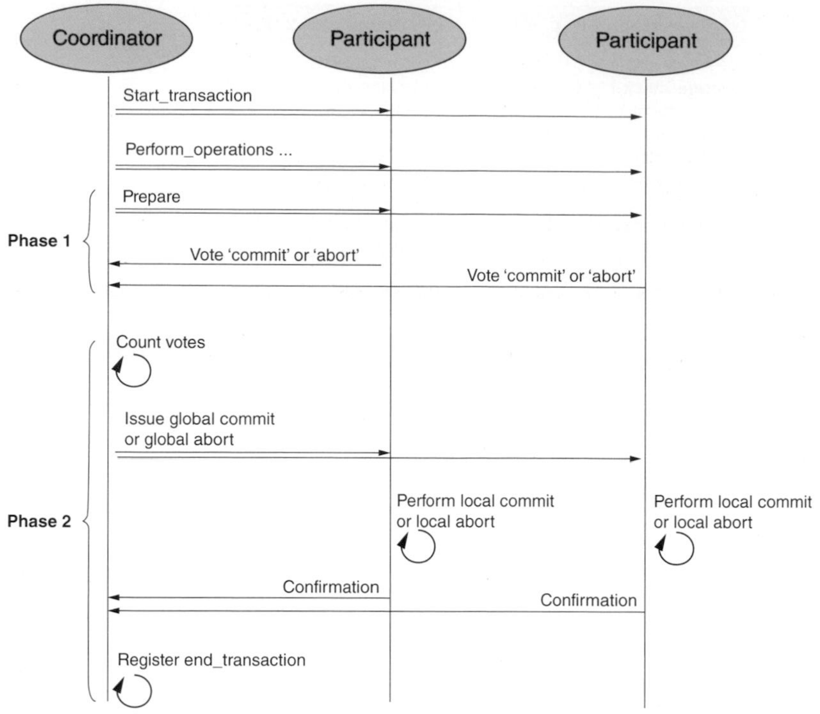


**Figure 16.10** Illustration of the Two-Phase Commit protocol.

abort" message to all participants, and enters the "aborted" state. Each participant then locally executes the global decision (commit in the first case and abort in the second) and returns a confirmation to the coordinator. Finally, the coordinator completes the transaction using an "end transaction" mark on the logfile.

The 2PC Protocol is supplemented by two additional protocols: a termination protocol and a recovery protocol. Given the distributed setting, care should be taken that neither the coordinator nor the participants can end up in an endless state, waiting for a message that will never come because of a communication malfunction or because the party that should send the message had faulted. Therefore, a site will wait no longer for incoming messages than for a fixed timeout period. If a timeout occurs, it will invoke a *termination protocol* (aka timeout protocol), which describes how to react to the timeout. If the timeout was caused by a calamity at one of the other locations, a *recovery protocol* describes how the faulty site should correctly resume operation after its malfunction.

### 16.6.4 Optimistic Concurrency and Loosely Coupled Systems

It was explained in Chapter 14 how optimistic concurrency protocols provide an alternative to pessimistic protocols such as 2PL if the chance of interference between concurrent transactions is limited. Therefore, optimistic protocols do not attempt to *prevent* such conflicts by postponing certain operations until conflict-free execution can be guaranteed because this inevitably affects throughput. Rather, they *resolve* the conflict before transaction commit, typically with an abort and rollback of the conflicting transaction(s). Optimistic concurrency can be appropriate in standalone systems where transactions do not often interfere, e.g., because update operations are scarce or because different transactions mostly pertain to disjoint subsets of the data. However, it is also advantageous in many distributed settings, where the loose coupling between the respective participants in a distributed transaction would render the previously mentioned approaches inappropriate.

Tightly coupled distributed systems often apply a pessimistic concurrency protocol, enforcing global transaction serializability by, across all participants, placing locks on the database objects that participate in the global transaction, as discussed in previous sections. Conflicting operations of other transactions are postponed until the locks are released. Obviously, the longer these locks are held, the higher the negative impact on transaction throughput. In a tightly coupled environment, transactions are typically sufficiently short-lived so as not to hold any locks for longer periods. A transaction either commits in a short time span, or the transaction coordinator, and the other participants, are notified promptly that a participant is not available or will not be able to commit its subtransaction, so the global transaction can be aborted and locks can be released across all participants. However, the situation is different in a loosely coupled setting, characterized by asynchronous communication and unpredictable response times of the transaction participants. This is even more pertinent if these participants are independent organizations or business units, who are not prepared to have their throughput and performance suffer from locks held by another participant, without knowing whether the latter is disconnected or otherwise unavailable. Therefore, pessimistic concurrency is mostly inappropriate and at least not very scalable in such a context.

A typical application of loose coupling and optimistic concurrency is the disconnected database paradigm as applied in, among others, ADO.NET DataSets. In this context, locks are only held during the brief period when a database connection is open, to exchange data between the database and the DataSet – for example, consider mobile sales teams, with partial replicas of product and sales data for their region on their mobile devices when they are on the road. Thanks to the replication, they can operate autonomously and register sales locally without a permanent database connection. Their local copies are periodically synchronized when they connect to the global database. Possible conflicts with other transactions are not prevented but are detected and handled upon transaction completion, possibly resulting in one or more transactions being rolled back.

However, whereas optimistic concurrency may considerably increase transaction throughput and overall data availability in a loosely coupled setting, because of the absence of locks, there is also a downside. For example, suppose application $A_1$ reads data from a database into a DataSet and then closes the database connection. After that, the data in the disconnected dataset can be processed and, possibly, updated locally. If these updates are to be propagated to the database afterward, a new connection is opened, again only for the brief time of the data exchange. However, there is no guarantee that the original data in the database was not altered by another application $A_2$ in the meantime. There, the updates by $A_1$ will be rejected, because they would overwrite $A_2$'s updates, which are unknown to $A_1$, resulting in a lost update. It would not be a solution to lock the original data in the database either since, in a disconnected setting, the DBMS would not know when (if ever) application $A_1$ will reconnect to release the locks, which is obviously unacceptable from a data availability and throughput perspective.

There exist different techniques to detect conflicting updates in an optimistic concurrency setting. A first possibility is the use of *timestamps*. In this approach, a "timestamp" column is added to any table that is open to disconnected access. The timestamps indicate the time of the most recent update of a row. If application $A_1$ retrieves rows from the database and then disconnects, the timestamp column is copied. At the moment when the application attempts to propagate its updates to the database, the timestamp associated with an updated row is compared to the timestamp of the

```
UPDATE  MYTABLE
SET     column1 = @currentValue1,
        column2 = @currentValue2,
        column3 = @currentValue3
WHERE   column1 = @originalValue1
AND     column2 = @originalValue2
AND     column3 = @originalValue3
```

**Figure 16.11** Illustration of optimistic concurrency in an ADO.NET DataSet.

corresponding row in the database. If both timestamps don't match, it means that the row in the database was updated by another application $A_2$ in the meantime, so the update by $A_1$ will be refused. If the timestamps match, the updated row can be propagated safely to the database, and a new timestamp value is stored in the database for the corresponding row.

A second possibility, which is the default technique in an ADO.NET DataSet, is to store two versions of each row in the disconnected entity: a "current" version and an "original" version. The "original" version contains the values as they were read from the database. The "current" version contains the values as they were (possibly) affected by local updates in the DataSet, which are not yet propagated to the database. Once the DataSet attempts to propagate updates to the database, for each locally updated row, the "original" values are compared to the values of the corresponding row in the database. If the values are identical, the row in the database will be updated with the "current" values of the corresponding row in the DataSet. If they are not identical, it means that the row in the database was updated by another application in the meantime and the update by the DataSet is rejected.

The second approach is illustrated in Figure 16.11. Suppose an ADO.NET DataSet was generated based on the rows in a database table MYTABLE consisting of column1, column2, and column3. An update to the database table will only be accepted if the column1, column2, and column3 values in the database are equal to the @originalValue values in the DataSet. In that case, the database row will be updated with the corresponding @currentValue values of the DataSet. If the values are not equal, which means that the rows in the database were already updated by another party, the WHERE condition is not satisfied, and no data will be updated. Note that in most cases one of the selected columns should be the primary key to uniquely identify the rows to be updated. This kind of code can be crafted manually, but is also generated automatically as part of a DataAdapter's UpdateCommand, which is a specific Command object that is used by the DataAdapter to propagate updates from the DataSet to the database. A similar approach is followed in JDBC's disconnected database construct, the CachedRowSet.

> **Connections**
>
> The overall functioning of the ADO.NET DataSet and DataAdapter is illustrated in Chapter 15.

### 16.6.5 Compensation-Based Transaction Models

A loosely coupled environment not only impacts the concurrency aspects of transaction management but also affects recovery and how transaction atomicity is to be guaranteed. Although optimistic concurrency assumes that transactions interfere only rarely, conflicts cannot be ruled out altogether. If upon transaction completion a concurrency problem is detected, the conflicting transaction should be rolled back. This is also the case if the transaction cannot be committed for any other reason, such as a timeout of a participant or another kind of calamity. Atomicity of a distributed transaction is relatively easy to realize using 2PC if the transactions are simple and

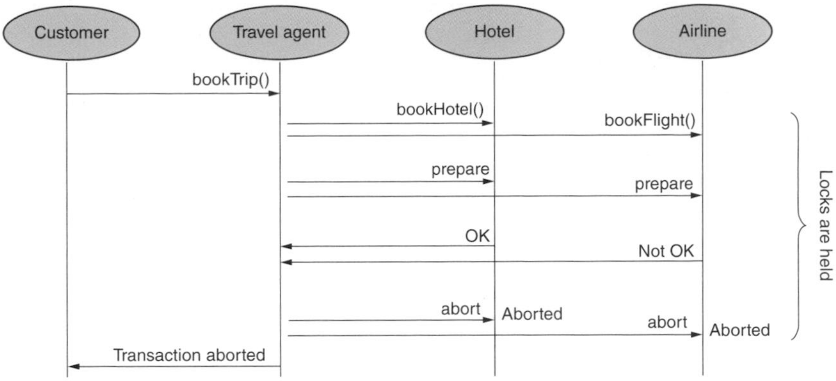


**Figure 16.12** Illustration of enforcing ACID properties on long-running transactions.

> **Connections**
>
> Chapter 10 provides an introduction to web services and related standards such as SOAP and WS-BPEL. The realization of business processes through web services orchestration is also discussed further in Chapter 18.

short-lived. However, many loosely coupled settings, such as web service environments, are characterized by **long-running transactions** (aka long-lived transactions). The duration of such transactions depends on the asynchronous interactions between participants in a business process (e.g., a WS-BPEL process, as described in Chapter 10) and can be extensive, as the name suggests.

Let's consider the example of a travel agent web service, where customers can book trips that consist of flight tickets and a hotel booking (see Figure 16.12). The "travel agent" service in its turn calls upon respectively an "airline" service and a "hotel" service to perform its task; in this context, it acts as the coordinator of a global transaction, in which the airline service and the hotel service are participants. Suppose the transaction is initiated by choosing a destination. It is possible that the customer then takes time to decide on an airline. Maybe the hotel service is temporarily unavailable. The global transaction will only be completed if all participants have done their part, but because of the loosely coupled, asynchronous character of the interaction, this may take from minutes to hours or even days. Enforcing actual ACID properties in such a context would be next to impossible. Also, it would be unadvisable to use a pessimistic concurrency protocol, because locks might be held for as long as the long-running transaction is active, with a dramatic impact on data availability and throughput. To make things worse, it could be that hotel data are locked within the hotel service, whereas it is actually the airline service, belonging to another organization, that causes the delay in transaction completion. On the other hand, pure optimistic concurrency may be inappropriate in this situation, because a coordinated rollback across participants representing independent organizations would be hard to realize if a concurrency issue is detected after a long-running transaction has been active for an extensive amount of time.

In the case of long-running transactions, a **compensation-based transaction model** is often more appropriate. It allows for undoing local effects of a transaction if the global long-running transaction is unsuccessful. The latter could be for reasons of transaction failure (e.g., a participant timed out), but just as well because of issues at the business-process level (e.g., a hotel was already booked, but there are no more flights available). An ACID transaction would require the entire transaction to be rolled back, including the successful hotel booking. However, a compensation-based transaction

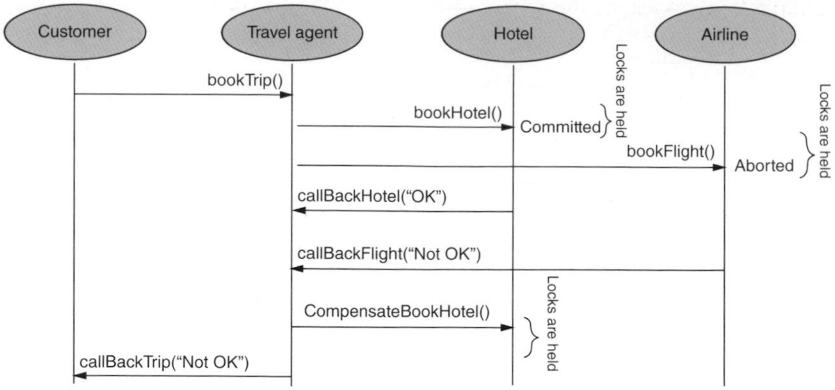


**Figure 16.13** Illustration of compensating transactions.

mechanism abandons the "atomicity" property of the long-running transaction. Local subtransactions within a single participant remain atomic and are committed as soon as possible, without waiting for a global commit notification. In this way, all locks held at that individual participant's premises can be released, with a positive effect on local transaction throughput and, even more important, it makes the participants less dependent on one another with respect to locking and data availability.

Let's examine the example in Figure 16.13. The global "book trip" transaction, which is coordinated by the travel agent service, is long running. Therefore, it may take some time to complete, and therefore it is undesirable to enforce atomicity. The transaction consists of two subtransactions, "book hotel" and "book flight", which reside entirely with an individual participant. Each participant will attempt to locally commit its subtransaction, without awaiting the outcome of the global transaction. Let's assume that the hotel service completes its subtransaction. The "book hotel" transaction is committed, all locks pertaining to the subtransaction are released, and the hotel service notifies the transaction coordinator of its successful completion of the subtransaction. However, suppose the airline service cannot commit the transaction (e.g., because there are no more flights available). It will abort and rollback the local transaction and notifies the transaction coordinator accordingly. However, a global rollback is no longer possible, since one of the local transactions was already committed. Instead, a compensation-based transaction mechanism will require each transaction participant to define its transaction-sensitive operations in pairs, with the second operation specifying a new local transaction that cancels out the effects of the first one: it literally "compensates for" the first transaction.

In this example, the hotel service will specify a bookHotel() operation along with a compensateBookHotel() operation, whereas the airline service specifies a bookFlight() and a compensate-BookFlight() operation. If the local "book hotel" transaction was committed, but the global transaction fails, then the compensating operation compensateBookHotel() will be invoked by the transaction coordinator. This compensating operation will not rollback the local transaction as such (this would not be possible since it was already committed) but will instead induce a new transaction that somehow makes up for the changes made by the first transaction. However, the logic about how to compensate the first transaction is not part of the actual transaction management system or even the DBMS: the compensating operation just specifies an interface that can be invoked by the transaction coordinator, but should have an implementation at application or business-process level. In this example, the compensation logic could consist of just inducing a new transaction that deletes the tuple that represents the hotel booking from the database but could also entail a business logic element, such as a cancelation fee.

A compensation-based transaction model will require that for each transaction-sensitive operation $O_i$ offered by a service, a compensating operation $C_i$ is specified. If a global transaction that invoked $O_i$ is aborted, $C_i$ will be invoked by the transaction coordinator. The implementation of $C_i$ should be "hand coded" by the developer. It is not an automated feature offered by the DBMS, using logfile registrations, as with traditional transaction recovery mechanisms. In this way, the global, long-running transaction is no longer atomic (i.e., some subtransactions can be locally committed whereas the global transaction fails). Note, however, that traditional ACID properties can still be enforced on the short-lived local subtransactions, as induced by $O_i$ and $C_i$. Compensation is the default transaction mechanism of languages such as WS-BPEL, which define long-running processes as orchestrations of individual web services.

As mentioned above, the implementation of the $C_i$ is provided by the developer and shouldn't be restricted to mechanically undoing previously made changes. Canceling a hotel booking could entail a cancelation fee, which could even be made dependent on the reason for the cancelation. Alternatively, the compensation could be taken care of at the level of the global transaction, e.g., by booking an alternative means of transportation, such as a rental car, to reach the destination. In this way, the global transaction can still be completed successfully, despite one or more failed subtransactions. The latter illustrates that the boundary between transaction management and business process modeling becomes considerably more vague than in tightly coupled systems with only short-lived transactions.

Finally, it is important to mention that a compensation-based transaction model does not guarantee transaction isolation (i.e., the "I" in "ACID"). For example, if a bookHotel() operation is followed by a compensateBookHotel() operation in a long-running transaction $T_1$, it is far from impossible that another transaction $T_2$ has read information about room availability between both operations. The availability information as read by $T_2$ may be inaccurate afterward, if one or more room bookings are undone by compensateBookHotel(). This availability of intermediate results is similar to the "uncommitted dependency" problem.

**Connections**

The "uncommitted dependency" problem was explained in Chapter 14.

In some loosely coupled settings, compensating transactions are the only technically feasible alternative, whereas, in others, the tradeoff can be considered between enforcing ACID properties and higher performance. An approach with pessimistic concurrency is preferable where many concurrent updates to the same data subsets are expected, especially if data consistency is important. In other situations, one will be prepared to sacrifice a certain measure of consistency, if this improves throughput, data availability, and scalability. There, optimistic concurrency and/or compensation can be considered, especially if the concurrent access to the same data subsets is rather limited or if the read operations largely outnumber the write operations. For example, in the hotel service, it is probably not too problematic if the reported number of available rooms is slightly off due to the "uncommitted dependency" problem.

**Retention Questions**

- Discuss and contrast primary site 2PL, primary copy 2PL, and distributed 2PL.
- Discuss and illustrate the Two-Phase Commit Protocol (2PC Protocol).
- Discuss the use of optimistic concurrency protocols in a distributed setting.
- Discuss compensation-based transaction models. Illustrate with an example.

The tradeoff between consistency and performance is also very pertinent to the divide between traditional relational databases and NoSQL databases. In particular, NoSQL databases often propose an alternative transaction paradigm, "BASE" transactions, in contrast to the "ACID" paradigm known from a relational database setting. This paradigm shift is dealt with in more detail in the next section.

**Drill Down**

This is also a good point to mention that concurrent systems, in general, are quite challenging to deal with, not only in the realm of databases, but also in the construction of programs themselves. Most computers these days come with multiple CPUs, which makes parallel execution possible, though not always easy due to similar reasons to the ones discussed above: writing programs that are both concurrent and consistent is hard. A well-known recent example of a concurrency-versus-consistency issue is that of a security researcher who was able to game the Starbucks gift cards system to generate unlimited amounts of money on them. The issue was a "race condition" problem in Starbucks' website in the section that was responsible for checking balances and transferring money to gift cards. Issues like this have spurred companies like Google to develop new programming languages (such as the Go language) that are designed to include robust concurrency mechanisms.

## 16.7 Eventual Consistency and BASE Transactions

As explained in Chapter 11, a new wave of database management systems, under the common denominator of NoSQL databases, aims to overcome the capacity limitations of RDBMSs and cater for the storage of Big Data. Although it is already clear that they are very diverse in nature and approach, there are some principles regarding data distribution and distributed transaction management that are prevalent in many of them. We discuss these principles below.

### 16.7.1 Horizontal Fragmentation and Consistent Hashing

Many NoSQL databases apply some form of horizontal fragmentation, referred to as **sharding** in a NoSQL setting. The horizontal fragments (called *shards*) are allocated to different nodes in a database cluster with a hashing mechanism applied to the data items' key. These consistent hashing schemes are conceived in such a way that there is no need to remap each key to a new node when nodes are added or removed. The data manipulation facilities are typically less rich compared to RDBMSs, with, for example, key–value stores only providing basic APIs to "put" and "get" a data item according to its key, the key value being mapped to a node using consistent hashing.

The sharding, which usually also entails a level of data replication, allows for parallel data access across the respective nodes, supporting massive amounts of data and very high volumes of read and write operations. Therefore, many NoSQL DBMSs approach linear horizontal scalability, which means that the performance increases nearly linearly with the number of nodes in the cluster. In addition to the performance, the combination of sharding and replication also yields high availability, with the workload being redistributed over the other nodes in case of failure of a node or network connection. The same levels of horizontal scalability and availability would never be achievable by traditional DBMSs executing ACID transactions over a cluster of nodes. The overhead induced by enforcing transactional consistency over the distributed and replicated data would undo much of the performance gain from including additional nodes. NoSQL databases therefore often resort to non-ACID transaction paradigms, as discussed in the following subsections.

### 16.7.2 The CAP Theorem

The CAP theorem was originally formulated by Eric Brewer and states that a distributed system can exhibit at most two of these three desirable properties:

- Consistency: all nodes see the same data, and the same versions of these data, at the same time.
- Availability: every request receives a response indicating a success or failure result.
- Partition tolerance: the system continues to work even if nodes go down or are added. The distributed system can cope with it being divided into two or more disjoint network partitions due to node or network failure.

As to standalone DBMSs, the choice of which property to abandon is trivial, as there is no network involved (or at least no network connecting different database nodes). Therefore, no partitions can occur, and the standalone system can provide both data consistency and availability with ACID transactions.

Traditional tightly coupled distributed DBMSs (e.g., an RDBMS distributed over multiple nodes), will often sacrifice availability for consistency and partition tolerance. The distributed DBMS still enforces ACID properties over the participants in a distributed transaction, bringing all the data involved (including possible replicas) from one consistent state into another upon transaction execution. If individual nodes or network connections are unavailable, the DBMS would rather not perform the transaction (or not provide a query result to a read-only transaction) than yield an inconsistent result or bring the database into a temporary inconsistent state.

Many NoSQL database systems will give up on consistency instead, the reason being twofold. First, in many Big Data settings, unavailability is costlier than (temporary) data inconsistency. For example, it is far preferable that multiple users get to see partially inconsistent versions of the same social media profile (e.g., with or without the latest status update), than having the system unavailable until all versions are synced, and all inconsistencies are resolved. In the event of node or network failure, the transaction will be executed, even if one or more nodes cannot participate, yielding a possibly inconsistent result or database state. Second, even if no failure occurs when executing the transaction, the overhead of locking all the necessary data, including replicas, and overseeing that consistency is guaranteed over all nodes involved in a distributed transaction has a severe impact on performance and transaction throughput.

**Connections**

NoSQL databases are discussed in Chapter 11, where the CAP theorem was also introduced.

Although the CAP theorem is widely referred to when explaining transaction paradigms for NoSQL databases, it can also be criticized. As became apparent from the previous discussion, it is not only the actual occurrence of network partitions that will result in the choice to abandon consistency. The performance degradation induced by the overhead of mechanisms that enforce transactional consistency *under normal system operation, even in the absence of network partitions* is often the true reason to abandon perpetual consistency. This overhead is further increased by the data replication that is necessary to guarantee availability and *to be prepared for failures*. This overhead exists even when no such failures occur. Also, one could argue that availability and performance are essentially the same concepts, with unavailability being an extreme case of high latency and low performance. Therefore, in many high-volume settings, the real tradeoff is between consistency and performance. Obviously, the result of this tradeoff will be different, depending on the setting: a bank will never allow its customers to receive an inconsistent overview of their savings accounts status just for the sake of performance.

### 16.7.3 BASE Transactions

Although many NoSQL databases make a different tradeoff between consistency and availability/performance than more traditional DBMSs, they do not give up on consistency altogether. There would be no point in maintaining a database if the quality and consistency of its content cannot be guaranteed in the long run. Rather, they position themselves on a continuum between high availability and permanent consistency, where the exact position on this continuum can often be configured by the administrator. This paradigm is called **eventual consistency**: the results of a database transaction will eventually be propagated to all replicas and if no further transactions are executed then the system will eventually become consistent, but it is not consistent at all times, as is the case with ACID transactions.

To contrast this approach to ACID transactions (and staying within the chemical jargon), this transaction paradigm was coined as BASE transactions. BASE stands for Basically Available, Soft state, Eventually consistent:

- Basically Available: measures are in place to guarantee availability under all circumstances, if necessary at the cost of consistency.
- Soft state: the state of the database may evolve, even without external input, due to the asynchronous propagation of updates throughout the system.
- Eventually consistent: the database will become consistent over time, but may not be consistent at any moment and especially not at transaction commit.

**Drill Down**

ACID and BASE both refer to concepts from chemistry. In that sense, it's not surprising that BASE was chosen as an acronym to contrast ACID.

Write operations are performed on one or at most a few of the replicas of a data item. Once these are updated, the write operation is considered as finished. Updates to the other replicas are propagated asynchronously in the background (possibly waiting for unavailable nodes or connections to become available again), so eventually all replicas receive the update. Read operations are performed on one or only a few of the replicas. If only a single replica is retrieved, there is no guarantee that this is the most recent one, but the eventual consistency guarantees it will not be too out of date either. If a read operation involves multiple replicas, these may not necessarily be consistent with one another. There are different options to resolve such inconsistencies:

- The DBMS contains rules to resolve conflicts before returning the retrieved data to the application. This often involves the use of timestamps (e.g., "last write wins"), which means that the most recently written version is returned. This approach can be used to retrieve the current session state, for example, if data pertaining to customer sessions of a web store are persisted in a NoSQL database.
- The burden of conflict resolution is shifted from the DBMS to the application. Here, the business logic can determine how conflicting replicas of the same data item can be reconciled. For example, the application may contain logic to combine the contents of two conflicting versions of the same customer's shopping cart into a single unified version.

### 16.7.4 Multi-Version Concurrency Control and Vector Clocks

The previous discussion illustrated that the moment of enforcing consistency on the database content, and especially on different versions of the same data item, is different for ACID versus BASE transactions. With ACID transactions, the database cannot be updated (i.e., some data cannot be written) if this may be a cause for conflicts. Therefore, the DBMS will lock certain data to postpone read or write operations until consistency can be guaranteed. With BASE transactions, conflict resolution does not necessarily happen at the moment of *writing* the data but may be postponed until the data are actually *read*. This approach is inspired by the concern of availability and transaction throughput: the database may need to be "always writable", and updates should not be prevented by locks or the risk of conflicts. For example, it would be unacceptable for a web store that the inability to write to the database induces missed sales transactions. Rather than postponing the write operation until the risk of conflicts is mitigated, a new version of the data item is created with the updated value. Meanwhile, another user or application may be inducing another write, resulting in yet another replica of the same data item. As a consequence, the DBMS may contain multiple inconsistent versions of this data item; conflict resolution between these versions is postponed until the data are actually retrieved.

The concurrency protocols that sustain this approach are called MVCC (Multi-Version Concurrency Control). Such protocols are typically based on these principles:

- A read operation returns one or more versions of a data item; there may be conflicts between these versions, which are resolved by the DBMS or the client application.
- A write operation results in the creation of a new version of a data item.
- A more elaborate kind of timestamp, called a vector clock, is used to discriminate between data item versions and to trace their origin. Each version of a data item is associated with such a vector clock.
- Versions of a data item that are obsolete according to their vector clock are garbage collected.[5] In some implementations, obsolete versions are archived for version management.

A vector clock consists of a list of [node, counter] pairs, with the node referring to the node that handled the write of that version and the counter denoting the version number of writes by that node. In this way, the entirety of vector clocks associated with versions of a data item represents the lines of descendance of the respective versions.

A read operation retrieves all conflicting versions of a data item, with the versions' vector clocks. A write operation creates a new version of a data item with a corresponding vector clock. If all counters in a version's vector clock are less-than-or-equal-to all counters in another version's clock, then the first version is an ancestor of the second one and can safely be garbage collected. Otherwise, both versions represent conflicting versions and should be retained. They may be reconciled afterward.

An example is provided in Figure 16.14. Suppose a client stores a new data item D into the database. The write is handled by node N1, which creates a first version $D_1$ of the data item. This results in the vector clock ([N1, 1]). Then, the client updates the data item, and the write is handled by the same node N1. A new version $D_2$ of the data item is created, and the vector clock becomes ([N1, 2]) since the same node N1 has created a second version. According to the vector clock, $D_2$ is a descendant of $D_1$, and therefore $D_1$ can be garbage collected.

[5] Garbage collection refers to the cleaning up of obsolete or unnecessary objects or versions of objects. The term may apply to objects in internal memory (e.g., as part of the memory management of a programming language) or to objects in persistent storage (e.g., as part of a database).

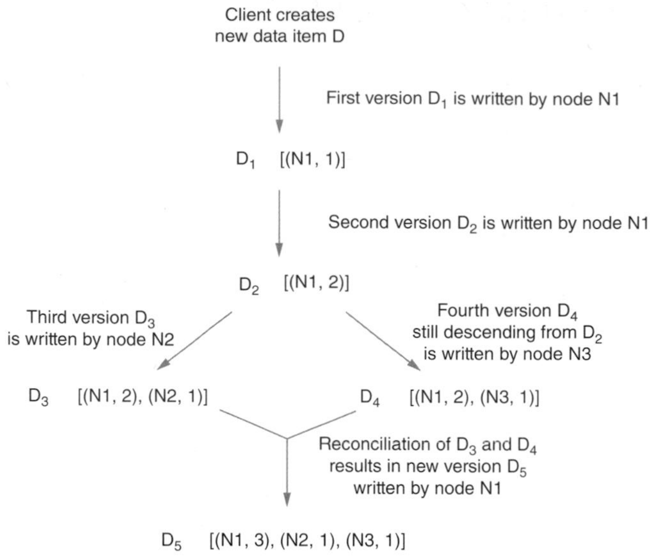


**Figure 16.14** Illustration of MVCC with vector clocks.

Then, once more, the client updates the data item, but now the write is handled by a different node N2. This results in a third version $D_3$ of the data item, which descends from $D_2$ and which is the first version written by N2. The vector clock therefore becomes ([N1, 2], [N2, 1]). Now suppose in the meantime another client reads D and receives version $D_2$. The client updates the data item, and the write is handled by yet another node N3. This results in a version $D_4$, which is a descendant of $D_2$. The vector clock becomes ([N1, 2], [N3, 1]).

Note that $D_2$ can be garbage collected because it is superseded by both $D_3$ and $D_4$, as is also represented in the respective vector clocks. Yet, both $D_3$ and $D_4$ need to be retained. Although they have a common ancestor in $D_2$, they do not descend from one another, and both $D_3$ and $D_4$ contain updates that are not reflected in the other. This is also represented in their vector clocks. However, at some point, both versions will be read and reconciled by a client or by the DBMS. The new version $D_5$ will be a descendant of both $D_3$ and $D_4$. Suppose the write is handled by N1 again. The vector clock then becomes ([N1, 3], [N2, 1], [N3, 1]). $D_3$ and $D_4$ can now be garbage collected.

### 16.7.5 Quorum-Based Consistency

As mentioned, many NoSQL database systems provide the administrator with the means to position the system on a continuum between high availability and permanent consistency. This position can be configured by manipulating the parameters in a quorum-based protocol. Quorum-based protocols essentially enforce consistency between replicas of the same data item using three configurable parameters N, R, and W, with $R \leq N$ and $W \leq N$:

- N represents the number of nodes to which a data item is replicated (e.g., in a consistent hashing ring). The higher N, the higher the redundancy and hence the smaller the risk of unavailability or data loss. A higher N also allows for more parallelism but increases the overhead if one needs to keep all N replicas permanently consistent.
- R refers to the minimum number of nodes that should respond before a read operation for a data item can be considered as completed. The higher R is, the slower the read performance since the

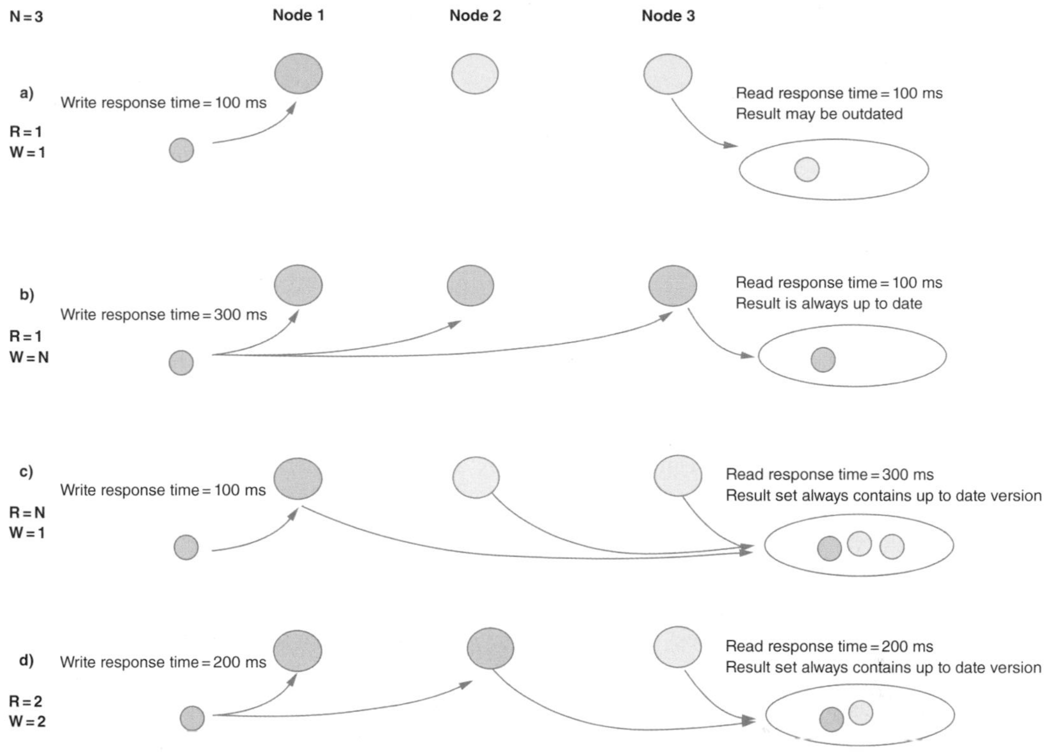


**Figure 16.15** Illustration of quorum-based consistency.

response time is determined by the slowest of these R nodes. A higher R increases the chance that the set of replicas returned by these R nodes contains an up-to-date version of the data item.

- W refers to the minimum number of nodes that should receive the updated value before a write operation for a data item can be considered as completed. The higher W is, the slower the write performance since the response time is determined by the slowest of these W nodes. A higher W increases the number of nodes that contain an up-to-date version of the data item, and therefore increases consistency of the database.

By manipulating R and W, the database administrator can decide on the tradeoff between performance and consistency, but also on the tradeoff between read performance and write performance. Some typical configurations are depicted in Figure 16.15. Four configurations are presented with each time N = 3 and with varying R and W. The circles represent replicas of a single data item, stored on node 1, node 2, and node 3, with a dark circle denoting an up-to-date replica and a light circle denoting an outdated replica. For the sake of simplicity, let's assume that a first node always responds after 100 milliseconds, a second node after 200 milliseconds, and a third node after 300 milliseconds. Let's also assume these figures hold for both read and write operations. In real-life situations, these values will fluctuate depending on the actual workload of every node.

Configuration (a) represents a situation in which both R = 1 and W = 1. A write operation is completed after a first node has received the updated value. This takes 100 ms. A read operation is completed once the response from one node is received; this takes 100 ms as well. However, the first responding node may not be the one with the most up-to-date replica of the data item, so the result may be (slightly) outdated. However, this may not be a problem in many Big Data contexts.

Configuration (b) represents a situation in which R = 1 and W = N. Now, a write operation is only completed after all three nodes received the updated value. For the slowest responding node, this is after 300 ms, so the write takes much longer than in configuration (a). A read operation is still considered as completed once the response from one node is received, so the read time remains at 100 ms. Since all nodes participated in the write and hence received the updated value, the response of even a single node is guaranteed to provide an up-to-date version of the data item. This configuration may be appropriate in settings with not too many writes but the need for many fast reads – for example, if the database contains fairly stable product catalog data.

Configuration (c) represents a situation in which R = N and W = 1. A write operation is completed after a first node has received the updated value, so the write time is back to 100 ms. Now a read operation is only completed once the response from all three nodes is received, so the read time increases to 300 ms. Since all replicas of the data item are retrieved with the read, the result set is guaranteed to contain the most up-to-date version, next to more outdated versions. Upon every read, the conflicting versions can be reconciled by the DBMS or by the application. Write performance will be better than read performance, so this configuration may be appropriate if the DBMS needs to be "always writable", e.g., in order not to miss any sales transactions because of too slow response times.

Configuration (d) represents a situation in which both R = 2 and W = 2. A write operation is completed after two nodes have received the updated value, so the write time is 200 ms. Now a read operation is completed once the response from two nodes is received, so the read time amounts to 200 ms as well. Since two out of the three replicas are retrieved with each read operation, and two out of the three nodes receive an up-to-date value with each write operation, the result set of each read is guaranteed to contain the most up-to-date version, possibly next to a more outdated version (although both versions in the result set could be up-to-date as well). The conflicting versions can be reconciled by the DBMS or by the application.

Note that any of the four configurations can be most appropriate, depending on the context and the need for retrieving up-to-date versions of the data at all times, and depending on the tradeoff between read and write performance. However, configuration (d), with W = 2 and R = 2, strikes a good balance between all concerns. A configuration with R + W > N is guaranteed to provide at least one up-to-date replica with each read operation. This is the case in configurations (b), (c), and (d). Configurations with R + W ≤ N will have better read and/or write performance, but it cannot be guaranteed that the result set of each read operation will contain an up-to-date replica. This situation was illustrated in configuration (a), which had the best overall performance.

To conclude this chapter, it is important to stress that not all NoSQL DBMSs use some form of BASE transactions and tolerate temporary inconsistent data. Many, and this is a growing tendency, do value consistency and hold on to an ACID transaction paradigm (e.g., using optimistic concurrency).

**Retention Questions**

- Discuss the key principles regarding data distribution and distributed transaction management in a NoSQL database setting.
- Explain the CAP theorem.
- Contrast BASE versus ACID transactions.
- What are the key principles of multi-version concurrency control?
- How do quorum-based protocols enforce consistency between replicas of the same data item? Illustrate with some examples.

## Summary

In this chapter, we dealt with distributed databases and specifically focused on distributed transaction management. We started with the rationale behind distributed systems and data distribution and discussed different architectural set-ups. Then, we discriminated between horizontal, vertical, and mixed fragmentation, and discussed data replication and different kinds of transparency. We overviewed the complexities of distributed query processing and query optimization. Finally, we introduced transaction paradigms for tightly coupled and more loosely coupled distributed settings, with examples of both pessimistic and optimistic concurrency. We focused on the extra coordination required to guarantee data consistency and transaction atomicity. Also, some paradigms sacrificed atomicity and/or consistency to a certain extent to reduce overhead and improve transaction throughput. An example here is compensation-based protocols. We concluded with a discussion of the BASE transaction paradigm, which is often applied in a NoSQL setting, and which can be complemented by multi-version concurrency control and quorum-based consistency.

### Scenario Conclusion

Sober has now learned about the impact of data distribution and distributed databases on query processing and optimization, transaction management, and concurrency control. The company now also knows the basic principles regarding data distribution and distributed transaction management in a NoSQL database setting. It will take into account all lessons learned as part of its strategic expansion plan.

## Key Terms

**access transparency**
**canonical form**
**compensation-based transaction model**
**data localization**
**decision phase**
**derived fragmentation**
**distributed 2PL**
**distributed database systems**
**eventual consistency**
**federated database**
**fragment query**
**fragmentation**
**fragmentation transparency**
**fragments**
**global deadlock**
**global query optimization**
**horizontal fragmentation**
**inter-query parallelism**
**intra-query parallelism**
**local query optimization**
**location transparency**
**long running transactions**
**loosely coupled**
**mixed fragmentation**
**parallel databases**
**participants**
**primary copy 2PL**
**primary site 2PL**
**query decomposition**
**replication transparency**
**shared-disk architecture**
**shared-memory architecture**
**shared-nothing architecture**
**tightly coupled**
**transaction coordinator**
**transaction transparency**
**transparency**
**Two-Phase Commit Protocol (2PC Protocol)**
**vertical fragmentation**
**voting phase**
**wrappers**

## Review Questions

**16.1.** Which statement is **correct**?

a. In a shared-memory architecture, multiple interconnected processors that run the DBMS software share the same central storage and secondary storage.
b. With a shared-disk architecture, each processor has its own central storage but shares secondary storage with the other processors.
c. In a shared-nothing architecture, each processor has its own central storage and hard disk units.
d. All statements are correct.

**16.2.** With horizontal fragmentation...

a. each fragment consists of a subset of the columns of the global dataset.
b. each fragment consists of rows that satisfy a certain query predicate.

**16.3.** Which statement is **not correct**?

a. Location transparency means that database users do not need to know on which node the required data reside.
b. Fragmentation transparency refers to the fact that users can execute global queries, without being concerned with the fact that distributed fragments will be involved, and need to be combined, to perform the query.
c. Transaction transparency refers to the fact that the distributed database can be accessed and queried in a uniform fashion, regardless of the different database systems and APIs that may be involved.
d. Replication transparency means that different replicas of the same data item will be automatically kept consistent by the database system and updates to one replica will be propagated transparently (be it synchronously or asynchronously) to the other copies of the same data item.

**16.4.** Which statement is **not correct**?

a. Primary site 2PL comes down to applying the centralized Two-Phase Locking Protocol in a distributed environment.
b. A disadvantage of primary site 2PL is that the central lock manager may become a bottleneck.
c. With distributed 2PL, every site has its own lock manager, which is responsible for managing all locking data pertaining to the fragments stored on that site.
d. Even if the database contains replicated data, applying the basic 2PL protocol still suffices to guarantee serializability.

**16.5.** A schedule in 2PL is deadlock free if...

a. both the local and global wait-for graphs contain no cycles.
b. the local wait-for graphs contain no cycles.
c. the global wait-for graph contains only a limited number of cycles.
d. the local wait-for graph contains only a limited number of cycles.

**16.6.** Optimistic concurrency may considerably increase transaction throughput and overall data availability in a...

a. tightly coupled setting.
b. loosely coupled setting.

**16.7.** Many NoSQL databases apply some form of...

a. vertical fragmentation.
b. horizontal fragmentation.

**16.8.** Eventual consistency in a NoSQL environment implies that...

a. the results of a database transaction will eventually be propagated to all replicas and if no further transactions are executed then the system will eventually become consistent.
b. the results of a database transaction will immediately be propagated to all replicas.
c. the database is consistent at all times.
d. the database is inconsistent at all times.

**16.9.** With BASE transactions, conflict resolution...

a. always happens at the moment of writing the data.
b. may be postponed until the data are actually read.

**16.10.** Quorum-based protocols essentially enforce consistency between replicas of the same data item by means of three configurable parameters N (the number of nodes to which a data item is replicated), R (the minimum number of nodes that should respond before a read operation for a data item can be considered as completed), and W (the minimum number of nodes that should receive the updated value before a write operation for a data item can be considered as completed), with $R \leq N$ and $W \leq N$. Which statement is **not correct**?

a. A higher N allows for more parallelism, but at the same time increases the overhead if one needs to keep all N replicas permanently consistent.
b. A higher R increases the chance that the set of replicas that is returned by these R nodes contains an up-to-date version of the data item.
c. The higher W is, the faster the write performance, since the response time is determined by the fastest of these W nodes.
d. By manipulating R and W, the database administrator can decide on the tradeoff between performance and consistency, but also on the tradeoff between read performance and write performance.

## Problems and Exercises

16.1E Discuss the most important architectural variants of distributed databases.

16.2E Illustrate vertical, horizontal, mixed, and derived fragmentation with an example.

16.3E Discuss the different types of transparency in a distributed database environment.

16.4E Work out an example of distributed query processing.

16.5E Discuss and contrast the following locking approaches: primary site 2PL, primary copy 2PL, and distributed 2PL.

16.6E Discuss different techniques to detect conflicting updates in an optimistic concurrency setting.

16.7E Discuss and illustrate a compensation-based transaction model.

16.8E What is meant by eventual consistency and BASE transactions?

16.9E What is meant by multi-version concurrency control?

16.10E What is quorum-based consistency? Illustrate with an example.

# Part IV

# Data Warehousing, Data Governance, and (Big) Data Analytics

# 17 Data Warehousing and Business Intelligence

## Chapter Objectives

In this chapter, you will learn to:

- understand the differences between operational and tactical/strategic decision-making;
- define a data warehouse in terms of its key characteristics;
- discern different types of data warehouse schemas;
- understand the key steps of the extraction, transformation, and loading process;
- define a data mart in terms of its key characteristics;
- understand the advantages and disadvantages of virtual data warehouses and virtual data marts;
- define an operational data store;
- discern the differences between data warehouses and data lakes;
- understand the applications of business intelligence by means of query and reporting, pivot tables, and on-line analytical processing.

### Opening Scenario

In addition to using its data for day-to-day operational activities, Sober wants to leverage it for both tactical and strategical decision-making. More specifically, the company wants to get a thorough insight in its sales numbers and how these vary on a quarterly basis, per type of service (ride-hailing versus ride-sharing) and per type of car (Sober car or not). By doing so, Sober wants to better understand where it can grow and identify interesting opportunities. The company does not believe it can use its existing relational data model for this since turning the above questions into SQL queries might be too cumbersome. The principals think a new type of data structure is needed to more efficiently answer the above business questions. Considering the limitations of its current model, what would you recommend Sober to do?

Until this point, we have largely focused on storing data in the most optimal way, ensuring their integrity, as much as possible, at all times. A next obvious question is what can we do with these data from a business perspective? In this chapter, we discuss how to take data and extract valuable new business insights from it. We start by zooming into the various levels of corporate decision-making and how this relates to data requirements that support these decisions. This will bring us to the concept of a data warehouse, a massive consolidated data store that we formally define and extensively discuss in terms of data model, design, and development. We contrast data warehousing with some newer developments, such as virtualization, data lakes, and indicate synergies. We then zoom into business intelligence (BI), discussing query and reporting, pivot tables, and on-line analytical processing (OLAP) as key techniques to better understand and unravel hidden patterns in your corporate data.

## 17.1 Operational versus Tactical/Strategic Decision-Making

Each company has different levels of decision-making, which have an important impact on the underlying supporting data infrastructure. The first is the **operational level**, where day-to-day business decisions are made – typically in real-time, or within a short time frame. Traditional databases were primarily developed for these operational decisions and have a strong transactional focus in which many transactions need to be processed in small units of time. Think of a **point-of-sale (POS)** application storing information about who buys what products in what store at what time, or a banking application processing daily money transfers. Operational database applications typically work with highly normalized data to avoid duplication or inconsistencies during transaction processing. They should incorporate advanced transaction and recovery management facilities at all times, guaranteeing the consistency and integrity during the simultaneous and distributed access of data. Given this strong focus on managing transactions, these systems are also commonly described as **on-line transaction processing (OLTP)** systems. Many firms adopt a mix of OLTP systems that have been designed with a strong application focus and are often based on a mixture of underlying data storage formats, such as relational databases, legacy databases such as CODASYL, or even flat files.

The next level of decision-making is the **tactical level**, where decisions are made by middle management with a medium-term focus (e.g., a month, a quarter, a year). As an example, think of a store manager who wants to know the monthly sales for all products to decide upon replenishment orders. Finally, at the **strategic level**, decisions are made by senior management with long-term implications (e.g., 1, 2, 5 years, or more). As an example, think about the chief executive officer who wants to inspect the geographical distribution of sales in order to make an investment decision about building a new store. The information systems needed at both the tactical and strategic level are often referred to as **decision support systems (DSS)** since their primary aim is to provide information to support decisions in either the medium or long term. Those DSSs require other types of data manipulation than traditional operational systems. More specifically, DSSs focus on data retrieval by answering complex ad-hoc queries (SELECT statements) in a user-friendly way. They should include facilities to represent data in a multidimensional way, support various levels of data aggregation or summarization, and provide interactive facilities for advanced data analysis. A DSS should also provide support for trend analysis by detecting patterns in a time series of data. These requirements are in strong contrast to operational systems which focus on simple INSERT, UPDATE, DELETE, and/or SELECT statements and where transaction throughput is one of the most important KPIs. Hence, given these different requirements in terms of data storage and manipulation, a new type of comprehensive data storage facility is needed to implement a DSS. A data warehouse provides this centralized, consolidated data platform by integrating data from different sources and in different formats. As such, it provides a separate and dedicated environment for both tactical and strategic decision-making. By doing so, we can avoid overloading the operational databases with complex queries and allow them to focus on their core activity: transaction processing. The data

> **Retention Questions**
>
> - What are the differences between operational, tactical, and strategic decision-making? Illustrate with examples.

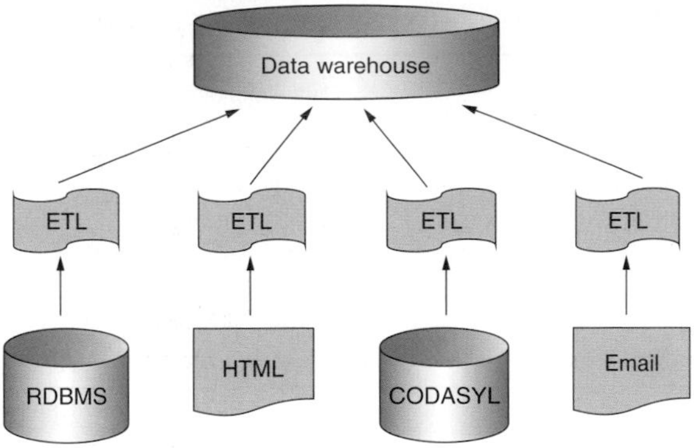


**Figure 17.1** Populating a data warehouse.

warehouse can then focus on providing the master data for doing advanced analyses such as OLAP and analytics, as we discuss in what follows.

## 17.2 Data Warehouse Definition

A **data warehouse** was first formally defined by Bill Inmon in 1996 as follows:[1]

A data warehouse is a subject-oriented, integrated, time-variant, and nonvolatile collection of data in support of management's decision-making process.

Let's discuss each of these properties in some more detail.

**Subject-oriented** implies that the data are organized around subjects such as customers, products, sales, etc. By focusing on the subjects rather than on the applications or transactions, the data warehouse is optimized to facilitate the analysis of the decision-makers by leaving out any data that are not relevant to the decision-making process.

The data warehouse is integrated in the sense that it integrates data from a variety of operational sources and a variety of formats such as RDBMSs, legacy DBMSs, flat files, HTML files, XML files, etc. To successfully merge and consolidate all of these data, the data warehouse needs to ensure that all data are named, transformed, and represented in a similar way. For example, consider the cases in which gender is encoded as male/female, 0/1, m/f; birth date is represented as dd/mm/yyyy, mm/dd/yyyy, dd/mm/yy; or sales are represented in dollars and euros in the underlying transaction data stores. The data warehouse harmonizes all these differences and adopts one integrated representation format. In other words, it establishes a common set of data definitions. These are then typically used during an extraction, transformation, and loading (ETL) process to populate the data warehouse with the harmonized data (Figure 17.1).

**Non-volatile** implies that the data are primarily read-only, and will thus not be frequently updated or deleted over time. Hence, the two most important types of data manipulation operations for a data warehouse are data loading and data retrieval. This has some implications for designing the data warehouse. For example, in a transactional system, integrity rules (e.g., ON UPDATE CASCADE,

[1] W.H. Inmon, *Building the Data Warehouse*, 2nd edition, Wiley, 1996.

**Table 17.1** Difference between transactional system and data warehouse

| | Transactional system | Data warehouse |
|---|---|---|
| Usage | Day-to-day business operations | Decision support at tactical/strategic level |
| Data latency | Real-time data | Periodic snapshots, including historical data |
| Design | Application oriented | Subject oriented |
| Normalization | Normalized data | (Sometimes also) denormalized data |
| Data manipulation | Insert/Update/Delete/Select | Insert/Select |
| Transaction management | Important | Less of a concern |
| Type of queries | Many, simple queries | Fewer, but complex and ad-hoc queries |

**Connections**

Normalization of relational data is discussed in Chapter 6. Transaction management is discussed in Chapters 14 and 16.

ON DELETE CASCADE) need to be carefully defined to guarantee data integrity upon update or removal of data. This is less of an issue in a data warehouse environment since data are only rarely updated or removed. Furthermore, to avoid duplication and inconsistencies, transactional systems always assume that the data are normalized (e.g., totals and other derived data elements will never be stored). This is in contrast to data warehouses, which often store aggregated/non-normalized data to speed up the analyses (see also Section 17.3). Finally, transaction management, concurrency control, deadlock detection, and recovery management are less of a concern for data warehouses since data are mostly retrieved.

**Time variant** refers to the fact that the data warehouse essentially stores a time series of periodic snapshots. Operational data are always up-to-date and represent the most recent state of the data elements, whereas a data warehouse is not necessarily up-to-date but represents the state at some specific moment(s) in time. Data are not updated or deleted as the business state changes, but new data are added, reflecting this new state. In this way, a data warehouse also stores state information about the past, called historical data. Therefore, every piece of data stored in the data warehouse is accompanied by a time identifier. The latter can then be used to do historical trend analysis.

**Retention Questions**

- What are the key characteristics of a data warehouse?
- Contrast a data warehouse to a transactional system.

**Drill Down**

According to the Guinness World of Records, the largest data warehouse contains 12.1 petabytes (12,100 terabytes) of raw data, achieved by a collaboration between SAP, BMMsoft, HP, Intel, NetApp, and Red Hat at the SAP Co-location Lab, Santa Clara, California, USA, on 17 February 2014.

Table 17.1 summarizes the key differences between a transaction system and a data warehouse.

## 17.3 Data Warehouse Schemas

Various conceptual data models or schemas can be adopted to design a data warehouse, which all involve the modeling of facts, as well as dimensions with which to analyze these facts. In what

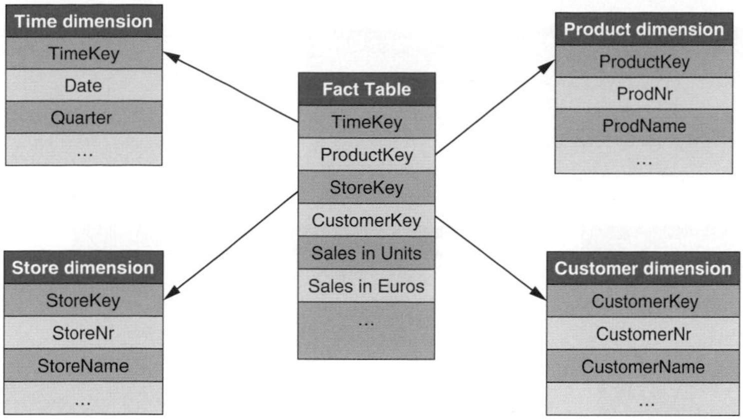


**Figure 17.2** Star schema.

follows, we discuss the most common schemas: a star schema, a snowflake schema, and a fact constellation schema.

### 17.3.1 Star Schema

As the name suggests, a **star schema** has one large central fact table that is connected to various smaller dimension tables. As illustrated in Figure 17.2, the fact table has multiple foreign keys referring to each of the dimension tables, implementing a 1:N relationship type. The primary key of the fact table consists of the composition of all these foreign keys. The fact table typically contains a tuple per transaction or event (i.e., a fact) and also contains measurement data (e.g., Sales in Units and Sales in Euros in our example). A dimension table stores further information about each of the facts in the fact table (e.g., Time, Store, Customer, Product). Additive measures can be summarized along all dimensions, using addition operators such as sum, average, etc. These are the most common type of measures encountered. In our example, Sales in Units and Sales in Euros can be meaningfully added across the Time, Store, Product, and Customer dimensions (e.g., sales per month, average sales per customer). Semi-additive measures can only be summarized using addition along some of the dimensions. For example, the measure inventory_quantity cannot be added across two different time periods since the quantities may be overlapping. Non-additive measures cannot be added along any of the dimensions. Examples are product price or cost.

The dimension tables contain the criteria for aggregating the measurement data and will thus be used as constraints to answer queries such as: What are the maximum sales during a particular quarter across all products, stores, and customers? What are the average sales per customer across all time periods, stores, and products? What is the minimum number of units sold in store XYZ during Quarter 2 across all products? To speed up report generation and avoid time-consuming joins, the dimension tables often contain denormalized data. In other words, the dimensional hierarchies (e.g., day, month, quarter, year), and therefore transitive dependencies, are less clear from the design since they are collapsed into one table and hidden in the columns. Since these dimensional tables are only seldom updated, we don't have to worry too much about the risk of inconsistent data. Hence, the only disadvantage of not normalizing the dimension tables is the duplicate storage of information, which is not that much of an issue given today's cheap (in terms of variable cost per gigabyte) storage solutions combined with the fact that most dimension tables take up less than 5% of the overall storage needed.

Fact table

| TimeKey | ProductKey | StoreKey | CustomerKey | Sales in Units | Sales in Euros |
|---|---|---|---|---|---|
| 200 | 50 | 100 | 20006010 | 6 | 167.94 |
| 210 | 25 | 130 | 20006012 | 3 | 54 |
| 180 | 30 | 150 | 20006008 | 12 | 384 |
| ... | | | | | |

Dimension tables

| TimeKey | Date | Quarter | ... |
|---|---|---|---|
| 200 | 08/03/2017 | 1 | ... |
| 210 | 09/11/2017 | 3 | |
| 180 | 27/02/2017 | 1 | |

| CustomerKey | CustomerNr | CustomerName | ... |
|---|---|---|---|
| 20006008 | 20 | Bart Baesens | ... |
| 20006010 | 10 | Wilfried Lemahieu | |
| 20006012 | 5 | Seppe vanden Broucke | |

| StoreKey | StoreNr | StoreName | ... |
|---|---|---|---|
| 100 | 68 | The Wine Depot | ... |
| 130 | 94 | The Wine Crate | |
| 150 | 69 | Vinos del Mundo | |

| ProductKey | ProdNr | ProdName | ... |
|---|---|---|---|
| 25 | 0178 | Meerdael, Methode Traditionnelle Chardonnay, 2014 | ... |
| 30 | 0199 | Jacques Selosse, Brut Initial, 2012 | |
| 50 | 0212 | Billecart-Salmon, Brut Réserve, 2014 | |

**Figure 17.3** Example tuples for the star schema of Figure 17.2.

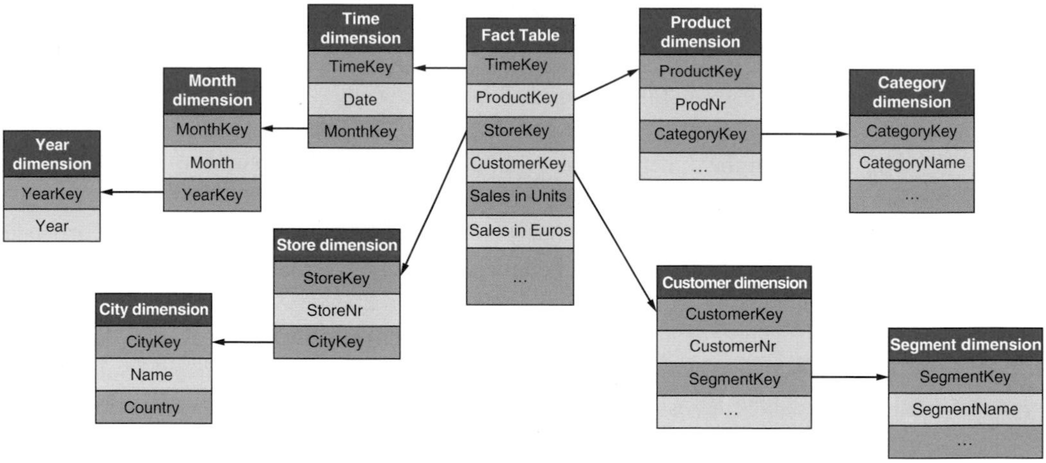


**Figure 17.4** Snowflake schema.

Figure 17.3 illustrates some example tuples for the star schema of Figure 17.2. It can be seen that for his birthday (on February 27), Bart (with CustomerKey = 20006008 and CustomerNr = 20) bought 12 bottles of Jacques Selosse, Brut Initial, 2012 (with ProductKey = 30 and ProdNr = 0199) in Vinos del Mundo (with StoreKey = 150 and StoreNr = 69).

## 17.3.2 Snowflake Schema

A **snowflake schema** normalizes the dimension tables, as you can see illustrated in Figure 17.4. By doing so, it essentially decomposes the hierarchical structure of each dimension. This creates more tables and primary–foreign key relationships, which may have a negative impact on report generation due to the many joins that need to be evaluated. This approach might, however, be considered if the dimension tables grow too large and a more efficient usage of storage capacity is required. It

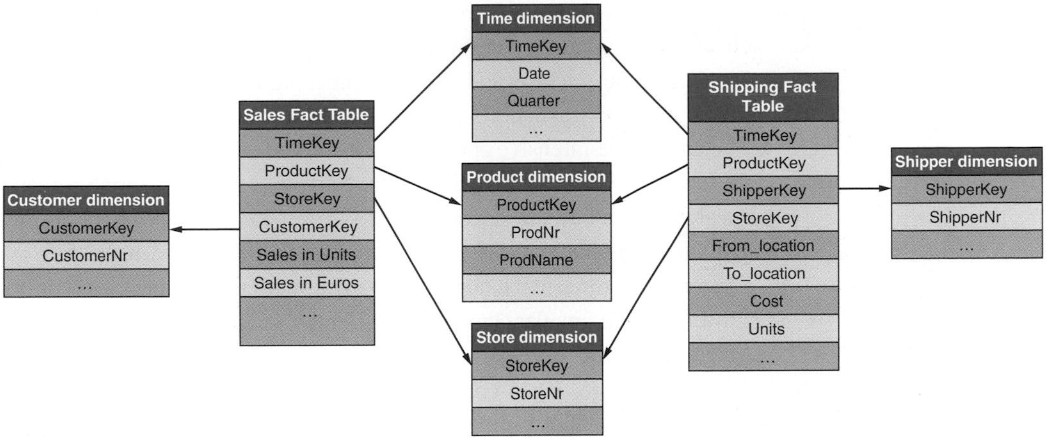


**Figure 17.5** Fact constellation.

may also be beneficial if it turns out that most queries don't make use of the outer-level dimension tables (e.g., Category dimension, Segment dimension) and only need access to the dimension tables directly connected to the fact table (e.g., Product dimension, Customer dimension). Since the latter dimension tables are now smaller compared to the corresponding (unnormalized) star schema, they can be more easily stored in internal memory.

## 17.3.3 Fact Constellation

A **fact constellation** schema has more than one fact table, as you can see illustrated in Figure 17.5. The two fact tables Sales Fact Table and Shipping Fact Table share the tables Time dimension, Product dimension, and Store dimension. This schema is sometimes also referred to as a collection of star schemas, or a galaxy schema.

The above three schemas are simply reference schemas and an organization may choose to adopt a mixture of these approaches by, for example, normalizing some dimensions and keeping the others denormalized (e.g., a starflake schema is a combination of a denormalized star schema with a normalized snowflake schema).

## 17.3.4 Specific Schema Issues

In this section, we elaborate on some specific schema issues. We discuss the use of surrogate keys and the granularity of the fact table. We introduce factless fact tables and give recommendations to optimize the dimension tables. We define junk dimensions and outrigger tables. We conclude with guidelines on dealing with slowly and rapidly changing dimensions.

### 17.3.4.1 Surrogate Keys

As you may have seen in our examples above, many of the dimension tables introduce new keys, called **surrogate keys**, such as StoreKey, ProductKey, ShipperKey, etc. These are typically meaningless integers used to connect the fact to the dimension tables. An obvious question is why we cannot simply re-use our existing natural or business keys such as StoreNr, ProdNr, ShipNr instead? There are various reasons for this. First, business keys usually have a business meaning in OLTP systems, such as social security number for Employee and VAT number for Company. Hence, they are tied to the business setting and requirements, and if these were changed (e.g., due to a merger or acquisition, or new legislation) then all tables using those keys would need to be updated, which may be a resource-intensive operation in a data warehouse environment, because not only the current state is stored, but also historical data. Surrogate keys essentially buffer the data warehouse from the operational environment by making it immune to any operational changes. They are used to relate the facts in the fact table to the appropriate rows in the dimension tables, with the business keys only occurring in the (much smaller) dimension tables to keep the link with the identifiers in the operational systems.

**Connections**

Indexes are part of the internal data model and are discussed in Chapters 12 and 13.

Furthermore, when compared to surrogate keys, business keys are usually larger, which will result in big indexes and slow down index traversal and, consequently, query execution time.

Therefore, using surrogate keys will save space and improve performance. This is especially true for the fact table, since most of its attribute types are foreign keys. For example, if the data warehouse contains data about 20,000 customers, who on average made 15 purchases, then the fact table will contain about 300,000 (small) surrogate key values, whereas the dimension table will contain 20,000 (large) business key values in addition to the same number of surrogate key values. Without surrogate keys, the fact table would contain 300,000 business key values.

Next, business keys are also often re-used over longer periods of time. For example, prodnr "123abc" may be a different product now than five years ago. Hence, they cannot be used as primary keys in a data warehouse storing multiple snapshots of the data across longer time periods. Finally, surrogate keys can also be successfully used to deal with slowly changing dimensions, as we discuss below.

### 17.3.4.2 Granularity of the Fact Table

Since the fact table contains the bulk of the data, it is important to design it at the appropriate level of **granularity** or grain. In other words, you should think carefully about the semantics in terms of the level of detail of one row of the fact table. Higher granularity implies more rows in the table, while lower granularity implies fewer rows. When determining the granularity, a tradeoff between the level of detailed analysis supported and the storage requirements (and hence query performance) needed should be evaluated. Note that it is always possible to obtain lower granularity from data stored with higher granularity (e.g., going from days to months) by using aggregation. If the data are stored at lower granularity (e.g., monthly), it is not possible to obtain more detailed information (e.g., daily). Examples of grain definitions could be:

- one tuple of the fact table corresponds to one line on a purchase order;
- one tuple of the fact table corresponds to one purchase order;
- one tuple of the fact table corresponds to all purchase orders made by a customer.

A first step when deciding upon the optimal grain entails identifying the dimensions. These are usually easy to determine since they directly stem from the business processes generating the data (e.g., common dimensions are customer, product, and time). A more challenging question concerns the grain at which these dimensions should be measured. For example, consider the Time

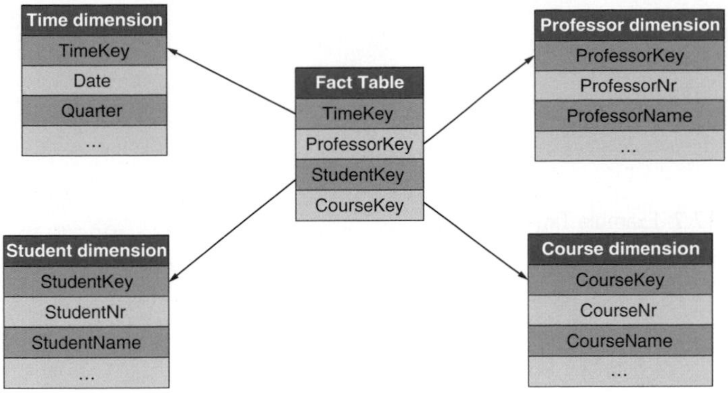


**Figure 17.6** Factless fact table.

dimension. Will we look at hourly, daily, weekly, or monthly sales? This is a decision that should be made in close collaboration with the end-users of the data warehouse. Hence, it is useful to know the type of reports and analyses that are needed for both tactical and strategic decision-making. Since a data warehouse is a long-term investment, it is important to anticipate future information needs when deciding upon the grain. A higher grain may mitigate the risk of not being able to provide the information at the right level of detail. If possible, it is highly recommended to define the grain at the atomic level, meaning at the highest granularity possible.

#### 17.3.4.3 Factless Fact Tables

A **factless fact table** is a fact table that contains only foreign keys and no measurement data. Although it is less common, it can be used to track events. Figure 17.6 shows an example of this for a course administration. The fact table only contains foreign keys to the Time, Professor, Student, and Course dimension tables. The fact table records the attendance of a student for a course taught by a professor at a specific moment in time. This data warehouse design allows you to answer questions such as:

- Which professor teaches the highest number of courses?
- What is the average number of students that attend a course?
- Which course has the maximum number of students?

Another use of a factless fact table is for analyzing coverage or negative reporting. Suppose we leave out all measurement data (i.e., Sales in Units and Sales in Euros) in Figure 17.2. The resulting factless fact table can then be used to answer questions such as:

- What is the average number of products sold by a store?
- Which customers did not purchase any products?
- Which stores did not sell any products during a particular period?

#### 17.3.4.4 Optimizing the Dimension Tables

A dimension table usually has a smaller number of rows compared to the fact table. The number of columns can get quite large, with many of them containing descriptive text. To improve query

| Time dimension |
|---|
| TimeKey |
| Date |
| DayOfWeek |
| DayOfMonth |
| DayOfYear |
| Month |
| MonthName |
| Year |
| LastDayInWeekFlag |
| LastDayInMonthFlag |
| FiscalWeek |
| HolidayFlag |
| WeekendFlag |
| Quarter |
| Season |
| ... |

**Figure 17.7** Example Time dimension.

execution time, the dimension tables should be heavily indexed because they contain the information that will be used as selection criteria. On average, the number of dimension tables is between five and ten. A popular dimension table is Time, which is included in almost every data warehouse or data mart (see Section 17.6). This is actually an example of a dimension that can be easily built upfront since, for example, ten years of data require only about[2] 3650 tuples to be stored if the most-fine grained level of Time is a single day. Figure 17.7 shows an example of the Time dimension definition. As you can see, it contains a lot of date attributes, such as information about fiscal periods, seasons, holidays, weekends, etc. which are not directly supported by the SQL Date function.

A large number of dimensions, say more than 25, is usually an indication that some of them can be aggregated into a single dimension because they are either overlapping or representing different levels in a hierarchy.

### 17.3.4.5 Defining Junk Dimensions

An interesting question is how to deal with low-cardinality attribute types such as flags or indicators. Consider the attribute types Online Purchase (Yes or No), Payment (cash or credit card), and Discount (Yes or No). We can either add these attribute types directly to the fact table or model them as three separate dimensions. Another interesting alternative might be to combine them into a **junk dimension**, which is a dimension that simply enumerates all feasible combinations of values of the low-cardinality attribute types as shown in Figure 17.8. Note that although $2^3 = 8$ combinations are theoretically possible, we left out the two impossible ones with Online Purchase = Yes and Payment = Cash, leaving us with six feasible combinations. We also introduce a new surrogate key, Junkkey1, to link this junk dimension table to the fact table.

The definition of junk dimensions greatly contributes to the maintainability and query performance of the data warehouse environment.

[2] Because of leap years.

| Junkkey1 | Online purchase | Payment | Discount |
|---|---|---|---|
| 1 | Yes | Credit card | Yes |
| 2 | Yes | Credit card | No |
| 3 | No | Credit card | Yes |
| 4 | No | Credit card | No |
| 5 | No | Cash | Yes |
| 6 | No | Cash | No |

**Figure 17.8** Defining a junk dimension.

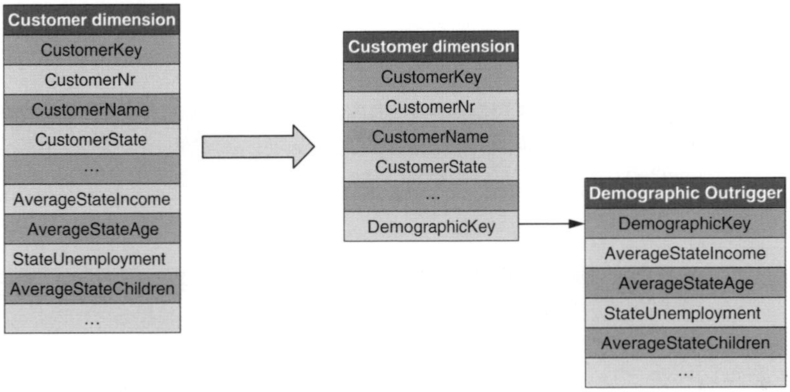


**Figure 17.9** Defining an outrigger table.

### 17.3.4.6 Defining Outrigger Tables

An **outrigger table** can be defined to store a set of attribute types of a dimension table which are highly correlated, low in cardinality, and updated simultaneously. As an example, suppose we have a Customer dimension table that also includes demographic data obtained from an external data provider. More specifically, attribute types are provided on a monthly basis, such as average income, average household size, unemployment rate, percentage female population, percentage population under 20/30/40/50/60, percentage homeownership, etc. in the geographical region (e.g., state, county) where the customer lives. If we were to keep this information in the Customer dimension table, it would imply a lot of duplication of information and, consequently, heavy data manipulation in the event of updates. A more attractive alternative is to put this information in a new table, an outrigger table, and link it through a foreign key with the Customer table (Figure 17.9). It is important to note that this outrigger table is not directly connected to the fact table. An advantage of this approach is that the Customer dimension table now has fewer attribute types and the outrigger table has a relatively small amount of rows since the demographic data are now only stored once per *region* instead of once per *customer*. A drawback is that an extra join is needed to combine both tables. Although a view can be defined to facilitate this, it is recommended to be careful and not define too many outrigger tables in your data warehouse design.

### 17.3.4.7 Slowly Changing Dimensions

As the term suggests, a **slowly changing dimension** is a dimension that changes slowly and irregularly over a period of time. As an example, consider a dimension table Customer that has

**Old status:**

| CustomerKey | CustomerNr | CustomerName | Segment |
|---|---|---|---|
| 123456 | ABC123 | Bart Baesens | AA |

**New status:**

| CustomerKey | CustomerNr | CustomerName | Segment |
|---|---|---|---|
| 123456 | ABC123 | Bart Baesens | AAA |

**Figure 17.10** Approach 1 to deal with slowly changing dimensions.

**Old status:**

| CustomerKey | CustomerNr | CustomerName | Segment | Start_Date | End_Date | Current_Flag |
|---|---|---|---|---|---|---|
| 123456 | ABC123 | Bart Baesens | AA | 27-02-2014 | 31-12-9999 | Y |

**New status:**

| CustomerKey | CustomerNr | CustomerName | Segment | Start_Date | End_Date | Current_Flag |
|---|---|---|---|---|---|---|
| 123456 | ABC123 | Bart Baesens | AA | 27-02-2014 | 27-02-2015 | N |
| 123457 | ABC123 | Bart Baesens | AAA | 28-02-2015 | 31-12-9999 | Y |

**Figure 17.11** Approach 2 to deal with slowly changing dimensions.

an attribute type customer segment ranging from AAA, AA, A, BBB, . . . to C, determined on a yearly basis. Assume now that we wish to upgrade a customer from AA to AAA. There are various ways to accommodate this slow (i.e., yearly) change in a data warehouse environment, based upon whether you want to store no historical, full historical, or partial historical information. A first approach is to simply overwrite the old segment value with the new one (Figure 17.10). Obviously, this implies a loss of information since no history of changes is kept. This approach can, however, be used to correct data errors (e.g., changing the incorrect value Baessens to the correct value Baesens) or when the original value is no longer relevant (e.g., a change in telephone number).

A second approach stores the historical information by duplicating the record and adding Start_Date, End_Date, and Current_Flag attribute types (Figure 17.11). A new surrogate key value is introduced (123457 in our case) and both tuples share the same value for the business key (ABC123 in our case). This clearly illustrates the benefit of using surrogate keys, since we now have two tuples referring to the same customer as indicated by the same business key (CustomerNr), but that can still be distinguished by the surrogate key. The Start_Date and End_Date attribute types are assigned default values of 31–12–9999 but can be updated as needed. Both indicate the so-called validity range, i.e., the time frame during which the other attribute values of the tuple are valid. The most recent tuple has its Current_Flag indicator set to Y. This allows for quick retrieval of the most recent information of a customer. This method works well if the dimension table is relatively small and the changes are not that frequent. The fact table refers to the dimension table by means of the surrogate key, so each fact will always be related to the correct "version" of the customer (i.e., with the Segment value as it was at the moment of the fact). In this way, full historical information is retained. This is not the case if the Segment value is just overwritten as in the first approach. In that case, facts from before 28–02–2015 are erroneously attributed to the "AAA" version of the customer, whereas in fact it was an "AA" customer. Analysis of the data would then result in the

**Old status:**

| CustomerKey | CustomerNr | CustomerName | Segment |
|---|---|---|---|
| 123456 | ABC123 | Bart Baesens | AA |

**New status:**

| CustomerKey | CustomerNr | CustomerName | Old Segment | New Segment |
|---|---|---|---|---|
| 123456 | ABC123 | Bart Baesens | AA | AAA |

**Figure 17.12** Approach 3 to deal with slowly changing dimensions.

**Customer:**

| CustomerKey | CustomerNr | CustomerName | Segment |
|---|---|---|---|
| 123457 | ABC123 | Bart Baesens | AAA |

**Customer_History:**

| CustomerKey | CustomerNr | CustomerName | Segment | Start_Date | End_Date |
|---|---|---|---|---|---|
| 123456 | ABC123 | Bart Baesens | AA | 27-02-2014 | 27-02-2015 |
| 123457 | ABC123 | Bart Baesens | AAA | 28-02-2015 | 31-12-9999 |

**Figure 17.13** Approach 4 to deal with slowly changing dimensions.

wrong conclusions. It would also become impossible to analyze the impact of certain changes in the customer's condition on the facts that occur over time (e.g., whether a change of segment impacts purchase behavior). Therefore, the first approach is not suitable for data whose historical value is relevant to the analysis.

A third approach is to add a new attribute type to the table (Figure 17.12). In this approach, only partial historical information is stored since it only keeps the most recent and previous value. The approach can be easily extended by also adding a Date attribute type indicating when the most recent change (i.e., update to AAA) took place. Also, caution is required not to draw any erroneous conclusions during analyses due to the loss of full historical information.

A fourth approach is to create two dimension tables: Customer and Customer_History. Both are linked to the fact table using their surrogate keys, but the former has the most recent information, whereas the latter contains the full history of updates. This is illustrated in Figure 17.13. Depending upon the type of information needed (most recent or historical), the right dimension table is selected.

Note that the above four approaches can also be combined.

#### 17.3.4.8 Rapidly Changing Dimensions

A **rapidly changing dimension** is a dimension that changes rapidly and regularly over a period of time. Let's now say that a customer's status gets updated on a weekly rather than yearly basis, based upon how much he/she purchased. Suppose we would like to keep the entire history of changes, then both approaches 2 and 4 discussed in the previous section will result in a lot of rows being added to the dimension table (either Customer or Customer_History), which may seriously hamper the performance. A better alternative might be to first split all customer information into stable (e.g., gender, marital status, ...) and rapidly changing information (e.g., segment). The latter can then be put into a separate so-called **mini-dimension table** (CustomerSegment) with a new surrogate key (SegmentKey). If the volatile information is continuous (e.g., income, credit score), you may opt to categorize it and store categories instead (e.g., income <1000, 1000–3000, 3000–5000, >5000) so

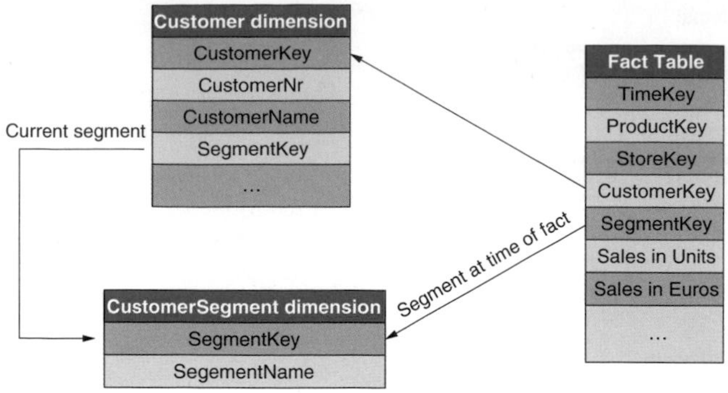


**Figure 17.14** Approach 1 to deal with rapidly changing dimensions.

## Retention Questions

- Discuss and contrast the following data warehouse schemas: star schema, snowflake schema, and fact constellation.
- What are the benefits of using surrogate keys in a data warehouse?
- How can we decide upon the granularity of the fact table and what is the impact thereof?
- What are factless fact tables and what can they be used for?
- Give recommendations to optimize the dimension tables.
- What are junk dimensions and what can they be used for?
- What are outrigger tables and what can they be used for?
- Discuss how slowly changing dimensions can be accommodated in a data warehouse. Illustrate with an example.
- Discuss how rapidly changing dimensions can be accommodated in a data warehouse. Illustrate with an example.

as to keep the size of the mini-dimension table manageable. To connect the Customer and CustomerSegment table, you cannot simply include the SegmentKey as a foreign key in Customer, since any change in the segment value of a customer would then necessitate the creation of a new record in the Customer table, which is obviously not what we want. To successfully make the connection between both tables, we can pursue two options. The first is by using the fact table as a connector. More specifically, we put an additional foreign key in the fact table referring to this mini-dimension (see Figure 17.14). As such, the fact table implicitly stores the historical information about the volatile customer data. Note that the customer segment can then only be updated when a new row is added to the fact table or, for example, when a new purchase is made. Additionally, as illustrated in Figure 17.15, it is also possible to include a foreign key in the Customer dimension referring to the current segment in the CustomerSegment mini-dimension. This is in contrast to the foreign key in the fact table, which refers to the CustomerSegment at the moment of the fact.

This is illustrated with some example tuples in Figure 17.15. Here you can see that the current segment of customer Bart (with CustomerKey = 1000) is B (with SegmentKey = 2), whereas the segment at the time of the most recent fact was C (with SegmentKey = 3). Also, for Seppe there is a difference: A is the most current segment, whereas it was D for his most recent fact. For Wilfried, the current segment is A, which is similar to the segment for his most recent fact.

Another alternative to connect both tables is by introducing an additional table Customer_CustomerSegment that includes both surrogate keys, together with the Start_Date and End_date attribute types (Figure 17.16). Whenever a customer's segment needs to be updated, a new row can be added to the Customer_CustomerSegment dimension table, essentially leaving all other tables unaffected. This allows us to keep full track of the rapidly changing dimension values while at the same time minimizing the storage requirements and safeguarding the performance. Note that the Customer_CustomerSegment table in this way embodies a many-to-many relationship type between Customer and CustomerSegment.

**Fact table**

| TimeKey | ProductKey | StoreKey | CustomerKey | SegmentKey | Sales in Units | Sales in Euros |
|---|---|---|---|---|---|---|
| 200 | 50 | 100 | 1200 | 1 | 6 | 167.94 |
| 210 | 25 | 130 | 1400 | 4 | 3 | 54 |
| 180 | 30 | 150 | 1000 | 3 | 12 | 384 |
| ... | | | | | | |

**Customer Dimension**

| CustomerKey | CustomerNr | CustomerName | SegmentKey |
|---|---|---|---|
| 1000 | 20 | Bart Baesens | 2 |
| 1200 | 10 | Wilfried Lemahieu | 1 |
| 1400 | 5 | Seppe vanden Broucke | 1 |

**CustomerSegment Dimension**

| SegmentKey | SegmentName |
|---|---|
| 1 | A |
| 2 | B |
| 3 | C |
| 4 | D |

**Figure 17.15** Example tuples for the approach suggested in Figure 17.14.

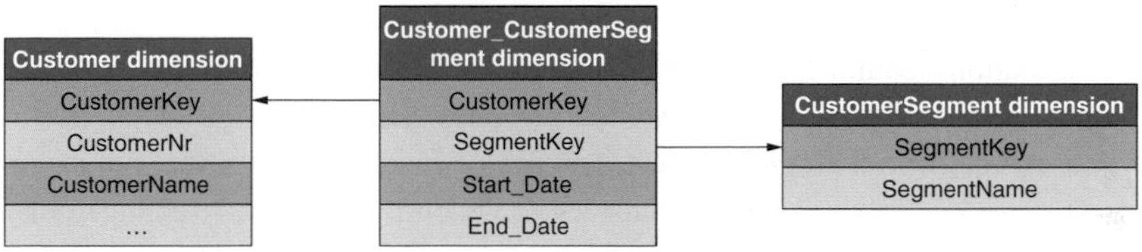


**Figure 17.16** Approach 2 to deal with rapidly changing dimensions.

> **Drill Down**
>
> Among the most popular commercial data warehousing vendors are Oracle, Teradata, Microsoft, IBM, and SAP.

## 17.4 The Extraction, Transformation, and Loading (ETL) Process

Once the data warehouse schema has been designed, we can start populating it with data from the operational sources. During this step, data will be extracted (E) from the source systems, transformed (T) to fit the data warehouse schema, and then loaded (L) into the data warehouse. Hence, this is commonly referred to as the **ETL step**. This is not an easy step, since many of the operational sources may be legacy applications or unstructured data that have been rather poorly documented. Some estimates state that the ETL step can consume up to 80% of all efforts needed to set up a data warehouse. It is also an iterative process that should be executed at regular points in time (e.g., daily, weekly, monthly) depending upon the tolerable data latency and/or desired refreshing frequency, in terms of the impact on source system performance. To decrease the burden on both the operational systems and the data warehouse itself, it is recommended to start the ETL process by dumping the data in a so-called staging area where all the ETL activities can be executed (see Figure 17.17). Note that this staging area cannot be used for any end-user queries or reporting; it is just an intermediate storage environment for the sake of transformation. In addition, some DBMS vendors propose a somewhat different approach, with the target DBMS providing facilities to perform part or all of the

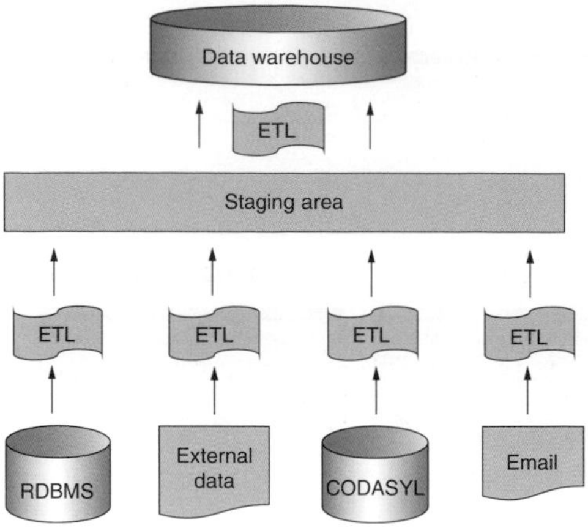


**Figure 17.17** The extraction, transformation, and loading (ETL) step.

transformations within the data warehouse, after loading the data. In that case, we speak of ELT (extract, load, transform), which we don't discuss further.

The **extraction strategy** can be either full or incremental. In the latter case, only the changes since the previous extraction are considered, which is also called "changed data capture" or CDC. Although this is a more efficient approach, it assumes the data in the source systems can be flagged for updates, which is often not possible since many of these operational systems have been carefully optimized and operate in a closed-box environment, thereby not allowing any intrusion. During extraction, it is important to properly accommodate the different types of data sources, operating systems, and hardware environments from where the data are sourced.

The transformation usually entails the following activities:

- formatting
- cleansing
- aggregation and merging
- enrichment.

**Formatting rules** specify how data should be consistently and uniformly encoded in the data warehouse. In the operational systems, gender can be coded as male/female, m/f, 0/1, etc. As another example consider the use of a different measurement basis (e.g., amount in dollars, GBP, or euros) or decimal separator (e.g., 1,000.50 versus 1.000,50). In the data warehouse, all these different formats should then be mapped to a single one.

**Connections**

Chapter 4 discusses various data quality dimensions such as accuracy, completeness, consistency, uniqueness and timeliness.

**Cleansing** will get rid of some of the inconsistencies or irregularities in the data. Examples are dealing with missing values or handling impossible values such as birth date is 01/01/1000. During this cleansing step, it is very important to report any irregularities to the business user to fully understand where they come from and how they should be properly treated. For example, a missing value for income might correspond to an unemployed customer, or a value of 01/01/1000 for birth date might correspond to the default setting of the attribute type. Ideally, any irregularities should be traced back to the operational source systems and data entry processes where appropriate actions can be taken to avoid similarly bad data from entering in the future. The ultimate aim is to provide the data warehouse with high-quality data in terms of accuracy, completeness, consistency, uniqueness, and timeliness.

It is not uncommon to find multiple records referring to the same entity in the operational data sources. This could be due to the usage of different attribute names (e.g., CustomerID, CustID, ClientID, ID), or data entry mistakes (e.g., Bart Baesens versus Bart Baessens). These should then be properly aggregated and merged before entering the data in the data warehouse. This feature is called **deduplication**. A somewhat similar problem is the situation in which different operational sources use different business keys to identify the same real-world entity (e.g., SSN versus CustomerID). Also in that case, the transformation should identify records referring to the same real-world entities, merge them correctly, and provide them with an appropriate and consistent unique identifier.

**Connections**

Chapters 12 and 13 discuss the design of the internal data model and the definition of indexes.

Finally, the data can also be enriched by adding derived data elements or external data. A straightforward example is calculating the age of a customer based upon the date of birth. Another example is enriching customer data with demographic information obtained from an external data provider. It is important that all these data transformation activities are executed with care, since this directly affects the quality and usability of the data stored in the data warehouse.

**Retention Questions**

- Summarize the key activities to be performed during the ETL process. Why is this process considered so important?

During the loading step, the data warehouse is populated by filling the fact and dimension tables, and thereby also generating the necessary surrogate keys to link it all up. Dimension rows should be inserted/updated before the fact rows can refer to them. Ideally, this should be done in a parallelized way to speed up the performance. Once this is completed, it should be closely followed up by adjusting all the indexes and corresponding table statistics. It might even be considered to drop all indexes first and then freshly rebuild them once loading of the new data has finished, to guarantee optimal performance.

**Connections**

Chapter 18 further discusses ETL as a data integration technique, along with other techniques such as federation and propagation.

Obviously, all decisions made during the ETL process should be carefully automated and documented to facilitate both maintenance and understanding of the data. An important aspect of this documentation is the generation of metadata about the data's structure (**structural metadata**) and, possibly, meaning (**semantic metadata**). This information can be persisted in a metadata repository, also called a catalog. Given the complexity of the entire process, commercial ETL tools might be considered instead of writing extensive routines in-house. Most of these tools allow you to visualize the entire ETL process as a flow of activities that can be easily adjusted or fine-tuned.

## 17.5 Data Marts

A **data mart** is a scaled-down version of a data warehouse aimed at meeting the information needs of a homogeneous small group of end-users such as a department or business unit (e.g., marketing, finance, logistics, HR, etc.). It typically contains some form of aggregated data and is used as the primary source for report generation and analysis by this end-user group. There are various reasons for setting up data marts. First of all, they provide focused content such as finance, sales, or

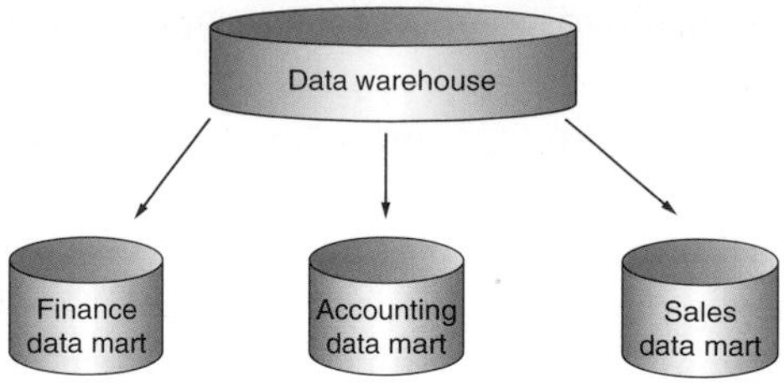


**Figure 17.18** Dependent data marts.

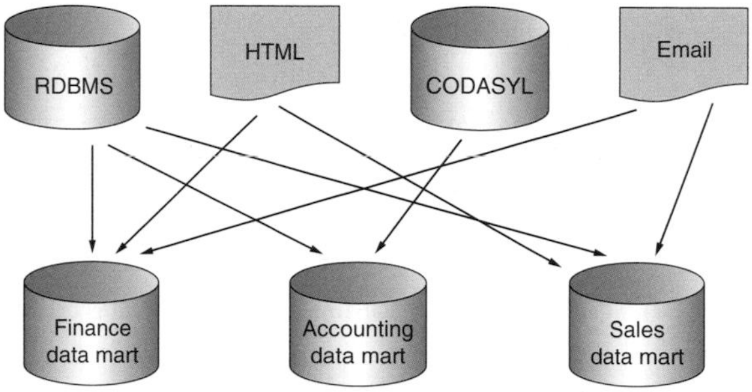


**Figure 17.19** Independent data marts.

accounting information in a format tailored to the user group at hand. They also improve query performance by offloading complex queries, and therefore workload, from other data sources (e.g., a data warehouse). Data marts can be located closer to the end-users, thereby alleviating heavy network traffic and giving them more control. Finally, certain reporting tools assume predefined data structures (e.g., a star schema) which can be provided by a customized data mart. In order to denote the contrast with a data mart, a full-blown data warehouse is often called an enterprise data warehouse, or EDW for short, to emphasize the organization-wide aspect.

A data mart can be physically implemented as an RDBMS, Cube (see Section 17.9.3.5), or a flat file (e.g., Excel file). Similar to a data warehouse, once the data mart schema has been defined, it can be fed data by using an ETL process. Depending upon the source of the data, a distinction can be made between dependent and independent data marts. **Dependent data marts** pull their data from a central data warehouse (Figure 17.18), whereas **independent data marts** are standalone systems drawing data directly from operational systems, external sources, or a combination of both (Figure 17.19).

### Retention Questions

- What are data marts and how do they compare against a data warehouse?
- What is the difference between dependent and independent data marts?
- Contrast the bottom-up with the top-down approach for data warehouse design.

Independent data marts are sometimes considered by firms who do not wish to make the substantial investment of a data warehouse. Dependent data marts have a more complex set-up, but provide the advantage that they all draw their data from the same formatted, cleansed, etc. data warehouse, thus avoiding inconsistencies across business units that share the same data. A well-known concept in this context is what we call **conformed dimensions**. It refers to a dimension that has exactly the same meaning and content across different fact tables and/or data marts. Two dimension tables can be considered as conformed if they are either identical or if one is a subset of the other. A typical candidate for conforming dimensions is the Time dimension, with a week running from Monday to Sunday in one data mart and from Saturday to Friday in another.

Although the benefits may seem attractive at first sight, setting up data marts is a decision that should be made by carefully considering the **total cost of ownership (TCO)** involved. More specifically, this entails development costs, operating costs, change management costs, and data governance and quality costs.

**Drill Down**

Bill Inmon and Ralph Kimball are considered the two pioneers of data warehousing. William H. (Bill) Inmon is an American computer scientist known as the father of data warehousing. He was the first to write a column on it, publish a book on it, and hold a conference on it. Ralph Kimball is the principal author of various best-selling books on data warehousing, such as *The Data Warehouse Toolkit, The Data Warehouse Lifecycle Toolkit*, and *The Data Warehouse ETL Toolkit*, all published by Wiley and Sons. Both disagree on the best way to design a data warehouse. Inmon's approach to data warehouse design is top-down, whereby the data warehouse is designed first, followed by various data marts. Kimball prefers a bottom-up design, starting from a set of data marts first and then aggregating them in a data warehouse.

## 17.6 Virtual Data Warehouses and Virtual Data Marts

A disadvantage of a physical data warehouse or data mart is that both consume physical storage and must be updated periodically. Hence, they never contain the most recent version of the data. One approach to deal with this is by using virtualization. The idea here is to use middleware to create a logical or **virtual data warehouse** (sometimes also called a federated database) or **virtual data mart**, which has no physical data but provides a uniform and consolidated single point of access to a set of underlying physical data stores. In other words, the data are left in their original source and are only accessed ("pulled") at query time. Because no data are stored or replicated physically, the risk of inconsistent or outdated data is not an issue when working with a virtual data warehouse or virtual data marts.

A virtual data warehouse can be built as a set of SQL views either directly on the underlying operational data sources (Figure 17.20), or as an extra layer on top of a collection of physical independent data marts (Figure 17.21). It should provide a uniform and consistent metadata model and data manipulation language (e.g., SQL). The metadata model contains the schema mappings between the schemas of the underlying data stores and the schema of the virtual data warehouse. Queries are then reformulated and decomposed using these schema mappings on the fly, whereby the underlying data are fetched and consolidated on demand. This provides the queries with a real-time perspective on the underlying evolving data. Figure 17.20 shows an example of a virtual data warehouse architecture. The wrappers are dedicated software components that receive queries from the upper level, execute them on the underlying data store, and convert the result to a format (e.g., relational tuples) that can be understood by the query processor. The complexity of the wrapper depends upon the data source. In the case of an RDBMS, the wrapper can make use of a database API such as JDBC. In the case of semi-structured data such as an HTML webpage, the wrapper needs to parse the HTML code into a set of tuples.

**Connections**

Database APIs such as JDBC are discussed in Chapter 15. Federation and virtualization as data integration techniques are discussed further in Chapter 18.

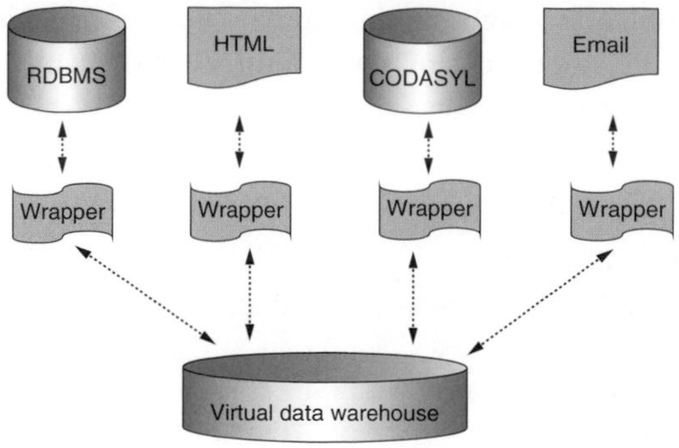


**Figure 17.20** Virtual data warehouse on top of operational data sources.

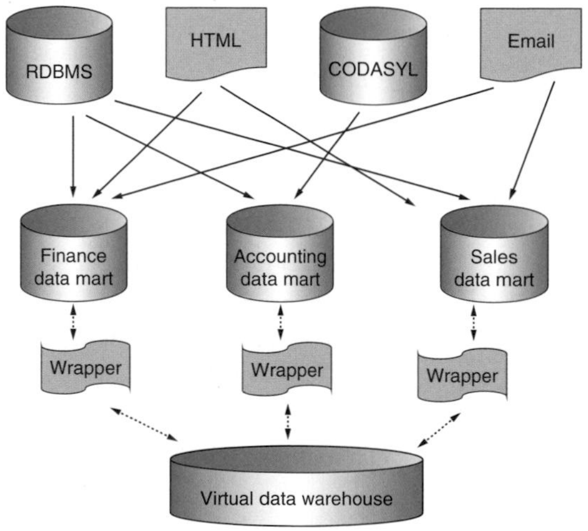


**Figure 17.21** Virtual data warehouse on top of data marts.

> **Connections**
>
> Chapter 7 introduced the concept of views and view materialization.

A virtual data mart is usually defined as a single SQL view. The view can be directly defined on physical operational source data (virtual independent data mart), or on a physical or virtual data warehouse (virtual dependent data mart). Since multiple virtual data marts may share data, it is important to carefully think about how the views are defined, in order to facilitate the overall maintenance.

A disadvantage of virtualization is that it requires extra processing capacity from the underlying (operational) data sources. Hence, it should only be considered in the case that the number of reports or queries is rather limited. The performance of the latter may then be optimized by using intelligent caching mechanisms and cache indexes, combined with materializing some of the views to speed up data access. Furthermore, it is not possible to keep track of historical data since old data are typically replaced by new data in the underlying data sources.

> **Retention Questions**
>
> - What is a virtual data warehouse and how can it be built?
> - What is a virtual data mart and how can it be built?
> - What is the key benefit of virtualization?

## 17.7 Operational Data Store

An **operational data store**, or ODS for short, is another way of dealing with the disadvantage of data warehouses not containing up-to-date data. To put it simply, an ODS can be considered as a staging area that provides query facilities. A normal staging area is only meant for receiving the operational data from the OLTP sources for the sake of transforming the data and loading it into the data warehouse. An ODS also offers this functionality, but in addition it can be queried directly. In this way, analysis tools that need data that are closer to real-time can query the ODS data as it is received from the respective source systems, before time-consuming transformation and loading operations. The ODS then only provides access to the current, fine-grained and non-aggregated data, which can be queried in an integrated manner without burdening the OLTP systems. However, more complex analyses requiring high-volume historical and/or aggregated data are still conducted on the actual data warehouse. In some configurations, the ODS and data warehouse together are overlaid with a virtualization layer, providing a single access point for queries on combined (near) real-time and historical data. Note that the ODS is still part of the data warehouse set-up and is not to be confused with the actual operational source systems.

**Retention Questions**

- What is an operational data source and what can it be used for?

## 17.8 Data Warehouses versus Data Lakes

Much more recent than data warehouses, the **data lake** concept became known as part of the Big Data and Analytics trend, as discussed in more detail in Chapters 19 and 20. Although both data warehouses and data lakes are essentially data repositories, there are some clear differences as listed in Table 17.2. A key distinguishing property of a data lake is that it stores raw data in its native format, which could be structured, unstructured, or semi-structured. This makes data lakes fit for more exotic and "bulk" data types that we generally do not find in data warehouses, such as social media feeds, clickstreams, server logs, sensor data, etc. A data lake collects data emanating from operational sources "as is", often without knowing upfront which analyses will be performed on it, or even whether the data will ever be involved in analysis at all. For this reason, either no or only very limited transformations (formatting, cleansing, etc.) are performed on the data before they enter the data lake. Consequently, when the data are tapped from the data lake to be analyzed, quite a bit of processing will typically be required before it is fit for analysis. The data schema definitions are only determined when the data are read (schema-on-read) instead of when the data are loaded (schema-on-write) as is the case for a data warehouse. Storage costs for data lakes are also relatively low because most of the implementations are open-source solutions that can be easily installed on low-cost commodity hardware. Since a data warehouse assumes a predefined structure, it is less agile compared to a data lake, which has no structure. Also, data warehouses have been around for quite some time already, which automatically implies that their security facilities are more mature. Finally, in terms of users, a data warehouse is targeted toward decision-makers at middle- and top-management level, whereas a data lake requires a data scientist, which is a more specialized profile in terms of data handling and analysis.

**Connections**

Chapter 20 discusses the data scientist job profile into more detail.

**Table 17.2** Difference between data warehouse and data lake

| | Data warehouse | Data lake |
|---|---|---|
| Data | Structured | Often unstructured |
| Processing | Schema-on-write | Schema-on-read |
| Storage | Expensive | Low cost |
| Transformation | Before entering the data warehouse | Before analysis |
| Agility | Low | High |
| Security | Mature | Maturing |
| Users | Decision-makers | Data scientists |

**Retention Questions**

- Contrast a data warehouse against a data lake.

To summarize, a data warehouse is not the same as a data lake. Both clearly serve different purposes and user profiles and it is important to be aware of their differences in order to make the right investment decisions.

**Drill Down**

Data warehousing solutions can also be offered in the cloud. A popular example of this is Amazon Redshift, which is part of the Amazon Web Services computing platform. It is based on Postgres, a well-known ORDBMS. Nasdaq migrated its legacy data warehouse in 2014 to Redshift. They load an average of 450 gigabytes per day (after compression) into Redshift. This includes data about orders, trades, quotes, markets, securities, and memberships. The Redshift costs turned out to be around 43% of the legacy budget for the same dataset (around 1100 tables). Also the query performance was substantially increased. This clearly illustrates the impact of cloud versus on-premise solutions for data warehousing.

## 17.9 Business Intelligence

The ultimate goal of setting up a data warehouse is to provide new insights for both tactical and strategic decision-making. The term **business intelligence (BI)** is often referred to as the set of activities, techniques, and tools aimed at understanding patterns in past data and predicting the future. In other words, BI applications are an essential component for making better business decisions through data-driven insights. These applications can be both mission critical or occasionally used to answer a specific business question.

Since data are the key ingredient to any BI application, it is important that they are appropriately stored and managed, and are of good quality. This is often referred to as the **garbage in, garbage out (GIGO)** principle, stating that bad data gives bad insights, which in turn leads to bad decisions. That's why we started this chapter by extensively discussing the data warehouse architecture. Note that although this is not a strict requirement, most BI systems are built upon an underlying relational data warehouse.

Various BI techniques can be used to extract patterns and provide new insights in data. Each of them differs in terms of sophistication, complexity, and computing resources needed. In what follows, we discuss query and reporting, pivot tables, and OLAP.

### 17.9.1 Query and Reporting

**Query and reporting** tools are an essential component of a comprehensive BI solution. They typically provide a user-friendly graphical user interface (GUI) in which the business user can graphically and interactively design a report. It is important to stress that it is not an IT expert doing the query and reporting, but a business user. Therefore, this approach is sometimes also referred to as self-service BI. Hence, the building blocks of the reports should preferably refer to business terms rather than technical IT artifacts such as database tables, views, indexes, etc. Some tools provide an intermediate **query by example (QBE)** facility that sits between the database and the business concepts. The idea is that a query is composed in a user-friendly way by visualizing database tables whereby the business user can enter conditions for each field that needs to be included in the query. This can then be translated to a formal data manipulation language such as SQL.

Once the report has been designed in terms of format and content, it can be refreshed at any time with up-to-date information from the underlying data store. If the latter is a data warehouse implemented using an RDBMS, the designed report will be translated to a set of SQL calls to retrieve the desired data. The reports can be either fixed or ad-hoc to answer a one-off business question, such as finding the root cause of a problem, or testing a specific hypothesis. Query and reporting tools implement innovative visualization techniques aimed at making interesting data patterns stand out more prominently. Although they are a useful first step to start exploring your data, other more advanced BI facilities are needed to unravel more complex patterns in the data.

### 17.9.2 Pivot Tables

A **pivot or cross-table** is a popular data summarization tool. It essentially cross-tabulates a set of dimensions in such a way that multidimensional data can be represented in a two-dimensional tabular format. An example is illustrated in Figure 17.22, where the dimensions region and quarter are summarized in terms of aggregated sales. A pivot table also contains row and column totals as depicted. The measurement data can be aggregated in various ways, such as in terms of count, sum, average, maximum, minimum, etc. BI tools also provide various user-friendly graphical facilities to customize the pivot table by dragging and dropping dimensions of interest. A first straightforward action is pivoting (hence the name), whereby rows and columns are rotated according to the business user's preference. Also drill-down facilities are provided whereby either a dimension is further de-aggregated into more detail (e.g., splitting up America into North America and South America in our example) or new dimensions are added (e.g., adding a product in our example). The idea here is to navigate from coarse to fine granularity to better see where interesting patterns may

| Sales | | Quarter | | | | Total |
|---|---|---|---|---|---|---|
| | | Q1 | Q2 | Q3 | Q4 | |
| Region | Europe | 100 | 200 | 50 | 100 | **450** |
| | Africa | 50 | 100 | 200 | 50 | **400** |
| | Asia | 20 | 50 | 10 | 150 | **230** |
| | America | 50 | 10 | 100 | 100 | **260** |
| | Total | **220** | **360** | **360** | **400** | **1340** |

**Figure 17.22** Pivot table.

| Array (key, value) | Q1 | Q2 | Q3 | Q4 | Total |
|---|---|---|---|---|---|
| Product A | (1,1) 10 | (1,2) 20 | (1,3) 40 | (1,4) 10 | (1,5) 80 |
| Product B | (2,1) 20 | (2,2) 40 | (2,3) 10 | (2,4) 30 | (2,5) 100 |
| Product C | (3,1) 50 | (3,2) 20 | (3,3) 40 | (3,4) 30 | (3,5) 140 |
| Product D | (4,1) 10 | (4,2) 30 | (4,3) 20 | (4,4) 20 | (4,5) 80 |
| Total | (5,1) 90 | (5,2) 110 | (5,3) 110 | (5,4) 90 | (5,5) 400 |

**Figure 17.23** Example MOLAP array.

originate. Removing dimensions, or roll-up, is also supported. In our example, we may want to roll-up the region dimension in order to get the full picture of sales across all quarters.

### 17.9.3 On-Line Analytical Processing (OLAP)

**On-line analytical processing (OLAP)** provides a more advanced set of techniques to analyze your data. More specifically, OLAP allows you to interactively analyze the data, summarize it, and visualize it in various ways. The term on-line refers to the fact that the reports can be updated with data almost immediately after they have been designed (or with negligible delay). The goal of OLAP is to provide the business user with a powerful tool for ad-hoc querying.

The key fundament of OLAP is a multidimensional data model that can be implemented in various ways. In what follows, we discuss MOLAP (multidimensional OLAP), ROLAP (relational OLAP), and HOLAP (hybrid OLAP).

#### 17.9.3.1 MOLAP

**Multidimensional OLAP (MOLAP)** stores the multidimensional data using a **multidimensional DBMS (MDBMS)**, whereby the data are stored in a multidimensional array-based data structure optimized for efficient storage and quick access. The dimensions represent the index keys of the array, whereas the array cells contain the actual fact data (e.g., sales). Aggregates are precomputed and also physically materialized. This is illustrated in Figure 17.23, where a two-dimensional array or matrix represents the sales for different products across different quarters. The element at row 2, column 3 of the array represents the sales of product B during quarter Q3. Note also that totals have been precomputed and stored in the array. The element at row 4, column 5 represents the total sales of product D across all quarters, whereas the element at row 5, column 5 represents the overall sales of all products across all quarters. A potential problem with this storage approach is that the array may become sparse with many zeros if only a limited number of combinations of dimension values occur. Ideally, an MDBMS should provide facilities for handling these sparse datasets efficiently.

Although MOLAP can be fast in terms of data retrieval, it needs more storage to accomplish this. Moreover, it scales poorly when the number of dimensions increases.

MDBMSs make use of proprietary data structures and data manipulation languages (DML), so no universal SQL-like standard is provided for data handling, which impedes their adoption. Furthermore, they are not optimized for transaction processing. Updating, inserting, or deleting data is usually quite inefficient. Finally, they are typically not very portable because of their tight integration with particular BI tools.

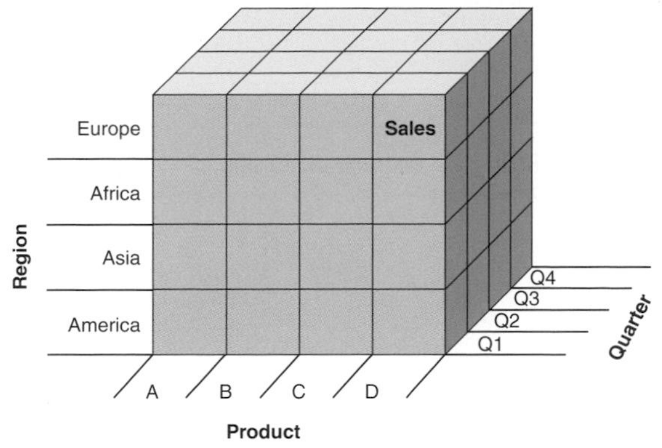


**Figure 17.24** OLAP Cube.

### 17.9.3.2 ROLAP

**Relational OLAP (ROLAP)** stores the data in a relational data warehouse, which can be implemented using a star, snowflake, or fact constellation schema. The advantage of this is that RDBMSs have been much better standardized and provide SQL as a universal data manipulation language. If it is feasible in terms of workload and performance, the same RDBMS can be used for both OLTP and OLAP applications. Furthermore, ROLAP scales better to more dimensions than MOLAP. The query performance may, however, be inferior to MOLAP unless some of the queries are materialized or high-performance indexes are defined.

### 17.9.3.3 HOLAP

**Hybrid OLAP (HOLAP)** tries to combine the best of both MOLAP and ROLAP. An RDBMS can then be used to store the detailed data in a relational data warehouse, whereas the pre-computed aggregated data can be kept as a multidimensional array managed by an MDBMS. The OLAP analysis can first start from the multidimensional database. If more detail is needed (e.g., during drill-down), the analysis can shift to the relational database. This allows you to combine the performance of MOLAP with the scalability of ROLAP.

### 17.9.3.4 OLAP Operators

Various OLAP operators can be used to interactively analyze the data and look for interesting patterns. In what follows, we illustrate them using the cube displayed in Figure 17.24. This cube has three dimensions:[3] Product, Region, and Quarter. The data in the cells represent the sales corresponding to each combination of dimension values.

**Roll-up** (or drill-up) refers to aggregating the current set of fact values within or across one or more dimensions. A distinction can be made between a hierarchical and a dimensional roll-up. The former aggregates within a particular dimension by climbing up the attribute hierarchy (e.g., going from day to week to month to quarter to year), whereas the latter aggregates across an entire

[3] The three-dimensional cube is very suitable as an example, as it can be represented as a real physical cube, but in practice an $n$-dimensional hypercube with more than three dimensions is very likely.

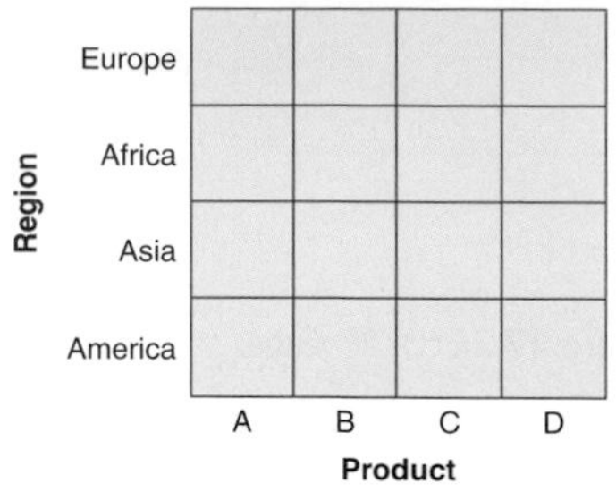


Figure 17.25 Rolling up the time dimension.

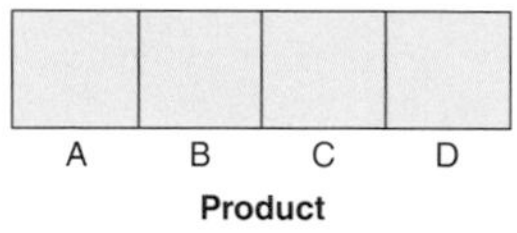


Figure 17.26 Rolling up the time and region dimension.

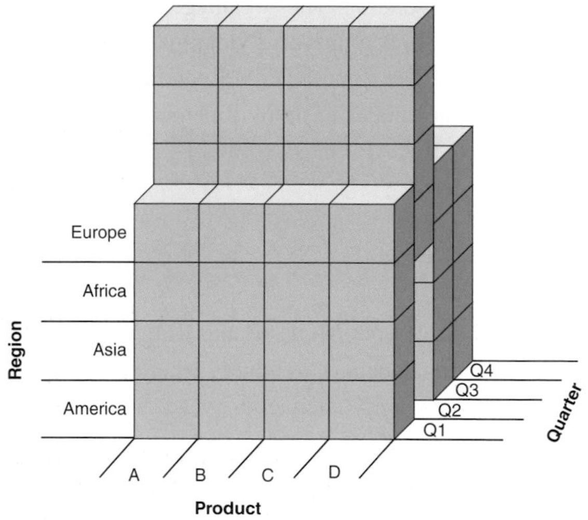


Figure 17.27 Slicing.

dimension and then drops it. Figure 17.25 shows the result of a dimensional roll-up of the time dimension which can then be further rolled up across region, as illustrated in Figure 17.26. The reverse process is referred to as **roll-down** (or drill-down). The idea is to de-aggregate by navigating from a lower level of detail to a higher level of detail. Again, a distinction can be made between hierarchical roll-down (e.g., going from year to quarter to month to week to day) and dimensional roll-down, in which a new dimension is added to the analysis.

**Drill-across** is another OLAP operation whereby information from two or more connected fact tables is accessed. Consider the fact-constellation schema in Figure 17.5. Adding shipping fact data to an analysis on sales fact data is an example of a drill-across operation.

**Slicing** represents an operation whereby one of the dimensions is set at a particular value. This is illustrated in Figure 17.27, where a slice is taken representing the sales in the second quarter for all products and regions. Both horizontal and vertical slicing are possible.

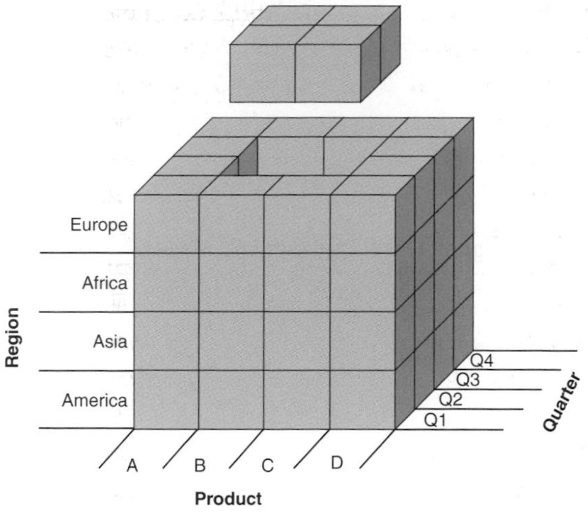


**Figure 17.28** Dicing.

**Dicing** corresponds to a range selection on one or more dimensions. In Figure 17.28, a dice is selected corresponding to the sales of products B and C, in quarters 2 and 3 in Europe.

#### 17.9.3.5 OLAP Queries in SQL

To facilitate the execution of OLAP queries and data aggregation, SQL-99 introduced three extensions to the GROUP BY statement: the CUBE, ROLLUP, and GROUPING SETS operators.

The **CUBE** operator computes a union of GROUP BYs on every subset of the specified attribute types. Its result set represents a multidimensional cube based upon the source table. Consider the following SALESTABLE depicted in Figure 17.29.

We can now formulate the following SQL query:

```
SELECT QUARTER, REGION, SUM(SALES)
FROM SALESTABLE
GROUP BY CUBE (QUARTER, REGION)
```

Basically, this query computes the union of $2^2 = 4$ groupings of the SALESTABLE, being: {(quarter,region), (quarter), (region), ()}, where () denotes an empty group list representing the total aggregate across the entire SALESTABLE. In other words, since Quarter has four values and Region has two values, the resulting multiset will have $4 \times 2 + 4 \times 1 + 1 \times 2 + 1 = 15$ tuples, as illustrated in Figure 17.30. NULL values have been added in the dimension columns Quarter and Region to indicate the aggregation that took place. They can be easily replaced by the more meaningful "ALL" if desired. More specifically, we can add two CASE clauses as follows

```
SELECT CASE WHEN grouping(QUARTER) = 1 THEN 'All' ELSE QUARTER END AS
QUARTER, CASE WHEN grouping(REGION) = 1 THEN 'All' ELSE REGION END AS
REGION, SUM(SALES)
FROM SALESTABLE
GROUP BY CUBE (QUARTER, REGION)
```

| PRODUCT | QUARTER | REGION | SALES |
|---|---|---|---|
| A | Q1 | Europe | 10 |
| A | Q1 | America | 20 |
| A | Q2 | Europe | 20 |
| A | Q2 | America | 50 |
| A | Q3 | America | 20 |
| A | Q4 | Europe | 10 |
| A | Q4 | America | 30 |
| B | Q1 | Europe | 40 |
| B | Q1 | America | 60 |
| B | Q2 | Europe | 20 |
| B | Q2 | America | 10 |
| B | Q3 | America | 20 |
| B | Q4 | Europe | 10 |
| B | Q4 | America | 40 |

**Figure 17.29** Examples SALESTABLE.

| QUARTER | REGION | SALES |
|---|---|---|
| Q1 | Europe | 50 |
| Q1 | America | 80 |
| Q2 | Europe | 40 |
| Q2 | America | 60 |
| Q3 | Europe | NULL |
| Q3 | America | 40 |
| Q4 | Europe | 20 |
| Q4 | America | 80 |
| Q1 | NULL | 130 |
| Q2 | NULL | 100 |
| Q3 | NULL | 40 |
| Q4 | NULL | 90 |
| NULL | Europe | 110 |
| NULL | America | 250 |
| NULL | NULL | 360 |

**Figure 17.30** Result from SQL query with the CUBE operator.

The grouping() function returns 1 in the case that a NULL value is generated during the aggregation and 0 otherwise. This distinguishes the generated NULLs and the possible real NULLs stemming from the data. We will not add this to the subsequent OLAP queries so as to not unnecessarily complicate them.

Also, observe the NULL value for Sales in the fifth row. This represents an attribute combination that is not present in the original SALESTABLE since apparently no products were sold in Q3 in Europe. Besides SUM(), other SQL aggregator functions such as MIN(), MAX(), COUNT(), and AVG() can be used in the SELECT statement.

The **ROLLUP** operator computes the union on every prefix of the list of specified attribute types, from the most detailed up to the grand total. It is especially useful to generate reports containing both subtotals and totals. The key difference between the ROLLUP and CUBE operators is that the former generates a result set showing the aggregates for a hierarchy of values of the specified attribute types, whereas the latter generates a result set showing the aggregates for all combinations of values of the selected attribute types. Hence, the order in

| QUARTER | REGION | SALES |
|---|---|---|
| Q1 | Europe | 50 |
| Q1 | America | 80 |
| Q2 | Europe | 40 |
| Q2 | America | 60 |
| Q3 | Europe | NULL |
| Q3 | America | 40 |
| Q4 | Europe | 20 |
| Q4 | America | 80 |
| Q1 | NULL | 130 |
| Q2 | NULL | 100 |
| Q3 | NULL | 40 |
| Q4 | NULL | 90 |
| NULL | NULL | 360 |

**Figure 17.31** Result from SQL query with ROLLUP operator.

which the attribute types are mentioned is important for the ROLLUP but not for the CUBE operator. Consider the following query:

```
SELECT QUARTER, REGION, SUM(SALES)
FROM SALESTABLE
GROUP BY ROLLUP (QUARTER, REGION)
```

This query generates the union of three groupings {(quarter,region), (quarter), ()}, where () again represents the full aggregation. The resulting multiset will thus have $4 \times 2 + 4 + 1 = 13$ rows and is displayed in Figure 17.31. You can see that the Region dimension is first rolled up followed by the Quarter dimension. Note the two rows that have been left out when compared to the result of the CUBE operator in Figure 17.30.

Whereas the previous example applied the GROUP BY ROLLUP construct to two completely independent dimensions, it can also be applied to attribute types that represent different aggregation levels (and hence different levels of detail) along the same dimension. For example, suppose the SALESTABLE tuples represented more detailed sales data at the individual city level and that the table contained three location-related columns: City, Country, and Region. We could then formulate the following ROLLUP query, yielding sales totals respectively per city, per country, per region, and the grand total:

```
SELECT REGION, COUNTRY, CITY, SUM(SALES)
FROM SALESTABLE
GROUP BY ROLLUP (REGION, COUNTRY, CITY)
```

**Connections**

Chapter 6 discusses transitive dependencies in the context of the third normal form (3 NF).

In this case the SALESTABLE would include the attribute types City, Country, and Region in a single table. Since the three attribute types represent different levels of detail in the same dimension, they are transitively dependent on one another, illustrating the fact that these data warehouse data are indeed denormalized.

The **GROUPING SETS** operator generates a result set equivalent to that generated by a UNION ALL of multiple simple GROUP BY clauses. Consider the following example:

```
SELECT QUARTER, REGION, SUM(SALES)
FROM SALESTABLE
GROUP BY GROUPING SETS ((QUARTER), (REGION))
```

| QUARTER | REGION | SALES |
|---|---|---|
| Q1 | NULL | 130 |
| Q2 | NULL | 100 |
| Q3 | NULL | 40 |
| Q4 | NULL | 90 |
| NULL | Europe | 110 |
| NULL | America | 250 |

**Figure 17.32** Result from an SQL query with the GROUPING SETS operator.

This query is equivalent to:

```
SELECT QUARTER, NULL, SUM(SALES)
FROM SALESTABLE
GROUP BY QUARTER
UNION ALL
SELECT NULL, REGION, SUM(SALES)
FROM SALESTABLE
GROUP BY REGION
```

The result is given in Figure 17.32.

Multiple CUBE, ROLLUP, and GROUPING SETS statements can be used in a single SQL query. Different combinations of CUBE, ROLLUP, and GROUPING SETS can generate equivalent result sets. Consider the following query:

```
SELECT QUARTER, REGION, SUM(SALES)
FROM SALESTABLE
GROUP BY CUBE (QUARTER, REGION)
```

This query is equivalent to:

```
SELECT QUARTER, REGION, SUM(SALES)
FROM SALESTABLE
GROUP BY GROUPING SETS ((QUARTER, REGION), (QUARTER), (REGION), ())
```

Likewise, the following query

```
SELECT QUARTER, REGION, SUM(SALES)
FROM SALESTABLE
GROUP BY ROLLUP (QUARTER, REGION)
```

is identical to:

```
SELECT QUARTER, REGION, SUM(SALES)
FROM SALESTABLE
GROUP BY GROUPING SETS ((QUARTER, REGION), (QUARTER),())
```

SQL2003 introduced additional analytical support for two types of frequently encountered OLAP activities: ranking and windowing. **Ranking** should always be done in combination with an SQL ORDER BY clause. Assume we have the following table depicted in Figure 17.33.

| PRODUCT | SALES |
|---|---|
| A | 50 |
| B | 20 |
| C | 10 |
| D | 45 |
| E | 40 |
| F | 30 |
| G | 60 |
| H | 20 |
| I | 15 |
| J | 25 |

**Figure 17.33** Example table for ranking.

| Product | Sales | RANK_SALES | DENSE_RANK_SALES | PERC_RANK_SALES | CUM_DIST_SALES |
|---|---|---|---|---|---|
| C | 10 | 1 | 1 | 0 | 0.1 |
| I | 15 | 2 | 2 | 1/9 = 0.11 | 0.2 |
| B | 20 | 3 | 3 | 2/9 = 0.22 | 0.4 |
| H | 20 | 3 | 3 | 2/9 = 0.22 | 0.4 |
| J | 25 | 5 | 4 | 4/9 = 0.44 | 0.5 |
| F | 30 | 6 | 5 | 5/9 = 0.55 | 0.6 |
| E | 40 | 7 | 6 | 6/9 = 0.66 | 0.7 |
| D | 45 | 8 | 7 | 7/9 = 0.77 | 0.8 |
| A | 50 | 9 | 8 | 8/9 = 0.88 | 0.9 |
| G | 60 | 10 | 9 | 9/9 = 1 | 1 |

**Figure 17.34** Result from the ranking SQL query.

Various ranking measures can now be calculated by using the following SQL query:

```
SELECT PRODUCT, SALES,
RANK() OVER (ORDER BY SALES ASC) as RANK_SALES,
DENSE_RANK() OVER (ORDER BY SALES ASC) as DENSE_RANK_SALES, PERCENT_RANK()
OVER (ORDER BY SALES ASC) as PERC_RANK_SALES,
CUM_DIST() OVER (ORDER BY SALES ASC) as CUM_DIST_SALES,
FROM SALES
ORDER BY RANK_SALES ASC
```

The result of this query is depicted in Figure 17.34. The RANK() function assigns a rank based upon the ordered sales value, whereby similar sales values are assigned the same rank. Contrary to the RANK() function, the DENSE_RANK() function does not leave gaps between the ranks. The PERCENT_RANK() function calculates the percentage of values less than the current value, excluding the highest value. It is calculated as (RANK() – 1)/(Number of Rows – 1). The CUM_DIST() function calculates the cumulative distribution or the percentage of values less than or equal to the current value.

All of these measures can also be computed for selected partitions of the data. The measures depicted in Figure 17.34 can also be computed for each region separately. Assuming the source table SALES now also includes a REGION attribute type, the query would then become:

```
SELECT REGION, PRODUCT, SALES,
RANK() OVER (PARTITION BY REGION ORDER BY SALES ASC) as RANK SALES,
DENSE_RANK() OVER (PARTITION BY REGION ORDER BY SALES ASC) as DENSE_RANK_SALES,
PERCENT_RANK() OVER (PARTITION BY REGION ORDER BY SALES ASC) as PERC_RANK_SALES,
```

| QUARTER | REGION | SALES |
|---|---|---|
| 1 | America | 10 |
| 2 | America | 20 |
| 3 | America | 10 |
| 4 | America | 30 |
| 1 | Europe | 10 |
| 2 | Europe | 20 |
| 3 | Europe | 10 |
| 4 | Europe | 20 |

**Figure 17.35** Example table for windowing.

| QUARTER | REGION | SALES | SALES_AVG |
|---|---|---|---|
| 1 | America | 10 | 15 |
| 2 | America | 20 | 13.33 |
| 3 | America | 10 | 20 |
| 4 | America | 30 | 20 |
| 1 | Europe | 10 | 15 |
| 2 | Europe | 20 | 13.33 |
| 3 | Europe | 10 | 16.67 |
| 4 | Europe | 20 | 15 |

**Figure 17.36** Result of windowing.

```
CUM_DIST() OVER (PARTITION BY REGION ORDER BY SALES ASC) as CUM_DIST_SALES,
FROM SALES
ORDER BY RANK_SALES ASC
```

**Windowing** allows calculating cumulative totals or running averages based on a specified window of values. In other words, windowing allows getting access to more than one row of a table without requiring a self-join. Consider the table depicted in Figure 17.35.

The following query calculates the average sales for each region and quarter on the basis of the current, previous, and next quarter.

```
SELECT QUARTER, REGION, SALES,
AVG(SALES) OVER (PARTITION BY REGION ORDER BY QUARTER ROWS
BETWEEN 1 PRECEDING AND 1 FOLLOWING) AS SALES_AVG
FROM SALES
ORDER BY REGION, QUARTER, SALES_AVG
```

The result is displayed in Figure 17.36.

The **PARTITION BY** REGION statement subdivides the rows into partitions, similar to a GROUP BY clause (see Chapter 7). It enforces that the windows do not reach across partition boundaries. In other words, the SALES_AVG values will always be computed within a particular region. As an example, the SALES_AVG value for quarter 2 in America will be calculated as $(10 + 20 + 10)/3 = 13.33$, whereas for quarter 4 in America it is calculated as: $(10 + 30)/2 = 20$.

These are just a few examples of ranking and windowing facilities available in SQL. It is highly recommended to check the manual of the RDBMS vendor for more information. Furthermore, note that not all RDBMS vendors support these extensions. The ones that do support them usually also provide a user-friendly and graphical environment to construct OLAP reports using point-and-click, which are then automatically translated by the tool into the corresponding SQL statements.

### Retention Questions

- Define business intelligence and illustrate with an example.
- What are query and reporting?
- Give an example of a pivot table and illustrate how it can be used for business intelligence.
- What is OLAP?
- Contrast MOLAP against ROLAP and HOLAP. Illustrate with an example.
- Discuss the various OLAP operators and illustrate with an example.
- Illustrate how the OLAP operators can be implemented in SQL.

Given the amount of data to be aggregated and retrieved, OLAP SQL queries may become very time-consuming. One way to speed up performance is by turning some of these OLAP queries into materialized views. For example, an SQL query with a CUBE operator can be used to pre-compute aggregations on a selection of dimensions of which the results can then be stored as a materialized view. A disadvantage of view materialization is that extra efforts are needed to regularly refresh these materialized views, although it can be noted that usually companies are fine with a close to current version of the data such that the synchronization can be done overnight or at fixed time intervals.

## Summary

In this chapter, we introduced data warehousing as an essential component to build enterprise wide business intelligence (BI) solutions. We extensively zoomed into various types of data warehouse schemas and modeling specifics, and also reviewed various issues related to their development. We discussed data marts, the important topic of virtualization, and contrasted data warehouses with data lakes, clearly stating that both technologies are complementary rather than substitutes.

The second part of this chapter zoomed into BI. More specifically, we covered query and reporting, pivot tables, and on-line analytical processing (OLAP). It is important to note that these BI techniques are verification-based since they heavily depend upon input provided by the business user to find interesting patterns or test hypotheses. In Chapter 20, we take BI to the next level by discussing discovery-based analysis techniques, also called data mining or analytics, where the generation of insights or new hypotheses can be automated without explicit user intervention.

### Scenario Conclusion

Now that Sober has learned about data warehousing and business intelligence, it is keen to pursue both technologies to support its tactical and strategic decision-making. More specifically, it has decided to first develop a data warehouse as depicted in Figure 17.37.

The star schema has one central fact table and four dimension tables. The Ride-Type attribute type indicates whether the ride concerns a ride-hailing or ride-sharing service. The Car-Type attribute indicates whether the car is a Sober or other car. Note the use of surrogate keys such as RideKey, CarKey, and CustomerKey. In the case of a ride-hail service, the sales in euros represents the total fee paid in euros. In the case of a ride-sharing service, it represents the fee per customer. Sober populates its data warehouse using a well-designed ETL process aimed at taking monthly snapshots from the operational systems. Given its relatively small size, the company decides not to develop any data marts yet. However, this may change as the company grows.

Once the data warehouse is up and running, Sober wants to start analyzing it using business intelligence applications. It will start with some basic query and reporting. The company also wants to use OLAP to interactively analyze the data and look for interesting patterns. More specifically, it was thinking about building the OLAP structure represented in Figure 17.38.

It can then perform the following types of OLAP operations:

- look at the total sales during Q2 of both types of rides and cars (slicing);
- look at the sales during Q2 and Q3 of both types of rides and cars (dicing);

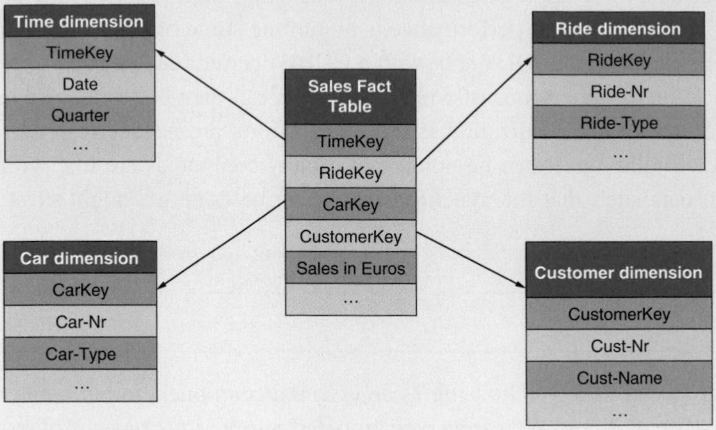

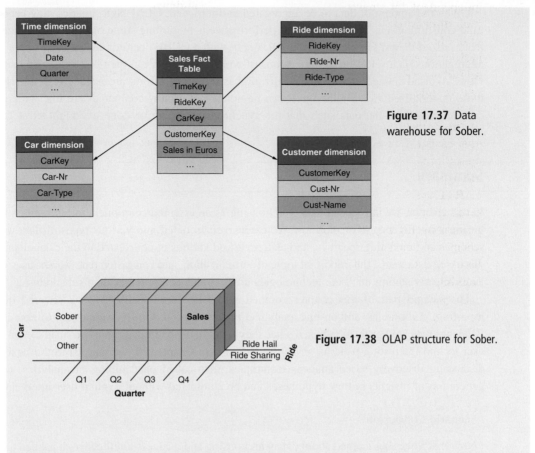

**Figure 17.37** Data warehouse for Sober.

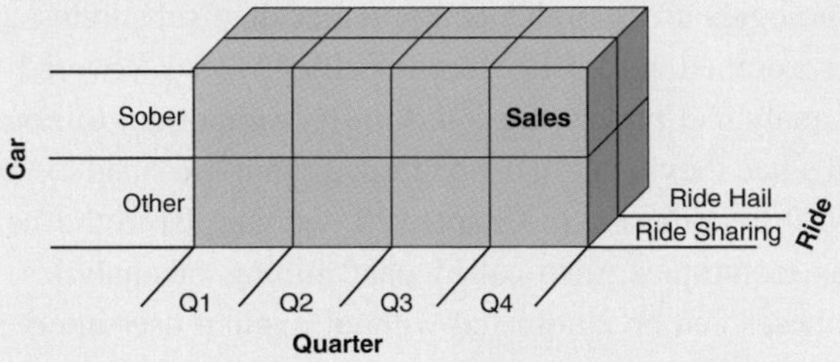


**Figure 17.38** OLAP structure for Sober.

- look at the aggregated sales across all quarters of both types of rides and cars (roll-up);
- look at the monthly sales during Q4 of both types of cars and rides (drill-down).

These analyses will allow Sober to get a thorough insight into its sales numbers and to identify interesting opportunities.

## Key Terms List

**business intelligence (BI)**
**cleansing**
**conformed dimensions**
**CUBE**
**data lake**
**data mart**
**data warehouse**
**decision support systems (DSS)**
**deduplication**
**dependent data marts**
**dicing**
**ETL (extract, transform, load)**
**extraction strategy**
**fact constellation**
**factless fact table**
**formatting rules**
**garbage in, garbage out (GIGO)**
**granularity**
**GROUPING SETS**
**hybrid OLAP (HOLAP)**

**independent data marts**
**junk dimension**
**mini-dimension table**
**multidimensional DBMS (MDBMS)**
**multidimensional OLAP (MOLAP)**
**non-volatile**
**on-line analytical processing (OLAP)**
**on-line transaction processing (OLTP)**
**operational data store (ODS)**
**operational level**
**outrigger table**
**PARTITION BY**
**pivot or cross-table**
**point-of-sale (POS)**
**query and reporting**
**query by example (QBE)**
**ranking**
**rapidly changing dimension**
**relational OLAP (ROLAP)**
**roll-down**
**ROLLUP**
**roll-up**
**self-service BI**
**semantic metadata**
**slicing**
**slowly changing dimension**
**snowflake schema**
**star schema**
**strategic level**
**structural metadata**
**subject-oriented**
**surrogate keys**
**tactical level**
**time variant**
**total cost of ownership (TCO)**
**virtual data mart**
**virtual data warehouse**
**windowing**

## Review Questions

**17.1.** Which of the following statements is **not correct**?

a. At the operational level, day-to-day business decisions are made, typically in real-time or with a short time frame.
b. At the tactical level, decisions are made by middle management with a medium-term (e.g., a month, a quarter, a year) focus.
c. At the strategic level, decisions are made by senior management with long-term implications (e.g., 1, 2, 5 years, or more)
d. A data warehouse provides a centralized, consolidated data platform by integrating data from different sources and in different formats. As such, it provides a separate and dedicated environment for operational decision-making.

**17.2.** Which of the following is not a characteristic of a data warehouse?

a. Subject-oriented.
b. Integrated.
c. Time-variant.
d. Volatile.

**17.3.** In terms of data manipulation, a data warehouse focuses on. . .

a. Insert/Update/Delete/Select statements.
b. Insert/Select statements.
c. Select/Update statements.
d. Delete statements.

**17.4.** Which statement is **correct**?

a. A star schema has one large central dimension table which is connected to various smaller fact tables.
b. The dimension tables of a star schema contain the criteria for aggregating the measurement data and will typically be used as constraints to answer queries.
c. To speed up report generation and avoid time-consuming joins in a star schema, the dimension tables need to be normalized.
d. The dimension tables in a star schema are frequently updated.

**17.5.** Which statement is **not correct**?

a. A snowflake schema normalizes the fact table of a star schema.
b. A fact constellation schema has more than one fact table which can share dimension tables.
c. Surrogate keys essentially buffer the data warehouse from the operational environment by making it immune to any operational changes.
d. A factless fact table is a fact table that only contains foreign keys and no measurement data.

**17.6.** Which statement is **not correct?**

a. Junk dimensions can be defined to efficiently accommodate low-cardinality attribute types such as flags or indicators.
b. An outrigger table can be defined to store a set of attribute types of a dimension table which are uncorrelated, high in cardinality, and updated simultaneously.
c. For slowly changing dimensions, surrogate keys can be handy to store the historical information by duplicating a record and adding, e.g., Start_Date, End_Date, and Current_Flag attribute types.
d. One way to deal with rapidly changing dimensions is by splitting the information into stable and rapidly changing information. The latter can then be put into a separate mini-dimension table with a new surrogate key. The connection can then be made by using the fact table or by introducing a new table connecting both.

**17.7.** Which statement about ETL is **not correct**?

a. Some estimates state that the ETL step can consume up to 80% of all efforts needed to set up a data warehouse.
b. To decrease the burden on both the operational systems and the data warehouse itself, it is recommended to start the ETL process by dumping the data in a staging area where all the ETL activities can be executed.
c. During the loading step, the data warehouse is populated by filling the fact and dimension tables, thereby also generating the necessary surrogate keys to link it all up. Fact rows should be inserted/updated before the dimension rows.
d. The extraction strategy can be either full or incremental. In the latter case, only the changes since the previous extraction are considered.

**17.8.** Which statement is **not correct**?

a. A data mart is a scaled-down version of a data warehouse aimed at meeting the information needs of a homogeneous small group of end-users such as a department or business unit (e.g., marketing, finance, logistics, HR, etc.).
b. Dependent data marts pull their data from a central data warehouse, whereas independent data marts are standalone systems drawing data directly from the operational systems, external sources, or a combination of both.
c. A virtual data warehouse (sometimes also called a federated database) or virtual data mart contains no physical data but provides a uniform and consolidated single point of access to a set of underlying physical data stores.

d. A key advantage of virtualization is that it requires no extra processing capacity from the underlying (operational) data stores.

**17.9.** Which statement is **correct**?

a. A key distinguishing property of a data lake is that it stores raw data in its native format, which could be structured, unstructured, or semi-structured.
b. A data lake is targeted toward decision-makers at middle- and top-management level, whereas a data warehouse requires a data scientist, which is a more specialized profile in terms of data handling and analysis.
c. In case of a data warehouse, the data schema definitions are only determined when the data are read (schema-on-read), whereas for data lakes they are fixed when the data are loaded (schema-on-write).
d. A data lake is less agile compared to a data warehouse, which has no structure.

**17.10.** Which statement is **not correct**?

a. Query and reporting tools are an essential component of a comprehensive business intelligence solution.
b. A pivot or cross-table is a popular data summarization tool. It essentially cross-tabulates a set of dimensions.
c. A key disadvantage of OLAP is that it does not allow you to interactively analyze your data, summarize it, and visualize it in various ways.
d. The key fundament of OLAP is a multidimensional data model which can be implemented in various ways.

**17.11.** Which statement is **not correct**?

a. Multidimensional OLAP (MOLAP) stores the multidimensional data using a multidimensional DBMS (MDBMS) whereby the data are stored in a multidimensional array-based data structure optimized for efficient storage and quick access.
b. Relational OLAP (ROLAP) stores the data in a relational data warehouse, which can be implemented using a star, snowflake, or fact constellation schema.
c. Hybrid OLAP (HOLAP) tries to combine the best of both MOLAP and ROLAP. An RDBMS can then be used to store the detailed data in a relational data warehouse, whereas the pre-computed aggregated data can be kept as a multidimensional array managed by an MDBMS.
d. MOLAP scales better to more dimensions than ROLAP. The query performance may, however, be inferior to ROLAP unless some of the queries are materialized or high-performance indexes are defined.

**17.12.** Which statement is **correct**?

a. Roll-up (or drill-up) refers to aggregating the current set of fact values within or across one or more dimensions.
b. Roll-down (or drill-down) de-aggregates the data by navigating from a lower level of detail to a higher level of detail.
c. Slicing represents the operation whereby one of the dimensions is set at a particular value.
d. Dicing corresponds to a range selection on one or more dimensions.
e. All of the above are correct.

## Problems and Exercises

17.1E Contrast operational versus tactical versus strategic decision-making. Illustrate with examples in
- an online retail setting (e.g., Amazon, Netflix, eBay);
- a bank setting;
- a university setting.

17.2E How is a data warehouse defined according to Bill Inmon? Elaborate on each of the characteristics and illustrate with examples.

17.3E Discuss and contrast each of the following data warehouse schemas:
- star schema;
- snowflake schema;
- fact constellation.

17.4E What are surrogate keys? Why would you use them in a data warehouse instead of using the business keys from the operational systems?

17.5E Discuss four approaches to deal with slowly changing dimensions in a data warehouse. Can any of these approaches be used to deal with rapidly changing dimensions?

17.6E Explain and illustrate the following concepts:
- independent data mart;
- virtual data warehouse;
- operational data store;
- data lake.

17.7E Consider the following OLAP Cube:

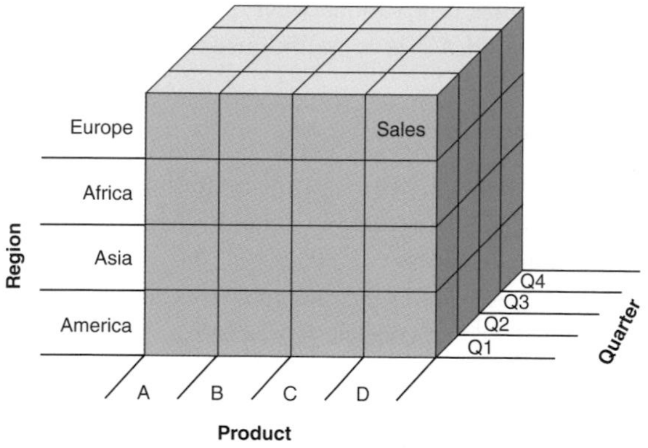


Give an example of a...

- roll-up operation;
- drill-down operation;
- slicing operation;
- dicing operation.

17.8E Given the following table:

| PRODUCT | QUARTER | REGION | SALES |
|---|---|---|---|
| A | Q1 | Europe | 10 |
| A | Q1 | America | 20 |
| A | Q2 | Europe | 20 |
| A | Q2 | America | 50 |
| A | Q3 | America | 20 |
| A | Q4 | Europe | 10 |
| A | Q4 | America | 30 |
| B | Q1 | Europe | 40 |
| B | Q1 | America | 60 |
| B | Q2 | Europe | 20 |
| B | Q2 | America | 10 |
| B | Q3 | America | 20 |
| B | Q4 | Europe | 10 |
| B | Q4 | America | 40 |

Consider the following queries:

```
SELECT PRODUCT, REGION, SUM(SALES)
FROM SALESTABLE
GROUP BY CUBE (PRODUCT, REGION)

SELECT PRODUCT, REGION, SUM(SALES)
FROM SALESTABLE
GROUP BY ROLLUP (PRODUCT, REGION)

SELECT PRODUCT, REGION, SUM(SALES)
FROM SALESTABLE
GROUP BY GROUPING SETS ((PRODUCT), (REGION))
```

What is the output of the above queries?
Can you reformulate each query using other SQL OLAP constructs?

17.8E What is windowing? Illustrate a query with windowing using the above table.

# 18 Data Integration, Data Quality, and Data Governance

## Chapter Objectives

In this chapter, you will learn to:

- identify the key challenges and approaches for data and process integration;
- understand the basic mechanisms of searching unstructured data within an organization and across the World Wide Web;
- define data quality as a multidimensional concept and understand how master data management (MDM) can contribute to it;
- understand different frameworks and standards for data governance;
- highlight more recent approaches in data warehousing, data integration, and governance.

### Opening Scenario

Things are going well at Sober. The company has set up a solid data environment based on a solid relational database management system used to support the bulk of its operations. Sober's mobile app development team has been using MongoDB as a scalable NoSQL DBMS to handle the increased workload coming from mobile app users and to provide back-end support for experimental features the team wants to test in new versions of their mobile app. Sober's development and database team is already paying attention to various data quality and governance aspects: the RDBMS is the central source of truth, strongly focusing on solid schema design and regular quality checks being performed on the data. The NoSQL database is an additional support system to handle large query volumes from mobile users in real-time in a scalable manner, but where all data changes are still being propagated to the central RDBMS. This is done in a manual manner, which sometimes leads to the two data sources not being in agreement with each other. Sober's team therefore wants to consider better data quality approaches to implement more robust quality checks on data and make sure that changes to the NoSQL database are propagated to the RDBMS system in a timely and correct manner. Sober also wants to understand how their data flows can be better integrated with their business processes.

In this chapter we will look at some managerial and technical aspects of data integration. We will zoom in on data integration techniques, data quality, and data governance. As companies often end up with many information systems and databases over time, the concept of data integration becomes increasingly important to consolidate a company's data to provide one, unified view to applications and users. Hence, constructing a data warehouse is one area in which data integration will be an important concern, but data integration is also important for many other use cases – consider two companies that wish to utilize each other's systems and data resources. In what follows, we will discuss different patterns for data integration. We will also focus on techniques to efficiently search unstructured data, both within an intra-enterprise data integration setting and across the World Wide Web.

Data integration is also closely related to data quality, so we will discuss this managerial concern, and master data management. Finally, we look at data governance standards that help companies to set up initiatives to measure, monitor, and improve data integration and quality practices.

## 18.1 Data and Process Integration

**Data integration** aims at providing a unified view and/or unified access over heterogeneous, and possibly distributed, data sources. In what follows, we discuss different approaches and patterns to realize this, with a different tradeoff between concerns such as data quality, performance, the ability to transform the data, etc. In addition, we introduce the concept of process integration. **Process integration** deals with the sequencing of tasks in a business process but also governs the data flows in these processes. In this way, the data flows in process integration are complementary to data integration because they aim at making the right data available to applications and human actors in order that they are able to perform their tasks with the appropriate input data. Therefore, ideally, both data and processes are considered in a data integration effort. We start, however, with the rationale behind the data integration needs in a contemporary data-processing context.

### 18.1.1 Convergence of Analytical and Operational Data Needs

Traditionally, applications and databases were organized around functional domains such as accounting, human resources, logistics, CRM, etc. (Figure 18.1). Every department or business unit worked with its own **data silo** (e.g., a file or database) with no cross-department integration. Operational processes used these data silos to answer simple queries or perform updates in (near) real-time on the detailed underlying data. A classical point-of-sale (POS) application storing product purchases or a trading system storing stock prices are examples of this.

Whereas the silos mainly aimed at operational support, a next phase saw the emergence of business intelligence (BI) and analytics applications, fueled by the need for data-driven tactical and

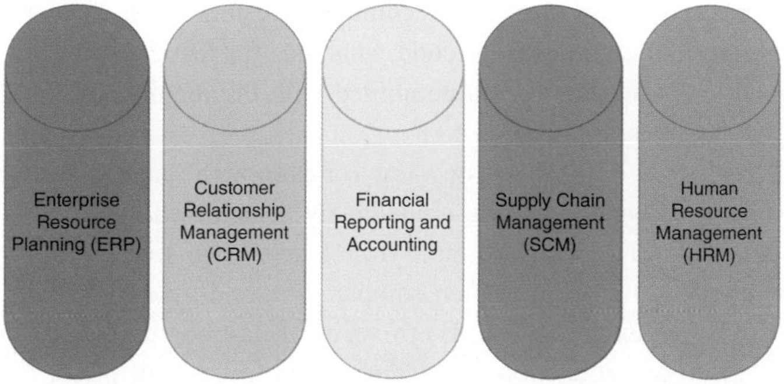


**Figure 18.1** Traditional "data silos", organized around functional domains.

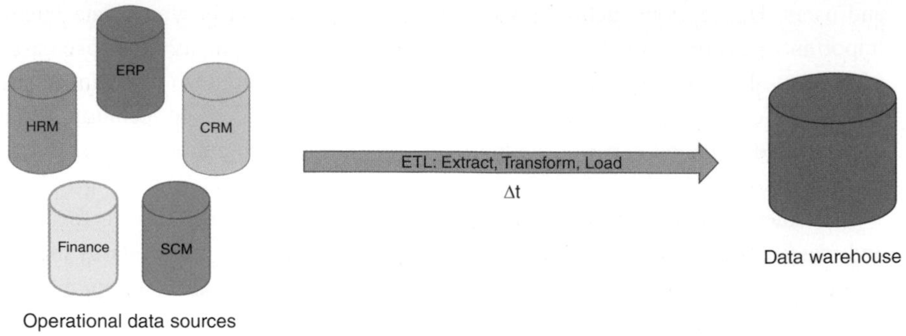


**Figure 18.2** Traditional data warehouse set-up.

**Connections**

Data warehousing and ETL were discussed in Chapter 17. Chapter 20 discusses analytics.

strategical decision-making, with a company-wide impact. To sustain this company-wide view, data from the silos were transformed, integrated, and consolidated into a company-wide data warehouse. ETL (extract, transform, load) processes supported the asynchronous data extraction and transfer from the source systems (the operational data silos) to the target data warehouse.

Because of this evolution, we were confronted for nearly two decades with a dual data storage and processing landscape, supported by two very distinct scenes of tool vendors and products. On the one hand, operational applications performed simple queries on operational data silos, containing an up-to-date "snapshot" of the business state in the domain at hand (HR, logistics, CRM, etc.). Business intelligence and analytics applications supported tactical and strategic decision-making by analyzing company-wide data in a data warehouse (Figure 18.2). The data warehouse contained not only detailed operational data but also historical, enriched, and aggregated data. However, the ETL process of extracting data from the source systems, transforming it into the appropriate format for analysis, and loading it into the data warehouse was time-consuming. Therefore, there was a certain latency between the up-to-date operational data stores and the slightly outdated data warehouse. This latency was tolerable: real-time business intelligence was not the goal in traditional data warehousing. The goal was to support business executives in their decision-making at ad-hoc moments in time (e.g., daily or monthly).

Nowadays, we see a complete convergence of the operational and tactical/strategic data needs of the corresponding data integration tooling. This trend was initiated by new marketing practices centered on proactive (instead of reactive) actions requiring a complete understanding of the customer, and quickly spread toward other functional domains. It culminates in the term **operational BI**, with a twofold meaning. First, analytics techniques are more and more used at the operational level as well by front-line employees. Second, analytics for tactical/strategic decision-making increasingly uses real-time operational data combined with the aggregated and historical data found in more traditional data warehouses.

In both cases, this operational usage of BI aims for a low (or even zero) latency so unexpected, business-altering events or trends in the data can be immediately detected and addressed with the appropriate response. The idea is to move more and more from batch processing to (near) real-time BI, where historical data are combined with, and often compared to, real-time trends and insights, and analyzed 24/7. To provide some examples, think of executive dashboards that monitor *KPIs* (Key Performance Indicators, such as production throughput, stock prices, oil price, etc.) in real time. Another example is *business process monitoring* and *business activity monitoring (BAM)* for the timely detection of anomalies or opportunities in business processes. Companies such as Netflix and Amazon detect cross-selling opportunities in real-time by a recommender system, and credit card processors detect credit card fraud soon after the transaction is initiated.

This evolution poses interesting challenges to the landscape of data storage and data integration solutions. This is especially true in Big Data analytics, where new insights are acquired by combining and enriching more traditional data types with "new" kinds of internal and external data, often with a very volatile structure and very extensive in size. Different data are drawn into the analysis, such as click stream data, server logs, sensor data, social media feeds, etc. Chapter 11 (NoSQL databases) and Chapter 19 (Big Data) discuss the solutions to cope with these evolving data storage needs. However, an equally big challenge is the integration of these diverse data types in such a way that they can be processed and analyzed efficiently, often with pressing constraints regarding the real-time character of the data or even the need to open so-called **streaming data** for analysis "on the fly". The result is typically a hybrid data integration infrastructure, combining different integration techniques catering for different quality of service (QoS) characteristics and data quality concerns. Many data integration vendors satisfy this need with extensive data integration suites, combining different tools and techniques. However, to make informed implementation choices, it is key to discern the generic data integration patterns that underlie these suites, and assess their inherent tradeoffs in QoS characteristics, such as real-time capabilities, performance, abilities to enrich and cleanse the data, the ability to retain historical data in addition to real-time data, etc. This is the focus of the next sections of this chapter.

## 18.1.2 Data Integration and Data Integration Patterns

Data integration aims at providing a unified and consistent view of all enterprise-wide data. The data themselves may be heterogeneous and reside in different resources (XML files, legacy systems, relational databases, etc.). The desired extent of data integration will highly depend upon the required QoS characteristics. Data will never be of perfect quality, so a certain level of inaccurate, incomplete, or inconsistent data may have to be tolerated for operational BI to succeed.

> **Connections**
>
> The dimensions of data quality have been discussed in Chapter 4.

Figure 18.3 illustrates the concept of data integration at a high level: the goal is to logically (and sometimes also physically) unify different data sources or data silos, as we called them above, to provide a single unified view which is as correct, complete, and consistent as possible. Different data integration patterns exist to provide this unified view. First, we discuss the following basic data integration patterns: data consolidation, data federation, and data propagation. Then, we deal with more advanced techniques and the interplay between data integration and process integration.

### 18.1.2.1 Data Consolidation: Extract, Transform, Load (ETL)

> **Connections**
>
> ETL was already discussed in the context of data warehousing in Chapter 17.

The essence of **data consolidation** as a **data integration pattern** is to capture the data from multiple, heterogeneous source systems and integrate it into a single persistent store (e.g., a data warehouse or data mart). This is typically accomplished using extract, transform, and load (ETL) routines (see Figure 18.4).

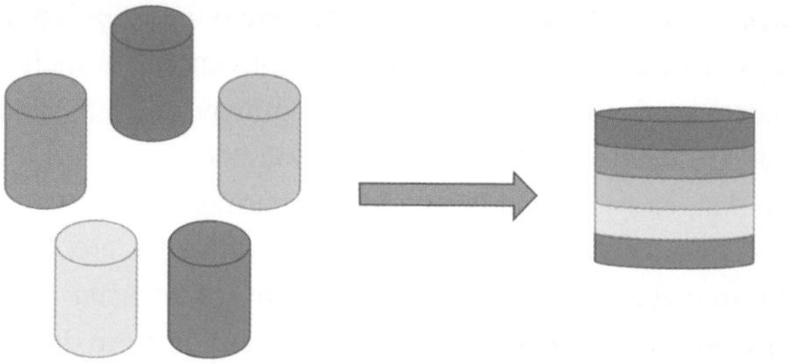

**Figure 18.3** The goal of data integration is to provide a unified and consistent view over different data sources.

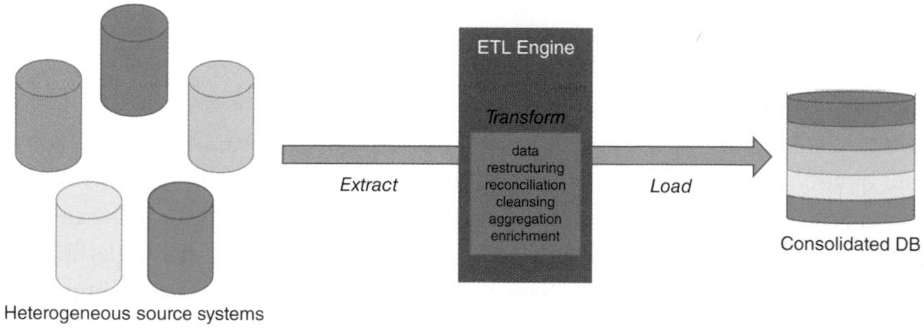


**Figure 18.4** An extract, transform, load (ETL) engine as a data consolidation solution.

As discussed in Chapter 17, ETL is a technology supporting the following activities:

- Extract data from heterogeneous data sources (including legacy and external sources);
- Transform the data to satisfy business needs;
- Load the transformed data into a target system (e.g., a data warehouse).

This approach with an ETL process feeding a store with consolidated data is very suitable for dealing with massive amounts of data and preparing them for analysis. There is room for extensive transformation, involving data restructuring, reconciliation, cleansing, aggregation, and enrichment steps. Therefore, this pattern has a positive impact on many data quality dimensions such as completeness, consistency, and interpretability. Another important advantage of the consolidation approach is that it caters for not only present information, but also historical data, since a changed business state does not result in updates to the data, but in additions of new data.

On the downside, the ETL process typically induces a certain measure of latency, so the timeliness dimension may suffer, with the data being slightly out of date. However, as we will discuss in Section 18.1.2.5, there exist techniques to at least contain this latency. The latency can be measured as the delay between the updates in the source systems and the updates in the target data store. It can be a few seconds, hours, or a couple of days depending upon the refreshment strategy. Consolidation also requires a physical target, so additional storage capacity is consumed. This allows for analytics workloads to be removed from the original data sources. That, with the fact that the data are already formatted and structured upfront to suit the analytical needs, guarantees acceptable performance levels.

There exist different variations on the ETL process, e.g., either a full update or an incremental refreshment strategy of the target data store can be adopted. Note that some vendors such as Oracle propose another variant, ELT (extract, load, transform), with the transformation being performed directly in the physical target system. Figure 18.4 illustrates the ETL process.

Besides the traditional set-up with ETL and a data warehouse, data lakes as discussed in Chapter 17 can also be an implementation of the consolidation pattern. However, in contrast to a data warehouse, the data are mostly consolidated in the native format they had in the source systems, with little transformation or cleansing. Therefore, the positive impact on the respective data quality dimensions will be limited compared to a data warehouse, but this is often less of an issue for the Big Data types typically stored in data lakes, where the formal structure is much more volatile or even completely absent. Analyzing the data may still require some preprocessing and restructuring, which would already have been performed upfront with a data warehouse.

#### 18.1.2.2 Data Federation: Enterprise Information Integration (EII)

**Data federation** also aims at providing a unified view over one or more data sources. Instead of capturing and integrating the data in one consolidated store, it typically follows a pull approach through which data are pulled from the underlying source systems on an on-demand basis. **Enterprise information integration (EII)** is an example of a data federation technology (Figure 18.5). EII can be implemented by realizing a virtual business view on the dispersed underlying data sources. The view serves as a universal data access layer. The data sources' internals are isolated from the outside world with *wrappers*. In this way, the virtual view shields the applications and processes from the complexities of retrieving the needed data from multiple locations, with different semantics, formats, and interfaces. No movement or replication of data is needed (except perhaps some caching for performance) since all data stay in the source systems. Hence, a federation strategy enables real-time access to current data, which was not the case for a data consolidation strategy.

Queries performed on the business view will be translated into queries on the underlying data sources that can then be further optimized using global and local query optimization techniques, also exploiting query parallelism (see also Chapter 16). The returned results will typically be rather small because the real-time characteristic is prohibitive to larger datasets. For the same reason, only limited transformation and cleansing capabilities are possible. Many EII technologies are read-only, but some also support update operations on the business view, which are then applied to the underlying data stores. However, as already discussed in Chapter 7, it is not always possible to map updates on a virtual view unambiguously to back-end relational tables, even in a standalone database. This is even more true in a distributed setting. EII is also less suitable for complex queries

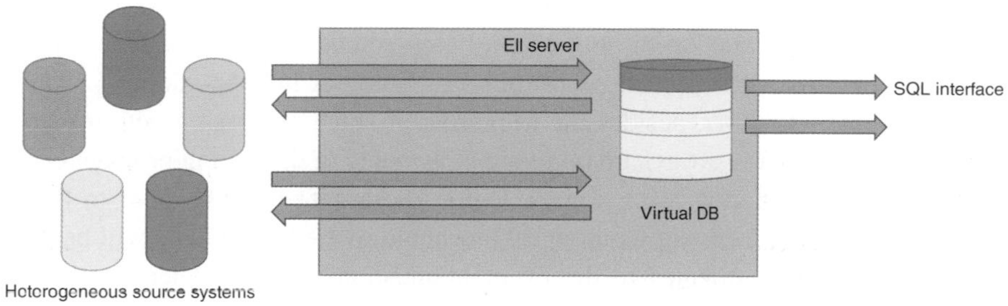


**Figure 18.5** Enterprise information integration (EII) as a data federation solution.

> **Connections**
>
> Chapter 7 discussed the requirements for relational views to be updatable. Chapter 16 deals with query parallelism.

including, e.g., joins between structured and unstructured data. Therefore, EII is often adopted by firms as a temporary measure following a merger or acquisition.

Data federation and EII can be beneficial as it leaves data in place that otherwise might dramatically increase overall storage requirements if a consolidated approach were to be followed. One important disadvantage to remember is the overall worse performance of EII. Since queries performed on the business view must be translated to underlying data sources, a performance hit is unavoidable. Parallelization and caching solutions (meaning that results of frequently executed queries are kept around for a while on the view) can help to overcome this, though when performance is a key issue a consolidated approach might be advisable instead. Another related issue is whether the source systems will continue to receive direct queries, i.e., queries that do not go through the federation layer. There, you must remember that the existing operational source systems will incur an increased utilization rate, as they now must handle both direct incoming queries and those coming from the federation layer, leading to a potential performance hit. Finally, note that EII solutions are limited in the number of transformation and cleansing steps they can perform on query result sets. In the event that data from multiple sources have to be transformed, aggregated, or cleansed before they can be ready for use, a data consolidation approach might be a better solution.

#### 18.1.2.3 Data Propagation: Enterprise Application Integration (EAI)

The **data propagation** pattern corresponds to the synchronous or asynchronous propagation of updates or, more generally, events in a source system to a target system. Regardless of the synchronous or asynchronous character, most implementations provide some measure of guaranteed delivery of the update or event notification to the target system. The data propagation pattern can be applied at two levels in a system architecture. It can be applied in the interaction between two applications or in the synchronization between two data stores. In an application interaction context, we speak of enterprise application integration (EAI), which is discussed below. In a data store context, we speak of enterprise data replication (EDR), as discussed in the next section.

The idea of **enterprise application integration (EAI)** is that an event in the source application requires some processing within the target application. For example, if an order is received in an order-handling application, this may trigger the creation of an invoice in the invoicing application. The event in the source system (an order is received) is notified to the target system to trigger some processing there (the creation of an invoice). There exist many distinct EAI technologies to realize this triggering, ranging from web services, .NET or Java interfaces, messaging middleware, event notification buses, remote procedure call technology, legacy application interfaces and adapters, etc. Different topologies may be adopted, such as point-to-point, hub, bus, etc. However, besides the triggering of some processing within the target application, such exchange nearly always involves small amounts of data being propagated from the source to the target application as well (Figure 18.6). These data provide input to the processing at the target application. Depending on the EAI technology used, these data will be part of the messages being exchanged; attributes to the event notifications; or parameters to the remote procedures being invoked. It would lead us too far to discuss all EAI technologies in detail, but they invariably entail some triggering of functionality at the target system because of an event at

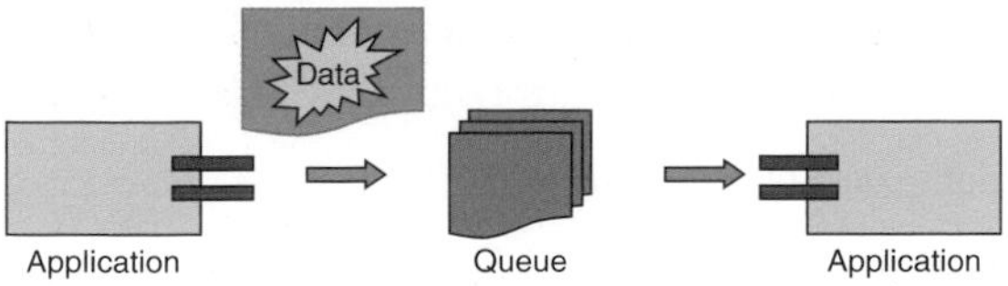


**Figure 18.6** Enterprise application integration (EAI).

the source system, and some data propagation that goes along with this triggering. In our example, the invoicing application would need at least the ID of the customer, the total amount of the order, etc. to create an invoice.

The data propagation in EAI may occur synchronously, so the message is sent, along with the data, at the moment the event occurs in the source system. The target system may respond immediately, but the message (or event notification or other format) may also be queued before being processed, resulting in asynchronous interaction. The advantage of an asynchronous approach is less interdependence between the respective systems, but the downside is a certain latency in responding to an event and processing the data that goes along with it.

Data propagation with EAI is usually employed for operational business transaction processing across multiple systems that act upon one another's events and therefore require (partially) the same data. Many EAI implementations provide facilities for message transformation, monitoring, and routing. A synchronous set-up allows for responding in real-time, whereas a two-way exchange of data is possible, which isn't the case with, e.g., consolidation and ETL. However, for most EAI technologies, the size of the data that can be exchanged is rather small, as the main focus is on the triggering of processing.

### 18.1.2.4 Data Propagation: Enterprise Data Replication (EDR)

The propagation pattern can also be applied at the level of the interaction between two data stores. In that case, we speak of **enterprise data replication (EDR)**. Here, the events in the source system explicitly pertain to update events in the data store. Replication means copying the updates in the source system in (near) real-time to a target data store, which serves as an exact replica (Figure 18.7). At the software level, this can be implemented by the operating system, DBMS, or a separate replication server. As an alternative, a separate hardware storage controller can be used. The respective options were already discussed in Chapters 13 and 16. EDR has been traditionally adopted for load balancing, ensuring high availability and recovery, but not data integration as such. However, recently it has been used more often for (operational) BI and to offload data from the source systems onto a separate data store, which is an exact replica. In this way, analytics can be performed on real-time operational data, without burdening the original operational source systems with additional workload. In this context, load balancing is the main driver for offloading the data to another data store, rather than the need for data transformation as with ETL.

Although they originally represent different patterns, the boundary between EDR and ETL is not always sharp. The event paradigm and real-time aspect of EDR can be combined with the consolidation and transformation elements of ETL, resulting in so-called near-real-time ETL. The latter is discussed in the next section.

**Connections**

Chapters 13 and 16 discussed several aspects and techniques regarding data replication.

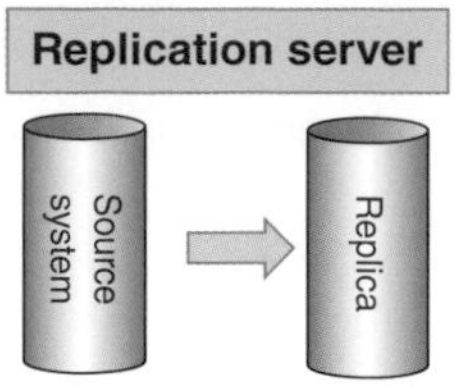


**Figure 18.7** Enterprise data replication (EDR).

### 18.1.2.5 Changed Data Capture (CDC), Near-Real-Time ETL, and Event Processing

A technology complementary to ETL, which adds the event paradigm to ETL, is **changed data capture (CDC)**. CDC technology can detect update events in the source data store, and trigger the ETL process based on these updates. In this way, a "push" model to ETL is supported: the ETL process is triggered by any significant change in the underlying data store(s). This is in contrast with traditional ETL, where data extraction occurs on scheduled time intervals or in periods with low system workload, but without considering actual changes in the source data.

This approach is often technically more complex, and its feasibility depends to a certain extent on the characteristics and openness of the source systems. It has several advantages. A first advantage is a real-time capability; changes in the source systems can be detected and propagated as they occur, rather than them being propagated with a certain latency, according to the fixed schedule of the ETL process. The approach may also reduce network load since only data that have actually changed are transferred.

Finally, the event notification pattern can also play other roles in a data-processing setting. Relevant events (updates to source data, but also other events with semantics at the business process level, e.g., an order being confirmed or a credit card purchase being made) can be notified to multiple components or applications that can act upon the event and trigger some processing, e.g., with EAI technology. Also, the events generated in this context are more and more also the focus of analytics techniques, especially in business activity monitoring and process analytics (see also Chapter 20). **Complex event processing (CEP)** refers to a series of analytics techniques that do not focus on individual events, but rather on the interrelationships between events and patterns within so-called event clouds. For example, a suddenly changing pattern in purchases made with a certain credit card may be an indication of fraud. Event notifications can be buffered, and in this way acted upon asynchronously, or they can be processed in real-time. The latter can be supported by technologies that can cope with so-called streaming data, as discussed in Chapter 19.

**Connections**

Chapter 19 focuses on Big Data, including methods for dealing with streaming data. Chapter 20 discusses different analytics techniques.

### 18.1.2.6 Data Virtualization

**Data virtualization** is a more recent approach to data integration and management that also aims (like the other approaches) to offer a unified data view for applications to retrieve and manipulate data without necessarily knowing where the data are stored physically or how they are structured and formatted at the sources. Data virtualization builds upon the basic data integration patterns discussed previously, but also isolates applications and users from the actual (combinations of) integration patterns used.

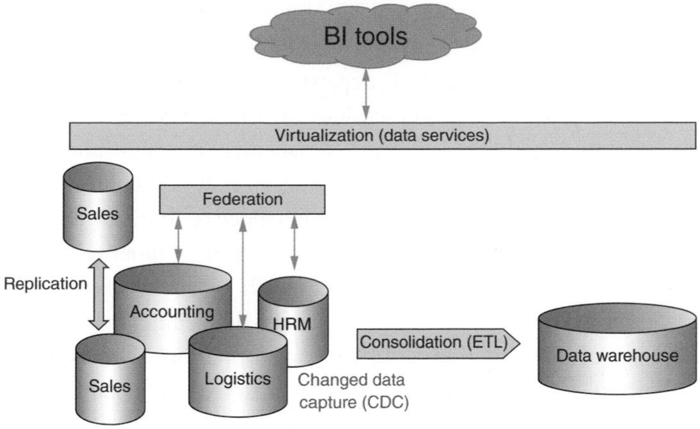


**Figure 18.8** Data integration practices often combine a variety of patterns and approaches.

The technologies underlying data virtualization solutions vary widely from vendor to vendor, but they often avoid data consolidation techniques such as ETL: the source data remain in place, and real-time access is provided to the source systems of the data. This approach hence seems familiar to data federation, but an important difference of data virtualization is that, contrary to a federated database as offered by basic EII, virtualization does not impose a single data model on top of the heterogeneous data sources. Virtual views (often structured as virtual relational tables) on the data can be defined at will and can be mapped top-down onto relational and non-relational data sources. Data virtualization systems can apply various transformations before offering the data to their consumers. Hence, they combine the best features of traditional data consolidation, such as the ability to provide data transformations, and the ability to provide data in real-time. To guarantee sufficient performance, virtual views are cached transparently, and query optimization and parallelization techniques are applied. However, for very large volumes of data, the combination of consolidation and ETL may still be the most efficient approach performance-wise. There, virtualization techniques can provide a unified view of the consolidated data and other data sources, e.g., to integrate historical data with real-time data. Hence, in many real-life contexts, a data integration exercise is an ongoing initiative within an organization, and will often combine many integration strategies and approaches. This is illustrated in Figure 18.8.

#### 18.1.2.7 Data as a Service and Data in the Cloud

The pattern of virtualization is often linked to the concept of **Data as a Service (DaaS)**, in which data services are offered as part of the overall **Service-Oriented Architecture (SOA)** in which business processes are supported by a set of loosely coupled software services. The data services can be invoked by different applications and business processes, which are isolated from how the data services are realized regarding location, data storage, and data integration technology. Many commercial data integration suites adhere to the SOA principles and support the creation of data services. Data services can be read-only or updatable, in which case they must be able to map the updates as issued by consumers of the data service to the underlying data stores in an unambiguous way. Most data integration suites also provide easy features for **data service composition**, in which data from different services can be combined and aggregated into a new, composite service.

The concept of data services and data services composition also raises questions concerning the boundary between the responsibility of the business user and the ICT provider. Data integration as such was traditionally the responsibility of the ICT department. However, exactly because the consumer is isolated from most technical details, data services cater for a degree of *self-service BI*, in which data services can be composed, and then subjected to data analytics algorithms, simply by a business user dragging and dropping icons representing data services in a graphical user interface. This self-service aspect is very appealing from a productivity perspective. It offers the business user the freedom to integrate data on demand and perform analyses on them, without relying on the ICT department to integrate and transform the required data, which often involves delays and/or coordination overhead. Experience shows that, exactly because all technical details are hidden, there is also the risk of leaving data integration and data transformation to end-users without a technical background, as they are unaware of the impact of different data integration patterns, cleansing activities, transformations, etc. on data quality. Therefore, offering self-service features regarding data integration and BI should not be avoided *per se*, but should nonetheless be considered with sufficient caution.

DaaS is in its turn often related to cloud computing. The "as a service" and "in the cloud" concepts are very related, with the former putting more emphasis on the consumer perspective (invocation of the service) and the latter mainly emphasizing the provisioning and infrastructure aspect. The (positive and negative) properties of cloud computing are as follows:

- Hardware, software, and/or infrastructure are provided "on demand" over a network.
- Clouds can be *public* (offered by an external cloud service provider), *private* (cloud technology being set up in-company), or *hybrid* (a mixture of both).
- An attractive property of public and hybrid clouds are the fading boundaries between one's own infrastructure and the service providers' infrastructure, hence removing capacity constraints and allowing for extending storage or processing capacity gradually and on demand, without having to make extensive investments upfront, in situations where the future workload is very unpredictable.
- The ability to convert fixed infrastructure costs, and upfront investments, into variable costs (payment per unit of time or volume, payment depending on features or service levels, etc.).
- A downside is the risk of vendor lock-in and/or unexpected switching costs.
- Another possible risk exists regarding performance guarantees, privacy, and security, which can be partially mitigated by scrupulously asserting formal Service Level Agreements (SLAs).
- The question of accountability of the cloud service provider, if a calamity occurs or damage is incurred (e.g., data loss or breach of privacy).

Different data-related services can be hosted in the cloud. Below, we provide a widely used classification of different cloud offerings (although other, not necessarily congruent, classifications exist as well), and indicate which data-related services could relate to them:

- **Software as a Service (SaaS)**: Full applications are hosted in the cloud, e.g., applications for analytics, data cleansing, or data quality reporting.
- **Platform as a Service (PaaS)**: Computing platform elements are hosted in the cloud, which can run and integrate with one's own applications, e.g., a cloud storage platform offering simple key–value store functionality, such as Amazon S3.
- **Infrastructure as a Service (IaaS)**: Hardware infrastructure (servers, storage, etc.) are offered as virtual machines in the cloud, e.g., cloud-hosted storage hardware.

- **Data as a Service (DaaS)**: Data services are hosted in the cloud, typically based on strict SLAs and sometimes with additional features such as data quality monitoring or cloud-based data integration tools, to integrate one's own data with data from external providers.

These respective cloud components can also be combined, e.g., to store, integrate, and analyze data in the cloud. The pros and cons of a cloud-based approach regarding analytics are discussed further in Chapter 20.

**Drill Down**

The below chart displays the projected growth in the As-a-Service sector based on a Gartner study.[1] Both PaaS and SaaS are projected to double in size, whereas IaaS is about to triple. These numbers demonstrate impressive growth during a three-year time period.

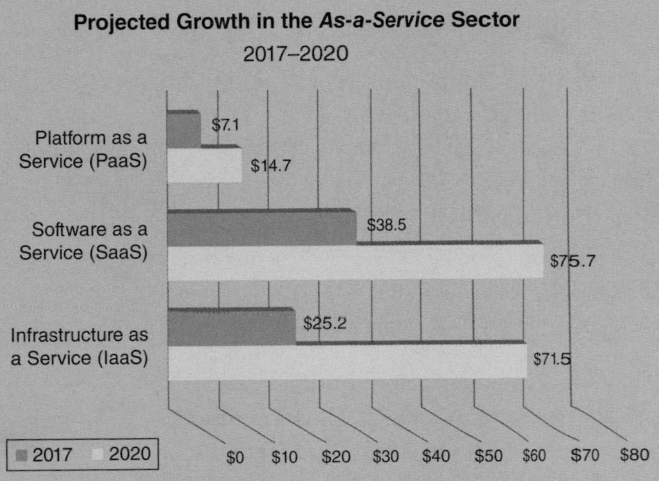

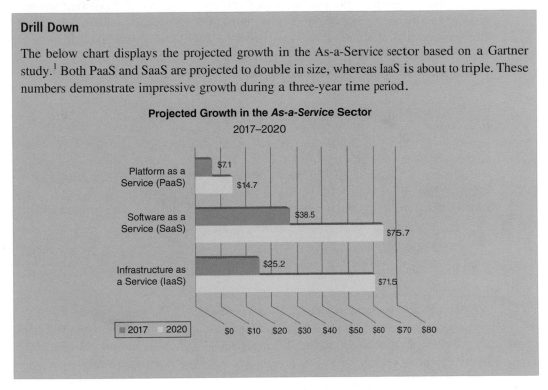

## 18.1.3 Data Services and Data Flows in the Context of Data and Process Integration

Complementary to data integration, the idea of process integration is to integrate and harmonize the business processes in an organization as much as possible. A **business process** is defined as a set of tasks or activities with a certain ordering that must be executed to reach a certain organizational goal. As an example, think of a loan approval process with various tasks such as filing a loan application, calculating the credit score, drafting the loan offer, signing the contract, etc. This also includes a data flow specifying the path of the data between these tasks. Business processes can be considered from two perspectives. The control flow perspective, on the one hand, specifies the correct sequencing of tasks (e.g., a loan offer can only be made when the credit score has been calculated). The data flow perspective, on the other hand, focuses on the inputs of the tasks (e.g., the interest rate calculation depends on the credit score). As to the actual implementation in an information system, task coordination/triggering, on the one hand, and task execution, on the other hand, are often intertwined in the same software code. However, among other things in a service-oriented

[1] Gartner, Forecast: Public Cloud Services, Worldwide, 2014–2020, 4Q16 Update, 2017.

context, there is a tendency to separate services with the purpose of task coordination from services that perform the actual task execution and from services that provide access to the necessary data. We come back to this divide later in this section.

#### 18.1.3.1 Business Process Integration

Due to the control flow perspective, which defines a sequence and ordering among tasks, the modeling of business processes is often performed using visual, flowchart-like languages such as Business Process Model and Notation (BPMN), Yet Another Workflow Language (YAWL), Unified Modeling Language (UML) Activity Diagrams, Event-driven Process Chain (EPC) diagrams, and so on. Figure 18.9 shows our loan approval process modeled using BPMN.

**Drill Down**

Most business process modeling languages are rigid and explicit in the sense that the ordering between tasks is defined so it does not allow for much deviation. In many business environments, this is seen as an advantage, as it allows for better control and monitoring of business activities, and removing room for ambiguities that might arise. Other practitioners and researchers, however, have argued this way of over-specifying processes is not capable of handling the deviations that arise in most business environments and is hence not very flexible. Other process modeling languages exist that only specify the crucial control flow constraints among activities, but leave the rest open to the parties executing the tasks in the process.

Once a business process is modeled, it can be used "as is" in manual processes by workers and employees, then acting as a prescriptive guide governing the executions of required steps to which the involved parties should adhere. In most settings, however, the idea is to use the modeled business process in such a way that it can drive the steps of an information system, hence aiding in the automation of the process at hand. In this context, the execution of the process is handled by a so-called **process engine**, which will oversee the steps in the process to ensure they are performed correctly. To do so, a process model is often translated into a declarative definition of an executable process that can then be understood and used by the process engine. One example of such an execution language is the Business Process Execution Language standard, **WS-BPEL**. Let's illustrate this concept again for our loan application process. After converting the process model into an executable WS-BPEL process definition, the business process engine can then use this definition to lead a clerk through different user-interfacing tasks by generating a user interface and consecutive data entry screens, making sure that the correct execution order is followed. It can also trigger the execution of automated tasks, e.g., by invoking a software component that implements an algorithm that calculates the credit score, based on the appropriate input parameters. In this way, WS-BPEL can also handle the data flow perspective, making sure, for instance, that a next step in the loan application process can only be started once all details have been filled out correctly in the current step. Note that in this way, the responsibility of task coordination (as performed by the process engine) is separated from the task execution (as performed by other software components and/or human actors).

Business processes can become complex, and several steps in a business process will often spawn subprocesses across departments. For instance, the review of the loan application was modeled as a

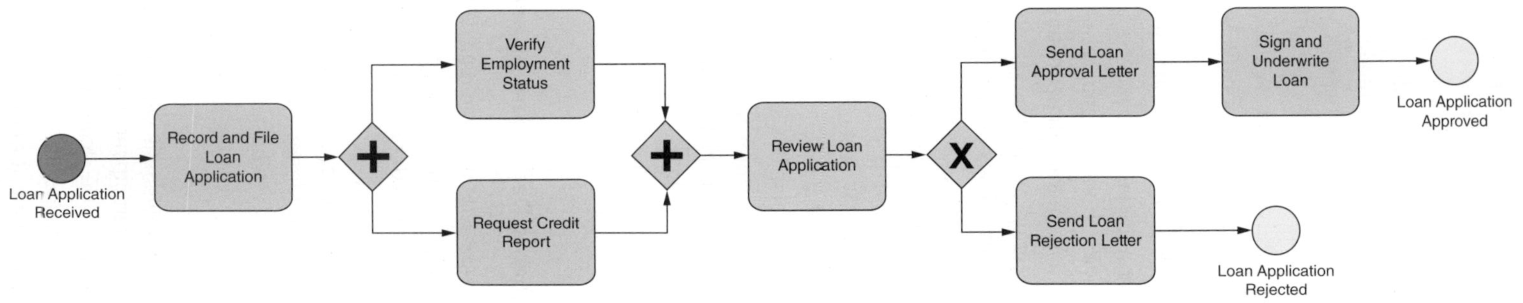


**Figure 18.9** Loan approval process expressed using the BPMN modeling language.

**Connections**

Web services and WS-BPEL were introduced in Chapter 10. Chapter 16 focuses on the transactional aspects of web services and WS-BPEL processes.

single activity in the process above, but might start off a new "review" process where several steps must be performed before reaching the outcome of the review. Integrating these business processes is hence an essential task for an organization where many of these processes depend on each other, and where many processes may span multiple organizational units, such as departments or even external partners. In modern business process set-ups, different business process tasks or subprocesses will hence be offered as services, which other parties can then invoke or utilize to achieve a certain goal, reach an outcome, or receive a result. A popular way of exposing such services both within and across organizations is web services technology, as discussed in Chapter 10.

Process execution languages such as WS-BPEL aim at managing the control flow and data flow across services that together perform the business process as expressed in the WS-BPEL document. Therefore, two types of dependencies should be appropriately managed to guarantee the successful overall process execution. First, a **sequence dependency** states that the execution of a service B depends on completing the execution of another service A, hence guaranteeing that all services are consumed in the right order. An example could be a loan proposal that can only be made after a positive credit score has been calculated. As another example, think of an order fulfillment process in which there is a sequence dependency between the payment service and the shipping service: an order can only be shipped after payment is arranged. A **data dependency**, on the other hand, specifies that the execution of a service B depends on data provided by a service A. An example could be the interest rate of a loan proposal that depends upon the credit score calculated during the credit check. Data dependencies should also be carefully managed to ensure that a service is always provided with all the data it needs to perform its task. Another example is the data dependency between a shipping service and a customer relationship service: the shipping service can only ship an order if it received the customer's address from the customer relationship service. In what follows, we discuss how to deal with data dependencies, given different possible patterns for data integration and process integration.

#### 18.1.3.2 Patterns for Managing Sequence Dependencies and Data Dependencies in Processes

Different patterns exist to manage the sequence and data dependencies in business processes. Many process engine vendors, and the WS-BPEL language, favor the **orchestration pattern**. Process orchestration assumes a single centralized executable business process (the orchestrator) that coordinates the interaction among different services and subprocesses. The control flow and data flow are described at a single, central place, and the orchestrator is responsible for invoking and combining the services, as illustrated in Figure 18.10. Compare this with a team of people with a central manager telling everyone exactly what and when something should be done. The team members do not care about the overall goal of the process, as the manager combines the outputs into a single deliverable.

Another pattern to manage sequence and data dependencies is **choreography**, which differs from orchestration because it relies on the participants themselves to coordinate their collaboration. It is hence a decentralized approach in which the decision logic and interactions are distributed, with no centralized point (Figure 18.11). Compare this again with a team of people, but now without a central manager. All the team members must know the overall process (the goal to be reached), so everyone knows when to do something and to whom to pass the work.

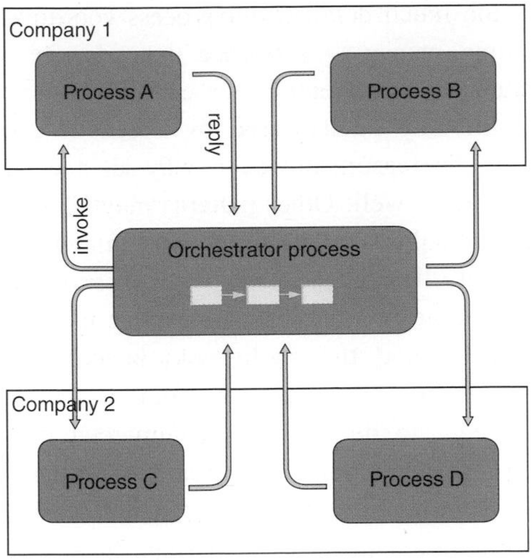


**Figure 18.10** Illustration of the orchestration pattern.

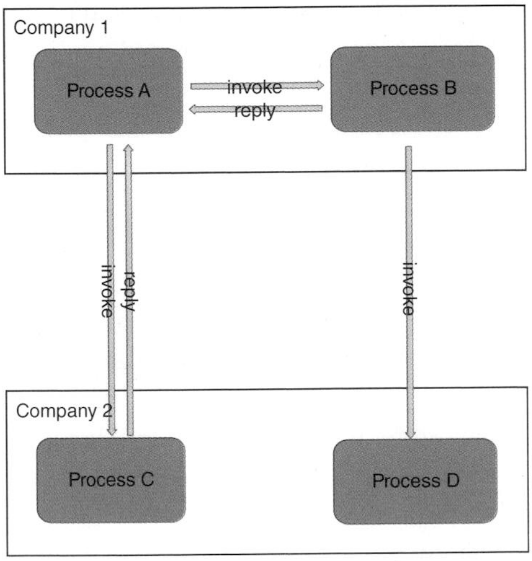


**Figure 18.11** Illustration of the choreography pattern.

Even though the central aspect of orchestration might look more appealing from a managerial point of view, many actual processes follow a more choreographed approach, and both come with their respective benefits and costs. In many real-life settings, a combination of both approaches will be applied, where, e.g., some processes are orchestrated by a central authority, and others might be easier to integrate using a choreography-inspired approach. However, a very important remark, given data management, is that in scientific literature and in most real-life contexts, the choice of a process integration pattern is primarily made based on considerations regarding optimally managing the sequence dependencies – i.e., according to which pattern service execution should be triggered. Data flow then just follows the same pattern as the control flow – i.e., the input data needed to perform a certain task are simply embedded in the message that triggers the task execution, e.g., as parameters in a SOAP message or method invocation.

Despite the above, and without going into too much detail about process coordination, it is important to stress that the decisions regarding managing sequence dependencies and data dependencies can be made, to a certain extent, independently. For example, a service that determines the interest rate of a loan proposal may be triggered by a central coordinator, according to the orchestration pattern. There is no reason, however, why all necessary input data should be provided in the triggering message as well. Other patterns may be chosen here, and the choice may even be different for different subsets of the input data. In addition, part of the data dependencies may be satisfied using data flow at the process level, and part may be satisfied by data integration technology. For example, the interest rate service may request the credit score directly from the service that calculated the credit risk, hence applying the choreography pattern for this data flow. However, it may be more appropriate for the interest rate service to retrieve other customer data, e.g., to decide on a commercial discount for excellent customers, directly from the database that contains all customer information, hence applying the "consolidation" data integration pattern. From this example, it is clear that data flow patterns at the process layer and data integration patterns at the data layer are complementary in satisfying a service's data needs. Therefore, data integration and (the data flow aspects of) process integration should be considered in a single effort. They both contribute to managing data dependencies and the respective pattern choices made at the level of the process layer and the data layer will together determine the data lineage and quality. The next section provides a unified perspective on the data flow in the process layer and on the data integration layer by identifying three types of services that deal with the processing and exchange of data.

#### 18.1.3.3 A Unified View on Data and Process Integration

Roughly speaking, a data dependency between service A and service B can be resolved in two ways. The first option is that the process provides a data flow between A and B, making sure that the necessary data are passed from service A to service B at the level of the business process. The other option is for service A to persist these data into a data store, which is also accessible through one of the aforementioned data integration techniques to service B to retrieve and use the data afterward. In this way, managing data dependencies is a shared responsibility of the process layer (where the control flow and data flow are handled) and the data layer (where data integration and data storage capabilities reside).

To analyze data flow at the process level and data integration at the data layer level in a unified way, we discriminate between three types of services: workflow services, activity services, and data services. In actual SOAs, these services will correspond to real separate software artifacts. For example, a workflow service may correspond to a process engine and an activity service may correspond to a web service. However, the analysis is also useful for architectures in which the implementation of these services is interwoven into monolithic software modules or even legacy code. Workflow and activity services needn't even be automated, but can also be performed manually, by human actors. Even if the three service types are just used as an instrument for analysis and do not correspond to actual software artifacts, they provide a means to assess the coordination functionality, the task execution functionality, and the data provisioning in any information system. In this way, they capture process-level data flow and data sharing through data integration technology into a unified perspective. We distinguish between the following three service types (Figure 18.12):

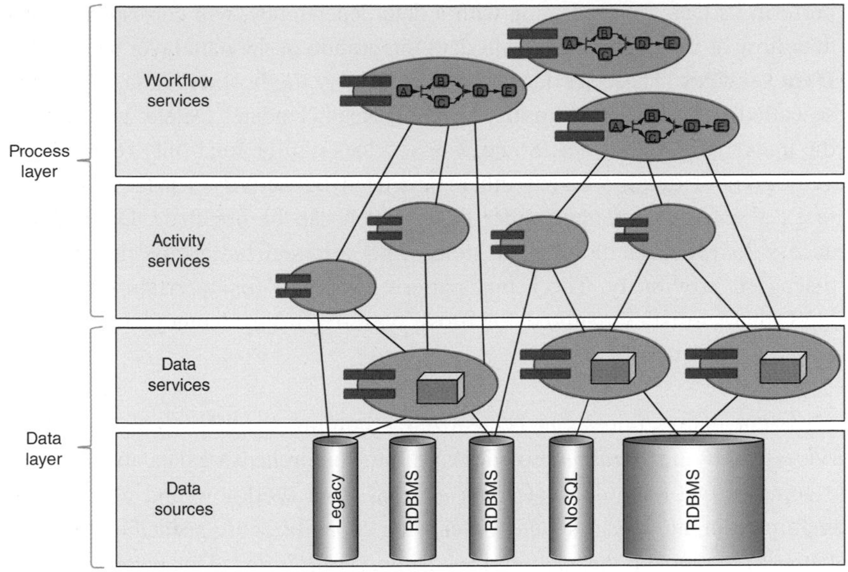


**Figure 18.12** Workflow services, activity services, and data services.

- **Workflow services**: These services coordinate the control flow and data flow of a business process by triggering its respective tasks in line with the sequence constraints in the process model, and according to an orchestration or choreography pattern. For example, workflow services will trigger the different tasks in a loan approval process. Some of these tasks will be human interfacing activities, e.g., a business expert assessing the risk of a complex loan request. There, the workflow service assigns the task to the appropriate human actor. For fully automated tasks, e.g., an algorithm that assesses the credit risk, the workflow service triggers an activity service (see below) to perform the task. This triggering occurs through, e.g., a message being sent or a method being invoked. Certain variables or parameters are passed as input along with this triggering message or method, e.g., containing the ID of the customer, the amount of the requested loan, etc. This passing of variables constitutes the **data flow** in a business process.
- **Activity services:** These services perform one task in a business process. They are triggered by a workflow service when the corresponding task is due in the process. They can also be triggered by different workflow services, for example in a situation in which different purchase processes (possibly even belonging to different organizations) make use of the same "credit card validation" activity service. The activity service is triggered (representing the control flow) and may receive input variables (representing the data flow). The activity service may just return a result to the workflow service (e.g., the result of a credit risk calculation), but it may also alter the business state, e.g., for an activity service that creates a new purchase order or that brings a loan into an "approved" state. This manipulation of business state occurs through interaction with the data services (see below) that provide access to the actual business data. Also, activity services may interact with the data services to retrieve business state not provided in their input variables. For example, whereas an activity service responsible for creating a transportation order may receive the CustomerID as an input variable, it may need to retrieve the CustomerAddress through the data services. This already illustrates that providing an activity service with the appropriate data to

perform its task, hence dealing with a data dependency, will correspond to an interplay between data flow at the process level and data integration at the data layer level.

- **Data services**: These services provide access to the business data. Their only logic consists of so-called **CRUDS functionality**: Create, Read, Update, Delete, and Search on data stored in the underlying data stores. Some data services will be read-only (e.g., an external service with demographic data), whereas others are used by activity services to alter the business state (e.g., a service containing order data, which can be updated). Data services provide unified access to the underlying data stores and are realized using the data integration patterns discussed previously. The actual pattern(s) chosen for a certain data service depend on the QoS characteristics required for those data, regarding latency, response time, completeness, consistency, etc.

Different data services can be realized according to different data integration patterns. Data services based on *federation* provide real-time, comprehensive data about the business state, hiding the complexity of the disparate data sources from workflow and activity services. If extensive transformation, aggregation, and/or cleansing capabilities are needed, or performance is an issue, it is better to implement the data services using *consolidation*. This pattern is also required if the data service should provide access to historical data. If only performance is a criterion without the need for transformation/cleansing or historical data, *replication* can be used to, e.g., offload analytical workload from source systems and provide access to zero-latency operational data for analysis. These basic patterns can be combined with approaches such as CDC and virtualization. In this way, a hybrid data integration landscape emanates. This is also facilitated by the contemporary data integration suites from the main vendors, which support different data integration patterns, and the possibility to publish data services formally.

The picture is only complete if the data services perspective and the process perspective are combined to provide activity services with the necessary input data. For example, the "order creation" activity service will receive part of its input through process-level data flow, as part of the task triggering. At least data that define the very task to be performed (e.g., the ID of the customer and the ordered product, and the ordered quantity) should be received from the process, embedded in the triggering message. This is none other than an application of the EAI pattern. The other data necessary to perform the task can be retrieved by the activity service from the data services. The balance between input through data flow and through data layer can differ from context to context: sometimes, all necessary input data will be provided as part of the triggering of the activity service, on top of what is minimally required. For example, all customer data can be provided within the triggering message, even if it is available in the data layer, so the activity service needn't contact any data services. We then speak of *comfort data*. There is always a tradeoff though: The more comfort data, the less the activity service depends on access to the data layer for its functioning. If such data, e.g., the customer address, were recently altered in the data layer by another process, the activity service may not be aware of this if the data are received as comfort data and will, therefore, work with outdated data.

The above discussion is closely related to the concept of **data lineage**. Data lineage refers to the whole trajectory followed by a data item, from its origin (data entry), possibly over respective transformations and aggregations, until it is ultimately being used or processed. Often, the same data will be copied and distributed to multiple business processes, users, and/or data stores, so what was originally entered as a single data item may result in many trajectories and paths down the line, making the lineage even more difficult to trace. And yet, if the data lineage is unknown or unclear, it

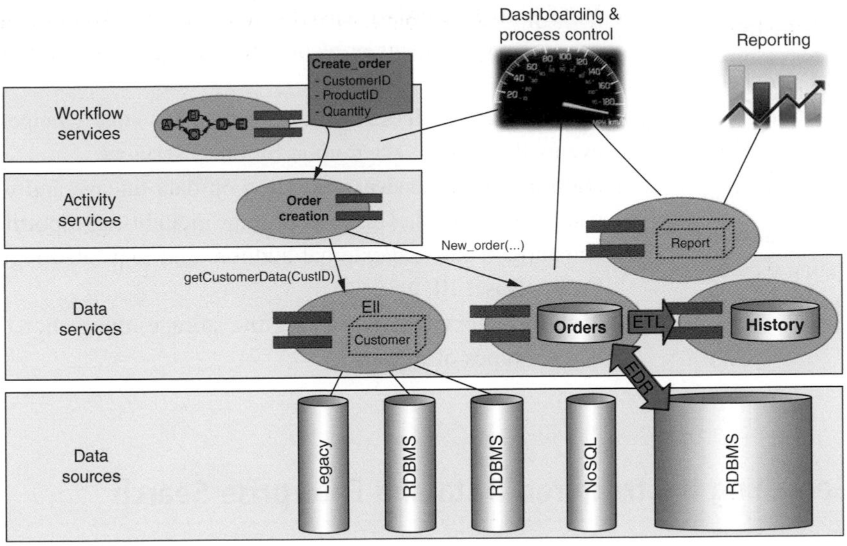


**Figure 18.13** Combining different patterns to resolve data dependencies.

is very difficult to assess the data's quality, since the quality is affected by all transformations and manipulations a data item underwent throughout its journey. In this respect, it is important to take data integration patterns at the data layer level, and data flow at the business processes level, into account to see the whole picture regarding data lineage and to assess the impact of the data's lineage on different data quality dimensions.

A rule of thumb is that *event data* (When was an order created? What is the order quantity? By whom was the stock replenished?) can be safely passed as data flow, as these data will never change after the actual event they describe. Other data, which refer to the *business state* (What is the customer's current address? What is the current stock? What is the client's current credit score?) should be treated with more care. It is safer that these data are retrieved through the data layer when needed unless the data are very stable or the impact of some of the data being somewhat outdated is limited. Therefore, ideally, different subsets of the input data for an activity service to perform its task may be provided through a combination of patterns at the process layer and data layer level, as illustrated in Figure 18.13.

Besides the data services that provide the actual data, most SOA-enabled data integration suites also provide different data-related infrastructure services that support the exploitation and management of data services. We provide some examples below. Many services are also related to data quality and data governance, which will be discussed in more detail in Sections 18.3 and 18.4.

- **Data profiling services**: providing automated support for assessing and understanding content, quality, and structure of enterprise data; relating data from various sources to one another based on the patterns and values in the data, e.g., by automatically detecting and matching foreign keys.
- **Data cleansing services**: ensuring the validity and consistency of data using name-and-address cleansing; resolving missing fields, poor formatting, and conflicting data; and standardization to various industry formats.
- **Data enrichment services**: enhancing the data by exploiting external data sources.

**Retention Questions**

- Why is data integration important?
- Discuss and contrast different patterns for data integration.
- What patterns are needed for managing sequence and data dependencies in processes?

- **Data transformation services**: transforming data to match the target application's requirements or reconciling between data items residing in different data sources.
- **Data event services**: monitoring data for state changes and rules, raising events that can be acted upon by other services.
- **Data auditing services**: reporting on data lineage and when/how/by whom data was changed. This is important in auditing, reporting, and meeting the demands of internal/external auditors and legislated regulations (Sarbanes–Oxley, Basel III, etc.)
- **Metadata services:** supporting the storage, integration, and exploitation of diverse types of metadata.

## 18.2 Searching Unstructured Data and Enterprise Search

The data integration patterns discussed in the previous sections are, in principle, applicable to structured, semi-structured, and unstructured data. However, with unstructured data, even if data integration technology yields unified access to collections of full-text documents or multimedia data, there remains the question of how to search these documents efficiently. As Google and others would tell you, making vast repositories of data searchable is a daunting task, especially when the majority of data consist of textual and other unstructured formats. Over the years, various database providers have worked on offering specialized features to tackle this problem, in full-text search engines. These can be systems of their own, or components of a DBMS, in particular to process CLOB (character large object; see also Chapter 9) data types. They allow quickly searching large volumes of unstructured text, stored as several "documents", and return documents based on how well they match a query.

The querying capabilities of such engines differ from those offered in SQL. Whereas SQL is primarily well suited to query structured collections of records, using such languages becomes hard when dealing with text fields. For example, writing out a query to match documents having something to do with "SQL" might be done as follows:

```
SELECT * FROM documents
WHERE text LIKE '%SQL%' OR text LIKE '%STRUCTURED QUERY LANGUAGE%'
```

This approach, however, comes with several questions. For instance, how can we sort the results based on some notion of relevancy? What about documents that do not mention the terms "SQL" or "Structured Query Language" but are still related to our topic? How do we extract matching fragments and show them to the user? Therefore, this section deals with the main principles of searching unstructured data, and full-text search in particular. We also zoom in to the specifics of searching collections of full text documents in the World Wide Web, with web search engines. We conclude these sections with a discussion of enterprise search, which applies the same techniques to organize and search distributed collections of both structured and unstructured content within an enterprise or organization.

### 18.2.1 Principles of Full-Text Search

So far, most of the query languages and search techniques we have discussed focused on structured data, expressed as collections of neatly organized records consisting of typed fields. Even NoSQL databases, which generally allow for more flexibility and emphasize less the aspect of a strict schema design, do assume some structure, e.g., in the form of records consisting of key–value pairs or dictionary-like data structures. However, in today's data-driven world, a lot of data are being captured and stored in an unstructured format. Taking text as an example, it is easy to imagine environments generating thousands of documents in the form of text files, PDFs, and so on. The internet itself consists of a huge amount of interlinked web pages, the majority of which follow no standard structure and just represent their content and information as "text", rendered by your web browser.

The main difference between structured and unstructured data was already explained in Chapter 1. Structured data can be described according to a formal logical data model. Individual characteristics of data items can be identified and formally specified, such as the number, name, address, and email of a student or the number and name of a course. The advantage in searching these kinds of data is that a query mechanism has fine-grained control over the data: it can, for example, discriminate between a series of characters representing a student's name and a student's address. In this way, it becomes possible to formulate fine-grained search criteria, such as all the names of students who live in New York. With unstructured data, there are no finer-grained components in a text document that can be interpreted in a meaningful way by the search mechanism. For example, given a collection of text documents containing the biographies of famous New York citizens, it is impossible to retrieve only those biographies of people who lived in New York as a student. One could search for documents containing the terms "name", "student", and "New York" occurring closely together, but such a search would also yield biographies of people born in New York, but who studied elsewhere, or maybe even people who the text explains that as a student they always wore the same sweater, with the imprint "New York" on it. The search result will always consist of entire biography documents, but it is impossible to retrieve, e.g., only the names and birth dates of the people mentioned in a biography.

And yet, given the huge amounts of unstructured text documents that may contain vital data (emails, contracts, manuals, legal documents, etc.), it is important to examine how the rudimentary search techniques available to these kinds of data can be exploited to the fullest. The main idea of full-text search is that individual text documents can be selected from a collection of documents according to the presence of a single search term or a combination of search terms in the document. This is also the basic principle behind web search engines like Google or Bing. An additional criterion can be *proximity*, i.e., the fact that some search terms occur closely together, or the *absence* of some terms. For example, searching for documents containing the term "python" may yield a completely different result than a search for documents containing the term "python" but not the term "monty". Often, the set of documents resulting from a full-text search is ordered according to *relevance*. A simple way of expressing the latter is the *frequency* with which the search term(s) occur(s) in the document, meaning that a document containing a term multiple times will be more relevant to the search than a document containing the term only once. Typically, this frequency is expressed in relative terms, i.e., relative to the frequency of occurrence of the term in the entire document collection.

### 18.2.2 Indexing Full-Text Documents

Whereas the most basic functionality of a full-text search engine is simple – receive a set of search terms as input and return a set of references to documents containing the search terms as a result – its implementation becomes less straightforward for document collections of a size that prohibits the documents being searched on the fly. The only option is to search the documents in advance for relevant terms and to capture the results in an index, relating search terms to documents. In this way, only the index must be searched on the fly, which is much more efficient.

The prevalent approach for indexing full-text documents is an inverted index, which was introduced in the context of structured data in Chapter 12. Basically, a single index is used, which is conceived as follows:

**Connections**

The distinction between structured and unstructured data was introduced in Chapter 1. Chapter 9 discussed the CLOB data type as a means to store full-text content in (extended) RDBMSs. Chapter 12 dealt with different index types, including inverted indexes, in the context of structured data.

- The document collection is parsed upfront, with only relevant terms being withheld – i.e., prepositions, articles, conjunctions, etc. are typically omitted.
- An index entry is created for every individual search term. The index entries consist of (search term, list pointer) pairs, with the list pointer referring to a list of document pointers. Each document pointer refers to a document that contains the corresponding search term.
- For a search term $t_i$ the list is typically of this format: [($d_{i1}$, $w_{i1}$), ... ($d_{in}$, $w_{in}$)]. A list item ($d_{ij}$, $w_{ij}$) contains a document pointer $d_{ij}$, referring to a document j that contains the search $t_i$, with j = 1..n. The list item also contains a weight $w_{ij}$, denoting how important term $t_i$ is to document j. The weight can be calculated in different ways, but often depends on the number of occurrences of $t_i$ in document j.
- In addition, most search engines contain a *lexicon*, which maintains some statistics per search term, e.g., the total number of documents that contain the term. These statistics can also be used by the ranking algorithm (see below), besides the weights.

A full-text search then comes down to providing one or more search terms. At that time, only the index is searched, not the document collection. For each search term, the corresponding index entry yields access to a list with pointers to documents that contain the search term. If multiple search terms are used (e.g., the terms "full" *and* "text"), the intersection of the two lists yields the pointers to all documents containing both terms. If the search pertains to all documents containing the terms "full" *or* "text", the union of both lists can be used. The ranking algorithm sorts the results in descending order of relevance, according to the combined weights and other statistical information in the lexicon. This is illustrated in Figure 18.14. In many cases, the result also contains a summary or description of the selected documents with the pointers to the full documents.

Many search engines extend this basic approach with additional features, such as the following:

- A *thesaurus*, allowing inclusion of documents containing synonyms or derived terms of the search terms in the search result.
- *Proximity*, allowing to enforce that only documents are included where particular search terms occur closely together.
- The use of *fuzzy logic* or *similarity measures* to also take into account terms very similar to the search terms, among other things to accommodate for misspellings (e.g., documents containing the term "dtaabases" would be retrieved when searching for "databases").
- The use of *text mining* techniques: these are advanced analytics techniques specifically focusing on unstructured, textual data, e.g., to automatically derive the most representative key terms from a document, or to classify documents according to similarity.

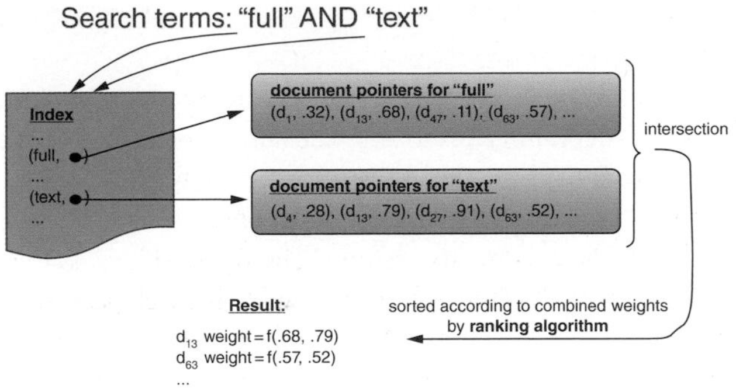


**Figure 18.14** Illustration of full-text search and inverted index.

In many cases, **document metadata** can also be included in the search criteria. Document metadata do not pertain to the actual document content, but to the properties of the document itself: file name, creator of the file, creation and last modification date of the file, file type (text, image, audio, etc.), for example. Using document metadata can improve search efficiency, as document metadata are themselves structured data,[2] so one can distinguish between, e.g., a date denoting when the document was created and a date denoting when it was last modified. Still, the search result will be entire documents, not individual fields, since the result still consists of unstructured data. In this way, it becomes possible to, e.g., search for all documents authored by Wilfried Lemahieu, modified after 8 June 2017, and containing the terms "database management".

## 18.2.3 Web Search Engines

The basic principles of web search engines are very similar to the ones described above, apart from obviously the larger scale of the document collection. This is illustrated in Figure 18.1. A first important component of web search technology is the **web crawler** or web spider, which continuously retrieves web pages, extracts their links (URLs) to other pages, and adds these URLs to a buffer that contains the links to pages yet to be visited. Each retrieved page is sent to an **indexer**, which extracts all relevant terms from the page and updates the inverted index structure we discussed previously. Each relevant term corresponds to an index entry, referring to a list with ($d_{ij}$, $w_{ij}$) pairs, with $d_{ij}$ representing the web page's URL and $w_{ij}$ denoting the weight of the corresponding search term to the page. If a user issues a web search with one or more search terms, the query engine searches the index according to the search terms and sends the matching pages, with their weights, to a **ranking module** that sorts the result set according to relevance. Finally, this ranked result, containing essentially a list of URLs (and possibly brief descriptions of the corresponding web pages) is returned to the user.

[2] To illustrate the difference between structured data and structured metadata, let's consider the example of a document containing book descriptions. If the document contains structured data, it would be possible to refer to the "author" field for each individual book in the document. If the document contains unstructured data, it would be possible to refer to the "author" of the document itself (which is metadata), but not to the author information of the individual books (which is unstructured content).

**Drill Down**

The ranking module for Google's search engine is based on the PageRank algorithm introduced by Page et al. in 1999.[3] The PageRank algorithm aims to simulate surfing behavior. Figure 18.15 represents a network of web pages linked to each other. Given the figure, what is the probability that a surfer will visit web page A? Assume for now that a surfer only browses web pages by following the links on the web page she/he is currently visiting. The figure shows that web page A has three incoming links. A surfer currently visiting web page B will visit web page A next with a probability of 20% (1/5). This is because web page B has five links to other web pages, among which is web page A. Analogously, if a surfer is currently on web page C or D, there is a probability of 33.33% and 50% respectively that web page A will be visited next. The probability of visiting a web page is called the PageRank of that web page. To know the PageRank of web page A, we must know the PageRank of web page B, C, and D. This is often called collective inference: the ranking of one web page depends on the ranking of other web pages; and a change in the ranking of one web page might affect the ranking of all other web pages.

Specifically, the main idea is that important web pages (i.e., web pages that appear at the top of the search results) have many incoming links from other (important) web pages. Hence, the ranking of a web page depends on (a) the ranking of web pages linking toward that web page; and (b) the number of outgoing links of the linking web pages. However, visiting web pages by following a random link on the current web page is not a realistic assumption. Surfers' behavior is typically more random: instead of following one of the links on a web page, they might also randomly visit another web page. Therefore, the PageRank algorithm includes this random surfer factor, which assumes that surfers might randomly jump to another web page. With a probability of $\alpha$ the surfer will follow a link on the web page she/he is currently visiting. However, with a probability $1 - \alpha$, the surfer visits a random other web page. The PageRank formula can then be expressed as follows:

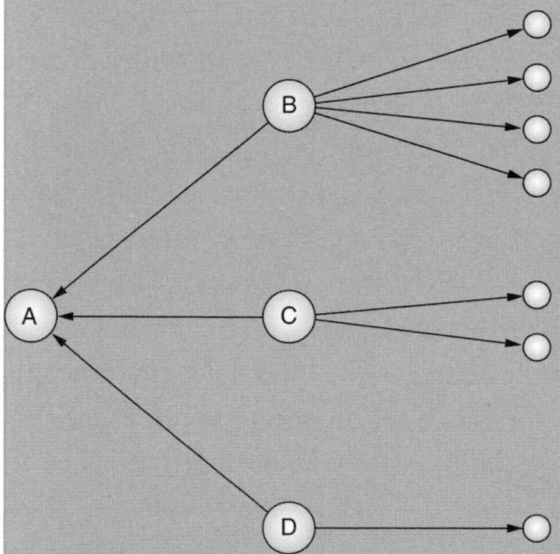


**Figure 18.15** The PageRank algorithm.

[3] Page L., Brin S., Motwani R., Winograd T., The PageRank citation ranking: Bringing order to the Web, *Proceedings of the 7th International World Wide Web Conference*, pp. 161–172. Brisbane, Australia, 1998.

$$PR(A) = \alpha \sum_{i \in N_A} \frac{PR(i)}{D_{out,i}} + (1-\alpha) \cdot e_A$$

where $PR(A)$ is the PageRank of web page A, $N_A$ is the pages linking to page A, $D_{out,i}$ is the number of outgoing links of web page $i$, $(1-\alpha)$ is the restart probability, and $e_A$ is the restart value for web page A, which is often uniformly distributed among all web pages. This equation requires the ranking of the neighboring web pages. One option is to start with a random PageRank value for every web page and iteratively update the PageRank scores until a predefined number of iterations is reached or a stopping criterion is met (e.g., when the change in the PageRank scores is marginal).

The above equation can be rewritten so the ranking is computed for all web pages simultaneously:

$$\vec{r} = \alpha \cdot \mathbf{A} \cdot \vec{r} + (1-\alpha) \cdot \vec{e}$$

where $\vec{r}$ is a vector of size $n$ containing the PageRanks of all $n$ web pages, $\mathbf{A}$ is the column-normalized adjacency matrix of size $n \times n$, $(1-\alpha)$ is the restart probability, and $\vec{e}$ is the restart vector. The restart vector is generally uniformly distributed among all web pages, and normalized afterwards.

Many variations are possible in this basic technology, also taking into account the particularities of the World Wide Web. For example, when calculating the weight of a term to a page, the HTML markup can be considered, e.g., attributing a higher weight to terms in bold or in headings, assuming that these terms are considered more important or more representative of the page. Also, the HTML markup contains document metadata such as the last modification date and the author of the document, which can be used as search criteria or to further refine the search results. Finally, given the huge number of web users, the behavior of these users can also be exploited to improve the search results. For example, links clicked upon in the past by many users using the same search terms as the ones at hand are probably very relevant to these search terms and should be ranked higher in the result, even if the terms occur not very frequently in the document. A complementary technique is the recognition and grouping of web pages with the same content into a single item in the result, so as not to clutter up the result set with too many similar pages. Such mechanisms show us that web search engines and recommender systems, which recommend products or items to users

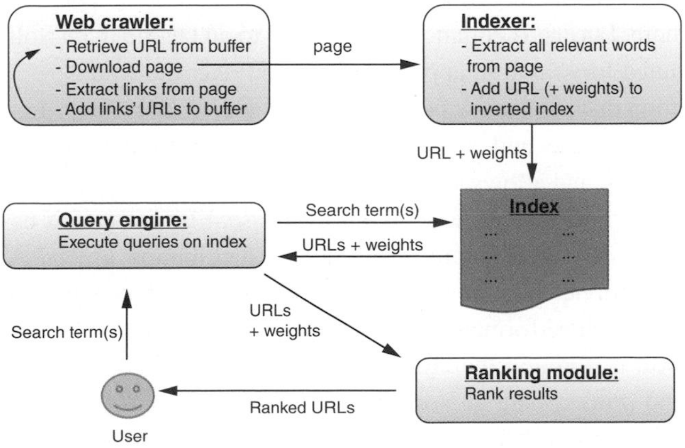


Figure 18.16 Illustration of the functioning of a web search engine.

according to their (predicted) interest, are very related technologies. Recommender systems are discussed in more detail in Chapter 20.

**Drill Down**

Search data themselves can also be a very relevant source of information. Website owners are interested to know when the search functionality on their website is invoked and what are the most popular search terms to understand the key interests of their visitors and improve the design of their website.

Google Trends is another example and shows how often a search term is entered relative to the total number of searches per region, time period, interest category, and type of search. Google Trends search data have been successfully used to forecast housing market trends, unemployment rates, and flu outbreaks based on searches for, e.g., buy house, employment benefits, and flu symptoms. The forecasts are especially good at predicting the present (also called nowcasting) or short-term future, which allows getting the measures of interest in a quicker way than having to wait for the statistical releases from the official (e.g., government) channels.

### 18.2.4 Enterprise Search

Another related concept is **enterprise search**, referring to the practice of making the content stemming from various distributed data sources (databases, but also plain files) in an organization searchable. Enterprise search technologies are strongly related to standard web search products and providers (such as Google and the like), but aim to offer tools that can be deployed and used internally, within an organization's boundaries and not exposed to the outside world.

The open-source technology that provided a lot of groundbreaking fundamental work for subsequent tools in full-text search was Apache Lucene. Originally written in 1999 in Java, it supported information retrieval from textual sources by offering indexing and search capabilities. At the center of Lucene's architecture is the idea of documents containing fields of text, be it from PDFs, HTML, Word files, or many others. These can be indexed in Lucene if their textual information can be extracted. Lucene offers a custom query syntax allowing for rich query expressions, including searching for keywords in named text fields, Boolean operators, wildcard matching, proximity matching, range searches, and so on.

Lucene has given rise to a large number of spinoff projects. Apache Solr, for instance, builds on top of Lucene and adds various APIs, highlighting matches, additional search capabilities, a web administration interface, and more. Lucene is commonly compared to an engine, with Solr being the car. Solr is particularly well-suited for search in applications served over the web.

Another popular search solution that has seen widespread adoption is Elasticsearch. Just like Solr, Elasticsearch is built on top of Lucene and adds additional APIs, distributed search support, grouping and aggregation in queries, and allows storing documents in a schema-free JSON format, which means Elasticsearch can also be described as a NoSQL database. Elasticsearch is based on the same inverted index principles as described before, but adds the distribution aspect. An Elasticsearch index consists of multiple individual Lucene indexes, which are distributed and replicated to cater for parallelism and, hence, search performance. Elasticsearch is frequently combined with two other applications that work with it (forming the "ELK stack" – Elasticsearch–Logstash–Kibana). Logstash is a tool to collect and process data to store it in a back-end system (not necessarily an Elasticsearch database, though it can be). It is hence typically used in the ETL process of a data

**Retention Questions**

- Discuss the basic principles of full-text search.
- How can full-text documents be indexed?
- How do web search engines work?
- Discuss the basic principles of Elasticsearch.

analysis exercise. Logstash comes with many typical parsing actions and predefined regular expression patterns that allow rapid development of parsing routines. The K in "ELK" stands for Kibana, which is a web-based analytics, visualization, and search interface for Elasticsearch. Kibana supports a large number of visualization types like area charts, data tables, line charts, pie charts, tag clouds, geographic maps, vertical bar charts, and time series charts with functions like derivatives and moving averages which can all be put in user-defined dashboards. These three tools together form a powerful data analysis framework that is open-source. The ELK stack is becoming increasingly popular, both in non-commercial environments and in large enterprises.

Although a lot of attention is being devoted to text as a form of unstructured data, other types of unstructured data exist as well, such as audio, imagery, or video data. Technology support in terms of providing database-like functionality for these types of data is not as developed as for full-text search, though some DBMSs support storing and querying images by means of image similarity matching or even computer-vision-based techniques.

## 18.3 Data Quality and Master Data Management

Not surprisingly, the aspect of data integration is also heavily related to that of data quality. As was introduced in Chapter 4, data quality can be defined as "fitness for use", meaning that the required level of quality of data depends on the context. Data quality is a multidimensional concept involving various aspects or criteria by which to assess the quality of a dataset or individual data record. In Chapter 4, the following data quality dimensions were already highlighted as being important:

- **Data accuracy**, referring to whether the data values stored are correct (e.g., the name of the customer should be spelled correctly).
- **Data completeness**, referring to whether both metadata and values are represented to the degree required and are not missing (e.g., a date of birth should be filled out for each customer).
- **Data consistency**, relating to consistency between redundant or duplicate values, and consistency among different data elements referring to the same or a related concept (e.g., the name of a city and postal code should be consistent).
- **Data accessibility**, which reflects the ease of retrieving the data.

Also, timeliness – the extent to which data are sufficiently up-to-date for the task at hand – has already been mentioned as an essential dimension in the respective data integration patterns.

**Connections**

Refer to Chapter 4 for more information regarding data quality and the dimensions of data quality.

Approached from the angle of data integration, it is important to mention that data integration can aid in improving data quality, but might also hamper it. We have seen how data consolidation and ETL allow performing different transformation and cleansing operations, so the consolidated view of the data should be of higher quality, but one might – appropriately so – wonder why it wouldn't be better to invest in data quality improvements at the source. The same remark holds for environments in which, throughout time, different integration approaches have been combined, leading to a jungle of legacy and newer systems and databases that now all must be maintained and integrated with one another.

This is a key challenge for many organizations and one that is indeed very difficult to solve. In these settings, master data management (MDM) is frequently mentioned as a management initiative to counteract these quality-related issues.

**Master data management (MDM)** comprises a series of processes, policies, standards, and tools to help organizations to define and provide a single point of reference for all data that are "mastered". Its key concern is to provide a trusted, single version of the truth on which to base decisions to ensure that organizations do not use multiple, potentially inconsistent versions of the same concept in different parts of their operations. The focus is on unifying company-wide reference data types such as customers and products. This might seem straightforward, but imagine the situation of a large bank in which one department is using an operational customer database for its day-to-day interactions, while the marketing department is setting up a campaign by selecting leads from a data warehouse using a BI tool, which, however, is running behind compared to the operational view. A customer that has just taken out a mortgage at the bank might receive a mortgage solicitation a week later, as the customer information used by the marketing department lacks fast or solid integration with the customer operational systems. Putting a data federation or virtualization solution on top can help, but converting all departments and applications to go through this newer layer can take years, let alone coming up with a clear mapping of the current data and systems overview and architecture. Modern information systems can be very complicated and entangled constructs, which should emphasize the necessity for master data management.

Setting up a master data management initiative involves many steps and tools, including data source identification, mapping out the systems architecture, constructing data transformation, cleansing and normalization rules, providing data storage capabilities, monitoring and governance facilities, and so on. Another key element is a centrally governed data model and metadata repository. Perhaps surprisingly, many vendor "solutions" to set up an MDM initiative look very similar to data integration solutions we discussed before – data consolidation, federation, propagation, or virtualization techniques. These integration approaches can be used as a method to achieve maturity in master data management. Note, however, that this assumes these solutions are used to set up a trusted, single version of the truth of the data on which decisions are based, and that no other representation of the data is used anywhere in the organization. The challenge hence lies in the execution: following these core principles is a daunting task, and integration officers must avoid adding yet another few strands of "spaghetti systems" and cross-links between data stores, causing the master data repository to become yet another half-integrated data silo.

**Retention Questions**

- How can master data management (MDM) contribute to data quality?

## 18.4 Data Governance

Due to data quality and integration concerns, organizations are increasingly implementing company-wide data governance initiatives to govern and oversee these concerns. To manage and safeguard data quality, a data governance culture should be put in place assigning clear roles and responsibilities. These roles (data owner, data steward, etc.) were already tackled in Chapter 4. Another important element is the ability to assess data lineage, as discussed earlier in this chapter. The ultimate aim of data governance is to set up a company-wide controlled and supported approach toward data quality, accompanied by data quality management processes. The core idea is to manage data as an asset rather than a liability, and adopt a proactive attitude toward data quality

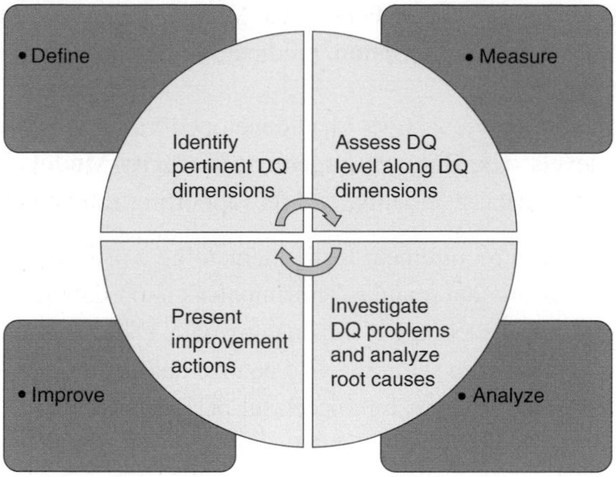


**Figure 18.17** Total Data Quality Management.

problems. To succeed, it should be a key element of a company's corporate governance and supported by senior management.

Different frameworks and standards have been introduced for data governance. Some are rooted in process maturity or quality management, while others focus explicitly on data quality or data integration. Other standards propose methods to organize the governance of IT and IT departments. In what follows, we summarize some notable data governance standards and frameworks.

### 18.4.1 Total Data Quality Management (TDQM)

The **Total Data Quality Management (TDQM)** framework is illustrated in Figure 18.17.[4] It presents a cycle consisting of four steps related to the management of data quality – Define, Measure, Analyze, and Improve – which are performed iteratively. The Define step identifies the pertinent data quality dimensions. These can then be quantified using metrics in the Measure step. Some example metrics are: the percentage of customer records with an incorrect address (accuracy); the percentage of customer records with a missing birth date (completeness); or an indicator specifying when customer data were last updated (timeliness). The Analyze step tries to identify the root cause of the diagnosed data quality problems. These can then be remedied in the Improve step. Example actions could be: automatic and periodic verification of customer addresses; the addition of a constraint that makes the date of birth a mandatory data field; and the generation of alerts when customer data have not been updated during the previous six months.

### 18.4.2 Capability Maturity Model Integration (CMMI)

The **Capability Maturity Model Integration (CMMI)** is a training and appraisal program geared toward the improvement of business processes. It was developed at Carnegie Mellon University (CMU) and is required by many United States Department of Defense and US Government contracts, especially in software development.

[4] Wang R.Y., A product perspective on total data quality management, *Communications of the ACM*, 1998; 41(2): 58–65.

CMMI defines the maturity of a process by five levels: Performed, Managed, Defined, Measured, and Optimized. Every level aims at improving the description, predictability, control, and measurement of the process at hand.

While CMMI focuses on a process-oriented view, CMU has developed various side-standards applying the same concept of maturity levels. The **Data Management Maturity Model** applies the five levels of maturity to the governance of data, its quality, and its supporting infrastructure:

- Level 1 – Performed: Data are managed as a requirement for implementing a project in a reactive manner, with little discipline or emphasis on data quality. The emphasis is on data repair.
- Level 2 – Managed: There is awareness of the importance of managing data. Data are understood to be a critical infrastructure asset. Some policies are set in place to control quality and monitor data.
- Level 3 – Defined: Data are treated as a critical asset for successful performance. Data quality is predictable, and policies are set in place to meet specific needs.
- Level 4 – Measured: Data are treated as a source of competitive advantage and seen as a strategic asset. Fully managed policies and formal specifications govern the quality of the data. A single source of truth is provided for the data.
- Level 5 – Optimized: Data are seen as critical to survival in a dynamic market. The organization is continuously improving its data governance initiatives and the quality of its data sources.

### 18.4.3 Data Management Body of Knowledge (DMBOK)

Inspired by the Project Management Body of Knowledge (PMBOK), a collection of processes, best practices, terminologies, and guidelines for project management overseen by the Project Management Institute (PMI), the **Data Management Body of Knowledge (DMBOK)** aims to offer a similar collection toward data management. DMBOK is overseen by DAMA International (the Data Management Association) and lists best practices toward data quality management, metadata management, data warehousing, data integration, and data governance. DMBOK is in its second version.

### 18.4.4 Control Objectives for Information and Related Technology (COBIT)

**Control Objectives for Information and Related Technologies (COBIT)** is a framework created by the international professional association ISACA for IT management and IT governance. As the name suggests, COBIT describes a series of implementable control sets and organizes them in a logical framework. The core goal of COBIT is to link business goals to IT goals, starting from business requirements and mapping these to IT requirements, and hence provides measurement tools, metrics, and maturity models to measure the effectiveness of these IT goals. Even though many of these focus on aspects such as data quality and integration, COBIT itself is a very large and comprehensive framework encompassing much more than just data governance. It is important to mention, however, that COBIT will often be positioned as an overall IT governance standard utilized at a high level, under which different standards, frameworks, and practices will be placed and aligned.

**Drill Down**

COBIT is sometimes called the "integrator standard" to integrate all other standards. There's perhaps a certain, Kafkaesque beauty in standards talking about integration requiring their own integration framework.

### 18.4.5 Information Technology Infrastructure Library

The Information Technology Infrastructure Library (ITIL) is a set of detailed practices for IT service management that focuses on aligning IT services with the needs and requirements of business. ITIL is published in five volumes, each of which covers a different IT service management lifecycle stage.

**Drill Down**

Recent versions of ITIL are just called "ITIL", without it being regarded as an acronym anymore.

**Retention Questions**

- What is data governance and why is it needed?
- Give two examples of data governance frameworks.

Just as with COBIT, ITIL also encompasses much more governance than just data quality and integration aspects, though puts a heavy emphasis on these elements in its fifth volume. The latter focuses on continuous service improvement, where several best practices are outlined toward benchmarking, monitoring, measuring, and improving the quality of IT services and hence also that of the underlying data sources. Other parts of ITIL deal with integration issues and their impact on different IT services.

## 18.5 Outlook

As infrastructure and data(base) requirements continue to change, it is only natural that managerial concerns regarding data integration, quality, and governance follow. To conclude our discussion on data integration, quality, and governance, it is interesting to highlight some more recent approaches to tackle these issues. It is remarkable how many vendors and cloud providers are trying to offer ways to handle the data integration issue in a world in which companies are either moving their data to the cloud or are shifting to a Big Data environment. Some examples include:

- Sqoop and Flume for Hadoop: Apache Sqoop is a tool designed for efficiently transferring data in bulk between Hadoop (an environment for Big Data processing we will discuss in Chapter 19) and "traditional" structured data stores such as relational databases. Apache Flume is a distributed system for efficiently collecting, aggregating, and moving large amounts of log data from many different sources to a centralized data store.
- Apache Kylin: An open-source analytics engine designed to provide an SQL interface and multidimensional analysis (OLAP) on top of Hadoop, supporting extremely large datasets. Think of it as a technology to define star schemas and analyze OLAP cubes on top of data stored in Hadoop.
- Google Cloud Dataflow and BigQuery ETL: Google is offering a managed service for developing and executing data processing and integration patterns, including ETL, to bring data to its Google Cloud platform.
- Amazon Redshift: A managed, cloud-based data warehouse solution that tries to integrate well with existing BI tools, but can run queries against petabytes of structured data.
- Amazon Relational Database Service (RDS): A managed web service that makes it easier to set up, operate, and automatically scale a relational database in the cloud without having to set up such a database yourself.

## 18.6 Conclusion

In this chapter, we have discussed some managerial aspects of data and databases, namely data integration, data quality, master data management, and data governance. Some had also a technical element, in particular the different data integration technologies and the complementary techniques to efficiently search unstructured data in a company-wide or World Wide Web setting. We have seen how these aspects play an important role as companies start using a multitude of databases and information systems over time, especially when the need arises to consolidate a company's data to provide a single, unified view, for instance, to construct a data warehouse to provide BI solutions.

Data, and BI, are fields still heavily evolving today. In recent years, we have seen companies being concerned not only with offering a unified view across their data sources, but also with looking for ways to tackle the Big Data challenge, i.e., looking for solutions to deal with incredibly large or even unstructured volumes of data. Also, analytics techniques have been developing rapidly, leading to several data science practices to perform both descriptive and predictive analytics. Big Data and analytics form the topics of the upcoming chapters.

### Scenario Conclusion

Based on a thorough analysis of their current data and process set-up, Sober's team implemented the following data quality and governance measures. First, regarding data quality, Sober plans to implement a checklist of various data quality checks routinely run over its relational database – e.g., to make sure street information is up-to-date, customer and driver details are entered correctly – in accordance with the Total Data Quality Management (TDQM) framework. Regarding the integration between the NoSQL database driving the mobile app and the RDBMS, Sober implements a changed data capture (CDC) solution in which all changes made to the NoSQL database are immediately propagated to the RDBMS. A queue is used to prevent overloading the RDBMS, and various checks are implemented to verify that the updates are executed correctly. Regarding experimental features, the mobile development team can continue to add NoSQL tables in an ad-hoc manner, but are requested to properly track and document the development of such features so the relational database schema can be modified later to also incorporate data from these features once they are vetted for a full release.

## Key Terms List

**activity services**
**business process**
**Capability Maturity Model Integration (CMMI)**
**changed data capture (CDC)**
**choreography**
**complex event processing (CEP)**
**Control Objectives for Information and Related Technologies (COBIT)**
**CRUDS functionality**
**data accessibility**
**data accuracy**
**Data as a Service (DaaS)**
**data auditing services**
**data cleansing services**
**data completeness**
**data consistency**
**data consolidation**

**data dependency**
**data enrichment services**
**data event services**
**data federation**
**data flow**
**data integration**
**data integration pattern**
**data lineage**
**Data Management Body of Knowledge (DMBOK)**
**Data Management Maturity Model**
**data profiling services**
**data propagation**
**data service composition**
**data services**
**data silo**
**data transformation services**
**data virtualization**
**document metadata**
**enterprise application integration (EAI)**
**enterprise data replication (EDR)**
**enterprise information integration (EII)**
**enterprise search**
**indexer**
**Information Technology Infrastructure Library (ITIL)**
**Infrastructure as a Service (IaaS)**
**master data management (MDM)**
**metadata services**
**operational BI**
**orchestration pattern**
**Platform as a Service (PaaS)**
**process engine**
**process integration**
**ranking module**
**service oriented architectures (SOA)**
**Software as a Service (SaaS)**
**streaming data**
**Total Data Quality Management (TDQM)**
**web crawler**
**workflow service**
**WS-BPEL**

## Review Questions

**18.1.** Ideally, data integration should include...

a. only data.
b. only processes.
c. both processes and data.

**18.2.** Which statement is **not correct**?

a. Analytics techniques are more and more used at the operational level as well by front-line employees.
b. Analytics for tactical/strategic decision-making increasingly uses real-time operational data combined with the aggregated and historical data found in more traditional data warehouses.
c. The operational usage of business intelligence aims for a low (or even zero) latency so interesting events or trends in the data can be immediately detected and accompanied with the appropriate response.
d. Nowadays, we see a complete divergence of the operational and tactical/strategic data needs and of the corresponding data integration tooling.

**18.3.** Which statement is **not correct**?

a. The essence of data consolidation as a data integration pattern is to capture the data from multiple, heterogeneous source systems and integrate it into a single persistent store (e.g., a data warehouse or data mart).
b. An important disadvantage of the consolidation approach is that it does not cater for historical data.

c. An ETL process typically induces a certain measure of latency, so the timeliness dimension may suffer, with the data being slightly out of date.
d. Besides the traditional set-up with ETL and a data warehouse, data lakes can also be considered an implementation of the consolidation pattern.

**18.4.** The federation pattern typically follows. . .

a. a pull approach.
b. a push approach.

**18.5.** Enterprise information integration (EII) is an example of. . .

a. data consolidation.
b. data integration.
c. data propagation.
d. data replication.

**18.6.** Enterprise application integration (EAI) and enterprise data replication (EDR) are examples of. . .

a. data consolidation.
b. data federation.
c. data propagation.
d. data virtualization.

**18.7.** Which statement is **not correct**?

a. Data virtualization isolates applications and users from the actual (combinations of ) data integration patterns used.
b. Data virtualization extensively uses data consolidation techniques such as ETL.
c. Contrary to a federated database as offered by basic EII, data virtualization does not impose a single data model on top of the heterogeneous data sources.
d. In many real-life contexts, a data integration exercise is an ongoing initiative within an organization, and will often combine a variety of integration strategies and approaches.

**18.8.** Which statement is **not correct**?

a. Process integration is to integrate and harmonize the various business processes in an organization as much as possible.
b. The control flow perspective of a business process specifies the correct sequencing of tasks (e.g., a loan offer can only be made when the credit score has been calculated).
c. The data flow perspective of a business process focuses on the inputs of the tasks (e.g., the interest rate offered depends on the credit score).
d. In a service-oriented context, there is a tendency to physically integrate services with the purpose of task coordination with services that perform the actual task execution and services that provide access to the necessary data.

**18.9.** Process execution languages such as WS-BPEL aim at managing. . .

a. only the control flow.
b. only the data flow.
c. both the control and data flow.

**18.10.** The choreography pattern to manage sequence and data dependencies is a. . .

a. centralized approach.
b. decentralized approach.

**18.11.** Which statement is **correct**?

a. The prevalent approach for indexing full-text documents is an inverted index.
b. SQL is well suited to query structured collections of records as well as unstructured data such as text.
c. It makes no sense to look at HTML markup when calculating the weight of a term to a page for web search.
d. Enterprise search technologies are strongly related to standard web search products and providers (e.g., Google), but aim to offer a series of tools that can be deployed and used externally such that an organization can expose itself to the outside world.

**18.12.** Which statement is **not correct**?

a. Master data management (MDM) compromises a series of processes, policies, standards, and tools to help organizations define and provide multiple points of reference for all data that are "mastered".
b. The focus of MDM is on unifying company-wide reference data types such as customers and products.
c. Setting up an MDM initiative involves a large number of steps and tools, including data source identification, mapping out the systems architecture, constructing data transformation, cleansing and normalization rules, providing data storage capabilities, monitoring and governance facilities, and so on.
d. A key element in MDM is a centrally governed data model and metadata repository.

## Problems and Exercises

18.1E Give some examples of operational business intelligence.

18.2E Conduct an illustrated SWOT analysis of data consolidation versus data integration versus data propagation.

18.3E What is data virtualization and what can it be used for? How does it differ from data consolidation, data federation, and data propagation?

18.4E What is meant by "Data as a Service"? How does this relate to cloud computing? What kind of data-related services can be hosted in the cloud? Illustrate with examples.

18.5E Discuss two types of dependencies that should be appropriately managed to guarantee the successful overall process execution. What patterns can be used to manage these dependencies?

18.6E Discuss and contrast the following three service types: workflow services, activity services, and data services. Illustrate with an example.

18.7E Discuss how different data services can be realized according to different data integration patterns.

18.8E How can full-text documents be indexed? Illustrate with an example.

18.9E How do web search engines work? Illustrate in the case of Google.

18.10E Discuss the impact of data lineage on data quality. Illustrate with examples.

18.11E What is data governance and why is it important?

18.12E Discuss and contrast the following data governance frameworks: Total Data Quality Management (TDQM); Capability Maturity Model Integration (CMMI); Data Management Body of Knowledge (DMBOK); Control Objectives for Information and Related Technology (COBIT); and Information Technology Infrastructure Library (ITIL).

# 19 Big Data

## Chapter Objectives

In this chapter, you will learn:

- what is meant by "Big Data" and its "5 Vs";
- to understand the differences between traditional database management systems and Big Data technologies such as Hadoop;
- to understand the differences between traditional data warehousing approaches and Big Data technologies;
- to identify the tradeoffs when opting to adopt a Big Data stack;
- what the links are between Big Data and NoSQL databases.

### Opening Scenario

Sober has made its first steps in setting up a data warehouse on top of its existing DBMS stack to kick-start its business intelligence activities, with the main goal of reporting purposes. However, Sober's management is hearing a lot lately about "Big Data" and "Hadoop" with regards to storing and analyzing huge amounts of data. Sober is wondering whether these technologies would offer an added benefit. So far, Sober is happy with its relational DBMS, which integrates nicely with its business intelligence tooling. The mobile development team, meanwhile, has been happy to work with MongoDB, a NoSQL database, to handle the increased workload from mobile users. Hence, the question for Sober is: what would a Big Data stack offer on top of this?

Data are everywhere. To give some staggering examples, IBM projects that every day we generate 2.5 quintillion bytes of data. Every minute, more than 300,000 tweets are created, Netflix subscribers are streaming more than 70,000 hours of video, Apple users download 30,000 apps, and Instagram users like almost two million photos. In relative terms, 90% of the data in the world have been created in the last two years. These massive amounts of data yield an unprecedented treasure of internal customer knowledge, ready to be analyzed using state-of-the-art analytical techniques to better understand and exploit customer behavior by identifying new business opportunities together with new strategies. In this chapter, we zoom into this concept of "Big Data" and explain how these huge data troves are changing the world of DBMSs. We kick-off by reviewing the 5 Vs of Big Data. Next, we zoom in on the common Big Data technologies in use today. We discuss Hadoop, SQL on Hadoop, and Apache Spark.

## 19.1 The 5 Vs of Big Data

Datasets are growing rapidly. We are living in a digitalized world, and the rise of internet giants such as Facebook, Google, and Twitter has led to an immense amount of data being generated each day, be it users posting pictures, tweets, messages, checking Google Maps, or talking to smart agents such as Siri, Alexa, or Google's assistant. Recent developments in research and technology have also brought along new devices, such as sensors or drones capturing high-resolution photographs, or 3D point maps user LIDAR (laser) scanners.

**Drill Down**

Another example of Big Data are Rolls Royce's airplane engines, which are packed with sensors generating hundreds of terabytes of data that can then be analyzed to improve fleet performance and safety. Another captivating example is Tesla's Autopilot, which has so far collected more than one billion miles of data and is being used by the company to continuously improve its self-driving software.

**Drill Down**

All these new devices and sensors generating data are often described as the "Internet of Things". Gartner says that 8.4 billion connected "Things" will be in use in 2017. Examples are automotive systems, smart TVs, digital set-top boxes, smart electric meters, and commercial security cameras. All these applications will generate a tremendous amount of sensor data.

Even though the term "Big Data" only became widespread in the last several years, it has been in use since the 1990s. It is hard to pinpoint exactly how the term was brought into existence, though many sources refer to John R. Mashey, chief scientist at SGI, making it popular by using it in his work around 1998. When people refer to Big Data, they usually refer to datasets with volumes beyond the ability of common tools to store, manage, or process in a reasonable amount of time. In addition, the Big Data philosophy encompasses both structured and highly unstructured forms of data.

In a 2001 research report, Gartner set out to define the scope of Big Data by listing its characteristics in the now-famous 3 Vs: **volume** (the amount of data, also referred to the data "at rest"); **velocity** (the speed at which data come in and go out, data "in motion"); and **variety** (the range of data types and sources that are used, data in its "many forms"). Many vendors and industry actors continue to use these Vs to describe Big Data today.

In recent years, vendors and researchers have also argued for a fourth V to be included in the description of Big Data: **veracity**, or data "in doubt". It describes the uncertainty due to data inconsistency and incompleteness, to ambiguities present in the data, as well as latency or certain data points that might be derived from estimates or approximations. Finally, to emphasize that being able to store or process these forms of data is not enough, many vendors, such as IBM, have also included an obvious though crucial fifth V: **value**. This is the end game – after spending a lot of time, effort, and resources in setting up a Big Data initiative, one needs to make sure that actual value is being derived from doing so. This V refers specifically to the economic value of Big Data as quantified using the total cost of ownership (TCO) and return on investment (ROI). This aspect has become especially important as many early adopters of the Big Data hype lost significant effort and time in setting up a Big Data initiative, without any advantages, insights, or efficiency gains to justify it in the end.

**Drill Down**

One can even find resources coming up with seven (!) Vs of Big Data: volume, velocity, variety, variability, veracity, visualization, and value. Variability here is seen as differing from variety; the latter describes the different types of data (from JSON to text to video to sound, for instance), whereas variability (data "in change") refers to the same type of data, but where the meaning and structure of the data shift over time. Our advice here is to stick to the 5 Vs, as this is the most widely adopted definition.

To illustrate the 5 Vs of Big Data in more detail, let's have a closer look at some example sources or processes generating Big Data. A traditional source is large scale enterprise systems such as enterprise resource planning (ERP) packages, customer relationship management (CRM) applications, and supply chain management (SCM) systems. Companies have been deploying these systems for about two decades now, yielding an unprecedented amount of data stored in various formats. The online social graph is another example. Consider the major social networks such as Facebook, Twitter, LinkedIn, Weibo, and WeChat. All together these networks capture information about two billion people, their friends, preferences, and other behavior, leaving a massive digital trail of data. With close to five billion handsets worldwide and with the mobile channel serving as the primary gateway to the internet in many developed and developing countries, this is another source of Big Data as every action taken by the user can be tracked and potentially geo-tagged. Also think about the Internet of Things (IoT) or the emerging sensor-enabled ecosystem that is going to connect various objects (e.g., homes, cars, etc.) with each other, and with humans. Finally, we see more and more open or public data such as data about weather, traffic, maps, macro-economy, etc.

All the above data-generating processes can be characterized in terms of the sheer volume of data being generated. This poses serious challenges in terms of setting up scalable storage architectures combined with a distributed approach to data manipulation and querying.

To illustrate variety, consider traditional data types or structured data such as employee name or employee date of birth, which are more and more complemented with unstructured data such as images, fingerprints, tweets, emails, Facebook pages, MRI scans, sensor data, GPS data, and so on. Although the former can be easily stored in traditional (e.g., relational) databases, the latter needs to be accommodated using the appropriate database technology facilitating the storage, querying, and manipulation of each of these types of unstructured data. Here, too, a substantial effort is required since it is claimed that at least 80% of all data are unstructured.

Velocity, the speed at which the data are generated, can be illustrated with streaming applications such as online trading platforms, YouTube, SMS messages, credit card swipes, phone calls, etc., which are all examples in which high velocity is a key concern. Successfully dealing with data velocity paves the way for real-time analytics, which can create substantial competitive advantage.

**Connections**

Refer to Chapters 4 and 18 for more details regarding data quality and veracity.

Veracity indicates the quality or trustworthiness of the data. Unfortunately, more data does not automatically imply better data, so the quality of the data-generating process must be closely monitored and guaranteed. As mentioned earlier (see Chapters 4 and 18), the degree of veracity required depends upon the business application.

Recall that value, finally, complements the 4 Vs framework from a business perspective. It refers specifically to the economic value of Big Data. This V refers to both an opportunity and a challenge. To provide an example: in 2016, Microsoft bought the professional social network site LinkedIn for $26.2 billion. Prior to the acquisition, LinkedIn had 422 million registered users and 100 million active users per month. Microsoft paid approximately $260 per monthly active user. This clearly illustrates why data are often branded as the new oil! Just as with oil, data need to be refined and treated to become valuable; just storing your piles of data without a clear business objective is not enough. This seems straightforward, but in recent years many organizations have reported on Big Data failures with projects coming with high expectations and high costs, but without a clear plan or process in place. The main root cause is failing to start with a clear business objective and jumping into Big Data due to an "us too" mentality, without first understanding your needs. The two most common pitfalls are the following. First, believing that one has huge volumes of data (millions of customer records), hence requiring a Big Data set-up, even though modern RDBMSs are perfectly capable of handling these. The data are structured, do not move at high velocities, and even the volume is still reasonable compared to the scale that companies such as Netflix and Google are working at.

**Connections**

NoSQL databases can be seen as one component in the whole Big Data technology ecosystem. Refer to Chapter 11 for a comprehensive discussion of NoSQL databases.

**Drill Down**

To provide another example of what constitutes high volume: eBay.com works with a data warehouse of 40 petabytes (that's 40,000 terabytes!).

Here, there might not be a true need to switch. In the chapter on NoSQL, we already discussed how traditional DBMSs are not good at extensive horizontal scaling. If you have the need for such a set-up, a NoSQL database can offer benefits, but potentially at the cost of consistency or querying capabilities.

A second pitfall concerns the fact that many Big Data technologies originally came around to handle unstructured, high-speed, or huge datasets, something which was simply not possible with traditional DBMSs. This does, however, not mean they are as easy to query, analyze, or derive insights from. The concept of data "analytics" frequently gets mentioned together with "Big Data", but one can just as well derive insights from reasonably sized and structured datasets. As we will illustrate throughout the remainder of this chapter, true Big Data stacks are often not that straightforward to work with or to derive insights from.

**Connections**

In this chapter, we focus on Big Data. In Chapter 20, we focus on the actual "analytics" aspects of data in general.

To put it another way: Big Data is first about managing and storing huge, high-speed, and/or unstructured datasets, but this does not automatically mean one can analyze them or easily leverage them to obtain insights. As we will discuss, this requires specialized skills and strong management follow-up. Analytics, on the other hand (or "data science") is about analyzing data and obtaining insights and patterns from it, but does not necessarily have to be applied on huge volumes or unstructured datasets.

**Retention Questions**

- What is meant by the 5 Vs of Big Data? What does each V mean or refer to?

## 19.2 Hadoop

It is impossible to talk about Big Data without mentioning Hadoop. **Hadoop** is an open-source software framework used for distributed storage and processing of big datasets. The main difference between Hadoop and other attempts to work with huge volumes of data that came before is that Hadoop can be set up over a cluster of computers built from normal, commodity hardware, instead of requiring specialized, expensive machines. Hadoop is designed with the fundamental assumption that hardware failures are common occurrences and should be gracefully handled.

Nowadays, Hadoop has almost become a synonym of "Big Data", even though Hadoop itself in its rawest form offers a relatively simple and limited set of features. Although Hadoop is managed by the Apache Foundation and is open-source, many vendors offer their implementation of a Hadoop stack, which all differ in features, extra components, and support offered. To understand what is going on, we will first look at the history of Hadoop and what it entails.

**Drill Down**

Amazon, Cloudera, Datameer, DataStax, Dell, Oracle, IBM, MapR, Pentaho, Databricks, Microsoft, Hortonworks, and many other vendors offer their own version of a Hadoop-based Big Data stack.

### 19.2.1 History of Hadoop

The genesis of Hadoop came from the Google File System paper published in 2003.[1] In this paper, researchers at Google introduced a new file system, meant to support Google's growing storage needs. The goal was to develop a file system that could be easily distributed across inexpensive commodity hardware while providing fault tolerance. This work led to another research paper from Google, called "MapReduce: Simplified Data Processing on Large Clusters".[2] Whereas the Google File System mainly concerned itself with distributing the storage of data across a cluster of computers, **MapReduce** introduced a programming paradigm to write programs that can be automatically parallelized and executed across a cluster of different computers. This way, Google not only had a way to distribute the storage of data, but could also write programs that were able to work on top of it. Consider a program working over a huge repository of web logs, simply counting the number of times a link is present. A simple task to express in SQL on top of a relational database, but a lot harder once one is dealing with a distributed set of files consisting of many petabytes of data.

**Connections**

In Chapter 11, when discussing MongoDB and other NoSQL databases, we have already encountered MapReduce as a way to construct more complicated queries.

Around the same time, Doug Cutting was developing a new web crawler prototype that would be better able to handle the growing web, called "Nutch". The project had its first version demonstrated in 2003, successfully handling 100 million web pages. To do so, the Nutch project had also implemented a MapReduce-based programming facility and a distributed file

[1] Ghemawat S., Gobioff H., Leung S.-T., The Google file system, *ACM SIGOPS Operating Systems Review*, 2003; 37(5).
[2] Dean J., Ghemawat S., MapReduce: Simplified data processing on large clusters, *Communications of the ACM*, 2008; 51(1): 107–113.

**Connections**

A web crawler (also called a web spider) is a program that systematically browses the World Wide Web, typically for the purpose of indexing the web. It is naturally one of the main components of a search engine. Refer back to Chapter 18 for more details on search.

system, called NDFS (Nutch Distributed File System), the latter encompassing barely 5000 lines of Java code. In 2006, Doug Cutting joined Yahoo!, who had taken an interest in his project, to work in its search engine division. The part of Nutch which dealt with distributed computing and processing (NDFS and the MapReduce subsystems) was split off and renamed to "Hadoop", named after the yellow toy elephant of Cuttings's son. The first version of Hadoop showed that it could successfully sort about two terabytes of data on 188 computers in two days, and Yahoo!'s Hadoop cluster quickly grew to include 1000 machines in the following months. In 2008, Yahoo! open-sourced Hadoop as "Apache Hadoop", since it was managed by the Apache Software Foundation, a US-based non-profit corporation overseeing a multitude of open-source projects, including the well-known Apache HTTP web server. Hadoop continues to be actively maintained and worked on by an ecosystem of developers across multiple organizations.

### 19.2.2 The Hadoop Stack

When talking about Hadoop in its "pure" form, with no additional components or technology, it is important to know that it describes a stack containing four modules. The first one is **Hadoop Common**, a set of shared programming libraries used by the other modules. The second is the **Hadoop Distributed File System (HDFS)**, a Java-based file system to store data across multiple machines, renamed from NDFS in the Nutch Project. The third module entails the MapReduce framework, a programming model to process large sets of data in parallel. **YARN (Yet Another Resource Negotiator)** forms the fourth module and handles the management and scheduling of resource requests in a distributed environment.

In the first versions of Hadoop (Hadoop 1), HDFS and MapReduce were tightly coupled, with the MapReduce component overseeing its own scheduling and resource request concerns. Since this didn't scale well to bigger clusters, the current versions of Hadoop (Hadoop 2) split up the resource management and scheduling tasks from MapReduce, which are now present in YARN (YARN was not present in Hadoop 1).

#### 19.2.2.1 The Hadoop Distributed File System

HDFS is the distributed file system used by Hadoop to store data across a cluster of commodity machines. It lets users connect to nodes over which data files are distributed, in a manner that allows for accessing and storing files as if it were one seamless file system (just as you would work with the hard drive in your own computer). HDFS puts a high emphasis on fault tolerance, since it assumes that commodity hardware will commonly fail.

**Drill Down**

Hard drives fail often. In 2007, Google already analyzed 100,000 drives in its data center and found that hard drives older than one year had an annual failure rate of 8%, meaning that every year 8000 drives would fail. That is about 21 failures every day!

Technology-wise, an HDFS cluster is composed of a NameNode, a server which holds all the metadata regarding the stored files. Think of this as a registry containing file names and their size, and where to find their contents in the cluster. A NameNode manages incoming file system operations such as opening, closing, and renaming files and directories. It is also responsible for mapping data blocks (parts of files) to DataNodes, which handle file read and write requests. DataNodes will create, delete, and replicate data blocks among their disk drives according to instructions from the governing NameNode. They continuously loop, asking the NameNode for instructions. Data replication is important to ensure fault tolerance. It is possible to specify how many replicas (or copies) of a file have to be created across different DataNodes at the time the file is created, a number that can also be changed after creation. The NameNode will make sure to then adhere to this request and distribute data blocks accordingly.

Since one of the main goals of HDFS is to support large files, the size of one data block is typically 64 megabytes. Each file that gets stored on HDFS is hence cut up into one or more 64 MB data blocks, which are then placed (in multiple copies) by the NameNode on multiple DataNodes. Finally, if a failure of the NameNode occurs (which also stores its register on its own disks), SecondaryNameNode servers can be provisioned. Figures 19.1–19.4 illustrate the operations of HDFS.

Figure 19.1 illustrates a basic metadata operation in action. The client consults the NameNode to find out which files are in the directory "/mydir/". The NameNode maintains a registry of files, and can immediately answer that one file is present with two replicas, and that the size is 1 GB.

Next, our client wishes to read out this file (Figure 19.2). It sends the NameNode a request to perform a read. The NameNode will look in its registry, and instruct the client that it can read the

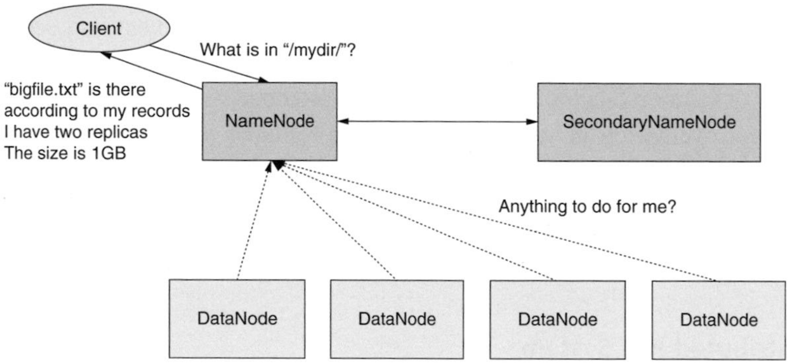


**Figure 19.1** A client requests metadata from the NameNode.

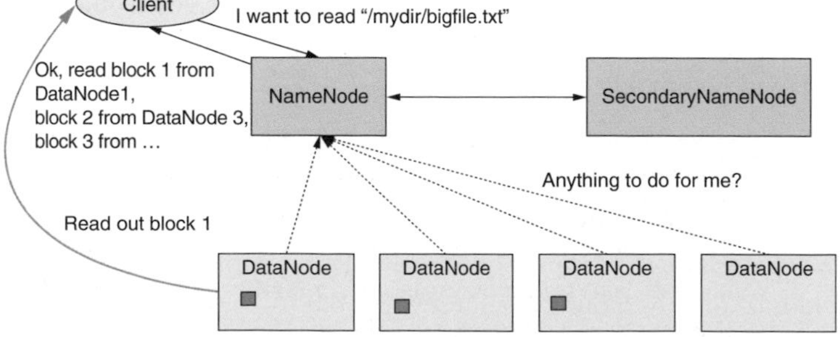


**Figure 19.2** A client wants to read out a file from the HDFS cluster.

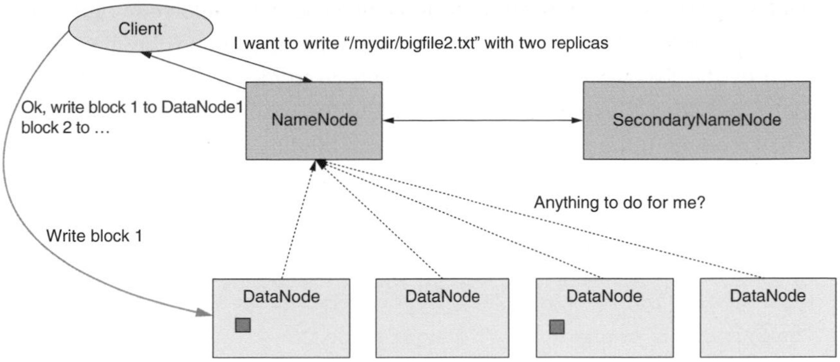


**Figure 19.3** A clients wants to write a file to the HDFS cluster.

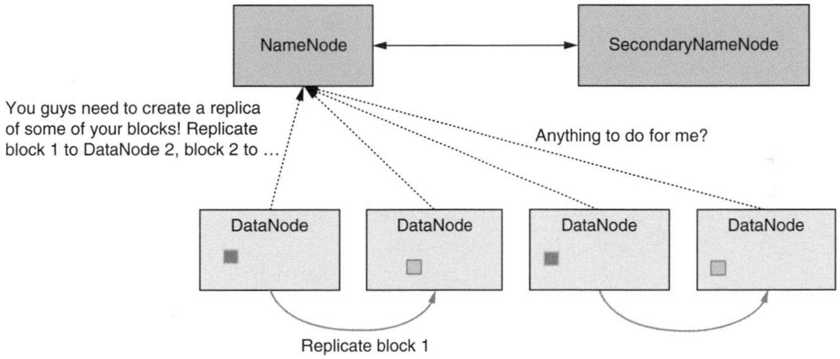


**Figure 19.4** A NameNode makes sure that replication is handled.

first 64 MB data block from DataNode 1, the next block from DataNode 3, and so on. The client can then contact each DataNode to receive the contents of the file.

In Figure 19.3, our client wants to create a new file, and indicates this once again through a request to the NameNode, together with the instruction to create two replicas. The NameNode responds with instructions regarding how to send the data blocks to the DataNodes. The client will then contact the DataNodes and start sending the contents of this new file.

The work of the NameNode is not done yet, however. Every few seconds, DataNodes will report in to the NameNode to indicate that they're still alive (i.e., send a "heartbeat") and to update the NameNode regarding the blocks they are storing. The NameNode now sees that our recently written file has not yet been replicated, and hence instructs the DataNodes to perform the replication (Figure 19.4).

If the NameNode stops receiving heartbeats from a DataNode, it presumes it is gone and that any data blocks it stores are gone. By comparing its registry with the reports it had been receiving from the dead node, the NameNode knows which copies of blocks died with the node and can then re-replicate those blocks to other DataNodes. Note, these figures describe a very basic set-up. In practice, DataNodes will also be organized in different "racks" holding several DataNodes. This allows for more efficient resource management and replication.

It is easy to see how the NameNode plays a crucial role within HDFS. Hence, to foresee a failure in the NameNode occurring, a SecondaryNameNode is often added to the cluster as well. The

SecondaryNameNode also occasionally connects to the NameNode (but less often than the DataNodes) and grabs a copy of the NameNode's registry. Should the main NameNode die, the files retained by the SecondaryNameNode can be used to recover the NameNode.

HDFS provides a native Java API to allow for writing Java programs that can interface with HDFS. Throughout the years, various ports and bindings have been created for other programming languages so they can communicate with HDFS. HDFS also comes with several command-line commands to interface with HDFS. The following code fragment shows a simple client program accessing HDFS from Java and reading out a file:

```
String filePath = "/data/all_my_customers.csv";
Configuration config = new Configuration();
# Connect to the HDFS filesystem
org.apache.hadoop.fs.FileSystem hdfs = org.apache.hadoop.fs.FileSystem.get(config);
# Create Path object using our file location string
org.apache.hadoop.fs.Path path = new org.apache.hadoop.fs.Path(filePath);
# Open the file on HDFS
org.apache.hadoop.fs.FSDataInputStream inputStream = hdfs.open(path);
# Create a byte array to store the contents of the file
# Warning: can exceed Java's memory in case the HDFS file is very large
byte[] received = new byte[inputStream.available()];
# Read the file into the byte array
inputStream.readFully(received);
```

This example shows off an important point when working with HDFS. Recall that the whole goal of HDFS is to split up potentially very large files and distribute them across machines. In this example, we're reading in a complete file and storing it in a byte array in the memory of the computer executing the Java program. When working with big files, the received file's size can easily exceed that of the client's available memory. Hence, it is important to construct programs in such a way that they can deal with files line by line, or in limited blocks, such as shown below:

```
// ...
org.apache.hadoop.fs.FSDataInputStream inputStream = hdfs.open(path);
byte[] buffer = new byte[1024]; // Only handle 1KB at once
int bytesRead;
while ((bytesRead = in.read(buffer)) > 0) {
    // Do something with the buffered block here
}
```

This shows (through a very simple example) how users aiming to do something with files stored on HDFS should still think of how best to approach the problem at hand, knowing that incoming files can potentially be very large.

Finally, we also provide a listing of the most common Hadoop HDFS command-line commands, which allow you to access an HDFS cluster from the command line:

| | |
|---|---|
| • hadoop fs -mkdir mydir | Create a directory on HDFS |
| • hadoop fs -ls | List files and directories on HDFS |
| • hadoop fs -cat myfile | View a file's content |
| • hadoop fs -du | Check disk space usage on HDFS |
| • hadoop fs -expunge | Empty trash on HDFS |

| | |
|---|---|
| • hadoop fs -chgrp mygroup myfile | Change group membership of a file on HDFS |
| • hadoop fs -chown myuser myfile | Change file ownership of a file on HDFS |
| • hadoop fs -rm myfile | Delete a file on HDFS |
| • hadoop fs -touchz myfile | Create an empty file on HDFS |
| • hadoop fs -stat myfile | Check the status of a file (file size, owner, etc.) |
| • hadoop fs -test -e myfile | Check if a file exists on HDFS |
| • hadoop fs -test -z myfile | Check if a file is empty on HDFS |
| • hadoop fs -test -d myfile | Check if myfile is a directory on HDFS |

#### 19.2.2.2 MapReduce

**MapReduce** forms the second main important component of Hadoop. MapReduce is a programming paradigm (a way to construct programs) made popular by Google and subsequently implemented by Apache Hadoop, as discussed above. It is important to note that the main innovative aspects of the MapReduce model do not come from the map-and-reduce paradigm itself, as these concepts were long known in functional programming circles, but rather from applying these functions in a manner that is scalable and fault-tolerant.

A map–reduce[3] pipeline starts from a series of values and maps each value to an output using a given mapper function. In many programming languages, this concept of applying a "mapping" exists natively, as this Python example illustrates:

```
>>> numbers = [1,2,3,4,5]
>>> numbers.map(lambda x : x * x) # Map a function to our list
[1,4,9,16,25]
```

The reduce operation then applies a reducing function to a series of values, but now operates on the list as a whole, instead of element-by-element. A list of values hence gets reduced to a single value:

```
>>> numbers.reduce(lambda x : sum(x) + 1) # Reduce a list using given function
16
```

These two components form the basics behind the Hadoop MapReduce programming model, although some differences are present here. First, a MapReduce pipeline in Hadoop starts from a list of key–value pairs, and maps each pair to one or more output elements. The output elements are also key–value pairs. This operation can easily be run in parallel over the input pairs. Next, the output entries are grouped so all output entries belonging to the same key are assigned to the same worker (in most distributed set-ups, workers will correspond to different physical machines, so that this step can also happen in parallel). These workers then apply the reduce function to each group, producing a new list of key–value pairs. The resulting, final outputs are then (optionally) sorted by their key to produce the final outcome.

There is another particularly important aspect to note when working with MapReduce in Hadoop: even though not all mapping operations have finished, reduce-workers can already get started on their work by applying their reduce function on a partial group of results with the same key. When new mapped results come in, the reduce operation can be applied again to form the ultimately resulting outcome. This has two important implications: first, the reduce function should output the same key–value structure as the one emitted by the map function, since this output can be

[3] We utilize "MapReduce" when referring to the specific implementation in Hadoop. "Map–reduce" is used when describing the general usage of the two mathematical functions "map" and "reduce".

**Connections**

In Chapter 11, when discussing MongoDB and other NoSQL databases, we saw how many databases have adopted MapReduce to construct more complicated queries. Refer to that chapter if you want to freshen up on more details regarding MapReduce. In what follows, we continue working with the MapReduce paradigm on Hadoop.

used again in an additional reduce operation. Second, the reduce function itself should be built in such a way that it provides correct results, even if called multiple times. Briefly: the MapReduce way of writing programs is "embarrassingly parallel", since both the map and reduce operations can be split over multiple machines, and the reducers can already get to work even when not all mappers have finished. MapReduce hence offers a powerful programming framework, but one that requires some clever thinking on the part of the programmer or analyst.

In Hadoop, MapReduce tasks are written using the Java programming language. Bindings for Python and other programming languages exist, but Java is still regarded as the "native" environment to construct programs. To run a MapReduce task, a Java program is packaged as a JAR archive and launched using the command:

```
hadoop jar myprogram.jar TheClassToRun [ args...]
```

Let's illustrate how a MapReduce task runs in a distributed cluster by constructing a Java program to count the appearance of a word in a file (imagine again an incredibly huge file with long lines). To keep things simple, we'll write our program using one Java class:

```
import java.io.IOException;
import org.apache.hadoop.conf.Configuration;
import org.apache.hadoop.fs.*;
import org.apache.hadoop.io.*;
import org.apache.hadoop.mapreduce.*;
import org.apache.hadoop.mapreduce.lib.input.TextInputFormat;
import org.apache.hadoop.mapreduce.lib.output.FileOutputFormat;

public class WordCount {
  // Following fragments will be added here
}
```

First, we need to define our mapper function. In Hadoop MapReduce, this is defined as a class extending the built-in Mapper<KeyIn, ValueIn, KeyOut, ValueOut> class, indicating which type of key–value input pair we expect and which type of key–value output pair our mapper will emit:

```
// Add this in the WordCount class body above:

public static class MyMapper extends Mapper<Object, Text, Text, IntWritable> {
        // Our input key is not important here, so it can just be any generic object
        // Our input value is a piece of text (a line)
        // Our output key will also be a piece of text (a word)
        // Our output value will be an integer

        public void map(Object key, Text value, Context context)
                    throws IOException, InterruptedException {
                // Take the value, get its contents, convert to lowercase,
                // and remove every character except for spaces and a-z values:
```

```
                String document = value.toString().toLowerCase()
                                        .replaceAll("[^a-z\\s]", "");
                // Split the line up in an array of words
                String[] words = document.split(" ");

                // For each word...
                for (String word : words) {
                        // "context" is used to emit output values
                        // Note that we cannot emit standard Java types such as int,
                        // String, etc. Instead, we need to use a
                        // org.apache.hadoop.io.* class such as Text
                        // (for string values) and IntWritable (for integers)[4]

                        Text textWord = new Text(word);
                        IntWritable one = new IntWritable(1);

                        // ... simply emit a (word, 1) key-value pair:
                        context.write(textWord, one);
                }
        }
}
```

The mapper in our basic word-counting example works like this. Our given input line will be split up in key–value pairs as follows: every line in the file will become one pair, with the key indicating the starting position of the line (which we won't need to use) and the value being the line of text itself. This will be mapped to multiple key–value output pairs. For each word we find, we emit a (word, 1) pair:

| Input key–value pairs | |
|---|---|
| Key <Object> | Value <Text> |
| 0 | This is the first line |
| 23 | And this is the second line, and this is all |

will be mapped to:

| Mapped key–value pairs | |
|---|---|
| Key <Text> | Value <IntWritable> |
| this | 1 |
| is | 1 |
| the | 1 |
| first | 1 |
| line | 1 |
| and | 1 |
| ... | ... |

[4] The reason behind this is a bit technical. MapReduce's types (say, "Text") are similar to Java's built-in types (like "String"), with the exception that they also implement a number of additional interfaces, like "Comparable", "Writable", and "WritableComparable". These interfaces are all necessary for MapReduce: the Comparable interface is used for comparing when the reducer sorts the keys, and Writable can write the result to the local disk.

This operation will happen in parallel. While our mappers are busy emitting output pairs, our reducers will start working. Also, the reducer function is specified as a class extending the built-in Reducer<KeyIn, ValueIn, KeyOut, ValueOut> class:

```
public static class MyReducer extends Reducer<Text, IntWritable, Text, IntWritable> {
        public void reduce(Text key, Iterable<IntWritable> values, Context context)
                        throws IOException, InterruptedException {
                int sum = 0;
                IntWritable result = new IntWritable();
                // Summarize the values so far...
                for (IntWritable val : values) {
                        sum += val.get();
                }
                result.set(sum);
                // ... and output a new (word, sum) pair
                context.write(key, result);
        }
}
```

Our reducer works as follows (keep in mind that the reducer works over a list of values and reduces them). Here, our list of values is a list of integer counts for a particular key (a word), which we sum and output as (word, sum). To see how this works, imagine that our mappers have already emitted these pairs:

Mapped key–value pairs

| Key <Text> | Value <IntWritable> |
|---|---|
| this | 1 |
| is | 1 |
| the | 1 |
| first | 1 |
| line | 1 |
| and | 1 |
| this | 1 |
| is | 1 |

Since we already have duplicate keys (for "this" and "is"), some reducers can already get started:

Mapped key–value pairs for "this"

| Key <Text> | Value <IntWritable> |
|---|---|
| this | 1 |
| this | 1 |

will be reduced to:

| Reduced key–value pairs for "this" | |
|---|---|
| Key <Text> | Value <IntWritable> |
| this | 1 + 1 = 2 |

When later additional mapped output pairs appear with the key "this", they can be reduced again to one output pair for "this":

| Reduced key–value pairs for "this" | |
|---|---|
| Key <Text> | Value <IntWritable> |
| this | 2 + 1 = 3 |

Finally, we also need to add a main method to our Java program to set everything up:

```
public static void main(String[] args) throws Exception {
        Configuration conf = new Configuration();

        // Set up a MapReduce job with a sensible short name:
        Job job = Job.getInstance(conf, "wordcount");

        // Tell Hadoop which JAR it needs to distribute to the workers
        // We can easily set this using setJarByClass
        job.setJarByClass(WordCount.class);

        // What is our mapper and reducer class?
        job.setMapperClass(MyMapper.class);
        job.setReducerClass(MyReducer.class);

        // What does the output look like?
        job.setOutputKeyClass(Text.class);
        job.setOutputValueClass(IntWritable.class);

        // Our program expects two arguments, the first one is the input file on HDFS
        // Tell Hadoop our input is in the form of TextInputFormat
        // (Every line in the file will become value to be mapped)
        TextInputFormat.addInputPath(job, new Path(args[0]));

        // The second argument is the output directory on HDFS
        Path outputDir = new Path(args[1]);
        // Tell Hadoop what our desired output structure is: a file in a directory
        FileOutputFormat.setOutputPath(job, outputDir);

        // Delete the output directory if it exists to start fresh
        FileSystem fs = FileSystem.get(conf);
        fs.delete(outputDir, true);
```

**Figure 19.5** Running a Hadoop MapReduce program.

```
    // Stop after our job has completed
    System.exit(job.waitForCompletion(true) ? 0 : 1);
  }
```

After compiling and packaging our program as a JAR file, we can now instruct the Hadoop cluster to run our word counting program:

```
hadoop jar wordcount.jar WordCount /users/me/dataset.txt /users/me/output/
```

Hadoop will start executing our MapReduce program and report on its progress (Figure 19.5).

When finished, the "/users/me/output/" will contain the following contents

```
$ hadoop fs -ls /users/me/output
Found 2 items
-rw-r—r--  1  root hdfs     0  2017-05-20  15:11  /users/me/output/_SUCCESS
-rw-r—r--  1  root hdfs  2069  2017-05-20  15:11  /users/me/output/part-r-00000
```

```
$ hadoop fs -cat /users/me/output/part-r-00000and 2
first    1
is       3
line     2
second   1
the      2
this     3
```

This is a very basic example. In Hadoop, a MapReduce task can consist of more than mappers and reducers, and can also include partitioners, combiners, shufflers, and sorters that specify in more detail how key–value pairs have to be shuffled around, distributed, and sorted across the computing nodes (one sorter is implicitly enabled and shown in our example above, as the output has been sorted by key).

What should be clear from this example is that constructing MapReduce programs requires a certain skillset in terms of programming. To tackle a problem, multiple ways of approaching it usually exist, all with different tradeoffs in terms of speed, memory consumption, and scalability over a set of computers. There is a reason most guides and tutorials never go much further than a basic word-counting or averaging example, and most organizations that have adopted the MapReduce framework in their data pipeline haven't been very eager to share their efforts.

#### 19.2.2.3 Yet Another Resource Negotiator

One question we still need to answer is how a MapReduce program gets distributed across different nodes in the cluster and how coordination among them happens. This is the job of YARN, the final "main" Hadoop component. In early Hadoop versions (Hadoop 1), YARN did not exist, and the MapReduce component itself was responsible for the setting up and organization of MapReduce programs. To do so, Hadoop 1 appointed one node in a cluster to be a JobTracker: a service that would accept incoming jobs and serve information about completed ones. Next, each node that needs to handle map and reduce tasks runs a TaskTracker service, which would launch tasks as instructed and governed by the JobTracker. This system worked for smaller clusters, but for larger set-ups, with many jobs being executed and submitted at once, the JobTracker could become overloaded.

In Hadoop 2, MapReduce was split up into two components: the MapReduce-specific programming framework remained MapReduce (see above), while the cluster resource management capabilities were put under a new component, called YARN. Three important services are present in YARN. First, the ResourceManager is a global YARN service that receives and runs applications (an incoming MapReduce job, for instance) on the cluster. It contains a scheduler to govern the order in which jobs are handled. Second, the JobTracker's function of serving information about completed jobs is now handled by the JobHistoryServer, keeping a log of all finished jobs. Finally, the TaskTracker service in Hadoop 1 is replaced by a NodeManager service, which is responsible to oversee resource consumption on a node. NodeManagers are responsible for setting up containers on a node, each of which can house a particular task, such as a single map or reduce task. By doing so, the NodeManager can also keep track of how "busy" a node is and whether it can accept more tasks at the moment.

Note that once an application (such as our word-count program above) gets accepted by the ResourceManager and is scheduled to start, the ResourceManager will delegate the responsibility to further oversee it by instructing one of the NodeManagers to set up a container with an Application Master for that job, which will handle the further management of that application. That way, the ResourceManager can free up resources to handle and schedule other incoming applications, without having to also follow-up on their execution.

The whole YARN set-up can look daunting. Let us provide a step-by-step example as follows. Figure 19.6 introduces a simple YARN cluster with four servers, one of which is running the ResourceManager, one of which is running the JobHistoryServer, and two of which are running NodeManagers.

Our client wishes to submit an application to the cluster (like we submitted our word-count program before). The client contacts the resource manager with the request to deploy and run a MapReduce program (Figure 19.7).

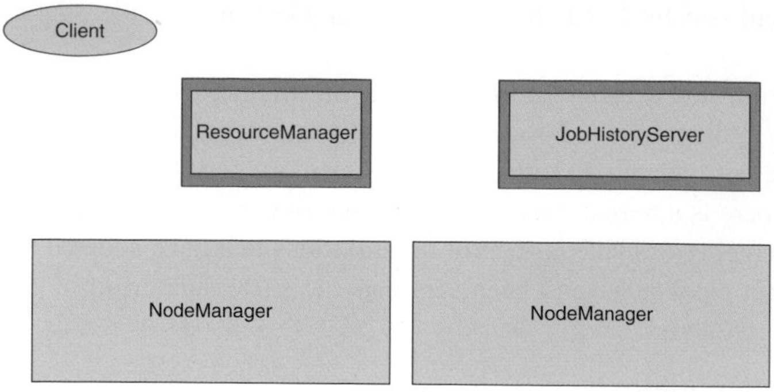


**Figure 19.6** A basic YARN cluster.

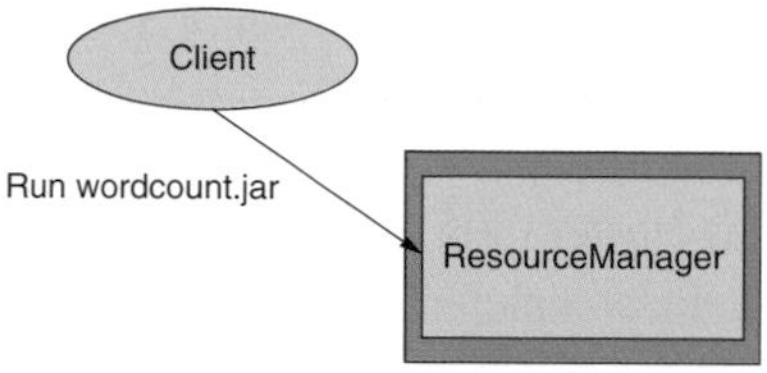


**Figure 19.7** A client submits an application to the ResourceManager.

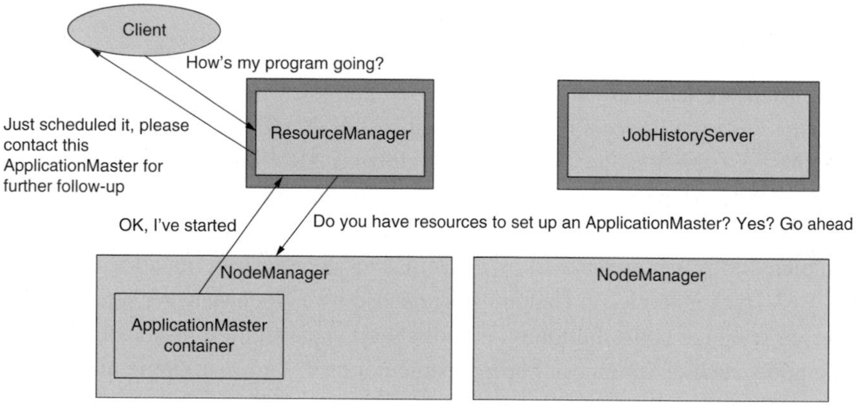


**Figure 19.8** The ResourceManager sets up an ApplicationMaster by negotiating with the NodeManager and passes the client the information.

The ResourceManager will keep our application in a queue until its scheduler determines that it is time to start our application. The ResourceManager will now negotiate with a NodeManager to instruct the setting up of a container in which to start the ApplicationMaster. The ApplicationMaster will register itself on startup with the ResourceManager, which can then be kept up-to-date with further job status information. This also allows us to relay this information to the client, which can then communicate directly with the ApplicationMaster for further job follow-up (progress updates, status) (Figure 19.8).

The ApplicationMaster will now handle the further execution of the submitted application, including setting up containers for map and reduce operations. To do so, the ApplicationMaster will ask the ResourceManager to negotiate with the NodeManagers (who all report-in regularly to the ResourceManager) to see which one is free. When a NodeManager is free, the

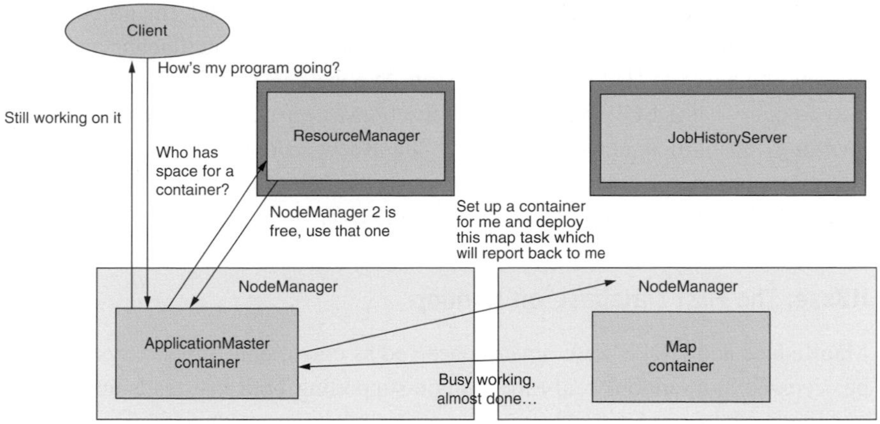


**Figure 19.9** The ApplicationMaster will set up containers for each subtask by first negotiating with the ResourceManager which NodeManager it should contact to do so.

ApplicationMaster will launch the container by providing necessary information to that NodeManager (Figure 19.9).

When a map or reduce container is finished, it will deregister itself by letting the ApplicationMaster know it is done. This continues until the application has completed, at which point also the ApplicationMaster will send a completion update to the client and deregister itself with the ResourceManager and shut down, allowing its container to be repurposed. The ResourceManager then contacts the JobHistoryServer to store a full execution log of this application in its archives.

YARN is a complex set-up, but the architecture comes with many advantages. By breaking up the JobTracker into different services, it avoids many of the scaling issues still present in Hadoop 1. In addition, YARN allows us to run programs and applications other than MapReduce on its cluster as well. That is, YARN can be used for coordination of any sort of task in which decomposition into parallel subtasks is beneficial. This will become especially useful once we move away from MapReduce, as we will see later. First, we will look at SQL on Hadoop.

**Retention Questions**

- Describe the Hadoop stack.
- What is HDFS? Describe the architecture and key components behind HDFS.
- How does a MapReduce pipeline work in Hadoop?
- What is YARN? Describe the architecture and key components behind YARN.

## 19.3 SQL on Hadoop

It should be clear that MapReduce does not form the most pleasant way to interact with and query datasets for end-users, even those with programming experience. The fact that MapReduce programs can operate in parallel over huge datasets is a strong advantage, as is the fact that it can work with HDFS, which can store large datasets in a distributed way without any structure imposed on the actual files (note that we have made no mention of a schema or structure when working with HDFS – it is simply a big distributed hard drive).

It seems, however, that we are far away from the benefits that, e.g., SQL offered us in terms of querying data, and even further from deriving business intelligence or analytical insights from it.

This is exactly the letdown many early adopters of Hadoop faced. Imagine working with a relational data warehouse that is tightly integrated with your business intelligence and reporting applications. Making the move to Hadoop does not seem like the best choice here: your data are structured and easy to query using SQL, whereas Hadoop offers an unstructured file system and no out-of-the-box querying capabilities, other than writing MapReduce programs. The benefits of Hadoop, such as being capable of working with huge amounts of data, were understood, but the need for a more database-like set-up on top of Hadoop became clear.

### 19.3.1 HBase: The First Database on Hadoop

MapReduce and HDFS were never conceived as operational support systems in which data had to be accessed in a random, real-time fashion supporting both fast reads and writes. Instead, Hadoop was primarily geared toward resource- and time-intensive batch-computing operations. That is, geared toward long-running MapReduce computing tasks that had to ensure the capability to restart subtasks (map or reduce operations) when a node went down, and where waiting times for a job to complete were assumed to easily lie in the days-to-weeks range. This presented a huge dichotomy from the thinking present in the business environment, coming from data warehouse-based set-ups together with business intelligence platforms. Businesses had hence invested in Hadoop hoping it would offer a faster, more feature-rich platform to gain insights into the data. To remedy this, the October 2007 release of Hadoop included the first version of **HBase**, the first Hadoop database inspired by Google's Bigtable, offering a DBMS that can be run on top of HDFS, handling very large relational tables. It hence puts some logical structure on top of HDFS. Note that HBase, with its focus on large datasets and emphasis on running in a distributed fashion, can be regarded as one of the older NoSQL databases. HBase is hence also more a "data storage platform" rather than a true DBMS as it still lacks many features you find in a relational DBMS such as typed columns, triggers, advanced query capabilities, and so on. Instead, HBase focuses on offering a simplified structure and query language in a way that is highly scalable and can tackle large volumes of data.

**Connections**

HBase was one of the main projects driving the NoSQL movement later on, as we discussed in Chapter 11. Many NoSQL databases aim to offer the same scalability, without running on top of Hadoop. Also, if you recall our discussion on consistency in Chapters 11 and 16 and wonder how HBase stands in this field, it is important to know that HBase is one of the few NoSQL databases that does not adopt eventual consistency. Instead, HBase offers strongly consistent reads and writes.

Just as a relational DBMS, HBase also organizes its data in tables that have rows and columns. Still, the similarities end there, as it is more helpful to think of HBase's tables as being multi-dimensional maps (or multidimensional arrays) as follows. An HBase table consists of multiple rows. A row consists of a row key and one or more columns with values associated with them. Rows in a table are sorted alphabetically by the row key, making the design of this key a crucial factor. The goal is to store data in such a way that related rows are near each other. For instance, if your rows relate to website domains, it might be helpful to define the key in reverse order, so that "com.mycorp.mail" and "com.mycorp.www" are closer to each other, rather than "www.mycorp.com" being closer to "www.yourcorp.mail".

Each column in HBase is denoted by a column "family" and an optional "qualifier", separated by a colon (:), e.g., "name:first" and "name:last". A column family physically co-locates a set of columns and their values. Each family has a set of storage properties, including whether its values should be cached, whether values should be compressed, and so on. Every row in a table has the same column families, but not all column families need to have a value filled in for each row. The column qualifier is added to the column family to provide an index of a certain piece of data. Each cell in a table is hence defined by a combination of the row key, column family and column qualifier, and a timestamp. The timestamp represents a value's version and is written alongside each value. Hence the comparison to data being stored as a multidimensional map, in which "data[table][row key][column family][column qualifier][timestamp] = value".

**Drill Down**

In the online playground, you can experiment with the HBase shell and follow along with the queries in the chapter (see the Appendix for more details).

To show how this works in practice, let's create a simple HBase table to store and query users using the HBase shell (started on the command prompt). The row key will be the user ID. We'll construct the following column "families:qualifiers":

- name:first
- name:last
- email (without a qualifier).

Let's start by creating our "users" table with two column families:

```
hbase(main):001:0> create 'users', 'name', 'email'
0 row(s) in 2.8350 seconds

=> Hbase::Table - users
```

Describe the table (this statement will return a lot of additional configuration information):

```
hbase(main):002:0> describe 'users'
Table users is ENABLED
users
COLUMN FAMILIES DESCRIPTION
{NAME => 'email', BLOOMFILTER => 'ROW', VERSIONS => '1', IN_MEMORY =>
'false', K
EEP_DELETED_CELLS => 'FALSE', DATA_BLOCK_ENCODING => 'NONE', TTL =>
'FOREVER', C
OMPRESSION => 'NONE', MIN_VERSIONS => '0', BLOCKCACHE => 'true',
BLOCKSIZE => '6
5536', REPLICATION_SCOPE => '0'}
{NAME => 'name', BLOOMFILTER => 'ROW', VERSIONS => '1', IN_MEMORY =>
'false', KE
EP_DELETED_CELLS => 'FALSE', DATA_BLOCK_ENCODING => 'NONE', TTL =>
'FOREVER', CO
MPRESSION => 'NONE', MIN_VERSIONS => '0', BLOCKCACHE => 'true',
BLOCKSIZE => '65
536', REPLICATION_SCOPE => '0'}
2 row(s) in 0.3250 seconds
```

Another way to list this table (the table itself, not its contents) is:

```
hbase(main):003:0> list 'users'
TABLE
users
1 row(s) in 0.0410 seconds

=> [ "users"]
```

We can now start inserting values. Since HBase represents data as a multidimensional map, we store values using "put" one by one by specifying the table name, a row key, column family and qualifier, and the value itself (note the deliberate misspelling of "first" as "firstt"):

```
hbase(main):005:0> put 'users', 'seppe', 'name:firstt', 'Seppe'
0 row(s) in 0.0560 seconds
```

Oops, we made a typo there, so let's insert the correct column family:qualifier instead:

```
hbase(main):006:0> put 'users', 'seppe', 'name:first', 'Seppe'
0 row(s) in 0.0200 seconds

hbase(main):007:0> put 'users', 'seppe', 'name:last', 'vanden Broucke'
0 row(s) in 0.0330 seconds

hbase(main):008:0> put 'users', 'seppe', 'email', 'seppe.vandenbroucke@kuleuven.be'
0 row(s) in 0.0570 seconds
```

Now list the full contents of this table (using scan):

```
hbase(main):009:0> scan 'users'
ROW                COLUMN+CELL
 seppe             column=email:, timestamp=1495293082872, value=seppe.vanden
                   broucke@kuleuven.be
 seppe             column=name:first, timestamp=1495293050816, value=Seppe
 seppe             column=name:firstt, timestamp=1495293047100, value=Seppe
 seppe             column=name:last, timestamp=1495293067245, value=vanden Br
                   oucke
1 row(s) in 0.1170 seconds
```

Give the information for row key "seppe" only (using "get" to select a single row key):

```
hbase(main):011:0> get 'users', 'seppe'
COLUMN          CELL
 email:         timestamp=1495293082872, value=seppe.vandenbroucke@kuleuven.be
 name:first     timestamp=1495293050816, value=Seppe
 name:firstt    timestamp=1495293047100, value=Seppe
 name:last      timestamp=1495293067245, value=vanden Broucke
4 row(s) in 0.1250 seconds
```

Our incorrectly spelled entry is still present. Let's try to delete it:

```
hbase(main):016:0> delete 'users', 'seppe', 'name:firstt'
0 row(s) in 0.1800 seconds
```

```
hbase(main):017:0> get 'users', 'seppe'
COLUMN          CELL
 email:         timestamp=1495293082872, value=seppe.vandenbroucke@kuleuven.be
 name:first     timestamp=1495293050816, value=Seppe
 name:last      timestamp=1495293067245, value=vanden Broucke
3 row(s) in 0.1750 seconds
```

We can change the email value by just running "put" again:

```
hbase(main):018:0> put 'users', 'seppe', 'email', 'seppe@kuleuven.be'
0 row(s) in 0.0240 seconds
```

Let's now retrieve this row again, but only for the column family "email":

```
hbase(main):019:0> get 'users', 'seppe', 'email'
COLUMN          CELL
 email:         timestamp=1495293303079, value=seppe@kuleuven.be
1 row(s) in 0.0330 seconds
```

What if we want to see earlier versions as well?

```
hbase(main):021:0> get 'users', 'seppe', {COLUMNS => ['email'], VERSIONS => 2}
COLUMN          CELL
 email:         timestamp=1495293303079, value=seppe@kuleuven.be
1 row(s) in 0.0220 seconds
```

That didn't work, we first need to instruct HBase to keep multiple versions for this column family:

```
hbase(main):024:0> alter 'users', {NAME => 'email', VERSIONS => 3}
Updating all regions with the new schema...
0/1 regions updated.
1/1 regions updated.
Done.
0 row(s) in 3.3310 seconds

hbase(main):025:0> put 'users', 'seppe', 'email', 'seppe.vandenbroucke@kuleuven.be'
0 row(s) in 0.0540 seconds

hbase(main):026:0> put 'users', 'seppe', 'email', 'seppe@kuleuven.be'
0 row(s) in 0.0330 seconds

hbase(main):027:0> get 'users', 'seppe', {COLUMNS => ['email'], VERSIONS => 2}
COLUMN          CELL
 email:         timestamp=1495294282057, value=seppe@kuleuven.be
 email:         timestamp=1495294279739, value=seppe.vandenbroucke@kuleuven.be
2 row(s) in 0.0480 seconds
```

We can delete all values pertaining to row key "seppe" in "users" as follows:

```
hbase(main):026:0> deleteall 'users', 'seppe'
0 row(s) in 0.0630 seconds
```

```
hbase(main):027:0> scan 'users'
ROW                          COLUMN+CELL
0 row(s) in 0.0280 seconds
```

We then try to delete the table:

```
hbase(main):029:0> drop 'users'
ERROR: Table users is enabled. Disable it first.
```

We first need to disable the table before it can be dropped:

```
hbase(main):001:0> disable 'users'
0 row(s) in 3.5380 seconds

hbase(main):002:0> drop 'users'
0 row(s) in 1.3920 seconds

hbase(main):003:0> list 'users'
TABLE
0 row(s) in 0.0200 seconds

=> [ ]
```

**Connections**

Refer back to Chapter 18 where data migration and integration were exhaustively discussed. Apache Sqoop and Flume were already mentioned there as interesting projects to gather and move data between relational databases and HDFS. Even though these tools can offer a lot of help in migration exercises, these kinds of projects still require a heavy investment in time and effort, as well as management oversight.

HBase's query facilities are very limited. Just as we saw in Chapter 11, HBase offers a column-oriented, key–value, distributed data store with simple get/put operations. Like MongoDB, HBase includes facilities to write MapReduce programs to perform more complex queries, but once again this comes at an extra cognitive overhead. When using HBase, make sure you really have that much data to warrant its usage in the first place, i.e., if you have hundreds of millions or billions of rows, then HBase is a good candidate. If you have only a few million rows, then using a traditional RDBMS might be a better choice because all your data might wind up on a few nodes in HBase anyway, and the rest of the cluster may be sitting idle.

Additionally, think about portability issues when trying to "migrate" your data from an existing RDBMS set-up to HBase. In this case, it is not as simple as changing a JDBC driver and being able to re-use the same SQL queries.

Finally – and this is also often forgotten when setting up a Big Data cluster – make sure you have enough hardware available. HBase, just as the rest of Hadoop, does not perform that well on anything less than five HDFS DataNodes with an additional NameNode. This is mainly due to the way HDFS block replication works, which only makes the effort worthwhile when you can invest in, set up, and maintain at least 6–10 nodes.

### 19.3.2 Pig

Although HBase somewhat helps to impose structure on top of HDFS and implements some, albeit basic, querying facilities, more advanced querying functionality must still be written using the

MapReduce framework. To mitigate this problem, Yahoo! Developed "Pig", which was also made open-source as Apache Pig in 2007. **Pig** is a high-level platform for creating programs that run on Hadoop (in a language called Pig Latin), which uses MapReduce underneath to execute the program. It aims to enable users to more easily construct programs that work on top of HDFS and MapReduce, and can somewhat resemble querying facilities offered by SQL. The following Pig Latin fragment shows how a CSV file (comma-separated values file) from HDFS can be loaded, filtered, and aggregated. The "$0", "$1", . . . refer to column numbers in the CSV file:

```
timesheet = LOAD 'timesheet.csv' USING PigStorage(',');
raw_timesheet = FILTER timesheet by $0 > 100;
timesheet_logged = FOREACH raw_timesheet GENERATE $0 AS driverId,
                                                  $2 AS hours_logged,
                                                  $3 AS miles_logged;
grp_logged = GROUP timesheet_logged by driverId;
sum_logged = FOREACH grp_logged GENERATE group as driverId,
  SUM(timesheet_logged.hours_logged) as sum_hourslogged,
  SUM(timesheet_logged.miles_logged) as sum_mileslogged;
```

While Pig offers several benefits compared to standard SQL, such as being able to store data at any point during the execution of its programs (allowing once again for failure recovery and restarting a query), some have argued that RDBMSs and SQL are substantially faster than MapReduce – and hence Pig – especially for reasonably sized and structured datasets and when working with modern RDBMS engines (which are capable of using multiple processing units in parallel). In addition, Pig Latin is relatively procedural, versus SQL's declarative way of working. In SQL, users can specify that two tables should be joined or an aggregate summary should be calculated, but not how this should be performed on the physical level, as it is up to the DBMS to figure out the best query execution plan. Programming with Pig Latin is similar to specifying a query plan yourself, meaning greater control over data flows, once again imposing some extra requirements on the part of the programmer. Pig has not seen wide adoption, and does not receive frequent updates (only one version was released in 2016). The question hence remains whether supporting SQL as-is on Hadoop is possible.

### 19.3.3 Hive

Supporting SQL on top of Hadoop is what Apache Hive set out to do. **Hive** is a data warehouse solution which – like HBase – runs on top of Hadoop but allows for richer data summarization and querying facilities by providing an SQL-like interface. Before Hive, traditional queries had to be specified in a MapReduce program. Hive provides the necessary abstraction layer to convert SQL-like queries to a MapReduce pipeline. Since most existing business intelligence solutions already work with SQL-based queries, Hive also aids portability as it offers a JDBC interface.

Hive was initially developed by Facebook, but was open-sourced later and is now being worked on by other companies as well, so it now can run on top of HDFS as well as other file systems such as Amazon's S3 cloud storage file system. Physical storage of tables is done in plain text files, or other (better suited) formats such as ORC, RCFile, and Apache Parquet, which try to organize data in a more efficient manner on the physical level compared to simple text files.

Architecturally, Hive puts several additional components on top of Hadoop. The Hive Metastore, its first component, stores metadata for each table such as their schema and location on HDFS. It is worth noting that these metadata are stored using a traditional RDBMS. By default, the embedded Apache Derby database is used, but other RDBMSs can be used for this task. The Metastore helps the rest of the Hive system to keep track of the data and is a crucial component. Hence, a backup server regularly replicates the metadata, which can be retrieved if data loss occurs.

Next, the Driver service is responsible for receiving and handling incoming queries. It starts the execution of a query and monitors the lifecycle and progress of the execution. It stores the necessary metadata generated during the execution of a query and acts as a collection point to obtain the query result. To run a query, the Compiler will first convert it to an execution plan, containing the tasks needed to be performed by Hadoop's MapReduce. This is a complex step in which the query is first converted to an abstract syntax tree, which, after checking for errors, is converted again to a directed acyclic graph representing an execution plan. The directed acyclic graph will contain a number of MapReduce stages and tasks based on the input query and data. The Optimizer also kicks into gear to optimize the directed acyclic graph, for instance by joining various transformations in a single operation. It can also split up tasks if it determines this will help performance and scalability once the directed acyclic graph runs as a series of map-and-reduce operations. Once the directed acyclic graph is compiled, optimized, and divided into MapReduce stages, the Executer will start sending these to Hadoop's resource manager (YARN, usually) and monitor their progress. It takes care of pipelining the stages by making sure that a stage gets executed only if all other prerequisites are done.

Finally, to interface with the system, Hive provides a set of command-line tools and a web-based user interface to allow users to submit queries and monitor running queries. The Hive Thrift server, finally, allows external clients to interact with Hive by implementing a JDBC and ODBC driver, greatly improving Hive's portability.

Though Hive queries strongly resemble SQL, HiveQL, as Hive's query language is named, does not completely follow the full SQL-92 standard. HiveQL offers several helpful extensions not in the SQL standard (such as allowing for inserts in multiple tables at once), but lacks strong support for indexes, transactions, and materialized views, and only has limited subquery support, so some very complex SQL queries might still fail when trying to execute them on Hive.

Nevertheless, Hive's ability to handle most SQL queries offers a huge advantage. Hive offering JDBC drivers made the project wildly successful. It was quickly adopted by various organizations that had realized they had taken a step back from their traditional data warehouse and business intelligence set-ups in their desire to switch to Hadoop as soon as possible. Hence, one can easily write this HiveQL query:

```
SELECT genre, SUM(nrPages) FROM books GROUP BY genre
```

which automatically gets converted to a MapReduce pipeline behind the scenes. In addition, the fact that Hive stores its data tables on top of HDFS also makes the query language particularly well suited when datasets other than structured tables need to be queried, as long as it is possible to express a statement to extract data out of them in a tabular format. For instance, this query illustrates the word-count example using HiveQL:

```
CREATE TABLE docs (line STRING); -- create a docs table

-- load in file from HDFS to docs table, overwrite existing data:
LOAD DATA INPATH '/users/me/doc.txt' OVERWRITE INTO TABLE docs;
```

```
-- perform word count
SELECT word, count(1) AS count
FROM ( -- split each line in docs into words
  SELECT explode(split(line, '\s')) AS word FROM docs
) t
GROUP BY t.word
ORDER BY t.word;
```

The storage and querying operations of Hive closely resemble those of traditional DBMSs, but it internally works in a different manner, since Hive utilizes HDFS and MapReduce as its file system and query engine. Designing structured tables is now possible using Hive, with the defined structure being kept in Hive's Metastore. One difference with traditional DBMSs, however, is that Hive does not enforce the schema at the time of loading the data. A traditional RDBMS, for instance, can store data with a schema already being defined, meaning you have to define your schema ahead of time. This is also called "schema on write": the schema is applied and checked when data are written to the data store. Hive, on the other hand, applies a "schema on read" approach, in which tables can just be defined over a series of input files, but where the schema check will occur as the data are being queried and read from the data store. In this way, you can quickly load your data into the data store and figure out how to parse and handle it later. To put it another way: a schema-on-write approach means you need to figure out the format of your data before you write it, whereas a schema-on-read approach means you can indicate what your data are first, before figuring out what their structure is. The former allows for early detection of corrupt data and better query time performance, since the schema is known and enforced at the time of executing a query. Hive, on the other hand, can load data dynamically, ensuring a fast and very flexible initial load, but where queries might fail when trying to access the data under certain assumptions about its structure. Queries may take a longer time to execute since Hive needs to assume that a data schema can change or be interpreted in different ways (e.g., in our word-count example, is every line one column in a table, or is every word a column?).

**Connections**

See Chapters 14 and 16 for an overview on transactions and transaction management, with Chapter 16 focusing on a distributed setting.

Transactions are another area where Hive differs from traditional databases. A typical RDBMS supports ACID transaction management (Atomicity, Consistency, Isolation, and Durability). Transactions in Hive were introduced in Hive 0.13 but were still limited. Only in a more recent version of Hive (0.14) was functionality added to support full ACID transaction management, albeit at a high performance cost, since Hadoop itself has a hard time enforcing immutability (i.e., preventing changes being made) on a row-level basis. To work around this issue, Hive creates a new table first which contains all changes, before locking it and replacing the old table.

Performance and speed of SQL queries still forms the main disadvantage of Hive today. Just as with HBase, Hive is meant to be used on top of truly large data repositories, i.e., together with a large HDFS cluster and tables having many millions of rows. Many datasets that customers work with are not that large. Since there is still a large overhead in setting up and coordinating a series of MapReduce tasks, even relatively simple Hive queries can take a few hours to complete. Some Hadoop vendors, such as Hortonworks, have pushed strongly toward the adoption of Hive, mainly by putting efforts behind Apache Tez, which provides a new back-end for Hive, through which queries are no longer converted to a MapReduce pipeline but where the Tez execution engine directly works with operational pipelines expressed as a directed acyclic graph. In 2012, Cloudera,

**Retention Questions**

- Can you run a DBMS on top of Hadoop? How?
- What is Hive and how does it enable SQL querying on Hadoop? Explain the advantages and disadvantages.

another well-known Hadoop vendor, introduced their own SQL on Hadoop technology, called "Impala". Also, Cloudera opted to forego the underlying MapReduce pipeline completely. Other vendors such as Oracle and IBM also offer their Hadoop platforms – including Hive – which often differ strongly in terms of which version of Hive they actually ship with, and custom modifications or add-ons that have been made or implemented to speed up Hive's execution. Thinking carefully before committing to a vendor, or even Hadoop altogether, remains a strong recommendation. Meanwhile, the Apache Foundation continues to work on new projects, such as the recently proposed Apache Drill initiative, which offers SQL not only on top of HDFS, but also on top of HBase, flat files, NoSQL databases such as MongoDB, and aims to offer a unified querying interface to work on these repositories simultaneously. Again, a great initiative when working in an environment consisting of many database types and huge amounts of both structured and unstructured data, but coming again at a cost of extra performance drawbacks.

**Drill Down**

Facebook itself was quick to release another project, called Presto, which works on top of Hive and is another "SQL on Hadoop" solution more suited toward interactive querying. Also here, queries are no longer converted to a MapReduce pipeline, but instead to a directed acyclic graph consisting of various subtasks.

## 19.4 Apache Spark

Although Apache Hive made it possible to execute SQL queries on top of Hadoop, the lack of performance still made it less suited for many operational tasks. End-users were still on the lookout for ways to go further with their data than performing queries, and wanted to perform analytics on top of them to extract patterns and drive decisions, something which is not an easy task when working with huge datasets. Another issue was the continuous underlying presence of MapReduce, which is primarily geared toward resource- and time-intensive batch-computing operations and offers efficiency in terms of data throughput, but not necessarily in terms of response time when waiting for an answer to come back.

To work around this issue, researchers at the University of California started working on an alternative to MapReduce in 2014: **Spark**, a new programming paradigm centered on a data structure called the resilient distributed dataset, or RDD, which can be distributed across a cluster of machines and is maintained in a fault-tolerant way. Spark was developed with the specific focus on offering a response to the limitations that MapReduce had. Whereas Spark still enforces a relatively linear and fixed data flow structure (i.e., mapping and reducing data), Spark's RDDs allow you to construct distributed programs in a way that a cluster's memory can be used as a shared, distributed resource, opening the possibility to construct a wide variety of programs. That is, RDDs can enable the construction of iterative programs that have to visit a dataset multiple times, as well as more interactive or exploratory programs, which is exactly the type of programs one would need to facilitate the querying of data. The Spark team showed this approach was many orders of magnitude faster than MapReduce implementations, and Spark has hence been extremely rapidly adopted by many Big Data vendors in recent years as the way forward for exploring, querying, and analyzing large datasets. Spark itself has also been made open-source under the Apache Software Foundation.

Spark is not completely different from Hadoop in terms of set-up. It still works with HDFS as a distributed storage system (or other storage systems such as Amazon's S3), and still requires a cluster manager such as YARN as well (or other alternative cluster managers such as Mesos or even its own cluster manager). The MapReduce component, however, is what Spark aims to replace, as well as offering additional components on top of the Spark Core to facilitate a number of data analysis practices. In what follows, we discuss these components in more detail.

### 19.4.1 Spark Core

**Spark Core** forms the heart of Spark, and is the foundation for all other components. It provides functionality for task scheduling and a set of basic data transformations that can be used through many programming languages (Java, Python, Scala, and R). To do so, Spark introduces a programming model based around the concept of resilient distributed datasets, the primary data abstraction in Spark. RDDs are specifically designed to support in-memory data storage and operations, distributed across a cluster so it is both fault-tolerant and efficient. The first is achieved by tracking the lineage of operations applied to coarse-grained sets of data, whereas efficiency is achieved through parallelization of tasks across multiple nodes while minimizing the number of times data get replicated or moved around between them. Once data are loaded into an RDD, two basic types of operations can be performed: transformation, which creates a new RDD through changing the original one; and actions (such as counts), which measure but do not change the original data. The chain of transformations gets logged and can be repeated if a failure occurs. One might wonder what makes this approach so much faster than the MapReduce pipeline. First, transformations are lazily evaluated, meaning they are not executed until a subsequent action has a need for the result. RDDs will also be kept in memory for as long as possible, greatly increasing the performance of the cluster. This is a big difference with MapReduce, as this approach writes and reads data a lot throughout its pipeline of map-and-reduce operations. Finally, a chain of RDD operations gets compiled by Spark into a directed acyclic graph (similar to how Hive did for HiveQL queries), but which is then spread out and calculated over the cluster by splitting up this computational graph into a set of tasks, instead of converting it to a set of map-and-reduce operations. This greatly helps to speed up operations. Figure 19.10 shows Spark's general approach.

A big advantage for end-users is that Spark's RDD API is relatively pleasant to work with compared to writing MapReduce programs. Even map-and-reduce operations can still be expressed through the concept of RDDs, which can hold a collection of any type of object, as this Python code sample shows:

```
# Set up connection to the Spark cluster
sconf = SparkConf()
sc = SparkContext(master='', conf=sconf)

# Load an RDD from a text file, the RDD will represent a collection of
# text strings (one for each line)
text_file = sc.textFile("myfile.txt")
```

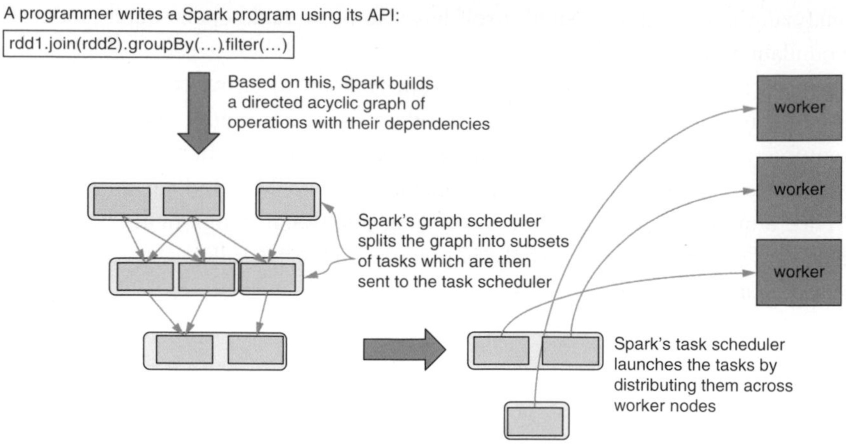
A programmer writes a Spark program using its API:
rdd1.join(rdd2).groupBy(...).filter(...)
Based on this, Spark builds a directed acyclic graph of operations with their dependencies
Spark's graph scheduler splits the graph into subsets of tasks which are then sent to the task scheduler
worker
worker
worker
Spark's task scheduler launches the tasks by distributing them across worker nodes

**Figure 19.10** Basic overview of Spark's architecture.

```
# Count the word occurrences: first split the lines into words, then
# apply map-reduce operators
counts = text_file.flatMap(lambda line: line.split(" ")) \
            .map(lambda word: (word, 1)) \
            .reduceByKey(lambda a, b: a + b)
print(counts)
```

### 19.4.2 Spark SQL

RDDs remain the primary data abstraction in Spark. At its core, an RDD is an immutable, distributed collection of elements, partitioned across nodes that can be operated upon in parallel using Spark's API, which offers a number of transactions and actions. Since an RDD imposes no preset structure in terms of what its elements should look like, it also offers a great way to deal with unstructured forms of data.

Nevertheless, Spark's RDD API can still be daunting when coming from an SQL background or if one is used to working with data that are structured, such as tabular data. To allow for a user-friendly way of working with such structured datasets, **Spark SQL** was devised as another Spark component that runs on top of Spark Core and introduces another data abstraction called DataFrames. DataFrames can be created from RDDs by specifying a schema on how to structure the data elements in the RDD, or can be loaded directly from various sorts of file formats such as CSV files, JSON files, from a JDBC query result, and even from Hive. Even though DataFrames continue to use RDDs behind the scenes, they represent themselves to the end-user as a collection of data organized into named columns. This is done to make processing of large but structured datasets easier. This code fragment shows Spark's DataFrames in action:

```
from pyspark.sql import SparkSession
spark = SparkSession.builder.appName("Spark example").getOrCreate()

# Create a DataFrame object by reading in a file
df = spark.read.json("people.json")
```

```
df.show()
# |  age|    name|
# +----+--------+
# |null|   Seppe|
# |  30|Wilfried|
# |  19|    Bart|
# +----+--------+

# DataFrames are structured in columns and rows:
df.printSchema()
# root
# |-- age: long (nullable = true)
# |-- name: string (nullable = true)

df.select("name").show()
# +--------+
# |    name|
# +--------+
# |   Seppe|
# |Wilfried|
# |    Bart|
# +--------+

# SQL-like operations can now easily be expressed:
df.select(df['name'], df['age'] + 1).show()
# +--------+---------+
# |    name|(age + 1)|
# +--------+---------+
# |   Seppe|     null|
# |Wilfried|       31|
# |    Bart|       20|
# +--------+---------+

df.filter(df['age'] > 21).show()
# +---+--------+
# |age|    name|
# +---+--------+
# | 30|Wilfried|
# +---+--------+

df.groupBy("age").count().show()
# +----+-----+
# | age|count|
# +----+-----+
# |  19|    1|
# |null|    1|
# |  30|    1|
# +----+-----+
```

Even though these statements resemble SQL, they (so far) are not completely alike. However, remember that underlying the DataFrame API which you can use in Python, Java, and other languages, the concept of RDDs is still being used to execute your operations. To do so, Spark implements a full SQL query engine that can convert SQL statements to a series of RDD transformations and actions. This is similar to how Hive converted SQL statements to a MapReduce pipeline. The difference is that Spark's "Catalyst" query engine is a powerful engine that can convert SQL queries in a very efficient RDD graph. All code examples we have just seen are converted to an SQL statement, which is then transformed to an RDD program. It is just as possible to directly write SQL in your programs to manipulate DataFrames if you prefer, hence the name "Spark SQL":

```
# Register the DataFrame as an SQL temporary view
df.createOrReplaceTempView("people")

sqlDF = spark.sql("SELECT * FROM people WHERE age > 21")
sqlDF.show()

# +---+---------+
# |age|     name|
# +---+---------+
# | 30| Wilfried|
# +---+---------+
```

Finally, besides integrating with Python, Java, Scala, and R programs, Spark also offers SQL command-line tools and an ODBC and JDBC server if you wish to execute queries that way.

**Drill Down**

Recent versions of Spark also offer another abstraction other than DataFrames: the Dataset. Like DataFrames, Datasets take advantage of the Spark Catalyst SQL engine, but extend this with compile-time type safety checks when using a type safe programming language such as Java or Scala. The main difference is that a DataFrame represents a collection of Rows, where a Row is a general structure of which it is known that it will contain several named columns with values that should be of a certain type. Type errors, however, can only be checked at runtime while the query or application is running. A Dataset represents a collection of objects containing a number of strongly typed fields (i.e., attributes having a specific type such as integer or decimal value), enabling extra checks at compile time. These objects still need to be able to be represented as a tabular row, however. To do so, the Dataset API introduces a new concept called an encoder, which can convert JVM (Java Virtual Machine) objects from and to a tabular representation in a way that is also fast and efficient. This is certainly another feat of engineering in Spark, but one you can only encounter and use when working with Java or Scala (as R and Python do not run on top of the Java Virtual Machine).

### 19.4.3 MLlib, Spark Streaming, and GraphX

The last Spark components we need to mention are MLlib, Spark Streaming, and GraphX. **MLlib** is Spark's machine learning library. Its goal is to make practical machine learning scalable and user-friendly, and even though there had been earlier initiatives to put machine learning algorithms on top of Hadoop (most notably through the Apache Mahout project), also here it was quickly discovered that many of these were not that easily ported to a MapReduce pipeline. MLlib can offer a solid set of algorithms that – once again – work on top of the RDD paradigm.

**Connections**

In Chapter 20, analytics and machine learning algorithms are discussed further, so we will not spend too much time discussing MLlib's included algorithms here.

MLlib offers classification, regression, clustering, and recommender system algorithms.

What is important to know is that MLlib was originally built directly on top of the RDD abstraction. In Spark version 2, the Spark maintainers announced that the old MLlib component would be gradually replaced with a new version of this component that works directly with Spark SQL's DataFrames-based API, as many machine learning algorithms assume data to be formatted in a structured, tabular format anyway. The RDD-based MLlib API is expected to be removed in Spark 3. This change makes sense, but has caused MLlib to be somewhat of a confusing offering today. A lot of Spark 1 code is still being used in production, and might not be that easy to update with the newer MLlib API.

**Spark Streaming** leverages Spark Core and its fast scheduling engine to perform streaming analytics. The way it does so is relatively simple, and although it is not as configurable or feature-rich as other Big Data real-time streaming technologies such as Flink or Ignite (two very recent projects), it offers a very approachable way to handle continuous data streams at high velocity. Spark Streaming provides another high-level concept called the DStream (discretized stream), which represents a continuous stream of data. Internally, however, a DStream is represented as a sequence of RDD fragments, with each RDD in a DStream containing data from a certain interval. Similar to RDDs, most of the same transformations can be applied directly on the DStream, allowing its data to be modified. DStreams also provide windowed computations, which allow applying transformations over a sliding window of data. Different DStreams can also easily be joined. This Python example shows a word-counting program that now works over a continuous stream of data:

```
from pyspark import SparkContext
from pyspark.streaming import StreamingContext
sc = SparkContext("local[ 2] ", "StreamingWordCount")
ssc = StreamingContext(sc, 1)

# Create a DStream that will connect to server.mycorp.com:9999 as a source
lines = ssc.socketTextStream("server.mycorp.com ", 9999)

# Split each line into words
words = lines.flatMap(lambda line: line.split(" "))

# Count each word in each batch
pairs = words.map(lambda word: (word, 1))
wordCounts = pairs.reduceByKey(lambda x, y: x + y)

# Print out first ten elements of each RDD generated in the wordCounts DStream
wordCounts.pprint()

# Start the computation
ssc.start()
ssc.awaitTermination()
```

It is important to note that the Spark Streaming component uses the concept of RDDs. But what about allowing for SQL statements that work on a stream? Again, to handle this aspect, Spark is working on a Structured Streaming component which would allow expressing streaming computation pipelines on top of DataFrames, and hence through SQL. The Spark SQL engine will take care of running it incrementally and will continuously update the final result as streaming data continue to arrive. However, Structured Streaming is still in its alpha stage in Spark 2.1, and the API is still considered experimental. Because of this, projects such as Flink, which offer richer and more fluent streaming capabilities, have seen increased adoption in the past year or so, though nowhere yet as much as Spark.

**Drill Down**

In earlier days, Apache Storm (acquired and open-sourced by Twitter) was also frequently used as a stream computation framework, which also has the idea of expressing a computational pipeline as a directed acyclic graph. However, the framework is no longer that widely chosen for newer projects. Its latest release dates from 2016 and, with its version 1.0.0, is considered a completed product. The fact that programs on top of Storm are – preferably – written through the Clojure programming language, which is not that well known, also caused the project to fall by the wayside.

**Retention Questions**

- What is Spark? Which benefits does it offer over Hadoop?
- What are RDDs? How are they used in Spark?
- Give a general overview of the different components of Spark.

**GraphX** is Spark's component implementing programming abstractions to deal with graph-based structures, again based on the RDD abstraction. To support common graph computations, GraphX comes with a set of fundamental operators and algorithms (such as PageRank) to work with graphs and simplify graph analytics tasks. Also here, work has been underway for Spark to provide the same graph-based abstractions on top of DataFrames (called GraphFrames), although this is still very much a work in progress.

**Drill Down**

If you are wondering how GraphX stacks up to Neo4j (a graph database seen in Chapter 11) and other graph databases, Neo4j and other graph databases focus on providing end-to-end online transaction processing capabilities with graphs being the primary structural construct. Graphs in Neo4j are stored in a way that is optimal to query them, which might not be the case when trying to load them in through GraphX (as they can still be stored in various ways on the underlying file system). On the other hand, Neo4j was not built specifically with the intent to perform high-intensity computing or analytical operations. However, various developers have extended Neo4j with plugins to provide more algorithms that can work on top of it, and it is also possible to export Neo4j graphs to GraphX, where they can be further analyzed. If your focus is graphs, and you want to store and query your data in this form, start with a graph database such as Neo4j first and then include GraphX if the need arises.

## 19.5 Conclusion

This chapter has discussed Big Data and the most common technology stacks supporting it. We have started our discussion from the 5 Vs of Big Data: volume, velocity, variety, veracity, and value. From there, we have reviewed various Big Data technologies, starting from Hadoop. We saw how Hadoop's raw stack is unable to support strong querying capabilities, leading to various solutions to "bring the DBMS to Hadoop", so to speak. HBase and Pig were among the first efforts in this space, with HBase being an example of a NoSQL database on top of Hadoop, but still offering limited query capabilities, and Pig trying to offer a friendlier programming language on top of MapReduce. Hive was introduced as the main project bringing the power of SQL to Hadoop, but still being limited by the MapReduce paradigm. Finally, Spark was introduced, doing away with MapReduce altogether and replacing it with a directed acyclic graph-based paradigm with a strong SQL engine offering performant query capabilities, and machine learning, streaming, and graph-based components.

The Big Data ecosystem continues to evolve at a rapid pace, however, with new projects being introduced every few months that promise to turn the field on its head. The field has become hard to navigate, and one must be careful regarding vendors and what, exactly, they provide, as even different versions of a project – say, Spark – can differ widely in terms of functionality. Many projects within the Big Data ecosystem can also be replaced or mixed-and-matched together. For instance, recent versions of Hive can also convert their HiveQL queries to a Spark-directed acyclic graph pipeline, just as Spark does itself! We have seen how Spark can use YARN to perform its resource negotiations in the cluster, but can also use Mesos or its own built-in resource manager, and so can many other Big Data products. Meanwhile, new projects such as Flink or Ignite promise richer querying capabilities surpassing those of Spark. Apache recently also announced Apache Kylin, another "extreme OLAP engine for Big Data", which also provides an SQL interface and business intelligence "cubes" on top of Hadoop (this time contributed by eBay). It works on top of Hive and HBase to store its data, but comes with its own query engine that is particularly well suited to query cubes, is SQL-standard compliant, and can integrate with existing tooling through ODBC and JDBC drivers.

**Drill Down**

There's also an abundance of projects concerning themselves with the "meta-management", maintenance, and governance of your Big Data cluster, such as Ambari (a web management portal), Oozie (an alternative scheduler that can be plugged into YARN), Zookeeper (a centralized service for maintaining configuration metadata), Atlas (a system to govern data compliance), and Ranger (a platform to define and manage security policies across Hadoop components).

There's also the aspect of machine learning and data analytics. Even though MLlib offers a solid set of algorithms, its offering cannot be compared with the number of algorithms included in proprietary and open-source tooling, which works with a whole dataset in memory in a non-distributed set-up. To reiterate our statement from the introduction: Big Data first concerns itself with managing and storing huge, high-speed, and/or unstructured datasets, but this does not automatically mean one can analyze them or easily leverage them to obtain insights. Analytics (or "data science") concerns itself with analyzing data and obtaining insights and patterns from it, but does not have to be applied on huge volumes or unstructured datasets. One interesting project to mention here is H2O, which also offers a distributed execution engine that can be somewhat less powerful than Spark's one, but offers a complete and strong collection of techniques to build descriptive and predictive analytics models on Big Data, and hence can offer a better alternative to the less mature MLlib. Recent versions of H2O also allow it to run on top of Spark's execution engine, which makes it a very strong add-on on top of Spark if your goal is to perform analytics, but other choices work just as well if you aren't working with Big Data. Again, the main question to consider is whether you have Big Data. If not, one can continue to use a relational DBMS, for instance, complete with strong query facilities, transaction management, and consistency, while then still being able to analyze it. What exactly is meant with "analytics algorithms" and "descriptive and predictive modeling" will form the topic of the next chapter.

### Scenario Conclusion

After looking at Big Data stacks such as Hadoop, Sober decides that, at this moment, there is no need to adopt any of these Big Data technology stacks. Sober is happy with its relational DBMS, and its business intelligence applications are running fine on top of it. To counteract the issue of scalability, the mobile team is already using MongoDB to handle the increased workload in this operational setting, so introducing additional technology components cannot be justified at the moment. Sober is getting interested, however, in investing further in analytics capabilities on top of the modestly sized amount of data they do have – for instance, to predict which users will churn from its service, or to optimize route planning of its cab drivers so there is always a cab nearby to a user. Sober will hence investigate whether analytics algorithms and tooling can be used to do so in the very near future, to go one step further from business intelligence reporting and move toward prediction and optimization.

## Key Terms List

**5 Vs of Big Data**
**GraphX**
**Hadoop**
**Hadoop Common**
**Hadoop Distributed File System (HDFS)**
**HBase**
**Hive**
**MapReduce**
**MLlib**
**Pig**
**Spark**
**Spark Core**
**Spark SQL**
**Spark Streaming**
**value**
**variety**
**velocity**
**veracity**
**volume**
**YARN (Yet Another Resource Negotiator)**

## Review Questions

**19.1.** What do the 5 Vs of Big Data stand for?

a. Volume, variety, velocity, veracity, value.
b. Volume, visualization, velocity, variety, value.
c. Volume, variety, velocity, variability, value.
d. Volume, versatile, velocity, visualization, value.

**19.2.** Which of the following statements is **not correct**?

a. Velocity in Big Data refers to data "in movement".
b. Volume in Big Data refers to data "at rest".
c. Veracity in Big Data refers to data "in change".
d. Variety in Big Data refers to data "in many forms".

**19.3.** Which components does the base Hadoop stack include?

a. NDFS, MapReduce, and YARN.
b. HDFS, MapReduce, and YARN.
c. HDFS, Map, and Reduce.
d. HDFS, Spark, and YARN.

**19.4.** Which of the following statements is **correct**?

a. DataNodes in HDFS store a registry of metadata.
b. The HDFS NameNode sends regular heartbeat messages to its DataNodes.
c. HDFS is composed of a NameNode, DataNodes, and an optional SecondaryNameNode.
d. Both the SecondaryNameNode and primary NameNode can simultaneously handle requests from clients.

**19.5.** Which of the following statements is **not correct**?

a. A mapper in Hadoop maps each element in a collection to one or more output elements.
b. A reducer in Hadoop reduces a collection of elements to one or more output elements.
c. Reducer workers in Hadoop will start once all mapper workers have finished.
d. A MapReduce pipeline in Hadoop can include an optional Sorter to sort the final output.

**19.6.** Which of the following statements is **not correct**?

a. Apart from handling MapReduce programs, YARN can also be used to manage other types of applications.
b. YARN's JobHistoryServer keeps a log of all finished jobs.
c. NodeManagers in YARN are responsible for setting up containers on the node hosting a particular (sub)task.
d. The YARN ApplicationMaster contains a scheduler which will hold submitted jobs in a queue until they are deemed ready to start.

**19.7.** Which of the following commands are not a part of HBase?

a. Place.
b. Put.
c. Get.
d. Describe.

**19.8.** Which of the following statements is **correct**?

a. HBase can be considered as a NoSQL database.
b. HBase offers an SQL engine to query its data.
c. MapReduce programs cannot be used with HBase. Data are accessed using simple put and get commands instead.
d. HBase works well on large clusters as well as small ones having a few nodes.

**19.9.** Pig is...

a. a programming language that can be used to query HDFS data.
b. a project offering a programming language to provide more user-friendliness compared to MapReduce programs.

c. a database that runs on Hadoop.
d. an SQL engine that runs on top of Hadoop.

**19.10.** Which of the following statements is **not correct**?

a. Hive offers an SQL engine to query Hadoop data.
b. Hive's query language is not as feature-complete as the full SQL standard.
c. Hive offers a JDBC interface.
d. Hive queries run much faster than hand-written MapReduce programs.

**19.11.** Which of the following schema-handling methods does Hive apply?

a. Schema on write.
b. Schema on load.
c. Schema on read.
d. Schema on query.

**19.12.** Which of the following statements is **not correct**?

a. RDDs allow for two forms of operations: transformations and actions.
b. RDDs represent an abstract, immutable data structure.
c. RDDs are structured and represent a collection of columnar objects.
d. RDDs offer failure protection by tracking the lineage of operations that are applied on them.

**19.13.** Which of the following is not one of the reasons why Spark programs are generally faster than MapReduce operations?

a. Because Spark tries to keep its RDDs in memory as long as possible.
b. Because Spark uses a directed acyclic graph instead of MapReduce.
c. Because RDD transformations are "lazily" applied.
d. Because Mesos can be used as a resource manager instead of YARN.

**19.14.** Which of the following statements is **not correct**?

a. Spark SQL exposes DataFrame and Dataset APIs which underlyingly use RDDs together with a performant SQL query engine.
b. Spark SQL can be used from within Java, Python, Scala, and R.
c. Spark SQL can be used through ODBC and JDBC interfaces.
d. Spark SQL DataFrames need to be created by loading a file.

**19.15.** Which of the following statements is **correct**?

a. One of the disadvantages of Spark is that it does not support streaming data.
b. One of the disadvantages of Spark is that its streaming and machine learning APIs are still mostly RDD-based.
c. One of the disadvantages of Spark is that it has no way to deal with graph-based data.
d. One of the disadvantages of Spark is that its streaming API does not allow joining multiple streams.

## Problems and Exercises

19.1E Discuss some application areas where the usage of streaming analytics (such as provided by Spark Streaming) might be valuable. Consider Twitter, but also other contexts.

19.2E Think about some examples of Big Data in industry. Try to focus on Vs other than the volume aspect of Big Data. Why do you think these examples qualify as Big Data?

19.3E Both Hortonworks (Hortonworks Hadoop Sandbox) and Cloudera (Cloudera QuickStart VM) offer virtual instances (for Docker, VirtualBox, and VMWare) providing a full Hadoop stack you can easily run contained in a virtual machine on a beefy computer. Try Googling for these and running these environments if you're interested in getting hands-on experience with the Hadoop ecosystem.

19.4E Some analysts have argued that Big Data is fundamentally about data "plumbing", and not about insights or deriving interesting patterns. It is argued that value (the fifth V) can just as easily be found in "small", normal, or "weird" datasets (i.e., datasets that would not have been considered before). Do you agree with this? Can you think of small or novel datasets that would provide value as well, without requiring a full-fledged Hadoop set-up?

19.5E If Spark's GraphX library provides a number of interesting algorithms for graph-based analysis, do you think that graph-based NoSQL databases are still necessary? Why? If you're interested, try searching the web on how to run Neo4j together with Spark – which roles do both serve in such an environment?

# 20 Analytics

## Chapter Objectives

In this chapter, you will learn to:

- understand the key steps of the analytics process model;
- identify the skill set of a data scientist;
- preprocess data for analytics using denormalization, sampling, exploratory data analysis, and dealing with missing values and outliers;
- build predictive analytical models using linear regression, logistic regression, and decision trees;
- evaluate predictive analytical models by splitting up the dataset and using various performance metrics;
- build descriptive analytical models using association rules, sequence rules, and clustering;
- understand the basic concepts of social network analytics;
- discern the key activities during post-processing of analytical models;
- identify the critical success factors of analytical models;
- understand the economic perspective on analytics by considering the total cost of ownership (TCO) and return on investment (ROI) and how they are affected by in- versus outsourcing, on-premise versus cloud solutions, and open versus commercial software;
- improve the ROI of analytics by exploring new sources of data, increasing data quality, securing management support, optimizing organizational aspects, and fostering cross-fertilization;
- understand the impact of privacy and security in a data storage, processing, and analytics context.

### Opening Scenario

Now that Sober has made its first steps in business intelligence, it is eager to take this to the next level and explore what it could do with analytics. The company has witnessed extensive press and media coverage on predictive and descriptive analytics and wonders what these technologies entail and how they could be used to its advantage. It is actually thinking about analyzing its booking behavior, but is unsure how to tackle this. Given that Sober is a startup, it also wants to know the economic and privacy implications of leveraging these technologies.

In this chapter, we extensively zoom into analytics. We kick-off by providing a bird's eye overview of the analytics process model. We then give examples of analytics applications and discuss the data scientist job profile. We briefly zoom into data pre-processing. The next section elaborates on different types of analytics: predictive analytics, descriptive analytics, and social network analytics. We also discuss the post-processing of analytical models. Various critical success factors for analytical models are clarified in the following section. This is followed by a discussion on the economic perspective of analytics. We also give recommendations of how to improve the ROI of analytics. We conclude by a discussion on privacy and security.

## 20.1 The Analytics Process Model

Analytics is a process that consists of various steps, as illustrated in Figure 20.1. The **analytics process model** starts with the raw data followed by pre-processing, analytics, and post-processing. As a first step, a thorough definition of the business problem is needed. Some examples are: customer segmentation of a mortgage portfolio; retention modeling for a postpaid telecom subscription; or fraud detection for credit cards. Defining the scope of the analytical modeling exercise requires close collaboration between the data scientist and business expert. Both need to agree on a set of key concepts, such as how to define a customer, transaction, churn, fraud, etc.

Next, all source data that could be of potential interest must be identified. This is a very important step as data are the key ingredient to any analytical exercise and the selection of data has a deterministic impact on the analytical models built in a later step. The golden rule here is: the more data, the better! The analytical model itself can later decide which data are relevant to the task at hand and which are not. All data will then be gathered in a staging area and consolidated into a data warehouse, data mart, or even a simple spreadsheet file. Some basic exploratory data analysis can be considered using, for example, OLAP facilities for multidimensional analysis (e.g., roll-up, drill-down, slicing, and dicing) (see Chapter 17). This can be followed by a data cleansing step to remove all inconsistencies, such as missing values, outliers, and duplicate data.[1] Additional transformations may also be considered, such as alphanumeric to numeric coding, geographical aggregation, logarithmic transformation to improve symmetry, etc.

**Connections**

One of the first steps toward analytics is usually data warehousing, OLAP, and BI, as discussed in Chapter 17.

In the analytics step, an analytical model is estimated on the pre-processed and transformed data. Depending upon the business problem, a particular analytical technique will be selected (see Section 20.5) and implemented by the data scientist.

Finally, once the model has been built, it will be interpreted and evaluated by the business experts. Trivial patterns (e.g., spaghetti and spaghetti sauce are often purchased together) that may be detected by the analytical model are interesting as they provide a validation of the model. But the key issue is to find the unknown but interesting and actionable patterns that can provide new insights into your data (sometimes also called knowledge diamonds, or nuggets). Once the analytical model has been appropriately validated and approved, it can be put into production as an analytics application (e.g., decision-support system, scoring engine, etc.). It is important to consider how to represent the model output in a user-friendly way, how to integrate it with other applications (e.g., marketing campaign management tools, risk engines, etc.), and how to ensure the analytical model can be appropriately monitored on an ongoing basis.

The process model outlined in Figure 20.1 is iterative, in the sense that one may have to go back to previous steps during the exercise. For example, during the analytics step, the need for additional

[1] If the data originate from a data warehouse, then the cleansing step has already been done as part of the ETL process (see Chapter 17).

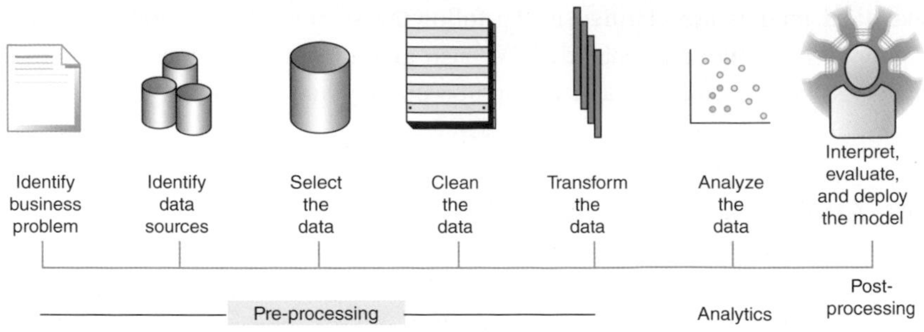


**Figure 20.1** The analytics process model.

data may be identified, which may necessitate additional cleansing, transformation, etc. Typically, the most time-consuming step is the data selection and pre-processing step, which usually takes around 80% of the total efforts needed to build an analytical model.

The analytics process is essentially a multidisciplinary exercise in which many job profiles must collaborate. First, there is the database or data warehouse administrator (DBA). He/she knows of all the data available within the firm, the storage details, and the data definitions. Hence, the DBA plays a crucial role in feeding the analytical modeling exercise with its key ingredient – data. Since analytics is an iterative exercise, the DBA may continue to play an important role as the modeling exercise proceeds.

Another important profile is the business expert. This could be a credit portfolio manager, fraud detection expert, brand manager, e-commerce manager, etc. He/she has extensive business experience and business common sense, which is very valuable. It is precisely this knowledge that helps steer the analytical modeling exercise and interpret its key findings. A key challenge is that much of the expert knowledge is tacit and may be hard to elicit at the start of the modeling exercise.

Legal experts are becoming more important since not all data can be used in an analytical model because of issues relating to privacy, discrimination, etc. In credit risk modeling, for example, one typically cannot discriminate good and bad customers based upon gender, national origin, or religion. In web analytics, information can be gathered with cookies, which are stored on the user's browsing computer. However, when gathering information using cookies, users should be appropriately informed. This is subject to regulation at various levels (both nationally and governing bodies like the European Commission). A key challenge here is that privacy and other regulations vary greatly, depending upon the geographical region. Hence, the legal expert should have good knowledge about what data can be used and when, and what regulation applies in which location.

Software tool vendors are also an important part of the analytics team. Different tool vendors can be distinguished here. Some vendors only provide tools to automate specific steps of the analytical modeling process (e.g., data pre-processing), whereas others sell software that covers the entire analytical modeling process. Also, cloud-based approaches, such as analytics-as-a-service (AaaS) solutions, are possible. The idea here is to lower the entry barrier to performing analytics by providing an easy-to-use web-based interface.

The data scientist, data miner, quantitative modeler, or data analyst is the person responsible for doing the actual analytics. He/she should possess a thorough understanding of all Big Data and analytical techniques involved, and should know how to implement them in a business setting using the appropriate technology. We elaborate more on the required skills of a data scientist in the next sections.

**Retention Questions**

- What are the key steps of the analytics process model? Illustrate with an example.

## 20.2 Example Analytics Applications

Big Data can be leveraged in various ways using analytics. Before we zoom in further, let's kick-off with some examples of how analytics can help optimize business decisions. In what follows, we discuss risk analytics, marketing analytics, recommender systems, and text analytics.

Two popular examples of **risk analytics** are credit scoring and fraud detection. Financial institutions use analytics to build credit scoring models to gauge the creditworthiness of their customers on all their credit products (mortgages, credit cards, installment loans, etc.). They use these analytical models to do debt provisioning, Basel II/Basel III capital calculation, and marketing (e.g., increase/decrease the limit on a credit card in the case of a good/bad credit score). Credit card companies use sophisticated analytical fraud-detection models to see whether payments are legitimate or fraudulent because of identity theft. The government uses fraud analytics to predict tax evasion, VAT fraud, or for anti-money laundering tasks.

Three popular types of **marketing analytics** are churn prediction, response modeling, and customer segmentation. **Churn prediction** aims at predicting which customers a firm is likely to lose. As an example, telecom operators estimate analytical churn prediction models using all recent call behavior data, to see whether customers are likely to churn or not in the next 1–3 months. The resulting retention score can then be used to set up marketing campaigns to prevent customers from churning (unless they would not be profitable). **Response modeling** tries to develop an analytical model that selects the customers who are most likely to respond (e.g., buy) to a marketing campaign (e.g., banner ad, email, brochure). In this way, marketing efforts can be directed toward these customers where they are most effective. **Customer segmentation** aims at segmenting a set of customers or transactions into homogeneous clusters that can be used for marketing purposes (e.g., targeted marketing, advertising, mass customization).

**Recommender systems** are another example of an analytics application. These systems aim at providing well-targeted recommendations to a user and are extensively used by companies like Amazon, Netflix, TripAdvisor, eBay, LinkedIn, Tinder, and Facebook. Various types of items can be recommended, such as products or services, restaurants, jobs, friends, and even romantic partners.

**Text analytics** aims at analyzing textual data such as reports, emails, text messages, tweets, web documents, blogs, reviews, financial statements, etc. Popular applications are text categorization and clustering. Facebook and Twitter posts are continuously analyzed using social media analytics to study both their content and sentiment (e.g., positive, negative, or neutral) to better understand brand perception, and/or further fine-tune product and/or service design. As our book details are made available online, it will be analyzed and categorized by Google and other search engines and (hopefully) included in their search results.

As these examples illustrate, analytics is all around, and even without us explicitly being aware of it, it is getting more and more pervasive and directly embedded into our daily lives. Businesses (ranging from international firms to SMEs) jump on the analytics bandwagon to create added value and strategic advantage. Without claiming to be exhaustive Table 20.1 presents examples of how analytics can be applied in various settings.

**Retention Questions**

- Give some examples of analytics applications.

**Table 20.1** Example analytics applications

| Marketing | Risk management | Government | Web | Logistics | Other |
|---|---|---|---|---|---|
| Response modeling | Credit risk modeling | Tax avoidance | Web analytics | Demand forecasting | Text analytics |
| Net lift modeling | Market risk modeling | Social security fraud | Social media analytics | Supply chain analytics | Business process analytics |
| Retention modeling | Operational risk modeling | Money laundering | Multivariate testing | | HR analytics |
| Market basket analysis | Fraud detection | Terrorism detection | | | Healthcare analytics |
| Recommender systems | | | | | Learning analytics |
| Customer segmentation | | | | | |

## 20.3 Data Scientist Job Profile

The **data scientist** job profile is relatively new and requires a unique skill set consisting of a well-balanced mix of quantitative, programming, business, communication, and visualization skills. Not surprisingly, these individuals are hard to find in today's job market.

As the name implies, data scientists work with data. This involves activities such as sampling and pre-processing of data, analytical model estimation, and post-processing (e.g., sensitivity analysis, model deployment, backtesting, model validation). Although many user-friendly software tools are on the market to automate this, every analytical exercise requires tailored steps to tackle the specificities of a particular business problem. To perform these steps, programming must be done. Therefore, a good data scientist should possess sound programming skills in such areas as Java, R, Python, SAS, etc. The programming language itself is not that important, as long as the data scientist is familiar with the basic concepts of programming and knows how to use these to automate repetitive tasks or perform specific routines.

Obviously, a data scientist should have a thorough background in statistics, machine learning, and/or quantitative modeling. The distinction between these various disciplines is becoming more blurred, and is not that relevant in many cases because they are more frequently used as a means to an end and not as a separate entity. They all provide a set of quantitative techniques to analyze data and find business-relevant patterns within a particular context (e.g., risk management, fraud detection, marketing analytics). The data scientist should know which techniques can be applied, when, and how. He/she should not focus too much on the underlying mathematical (e.g., optimization) details but have a good understanding of what analytical problem a technique solves, and how its results should be interpreted. Also important in this context is to spend enough time validating the analytical results obtained to avoid situations often called data massage and/or data torture whereby data are (intentionally) misrepresented and/or too much focus is spent discussing spurious correlations.

Essentially, analytics is a technical exercise. There is often a huge gap between the analytical models and business users. To bridge this gap, communication and visualization facilities are key. A data scientist should know how to represent analytical models, statistics, and reports in user-friendly ways by using traffic-light approaches, OLAP (on-line analytical processing) facilities, if–then business rules, etc. The data scientist should be able to communicate information without getting lost in complex details (e.g., statistical) that inhibit a model's successful deployment. Business users can then better understand the characteristics and behavior in the (big) data, which will improve their attitude toward, and acceptance of, the resulting analytical models. Educational institutions must learn to balance between theory and practice, since many academic degrees form students skewed to either too much analytical or too much practical knowledge.

While this might seem obvious, many data science projects have failed because the analyst(s) did not properly understand the business problem at hand. By "business" we refer to the respective application areas, which could be churn prediction or credit scoring in a real-world business context, astronomy, or medicine if the data to be analyzed stem from such areas. Knowing the characteristics of the business process, its actors, and performance indicators is an important prerequisite for analytics to succeed.

A data scientist needs creativity on at least two levels. On a technical level it is important to be creative regarding data selection, data transformation, and cleansing. The steps of the standard analytical process must be adapted to each specific application and the "right guess" could often make a big difference. Second, analytics is a fast-evolving field. New problems, technologies, and corresponding challenges pop up on an ongoing basis. It is important that a data scientist keeps up with these new evolutions and technologies and has enough creativity to see how they can yield new business opportunities.

**Retention Questions**

- What are the key characteristics of a data scientist?

## 20.4 Data Pre-Processing

Data are the key ingredient for any analytical exercise. It is imperative to thoroughly consider and list all data sources that are of potential interest and relevant before starting the analysis. Large experiments, and our own experience in different fields, indicate that when it comes to data, bigger is better. However, real-life data can be (and typically are) dirty because of inconsistencies, incompleteness, duplication, merging, and many other problems. Throughout the analytical modeling steps, various **data pre-processing** checks are applied to clean-up and reduce the data to a manageable and relevant size. Worth mentioning here is the garbage in, garbage out (GIGO) principle, which essentially states that messy data yields messy analytical models. Hence, it is of critical importance that every data pre-processing step is carefully justified, carried out, validated, and documented before proceeding with further analysis. Even the slightest mistake can make the data unusable for further analysis and the results invalid and of no use. In what follows, we briefly zoom into some of the most important data pre-processing activities.

### 20.4.1 Denormalizing Data for Analysis

The application of analytics typically requires or presumes the data will be presented in a single table containing and representing all the data in a structured way. A structured data table enables straightforward processing and analysis. Typically, the rows of a data table represent the basic entities to which the analysis applies (e.g., customers, transactions, enterprises, claims, cases). The rows are also called instances, observations, or lines. The columns in the data table contain information about the basic entities. Plenty of synonyms are used to denote the columns of the data table, such as (explanatory) variables, fields, characteristics, indicators, features, etc.

| Transactions | | |
|---|---|---|
| ID | Date | Amount |
| XWV | 2/01/2015 | 52 € |
| XWV | 6/02/2015 | 21 € |
| XWV | 3/03/2015 | 13 € |
| BBC | 17/02/2015 | 45 € |
| BBC | 1/03/2015 | 75 € |
| VVQ | 2/03/2015 | 56 € |

| Customer data | | |
|---|---|---|
| ID | Age | Start date |
| XWV | 31 | 1/01/2015 |
| BBC | 49 | 10/02/2015 |
| VVQ | 21 | 15/02/2015 |

| Non-normalized data table | | | | |
|---|---|---|---|---|
| ID | Date | Amount | Age | Start date |
| XWV | 2/01/2015 | 52 € | 31 | 1/01/2015 |
| XWV | 6/02/2015 | 21 € | 31 | 1/01/2015 |
| XWV | 3/03/2015 | 13 € | 31 | 1/01/2015 |
| BBC | 17/02/2015 | 45 € | 49 | 10/02/2015 |
| BBC | 1/03/2015 | 75 € | 49 | 10/02/2015 |
| VVQ | 2/03/2015 | 56 € | 21 | 15/02/2015 |

**Figure 20.2** Aggregating normalized data tables into a non-normalized data table.

**Denormalization** refers to the merging of several normalized source data tables into an aggregated, denormalized data table. Merging tables involves selecting information from different tables related to an individual entity, and copying it to the aggregated data table. The individual entity can be recognized and selected in these tables by making use of (primary) keys, which have been included in the table to allow identifying and relating observations from different source tables pertaining to the same entity. Figure 20.2 illustrates merging two tables (i.e., transaction data and customer data) into a single denormalized data table by using the key attribute type ID that connects observations in the transactions table with observations in the customer table. The same approach can be followed to merge as many tables as required, but the more tables are merged, the more duplicate data might be included in the resulting table due to the denormalization. It is crucial that no errors are introduced during this process, so checks should be applied to control the resulting table and to make sure that all information is correctly integrated.

**Connections**

Normalization and the risks of working with denormalized data are discussed in Chapter 6.
Chapter 17 discussed why denormalization may be appropriate in a data warehousing context, and why it is less problematic compared to denormalization in an operational database setting.

## 20.4.2 Sampling

**Sampling** takes a subset of historical data (e.g., past transactions) and uses that to build an analytical model. A first obvious question that comes to mind concerns the need for sampling. It is true that, with the availability of high-performance computing facilities (e.g., grid and cloud computing), one could also try to directly analyze the full dataset. However, a key requirement for a good sample is that it should be representative for the future entities on which the analytical model will be run. The timing becomes important since transactions of today are more like transactions of tomorrow than transactions of yesterday. Choosing the optimal time window of the sample involves a tradeoff between lots of data (and hence a more robust analytical model) and recent data (which may be more representative). The sample should also be taken from an average business period to get an accurate picture of the target population.

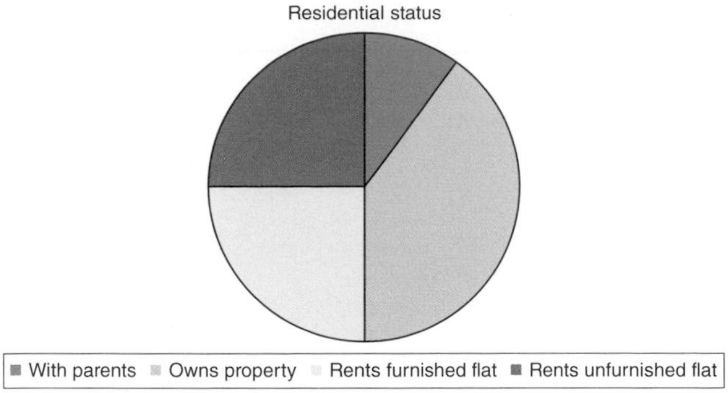


**Figure 20.3** Pie chart for residential status.

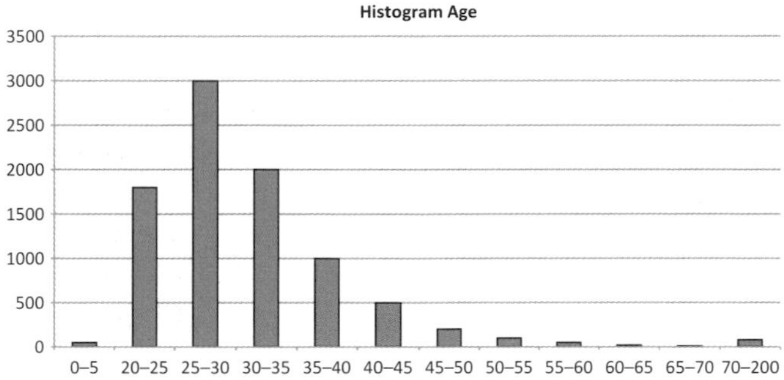


**Figure 20.4** Histogram for age.

### 20.4.3 Exploratory Analysis

**Exploratory analysis** is a very important part of getting to know your data in an "informal" way. It allows gaining initial insights into the data that can be usefully adopted throughout the analytical modeling stage. Different plots/graphs can be useful here, such as bar charts, pie charts, histograms, scatter plots, etc. Figure 20.3 shows an example of a pie chart for a residential status variable; Figure 20.4 shows an example histogram for the age variable.

The next step is to summarize the data by using some descriptive statistics that provide information regarding a particular characteristic of the data. Basic descriptive statistics are the mean and median value of continuous variables, with the median value less sensitive to extreme values but not providing as much information regarding the full distribution. Complementary to the mean value, the variation or the standard deviation provide insight into how much the data are spread around the mean value. Likewise, percentile values such as the 10th, 25th, 75th, and 90th percentile provide further information about the distribution and are complementary to the median value. For categorical variables, other measures need to be considered, such as the mode or most frequently occurring value. It is important to note that all these descriptive statistics should be assessed together (i.e., in support and completion of each other). For example, comparing the mean and median can give insight into the skewness of the distribution and outliers.

### 20.4.4 Missing Values

**Missing values** (see Table 20.2) can occur for various reasons. The information can be non-applicable. For example, when modeling the amount of fraud, this information is only available

**Table 20.2** Missing values

| ID | Age | Income | Marital status | Credit bureau score | Fraud |
|---|---|---|---|---|---|
| 1 | 34 | 1800 | ? | 620 | Yes |
| 2 | 28 | 1200 | Single | ? | No |
| 3 | 22 | 1000 | Single | ? | No |
| 4 | 60 | 2200 | Widowed | 700 | Yes |
| 5 | 58 | 2000 | Married | ? | No |
| 6 | 44 | ? | ? | ? | No |
| 7 | 22 | 1200 | Single | ? | No |
| 8 | 26 | 1500 | Married | 350 | No |
| 9 | 34 | ? | Single | ? | Yes |
| 10 | 50 | 2100 | Divorced | ? | No |

for the fraudulent accounts and not for the non-fraudulent accounts since it is not applicable there. The information can also be undisclosed, such as a customer who has decided not to disclose his or her income for privacy reasons. Missing data can also originate from an error during merging (e.g., typos in a name or ID). Missing values can be very meaningful from an analytical perspective because they may indicate a pattern. As an example, a missing value for income could imply unemployment, which may be related to loan default. Some analytical techniques (e.g., decision trees) can directly deal with missing values. Other techniques need additional pre-processing. Popular missing value handling schemes are removal of the observation or variable, and replacement (e.g., by the mean/median for continuous variables and by the mode for categorical variables).

### 20.4.5 Outlier Detection and Handling

**Outliers** are extreme observations that are very dissimilar to the rest of the population. Two types of outliers should be considered: valid observations (e.g., the CEO's salary is $1,000,000) and invalid observations (e.g., age is 300 years). Two important steps in dealing with outliers are detection and treatment. A first check for outliers is to calculate the minimum and maximum values for each of the data elements. Various graphical tools can also detect outliers, such as histograms, box plots, and scatter plots. Some analytical techniques, like decision trees, are robust with respect to outliers. Others, such as linear/logistic regression, are more sensitive to them. Various schemes exist to deal with outliers. It depends upon whether the outlier represents a valid or invalid observation. For invalid observations (e.g., age is 300 years), one could treat the outlier as a missing value by using any of the schemes (i.e., removal or replacement) discussed in the previous section. For valid observations (e.g., income is $1,000,000), other schemes are needed, such as capping, in which a lower and upper limit are defined for each data element.

**Retention Questions**

- What is meant by "denormalizing data for analytics"?
- Why is sampling needed?
- Give some examples of plots and statistics that can be meaningful during exploratory analysis.
- How can missing values be treated?
- How can outliers be detected and handled?

## 20.5 Types of Analytics

Once the pre-processing step is finished, we can move on to **analytics**. Synonyms of analytics are data science, data mining, knowledge discovery, and predictive or descriptive modeling. The aim here is to extract valid and useful business patterns or mathematical decision models from a pre-processed dataset. Depending upon the aim of the modeling exercise, various analytical techniques from a variety of background disciplines, such as machine learning, statistics, etc. can be used. In what follows, we discuss predictive analytics, descriptive analytics, survival analysis, and social network analytics.

### 20.5.1 Predictive Analytics

In **predictive analytics**, the goal is to build an analytical model predicting a target measure of interest. The target is then typically used to steer the learning process during an optimization procedure. Predictive analytics is therefore also called supervised learning. Two types of predictive analytics can be distinguished: regression and classification. In **regression**, the target variable is continuous. Popular examples are predicting customer lifetime value (CLV), sales, stock prices, or loss given default (LGD). In **classification**, the target is categorical. There are two types of classification: binary (often yes/no or true/false) and multiclass. Popular examples of binary classification are predicting churn, response, fraud, and credit default, whereas predicting credit ratings (AAA, AA, A, BBB, ..., D) is an example of multiclass classification in which the target consists of more than two categories. Different types of predictive analytics techniques have been developed. In what follows, we discuss a selection of techniques, focusing on the practitioner's perspective.

#### 20.5.1.1 Linear Regression

**Linear regression** is the most commonly used technique to model a continuous target variable. For example, in a CLV context, a linear regression model can be defined to model the CLV in terms of the age of the customer, income, gender, etc.:

$$CLV = \beta_0 + \beta_1 Age + \beta_2 Income + \beta_3 Gender + \ldots$$

The general formulation of the linear regression model then becomes:

$$y = \beta_0 + \beta_1 x_1 + \ldots + \beta_k x_k$$

where $y$ represents the target variable and $x_1, \ldots x_k$ are the explanatory variables. The $\boldsymbol{\beta} = [\beta_1; \beta_2; \ldots; \beta_k]$ parameters measure the impact on the target variable $y$ of each of the individual explanatory variables.

Let us now assume we start with a dataset $D = \{(\boldsymbol{x}_i, y_i)\}_{i=1}^{n}$ with $n$ observations and $k$ explanatory variables structured as depicted in Table 20.3.[2]

The $\boldsymbol{\beta}$ parameters of the linear regression model can then be estimated by minimizing the following squared error function:

[2] We use the notation $x_i$ to refer to variable $i$ (e.g., age, income), whereas $\mathbf{x}_i$ refers to the vector with the values for all variables for observation $i$. $\mathbf{x}_i(j)$ refers to the value of variable $j$ for observation $i$.

**Table 20.3** Dataset for linear regression

| Observation | $x_1$ | $x_2$ | ... | $x_k$ | $y$ |
|---|---|---|---|---|---|
| $\boldsymbol{x}_1$ | $\boldsymbol{x}_1(1)$ | $\boldsymbol{x}_1(2)$ | ... | $\boldsymbol{x}_1(k)$ | $y_1$ |
| $\boldsymbol{x}_2$ | $\boldsymbol{x}_2(1)$ | $\boldsymbol{x}_2(2)$ | | $\boldsymbol{x}_2(k)$ | $y_2$ |
| ... | ... | ... | ... | ... | ... |
| $\boldsymbol{x}_n$ | $\boldsymbol{x}_n(1)$ | $\boldsymbol{x}_n(2)$ | | $\boldsymbol{x}_n(k)$ | $y_n$ |

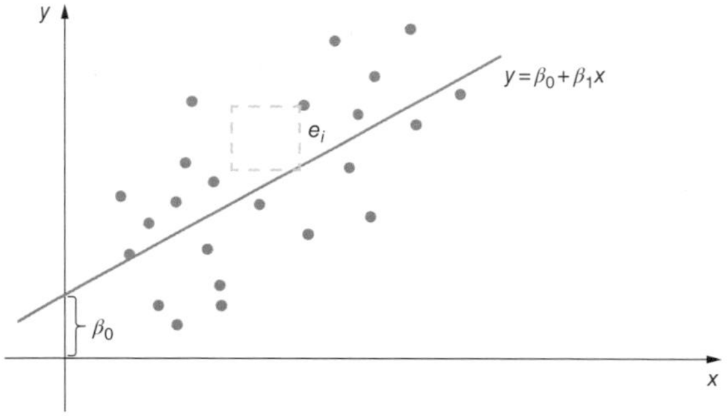


**Figure 20.5** Ordinary least squares regression.

$$\frac{1}{2}\sum_{i=1}^{n} e_i^2 = \frac{1}{2}\sum_{i=1}^{n} (y_i - \hat{y}_i)^2 = \frac{1}{2}\sum_{i=1}^{n} \left(y_i - (\beta_0 + \boldsymbol{\beta}^T\boldsymbol{x}_i)\right)^2,$$

where $y_i$ represents the (observed) target value for observation $i$, $\hat{y}_i$ the prediction made by the linear regression model for observation $i$, $\boldsymbol{\beta}^T$ is the transpose of $\boldsymbol{\beta}$, and $\boldsymbol{x}_i$ the vector with the explanatory variables. Graphically, this idea corresponds to minimizing the sum of all error squares, as presented in Figure 20.5, for a regression model with a single explanatory variable $x$.

Straightforward mathematical calculus then yields the following closed-form formula for the weight parameter vector $\hat{\boldsymbol{\beta}}$:

$$\hat{\boldsymbol{\beta}} = \begin{bmatrix} \hat{\beta}_0 \\ \hat{\beta}_1 \\ \cdots \\ \hat{\beta}_k \end{bmatrix} = \left(\boldsymbol{X}^T\boldsymbol{X}\right)^{-1}\boldsymbol{X}^T\boldsymbol{y},$$

where $\boldsymbol{X}$ represents the matrix with the explanatory variable values augmented with an additional column of 1s to account for the intercept term $\beta_0$, and $\boldsymbol{y}$ represents the target value vector. This model and corresponding parameter optimization procedure are often referred to as **ordinary least squares (OLS)** regression.

A key advantage of OLS regression is that it is simple and easy to understand. Once the parameters have been estimated, the model can be evaluated in a straightforward way, contributing to its operational efficiency.

More sophisticated variants have been developed, such as: ridge regression, lasso regression, time series models (ARIMA, VAR, GARCH), multivariate adaptive regression splines (MARS). Most of these relax the linearity assumption by introducing additional transformations, albeit at the cost of increased complexity.

### 20.5.1.2 Logistic Regression

**Logistic regression** extends linear regression to model a categorical target variable. Consider a classification dataset in a response modeling setting as depicted in Table 20.4.

When modeling the binary response target using linear regression, one gets:

$$y = \beta_0 + \beta_1 Age + \beta_2 Income + \beta_3 Gender$$

When estimating this using OLS, two key problems arise:

- The errors/target are not normally distributed but follow a Bernoulli distribution with only two values.
- There is no guarantee that the target is between 0 and 1, which would be handy since it can then be interpreted as a probability.

Consider the following bounding function:

$$f(z) = \frac{1}{1 + e^{-z}}$$

which looks as illustrated in Figure 20.6.

For every possible value of $z$, the outcome is always between 0 and 1. Hence, by combining the linear regression with the bounding function, we get the following logistic regression model:

**Table 20.4** Example classification dataset

| Customer | Age | Income | Gender | ... | Response | y |
|---|---|---|---|---|---|---|
| John | 30 | 1200 | M | | No | 0 |
| Sarah | 25 | 800 | F | | Yes | 1 |
| Sophie | 52 | 2200 | F | | Yes | 1 |
| David | 48 | 2000 | M | | No | 0 |
| Peter | 34 | 1800 | M | | Yes | 1 |

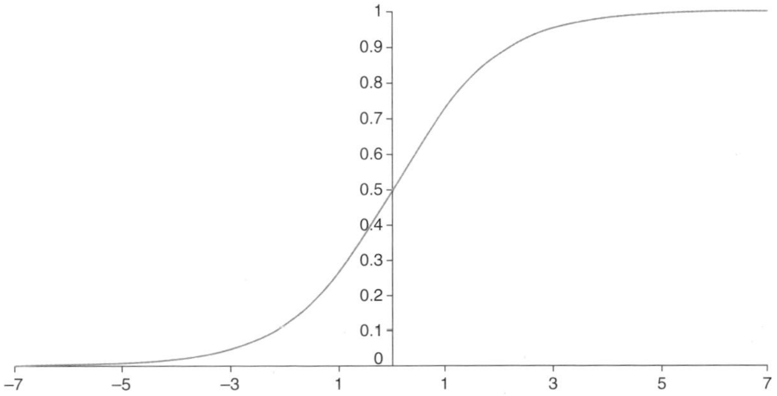


**Figure 20.6** Bounding function for logistic regression.

$$p(response = yes|Age, Income, Gender) = \frac{1}{1 + e^{-(\beta_0+\beta_1 \text{Age}+\beta_2 \text{Income}+\beta_3 \text{Gender})}}$$

The outcome of the above model is always bounded between 0 and 1, no matter which values of *Age, Income*, and *Gender* are being used, and can as such be interpreted as a probability.

The general formulation of the logistic regression model then becomes:

$$p(y = 1|x_1, \ldots, x_k) = \frac{1}{1 + e^{-(\beta_0+\beta_1 x_1+\cdots+\beta_k x_k)}}$$

Since $p(y = 0|x_1, \ldots, x_k) = 1 - p(y = 1|x_1, \ldots, x_k)$, we have

$$p(y = 0|x_1, \ldots, x_k) = 1 - \frac{1}{1 + e^{-(\beta_0+\beta_1 x_1+\cdots+\beta_k x_k)}} = \frac{1}{1 + e^{(\beta_0+\beta_1 x_1+\cdots+\beta_k x_k)}}$$

Hence, both $p(y = 1|x_1, \ldots, x_k)$ and $p(y = 0|x_1, \ldots, x_k)$ are bounded between 0 and 1.

Reformulating in terms of the odds, the model becomes:

$$\frac{p(y = 1|x_1, \ldots, x_k)}{p(y = 0|x_1, \ldots, x_k)} = e^{(\beta_0+\beta_1 x_1+\cdots+\beta_k x_k)}$$

or in terms of the log odds, also called the *logit*:

$$\ln\left(\frac{p(y = 1|x_1, \ldots, x_k)}{p(y = 0|x_1, \ldots, x_k)}\right) = \beta_0 + \beta_1 x_1 + \cdots + \beta_k x_k$$

The $\boldsymbol{\beta}$ parameters of a logistic regression model are then estimated using the idea of maximum likelihood. Maximum likelihood optimization chooses the parameters in such a way that it maximizes the probability of getting the sample at hand.

### *Logistic Regression Properties*

Since logistic regression is linear in the log odds (logit), it basically estimates a **linear decision boundary** to separate both classes. This is illustrated in Figure 20.7 in which Y (N) corresponds to Response = Yes (Response = No).

To interpret a logistic regression model, one can calculate the **odds ratio**. Suppose variable $x_i$ increases by one unit with all other variables being kept constant (*ceteris paribus*), then the new logit becomes the old logit increased by $\beta_i$. Likewise, the new odds become the old odds multiplied by $e^{\beta_i}$. The latter represents the odds ratio, i.e., the multiplicative increase in the odds when $x_i$ increases by 1 (*ceteris paribus*). Hence:

- $\beta_i > 0$ implies $e^{\beta_i} > 1$ and the odds and probability increase with $x_i$;
- $\beta_i < 0$ implies $e^{\beta_i} < 1$ and the odds and probability decrease with $x_i$.

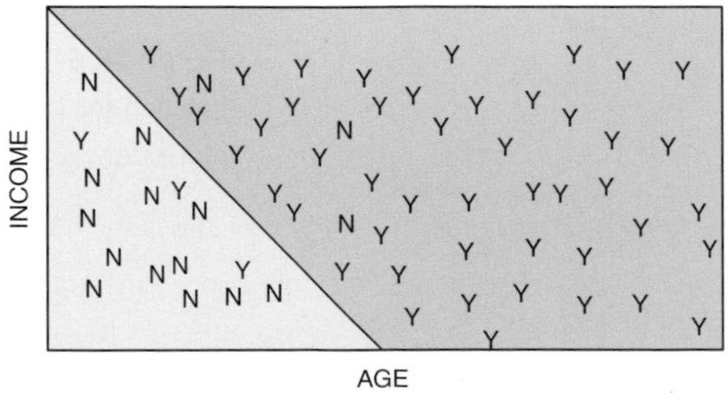


**Figure 20.7** Linear decision boundary of logistic regression.

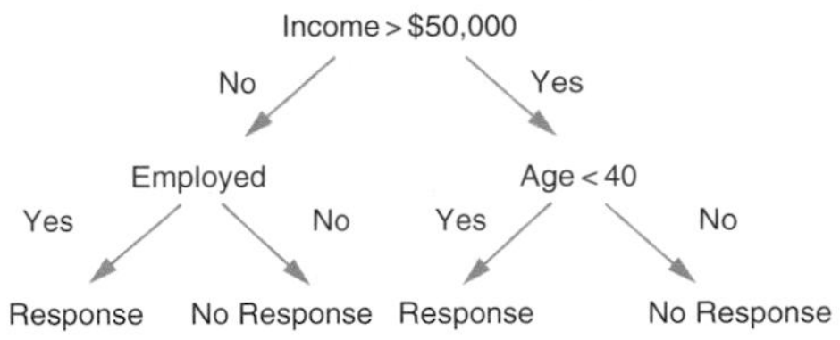


**Figure 20.8** Example of a decision tree.

Another way of interpreting a logistic regression model is by calculating the **doubling amount**. This represents the amount of change required for doubling the primary outcome odds. It can be easily seen that, for a particular variable $x_i$, the doubling amount equals $\log(2)/\beta_i$.

#### 20.5.1.3 Decision Trees

**Decision trees** are recursive partitioning algorithms (RPAs) that come up with a tree-like structure representing patterns in an underlying dataset. Figure 20.8 provides an example of a decision tree in a response modeling setting.

The top node is the root node, specifying a testing condition of which the outcome corresponds to a branch leading to an internal node. The terminal nodes, also called leaf nodes, assign the classifications (in our case response labels). Many algorithms have been suggested to construct decision trees. Among the most popular are C4.5 (See5),[3] CART,[4] and CHAID.[5] These algorithms differ in the ways they answer the key decisions to build a tree, which are:

- ***Splitting decision***: which variable to split at what value (e.g., *Income* is $>$ \$50,000 or not, *Age* is $<$ 40 or not, *Employed* is Yes or No).
- ***Stopping decision***: when to stop adding nodes to the tree? What is the optimal size of the tree?
- ***Assignment decision:*** what class (e.g., response or no response) to assign to a leaf node?

Usually, the assignment decision is the most straightforward to make, since one typically looks at the majority class within the leaf node to make the decision. This idea is also called winner-take-all learning. Alternatively, one may estimate class membership probabilities in a leaf node equal to the observed fractions of the classes. The other two decisions are less straightforward and are elaborated upon in what follows.

##### *Splitting Decision*

To address the splitting decision, one needs to define the concept of **impurity** or chaos. Consider the three datasets in Figure 20.9, each containing good customers (e.g., responders, non-churners, legitimates) represented by the unfilled circles, and bad customers (e.g., non-responders, churners, fraudsters) represented by the filled circles.[6] Minimal impurity occurs when all customers are either

[3] Quinlan J.R., *C4.5 Programs for Machine Learning*, Morgan Kauffman Publishers, 1993.

[4] Breiman L., Friedman, J.H., Olshen R.A., Stone, C. J., *Classification and Regression Trees*, Wadsworth & Brooks/Cole Advanced Books & Software, 1984.

[5] Hartigan J.A., *Clustering Algorithms*, Wiley, 1975.

[6] One often also uses the term "positives" to refer to the minority class (e.g., churners, defaulters, fraudsters, responders) and "negatives" to refer to the majority class (e.g., non-churners, non-defaulters, non-fraudsters, non-responders).

**Figure 20.9** Example datasets for calculating impurity.

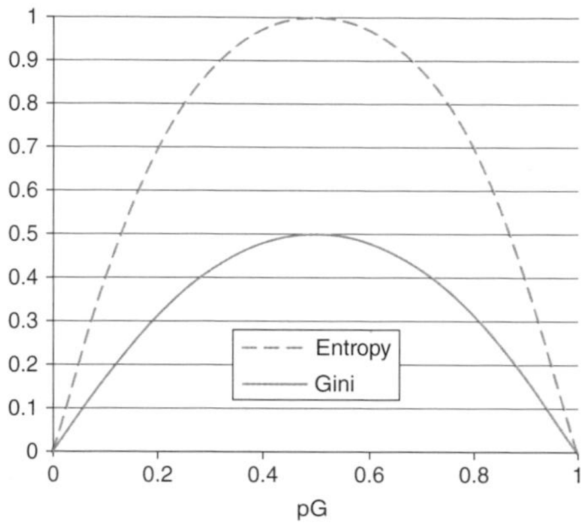


**Figure 20.10** Entropy versus gini.

good or bad. Maximal impurity occurs when one has the same number of good and bad customers (i.e., the dataset in the middle).

Decision trees aim at minimizing the impurity in the data. To do so appropriately, one needs a measure to quantify impurity. Various measures have been introduced in the literature, and the most popular are:

- Entropy: $E(S) = -p_G \log_2(p_G) - p_B \log_2(p_B)$ (C4.5/See5);[7]
- Gini: $Gini(S) = 2p_G p_B$ (CART); and
- Chi-squared analysis (CHAID),

with $p_G$ ($p_B$) being the proportions of good and bad, respectively. Both measures are depicted in Figure 20.10, where the entropy (gini) is minimal when all customers are either good or bad, and maximal if the number of good and bad customers is the same.

To address the splitting decision, various candidate splits are evaluated in terms of their decrease in impurity. Consider, for example, a split on age as depicted in Figure 20.11.

The original dataset had maximum entropy since the amounts of goods and bads were the same. The entropy calculations now become:

- Entropy top node $= -1/2 \times \log_2(1/2) - 1/2 \times \log_2(1/2) = 1$
- Entropy left node $= -1/3 \times \log_2(1/3) - 2/3 \times \log_2(2/3) = 0.91$
- Entropy right node $= -1 \times \log_2(1) - 0 \times \log_2(0) = 0$.

The weighted decrease in entropy, also known as the **gain**, can then be calculated as follows:

[7] See5 is a more recent, improved version of C4.5.

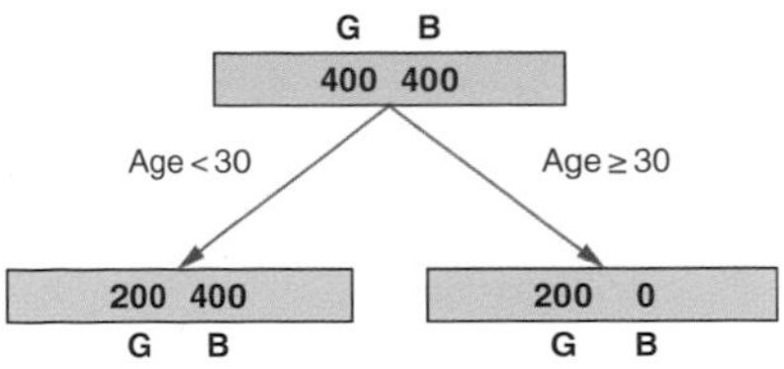


**Figure 20.11** Calculating the entropy for age split.

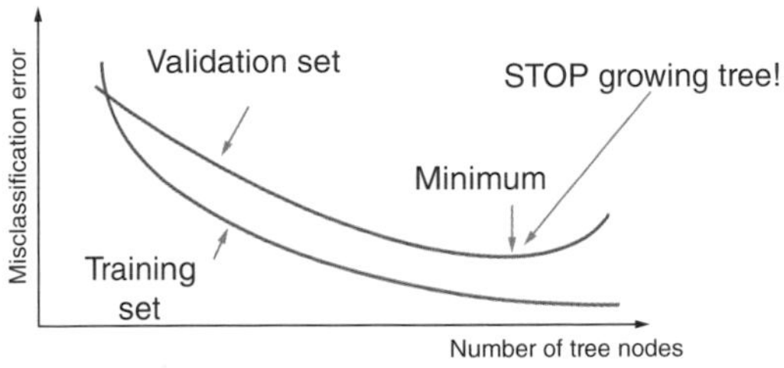


**Figure 20.12** Using a validation set to stop growing a decision tree.

$$\text{Gain} = 1 - (600/800) \times 0.91 - (200/800) \times 0 = 0.32$$

The gain measures the weighted decrease in entropy due to the split. It speaks for itself that a higher gain is to be preferred. The decision tree algorithm now considers different candidate splits for its root node and adopts a greedy strategy by picking the one with the biggest gain. Once the root node has been decided upon, the procedure continues in a recursive way, each time adding splits with the biggest gain. This can be perfectly parallelized and both sides of the tree can grow in parallel, increasing the efficiency of the tree construction algorithm.

### *Stopping Decision*

The third decision relates to the stopping criterion. If the tree continues to split it will become very detailed, with leaf nodes containing only a few observations. In the most extreme case, the tree will have one leaf node per observation and will perfectly fit the data. However, by doing so, the tree will start to fit the specificities or noise in the data, which is also referred to as **overfitting**. The tree has become too complex and fails to correctly model the noise-free pattern or trend in the data. It will generalize poorly to new data. To avoid this happening, the data will be split into a training sample and a validation sample. The training sample will be used to make the splitting decision. The validation sample is an independent sample, set aside to monitor the misclassification error (or any other performance metric such as a profit-based measure) as the tree is grown. A commonly used split is a 70% training sample and 30% validation sample. One then typically observes a pattern, as depicted in Figure 20.12.

The error on the training sample keeps on decreasing as the splits become more and more specific and tailored toward it. On the validation sample, the error will initially decrease, which indicates that the tree splits generalize well. However, at some point the error will increase because the splits become too specific for the training sample as the tree starts to memorize it. Where the validation set curve reaches its minimum, the procedure should be stopped as otherwise overfitting will occur. As already mentioned, besides classification error, one might also use accuracy- or profit-based

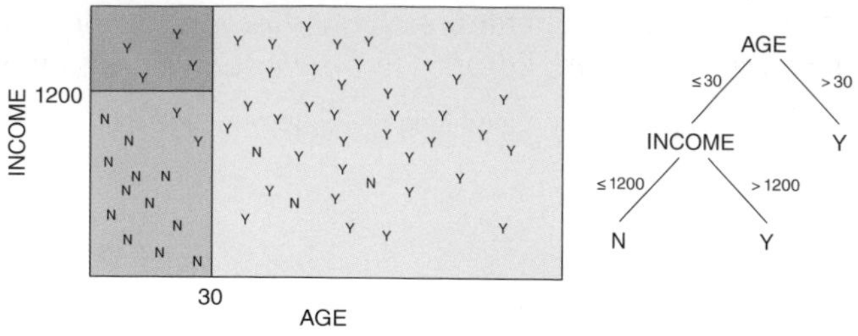


**Figure 20.13** Decision boundary of a decision tree.

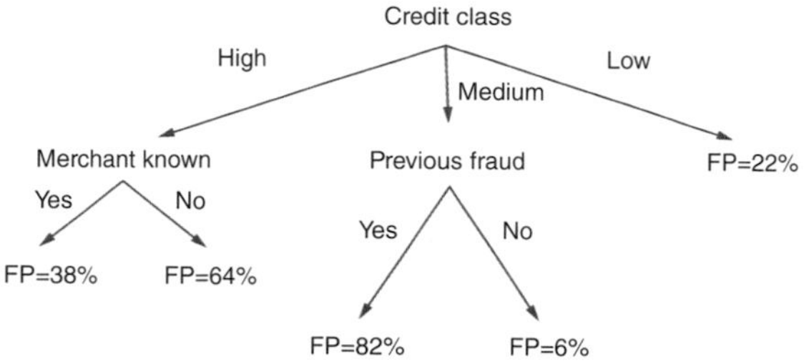


**Figure 20.14** Example regression tree for predicting the fraud percentage.

measures on the *y*-axis to make the stopping decision. Sometimes simplicity is preferred above accuracy, and one can select a tree that does not necessarily have minimum validation set error, but a lower number of nodes or levels.

### *Decision Tree Properties*

In the example given in Figure 20.8, every node had only two branches. The advantage of this is that the testing condition can be implemented as a simple yes/no question. Multiway splits allow for more than two branches and can provide trees that are wider but less deep. In a read-once decision tree, a particular variable can be used only once in a certain tree path. Every tree can also be represented as a rule set, since every path from a root node to a leaf node makes up a simple if–then rule. For the tree depicted in Figure 20.8, the corresponding rules are:

**If** *Income* $>$ \$50,000 **And** *Age* $<$ 40 **Then** Response = Yes
**If** *Income* $>$ \$50,000 **And** *Age* $\geq$ 40 **Then** Response = No
**If** *Income* $\leq$ \$50,000 **And** *Employed*=Yes **Then** Response = Yes
**If** *Income* $\leq$ \$50,000 **And** *Employed*=No **Then** Response = No

These rules can then be easily implemented in many software packages (e.g., Microsoft Excel).

Decision trees essentially model decision boundaries orthogonal to the axes. This is illustrated in Figure 20.13 for an example decision tree.

### *Regression Trees*

Decision trees can also be used to predict continuous targets. Consider the example of Figure 20.14, in which a **regression tree** is used to predict the fraud percentage (FP). This percentage can be expressed as the percentage of a predefined limit based upon, for example, the maximum transaction amount.

Other criteria now need to be used to make the splitting decision, since the impurity will need to be measured in another way. One way to measure impurity in a node is by calculating the mean squared error (MSE) as follows:

$$\text{MSE} = \frac{1}{n}\sum_{i=1}^{n}(y_i - \bar{y})^2$$

where $n$ represents the number of observations in a leaf node, $y_i$ is the value of observation $i$, and $\bar{y}$ is the average of all values in the leaf node. It is desirable to have a low MSE in a leaf node since this indicates that the node is more homogeneous.

Another way to make the splitting decision is by conducting a simple analysis of variance (ANOVA) test and then calculating an F-statistic as follows:

$$F = \frac{SS_{between}/(B-1)}{SS_{within}/(n-B)} \sim F_{n-B,B-1}$$

where:

$$SS_{between} = \sum_{b=1}^{B} n_b(\bar{y}_b - \bar{y})^2$$

$$SS_{within} = \sum_{b=1}^{B}\sum_{i=1}^{n_b}(y_{bi} - \bar{y}_b)^2$$

with $B$ as the number of branches of the split, $n_b$ the number of observations in branch $b$, $\bar{y}_b$ the average in branch $b$, $y_{bi}$ the value of observation $i$ in branch $b$, and $\bar{y}$ the overall average. Good splits favor homogeneity within a node (low $SS_{within}$) and heterogeneity between nodes (high $SS_{between}$). In other words, good splits should have a high $F$-value, or low corresponding $p$-value, which is the probability of obtaining the same or a more extreme value in the case that the null hypothesis of similarity is true.

The stopping decision can be made in a similar way to classification trees, but using a regression-based performance measure (e.g., MSE, mean absolute deviation, R-squared) on the $y$-axis. The assignment decision can be made by assigning the mean (or median) to each leaf node. Note that standard deviations, and confidence intervals, may also be computed for each of the leaf nodes.

#### 20.5.1.4 Other Predictive Analytics Techniques

Linear regression, logistic regression, and decision trees are commonly used predictive analytics techniques. Their success stems from their good performance and high interpretability. Other more complex predictive analytics techniques have been developed. Ensemble methods aim at estimating multiple analytical models instead of using only one. The idea here is that multiple models can cover different parts of the data input space and complement each other's deficiencies. Popular examples of ensemble techniques are: bagging, boosting, and random forests. Neural networks and support vector machines (SVMs) are also predictive analytics techniques. Both are capable of building very sophisticated, highly nonlinear predictive analytics models. However, the resulting models are based upon complex mathematics and are often difficult to

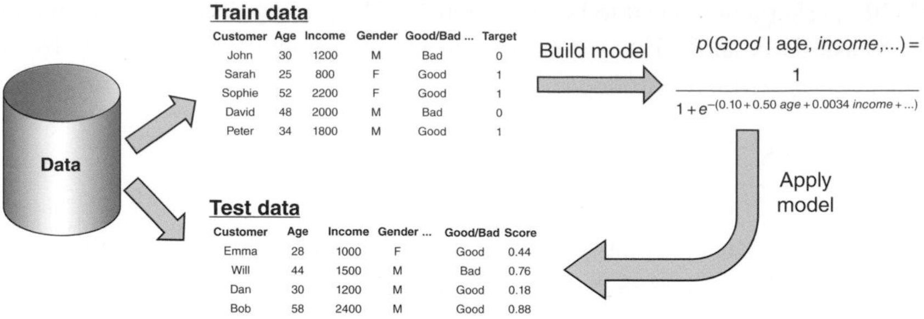


**Figure 20.15** Training versus test sample set-up for performance estimation.

understand for business users. Refer to the literature for more information about ensemble methods, neural networks, and SVMs.[8]

## 20.5.2 Evaluating Predictive Models

In this section we discuss how to evaluate predictive models. We start by reviewing various procedures for splitting up the dataset to get a good performance estimate. This is followed by an overview of performance measures for classification and regression models. We conclude by elaborating on other performance measures.

### 20.5.2.1 Splitting Up the Dataset

When evaluating predictive models, two key decisions need to be made. The first decision concerns the dataset split, which specifies on what part of the data the performance will be measured. A second decision concerns the performance metric. In what follows, we elaborate on both.

The decision on how to split up the dataset for performance measurement depends upon its size. In large datasets (say, more than 1000 observations), the data can be split up into a training and a test sample. The training sample (also called development or estimation sample) will be used to build the model, whereas the test sample (also called the hold-out sample) will be used to calculate its performance (see Figure 20.15). A commonly applied split up is a 70% training sample and a 30% test sample. There should be a strict separation between training sample and test sample. No observation used for model development can be used for independent testing. Note that with decision trees, the validation sample is a separate sample, since it is actively being used during model development (i.e., to make the stopping decision). A typical split is a 40% training sample, 30% validation sample, and 30% test sample.

In small datasets (say, fewer than 1000 observations) special schemes need to be adopted. A popular scheme is cross-validation (Figure 20.16). In **cross-validation**, the data are split into $K$ folds (e.g., five or ten). An analytical model is then trained on $K-1$ training folds and tested on the remaining validation fold. This is repeated for all possible validation folds resulting in $K$ performance estimates that can then be averaged. A standard deviation and/or confidence interval can be calculated if desired. In its most extreme cases, cross-validation becomes leave-one-out cross-validation whereby every observation is left out in turn and a model is estimated on the remaining

[8] E.g., Baesens B., *Analytics in a Big Data World*, Wiley, 2014.

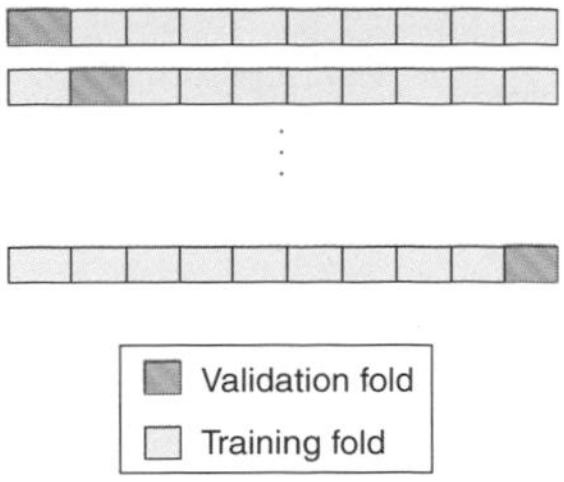


**Figure 20.16** Cross-validation for performance measurement.

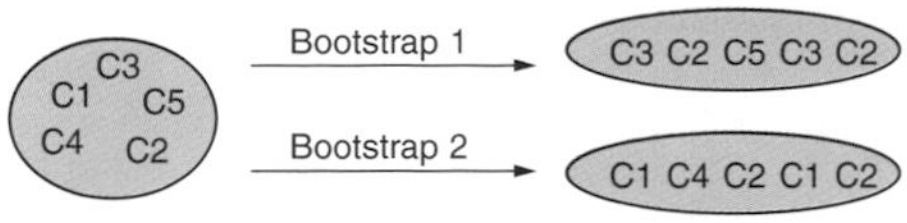


**Figure 20.17** Bootstrapping.

$K - 1$ observations. This gives $K$ analytical models in total. Consider three observations: Bart, Wilfried, and Seppe. A leave-one out cross-validation estimates three models: one on Bart and Wilfried which is evaluated on Seppe; one on Bart and Seppe which is evaluated on Wilfried; and one on Wilfried and Seppe which is evaluated on Bart.

A key question to answer when doing cross-validation is what the final model being outputted from the procedure should be. Since cross-validation gives multiple models, this is not an obvious question. One could let all models collaborate in an ensemble set-up by using a (weighted) voting procedure. A more pragmatic answer would be to, for example, do leave-one-out cross-validation and pick one model at random. Since the models differ up to one observation only, they will be similar anyway. Alternatively, one may also build one final model on all observations, but report the performance coming out of the cross-validation procedure as the best independent estimate.

For small samples, one may also adopt **bootstrapping** procedures. In bootstrapping, one takes samples with replacement from a dataset D. An example with five observations, representing five customers C1 to C5, is represented in Figure 20.17.

The probability that a customer is sampled equals $1/n$, with $n$ the number of observations in the dataset. The probability that a customer is not sampled equals $1 - 1/n$. Assuming a bootstrap with $n$ sampled observations, the fraction of customers not sampled equals:

$$\left(1 - \frac{1}{n}\right)^n$$

We then have:

$$\lim_{n \to \infty} \left(1 - \frac{1}{n}\right)^n = e^{-1} = 0.368$$

whereby the approximation already works well for small values of $n$. So, 0.368 is the probability that a customer does not appear in the sample and 0.632 is the probability that a customer appears. If we then take the bootstrap sample as the training set and the test set as all samples in $D$, excluding the samples in the bootstrap (e.g., for the first bootstrap of Figure 20.17, the test set consists of C1 and C4), we can approximate the performance as follows:

**Table 20.5** Example dataset for performance calculation

| | Churn | Score |
|---|---|---|
| John | Yes | 0.72 |
| Sophie | No | 0.56 |
| David | Yes | 0.44 |
| Emma | No | 0.18 |
| Bob | No | 0.36 |

| | Churn | Churn score |
|---|---|---|
| John | Yes | 0.72 |
| Sophie | No | 0.56 |
| David | Yes | 0.44 |
| Emma | No | 0.18 |
| Bob | No | 0.36 |

Cutoff= 0 .50

| | Churn | Churn score | Predicted |
|---|---|---|---|
| John | Yes | 0.72 | Yes |
| Sophie | No | 0.56 | Yes |
| David | Yes | 0.44 | No |
| Emma | No | 0.18 | No |
| Bob | No | 0.36 | No |

**Figure 20.18** Calculating predictions using a cutoff.

**Table 20.6** The confusion matrix

| | | Actual status | |
|---|---|---|---|
| | | Positive (churn) | Negative (no churn) |
| **Predicted status** | **Positive (churn)** | True positive (John) | False positive (Sophie) |
| | **Negative (no churn)** | False negative (David) | True negative (Emma, Bob) |

$$\text{Error estimate} = 0.368 \text{ error(training)} + 0.632 \text{ error(test)}$$

where a higher weight is being put on the test set performance. As illustrated in Figure 20.17, multiple bootstraps can then be considered to get the distribution of the error estimate.

#### 20.5.2.2 Performance Measures for Classification Models

Consider this churn prediction example for a five-customer dataset. The first column in Table 20.5 depicts the churn status, while the second column depicts the churn score as it comes from a logistic regression or decision tree.

One can now map the scores to a predicted classification label by assuming a default cutoff of 0.5, as shown in Figure 20.18.

A confusion matrix can now be calculated, as shown in Table 20.6.

Based upon this matrix, one can now calculate the following performance measures:

- Classification accuracy = (TP + TN)/(TP + FP + FN + TN) = 3/5
- Classification error = (FP + FN)/(TP + FP + FN + TN) = 2/5
- Sensitivity = Recall = Hit rate = TP/(TP + FN) = 1/2
- Specificity = TN/(FP + TN) = 2/3
- Precision = TP/(TP + FP) = 1/2
- F-measure = 2 × (Precision × Recall)/(Precision + Recall) = 1/2.

**Table 20.7** Table for ROC analysis

| Cutoff | Sensitivity | Specificity | 1-Specificity |
|---|---|---|---|
| 0 | 1 | 0 | 1 |
| 0.01 | | | |
| 0.02 | | | |
| …. | | | |
| 0.99 | | | |
| 1 | 0 | 1 | 0 |

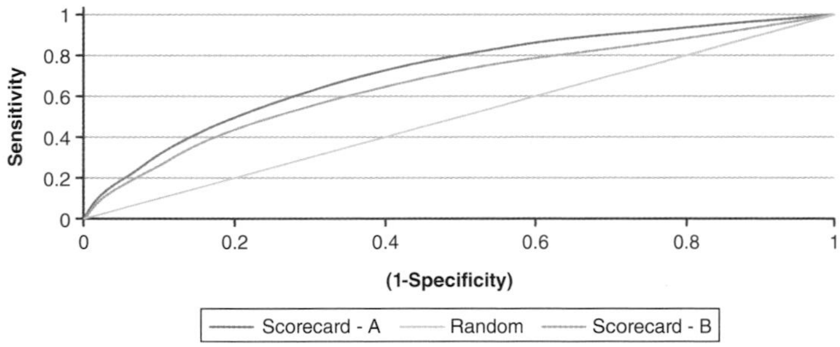


**Figure 20.19** The receiver operating characteristic curve.

The **classification accuracy** is the percentage of correctly classified observations. The classification error is the complement thereof and referred to as the **misclassification rate**. The **sensitivity**, recall, or hit rate measures how many of the churners are correctly labeled by the model as a churner. The **specificity** looks at how many of the non-churners are correctly labeled by the model as non-churners. The **precision** indicates how many of the predicted churners are actually churners.

All these classification measures depend upon the **cutoff**. For example, for a cutoff of 0 (1), the classification accuracy becomes 40% (60%), the error 60% (40%), the sensitivity 100% (0%), the specificity 0% (100%), the precision 40% (0%), and the F-measure 57% (0%). Given this dependence, it would be nice to have a performance measure independent from the cutoff. One could construct a table with the sensitivity, specificity, and 1-specificity for various cutoffs, as shown in Table 20.7.

The **receiver operating characteristic (ROC) curve** then plots the sensitivity versus 1-specificity as illustrated in Figure 20.19.

A perfect model detects all the churners and non-churners at the same time, resulting in a sensitivity of 1 and a specificity of 1, and is represented by the upper left corner. The closer the curve approaches this point, the better the performance. In Figure 20.19, model A has a better performance than model B. A problem arises if the curves intersect. Here, one can calculate the **area under the ROC curve (AUC)** as a performance metric. The AUC provides a simple figure-of-merit for the performance of the constructed classifier; the higher the AUC the better the performance. The AUC is always bounded between 0 and 1 and can be interpreted as a probability. It represents the probability that a randomly chosen churner gets a higher score than a randomly chosen non-churner.[9] The diagonal represents a random scorecard, whereby sensitivity equals 1-specificity for

[9] Hanley, J.A., McNeil, B.J., The meaning and use of area under the ROC curve, *Radiology*, 1982; 143: 29–36.

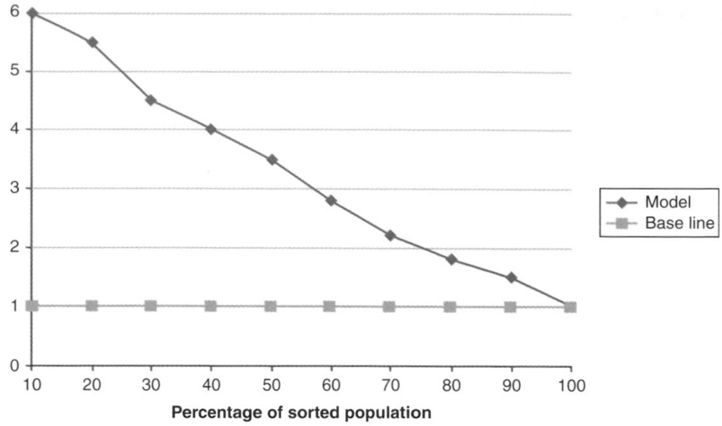


**Figure 20.20** The lift curve.

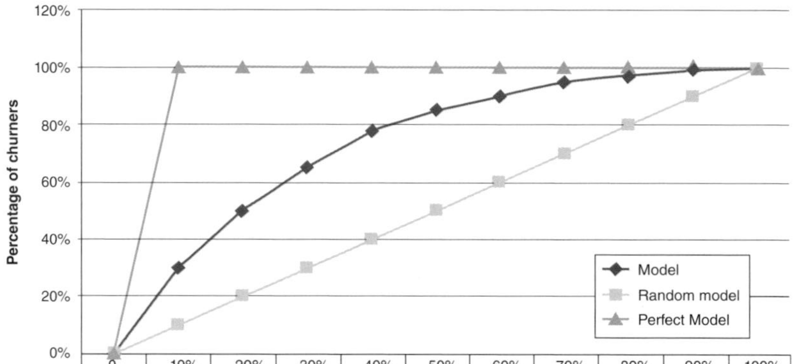


| | 0 | 10% | 20% | 30% | 40% | 50% | 60% | 70% | 80% | 90% | 100% |
|---|---|---|---|---|---|---|---|---|---|---|---|
| Model | 0% | 30% | 50% | 65% | 78% | 85% | 90% | 95% | 97% | 99% | 100% |
| Random model | 0% | 10% | 20% | 30% | 40% | 50% | 60% | 70% | 80% | 90% | 100% |
| Perfect Model | 0% | 100% | 100% | 100% | 100% | 100% | 100% | 100% | 100% | 100% | 100% |

Percentage of sorted population

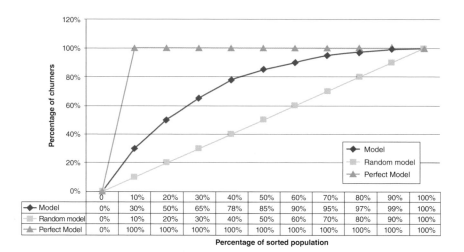

**Figure 20.21** The cumulative accuracy profile.

all cutoff points. Hence, a good classifier should have an ROC above the diagonal and AUC bigger than 50%.

A **lift curve** is another important performance evaluation approach. The lift curve represents the cumulative percentage of churners per decile, divided by the overall population percentage of churners. It starts by sorting the population from high score to low score. Suppose that in the top 10% highest scores there are 60% churners, whereas the total population has 10% churners. The lift value in the top decile then becomes 60%/10% = 6. Using no model, or a random sorting, the churners would be equally spread across the entire range and the lift value would always equal 1. The lift curve typically decreases as one cumulatively considers bigger deciles, until it reaches 1. This is illustrated in Figure 20.20. A lift curve can also be expressed in a non-cumulative way, and is also often summarized by reporting top decile lift.

The **cumulative accuracy profile (CAP)** (also called Lorenz or power curve) is closely related to the lift curve (Figure 20.21). It also starts by sorting the population from high score to low score and then measures the cumulative percentage of churners for each decile on the *y*-axis. The perfect

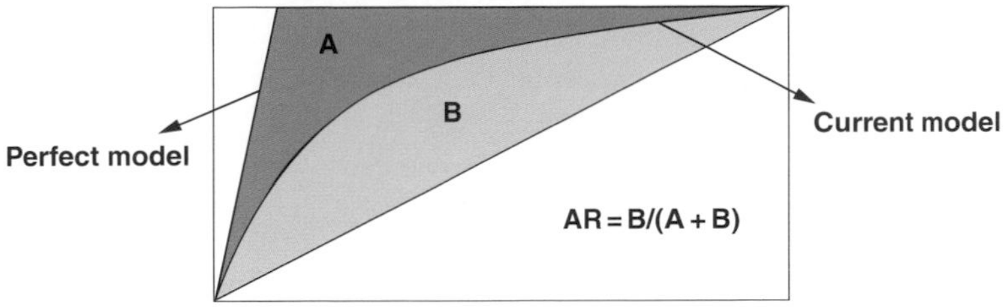


Figure 20.22 Calculating the accuracy ratio.

model gives a linearly increasing curve up to the sample churn rate and then flattens out. The diagonal again represents the random model.

The CAP curve can be summarized in an **accuracy ratio (AR)**, as depicted in Figure 20.22. The accuracy ratio is then defined:

$$(\text{Area below CAP curve for current model} - \text{Area below CAP curve for random model}) / \\ (\text{Area below CAP curve for perfect model} - \text{Area below CAP curve for random model})$$

A perfect model will have an AR of 1 and a random model an AR of 0. The AR is also often called the Gini coefficient. There is also a linear relation between the AR and the AUC: $AR = 2 \times AUC - 1$.

**Drill Down**

The following table illustrates some typical AUC performance benchmarks for credit scoring, churn prediction in telco, and insurance fraud detection. It also includes an indication of the number of variables in each model.

| Application | Number of variables | AUC range |
|---|---|---|
| Credit scoring | 10–15 | 70–85% |
| Churn prediction (telco) | 6–10 | 70–90% |
| Fraud detection (insurance) | 10–15 | 70–90% |

### 20.5.2.3 Performance Measures for Regression Models

A first way to evaluate the predictive performance of a regression model is by visualizing the predicted target against the actual target using a scatter plot (Figure 20.23). The more the plot approaches a straight line through the origin, the better the performance of the regression model. It can be summarized by calculating the **Pearson correlation coefficient**:

$$corr(\hat{y}, y) = \frac{\sum_{i=1}^{n} (\hat{y}_i - \bar{\hat{y}})(y_i - \bar{y})}{\sqrt{\sum_{i=1}^{n} (\hat{y}_i - \bar{\hat{y}})^2} \sqrt{\sum_{i=1}^{n} (y_i - \bar{y})^2}}$$

where $\hat{y}_i$ represents the predicted value for observation $i$, $\bar{\hat{y}}$ the average of the predicted values, $y_i$ the actual value for observation $i$, and $\bar{y}$ the average of the actual values. The Pearson correlation always varies between –1 and +1. Values closer to +1 indicate better agreement and better fit between the predicted and actual values of the target variable.

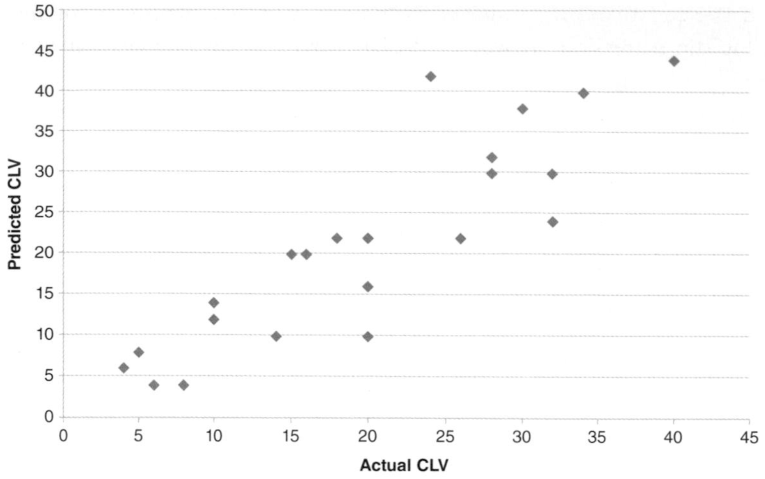


**Figure 20.23** Scatter plot.

Another key performance metric is the **coefficient of determination** or $R^2$, defined as:

$$R^2 = \frac{\sum_{i=1}^{n}(\hat{y}_i - \bar{y})^2}{\sum_{i=1}^{n}(y_i - \bar{y})^2} = 1 - \frac{\sum_{i=1}^{n}(y_i - \hat{y}_i)^2}{\sum_{i=1}^{n}(y_i - \bar{y})^2}$$

The $R^2$ always varies between 0 and 1, and higher values are to be preferred. Basically, this measure tells us how much better we can predict by using the analytical model to compute $\hat{y}_i$ than by using the mean $\bar{y}$ as the predictor. To compensate for the variables in the model, an adjusted $R^2$, $R^2_{adj}$, has been suggested:

$$R^2_{adj} = 1 - \frac{n-1}{n-k-1}\left(1 - R^2\right) = 1 - \frac{n-1}{n-k-1}\frac{\sum_{i=1}^{n}(y_i - \hat{y}_i)^2}{\sum_{i=1}^{n}(y_i - \bar{y})^2}$$

whereby $k$ represents the number of variables in the model. Although $R^2$ is usually a number between 0 and 1, it can also have negative values for non-OLS models when the model predictions are worse than always using the mean from the training set as the prediction.

Two other popular measures are the mean squared error (MSE) and mean absolute deviation (MAD) defined as:

$$\text{MSE} = \frac{\sum_{i=1}^{n}(y_i - \hat{y}_i)^2}{n},$$

$$\text{MAD} = \frac{\sum_{i=1}^{n} | y_i - \hat{y}_i |}{n}.$$

A perfect model would have an MSE and MAD of 0. Higher values for both MSE and MAD indicate lower performance. The MSE is sometimes also reported as the root mean squared error (RMSE): $\text{RMSE} = \sqrt{\text{MSE}}$.

### 20.5.2.4 Other Performance Measures for Predictive Analytical Models

As already mentioned, statistical performance is just one aspect of model performance. Other important criteria are comprehensibility, justifiability, and operational efficiency. Although comprehensibility is subjective and depends on the background and experience of the business analyst, linear and logistic regression, as well as decision trees, are commonly called white box, comprehensible techniques. Other techniques such as neural networks and random forests methods are essentially opaque models and much harder to understand. However, in settings in which statistical performance is superior to interpretability, they are the method of choice. Justifiability goes one step further and verifies to what extent the relationships modeled are in line with prior business knowledge and/or expectations. In a practical setting, this often boils down to verifying the univariate impact of a variable on the model's output. For example, for a linear/logistic regression model, the signs of the regression coefficients will be verified. Finally, the operational efficiency can also be an important evaluation criterion to consider when selecting the optimal analytical model. Operational efficiency represents the ease with which one can implement, use, and monitor the final model. For example, in a (near) real-time fraud environment, it is important to be able to quickly run the fraud model using new cases. With regards to implementation, rule-based models excel because implementing rules can be done easily, even in spreadsheet software. Linear models are also easy to implement whereas nonlinear models are much more difficult to implement due to the complex transformations being used by the model.

## 20.5.3 Descriptive Analytics

In descriptive analytics, the aim is to describe patterns of customer behavior. Contrary to predictive analytics, there is no real target variable available (e.g., churn, response, or fraud indicator). Hence, descriptive analytics is often called unsupervised learning since there is no target variable to steer the learning process. The three most common descriptive analytics techniques are association rules, sequence rules, and clustering.

### 20.5.3.1 Association Rules

**Association rules** are rules aimed at detecting frequently occurring associations between items. In what follows, we first introduce the basic setting. We then define the support, confidence, and lift measures. We conclude by discussing post-processing of association rules.

*Basic Setting*

Association rules typically start from a database of transactions $D$. Each transaction consists of a transaction identifier and a set of items (e.g., products, web pages, courses) $\{i_1, i_2, ...\}$ selected from all possible items $I$. Table 20.8 gives an example of a transactions database in a supermarket setting.

An association rule is then an implication of the form $X \Rightarrow Y$, whereby $X \subset I$, $Y \subset I$, and $X \cap Y = \emptyset$. $X$ is the rule antecedent, whereas $Y$ is the rule consequent. The following are examples of association rules:

- If a customer buys spaghetti, then the customer buys red wine in 70% of cases.
- If a customer has a car loan and car insurance, then the customer has a checking account in 80% of cases.
- If a customer visits web page A, then the customer will visit web page B in 90% of cases.

It is important to note that association rules are stochastic in nature; that means they should not be interpreted as a universal truth and are characterized by statistical measures quantifying the strength

**Table 20.8** Example transaction dataset

| Transaction identifier | Items |
|---|---|
| 1 | Beer, milk, diapers, baby food |
| 2 | Coke, beer, diapers |
| 3 | Cigarettes, diapers, baby food |
| 4 | Chocolates, diapers, milk, apples |
| 5 | Tomatoes, water, apples, beer |
| 6 | Spaghetti, diapers, baby food, beer |
| 7 | Water, beer, baby food |
| 8 | Diapers, baby food, spaghetti |
| 9 | Baby food, beer, diapers, milk |
| 10 | Apples, wine, baby food |

of the association. Also, the rules measure correlational associations and should not be interpreted in a causal way.

### *Support, Confidence, and Lift*

Support and confidence are two key measures to quantify the strength of an association rule. The **support** of an item set is defined as the percentage of total transactions in the database that contains the item set. Therefore, the rule $X \Rightarrow Y$ has support $s$ if $100s\%$ of the transactions in $D$ contain $X \cup Y$. It can be formally defined as follows:

$$support(X \cup Y) = \frac{number\ of\ transactions\ supporting\ (X \cup Y)}{total\ number\ of\ transactions}$$

When considering the transaction database in Table 20.8, the association rule baby food and diapers ⇒ beer has support 3/10 or 30%.

A frequent item set is an item set for which the support is higher than a minimum support threshold (minsup) which is typically specified upfront by the business user or data analyst. A lower (higher) minsup will generate more (less) frequent item sets. The **confidence** measures the strength of the association and is defined as the conditional probability of the rule consequent, given the rule antecedent. The rule $X \Rightarrow Y$ has confidence $c$ if $100c\%$ of the transactions in $D$ that contain $X$ also contain $Y$. It can be formally defined as follows:

$$confidence(X \rightarrow Y) = p(Y|X) = \frac{support(X \cup Y)}{support(X)}$$

Again, the data analyst must specify a minimum confidence (minconf) for an association rule to be considered interesting. In Table 20.8, the association rule baby food and diapers ⇒ beer has confidence 3/5 or 60%.

Consider the example from a supermarket transactions database shown in Table 20.9.

Let us now evaluate the association rule Tea ⇒ Coffee. The support of this rule is 150/1000 or 15%. The confidence of the rule is 150/200 or 75%. At first sight, this association rule seems very appealing, given its high confidence. However, closer inspection reveals that the prior probability of buying coffee equals 900/1000 or 90%. Hence, a customer who buys tea is less likely to buy coffee than a customer about whom we have no information. The **lift**, also referred to as the interestingness

**Table 20.9** The lift measure

| | Tea | Not tea | Total |
|---|---|---|---|
| Coffee | 150 | 750 | 900 |
| Not coffee | 50 | 50 | 100 |
| **Total** | 200 | 800 | 1000 |

measure, takes this into account by incorporating the prior probability of the rule consequent as follows:

$$Lift(X \rightarrow Y) = \frac{support(X \cup Y)}{support(X) \times support(Y)}$$

A lift value less (greater) than 1 indicates a negative (positive) dependence or substitution (complementary) effect. In our example, the lift value equals 0.89, which clearly indicates the expected substitution effect between coffee and tea.

*Post-Processing Association Rules*

Typically, an association rule modeling exercise will yield lots of association rules, so post-processing will become a key activity. Example steps that can be considered here are:

- Filter out the trivial rules that contain already known patterns (e.g., buying spaghetti and spaghetti sauce). This should be done in collaboration with a business expert.
- Perform a sensitivity analysis by varying the minsup and minconf values. Particularly for rare but profitable items (e.g., Rolex watches), it could be interesting to lower the minsup value and find the interesting associations.
- Use appropriate visualization facilities (e.g., OLAP-based) to find the unexpected rules that might represent novel and actionable behavior in the data.
- Measure the economic impact (e.g., profit, cost) of the association rules.

#### 20.5.3.2 Sequence Rules

Given a database $D$ of customer transactions, the goal of mining **sequence rules** is to find the maximal sequences among all sequences that have certain user-specified minimum support and confidence. Important to note here is that, contrary to association rules that work with sets, the order of the items in a sequence is important. An example could be a sequence of web page visits in a web analytics setting:

Home page ⇒ Electronics ⇒ Cameras and Camcorders ⇒ Digital Cameras ⇒ Shopping cart ⇒ Order confirmation ⇒ Return to shopping.

A transaction time or sequence field will now be included in the analysis. While association rules are concerned with what items appear together at the same time (intra-transaction patterns), sequence rules are concerned about what items appear at different times (inter-transaction patterns).

Consider the example of a transactions dataset in a web analytics setting shown in Table 20.10. The letters A, B, C, etc. refer to web pages.

**Table 20.10** Example transactions dataset for sequence rule mining

| Session ID | Page | Sequence |
|---|---|---|
| 1 | A | 1 |
| 1 | B | 2 |
| 1 | C | 3 |
| 2 | B | 1 |
| 2 | C | 2 |
| 3 | A | 1 |
| 3 | C | 2 |
| 3 | D | 3 |
| 4 | A | 1 |
| 4 | B | 2 |
| 4 | D | 3 |
| 5 | D | 1 |
| 5 | C | 1 |
| 5 | A | 1 |

A sequential version can then be obtained:

Session 1: A, B, C
Session 2: B, C
Session 3: A, C, D
Session 4: A, B, D
Session 5: D, C, A

One can now calculate the support in two ways. Consider the sequence rule A ⇨ C. One approach would be to calculate the support whereby the consequent can appear in any subsequent stage of the sequence. Here, the support becomes 2/5 (40%). Another approach would be to consider only sessions in which the consequent appears right after the antecedent. Here, the support becomes 1/5 (20%). A similar reasoning can now be followed for the confidence, which can then be 2/4 (50%) or 1/4 (25%), respectively.

Remember that the confidence of a rule $A_1 \Rightarrow A_2$ is defined as the probability $p(A_2|A_1) = support(A_1 \cup A_2)/support(A_1)$. For a rule with multiple items, $A_1 \Rightarrow A_2 \Rightarrow \ldots A_{k-1} \Rightarrow A_k$, the confidence is defined as $p(A_k|A_1, A_2, \ldots, A_{k-1}) = support(A_1 \cup A_2 \cup \ldots \cup A_{k-1} \cup A_k)/support(A_1 \cup A_2 \cup \ldots \cup A_{k-1})$.

### 20.5.3.3 Clustering

The aim of clustering, or segmentation, is to split a set of observations into clusters so the homogeneity within a cluster is maximized (cohesive), and the heterogeneity between clusters is maximized (separated). Clustering techniques can be categorized as either hierarchical or nonhierarchical (Figure 20.24). In what follows, we elaborate on hierarchical and k-means clustering. Refer to textbooks on analytics for a discussion of self-organizing maps (SOMs).[10]

[10] Kohonen, T., *Self-Organizing Maps*, Springer, 2000.

### *Hierarchical Clustering*

In what follows, we first discuss **hierarchical clustering**. **Divisive hierarchical clustering** starts from the whole dataset in one cluster and then breaks it up, each time into smaller clusters until one observation per cluster remains (right to left in Figure 20.25). **Agglomerative hierarchical clustering** works the other way around, starting from all observations in individual clusters, then merging the ones that are most similar until all observations make up a single big cluster (left to right in Figure 20.25). The optimal clustering solution lies somewhere between the extremes to the left and right, respectively, in Figure 20.25.

To decide upon the merger or splitting, a distance measure is needed to assess the distance between two observations. Examples of popular distance measures are the Euclidean distance and Manhattan (city block) distance. Figure 20.26 illustrates two customers characterized by the recency

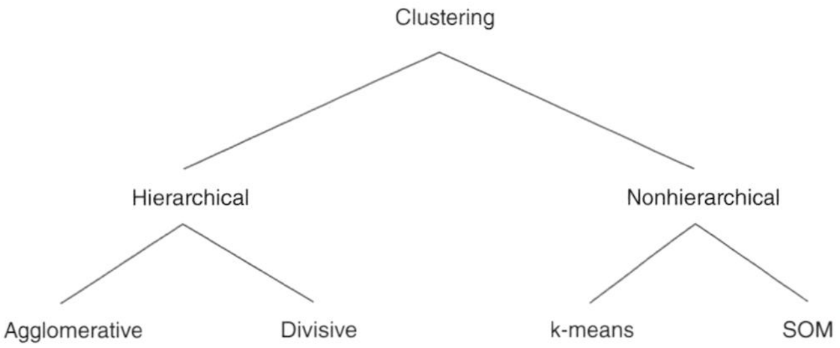


**Figure 20.24** Hierarchical versus nonhierarchical clustering techniques.

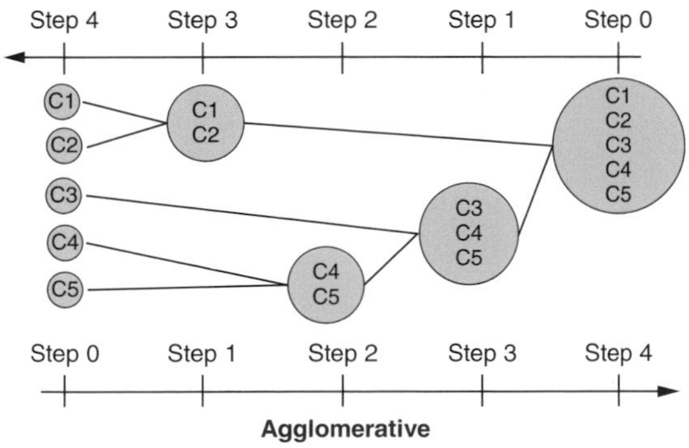


**Figure 20.25** Divisive versus agglomerative hierarchical clustering.

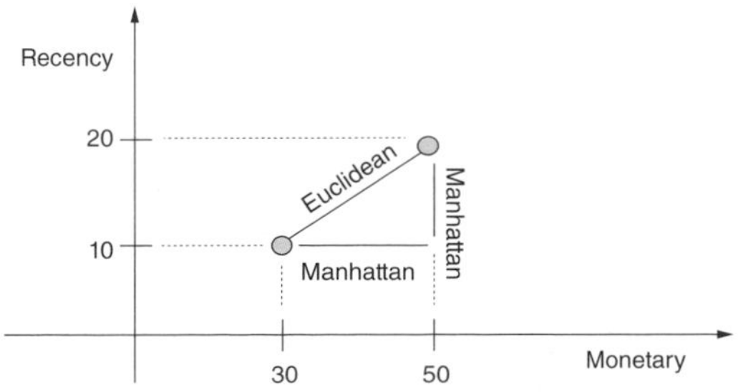


**Figure 20.26** Euclidean versus Manhattan distance.

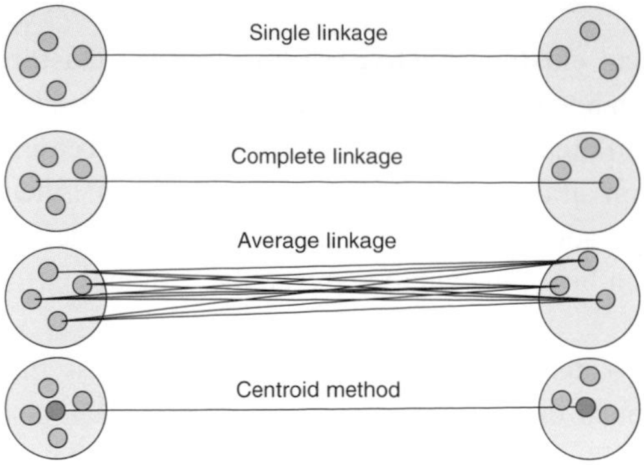


**Figure 20.27** Calculating distances between clusters.

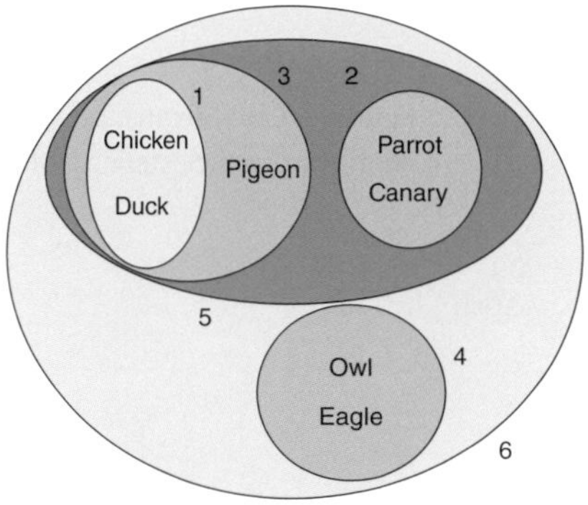


**Figure 20.28** Example for clustering birds. The numbers indicate the clustering steps.

(i.e., number of days ago) and average monetary value of their purchases. The distance measures can be calculated as follows:

$$\text{Euclidean}: \sqrt{(50-30)^2 + (20-10)^2} = 22$$

$$\text{Manhattan}: \mid 50-30 \mid + \mid 20-10 \mid = 30$$

The Euclidean distance will always be shorter than the Manhattan distance.

Various schemes can now be adopted to calculate the distance between two clusters (see Figure 20.27). The single linkage method defines the distance between two clusters as the shortest possible distance, or the distance between the two most similar observations. The complete linkage method defines the distance between two clusters as the biggest distance, or the distance between the two most dissimilar objects. The average linkage method calculates the average of all possible distances. The centroid method calculates the distance between the centroids of both clusters.

To decide upon the optimal number of clusters, one could use a **dendrogram**. A dendrogram is a tree-like diagram that records the sequences of merges. The vertical (or horizontal) scale then gives the distance between two amalgamated clusters. One can then cut the dendrogram at the desired level to find the optimal clustering. This is illustrated in Figure 20.28 and Figure 20.29 for a birds clustering example.

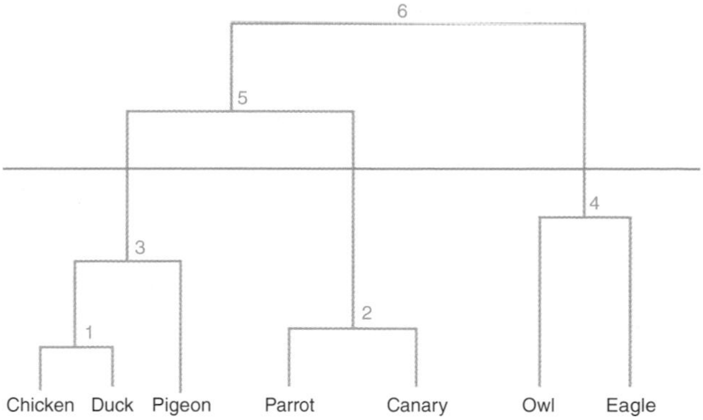


**Figure 20.29** Dendrogram for the birds example. The horizontal line indicates the optimal clustering.

A key advantage of hierarchical clustering is that the number of clusters need not be specified prior to the analysis. A disadvantage is that the methods do not scale well to large datasets. Also, interpreting the clusters is often subjective and depends upon the business expert and/or data scientist.

*K-means Clustering*

**K-means clustering** is a non-hierarchical procedure that works along these steps:

1. Select *K* observations as the initial cluster centroids (seeds).
2. Assign each observation to the cluster that has the closest centroid (for example, in the Euclidean sense).
3. When all observations have been assigned, recalculate the positions of the *K* centroids.
4. Repeat until the cluster centroids no longer change.

A key requirement here is that the number of clusters, *K*, needs to be specified before the start of the analysis. It is also advised to try out different seeds to verify the stability of the clustering solution. This decision can be made using expert-based input or based on the result of another (e.g., hierarchical) clustering procedure. Typically, multiple values of *K* are tried out and the resulting clusters are evaluated in their statistical characteristics and interpretation.

### 20.5.4 Social Network Analytics

In recent decades, the use of social media websites in everybody's daily life is booming. People can continue their conversations on social networking sites like Facebook, Twitter, LinkedIn, Google+, Instagram, etc., and share their experiences with their acquaintances, friends, family, etc. It takes only one click to update your whereabouts to the rest of the world. There are plenty of options to broadcast your current activities: by picture, video, geo-location, links, or just plain text.

Users of online social networking sites explicitly reveal their relationships with other people. Consequently, social networking sites are a nearly perfect mapping of the relationships that exist in the real world. They know who you are, what your hobbies and interests are, to whom you are married, how many children you have, your buddies with whom you run every week, your friends at the wine club, etc. This massive interconnected network of people knowing each other in some way is an interesting source of information and knowledge. Marketing managers no longer need to guess who might influence whom to create the appropriate campaign. It is all there – which is the problem. Social networking sites acknowledge the richness of the data sources they have, and are not willing to share them free of charge. Those data are often privatized and regulated, and well hidden from commercial use. On the other hand, social networking sites offer many built-in facilities to managers and other interested parties to launch and manage their marketing campaigns by exploiting the social network, without publishing the exact network representation.

However, companies often forget that they can reconstruct a portion of the social network using in-house data. Telecommunication providers, for example, have a massive transactional database in which they record call behavior of their customers. Under the assumption that good friends call each other more often, we can recreate the network and indicate the tie strength between people based on the frequency and/or duration of calls. Internet infrastructure providers might map the relationships between people using their customers' IP addresses. IP addresses that frequently communicate are represented by a stronger relationship. In the end, the IP network will envisage the relational structure between people from another point of view, but to a certain extent, as observed in reality. Many more examples can be found in the banking, retail, and online gaming industries. In this section, we discuss how social networks can be leveraged for analytics.

#### 20.5.4.1 Social Network Definitions

A **social network** consists of both nodes (vertices) and edges. Both must be clearly defined at the outset of the analysis. A **node** (vertex) could be defined as a customer (private/professional), household/family, patient, doctor, paper, author, terrorist, webpage, etc. An **edge** can be defined as a "friends" relationship, a call, transmission of a disease, a "follows" relationship, a reference, etc. The edges can also be weighted based upon interaction frequency, importance of information exchange, intimacy, emotional intensity, and so on. For example, in a churn prediction setting, the edge can be weighted according to the (total) time two customers called each other during a specific period. Social networks can be represented as a **sociogram**. This is illustrated in Figure 20.30, where the color of the nodes corresponds to a specific status (e.g., churner or non-churner).

Sociograms are useful for representing small-scale networks. For larger-scale networks, the network is typically represented as a matrix (Table 20.11). These matrices will be symmetrical and typically very sparse (with lots of zeros).[11] The matrix can also contain the weights if weighted connections occur.

#### 20.5.4.2 Social Network Metrics

A social network can be characterized by various **centrality metrics**. The most important centrality measures are depicted in Table 20.12. Assume a network with $g$ nodes $N_i, i = 1, \ldots, g$. $g_{jk}$ represents the number of geodesics from node $N_j$ to node $N_k$, whereas $g_{jk}(N_i)$ represents the number of geodesics from node $N_j$ to node $N_k$, passing through node $N_i$. The formulas each time calculate the metric for node $N_i$.

[11] This is only the case for undirected networks. For directed networks, representing, e.g., a "follows" relationship that is not necessarily reciprocal, the matrix will not be symmetrical.

**Table 20.11** Matrix representation of a social network

| | C1 | C2 | C3 | C4 |
|---|---|---|---|---|
| **C1** | – | 1 | 1 | 0 |
| **C2** | 1 | – | 0 | 1 |
| **C3** | 1 | 0 | – | 0 |
| **C4** | 0 | 1 | 0 | – |

**Table 20.12** Network centrality measures

| | | |
|---|---|---|
| Geodesic | Shortest path between two nodes in the network. | |
| Degree | Number of connections of a node (in- versus out-degree if the connections are directed). | |
| Closeness | The average distance of a node to all other nodes in the network (reciprocal of farness). | $\left[\frac{\sum_{j=1}^{g} d(N_i,N_j)}{g}\right]^{-1}$ |
| Betweenness | Counts the number of times a node or edge lies on the shortest path between any two nodes in the network. | $\sum_{j<k} \frac{g_{jk}(N_i)}{g_{jk}}$ |
| Graph theoretic center | The node with the smallest maximum distance to all other nodes in the network. | |

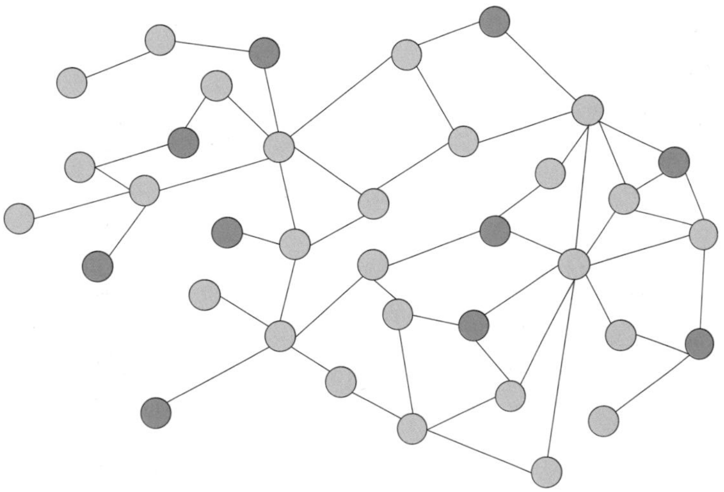

**Figure 20.30** Example sociogram.

These metrics can now be illustrated with the Kite network toy example depicted in Figure 20.31.[12]

Table 20.13 reports the centrality measures for the Kite network. Based on degree, Diane is most central since she has the most connections. She works as a connector, or hub. Note, however, that

[12] Krackhardt, D., Assessing the political landscape: Structure, cognition, and power in organizations, *Administrative Science Quarterly*, 1990; 35: 342–369.

**Table 20.13** Centrality measures for the Kite network

| Degree | | Closeness | | Betweenness | |
|---|---|---|---|---|---|
| 6 | Diane | 0.64 | Fernando | 14 | Heather |
| 5 | Fernando | 0.64 | Garth | 8.33 | Fernando |
| 5 | Garth | 0.6 | Diane | 8.33 | Garth |
| 4 | Andre | 0.6 | Heather | 8 | Ike |
| 4 | Beverly | 0.53 | Andre | 3.67 | Diane |
| 3 | Carol | 0.53 | Beverly | 0.83 | Andre |
| 3 | Ed | 0.5 | Carol | 0.83 | Beverly |
| 3 | Heather | 0.5 | Ed | 0 | Carol |
| 2 | Ike | 0.43 | Ike | 0 | Ed |
| 1 | Jane | 0.31 | Jane | 0 | Jane |

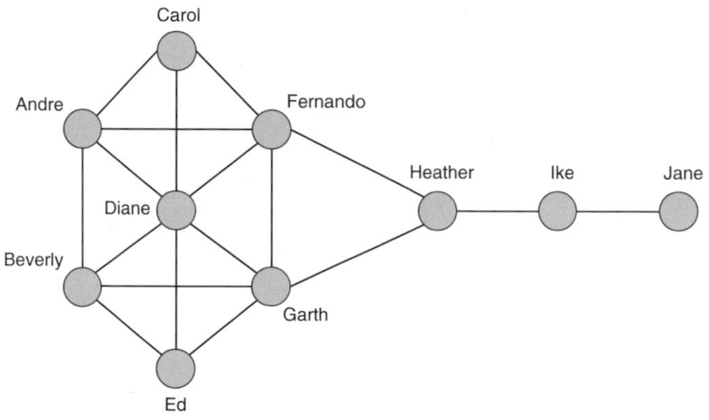


**Figure 20.31** The Kite network.

she only connects those already connected to each other. Fernando and Garth are the closest to all others. They are the best positioned to communicate messages that must flow quickly through to all other nodes in the network. Heather has the highest betweenness. She sits between two important communities (Ike and Jane versus the rest). She plays a broker role between both communities, but is also a single point of failure. Note that the betweenness measure is often used for community mining. A popular technique here is the Girvan–Newman algorithm, which works as follows:[13]

1. The betweenness of all existing edges in the network is calculated first.[14]
2. The edge with the highest betweenness is removed.
3. The betweenness of all edges affected by the removal is recalculated.
4. Steps 2 and 3 are repeated until no edges remain.

The result is essentially a dendrogram, which can then be used to decide upon the optimal number of communities.

[13] Girvan M., Newman M.E.J., Community structure in social and biological networks, *Proceedings of the National Academy of Sciences, USA*, 2002; 99: 821–826.

[14] The betweenness can be calculated for both nodes and edges.

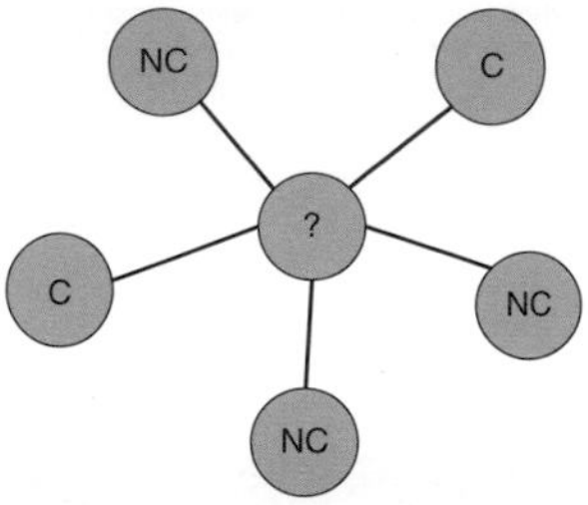


| Customer | Age | Income | ... | Mode link | Frequency no churn | Frequency churn | Binary no churn | Binary churn |
|---|---|---|---|---|---|---|---|---|
| Bart | 38 | 2400 | | NC | 3 | 2 | 1 | 1 |

**Figure 20.32** Relational logistic regression.

### 20.5.4.3 Social Network Learning

In **social network learning**, the goal is to compute the class membership probability (e.g., churn probability) of a specific node, given the status of the other nodes in the network. Various important challenges arise when learning in social networks. A key challenge is that the data are not independent and identically distributed (IID), an assumption often made in classical statistical models (e.g., linear and logistic regression). The correlational behavior between nodes implies that the class membership of one node might influence the class membership of a related node. Next, it is not easy to come up with a split into a training set for model development and a test set for model validation, since the whole network is interconnected and cannot just be cut into two parts. Many networks are huge in scale (e.g., a call graph from a telecom provider), and efficient computational procedures need to be developed to do the learning. Finally, one should not forget the traditional way of doing analytics using only node-specific information (i.e., without the network aspects), since this can still be very valuable information for prediction as well.

A straightforward way to leverage social networks for analytics is by summarizing the network in a set of features that can then be combined with local characteristics (i.e., non-network characteristics) for predictive modeling. A popular example of this is relational logistic regression as introduced by Lu and Getoor.[15] This approach basically starts off from a dataset with local node-specific characteristics and adds network features to it as follows:

- most frequently occurring class of neighbor (mode-link);
- frequency of the classes of the neighbors (frequency-link);
- binary indicators indicating class presence (binary-link).

This is illustrated in Figure 20.32 for customer Bart.

A logistic regression model is then estimated using the dataset with both local and network characteristics. There is some correlation between the network characteristics added, which should be filtered out during an input selection

**Retention Questions**

- What is the difference between predictive and descriptive analytics?
- Contrast linear regression versus logistic regression versus decision trees.
- How can predictive models be evaluated?
- What are the different types of descriptive analytics?
- Give some examples of social network analytics.

[15] Lu Q., Getoor L., Link-based classification, *Proceeding of the Twentieth Conference on Machine Learning (ICML-2003)*, Washington DC, 2003.

| Customer | Age | Recency | Number of contacts | Contacts with churners | Churn |
|---|---|---|---|---|---|
| John | 35 | 5 | 18 | 3 | Yes |
| Sophie | 18 | 10 | 7 | 1 | No |
| Victor | 38 | 28 | 11 | 1 | No |
| Laura | 44 | 12 | 9 | 0 | Yes |

**Figure 20.33** Example of featurization with features describing target behavior of neighbors.

| Customer | Age | Avg duration | Avg revenue | Promotions | Avg age friends | Avg duration friends | Avg revenue friends | Promotions friends | Churn |
|---|---|---|---|---|---|---|---|---|---|
| John | 35 | 50 | 123 | X | 20 | 55 | 250 | X | Yes |
| Sophie | 18 | 65 | 55 | Y | 18 | 44 | 66 | Y | No |
| Victor | 38 | 12 | 85 | None | 50 | 33 | 50 | X, Y | No |
| Laura | 44 | 66 | 230 | X | 65 | 55 | 189 | X | No |

**Figure 20.34** Example of featurization with features describing local node behavior of neighbors.

procedure. Creating network features is also called **featurization**, since the network characteristics are basically added as special features to the dataset. These features can measure the behavior of the neighbors in terms of the target variable (e.g., churn or not) or in terms of the local node-specific characteristics (e.g., age, promotions, etc.). Figure 20.33 provides an example in which a feature is added, describing the number of contacts with churners. The final column labeled "Churn" is the target variable. Figure 20.34 provides an example in which features are added describing the local node behavior of the neighbors.

## 20.6 Post-Processing of Analytical Models

The analytical process is concluded with the post-processing step. The first key activity of post-processing is the interpretation and validation of the analytical model by the business experts. Analytical models will detect both trivial or known patterns, and unexpected, unknown, potentially interesting patterns. An example of a trivial pattern in a credit scoring setting is: customers with higher debt are more likely to default. Although this pattern is not surprising, it is a good validation of the exercise, since it would be weird – or even suspicious – if this pattern was not found. Obviously, the business expert will be especially interested in the unexpected patterns since these may represent new insights that could lead to new strategies or actions.

Sensitivity analysis should be undertaken during post-processing. The idea is to verify the robustness of the analytical model and see how sensitive it is with respect to sample characteristics, assumptions, data quality, and/or model parameters.

Once approved by the business expert, the analytical model can be deployed into a business setting. It is important to note here that the model output should be represented in a user-friendly way, so it can be easily interpreted and used. Also, the output of the analytical model should be directly fed to the business applications, such as marketing campaign management tools and fraud engines.

**Retention Questions**

- Discuss the key activities during post-processing of analytical models. Illustrate with an example.

Finally, once the model has been brought into production it should be continuously monitored and backtested. Backtesting means that the model output should be compared to actual observed or realized numbers once they are available, so it can be determined when the model starts to degrade in performance and a new analytical model needs to be built.

## 20.7 Critical Success Factors for Analytical Models

To succeed, an analytical model needs to satisfy several requirements. A first key requirement is business relevance. The analytical model should solve the business problem it was developed for! It makes no sense to have a high-performing analytical model sidetracked from the original business problem. If the business problem is detecting insurance fraud, then the analytical model must detect insurance fraud. Obviously, this requires thorough business knowledge and understanding of the problem before any analytics can start.

Another important success factor is statistical performance and validity. The analytical model should make sense statistically. It should be significant and provide good predictive or descriptive performance. Depending on the type of analytics, various performance metrics can be used. In customer segmentation, statistical evaluation measures will contrast intra-cluster similarity with inter-cluster dissimilarity. Analytical churn prediction models will be evaluated in their ability to assign high churn scores to the most likely churners.

Interpretability refers to the fact that the analytical model should be comprehensible or understandable to the decision-maker (e.g., marketer, fraud analyst, credit expert). Justifiability indicates that the model aligns with the expectations and business knowledge of the expert. Both interpretability and justifiability are subjective and depend on the knowledge and experience of the decision-maker. They often must be balanced against statistical performance, which implies that complex, non-interpretable models (e.g., neural networks) are often better performing in a statistical sense. In settings like credit risk modeling, interpretability and justifiability are very important because of the societal impact of these models. However, in settings like fraud detection and marketing response modeling, they are typically less of an issue.

Operational efficiency relates to the effort needed to evaluate, monitor, backtest, or rebuild the analytical model. In settings like credit card fraud detection, operational efficiency is important because a decision should be made within a few seconds after the credit card transaction is initiated. In market basket analysis, operational efficiency is less of a concern.

Economical cost refers to the cost incurred to gather the model inputs, run the model and process its outcome(s). Also, the cost of external data and/or analytical models should be considered here. This will allow calculating the economic return on the analytical model, which is typically not a straightforward exercise (see Section 20.8).

Finally, regulatory compliance is becoming more and more important. This refers to the extent to which the analytical model complies with regulation and legislation. In a credit risk modeling setting, the models should comply with the Basel II and III regulations. In an analytical insurance setting, the Solvency II accord must be respected. Also, privacy is an important issue here (see Section 20.10).

**Retention Questions**

- What are critical success factors when building an analytical model? Illustrate with an example.

## 20.8 Economic Perspective on Analytics

In this section, we zoom out and provide an economic perspective on analytics. We start by introducing total cost of ownership (TCO) and return on investment (ROI). We discuss in- versus outsourcing and on-premises versus cloud solutions. We also contrast the use of open-source versus commercial software.

### 20.8.1 Total Cost of Ownership (TCO)

The **total cost of ownership (TCO)** of an analytical model refers to the cost of owning and operating the analytical model over its expected lifetime, from inception to retirement. It should consider both quantitative and qualitative costs and is a key input to make strategic decisions about how to optimally invest in analytics. The costs involved can be decomposed into: acquisition costs, ownership and operation costs, and post-ownership costs, as illustrated with some examples in Table 20.14.

TCO analysis tries to involve a comprehensive view of all costs. From an economic perspective, this should also include the timing of the costs through proper discounting using the weighted average cost of capital (WACC) as the discount factor. It should help identify any potential hidden and/or sunk costs. In many analytical projects, the combined cost of hardware and software is subordinate to the people cost that comes with the development and usage of the models, such as training, employment, and management costs.[16] The high share of personnel cost can be attributed to three phenomena: an increase in the number of data scientists; a greater use of open-source tools (see Section 20.8.5); and cheaper data storage and sharing solutions.

TCO analysis pinpoints cost problems before they become material. For example, the change management costs to migrate from a legacy model to a new analytical model are often largely underestimated. TCO analysis is a key input for strategic decisions, such as vendor selection, in- versus outsourcing, on premises versus cloud solutions, overall budgeting, and capital calculation. When making these investment decisions, it is also very important to include the benefits in the analysis, since TCO only considers the cost perspective.

### 20.8.2 Return on Investment

**Return on Investment** is defined as the ratio of the net benefits or net profits over the investment of resources that generated this return. The latter essentially comprises the TCO (see Section 20.8.1) and all follow-up expenses such as costs of marketing campaigns, fraud handling, bad debt collection, etc. ROI analysis is an essential input to any financial investment decision. It offers a common firm-wide language to compare multiple investment opportunities and decide which one(s) to go for.

Companies like Facebook, Amazon, Netflix, Uber, and Google continuously invest in new analytical technologies because even an incremental new insight can translate into a competitive advantage and significant profits. The Netflix competition in which Netflix provided an anonymized

[16] Lismont J., Vanthienen J., Baesens B., Lemahieu W., Defining analytics maturity indicators: A survey approach, *International Journal of Information Management*, 2017; 34(3): 114–124.

**Table 20.14** Example costs for calculating total cost of ownership (TCO)

| Acquisition costs | Ownership and operation costs | Post-ownership costs |
|---|---|---|
| • Software costs including initial purchase, upgrade, intellectual property and licensing fees<br>• Hardware costs including initial purchase price and maintenance<br>• Network and security costs<br>• Data costs including costs for purchasing external data<br>• Model developer costs such as salaries and training | • Model migration and change management costs<br>• Model set-up costs<br>• Model execution costs<br>• Model monitoring costs<br>• Support costs (troubleshooting, helpdesk, etc.)<br>• Insurance costs<br>• Model staffing costs such as salaries and training<br>• Model upgrade costs<br>• Model downtime costs | • De-installation and disposal costs<br>• Replacement costs<br>• Archiving costs |

dataset of user ratings for films, and awarded $1 million to any team of data scientists that could beat its own recommender system with at least 10% improvement in performance, is a nice illustration of this.

For traditional firms in financial services, manufacturing, healthcare, pharmaceutics, etc., the ROI of analytics may be less clear-cut and harder to determine. Although the cost component is usually not that difficult to approximate, the benefits are much harder to quantify precisely. One reason is that the benefits may be spread over time (short term, medium term, long term) and across the various business units of the organization. Examples of benefits of analytical models are:

- increase of sales (e.g., because of a response modeling or up-/cross-selling campaign);
- lower fraud losses (e.g., because of a fraud detection model);
- fewer credit defaults (e.g., because of a credit scoring model);
- identification of new customer needs and opportunities (e.g., because of a customer segmentation model);
- automation or enhancement of human decision-making (e.g., because of a recommender system);
- development of new business models (e.g., because of data poolers that gather data and sell the results of analyses).

When it comes to altering human behavior, the benefits are less compelling and harder to quantify. Many analytical models yield intangible benefits that are hard to include, yet substantial, in an ROI analysis. Think about social networks. Analytically modeling word-of-mouth effects (e.g., in a churn or response setting) can have material economic impacts, but the precise value thereof is hard to quantify. The benefits may also be spread across multiple products and channels, and in time. Think about a response model for mortgages. The effect of successfully attracting a mortgage customer could create cross-selling effects toward other bank products (e.g., checking account, credit card, insurance). Since a mortgage is a long-term engagement, the partnership may be further deepened in time, contributing to the customer's lifetime value. Untangling all these profit contributions is a challenging task, complicating the calculation of the ROI of the original mortgage response model.

**Drill Down**

A vast majority of the implementations of Big Data and analytics have reported significant returns. A study by Nucleus Research in 2014 found that organizations from various industries obtained returns of $13.01 for every dollar invested, which increased from $10.66 in 2011.[17] PredictiveanalyticsToday.com conducted a poll from February 2015 to March 2015 with 96 valid responses.[18] The results are displayed in Figure 20.35. From the pie chart, it can be concluded that only a minority (10%) reported no ROI of Big Data and analytics. Other studies have also reported strong positive returns, although the ranges typically vary.

Critical voices have been heard questioning positive returns of investing in Big Data and analytics. The reasons often boil down to the lack of good-quality data, management support, and a company-wide data-driven decision culture as we discuss in Section 20.9.

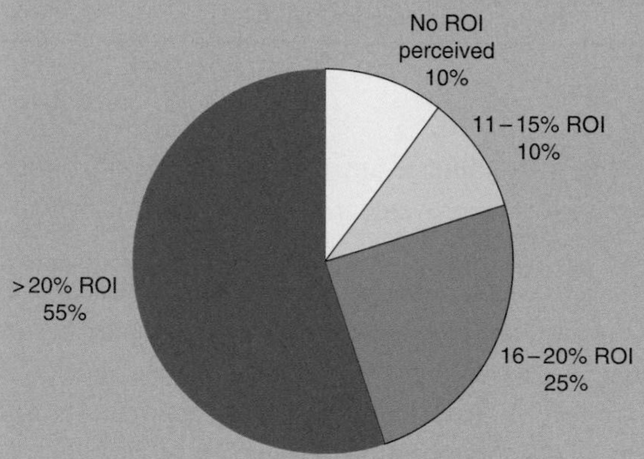


**Figure 20.35** ROI of analytics.

## 20.8.3 In- versus Outsourcing

The growing interest and need for analytics, combined with the shortage of skilled talent and data scientists in Western Europe and the USA, has triggered the question of outsourcing analytical activities. This need is further amplified by competitive pressure on reduced time-to-market and lower costs. Companies need to choose between **insourcing**, building the analytical skillset internally at the corporate or business-line level, **outsourcing** all analytical activities, or going for an intermediate solution in which only part of the analytical activities is outsourced. The dominant players in the outsourcing analytics market are India, China, and Eastern Europe, with some other countries (e.g., Philippines, Russia, South Africa) gaining ground.

Various analytical activities can be considered for outsourcing, ranging from the heavy-lifting grunt work (data collection, cleaning, and pre-processing), setting up of analytical platforms (hardware and software), training and education, to the more complex analytical model development, visualization, evaluation, monitoring, and maintenance. Companies may grow conservatively and start by outsourcing the analytical activities step by step, or immediately go for the full package

[17] http://nucleusresearch.com/research/single/analytics-pays-back-13-01-for-every-dollar-spent/
[18] www.predictiveanalyticstoday.com/return-of-investment-from-predictive-analytics/

of analytical services. It speaks for itself that the latter strategy has more risk associated with it and should be more carefully and critically evaluated.

Despite the benefits of outsourcing analytics, it should be approached with a clear strategic vision and critical reflection with awareness of all risks involved. First, the difference between outsourcing analytics and traditional ICT services is that analytics concerns a company's front-end strategy, whereas many ICT services are part of a company's back-end operations. Another important risk is the exchange of confidential information. Intellectual property (IP) rights and data security issues should be investigated, addressed, and agreed upon. All companies have access to the same analytical techniques, so they are only differentiated by the data they provide. Hence, an outsource service provider should provide clear guidelines and guarantees about how intellectual property and data are managed and protected (e.g., encryption techniques, firewalls, etc.), especially if it also collaborates with other companies in the same industry sector. Another important risk is the continuity of the partnership. Offshore outsourcing service providers are often subject to mergers and acquisitions, sometimes with other companies collaborating with the competition, diluting any competitive advantage. Many of these companies face high employee turnover rates due to intensive work schedules, the boredom of performing low-level data pre-processing activities daily, and aggressive headhunters chasing hard to find data science profiles. This attrition problem inhibits a long-term thorough understanding of a customer's analytical business processes and needs. Another often-cited complexity is a cultural mismatch (e.g., time management, time difference, different languages, local versus global issues) between the buyer and outsource service provider. Exit strategies should be clearly agreed upon in advance. Many analytical outsourcing contracts have a maturity of 3–4 years. When these contracts expire, it should be stipulated how the analytical models and knowledge can be transferred to the buyer to ensure business continuity. Finally, the shortage of data scientists in the USA and Western Europe also applies, and might even be worse, in the countries providing outsourcing services. These countries typically have universities with good statistical education and training programs, but their graduates lack the business skills, insights, and experience to contribute with analytics.

Given the above considerations, many firms are critical of outsourcing and prefer to keep all analytics in-house. Others adopt a partial outsourcing strategy, where baseline, operational analytical activities, such as query and reporting, multidimensional data analysis, and OLAP are outsourced, and the advanced descriptive and predictive analytical skills are developed and managed internally.

### 20.8.4 On-Premises versus Cloud Solutions

Most firms developed their first analytical models using on-premises architectures, platforms, and solutions. However, given the significant amount of investment in installing, configuring, upgrading, and maintaining these environments, many companies are looking at **cloud-based solutions** for analytics as a budget-friendly alternative to further boost the ROI. In what follows, we elaborate on the cost and other implications of deploying analytics in the cloud.

> **Connections**
>
> A more general discussion on data in the cloud and different "As a Service" configurations was already provided in Chapter 18.

An often-cited advantage of **on-premises analytics** is that you keep your data in-house, giving you better security and full control. However, this is a double-edged sword because it requires firms to continually invest in high-end security solutions to thwart data breach attacks by hackers, which are becoming ever more sophisticated. It is because of this security concern that many companies start looking at the cloud. Another driver is the scalability and economies of scale offered by cloud providers because they pledge to provide customers with state-of-the-art platforms and software solutions. The computation power needed can be tailored specifically to the customer, whether it is a Fortune 500 firm or an SME. More capacity (e.g., servers) can be added on the fly, whenever needed. On-premises solutions need to carefully anticipate the computational resources needed and invest accordingly; the risk of over- or under-investment significantly jeopardizes the ROI of analytical projects. In other words, up- or downsizing on-premises systems is much more expensive and time-consuming.

Another key advantage relates to the maintenance of the analytical environment. Average on-premises maintenance cycles typically range around 18 months. These can get costly and create business continuity problems because of backward compatibility issues, new features added, old features removed, new integration efforts needed, etc. When using cloud-based solutions, these issues are taken care of, and maintenance or upgrade projects may even go unnoticed.

The low-footprint access to analytical platforms will also positively affect the time to value and accessibility. There is no need to set up expensive infrastructure (e.g., hardware, operating systems, NoSQL databases, analytical solutions), upload and clean data, integrate data, etc. Using the cloud, everything is readily accessible. It lowers the entry barrier to experiment with analytics, try out new approaches and models, and combine various data sources in a transparent way. This contributes to the economic value of analytical modeling and facilitates serendipitous discovery of interesting patterns.

Cloud-based solutions catalyze improved collaboration across business departments and geographical locations. Many on-premises systems are loosely coupled, or not integrated at all, inhibiting any firm-wide sharing of experiences, insights, and findings. The resulting duplication efforts negatively affect the ROI at the corporate level.

Cloud-based solutions have a substantial impact in terms of TCO and ROI of your analytical projects. However, as with any new technology, it is advised to approach them with a thoughtful strategic vision and the necessary caution. One risk to be considered is vendor lock-in, where a company becomes highly dependent upon a specific cloud vendor. Some firms adopt a mixed approach by gently migrating some of their analytical models to the cloud to get their toes wet and see the potential pros and cons of this technology. It can, however, be expected that given the many advantages offered, cloud-based analytics will continue to grow.

**Drill Down**

Amazon Web Services (Amazon WS) is a popular example of a cloud solution for Big Data and analytics. It offers hosted relational databases (e.g., MySQL, Oracle, SQL Server), a NoSQL database (Amazon DynamoDB), a data warehousing platform (Amazon Redshift), a Hadoop/MapReduce environment (Amazon Elastic MapReduce), and a machine learning solution (Amazon Machine Learning) supporting various analytical techniques.

### 20.8.5 Open-Source versus Commercial Software

The popularity of open-source analytical software, such as R and Python, has sparked the debate about the added value of commercial tools such as SAS, SPSS, MATLAB, etc. Both commercial and open-source software have their merits, which should be evaluated before any software investment decision is made.

First, the key advantage of open-source software is that it is available for free, which lowers the entry barrier for use. This may be especially relevant to smaller firms who wish to kick-off with analytics without making big investments. However, this poses a danger as well, since anyone can contribute to open-source software without any quality assurance or extensive prior testing. In heavily regulated environments, such as credit risk (the Basel Accord), insurance (the Solvency Accord), and pharmaceuticals (FDA regulation), the analytical models are subject to external supervisory review because of their strategic impact on society, which is bigger than ever before. Therefore, in these settings, many firms prefer to rely on mature commercial solutions that have been thoroughly engineered and extensively tested, validated, and completely documented. Many solutions also include automatic reporting facilities to generate compliant reports in each setting mentioned. Open-source software solutions may come without any kind of quality control or warranty, which increases the risk of using them in regulated environments.

Another key advantage of commercial solutions is that the software offered is no longer centered around dedicated analytical workbenches for data pre-processing, data mining, etc., but on well-engineered business-focused solutions that automate the end-to-end activities. As an example, consider credit risk analytics, which start from framing the business problem to data pre-processing, analytical model development, model monitoring, stress testing, and regulatory capital calculation. To automate this entire chain of activities using open-source options would require various scripts, likely originating from heterogeneous sources, to be matched and connected, resulting in a melting pot of software in which the overall functionality can become unstable and unclear.

Contrary to most open-source software, commercial software vendors also offer extensive help facilities such as FAQs, technical support lines, newsletters, professional training courses, etc. Another key advantage of commercial software vendors is business continuity. The availability of centralized R&D teams (as opposed to worldwide loosely connected open-source developers) that closely follow-up on new analytical and regulatory developments provides a better guarantee that new software upgrades will provide the facilities required. In an open-source environment, you must rely on the community to voluntarily contribute, which provides less of a guarantee.

A disadvantage of commercial software is that it usually comes in prepackaged, black box routines which, although extensively tested and documented, cannot be inspected by the more sophisticated data scientist. This contrasts with open-source solutions, which provide full access to the source code of each of the scripts contributed.

Both commercial and open-source software have their strengths and weaknesses. It is likely that both will continue to coexist, and interfaces should be provided for both to collaborate as is the case for SAS and R/Python.

**Retention Questions**

- What are the key components of TCO and ROI?
- Contrast the following:
  - in- versus outsourcing;
  - on-premises versus cloud solutions;
  - open-source versus commercial software.

**Drill Down**

In 2016, the well-known analytics portal site KDnuggets (www.kdnuggets.com) conducted a poll on analytics software, asking the following question:[19]

What software have you used for Analytics, Data Mining, Data Science, Machine Learning projects in the past 12 months?

[19] www.kdnuggets.com/2016/06/r-python-top-analytics-data-mining-data-science-software.html

The poll was answered by 2895 voters. The results are displayed in the table.

| Tool | 2016 percentage share | percentage change |
|---|---|---|
| R | 49% | +4.5% |
| Python | 45.8% | +51% |
| SQL | 35.5% | +15% |
| Excel | 33.6% | +47% |
| RapidMiner | 32.6% | +3.5% |
| Hadoop | 22.1% | +20% |
| Spark | 21.6% | +91% |
| Tableau | 18.5% | +49% |
| KNIME | 18.0% | –10% |
| scikit-learn | 17.2% | +107% |

From the table, it can be concluded that both open-source packages R and Python are most popular, with Python growing especially quickly. Surprisingly, SQL and Excel rank third and fourth, which clearly illustrates their impact. About 25% of the respondents used only commercial software, whereas 13% used only open-source software. A majority (61%) used both free and commercial software.

## 20.9 Improving the ROI of Analytics

### 20.9.1 New Sources of Data

The ROI of an analytical model is directly related to its predictive and/or statistical power. The better it can predict or describe customer behavior, the better the effectiveness of the resulting actions. One way to boost this is by investing in new sources of data that can help to further unravel complex customer behavior and improve key analytical insights. In what follows, we briefly explore various types of data sources that could be worthwhile to pursue to squeeze more economic value out of analytical models.

One option is the exploration of network data by carefully studying relationships between customers. These relationships can be explicit or implicit. Examples of explicit networks are calls between customers, shared board members between firms, and social connections (e.g., family, friends, etc.). Explicit networks can be readily distilled from underlying data sources (e.g., call logs) and their key characteristics can then be summarized using featurization procedures as discussed in Section 20.5.4.3. In our previous research, we found network data to be highly predictive for both customer churn prediction and fraud detection.[20] Implicit networks, or pseudo-networks, are networks that are not based upon explicit ties and are more challenging to define and featurize. Martens and Provost built a network of customers where links were defined based upon which customers transferred money to the same entities (e.g., retailers) using

[20] Verbeke W., Martens D., Baesens B., Social network analysis for customer churn prediction, *Applied Soft Computing*, 2014; 14: 341–446, 2014. Baesens B., Verbeke W., Van Vlasselaer V., *Fraud Analytics Using Descriptive, Predictive and Social Network Techniques: A Guide to Data Science for Fraud Detection*, Wiley, 2015.

data from a major bank.[21] When combined with non-network data, this innovative way of defining a network based upon similarity instead of explicit social connections gave a better lift and profit for almost any targeting budget. In another, award-winning study they built a geosimilarity network among users based upon location-visitation data in a mobile environment.[22] Two devices are considered similar, and thus connected, when they share at least one visited location. They are more similar if they have more shared locations and if these are visited by fewer people. This implicit network can then be leveraged to target advertisements to the same user on different devices or to users with similar tastes, or to improve online interactions by selecting users with similar tastes. Both examples illustrate the potential of implicit networks as an important data source. A key challenge here is to think creatively about how to define these networks based upon the goal of the analysis. Recall our discussion in Chapter 11 on various NoSQL niche databases, geared specifically toward storing and querying special types of data or structures. For network structured data, we have seen how graph databases are becoming increasingly important, since they do away with traditional RDBMS-based relational structures and allow users to express densely connected structures directly as a graph. Such databases offer advantages for performing analytics, since they often allow for fast and easy querying of graphs, with applications as mentioned above in marketing analytics and fraud analytics, among others. An interesting and eye-catching recent example of graph databases being applied in analytics combines text analytics (text is, by nature, unstructured data) with Neo4j (a popular graph database) to analyze links between companies, documents, and persons contained in the Panama Papers, the 11 million leaked documents that contained detailed financial information of offshore entities.

**Connections**

Graph databases were discussed in Chapter 11.

Data are often branded as the new oil. Data-pooling firms capitalize on this by gathering various types of data, analyzing it in innovative and creative ways, and selling the results. Popular examples are Equifax, Experian, Moody's, S&P, Nielsen, Dun & Bradstreet, etc. These firms consolidate publicly available data, data scraped from websites or social media, survey data, and data contributed by other firms. By doing so, they can perform a variety of aggregated analyses (e.g., geographical distribution of credit default rates in a country, average churn rates across industry sectors), build generic scores (e.g., the FICO score in the USA – see below) and sell these to interested parties. Because of the low entry barrier in terms of investment, externally purchased analytical models are sometimes adopted by smaller firms to take their first steps in analytics. In addition to commercially available external data, open data can also be a valuable source of external information. Examples are industry and government data, weather data, news data, and search data. As an example of the latter, Google Trends data have been used to predict unemployment and flu outbreaks. It has been empirically shown that both commercial and open external data can boost the performance and economic return of an analytical model.

Macroeconomic data are another valuable source of information. Many analytical models are developed using a snapshot of data at a specific moment in time. This is conditional on the external environment at that moment. Macroeconomic up- or down-turns can have a significant impact on the performance, and thus ROI, of the model. The state of the macro-economy can be summarized

[21] Martens D., Provost F., Mining massive fine-grained behavior data to improve predictive analytics, *MIS Quarterly*, 2016; 40(4): 869–888.

[22] Provost F., Martens D., Murray A., Finding similar mobile consumers with a privacy-friendly geosocial design, *Information Systems Research*, 2015; 26(2): 243–265.

using measures such as gross domestic product (GDP), inflation, and unemployment. Incorporating these effects will further improve the performance of analytical models and make them more robust against external influences.

Textual data are also an interesting type of data to consider. Examples are product reviews, Facebook posts, Twitter tweets, book recommendations, complaints, legislation, etc. Textual data are difficult to process analytically since they are unstructured and cannot be directly represented in a table or matrix format. Moreover, they depend upon the linguistic structure (e.g., type of language, relationship between words, negations, etc.) and are typically quite noisy data due to grammatical or spelling errors, synonyms, and homographs. However, these data can contain relevant information for your analytical modeling exercise. Just as with network data, it will be important to find ways to featurize text documents and combine them with your other structured data. A popular way of doing this is by using a document term matrix indicating what terms (similar to variables) appear and how frequently in which documents (similar to observations). This matrix will be large and sparse. Dimension reduction tries to make this matrix more compact by conducting these activities:

- represent every term in lower case (e.g., PRODUCT, Product, and product become product);
- remove terms that are uninformative, such as stop words and articles (e.g., "the product", "a product", and "this product" become product);
- use synonym lists to map synonym terms to one single term (product, item, and article become product);
- stem all terms to their root (products and product become product);
- remove terms that only occur in a single document.

Even after the above activities have been performed, the number of dimensions may still be too big for practical analysis. Singular value decomposition (SVD) offers a more advanced means to do dimension reduction.[23] It essentially summarizes the document term matrix into a set of singular vectors, also called latent concepts, that are linear combinations of the original terms. These reduced dimensions can then be added as new features to your existing, structured dataset.

Besides textual data, other types of unstructured data, such as audio, images, videos, fingerprint, location (GPS), geospatial, and RFID data can be considered as well. To leverage these data in your analytical models, it is of key importance to think carefully about creative ways of featurizing it. When doing so, it is recommended to consider any accompanying metadata. For example, not only the image itself might be relevant, but also who took it, where, at what time, etc. This information could be very useful for fraud detection, for example.

**Drill Down**

In the USA, three popular credit bureaus are Experian, Equifax, and TransUnion, which each cover their own geographical region. All three provide a FICO credit score that ranges between 300 and 850, with higher scores reflecting better credit quality. A FICO score essentially relies on the following five data sources to determine creditworthiness:

[23] Meyer C.D., Matrix analysis and applied linear algebra, SIAM, Philadelphia, 2000.

**Payment history**: Has the customer any delinquency history? This accounts for 35% of the FICO score.
**Amount of current debt**: How much credit does the customer have in total? This accounts for 30% of the FICO score.
**Length of credit history**: How long has the customer been using credit? This accounts for 15% of the FICO score.
**Types of credit in use**: What kind of loans does the customer have (e.g., credit cards, installment loans, mortgage)? This accounts for 10% of the FICO score.
**Pursuit of new credit**: How much new credit is the customer applying for? This accounts for 10% of the FICO score.

These FICO scores are commonly used in the USA, not only by banks, but also by insurance providers, telco firms, landlords, utilities companies, etc.

### 20.9.2 Data Quality

**Connections**

In Chapters 4 and 18 we defined data quality as "fitness for use" and discussed the underlying dimensions.

Besides volume and variety, the veracity of the data is also a critical success factor in generating a competitive advantage and economic value from data. Quality of data is key to the success of any analytical exercise as it has a direct and measurable impact on the quality of the analytical model and hence its economic value. The importance of data quality is nicely captured by the well-known *GIGO* or *garbage in garbage out* principle introduced before: bad data yield bad analytical models.

Most organizations are learning of the importance of data quality and are looking at ways to improve it. However, this often turns out to be harder than expected, more costly than budgeted, and definitely not a one-off project, but a continuous challenge. The causes of data quality issues are often deeply rooted within the core organizational processes and culture, and the IT infrastructure and architecture. Whereas only data scientists are often directly confronted with the consequences of poor data quality, resolving these issues, and more importantly their causes, typically requires cooperation and commitment from almost every level and department within the organization. It most definitely requires support and sponsorship from senior executive management to increase awareness and set up data governance programs that tackle data quality in a sustainable and effective manner, as well as to create incentives for everyone in the organization to take their responsibilities seriously.

Data pre-processing activities such as handling missing values, duplicate data, or outliers are corrective measures for dealing with data quality issues. However, these are short-term remedies with relatively low costs and moderate returns. Data scientists must keep applying these fixes until the root causes of the issues are resolved in a structural way. To avoid this, data quality programs need to be developed that aim at detecting the key problems. This will include a thorough investigation of where the problems originate, to find and resolve them at their very origin by introducing preventive actions to complement corrective measures. This obviously requires more substantial investments and a strong belief in the added value and return thereof. Ideally, a data governance program should be put in place assigning clear roles and responsibilities regarding data quality. Two roles essential in rolling out such a program are data stewards and data owners. Though we already extensively discussed both profiles in Chapter 4, we briefly refresh here. Data stewards are the data quality experts who oversee assessing data quality by performing extensive and regular data quality checks. They initiate remedial actions whenever needed. Data stewards, however, are not in charge of correcting the data themselves. This is the task of the data owner. Every data field in every database of the organization should be owned by a data owner, who can enter or update its value. Data stewards can request data owners to check or complete the value of a field, therefore correcting the issue. A transparent and well-defined collaboration between data stewards and data owners is key to improving data quality in a sustainable manner, and as such to the long-term ROI in analytics!

### 20.9.3 Management Support

To capitalize on Big Data and analytics, it should conquer a seat in the board of directors. This can be achieved in various ways. Either an existing chief-level executive (e.g., the CIO) takes the responsibility or a new CXO function is defined, such as chief analytics officer (CAO) or chief data officer (CDO). To guarantee maximum independence and organizational impact, it is important that the latter directly reports to the CEO instead of another C-level executive. A top-down, data-driven culture in which the CEO and his/her subordinates make decisions inspired by data combined with business acumen will catalyze a trickledown effect of data-based decision-making throughout the entire organization.

**Drill Down**

Given the surging importance of data to all organizations, not just business, many institutions are hiring chief data officers. For example, in the USA the National Institutes of Health and the state of California each have a CDO.

The board of directors and senior management should be actively involved in the analytical model building, implementation, and monitoring processes. One cannot expect them to understand all underlying technical details, but they should be responsible for sound governance of the analytical models. Without appropriate management support, analytical models are doomed to fail. Hence, the board and senior management should have a general understanding of the analytical models. They should demonstrate active involvement on an ongoing basis, assign clear responsibilities, and put into place organizational procedures and policies that will allow the proper and sound development, implementation, and monitoring of the analytical models. The outcome of the model monitoring exercise must be communicated to senior management and, if needed, accompanied by appropriate response. Obviously, this requires a careful rethinking of how to optimally embed Big Data and analytics in the organization.

### 20.9.4 Organizational Aspects

In 2010, Davenport, Harris, and Morison wrote:[24]

> There may be no single right answer to how to organize your analysts, but there are many wrong ones.

Investments in analytics only bear fruit when a company-wide data culture is in place to do something with all these new data-driven insights. If you were to put a team of data scientists in

[24] Davenport T.H., Harris J.G., Morison R., *Analytics at Work: Smarter Decisions, Better Results*, Harvard Business Review Press, 2010.

a room and feed them with data and analytical software, then the chances are small that their analytical models and insights will add economic value to the firm. One hurdle concerns the data, which are not always readily available. A well-articulated data governance program is a good starting point (see Chapter 18). Once the data are there, any data scientist can find a statistically meaningful analytical model from it. However, this does not necessarily imply that the model adds economic value, since it may not be in sync with the business objectives. And suppose it were, how do we sell it to our business people so that they understand it, trust it, and start using it in their decision-making? This implies delivering insights in a way that is easy to understand and use by representing them in simple language or intuitive graphics.

Given the corporate-wide impact of Big Data and analytics, it is important that both gradually permeate into a company's culture and decision-making processes, becoming part of a company's DNA. This requires a significant investment in awareness and trust that should be initiated top-down from the executive level, as discussed above. In other words, companies need to think thoroughly about how they embed Big Data and analytics in their organization to successfully compete using both technologies.

Lismont et al. conducted a worldwide, cross-industry survey of senior-level executives to investigate modern trends in the organization of analytics.[25] They observed various formats used by companies to organize their analytics. Two extreme approaches are centralized – where a central department of data scientists handles all analytics requests – and decentralized – where all data scientists are directly assigned to the respective business units. Most companies choose a mixed approach combining a centrally coordinated center of analytical excellence with analytics organized at the business unit level. The center of excellence provides firm-wide analytical services and implements universal guidelines in model development, model design, model implementation, model documentation, model monitoring, and privacy. Decentralized teams of 1–5 data scientists are then added to each of the business units for maximum impact. A suggested practice is to rotationally deploy the data scientists across the business units and center to foster cross-fertilization opportunities between the different teams and applications.

### 20.9.5 Cross-Fertilization

Analytics has matured differently across the various business units of an organization. Triggered by the introduction of regulatory guidelines (e.g., Basel II/III, Solvency II), many firms, especially financial institutions, have invested in analytics for risk management for quite some time now. Years of analytical experience and perfecting contributed to very sophisticated models for insurance risk, credit risk, operational risk, market risk, and fraud risk. The most advanced analytical techniques such as random forests, neural networks, and social network learning have been used in these applications. These analytical models have been complimented with powerful model monitoring frameworks and stress-testing procedures to leverage their potential.

Marketing analytics is less mature, with many firms deploying their first models for churn prediction, response modeling, or customer segmentation. These are typically based on simpler analytical techniques such as logistic regression, decision trees, or k-means clustering. Other application areas, such as HR and supply chain analytics, are starting to gain traction, though few successful case studies have been reported yet.

[25] Lismont J., Vanthienen J., Baesens B., Lemahieu W., Defining analytics maturity indicators: A survey approach, *International Journal of Information Management*, 2017; 34(3): 114–124.

**Retention Questions**

- Give examples of new sources of data that could boost the ROI of an analytical model.
- How can data quality affect the ROI of an analytical model?
- What is the impact of management support and organizational aspects on the ROI of an analytical model?
- How can cross-fertilization contribute to the ROI of analytical models?

The disparity in maturity creates a tremendous potential for cross-fertilization of model development and monitoring experiences. After all, classifying whether a customer is creditworthy or not in risk management is analytically the same as classifying a customer as a responder or not in marketing analytics, or classifying an employee as a churner or not in HR analytics. The data pre-processing issues (e.g., missing values, outliers), analytical techniques (e.g., decision trees), and evaluation measures are all similar. Only the actual variables, interpretation, and usage of the models are different. The cross-fertilization also applies to model monitoring since most challenges and approaches are essentially the same. Finally, gauging the effect of macroeconomic scenarios using stress testing (which is a common practice in credit risk analytics) could be another example of sharing useful experiences across applications.

To summarize, less mature analytical applications (e.g., marketing, HR, and supply chain analytics) can substantially benefit from many of the lessons learned by more mature applications (e.g., risk management), as such avoiding many rookie mistakes and expensive beginner traps. Hence, the importance of rotational deployment (as discussed in the previous section) to generate maximum economic value and return.

## 20.10 Privacy and Security

Privacy and security of data are important concerns when developing, implementing, using, and maintaining analytical models. There are two parties involved: the business and the data scientists. The ownership of the data is typically acquired by the business. This means that the business has a complete view of the data, how they are collected, and how it has to interpret them. Data scientists are not provided with the full dataset, but only the data that might be useful for the analytical models. It is the business that decides which data the data scientist may see and use, for how long, on which level of detail, etc. In what follows, we first overview the main points of attention with respect to privacy and security that are pertinent in any data storage and processing context. After that, we focus in more detail on tools and techniques that are relevant to an analytics setting.

### 20.10.1 Overall Considerations Regarding Privacy and Security

Privacy and security are two related concepts, but they are not synonyms. Data security can be defined as the set of policies and techniques to ensure the confidentiality, availability, and integrity of data. Data privacy refers to the fact that the parties accessing and using the data do so only in ways that comply with the agreed-upon purposes of data use in their role. These purposes can be expressed as part of a company's policy, but are also subject to legislation. In this way, several aspects of security can be considered as necessary instruments to guarantee data privacy.

More concretely, data security pertains to the following concerns:

- *Guaranteeing data integrity*: Preventing data loss or data corruption as a consequence of malicious or accidental modification or deletion of data. Here, the replication and recovery facilities of the DBMS play important roles. These were discussed in detail in Chapters 13, 14, and, for a distributed setting, Chapter 16.

- *Guaranteeing data availability*: Ensuring that the data are accessible to all authorized users and applications, even in the occurrence of partial system malfunctions. This was discussed in the context of enterprise storage subsystems and business continuity in Chapter 13.
- *Authentication and access control*: Access control refers to the tools and formats to express which users and applications have which type of access (read, add, modify, etc.) to which data. Relevant techniques here are *SQL privileges* and *views*, both discussed in Chapter 7. We also deal with access control in more detail in Section 20.10.3. An important condition for adequate access control is the availability of *authentication* techniques, which allow for unambiguously identifying the user or user category for which the access rights are to be established. The most widespread technique here is still the combination of a user ID and password, although several other approaches are gaining ground, such as fingerprint readers or iris scanning.
- *Guaranteeing confidentiality*: This is the flipside of access control, guaranteeing that users and other parties cannot read or manipulate data to which they have no appropriate access rights. This is the data security concern most closely related to privacy. One possible technique here, especially in the context of analytics, is *anonymization*, as discussed in Section 20.10.3.1. Another important tool is *encryption*, rendering data unreadable to unauthorized users that do not possess the appropriate key to decrypt the data back into a readable format.
- *Auditing*: Especially in heavily regulated settings such as the banking and insurance sector, it is key to keep track of which users performed which actions on the data (and at what time). Most DBMSs automatically track these actions in a rudimentary fashion by means of the logfile (see Chapter 14). Regulated settings require a much more advanced form of auditing, with extensive tracking and reporting facilities, maintaining a detailed inventory of all database accesses and data manipulations, including the users and user roles involved.
- *Mitigating vulnerabilities*: This class of concerns pertains to detecting and resolving shortcomings or downright bugs in applications, DBMSs, or network and storage infrastructure that yield malicious parties opportunities to circumvent security measures with respect to the aforementioned concerns. Examples here are wrongly configured network components or bugs in application software that provide loopholes to hackers. A very important concept in the context of DBMSs is avoiding SQL injection, as discussed in Chapter 15. Finally, the three-layer database architecture introduced in Chapter 1 is also instrumental to this purpose. By hiding implementation details from users and the outside world by means of logical and physical data independence, it becomes much harder to discover and exploit potential vulnerabilities.

**Connections**

Several tools and techniques regarding data security were already discussed in previous chapters: Chapter 1 presented the three-layer architecture. Chapter 7 explained SQL privileges and views. Chapter 13 dealt with replication and data availability in the context of enterprise storage subsystems and business continuity. Chapters 14 and 16 discussed recovery techniques and logging. Chapter 15 dealt with SQL injection.

The rest of this chapter focuses in more detail on some techniques with respect to privacy and security that are particularly relevant to the context of data analytics.

## 20.10.2 The RACI Matrix

To understand the impact of privacy, we must start by outlining the different roles in analytical model development into a RACI matrix (Figure 20.36). The acronym **RACI** stands for:

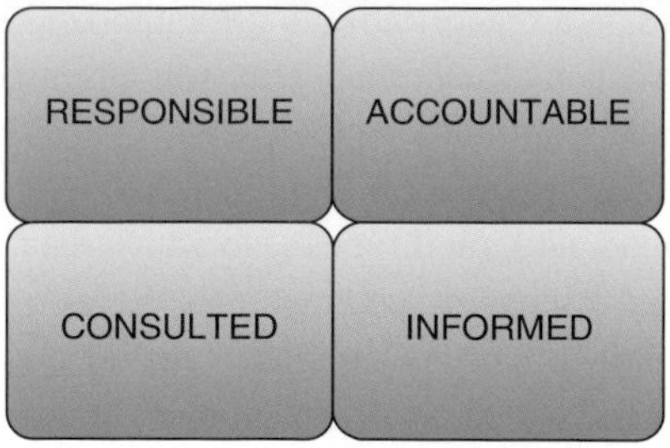


**Figure 20.36** RACI matrix.

- *Responsible*: whoever is responsible for developing the analytical model. These are the data scientists. The data scientists must get the necessary data from other parties.
- *Accountable*: this role refers to the people who delegate the work and decide what should be done. They approve the task at hand and provide the required data to the data scientists. This part is especially fulfilled by the business (e.g., the management, government, etc.).
- *Consulted*: often, a profound domain expertise is necessary to tune and polish analytical models. Experts and specialized profiles advise the business and data scientists with their valuable expertise and insights.
- *Informed*: certain people should be kept up-to-date of the output of the work as the result might affect their working process. Customer service, for example, must be informed about the changes imposed by the results of analytical models.

The roles of certain people can overlap (e.g., business people that also fulfill the consulting role) and change over time (e.g., certain experts are consultants in earlier phases of model development and should only be informed during later phases). As the RACI matrix is dynamic, the different roles should be re-evaluated regularly. The RACI matrix can be extended to the RASCI or CAIRO matrix. The RASCI matrix includes the role of support (S) to indicate whoever helps to complete the analytical model. Out-of-the-loop (O) in the CAIRO matrix explicitly mentions people not part of the analytical model development.

### 20.10.3 Accessing Internal Data

Before a data scientist starts an analysis for the development of analytical models, she or he should file a *data access request*. The data access request specifies which data are needed for which purpose and for which time period. A request to access internal data is approved by the internal privacy commission of the company. The privacy commission investigates whether the request can be granted or not, and answers these questions

- Which variables are sensitive?
- Which variables (columns) and instances (rows) should be shared?
- Which user or user group should be authorized to access the data?

To answer the above questions, various actions can be undertaken such as anonymization of data, the creation of SQL views or using Label Based Access Control (LBAC). We discuss each of these in more detail below.

#### 20.10.3.1 Anonymization

**Anonymization** is the process of transforming sensitive data so the exact value cannot be recovered by other parties, such as the data scientist. Unique or key attribute types are often converted into other values. Key attribute types are needed to link different databases to each other. For example, a company's VAT number uniquely identifies the company in various databases. The VAT number is public information that is available in many other data sources, such as the company's website, company registers, etc. Providing the VAT number enables de-anonymization and identification of the company. The conversion of a VAT number into another random number (ID) prevents the misuse of the data. The untransformed key is the *natural key* and reveals the identity of the instance. The **technical key** is a conversion of the natural key so that tables can be joined with each other, but protects the true identity of the instance. It is extremely important to preserve consistency among the different databases. The conversion of a natural key (e.g., VAT number) in database A should cause the same technical key as the conversion of the natural key (VAT number) in database B. Also, the conversion should be random and cannot follow the order in which the data appear in the database. New data instances are often inserted at the end of the database. In our company example, this means that the oldest companies appear at the top of the list, while the youngest companies end the list. Incrementally increasing the ID value is therefore strongly discouraged, as this can reveal the sequence in which companies were founded.

To anonymize other variables, different techniques can be used:

- aggregation
- discretization
- value distortion
- generalization.

If the privacy commission approves the request, they decide whether to provide raw or aggregated data. *Aggregated* data report summary statistics of the data without compromising data about individuals. Summary statistics that are derived include, among others, minimum, mean, maximum, standard deviation, *p*th percentile, and count. Raw data contain data of each individual/instance in the dataset. To preserve privacy of raw data items, the data should be further anonymized.

Anonymization of numeric variables can be achieved by *discretization*. Instead of specifying the exact value of the variable, it is partitioned into a set of disjoint, mutually exclusive classes. For example, rather than providing the exact income of a person, the income can be discretized by specifying the interval in which the value lies. Those intervals (mean, quantiles, quintiles, deciles, etc.) can be defined using an internal mapping schema or regional, national, or global summary statistics.[26] Alternatively, data can be anonymized by adding noise to sensitive variables. *Value distortion* is achieved by returning a value $x_i + e$ instead of $x_i$. The value of $e$ is randomly drawn from a predefined distribution (e.g., uniform, Gaussian). Another approach is to *generalize* a specific value description into a less specific but semantically consistent description. Using address records, for example, might positively affect an analytical model, but allows identification of a person/company. Therefore, the address can be generalized into the corresponding city, region, country, etc.

[26] Summary statistics for countries in the EU can be found at http://appsso.eurostat.ec.europa.eu/nui/show.do?dataset=ilc_di01&lang=en and for the US at https://dqydj.com/income-percentile-calculator.

*Company's demographics*

| VAT | Name | Address | Size | Creation date | Revenue | Sector |
|---|---|---|---|---|---|---|
| 532.581.34 | Mony Bank | Main Street 1943, Brussels | 592 | 09/05/1989 | € 9,900,000 | banking |
| 532.582.26 | Villa Bella | Av. Elisa 66, Liege | 6 | 12/08/1990 | € 25,000 | cleaning |
| 532.582.49 | The Green Lawn | Lawnstreet 1, Ghent | 63 | 24/02/2004 | € 185,000 | agriculture |
| 532.585.71 | Salad Palace | Main Street 1472, Brussels | 18 | 25/02/2007 | € 235,000 | catering |
| 532.586.52 | Bart&Co. | Main Street 239, Brussels | 37 | 04/02/2009 | € 1,700,000 | transport |
| 532.586.55 | Elisa's Bar | Shortstreet 5, Antwerp | 12 | 07/12/2011 | € 5,000 | catering |
| 532.590.00 | Transport John | Av. Lovanias 31, Antwerp | 104 | 18/12/2013 | € 34,000 | transport |
| ... | ... | ... | ... | ... | ... | ... |

*natural key*

*Personnel records*

| VAT | NAME | Income | Recruitment | Resignation |
|---|---|---|---|---|
| 532.586.52 | Gerry Hill | € 1,500 | 14/09/2012 | - |
| 532.586.52 | Niel Tenson | € 1,500 | 07/12/2009 | - |
| 532.586.52 | Daisy Astalos | € 1,800 | 26/03/2009 | 22/12/2009 |
| 532.586.52 | William Wheately | € 2,000 | 26/04/2014 | - |
| 532.586.52 | Tom Book | € 1,600 | 03/05/2010 | 14/01/2011 |
| 532.586.52 | John Angeles | € 1,750 | 17/05/2009 | 04/02/2015 |
| ... | ... | ... | ... | ... |

*Anonymized view*

| ID | Province | Size | Maturity | Revenue | Sector | Empl.Q1 | Empl.Q2 | Empl.Q3 | Empl.Q4 | Avg. wage |
|---|---|---|---|---|---|---|---|---|---|---|
| 19649524 | P7 | 3 | A | € 200,000 | agriculture | 2 | 4 | 0 | 0 | € 1,550 |
| 27499423 | P2 | 4 | Y | € 30,000 | transport | −5 | −5 | −3 | −5 | € 1,650 |
| 31865139 | P1 | 2 | A | € 2,000,000 | transport | 5 | 5 | 5 | −5 | € 1,600 |
| 39174842 | P1 | 2 | A | € 250,000 | catering | −1 | 2 | 0 | 2 | € 1,500 |
| 59135796 | P5 | 1 | M | € 30,000 | cleaning | 0 | 0 | 0 | 0 | € 1,400 |
| 73591064 | P1 | 5 | M | € 10,000,000 | banking | 10 | 10 | 5 | 5 | € 1,800 |
| 91245975 | P2 | 2 | Y | € 10,000 | catering | 0 | −2 | 0 | 1 | € 1,350 |
| ... | ... | ... | ... | ... | ... | ... | ... | ... | ... | ... |

**Figure 20.37** Anonymizing a dataset for analytics.

Figure 20.37 illustrates the anonymization process for social security fraud (i.e., tax evasion by companies). The business has two databases at its disposal. One contains the company's demographics, the other reports the company's personnel records. Both databases are linked to each other with the VAT number. Before they can be used safely by the data scientists, the databases must be anonymized. The company's demographics are converted as follows: the VAT is converted into a new identifier (ID), randomly chosen. The name of the company is excluded from the data scientists' view. The company size is categorized into discrete intervals ranging from one to five. The creation date is converted into three categories: young, adolescent, and mature. The mapping of both the size and the age is defined by the business, but is concealed for the data scientists. The value of the company's revenue is distorted by rounding the revenue using experts' domain knowledge. The address is generalized into the province. The sector is directly included in the view with no changes. The company's personnel records are aggregated on the company level. It now specifies quarterly employee turnover, and their average wage. Note that the rows in the anonymized table are sorted according to the randomly generated ID, and do not follow the sequence of the base tables.

The above-discussed anonymization techniques can create a k-anonymized dataset whereby every observation/record/tuple is indistinguishable from at least k − 1 other observations/tuples/records regarding the privacy-sensitive variables. K-anonymization aims at guaranteeing that subjects can no longer be re-identified while making sure that the data remain useful for analytics. Note, however, that a k-anonymized dataset might still be vulnerable to privacy attacks and, depending upon the application, other more ambitious anonymization goals might have to be set.

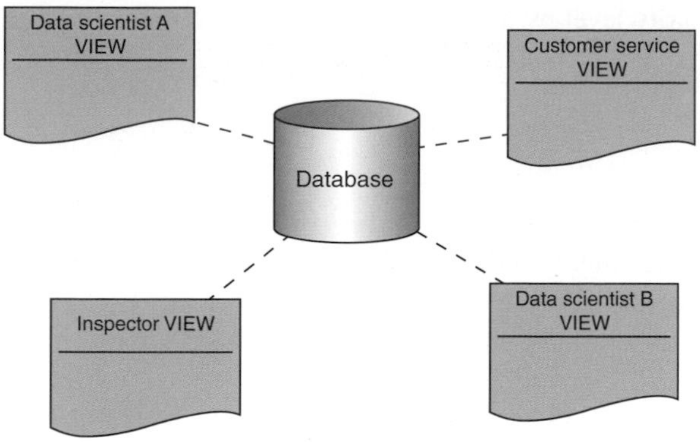


**Figure 20.38** Different SQL views defined for a database.

### 20.10.3.2 SQL Views

As discussed in Chapter 7, *SQL views* can be seen as virtual tables without physical tuples (Figure 20.38). A view definition consists of a formula that determines which data from the *base tables* are to be shown upon invocation of the view. The view's content is generated upon this invocation. Views enable extracting part of the data tables, aggregating values where necessary, and sharing (only) the data authorized by the internal privacy commission.

Consider this example of an SQL view that combines both anonymized and not-anonymized information:

```
CREATE VIEW FRAUD_INPUT
AS SELECT C.ANON_VAT, C.PROVINCE, C.ANON_SIZE, C.ANON_REVENUE, C.SECTOR,
C.ANON_AGE, AVG(P.WAGE), COUNT(*)
FROM COMPANIES C, PERSONNEL P
WHERE C.ANON_VAT = P.ANON_VAT
GROUP BY C.ANON_VAT;
```

This view retrieves anonymized VAT, size, revenue, and age information, whereas the province, sector, and wage information are not anonymized. Views contribute not only to privacy, but also to data security, by hiding the logical database structure from internal or external users, hence rendering malicious manipulation of the database or the data more difficult.

### 20.10.3.3 Label-Based Access Control

**Label-Based Access Control (LBAC)** is a control mechanism to protect your data against unauthorized access and can differentiate between the level of authorization that is granted to users. LBAC can grant read and write access to specific tables, rows, and columns. For example, data items (e.g., individual rows) that are inserted by users with a higher security level cannot be seen by users with a lower security level. Using LBAC comes in as a handy alternative when there are many views on a table, and when specific users can only access data with the same security level or lower. LBAC is implemented by many governments and companies that use strict hierarchical classification labels such as TOP SECRET, SECRET, and CONFIDENTIAL.

Protected data are assigned a security level by a security administrator responsible for:

- creating security label components;
- creating security policies;
- creating security labels; and
- granting security labels to users.

A security label component defines the criteria to decide who can access the data. As an example, we can create this security label component:

```
CREATE SECURITY LABEL COMPONENT my_sec_label_comp
    ARRAY [ confidential, unclassified] ;
```

The array represents a simple hierarchy. In this example, read and write access are blocked when a user's security label (e.g., unclassified) is lower than the protecting label (e.g., confidential). Note that LBAC also supports more complex tree-based hierarchies.

A security policy defines how a table is protected using LBAC. A table can have only one security policy specifying which security label components are used in the security labels that are part of the policy and what rules are used to compare security label components. The rows and columns of the table can only be protected by security labels that belong to the security policy. As an example, we create this security policy based upon our earlier defined "my_sec_label_comp" security label component:

```
CREATE SECURITY POLICY my_sec_policy
COMPONENTS my_sec_label_comp
WITH DB2LBACRULES;
```

Note that we hereby make use of the IBM DB2 implementation of LBAC.[27] The keyword DB2LBACRULES refers to a set of predefined DB2 rules for comparing the values of security label components.

A security label describes a set of security criteria to protect data against unauthorized access. It can be granted to users or groups. A user's security label will then be compared to the security label protecting the data (e.g., a table row or column) to decide whether access can be granted. A security label is part of exactly one security policy and a security label must exist for each security label component used by the security policy. A security label can be defined as follows:

```
CREATE SECURITY LABEL my_sec_policy.confidential
COMPONENT my_sec_label_comp confidential;

CREATE SECURITY LABEL my_sec_policy.unclassified
COMPONENT my_sec_label_comp unclassified;
```

Security labels can then be granted to users:

```
GRANT SECURITY LABEL my_sec_policy.unclassified TO USER BartBaesens FOR ALL
ACCESS;
```

27 www.ibm.com/support/knowledgecenter/SSEPGG_9.7.0/com.ibm.db2.luw.admin.sec.doc/doc/c0021114.html.

```
GRANT SECURITY LABEL my_sec_policy.unclassified TO USER SeppevandenBroucke FOR
READ ACCESS;

GRANT SECURITY LABEL my_sec_policy.confidential TO USER WilfriedLemahieu FOR
ALL ACCESS;
```

The above statement specifies that user BartBaesens has read and write access to all data labeled as unclassified. User SeppevandenBroucke has only read access to all data labeled as unclassified. User WilfriedLemahieu has read and write access to all data with an unclassified or confidential label.

Once the security label components, security policy, and security labels have been defined, they can protect individual rows, individual columns, or a combination of both. When a user tries to access protected data, his/her LBAC credentials will be compared to the security labels of the security policy protecting the table to determine whether the access can be granted. Consider this example of an EMPLOYEE table:

```
CREATE TABLE EMPLOYEE
     (SSN CHAR(6) NOT NULL PRIMARY KEY,
     NAME VARCHAR(40) NOT NULL,
     SALARY INT SECURED WITH confidential,
     ...
SECURITY POLICY my_sec_policy)
```

The salary column has been protected using the confidential label. Hence, only user WilfriedLemahieu will have access to it.

**Drill Down**

A complementary way to enforce security is by means of encryption. The idea is to encode (encrypt) plain data using a secret key (encryption key) into ciphertext that can only be read by people who possess the key. Two popular types of encryption are symmetric and asymmetric encryption. Symmetric encryption uses the same key to encrypt and decrypt the data. This implies that the key must be exchanged beforehand between the parties involved, which poses a security risk.

Asymmetric encryption uses two keys: a public key and a private key. Public keys can be exchanged publicly (using, e.g., a repository) whereas private keys are only known to the owner. Both keys are mathematically related. Only the holder of the paired private key can decrypt a message encrypted with the public key, which solves the key distribution problem. RSA (developed by R. Rivest, A. Shamir, and L. Adleman, hence the name) is a popular example of an asymmetric encryption algorithm.

### 20.10.4 Privacy Regulation

In recent years, we have seen a dramatic increase in regulatory attention being put toward ensuring privacy and data protection concerns, both in the USA and the EU. The emergence of Big Data and analytics has stimulated a lot of new opportunities to understand patterns in customer behavior, but the ever-increasing thirst to capture and store data has also uncovered new privacy concerns and a call to construct ethical frameworks for data scientists. The White House, for instance, recently released a report, "Big Data: A Report on Algorithmic Systems, Opportunity, and Civil Rights",[28] laying out a national perspective regarding data science ethics. Other authors have also warned against ways that Big Data can harm minorities and the underprivileged. Finally, the increased awareness regarding cyber security has also raised concerns regarding how data are stored and analyzed.

In the European Union, these concerns led to introducing Regulation (EU) 2016/679 (the **General Data Protection Regulation**, or "GDPR"), published in May 2016 with enforcement starting in May 2018. The GDPR represents a significant step in developing privacy, and law-makers predict that almost every organization based in the EU or that does business in the EU will be affected. The GDPR raises the bar for compliance, openness, and transparency. Some key articles in the regulation include: the right to be informed about how your personal data will be used; the right to access and rectify your personal data; the right to erase your personal data (this replaces the stricter regulation on the right to be forgotten in the Directive); and the right for human intervention in automated decision models, such as analytical prediction models. The GDPR will impact a huge range of companies and data processors. Education in data protection and privacy laws will hence become a critical success factor in the years to come.

In the USA, data privacy is not highly regulated. Access to personal data contained in credit reports (provided by Experian, Equifax, TransUnion, etc.), for example, may be retrieved by third parties when seeking employment or medical care, or making purchases on credit terms. There is no all-encompassing law regulating the acquisition, storage, or use of personal data in the USA, although partial regulation exists, such as the Privacy Act of 1974, which establishes a code of fair practice to govern the collection of personal data, the Health Insurance Portability and Accountability Act of 1996 (HIPAA) to protect health information privacy rights, and the Electronic Communications Privacy Act (ECPA) of 1986 that establishes sanctions for interception of electronic communications.

Unlike the US approach to privacy protection, which relies on industry-specific legislation and self-regulation, the EU relies on comprehensive privacy legislation (see the Directive and the GDPR above). To bridge these different privacy approaches, the US Department of Commerce in consultation with the European Commission developed the EU–US Privacy Shield. The EU–US Privacy Shield is a framework for transatlantic exchanges of personal data between the EU and the USA. Considering the now-upcoming GDPR, however, law-makers have raised the issue that the newer regulation is deemed incompatible with the EU–US Privacy Shield legislation, as it would no longer permit processing EU personal data by US companies. It remains to be seen how the two sets of legal provisions can be harmonized. To provide an example, in the USA the right to erasure is more limited and only seen in case law (i.e., the law as established by the outcome of former cases, also called precedents), unlike in the GDPR, which guarantees that right to any EU subject. As a result, coming to an agreement will be difficult. The current plan is to perform a joint annual review of the Privacy Shield by EU and US authorities, so changes will likely be made. Although broad EU rules try to

### Retention Questions

- What is a RACI matrix and how can it contribute to privacy and security?
- How can the following concepts contribute to privacy and security?
  - Anonymization
  - SQL views
  - Label-Based Access Control (LBAC)
- Contrast the privacy regulation in the USA versus the EU.

[28] https://obamawhitehouse.archives.gov/sites/default/files/microsites/ostp/2016_0504_data_discrimination.pdf.

unify the privacy regulation within the European Union, we conclude that there is still a lack of a clear international agreement on privacy. There is a strong need for a unified organism that regulates cross-border privacy and data protection, with a focus on integration and transparency.

## 20.11 Conclusion

In this chapter we zoomed into analytics. We provided a bird's eye overview of the analytics process model, reviewed example applications, and zoomed in on the skill set of a data scientist. This was followed by a discussion on data pre-processing. Next, we elaborated on different types of analytics: predictive analytics, descriptive analytics, and social network analytics. We highlighted various activities during post-processing of analytical models.

We enumerated various critical success factors for analytical models, such as statistical performance and validity, interpretability, operational efficiency, economical cost, and regulatory compliance. Next, we elaborated on the economical perspective and discussed total cost of ownership, return on investment, in- versus outsourcing, on-premises versus cloud solutions, and open-source versus commercial software.

We also gave recommendations to improve the ROI of analytical projects by considering new sources of data, improving data quality, introducing management support, adequate organizational embedding, and fostering cross-fertilization opportunities between business departments. We concluded with the very important aspects of privacy and security whereby privacy-preserving analytical techniques and the relevant US/EU regulation were covered.

### Scenario Conclusion

Now that Sober understands the basic concepts of analytics, the company is even more convinced of the potential of this technology in its business setting. Sober sees various applications of predictive, descriptive, and social network analytics.

A first example is predicting booking behavior. Based upon customer characteristics and previous services booked, Sober wants to develop a predictive analytics model predicting who is likely to book a service in the next three months. Since the company considers interpretability as very important, it will use decision trees to develop these models. It will evaluate the decision trees estimated in terms of their classification accuracy, sensitivity, specificity, and lift.

In terms of descriptive analytics, the company is thinking about clustering its customers based on their purchasing behavior. It is thinking about clustering based upon this information:

- Recency (R): How long has it been since a customer booked either a ride-hail or ride-sharing service?
- Frequency (F): What is the average number of ride-hail or ride-sharing services booked per month?
- Monetary (M): What is the average amount paid for a ride-hail or ride-sharing service?

Sober will first calculate each of these RFM features for its entire customer base. It will then run a k-means clustering exercise with varying values for k (e.g., $k = 5$ to $k = 20$). Based upon the clusters detected, Sober will then see how to target each cluster using the appropriate marketing campaign.

Also, social network analytics is a technology Sober considers as interesting. It is thinking about using it to analyze its sharing services. It is planning to build a network of customers that jointly booked ride-sharing services. It can then analyze this network and see whether there are any communities of customers that frequently book ride-sharing services together. With this information, Sober can better tailor its marketing efforts to each of these communities. In a next step, it can featurize the network and add the features to its decision tree predicting booking behavior.

Since Sober is taking its first steps in analytics, it prefers to do it all in-house, using the data scientist it hired earlier. It will use the open-source package R to do all data pre-processing and descriptive, predictive, and social network analytics. In the long run, it also plans to explore new sources of data, especially weather and traffic data, which are sources the company considers as very interesting, since both undoubtedly affect its customers' behavior.

Given the relatively small size of its database, Sober will enforce privacy and security using SQL views. The company will also closely follow up any new regulation on the matter.

## Key Terms List

**accuracy ratio (AR)**
**agglomerative hierarchical clustering**
**analytics**
**analytics process model**
**anonymization**
**area under the roc curve (AUC)**
**association rules**
**bootstrapping**
**centrality metrics**
**churn prediction**
**classification**
**classification accuracy**
**cloud-based solutions**
**coefficient of determination**
**confidence**
**cross-validation**
**cumulative accuracy profile (CAP)**
**customer segmentation**
**cutoff**
**data pre-processing**
**data scientist**
**decision trees**
**dendrogram**
**denormalization**
**divisive hierarchical clustering**
**doubling amount**
**edge**
**exploratory analysis**
**featurization**
**gain**
**General Data Protection Regulation (GDPR)**
**hierarchical clustering**
**impurity**
**insourcing**
**k-means clustering**
**Label-Based Access Control (LBAC)**
**lift**
**lift curve**
**linear decision boundary**
**linear regression**
**logistic regression**
**marketing analytics**
**mean absolute deviation (MAD)**
**mean squared error (MSE)**
**misclassification rate**
**missing values**
**node**
**odds ratio**
**on-premises analytics**
**ordinary least squares (OLS)**

**outliers**
**outsourcing**
**overfitting**
**Pearson correlation coefficient**
**precision**
**predictive analytics**
**RACI matrix**
**receiver operating characteristic curve (ROC curve)**
**recommender systems**
**regression**
**regression tree**
**response modeling**
**return on investment (ROI)**
**risk analytics**
**sampling**
**sensitivity**
**sequence rules**
**social network**
**social network learning**
**sociogram**
**specificity**
**support**
**technical key**
**text analytics**
**total cost of ownership (TCO)**

## Review Questions

**20.1.** OLAP (on-line analytical processing) can help in which of the following steps of the analytics process?

a. Data collection.
b. Data visualization.
c. Data transformation.
d. Data denormalization.

**20.2.** The GIGO principle mainly relates to which aspect of the analytics process?

a. Data selection.
b. Data transformation.
c. Data cleaning.
d. All of the above.

**20.3.** Which of the following statements is **correct**?

a. Missing values should always be replaced or removed.
b. Outliers should always be replaced or removed.
c. Missing values and outliers can potentially provide useful information and should be analyzed before they are removed/replaced.
d. Missing values and outliers should both always be replaced or removed.

**20.4.** Which of the following strategies can be used to deal with missing values?

a. Keep.
b. Delete.
c. Replace/impute.
d. All of the above.

**20.5.** Outlying observations which represent erroneous data are treated using...

a. missing value procedures.
b. truncation or capping.

**20.6.** Examine the following decision tree:

According to the decision tree, an applicant with *Income* > \$50,000 and *High Debt* = Yes is classified as:

a. Good risk.
b. Bad risk.

**20.7.** Decision trees can be used in the following applications:

a. Credit risk scoring.
b. Credit risk scoring and churn prediction.
c. Credit risk scoring, churn prediction, and customer profile segmentation.
d. Credit risk scoring, churn prediction, customer profile segmentation, and market basket analysis.

**20.8.** Consider a dataset with a multiclass target variable as follows: 25% bad payers, 25% poor payers, 25% medium payers, and 25% good payers. In this case, the entropy will be...

a. minimal.
b. maximal.

**20.9.** Which of the following measures cannot be used to make the splitting decision in a regression tree?

a. Mean squared error (MSE).
b. ANOVA/F-test.
c. Entropy.

**20.10.** Bootstrapping refers to...

a. drawing samples with replacement.
b. drawing samples without replacement.

**20.11.** Clustering, association rules, and sequence rules are examples of...

a. predictive analytics.
b. descriptive analytics.

**20.12.** Given the following five transactions:

T1 {K, A, D, B}
T2 {D, A, C, E, B}
T3 {C, A, B, D}
T4 {B, A, E}
T5 {B, E, D},

consider the association rule R: A ➔ BD.
Which statement is **correct**?

a. The support of R is 100% and the confidence is 75%.
b. The support of R is 60% and the confidence is 100%.

c. The support of R is 75% and the confidence is 60%.
d. The support of R is 60% and the confidence is 75%.

**20.13.** The aim of clustering is to come up with clusters such that the...

a. homogeneity within a cluster is minimized and the heterogeneity between clusters is maximized.
b. homogeneity within a cluster is maximized and the heterogeneity between clusters is minimized.
c. homogeneity within a cluster is minimized and the heterogeneity between clusters is minimized.
d. homogeneity within a cluster is maximized and the heterogeneity between clusters is maximized.

**20.14.** Which statement about the adjacency matrix representing a social network is **not correct**?

a. It is a symmetric matrix.
b. It is sparse since it contains a lot of non-zero elements.
c. It can include weights.
d. It has the same number of rows and columns.

**20.15.** Which statement is **correct**?

a. The geodesic represents the longest path between two nodes.
b. The betweenness counts the number of the times that a node or edge occurs in the geodesics of the network.
c. The graph theoretic center is the node with the highest minimum distance to all other nodes.
d. The closeness is always higher than the betweenness.

**20.16.** Featurization refers to...

a. selecting the most predictive features.
b. adding more local features to the dataset.
c. making features (= inputs) out of the network characteristics.
d. adding more nodes to the network.

**20.17.** Which of the following activities are part of the post-processing step?

a. Model interpretation and validation.
b. Sensitivity analysis.
c. Model representation.
d. All of the above.

**20.18.** Is the following statement true or false? "All given success factors of an analytical model, i.e., relevance, performance, interpretability, efficiency, economical cost, and regulatory compliance, are always equally important."

a. True.
b. False.

**20.19.** Which role does a database designer have according to the RACI matrix?

a. Responsible.
b. Accountable.
c. Support.
d. Consulted.
e. Informed.

**20.20.** Which of the following costs should be included in a total cost of ownership (TCO) analysis?

a. Acquisition costs.
b. Ownership and operation costs.
c. Post-ownership costs.
d. All of the above.

**20.21.** Which of the following statements is **not correct**?

a. ROI analysis offers a common firm-wide language to compare multiple investment opportunities and decide which one(s) to go for.
b. For companies like Facebook, Amazon, Netflix, and Google, a positive ROI is obvious since they essentially thrive on data and analytics.
c. Although the benefit component is usually not that difficult to approximate, the costs are much harder to precisely quantify.
d. Negative ROI of analytics often boils down to the lack of good-quality data, management support, and a company-wide data-driven decision culture.

**20.22.** Which of the following is not a risk when outsourcing analytics?

a. The fact that all analytical activities need to be outsourced.
b. The exchange of confidential information.
c. Continuity of the partnership.
d. Dilution of competitive advantage due to, e.g., mergers and acquisitions.

**20.23.** Which of the following is not an advantage of open-source software for analytics?

a. It is available for free.
b. A worldwide network of developers can work on it.
c. It has been thoroughly engineered and extensively tested, validated, and completely documented.
d. It can be used in combination with commercial software.

**20.24.** Which of the following statements is **correct**?

a. When using on-premises solutions, maintenance or upgrade projects may even go by unnoticed.
b. An important advantage of cloud-based solutions concerns the scalability and economies of scale offered. More capacity (e.g., servers) can be added on the fly whenever needed.
c. The big footprint access to data management and analytics capabilities is a serious drawback of cloud-based solutions.
d. On-premises solutions catalyze improved collaboration across business departments and geographical locations.

**20.25.** Which of the following are interesting data sources to consider to boost the performance of analytical models?

a. Network data.
b. External data.
c. Unstructured data such as text data and multimedia data.
d. All of the above.

**20.26.** Which of the following statements is **correct**?

a. Quality of data is key to the success of any analytical exercise since it has a direct and measurable impact on the quality of the analytical model and hence its economic value.
b. Data pre-processing activities such as handling missing values, duplicate data, or outliers are preventive measures for dealing with data quality issues.
c. Data owners are the data quality experts who are in charge of assessing data quality by performing extensive and regular data quality checks.
d. Data stewards can request data scientists to check or complete the value of a field.

**20.27.** To guarantee maximum independence and organizational impact of analytics, it is important that...

a. the chief data officer (CDO) or chief analytics officer (CAO) reports to the CIO or CFO.
b. the CIO takes care of all analytical responsibilities.

c. a chief data officer or chief analytics officer is added to the executive committee who directly reports to the CEO.
d. analytics is supervised only locally in the business units.

**20.28.** What is the correct ranking of the following analytics applications in terms of maturity?

a. Marketing analytics (most mature), risk analytics (medium mature), HR analytics (least mature).
b. Risk analytics (most mature), marketing analytics (medium mature), HR analytics (least mature).
c. Risk analytics (most mature), HR analytics (medium mature), marketing analytics (least mature).
d. HR analytics (most mature), marketing analytics (medium mature), risk analytics (least mature).

## Problems and Exercises

20.1E Discuss the key activities when pre-processing data for credit scoring. Remember, credit scoring aims at distinguishing good payers from bad payers using application characteristics such as age, income, and employment status. Why is data pre-processing considered important?

20.2E What are the key differences between logistic regression and decision trees? Give examples of when to prefer one above the other.

20.3E Consider the following dataset of predicted scores and actual target values (you can assume higher scores should be assigned to the goods).

| Score | Actual good/bad |
|---|---|
| 100 | Bad |
| 110 | Bad |
| 120 | Good |
| 130 | Bad |
| 140 | Bad |
| 150 | Good |
| 160 | Bad |
| 170 | Good |
| 180 | Good |
| 190 | Bad |
| 200 | Good |
| 210 | Good |
| 220 | Bad |
| 230 | Good |
| 240 | Good |
| 250 | Bad |
| 260 | Good |
| 270 | Good |
| 280 | Good |
| 290 | Bad |
| 300 | Good |
| 310 | Bad |
| 320 | Good |
| 330 | Good |
| 340 | Good |

- Calculate the classification accuracy, sensitivity, and specificity for a classification cutoff of 205.
- Draw the ROC curve. How would you estimate the area under the ROC curve?

- Draw the CAP curve and estimate the AR.
- Draw the lift curve. What is the top decile lift?

20.4E Discuss how association and sequence rules can be used to build recommender systems such as the ones adopted by Amazon, eBay, and Netflix. How would you evaluate the performance of a recommender system?

20.5E Explain *k*-means clustering using a small (artificial) dataset. What is the impact of *k*? What pre-processing steps are needed?

20.6E Discuss an example of social network analytics. How is it different from classical predictive or descriptive analytics?

20.7E The Internet of Things (IoT) refers to the network of interconnected things such as electronic devices, sensors, software, and IT infrastructure that create and add value by exchanging data with various stakeholders such as manufacturers, service providers, customers, other devices, etc., hereby using the World Wide Web technology stack (e.g., WiFi, IPv6). In terms of devices, you can think about heartbeat monitors; motion, noise, or temperature sensors; smart meters measuring utility (e.g., electricity, water) consumption; and so on. Some examples of applications are:

- smart parking: automatically monitoring free parking spaces in a city;
- smart lighting: automatically adjusting street lights to weather conditions;
- smart traffic: optimizing driving and walking routes based upon traffic and congestion;
- smart grid: automatically monitoring energy consumption;
- smart supply chains: automatically monitoring goods as they move through the supply chain;
- telematics: automatically monitoring driving behavior and linking it to insurance risk and premiums.

It speaks for itself that the amount of data generated is enormous and offers an unseen potential for analytical applications.

Pick one particular type of application of IoT and discuss the following:

- how to use predictive, descriptive, and social network analytics;
- how to evaluate the performance of the analytical models;
- key issues in post-processing and implementing the analytical models; and
- important challenges and opportunities.

20.8E Many companies nowadays are investing in analytics. Also, for universities, there are plenty of opportunities to use analytics for streamlining and/or optimizing processes. Examples of applications where analytics may have a role to play are:

- analyzing student fail rates;
- timetabling of courses;
- finding jobs for graduates;
- recruiting new students;
- meal planning in the student restaurant.

Identify some other possible applications of analytics in a university context. Discuss how analytics could contribute to these applications. In your discussion, make sure you clearly address:

- the added value of analytics for analyzing the problems considered;
- the analytical techniques to be used;
- key challenges; and
- new opportunities.

# APPENDIX USING THE ONLINE ENVIRONMENT

Here, we will show you how you can use the online environment for this book to play around with several types of database management systems and database query languages.

## How to Access the Online Environment

1. Navigate to www.pdbmbook.com/playground.
2. If this is your first time accessing the environment, you'll need to register first. Click on the "register" link and enter your details.
3. You'll receive a confirmation email with a unique link you need to open to verify your account.
4. Afterwards, you can log-in and see the following overview of interactive environments:[1]

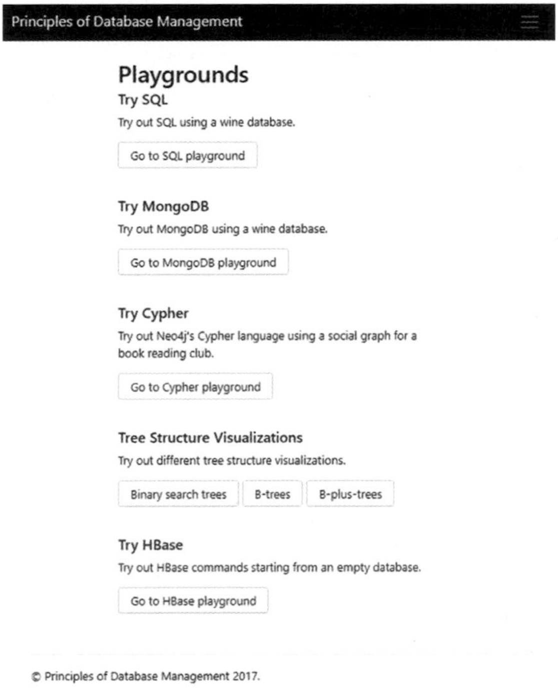


[1] The online environment may be further expanded in the future, so the actual overview could be somewhat different from the one depicted here.

## Environment: Relational Databases and SQL

In Chapter 7 on the Structured Query Language, a wine database was introduced. You can follow along with the queries by navigating the SQL environment.

For instance, to select all information from the SUPPLIER table, you can execute:

```
SELECT * FROM SUPPLIER
```

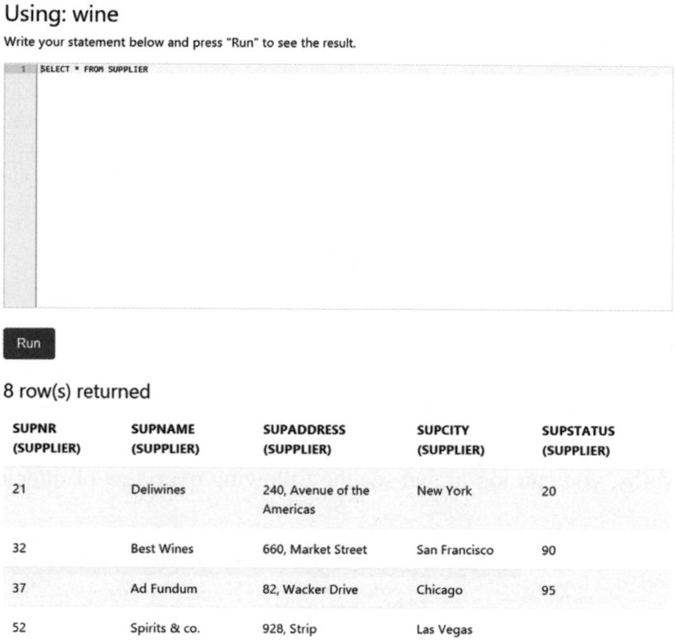
Using: wine
Write your statement below and press "Run" to see the result.
SELECT * FROM SUPPLIER
Run
8 row(s) returned

| SUPNR (SUPPLIER) | SUPNAME (SUPPLIER) | SUPADDRESS (SUPPLIER) | SUPCITY (SUPPLIER) | SUPSTATUS (SUPPLIER) |
|---|---|---|---|---|
| 21 | Deliwines | 240, Avenue of the Americas | New York | 20 |
| 32 | Best Wines | 660, Market Street | San Francisco | 90 |
| 37 | Ad Fundum | 82, Wacker Drive | Chicago | 95 |
| 52 | Spirits & co. | 928, Strip | Las Vegas | |

Feel free to execute INSERT, UPDATE, and DELETE queries as well. The following example removes the product tuple with product number 0119 from the PRODUCT table:

```
DELETE FROM PRODUCT WHERE PRODNR = '0119'
```

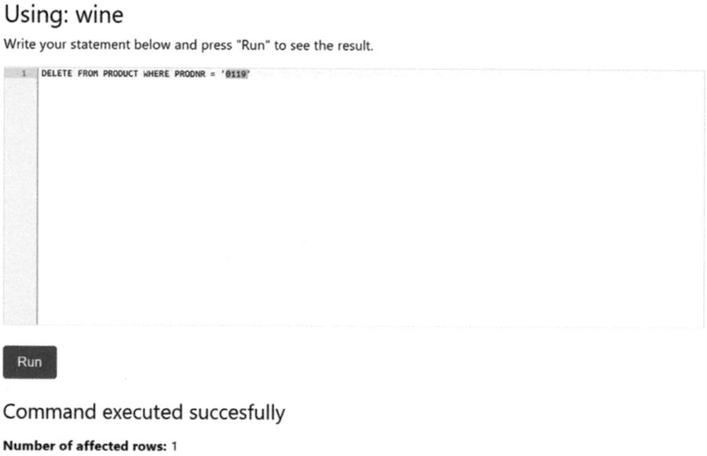
Using: wine
Write your statement below and press "Run" to see the result.
DELETE FROM PRODUCT WHERE PRODNR = '0119'
Run
Command executed succesfully
Number of affected rows: 1

If you want to start over with a fresh database (helpful if you just deleted a complete table), you can press the "reset" link to reset the database to its initial state.

## Environment: MongoDB

In Chapter 11 on NoSQL databases, we discussed MongoDB as an example of a document store. The respective online environment contains a MongoDB version of the wine database, which you can query through its JavaScript shell. Some interesting commands to play around with are the following.

Retrieve all documents in the "products" collection:

```
db.products.find();
```

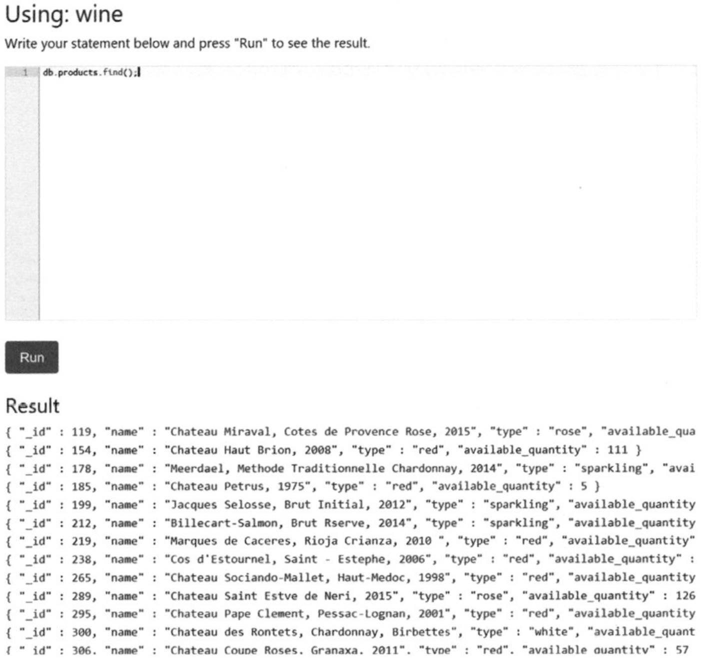
Using: wine
Write your statement below and press "Run" to see the result.
1
db.products.find();
Run
Result
{ "_id" : 119, "name" : "Chateau Miraval, Cotes de Provence Rose, 2015", "type" : "rose", "available_qua
{ "_id" : 154, "name" : "Chateau Haut Brion, 2008", "type" : "red", "available_quantity" : 111 }
{ "_id" : 178, "name" : "Meerdael, Methode Traditionnelle Chardonnay, 2014", "type" : "sparkling", "avai
{ "_id" : 185, "name" : "Chateau Petrus, 1975", "type" : "red", "available_quantity" : 5 }
{ "_id" : 199, "name" : "Jacques Selosse, Brut Initial, 2012", "type" : "sparkling", "available_quantity
{ "_id" : 212, "name" : "Billecart-Salmon, Brut Rserve, 2014", "type" : "sparkling", "available_quantity
{ "_id" : 219, "name" : "Marques de Caceres, Rioja Crianza, 2010 ", "type" : "red", "available_quantity"
{ "_id" : 238, "name" : "Cos d'Estournel, Saint - Estephe, 2006", "type" : "red", "available_quantity" :
{ "_id" : 265, "name" : "Chateau Sociando-Mallet, Haut-Medoc, 1998", "type" : "red", "available_quantity
{ "_id" : 289, "name" : "Chateau Saint Estve de Neri, 2015", "type" : "rose", "available_quantity" : 126
{ "_id" : 295, "name" : "Chateau Pape Clement, Pessac-Lognan, 2001", "type" : "red", "available_quantity
{ "_id" : 300, "name" : "Chateau des Rontets, Chardonnay, Birbettes", "type" : "white", "available_quant
{ "_id" : 306, "name" : "Chateau Coupe Roses, Granaxa, 2011", "type" : "red", "available_quantity" : 57

Retrieve all documents in the "products" collection where the id matches 119:

```
db.products.find({ _id: 119 });
```

Using: wine
Write your statement below and press "Run" to see the result.
1
db.products.find({ _id: 119 });
Run
Result
{ "_id" : 119, "name" : "Chateau Miraval, Cotes de Provence Rose, 2015", "type" : "rose", "available_qua

Retrieve all documents in the "products" collection where the type matches "rose":

```
db.products.find({ type: 'rose' });
```

Using: wine
Write your statement below and press "Run" to see the result.
1 db.products.find({ type: 'rose' });
Run
Result
{ "_id" : 119, "name" : "Chateau Miraval, Cotes de Provence Rose, 2015", "type" : "rose", "available_qua
{ "_id" : 289, "name" : "Chateau Saint Estve de Neri, 2015", "type" : "rose", "available_quantity" : 126
{ "_id" : 668, "name" : "Gallo Family Vineyards, Grenache, 2014", "type" : "rose", "available_quantity"

Retrieve all documents in the "products" collection where the available quantity is greater than 100:

```
db.products.find({ available_quantity: { $gt: 100 } });
```

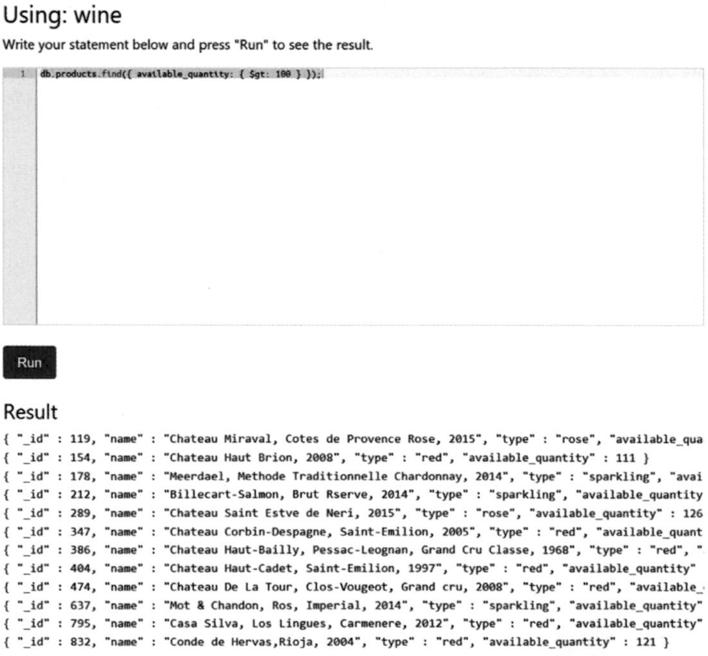
Using: wine
Write your statement below and press "Run" to see the result.
1 db.products.find({ available_quantity: { $gt: 100 } });
Run
Result
{ "_id" : 119, "name" : "Chateau Miraval, Cotes de Provence Rose, 2015", "type" : "rose", "available_qua
{ "_id" : 154, "name" : "Chateau Haut Brion, 2008", "type" : "red", "available_quantity" : 111 }
{ "_id" : 178, "name" : "Meerdael, Methode Traditionnelle Chardonnay, 2014", "type" : "sparkling", "avai
{ "_id" : 212, "name" : "Billecart-Salmon, Brut Rserve, 2014", "type" : "sparkling", "available_quantity
{ "_id" : 289, "name" : "Chateau Saint Estve de Neri, 2015", "type" : "rose", "available_quantity" : 126
{ "_id" : 347, "name" : "Chateau Corbin-Despagne, Saint-Emilion, 2005", "type" : "red", "available_quant
{ "_id" : 386, "name" : "Chateau Haut-Bailly, Pessac-Leognan, Grand Cru Classe, 1968", "type" : "red", "
{ "_id" : 404, "name" : "Chateau Haut-Cadet, Saint-Emilion, 1997", "type" : "red", "available_quantity"
{ "_id" : 474, "name" : "Chateau De La Tour, Clos-Vougeot, Grand cru, 2008", "type" : "red", "available_
{ "_id" : 637, "name" : "Mot & Chandon, Ros, Imperial, 2014", "type" : "sparkling", "available_quantity"
{ "_id" : 795, "name" : "Casa Silva, Los Lingues, Carmenere, 2012", "type" : "red", "available_quantity"
{ "_id" : 832, "name" : "Conde de Hervas,Rioja, 2004", "type" : "red", "available_quantity" : 121 }

Aggregate some documents in the “products” collection as follows: take all products with an available quantity greater than 100, group these by their “type”, and create a “total” field by summing “1” per record in each group. Finally, sort descending on “total”:

```
db.products.aggregate([
    { $match: { available_quantity: {$gt: 100} } },
    { $group: { _id: "$type", total: { $sum: 1 } } },
    { $sort: { total: -1 } }
]);
```

Using: wine
Write your statement below and press "Run" to see the result.
db.products.aggregate([
{ $match: { available_quantity: {$gt: 100} } },
{ $group: { _id: "$type", total: { $sum: 1 } } },
{ $sort: { total: -1 } }
])
Run
Result
{ "_id" : "red", "total" : 8 }
{ "_id" : "sparkling", "total" : 3 }
{ "_id" : "rose", "total" : 2 }
{ "_id" : "white", "total" : 1 }
{ "_id" : "sparling", "total" : 1 }

If you want to start over with a fresh MongoDB instance, you can press the “reset” link to reset the database to its initial state.

## Environment: Neo4j and Cypher

In Chapter 11 on NoSQL databases, we discussed Neo4j as an example of a graph database. The online environment contains a Neo4j database for our book-reading club. You can use the same queries as the ones in the chapter to follow along.

For instance: who likes romance books?

```
MATCH (r:Reader)--(:Book)--(:Genre {name:'romance'})
RETURN r.name
```

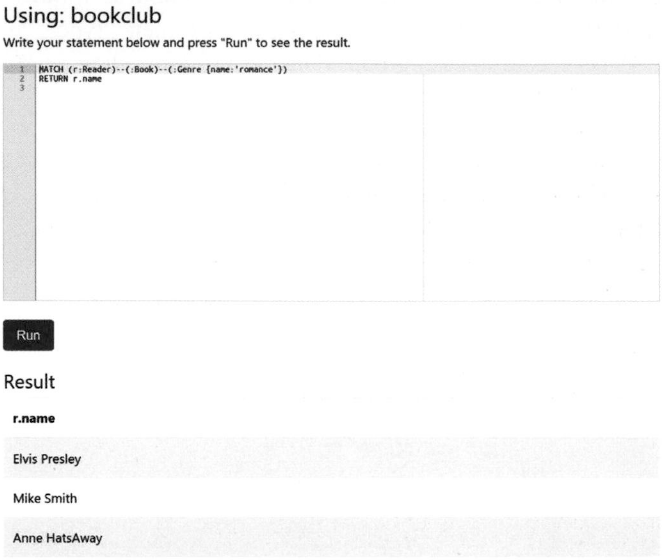


Show Bart and Bart's friends that liked humor books:

```
MATCH (me:Reader)--(friend:Reader)--(b:Book)--(g:Genre)
WHERE g.name = 'humor'
  AND me.name = 'Bart Baesens'
RETURN me, friend
```

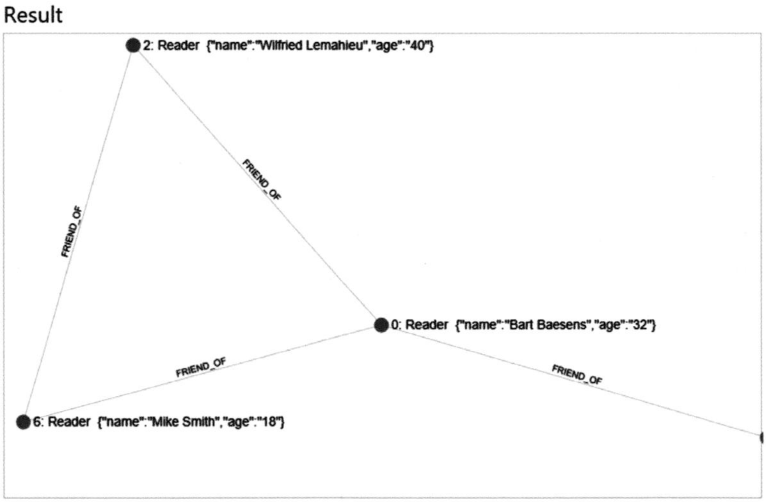


If you want to start over with a fresh Neo4j instance, you can press the "reset" link to reset the database to its initial state.

## Environment: Tree Structure Visualizations

This environment provides visualization of several tree-based data structures as discussed in Chapter 12 (i.e., binary search trees, B-trees, and $B^+$-trees).

A binary search tree is a physical tree structure in which each node has at most two children. Each tree node contains a search key value and (at most) two pointers to children. Both children are the root nodes of subtrees, with one subtree only containing key values that are lower than the key value in the original node, and the other subtree only containing key values that are higher.

To see how this works, you can try inserting the following elements individually in the online environment:

20, 8, 28, 3, 16, 24, 30, 7, 11, 17, 26, 12

You will obtain a similar view to the tree shown in the chapter:

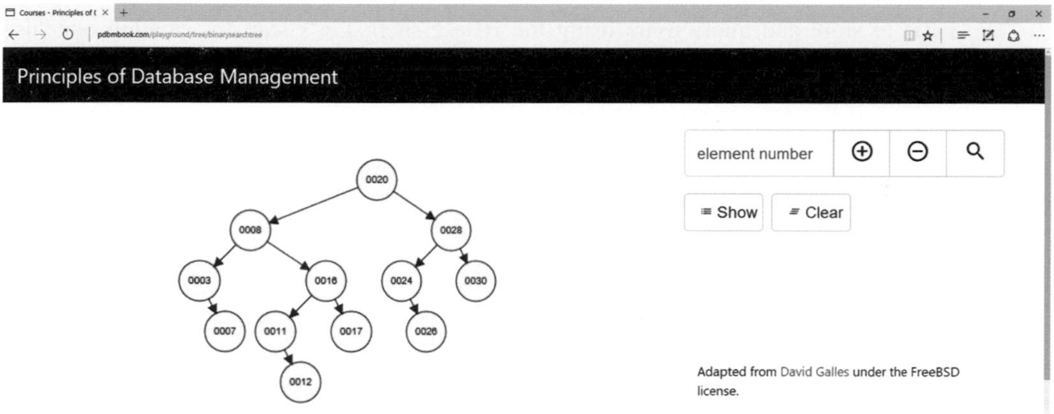


Navigating a binary search tree is very efficient, as half of the search key values can be skipped with every step, rather than linearly navigating all key values. To illustrate this, try using the "find" button to look for key 11. An animation will play showing how the tree is traversed:

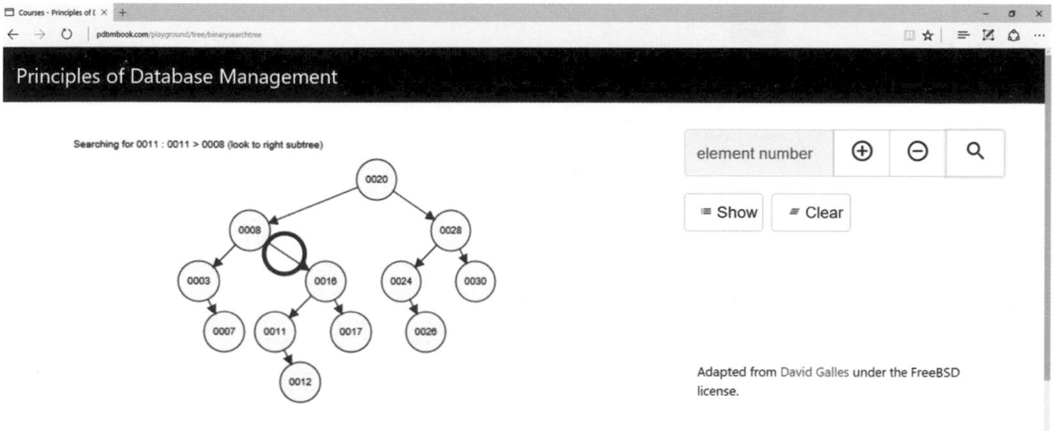


The performance could be increased even further if each node would contain more than one key value and more than two children. In that case, with an equal total number of key values, the height of the tree would be reduced and therefore the average and maximal number of steps would be lower.

This exact consideration is at the basis of the B-tree concept. B-trees and $B^+$-trees can be considered as variations of search trees that are explicitly designed for hard disk storage. Every node contains a set of search key values, a set of tree pointers that refer to child nodes, and a set of data pointers that refer to data records that correspond to the search key values. The data records are stored separately and are not part of the B-tree. You can play around with B-trees and $B^+$-trees in the environment as well.

## Environment: HBase

In Chapter 19 on Big Data, we discussed HBase as a first, key–value based data store that runs on top of Hadoop. In the online environment, you can experiment with the HBase shell and follow along with the queries in the chapter.

We start with an empty HBase set-up in this environment, so let's create a simple HBase table to store and query users using the HBase shell. Let's start by creating our "users" table with two column families (note: the HBase environment can take some time to parse each command!):

```
create 'users', 'name', 'email'
```

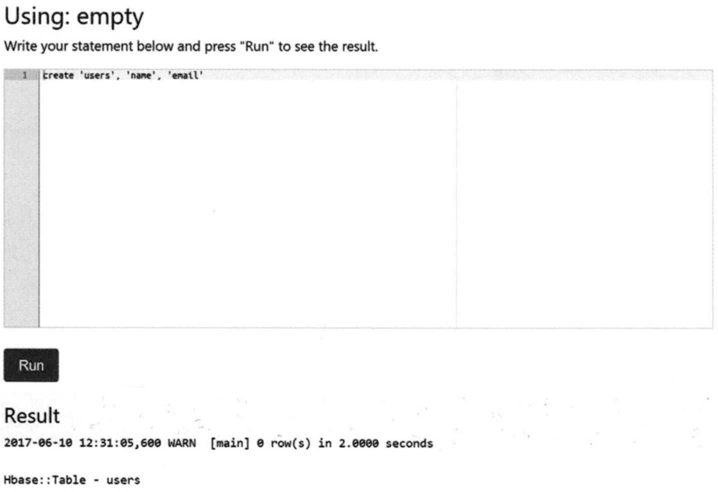
Using: empty
Write your statement below and press "Run" to see the result.
1 create 'users', 'name', 'email'
Run
Result
2017-06-10 12:31:05,600 WARN [main] 0 row(s) in 2.0000 seconds
Hbase::Table - users

Describe the table:

```
describe 'users'
```

Result

```
2017-06-10 12:32:31,156 WARN  [main] Table users is ENABLED
users
COLUMN FAMILIES DESCRIPTION
{NAME => 'email', BLOOMFILTER => 'ROW', VERSIONS => '1', IN_MEMORY => 'false', KEEP_DELETED_CELLS => 'FA
{NAME => 'name', BLOOMFILTER => 'ROW', VERSIONS => '1', IN_MEMORY => 'false', KEEP_DELETED_CELLS => 'FAL
2 row(s) in 1.3410 seconds

nil
```

List this table (the table itself, not its contents):

```
list 'users'
```

We can now insert values. Since HBase represents data as a multidimensional map, we store values using "put" one by one by specifying the row key, column family:qualifier, and the value itself. Note you can enter multiple statements by just entering them line-by-line:

```
put 'users', 'seppe', 'name:first', 'Seppe'
put 'users', 'seppe', 'name:last', 'vanden Broucke'
put 'users', 'seppe', 'email', 'seppe.vandenbroucke@kuleuven'
```

Now list the full contents of this table using the "scan" command:

```
scan 'users'
```

Result

```
2017-06-10 12:36:29,150 WARN  [main] ROW  COLUMN+CELL
 seppe column=email:, timestamp=1497112543342, value=seppe.vandenbroucke@kuleuven
 seppe column=name:first, timestamp=1497112543161, value=Seppe
 seppe column=name:last, timestamp=1497112543274, value=vanden Broucke
1 row(s) in 0.6330 seconds

nil
```

Give the information for row key "seppe" only:

```
get 'users', 'seppe'
```

Result

```
2017-06-10 12:38:28,163 WARN  [main] COLUMN  CELL
 email: timestamp=1497112543342, value=seppe.vandenbroucke@kuleuven
 name:first timestamp=1497112543161, value=Seppe
 name:last timestamp=1497112543274, value=vanden Broucke
3 row(s) in 0.7000 seconds

nil
```

We can change the email value by just running put again:

```
put 'users', 'seppe', 'email', 'seppe@kuleuven.be'
```

Let's now retrieve this row again, but only for the column family "email":

```
get 'users', 'seppe', 'email'
```

Result

```
2017-06-10 12:39:41,915 WARN  [main] 0 row(s) in 0.8180 seconds

nil
COLUMN  CELL
 email: timestamp=1497112786182, value=seppe@kuleuven.be
1 row(s) in 0.0870 seconds

nil
```

We can delete all values pertaining to row key “seppe” in “users” as follows and scan the table to confirm that the data are deleted:

```
deleteall 'users', 'seppe'
scan 'users'
```

Result

```
2017-06-10 12:41:02,753 WARN  [main] 0 row(s) in 0.8420 seconds

nil
ROW  COLUMN+CELL
0 row(s) in 0.0640 seconds

nil
```

If you want to start over with a fresh HBase instance, you can press the “reset” link to reset the database to its initial, empty state.

# GLOSSARY

**5 Vs of Big Data** a description of Big Data that defines its scope by listing its characteristics. Initially defined as the 3 Vs – volume, velocity, and variety – researchers have argued for the inclusion of two additional characteristics, veracity and value.

**aborted** when a transaction completed unsuccessfully because of an error or anomaly that occurred during the transaction's execution and the transaction needs to be canceled.

**absolute address** a translation of a relative block address into a device number, cylinder number, track number, and block number.

**abstraction** see generalization.

**access category** a DQ framework category that represents the extent to which data are available and obtainable in a secure manner.

**access modifiers** specify who can have access to a variable or method.

**access path** the path chosen by the DBMS to retrieve data in response to a query.

**access transparency** when the distributed database can be accessed and queried uniformly, regardless of the different database systems and APIs that may be involved.

**accessibility** a DQ dimension that reflects the ease of retrieving data from the underlying data sources.

**accessor methods** in object-oriented programming, methods that give access of the state of an object to another object. Common examples are the getter and setter methods.

**accuracy** a DQ dimension that refers to whether the data values stored for an object are the correct values.

**accuracy ratio (AR)** the ratio between the area below the CAP curve for the current model minus the area below the CAP curve for the random model and the area below the CAP curve for the perfect model minus the area below the CAP curve for the random model. Can also be calculated as $2 \times AUC - 1$.

**ACID** denotes the four desirable properties of database transactions: **A**tomicity, **C**onsistency, **I**solation, and **D**urability.

**active** a DBMS, such as a modern RDBMS, that autonomously takes the initiative for action if specific situations occur.

**ActiveX Data Objects (ADO)** a set of components defined by Microsoft to access data sources, based on the Component Object Model (COM) framework.

**activity services** perform one task in a business process and are triggered by a workflow service when the corresponding task is due.

**actuator** a component of a disk that moves the read/write heads.

**ADO.NET** a set of components defined by Microsoft to access data sources, based on the .NET framework.

**after images** a copy of the new values, after the update by a transaction; kept to redo changes that were not adequately persisted in the physical database files in the first place.

**after trigger** a trigger that is activated after the triggering event took place.

**agglomerative hierarchical clustering** a clustering technique that begins with observations in individual clusters and merges similar observations/clusters until all observations make a single cluster.

**aggregate functions** functions used to summarize information from database tuples. Popular examples are COUNT, SUM, AVG, VARIANCE, MIN/MAX, and STDEV.

**aggregation** entity types related by a particular relationship type can be combined into a higher-level aggregate entity type.

**ALL** an operator that compares a single value to a multiset and returns TRUE only if all values in the subquery match.

**ALTER** an SQL command that modifies table column definitions.

**alternative key** any candidate key not chosen as a primary key.

**analytics** the extraction of valid and useful business patterns, or mathematical decision models from a preprocessed dataset.

**analytics process model** a structured, iterative model that puts analytics in a three-stage process (pre-processing, analytics, and post-processing) with seven steps (identify business problem, identify data sources, select data, clean data, transform data, analyze, and interpret, evaluate, and deploy model).

**anonymization** transforming sensitive data so the exact value cannot be recovered by other parties, such as the data scientist.

**ANY** an operator that compares a single value to a multiset and returns TRUE if any value in the subquery matches.

**application programming interface (API)** exposes an interface with functions of an application or service; clients can then access those functions through this interface.

**archiving** when database files are periodically copied to other storage media, such as tape or another hard disk.

**area under the ROC curve (AUC)** performance metric that provides a simple figure-of-merit for the performance of the constructed classifier; the higher the AUC the better the performance. Can also be interpreted as the probability that a randomly chosen positive (e.g., churner) gets a higher score than a randomly chosen negative (e.g., non-churner).

**association class** an association with variables and/or methods of its own.

**association rules** rules to detect frequently occurring associations between items.

**association** UML construct which corresponds to a relationship type in the ER model whereas a specific occurrence of an association is referred to as a link that corresponds to a relationship in the ER model.

**associative query** a query that returns a collection (e.g., a set or bag) of objects located by the OODBMS.

**Asynchronous JavaScript and XML (AJAX)** a method used by many modern websites to dynamically update parts of a web page without triggering a full page refresh. Commonly implemented by means of an ActiveX component or as the "XMLHttpRequest" JavaScript object.

**atomic attribute type** an attribute type that is indivisible; cannot be further divided or decomposed further into other meaningful attribute types.

**atomic literal** in ODMG, a constant value of type short (short integer), long (long integer), double (real number), float (real number), Boolean (true or false), char, or string.

**attribute type** representation of a specific, defined property of an entity type.

**authorization identifier** indicates the user, or user account, who owns the schema.

**AVG** an SQL operator used in aggregate functions that provides the average of all values in the selected column.

**$B^+$-tree** a tree-structured index in which only the leaf nodes contain data pointers and all key values that exist in the non-leaf nodes are repeated in the leaf nodes, so every key value occurs in a leaf node with a corresponding data pointer. The higher-level nodes only contain a subset of the key values present in the leaf nodes and every leaf node of a $B^+$-tree has one tree pointer, pointing to its next sibling.

**Bachman diagram** a visual representation of the CODASYL model using a network developed by Charles Bachman.

**backup** a copy of archived data kept as part of a recovery strategy in case catastrophic events occur.

**backup and recovery utility** a means to backup and recover the database in the event of a crash or failure.

**BASE principle** used by NoSQL this alternative to the traditional transactional model (ACID) enforces the following three principles: **B**asic **A**vailability, **S**oft state, and **E**ventual consistency.

**before images** a copy of the original values, before the records were updated; kept for the purpose of undoing unwanted effects of failed transactions.

**before trigger** trigger that is activated before the triggering event takes place.

**begin_transaction** an instruction that serves as the notification of the first operation of a new transaction.

**BETWEEN** an SQL operator used with the WHERE clause that specifies a range of values from which to return results.

**bidirectional association** an association in which two ways of navigating are indicated by an arrow in the UML model.

**binary large object (BLOB)** data collected and stored as a single large object in a DBMS; BLOBs are typically multimedia files (e.g., image, audio, video).

**binary search** an efficient algorithmic search for a record in an ordered list performed recursively by halving the search interval with each iteration.

**binary search tree** a physical tree structure in which each node has at most two children. Each tree node contains a search key value and a maximum of two pointers to children. Both children are the root nodes of subtrees, with one subtree only containing key values that are lower than the key value in the original node, and the other subtree only containing key values that are higher.

**bitmap index** contains a row ID and a series of bits – one bit for each possible value of the indexed attribute type; mostly efficient for attribute types with only a limited set of possible values.

**BLOB (binary large object)** see binary large object.

**block pointer** refers to the physical block address of a corresponding record.

**blocking factor** indicates how many records are stored in a single disk block; determines how many records are retrieved with a single read operation, without intermediate seeks and/or rotational delay.

**blocking factor of the index (BFI)** denotes how many index entries fit within a single disk block, resulting in a single entry for a higher-level index.

**block-level I/O protocol** the I/O commands are defined at the level of requests for individual blocks on the storage device.

**bootstrapping** when one takes samples with replacement from a dataset.

**Boyce–Codd normal form (BCNF)** a normal form such that for each of the non-trivial functional dependencies $X \rightarrow Y$, X is a superkey.

**B-tree** a tree-structured index in which each node corresponds to a disk block and nodes are kept between half-full and full to cater for a certain dynamism of the index.

**bucket** a contiguous area of record addresses that contains one or more stored record slots.

**buffer manager** manages the buffer memory. Intelligently caches data in the buffer for quick access and monitors the buffer to determine what should be added or deleted.

**business continuity** an organization's ability to guarantee its uninterrupted functioning, despite possible planned or unplanned downtime of the hardware and software supporting its database functionality.

**business intelligence (BI)** the set of activities, techniques, and tools aimed at understanding patterns in past data and predicting the future.

**business process** a set of tasks or activities with a certain ordering that must be executed to reach a certain organizational goal.

**call-level API** an API that allows SQL instructions to be passed to the DBMS by direct calls to functions, procedures, or methods to perform necessary actions.

**candidate key** the attribute type(s) of a relation that are unique, such as a unique product number.

**canonical form** a mathematical expression of a query, according to the relational algebra that provides the mathematical underpinning of the relational model.

**CAP theorem** formulated by Eric Brewer, this theorem states a distributed computer system cannot guarantee the following three properties simultaneously: **C**onsistency, **A**vailability, and **P**artition tolerance.

**Capability Maturity Model Integration (CMMI)** a training and appraisal program developed by Carnegie Mellon University geared toward the improvement of business processes.

**cardinalities** specify the minimum or maximum number of relationship instances in which an individual entity can participate; the minimum cardinality can be either 0 or 1 and the maximum cardinality can be either 1 or N.

**cascading rollback** a recursive rollback in which transactions that read data written by transactions marked for rollback in the previous step have to be rolled back as well, and so on.

**catalog** a repository for data definitions generated by the DDL compiler, integrity rules, metadata, and other information such as users, user groups, and statistics about data and storage.

**categorization** representing a collection of entities that is a subset of the union of the superclasses; represented in the EER model by a circle with a letter "u" (from union) in it.

**central storage** part of the storage hierarchy; consists of memory chips (also called random access memory, or RAM) of which each individual byte has its own address, which is directly referable by the operating system. Also called internal memory or main memory.

**centrality metrics** characterize how central a node is in a network from different perspectives. Examples are degree, closeness, and betweenness.

**centralized DBMS architecture** data are maintained on a centralized host (e.g., a mainframe) system. All queries then have to be processed by this single host.

**centralized system architecture** a database architecture in which all responsibilities of the DBMSs are handled by a single centralized entity; a system in which the DBMS logic, the data themselves, and the application logic and presentation logic (also called the user interface), are all handled by the same system.

**chaining** an overflow-handling technique in which overflow records are stored in a separate overflow area, with subsequent records that overflow from the same bucket being chained together by pointers.

**changeability property** specifies the type of operations allowed on either variable values or links.

**changed data capture (CDC)** data integration technology that can detect update events in the source data store, and trigger the ETL process based on these updates.

**CHECK constraint** used to define a constraint on the column values of a relational table.

**checkpoint** synchronization point denoting the moment when buffered updates by active transactions, as present in the database buffer, are written to disk at once.

**choreography** a decentralized sequence and data dependency management pattern that relies on the participants themselves to coordinate their collaboration in the context of a business process.

**churn prediction** predicting which customers a firm is likely to lose.

**class** a blueprint definition for a set of objects.

**class invariant** a constraint that holds for all objects of a class.

**classification** a type of predictive analytics in which the target variable is categorical. Classification can be binary or multiclass.

**classification accuracy** the percentage of correctly classified observations.

**cleansing** removing some inconsistencies or irregularities in the data (e.g., missing or impossible values).

**client–server DBMS architecture** active clients request services from passive servers. A *fat client variant* stores more processing functionality on the client, whereas a *fat server variant* puts more on the server.

**client-side scripting** scripts are embedded inside HTML documents then interpreted and run directly inside the browser on the user's computer.

**CLOB (character large object)** variable-length character string made up of single-byte characters.

**cloud DBMS architecture** both the DBMS and database are hosted by a third-party cloud provider. The data themselves can then be distributed across multiple nodes in a cluster.

**cloud-based solution** a solution in which a requested service is offered via the internet by a cloud computing provider.

**clustered index** similar to a primary index but where the ordering criterion, and therefore the search key, is a non-key attribute type or set of attribute types, instead of a primary or candidate key.

**clustering** (1) *In analytics*: splitting up a set of observations into clusters so the homogeneity within a cluster is maximized (cohesive), and the heterogeneity between clusters is maximized (separated). (2) *In failover*: multiple interconnected computer systems working together to be perceived, in certain aspects, as a unity for improved performance by means of parallelism and/or availability through redundancy in hardware, software, and data.

**CODASYL model** an early data model developed by the Data Base Task Group of the **CO**nference on **DA**ta **SY**stem **L**anguages in 1969. The CODASYL model only includes record types, set types, and 1:N relationship types.

**coefficient of determination** performance measure of a regression model specifying how much better the model predicts than the average; varies between 0 and +1.

**collection literal** in ODMG, a collection of elements such as a set, bag, list, array, or dictionary.

**collision** happens when several records are assigned to the same bucket in random file organization.

**column-oriented DBMS** a database management system that stores data tables as sections of columns, rather than as rows of data.

**combined approach** in the context of XML storage; a storage technique that combines both the document- and data-oriented approach for storing XML documents. Some parts of the XML document will be stored as BLOBs, CLOBs, or XML objects, whereas other parts will be shredded and stored in relational tables.

**committed** when a transaction completed successfully and all changes made by the individual operations belonging to that transaction can be made permanent.

**common gateway interface (CGI)** a standard protocol that allows web servers to construct dynamic pages by executing a program at the server level responsible for generating the content and sending it to the user.

**compatibility matrix** in transaction management, a matrix which indicates which request will be granted for a particular database object based on the locks currently in place on that same object.

**compensation-based transaction model** transaction model that allows for undoing local effects of a transaction if the global long-running transaction is unsuccessful; defines compensating operations for each transaction-sensitive operation.

**completeness** a DQ dimension that refers to the extent to which data are not missing and cover the needs of and are of sufficient breadth and depth for the task being performed.

**completeness constraint** indicates whether all entities of the superclass should belong to one of the subclasses.

**complex event processing (CEP)** analytics techniques that do not focus on individual events, but rather on the interrelationships between events and patterns within so-called event clouds.

**composite attribute type** an attribute type that is divisible; can be decomposed into other meaningful attribute types.

**conceptual data model** a high-level description of data items, characteristics, and relationships. Used for communication between information architect and business user to ensure data requirements are properly captured and modeled.

**concurrency control** the coordination of transactions that execute simultaneously on the same data so they do not cause inconsistencies in the data because of mutual interference.

**confidence** measures the strength of the association; the conditional probability of the rule consequent, given the rule antecedent.

**conformed dimensions** a dimension that has the same meaning and content across different fact tables and/or data marts.

**connection manager** provides the facilities to set up a connection to a database by verifying credentials and returning a connection handle. Connections can be set up locally or through a network.

**connectivity** the way in which storage devices are connected to processors and/or servers.

**conservative 2PL** see static 2PL.

**consistency** a DQ dimension that refers to the extent to which data are continuously presented in the same format.

**consistent hashing** hashing schema that avoids having to remap each key to a new node when nodes are added or removed.

**constructor** in object-oriented programming, a method that creates and returns a new object of a class.

**contextual category** a DQ framework category that measures the extent to which data are appropriate to the task of the data consumer.

**contingency plan** a formal plan outlining recovery objectives and strategic priorities if a calamity occurs, jeopardizing business continuity.

**Control Objectives for Information and Related Technologies (COBIT)** a framework created by the international professional association ISACA for information technology (IT) management, and IT governance.

**correlated nested queries** a condition in which the WHERE clause of a nested query references a column of a table declared in the outer query; the nested query is evaluated once for each tuple, or combination of tuples, in the outer query.

**cost-based optimizer** a query optimizer that calculates the optimal access plan according to a set of built-in cost formulas.

**COUNT** an SQL operator used in aggregate functions to count the number of tuples.

**cross-validation** performance estimation method where the data are split into $K$ folds (e.g., five or ten). An analytical model is then trained on $K-1$ training folds and tested on the remaining validation fold. This is repeated for all possible validation folds, resulting in $K$ performance estimates that can then be averaged.

**CRUDS functionality** data manipulation activities that will Create, Read, Update, Delete, or Search on data stored in the underlying data stores.

**CUBE** an SQL operator that computes a union of GROUP BYs on every subset of the specified attribute types, with results representing a multidimensional cube based upon the source table.

**cumulative accuracy profile (CAP)** sorts the population from high score to low score and then measures the cumulative percentage of positives (e.g., churners) for each decile on the $x$-axis.

**cursor mechanism** similar to a textual cursor, a database cursor keeps track of where we are in the result set, so that the tuples that result from an SQL query can be traversed and are presented to the application code one by one.

**customer segmentation** the segmentation of a set of customers or transactions into homogeneous clusters that can be used for marketing purposes.

**cutoff** number used to map class probabilities to class labels.

**cylinder** a set of tracks with the same diameter (distance from the center) on different platters of a hard disk.

**Cypher** a graph-based query language introduced by Neo4j, one of the most popular graph databases.

**DAS (directly attached storage)** storage devices directly connected to individual servers.

**Data as a Service (DaaS)** data services are offered as part of an overall service oriented architecture (SOA) or cloud architecture.

**data accessibility** see accessibility.

**data accuracy** see accuracy.

**data auditing services** report on data lineage and when/how/by whom data were changed.

**data cleansing services** ensure the validity and consistency of data using name-and-address cleansing by resolving missing fields, poor formatting, and conflicting data, and standardization to various industry formats.

**data completeness** see completeness.

**data consistency** see consistency.

**data consolidation** a data integration pattern that captures the data from multiple, heterogeneous source systems and integrates them into a single, persistent data store (e.g., a data warehouse or data mart).

**data definition language (DDL)** language used by the database administrator to express the database's external, logical, and internal data models.

**data dependency** specifies that the execution of a service B depends on data provided by a service A.

**data enrichment services** enhance the data by exploiting external data sources.

**data event services** monitor data for state changes and rules, raising events that can be acted upon by other services.

**data federation** a data integration pattern to provide a unified view over one or more data sources through a pull approach in which data are pulled from the underlying source systems on an on-demand basis.

**data flow** specifies the path of the data between business activities or tasks in a business process.

**data governance** the proactive management of data as an asset; a company-wide controlled and supported approach toward data quality accompanied by a data quality management process.

**data independence** when changes in data definitions in one layer of the database architecture have minimal to no impact on the other layers.

**data integration** a process with the purpose of providing a unified view and/or unified access over heterogeneous, and possibly distributed, data sources.

**data integration pattern** method to provide a single unified view on a set of underlying data sources.

**data item** a collection of bits or characters that represent a specific value on a physical storage medium. Also called a field.

**data lake** a large data repository that holds data in their raw format, which can be structured, unstructured, or semi-structured.

**data lineage** the whole trajectory followed by a data item, from its origin (data entry), possibly over respective transformations and aggregations, until it is ultimately used or processed.

**data localization** a step in distributed query processing in which the query is transformed into a fragment query.

**data management** proper management of data and corresponding data definitions or metadata to ensure good quality for effective and efficient decision-making.

**Data Management Body of Knowledge (DMBOK)** overseen by DAMA International (the Data Management Association), this collection of processes lists best practices toward data quality management, metadata management, data warehousing, data integration, and data governance.

**Data Management Maturity Model** a model that applies five levels of maturity to the governance of data, their quality, and their supporting infrastructure.

**data manipulation language (DML)** used to retrieve, insert, delete, and modify data in a database. DML statements can be embedded in a general-purpose programming language, or entered through a front-end querying tool.

**data mart** a scaled-down version of a data warehouse aimed at meeting the information needs of a small homogeneous group of end-users such as a department or business unit.

**data owner** person with the authority to ultimately decide on the access to, and usage of, the data; can be the original producer of the data, one of its consumers, or a third party.

**data pointers** pointers that refer to data records, or blocks with data records, that correspond to the search key values.

**data pre-processing** set of activities to prepare data for analysis, including sampling and data cleaning.

**data profiling services** provide automated support for assessing and understanding content, quality, and structure of enterprise data and relate data from various sources to one another based on the patterns and values in the data.

**data propagation** a data integration pattern corresponding to the synchronous or asynchronous propagation of updates, or events in a source system to a target system.

**data quality (DQ)** a set of contextual rules that determine the fitness of data for use in a business application; determines the intrinsic value of the data to a business.

**data redundancy** when additional (redundant) copies of the files or data are stored on offline media (e.g., a tape vault) or online media (e.g., on an online backup hard disk drive, or even in a full-blown redundant database node), e.g., for recovery purposes in case of failures or crashes; see also replication.

**data replication** the act of propagating data written to one device over a network onto another device. This can be done synchronously or semi-synchronously, or asynchronously.

**data scientist** a relatively new profession in which a person uses quantitative, programming, business, communication, and visualization skills to analyze complex data using activities such as sampling and preprocessing of data, analytical model development, and post-processing.

**data service composition** when data from different services can be combined and aggregated into a new, composite, service.

**data services** provide access to the business data.

**data silo** a set of data specific to a business domain not integrated with an organization's global data infrastructure.

**data steward** DQ expert in charge of ensuring the quality of both the actual business data and the corresponding metadata by performing extensive and regular data quality checks.

**data striping** technique applied in RAID in which subsections of a data file (called strips, consisting of individual bits or entire disk blocks) are distributed over multiple disks to be read and written in parallel.

**data transformation services** transform data to match the target application's requirements or reconcile data items residing in different data sources.

**data virtualization** a data integration technique that uses basic data integration patterns and isolation of applications and users from the actual (combinations of) integration patterns used to produce a unified data view for applications to retrieve and manipulate data without knowing where the data are stored physically or how they are structured and formatted at the sources.

**data warehouse** As defined by Bill Inmon: *"A data warehouse is a subject-oriented, integrated, time-variant, and nonvolatile collection of data in support of management's decision-making process."*

**database** a collection of related data items within a specific business process or problem setting stored on a computer system through the organization and management of a database management system.

**database administrator (DBA)** responsible for the implementation and monitoring of the database; closely collaborates with network and system managers.

**database approach** a data management approach in which all data are stored centrally and managed by a DBMS. Each application has access to the data it needs through the DBMS, resulting in fewer instances of duplicate data or data with errors.

**database designer** translates the conceptual data model into a logical and internal data model.

**Database Management System (DBMS)** a software package consisting of several software modules used to define, create, use, and maintain a database.

**database management system architecture** a conceptual specification of the various modules that interact with one another to make up a DBMS.

**database model** the description of the database data at different levels of detail, specifying the data items, their characteristics and relationships, constraints, storage details, etc.

**database schema** see database model.

**database state** a representation of the data in a database at a given moment that changes on an ongoing basis with data manipulation, such as adding, updating, or removing data.

**database system** the combination of a database and database management system.

**data-oriented approach** a storage technique in which an XML document is decomposed into its constituting data parts, which are spread across a set of connected (object-)relational tables.

**DBCLOB (double byte character large object)** variable-length character string made up of double-byte characters.

**DDL compiler** compiles and processes the data definitions and commands specified by the data definition language.

**DDL statements** also called data definition language statements. Create data definitions stored in the catalog that define or alter the database model.

**deadlock** occurs if two or more transactions are waiting for one another's locks to be released. Each transaction holds one or more locks required by another transaction to continue, resulting in all transactions remaining in an endless wait state.

**deadlock detection and resolution** strategy adopted to first find out if a deadlock occurred and then resolve it afterwards.

**deadlock prevention** strategy adopted to prevent deadlocks from occurring.

**decision phase** the second phase of the 2PC Protocol in which the transaction coordinator makes the final decision about the outcome.

**decision support systems (DSS)** the information systems needed at both the tactical and strategic level to provide information supporting decisions in either the mid- or long-term range.

**decision trees** recursive partitioning algorithms (RPAs) that come up with a tree-like structure representing patterns in an underlying dataset.

**declarative DML** type of DML that improved upon procedural DML. Specifies *which* data should be retrieved or *what* changes should be made without the need to specify the *how*.

**deduplication** aggregating and merging different attribute types (e.g., CustomerID, CustID, ClientID, ID) or attribute values (e.g., Bart Baesens versus Bart Baessens) into one attribute type or value.

**deep equality** implies that objects have the same values for their variables and all their referred objects have the same values for their variables.

**DEFAULT constraint** can be used in SQL to set a default value for a column.

**deferred update** database buffer flushing policy in which only pending updates from already committed transactions are written to disk; there will never be a need for UNDO operations, but REDO operations may still be required. Also called NO-UNDO/REDO policy.

**degree** corresponds to the number of entity types participating in the relationship type (e.g., a binary relationship type has a degree of two).

**DELETE** an SQL statement that removes data from a relational database.

**deletion anomaly** an issue encountered when a tuple in an unnormalized table is deleted, resulting in the deletion of all corresponding data.

**delimiters** one or more characters to mark the beginning or end of a unit of data.

**delineate** to specify the transaction boundaries.

**dendrogram** a tree-like diagram that records the sequences of merges in hierarchical clustering.

**denormalization** the merging of several normalized source data tables into an aggregated, denormalized data table.

**dense index** an index with an index entry for every possible value of the search key it indexes.

**dependency** defines a "using" relationship that states that a change in the specification of a UML modeling concept may affect another modeling concept that uses it; denoted by a dashed line in the UML diagram.

**dependent data marts** data marts that pull their data from a central data warehouse.

**derived attribute type** an attribute type that can be derived from another attribute type.

**derived fragmentation** when the fragmentation criteria belong to another table.

**dicing** an OLAP operation corresponding to a range selection on one or more dimensions.

**direct attach** storage devices with a one-to-one connection between server and storage device.

**directly accessible storage device (DASD)** storage device on which every location should be individually addressable and directly reachable to access its content.

**directory** a file that defines the relationships between the records in another file.

**disaster tolerance** refers to an organization's endurance against human- or nature-induced disasters.

**disjoint specialization** a specialization whereby an entity can be a member of at most one of the subclasses.

**disjointness constraint** specifies what subclasses an entity of the superclass can belong to.

**disk block** a single sector or multiple physically adjacent sectors which a disk reads as a single unit, increasing read speed and efficiency; also called cluster, page, or allocation unit.

**disk mirroring** a (near) real-time approach that writes the same data simultaneously to two or more physical disks (e.g., in a RAID set-up).

**dissemination** mechanism used to specify how information flows between nodes in a network.

**DISTINCT** an SQL operator used in aggregate functions that filters out duplicates.

**distinct data type** a user-defined data type that specializes a standard, built-in SQL data type, inheriting all the properties of the SQL data type used for its definition.

**distributed 2PL** a distributed version of 2PL in which every site has its own lock manager, which manages all locking data pertaining to the fragments stored on that site.

**distributed database system** a database system in which data and data retrieval functionality are distributed over multiple data sources and/or locations.

**divisive hierarchical clustering** a clustering technique that starts with one cluster and splits recursively until one observation per cluster remains.

**DML compiler** compiles the data manipulation statements specified in the DML. Translates the DML statements into a set of simple constructs to select, insert, update, and delete data.

**document metadata** metadata that refer to the properties of the document itself: file name, creator of the file, creation, and last modification date of the file, file type (text, image, audio, etc.).

**document store** type of NoSQL database that stores a collection of attributes labeled and unordered, representing items that are semi-structured.

**Document Type Definition (DTD)** a formal specification of the structure of an XML document that defines the tag set, the location of each tag, and how they are nested. See also XML Schema Definition.

**document-oriented approach** a storage technique in which an XML document is stored as either a BLOB (binary large object) or a CLOB (character large object) in a table cell.

**DOM API** a tree-based API that represents the XML document as a tree in internal memory.

**domain** specifies and organizes the range of admissible values for an attribute type.

**doubling amount** the amount of change required for doubling the primary outcome odds in a logistic regression.

**DQ framework** categorizes the dimensions of data quality; a methodology developed to determine the measures of data quality.

**drill-across** an OLAP operation where information from two or more connected fact tables is accessed.

**DROP** an SQL command that removes database objects.

**dummy record type** record type needed in the CODASYL model to model N:M or recursive relationship types.

**dynamic binding** in object-oriented programming, the binding of a method to its implementation at runtime, based on the object and its class. Also known as virtual method invocation.

**dynamic hashing** a hashing procedure that allows for a file to shrink or grow without the need for it to be completely rearranged.

**early binding** queries are translated into an executable format ("bound") before compiling the host language. In this way, the queries can be checked for correctness, but they have the disadvantage that they cannot be constructed dynamically during runtime.

**edge** one of the primary components of graphs, consisting of arcs or lines that connect nodes.

**electronic vaulting** backup method in which backup data are transmitted over a network to hard disk or tape devices at a secure vaulting facility or at an alternate data center.

**embedded API** an API with SQL statements embedded in the host programming language so the SQL statement(s) will be an integral part of the source code of a program.

**embedded DBMSs** a DBMS containing a single library embedded, or tightly integrated, with an application so it becomes an integral part of the application.

**embedded DML statements** also called embedded data manipulation language statements, this is how applications are able to interact with the DBMS.

**embedded documents** used in MongoDB to embed related data as subdocuments in a document.

**embedded identification** a record organization technique in which data items representing attributes are always preceded explicitly by the attribute type; only non-empty attributes of the records are included.

**encapsulation** see information hiding.

**end_transaction** an instruction that indicates the end of a transaction.

**Enhanced Entity Relationship Model (EER)** an extension of the ER model that includes all the modeling concepts of the ER model, plus additional semantic data modeling concepts: specialization/generalization, categorization, and aggregation.

**enterprise application integration (EAI)** the set of activities aimed at integrating applications within a specific enterprise environment. It often applies a data propagation pattern in the interaction between two applications (e.g., when an event in a source application requires processing within a target application).

**enterprise data replication (EDR)** data propagation pattern applied in the synchronization between two data stores where updates in a source system are copied in (near) real-time to a target data store which serves as an exact replica.

**enterprise information integration (EII)** a data federation technology implemented by realizing a virtual business view on the dispersed underlying data sources.

**Enterprise JavaBeans (EJB)** business components that run within the Java Enterprise Edition (Java EE) platform. Each EJB defines a modular piece of business logic which can be used and re-used in business applications.

**enterprise search** the practice of making content stemming from various distributed data sources (databases, but also plain files) in an organization searchable.

**Entity Relationship (ER) model** a data model that shows the relationship among data items through entity types, attribute types, and relationship types. Visualized through an attractive and user-friendly graphical notation.

**entity type** representation of a business concept with an unambiguous meaning to a specific set of users.

**Ethernet** the long-standing standard medium for local area networks (LANs) and sometimes wide area networks (WANs), mostly in combination with the internet protocol stack TCP/IP.

**ETL (extract, transform, load)** step of a data warehouse development process in which data are extracted (E) from the source systems, transformed (T) to fit the data warehouse schema, and then loaded (L) into the data warehouse.

**eventual consistency** data and respective replicas of the same data item become consistent over time after each transaction, but continuous consistency is not guaranteed.

**EXCEPT** an SQL set operation that returns a table that includes all tuples that are in the first SELECT block but not in the second.

**exclusive lock** a lock in which a single transaction acquires the sole privilege to interact with the locked database object; no other transactions may read from it or write to it until the lock is released.

**existence dependency** see total participation.

**EXISTS** an SQL function that checks whether the result of a correlated nested query is empty or not, returning TRUE or FALSE.

**exploratory analysis** data analysis activities that summarize and visualize characteristics of a dataset to provide initial insights into the data that can be usefully adopted throughout the analytical modeling stage.

**extended relational DBMS (ERDBMS)** see object-relational DBMS (ORDBMS).

**Extensible Markup Language (XML)** a markup language for the storage and exchange of complex, structured, and semi-structured documents; designed to be both human and machine readable. It was introduced by the World Wide Web Consortium (W3C) in 1997.

**Extensible Stylesheet Language (XSL)** collection of languages that can be used to transform XML documents.

**external data model** the subsets of the data items in the logical model, also called views, tailored toward the needs of specific applications or groups of users.

**external scalar function** function written in an external host language (e.g., Java, C, Python) that returns a single value or scalar.

**external table function** function written in an external host language (e.g., Java, C, Python) that returns a table of values.

**extraction strategy** strategy adopted to extract data from the source systems and load them into the data warehouse; can be either full or incremental.

**fact constellation** a conceptual data model of a data warehouse that has more than one fact table, and which share some dimension tables.

**factless fact table** a fact table that contains only foreign keys and no measurement data.

**failover time** time needed to have a backup system up and running, with up-to-date data, after, e.g., a media malfunction.

**failure detection** mechanism used to find out if a node in a network has gone down.

**featurization** mapping of network characteristics into explanatory variables (also called features) for each node.

**federated database** see federated DBMS.

**federated DBMS** provides a uniform interface to underlying data sources such as other DBMSs, file systems, and document management systems. Hides the underlying storage details to facilitate data access.

**Fibre Channel (FC)** medium developed specifically to connect high-end storage systems to servers. Originally, it was based on fiber-optic cable (hence the name), but nowadays it also supports other cabling such as copper wire.

**file-based approach** a data management approach common in the early days of computing, in which every application stored its data in its own dedicated files, which resulted in multiple instances of duplicate data or data with errors.

**file-level I/O protocol** the I/O commands are defined at the level of requests for entire files on the storage device.

**filter factor (FF)** the fraction of the total number of rows that is expected to satisfy the predicate associated with an attribute type.

**first normal form (1 NF)** states that every attribute type of a relation must be atomic and single-valued. Hence, no composite or multi-valued attribute types are tolerated.

**FLWOR** the formulation of an XQuery statement that represents **F**or, **L**et, **W**here, **O**rder By, and **R**eturn.

**foreign key** an attribute type or attribute types of one relation that is/are referring to the primary key of another.

**formatting rules** specify how data should be consistently and uniformly encoded in the data warehouse.

**fourth normal form (4 NF)** when Boyce–Codd normal form is satisfied and for every non-trivial multi-valued dependency $X \rightarrow\rightarrow Y$, X is a superkey.

**fragment query** the transformation of a query to a query on physical fragments based on the data distribution; the result of the data localization step in distributed query processing.

**fragmentation** the act of partitioning the global dataset into fragments.

**fragmentation transparency** when users can execute global queries, without being concerned with the fact that distributed fragments will be involved, and need to be combined, to perform the query.

**fragments** data that have been partitioned into subsets in a distributed database.

**free-form language** a language in which no special indentation is required, in contrast to languages such as Python or COBOL.

**FROM** part of an SQL statement that specifies which table(s) are used for data retrieval.

**full backup** a backup of the entire database, including data and all changes from transactions.

**full functional dependency** exists if there is a dependency between two sets of attribute types X and Y and when the removal of any attribute type A from X means that the dependency does not hold anymore.

**full outer join** an SQL join query in which each row of both tables is kept in the result, if necessary completed with NULL values.

**full-text search** a technique for searching XML data that treats the XML document as textual data, ignoring tag structure and information.

**functional dependency** a constraint in which one value of an attribute type determines the value of another.

**gain** the weighted decrease in entropy. Used to decide on node splits when growing a decision tree.

**garbage in, garbage out (GIGO)** a principle that states that bad data give bad insights, which lead to bad decisions.

**General Data Protection Regulation (GDPR)** regulation in the European Union with rules for compliance, openness, and transparency regarding the use of an individual's personal data.

**generalization** the reverse process of specialization; a bottom-up process of conceptual synthesis.

**global deadlock** a deadlock spanning several locations that cannot be detected by individual local lock managers.

**global query optimization** a step in distributed query processing in which a cost model, based on statistical evidence, is used to evaluate different global strategies for query execution.

**granularity** the level of depth of the data represented in a fact table. High granularity means deep depth and low granularity means shallow depth.

**graph theory** a theory that uses the mathematical structures of graphs to model pairwise relations between objects.

**graph-based database** type of NoSQL database that applies the mathematical graph theory to the storage of records. Data are stored in graph structures using the elements of nodes and edges.

**GraphX** Spark's component implementing programming abstractions to deal with graph-based structures. It comes with a set of fundamental operators and algorithms to work with graphs and simplify graph analytics tasks.

**GROUP BY** an SQL clause in which rows are grouped when they have the same value for one or more columns and the aggregation is applied to each group separately.

**GROUPING SETS** an SQL operator that generates a result set equivalent to one created by a UNION ALL of several simple GROUP BY clauses.

**Hadoop** a popular open-source software framework used for distributed storage and processing of big datasets that can be set up over a cluster of computers built from normal, commodity hardware, instead of requiring specialized, expensive machines.

**Hadoop Common** a set of shared programming libraries used by the other Hadoop modules; the first module of the Hadoop stack.

**Hadoop Distributed File System (HDFS)** a Java-based file system to store data across multiple machines; the second module of the Hadoop stack.

**hard disk backup** backup method in which database files are copied periodically to a hard disk for safekeeping.

**hard disk controller** circuitry that oversees a drive's functioning and interfaces between the disk drive and the rest of the system.

**hash function** a function that takes an arbitrary value of arbitrary size and maps it to a key with a fixed size, which is called the hash value, hash code, hash sum, or simply the hash.

**hash index** a secondary file organization method that combines hashing with indexed retrieval; index entries have the same format as with a normal secondary index, but the index is organized as a hash file.

**hash join** technique to physically implement a join, in which a hashing algorithm is applied to the values of the attribute types involved in the join condition for a table R. Based on the resulting hash values, the corresponding rows are assigned to buckets in a hash file. The same hashing algorithm is then applied to the join attribute types of the second table S. If a hash value for S refers to a non-empty bucket in the hash file, the corresponding rows of R and S are compared according to the join condition.

**hashing** a key-to-address transformation, such that a record's physical address can be calculated from its key value.

**HBase** the first Hadoop database inspired by Google's Bigtable, offering a DBMS that can be run on top of HDFS, handling very large relational tables.

**heap file** a primary file organization method in which new records are inserted at the end of the file. There is no relationship between a record's attributes and its physical location, which is not efficient for record retrieval.

**Hibernate** a framework for the Java programming language that handles object persistence through object-relational mapping.

**hierarchical clustering** a clustering technique that builds a hierarchy of clusters; can work in a divisive or agglomerative way.

**hierarchical DBMS** one of the earliest DBMS types. It is record oriented, using a tree-style model with procedural DML and no query processor. Examples include IMS and the Windows Registry.

**hierarchical model** one of the earliest data models developed, originating during the Apollo missions. As a tree-structured model it must have 1:N relationship types. Parent records can have multiple child records, but a child record can have only one parent.

**Hive** a data warehouse solution which – like HBase – runs on top of Hadoop, but allows for richer data summarization, and querying facilities by providing an SQL-like interface.

**horizontal fragmentation** when each fragment in a distributed database consists of rows that satisfy a certain query predicate.

**horizontal scaling** a way to increase capacity by arranging multiple database servers in a cluster.

**hybrid OLAP (HOLAP)** combines elements of both MOLAP and ROLAP, allowing an RDBMS to store the detailed data in a relational data warehouse, whereas the pre-computed aggregated data can be kept as a multidimensional array managed by a MDBMS.

**I/O** input/output; the exchange of data between secondary and primary storage supervised by the operating system.

**I/O boundary** boundary between primary (volatile) and secondary (persistent) storage.

**immediate update policy** database buffer flushing policy in which the database may be updated before a transaction is committed.

**implementation** in object-oriented programming, the implementation of methods' signatures.

**impurity** the distribution of classes in a classification context. Maximum impurity means balanced class distribution, whereas minimum impurity means one class dominates the other(s).

**IN** an SQL operator used with the WHERE clause that can specify multiple values, creating a set.

**inconsistent analysis problem** when a transaction reads partial results of another transaction that simultaneously interacts with (and updates) the same data items.

**incremental backup** a backup of only the data changed since the last backup.

**independent data mart** standalone system that draws data directly from the operational systems, external sources, or a combination of both, and not from a central data warehouse.

**index** a stored, ordered list of key values that is part of the internal data model and that provides a fast access path to the physical data to speed up the execution time of a query.

**index entry** a representation of an interval that contains the search key value of the first record in the interval, and a pointer to the physical position of the first record in the interval.

**index space** a space in the storage structure separate from the tablespace in which indexes are stored.

**indexed sequential file organization** primary file organization method in which a sequential file is combined with one or more indexes.
**indexer** a web search component that extracts all relevant terms from the page and updates the inverted index structure.
**indexing** primary or secondary file organization method that makes use of an index to specify a relationship between a record's search key and its physical location.
**information analyst** see information architect.
**information architect** designs the conceptual data model; bridge between business process and IT environment; collaborates closely with the database designer.
**information hiding** states that the variables of an object can only be accessed through either getter or setter methods; also called encapsulation.
**Information Technology Infrastructure Library (ITIL)** a set of detailed practices for IT service management that focuses on aligning IT services with the needs and requirements of business.
**Infrastructure as a Service (IaaS)** hardware infrastructure (servers, storage, etc.) are offered as virtual machines in the cloud, e.g., cloud-hosted storage hardware.
**inheritance** in the case of categorization corresponds to an entity inheriting only the attributes and relationships of that superclass of which it is a member. In the case of object-oriented programming, represents an IS-A relationship in which a subclass inherits variables and methods from a superclass.
**in-memory DBMS** stores all data in internal memory instead of slower external storage such as disk. Often used for real-time purposes, such as in telecom or defense applications.
**inner join** an SQL join query in which matching tuples from two different tables are joined. An exact match is a requirement; tuples that do not match any other tuple are not included.
**INSERT** an SQL statement that adds data to a relational database.
**insertion anomaly** an issue encountered when a tuple is inserted into an unnormalized table resulting in data needing to be reentered repeatedly.
**insourcing** building a skill set internally at the corporate or business-line level.
**intention exclusive lock (ix-lock)** lock introduced by the MGL protocol that conflicts with both x-locks and s-locks.
**intention lock** lock placed on all coarser-grained database objects that encompass an object to be locked in the MGL protocol.
**intention shared lock (is-lock)** lock introduced by the MGL protocol that only conflicts with x-locks.
**inter-query parallelism** when many simple queries are executed in parallel.
**interactive queries** the manner in which a user can ask to retrieve or update data from the DBMS. Usually executed from a front-end tool, such as a GUI or command line.
**interface** in object-oriented programming, refers to the signatures of the methods of an object.
**internal data model** a representation of a database's physical storage details.
**internal layer** specifies how the data are stored or organized physically.
**INTERSECT** an SQL set operation that returns a table that includes all tuples that are in both SELECT blocks.
**interval** part of a file that is represented as an index entry in the indexed sequential file organization method; also called partition.
**intra-query parallelism** when different subsets of the data are searched in parallel in the context of a single, complex query.
**intrinsic category** a DQ framework category that represents the degree of conformance between the data values and the actual or true values.
**inverted file** defines an index over a non-unique, non-ordering search key of a dataset. The index entries refer to the address of a block containing pointers to all records with that particular key value. The same approach is used for indexing unstructured text documents, with one index entry per search term, referring to a block with pointers to all documents that contain the search term.
**iSCSI** network for storage-related data transfer using Ethernet as a medium.
**Java applet** a Java program that runs in a special sandbox in a web browser, stripping many permissions a normal Java program would have.
**Java Bean** Java's term to refer to re-usable, modular, object-oriented software components.
**Java Data Objects (JDO)** a set of standardized Java components to access data sources.
**Java DataBase Connectivity (JDBC)** a universal database API written in Java to access a variety of SQL databases.
**Java Persistence API** the replacement for the entity Beans in Enterprise JavaBeans 3.0. A standard that can be implemented by vendors to facilitate access to data sources.
**JavaScript** a programming language originally meant to be embedded in web pages and

executed by the web browser to enhance the user experience on a particular web page.

**JavaScript Object Notation (JSON)** a simple, human-readable, data description language based on Java in which objects are described as name–value pairs and which is optimized for data interchange and serialization.

**join index** a multicolumn index that combines attribute types from two or more tables so it contains the pre-calculated result of a join between these tables.

**join query** allows the user to combine, or join, data from multiple tables.

**JSONB** one of the two JSON data types, in which data are stored in a decomposed binary format which is slower to store but significantly faster to process in subsequent calls, as no reparsing is needed.

**junk dimension** a dimension that simply enumerates all feasible combinations of values of the low cardinality attribute types.

**key attribute type** an attribute type with distinct values for each individual entity; a key attribute type can uniquely identify each entity.

**key-to-address transformation** a transformation defined by a hashing algorithm to determine a record's physical address from its key value.

**key–value store** a database storing data as (key, value) pairs.

**keyword-based search** a technique for searching XML data that assumes the XML document is complemented with a set of keywords describing the document metadata, such as file name, author name, date of last modification, keywords summarizing document content, etc.

***K*-means clustering** popular non-hierarchical clustering method that estimates *K* clusters using an iterative procedure.

**Label-Based Access Control (LBAC)** a control mechanism to protect data against unauthorized access; can differentiate between the level of authorization granted to users.

**language-integrated querying** a way to write queries using a programming language's native facilities instead of, e.g., writing them using SQL.

**language-native query expression** query expression based on programming language-specific syntax.

**large objects (LOBs)** data structures created in an ORDBMS to deal with large objects such as multimedia; stored in a separate table and tablespace to improve physical storage efficiency.

**late binding** queries are only translated into an executable format ("bound") at runtime. When compiling the programming code, the queries are treated as text strings and therefore cannot be checked for correctness, but they have the benefit that they can still be constructed dynamically during runtime.

**latency** see rotational delay.

**left outer join** an SQL join query in which each row from the left table is kept in the result; if no match is found in the other table it will return NULL values for these columns.

**legacy** anything hardware, software, or system left over from a previous iteration or technology, often with little or no documentation or support from the creator.

**lift** indicates a negative (lift smaller than 1) or positive (lift bigger than 1) dependence between the antecedent and consequent of an association rule.

**lift curve** represents the cumulative percentage of positives (e.g., churners) per decile, divided by the overall population percentage of positives.

**LIKE** an SQL operator used with the WHERE clause that uses wildcards to find patterns.

**linear decision boundary** linear separating line (or plane) between the classes of a classification problem.

**linear list** a list in which each element has exactly one successor, except for the last element.

**linear regression** the most commonly used technique to model a continuous target variable. Assumes a linear relationship between the target variable and the explanatory variables.

**linear search** a search that sequentially retrieves and assesses each record in a file against a search key.

**linked data** a mechanism to mash distributed and heterogeneous data into one overall semantic model using a simple representation to connect existing information via the re-use of URIs.

**linked list** a structure in which items (e.g., records) are connected sequentially by pointers, representing some logical ordering.

**list** an ordered set of elements.

**literal** in an OODBMS, a constant value, typically embedded in an object, with no OID and which cannot exist on its own.

**loading factor** the average number of records in a bucket divided by the bucket size; indicates how "full" every bucket is on average.

**loading utility** supports the loading of the database with information from a variety of sources, such as another DBMS, text fields, Excel files, etc.

**local query optimization** a step in distributed query processing that determines the optimal strategy for local query execution.

**location transparency** when database users do not need to know on which node the required data reside.

**lock manager** provides concurrency control to ensure data integrity at all times by assigning and releasing locks that specify what types of data operations a transaction can perform on a certain database object.

**lock table** contains information about which locks are currently held by which transaction; which transactions are waiting to acquire certain locks, etc.

**locking** mechanism used to manage simultaneous access to data by granting and releasing locks that specify access rights (e.g., read or write access).

**locking protocol** a mechanism used by the lock manager that specifies the rules and conditions of when to lock and unlock database objects.

**log record** a record of a transaction or operation in a database; stored in a logfile.

**logfile** a sequential file, consisting of log records that contain information such as before and after images of all records involved in a transaction, which is vital to transaction management and recovery.

**logical data independence** the ability to make changes to the conceptual/logical layer with minimal impact on the external layer.

**logical data model** the translation or mapping of the conceptual data model toward a specific implementation environment.

**logistic regression** an extension of linear regression used to model a categorical target variable.

**long-running transactions** transactions of which the duration can be extensive as it, e.g., depends on the asynchronous interactions between participants in a business process (e.g., a WS-BPEL process), also referred to as long-lived transactions.

**long-term lock** lock granted and released according to a protocol, and held for a longer time, until the transaction is committed.

**loosely coupled** with only limited interdependence.

**lost update problem** when an otherwise successful update of a data item by a transaction is overwritten by another transaction that wasn't "aware" of the first update.

**manual failover** a failure safeguarding technique in which a backup server with DBMS software is on standby, possibly with shared access to the same storage devices as the primary server. If a calamity occurs, the spare server is manually started up and the workload transferred from the primary to the backup.

**MapReduce** a programming model, primarily seen in Hadoop, that is a highly scalable implementation of both a map function (the conversion of a dataset broken down into tuples of key–value pairs), and a reduce function, which reduces the output of the map into a smaller set of tuples. The third module of the Hadoop stack.

**marketing analytics** using analytics for marketing purposes such as churn prediction, response modeling, and customer segmentation.

**master data management (MDM)** series of processes, policies, standards, and tools to help organizations to define and provide a single point of reference for all data that are "mastered". The focus is on unifying company-wide reference data types such as customers and products.

**mean absolute deviation (MAD)** mean absolute deviation between the predictions and actual values of a target variable.

**mean squared error (MSE)** mean squared deviation between the predictions and actual values of a target variable.

**media failure** failure that occurs when the secondary storage that contains the database files, and possibly the logfile, is damaged or inaccessible due to a disk crash, a malfunction in the storage network, or other catastrophic event.

**member record type** record type at the N-side of a 1:N relationship type in the CODASYL model.

**membership protocol** set of rules to specify how nodes remain informed at all times of the other nodes in the network.

**Memcached** a NoSQL database that implements a distributed memory-driven hash table that is placed in front of a traditional database to speed up queries by caching recently accessed objects in internal memory.

**message-oriented middleware (MOM)** an alternative to RPC that is more suitable in a heterogeneous environment; integration is established by exchanging XML messages between involved parties.

**metadata** the data definitions stored in the catalog of the DBMS.

**metadata services** support the storage, integration, and exploitation of diverse types of metadata.

**metamodel** a data model for metadata that determines the type of metadata that can be stored.

**method overloading** in object-oriented programming, using the same name for more than one method in the same class. The OO language environment can then determine which method you're calling, provided the number or type of parameters is different in each method.

**method overriding** in object-oriented programming, a process that allows subclasses or child classes to provide a specialized implementation of a method that is previously present in one of its superclasses or parent classes.

**mini-dimension table** a separate dimension table with a new surrogate key, often used to store rapidly changing information.

**mirroring** the act of performing the same write operations on two or more identical disks simultaneously. This is always done synchronously.

**misclassification rate** the share of misclassified observations.

**missing values** when some values are not included in a dataset. Missing values can occur for many reasons, such as they were undisclosed, or due to a merging error.

**mixed file** a file that combines stored records representing different real-world concepts.

**mixed fragmentation** the combination of both vertical and horizontal fragmentation in a distributed database.

**MLlib** Spark's machine learning library. It makes practical machine learning scalable and user-friendly and includes algorithms for classification, regression, clustering, and recommender systems.

**mobile DBMS** database that runs on smartphones. Must have a small footprint, always be online, and have limited processing power, storage, and impact on battery life. Often connects and synchronizes with a central DBMS.

**multicolumn index** index based on the values of multiple columns in a table.

**multidimensional DBMS (MDBMS)** a DBMS that supports multidimensional OLAP.

**multidimensional OLAP (MOLAP)** stores the multidimensional data in a multidimensional array-based data structure optimized for efficient storage and quick access.

**multilevel index** an index-to-an-index for an index that has grown too large to be searched efficiently.

**multimedia DBMS** stores multimedia data such as text, images, audio, video, 3D games, CAD designs, etc., and provides content-based query facilities.

**Multiple Granularity Locking Protocol (MGL)** locking protocol that ensures that the respective transactions that acquired locks on database objects interrelated hierarchically (e.g., tablespace – table – disk block – tuple) cannot conflict with one another.

**multiset** a collection type that can have duplicate elements without order.

**multi-user database** a database that many applications and users can access in parallel.

**multi-user system** see multi-user database.

**multi-valued attribute type** an attribute type that can have multiple values at any given time.

**multi-valued dependency** a dependency $X \rightarrow\rightarrow Y$, such that each X value exactly determines a set of Y values, independently of the other attribute types.

**named row type** a user-defined data type that groups a coherent set of data types into a new composite data type and assigns a meaningful name to it.

**namespace** prefixes to XML elements that provide a unique, unambiguous identification of their meaning.

**NAS (network attached storage)** a specialized device for file storage that can be "plugged" straightforwardly into a TCP/IP-based LAN or WAN via Ethernet.

**NAS gateway** similar to a NAS device, but without the hard disk drives; it consists of only a processor and a stripped-down operating system. The gateway is plugged into a TCP/IP-based LAN or WAN and connected to external disk drives by either DAS or SAN.

**navigational query** a query that navigates from one object to another in an OODBMS.

**nested query** a query that appears within, or "nested" inside, a different query. Also called a subquery or inner query.

**nested-loop join** technique to physically implement a join in which one of the tables is denoted as the inner table and the other becomes the outer table. For every row in the outer table, all rows of the inner table are retrieved and compared to the current row of the outer table. If the join condition is satisfied, both rows are joined and put in an output buffer.

**network attach** storage devices in a many-to-many connection with the corresponding servers through network technology.

**network DBMS** a record-oriented DBMS with a procedural DML and no query processor. Uses a network data model to link records within the database. More flexible than a hierarchical DBMS because it can make connections in more than one direction.

**node** key component of a network which is connected to other nodes using edges or vertices.

**nonlinear list** any list that does not fit the criteria of a linear list.

**nonrepeatable read** when a transaction $T_1$ reads the same row multiple times, but obtains different subsequent values, because another transaction $T_2$ updated this row in the meantime.

**non-volatile** a property of a data warehouse that implies that the data are primarily read-only, and will not be frequently updated or deleted.

**normalization** the process of analyzing the relations to ensure that they contain no redundant data in order to avoid anomalies that can occur during data insertion, deletion, or update.

**NOT EXISTS** an SQL function that returns TRUE if there are no tuples in the result of the nested query, or otherwise returns FALSE.

**NOT NULL constraint** prohibits null values for a column.

**Not-only SQL (NoSQL)** databases that store and manipulate data in other formats than tabular relations (i.e., non-relational databases). Can be classified according to data model into key–value stores, tuple or document stores, column-oriented databases, and graph databases. Very popular for Big Data.

**n-tier architecture** a database system architecture in which the applications on an application server or the functionality of other tiers are spread out over multiple tiers. Also known as multi-tier architecture.

**object** an instance of a class. An object encapsulates both data and functionality.

**object constraint language (OCL)** used to specify various types of constraints, defined in a declarative way; specify what must be true, but not how this should be accomplished.

**Object Data Management Group (ODMG)** A group of OODBMS vendors formed in 1991 to define standards for working with OODBMSs. Originally called Object Database Management Group, the consortium changed its name to The Object Data Management Group with the release of the ODMG 3.0 standard, to emphasize the shift from object database standard toward object storage API standard.

**object definition language (ODL)** a data definition language (DDL) independent of any programming language, that defines the object types that conform to the ODMG Object Model for an OODBMS.

**object equality** in an OODBMS, when the values of two objects' variables are the same.

**object identifier (OID)** a unique and immutable identifier for an object in an OODBMS.

**object identity** in object-oriented programming, refers to the fact that every object can be identified in a unique way.

**Object Management Group (OMG)** an international open membership consortium to develop and advance standards with respect to object orientation and model-based development. One of the most important standards under OMG governance is the Unified Modeling Language (UML).

**object model** consisting of objects and literals, provides a common model to define classes, variables or attributes, behavior, and object persistence in an OODBMS.

**object persistence** a general term referring to saving objects on a persistent medium where they can be retrieved from later on.

**object query language (OQL)** a declarative, non-procedural query language for OODBMSs.

**object-relational mapping (ORM)** a technique to map and convert objects (the core concepts in object-oriented programming languages) and queries on such objects to a relational structure as found in an RDBMS.

**object-oriented (OO)** a programming paradigm in which an application consists of a series of objects that request services from each other.

**object-oriented DBMS (OODBMS)** DBMS based on the object-oriented data model. An object encapsulates both data and functionality.

**object-relational DBMS (ORDBMS)** uses a relational model extended with object-oriented concepts, such as user-defined types, user-defined functions, collections, inheritance, and behavior. Shares characteristics with both an RDBMS and an OODBMS.

**odds ratio** multiplicative increase in the odds when an explanatory variable increases with one unit, *ceteris paribus*.

**OLE DB** a follow-up specification to ODBC that allows uniform access to a variety of data sources using Microsoft's Component Object Model (COM).

**ON DELETE CASCADE** a referential integrity constraint that says a removal should be cascaded to all referring tuples.

**ON UPDATE CASCADE** a referential integrity constraint that says an update should be cascaded to all referring tuples.

**one-way linked list** a linked list in which records are physically stored in an arbitrary order, or sorted according to another search key. A logical sequential ordering is then represented by means of pointers, with each record containing a "next" pointer to the physical location of its logical successor.

**on-line analytical processing (OLAP)** refers to an advanced set of techniques to interactively analyze data, summarize it, and visualize it in various ways.

**on-line analytical processing (OLAP) DBMS** DBMS containing data in support of tactical or strategical decision-making. A limited number of users formulate complex queries to analyze huge amounts of data along different dimensions.

**on-line transaction processing (OLTP)** the processing of lots of simple, online transactions in an efficient way.

**On-Line Transaction Processing (OLTP) DBMS** manages operational or transactional data; queries are initiated in real-time, simultaneously, by many users and applications, such as a point-of-sale system.

**on-premises analytics** keeping data and analytical activities in-house for security and full control.

**opaque data type** an entirely new, user-defined data type in an ORDBMS that is not based upon any existing SQL data type.

**open addressing** overflow-handling technique in which overflow records are stored in the next free slot in the primary area, after the full bucket where the record would normally have been stored according to the key-to-address transformation.

**Open Database Connectivity (ODBC)** a Microsoft universal database API that allows access to SQL databases.

**open-source DBMS** a DBMS for which the source code is publicly available and can be extended and redistributed by anyone.

**operational BI** term with a twofold meaning: analytics used at the operational level (e.g., by front-line employees) or analytics for tactical/strategic decision-making based on real-time operational data combined with the aggregated and historical data in traditional data warehouses.

**operational data store (ODS)** a staging area that provides direct querying facilities.

**operational level** the business decision-making level where day-to-day business decisions are made – typically in real-time, or within a short time frame.

**optimistic protocol** a scheduling protocol managed by a scheduler that assumes conflicts between simultaneous transactions are exceptions.

**orchestration pattern** a sequence and data dependency management pattern that assumes a single centralized executable business process (the orchestrator) coordinates the interaction among different services and subprocesses.

**ORDER BY** an SQL statement that orders the tuples in the result of a query by the values of one or more columns.

**ordinary least squares (OLS)** an optimization method for estimating the parameters of a linear regression model by minimizing the sum of squared errors.

**outliers** extreme observations, very dissimilar to the rest of the population.

**outrigger table** stores a set of attribute types of a dimension table which are highly correlated, low in cardinality, and updated simultaneously.

**outsourcing** hiring an outside company to build a skill set.

**overfitting** when an analytical model (e.g., a decision tree) fits the specificities or noise in the data.

**overflow** happens when there are more synonyms than slots for a certain bucket in random file organization.

**overflow area** the address space that only contains overflow records in random file organization.

**overflow-handling technique** the way in which overflow records are stored and retrieved in random file organization.

**overlap specialization** a specialization whereby an entity can be a member of more than one subclass.

**owner entity type** an entity type from which an attribute type is borrowed by a weak entity type.

**owner record type** record type at the 1-side of a 1:N relationship type in the CODASYL model.

**parallel database** data distribution with only one purpose: performance. The performance gain is achieved through parallel access to the distributed data.

**partial categorization** only some entities of the superclasses belong to the subclass.

**partial participation** a situation in which some entities may not participate in the relationship.

**partial shredding** another term for the combined approach to storage of an XML document.

**partial specialization** allows an entity to only belong to the superclass and to none of the subclasses.

**participants** participate in transactions in a distributed setting.

**partition** see interval.

**PARTITION BY** an SQL operator that subdivides the rows into partitions, similar to a GROUP BY clause.

**passive** a DBMS, such as a traditional RDBMS, that only executes transactions explicitly invoked by users and/or applications.

**Pearson correlation coefficient** measures the linear relationship between two variables; varies between –1 and +1.

**performance monitoring utilities** monitor and report key performance indicators (KPIs) of the DBMS, such as storage space used/available, query response times, and transaction throughput rates.

**persistence by class** in object-oriented programming, implies that all objects of a particular class will be made persistent.

**persistence by creation** in object-oriented programming, the extension of the syntax for creating objects to indicate at compile time that an object should be made persistent.

**persistence by inheritance** in object-oriented programming, indicates that the persistence capabilities are inherited from a predefined persistent class.

**persistence by marking** in object-oriented programming, implies that all objects will be created as transient and may be marked as persistent during program execution.

**persistence by reachability** in object-oriented programming, implies that all objects referred to (either directly or indirectly) by predefined persistent root object(s) will be made persistent as well.

**persistence independence** the persistence of an object is independent of how a program manipulates it; the same code fragment or function can be used with both persistent and transient objects.

**persistence orthogonality** in object-oriented programming, implies these properties: persistence independence, type orthogonality, and transitive persistence.

**persistent object** in object-oriented programming, an object that should survive program execution.

**persistent storage media** memory that retains its content even without being powered.

**pessimistic protocol** a scheduling protocol managed by a scheduler that assumes it is likely that transactions will interfere and cause conflicts.

**phantom reads** when a transaction $T_2$ is executing insert or delete operations on a set of rows being read by a transaction $T_1$. If $T_1$ reads the same set of rows a second time, additional rows may turn up, or previously existing rows may have disappeared, because they have been inserted or deleted by $T_2$ in the meantime.

**physical data independence** the ability to physically reorganize the data with minimal impact on the conceptual/logical or external layer.

**physical database** an integrated collection of stored files consisting of data items and stored records describing different real-world entities and their interrelationships. Also called a stored database.

**physical file** a collection of stored records that represent similar real-world entities (e.g., students, wines, or purchase orders); also called a dataset.

**Pig** a high-level platform for creating programs that run on Hadoop (in a language called Pig Latin), which uses MapReduce underneath to execute the program. It enables users to more easily construct programs that work on top of HDFS and MapReduce, and can somewhat resemble querying facilities offered by SQL.

**pivot or cross-table** a data summarization tool that cross-tabulates a set of dimensions in such a way that multidimensional data can be represented in a two-dimensional tabular format.

**Platform as a Service (PaaS)** computing platform elements hosted in the cloud, which can run and integrate with one's own applications.

**pointer** reference to a storage location.

**point-of-sale (POS)** a system that collects and stores information about who buys what products in what store at what time.

**polymorphism** the ability of objects to respond differently to the same method; closely related to inheritance in object-oriented programming.

**precedence graph** a graph in which nodes represent transactions and edges are based on read/write operations; can be used to test a schedule for serializability.

**precision** measures how many of the predicted positives (e.g., churners) are actually positives.

**predictive analytics** building an analytical model predicting a target measure of interest.

**primary area** the address space that contains the non-overflow records in random file organization.

**primary copy 2PL** extension of primary site 2PL, which aims at further reducing the disadvantages of the latter. Uses lock managers implemented at different locations that maintain locking information pertaining to a predefined subset of the data.

**primary file organization methods** the methods that determine the physical positioning of stored records on a storage medium. Examples are heap files, random file organization, and indexed sequential file organization.

**primary index** when a data file is ordered on a unique key and an index is defined over this unique search key.

**primary key** a selected candidate key that identifies tuples in the relation and is used to establish connections to other relations; must be unique within the relation.

**primary site 2PL** concurrency control technique which applies the centralized Two-Phase Locking protocol in a distributed environment.

**primary storage** the top of the storage hierarchy, consisting of the CPU, cache, and central storage.

**prime attribute type** an attribute type that is part of a candidate key.

**privilege** defines a user's right to use certain SQL statements such as SELECT, INSERT, etc. on one or more database objects.

**procedural DML** early type of DML that explicitly specifies *how* to navigate in the database to locate and modify the data. Focuses on the *procedure* of interaction.

**process engine** a software service that executes a business process and ensures all steps in the process are performed correctly.

**process integration** a process that deals with the sequencing of tasks in a business process and governs the data flows in these processes.

**proprietary API** vendor-specific API; developed for, and particular to, a specific type of DBMS.

**qualified association** a special type of association that uses a qualifier to further refine the association.

**query and reporting** a business intelligence tool that provides a GUI in which the business user can graphically and interactively design a report.

**query by example (QBE)** a facility that sits between the database and the business concepts, in which a query is composed in a user-friendly way by visualizing database tables so the business user can enter conditions for each field that needs to be included in the query.

**query cardinality (QC)** the number of rows selected by the query.

**query decomposition** a step in distributed query processing in which the query is first analyzed for correctness. The query is then represented in relational algebra and transformed into a canonical form, which is most appropriate for further processing.

**query executor** executes the query by calling on the storage manager to retrieve or update the requested data.

**query optimizer** optimizes the queries based upon current database state and metadata. Can use predefined indexes that are part of the internal data model to provide quick access to data.

**query parser** checks the query for syntactical and semantical correctness and decomposes the query into an *internal representation format* that can then be further evaluated by the system.

**query predicate** specifies the selection condition with respect to a particular attribute type in a query.

**query processor** assists in the execution of database queries. Consists of multiple components, such as the DML compiler, query parser, query rewriter, query optimizer, and query executor.

**query rewriter** using predefined rules and heuristics specific to the DBMS, optimizes the query independent of the current database state.

**RACI Matrix** RACI stands for Responsible, Accountable, Consulted, and Informed. It is a matrix used to determine roles and responsibilities of a project or job.

**RAID controller** either hardware or software that manages an array of hard drives to appear as a single logical drive.

**RAID levels** different possible RAID configurations using different combinations of data striping, redundancy, and data mirroring, each resulting in different performance and reliability.

**random file organization** primary file organization method in which a record's physical location is directly related to the value of a search key using a hashing procedure; also called direct file organization or hash file organization.

**ranking** the ordering of values, either ascending or descending.

**ranking module** a web search component that sorts the result set according to relevance.

**rapidly changing dimension** a dimension that contains information that changes rapidly and regularly over a period of time.

**RDF Schema** an extension of RDF through more robust vocabulary with classes and subclasses, properties and subproperties, and typing of properties.

**read committed** isolation level that uses long-term write locks, but short-term read locks; resolves the lost update as well as the uncommitted dependency problem.

**read lock** allows a transaction to read a database object. Assigned by the lock manager.

**read uncommitted** lowest isolation level in which long-term locks are not taken into account; assumes that concurrency conflicts do not occur.

**read/write heads** components of a hard disk drive that sit on actuators and move in and out from the center of the disk to each readable or writeable surface on the platter.

**receiver operating characteristic curve (ROC curve)** plots the sensitivity versus 1-specificity for various cutoffs. The closer the curve approaches to a sensitivity of 1 and a specificity of 1, the better the performance.

**recommender system** application that provides well-targeted recommendations based on customer behavior, input, or past purchases.

**record organization** the organization of data items into stored records.

**record pointer** the combination of a block address and a record ID or offset within this block referring to an actual record.

**record type** a set of records describing similar entities.

**record-at-a-time DML** see procedural DML.

**recovery** the activity of ensuring that, whichever problem occurs during transaction execution, the database is returned to a consistent state without any data loss afterwards.

**recovery manager** supervises the correct execution of database transactions by keeping a logfile of all database operations. Will be called upon to undo actions of aborted transactions or during crash recovery.

**redundancy** see data redundancy.

**Redundant Array of Independent Disks (RAID)** technology in which standard HDDs are coupled to a dedicated hard disk controller (the RAID controller) to make them appear as a single logical drive.

**regression** a type of predictive analytics in which the target variable is continuous.

**regression tree** decision tree in which the target variable is continuous (e.g., sales, CLV, LGD).

**relation** a set of tuples that each represent a similar real-world entity.

**relational database management system (RDBMS)** a DBMS based on the relational data model.

**relational model** a formal data model with a sound mathematical foundation, based on *set theory* and *first order predicate logic* in which a database is represented as a collection of relations.

**relational OLAP (ROLAP)** stores data in a relational data warehouse, which can be implemented using a star, snowflake, or fact constellation schema.

**relationship** an association between two or more entities.

**relationship type** a set of relationships among instances of one, two, or more record or entity types; indicated using a rhombus symbol in the ER model.

**relative block address** an address that is relative to the first block of a file.

**relative location** a record organization technique in which only attributes are stored; attribute types are not stored and are determined implicitly by the relative ordering in which the data items occur, based on metadata about record structure in the catalog.

**Remote Procedure Call (RPC)** technology in which communication between applications is established through procedure calls; an object invokes a method from a remote object on another server.

**reorganization utility** improves performance through automatic data reorganization for efficiency.

**repeatable read** isolation level that uses both long-term read locks and write locks; phantom reads can still occur with this isolation level.

**repeated group** a composite data item for which a record can have multiple values or a composite multi-valued attribute type. Common to the CODASYL model.

**replicas** the different virtual nodes that correspond to the same physical node in a consistent hashing ring.

**replication** see data replication.

**replication transparency** when different replicas of the same data item will be automatically kept consistent by the database system and updates to one replica will be propagated transparently (be it synchronously or asynchronously) to the other copies of the same data item.

**representation category** a DQ framework category that indicates the extent to which data are presented in a consistent and interpretable way.

**representational state transfer (REST)** a web service API architecture that bases itself on HTTP to handle requests between the service and its clients.

**request coordinator** the responsible party that routes requests to the appropriate destination node and relays back the result status of the operation in a distributed system.

**requirement collection and analysis** the identification and determination of needs, conditions, and stakeholders required to understand the data needs and functionalities of the process and/or application under development.

**Resource Description Framework (RDF)** provides the data model for the semantic web through encoding graph-structured data by attaching a semantic meaning to the relationships.

**response modeling** the development of an analytical model that selects the customers who are most likely to exhibit the desired response to a marketing campaign.

**REST (representational state transfer)** see representational state transfer.

**RESTRICT** a referential integrity constraint in which the update or removal is halted if referring tuples exist.

**return on investment (ROI)** the ratio of the net benefits or net profits over the investment of resources that generated this return.

**right outer join** an SQL join query in which each row from the right table is kept in the result; if no match is found in the other table it will return NULL values for these columns.

**rigorous 2PL** a 2PL variant that specifies that a transaction holds all its locks until it is committed.

**ring topology** network topology in which each node occupies a position in a closed range of numbers.

**risk analytics** using analytics techniques to measure, predict, and mitigate risk.

**roles** indicate the various directions that can be used to interpret a relationship type.

**rollback** when all changes made by the transaction's respective operations should be undone in such a way that, after completion of the rollback, it appears as if the faulty transaction never happened.

**roll-down** an OLAP operation that is the de-aggregation of the current set of fact values by navigating from a lower level of detail to a higher level of detail.

**rollforward recovery** when the archived data from the backup copy is restored and then complemented with (a redo of) the more recent transactions as recorded in the mirrored logfile.

**roll-up** an OLAP operation that is the aggregation of the current set of fact values within or across one or more dimensions.

**ROLLUP** an SQL operator that computes the union on every prefix of the list of specified attribute types, from the most detailed up to the grand total.

**rotational delay** once read/write heads are in place above the specified track, the time to rotate the platter surface until the desired sector on the platter surface is located. Also known as latency.

**sampling** taking a relevant subset of historical data to build an analytical model.

**SAN (storage area network)** dedicated network for storage related data transfer.

**SAX API (simple API for XML)** an event-based API that represents an XML document as a stream of events.

**schedule** a set of *n* transactions, and a sequential ordering over the statements of these transactions, for which the following property holds: for each transaction T that participates in a schedule S and for all statements $s_i$ and $s_j$ that belong to the same transaction T: if statement $s_i$ precedes statement $s_j$ in T, then $s_i$ is scheduled to be executed before $s_j$ in S.

**scheduler** a component of the transaction manager that plans the start of the transactions and the execution of their respective operations, aiming at optimizing KPIs such as query response times and transaction throughput rates.

**schema-aware mapping** transforms an XML document into a relational structure based on an already existing DTD or XSD.

**schema-level triggers** also called DDL triggers, RDBMS triggers that are fired after changes are made to the DBMS schema (such as creating, dropping, or altering tables, views, etc.).

**schema-oblivious mapping/shredding** transforms an XML document into a relational structure without the availability of a DTD or XSD.

**search key** a single attribute type, or set of attribute types, whose values determine the criteria according to which records are retrieved. These criteria are generally formulated with a query language, such as SQL.

**search key values** values of a search key.

**search tree** a tree structure used for locating a record in which each navigation downwards in the tree reduces the search interval.

**second normal form (2 NF)** when 1 NF is satisfied and every non-prime attribute type A in R is fully functionally dependent on any key of R.

**secondary file organization methods** the methods that provide constructs to efficiently retrieve records according to a search key not used for the primary file organization.

**secondary index** an index created for secondary file organization methods and therefore with no impact on a record's physical location.

**secondary storage** the bottom half of the storage hierarchy, consisting of persistent storage media, such as a hard disk drive, solid state drive, and tape or optical media.

**sector** the smallest addressable individual unit on a hard disk drive on which data can be written or read; multiple sectors make up tracks.

**seek time** the time to locate and position the actuator of a disk drive over a specific track.

**SELECT** an SQL statement that retrieves data from a relational database.

**selective inheritance** see inheritance in categorization.

**self-service BI** business intelligence in which a business user, not an IT expert, can do the query and reporting, often through a graphical user interface.

**semantic metadata** metadata about the data's meaning.

**semantic search** methods that allow formulating semantically complicated queries.

**semi-structured data** data which have a certain structure, but the structure may be very irregular or highly volatile. Examples are individual users' web pages on a large social media platform, or resumé documents.

**sensitivity** measures how many of the positives (e.g., churners) are correctly labeled by the analytical model as a positive.

**sensor DBMS** manages sensor data such as biometric data obtained from wearables, or telematics data which continuously records driving behavior.

**sequence rule** a rule specifying a sequence of events (e.g., item purchases, web page visits).

**sequential file organization** a primary file organization method in which records are stored in ascending or descending order of a search key.

**serializable** when a non-serial schedule is equivalent to (i.e., yields the same outcome as) a serial schedule.

**serialization** in object-oriented programming, the translation of an object's state into a format that can be stored (for example, in a file) and reconstructed later.

**serially** when actions, such as transactions, are executed in a sequence.

**service oriented architecture (SOA)** software architecture in which business processes are supported by a set of loosely coupled software services.

**SET DEFAULT** a referential integrity constraint in which the foreign keys in the referring tuples should be set to their default value.

**SET NULL** a referential integrity constraint in which all foreign keys in the referring tuples are set to NULL.

**set type** models a 1:N relationship type between an owner record type and a member record type.

**set-at-a-time DML** see declarative DML.

**shallow equality** implies that two objects have the same values for their variables.

**shard** an individual partition.

**sharding** also known as horizontal fragmentation or partitioning, where data are partitioned into separate sets, each of which are attributed to a different node in a distributed DBMS.

**shared and intention exclusive lock (six-lock)** lock introduced by the MGL protocol that conflicts with all other MGL lock types, except for an is-lock.

**shared-disk architecture** distributed database system architecture in which each processor has its own central storage but shares secondary storage with the other processors.

**shared lock** a lock in which a transaction gets the guarantee that no other transactions will update the locked object for as long as the lock is held. The transaction can then read from the locked object without the risk of conflicts with other transactions that write to it.

**shared-memory architecture** distributed database system architecture in which multiple interconnected processors that run the DBMS software share the same central storage and secondary storage.

**shared-nothing architecture** distributed database system architecture in which each processor has its own central storage and hard disk units. Data sharing occurs through the processors communicating with one another over the network, not by the processors directly accessing one another's central storage or secondary storage.

**short-term lock** lock only held during the time interval needed to complete the associated operation.

**shredding** another term for a data-oriented approach to storage of an XML document.

**Simple Object Access Protocol (SOAP)** see SOAP.

**simple attribute type** see atomic attribute type.

**simultaneous access** also known as concurrent access. Allowing more than one user access to a DBMS at a time.

**single point of failure** a single component failure that can cause an entire system failure. Single points of failure in database management include availability and accessibility of storage devices, availability of database functionality and availability of the data.

**single-user system** allows only one user at a time to work with a DBMS.

**single-valued attribute** an attribute type with only one value for a particular entity at any given time.

**slicing** an OLAP operation in which one dimension is set at a particular value.

**slowly changing dimension** a dimension that changes slowly and irregularly over a period of time.

**Small Computer Systems Interface (SCSI)** popularly pronounced "scuzzy", SCSI is a standard parallel connection between devices such as peripheral hard drives and high-capacity workstations and servers. The SCSI specification involves two elements: on the one hand a command set to communicate with storage devices, and on the other hand specifications for a low-level protocol and cabling to transfer SCSI commands and data between servers and storage devices.

**snowflake schema** a conceptual data model of a data warehouse that normalizes the dimension tables.

**SOAP** originally "Simple Object Access Protocol"; a web service interaction protocol that uses XML-based messages to exchange requests between the service and its clients.

**social network** consists of a network of nodes (vertices) and edges. Examples are a friends network, a family network, or a call network.

**social network learning** inferencing in a social network. An example is computing class membership probability (e.g., churn probability) of a specific node, given the status of the other nodes in the network.

**sociogram** a visual representation of an entity's (person, business, etc.) social network, showing links and relationships between individuals and groups.

**Software as a Service (SaaS)** full applications hosted in the cloud (e.g., applications for analytics, data cleansing, or data quality reporting).

**sort-merge join** technique to physically implement a join in which the tuples in both tables are first sorted according to the attribute types involved in the join condition. Both tables are then traversed in this order, with the rows that satisfy the join condition being combined and put in an output buffer.

**sourced function** a user-defined function in an ORDBMS that is based on an existing, built-in function.

**Spark** a new programming paradigm centered on a data structure called the resilient distributed dataset, or RDD, which can be distributed across a cluster of machines and is maintained in a fault-tolerant way.

**Spark Core** the heart of Spark, it forms the foundation for all other components. It provides functionality for task scheduling and a set of basic data transformations that can be used through many programming languages (Java, Python, Scala, and R).

**Spark SQL** Spark component that runs on top of Spark Core and introduces another data abstraction called DataFrames, which represent themselves to the end-user as a collection of data organized into named columns.

**Spark Streaming** leverages Spark Core and its fast scheduling engine to perform streaming analytics.

**SPARQL** a recursive acronym for "SPARQL Protocol and RDF Query Language"; it is a query language based on matching graph patterns against RDF graphs.

**sparse index** an index with an index entry for only some of the search key values; each entry refers to a group of records. Contains fewer index entries than a dense index.

**spatial DBMS** supports the storage and querying of spatial data, including both 2D objects (e.g., points, lines, and polygons) and 3D objects. Spatial operations like calculating distances or relationships between objects are provided. Key building block of geographical information systems (GIS).

**specialization** the process of defining a set of subclasses of an entity type; a top-down process of conceptual refinement.

**specificity** measures how many of the negatives (e.g., non-churners) are correctly labeled by the analytical model as a negative.

**spindle** the component of a hard disk drive on which the platter is secured, and which rotates at a constant speed.

**SQL** see Structured Query Language.

**SQL injection** an attack in which malicious fragments are injected into normal-looking SQL statements, which can cause a wide range of harm. Many websites and applications are vulnerable to SQL injections.

**SQL schema** a grouping of tables and other database objects such as views, constraints, and indexes that logically belong together.

**SQL/XML** an extension of SQL that introduces an XML data type and constructor to treat XML documents as cell values in a common relational table, a set of operators for the XML data type, and a set of functions to map relational data to XML.

**SQLJ** Java's embedded, static database API.

**stabilization** an operation that repartitions hashes over nodes if nodes are added or removed.

**star schema** a conceptual data model of a data warehouse with one large central fact table that is connected to various smaller dimension tables.

**starvation** a situation in which some transactions wait endlessly for the required exclusive locks, whereas the other transactions continue normally.

**static 2PL** a 2PL variant that specifies that a transaction acquires all its locks right at the start of the transaction; also called conservative 2PL.

**static binding** in object-oriented programming, that the binding of methods to the appropriate implementation is resolved at compile time.

**StAX (streaming API for XML)** XML API defined as a compromise between DOM and SAX and originated from the Java programming community.

**storage manager** governs physical file access and supervises correct and efficient data storage. Consists of a transaction manager, buffer manager, lock manager, and recovery manager.

**stored data manager** coordinates the I/O instructions and the physical interactions with the database files.

**stored procedure** a piece of SQL code consisting of declarative and/or procedural instructions and stored in the catalog of the RDBMS. It must be invoked explicitly by calling it from an application or command prompt.

**stored record** a collection of data items related to the same real-world entity that represents all attributes of the entity; physical representation of a tuple in a relational table.

**stored table** a physical representation of a logical table that occupies one or more disk blocks or pages in a tablespace.

**strategic level** the business decision-making level at which decisions are made by senior management, with long-term implications (e.g., 1, 2, 5 years, or more).

**streaming data** continuous, high-velocity data generated by multiple sources.

**stretched cluster** a clustering technique in which both the primary and the backup DBMS are conceived as nodes in a cluster that spans both the primary and remote data centers.

**strong entity type** an entity type with its own key attribute type(s).

**structural metadata** metadata about the data's structure (e.g., column definitions in a relational database or tags in an XML document).

**structured data** data in which the individual characteristics of data items (such as the number, name, address, and email of a student) can be identified and formally specified.

**structured literal** in ODMG, consists of a fixed number of named elements which can be predefined (e.g., Date, Interval, Time, and TimeStamp) or user-defined.

**Structured Query Language (SQL)** the language used for both data definition and data manipulation in a relational database management system.

**structured search** refers to query methods that make use of structural metadata, which relates to the actual document content.

**subject-oriented** a property of a data warehouse that implies that the data are organized around subjects such as customers, products, sales, etc.

**SUM** an SQL operator used in aggregate functions that provides the sum of all values in the selected column.

**superkey** a subset of attribute types of a relation R with the property that no two tuples in any relation state should have the same combination of values for these attribute types. Specifies a uniqueness constraint in the sense that no two distinct tuples in a state can have the same value for the superkey.

**support** support of an item set is the percentage of total transactions in the database that contains the item set.

**surrogate key** meaningless integer used to connect facts to the dimension table.

**synonyms** records that are assigned to the same bucket in random file organization.

**system failure** failure that occurs when an operating system or database system crashes due to a bug, power outage, or similar event, that may cause loss of the primary storage's content and, therefore, the database buffer.

**table cardinality (TC)** the number of rows in the table.

**table data type** defines the type of a table in an ORDBMS, much like a class in OO.

**table-based mapping** transforms an XML document into a relational structure, specifying strict requirements to the structure of the XML document: it should be a perfect reflection of the database structure.

**tablespace** a physical container of database objects consisting of one or more physical files, often with the option of distributing the files over multiple storage devices.

**tactical level** the business decision-making level at which decisions are made by middle management with a medium-term focus (e.g., a month, a quarter, a year).

**tape backup** backup method in which database files are copied periodically to a tape storage medium for safekeeping.

**technical key** a conversion of the natural key so tables can be joined with each other while protecting the true identity of the instance.

**template-based mapping** an XML mapping technique in which SQL statements can be directly embedded in XML documents using a tool-specific delimiter.

**temporal constraint** constraint spanning a particular time interval.

**ternary relationship type** relationship type with three participating entity types.

**text analytics** the analysis of textual data such as reports, emails, text messages, tweets, web documents, blogs, reviews, or financial statements.

**third normal form (3 NF)** when 2 NF is satisfied and no non-prime attribute type of R is transitively dependent on the primary key.

**three-layer architecture** a description of how the underlying data models of a database are related. The three layers are external, conceptual/logical, and internal.

**three-tier architecture** a database system architecture in which a client connects to an application server that then queries a database server hosting the DBMS.

**tiered system architecture** a decentralized approach to database system architecture in which the computing capabilities of powerful central computers acting as a passive server are combined with the flexibilities of PCs that act as active clients.

**tightly coupled** based on a strong interdependence.

**time variant** a property of a data warehouse that refers to the fact that the data warehouse essentially stores a time series of periodic snapshots.

**timeliness** a DQ dimension that refers to the extent to which data are sufficiently up-to-date for the task being performed.

**timestamping** a concurrency control technique in which database objects have attributes that indicate the last time the object was read and/or the last time it was written.

**total categorization** all entities of the superclasses belong to the subclass.

**total cost of ownership (TCO)** the cost of owning and operating a system during its expected lifetime, from inception to retirement – including development, operating, change management, data governance, and quality costs.

**Total Data Quality Management (TDQM)** a data governance framework that presents a cycle consisting of four steps related to the management of data quality – Define, Measure, Analyze, and Improve – which are performed iteratively.

**total participation** a situation in which all entities need to participate in the relationship; the existence of an entity depends upon the existence of another.

**total specialization** a specialization whereby every entity in the superclass must be a member of some subclass.

**track** one of multiple concentric circles on the platter of a hard disk consisting of individual sectors on which data are written and read.

**transaction** a set of database operations induced by a single user or application, that should be considered as one undividable unit of work. An example is a sequence of SQL statements in a relational database setting.

**transaction coordinator** coordinates transactions in a distributed setting.

**transaction failure** failure that results from an error in the logic that drives a transaction's operations (e.g., wrong input, uninitialized variables, incorrect statements, etc.) and/or in the application logic.

**transaction management** the management of transactions typically in a database application.

**transaction manager** supervises execution of database transactions. Creates a schedule with interleaved read/write operations to improve efficiency and execution performance; guarantees atomicity, consistency, isolation, and durability (ACID) properties in a multi-user environment.

**transaction recovery** to restore the context of transactions that were ongoing in the event of calamities.

**transaction transparency** a type of transparency in which a DBMS transparently performs distributed transactions involving multiple nodes as if they were transactions in a standalone system.

**transfer time** the time to transfer the data from the disk drive to the host system. Transfer time is dependent on block size, density of magnetic particles, and rotational speed of the disks.

**transient object** in object-oriented programming, an object only needed during program execution and discarded upon program termination.

**transitive dependency** when the dependency concerns a set of attribute types Z that is neither a candidate key nor a subset of any key of R, and both $X \rightarrow Z$ and $Z \rightarrow Y$ hold.

**transitive persistence** see persistence by reachability.

**transparency** in distributed databases, refers to the property that the user is insulated from one or more aspects of the distribution.

**tree pointer** pointer that refers to a node in a tree.

**trigger** a piece of SQL code consisting of declarative and/or procedural instructions and stored in the catalog of the RDBMS. It is automatically activated and run (fired) by the RDBMS whenever a specified event (e.g., insert, update, delete) occurs and a specific condition is evaluated as true.

**trivial functional dependency** a functional dependency $X \rightarrow Y$ where Y is a subset of X.

**tuple** an ordered list of attributes that each describe an aspect of a relation.

**tuple store** similar to a key–value store, a tuple store stores a unique key with a vector of data instead of a pairwise combination of a key and a value.

**Two-Phase Commit Protocol (2PC Protocol)** developed for transaction recovery in a distributed environment, derives its name from the fact that global transaction completion involves two phases: a voting phase in which all transaction participants "vote" about transaction outcome; and a decision phase in which the transaction coordinator makes the final decision about the outcome.

**Two-Phase Locking Protocol (2PL Protocol)** a popular locking protocol that applies a compatibility matrix and determines when lock and unlock instructions are allowed in a transaction's lifecycle; specifies that acquiring and releasing locks occurs in two phases for each transaction.

**two-tier architecture** also known as client–server architecture, where a PC acts as a client making requests of a database server where the DBMS sits.

**type orthogonality** in object-oriented programming, ensuring that all objects can be made persistent, despite their type or size.

**uncommitted dependency problem** when one transaction is ultimately aborted and rolled back, so another transaction ends up in a situation in which it has read tentative values it never should have "seen".

**unidirectional association** an association in which only a single way of navigating is indicated by an arrow in the UML model.

**Unified Modeling Language (UML)** a modeling language that assists in the specification, visualization, construction, and documentation of artifacts of a software system; an OO system modeling notation which focuses not only on data requirements, but also on behavioral modeling, process, and application architecture.

**uniform distribution** equal spreading of data (e.g., records) over a range (e.g., set of buckets).

**UNION** an SQL set operation that returns a table that includes all tuples that are in one of the SELECT blocks, or both.

**UNIQUE constraint** defines an alternative key of a table.

**universal API** a vendor agnostic API that hides vendor-specific details to allow applications to be easily ported between multiple database systems.

**unnamed row type** type which allows to use unnamed tuples as composite values in a table.

**unrepeatable read** see nonrepeatable read.

**unstructured data** data with no finer-grained components that have been formally specified. A long text document is an example.

**UPDATE** an SQL statement that modifies data to a relational database.

**update anomaly** an issue encountered when a tuple in an unnormalized table is updated, causing the need to make multiple updates with the risk of inconsistency.

**user interface** the front-facing means in which a user interacts with an application or a DBMS.

**user management utilities** tools that support the creation and assignment of privileges to user groups and accounts.

**user-defined function (UDF)** allows users to extend built-in ORDBMS functions by explicitly defining their own functions to enrich the functional capability of the ORDBMS, similar to methods in OODBMSs.

**user-defined type (UDT)** defines a customized data type with specific properties.

**valid** a designation of an XML document that complies with the structural prescriptions of a specific document type as expressed in a DTD of XML Schema; a higher certification than well-formed.

**value** the fifth of the 5 Vs of Big Data; the economic value of Big Data as quantified using the total cost of ownership (TCO) and return on investment (ROI).

**variable length record** a situation in record organization in which a record has no fixed length; can be due to data types with variable length (e.g., VARCHAR), multi-valued attribute types, optional attribute types, or a mixed file.

**VARIANCE** an SQL operator used in aggregate functions that provides the variance of all values in the selected column.

**variety** the third of the 5 Vs of Big Data; the range of data types and sources that are used, data in its "many forms".

**vector** a multi-valued attribute type; part of the CODASYL model.

**velocity** the second of the 5 Vs of Big Data; the speed at which data comes in and goes out, data "in motion".

**veracity** the fourth of the 5 Vs of Big Data; data "in doubt". Describes the uncertainty due to data inconsistency and incompleteness, ambiguities present in the data, and latency or certain data points that might be derived from estimates or approximations.

**vertical fragmentation** when every fragment in a distributed database consists of a subset of the columns of the global dataset.

**vertical scaling** a way to increase data capacity by the extension of storage capacity and/or CPU power of a database server; also called scaling up.

**victim selection** choosing and aborting one transaction involved in a deadlock.

**view** a subset of the data items in the logical model tailored toward the needs of a specific application or group of users. Often called a virtual table in a relational setting.

**virtual child record type** child record type needed to model an N:M relationship type in the hierarchical model.

**virtual data mart** data mart that has no physical data but provides a uniform and consolidated single point of access to a set of underlying physical data stores.

**virtual data warehouse** data warehouse that has no physical data but provides a uniform and consolidated single point of access to a set of underlying physical data stores.

**virtual nodes** see replicas.

**virtual parent record type** parent record type needed to model an N:M relationship type in the hierarchical model.

**virtual parent–child relationship type** relationship type needed to model an N:M relationship type in the hierarchical model.

**volatile memory** memory of which the content is cleared when the power is turned off.

**volume** the first of the 5 Vs of Big Data; the amount of data, also referred to the data "at rest".

**voting phase** the first phase of the 2PC Protocol in which all transaction participants "vote" about transaction outcome.

**wait-for graph** graph in which nodes represent active transactions and a directed edge from $T_i \rightarrow T_j$ indicates that transaction $T_i$ is waiting to acquire a lock currently held by transaction $T_j$. Can be used to detect deadlocks if the wait-for graph contains a cycle.

**weak entity type** an entity type without a key attribute type of its own.

**web crawler** a web search component that continuously retrieves web pages, extracts their links (URLs) to other pages, and adds these URLs to a buffer that contains the links to pages yet to be visited.

**Web Ontology Language (OWL)** an expressive ontology language that implements various sophisticated semantic modeling concepts.

**web service** self-describing software component that can be published, discovered, and invoked through the web.

**Web Services Description Language (WSDL)** an XML-based language used to describe the interface or functionalities offered by a web service.

**well-formed** an XML document that satisfies the proper XML formatting rules; a certification lower than valid.

**WHERE** an SQL clause that when added to a statement specifies selection conditions to indicate which table rows should be selected.

**windowing** refers to calculating the cumulative totals or running averages based on a specified window of values.

**workflow service** coordinates the control flow and data flow of a business process by triggering its respective tasks in line with the sequence constraints in the process model, and according to an orchestration or choreography pattern.

**wrappers** an additional layer of an API that forms a shell around the respective data sources, insulating the users and applications from their heterogeneity to provide a virtual unified database model over the distributed data sources.

**write ahead log strategy** registering updates on the logfile before they are written to disk.

**write lock** allows a transaction to update a database object. Assigned by the lock manager.

**WS-BPEL** Web Services Business Process Execution Language; an execution language that allows converting a process model into an executable process definition based on web services that can then be understood and used by a process engine.

**XML DBMS** Uses the XML data model to store data; represents data in a hierarchical, nested, way.

**XML element** the combination of a start tag, content, and end tag, such as <term>content</term>.

**XML Schema Definition (XSD)** a formal specification of the structure of an XML document that defines the tag set, the location of each tag, and how the tags are nested. See also Document Type Definition (DTD).

**XML-enabled DBMS** DBMS with facilities to store XML data using a document-oriented, data-oriented, or combined approach.

**XPath** a simple, declarative language that uses path expressions to refer to parts of an XML document.

**XQuery** a language that formulates structured queries for XML documents.

**XSL Formatting Objects (XSL-FO)** a component of XSL that specifies formatting semantics (e.g., to transform XML documents to PDFs).

**XSL Transformations (XSLT)** a component of XSL that transforms XML documents into other XML documents, HTML web pages, or plain text.

**YAML Ain't a Markup Language (YAML)** a superset of JSON with additional capabilities such as support for relational trees, user-defined types, explicit data typing, lists, and casting; designed for better object serialization.

**YARN (Yet Another Resource Negotiator)** handles the management and scheduling of resource requests in a distributed environment; the fourth module of the Hadoop stack.

# INDEX

# ENDORSEMENTS

"As we are entering a new technological era of intelligent machines powered by data-driven algorithms, understanding fundamental concepts of data management and their most current practical applications has become more important than ever. This book is a timely guide for anyone interested in getting up to speed with the state of the art in database systems, Big Data technologies and data science. It is full of insightful examples and case studies with direct industrial relevance."

– Nesime Tatbul, *Intel Labs and MIT*

"It is a pleasure to study this new book on database systems. The book offers a fantastically fresh approach to database teaching. The mix of theoretical and practical contents is almost perfect, the content is up to date and covers the recent databases, the examples are nice, and the database testbed provides an excellent way of understanding the concepts. Coupled with the authors' expertise, this book is an important addition to the database field."

– Arnab Bhattacharya, *Indian Institute of Technology, Kanpur*

"*Principles of Database Management* is my favorite textbook for teaching a course on database management. Written in a well-illustrated style, this comprehensive book covers essential topics in established data management technologies and recent discoveries in data science. With a nice balance between theory and practice, it is not only an excellent teaching medium for students taking information management and/or data analytics courses, but also a quick and valuable reference for scientists and engineers working in this area."

– Chuan Xiao, *Graduate School of Informatics, Nagoya University*

"Data science success stories and Big Data applications are only possible because of advances in database technology. This book provides both a broad and deep introduction to databases. It covers the different types of database systems (from relational to NoSQL) and manages to bridge the gap between data modeling and the underlying basic principles. The book is highly recommended for anyone who wants to understand how modern information systems deal with ever-growing volumes of data."

– Wil van der Aalst, *RWTH Aachen University*

"The database field has been evolving for several decades and the need for updated textbooks is continuous. Now, this need is covered by this fresh book by Lemahieu, vanden Broucke and Baesens. It spans from traditional topics – such as the relational model and SQL – to more recent topics – such as distributed computing with Hadoop and Spark, as well as data analytics. The book can be used as an introductory text and for graduate courses."

– Yannis Manolopoulos, *Data Science & Engineering Lab., Aristotle University of Thessaloniki*

"I like the way the book covers both traditional database topics and newer material such as Big Data, NoSQL databases and data quality. The coverage is just right for my course and the level of the material is very appropriate for my students. The book also has clear explanations and good examples."

– Barbara Klein, *University of Michigan*

"This book provides a unique perspective on database management and how to store, manage and analyze small and big data. The accompanying exercises and solutions, cases, slides and YouTube lectures turn it into an indispensable resource for anyone teaching an undergraduate or postgraduate course on the topic."

– Wolfgang Ketter, *Erasmus University Rotterdam*

"This is a very modern textbook that fills the needs of current trends without sacrificing the need to cover the required database management systems fundamentals."

– George Dimitoglou, *Hood College*

"This book is a much-needed foundational piece on data management and data science. The authors successfully integrate the fields of database technology, operations research and Big Data analytics, which have often been covered independently in the past. A key asset is its didactical approach that builds on a rich set of industry examples and exercises. The book is a must-read for all scholars and practitioners interested in database management, Big Data analytics and its applications."

– Jan Mendling, *Institute for Information Business, Vienna*

"*Principles of Database Management* creates a precious resource for researchers, industry practitioners, and students of databases and Big Data alike. This easy-to-read, well-organized book provides coverage of a number of important topics and techniques about storing, managing and analyzing big and small data that are specifically not covered in most database or data-analytics books. If you work in the area of scalable data management and analysis, you owe it to yourself to read this book."

– Kunpeng Zhang, *University of Maryland*

"Database and Big Data analytics are transforming our daily lives, businesses and society at large. To achieve competitive advantage in this new environment, we should be able to collect, manage and analyze a variety of datasets using database systems. This book, written by database and analytics experts, provides a comprehensive view of database technologies from fundamental principles to cutting-edge applications in business intelligence and Big Data analytics."

– Gene Moo Lee, *University of British Columbia*

"The book will provide readers with relevant concepts for today's databases at a perfect reading and technical level."

– Douglas Hawley, *Northwest Missouri State University*

"Here is a book with a strong practical orientation, which covers the recent database management topics relevant to industry. It is a good book with a logical structure, to use in an undergraduate database management course."

– Faruk Arslan, *University of Houston–Clear Lake*

"Lemahieu *et al.*'s *Principles of Database Management* is a wonderful, and the most comprehensive, database book covering both the technical and organizational aspects of data management. It shows technical details and practical examples of how to implement databases. This book also addresses in a timely manner new Big Data and analytics technologies such as NoSQL and Hadoop. I strongly recommend it to anyone who wants to study database technology."

– Bin Zhang, *Eller College of Management, University of Arizona*